Based on the Latest Syllabi for MBA, MFC, MBE, and M.Com. of Indian Universities and Management Institutes

Economic Environment of Business

AN IN-DEPTH STUDY OF

- **Business Environment (External and Internal), Corporate Governance and Social Responsibility**
- **New Economic Policy of Liberalisation, Privatisation and Globalisation**
- **Macroeconomic Environment : Major Issues, Macroeconomic Theories and Policies, Problems of Business Cycles, Inflation and Economic Growth**
- **International Business Environment and Global Financial Crisis**
- **Important Aspects of Indian Business Environment**
- **Growth Models and Economic Planning in India**
- **Environment, Climate Change and Sustainable Development**

Dr H L AHUJA
M.A., Ph.D. (DSE)
Former Senior Reader
Department of Economics
Zakir Husain Delhi College
University of Delhi
and
Former Visiting Professor of Managerial Economics
Maharishi Institute of Management
Noida

S. CHAND
PUBLISHING

S Chand And Company Limited
(ISO 9001 Certified Company)

S Chand And Company Limited

(ISO 9001 Certified Company)

Head Office: D-92, Sector–2, Noida – 201301, U.P. (India), Ph. 91-120-4682700

Registered Office: A-27, 2nd Floor, Mohan Co-operative Industrial Estate, New Delhi – 110 044, Phone: 011-49731800

www.**schandpublishing.com**; e-mail: **info@schandpublishing.com**

Marketing Offices:

Chennai : Ph: 23632120; chennai@schandpublishing.com
Guwahati : Ph: 2738811, 2735640; guwahati@schandpublishing.com
Hyderabad : Ph: 40186018; hyderabad@schandpublishing.com
Jalandhar : Ph: 4645630; jalandhar@schandpublishing.com
Kolkata : Ph: 23357458, 23353914; kolkata@schandpublishing.com
Lucknow : Ph: 4003633; lucknow@schandpublishing.com
Mumbai : Ph: 25000297; mumbai@schandpublishing.com
Patna : Ph: 2260011; patna@schandpublishing.com

First Edition 2005
Subsequent Editions and Reprints 2006, 2007, 2008, 2009, 2010, 2012, 2013
Seventh Revised Edition 2014
Reprint 2018, 2020, 2022

Reprint 2025

ISBN: 978-81-219-2487-0 **Product Code:** H8ECB60ECON10ENAG14O

PRINTED IN INDIA

By Vikas Publishing House Private Limited, Plot 20/4, Site-IV, Industrial Area Sahibabad, Ghaziabad – 201 010 and Published by S Chand And Company Limited, A-27, 2nd Floor, Mohan Co-operative Industrial Estate, New Delhi – 110 044.

PREFACE TO THE SEVENTH EDITION

It gives me great satisfaction to bring out the seventh edition of the book. I may reiterate that in this book I have not merely described the various aspects of business environment and Government's business-related policies but have also given the theoretical background and made analytical analysis of the issues. Accordingly, this work has made an in-depth and analytical analysis of the following aspects of business environment :

1. **Business Environment (External and Internal)** and Strategic Management.
2. **Corporate Governance and Corporate Social Responsibility.**
3. A Critical Analysis of **New Policy of Liberalisation, Privatisation and Globalisation.**
4. **Macroeconomic Environment** : Major Issues, Macroeconomic Theories and Policies, Problems of Business Cycles, Inflation and Economic Growth.
5. **International Business Environment.** Foreign Trade and Policy, Foreign Investment (FDI and Portfolio), BoP and Foreign Exchange Rate, IMF, World Bank, WTO, External Sector Reforms.
6. **Aspects of India's Business Environment:** Monetary and Fiscal Policies, New Industrial Policy, Industrial Sickness, Consumer Protection, Role of Public Sector, Financial Sector Reforms.
7. **Globalisation :** Its Advantages and Risks, Global Financial Crisis and its Impact.
8. **Growth Models and Economic Planning in India.**
9. **Environment, Climate Change and Sustainable Development.**

In the revision for the present seventh edition we have made the following changes :

(*a*) In Chapter 2, dealing with **Macroeconomic Environment,** latest data of India's unemployment, poverty, balance of payments (especially, widening of current account deficit) and exchange rate instability have been explained.

(*b*) **In Chapter 3, Highlights of the New Companies Bill, 2011 and Corporate Social Responsibility have been discussed under it.**

(*c*) Chapter 9 concerning Consumption Function has been extensively revised and **Keynes' Psychological Law of Consumption and Modigliani's Life Cycle Theory and Friedman's Permanent Consumption hypothesis have been discussed.**

(*d*) In Chapter 11, which explains investment demand, I have included **Tobin's Q Theory of Investment** according to which investment also depends on changes in stock market Indices.

(*e*) In Chapter 12, I have updated **Monetary Policy of Reserve Bank of India incorporating** the recent changes in it to control inflation and to prevent rapid depreciation of rupee.

(*f*) Important changes have been made in Chapter 20 that explains **IS-LM curve model** where with this model we have explained the **effectiveness of monetary and fiscal policies to raise the level of national income.**

(*g*) As a background to explain inflation, a new Chapter 22 concerning ***AD-AS model** with price flexibility* has been given where it has been shown how rightward shift in AD curve leads to demand-pull inflation and leftward shift in AS curve causes **stagflation.**

(*h*) Chapter 22A has been rewritten where it has been shown how persistent or continuous inflation occurs, both in demand-pull and cost-push inflation theories. Besides, in this, **social cost of inflation and its adverse effect on long-term economic growth** have been explained.

(*i*) Major changes in Part-VI dealing with *International Business Environment* have been made. In this regard, special mention may be made of **export diversification and**

changes in composition of exports and imports, and India's export performance including progress of Special Economic Zones (SEZ), volatility in exchange rate of rupee, especially sharp depreciation of rupee in June-August 2013, changes in foreign investment (both FDI and portfolio), widening of current account deficit of balance of payments in recent years and steps taken to reduce current account deficit and changes in foreign capital flows and their impact on macroeconomic stability.

Besides, advantages and risks of globalisation of the Indian economy have been explained. Failure of WTO Doha Round of negotiations and as a result India's effort to pursue **bilateral and regional trade cooperation** to promote its exports has also been discussed.

(*i*) In part-VII concerning **Important aspects of India's Business Environment** mention may be made of changes in India's fiscal policy and measures taken for fiscal consolidation, relationship between fiscal deficit, inflation and economic growth have been explained at length. Further, critical analysis of planning in India both in the pre-reform and post-reform periods has been made. Besides, **global financial crisis of 2008-09 and Eurozone crisis and their impact** on the Indian economy have been discussed at length in Chapter 43. Besides, Appendix to Chapter 42 regarding a **Critical Analysis of Twelfth Five Year Plan has been given.**

(*j*) Last but not the least a comprehensive Chapter on **Environment, Climate Change and Sustainable Development** has been revised in the light of new facts and developments.

With the above changes and additions, I hope the students of Business Environment will find this extensively revised edition highly useful and instructive. Suggestions for further improvement of the book from fellow teachers will be heartily welcomed.

The author can be approached on the address given below and also if they like through e-mail: drhlahuja@gmail.com.

Dr. H.L. AHUJA

69, Vaishali
Pitampura
Delhi – 110 088

PREFACE TO THE FIRST EDITION

In recent years a highly useful subject of '*Economic Environment of Business*' (or alternatively a wider subject of '*Business Environment*') has been introduced for classes of MBA, M.Com, MFC, MBE of Indian Universities and for PGDBM of IIMs and other Management Institutes. The courses of the subject of various Universities and Management Institutes vary a good deal. However, a prominent feature of these courses is integration of macroeconomic analysis of the economy with business environment of India. This approach to the subject will enable the future managers and executives of business firms to gain thorough understanding of the problems and policies of macroeconomic business environment in India.

Another important feature of the courses is the incorporation of *International Business Environment* whose understanding is essential in the context of rapid globalisation of the Indian economy. Therefore, an in-depth study of international business environment has been made in this book.

I have been teaching the subject in a number of prominent management institutes in Delhi for over a decade now. I thought it would be useful if I share my little knowledge of the subject with a larger audience of the student community in India. Hence, the publication of this book. Every possible effort has been made to explain the subject matter in a lucid and easily understandable style and language. This book has been divided into the following seven parts.

The Part I is concerned with the study of *concept and scope of business environment*. In this part the nature of various economic issues such as economic growth, inflation, employment and unemployment, balance of payments and foreign exchange rate has also been explained at length. Besides, the role of planning in India, growth models in Indian planning, structural adjustment economic reforms initiated in India since 1991 have been discussed at length in this part.

The Part II deals with the *analysis of determination of national income and employment* in the economy. The study of two sectors, three sectors and four sectors models of an economy has been made with a good number of solved numerical problems. It is worth noting that my approach is not merely to make analysis of macroeconomic environment of industrialised developed economies but also that of India's emerging economy. In the analysis of the working of investment multiplier, investment behaviour of business firms and consumption behaviour of households, determination of employmnt and rate of inflation, fiscal and monetary policies their relevance and limitations for India's macroeconomic environment have been highlighted.

In Part III of the book we explained the *causes of business cycles* in a free market economy and role of fiscal policy for achieving stabilisation. In this context the concepts of balanced budget multiplier and automatic stablisers have been analysed.

Part IV deals with the analysis of monetary sector where we explain the demand for and supply of money and monetary equilibrium. Besides, in this part we have critically examined the role of monetary policy for economic stabilisation and promotion of economic growth.

Part V is concerned with how *goods market and money markets are integrated through IS–LM Model* to explain the joint determination of national income and rate of interest. With *IS–LM* model we have explained at length how intervention by Government through fiscal and monetary policies affects business environment. Besides, the problem of trade- off between inflation and unemployment as described by Phillips curve concept has also been analysed in this part. Further, analysis of inflation with special reference to India has been made in this part.

Of greater significance is Part VI which deals with the critical analysis of *International Business Environment* which occupies quite a large space of the book. In this part theories of international trade, gains from trade, balance of payments, foreign exchange rate, foreign trade multiplier have been discussed at length. A special mention may be made of the inclusion of the study of *International Linkages and Mundell-Fleming Linkage Model* which explains capital flows in an open economy. India's foreign trade and Export-Import Policy and its impact on growth trends in India's exports and imports over a last decade have been dealt with at length.

Finally, some important aspects of India's business environment, namely, India's fiscal policy, fiscal deficit and fiscal consolidation, disinvestment of public sector enterprises, recent financial sector reforms and India's new industrial policy initiated since 1991 have been discussed in detail in Part VII.

It may be noted that we have confined ourselves to the *analysis of economic environemnt of business (including international business environment)*. Political-legal environment, socio-cultural environment, natural and demographic environment of business have not been discussed at length in this book. However, in the introductory chapter we have briefly explained them.

I am grateful to Mrs. Bimla Vohra, Reader in Economics, Kalindi College, University of Delhi for having contributed the following Chapters in this book :

1. Planning in India
2. India's Economic Reforms, Structural Adjustment and Economic Growth
3. Industrial Policy in India
4. Public Sector and Privatisation

Every effort has been made to make the book quite comprehensive so as to cover syllabi of various Indian Universities and Management Institutes. Suggestions from fellow teachers and students for further improvement of the book will be heartily welcomed.

69, Vaishali
Pitampura
Delhi – 110 088

H.L. AHUJA

CONTENTS

PART —1

BUSINESS ENVIRONMENT : AN INTRODUCTION

PART — III
BUSINESS CYCLES AND ECONOMIC STABILISATION

PART — IV
ANALYSIS OF MONETARY SECTOR

PART — I

BUSINESS ENVIRONMENT : AN INTRODUCTION

- Business Environment : Concept and Scope
- Macroeconomic Environment : Major Issues
- Planning in India
- Growth Models in Indian Planning
- India's Economic Reforms, Structural Adjustment and Economic Growth

Chapter 1
Business Environment : Concept and Scope

Introduction

A business organisation does not exist in a vaccum. It is in fact dependent on external environment. For efficient and rational decision making a business organisation must understand its relationship with its environment. A business firm is an *open* system as it affects and is affected by outside events and factors which make up the external environment. Apart from external forces a business firm is affected by a number of internal factors, that is, forces inside the business organisation. While top management is generally concerned with external evironment, middle level and lower level managements are more intimately concerned with internal environment. Thus, *business environment consists of all those external and internal factors that have a bearing on the business.*

A business organisation is a part of a large system such industry to which it belongs, the economy and the society. The relation of a business enterprise with its environment can be better understood

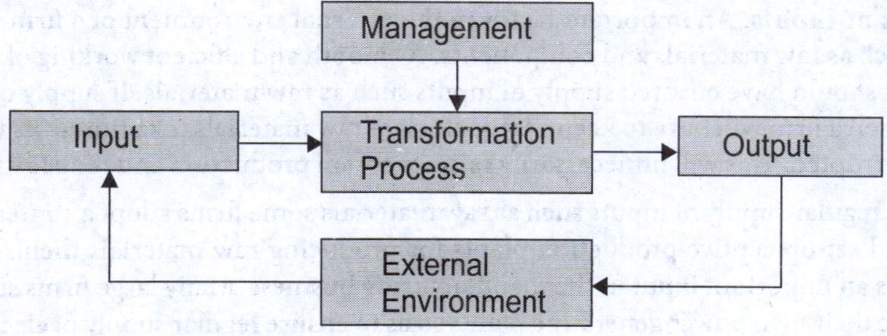

Fig. 1.1. *Business System : Input-Output Model*

from the input-output model of business system as shown in Figure 1.1. The task of the management of a business enterprise is to receive inputs from external environment, converts them into output which is then sold to the external environment. However, this simple model of business organisation needs to be further expanded into a model of operational management which shows how the transformation process is planned, organised and controlled by managers. This organisation and management of the transformation is affected both by internal and eternal environment, though the term business environment is sometimes used in the sense of external environment. In what follows we explain both the external and internal environment.

EXTERNAL ENVIRONMENT

External environment consists of those factors that affect a business enterprise from outside. External environment includes shareholders, competitors, customers, society, government laws and regulations, publics and technology. External environment is generally classified into micro environment and macro envrionment "*The micro environment consists of actors in the company's immediate environment that affects the performance of the company. these include the suppliers, marketing intermediaries, competitors, customers and the publics.*" [1]

1. Philip Kotler, *Marketing Management,* Prentice Hall of India, New Delhi, 1998, p. 127.

Thus, micro external environment includes all those players whose decisions and actions have a direct bearing on the activities of business firms. Since modern business firm has two aspects, namely, production and sale of goods, micro-environment of business can also be divided into two types of players. One, which affects the production of a firm such as input suppliers. Second, the factors which influence sales of the firm and include customers, competitors and market intermediaries.

On the other hand, macro external environment includes larger social forces such as economic, demographic, technological, political, natural and cultural factors. They affect all the actors in the company's micro environment.

We explain below micro and macro types of external environment of business.

External Micro Environment

Micro external forces have an important effect on business operations of a firm. However, all micro forces may not have the same effect on all firms in the industry. For example, suppliers, an important element of micro level environment, are often willing to provide the materials at relatively lower prices to big business firms. They do not have the same attitude towards relatively small business firms. Similarly, a competitive firm will start a price war if its rival firm in the industry is relatively small. If the rival firm is a big one which is a capable of retaliating any adverse action from its rival, a competitive firm will hesitate to start a price war. We explain below important factors or forces of micro-level external environment.

Suppliers of Inputs. An important factor in the external environment of a firm is the suppliers of its inputs such as raw materials and components. A smooth and efficient working of a business firm requires that it should have ensured supply of inputs such as raw materials. If supply of raw materials is uncertain, then a firm will have to keep a large stock of raw materials to continue its transformation process uninterrupted. This will unnecessarily raise its cost of production and reduce its profit margin.

To ensure regular supply of inputs such as raw materials some firms adopt a strategy of *backward integration* and set up captive production plants for producing raw materials themselves. Furtheir, energy input is an important input in the manufacturing business. Many large firms such as Reliance industries have their own power generating plants so as to ensure regular supply of electricity for their manufacturing business. However, small firms cannot adopt this strategy of vertical integration and have to depend on outside sources for supply of needed inputs.

Further, it is not a good strategy to depend on a single suuplier of inputs. If there is disruption in production of the supplier firm due to labour strike or lock-out, it will adversely affect the production work of a firm. Therefore, to reduce risk and uncertainty business firms prefer to keep multiple suppliers of inputs.

Customers. The people who buy and use a firm's product and services are an important part of external micro-environment. Since sales of a product or service is critical for a firm's survival and growth, it is necessary to keep the customers satisfied. To take care of customer's sensitivity is essential for the success of a business firm. A firm has different categories of customers. For example, a car manufacturing firm such as Maruti Udyog has individuals, companies, institutions, government as its customers. Maruti Udyog, therefore, has cater to the needs of all these types of customers by producing different varieties and models of cars.

Besides, a business firm has to compete with rival firms to attract customers and thereby increase the demand and market for its product. In the present day of intense competition a firm has to spend a lot on advertisements to promote the sales of its product by creating new customers and retaining the old ones. For this purpose, a business firm has also to launch new products or models. With increasing globalisation and liberalisation the customers' satisfaction is of paramount importance because the consumers have the option of buying imported products. Therefore, to survive and succeed a firm has to make continuous efforts to improve the quality of its products.

Marketing Intermediaries. In a firm's external environment marketing intermediaries play an essential role of selling and distributing its products to the final buyers. Marketing intermediaries include agents and merchants such as distribution firms, wholesalers, retailers. Marketing intermediaries are responsible for stocking and transporting goods from their production site to their destination, that is, ultimate buyers. There are marketing service agencies such as marketing research firms, consulting frims, advertising agencies which assist a business firms in targeting, promoting and selling its products to the right markets.

Thus, marketing is an important link between a business firm and its ultimate buyers. A dislocation of this link will adversely affect the fortune of a company. A few years ago chemists and druggists in India declared a collective boycott of a leading pharma company because it was providing a low retail margin. They succeeded in raising this margin. This shows that a business firm must take care of its intermediaries if it has to succeed in this age of intense competition.

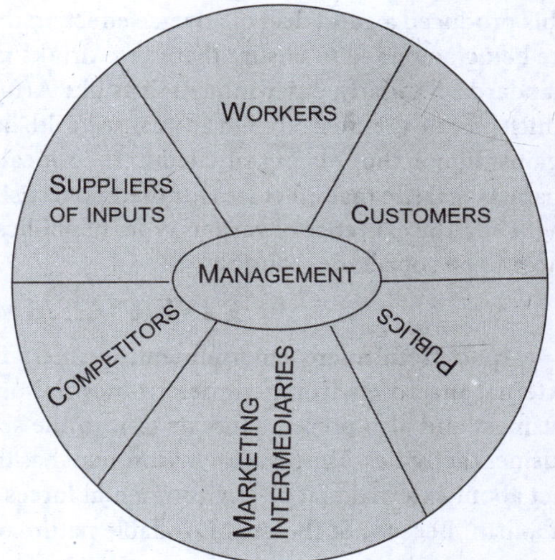

Figure 1.2. *External Micro Environment*

Competitors. Business firms compete with each other not only for sale of their products but also in other areas. Absolute monopolies in case of which competition is totally absent are found only in the sphere of what are called *public utilities* such as power distribution, telephone service, gas distribution in a city etc. More generally, market forms of monopolistic competition and differentiated oligopolies exist in the real world. In these market forms different firms in an industry compete with each other for sale of their products. This competition may be on the basis of pricing of their products. But more frequently there is *non-price competition* under which firms engage in competition through competitive advertising, sponsoring some events such as cricket matches for sale of different varieties and models of their products, each claiming the superior nature of its products. The readers will be witnessing how intense is the competition between Coca Cola and Pepsi Cola. Sometimes there has been price war between them to capture new markets or enlarge their market share. Likewise, there is severe competition between the manufacturers of Aerial and Surf washing powders, between manufacturers of various brands of colour TV. This type of competition is generally referred to as *brand competition as it relates to producing and selling different brands of a product.*

But not only is there a competition among the producers producing different varieties or brands of a product but also among firms producing quite diverse products as all products ultimately compete for attracting spending by the consumers of their disposable incomes. For example, competition for a firm producing TVs does not come only from other brands of TV manufacturers but also from manufacturers of air conditioners, refrigerators, cars, washing machines etc. All these goods compete for attracting disposable incomes of the final consumers. Competition among these diverse products is generally referred to as *desire competition* as all these goods fulfil the various desires of the consumers who have limited desposable incomes.

As a consequence of liberalisation and globalisation of the Indian economy since the adoption of economic reforms there has been a significant increase in competitive envrionment of business firms. Now, Indian firms have to compete not only with each other but also with the foreign firms whose products can be imported. For example, in the USA American firms faced a lot of competition from the Japanese firms producing electronic goods and automobiles. Similarly, the Indian firms are facing a lot of competition from Chinese products. It is important to note that for successful competition the Indian firms have to improve not only the quality of the products but also to enhance their productivity so that cost per unit can be reduced.

Publics. Finally, publics are an important force in external micro environment. Public, according to Philip Kotler "is any group that has an actual or potential interest in or impact on a company's ability to achieve its objective"[2]. Environmentalists, media groups, women associations, consumer protection groups, local groups, citizens associations are some important examples of publics which have an important bearing on environment of the firms. For example, a consumer protection firm in Delhi headed by Sunita Narain came out with an amazing fact that cold drinks such as Coca Cola, Pepsi Cola, Limca, Fanta had a higher contents of pesticides which posed threat to human health and life. This produced a good deal of adverse effect on the sale of these products in 2003-04. The Indian laws are being amended to ensure that these drinks must not contain pesticides beyond European safety standards. Similarly, environmentalists like Arundhi Roy have been compaigning against industries which pollute the environment and cause health hazards. Women in some villages of Haryana protested against liquor shops being situated in their localities. Many citizen groups are actively compaigning against cigarette manufactures for their advertising compaigns luring the people to indulge in smoking. Thus, the existence of various types of publics influence the working of business firms and compel them to be socially responsible.

EXTERNAL MACRO ENVIRONMENT

Apart from micro-environment, business firms face large external environmental forces. The external macro environment determines the opportunities for a firm to exploit for promoting its business and also presents threats to it in the sense that it can put restrictions on the expansion of business activities. The macro-environment has thus both positive and negative aspects. An important fact about external macro-environmental forces is that they are *uncontrollables* by the management of a firm. Because of the uncontrollable nature of macro forces a firm has to adjust or adapt itself to these external forces.

External macro-envrionemental factors are classified into (1) economic, (2) social, (3) technological, (4) political and legal, and (5) demographic. We explain below all these factors determining external macro-environment.

Economic Environment

Economic environment includes the type of economic system that exists in the economy, the nature and structure of the economy, the phase of the business cycle (for example, the conditions of boom or recession), the fiscal, monetary and financial policies of the Government, foreign trade and foreign investment policies of the government. These economic policies of the government present both the opportunities as well as the threats (i.e. restrictions) for the business firms.

The type of the economic system, that is, socialist, capitalist or mixed provides institutional framework within which business firm have to work. For example, before 1991, the Indian economic system was of the type of a mixed economy with pronounced orientation towards the public sector. Prior to 1991 private sector's role in India's mixed economy was greatly restricted. Many industries were reserved exclusively for investment and production by the public sector. Private sector operations were limited mainly to the consumer goods industries. Even in these goods the private sector production and operation was controlled by industrial licensing system, Monopolistic and Restrictive Trade Practices (MRTP) Commission. The private sector was also subjected to various export and import-restrictions. High tariffs were imposed to protect domestic industries and to pursue import substitution strategy of industrial growth.

---

2. Philip Kotler, *Marketing Management*, Prentice Hall of India, New Delhi, 1998.

Now, there has been significant changes in the economic policies since 1991 which have changed the macroeconomic environment for private sector firms. Far-reaching structural economic reforms were carried out by Dr. Manmohan singh during the period 1991-96 when he was the Finance Minister. Industrial licensing has been abolished and private sector can now invest and produce many industrial products without getting license from the government. Many industries, except only a few industries of strategic importance, which were earlier reserved for the public sector have been thrown open for the private sector. Import duties have been greatly reduced due to which domestic industries face competition from the imported products. Incentives have been given to boost exports. Rupee has been made convertible into foreign currencies on current account. It is thus evident that new economic reforms carried out since 1991 has significantly changed the business environment.

Social and Cultural Environment

Members of a society wields important influence over business firms. People these days do not accept the activities of business firms without question. Activities of business firms may harm the physical envrionment and impose heavy social costs. Besides, business practices may violate cultural ethos of a society. For example, advertisement by business firms may be nasty and hurt the ethical sentiments of the people.

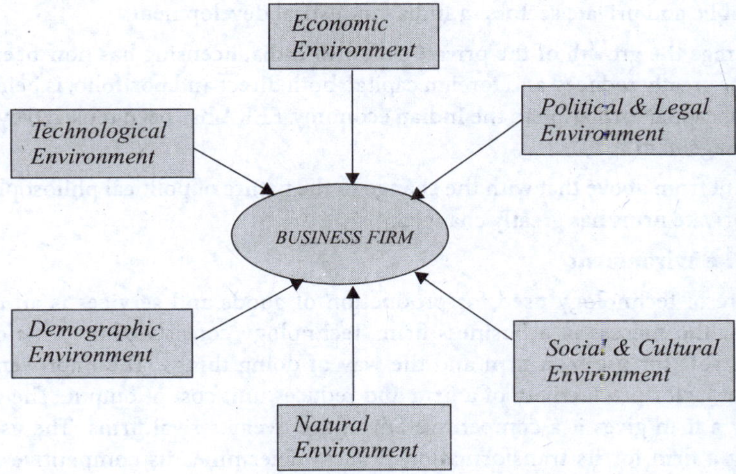

Fig. 1.3. *External Macro Environment*

Businesses should consider the social implications of their decisions. This means that companies must seriously consider the impact of its actions on the society. *When a business firm in their decision making take care of social interests, it is said to be socially responsible.* Social responsibility is the felt obligation or self-encforced duty of business firms to serve or protect social interests. By doing so they promote social well being. Good corporate governance should be judged not only by the productivity and profits earned by a business firm but also by its social-welfare promoting activities.

It is worth noting that in modern management science a new concept of *social responsiveness* has been developed. By social responsiveness we mean "the ability of a corporate firm to relate its operations and policies to social environment in way that are mutually beneficial to the company and society at large"[3]. It may be noted that social responsibility or social responsiveness is related to ethics. The discipline of ethics deals with what is good and bad, or right and wrong or with moral duty and obligation. Further, even if managers enjoy full freedom to adopt actions and policies in accordance with the conceived notion of social responsibility, they may not do so if standards

3. Keith Davis, and William Frederich, *Business Society* (New York, MacGraw Hill Company, 1984) p. 564.

applied to evaluate their performance are quite different. Every manager would like its performance to be positively appraised. Therefore, if the performance of managers of business firms are judged by the amount of profits they make for the owners of the firms, it is then not proper to expect socially responsible actions from them.

Political and Legal Environment

Businesses are closely related to the government. The political philosophy of the government wields a great influence over business policies. For example, after indpendence under the leadership of Jawahar Lal Nehru India adopted '*democratic socialism*' as its goal. In the economic sphere it implied that public sector was to play a vital role in India's economic development. Besides, it required that working of the private sector were to be controlled by a suitable industrial policy of the government. In this political framework proviate business firms worked under various types of regulatory policies which sought to influence the directions in which private business enterprises had to function. Thus, Industrial Regulation Act 1951, Industrial Policy Resolution 1956, Foreign Exchange Regulation Act (FERA), Monopolistic and Restrictive Practices (MRTP) Act were passed to control the business activities of the private sector. Besides, role of foreign direct investment was restricted to only few spheres. However, since 1991 several structural economic reforms have been undertaken following a change in political philosophy in favour of a free market economy. The collapse of socialism in Soviet Russia, China and East European Countries has brought about a change in political thinking about the roles of public and private sectors in India's industrial development.

To encourage the growth of the private sector in India, licensing has now been abolished, role of public sector greatly reduced and foreign capital, both direct and portfolio, is being encouraged to raise the rate of capital formation in the Indian economy. FERA has been replaced by FEMA (Foreign Exchange Management Act)

It is evident from above that with the change in the nature of political philosophy business environment for private firms has greatly changed.

Technological Environment

The nature of technology used for production of goods and services is an important factor responsible for the success of a business firm. Technology consists of the type of machines and processes avaitable for use by a firm and the way of doing things. The improvement in technology raises total factor productivity of a firm and reduces unit cost of output. The use of a superior technology by a firm gives it a competitive advantage over its rival firms. The use of a particular technology by a firm for its transformation process determines its competitive strength. In this age of globalisation the firms have to compete in the international markets for sales of their products. The firms which use outdated technologies cannot compete globally. Therefore, technological development plays a vital role in enhancing the competitive strength of business firms.

It has been generally observed that the competition between firms in the domestic economy and in international markets ensures that the firms will try to improve the technology they use because failure to do so would pose a threat to their survival. In the protected markets, technological improvements are slow and firms are able to survive for a long period without making technological changes. This is quite evident from the experience of automobile industry in India. Manufacturers of Ambassadors and Fiat Cars not only made no significant changes in their models, but also did not make any improvement in technology for decades because of absence of competition. The users had no choice and Ambassador and Fiat cars survived for decades in the protected environment. It is when Maruti Udyog Ltd. was started in India using superior technology and introducing more attractive models that there has been significant improvements in car manufacturing. With libersalisation of the Indian economy new car manufacturing firms have entered the industry and are producing different varities and models of cars with improved technology.

Besides, the cotton textile industry is an other important example of an industry which due to protection provided to it by imposing high tariffs on imports of cotton textiles became sick. Following trade liberalisation many cotton textile firms have closed down because they could not withstand competition. Technological environment affects the success of firms and the need for technological advancement cannot be ignored.

Demographic Environment

Demographic environment includes the size and growth of population, life expectancy of the people, rural-urban distribution of population, the technological skills and educational levels of labour force. All these demographic features have an important bearing on the functioning of business firms. Since new workers are recruited from outside the firm, demographic factors are considered as parts of external environment. The skills and ability of a firm's workers determine to a large extent how well the organisation can achieve its mission. The labour force in a country is always changing. This will cause changes in the work force of a firm. The business firms have to adjust to the requirements of their employees. They have also to adapt themselves to their child care services, labour welfare programmes etc.

The demographic environment affects both the supply and demand sides of business organisations. As mentioned above, firms obtain their working force from the outside labour force. The technical and education skills of the workers of a firm are determined mostly by human resources available in the economy which are a part of demographic environment. On the other hand, the size of population and its rural-urban distribution determine the demand for the products of industrial firms. For example, when there is good monsoon in India causing increase in incomes of rural population dependent on agriculture, demand for industrial products greatly increases.

In the wake of economic reforms initiated in the early nineties when foreign investors were allowed to make investment in India, they were prompted to invest in India by pointing out that the size of Indian market was quite large. They were told that 200 million Indian people could afford to buy the industrial products and this constituted quite a large market which could be profitably exploited.

Besides, the growth rate of population and age composition of population determine the demand pattern of goods. When the population of a country is growing at a high rate, its child population will be relatively large. This means demand for products such as baby food which cater to the needs of children will be relatively high. On the other hand, if population of a country is stable and life expectancy of the people is high, this will cause greater proportion of elderly aged people in the population of a country. This means different demand pattern of goods. Thus business firms have to consider all these demographic factors in their planning for production of goods and services and formulation of marketing strategies for sale of their products.

Demographic environment is also important for business firms as it determines the *choice of technology* by them. Other things being equal, if labour is abundant and relatively chapter than capital, business firms will prefer relatively labour-intensive techniques for production of goods. However, for various reasons such as rigid labour laws and low productivity of labour, various tax concessions on investment in capital equipment and machinery, business firms in India are generally seem to be using capital-intensive technologies imported from abroad. This has resulted in the increase in unemployment of labour, especially among the young workers. Therefore, social and government pressure is increasing on the business firms to create more employment opportunities for labour so as to render help in solving the problem of unemployment. It is quite interesting to note here that to take advantages of relatively cheap labour in India and China that foreign MNCs are setting up manufacturing plants in these countries.

It is evident from above that demographic factors play a crucial role in determining the productive activity of business firms.

Natural Environment

Natural environment is the ultimate source of many inputs such as raw materials, energy which business firms use in their productive activity. In fact, availability of natural resources in a region or country is a basic factor in determining business activity in it. Natural environment which includes geographical and ecological factors such as minerals and oil reserves, water and forest resources, weather and climatic conditions, port facilities are all highly significant for various business activities. For example, the availability of minerals such as iron, coal etc. in a region influence the location of certain industries in that region. Thus, the industries with high material contents tend to be located near the raw material sources. For example, steel producing industrial units are set up near coal mines to save cost of transporting coal to distant locations.

Besides, certain weather and climatic conditions also affect the location of certain business units. For example, in India the firms producing cotton textiles are mostly located in Bombay, Madras, West Bengal where weather and climatic conditions are conducive to the production of cotton textiles.

Natural environment also affects the demand for goods. For example, in regions where there is high temperature in summer there is a good deal of demand for dessert coolers, air conditioners, business firms set up industrial units producing these products. Similarly, weather and climatic conditions influence the demand pattern for clothing, building materials for housing etc. Furthermore, weather and climatic conditions require changes in design of products, the type of packaging and storage facilities.

It may however be noted that resource availability is not a sufficient condition for the growth of production and business activities. For instance, India through rich in natural resources remained poor and underdeveloped because available resources had not been put to use due to lack of adequate capabilities of Indian business class. Thus, it is not the availability of natural resources alone but also the technology and ability to being them into use that determines the growth of business and the economy.

Ecological Effects of Business

Until recently businesses had generally overlooked the serious ecological effects of its activities. Driven purely by the motive of maximising profits, they cause irreparable damage to the exhaustible natural resources, especially minerals and forests. By their careless attitude they caused pollution of environment, especially air and water which posed health hazards for the people. By creating external detrimental diseconomies they imposed heavy costs on the society. Thanks to the efforts by environmentalists and international organisations such as World Bank, the people and the governments have now became conscious of the *adverse effects of depletion of exhaustible natural resources and pollution of environment by business activity.* Accordingly, laws have been passed for conservation of natural resources and prevention of environment pollution. These laws have imposed additional responsibilities and costs for business firms. But it is socially desirable that these costs are borne by business firms if we want sustainable economic growth and also healthy environment for human beings.

INTERNAL ENVIRONMENT

Having discussed various external environmental factors we now turn to explain the factors which determine internal environment of a business firm. Some management experts confine the term business environment to external environment only. However, the recent view is to include both external and internal factors determining business environment. *Internal environment includes such factors as value system, mission and objectives of the firm, management structure, quality of its human resources, physical assets, technological development, financial position and capital structure of the firm.* It is worth noting that internal environmental factors are to a good extent *controllable* factors because the firm can change or modify these factors to improve its efficiency. However, the firm may not be able to change all the internal factors. We explain below some crucial internal environmental factors.

Value System. The value system of an organisation means the ethical beliefs that guides the organisation in achieving its mission and objective. The value system of a business organisation also determines its behaviour towards its employees, customers and society at large. The value system of the promoters of a business firm has an important bearing on the choice of business and the adoption of business policies and practices. Due to its value system a business firm may refuse to produce or distribute liquor for it may think morally wrong to promote the consumption of liquor. The value system of a business organisation makes an important contribution to its success and its prestige in the world of business. For instance, the value system of J.R.D. Tata, the founder of Tata group of industries, was its self-imposed moral obligation to adopt morally just and fair business policies and practices which promote the interests of consumers, employees, shareholders and society at large. This value system of J.R.D. Tata was voluntarily incorporated in the articles of association of TISCO, a premier Tata company.

Infosys Technologies which won the first national corporate governance award in 1999 attributes its success to its high value system which guides its corporate culture. To quote one of its report, "*our corporate culture is to achieve our objectives in environment of fairness, honesty, transparency and courtsy towards our customers, employees, vendors and society at large.*"

Thus value system of a business firm has an important bearing on its corporate culture and determines its behaviour towards its employees, shareholders and society as a whole.

Mission and Objectives. The objective of all firms is assumed to be maximisation of long-run profits. But mission is different from this narrow objective of profit maximisation. Mission is defined as the *overall purpose or reason for its existence* which guides and influences its business decision and economic activities. The choice of a business domain, direction of its development, choice of a business strategy and policies are all guided by the overall mission of the company. For example, "to become a world-class company and to achieve global dominance has been the mission of '*Reliance Industries of India*'. Similarly "*to become a research based international pharma company*" has been stated as mission of *Ranbaxy Laboritories* of India.

Organisation Structure. Organisation structure means such things as composition of board of directors, the number of independent directors, the extent of professional management and share -holding pattern. The nature of organisational structure has a significant influence over decision making process in an organisation. An efficient working of a business organisation requires that its organisation structure should be conducive to quick decision making. Delays in decision making can cost a good deal to a business firm.

The board of directors is the highest decision making body in a business organisation. It takes general policy decisions regarding direction of growth of business of the firm and supervises its overall functioning. Therefore, the managerial capability of the board of directors is of crucial importance for the functioning of a business firm and for achievement of its overall mission and objectives. For efficient and transparent working of the board of directors in India it has been suggested that the number of independent directors be increased.

Many private corporate firms in India are managed by family members of their promoters which is not conducive to the efficient working of these firms.

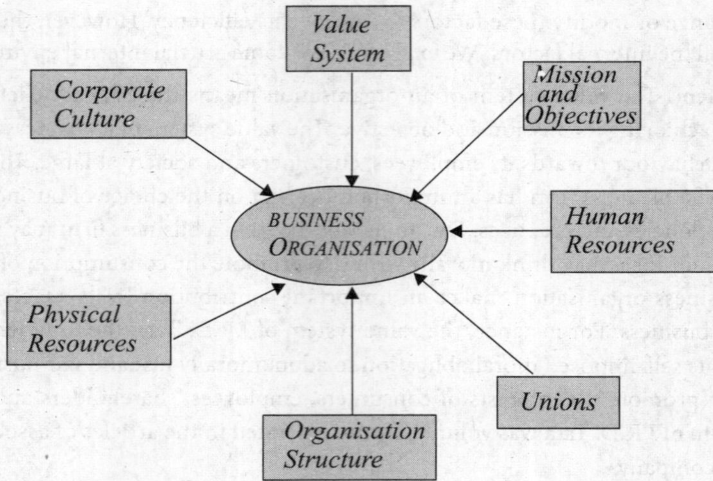

Fig. 1.4. *Internal Environment*

It is therefore highly desirable to increase the extent of professional management of private corporate companies. The share holding pattern has also an important implication for business management. In some Indian companies the majority of shares is held by the promotors of the company themselves. In some others share-holding pattern is quite diversified among the public. In India financial institutions such as UTI, LIC, GIC, IDBI, IFC etc. have large share holdings in prominent Indian corporate companies and the nominees of these financial institutions play a critical role in making major business policy decisions of these corporate companies.

Technically, share holders elect directors who make up the board of directors. The directors then appoint company's top managers who take various business decisions. However, most of the shareholders delegate the voting rights to the management or do not attend the general body meeting. Thus, most of the shareholders regard ownership of the company as a purely financial investment. However, in recent years in developed countries like the United States the shareholders have come to wield a great influence. The bankruptcy of business giants such as Enron, World Com. in the United States have created great awareness as well as mistrust among shareholders. In the last few years there has been frequent law suits filed by shareholders against directors and managers for ignoring the interests of shareholders or in fact cheating them by not declaring dividends[4]. That is why there is worldwide debate on proper corporate governance of business firms.

Corporate Culture and Style of Functioning of Top Management. Corporate culture and style of functioning of top managers is important factor for determining the internal environment of a company. Corporate culture is generally considered as either *closed and threatening* or open and participatory. In a closed and threatening type of corporate culture the business decisions are taken by top-level managers, while middle level and work-level managers have no say in business decision making. There is lack of trust and confidence in subordinate officials of the company and secrecy pervades throughout in the organisation. As a result, among lower level managers and workers there is no sense of belongingness to the company.

On the contrary, in an open and participatory culture, business decisions are taken at lower levels of management, and top management has a high degree of trust and confidence in the subordinates.

4. A study by '*Society for Capital Market Research and Development*' concludes that for the 6,330 BSE listed companies taken as a whole, the estimated proportion of companies which paid dividend in 2002-03 was 21.4%". With regard to capital appreciation, this study shows that "a vast majority of the Indian listed comapnies have destroyed shareholders value". Quoted by Dr. L.C. Gupta in 'Corporate Governance, Indian Style, *The Economic Times*, March 17, 2004.

Free communication between the top level management and lower-level managers is the rule in this open and participatory type of corporate culture. In this open and participatory system the participation of workers in managerial tasks is encouraged.

Closely related to corporate culture is the style of functioning of top management. Some top managers believe in just giving orders and want them to be strictly followed without holding consultations with lower level managers. This style of functioning is not conducive to the adaptability and flexibility in dealing with the changing external environment of business.

Quality of Human Resources. Quality of employees (*i.e.* human resources) of a firm is an important factor of internal environment of a firm. The success of a business organisation depends to a great extent on the skills, capabilities, attitudes and committment of its employees. Employees differ with regard to these characteristics. It is difficult for the top management to deal directly with all the employees of the business firm. Therefore, for efficient management of human resources, employees are divided into different groups. The manager may pay little attention to the technical details of the job done by a group and encourage group cooperation in the interests of a company.

Due to the importance of human resources for the success of a company these days there is a special course for managers how to select and manage efficienly human resources of a company.

Labour Unions. Labour unions are other factor determining internal environment of a firm. Unions collectively bargain with top managers regarding wages, working conditions of different categories of employees. Smooth working of a business organisation requires that there should be good relations between management and labour union. Each side must implement the terms of agreement reached. Sometimes, a business organisation requires restructuring and modernisation. In this regard, the terms and conditions reached with the labour union must be implemented in both letter and spirit if cooperation of workers is to be ensured for the reconstruction and modernisation of business.

Physical Resources and Technological Capabilities. Physical resources such as plant and equipment, and technological capabilities of a firm determine its competitive strength which is an important factor determining its efficiency and unit cost of production. R and D capabilities of a company determine its ability to introduce innovations which enhance productivity of workers.

It is however important to note that rapid technological progress, especially unprecedented growth of *information technology* in recent years has increased the relative importance of '*intellectual capital*' and human resources as compared to physical resources of a company. The growth of Bill Gates *Microsoft Company* and *Murthy's Infosys Technologies* is mostly due to the quality of human resources and intellectual capital than to any superior physical resources.

BUSINESS ENVIRONMENT, SOWT ANALYSIS AND MANAGEMENT STRATEGY

The nature of business environment facing a firm plays an important role in the formulation of management strategy and policy. *Management strategy is defined as the set of decisions and actions adopted to achieve the corporate objectives*. After carefully scanning and evaluating the environment a manager adopts a certain set of policies or a course of action which helps to achieve its mission and objective. From evaluation and scanning of external environment, the management can identify the *opportunities and threats* presented by the external environment and *strengths and weaknesses* of the firm as revealed by its internal environment. This analysis of *strengths* (*S*) *and opportunities* (*O*) on the one hand and *Weaknesses* (*W*) and *threats* (*T*) on the other of business environment is generally called ***SOWT analysis*** which has a great significance for formulation of optimal coruse of action to achieve the objective of business organisation.

The environment of a firm may present many opportunities for its growth but it may not be able to use it to its advantage due to internal weaknesses. Similarly, environment may pose threats to the survival of the firm. For example, competitors may adopt aggressive advertising campaigns or start a price war to drive it out of business. Thus, business environment presents both opportunities and threats for the firm. These opportunities and threats of business environment have to be *scanned and evaluated* in the light of the internal factors such physical resources, technology of production, managerial efficiency, its technological development, the quality of its human resources, marketing capabilities. The ability of a company to take advantage of the opportunities and to successfully meet the threats depends on the strength of these factors.

The economic reforms aimed at liberalisation and globalisation of the Indian economy have changed the business environment for the Indian firms. As a result, domestic competition has increased as well as the Indian firms face threats from the imported products. Some Indian firms have made adjustments in their product lines in response to the changed business environment. Due to the lack of competitive strength, some have been forced to exit the industries. On the other hand, some firms such as Reliance Industries, Infosys Technologies, Ranbaxy Laboratories, WIPRO have identified their opportunities thrown up by economic liberalisation for becoming global and have therefore set up their production and business units abroad.

It is interesting to note here that some Chinese firms saw opportunities for the sales of the various kinds of products and flooded the Indian markets with cheap Chinese industrial products. For sometime they posed a serious threat to the Indian business firms. But it is happy to note that Indian firms succeeded in meeting this challenge of Chinese products.

The story of Japanese products capturing the American markets makes an interesting reading. The success of Japanese products in the American markets is due to the right choice of products, better quality of products, lower prices due to efficient internal business environment of Japanese firms. In the context of grand success of Japanese products in the world markets, Kotler brings out quite vividly the significance of business environment. He writes "the Japense government and companies work hard to identify attractive global markets. They favour industries that require high skills, high labour intensity and only small quantities of natural resources : candidates include consumer electronics, cameras, watches, motor cycles and pharmaceuticals. They prefer product markets that are in a state of technological evolution. They like product markets where consumers around the world would be willing to buy the same product designs. They look for industries where the market leaders are complacent or under-financed"[5].

5. Philip Kotler, *Marketing Management,* Prentice Hall of India, New Delhi, 1998, p. 658.

APPENDIX TO CHAPTER 1

Business Environment and Strategic Management

Strategic Management : Meaning

In the analysis of business environment, it is important to explain the concept of strategic management. The analysis of strengths and weakness of the companies and opportunities and threats it is confronting plays a crucial role in determining *strategic management policy* or what is also called *strategic planning*. Strategic management needs to be distinguished from the general or routine management of the business firm. The *strategic management is concerned with the determination, given the business environment it confronts, of long-term goals and objectives and allocation of substantial amount of resources and the adoption of action plan to achieve these goals. Thus, according to William Glueck*, "strategic management is that set of decisions and actions which leads to the development of an effective strategy or strategies to help achieve corporate objectives"[1]. Elaborating the concept of strategic management Paine and Naumes write, "Strategic management involves the decision making and the activities in an organisation which (1) have wider ranifications, (2) have a long-term perspective, (3) use critical resources towards perceived opportunities and threats in a changing environment[2].

Strategic Management Process

From above it is evident that strategic management or strategic planning process requires :

1. Deciding about the *mission* and setting of *long-term objectives* of the business firm;
2. *Scanning and evaluation of environment* for determining and identifying opportunities for investment or trade and threats to be faced;
3. On the basis of environmental analysis (i.e., scanning and evaluating the business environment), setting of *specific objectives* of the enterprise and the formulation of strategies to accomplish the objectives or goals;
4. Implementation of the strategy designed and resource allocation accordingly;
5. In the light of experience reformulation of the firm's objectives or strategy if required.

We explain below these five processes of strategic management

Determination of Mission

The first task in the strategic management process is the determination of corporate mission, that is, what the management seeks to accomplish. In other words, what is the *purpose* of the organisation ? Should it maximise profits so that shareholders receive higher dividends and share prices of the company rise. Alternatively, should it stabilise the earnings of the company so as to promote employee's security. The present thinking among the top management of the corporate world is to *achieve maximum growth in earnings*. Besides, determination of mission of the organisation is also concerned with the decision about the *guiding principles* on which the management decisions will be

1. William F. Glueck, *Business Policy and Strategic Management*, McGraw-Hill International Book Company, Auckland, 1972, p. 19.
2. Frank T. Paine and William Naumes, *Organisational Strategy and Policy*, Dryden Press, Chicago, 1982. p.4.

based. Will the organisation adopt honourable or dishonourable behaviour or will it have considerate or ruthless or straight forward attitude in dealing with others. The decisions taken in this regard become a part of corporate culture of the organisation which determines its mission.

Strategic Management Process

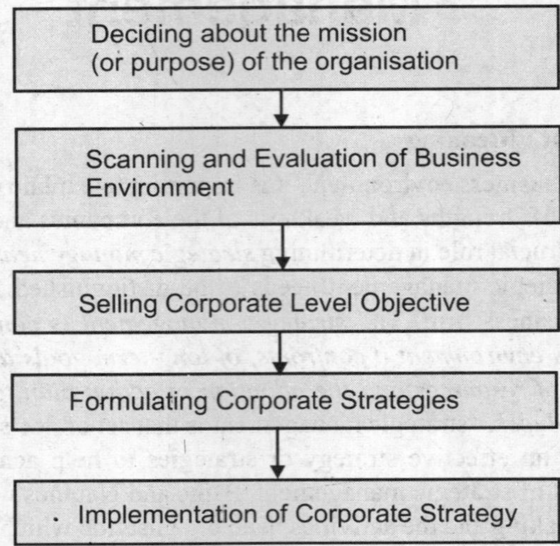

Scanning and Evaluation of Business Environment

The importance of environmental scanning for strategic management or corporate planning is now well recognised[3]. The existing and potential opportunities, threats and constraints for the operation of the corporation are left to be shaped by the external conditions of environment with which it has to live. Even in the present business environment in India characterised by liberalisation and privatisation, the Government attempts to influence the level of economic activity in the country so as to achieve *inclusive growth*, that is, growth with social justice. Therefore, a business firm for the purpose of expansion of its capacity or diversification of its product line, it has to scan and analyse the external conditions of environment for formulating its strategic planning. Thus Mondy, Sharplin and Premeaux write "Making strategic plan involves information flows from both the internal and external environment. From inside comes information about organisation's competencies, strengths and weaknesses. Scanning the external environment allows organisational stratagies to identify threats and opportunities as well as constraints. In brief, the job in the planning phase is to develop strategies that take advantage of the company's strengths and minimise its weakness in order to grasp opportunities and avoid threats"[4].

It has now been found in India that the following macroeconomic factors and policies have a significant effect for the formulation of strategies for management by corporate business firms.

1. Infrastructure spending by the Government on power, steel, ports, highways.
2. Level of fiscal deficit and Government borrowing which affect market rate of interest and availability of funds for the private sector.
3. The current rate of economic growth and its future forecasts.
4. Foreign trade situation and capital flows in the Indian economy.

3. See F.J. Agullar, *Scanning the Business Environment*, The MacMillan Co. The New York, 1967,
4. R. Wayne Mondy, Arthur Sharplin, Shane R. Premeaux, *Management : Concepts, Practices and Skills*. Needham Heights, Massachusetts, 5th edition, 1991, p. 174.

5. Monetary policy of RBI and fiscal, policy (i.e. policies regarding taxation and expenditure) the government.

But given the macroeconomic environment as mentioned above there are selected microeconomic factors which affect the various individual enterprises which need to be scanned and evaluated for strategic management.

Globalization and Strategic Management. Besides, in the context of globalisation the opportunities regarding trade with other countries and investment possibilities abroad by the Indian business firms and threats such as tariff protection and provision of subsidies by foreign countries to their domestic firms are the global factors that have to be scanned and evaluated by the business enterprises for formulation of their long-term strategies.

Setting Specific Objectives

In his path-breaking work "*Management by objectives*" in the 1950s, Peter Drucker explained that setting of objectives by an organisation improves the process of management. Peter Druck's idea of setting specific objectives is now generally accepted in the corporate world and is considered essential for effective corporate management. It is now recognised that corporate objectives should be challenging but achievable. This means that objectives should be neither easily attainable nor should they be beyond one's ability. Thus corporate objectives should be such that offer a reasonable opportunity for achievement.

Besides, the objectives set should be *specific and preferably quantifiable and measurable*. For example, the objective of '*maximising profits*' is of little help if it is not specified what exactly should be the profits. To make the profits of say 5 crore per year or increase profits by 5 per cent per annum over the previous year's level is the specific target or objective. Setting of specific objective will greatly help in achievening it.

Satisficing Vs. Maximising. It is worthwhile to mention here Herbert Simon's view of management objective. In an important study he suggests that corporate managers in general do not maximise profits. Instead, he believes the managers only *satisfice*. By *satisficing* he means the corporate managers accept the first 'satisfactory outcome' they are offered. For example, if 12 per cent return on investment is considered reasonable, then they are likely to accept any return on investment that exceeds 12 per cent as an objective. In fact, according to Simon, many corporate-level managers are more concerned with *setting the direction* rather than achieving specific objectives.

Choice of a Corporate Growth Strategy

After the scanning and evaluation of external environment opportunities and threats it is confronting and the internal organisational structure, strengths and weakness of the enterprise the next step in the strategic management is the choice of most appropriate strategy to achieve the objective. To do so the top management at the corporate level of an enterprise has to consider several alternatives from which it has to make a choice. Several alternatives confronting the corporate enterprise may be the following from which it has to make a choice.

(a) Should the firm or enterprise continue doing the same business or exit, given the business environment for it.

(b) In case of continuing in the same business it has to decide whether it should grow or expand further. If it decide to grow, should it grow by *expanding its existing business unit* or *setting up new business establishments* or by *taking over or acquiring other establishments in the same industry*.

(c) Growth by diversification. When corporate top management decides in favour of growth of the enterprise it can decide to grow through diversification of its product line. In case of diversification it has further to decide whether to diversify into related areas or the unrelated ones. In case of diversification related to the firm's current business, it will produce a variety of goods or services. This diversification of a company has the advantage that it reduces risk of the enterprise. In this case, as when some type of business declines, some other one may increase. Thus through diversification a company avoids putting all its eggs in one basket.

Growth through Integration. *A usual strategy of growth often chosen by corporate managers is of integration. Integration means bringing under unified control a number of successive or similar operations*. The combining different firms or companies is also a form of integration. Integration takes place when a company takes over a portion of industrial process that was previously done by another company. For example, when a publishing company takes over the printing work presently done by others, it is a form of *backward integration.* Similarly, the company may overtake the control of stores which sell or market its goods. Such an integration is called *forward integration.* For example, if Reliance or Tata Motors open own-sale stores or takes control of them it will be a sort of *forward integration.*

Note that integration can also occur when a corporate company acquires a firm overseas or abroad. This is a case of globalisation of a company.

Besides, there is a *horizontal integration* which occurs when a company acquires or takes over control of competitors *at the same level in the production and marketing process*. For example, if Maruti Company acquires or takes over Tata Motors, it will be an example of horizontal integration.

The strategy of integration has the following advantages.

1. Integration leads to the improvement in the marketing of products causing expansion in its sales.

2. Integration helps to take advantage of economies of scale which reduce cost of production of goods or services produced by a company.

3. Integration ensures superior control by the company over its economic environment

4. Integration when it takes place by taking over other firms producing similar products or services it leads to product differentiation which satisfies the wants of the buyers for variety.

Each kind of integration is a strategy for achievement of a different objective. If the aim is to reduce cost of using inputs, then a company can acquire companies that make profits by producing its inputs. This is the strategy of backward integration. If the objective is to increase its market share of a product, then strategy of horizontal integration may be adopted. Thus, to quote Mondy, Sharplin, and Premeaux, "Backward and forward integration are usually designed to accomplish both of two purposes; capturing additional profits and obtaining better control. Backward integration does this for the supply channels and forward integration does it for the distribution channels. Obviously, if either a supplier or an intermediate customer is making exorbitant profits a vertical integration may be justified on this basis alone. Vertical integration may also be justified when a company believes it can perform the functions of suppliers or intermediate customers effectively and efficiently.

Implementation of Strategy

Once the strategy has been determined it must be implemented. Implementation of strategy is a difficult task but a very important part of strategic management. A creative and well formulative strategy will not be of much use if it is wrongly implemented. Implementation of strategy requires changes in the various aspects of the organisation such as changes in leadership's ability, organisation structure, information and control system, production technology and human resources[6].

Leadership. The task of the leadership is to get work done by others. Top level management has to influence other members of the organisation such as lower level manages, supervisors and employees to adopt the behaviour and do work required for the implementation of strategy that

5. *Op.cit.* p. 181
6. See Jay, R. Galbraith and Robert Kazanjian, "*Strategy Implementation: Structure, System and Process*", 2nd edition, West Publishing, 1986.

has been determined. If leaders (i.e. top level managers) involve departmental managers in the formulation of strategy, it will be easier to get the strategy implemented. Leadership has to motivate employees to adopt such behaviour and attitudes that are required to implement the strategy.

Organisation Structure. Organisation structure consists of departmental manager's responsibility and degrees of authority over their subordinates or employees of the departments. It also involves the degree of centralisation and decentralisation of the decision-making in various tasks to be performed in the implementation of strategies. As a corporate company grows through diversification or integration it alters its organisation structure to meet the required needs of a big concern.

Technology. Technology consists of technical knowledge, tools and equipment to do the required production work as per the strategy determined. For instance, if strategy of producing a new product has been selected, then to implement this strategy the top management must assign and reallocate jobs according to the abilities and technical skills of various employees and make appropriate changes in the building and facilities so as to make the new product.

Human resources. The organisation's human resources are its employees who may be ordinary workers, skilled technical personnel, departmental managers. The new strategy may require fresh recruitment, selection and training the existing staff, transfer and promotion. It may require retrenchment of some employees which, given the labour protection legistation, is quite difficult. More important is training the existing staff for performing new tasks required by new strategy formulated.

We have explained above the various processes required for strategic management. An efficient and effective strategic management is of crucial importance for the working and growth of a corporate enterprise and to satisfy its shareholders

The importance of Strategic Management

There is growing realisation on the part of professional managers of the importance of strategic management to achieve higher growth and profitability of the business enterprise. It is also important to ensure job security to the employees and financial security to the investors of the company. For example, Infosys is a prime example of a well-managed company that has adopted strategic planning to achieve its mission and goals. It pays its workers well and provides them job security and gives them rewards and other incentives to perform well to achieve its objectives.

When as a result of strategic management the mission of the company and its objectives are clearly defined, employees and managers at lower levels of the organisation put forth maximum effort to attain the company's objective. Besides, with strategic management, the firm is most likely to succeed in responding to the changing business environment. Several research studies have found that the firms that adopt strategic management or planning show greater profitability.

However strategic planning and management is not without some drawbacks. The strategic planning creates a bureaucracy of "managers" at different levels of the organisation who are likely to lose touch with the various markets the enterprise is attempting to serve. Further, too much emphasis on formality in strategic management is likely to show down the decision-making process. Managers may try to make rational, risk-minimising decision, but their efforts may discourage introduction of innovations and exploration of lucrative business possibilities.

Chapter 2
Macroeconomic Environment : Major Issues

Introduction

Having discussed the nature and scope of business environment, we will now discuss the major macroeconomic issues which are considerd by business firms while taking business decisions. The important macroeconomic issues are the rate economic growth of the country, the magnitude of employment generation in the economy and the extent of unemployment prevailing in the economy, the rate of inflation in the economy, foreign exchange rate of the national currency and balance of payments situation of the country. All these macroeconomic issues have an important bearing on the business decision-making by the firms. The study of these issues in the context of Indian macroeconomic environment is made below :

ECONOMIC GROWTH

Meaning

Economic growth has been defined in two ways. In the first place, *economic growth is defined as increase in an economy's real national income or gross national product (*GNP*) over a period of time*. In other words, economic growth means rising trend of national product at constant prices. This definition has been criticized by some economists as inadequate and unsatisfactory. They argue that total national income may be increasing and yet the standard of living of the people may be falling. This can happen when the population is increasing at a faster rate than total national income. For instance, if national income is rising by 1.5 per year and population is increasing at 2% per year, the standard of living of the people will tend to fall. This is so because when population is increasing more rapidly than national income, per capita income will go on falling.

Therefore, the second and better way of defining economic growth is to do so in terms of per capita income. Thus, *economic growth means the annual increase in real per capita income of a country*. Professor Arthur Lewis writes that "*economic growth means the growth of output per head of population*". Since the main aim of economic growth is to raise the standard of living of the people, the second way of defining economic growth which runs in terms of per capita income is considered to be better. However, the concept of economic growth is generally used in both these senses, that is, in the sense, of increase In GNP or in per capita real income over a period. Economic growth of a country is a major measure of macro economic performance of a country.

Another point which is worth mentioning in regard to the definition of economic growth is that the increase in national income or increase in per capita income must be a '*sustained increase*' if it is to be called economic growth. By sustained increase in per capita income is meant the *upward or rising trend in per capita income over a long period of time*. A mere short-period rise in per capita income, such as that occurs within a business cycle, cannot be validly called economic growth.

Now, almost universally, rates of economic growth are measured both in terms of increase in overall Gross National Product (GNP) or Net National Product (NNP) and increase in per capita income. While Gross National Product (GNP) measures the value of total output of goods and services which an economy is capable of producing, per capita income measures how much of the total value of goods and services which an *average person* of the community will have for consumption and investment, that is, average level of living of a citizen of a country.

Thus, world organisations such as World Bank, and IMF have been employing both these measures of economic growth in their annual *World Development Reports* for comparing growth and levels of living of the developed and the developing countries. In India also our Planning Commission, Central Statistical Organization (CSO), and Reserve Bank of India have been measuring economic growth on the basis of both overall GNP or GDP or NNP and per capita income. The recent estimates of annual growth in GNP and per capita income are given in Table 3.1. This table reveals an interesting feature that economic growth achieved in recent years is higher in the developing countries than in the developed countries. However, it should be noted that in the past several decades the present-day developed countries recorded much higher growth rates than the developing countries which remained static for a long period. As a result, per capita income and levels of living of the people of the developed countries are now much higher as compared to those of the developing countries. The problem of the developing countries is to catch up with the developed countries through attaining rapid economic growth so as to enjoy higher levels of living.

Table 3.1. GNP Per Capita, Growth Rate and Population in Some Developed and Developing Countries

Country	Population (millions) 2009	GNP per Capita in 2009 (US Dollars)	Growth Rate of GNP		
			1980-90	1990-2000	2000-09
Developed Countries					
U.S.A.	307	46,360	3.0,	3.5	2.0
Australia	22	43,770	3.5	3.9	3.3
U.K.	62	41,378	3.2	3.7	2.0
Canada	34	41,980	3.4	3.1	2.0
Japan	128	38,080	4.1	1.3	1.1
Developing Countries					
India	1155	1,230	5.8	6.0	7.9
China	1331	3,650	10.2	10.6	10.9
Pakistan	170	1,000	6.3	3.8	5.2
Bangladesh	162	580	4.3	4.8	5.9
Sri Lanka	20	1,990	4.2	5.3	5.8

Source: World Bank, *World Development Indicators*, 2011

The World Bank and IMF have been estimating economic growth rates of the world as a whole (i.e. global growth rate) and the growth rates of the major economies of the world. In its latest '*Global Economic Prospects*' report published in June 2013, the World Bank said that India's gross domestic product (GDP) at factor cost is estimated to grow at 5.7% in fiscal year 2013-14 and then accelerate to 6.5% in 2014-15 and 6.7% in 2015-16. This World Bank report also cuts its outlook for global growth as well. For the fiscal year 2013-14 it estimated that the world economy will grow at 2.2 per cent. For this slower world growth rate it cited lower than expected growth in China, India and Brazil and a stubborn contraction in Europe as reasons for the slower growth.

According to the report, India's greater dependence on foreign investment inflows to finance its significantly larger current account deficit compared to the past has increased its vulunerability to a sudden reversal of investor sentiment. "Several factors could result in a slowing or reversal of investment inflows – an unanticipated monetary tightening in some high income countries; resurgence of debt tensions; escalation of geopolitical conflict; and even disenchantment with the pace or nature of domestic reforms" it said.

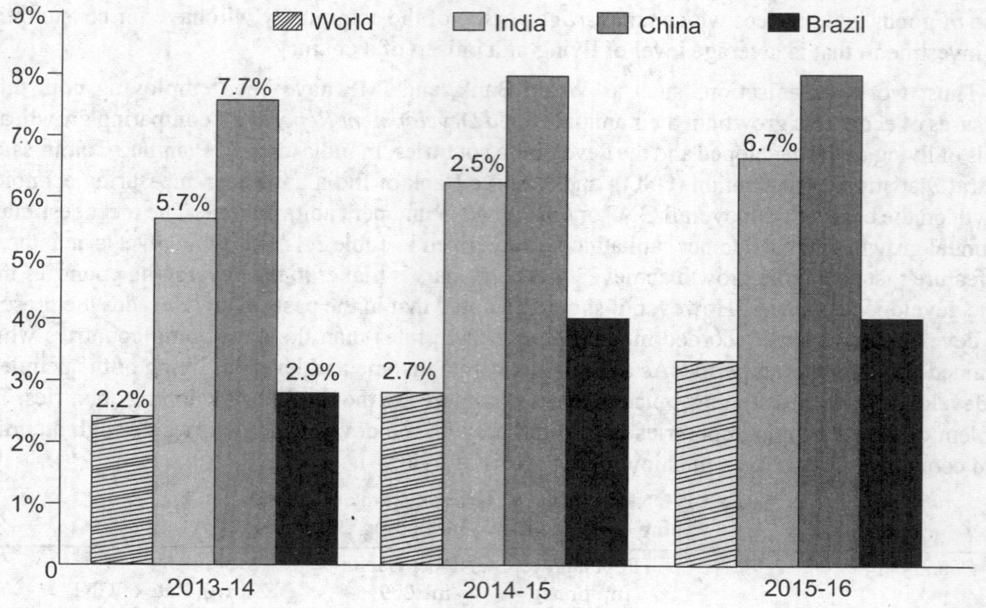

Fig. 2.1. *Real GDP Growth World Bank Estimates for 2013-14, 2014-15 and 2015-16 June, 2013 Estimates*

The World Bank, however; feels that the continued progress in implementing reforms that relieve supply-side constraints, such as reducing energy supply bottlenecks, labour market reforms, improving the business climate, and investing in education, health and infrastructure would be the key to growth.

Economic Growth and Economic Development

No distinction was drawn between economic growth and development in the beginning of the evolution of economics of development. However, since the seventies it has been thought necessary to distinguish between economic growth and economic development. There are two views even about the concept of economic development. The traditional view has been to interpret it in terms of changes in the structure of national product and the occupational pattern of labour force and the institutional and technological changes that bring about such changes or accompany such changes[1]. In this view share of agriculture in both national product and employment of labour force declines and that of industries and services increases. Various strategies of development which were suggested until 'seventies' generally focussed on rapid industrialisation so that *structural transformation* could be achieved. For this purpose appropriate institutional and technological changes were recommended to bring about such structural changes. Thus, C.P. Kindleberger writes, "*economic growth means more output and economic development implies both more output and changes in the technical and institutional arrangements by which it is produced.*"[2]

Thus, *according to this view, economic development implies growth plus structural change.* Structural changes refer to changes in technological and institutional factors which cause shift of labour from agriculture to modern manufacturing and services sectors and also generate self-sustaining growth of output. An aspect of structural change which is of special mention is that during the process of economic development there occurs a shift of working population from low productivity employment in agriculture to the modern industrial and services sectors having higher levels of productivity of labour. That is, during the process of economic development percentage share of

1. It may be noted that Kuznets in his study of "*Modern Economic Growth*" interpreted the process of modern economic growth which involves these structural changes.
2. C.P. Kindleberger, *Economic Development*.

working population in agriculture sharply falls whereas percentage shares of working population employed in modern industrial and services sectors substantially increase. Along with this change in sectoral distribution of labour force there occurs a change in sectoral composition of national income in which while percentage contribution of agriculture to national income declines, percentage contributions to national income of industrial and services sectors increase. This occurs due to the change in pattern of consumption of the people as economy grows and people's income increases as well as due to the changes in levels of productivity in the different sectors of the economy.

It is worth mentioning that in this view casual references were made to the role of some social factors such as growth of literacy, education and good health in economic development but they were considered to be of secondary importance. On the whole, in this view of economic development which generally prevailed till seventies, development was considered to be an economic phenomenon in which benefits from growth in overall GNP or per capita GNP and the structural changes accompanying it would trickle down to the poor and unemployed. No separate or special attention was paid to eliminate mass poverty and unemployment and to reduce inequalities in income distribution.

The Concept of Economic Development: The Modern View

The experience of the developing countries during the sixties and seventies showed that whereas target rates of economic growth were in fact achieved trickle-down effect of economic growth in the form of creation of more employment opportunities, rise in wages and improvement in income distribution did not operate. The problems of poverty, unemployment and income inequality further worsened instead of getting reduced during the process of growth in the Fifties and Sixties in the developing countries. For instance, in India Dandekar and Rath[3] found that 40 per cent of rural population in India lived below the poverty line in 1968-69. Using somewhat different approach, B.S. Mimhas[4] estimated that 37 per cent of rural population in India lived below the poverty line in 1967-68. Similarly, the magnitude of unemployment and the extent of income inequalities also increased in many other developing countries.

Thus, due to the failure of traditional strategies of development in solving the problems of poverty, unemployment and inequality, it was realised in the seventies that the concept of development should be broadened so that it should signify that well-being of the people has increased. This led to the view that economic development should not be judged on the basis of "*growth in GNP alone*". Therefore, when we regard the well-being of the masses as the ultimate objective of development, we have to see whether poverty and unemployment are decreasing and how the increases in gross national product or national income are being distributed among the population. Economic development will take place in true terms only if the poor people are raised above the poverty line. Late Prof. Sukhamoy Chakravarty rightly writes, "*The rate of growth strategy is by itself an inadequate device to deal with the problems of generating employment opportunities and for reducing economic disparities. Much depends on the composition of the growth process and how growth is financed and how benefits from growth process are distributed.*"[5]

It is worth mentioning that there is no guarantee that when there is increase in GNP, employment will also increase. It can happen that with the use of more capital-intensive technique while production may be increasing at a rapid rate, employment may be falling instead of rising. According to the modern perception of economic development, rapid increase in GNP secured through displacing labour by the use of capital-intensive technology and thus causing rise in unemployment and underemployment cannot be called true economic development. Professor Dudley Seers makes the meaning of economic development according to the new perception in the following words :

---

3. Dandekar and Rath, *Poverty in India*, 1971.
4. B.S. Minhas, Poverty, Land Redistribution and Development Strategy, *Indian Economic Review, 1971.*
5. Sukhamoy Chakravarty, Some Observations on Growth Process, *Seminar*, 1971.

"The question to ask about a country's development are therefore: What has been happening to poverty? What has been happening to unemployment? What has been happening to inequality? If all three of these have declined from high levels, then beyond doubt this has been a period of development for the country concerned. If one or two of these central problems have been growing worse, especially if all three have, it would be strange to call the result "development" even if per capita income doubled."[6]

Recently, the concept of economic development has been further widened so that it now involves not only reduction in poverty, inequality and unemployment but also requires *improvement in quality of life* which includes cleaner environment, better education, good health and nutrition. Thus World Development Report 1991, published by World Bank asserts: "*the challenge of development is to improve the quality of life. Especially in the World's poor countries, a better quality of life generally calls for higher incomes–but it involves much more. It encompasses as ends in themselves better education, higher standards of health and nutrition, less proverty, a cleaner environment, more equality of opportunity.*"[7] Thus the concept of economic development has been greatly broadened. Today, economic development is interpreted as not only in more growth in economic well-being but also in terms of good quality of life which, according to Prof. Amartya Sen, consists in *enlargement of opportunities for people and freedom of human choices*. This new concept of development includes achievement of freedom from servitude to ignorance and illiteracy. It also includes enjoyment of human rights. Thus United Nations '*Human Development Report*' of 1994 in the writing of which Prof. Amartya Sen made a significant contribution, asserts, "Human beings are born with certain potential capabilities. The purpose of development is to create an environment in which all people can expand their capabilities, and opportunities can be enlarged for both present and future generations..... .Wealth is important for human life. but to concentrate on it exclusively is wrong for two reasons. First, accumulating wealth is not necessary for the fulfillment of some important human choices .... Second, human choices extend far beyond economic well being". In his recent book, Amartya Sen writes "*Economic growth cannot be sensibly treated as an end in itself. Development has to be more concerned with enhancing the lifes we lead and the freedoms we enjoy.*"[8]

On the basis of various ingredients of good quality of life and other criteria such as enlargement of human choices and freedom a human *development index* is prepared by United Nations Development Programme (UNDP). This human development index is considered as a better indicator of economic development. We now explain below the concept of human development index and to show where India stands in the ranking in terms of this human development index.

Poverty and Economic Growth

Despite significant economic growth achieved during the last half a century, there still prevails widespread poverty in developing countries. The poor people suffer from under-nourishment, poor health, illiteracy. Freedom from underishment, freedom from illness and freedom from illiteracy are the essential requirements of economic development. *It is the building up capabilities of the poor to gain freedoms in these respects which Amartya Sen calls development.*[9] Now, an important question is whether faster economic growth will necessarily solve the problems of poverty and development. In the fifties and sixties of the last century it was widely held that benefits of economic growth would trickle down to the poor. This is generally referred to as '*trickle down theory*'. It was then maintained that if you take care of economic growth, poverty will take care of itself.

---

6. Dudley Seers, "The Meaning of Development" presented at the Eleventh World Conference of the Society for International Development, (New Delhi), 1969.
7. United Nations, *Measures for Economic Development of Under-developed Countries,* 1951.
8. See Amartya Sen, *Development as Freedom*, Oxford University Press, 2001, 175
9. See Amartya Sen, *Development as Freedom*, Alfred Knoph, New York 1999. p.43

But in the nineteen seventies there was a drastic change in the views of prominent development economists. They pointed that economic growth of GNP though necessary was not sufficient for eliminating poverty. This has been generally referred to as '*Dethronement of* GNP'. Therefore, to remove poverty measures for making '*direct attack on poverty*' were suggested. For this purpose development economists suggested special anti-poverty schemes such as starting of employment schemes, especially construction of rural public works and strengthening of public distribution system for providing to the poor the foodgrains and some other essential commodities at subsidised prices. However, in the late eighties and nineties some world bank economists with the officials of US Government at Washington again reverted to the old view that economic growth benefits poor substantially even if no special pro-poor measures are adopted[10]. This provided a rationale for what is popularly called **Washington Consensus** which envisaged fiscal and structural adjustment reforms to accelerate economic growth in developing countries, first imposed on the Latin American countries and then on the developing countries of Malaysia, Indonesia and India. In India there was an economic crisis in 1990-91 resulting from serious balance of payments problem and reduction of foreign exchange reserves to a very low level and flight of capital abroad. There was an urgent need for foreign aid from IMF and World Bank to tide over the crisis. But IMF and World Bank provided aid only if certain conditionalities were fulfilled. These conditionalities were nothing but implementation of fiscal and structural adjustment programme (SAP) as contained in Washington Consensus. These economic reforms of fiscal consolidation and structural adjustment involved reduction in fiscal deficit and carrying out the policies of economic liberalisation and privatisation. In 1991-94 most of these policies were implemented in India to accelerate economic growth and thereby to reduce poverty.

It may however be noted that the data collected by World Bank reveals that economic growth has led to the reduction in absolute poverty where it has been accompanied by *more equal distribution of assets*, especially land. Stressing this point Michael Bruno and Lyn Squire, two development economists of World Bank write."*Using the new data, we found that developing countries with a more equal distribution of assets—specifically land – grew more rapidly than countries with a less equal distribution of assets. Why is a more equal distribution of assets good for growth? One likely explanation involves credit. We know that investment is crucial for growth. The poor often cannot invest because they lack capital and they lack the collateral to borrow. In countries with a very unequal distribution of assets, many people find it difficult or impossible to invest, even in their own health or education.*"[11] They further write, "Economies in East Asia that had comparatively equal land distribution and aggressively pursued economic growth have achieved dramatic reductions in poverty. In Latin America, land distribution has generally been less equal, growth has been slower and less consistent, and poverty has remained stubbornly high".[11] To reduce absolute poverty and to accelerate progress in human development, economic growth is of course necessary but not enough. World Development Report 2004 by World Bank rightly stresses that broad improvements in human welfare will not occur unless poor people receive wider access to affordable, better quality services in health, education, water sanitation, and electricity. Without such improvements in services, freedom from illness and freedom from illiteracy — two of the most important ways poor people can escape poverty – will remain elusive to many.

---

10. Author of the various provisions of Washington Consensus John Williamson writes, "The evidence says pretty clearly that growth benefits the poor, even if nothing is consciously done to make it pro-poor growth. *Benefits do trickle down.*" in 'Washington Consensus and Beyond', *EPW*, April 12, 2003.
11. Michal Bruno and Lyn Squire, "Why Worry about Inequality," *The Economic Times*, Oct. 8, 1996.

As we shall see below poverty in India declined during the nineties but to attribute this decline in poverty to economic growth alone is not correct. In fact various special employment schemes, promotion of literacy, strengthening of public distribution system to provide foodgrains at subsidised prices and keeping inflation under control have also made important contribution to reduction in poverty. Besides, as we shall see below, to what extent poverty has declined is also a matter of great controversy because changes in methodology used for collecting household consumption expenditure data in NSS survey for 1999-2000.

TOTAL FACTOR PRODUCTIVITY AND ECONOMIC GROWTH

Growth in Gross Domestic Product (GDP) depends on supply of resources such as labour, capital, natural resources. Many economists use *production function approach* to explain the importance of various factors for determining growth rate. The following type of production function has been used to measure the contributions of different factors to economic growth.

$$Y = AF(L, K, N)$$

where Y = Gross domestic product (GDP)

A = Total factor productivity

L = The quantity of labour input

K = The size of capital stock

N = The quantity of natural resources.

In the studies of sources of growth, the natural resources are taken as constant and human capital is added as a separate factor for determining growth in Gross Domestic Product. With these changes then the production function becomes

$$Y = AF(L, K, H)$$

where H represents the quantity of human capital.

An important way to assess the contribution of a resource to the production of goods and services is its productivity. By *productivity we mean the ratio of output produced to the quantity of input used to produce it.* We can measure productivity of a single factor such as labour or capital. To measure the productivity of all inputs together the concept of *total factor productivity* (TFP) is employed. The total factor productivity means the ratio of output produced to the amount of *all inputs used.* Total factor productivity is index of overall productivity of the economy. In fact, *technical progress in the economy* is measured by the annual increase in total factor productivity.

Now, the economic growth depends on the increase in factor inputs and technological progress that is taking place in the economy. Improvement in technology makes factor inputs or resources more productive. If the quantity of resources is increasing and total factor productivity is rising, then output would grow faster than the increase in the quantity of resources. Therefore, rate of economic growth achieved will depend on the growth in resources (i.e. factor inputs such as labour, capital and the rate of increase in total factor productivity. Thus

Economic growth = growth rate of supply of resources + rate of increase in total factor productivity

Now, the amount by which output increases due to the increase in labour input depends on the contribution of labour to it. Similarly, the amount by which output increases due to accumulation of capital depends on the contribution of capital to it. Assuming no change in natural resources and

12. Robert Solow, "A Contribution to the Theory of Economic Growth" *Quarterly Journal of Economics*, vol. 70 Feb. 1956.

13. J.E. Meade, *A Neoclassical Theory of Economic Growth*. 1961

taking two factor production function, then the growth in real output resulting from the increases in labour and capital inputs can be obtained from multiplying the increases in labour and capital by their respective contributions to the production of output. Following the neoclassical economists such as Solow[12], and Meade[13] the economists generally use the shares in national income (GDP) of labour and capital to measure their contributions to output. From the recent production function studies conducted for the US economy it has been found that labour's share is about 70 per cent and capital's share is about 30 per cent of national income. We can obtain the growth in output, (i.e. GDP) by using the following growth equation.

$$\% \Delta \text{GDP} = \% \ \ \Delta \text{TFP} + 0.70 \ (\% \ \Delta L) + 0.30 \ (\% \ \Delta K)$$

where

GDP = Gross Domestic Product

ΔTFP = Change in total factor productivity

ΔL = Increase in the quantity of labour

ΔK = Increase in the capital stock

The above growth equation shows how growth in GDP depends on changes in total factor productivity (TFP) and changes in quantities of factors such as labour and capital. Recall that *change in total factor productivity measures technological progress* that is taking place in the economy. As explained earlier, technical progress, that is, changes in total factor productivity is a crucial factor in determining growth of output. For example, if total factor productivity is increasing at the rate of 2 per cent per annum, then even with capital stock and labour force being held constant, gross domestic product (GDP) will increase at the rate of 2 per cent per annum. If labour input increases by 2 per cent and capital stock increases by 3 per cent per annum each, then applying the above growth equation :

$$\begin{aligned} \% \Delta \text{GDP} &= 2 + 0.70 \ (2) + 0.30 \ (3) \\ &= 2 + 1.40 + 0.90 \ = 4.3 \end{aligned}$$

Thus, GDP will grow at the rate of 4.3 per cent per annum.

It is worth noting here that higher growth rate achieved by Japan in the past was not only due to rapid growth rate of capital stock but also because of relatively higher growth rate in total factor productivity (TFP), that is, technological progress. Further, from 1973 to mid nineties, lower growth rate in the United States has been due to slowdown in growth in total factor productivity. It may be further noted that differences in growth rates across countries can be explained in terms of differences in growth rates of capital stock and of total factor productivity.

ARE NATURAL RESOURCES A LIMIT TO GROWTH ?

World's population is larger today than it was a century ago. Increase in population has used more resources to expand production and to achieve a higher rate of economic growth. As a result of economic growth, living standards of the people have greatly increased. Now, the increase in production to meet the growing needs of population and to raise living standards of the people uses up natural resources. Now a pertinent question has been asked whether economic growth and living standards will continue rising in future or the depletion of non-renewable natural resources will limit it. About 50 years ago a group of economists called *Club of Rome* argued that non-renewable natural resources such as oil and minerals put a limit to how much economies of the world could grow. This is because exponential economic growth will eventually use up the fixed stock of these natural resources. When this stage occurs economic growth will come to halt and living standards may fall if population goes on increasing.

Though the above argument apparently seems to be plausible but in fact it is not true to assert that natural resources will limit economic growth. Two factors save us from this disaster of depletion of natural resources that results in halting the process of economic growth. First, technological progress helps us to produce more using fewer resources. Progress in technology enables us to improve the ways in which natural resources are used. Thus, modern cars have better petrol mileage than the cars of fifty years ago. Energy efficiency of room lighting and heating has greatly increased. Besides, recycling permits some non-renewable resources to be used again.

Second, as shortage of some specific natural resources was felt, their prices rose which led to the discovery and use of their substitutes. For example, some fifty years ago, it was feared that due to excessive use of tin and copper, their natural stocks would soon be depleted posing great problems. These were than essential commodities Tin was used to make various types of food containers and copper was used to make telephone wires. Today, plastic has replaced tin for making food containers and telephones now use fiber-optic cables which are made from sand. Ethanol is being used as substitute for gasoline. It follows from above that technological progress and growing ability to find synthetic substitutes for natural products show that there is no reason to believe that natural resources are a limit to economic growth.

ASIAN TIGERS AND ECONOMIC GROWTH

In recent years (between mid-sixties to the end of eighties, that is, during 1966-1990), the rate of economic growth in the four Asian countries, namely, Hong Kong, Singapore, South Korea and Taiwan has been so remarkable that they are popularly known as Asian Tigers. It will be seen from Table 2.2 that growth rate in GDP per capita in these countries has been within the range of 5.7 to 6.8 per cent per annum1[14]. It has been mentioned with pride by some leaders of these four Asian countries that they have learned a 'special trick' to grow more rapidly that is worthy of emulation by the other poor developing countries.

Table 2.2: Economic Growth in Asian Tigers (Per cent per annum)

	Hong Kong (1966-1991)	Singapore (1966-1990)	South Korea (1966-1990)	Taiwan (1966-1990)
Growth in GDP Per Capita	5.7	6.8	6.8	6.7
Change in Labour Force Participation (%)	38 → 49	27 → 51	27 → 36	28 → 37
Change in Secondary Education or Higher (%)	27.2 → 71.4	15.8 → 66.3	26.5 → 75.0	25.8 → 67.6
TFP growth (%)	2.3	0.2	1.7	2.6

Source : Alwyn Young, The Tyranny of Numbers: Confronting the Statistical Realities of the East Asian Growth Experience, *Quarterly Journal of Economics*, August 1995.

However, some economists, especially Alwyn Young have found that there are no 'special tricks' used by these countries to achieve remarkably high rates of growth in per capita income. Instead, they have relied on well-known factors determining growth, namely, using more labour input, saving and investing more, and expanding education of work force and thereby building more human capital. An important fact about determinants of growth which is noteworthy is that that growth in total factor productivity (TFP) (by which technical progress is generally measured) has been high but not remarkably high. We give data about these variables of growth of these so called Asian Tigers in Table 2.2. It will be seen that all these four countries have remarkably high growth rates in GDP per capita but their growth is explained by increased inputs (that is, by use of more labour input, more human capital, i.e. increase in education and correspondingly more physical capital) and not by much higher increase in total factor productivity (TFP). It may be noted that change in total factor productivity measures the change in output per unit increase in inputs and represents technological

14. In contrast, it may be noted that annual *growth rate of per capita income in India* during this period (1965–90) was only about 2 to 2.5 per cent.

progress. Although the change in total factor productivity in these countries (except Singapore) is high but not remarkably high and therefore cannot explain remarkably high growth rate in per capita GDP achieved by them. Total factor productivity growth rate in Singapore is very small but still its growth in per capita GDP has been very high (6.8 per cent per annum).

It will be seen from Table 2.2 that in all these four countries there has been a very large increase labour force participation rate indicating use of more labour input in the production of goods and services. It is noteworthy that much of this increase in labour force participation rate has been due to more women joining the labour force. Each of these countries substantially increased its human capital. In fact education level of these countries reached close to those of rich industrialised countries.

Another important feature of these East Easian countries is that they have pursued *outward-looking economic strategy* (*i.e.* promoting exports to generate growth) and followed *laissez-faire* free market policies with emphasis on competition as driving force of growth with the exception of Singapore where Government played a significant role in regulating and controlling private enterprise and direction of investment. Moreover, Singapore relied on foreign direct investment to bring in new technologies.

To sum up, in the history of economic development these four Asian Tigers have achieved extraordinary high growth rates, and that too with the well-known way through using more labour input, more investment in capital, both physical and human, and fostering competition. It is reassuring to note that these former poor countries will soon catch up with the developed industrialised countries in per capita income level. Singapore has already achieved per capita income level of the rich industrialised nations of the world. It is important to note that *since 1991, China and India too have registered a higher growth rate and have become the two fastest growing economies of the world.* India achieved 6.2 per cent growth in GDP during 1992-2006 and further its annual growth rate during three year period, 2004-2007 rose to over 9 per cent per annum. In 2009-10 and 2010-11, India's growth of GDP has been 8% and 8.6% respectively. In fact India is now the second fastest growing country of the world, next only to China.

INFLATION

Another important factor which determines macroeconomic environment is the rate of inflation in the economy. Whereas economic growth is a major yardstick of macroeconomic performance of a country, low rate of inflation is generally regarded as the indicator of macroeconomic stability. By inflation we mean *a general rise in prices*. To be more correct, inflation is a *persistent rise in general price level* rather than a once-for-all rise in it. Rate of inflation is either measured by the the percentage change in wholesale price index number (WPI) over a period or by percentage change in consumer price index number (CPI). Opinion surveys conducted in India and the United States reveal that inflation is the most important concern of the people as it affects their standard of living adversely A high rate of inflation erodes the real incomes of the people. A high rate of inflation makes the life of the poor people miserable. It is therefore described as *anti-poor*. Inflation redistributes income and wealth in favour of the rich. Thus, it makes the rich richer and the poor poorer. Above all, a high rate inflation adversely effects output and encourages investment in unproductive channels such as purchase of gold, silver, jewellery and real estate. Therefore, it adversely affects long-run economic growth, especially in developing countries like India. Inflation has therefore been described '*as enemy number one*'.

Measurement of Rate of Inflation

Inflation has been one of the important problems facing the economies of the world. Precisely stated, inflation is the rate of change of general price level during a period of time. And the general price level in a period is the result of inflation in the past. Through rate of inflation economists measures the *cost of living* in an economy. Let us explain how rate of inflation is measured. Suppose P_{t-1} represents the price level on 31st March 2006 and P_t represents the price level on 31st March

2007. Then the rate of inflation in year 2006-07 will be equal to

$$\pi = \frac{P_t - P_{t-1}}{P_{t-1}}$$

where *P* represents rate of inflation. Suppose Consumer Price Index (CPI) on March 31, 2006 which was 250, it rose to 275 on March 31, 2007, rate of inflation in 2006-07 will be

$$\pi = \frac{275-250}{250} \times 100 = \frac{25}{250} \times 100 = 10\%$$

Thus, rate of inflation during 2006-07 will be 10 per cent. This is called *point-to-point inflation rate*. There are 52 weeks in a year, average of price indexes of 52 weeks of a year (say 2005-06) can be calculated to compare the average of price indexes of 52 weeks of year 2006-07 and find the inflation rate on the basis of average weekly price levels of a year. In both these ways rate of inflation in different years is measured and compared.

It is evident from above that price level in a period is measured by a price index. There are several commodities in an economy which are produced and consumed by the people. It is through construction of a weighted price index that economists aggregate money prices of several commodities which are assigned different weights.

In India the wholesale price Index (WPI) of all commodities with base year 1993-94 price level at the end of fiscal year is used to measure rate of inflation and is widely reported in the media. Since the wholesale price index does not truly indicate the cost of living, separate Consumer Price Index (CPI) for agricultural labourers and Consumer Price Index (CPI) for industrial workers (with base 1982 = 100) at the end of fiscal year are constructed to measure rate of inflation. In constructing the Consumer Price Index (CPI) the price of a *basket* of goods which a typical consumer, industrial worker or agricultural labourer as the case may be are taken into account. We will explain the nature and causes of inflation in detail in a separate chapter. Here we shall explain them briefly.

What Causes Inflation ?

Classical economists thought that it was the quantity of money in the economy that determined the general price level in the economy. According to them, rate of inflation depends on the growth of money supply in the economy. Keynes criticised the '*Quantity Theory of Money*' and showed that expansion in money supply did not always lead to inflation or rise in price level. Keynes who before the Second World War explained that involuntary unemployment and depression were due to the deficiency of aggregate demand, during the war period when price rose very high he explained that inflation was due to excessive aggregate demand. Thus, Keynes put forward what is now called *demand-pull theory of inflation.*

Demand - Pull Inflation : Keynes's View. Thus, according to Keynes, *inflation is caused by a situation whereby the pressure of aggregate demand for goods and services exceeds the available supply of output (both beging counted at the prices ruling at the beginning of a period)*. In such a situation, rise in price level is the natural consequence. Now, this imbalance between aggregate demand and supply may be the result of more than one force at work. As we know aggregate demand is the sum of consumers' spending on consumer goods and services, government spending on consumer goods and services and net investment being planned by the entrepreneurs.

But excess of aggregate demand over aggregate supply does not explain *persistent rise in prices*, year after year. An important factor which feeds inflation is *wage-price spiral*. Wage-price spiral operates as follows : A rise in prices reduces the real consumption of the wage earners. They will, therefore, press for higher money wages to compensate them for the higher cost of living. Now, an increase in wages, if granted, will raise the prime cost of production and, therefore, entrepreneurs will raise the prices of their products to recover the increment in cost. This will add fuel to the inflationary fire. A further rise in prices raises the cost of living still further and the workers ask for still higher wages. In this way, wages and prices chase each other and the process of inflationary rise in prices gathers momentum. If unchecked, this may lead to *hyper-infaltion* which signifies a state of affairs where wages and prices chase each other at a very quick speed.

Cause of Inflation : Monetarist View. We have explained above the Keynesian explanation of demand-pull inflation. It is important to note that both the original quantity theorists and the modern monetarists, prominent among whom is Milton Friedman, explain inflation in terms of excess demand for goods and services. But there is an important difference between the monetarist view of demand-pull inflation and the Keynesian view of it. Keynes explained inflation as arising out of real sector forces. In his model of inflation excess demand comes into being as a result of *autonomous* increase in expenditure on investment and consumption or increase in government expenditure. That is, the increase in aggregate expenditure or demand occurs independent of any increase in the supply of money. On the other hand, monetarists explain the emergence of excess demand and the resultant rise in prices on account of the increase in money supply in the economy. To quote Milton Friedman, a Nobel Laureate in economics. "*Inflation is always and everywhere a monetary phenomenon..... and can be produced only by a more rapid increase in the quantity of money than in output.*"[15]

Friedman holds that when money supply is increased in the economy, then there emerges an excess supply of real money balances with the public over their demand for money. This distrubs the monetary equilibrium. In order to restore the equilibrium the public will reduce the money balances by increasing expenditure on goods and services. Thus, according to Friedman and other modern quantity theorists, the excess supply of real monetary balances results in the increase in aggregate demand for goods and services. If there is no proportionate increase in output, then extra money supply leads to excess demand for goods and services. This causes inflation or rise in prices. Thus, according to monetarists let by Prof. Milton Friedman, excess creation of money supply is the main factor responsible for inflation.

Cost-Push Inflation. Even when there is no increase in aggregate demand, prices may still rise. This may happen if the costs, particularly the wage costs, increase. Now, as the level of employment increases, the demand for workers rises progressively so that the bargaining position of the workers is enhanced. To exploit this situation, they may ask for an increase in wage rates which are not justifiable either on grounds of a prior rise in productivity or cost of living. The employers in a situation of high demand and employment are more agreegable to concede to these wage claims because they hope to pass on these rises in costs to the consumers in the form of rise in prices. Therefore, when inflation is caused by rise in wages or hike in other input costs such as rise in prices of raw materials, rise in prices of petroleum products, it is called *cost-push inflation.* If this happens we have another inflationary factor at work.

Besides the increase in wages of labour without any increase in its productivity, or rise in costs of other inputs there is another factor responsible for cost-push inflation. This is the increase in the *profit margins* by the firms working under monopolistic or oligopolistic conditions and as a result charging higher prices from the consumers. In the former case when the cause of cost-push inflation is the rise in wages it is called *wage-push inflation* and in the latter case when the cause of cost-push inflation is the rise in profit margins, it is called *profit-push inflation.*

In addition to the rise in wage rate of labour and increase in profit margin, in the seventies the other cost-push factors (also called *supply shocks*) causing increase in marginal cost of production became more prominent in bringing about rise in prices. During the seventies, rise in prices of raw materials, especially energy inputs such a hike in crude oil prices made by OPEC resulted in rise in prices of petroleum products. For example, sharp rise in world oil prices during 1973-75 and again in 1979-80 produced significant cost-push factor which caused infaltion not only in Indian but all over the world. Now, in June-August 2004 again the world oil prices have greatly risen. As a result, in India prices of petrol, diesel, cooking gas were raised by petroleum companies. This is tending to raise the rate of inflation.

15. Milton Friedman, The Role of Monetary Policy, *American Economic Review*, 1968

EMPLOYMENT AND UNEMPLOYMENT

Another important macroeconomic issue is what determines the level of employment in the economy and what causes involuntary unemployment. *Involuntary unemployment is defined as the situation when in the country there are a large number of workers who are willing to work at the current wage rates but are unable to get employment.* In times of depression, the level of employment declines very low with the result that a large number of persons become involuntarily unemployed

Say's Law and Employment

Classical economists were of the view that there was always full employment in a free-market economy. According to them, if there are lapses from the full employment level, then some forces would work automatically to restore full employment. Their view was based upon their faith in *Say's Law of Markets*. According to Say's law, there is always enough expenditure or aggregate demand to purchase the total output produced with full-employment of resources. In other words, in their theory, the classical economists neglected the problem of deficiency of demand for purchasing goods produced at full-employment level of resources. Even when deficiency of aggregate demand arises, according to them, prices and wages would change in such a way that real production, employment and income will not decline.

J.B. Say was the famous French economist of the 19th century. Say's Law is based on the fact that every production of goods also creates incomes for the factors of production equal to the value of goods produced by them. Incomes earned by the factors are spent on purchasing goods produced. In other words, production of goods creates purchasing power for itself. Therefore, Say's law is expressed as "*supply creates its own demand*", that is, the supply of goods produced creates demand for it equal to its own value. As a result, the problem of general overproduction and unemployment of resources do not arise. In this way, in Say's law, the possibility of lack of aggregate demand had been ignored.

We thus see that according to Say's law, aggregate demand for goods will always be adequate so as to ensure that all resources are fully employed. The factors which participate in productive activity and earn incomes from it, spend a good part of their incomes on consumer goods and save some part of them. But, according to classical economists, savings by the individuals are automatically spent on investment or capital goods. Therefore, since saving becomes another form of expenditure (that is, investment expenditure), in classical theory the whole income is spent, partly on consumption and partly on investment. There is thus no reason for any leakage in the income stream and therefore supply creates its own demand.

According to classical theory, it is the rate of interest which makes investment equal to saving. When savings of the people increase, rate of interest declines. As a result of fall in the rate of interest, demand for investment increases and in this way investment expenditure becomes equal to the increased savings. Hence, according to classical economists, it is changes in the interest rate that bring about equality between saving and investment and therefore Say's law applies in spite of savings by the people. This guarantees full employment of resources in the economy. In other words, it is changes in the rate of interest due to which the withdrawal of some money from the income stream as a result of savings automatically comes back to it in the form of investment expenditure and therefore income flow continues unchanged and supply goes on creating its own demand.

Flexibility in Prices and Wages and Full Employment : The View of Classical Economists

Classical economists also proved the validity of the assumption of full employment with another reasoning. According them, especially the then living British Classical economist, A.C. Pigou, if changes in rate of interest somehow fail to bring about equality between savings and investment and as a result deficiency of aggregate demand or expenditure arises, even then the problem of overproduction and involuntary unemployment will not arise. This is because they thought that the deficiency in aggregate demand would be made up by changes in the price level. When, due to the increase in savings by the people, the expenditure of the people declines, it will affect the prices of products. As a result of fall in aggregate expenditure or demand, prices of products would decline and at reduced prices their quantity demanded will increase. As a result, all the quantity produced of goods will be sold out at lower prices.

Thus, Classical economists thought that a free-market capitalist economy works in a self-correcting manner and when aggregate expenditure on goods or aggregate demand for them declines, then various sellers and producers will reduce prices of their products so as to avoid the excessive accumulation of stocks of goods with them. Hence, according to them, when aggregate demand declines due to investment expenditure falling short of saving the prices of products will decline, the level of production and employment remaining unaffected. Further, to make their business profitable producers will have to reduce the prices of the factors of production such as labour. With a fall in wages of labour, all labourers who are willing to work at the new prevailing wages will get employment and all those who want to work at the lower wages will get employment.

If some workers do not want to work at lower wages, they will not get any job or employment and therefore will remain unemployed. But, according to Classical economists, those workers who do not want to work at lower wages and thus remain unemployed are only *voluntarily unemployed.* This voluntary unemployment is not real unemployment. According to the classical thought, it is *involuntary unemployment* which is not possible in a free-market capitalist economy. All those labourers who want to work at the prevailing wage rate determined by market forces will get employment.

During the period 1929-33 when there was a great depression in capitalist economies, eminent classical economist A.C. Pigou suggested a cut in wage rates in order to remove huge and widespread unemployment prevailing at that time. According to him, the cause of depression and unemployment was that the Government and trade unions of workers were preventing the free working of the capitalist economy and were artificially keeping the wage rates at high levels. He expressed the view that if wage rates were cut down, the demand for labour would increase so that all would get employment. It was at this time that J.M. Keynes challenged the classical theory and put forward a new theory of income and employment. *He brought about a basic change in economic thought regarding the determination of income and employment. Therefore, it is often said that Keynes brought about a revolution in economic theory.* Keynes made a genuine break and a basic departure from the Classical economics. His macro-economic theory is therefore called *Keynesian Revolution* or *New Economics.*

Keynes on Employment and Unemployment

Towards the close of the nineteen twenties and early nineteen thirties (1929-33) free-market capitalist economies experienced severe depression rendering a large number of workers unemployed. For example, in the USA unemployment of labour increased from 3.2 per cent in 1929 to 25 per cent of labour force in 1933 and national income declined by 30 per cent during this period. This huge unemployment of labour persisted for a long time and full employment did not get automatically restored. Therefore, it became evident that there was something wrong with Classical economics which believed in self-correcting nature of a free market economy to eliminate involuntary unemployment. It was at this time that the English economist John Maynard Keynes challenged the classical theory of full employment, especially Say's law and Pigou's proposal to cut down wages to restore full employment. He put forth a new theory in his book "*A General Theory of Employment, Interest and Money*". Keynes laid a great stress on macro-economic analysis. He showed how incorrect was the view that involuntary unemployment could not prevail in a free-market capitalist economy. We explain below how he proved that Say's law and Pigou's view regarding wage-employment relationship was wrong.

Keynes challenged the correctness of Say's law that supply creates its own demand. He also criticised Pigou's view that a general cut in wages during depression and unemployment would restore full employment in the economy. As explained above, according to Say's law, every supply of production creates its own demand. Therefore, problems of demand deficiency and unemployment do not arise. It is, of course, true that supply creates demand for goods because the various factors which are employed in a productive activity earned incomes from it, which are spent on goods. But the incomes earn by the various factors of production are not wholly spent on the output of goods produced. A part of the income that is saved does not create demand. If entrepreneurs do not invest equal to the desired savings by the people, then aggregate demand which consists of demand for consumer goods and capital goods, will not be enough to purchase available supply of output. If aggregate demand is not sufficient to purchase the entire supply of goods, the producers would be unable to sell their whole output. As a result, their *inventories of goods will increase beyond their desired level.* This will cause the producers to reduce their level of production giving rise to unemployment in the economy.

Keynes showed that there was no guarantee that investment expenditure by entrepreneurs would be equal to the desired savings by the people. Saving and investment are generally made by two different classes of the people. While savings are done by individuals and households, investment expenditure is made by entrepreneurs. Further, while savings depend on various subjective factors such as willingness to save for old age, for periods of sickness and unemployment, for education and marriage of their children, for amassing wealth to leave behind a large estate etc. Apart from these subjective factors savings depend on level of prices, rate of inflation, rate of interest, taxation policy of the Government, distribution of income and wealth in the society and expectations of future income. On the other hand, investment by the entrepreneurs are determined by rate of interest and expected rate of profits in the short run and progress in technology, growth in population in the long run. Therefore, it is not likely that investment will be automatically equal to savings at full-employment level of income and output. As a result, problem of demand deficiency arises which causes involuntary unemployment.

Keynes also challenged the classical viewpoint regarding the impact of all-round cut in money wages on output and employment of labour. According to him, *while in case of the analysis of price and output determination of an individual industry, it is justified to assume that a cut in wages by the industry would not significantly affect the demand for the product of that industry because most of the demand for the product of that industry comes from the workers and persons employed in other industries.* However, to assume that demand curve for output of *all industries* will remain unchanged when a *simultaneous cut in wages in all industries together* is made is not valid. In other words, to apply the result of micro analysis of the determination of price, output and employment in an individual industry to the economy as a whole is quite misleading and invalid. This is because *wages are not only costs for the individual industries, they also constitute incomes of the workers and these incomes determine the demand for the products of various industries.* When all-round cut in wages is made in all industries, it will reduce aggregate demand for the products because workers would have now less incomes and therefore would spend less on goods and services. With reduced demand for the products of industries smaller output will be produced. As a result, smaller amount of labour will be demanded and employed.

Keynes explained that level employment was determined by aggregate demand and aggregate supply. He further showed that equilibrium level of income and employment could well be established at less than full-employment level of national income. Thus, according to him, lack of aggregate demand can cause involuntary unemployment of labour and unutilised productive capacity. In a later chapter we will explain in detail how, according to Keynes, levels of employment and income are determined.

UNEMPLOYMENT AND EMPLOYMENT IN INDIA

We want to caution the readers that they should not think that unemployment prevailing in India is mainly Keynesian cyclical unemployment. The unemployment in developing countries like India is of quite different nature. The main cause of unemployment and underemployment prevailing in the developing countries such as India is *deficiency of the stock of physical capital* with which to employ the growing labour force. Due to the lack of physical capital, it has not been possible to absorb the growing labour force in productive employment. The result has been the emergence of *long-term or chronic unemployment*.

Apart from the relative low rate of capital formation as compared to the growth in labour force, the use of *capital-intensive techniques* in the industries mostly imported from the Western developed countries is another important factor causing unemployment in developing countries like India. Besides, in agriculture, despite the existence of surplus labour *reckless mechanisation of various* agricultural operations has reduced the employment opportunities in agriculture. Another important reason of rural unemployment prevailing in the developing countries like India is extremely unequal distribution of land so that many agricultural households have no *adequate access to land* for production and self-employment in agriculture.

Lack of infrastructure such as roads, power, telecommunications, highways, irrigation facilities in agriculture is also responsible for the existence of huge unemployment in India. Inadequate availability of infrastructure is a great obstacle for the generation of opportunities for productive employment.

In a later chapter we will explain in detail the causes of unemployment in India and what strategies can be adopted to solve it.

Growth of Employment in India : A Case of Jobless Growth

An important objective of planning in India has been to generate enough employment opportunities not only to provide jobs to the backlog of unemployed but also to the new annual additions to the labour force. The new economic reforms initiated in India in 1991 visualised that acceleration of economic growth would also lead to rapid growth of employment opportunities. The total growth rate of employment (*on usual principal status*) which was 2 per cent per annum in the period 1983-94, fell to about 1.57 per cent annum during the post-reform period, 1993-94 to 1999-2000. However, it recorded a higher growth rate of 2.48 per cent per annum in 1999-2000 to 2004-05. The *organised sector employment* which grew 1.2 per cent per annum during 1983-94 recorded much less growth (0.05 per cent) during the post-reform period (1994-2008). However, growth rate of GDP accelerated from 5.4 per cent in 1983-1994 to 7.2 per cent in 1994-2011. Thus, *higher output growth failed to generate higher employment* in the nineties and in the first decade of the present century 1994-2011. During 1994 to 2004-08 there was a *negative* growth in employment in the organised public sector (–0.65 per cent per annum), whereas in the organised private sector employment increased at the rate of 1.75 per cent per annum. Thus, in the organised private sector, the growth in employment was not sufficient to make up for the loss of jobs in the public sector. As a result, there was a decline in employment (–0.05 per cent per annum) in the organised sector in 1999-2000 to 2004-08 despite a quite high growth of output in it. The much lower growth of employment opportunities is due to the fact that the *employment elasticity of output growth* in the organised private sector has sharply declined in the recent years[17] as a result of *increase in capital intensity*. It means fewer people have been able to participate in and benefit from the growth process in the organised sector in the post-reform period.

It may however be noted that despite higher growth in employment in the 10th plan period (*though in the unorganised sector*), unemployment rate on *usual principal status* (UPS) basis was higher at 3.06 per cent of the labour force in 2004-05 compared to 2.78 in 1999-2000.[18] Besides, average *daily status unemployment rate* also increased from 7.3% in 1999-2000 to 8.3 per cent in 1999-2000. According to Approach to the 11th plan, worsening of unemployment situation was due

17. Note that employment elasticity with respect to output growth means percentage growth in employment resulting from one per cent growth in output.
18. Planning Commission, *Eleventh Five Year Plan* (2007-12).

to *faster growth in labour force*. However, in our opinion, the fact that there was decline in increase in employment in the organised sector despite of higher growth in GDP shows the ulter failure of the strategy of employment generation. Employment growth in the organised sector (both public and private combined) inreased during the post-reform period 1994-2008 at the rate of only 0.05 per cent per annum as against 1.20 per cent during 1983-94 (see Table 2.3).

Table 2.3. Rate of Growth of Employment in the Organised Sector

(per cent per annum)

	1983-94	1994-2008	2010/09	2011/10
Public Sector	1.53	-0.65	0.4	–1.8
Private Sector	0.44	1.75	4.5	5.6
Total Organised Sector	1.20	0.05	1.9	1.0

Source: Planning Commission and Directorate General of Employment and Training (DGET), GOI, *Economic Survey, 2012-13*, p. 275

In the recent years employment growth in the organised sector (both public and private sector) increased by 1.0 per cent in 2011/2010 as against 1.9 per cent in 2010/2009.[19] The annual growth in employment in the private sector was 5.6 per cent 2011/2010 whereas that in the public sector it was negative (–1.8%). The share of women in organised sector employment was around 20.5 per cent during 2009-11 and has remained nearly constant in recent years.

That there has been jobless growth is revealed by Report of 68th round of NSSO, especially conducted by the government in 2011-12, after the regularly five yearly survey carried out in 2009-2010 showed a dramatic dip in employment creation. According to this special unemployment survey in 2011-12, overall employment rate in the Indian economy on the basis of usual status (both principal and subsidiary), has fallen to 38.6 per cent of population in 2011-12 from 39.2 per cent of population in 2009-10. In 2004-05 the employment rate was 42 per cent of population. The number of unemployed persons rose to 10.8 million in January 2012 from 9.8 in million January 2010, that is, one million increase in unemployment in just 2 years. The data of 68th round of NSSO showed that just 2.7 million jobs were created in the five years period between 2004-05 and 2009-10 despite 8 per cent plus growth in GDP per annum during this period as against 60 million jobs created in the previous five years period (1999-2000 to 2004-05). Blaming the global financial crisis and its consequent global slowdown in 2008-09 and 2009-10 the government thought that it was due to drought conditions in 2009-10 and economic slowdown that unemployment survey in 2009-10 did not show better conditions regarding employment, it decided to conduct special employment-unemployment survey for 2011-12. But 2011-12 survey shows that situation regarding employment and unemployment worsened in the two year period between 2009-10 and 2011-12. The *usual status unemployment rate* (principal status) went up from 2.5 per cent of labour force in 2009-10 to 2.7 per cent in 2011-12. An important finding of 2011-12 survey is that labour force participation rate declined to 39.5 per cent of population in 2011-12 from 40 per cent in 2009-10 suggesting the lack of job opportunities forcing people to study longer or drop out of labour force.

However, unemployment rate on current daily status basis which was increasing before 2004-05 fell sharply from 8.2 per cent in 2004-05 to 6.6 per cent in 2009-10 and further to 5.6 per cent in 2011-12. This implies that in terms of man-days employment increased at a higher rate both between 2004-05 and 2009-10 and between 2009-10 and 2011-12. This has been explained by the fall in labour force participation rate because the relatively more young population has opted for getting more education rather than participation in labour force. However, in our view, this is only a part of the story. Under the newly started MGNREA scheme, a large number of mandays of employment has been created resulting in the persons in rural households getting relatively full employment (*i.e.*, more man days of employment). But employment generated under MGNREA scheme is neither

19. *Economic Survey, 2012-13*, p.275.

stable nor creating any durable assets which can sustain further growth of employment.

This lower rate of growth of employment in the organised sector has been there even in the post-reform period despite the fact that there has been very high rate of growth of output, both in the organised industrial and services sector. Obviously, this is bound to increase the problem of unemployment in the country.

Employment Strategy to Reduce Unemployment

The following measures should be adopted if unemployment problem is to be solved

Use of Labour-Intensive Technology. Both the organised and unorganised sectors must adopt *labour-intensive technology* if sufficient employment opportunities are to be generated in both the rural and urban sectors of the economy. The decline in employment elasticity of output growth is primarily due to the *increasing trend in capital intensity* in the organised industrial sector as well as in agriculture. Increasing mechanisation of agriculture in various states has lowered the employment elasticity of growth of agricultural output. Therefore, for raising labour intensity, suitable monetary and fiscal measures need to be adopted to discourage the use of capital-intensive techniques. Of course, the use of labour-intensive techniques with lower productivity of workers in the industry and agriculture may lower the growth of output. Thus, there might be same *trade off between employment and growth of output*. In our view due to the seriousness of unemployment problem some output growth should be sacrificed for the sake of more employment.

Accelerating Investment in Agriculture. Second, an important reason for slow growth of employment in agriculture and rural sector has also been a *shortfall in investment or capital formation in agriculture*. Both the public and private sector investment in agriculture has declined since the early nineties. Of special importance from the viewpoint of employment generation is investment in irrigation, rural roads, flood control projects, power generation and other infrastructure. It is worth noting that investment not only generates employment directly but also has a multipier effect which operates through backward and forward linkages. Therefore, UPA government's Common Minimum Programme (CMP) which provides for stepping up of investment in agriculture and rural infrastructures is a greatly welcome step for employment generation. The announcement by the government *to furnish more credit to farmers at lower than market rates of interest* from commercial banks will also ensure that the small and medium farmers will be able to buy fertilizers, other high-yielding imputs, and arrange for their irrigation. This will raise their productivity and tend to reduce under-employment and disguised unemployment. Despite more than five decades of planned industrial development, agriculture continues to be principal source of employment in the Indian economy. Though the share of GDP from agriculture has come down to around 22 per cent, still about 58 per cent of labour force continues to be employed in agriculture. In fact, agriculture continues to be the parking lot of the unemployed in the country. But a good number of persons engaged in agriculture and related activities are not productively employment. In fact there is widespread under-employment and disguised unemployed. Economic reforms initiated in 1991 has by and large neglected agriculture which even now does not get enough credit from commercial banks.

No wonder that there has been a fall in investment or capital formation in agriculture both by the private and public sectors. This is an important reason why employment opportunities in agriculture have not risen much causing increase in rural unemployment. Now, UPI (United Progressive Alliance) government with Dr. Manmohan Singh as Prime Minister, has set before itself the task of making substantial investment in agriculture so as to generate enough employment opportunities in this sector.

Diversification of Agriculture. Besides there is urgent need for diversification of agriculture. For example, there is an urgent need for a relative shift from growing of crops to horticulture, vegetable production, floriculture, animal husbandry, fisheries etc. which are more labour absorbing and higher income-yielding. In addition to this, promotion of agro-processing industries for export purposes has a large employment potential.

For the rapid growth of employment opportunities in agriculture and related sectors and agro-processing industries, investment in infrastructure including irrigation, rural reads, power supply, and development of agricultural markets are required.

Labour-Intensive Industrial Growth. For solving unemployment problem in the urban areas, the organised industrial sector must also absorb a sufficient number of workers. The failure of the organised industrial sector to generate enough employment opportunities is due to the use of capital-intensive technologies imported from abroad. The tendency to use the higher capital-intensive technology by the Indian industries in the post reform period has been intensified because they are trying *to improve competitiveness to face competition from imported commodities*. The other factor responsible for the use of higher capital intensive technologies is the *factor-price distortions* such as cheap capital and relatively higher wages of workers who have strong labour unions. Capital has become relatively cheap due to various fiscal concessions such as liberal depreciation and investment allowance and low interest rates on borrowed funds for investment. Consequent to the use of high capital-intensive technologies in our industries the labour productivity has been increasing while employment has been growing at a snail pace. Therefore, to encourage the use of relatively more labour-intensive technologies and thereby to generate more employment opportunities, fiscal and monetary concessions mentioned above on use of capital must be withdrawn. In this case there is bound to be some loss of workers' productivity. Therefore, this will involve some trade-off between employment and output. In our view, because unemployment problem is very serious and greatly hurts people's welfare, some growth of output is worth sacrificing for more employment opportunities.

Services and Employment Growth. The growth of services in India has a large employment potential. In 1993-94 to 1999-2000, next to the construction sector the employment elasticity of output growth in services was higher and was estimated at about 0.50. Of special mention are software services and BPO (Business Processing Outsourcing) which have a lot of employment potential, especially for the educated youth of the country. The other services such as finance, insurance, trade, hotels, and restaurants have also a lot of employment potential. But an important thing to note is that growth of these services is dependent on industrial and agricultural growth in the economy.

Education, Health and Employment Generation. Lastly, the expansion of education and health care not only promotes accumulation of human capital and thereby contributes to growth of output, it will also generate a good deal of employment opportunities. More schools, hospitals, health care clinics in the rural and urban areas will not only create employment during their construction but also, and more important, when they start working to provide education and health services. Their working provides employment to both the educated and unskilled persons. Therefore, a higher allocation of resources is required to be made for them in government budgets and in our future plans.

BALANCE OF PAYMENTS

In the modern world, there is hardly any country which is self-sufficient in the sense that it produces all the goods and services it needs. Every country imports from other countries the goods that cannot be produced at all in the country or can be produced only at an unduly high cost as compared to the foreign supplies. Similarly, a country exports to other countries the commodities which those countries prefer to buy from abroad rather than producing at home. Besides, trade of goods and services, there are *flows of capital*. Foreign capital flows are in the form of portfolio investment by foriegn institutional investors or in the form of foreign direct investment. *The balance of payments is a systematic record of all economic transactions of residents of a country with the rest of the world during a given period of time.*

This record is so prepared as to measure the various components of a country's external economic transactions. Thus, the aim is to present an account of all receipts and payments on account of goods exported, services rendered and capital received by the residents of a country, and goods imported, services received and capital transferred by residents of the country. The main purpose of keeping these records is to know the international economic position of a country which helps the Government in making decisions on monetary and fiscal policies on the one hand, and trade and payments policies on the other.

Balance of Trade and Balance of Payments. Balance of trade and balance of payments are two related terms but they should be carefully distinguished from each other because they do not have exactly the same meaning. *Balance of trade refers to the difference in values of imports and exports of commodities only, i.e., visible items only.* Movement of goods between countries is known as visible trade because the movement of goods is open and and visible and can be verified by the custom officials.

During a given period of time, the exports and imports may be exactly equal, in which case the *balance of trade is said to be in balance.* But this is not necessary because those who export and import are not necessarily the same persons. If the value of exports exceeds the value of imports, the country is said to have an *export surplus.* On the other hand, if the value of its imports exceeds the value of its exports, the country is said to have a *deficit balance of trade.*

Distinction between Current Account and Capital Account. The distinction between the current account and capital account of the balance of payment may be noted. The current account deals with payment for *currently produced goods and services*. It includes also interest earned or paid on claims and also gifts and donations. *The capital account, on the other hand, deals with capital receipts and payments of debts and claims.* The current account of the balance of payments affects the level of national income directly. For instance, when India sells its currently produced goods and services to foreign countries, the producers of those goods get income from abroad. In other words, current account receipts have the effect of increasing the flow of income in the country. On the other hand, when India imports goods and services from foreign countries and pays them money which would have been used to demand goods and services within the country money flows out to foreign countries. Thus, current account payments to foreigners involve reduction of the flow of income within the country and constitute a leakage. Thus, the current account of the balance of payments has a direct effect on the level of income in a country. The capital account, however, does not have such a *direct effect* on the level of income; it *influences the volume of assets which a country holds.*

Balance of Payments on Current Account

Two types of Balance of Payments are distinguished: (1) Balance of Payments on Current Account, and (2) Balance of Payments on Capital Account. We first explain the meaning and components of balance of payments on current account.

Balance of payments on current account is more comprehensive in scope than balance of trade. It includes not only imports and exports of goods which are visible items but also *invisible items* such as foreign travel, transportation (shipping, air transport etc.), insurance, tourism, investment income (e.g. interest on investments), transfer payments i.e. donations, gifts, etc.

A country, say India, has to make payments to the other countries not only for its imports of merchandise but also for tourists travelling abroad, insurance and shipping services rendered by other countries. Further, it has to pay the royalties to foreign firms, expenditure of Indians in foreign countries, interest on foreign investment in India. These are debit items for India, since the transactions involve *payments made to the rest of the world.* In the same way, foreign countries import goods from India, make use of Indian films and so on, for all of which they make payments to India.

An important item which has recently emerged as *an item of invisible exports is software exports* which has become good foreign exchange earner. These are the credit items for India as the latter receives payments. Balance of payments thus gives a comprehensive picture of all such transactions including imports and exports of goods and services concerned.

The Table 2.4 (given below) gives the position of India's balance of payments on current account for the years 2007-08 to 2011-12. In this table balance of payments the visible as well as invisible items of trade are given. The *visible items* are export-import of goods and the *invisible items* of balance of payments on current account are travel, transportation and insurance, interest on loans given and other investment income on private and official transfers. Both visible and invisible items together make up the current account. Interest on loans, tourist expenditure, banking and insurance charges, software services etc., are similar to visible trade since receipts from selling such services to the foreigners are very similar in their effects to the receipts from sales of goods; both provide income to the people who produce the goods or services.

Table 2.4. India's Balance of Payments on Current Account (in Billion US $)

S.No.	Items	2007-08	2008-09	2009-10	2010-11	2011-12	2012-13
1.	Exports	166.2	189.0	182.2	256.2	309.8	306.6
2.	Imports	257.6	307.6	300.6	383.5	499.5	592.2
3.	Trade Balance	–91.5	–118.6	–118.4	–127.3	–189.9	–195.7
		(–7.4)	(–9.8)	(–8.6)	(–7.8)	(–10.1)	(–10.8)
4.	Invisibles (Net)	75.7	89.9	79.9	79.3	111.6	64.9
	(*i*). Non-factor Services	38.9	49.6	35.7	44.1	64.1	–
	(*ii*). Investment Income	–5.1	–4.0	–8.0	–17.9	–16.0	–
	(*iii*). Private Transfers	41.7	44.6	52.3	53.1	63.5	–
5.	Goods and Services Balance	–52.6	–69.0	–83.0	–83.2	–125.7	–130.7
6.	Current Account Balance (Net)	–15.7	–28.7	–38.4	–48.1	–78.2	–87.8
		(–1.3)	(–2.4)	(–2.8)	(–2.7)	(–4.2)	(4.8)

Source : RBI

Note: *Goods and Services balance indicates balance on goods and non-factor services*

Note : *Figures in brackets show per cent of GDP at market prices.*

It will be noted from Table 2.4 above that the most important item in the balance of payments on current account is balance of trade which refers to imports and exports of goods. In Table 2.4 balance of trade does not balance and shows a deficit in all the seven years. In the years 2011-12 and 2012-13 trade deficit has substantially increased. Trade deficit was over 10 per cent of GDP in both these years. In fact, it is huge trade deficit in these two years that has caused huge current account deficit of over 4% of GDP in these two years. Economic slowdown in advanced countries and its spillover effects in Emerging Market Economies coupled with high crude oil and gold prices were responsible for sharp increase in trade deficit. Due to surplus in invisbles account, there was a surplus on current account during 2001-2002, 2002-03 and 2003-04. In India's balance of payments on current account from 2004-05 onwards there has been a deficit. Contrary to popular perception, deficit on current account is not always bad provided it is within reasonable limits and can be easily met by non-debt capital receipts. In fact, deficit on current account represents the extent of absorption of capital inflows in India during a year.

It may be noted that when there is deficit on the current account, it is financed either by using foreign exchange reserves held by Reserve Bank of India or by capital flows that come into the country in the form of foreign direct investment (FDI) and portfolio investment by FIIs, external commercial borrowing (ECB) from abroad and by NRI deposits in foreign exchange account in our banks. However, due to global financial crisis in 2008-09, there was first slowdown and then decrease in exports. As a result, there was a large deficit of 2.4 of per cent of GDP on current account which could not be met by capital inflows as they were quite meagre ($ 8.6 billion) as a result of global financial crisis. Therefore, to finance the deficit on current account in 2008-09 we had to withdraw US $ 20 billion from our foreign exchange reserves. Again, in the two years 2011-12 and 2012-13 the current account deficit (CAD) had been quite high. It may be noted that high current deficit tends to weaken the rupee by raising the demand for US dollars. In 2011-12, the current account deficit tended to weaken the rupee by raising the demand for US dollars. In 2011-12, the current account deficit was 4.2 per cent of GDP. Since capital inflows in this year were not adequate to finance the current account deficit, RBI had to withdraw 12.8 billion US dollars from its foreign exchange reserves to meet the demand for US dollars. In the year 2012-13 the current account deficit has been estimated to be even higher at 4.8 per cent of GDP, capital inflows through portfolio investment by FIIs had picked up in the latter half of 2012-13 but capital inflows through FDI had fallen. However, we managed to meet such large account deficit through capital inflows. In fact we added to our foreign exchange reserves by $3.8 billion in 2012-13. Thus current account deficit poses serious challenge to macroeconomic management of the economy. The dependence on volatile capital inflows through FIIs to meet the current account deficit is unsustainable as these capital flows go back when global situation worsens and thereby cause sharp depreciation in exchange rate of rupee and crash in stock market prices.

Since in the recent years, 2011-12 and 2012-13 current account deficit has widened, this has increased the balance of payments vulnerability to sudden reversal of capital flows, especially when sizable flows comprise debt and volatile portfolio investment by FIIs. The priority has therefore been to reduce current account deficit (CAD) through improving trade balance. Efforts have been made to promote exports by diversifying the export commodity basket and export destinations. One way to limit imports is to bring domestic prices up to the international level so that users bear the full cost. Accordingly, petrol has been decontrolled and diesel prices have been revised upward in Jan. 2013 to curtail subsidy on it. To discourage the imports of gold which has played a significant role in causing trade deficit, customs duty on its import was raised from 6% to 8% and further to 10% in July 2013.

Further, to improve the current account deficit emphasis has been on facilitating remittances and encouraging software exports that have been responsible for surplus on the invisible account. In recent years this surplus has lowered the impact of widening trade deficit on current account deficit (CAD) significantly. The two components together met nearly two-thirds of the trade deficit that was more than 10 per cent of GDP in 2011-12. Remittances particularly are known to exhibit resistance when the country is hit by external shock as was evident during the global crisis of 2008

Balance of Payments on Capital Account

In the balance of payments on capital account given in Table 2.5 important items are borrowings from foreign countries and lending funds to other countries. This takes two forms: (i) *External assistance* which means borrowing from foreign countries under concessional rate of interest; (ii) *Commercial borrowing* under which the Indian Government and the private sector borrow funds from world money market at higher market rate of interest. Besides *non-resident deposits* are another important item in capital account. These are the deposits made by non-resident Indians (NRI) who keep their surplus funds with Indian Banks. Another important item in balance of payments on capital account is *foreign investment* by foreign companies in India. There are two types of foreign investment. First is *portfolio investment* under which foreign institutional investors (FIIs) purchase shares (equity) and bonds of Indian companies and Government. The second is *foreign direct investment* (FDI) under which foreign companies set up plants and factories on their own or in collaboration with the Indian companies. Still another item in capital account is other capital flows in which the important source of funds is *remittances from abroad* sent by the Indian citizens working in foreign countries. Table 2.5 gives the position of India's capital account for the years 2007-08 to 2012-13.

Capital inflows in the capital account can be classified into *debt creating and non-debt creating*. Foreign investment (both direct and portfolio) represents non-debt creating capital inflows, whereas external assistance (i.e. concessional loans taken from abroad), external commercial borrowing (ECB) and non-resident deposits are debt-creating capital inflows.

Table 2.5. India's Balance of Payments on Capital Account (in Billion US $)

	2007-08	2008-09	2009-10	2010-11	2011-12	2012-13
External Assistance (Net)	2.1	2.6	2.9	4.93	2.3	–
Commercial Borrowing (Net)	22.6	7.0	2.8	11.8	10.3	–
Non-Resident Deposits (Net)	0.2	– 4.3	N.A	3.18	11.9	–
Foreign Investment (Net) of which	43.3	3.5	51.2	44.18	39.3	–
(*i*) FDI net	15.9	17.5	18.8	7.1	22.1	–
(*ii*) Portfolio Investment (Net)	27.4	–15.0	32.4	37.2	17.2	–
(*iii*) Other capital flows (Net)	39.7	–9.7	–13.1	–10.36	–	–
Capital Account Total (Net)	107.9	8.6	53.4	59.7	67.8	–
Use of Exchange Reserves*	–92.2	+20.1*	–13.4*	(–13.1)	(+12.8)	–3.8

* Also includes errors and omissions

Source: RBI, *Annual Report 2012-13*. Use of foreign exchange reserves (–indicates increase of reserves, and + indicates decrease of reserves on BOP basis.

It will be seen from Table 2.5 that during 2007-08, there was net capital inflow of 43.3 billion US dollars on account of foreign investment (both direct and portfolio). Table 2.5 gives the position of India's balance of payments in capital account for seven years, 2007-08, 2008-09, 2009-10, 2010-11, 2011-12 and 2012-13. When all items of balance of payments on capital account are taken into account we had a surplus of 107.9 billion US dollars in 2007-08. Taking into current account deficit of $ 15.7 billion on current account in year 2007-08 there was accretion to our foreign exchange reserves by $ 92.2 billion in 2007-08. Global financial crisis affected our capital account balance as there was *reversal of capital flows after Sept. 2008* with the result that we used $ 20.1 billion of our foreign exchange reserves in 2008-09 resulting in decrease of our foreign exchange reserves. That is, because we used our foreign exchange reserves equal to $ 20.1 billion, there was decline in our foreign exchange reserves by $ 20 billion in 2008-09. The situation improved in 2009-10 as foreign direct investment (FDI) and portfolio investment by FIIs picked up. As a result there was net capital account surplus of $ 53.4 billion in 2009-10 and after meeting the current account deficit of $ 38 billion there was addition to our foreign exchange reserves by $ 13.4 billion in 2009-10. In 2010-11 also there was surplus on capital account of $ 59.7 billion and after meeting current deficit we added $ 13.1 billion in our foreign exchange reserves in 2010.11.

However, in 2011-2012 and 2012-13 the situation regarding capital flows changed significantly and capital flows were not sufficient to meet the large current account deficit (CAD). Consequently, in 2011-12 withdrawal from foreign exchange reserves of 12.8 million US dollars was made.

Capital flows are driven by pull factors such as economic fundamentals of recipient countries and push factors such as policy stance of source countries. The capital flows have implications for exchange rate management, overall macroeconomic and financial stability including liquidity conditions. Capital account management therefore needs to emphasize promoting foreign direct investment (FDI) and reducing dependence on volatile portfolio capital inflows. This would ensure that to the extent current account defect is bridged through capital surplus it would be better if it is done through stable and growth-enhancing foreign direct investment flows. In the present international financial situation, reserves are the first line of defence against the volatile capital flows. However, the decline in reserves as a percentage of GDP is a source of concern.

When all items of balance of payments of capital account are taken into account we had a surplus of 6.8, 53.9 and 59.7 billion US dollars in 2008-09, 2009-10 and 2010-11. Small size surplus on capital account of 6.8 billion US dollars in 2008-09 was due to large portfolio capital outflows by FII, which occurred because of global financial crisis in 2008-09. As a result of this, capital flows fell short of current account deficit of 27.9 billion US dollars resulting in deficit of 20.1 billion US dollars in 2008-09. As a consequence our foreign exchange reserves declined by $ 20.1 billion in 2008-09. However, in 2009-10 and 2010-11, there was enough capital account surplus so that after meeting current account deficit we added to our foreign exchange reserves by $ 13.4 and $ 13.1 billion in our foreign exchange reserves in 2009-10 and 2010-11.

Further, it is important to note that surplus on capital account is mainly due to foreign investment in India, external commercial borrowing and NRI deposits which do not belong to us. These investment funds, especially foreign institutional investment funds and Non-Resident Deposits, can flow out of India if situation in India is not favourable. This in fact happened in the year 2008-09 when as a result of global financial crisis FIIs (Foreign Institutional Investors) sold corporate shares in the Indian stock market and capital outflow from India took place on a large scale.

Determinants of Balance of Payments

It may be further noted that when there is a deficit in the current account, it has to be financed either by *using foreign exchange reserves* with Reserve of Bank, if any, or by *capital inflows* (in the form of foreign assertance, commercial borrowing from abroad, non-residential deposits). There are several variables which determine the balance of payments position of a country, viz., national income at home and abroad, the prices of goods and factors, the supply of money, the rate of interest, etc. all of which determine exports, imports, and demand and supply of foreign currency. At the back of these variables lie the supply factors, production function, the state of technology, tastes, distribution of income, economic conditions, the state of expectations, etc. If there is a change in any of these variables and there are no appropriate changes in other variables, disequilibrium will be the result.

The main cause of disequilibrium in the balance of payments arises from imbalance between exports and imports of goods and services that is, deficit or surplus in balance of payments. When for one reason or another exports of goods and services of a country are smaller than their imports, disequilibrium in the balance of payments is the likely result. Exports may be small due to the lack of exportable surplus which in turn results from low production or the exports may be small because of the high costs and prices of exportable goods and severe competition in the world markets. Important causes of small exports are the inflation or rising prices in the country or over-valued exchange rate. When the prices of goods are high in the country, its exports are discouraged and imports encouraged. If it is not matched by other items in the balance of payments, disequilibrium emerges.

Does Balance of Payments must always balance ?

It is often said that balance of payments must always balance. What does it mean ? The individuals and business firms of an economy have to pay for the imports from abroad. If exports are not sufficient to pay for the imports, then how the balance of payments will be in balance. For example, the balance of payments on current account of India has been in deficit for most of the years till 2000-01. Deficit on current account implies that the residents of a country are spending more on imports of goods and services than the incomes they are earning from exports of goods and services. For the overall balance of payments to be in balance, this deficit in the current account of the balance of payments must by financed by selling capital assets of such as shares and bonds of companies or other assets such as gold or foreign exchange reserves of a country or by borrowing from abroad. Both by selling assets or by borrowing from abroad, foreign capital flows into the country as has been happening in the last several years in India. These foreign capital inflows are shown in the capital account of the balance of payments which must be in surplus to finance the deficit in the current account. Thus

$$\textit{current account} + \textit{capital account surplus} = 0. \qquad \ldots (i)$$

The above fact has an important lesson that must be borne in mind. If a country has no foreign currency reserves or it has no assets to sell to pay for the imports and if no body is willing to lend to it, it will have to cut down its imports which will reduce productive activity in the economy and adversely affect economic growth of the country. Such a crisis situation arose in India in 1991 when our foreign exchange reserves had fallen to a very low level and no one was willing to lend to us or give us aid. In fact, due to loss of confidence of foreign investors, *capital outflows* were taking place.

Therefore, in 1991 India had to mortgage gold to Bank of England and Central Bank of Japan to get the necessary foreign exchange to pay for the needed imports. We had to accept the pre-conditions of IMF for providing us assistance to tide over the crisis. It is interesting to note this was done under the guidance of Dr. Manmohan Singh who was then the Finance Minister.

Capital Flows and Globalisation

The globalization of the Indian economy has an important consequence with regard to capital flows into the economy. Suppose India faces given prices of its imports and a given demand for its exports of goods and services. Under these circumstances, if domestic rate of interest is higher as compared to what exists abroad, then given the mobility of capital, capital will flow into the Indian economy to a very large extent. This principle can be expressed as follows.

$$BP = NX(Y_d, Y_f, R) + CF(I_f - I_d) \qquad \ldots (ii)$$

where BP = balance of payments, NX is net exports (*i.e.* exports–imports which is also called trade balance, CF stands for surplus in the capital account of the balance of payments, that is, capital flows.

The above equation reveals that trade balance (NX) is a function of level of domestic income (Y_d) and foreign income (Y_f) and real rate of exchange (R). An increase in the domestic income due to higher industrial growth or fall in real exchange rate of rupee will adversely affect the trade balance (NX) by increasing imports. $I_f - I_d$ in equation (*ii*) measures net foreign investment, *i.e.* net capital inflows. Further, the above equation shows that higher interest rate in India as compared to that in the foreign country such as the United States will cause large capital inflows into India. Such capital inflows actually took place in India 2009-10 and 2010-11. Due to large capital inflows into the Indian economy our foreign exchange reserves increase. However, when there are large capital outflows as occurred during 2008-09, our foreign exchange reserves decline.

We shall explain in detail the balance of payments problem in a later part concerning the external sector of the economy.

FOREIGN EXCHANGE RATE

Related to the problem of balance of payments is the macro issue of foreign exchange rate. The balance of payments is influenced by the foreign exchange rate. *Exchange rate is the value of national currency in terms of a foreign currency.* Thus, currently (September 20, 2013) one US dollar is exchanged for around ₹ 62. Thus ₹ 62 to a dollar is the foreign exchange rate of rupee in terms of US dollars. Changes in foreign exchange rate affect the prices of exports and imports which in turn determine their volume and thereby determine balance of payments of a country. Since exchange rate is a price, its determination can be explained through demand for and supply of foreign exchange. However, in the long run the foreign exchange rate between the two currencies is determined by the purchasing powers of the two currencies in the domestic economies. In the short run, the demand for imports and exports of goods and services (that is, both visible and invisible items), magnitude of capital flows between the countries affect demand for and supply of foreign exchange and thereby determine the exchange rate between the currencies. *The system of exchange rate in which the value of a currency is allowed to adjust freely or to float as determined by demand for and supply of foreign exchange is called a flexible exchange rate system.* The flexible exchange rate system is also called *floating exchange system*. At present, in most of the countries of the world (including India), the flexible exchange rate system prevails.

On the other hand, if foreign exchange rate, instead of being determined by demand for and supply of foreign exchange, is fixed by the government, it is called the fixed exchange rate system which prevailed in the world under an agreement reached at Bretton Woods in New Hampshire in July 1944. Therefore, fixed exchange rate is also often called Bretton Woods System. Under the Bretton Woods fixed exchange rate system, exchange rate is not determined by demand for and supply of foreign exchange but is pegged at a certain rate. At the fixed exchange rate, if there is disequilibrium in the balance of payments giving rise to either excess demand or excess supply of foreign exchange, the Central Bank of the country has to buy or sell the required quantities of foreign exchange to eliminate the excess demand or supply. But in the mid seventies Bretton Woods system of fixed exchange rate system in which US dollar played a key role collapsed as the USA could not keep constant the price of US dollar in terms of gold.

As mentioned above, in a fixed exchange rate system the government has to buy or sell foreign exchange in order to maintain the rate at the controlled level. However, under the fixed exchange rate system, the value of one's currency can be changed occasionally. For instance, in June 1966, the value of rupee in terms of US dollar and U.K's pound sterling was lowered. Again in July 1991 India reduced its value of rupee in terms of US dollar by about 20 per cent. Such a *one-time lowering of value of its currency in terms of foreign exchange occasionally by a country is called devaluation as distinguished from depreciation which under flexible exchange rate system can often take place under the influence of changes in demand for and supply of a currency.* On the other hand, with a fixed rate exchange system if a country raises the value of its currency in terms of foreign currency, it is called *revaluation*. It should be noted that since March 1993 India has adopted flexible exchange rate system and has also now made its rupee convertible into a foreign currency. In fact, at present the Indian rupee can appreciate or depreciate every day depending on the demand for and supply of US dollar and other foreign currencies and demand for and supply of the Indian rupee. In a later chapter we will explain at length how the exchange rate is determined by demand for and supply of foreign exchange and the factors which can cause changes in it.

Foreign Exchange Rate, Balance of Payments and Capital Inflows and Outflows

Changes in foreign exchange rate have an important effect on the balance of payments of a country. When there is depreciation or devaluation in the currency of a country, its exports become cheaper and imports costlier than before. This causes exports to increase and imports to decrease causing reduction in deficit in balance of payments. Thus in order to check increase in deficit in balance of payment and to restore equilibrium in it, devaluation or depreciation of the domestic currency against foreign currencies is often undertaken.

Besides, the foreign exchange inflows in various forms such as those resulting from rising exports, portfolio investment by FIIs (Foreign Institutional Investors), foreign direct investment (FDI) not only causes appreciation of exchange rate of the domestic currency but also leads to the increase in money supply in the economy and therefore inflationary situation in the country.

Thus higher appreciation in the value of rupee against US dollar in 2007-08 in India was the direct result of large capital inflows in India. The price of Indian rupee against US dollar rose from around ₹ 45 in January 2007 to 39.5 in Sept. 2007, that is, over 11 per cent appreciation in the year 2007 alone. This appreciation of rupee was driven by foreign exchange inflows partly by rising software exports but more importantly inflows by FIIs coming in large quantity to take advantage of the stock market boom in India. Besides, foreign exchange inflows through NRI deposits lured by higher interest rates in India than those prevailing in their country of residence took place. Further, large capital inflows through foreign direct investment (FDI) in India also increased in 2006-07 and 2007-08.

These large inflows of foreign exchange in India through its effect on the supply of dollars in foreign exchange market would have caused a very high appreciation of rupee vis-a-vis US dollar but RBI did buy some dollars from market from time to time to prevent it and built up reserves of foreign exchange. But RBI could not buy dollars as fast as the large inflows came in. This resulted in appreciation of rupee in 2007-08. RBI could not ensure foreign exchange rate stability in situation of large capital inflows by buying sufficient amount of dollars from the market.

Again in Sept. 2011 there had been large capital outflows from the Indian economy resulting in increase in demand for US dollars and therefore depreciation of Indian rupee. The value of Indian rupee which was ₹ 43 to a US dollar in July 2011 declined to around ₹ 53 to a US dollar in the second week of December 2011. To prevent excessive depreciation of the Indian rupee RBI intervenced and sold US dollars from its foreign exchange reserves.

Further from May 2013 FIIs started withdrawing capital from debt market and capital markets as a result of which demand for US dollars rose for sending it for investment in the US. This was triggered by the statement of the governor Ben Bernanke of the US Federal Reserve that as the US economy had revived, it would start unwinding the *quantitative easing* (QE) which was adopted to give stimulus to the US economy. This led to capital outflows from the emerging economies including India to the US. Besides, India's large current account deficit which was estimated at a very high level of 4.8 per cent of GDP in 2012-13 was caused by rapid growth of imports, especially of gold and crude oil on the one hand and stagnant exports on the other also lead to the net increase in demand for US dollars. In the months of May and June 2013 about 9 billion US dollars were withdrawn from India and contributed to capital outflows from India. Thus large capital outflows by FIIs and large current account deficit (CAD) led to the sharp depreciation of the value of Indian rupee which was around ₹ 56 to a US dollar in the first week of June 2013 fell to 61.21 to a US dollar on July 8, 2013 and further hit a record low level ₹ 68.83 to a US dollar on August 28, 2013. This prompted Reserve Bank of India to take steps to squeeze liquidity in the Indian banking system whose funds were being used for speculative activities in the foreign exchange market. Though depreciation of a currency is considered to be desirable as it boosts exports and reduces imports. But a sharp depreciation of rupee in the present macro-economic situation has a serious consequences. Not only will it make imports costlier and fuel another round of inflation, it will also restrain the RBI from pushing through the cuts in repo rate and cash reserve ratio urgently needed for kick-starting investments and boosting growth Breaking out of this policy logjam requires that the government should curtail current account deficit (CAD) by taking steps to boost exports by increasing its competitiveness and undertaking its diversification and also cut imports by imposing high tariffs on luxury imports, as it has already raised imports duty on gold from 6% to 10%. Besides, it should make reforms in foreign direct investment policy so that stable capital inflows are attracted to the Indian economy.

It follows from above that portfolio capital flows result in a lot of instability in foreign exchange rate of rupee which adversely affects our real economy through its effects on our exports and imports. Dr. Manmohan Singh who is considered as votary of globalisation in its address to the United Nations General Assembly in Sept. 2011 called the attention of world leaders to its risks. He said, "*Today we are being called upon to cope with negative dimension of globalisation and global inter-dependence*". He further said that US, Europe and Japan faced with economic slowdown are affecting confidence in world financial and capital markets creating a lot of economic instability which has a negative impact on emerging economies like India. He added that world had taken for granted the benefits of globalisation and it is time that UN asks its development agencies (World Bank, IMF) to ensure inclusive and sustainable development for vast sections of humanity. He rightly warned against protectionist measures as a response to the global economic crisis, which he said has "deepened even further since 2008, in many respects." Calling for better coordination of macroeconomic policies of major economies, Singh said: "We should not allow the global economic slowdown to become a trigger for building walls around ourselves through protectionism or erecting barriers to movement of people, services and capital."

Another conclusion which follows from above is that there is a **clash between foreign exchange rate stability and domestic price stability** and RBI has been attempting to strike a balance between foreign exchange rate stability and domestic price stability. If in order to ensure foreign exchange rate stability RBI mops up sufficient dollars, it will result in pumping large sum of Indian rupees into the economy which will lead to the large increase in money supply causing a high rate of inflation. If to check inflation and ensure price stability, it does not mop up dollars from the market and let dollar inflows, this will result in appreciation of rupee. Thus it has to strike a balance in buying dollars from the market so as to check inflation one the hand and to prevent too much appreciation of rupee. It is important to note that appreciation of rupee adversely affects India's exports and leads to loss of jobs. Appreciation of rupee also makes imports cheaper causing increase in them. Fall in exports and rise in imports adversely affects balance of payments on current account. However, more imports brought in through appreciation of rupee adds to aggregate supply of output and help in controlling inflation. On the other hand, too much depreciation of rupee is also bad because it makes imports costlier, especially of fuel oil. Higher value of imports also adversely affects balance payments.

Chapter 3
Corporate Governance and Social Responsibility of Business

The Concept of Corporate Governance

In the corporate governance we deal with the problem of producing best results for its shareholders by the corporate enterprise, while at the same time promoting the interests of other stakeholders such as employees, consumers and lenders. When there is sole proprietorship form of business organisation, the sole owner manages a concern and, according to the standard economic theory, he will tend to maximise his profits or wealth. For achieving this objective he will try to achieve efficiency in the use of resources to minimise costs for a given level of output. The market forces will compel him to produce goods or services for satisfying consumer wants. So in a sole proprietorship there is no clash of interests between persons.

However, in a corporate business enterprise there is a separation of ownership from management, that is, shareholders of the firms from the board of directors and managers who conduct business and take various business decisions. In theory, shareholders control board of directors and top management and can change if they find they are not working in their best interests. However, the reality is quite different. Shareholders are spread over a wide area, and they generally do not attend the general body meetings of the corporate company. As a result, they have no effective control over the working of board of directors and management of corporate enterprise. This often causes clash of interests. Thus, while in theory the objective of board of directors and management is to maximise profits or shareholders value and wealth, but in practice this does not happen. The board of directors and top management in the context of separation of ownership may pursue their own interests by pursuing, for example, very risky or imprudent projects and misappropriate funds raised from investors and use them in promoting their own interests. Ishkander and Chamlou in a World Bank study of the problem writes, "The interests of those who have effective control over a firm can differ from the interests of those who supply the firm with external finance. The problem commonly known as a principal-agent problem grows out of the separation of ownership and control and corporate outsiders and insiders".[1]

Similarly, Mr. Justice Arijit Pasayat in his speech at 5th LAWASIA Business Law Conference, New Delhi, states, "When ownership is separated from control, the manager's self-interest may lead to the misuse of corporate assets, for example, through the pursuit of overly risky or imprudent projects. *Corporate financier* (whether they are individuals or pension funds, mutual funds, banks and other financial institutions, or even government) *need assurances that their investment will be protected from misappropriation and used as intended for the agreed corporate objective*. These assurances are at the heart of what effective corporate governance is all about".[2] The objective in a corporate, as stated above, is the maximisation of shareholders value subject to the protection of interests of other stakeholders. Committee on Corporate governance set up by SEBI and headed by Kumar Manglam Birla righly states that the objective of corporate governance is the "*enhancement of long-term shareholders' value while at the same time protecting the interests of other stakeholders.*

To achieve the objectives of the protection of investment of individuals from misappropriation of

1. Magdi R. Ishkander and Naderch Chamlou, "*Corporate Governance : A Framework for Implementation*", World Bank Group, Washington DC, 2000.
2. Italics added.

funds by management of a corporate enterprise and maximisations of long-term shareholders' value, it is required that practices of good corporate governance, namely, *transparency in the transactions of corporates with stakeholders, accountability and responsibility for the decisions taken, keeping of accurate accounts and fairness in treatment should be adopted if the objective of the corporate is to be attained.* The corporate governance is affected by the relationship among various participants in the governance system. The shareholders, especially those who can hold bulk of shares and are in controlling position can influence corporate behaviour, institutional investors (such as banks, mutual funds) are increasingly having a larger say in corporate governance of some companies. Creditors also demand an important role in the corporate governance and employees can also play an important role in contributing to the good performance of the corporation and realisation of its long-term objective.

It is worth mentioning that the *focus of good corporate governance is on the voluntary adoption of ethical code of conduct in business decision-making and financial transactions* in a corporate enterprise for its long-term success and performance, while the government can establish the overall legal framework.

The board of directors and top management is central to the concept of corporate governance and it is their accountability and transparency in the dealings with shareholders and other stakeholders that underlie good corporate governance. The practices of good corporate governance are expressed as ethical code of conduct and are mainly self-regulated and not imposed by laws or legislation. Of course, as mentioned above, the government can establish overall institutional and legal framework so that corporate enterprises do not indulge in patently corrupt practices and fleece shareholders and customers.

THE NEED AND IMPORTANCE OF CORPORATE GOVERNANCE

The need for corporate governance has arisen because of the increasing concern about the non-compliance of standards of financial reporting and accountability by boards of directors and management of corporates inflicting heavy losses on investors. The collapse of international gaints like Enron, World Com of the US and Xerox of Japan are said to be due to the absence of good corporate governance and corrupt practices adopted by management of these companies and their financial consulting firms. The failures of these multinational giants bring out the importance of good corporate governance structure making clear the distinction of power between the Board of Directors and the management which can lead to appropriate governance processes and procedures under which management is free to manage and board of directors is free to monitor and give policy directions.

In India, SEBI realised the need for good corporate governance and for this purpose appointed several committees such as Kumar Manglam Birla Committee, Naresh Chandra Committee and Narayana Murthy Committee. A good system of corporate governance is important on account of the following.

1. Investors and shareholders of a corporate company need protection for their investment due to lack of adequate standards of financial reporting and accountability. It has been noticed in India that companies raised capital from the market at high valuation of their shares by projecting wrong picture of the company's performance and profitability. The investors suffered a lot due to unscrupulous management of corporates that performed much less than reported at the time of raising capital. "Bad governance was also exemplified by allotment of promoters' share at preferential prices disproportionate to market value affecting minority holders interest".[3]

There is increasing awareness and consensus among Indian investors to invest in companies which have a record of observing practices of good corporate governance. Therefore, for encouraging Indian investors to make adequate investment in the stock of corporate companies and thereby

3. Ranjana Kumar, "Corporate Governance : Need for Mindset Change and Transparency" ***The Economic Times***, Nov. 20. 2007

boosting up rate of growth of the economy, the protection of their interests from fraudulent practices of corporate of boards of directors and management are urgently needed.

2. Corporate governance is considered as an important means for paying heed to investors' grievances. Kumar Manglam Birla Committee on corporate governance found that companies were not paying adequate attention to the timely dissemination of required information to investors in by India. Though some measures have been taken by SEBI and RBI but much more required to be taken by the companies themselves to pay heed to the investors grievances and protection of their investment by adopting good standards of corporate governance.

3. The importance of good corporate governance lies in the fact that it will enable the corporate firms to (1) attract capital and (2) perform efficiently. This will help in winning investors confidence. Investors will be willing to invest in the companies with a good record of corporate governance. New policy of liberalisation and deregulation adopted in India since 1991 has given greater freedom to management which should be prudently used to promote investors' interests. In India there are several instances of corporates' failures due to lack of transparency and disclosures and instances of falsification of accounts. This discourages investors to make investment in the companies with poor record of corporate governance.

3. **Global Perspective.** The extent to which corporate enterprises observe the basic principles of good corporate governance has now become an important factor for attracting foreign investment. In this age of globalisation when quantitative restrictions have been removed and trade barriers dismantled, the relationship between corporate governance and flows of foreign investment has become increasingly important. Studies in India and abroad show that foreign investors take notice of well-managed companies and respond positively to them. capital flows from foreign institutional investors (FII) for investment in the capital market and foreign direct investment (FDI) in joint ventures with Indian corporate companies will be coming if they are convinced about the implementation of basic principles of good corporate governance. Thus, "International flows of capital enable companies to access financing from a large pool of investors. If countries are to reap the full benefits of the global capital markets, and if they are to attract long-term capital, corporate governance arrangements must be credible and well understood across borders"[4]. The large inflows of foreign investment will contribute immensely to economic growth.

4. **Indespensable for healthy and vibrant stock market.** An important advantage of strong corporate governance is that it is indispensable for a vibrant stock market. A healthy stock market is an important instrument for investors protection. A bane of stock market is *insider trading*. Insider trading means trading of shares of a company by insiders such directors, managers and other employees of the company *on the basis of information which is not known to outsiders of the company*. It is through insider trading that the officials of a corporate company take undue advantage at the expense of investors in general. Insider trading is a kind of fraud committed by the officials of the company. One way of dealing with the problem of insider trading is enacting legislation prohibiting such trading and enforcing criminal action against violators. In India, insider trading has been rampant and therefore it was prohibited by SEBI. However, the experience shows prohibiting insider trading by law is not the effective way of dealing with the problem of insider trading because legal process of providing punishment is a lengthy process and conviction rate is very low.[5] According to Sandeep Parekh, an advocate (Securities and Financial Regulations), the effective way of tackling the problem is by encouraging the companies to practice self regulation and taking prophylactic action. This is inherently connected to the field of corporate governance. It is a means by which the company signals

4. Ajith Nivard Cabraal, *Corporate Governance, Transparency and Accounabiliy*" A paper read at 5th LAWASIA, Business Law Conference, New Delhi, January 2003.
5. Sandeep Parekh, '*Prevention of Insider Trading and Corporate Good Governance*' A paper read at 5th LAWASIA Business Law Conference, New Delhi, Jan. 2003

to the market that effective self-regulation is in place and that investors are safe to invest in their securities. In addition to prohibiting inappropriate actions (which might not necessarily be prohibited) self-regulation is also considered an effective means of creating shareholders value. Companies can always regulate their directors/officers beyond what is prohibited by the law"[6]

Conclusion

It is evident from above that it is essential that good governance practices must be effectively implemented and enforced preferably by self-regulation and voluntary adoption of ethical code of business conduct and if necessary through relevant regulatory laws and rules framed by Government or its agencies such as SFBI, RBI. The effective implementation of good governance practices would ensure investors confidence in the corporate companies which will lead to greater investment in them ensuring their sustained growth. Thus good corporate governance would greatly benefit the companies enabling them to thrive and prosper.

Further, in the context of liberalisation and globalisation there is growing realalisation in the emerging economies including India that a country's business environment must be maintained and operated in a manner that is conducive to investors' confidence so that both domestic and foreign investors are induced to make adequate investment in corporate companies. This will be conducive to rapid capital formation and sustained growth of the economy.

Some persons regard certain good corporate practices as 'irritants' to the growth of their businesses since they require the implementation of minimum standards of corporate governance. However, fact of the matter is that the observance of practices of good corporate governance will ensure investors' confidence in the companies which have record of good corporate governance.

Further, it needs to be emphasised that practices and principles of good corporate governance have been evolved which stimulate business rather than stifle it. In fact in good corporate governance structure what is ensured is that companies must preferably follow voluntarily ethical code of business conduct which are conducive to the expansion of investment in them and ensure good outcome in terms of rates of return.

PRINCIPLES OF GOOD CORPORATE GOVERNANCE

There is no single model of a good corporate governance. However, Organisation for Economic Cooperation and Development (OECD) analysing the works carried out in member countries has formulated some important principles of good corporate governance. The principles are stated to be evolutionary in nature and should be reviewed in the light of significant changes in circumstances. Ideally , since the corporate governance is primarily based on ethical code of business conduct, the principles of good corporate governance should be non-binding on the corporate companies. However, the government has important responsibility for regulating practices so that the misappropriation of funds and frauds do not occur. Subject to these regulations, corporate enterprises are allowed freedom in functioning so that they can promote the interests of shareholders and other stakeholders in a framework of free markets for both securities and products.

A. Rights of Shareholders and Fair Treatment of Them

An important principle of good corporate governance is that it *should protect shareholders rights*. Second, the corporate enterprise should ensure *fair treatment to all stakeholders* including minority shareholders and foreign shareholders. Third, all shareholders must have opportunity for effective redress of their grievances regarding violation of their rights including the rights to information. Above all, the corporate governance structure should recognise the rights of shareholders in creating value, employment and the working of enterprises in a financially sound manner.

6. *Op.cit.*
7. See UNDP, *Human Development Report*, 1998, p.11
8. This paper was read at 5th LAWASIA Business Law Conference, New Delhi Jan. 2003.

B. **Corporate Transparency.** The principle of corporate transparency requires timely and accurate disclosure of information by a corporate company on all matters regarding the corporation including its financial situation, performance and ownership.

C. **Corporate Accountability.** According to this principle the corporate governance system as shaped by the board of directors must ensure the effective monitoring of management by the board and above all responsibility of the Board and top management to the shareholders and other shakeholders for any transactions made and productive activities performed by the company.

Let us explain the two important principles of corporate transparency and accountability in some detail

Corporate Transparency

Inefficiency and lack of transparency in corporate governance that often leads to scandals and frauds are major challenges facing the corporate world. These have hampered the smooth functioning of companies and stock markets and have adversely affected long-term investment which is crucial for sustained growth of the economy. The failure of international giants like Enron, World Com., Xerox have been said to be caused by the absence of effective corporates transparency. To eradicate poor and ineffective corporate governance, there is a paramount need for transparency in the conduct of business by corporates. In response to the poor and ineffective corporate governance several initiatives have been taken in the past some years to make the working of corporates effective and transparent. Among them are codes of conduct, rules of business ethics to be self imposed by the companies to furnish complete information, disclosures regarding the financial position, performance of the company regarding its profitability, ownership and governance of the company to its shareholders and other stakeholders. Ajith Nivard Carbaal in his paper on "*Corporate Governance, Transparency and Accountability*"[8] writes, "Transparency involves the determination of information and data in as a complete manner as possible so as to provide, furnish and transmit information and data in a timely manner and in an understandable and knowledgeable form to shareholders about a relevant system. Transparency ensures that those who are in charge of systems, disclose the selected, specified information and its working at the given times in the pre-determined manner. Through the dissemination of such information it is believed that those who have interest in the particular system would be able to obtain an understanding and knowledge which is at least close to, if not equal to, that of those who are involved within the system."

The transparency is important for two reasons. First, the Board of directors and top management of corporate enterprises required to provide pre-determined information will become more conscious to ensure that their business transactions are proper and above board. This will reduce the chances of their committing frauds on shareholders, financiers and investors. Second, the recipients having gained access to the required information and data will be better able to evaluate in which company to invest to get good return from their investment. This will enable companies not only to attract domestic investors but also foreign capital inflows. Thus, with transparency good corporate governance can be achieved which will be of great help in promoting long-term investment and sustained growth of the corporate company.

Corporate Accountability

The principle of accountability is defined as the assignment of responsibility to specified persons or groups within the corporate enterprise for undertaking definite tasks to produce certain results or outcome and holding such persons or groups responsible for doing the assigned tasks properly. The accountability of a corporate company to its shareholders, financiers, investors is of crucial importance to win investors confidence. It is the board of directors and top managers who are held accountable for any wrongs committed in disclosures, financial reporting and business decisions taken by them.

The accountability of different persons within the corporate system is established codes of best practices, rules and regulations to be followed in discharge of their duties. It has been observed that despite several measures taken by the government, guidelines issued by SEBI and RBI, the accountability in the corporate sector has not been achieved to any significant degree. As a result, shareholders and investors, lenders to the corporate firms have suffered a lot due to the lack of accountability. In the South Asian countries including India there is concern about standards of financial reporting and accountability. As mentioned earlier, several companies in India raised funds from market projecting inflated picture of their past performance and profitability. But actually they performed much worse than the past reported figures. As a result, shareholders and investors suffered due to corrupt management and their investment in highly risky investments projects. Fraudulent practices were also adopted in allotting promoters shares at preferential prices disproportionate to market value. These practices adversely affected the minority holders interest.

But, at least in India, no sense of accountability has been shown to the investors and losses suffered by them. However, in the USA following the failures of reputed corporate companies like Enron, World Com. which caused heavy losses to the investors due to their wrong financial reporting, the Sarbanes - Oxley Act 2002 was passed to address the issues concerning accountability. Under this Act, the Securities and Exchange Commission initiated action against multinational accounting firms for failure to detect blatant violations of accounting standards and penalties running to several million dollars were recovered from certain multinational consultantancy firms. But in India there is acute lack of accountability of corporate firms and they often indulge in corrupt practices to dupe the investors. This is still happening despite the recommendations of Kumar Manglam Birla Committee, Naresh Chandra Committee, the Sebi Committee on Corporate Governance regarding the adoption of best practices of governance for protecting interests of shareholders and other stakeholders. Therefore, in case of India also the law on the lines of the US Sarbanes-Oxley-Act 2002 needs to be passed and strictly enforced if accountability of corporate companies is to be ensured .

Generally, in management science, accountability means ensuring that the person or division of the company who is assigned to perform a task actually performs it effectively and honestly. A corporate can easily lack accountability if various so called 'Profit Centres' in it do not perform well according to the established standards. Any business enterprise is run by managers of different divisions or departments (often called profit centres) and are given the resources (*i.e.* inputs) needed to accomplish the assigned task and therefore they are held accountable if things go wrong and they do not produce the expected results or outcome (*i.e.* output). According to Ajit Nivard Cabraal, "Organisations tends to focus on the quantum of funds that are allocated to respective departments or divisions without considering carefully as to what "*outcomes*" are expected from such '*inputs*'.. This shortcoming invariably leads to those divisions or departments not having to or being asked to account to the organisation for the funds entrusted to them. Even if there are some seemingly transparent controls in the *application and disbursement of the funds, but if there are no clear performance or output criteria* set out and expected outcomes identified, it is almost impossible to hold the responsible official accountable for the funds "thus expanded"[9].

However, the concept of corporate governance generally applies to the accountability of board of directors and top management who control and supervise the corporate enterprise and have sufficient authority to get things done properly. They are expected to adopt good and healthy principles and codes of good governance and avoid corruption in their dealings, especially with the shareholders and investors. They are expected to observe established standards of financial probity.

Corporate Governance and New Companies Bill

After Satyam fiasco in January 2009, the Government was under pressure to improve the governance of corporate companies and fix roles and responsibility of corporate management. On August 3, the Government introduced the Campanies Bill in the Lok Sabha which will replace the

9. *Op.cit.*

Campanies Act of 1956.

The new bill provides for articulation of shareholders democracy with *protection of rights* of *minority stakeholders* and responsible self-regulation with disclosures and accountability. "Shareholders associations or group of shareholders will be enabled to take legal action in case of any fraudulent action on part of the company and to take part in investor protection activities in *class action suits*," the bill said. Under current norms, a person holding shares worth ₹ 1 lakh or less in a company is categorised as a small investor. However, while large investors can question corporate strategies through voting rights and other means, small investors do not have any specific instrument to hold promoters of companies accountable.

The provision of class action suit is aimed at suitably **empowering small and minority stakeholders** in case of any wrong doing by promoters or management of a firm. A class action or a representative action is a form of lawsuit where large groups of people collectively bring a claim to court.

The bill has also proposed several provisions; apart from **setting accounting and auditing standards** it also **defines the role and responsibilities of an independent director.** An "independent director" according to the bill, should be a person of integrity with relevant experience and **should not have any monetary relationship** or **transaction with the company, its subsidiaries, or promoters.**

A single forum for approval of mergers and acquisitions along with a shorter merger process for holding and wholely-owned subsidiary companies has also been introduced in the new companies act.

Highlights of the Changes Made in the New Amended Companies Bill 2011

To ensure good corporate governance, the new amended Companies Bill 2011 which was passed by parliamnet in Aug. 2013 has made several important changes for the working of corporate companies. Some important changes are the following :

1. Social Responsibility for Companies. It is stipulated in the new companies act that companies will have to spend 2% their average net profit during three years on corporate social responsibility (CSR) activities in the local areas of their operations. In case of non-compliance, the broad of a company will have to explain why spending on CSR activities has fallen short in a particular year.

2. Independent Directors. To improve the proper and impartial working of the corporate companies it has been provided that every board of a listed company will have at least one-third of its directors as independent directors. *Listed companies can have one independent director representing small shareholders*. Further, no director can be on the boards of more than 20 companies.

3. Tightening of Rules for Auditors. To ensure strict financial control over the companies to prevent any financial bungling by the companies it has been had down that auditors can be appointed for 5 years at a time. Besides, in a limited company an auditor cannot get two consecutive 5 year terms. Further, one auditor cannot audit more than 20 companies.

4. More Powers to Shareholders. Shareholders can taken legal action against a company for fraud, shareholders or depositors of the companies can file **class-action suits** against a company in case of any fraud done with them. However, banking companies have been exempted from this.

5. Measures to Check Corporate Frauds. Fraud and wrongful gain has been defined first time in this new amended company bill. Serious fraud intestigation office (SFIO) has received statutory recognition. Once SFIO starts investigating any alleged case of fraud no other agency can be involved. The new bill allows assets of companies under investigation to be frozen for use as evidence. As mentioned above, shareholders can take legal action against the company for fraud.

6. Employees Protection in Failed Companies. If a company winds up its operations, it must pay two years' salary to its employees. Rights of employees will supersede even those of even secured creditors. Companies law tribunal will have powers to sanction compromise solutions among various stakeholders.

7. Strict Rules for Raising Funds. In the new bill tighter rules for raising funds have been laid down. Only banking companies, non-banking financial companies (NBFCs) and firms allowed by regulators can accept deposits from the public. For violation of this rule strict penalties with minimum of ₹ 1 crore can be imposed.

8. Transparency in Managerial Remuneration. Listed companies will have to disclose ratio of each director's remuneration to median salary. Besides, a director's remuneration should not exceed five per cent of a company's net profit.

The implementation of above rules, both in letter and spirit, will go a long way in ensuring transparency in working of corporate companies and better corporate governance with social service responsibility.

SOCIAL RESPONSIBILITY OF BUSINESS

Meaning

Social responsibility of business implies the obligations of the management of a business enterprise to protect the interests of the society. According to the concept of social responsibility the objective of managers for taking business decisions is not merely to maximise profits or shareholders' value but also to serve and protect the interests of other members of a society such as workers, consumers and the community as a whole. Thus, Sachar Committee on Companies and MRTP Acts appointed by Government of India states, "In the development of corporate ethics we have reached a stage where the question of social responsibility of business to the community can no longer be scoffed at or taken lightly. *In the environment of modern corporate economic development, the corporate sector no longer functions in isolation. If the plea of the companies that they are performing a social purpose is to be accepted, it can only be judged by the test of social responsivess shown to the needs of the society*".[10] It may be noted that some Indian sociologists and economists relate the idea of social responsibility of business of the Gandhian concept of trusteeship. According to Mahatma Gandhi, capitalist class owns wealth or capital as trustees of the society. The resources and capital they use for production of goods and services, according to him, should be used not to maximise profits for them but for the larger benefit of the society.

However, in our view, it will be too idealistic to expect that business enterprises will be purely guided by the benefits they confer on the society by their activities. The concept of social responsibility as used in management science is that businesses should maximise their profits subject to their working in a socially responsible manner to promote the interests of the society. Their business activities should not harm other groups such as consumers, workers, and public at large. Mr. N.R. Narayana, Chairman of Infosys makes the idea of social responsibility of business quite clear when in a conference on corporate social responsibility he said, "*Corporate's foremost social responsibility is to create maximum shareholders' value working in a way which is fair to all its stakeholders — workers, consumers, the community, government and the environment.*[11] *He further points out, "Working in harmony with the community and environment around us and not cheating our customers and workers we might not gain anything in the short run but in the long term it means greater profits and shareholders value*"[12]

Social Responsibility of Business and Social Contract

It is evident from above, the social responsibility of business implies that a corporate enterprise has to serve interests other than that of common shareholders who, of course, expect that their rate of return, value or wealth should be maximised. But in today's world the interest of other stakehold-

10. GOI, Report of Expert Committee on Companies and MRTP Acts 1978. This Committee was chaired by Justice Sachar.
11. N.R. Narayana Murthy, Reported in *The Economic Times*, December 5, 2001.

ers, community and environment must be protected and promoted. Social responsibility of business enterprises to the various stakeholders and society in general is considered to be the result of a *social*

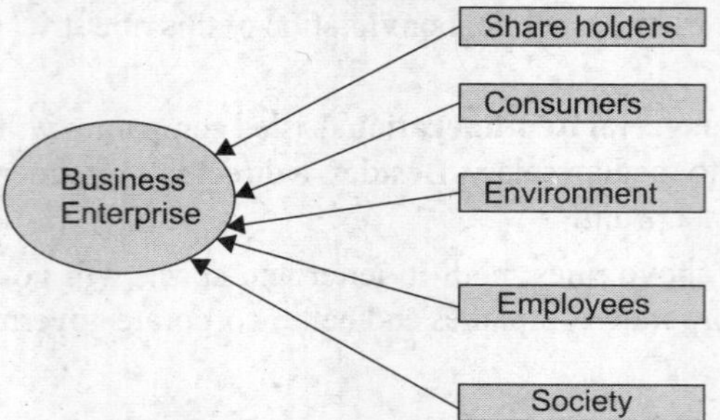

Fig. 3.1. *Responsibility of Business Enterprises towards Stakeholders and Society in General.*

contract. Social contract is a set of rules that defines the agreed interrelationship between various elements of a society. The social contract often involves a quid pro quo (*i.e.* something given in exchange for another). In the social contract, one party to the contract gives something and expects a certain thing or behaviour pattern from the other. In the present context the social contract is concerned with the relationship of a business enterprise with various stakeholders such as shareholders, employees, consumers, government and society in general. The business enterprises happen to have resources because society consisting of various stakeholders has given them this right and therefore it expects from them to use them to for serving the interests of all of them. Though all stakeholders including the society in general are affected by the business activities of a corporate enterprise, managers may not acknowledge responsibility to them. Social responsibility of business implies that corporate managers must promote the interests of all stakeholders not merely of shareholders who happen to be the so called owners of the business enterprises. We have depicted in Figure 40.1 the various stakeholders whose interests have to be served by the corporate enterprises. In what follows we explain in detail how the interests of various stakeholders are to be served and promoted.

Responsibility to Shareholders

As explained above in the context of good corporate governance a corporate enterprise must recognise the rights of shareholders and protect their interests. It should respect shareholders' right to information and respect their right to submit proposals to vote and to ask questions at the annual general body meeting. The corporate enterprise should observe the best code of conduct in its dealings with the shareholders. However, the corporate Board and management try to increase profits or shareholders' value but in pursuing this objective, they should protect the interests of employees, consumers and other stakeholders. Its special responsibility is that in its efforts to increase profits or shareholders' value it should not pollute the environment.

Responsibility to Employees

The success of a business enterprise depends to a large extent on the morale of its employees. Employees make valuable contribution to the activities of a business organisation. The corporate enterprise should have good and fair employment practices and industrial relations to enhance its productivity. It must recognise the rights of workers or employees to freedom of association and free collective bargaining. Besides, it should not discriminate between various employees.

The most important responsibility of a corporate enterprise towards employees is the *payment of fair wages to them and provide healthy and good working conditions*. The business enterprises should recognise the need for providing essential labour welfare activities to their employees, especially they should take care of women workers. Besides, the enterprises should make arrangements for proper training and education of the workers to enhance their skills.

However, it may be noted that very few companies in India follow many of the above good practices. While the captains of Indian industries generally complain about low productivity of their employees, little has been done to address their problems. Ajith Nivard Cabraal rightly writes, "It should perhaps be realised that corporations can only be as effective and efficient as its employees and therefore steps should be taken to implement such reforms in a pro-active manner, rather than merely attempting to comply with many labour laws that prevail in the country. This is probably one area where good governance practices could make a significant impact on the country's business environment."[13]

Responsibility to Consumers

Some economists think that consumer is a king who directs the business enterprises to produce goods and services to satisfy his wants. However, in the modern times this may not be strictly true but the companies must acknowledge their responsibilities to protect their interests in undertaking their productive activities. Invoking the notion of social contract, the management expert Peter Drucker observes, "*The customer is the foundation of a business and keeps it in existence. He alone gives employment. To meet the wants and needs of a consumer, the society entrusts wealth-producing resources to the business enterprise*".

In view of above, the business enterprises should recognise the rights of consumers and understand their needs and wants and produce goods or services accordingly. The following responsibilities of business enterprises to consumers are worth mentioning.

1. They should supply goods or services to the consumers at reasonable prices and do not try to exploit them by forming cartels. This is more relevant in case of business enterprises producing essential goods such as life-saving drugs, vegetable oil and essential' services such as electricity supply and telephone services.

2. They should not supply to the consumers' shoddy and unsafe products which may do harm to them.

3. They should provide the consumers the required after-sales services.

4. They should not misinform the consumers through inappropriate and misleading advertisements.

5. They should make arrangements for proper distribution system of their products so as to ensure that black-marketing and profiteering by traders do not occur.

6. They should acknowledge the rights of consumers to be heard and take necessary measures to redress their genuine grievances.

Despite the above responsibilities which are generally regarded as good marketing practices by management experts the business enterprises in India generally do not pay heed to them and as a result consumers are dissatisfied or disappointed in a large number of cases. There has been a growing awareness of consumer rights. The organised movement to protect consumer rights which is termed as *consumerism* has been the result of the negligence of business enterprises to their responsibilities to consumers. Besides, due to the indifferent attitude of business enterprises to consumer rights, Government has been compelled to enact *Consumer Protection Act* to protect consumers' rights and to prevent their exploitation by the businesses.

Obligation towards the Environment

The foremost responsibility of business enterprises is to ensure that they should not damage the environment and for this purpose *they should reduce as much as possible air and water pollution by their productive activities*. They should not dump their toxic waste products in rivers and streams to avoid their pollution. Pollution of environment poses a great health hazard for the people and is a cause of several respiratory and skin diseases. In economic theory pollution of environment is regarded as social cost that must be minimised. There is now a growing awareness towards reduction

---

13. *Op.cit.*

in environment pollution. According to the recent findings the *climate change* is occurring due to greater emission of carbon dioxide and other pollutants. Therefore, the corporate enterprises should adopt high standards of environmental protection and ensure that they are implemented regardless of enforcement of any environment laws passed by the government. Many countries including India have passed laws to protect the environment but they are not properly and strictly enforced. Business enterprises in their attempt to maximise profits recklessly and negligently pollute the environment. Therefore, it is required that government should take tough measures and enforce environment laws strictly if environment is to be protected.

Responsibility to Society in General

Business enterprises function by public consent with the basic objective of producing goods and services to meet the needs of the society and provide employment to the people. The traditional view is that in performing this function businesses maximise profits or shareholders' value and doing so they do not behave in any socially irresponsible way. According to Adam Smith whose invisible hand theorem is often quoted that while maximising their profits, businessmen are *led by an invisible hand* to promote the interests of the society. To quote him, "*An individual or business generally, indeed neither intends to promote the public interest, nor knows how much he is promoting it.... He intends only his own gains, and he is in this, as in many other cases, led by an invisible hand to promote an end which was no part of his intention, ... By pursuing his own interest he frequently promotes that of the society more effectively than when he really intends to promote it*".[14]

In the present world where there are monopolies, oligopolies in product and factor markets and also there are externalities, especially detrimental externalities such as environment pollution by the activities of business enterprises maximisation of private profits does not always lead to the maximisation of social benefit. In fact in such imperfect market conditions, consumers are exploited by raising of prices much above the cost of production, workers are exploited as they are not paid fair wages equal to the value of their marginal product. Besides, there are harmful external effects to which are not given due considerations by private enterprises in making their business decisions. Therefore, there is urgent need to make business enterprises behave in a socially responsible manner and to work for promoting social interests.

In view of the above in the context of modern developments, it is hard to agree with Milton Friedman, a winner of Nobel Prize in economics, who called the idea of corporate social responsibility as a "fundamentally subversive doctrine". Friedman writes, "*There is one and only one social responsibility of business – to use its resources and engage in activities designed to increase its profits so long as it stays within the rules of the game, which is to say, engages in open and free competition without deception or fraud*".[15]

However, few economists and rational thinkers will subscribe to Friedman's views like that of Adam Smith. Thus, authors of a noted textbook on management write, "It is true that Friedman sets a rather high standard when he suggests that businesses should operate within the 'rules of the game', practising neither deception nor fraud. The rules of the game obviously include accepted ethical practices, in addition to international, national and other laws. *How many corporations are willing to tell the absolute truth in the advertisements and to engage in open and fair competition avoiding collusion, price fixing and so forth. The fact is that few subscribe to Friedman's hard-line views today*".[16]

Expressing the same sentiments, Dr. Manmohan Singh, who has been instrumental in initiating economic reforms promoting liberalisation and privatisation, in his recent speech while inaugurating

14. Adam Smith, *The Wealth of Nations*, 1776, New York : Modern Library edition, 1937, p. 36
15. Milton Friedman, Capitalism and Freedom (Chicago : University of Chicago Press, 1962), p.123.
16. R. Wayne Mondy, Arthur Sharplin, Shane R. Premeaux, *Management Concepts, Practices and Skills*, Allyn and Bacon, 1991, 5th edition, p.88 (italics added)

the campus of Institute for Studies in Industrial Development on May 1, 2007 said, "*I was struck by a comment in the media that most of the billionaires among India's top business leaders operate in oligopolistic markets and in sectors where the government has conferred special privileges on a few. This sounds like a crony capitalism . . . . . Are we doing enough to protect consumers and small businesses from the consequences of modern capitalism in our country*" Later, on May 24, 2007, while giving inaugural address at the Annual Session of CII he urged the captains of Indian industry to break cartels and abstain from greed in their quest for profit maximisation. To quote him, "*The operation of cartels by groups of companies to keep prices high must end.* It is unacceptable to obstruct the forces of competition from having free play. It is even more distressing in a country where the poor are severely affected by rising commodity prices. Cartels are a crime and go against the grain of an open economy". More importantly, he further adds, "*Maximisation of profits should be within the bounds of decency and greed*".

The above views of Dr. Manmohan singh show that corporate businesses in India do not show any sense of social responsibility and due to oligopolies, informal collusion and other malpractices fleece the customers by charging higher prices in order to maximise their profits. This is clearly refutation of Friedman's view that profit maximisation always implies social responsibility of business.

Business enterprises have a lot of responsibility to the society at large. We mention below some of them.

1. To take appropriate measures to reduce level of pollution and adopt eco-friendly technologies.

2. To generate sufficient employment opportunities so as to make good contribution to the reduction of poverty in the country.

3. Respect the rights of workers and other employees and take appropriate measures to ensure their safety and to improve their working conditions.

4. To provide quality healthcare to their employees.

5. To invest adequately in the research and development so as to make innovations to improve their productivity.

Dr. Manmohan Singh in the speeches referred to above adds the following social responsibilities of the corporate enterprises in India :

6. Do not pay excessive remuneration to promoters and senior executives as it creates social resentment.

7. To end cartels that keep prices highl

8. To implement affirmative action and to provide jobs to SCs, STs and OBCs. Besides, Dr. Manmohan Singh wants the private corporate sector to give preference to minorities, especially Muslims in providing employment.

9. To resist to pay bribes to officials and therefore do not promote corruption. He thus says, "Corruption need not be the grease that oils wheels of progress. There are many successful companies today that have refused to yield to this temptation. Others must follow ".

Conclusion. Social responsibility is related to the concept of ethics. Ethics is the discipline that deals with moral duties and obligations. Social responsibility implies corporate enterprises should follow business ethics and work for not only to maximise their profits or shareholders' value but also to promote the interests of other stakeholders and the society as a whole.

Two instances of lack of social responsibility of business witnessed in India are worth mentioning. One refers to ***Bhopal Gas Leak Tragedy***. On Dec. 2, 1984 in a pesticide factory located in Bhopal and owned by a multinational corporation 'Union Carbide Limited (UCL), there was a leakage of poisonous gas from factory which resulted in the death of more than 2000 poor people and about 2 lakh persons were badly injured and crippled. This was due to the non-installation of safety measures by the company. Union Carbide tried to show that it was not responsible . A long legal battle was fought and ultimately Union Carbide was held responsible by the court and was asked to pay $650 millions to the victims as damages.

Another recent case of lack of corporate social responsibility in India and failure of good corporate governance in India is provided by *Satyam Saga*. Ramalinga Raju, chairman of Satyam Computers committed fraud running into several thousand crores inflicting heavy losses to the shareholders and lenders of the company. For this criminal act Raju is in Jail and his company has been taken over by Mahindera. This Satyam fraud raises the question of failure of corporate governance in India, especially the role of *independent directors* in ensuring good governance of the corporates.

The above two examples should serve as a wake-up call for Indian corporate businesses that they should discharge their responsibility to their customers, employees, other stakeholders and society at large.

Corporate Social Responsibility (CSR) Under the Amended Companies Bill 2011

An important provision of the new Companies Bill 2011 is that it requires the profit-making corporate companies to spend 2 per cent of their average net profits during preceding three years on social responsibility activities if they have net profit of ₹ 5 crore or more or net worth more than ₹ 500 crore or turnover of 1000 crore in a year. *The expenditure on CSR activities has to be spent only in the local areas*. This spending on CSR activities on is not mandatory, but in case of non-compliance to spend 2% of average profits of preceding three years on CSR activities in local areas the company's board will have to explain why spending on CSR activities has fallen short in a particular year. This provision for corporate companies to spend 2% of their net profit on CSR activities is a landmark measure to make the Indian corporate companies to spend adequate amount on CSR activities. The performance of Indian companies in case of CSR has been pathetic as they have failed in their role of being a good corporate citizen. They are found to be doing more of lip service rather than actual initiatives in and around the areas of their operations.

Estimates made by ET Intelligence group reveal that the bulk of CSR expenditure – nearly 5000 crore will be spent by the Nifty 50 Index of Bombay Stock Exchange. So far record of Indian companies for spending social responsibility activities is dismal. Only 2 companies Ambuja Cement, ITC companies, currently spend 2% of their net profits on CSR. Even noted company Infosys spend only 1% of its net profit on CSR activities. Spending on CSR activities by some companies in year 2010-11 is shown in Table 3.1.

Table 3.1. Spending by Companies on Corporate Social Responsibility (CSR) Activities

Companies	*Amount spent (in crores)*	*% of Net Profit*
Ambuja Cement	32.5	2.6
Axis Bank	85.7	–
ICICI Bank	11.2	0.2
ITC	88.0	2.1
M&M (Group)	72.0	1.3
NTPC	50.0	0.5
Sesa Goa (Vedanta Group)	230.0	1.8
State Bank of India	71.2	0.7
UltraTech Cement	18.2	0.8
Infosys	–	1.0

Source : Study by ET Intelligence Group

In our view spending on CSR activities by companies is spending for a social cause and they will benefit immensely from it goodwill for it that will be generated because of engaging with the community around their areas of operations. To ensure the compliance by the companies to spend 2 % of their average profit in three preceding years requires the government to watch their required spending on CSR activities prescribed in the new amended Companies Act, 2011.

CHAPTER 3A

Alternative Economic System

Introduction

A business firm works in a certain institutional framework defined by an economic system. The important economic systems that have prevailed in the world are a free market economic system (also called capitalism), command economy system represented by communism or authoritarian socialist system and mixed economic system that prevails in India and where both private and public sectors play a role in determining production, exchange, investment and distribution of national income. Business economics has been evolved and developed in the framework of a free market economy in which the resources of a society are privately owned by individuals and firms. Thus, a market economy recognises and protects *property rights*, that is, the rights that govern the ownership, use and disposal of resources and the goods and services produced with their help. Historically, such a social arrangement in which resources are privately owned and consumers (i.e. individuals or households) and producing firms interact to determine the choices regarding production and distribution of goods and services has been called capitalism. Thus, according to W.N. Loucks, "*Capitalism is a system of economic organisation featured by the private ownership of and the use of man-made and nature-made capital*"[1].

In the basic model of a market economy we also assume that competitive markets prevail in a market economy in which no individual consumer and firm exercises any control over the prices of products and resources. Hence we call this model of a market economy as *basic competitive model*. In what follows we will first explain the essential features of a competitive market economy and the basic competitive model.

CHIEF FEATURES OF A FREE MARKET (CAPITALIST) ECONOMY

The efficient working of a free market economy requires that the producer firms must have incentives to work hard and produce goods and services at the lowest possible cost per unit of output Market economies provide incentives to the firms and individuals by recognising and enforcing the property rights of the individuals and firms to own the resources and goods and services produced by using them. It also allows the individuals and firms to use the resources owned by them for making profits. *Earning of profits from using resources owned by them also provides incentives to the firms and individuals to produce goods and services efficiently*. Profits depend on cost per unit incurred and price charged of goods and services produced. The prices of goods and resources provide information to the individuals and firms about the relative scarcity of different goods and services. Thus property rights, profits, prices and incentives play a crucial role in the functioning of a market economy. We briefly explain them below.

Property Rights

Property rights are social institutions that govern the ownership, use and disposal of resources, goods and services. There are different types of property which individuals and firms can privately own. (1) *Real property* which includes land, buildings, durable goods such as plant, capital equipment etc. (2) *Financial property* which includes shares and bonds, bank deposits, money kept at home. (3) *Intellectual property*, which is the latest addition to the list of property, represents the products of creative effort and includes books written, audio and video material, computer programmes. It

1. W. N. Loucks, *Comparative Economic Systems*.

is interesting to note here that Bill Gates have become the richest man of the world by possessing intellectual property in the form of computer programmes such as windows, Miscrosoft Office.

The right of private property is a fundamental feature of a capitalist economy. The right of private property means that productive resources such as land, factories, machinery, mines, etc. are under the private ownership. In other words, an individual has a right to acquire and to use the means of production. Besides, the owner is free to sell or dispose of his property in any way he likes. Because of this right of private property, goods like land, factories, mines, machinery, houses, and other producer and consumer goods are privately owned by the people. They use these means of production for their individual benefit. Moreover, the right of private property includes in itself the **right of inheritance**. The right of inheritance means that on the death of a person, his sons or daughters or some relatives become the owners of his property. No doubt, there are always some restrictions on the right to private property imposed by the Government for social harmony and benefit. But, except for some restrictions capitalist economic system tries to protect and enforce the right of private property. The two attributes of property rights, namely, *the right of the owner to use the property as he likes and the right to sell it provide incentives to the owners to use their property efficiently.*

It is important that government should enforce the property rights. If property rights are not enforced, then the incentives to use the property efficiently is weakened and the potential gain from its efficient use will be lost. *Enforcing intellectual property rights is proving to be a big challenge these days* in view of the modern technologies that make it relatively easy to copy books, audio and video material and computer programmes.

Freedom of Private Enterprise

Allied to the property rights is freedom of enterprise which is another basic feature of a market economy. Freedom of enterprise means that everybody is free to engage in whatever economic activity he pleases. In other words, he is free to choose to work in any industry he likes or adopts any occupation or trade he desires. More specifically, freedom of enterprise means that an entrepreneur is free to set up any firm or business unit to produce goods or make investment in shares or bonds of corporate sector. True , he may not have enough capital to invest in business or a productive unit like factory or he may not have enough ability or training to follow certain occupations. But subject to these limitations and to the laws passed by the Government in public interest, an individual or firm is free to engage in any economic activity he feels most desirable or profitable. In India before 1991, there was a *system of industrial licensing* which restricted the freedom of enterprise. For setting up industrial units in various industries, the private sector firms had to obtain licenses which were not easily available. Similarly, for procuring necessary raw materials and inputs such as steel, cement, businessmen had to get *permits* from the government to purchase these products and to get permits businessmen had to bribe the government officials. This license-permit system greatly restricted the freedom of enterprise of the private sector firms. This not only caused allocative inefficiency but also obstructed economic growth of the country. Under the structural economic reforms initiated in 1991 by Dr. Manmohan Singh who was then Finance Minister ,industrial licensing has been largely abolished and the system of permits has been done away with. Grant of licenses to import goods, machines and raw materials has been greatly liberalised and custom duties have been drastically reduced. As a result, private sector now enjoys greater freedom to invest in industries they think it profitable and diversify their productive capacity by producing multiple products.

Abolition of industrial licensing system and liberalisation of imports and ending of permit system has tended to promote competition in the Indian economy. The greater competition has helped to keep inflation under check and to achieve higher industrial growth rate.

Profits and Prices : Incentives and Information

No individuals would work and save if adequate incentives are not provided to them in the form of wages and interest respectively. Similarly, the firms will not produce goods and services and bear risk of losing money if sufficient incentives are not given to them. Profits are earned from undertaking the task of producing goods and services and introducing new products and new techniques of production. Profits earned by the firm depend on prices of goods and services produced and cost incurred. As seen above, in a perfectly competitive market firms are price takers, that is they take price of a product or service as given. With a given price, firm's profits will be larger, if cost per unit of output is smaller. Therefore, in order to maximise profits, firms try to minimise cost for producing a given level of output. *Thus profits serve as incentive for the firm to produce efficiently.*

The working of price system ensures that those individuals and firms will get goods who are willing and able to pay for them. Prices of goods and services indicate how much money individuals are prepared to pay for them. In other words, *prices convey information to the firms about how individuals value different goods and services.* The goods and resources which are relatively more scarce, will have higher prices in the market. On the other hands, the goods and resources which are relatively less scarce will have low market prices. The profit motive induces firms to respond to the prices of different goods. The firms will earn more profits if they produce goods which people want most efficiently, that is, economise the use of scarce resources and use relatively more those resources which are relatively less scarce in supply. Thus, by producing efficiently the firms are able to increase profits. It is important to note that for profit motive to be effective the firms must be allowed to keep a good part of the profits earned by them and not taxed away by government. As seen above, this is implied by property rights enjoyed by the firms. Similarly, if incentives to individuals or households have to be provided to work hard and acquire skills and training, they should be permitted to retain a good amount of what they earn from their work or what they receive as a return on their investments.

Importance of Information and Incentives. It follows from above that *for market economies to solve its basic economic problems and work efficiently individuals and firms must have adequate information and have incentives to act on the available information.* In market economies it is prices through which individuals and firms get information about the relative scarcity of goods and resources. Relatively more scarce goods and resources tend to have higher prices than the relatively less scarce resources. Further, in market economies incentives play a crucial role for the working of individuals and firms. Professor Stiglitz, a Nobel laureate in economics writes, "*incentives can be viewed as being at the heart of economics. Without incentives, why would individuals go to work in the morning? Who would undertake the risks of bringing out new products ? Who would put aside savings for a rainy day*?"[2] Emphasising the importance of incentives he further writes, "Providing appropriate incentives is a fundamental economic problem. In modern market economies, profits provide incentives for firms to produce the goods individuals want and wages provide incentives for individuals to work, property rights also provide people with important incentives not only to invest and to save but also to put their assets to the best possible use."[3]

It follows from above that property rights are important features of market economies and play a significant role in their efficient working.

Incentives vs. Inequality. While incentives play a significant role in market economies for their working efficiently to solve the basic problems of what to produce, how to produce, for whom to produce and how much to invest for bringing about economic growth, but they involve a cost which must be taken into account. *The cost of providing incentives is the inequality in the economy they cause.* Any system of incentives must provide compensation to individuals and firms in terms of higher wages, larger profits, higher return on investment for better performance or higher efficiency. If pay for work, return on investment is tied to performance etc. then since performances differ, the compensation for them too will differ and this will bring about inequality in incomes. This raises the question how much incentives should be given for better performance or higher efficiency so that inequality of incomes is not much higher. Since the greater the incentives given, the greater will be the inequality of incomes, there is *incentive -inequality trade-off*. If a society provides greater

2. Joseph Stiglitz. *Principles of Economics*, p.25.
3. *Op. cit.*, p. 26.

incentives to promote efficiency and growth, there is likely to be more inequality of incomes.

It may be noted that one basic problem facing governments of market economies is to devise a tax system (*i.e.* kinds of taxes and rates of taxes) that tends to reduce incentives on the one hand but provide revenue to finance welfare programmes for those who have low incomes. Thus, providing incentives to earn higher wages or return and profits encounters serious problem of increasing inequalities of income in a society.

Competitive Markets

In ordinary speech the word *market* means a place where buyers and sellers meet to buy and sell goods. In economics, market has a wider meaning and is interpreted to mean any arrangement that enables buyers and sellers to exchange things; they may contact each other through telephone, fax or direct computer link to negotiate prices of goods they buy and sell. In our above example, rational and self-interested consumers and profit-maximising firms contact each other through any media and buy and sell things on the negotiated price.

The self-interested consumers are interested in low prices of goods they buy and, on the other hand, the profit-maximising firms will be interested in charging a higher price of the goods they produce and offer for sale in the market. However, through their interaction they may agree to buy and sell goods at the agreed price.

In the basic competitive model of a market economy, it is assumed that neither the consumers, nor the firms have any market power to influence the prices of the goods and services they want to buy and sell. In fact, the economists generally assume that *perfect competition* prevails in the market. Under perfect competition, there are a large number of firms producing a good and since no one is in a position to influence the price, they take prices of goods as given and constant, that is, each firm is a *price taker*. Each firm must accept the price prevailing in the market. This prevailing price is determined by the interaction of *all* firms and buyers. We will see in a later chapter how demand for a good by all the consumers who want to buy the goods and supply by all the firms who produce and supply a good together determine the market price of the goods. Suffice it to say here, if a firm in this perfectly competitive market charges a higher than the prevailing price, it will not be able to sell any quantity of the goods because his customers will switch to other firms producing and supplying the same good.

Similarly, in such a perfectly competitive market since each consumer cannot influence the market price, it must accept it as given and make a choice about how much to buy the various goods and services, given his budget constraint and preferences for different goods. Thus, in the basic competitive model of a market economy, rational and self-interested consumers and profit-maximising firms interact to determine prices of goods and resources. As will be explained later, these prices play a crucial role in determining social choices regarding what, how and for whom to produce.

COMMAND ECONOMY

In the foregoing analysis we have explained how the free market economic system which is historically called *capitalism* works and what are its merits and drawbacks. We have also studied how at present in the market economies government plays a role in improving the functioning of market economic system. Now, an important question is if there is any altenative economic system that can solve the basic economic problem faced by the nations. In fact an alternative economic system known as authoritarian socialist system or *command economy* was adopted in erstwhile Soviet Russia, China, East European countries such as Poland, Czechoslovakia. In this authoritarian socialist system or command economy basic economic problem of what, how and for whom to produce etc. are resolved through a combination of state ownership of productive enterprises and centralised planning. It is government or any central authority set up by it that decides output targets for each public enterprise, allocates resoures to them and fixes prices of various goods and services and incomes (wages, salaries) of various types of workers.

In a centrally planned socialist economy, there exists a central planning authority, which organises and regulates the various economic activities. Thus it is the central planning authority which determines what the various production units shall produce, what the various individuals shall obtain for consumption and as a result what shall be left for investment. Further, it decides what type of investment shall be made.

It should be realised that the organization of the various economic activities by one planning authority is full of administrative and economic difficulties. The authority is faced with the political and administrative problems of getting their decisions implemented. In other words, there are problems of putting the various decisions into effect. Moreover, the planning authority is faced with an overall economic problem, namely, how to use the limited productive resources for achieving the best possible results. The particulars purposes for which resources are to be used have to be decided. In other words, allocation of resources as between various kinds of consumer goods, and as between consumer goods and capital goods, and as between civilian goods and war goods, has to be decided. Taking of all these decisions is indeed a very difficult task. Besies, decisions have to be taken about the particular techniques with which various products are to be produced and about distributing goods among the people.

It may be noted that planning of actual production of various products is greatly difficult due to the fact that technical relations between different kinds of products are very much complicated. For example, to build ships it apparently seems that only steel and other materials which make up ships are required. But little more thinking will reveal that arrangements for the complicated process of production of steel and other materials have to be made before steel and other materials become available for use in ship building. Moreover, various types of machinery would have to be made for converting iron ore into steel as well as converting steel into ships. Further, the arrangements for coal, electricity and transport have to be made if the production of steel and ships is to become possible. Thus, technical relations between different kinds of output are so complicated that for carrying out the decision to produce more of one kind of product, adjustments on several other lines have to be made.

Collapse of the Command Economy or Authoritarian Socialist System

It is obvious from what has been said above that the planning of productive activity by one central authority is a very difficult task. The planning authority in the centrally planned economies like those of erstwhile Soviet Russia and East European countries which used to plan production with the aid of several technical experts before the system broke down in the late eighties. In the late eighties the socialist countries, Soviet Russia and countries of Eastern Europe such as Poland, Czechoslovakia had to face severe economic problems which led to the collapse of Soviet-type authoritarian socialism or what is called command economy. *In its place the market system has been introduced and this is proclaimed as victory of capitalism over socialism.*

There is more than one reason for the collapse of the command economy in Soviet Russian and Eastern Europe. The important reason for the collapse of socialism and centralised planning *was lack of efficiency in reasource allocation.* It was found that for a central planning authority consisting of bureaucrats it was difficult to make right decisions to allocate scarce resources according to the wants and perferences of the people. As result, shortage in some goods and surplus in others emerged. These could not be easily corrected due to corrupt, inefficient and unresponsive government officials. This caused a lot of wastage of national resources. The most glaring example of inefficiency in allocation of resources in Soviety Russia and othe command economies was the emergence of *acute scarcity of essential consumer goods*. This led to *long-queues* of the people at the consumer stores to get these goods.

This acute scarcity of consumer goods led to the lack of faith in socialism to deliver the goods. Indeed, it was said that Soviet-type authoritarian socialism promised bread at the expense of liberty of the people. But in actual practice people got neither bread nor liberty. Since by the late nineteen eighties the then Soviet President Mickhail Gorbachev had introduced some freedom for the people, the wide expression of resentment about the scarcity of consumer goods could not be suppressed. This led to the collapse of authoritarian socialism and introduction of reforms aimed at introduction of private enterprise and the market system.

The other important reason for the failure of centralised planning was that the managers of public enterprises *lacked incentives to improve productivity and efficiency*. This was due to the absence of profit motive on the part of managers of public enterprises. This caused inefficiency in the use and allocatiion of scarce resources.

The most important economic problem faced by these socialist countries was *slowdown in economic growth* in these countries. In Soviet Russia the growth rate which in the post-war period averaged about 7 per cent in 1950s and about 5 per cent in 1960s slipped into 3 per cent range during the 1970s and was nearly zero in the 1980s. Similar experience of slowdown in economic growth rate was observed in other socialist countries of Eastern Europe. Now, when growth rate in them was higher, more employment opportunities were increasing and more goods were forthcoming which enabled people to improve their levels of living. However, when there was sharp slowdown in economic growth, to satisfy the ever-rising wants of the people for goods became difficult and a strong need was felt to make a switch over to the market system to speed up the rate of economic growth.

Lastly, *problems of centralised planning with its inflexibility and inefficiency* have been present throughout in the post revolution period in Soviet Russia. Lacking profit-motive the managers of productive enterprises did not have sufficient incentives to produce the right type of goods in the most efficient way. This causes inefficiency in the use and allocation of resources which accounted for *low productivity and efficiency* in the socialist countries. Owing to lack of incentives managers of productive enterprises were more concerned with fulfilling the quotas assigned to them (which they succeeded in achieving them by deliberately setting them at lower levels) rather than improving efficiency. But still deeper problem posed by the absence of profit motive was *managers of state enterprises lacked incentives to introduce innovations and undertake risks* which caused inefficiency and slow economic growth and ultimately stagnation.

To conclude, the above problems led to the downfall of authoritarian socialism or command economy system in Soviet Russia and other socialist countries. This led to the process of liberalisation of Soviet Russia and other socialist countries. It is because of these problems of economic inefficiency and slowdown in economic growth that even China and India introduced economic reforms which lay stress on privatisation and greater role of market mechanism for solving the economic problems. It may be noted here tha India has adopted the path of a mixed economy. In India's mixed economy both private sector and economic planning by the Government play roles in the working of the Indian eocnomy.

MIXED ECONOMIC SYSTEM

In the real word today a pure free market economy and pure command economy or a centrally planned economic system are not found. Almost all economies have now become mixed economic system in which government plays an important role in allocation of resources and distribution of income. Thus mixed economy or mixed economic system refers to an economic system in which both free market and Government have significant roles in the working of the economy. In a mixed economy elements of both free market system and control or regulation by the Government are present. The proportion of free market working and Government regulation varies from country to country.

Many economies of the present-day world are examples of mixed economy. Mixed economy functions through private enterprise as well as Government. The Government interferes with or regulates the private enterprise in various ways. It has now been realised that the free and unfettered functioning of the private enterprise gives rise to many evils. As a result of free working of the private enterprise, there are violent fluctuations in economic activities; sometimes the conditions of depression and unemployment are created and sometimes the conditions of boom and inflation emerge. Thus a free-market economy suffers from what are called business cycles, with all their consequent evils. Besides, as a result of free functioning of the private enterprise and price mechanism, extreme inequalities of income and wealth are produced. The following of '*Laissez Faire*' policy by the Government, weaker sections of the society are not protected. On the other hand, the command economic system in which resource allocation and income distribution is decided through centralised planning collapsed due to various deficiencies and failures as explained above. Therefore, in both Russia and China free-market economic system along with some government control has been adopted.

In has also been realised that in a developing country like India, desired rate of economic growth cannot be achieved under free private enterprise. Therefore, in order to avoid the above-mentioned evils of the free private enterprise and free functioning of the market mechanism and to achieve the desired rate of economic growth the Government takes an active part in the functioning of the economic system in most economies of the world. Today all the capitalist economies have become mixed form of economies, because in all of them economic role of the Government has greatly increased. '*Laissez Faire*' policy advocated by Adam Smith and other classical economists has now been given up because of its several shortcomings and evils. Therefore, the economies of the United States of America and Britain have also become mixed systems. Paul Samuelson and A.H. Hansen, eminent American economists, have called the economies of America, Britain and France as '*Mixed Capitalist System*' or '*Mixed Enterprise System*', because in them the Government now interferes in the economic activities and takes active part in the functioning of the economic system and regulates and controls the private enterprise by various methods.

Two Forms of Mixed Economic Systems

It is worth noting that mixed economies can be classified into two forms. One form of mixed economy is that in which means of production are in the ownership of private sector and the Government regulates and controls the activities of private enterprise through direct controls (such as price control, licensing system, control over imports, etc.) as well as through monetary and fiscal policies. In such a type of economy, the government does not take over the means of production, and if it does, it does so relatiely on a small scale. That is why such a type of 'mixed system' has been called *Mixed Capitalist System* because such an economic system is basically capitalist and the Government regulates and controls the economic activities through various types of controls and various measures of monetary and fiscal policies so that the various evils of the free working of the private enterprise and the price mechanism are avoided and the economic system is directed towards the desired goals. In such a type of 'mixed economy,' Government itself does not undertake the work of production on a large scale. Government's production work is merely confined to the production of equipments and materials for the army and the working of the public utility services. Such a type of mixed economic system is also called *controlled capitalism*.

Indian Economy as a Mixed Economic System

The second form of a mixed economy is that in which the Government not only regulates and controls the private enterprise through various types of direct controls and appropriate monetary and fiscal policies, *it also directly participates in the production of various goods and services*. In such a type of mixed economy, various basic industries and infrastructure industries are generally in the ownership of the public sector and it is the government which organises and runs them. The remaining industries are in the ownership of private enterprise and it is the private enterprise which is assigned the task of production in them. But it is worth remembering that the government regulates and controls the private enterprise in such industries also through direct control and appropriate monetary and fiscal measures.

The economies of the United States of America and Britain have also become mixed economies. But the nature of mixed economy of India is quite different from them, because in the mixed economy of India the public sector takes more active, more important and more extensive part in the working and growth of the economy. Whereas the mixed economies of the USA and England are biased towards capitalism, the mixed economy of India is biased towards socialism.

Functioning of a Mixed Economy

A mixed economy functions through both price mechanism and planning by the Government. So far as the industries in the public sector are concerned the price, output and investment decisions are taken by the government or the authorities appointed by the government according to the strategy and policy frame of the development plans. But the private sector of the mixed economy is governed and regulated by the price and market mechanism and therefore in regard to the industries in the private sectors, the decisions regarding price, output and investment are taken by the private entrepreneurs or the industrialists with a view to making profits and these decisions are mainly based on price mechanism. The private sector in the mixed economy is, however, influenced, regulated and controlled by the government through monetary and fiscal measures as well as through direct or physical controls.

Prior to 1991 in India, there was a 'licensing system' according to which to start and establish factories in certain industries, the government's permission or licence was necessary. However, under the economic reforms initiated since 1991 in India, licensing and permit system has been done away with and private sector has been given a lot of freedom for deciding about production and expansion in their enterprises. Even foreign investment by multinational companies has been allowed to make investment in India and repatriate the profits to their home countries. However the government also regulates and controls the investment and production in the private sector through appropriate monetary and fiscal measures. By providing concessions in taxation, and by making available cheap credit facilities, the government provides incentives to private entrepreneurs for investment in the desired lines of production decided in development plans.

Role of Government in a Mixed Economic System

As noted above, in the mixed economic system the Government plays a significant role in allocation of scarce resources and distribution of income. However, despite the important role of Government, the people and private enterprises are free to make economic transactions. They voluntarily decide whether or not to transact, have the right to buy and sell what they want. Workers are free to accept or refuse any work they do not want to do, free to move to different places for employment of their choice. **The right to own property and freedom of contract are maintained by the Government.** The Government makes laws which provide right to ownership of property and freedom of contract and courts are set up by it to enforce these laws. Besides, the Government maintains law and order to protect life and liberty of the people and to enforce property rights of the people. It also makes arrangements for defence of the country against foreign aggression.

Besides the above basic functions, Government intervenes in the economy to correct what are called ***market failures.*** These are the situations in which free market does not work efficiently. For example, natural resources such as forests, mines, common pastures tend to be overexploited resulting in their destruction under free market conditions. Further, some goods, called *public goods* such as defence, law and order are not produced at all by private enterprises which are driven by profit motive. This is because once produced the people who do not even pay for them cannot be prevented from using them.

Moreover, private enterprises while producing goods often impose costs that are called ***detrimental externalities*** on others by their economic activities. For example, the production of goods in factories *pollute air and water* surrounding them. This *environment pollution* causes a lot of harm to the people but the private enterprises do not have to pay for the harms they do to others. Nor do they take into account these externalities in their cost calculations while making their investment decisions. As a result, there is overproduction of such goods whose production pollutes environment and impose costs on others and this causes misallocation of resources. The Government can prevent them by imposing taxes on private enterprises which pollute environment.

Above all, the Government in modern mixed economic systems takes fiscal and monetary policies to ***stabilise the economy*** against fluctuations in national income, employment and prices. Recession causes huge unemployment which deprives people of their livelihood. On the other hand, when there is inflation, cost of living of the people rises and as result there is a lot of human suffering. Inflation is a tax that hurts the poor people most. Following J.M. Keynes the Government adopts discretionary fiscal and monetary policies to lift the economy out of recession. For example, recently in 2007-09 when due to global financial crisis originated in the US due to bursting of sub-prime housing loan bubble which caused global recession and meltdown, the Governments in the US, Britain, Japan, France and India too increased public expenditure and cut taxes to revive their economies. In the US and other free market economies the Government even helped private banks with funds to bail them out of the turmoil. In India the Government borrowed heavily in 2008-09 and 2009-10 to increase its expenditure and also to cut taxes to prevent slowdown of the Indian economy due to the impact of global financial crisis. Similarly, when there is inflation the Central Bank of a country adopts tight monetary policy and the Government adopts contractionary fiscal policy to control rise in prices.

Last but not the least, it is a vital function of the modern Government to ***promote economic growth.*** Economic growth requires capital accumulation, progress in technology and investment in social sectors such as education and health. Besides, in developing countries like India the Government has to adopt measures ***to eradicate poverty*** that prevails on a large scale in these countries. For example, the Indian Government has started Mahatma Gandhi National Rural Employment Guarantee Scheme (MNREGS) under which it provides guaranteed employment to the poor households. Further, to help the poor. The Government in India has also begun Public Distribution System under which it provides subsidised foodgrains to the poor households. Just as there are ***market failures***, there are ***Government failures too.*** Mixed economy represents a middle path between a purely free-market economy and purely command economy.

CHAPTER 4
Growth Models in Indian Planning

Harrod-Domar Model of Growth

Keynes in his General Theory was concerned with the determination of income and employment in the short run. He explained that since in the short-run situation of developed capitalist economies aggregate demand was deficient in relation to the aggregate supply of output, the equilibrium will be established at less than full employment level. He did not go into the question of the long-run growth of the economy. In fact, he overlooked the effect of investment in a given period on the increase in productive capacity. However, *investment has a dual effect.*[1] First, investment increases aggregate demand and income of the people through the multiplier process, and secondly, it raises the productive capacity of the economy through the addition it makes to the stock of capital. Indeed, investment by very definition means the addition to the stock of capital. While Keynes took into account the demand effect of investment, he ignored the capacity effect of investment. It is because of the capacity effect of investment that Harrod-Domar model has been extensively used in Indian Planning. In India for setting growth target in terms of percentage increase in GDP per year during a plan period, estimates of rate of saving and investment and incremental capital-output ratio are made. Rate of economic growth in a plan period depends on rate of investment and incremental capital-output ratio.

Harrod[1] and Domar[2] extended the Keynesian analysis of income and employment to long-run setting and therefore considered both the income and capacity effects of investment. Harrod and Domar models of *economic growth explained at what rate investment should increase so that steady growth is possible in an advanced capitalist economy*. In the growth models of Harrod and Domar, the rate of capital accumulation plays a crucial role in the determination of economic growth. The problem of present-day mature economies lies in averting both secular stagnation and secular inflation. It were the pioneer works of Harrod and Domar that set the ball rolling in regard to this issue, i.e., the maintenance of steady growth in advanced industrialised countries. *Harrod and Domar models seek to determine the unique rate at which investment and income must grow so that full employment level is maintained over a long period of time, i.e., equilibrium growth is achieved.*

Harrod and Domar[2] developed their models of steady growth quite separately, though Harrod published his theory earlier than Domar. Although their models of steady growth differ in details, yet the underlying basic idea is the same. Both of them assigned to capital accumulation a crucial role in the development process. But they emphasised the double role of the investment process, viz., generating income (increasing demand) and adding to the productive capacity of the economy. The classical economists confined their attention to the capacity side only, whereas the earlier Keynesian economists studied the problem of demand only. Harrod and Domar consider both sides. It may be noted that we will confine ourselves to explain Domar's version of Harrod-Domar model of growth.

They start with full employment equilibrium level of income. According to them, to maintain full employment equilibrium, demand (total spending) generated by investment must be sufficient to be the additional output caused by this investment. To ensure steady growth with full employment the absolute amount of net investment must keep increasing and there must also be continuous growth of real national income. Because if demand and income do not increase while annual investment goes

1. R.F. Harrod *Towards a Dynamic Economics*, Macmillan & Co. London, 1948.
2. E. Domar, Capital Expansion, Rate of Growth and Employment, *Econometrica* Vol. 14, 1946.

on occurring, the additions made to the capital stock would remain unutilised and also employment could not be provided to the growing labour force which would result in unemployment of these two major resources. Obviously, such a situation is not conducive to steady economic growth.

Harrod-Domar Model : Capacity Effect of Investment

Let us first consider the supply side of Harrad-Domar growth model, that is, the capacity effect of investment. Increase in national output or national income of an economy during a period depends upon the increase in the stock of capital (which is represented by ΔK) during a period and the output-capital ratio or the productivity of capital. Assuming that both national income and the capital stock are measured in money, output-capital ratio can be written as $\Delta Y/\Delta K$, where ΔY stands for the increase in the national income and ΔK for the increase in the stock of capital. Thus, if ₹. 4 worth of capital goods is required to produce one rupee worth of real output, marginal output-capital ratio is equal to 1/4 or 0.25. Note that marginal output-capital ratio $\left(\frac{\Delta Y}{\Delta K}\right)$ is reciprocal of incremental capital-output (ICOR) which can be written as $\frac{\Delta K}{\Delta Y}$. Thus, the absolute increase in national income during a period (ΔY) can be obtained from increment in stock of capital ΔK multiplied by output Capital ratio $\left(i.e. \frac{\Delta Y}{\Delta K}\right)$. In symbolic terms we may express this as follows:-

$$\Delta y = \Delta K.\frac{\Delta Y}{\Delta k} \quad \text{...}(i)$$

Now, change in capital stock (ΔK) is nothing else but investment. Therefore, following Domar in place of ΔK we can write I. The marginal output-capital ratio $\Delta Y/\Delta K$ which is assumed to be constant as well as equal to average output-capital ratio by Domar and Harrod, can be denoted by σ. Thus, as Domar puts it, growth of capacity output can be written as under:

$$\Delta Y = I\sigma \quad \text{... }(ii)$$

It may be noted that output-capital ratio (σ) is reciprocal of capital-output ratio $\left(i.e \frac{\Delta k}{\Delta Y} or \frac{k}{y}\right)$. Let us give an example. If Rs. 500 crores are invested in a year and capital-output ratio is 4 (i.e. output-capital ratio will be 1/4), then growth of output in a year will be.

$$\Delta y = 500 \times 1/4$$

$$= 125 \text{ crores}$$

Demand or Income Effect of Investment

Now, according to Domar, growth in capacity output will be realised only if demand or income of the people increases by a sufficient amount. The increase in aggregate demand or income is explained by the Keynesian theory of multiplier. Domar has based his analysis of demand or income effect of investment on the Keynesian theory of multiplier and income determination. According to this, increase in income (or aggregate demand) is given by the increase in investment (ΔI) multiplied by the size of multiplier, *i.e.* $1/s$ where s is the marginal propensity to save (assumed by Domar to be equal to the average propensity to save). Thus, according to income effect of investment,

$$\Delta y = \frac{1}{s}.\Delta I \qquad \ldots (iii)$$

Note that $\frac{1}{s}$ represents the size of multiplier

The growth in income (ΔY) must be large enough to generate demand equal to capacity growth in output as explained above.

Domar's Growth Equation in Terms of Rates of Growth

It is greatly helpful to express the above growth equation in terms of *rates of growth of income and capital*. That is, growth in income and capital should be expressed as ratios of total income. For doing so we divide both sides of equation (*i*) above by Y and obtain :

$$\frac{\Delta y}{y} = \frac{\Delta K}{y}.\frac{\Delta y}{\Delta K} \qquad \ldots (iv)$$

$\frac{\Delta y}{y}$ represents the rate of growth of income and is therefore written as simply G_y. Besides, ΔK stands for increment in capital during a given time period and is nothing else but investment. Therefore, for ΔK in the equation (*iv*) we can write I which represents investment. With these changes, we get the following equation :

$$G_y = \frac{I}{y}.\frac{\Delta y}{\Delta K}$$

If it is further assumed that output-capital ratio remains constant, then the marginal output-capital ratio $\left(\frac{\Delta y}{\Delta k}\right)$ will be equal to average output-capital ratio $\left(\frac{y}{k}\right)$. With this assumption and also expressing output-capital ratio by σ we can write the above equation as follows

$$G_y = \frac{I}{y}.\frac{\Delta y}{\Delta k} \qquad \ldots (v)$$

Where G_y = Growth rate of output or income

$\frac{I}{y}$ = Rate of investment as ratio of national income

σ = Output-capital ratio

From the growth equation (*v*) above, it is clear that, *given the output-capital ratio, rate of growth of output depends upon the rate of investment; the greater the rate of investment, the greater the rate of growth of output or income*. To maintain full-employment equilibrium as the economy grows at a steady rate, rate of saving $\frac{s}{y}$ must remain equal to rate of investment $\frac{I}{y}$. Therefore, in equation (v) we can write $\frac{s}{y}$ for $\frac{I}{y}$. By doing so and rewriting equation (*v*) we have

$$G_y = \frac{s}{y}\sigma$$

Since $\frac{s}{y}$ represents ratio of savings to national income, we can write it as *s*. With rewriting the above equation we have,

$$G_y = s\,\sigma \qquad \text{... (vi)}$$

The above eqution (*vi*) represents the productive capacity effect of investment or saving and therefore represents the supply side of the growth problem.

The Condition for Equilibrium Growth

To achieve and maintain equilibrium growth aggregate demand (*i.e.* aggregate expenditure) must increase at the rate which is large enough to absorb the increase in capacity-output. We have explained above (equation, *iii*) that aggregate demand or income increases at the rate $\frac{1}{s}\,.\,\Delta I$ where *s* is propensity to save and ΔI is the absolute increase in investment. On the other hand, as explained above, the increase in capacity output occurs at the rate of $I\sigma$ where I is the absolute investment in a period and σ is the output-capital ratio. Thus, steady equilibrium growth rate will be achieved only if rate of growth of aggregate expenditure (demand or income) equals the rate of growth in capacity output.

Thus, it follows that to *maintain full-employment equilibrium growth of output* the following condition must hold.

$$\frac{1}{s}.\Delta I = I\sigma$$

$$\frac{\Delta I}{I} = s\,\sigma \qquad \text{. . . (vii)}$$

where $\frac{\Delta I}{I}$ represents the rate of growth of investment.

As seen above in equation (*vi*), rate of growth of income $\left(\frac{\Delta y}{y} \text{ or } G_y\right)$ is also equal to $s\sigma$, it follows that for equilibrium growth $G_y = \frac{\Delta y}{y} = \frac{\Delta I}{I}\; s\sigma$

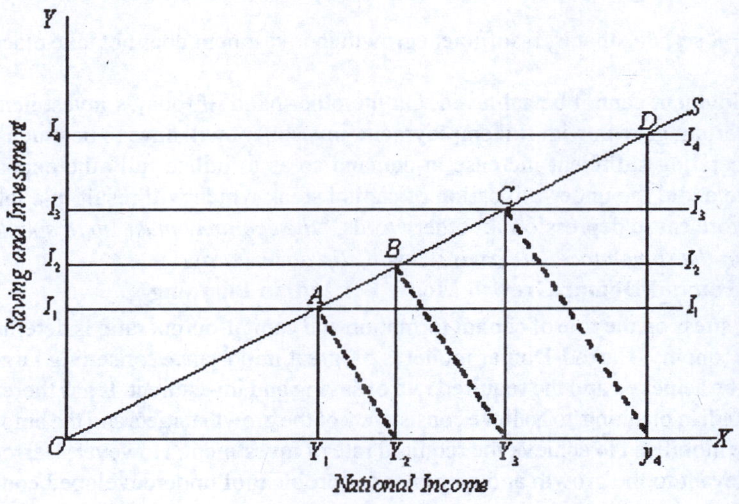

Fig. 4.1. *Harrod-Domar Model of Equilibrium Growth*

Thus, the essential condition for maintaining a continuous equilibrium state of full employment is that investment and real income must both grow at a constant annual rate. This rate should be equal to the propensity to save (s) multiplied by output-capital ratio, (σ) *i.e.*, $s\sigma$.

We can explain the model in geometrical terms with the help of the Fig. 4.1 given above. Here real income is measured along the horizontal axis, while saving and investment (in real terms) are measured along the vertical axis. The saving function is represented by the line OS starting from the origin. Its slope is given by the marginal propensity to save (s) which is assumed to remain constant for a considerable period of time. The initial investment demand is represented by curve I_1I_1. This intersects the saving function OS at the point A so that the corresponding equilibrium level of income is Y_1. We assume that it corresponds to the full-employment level of national inocme.

Now, the new capital so created (represented by OI_1) will lead to the increase in productive capacity as determined by output-capital ratio. Given the output-capital ratio, investment OI_1 leads to Y_1Y_2 increase in output or income. As a result, national income will increase to Y_2. The ratio between the increase in income (ΔY or Y_1Y_2) and the increase in investment (OI_1) is given by the 'output-capital' ratio σ. But the new equilibrium level of income Y_2 will be relalised or maintained only if the investment demand function shifts upward to I_2I_2 and intersects the saving function OS at the point B, which is vertically above Y_2.

However, as soon as the new capital equipment represented by the higher level OI_2 starts producing goods, capacity output or income will rise to Y_3 (indicating an increase by an amount σ times OI_2 over the previous level of income (Y_2). But the new level of income Y_3 will be maintained only if investment increases so much that the new investment demand curve I_3I_3 intersects the saving function OS at C. In this way, the process will continue so long as the investment increases by the appropriate amount in each period. The income would successively go on rising by an amount σ times the previous period's investment. And the investment in each period would rise by s times the output-capital ratio. Thus, income would continue to grow at the steady rate of $s\sigma$.

It is evident from the basic equation $\frac{\Delta I}{I} = s\sigma$ that greater the saving rate(s), the greater will be the growth of investment needed to maintain the steady growth with full employment. Similarly, greater the value of σ (*i.e.* the output-capital ratio), the greater should be the increase in income to avoid emergence of excess capacity. But greater income is possibly only through greater investment. Hence, if income is to grow, investment must also grow at the annual rate given by $s\sigma$.

If $\frac{\Delta I}{I} < s\sigma$, *i.e.*, that is, if sufficient growth in investment does not take place, steady growth with full employment cannot be achieved. On the other hand, if today's investment is sufficient to achieve equilibrium growth with full employment, investment will have to be much more in the next period for generating sufficient increase in demand so as to utilise fully the expanded production capacity and to avoid the under-utilisation of capital stock which will result in a fall in investment, and will therefore cause depression. In other words, "*the economy must, so to speak, run faster and faster to stay in the same place, otherwise, it will slip downwards.*"

Relevance of Harrod-Domar Growth Model For Indian Planning

By laying stress on the role of capital formation and capital-output ratio is determining economic growth of an economy, Harrod-Domar model is of great importance for setting targets of economic growth rate to be achieved and the required rate of saving and investment. It has therefore been extensively used in Indian planning to achieve consistency of the growth targets and the amount of additional resources to be mobilised to achieve the required rate of investment. However, Harrod-Domar model is not fully relevant to the growth and employment problem of underdeveloped country like India.

First, the usefulness of models based on the concept of capital-output ratio is of little operational significance in developing economies. Depending on the nature and degree of various shortages, bottlenecks and market imperfections, the productivity of capital is amenable to considerable fluctuations. It is indeed very difficult to have an accurate and valid estimate of a concept like capital-output ratio under such fluid conditions. Commenting in this regard, Prof. Hirschman[3] remarks that the predictive and operational significance of a model based on the concept of *capital-output* ratio is far less for an underdeveloped economy than for advanced economies. Models such as these, therefore, cannot explain the mechanism through which economic growth can get under way and could be carried forward on a sustained basis in the present-day developing economies.

Secondly, in Harrod-Domar model, growth variables are aggregative in nature and, therefore, fail to show the sectorial interrelationship. The processes of development of the developing economies are as is being increasingly acknowledged, fundamentally linked with structural and institutional changes. Their highly aggregative nature, comments Prof S. Chakravarty[4], 'prevents them from being used as a tool in detailed quantitative policy making and conceals many structural aspects of the problem of a steady rate of growth.

Thirdly and very importantly, these models can at best offer counter-cyclical and counter-stagnation policy formulation. They are in no way any guide to industrialisation programming for growth which is the dire necessity of developing countries. For instance, in Harrod's model, the deviations between the actual, warranted and natural rates of growth indicate that the advanced economies are subject to cyclical fluctuations and secular stagnation. Harrod is of the view that chronic deflation is a far greater possibility in advanced countries on account of the fact that these countries save more than the investment can absorb. Domar has also presented a similar reasoning. He similarly maintains that the likelihood of effective demand falling short of productive capacity is more pronounced. Of course, even in developing countries, the problems of growth of effective demand falling short of growth in capacity output cannot be denied but the developing countries face more severe problems of low savings and low productivity of investment.

Finally, Harrod excludes autonomous investment as an explicit variable in his formulation of *'warranted'* saving-investment equality. But the exclusion of autonomous investment as an important factor in determining growth by Harrod in his growth model renders Harrod's concept of 'warranted' growth rate analytically inadequate for the purpose of developing countries. The apparent reason for this exclusion is to be partly found in Harrod's desire to make place for the acceleration principle in his growth model. He also ignored the public investments to which Keynes assigned a crucial role. But, autonomous investments, whether public or private, are of pivotal importance to the developing countries. Besides, Harrod-Domar growth models assume that propensity to save and the capital-output ratio are constant. But actually they are likely to change over the longrun. Further, if the proportion of factors can be changed as labour may be substituted for capital, then adjustment within the economy can be easily made and steady growth made possible without any rigid conditions.

However, in spite of the fact that this model has limitations in the context of labour-surplus developing countries it highlights the crucial issues involved in the development process of these economies. They are useful in fixing the overall targets of income, investment and savings and in checking the consistency of such targets. Prof. Kurihara states that "Harrod and Domar have made the essential nature of the growth mechanism operationally significant, for they stress saving ratio and the capital-output ratio (or its reciprocal) as measurable strategic variables to investigate and possibly to manipulate for a desired rate of growth. Because of the universal character of these strategic variables, the growth mechanism discussed by Harrod and Domar is applicable to all economic systems, albeit with the modification" [5]

3. Hirschman, *Strategy of Economic Development,* 1957.
4. S. Chakravarty, *Op. cit.*
5. *K.K. Kurihara, The Keynesian Theory of Development,* 1959, p.185.

The use of these models has actually been made in the developing countries. For instance, in the First Five Year Plan of India, the rate of saving was planned to be raised through keeping the marginal rate of saving above the average rate of saving. And the current rate of capital formation and therefore growth of the economy was sought to be maximised through raising the marginal rate of saving. Thus, these models served to guide the planners in determining the growth rate of the Indian economy. Commenting on these models, Prof. S. Chakravarty remarks that "*The great service that these models perform is to indicate very roughly the dimensions of the problem involved in raising the per capita income level in an underdeveloped country*".[6] Further, prof. Kurihara contends that the growth model has this positive lesson for under-developed economies, that state should be allowed to play not only a stabilizing role but also a developmental role, if these economies are to industrialise more effectively and rapidly than the now industrialised economies did in conditions of *laissez faire.* [7]

MAHALANOBIS GROWTH MODEL AND HEAVY-INDUSTRY STRATEGY OF DEVELOPMENT

Having discussed Harrod-Domar model of growth we proceed to discuss an alternative nodel of growth and strategy of development which have been the subjects of a good deal of controversy in India. The strategy of development pursued in India's second and third five year plans accorded top priority to basic and heavy industries. This basic heavy industry model of development was put forward by a renowned statistician Late Professor P.C. Mahalanobis who was friend and adviser to Late Prime Minister Jawaharlal Nehru and who was one time member of the Planning commision. At the time of the formulation of the Second Five Year Plan, Prof. Mahalanobis prepared a growth model with which he showed that to achieve a rapid long-term rate of growth it would be essential to devote a major part of the investment outlay to building of basic heavy industries. Mahalanobis strategy of development emphasising basic heavy industries which was adopted first of all in the Second Plan also continued to hold the stage in Indian planning right up to the Fifth Plan which was terminated by the Janata Government in March 1978, a year before its full term of five years.

In critique of the Mahalanobis heavy-industry development strategy, Professors Vakil and Brahmanand of Bombay University put forward a *wage-goods model of development* and suggested a development strategy which accorded a top priority to agriculture and other wage-goods industries in sharp contrast to the Mahalanobis heavy-industry biased strategy of development. In what follows chapter we shall critically examine the heavy-industry biased strategy of development.

Mahalanobis Model of Growth

It will be useful to explain first Mahalanobis model of growth which provided a rationale for the heavy industry biased development strategy. An important point to note is that Mahalanobis identifies the rate of growth of investment in the economy not with rate of growth of savings as is usually considered by the economists but with rate of growth of output in the capital goods sector within the economy. The growth of capital goods sector in turn depends upon the proportion of total investment allocated to the capital goods sector and output-capital ratio in the capital goods sector. Given the output-capital ratio in capital goods sector (*i.e.* heavy industries), he proves that if the proportion of total investment allocated to the capital goods is relatively greater, the rate of growth of output of capital goods will be greater and hence, given the Mahalanobis assumption, the future rate of growth of investment in the economy will be greater. Now, the greater the rate of investment, the greater will be the long-term rate of growth. We thus see that with the rate of growth of output of capital goods industries. Mahalanobis shows that the proportion of total investment resources allocated to the capital goods industries for each year is the most important factor determining the long-term rate of growth of national income. Let us represent his two-sector model in the mathematical form.

6. Sukhamoy Chakravarty, *The Logic of Investment Planning,* p.43.
7. K.K. Kurihara, op. cit.

In his basic two-sector model Mahalanobis divides the economy into two sectors—the sector *C* produces consumer goods and sector *K* produces capital goods.

Let

I_0 = Initial rate of investment.

λ_k and λ_c = Proportions of total investment allocated to capital goods and consumer goods sectors respectively.

Therefore $\lambda_k + \lambda_c = 1$

β_k and β_c = Marginal output-capital ratio in the capital goods and consumer goods sectors respectively. In other words, they represent ratio of increment of income to investment in the sector *K* and sector *C* respectively.

Y_0, C_0, I_0 = The national income, consumption and investment in the base period.

Y_t, C_t, I_t = The national income, consumption and investment respectively in period *t*.

In Mahalanbis model, the net investment in any period can be divided into two components; the one $\lambda_k I_t$, going to capital goods sector *K* and $\lambda_c I_t$ going to consumer goods sector *C*. Therefore it follows that,

$$I_t = \lambda_k I_t + \lambda_c I_t$$

Let ΔI_t stands for increase in investment (*i.e.* addition to the stock of capital goods) and ΔC_t for increase in consumer goods in any period *t* which depend on the net investment in the previous period *t*–1. Now, given the output-capital ratios, β_k an β_c of the captial goods and consumer goods sectors respectively, the relationship between investment and the resultant increment in output in capital goods can be worked out as follows:

$$\Delta I_t = \beta_k \lambda_k I_{t-1} \text{ Or } I_t - I_{t-1} = \beta_k \lambda_k I_{t-1} \quad \text{... }(i)$$

This implies that the increase in investment in period *t* is equal to the increment in output of capital goods. The increase in output of capital goods ($\beta_K \lambda_K I_{t-1}$) in period *t* is given by investment in period I_{t-1} multiplied by the proportion of it going to capital-goods sector (λ_k) and the output-capital ratio (β_k) in the capital goods sector.

It is clear from above that Mahalanobis takes into account only the physical aspect of investment and makes it dependent on the proportion of investment allocated to capital goods sector λ_k and output-capital ratio β_k in the capital goods sector.

Similar to equation (*i*) we can also write:

$$\Delta C_t = \beta_c \lambda_c I_{t-1}$$

$$C_t - C_{t-1} = \beta_c \lambda_c I_{t-1} \quad \text{... }(ii)$$

and also

$$\Delta I_{t-1} = \beta_k \lambda_k I_{t-2}$$

Now, income in a period *t* is the sum of consumption and investment, therefore:-

$$Y_t = I_t + C_t$$

$$Y_t = \beta_k \lambda_k I_{t-1} + \beta_c \lambda_c I_{t-1}$$

By further manipulation, Mahalanobis derives the following formula:

$$y_t = y_0 \left[1 + \alpha_0 \frac{\beta_c \lambda_c + \beta_k \lambda_k}{\lambda_k + \beta_k} (1 + \lambda_k \beta_k)^{t-1} \right] \quad \text{... }(iii)$$

where α_0 is the initial rate of investment expressed as percentage of income. that is,

$$\alpha_0 = \frac{I_0}{Y_0}$$

It is worth noting that Mahalanobis recognises that output-capital ratio β_c in the consumer goods sector is greater than the output-capital ratio β_k in the captial goods sector. If this is the case, then it apparently implies that growth of output or income will be greater if more investment is made in the consumer goods sector. But, according to Mahalanobis, in this case the higher rate of growth of income will be only in the short run. As growth equation (*iii*) above shows that after a critical range of time, the larger the investment allocated to capital goods industries (λ_k), the higher will be growth in output or income. Elaborating this point Prof. Raj states, "The *logic here is the same as the more common proposition that a higher rate of investment (i.e., a larger proportion of the productive factors used for accumulation) would result in a smaller volume of output being available for consumption in the short run but that over a longer period, it would result in higher rate of growth of consumption; the difference is that the choice is here stated as between investment in capital goods and investment in consumer goods industries*."[1]

Rationale of Mahalanobis Growth Model

The rationale of Mahalanobis growth model and development strategy can be expressed in simple words without mathematical language. According to Mahalanobis, rate of economic growth depends upon the capital formation or real investment. The greater the rate of capital formation, the greater the rate of economic growth. The rate of capital formation in an economy, according to Mahalanobis, depends upon the capacity of the economy to produce capital goods. Thus, according to him, given a closed economy, the rate of real capital formation depends not upon the savings of the economy but on the capacity to produce capital goods. Even if the rate of savings was substantially raised in order to accelerate the rate of capital formation, it would be futile, for required capital goods would not be there if there is a lack of capacity to produce capital goods. Of course, this is based on *closed economy* assumption.

Thus, according to him, if large investment is not made in the basic heavy industries producing capital goods, the country will for ever remain dependent on foreign countries for the imports of steel and capital goods like machinery for real capital formation. Since it is not possible for India to earn sufficient foreign exchange by increasing exports, the capital goods cannot be imported in sufficient quantities owing to foreign exchange constraint. The result will be that the rate of real capital formation and the rate of economic growth in the country will remain low. Thus, Mahalanobis was of the opinion that without adequate investment in basic heavy industries, it would not be possible to achieve rapid self-reliant economic growth. Therefore according to him, to achieve rapid economic growth and self-reliance, it would be necessary to give the highest priority to basic capital goods industries in the development strategy of a plan.

Employment Generation in Mahalanobis Model. It is necessary in this connection to mention Prof. Mahalanobis' views on increasing employment opportunities and to achieve a stage of full employment. According to him, productive employment can be increased only by increasing the production of capital goods like steel, electricity, machinery, fertilizers, etc. Whether it is increase in employment in the industrial sector or in the agricultural sector it cannot be achieved without increasing the output of capital goods. To quote him, "*The only way of eliminating unemployment in India is to build up a sufficiently large stock of capital which will enable all unemployed persons being absorbed into productive capacity. Increasing the rate of investment is, therefore, the only fundamental remedy for unemployment in India*."[2] Thus, in Prof. Mahalanobis' opinion, not only to achieve the objective of rapid economic growth but also to achieve the goal of full employment, it is necessary to accord high priority to capital goods industries in the development strategy.

Import-substituting Industrialisation. Mahalanobis' emphasis on basic heavy industries was also due to his objective of meeting the requirements of higher rate of capital accumulation from

1. K.N. Raj, Growth Models in Indian Planning, *The Indian Economic Review*, Feb. 1961. Reprinted in C.D. Wadhwa, "*Some Problems of India's Economic Policy*, Tata Publishing Co. Ltd., Bombay.
2. P.C. Mahalanobis, The Approach of Operational Research to Planning in India. *Sankya*, Vol. 16. December 1953.

within the economy and therefore enabling the economy to stop imports of foreign capital equipment and machines. To quote him, "The proper strategy would be to bring about a rapid development of the industries producing investment goods in the beginning by increasing appreciably the proportion of investment in the basic heavy industries. As the capacity to manufacture both heavy and light machinery and other capital goods increases, the capacity to invest by using domestically produced capital goods would also increase steadily and India would become more and more independent of the imports of foreign machinery and capital."[1] In fact, Mahalanobis growth model advocated import-substitution type of industrial development strategy.

It is important to note that Mahalanobis assumed though implicitly that export earnings of India cannot be sufficiently increased. If this asumption is not valid, as has been pointed out by several critics, then he could not justifiably identify rate of investment in the economy with the domestic output of capital goods. If exports of a country can be adequately raised, the various capital goods can be imported in exchange for exports. In that case rate of investment or rate of capital accumulation in the economy can be stepped up without giving high priority to the basic heavy industries provided the exports can be adequately increased. Thus the assumption of stagnant exports is crucial in the Mahalanobis growth model for providing the rationale for a general shift in the investment pattern to the domestic production of capital goods.

Mahalanobis Growth Model and Development Strategy in India's Five-Year Plans

As pointed out above, Mahalanobis heavy industry first strategy of development was put into actual practice in India's Five-Year Plans beginning from the Second Plan. India started its planned development of its economy in 1951 when First Five-Year Plan was started. However, the Five year Plan did not propose any explicit strategy of development; it took over several projects which had been worked out earlier and some of them were already in the process of being carried out. It laid emphasis on stepping up the rate of saving and therefore investment and growth by maintaining the marginal rate of saving at a substantially higher level than the average rate of saving. Although it did not present any explicit formulation of development strategy regarding the pattern of investment its emphasis was on agriculture, irrigation, power and transport aimed at creating the base for more rapid industrialisation of the economy in the future.

Second Five Year Plan, based as it was on Mahalanobis growth model, proposed an explicit strategy of development which gave top priority to basic heavy industries. Not only the objectives of rapid rate of economic growth and employment generation but also the aim of self-reliant and self-generating economy were sought to be achieved by *"the building up of economic and social overheads, exploration and development of minerals and the promotion of basic industries like steel, machine building, coal and heavy chemicals."*[2] Identifying under-development with dependence on agriculture and thinking industrial growth especially the development of heavy industries as the core of development underlied the approach and strategy of the Second Five-Year Plan. To quote from Second Plan again. "low or static standards of living, under-employment and unemployment, and to a certain extent even the gap between the average incomes and the highest incomes are all manifestations of the basic under-development which characterises an economy depending mainly on agriculture. Rapid industrialisation and diversification of the economy is thus the core of development. But *if industrialisation is to be rapid enough, the country must aim at developing basic industries and industries which make machines to make the machines needed for further development."*[3]

It is clear from above that in the Second Plan there was clear shift of priorities from agriculture to industries and within industries to basic heavy industries. As mentioned above, the logic of Ma-

1. *Ibid*, p.22

2. Government of India, Planning Commission, *Second Five Year Plan*, 1956, p.24.

3. *Ibid*, p.25.

halanobis in emphasizing heavy industries was that the growth of basic heavy industries will enable the economy to accelerate the rate of capital formation and therefore economic growth. In fact, he identified the rate of growth of investment in the economy with the rate of growth of output in the capital goods (sector) industries within the economy.

Mahalanobis' Four Sector Model. Mahalanobis realised that the basic heavy industries being capital-intensive will not ensure rapid expansion of employment opportunities and to bring the employment aspect into sharp focus he put forward a four sector growth model in which he kept heavy industry sector (*i.e.* *K*-sector) intact but divided the *C*-sector (*i.e.* consumption goods sector) into three sub-sectors : C_1, C_2, and C_3 (sector C_1 represented factory enterprises using mechanised techniques and producing consumer goods; Sector C_2 represented the household and small-scale enterprises also producing consumer goods and Sector C_3 represented provision of services). It was sector C_2 representing households and small-scale industries which in Mahalanobis four sector model was visualised to ensure the increased supply of consumer goods to meet their rising demand for them and also to ensure, being labour intensive, expansion of employment opportunities. In keeping with this approach, Second Five Year Plan put restrictions on the growth of capacity in factory enterprises engaged in commodity production. However, since for these household or cottage enterprises, adequate resources were not provided, nor any effort was made to improve their productivity, they could neither fulfil their largest of production of consumer goods nor of generating enough employment opportunities.[1]

In the Third Plan (1961–66) also the strategy of Second Plan was continued as is clear from the following: "In the Third Plan, as in the Second, the development of basic industries such as steel, fuel and power and machine building and chemical industries is fundamental to rapid economic growth. These industries largely determine the pace at which the economy can become self-reliant and self-generating."[2] Though, "to achieve self-sufficiency in foodgrains and increase agricultural production to meet the requirements of industry and exports" was stated to be one on the objectives of the Third Plan, actual allocation of resources between agriculture and other sectors did not exihibit any significant difference from that of the Second Plan. Therefore, the concern for food and agriculture in the Third Plan appears to be mere verbal and was not built into the strategy of development.

The Fourth Five-Year Plan (1969–74) which was prepared under the Deputy Chairmanship of Late Prof. D.R.Gadgil, tried to give new shape to the planning strategy and emphasis was sought to be placed on the common man the weaker sections and the less privileged. However, the Fourth Plan slightly raised the allocation of Public Sector outlay to agriculture and irrigation to about 23 per cent as against 20 per cent in the Second Plan and the Third Plan, and a good deal of hang-over of the heavy industry biased strategy still prevailed in this plan too.

Despite all talk of Garibi Hatao and direct attack on poverty which preceded the formulation of the Fifth Plan, in the Fifth Plan allocation of public sector investment to agriculture and irrigation was once again reduced to about 20 per cent and the same old heavy-industry bias prevailed in the Fifth Plan's development strategy.

Critical Evaluation of Mahalanobis Heavy Industry Strategy of Development

Mahalanobis 'heavy industry first' strategy of development has come in for severe criticism right from the time of formulation of the Second Plan. First, **a serious mistake in Mahalanobis model is that he identified investment with saving**. That indicates lack of knowledge of economics. Economists have been emphasizing especially in the context of developing countries that increase in the rate of investment is governed by the increase in the rate of savings. If planned investment

1. Amlan Datta, *Strategy of Economic Development*, 1973. In the spinning of cotton, main emphasis was on Ambar Charkha. Ambar Charkha experiment failed because productivity and earning capacity per person engaged in it was found to be too low.

2. Government of India, Planning Commission, *Third Five Year Plan*. 1961, p. 50.

is not matched by savings, then inflationary gap will emerge which will cause prices to rise. It is bad economics to identify investment with savings. Savings in an economy are determined by behavioural characteristics of the decision-making units such as households, the corporate sector and the Government. Saving by the households depends upon the propensity to consume which in turn depends upon various subjective and objective factors. Savings by the corporate sector depend upon the policies regarding depreciation, distribution of dividends and undistributed profits. Savings of the Government are governed by its policies regarding taxation and consumption expenditure, efficiency and profitability of public enterprises. Thus, when the planning authority allocates relatively more resources to heavy capital goods industries, as is envisaged in Mahalanobis growth model, it will lead to more physical investment or growth of capital stock. But there is no guarantee that savings, governed as they are by various behavioural characteristics of decision-making units, will rise to the level of planned investment. Therefore, by envisaging higher rate of physical investment without considering how savings of the community could be raised to the planned investment, Mahalanobis model contained built-in inflationary potential. Therefore, being unmatched by savings to fulfil the investment targets of the plan, recourse in actual practice had to be made to deficit financing. No wonder that due to the existence of inflationary gap in India's Five Year Plan prices began to rise from the very beginning of the Second Plan so much so that during the Fourth Plan period (1969–74) rate of inflation assumed serious proportion reaching as high as about 30% during 1973–74, the last year of the Fourth Plan.

A crucial weakness of Mahalanobis heavy industry strategy of development was pointed out by Professors Vakil and Brahmananda. They criticised heavy-industry strategy in their now well known joint work, "*Planning for an Expanding Economy*." According to them, growth of national income and employment is determined by the supply of wage goods. They pointed out that when disguised unemployed are employed in productive work on the wage basis, the demand for wage goods will increase and unless the adequate amount of wage goods are not available, the disguised unemployed and openly unemployed cannot be put to work on the wage basis. According to them, there exists a *wage-goods gap* in under-developed countries like India and the basic cause of unemployment and disguised unemployment in them is the existence of this wage-goods gap. Wage goods act as a constraint on the growth of industrialisation and non-agricultural growth. Thus, in the determination of growth of income and employment, while Mahalanobis emphasised '*fixed capital*', Brahmananda and Vakil laid stress on the wage goods which are also called '*circulating capital*'. As mentioned earlier, Vakil and Brahmananda put forward a growth model in which wage goods played a key role. Accordingly, they suggested a developed strategy in which top priority was given to the agriculture which produces most important form of wage goods *i.e.*, foodgrains.

There is no doubt that **Mahalanobis "heavy industry" strategy overlooked the importance of agriculture or wage goods in the growth process of the economy**. This manifested itself in the rapid rise of prices from the very beginning of the Second Plan. While a relatively large investment in the basic industries resulted in the creation of money incomes and consequently in a large increase in demand for wage goods, the supply of wage goods did not adequately increase due to the continued neglect of agriculture in India's planning strategy. This caused imbalance between demand for and supply of wage goods which has been responsible for inflationary situation in the Indian economy. The continued neglect of wage goods in the development strategy of Indian Plans, right up to the Fifth Plan is quite surprising since, as pointed out above, this weakness of the strategy was pointed out by Professors Vakil and Brahmananda at the time of the formulation of the Second Plan.

The larger allocation of resources to the basic heavy industries deprived agriculture (including irrigation) and rural industries of enough resources required for their growth. It is now well-known as brought out by Professor Lipton, B.S. Minhas that India's Five Year Plans beginning from the Second one, based as they were on Mahalanobis growth model with its emphasis on heavy industries, suffered from '*relative neglect of agriculture*'. The view that there has been relative neglect of agriculture in Indian Plans has been forcefully and effectively expressed and provided by Professor Michael Lipton. He writes : "*We have seen that neither allocations of public money, nor incentives to the movement of persons and other resources, have favoured agricultural development; that 70 per cent of the workers get less than 35 per cent of investment finance and a far smaller share of human skills. Several types of pressures on opinion and policy have combined to bias the allocation of cash, effort, personnel and research away from rural needs.*"[1]

Like Professor Lipton, B.S. Minhas also holds similar view about relative neglect of agriculture in Indian Planning. He thus states, "In practical terms the most unfortunate consequences of our adherence to this philosophy of development has been the appalling neglect of agriculture and rural development."[2] Before Lipton and Minhas, Professors, C.N. Vakil and P.R. Brahmananda, as mentioned above have been consistently expressing the view, about the low priority assigned to agriculture since the beginning of Second Plan. Recently, C.H. Hanumantha Rao has also deplored the neglect of agriculture in the strategy of Indian Plans. He writes, "*The failure of the present strategy to step up public investment for agricultural development has accentuated the problem of unemployment in rural areas.*"

A serious failure of Mahalanobis development strategy with its emphasis on basic heavy industries is that **it failed to generate adequate amount of employment opportunities.** Pattern of industrialization has been based on capital-intensive technology imported from abroad and has been oriented towards urban large-scale industries. If the emphasis were on rural-oriented industrialization promoting cottage and small-scale industries, using intermediate technologies, the problem of labour-surplus and unemployment would not have been as acute as it is now. Besides this, attention was not paid to absorb labour in the agricultural sector, and the agricultural development strategy that could absorb more labour in productive employment was not adopted. Necessary technological and institutional changes for designing such an agricultural strategy required to create more employment were not in actual practice made. Many land reform measures, apart from abolition of big Zamindars and Jagirdars, remained mostly on paper. Legislations regarding tenancy reforms and ceiling on land holdings were not actually enforced and implemented. Being highly capital-intensive the basic heavy industries themselves created very little employment opportunities.

It is no doubt true that certain products of heavy industries such as fertilizers, steel, cement, etc. are certainly required for the growth of agriculture, especially in the context of new agricultural technology and should, therefore, be produced, but Mahalanobis strategy envisaged achievement of self-sufficiency all along the line, involving production of highly sophisticated machines to make machines. This *autarkic* nature of Mahalanobis development strategy has been rightly criticised. B.S. Minhas rightly writes[3], "*The logic of the Heavy Industry First Strategy in India sprouted from a number of philosophical riddles. One important conundrum runs as follows: should you import food, or import fertilisers to produce food at home ? Rather than import fertilisers, should you not import fertiliser materials and machinery in order to make fertilisers at home? But why import fertiliser machinery? Should you not import machines to make fertiliser machinery at home? On and on goes the riddle?*"[17]

In view of the limited resources available for investment, the inclusion of highly capital-intensive industries producing machines and mother machines, exhaust a great deal of resources, leaving rela-

1. M. Lipton, Strategy for Agriculture: Urban Bias and Rural Planning, Printed in P. Streeman and M. Lipton (ed.) *The Crisis of Indian Planning*, Oxford University press, 1960, p. 130.

2. B.S. Minhas, *Self-reliance and India's Planning Strategy*, Indian Statistical Institute (Discussion Paper No. 138), March 1976, p.14

3. B.S. Minhas, *op.cit.* p.12.

tively little for agriculture and rural industries which contain large employment potential. Therefore, in our view, in initial stages of development some intermediate products, machines, and capital goods should be imported if they are urgently needed for some industries, even if in their case, we possess comparative advantage in the dynamic context.

However, it needs to be emphasised again that the form of capital is crucial for employment generation. What is required is the small and simple types of machines and tools which are required for the growth of agriculture and small-scale rural industries. Further, the production of those types of intermediate goods such as fertilizers, pesticides, cement which will help in raising agricultural production and·employment need to be expanded. Some large-scale industries, if their large size is necessary in view of technological considerations, should play a supporting role to the development of agriculture and rural industries. Thus, *the strategy of growth in India should be reoriented so that agriculture and rural industries constitute the main thrust of the development effort.*

From the foregoing analysis, it follows that if the mounting unemployment problem is to be tackled, the strategy of development adopted need to be revised and modified. In the new strategy, agriculture has to play a key role in generating enough employment opportunities for a long time to come. The fact that about 60 per cent of the Indian labour force and majority of the unemployed and underemployed reside in the rural areas and further that the employment potential of the industries of large-scale type is very little, the promotion of agricultural and rural development must be made the springboard and the leading sector for generating productive employment for millions. Therefore, *the strategy for agricultural development should be such as will absorb productively the largest possible number of workers.*

Another weakness of the "heavy industry first" strategy and development was that it chose pattern of investment with *higher capital-output ratio.* In basic heavy industries capital-output ratio was admittedly high and in agriculture and related activities, capital output ratio was low. Thus, the highest priority to basic heavy industries and low priority to agriculture in the pattern of investment meant the choice of high macro-value of incremental capital output ratio (ICOR). As has been made clear in earlier chapters that if a higher growth rate is desired, given the initial value of a rate of saving and annual increments therein over the projected period, then the criterion should be to choose a pattern of investment with a lower macro-value of capital-output ratio. In the case of India, this would have implied a high priority to be given to agricultural and related sectors over a long period of time. Therefore, the choice of the pattern of investment containing a high priority to basic heavy industries and low priority to agriculture meant a low rate of economic growth. As has been pointed out above, Mahalanobis and others supporting his strategy contended that their strategy would ensure high rate of growth in the long run. But in actual practice even in 25 years (1956-80) Mahalanobis development strategy of 1955–56 failed to ensure more than 3.5 per cent average annual rate of growth. In the meantime people suffered a lot due to the inflation generated by the strategy and the non-availability of requisite amount of essential consumer goods.

Mahalanobis heavy industry strategy suffered from another weakness in that *it heavily depended upon foreign exchange requirements.* Though the strategy assumed that exports from the Indian economy could not be sufficiently increased it required a large amount of foreign exchange resources to establish a network of heavy capital goods industries which required the imports of capital equipment and machinery on a large scale from other countries. For a self-contained growth model framed in the context of a closed economy or stagnant exports, this was an inner contradiction. This also had two evil effects. Becasue of the low priority to agriculture and consumer goods industries which had export potentials, export could not rise much, and secondly, due to the highest priority to heavy capital goods industries large imports of capital equipment and materials had to be made. Such was the large requirement of foreign exchange to import capital equipment that despite the liberal foreign aid received from countries especially the U.S.A. even then the country had to face a serious foreign exchange crisis.

It was said in the defence of the heavy industry strategy that it would ultimately help in substituting imports of heavy industrial products such as steel, cement, various kinds of machines, fertilizers etc. This implies that import substitution when accomplished would enable the economy to dispense with foreign aid. However, it was said that in the mean time aid was required to import equipment and materials to set up heavy capital goods industries. Thus it was claimed that the heavy industry strategy envisaged getting "*aid to end aid*".

However, the fact remains that far from moving the economy towards self-reliance, the heavy industry strategy increased the dependence on foreign aid. Because of low priority to agriculture in the strategy, production of foodgrains did not increase adequately and as a result the imbalance between population and foodgrains further increased during the planning period. In order to correct this imbalance foodgrains had to be imported on a large scale from other countries. Whereas the imports of foodgrains into India during the First Plan period were of the order of 12 million tonnes, it rose to 17 million tonnes in the Second Plan period. The situation worsened in the Third Plan period as the implementation of heavy industry strategy further proceeded and 26 million tones of foodgrains were imported during the Third Plan period. During the three years of plan-holiday period (1966–69), the imports of foodgrains jumped to 25 million in *three* years period. In the Fourth Plan period in which hangover of the heavy industry strategy peristed, foodgrains imports continued unabated with the exception of the Year 1972. During the six years period 1970–76, 26.4 million tonnes of foodgrains were imported.[1]

It is thus clear that the imbalance between foodgrains and population was the direct result of the neglect of agriculture in India's heavy industry first strategy. Thus the most distressing effect of the strategy was that the country came to be dependent on even foodgrains. But for the imports of foodgrains under PL 480 and liberal foreign aid which was made available, India could not have been able to implement the Mahalanobis strategy for its inner contradictions and its inappropriateness to the Indian reality would have come to surface much earlier. The situation in the beginning of the Fifth Plan, *i.e.* in 1974 was that India's large foreign exhange resources were being used to meet the needs of current consumption (*i.e.*, to import foodgrains) rather than to import capital equipment and materials to sustain *new investment* or capital accumulation. Thus for stepping up the rate of capital accumulation and therefore economic growth we came to be dependent on all the three types of commodities (i) capital equipment, (ii) raw materials, and (iii) foodgrains. Thus, despite the objective of achieving self-reliance, the strategy adopted drove the economy away from it. The philosophy of "*aid to end aid*" proved to be myth.

Heavy industry strategy has also been criticised for its *ignoring the relevance of the principle of comparative advantage* and the gains to be obtained from specialisation in some selected fields. As mentioned before, Mahalanobis formulated his growth model on the assumption that exports could not be expanded sufficiently. With the help of his model he showed that it is through the adoption of the strategy of substituting imports by domestic production of heavy industry products such as steel, fertilizers, various kinds of machines and machines to make machines, heavy chemicals that high long-term rate of growth could be achieved. Thus Mahalanobis strategy involved industrialisation of import-substitution type. The question whether the new heavy industries would have a comparative advantage or not was not considered as a relevant consideration. The reckless pursuit of import substitution all along the line and accordingly setting up of all basic heavy industries such as steel, fertilizers, heavy chemicals, machine building and also industries which make machines to make machines (*i.e.*, industries producing mother machines), and so on without considering whether we had comparative advantage in their production. If we had comparative advantage in *some* basic heavy industries we should have concentrated our resources and enjoyed advantages of quick specialisa-

1. Government of India, *Economic Survey*, 1977–78, p. 69.

tion in selected lines rather than *thinly* spreading our resources on all types of basic heavy industries irrespective of whether we have comparative advantage or not in them caused misuse of scarce investment resources. As seen above, as a result of this strategy of all-round import substitution to build basic heavy industries we came to be dependent on imports from the rest of the world than we ever were or needed to be.

It may also be pointed out that in the Mahalanobis heavy industry strategy alternative policy of development of industries which had large export potential was not at all given any consideration. That supplies of some capital goods could be procured from abroad by development of export industries was ruled out. In this connection it was pointed out by the followers of Mahalanobis that the expansion of India's exports would mean the decline in its terms of trade. In our view, the contention that the increase in India's exports would necessarily mean decline in terms of trade was not justified. In fact, up to 1972 (*i.e.* before the oil crisis) the terms of trade had been in India's favour. It may be pointed out that declining terms of trade argument was advanced by supporters of Mahalanobis strategy only after the Mahalanobis model had been accepted and put into actual practice.

Finally, it may be noted that for achieving high long-term rate of economic growth Mahalanobis and later Raj and Sen[1] and Gautam Mathur[2] laid the greatest stress upon high magnitude of the ratio of incremental plough back of heavy industry products to the expansion of heavy industries sector itself as compared to all other sectors. This pattern of industrialisation, according to them, would automatically raise the saving-income ratio and generate a high rate of economic growth in the long run. However this argument is full of deficiencies and infirmities. The all-round development of heavy industry sector and the highest ratio of plough back of heavy industry products to the heavy industry sector involves, given the scarcity of resources, not only the appalling neglect of agriculture and rural development but also the neglect of the development of export industries and thereby enjoying the benefits of specialisation.

19. K.N. Raj and A.K. Sen, Alternative Patterns of Growth under Conditions of Export Earnings, *Oxford Economic Papers,* Feb. 1961

20. Gautam Mathur, *Planning for Steady Growth*, Oxford University Press, 1965.

CHAPTER 5

New Economic Policy : Liberalisation, Privatisation and Globalisation

Rationale for New Economic Policy of Economic Reforms

An important issue in the development policy has been whether the economic growth should be promoted by adopting planning and controls or through free market system in which private sector and foreign investors are permitted to play an important role. In the fifties and sixties, this issue was resolved in favour of planning and regulation of the private sector. It was felt that intervention by the Government was essential to initiate the process of development and thereby to break the vicious circle of poverty. However, in the eighties it was felt that excessive regulation and control of the private sector by the Government and high importance given to the public sector in the strategies of development of the developing countries were obstructing economic growth and *promoting inefficiency*. As a result, there was a slowdown in growth of these countries and further they experienced serious problems of large fiscal deficit resulting in a high rate of inflation and deficits in the balance of payments resulting in heavy indebtedness of the developing countries. To overcome the these problems some economists such as I.M.D. Little, Jagdesh Bhagwati, Bela Balassa who had been advisors to the World Bank and IMF argued for the adoption of the policy of economic liberalisation by the developing countries to promote economic growth, check inflation and solve the problem of balance of payments. They advocated that free markets and greater role of private sector (including foreign investors) would ensure efficiency by encouraging competition. Under these reforms direct controls had to be given up, the role of planning and public sector to be greatly diluted. Further, liberalisation of imports was suggested by drastically cutting down tariffs. Foreign private investment had been given greater importance and incentives had to be provided to attract them.

We explain below these structural adjustment reforms, with special reference to India. After independence, India avoided the extremes of both capitalism and socialism and opted for a mixed economy where planning and the public sector played an important role in the economic development of the country. The experiment of a mixed economy as evolved in India seemed to be a success in the beginning but during the seventies and eighties several shortcomings of its working had been noticed.

Inefficient Working of Public Enterprises. First, the public sector which was expected to generate adequate resources for the growth of the economy not only failed to do so but in fact was incurring huge losses which raised the expenditure of the Government. The losses of the public sector were said to be due to the *inefficiency in the working of public enterprises*. Secondly, the problem of *macroeconomic imbalances*, both in the internal and external sectors, emerged and assumed serious proportions in 1990-91. The huge deficits in the successive budgets of the government due to internal imbalance of Government expenditure and revenue led to the creation of more money supply which created the serious problem of rising prices, so much so that rate of inflation went up to about 17 per cent per annum during August 1991. This compelled the newly elected Congress government to reduce Government expenditure and fiscal deficit for stabilising prices.

Balance of Payments Crisis. In the external sector, *the huge deficits in the balance of payments due to the rising imports and sluggish exports persisted for a long time and, to meet* *this deficit, the Government resorted to commercial borrowing from abroad at higher market rates of interest.* As a result of persistent deficits on the current account, the foreign exchange reserves declined to a very small sum in June 1991 which could last for payments for necessary imports only for about few weeks. This compelled the Government to approach IMF (International Monetary Fund) for loans to make necessary payments and enhance the foreign exchange reserves.

Thirdly, though the annual growth of national income *during the eighties* went up to over 5 per cent and of the industrial sector to 8 per cent, which was considered to be a good performance, but due to macro-economic imbalances which emerged in the economy they could no longer be sustained any more. In the external sector, the situation became so worse in 1991 that India came to the brink of default. To avoid the default and to win over the confidence of international business community, the Government had to sell a part of its gold reserves and a certain amount of gold was even pledged with Bank of England to obtain the foreign exchange reserves to meet its obligations. Further, it had to approach the IMF for loans to tide over the foreign exchange crisis.

Excessive Government Controls over Private Sector. Besides, excessive Government regulation and control over the private sector proved to be counter-productive. The following drawbacks of excessive regulation of the private sector were emphasised and case for liberalisation of private sector was built up, especially by Jagdish Bhagwati and T.N. Srinivasan, the two economists associated with World Bank and International Monetary Fund. The following arguments were given in favour of dereguation of the private sector and assigning to it a greater role in economic growth of the Indian economy.

1. The industrial licensing and controls had degenerated into arbitrary bureaucratic controls on the allocation of resources in competing industries. The licenses were issued to make investment in those industries which bureaucrats chose in tune with the policies they administered. This licensing system replaced the efficient market system of resource allocation by personal system of resource allocation. Thus excessive regulation of the private sector, according to the advocates of economic reforms, had resulted in the sub-optimal resource allocation in industries. Hence, there was a need for liberalisation.

2. The Industrial licensing system had stiffled private initiative and enterprise because this system had left no scope for private initiatives in investment planning and investment decisions. In fact, the industrial licensing system did not allow the competitive economic environment to operate. As a result of this, the entrepreneurs had become attuned to secure *monopoly rent*, rather than to earn profits through enterprise and skills. Jagdish Bhagwati and T.N. Srinivasan identified licensing and control regime as the causative factor responsible for low productivity and high capital-output ratio. Hence, industrial liberalisation became an imperative condition for the growth of forces of competition to ensure high efficiency and productivity in Indian industries.

3. Under the regime of licensing, the industrial units which tried to increase output by making full utilisation of *installed capacity*, were penalised on the ground that their production exceeded the *licensed capacity* even if goods produced were much needed and were in short supply. Hence, industrial liberalisation became essential from the point of view of promoting industrial growth by the creation of additional productive capacity and its optimal utilisation.

4. The industrial licensing policy had failed to achieve its objectives of balanced regional industrial development and prevention of concentration of economic power. In fact, during licensing regime, the regional industrial imbalances and concentration of economic power had got intensified. Hence, there was a strong case for scrapping licensing system and switching over to market system.

WASHINGTON CONSENSUS, DEVELOPMENT POLICY AND STRUCTURAL ADJUSTMENT REFORMS

Before explaining the economic reforms initiated in 1991 under the pressure of IMF and World Bank, it may be mentioned that these reforms mainly constituted what is now labelled as *Washington Consensus*. This consensus was formulated by John Williamson, with the other officials of World Bank, IMF and key US government agencies. This consensus contains 10 elements of development policy which were suggested to promote economic growth in the developing countries and also help them solve their problems of indebtedness, balance of payments difficulties and high rate of inflation. It is noteworthy that this Washington Consensus followed a free market approach to development and, contrary to the views of many development economists, it did not emphasise elimination of poverty and reducing inequalities to achieve real development, as it is now widely understood. The Washington Consensus and fiscal and structural reforms it envisages views that poverty will be automatically removed if rapid economic growth is achieved. Its message is 'take care of growth, poverty will take care of itself'.

Let us list below the various elements of Washington Consensus.

1. **Fiscal Adjustment.** This means that developing countries should take steps to reduce fiscal deficit through curtailing Government expenditure by drastically reducing explicit and implicit subsidies provided by the Government of developing countries.

2. **Tax Reforms.** It was suggested that tax rates should be cut substantially to promote saving and private investment. This will promote investment and ensure a higher rate of economic growth. This was in line with supply-side economics. In fact, Jagdish Bhagwati and T.N. Srinivasan invoked *Laffer Curve* Concept of supply-side economics to argue that reduction in rates of taxes would cause not only greater private saving and investment but will lead to greater revenue for the government.

Besides, it was suggested to broaden the tax base by withdrawing exemptions and plugging the loopholes in taxes.

3. **Deregulation.** This was most significant policy measure under which it was recommended that industrial licensing controls be abolished but also such measures as Monopolistic and Restrictive Trade Practices Commission (MRTPC) and FERA (Foreign Exchange Regulation Act) be done away with so that private sector should grow without any obstructions.

4. **Privatisation.** This is another significant measure of development policy under which it was proposed that there should be disinvestment of public sector enterprises and accordingly either they should be sold outrightly to the private sector or Government stake should be reduced and its shares sold or transferred to private enterprises.

5. **Trade Liberalisation.** Under this it was suggested that tariffs on imports should be drastically reduced *to promote free trade*. Besides, all quantitative restrictions on imports were also to be eliminated to permit free trade.

6. **Competitive Exchange Rate.** Under this it was recommended that developing countries like India should devalue their over-valued currencies and ultimately adopt flexible exchange rate system. Besides, it was suggested to make the currency convertible so that obstacles to growth of free trade and capital mobility be removed.

7. **Removal of Barriers to Foreign Investment.** It was stressed that economic growth in developing countries could be accelerated through larger foreign direct investment (FDI). Therefore, all barriers put up by developing countries should be eliminated to attract foreign investment in their countries. To facilitate foreign investment it was also suggested to adopt *Convertivibility of currency on current account as well as on capital account*.

8. **Financial Reforms.** They involve reforms in the banking and insurance system and also in capital market.

9. **Protection of Property Rights.** According to this, suitable legislative measures should be taken to protect property rights. Besides, labour law should be amended so that it becomes easy for *private enterprise to enter and exit* the industries. In this, *freedom to exit* was emphasised and it was recommended that labour laws be made flexible so that it should be easy to retrench workers.

10. **Redirection of Public Sector Investment.** Lastly, it was emphasised that public sector investment should be redirected towards education, health and infrastructure only and also leave these and other fields open to private sector operation.

VARIOUS REFORMS UNDER NEW ECONOMIC POLICY

However, to evolve a long-term solution to promote price stability, to bring about equilibrium in balance of payments and, above all, to ensure higher rate of economic growth, the newly elected Congress Government with Dr. Manmohan Singh as Finance Minister adopted in 1991 what is popularly called *New Economic Policy* on the advice of IMF and World Bank. According to this policy, the Government was to prune down its expenditure so as to *recue budget deficits for achieving price stability. But more important element of new economic policy is the adoption of what are called Structural Adjustment Reforms* which sought to change the nature of Indian economic system by ultimately establishing *a free market economy*. Under this structural adjustment programme, the role of public sector in economic development had been diluted and that of private sector enhanced and expanded.

It may be noted that the policy of free-market economy also got strong stimulus due to the collapse of socialist system in Soviet Russia and other centrally planned socialist economies in the Eastern Europe. Accordingly, under the new economic policy, the idea of the predominant role of the public sector was abandoned and the private sector was given a greater role in promoting economic growth through competition and efficiency. Instead of being directed by the planning and licencing, the private sector would now be governed by the market forces, that is, by the free play of demand and supply of commodities and factors. We describe below the new economic reforms undertaken in India since 1991 under the *New Economic Policy or Structural Adjustment Programme.*

De-reservation of Industries of the Public Sector

The new industrial policy 1991 has been adopted under which far-reaching structural reforms have been initiated to lift excess direct controls and regultions on industries and to ensure a free-market oriented economic system. The list of industries reserved for the public sector has been pruned. Now, only 6 industries remain reserved for the public sector. Among the industries reserved earlier for the public sector were many core industries like iron and steel, electricity, air transport, ship building, heavy machinery industries such as heavy chemical plants and telecommunication cables and instruments. The new industrial policy of 1991 threw open all these industries for the private sector for investment and growth. Thus the new policy indicates the Government's intention to invite a greater degree of participation by the private sector in important areas of the economy. The six industries which continue to be reserved for the public sector are in areas where security and strategic considerations predominate. According to the new policy, the resources in the public sector will now be used for the development of strategic, high-technology industries and essential infrastructure areas and for social sectors such as education, public health and poverty alleviation programmes.

Liberalisation: Abolition of Industrial Licensing System

Until 1991 the Indian industrial sector had functioned under a system of tight controls and regulations represented by industrial licencing which meant to allocate the scarce resources towards building the industrial base of the economy. By the year 1991 the Indian industrial economy had a quite wide and diversified base, the new policy abolished all industrial licencing irrespective of the level of investment except for 15 industries for which licence was still required. These industries are those which are essential for security and safety purposes and for protection of environment. For granting of licence for even these 15 industries procedure has been greatly simplified. For getting licences only certain locational guidelines are to be fulfilled so that polluting industries should not cluster around the major urban centres. Besides, restrictions by Monopolistic and Restrictive Act (MRTPA) for expansion of big firms were also relaxed.

Privatisation of Public Sector Enterprises

An important aspect of new industrial policy of the Government is that it should not operate commercial enterprises. With that end in view the Government decided to disinvest the public enterprises. The Government can sell its enterprises completely to the private sector or disinvest a part of its equity capital held by it to the private sector companies or in the open market. Therefore *this policy of public sector disinvestment has also been called the policy of privatisation.* Through disinvestment or privatisation, the Government can mop up a good amount of resources which can be used for various purposes. The released resources can be used to restructure and strengthen the public sector enterprises which are potentially viable. These resources can also be used to pay back a part of public debt. These resources can also be used to finance budget deficits.

What are the reasons for the policy of privatisation or public sector disinvestment. First, resources available with the Government are scarce. The Government needs resources to reduce its budget deficit. The Government urgently requires resources to make investment in infrastructure, education, public health and for poverty alleviation programmes. Resources released through disinvestment can be used for investment in these crucial sectors. Second, a good number of existing public enterprises are working inefficiently and incurring huge losses.

Accordingly, a part of the economic reforms policy, the Government started reforms in public sector enterprises. The main elements of Government policy towards Public Sector Enterprises (PSU) are:

(1) Disinvestment of Government equity in all *non-strategic* Public Sector Undertakings (PSU) to 26 per cent or lower if necessary.

(2) Those public sector enterprises which are potentially viable have to be restructured and revived.

(3) Those Public Sector Undertakings (PSU) which cannot be revived would be closed down.

Table 5.1. Disinvestment of Public Sector Undertakings in India Since 1991

Year	*Target (₹ Crores)*	*Actual Receipts (₹. Crores)*
1991-92	2,500	3,038
1992-93	2,500	1,913
1993-94	3,500	NIL
1994-95	4,000	4,843
1995-96	7,000	168
1996-97	5,000	380
1997-98	4,800	910
1998-99	5,000	5.371
1999-2000	10,000	1,860
2000-01	10,000	1,871
2001-02	12,000	5,632
2002-03	12,000	3,348
2003-04	14,500	15,547
2004-05	4,000	2765
2005-06	no target	1568
2007-08	no target	2367
2008-09	no target	546
2009-10	no target	1120
2010-11	40,000	13,854
2012-13	30,000	NA

The Government has now evolved a fair, transparent and equitable procedure for disinvestment in selected public sector enterprises. The achievement made with regard to disinvestment of Public Sector Undertakings which started in 1991-92 with the sale of minority stakes in some public sector undertakings are given in Table 5.1. From 1999-2000 to March 2003 the disinvestment of public enterprises was mainly through sale of Government equity to *strategic private partners*. Under this policy of disinvestment through strategic sales, 100 per cent equity of Modern Food was sold to Hindustan Lever. 51 per cent of Government equity holding of BALCO was sold to private sector firm Sterlite Industries, 51 % of Government equity holdings in CMC was sold to TATA, 25% of Government equity in VSNL was sold to TATA. 25 per cent of Government Equity in IPCL was sold to Reliance Industries at ₹ 1490 crores. However, in the year 2003-04 policy of disinvestment through *public sale of government shares in market* of various public enterprises was adopted. Under it in August 2003 Government raised Rs. 900 crores by selling its equity in Maruti Udyog Ltd. to the general public in the open market. Similarly, in 2003-04 public sale of a part of government equity shares of public sector undertakings; IBP Ltd., DCIL, GAIL, ONGC was made and a good amount of resources was raised. As a result in 2003-04, Government's disinvestment receipts of ₹ 15,545 exceeded the target. After 2003-04, under UPA in 2003-04 Government process of disinvestment slowed down due to the opposition by Left Parties which were then alies of the government. In 2004-05 only ₹2765 crores and in 2005-06 ₹ 1568 crores were raised through public sector disinvestment, 2006-07 public sector disinvestment was kept on hold due to stiff opposition by the left parties except that disinvestment in Maruti-Udyog Ltd was undertaken and ₹ 2367 crores were raised.

Globalisation

The following measures for globalisation of the Indian economy were taken.

Welcoming Private Foreign Investment and Foreign Technology. Till 1991, foreign investment and import of foreign technology was regulated tightly in India. In the case of foreign technology agreements sought by Indian firms as well as foreign investment, it was necessary to obtain specific prior approval from the government for each project. This involved delays and hampered business decision making in the import of technology by Indian firms. Under the new economic policy for a selected list of high technology and high investment priority industries, firms receive *automatic approval* to make foreign technology agreements within certain guidelines. This policy measure is expected to remove the delay and uncertainty which earlier clouded the relationships between Indian and foreign firms.

Further, the government has *liberalised its policy regarding foreign investment*. To attract private foreign investment,it has been decided to grant *automatic permission to private foreign investors to invest up to 51 per cent of the total equity shares in 34 high priority industries if certain norms are fulfilled*. This facility will be available to those firms which are able to finance their capital equipment imports through their foreign equity. This is a major departure from the previous policies which required case-by-case approval of foreign investment normally limited to 40 per cent equity participation. The priority sector includes power generation and petroleum refining. Further, the government has given a guarantee of 16 per cent return on foreign investment in priority sectors. There is also proposal to allow automatic clearance for foreign *financial* and technical collaboration with Indian firms.

Trade Liberalisation. In a bid to open up the economy, under the new economic policy *quantitiave restrictions*, that is, import licencing for imports of goods have been removed. Further, to promote competitiveness, efficiency and globalisation of the Indian economy import duties have been reduced to the 20 per cent (excluding agricultural and dairy products) with effect from Jan. 9, 2004. The new thinking is that with the cheapening of imported goods, the Indian firms will try to increase their efficiency and reduce costs so that their products can compete with the foreign products. In this way they will be able to expand their exports.

Currency Convertibility and Floating of Indian Rupee. Another major step taken towards libralisation of the Indian economy has been to make the Indian rupee fully convertible on current account since March 1993. This implies that for the purpose of foreign trade and travel you can convert the rupees into dollars and dollars into rupees in the foreign exchange market at the market determined exchange rate. That is, the foreign exchange rate of rupee is now not fixed but liable to change as demand for and supply of foreign exchange change. In July 1991, the Indian rupee was devalued by about 20 per cent. But now with market-determined exchange rate, the Indian rupee can depreciate or appreciate depending upon demand and supply conditions.

NEW ECONOMIC REFORMS : A CRITICAL EVALUATION

It is evident from the reforms introduced in the Indian economy that from a planned economy it has moved towards a free-market economy. Though we still have mixed economy with both the public and private sectors coexisting but the role of private sector which is governed by market forces has been greatly increased and that of the public sector greatly diluted. So we now have a mixed economy with greater orientation towards a free market and private sector.

More than a decade and a half has passed when we initiated economic reforms in 1991 laying greater emphasis on liberalisation and privatisation. Now, the pertinent question is whether these economic reforms have ensured higher and sustained economic growth which the supporters of these reforms argued that they would, whether these reforms have led to a higher growth rate and to the greater reduction of poverty and unemployment which was expected of them.

Rise in Foreign Exchange Reserves and Growth in Exports

It may be said in favour of economic reforms that today we face no longer any foreign exchange crisis which prompted the initiation of these reforms. Foreign exchange resources which had gone too low in 1991 have substantially increased in the post-reforms period. Foreign exchange resources rose to 100 billion US dollars in Dec. 2003 and further to about 145 billion US dollars in March 2006 and on end-March, 2008, the foreigen exchange reserves stood at 310 billion US dollars. During 2008-09 there was capital outflow from India due to global financial crisis and as a result foreign exchange reserves fell to US $ 252 billion in March-end 2009. However, during 2009-10 there was reversal of capital flows and as a result foreign exchange reserves rose to US $ 270 billion on end-March 2010 and to US $ 300 billion in end-March 2011. Foreign exchange reserves were $ 275 billion in September, 2013.

New economic reforms, especially trade liberalisation, removal of excessive control over private sector and devaluation of rupee in July 1991 (and later floating of rupee) had a beneficial effect on growth of Indian exports. The growth rate of merchandise exports picked up during 1991-97 when on an average growth rate of 11,7 per cent per annum was registered. However, during the Ninth Plan period (1997-2002) rate of growth of exports fell to 6 per cent per annum due to global recession during this period. After 2002, growth rate of exports substantially increased and during 2003-04 to 2007-08 growth rate of 25.4 per cent per annum in exports was achieved. Thus reforms in the external sector have yielded good results in growth of exports and invisibiles (i.e., services and private transfers). However, growth of imports also increased due to liberalisation of trade through reduction of tariffs and elimination of quota restrictions. Even with the growth of imports balance of payments on current account improved; deficit in current account which was 3.1% of GDP in 1990-91 fell to 1.4% in 1997-98 and to 0.5 in 2000-01. For these years (2001-02, 2002-03 and 2003-04, there was surplus in balance of payments, that is, there was net investment abroad by the Indians. With 2004-05 onwards there has been again deficit on current balance of payments which was 1.2%, 1.1% and 1.5% of GDP in 2005-06, 2006-07 and 2007-08 respectively which was quite small. This represents *net inflow of capital* and is a good thing.

Control over Inflation

The annual rate of inflation as measured by the change in wholesale price index (WPI) which was brought down from about 17 per cent in August 1991 to 4.5 per cent in 1997-98, again went up to year-on-year basis to 7.1 per cent in 2000-01. But it ceme down to 3.6 per cent in 2001-02, 3.4 per cent in 2002-03 and went up to 5.5 per cent in 2003-04 and 6.5 per cent in 2004-05. Average annual inflation rate (based on WPI, 1993-94 = (100) was estimated at 4.4 per cent in 2005-06 and around 5.4 percent in 2006-07. Thus, inflation was brought under control. It may however be noted that for controlling inflation, credit must be given to prudent monetary policy produced by the Reserve Bank of India. Even after economic reforms with exception of few years fiscal deficit has been quite large which generated inflationary pressures in the Indian economy. Tight monetary policy of the RBI succeeded in neutralising to a great extent the possible inflationary impact of the large fiscal deficit.

However, inflationary pressures were built up during 2006-07 and 2007-08 though with the adoption of proper monetary measures by RBI and reduction in fiscal deficit by the Government, they were kept under check. But from march 2008, inflation rate as measured by WPI flared up and year-on-year inflation rate crossed 9 per cent in June 2008 and continued unabated and crossed 11 per cent in August 2008 and reached a peak level of 12.6 per cent in mid-Sept. 2008. As a result of supply-side measures adopted by the government and tight monetary policy adopted by RBI, inflation rate on year-on-year basis came down to 11.4 per cent in October and to 8.5 per cent in end-November 2008.

However, from the second half of 2009-10 inflation rate again started rising and became a matter of concern. The financial year 2010-11 started with a double digit headline inflation of 11.0 per cent in April 2010. After remaining in double digits from April to July 2010, inflation started falling for the whole financial year 2010-11, WPI inflation was measured at around 9 per cent which was quite a high level. In spite of good monsoon in 2010-11 and high agricultural growth rate of 6.6 per cent in this year, food inflation jumped to double-digit level and stood at 13.6 per cent in Dec. 2010. During FY 2011-12 also both WPI inflation and food inflation continued at an elevated levels and was around 7.3 per cent. However, inflation as measured by consumer price index (CPI) remained at a high level of 9.8% per cent Y-O-Y basis in March 2013. Food inflation rose to 18 per cent Y-O-Y basis in August 2013 despite 70 million tonnes of stocks of foodgrains with government. Nearly double digit inflation rates in terms of consumer price index (CPI) and and a very high rate of food inflation is a matter of serious concern as it erodes the real income of the common man. It hits the poor man badly.

However, it is important to note that current inflation rate is not due to economic reforms undertaken since 1991. It is the result of both supply-side and demand-side pressures presently operating in the Indian economy and both domestic and external factors are responsible for it. We will explain the causes of inflation in a market economy in detail in a later chapter.

Acceleration of Economic Growth. Though economic reforms have not ensured sustained economic growth during the over two decades since 1991, the overall picture that emerges is that rate of growth of GDP has gone up. We present in Table 5.2 below the overall growth of GDP and of various sectors in the Indian economy.

Table 5.2 : Average Annual Sectoral Growth Rate

	1980-81 to 1990-91	1992-93 to 2000-01	1997-98 to 2002 9th Plan	2002-07 10th Plan	2007 -08	2008 -09	2009 -10	2010 -11	2011 -12	2012 -13
Agriculture	3.4	3.2	2.0	2.5	2.5	–0.1	0.8	6.6	3.6	1.9
Industry	6.6	6.4	4.6	8.6	9.0	3.2	8.3	7.8	2.6	1.2
Services	6.7	7.8	8.1	9.3	10.2	10.9	9.7	9.2	7.8	6.6
GDP at factor cost	5.6	6.1	5.7	7.8	9.3	6.7	8.6	9.3	6.2	5.0

Source : 1. Dr. Shankar Acharya, Growth has slowed, *Economic Times*, 22 May, 2001
2. GOI, *Economic Survey* 2005-06, 2006-07, 2007-08, 2010-11, 20120-13

It may be noted that *growth rate of industry* where major reforms were undertaken, was estimated to be higher at 7.6 per cent per annum in the five year period during 1992-93 - 1996-97 (omitting the year 1991-92) as compared to 6.6 per cent achieved in the pre-reform decade 1980-81-1990-91. The growth rate of 6.7 per cent per annum in GDP achieved during the period 1992-93 to 1996-97 was also higher as compared to the eighties. However, during the Ninth Plan period (1997-2002), the growth rate of industry declined to 4.6 which is far less than the industrial growth in the pre-reform period. The overall *growth rate in GDP* during the five year period of Ninth Plan, 1997-98-2001-02 was 5.5 per cent which was also less than that of pre-reform period. The lower industrial growth during 1997 to 2002 resulted from global recession and also sluggish domestic demand conditions which arose due to decline in public sector investment and lower growth rate of agriculture.

However, during the Tenth Plan period (2002-07) annual growth rate of industry rose to 8.6 per cent and of GDP to 7.8 per cent. In the four year period 2003-04 to 2007-08, *average annual growth rate of GDP has been over 9 per cent*. Due to global financial crisis, growth rate in 2008-09 fell to 6.7% but it again went up to 8.6 per cent in 2009-10 and 9.3 per cent in 2010-11. In fact, in the four years (2005-06, 2006-07, 2007-08 and 2010-11) annual average growth rate in GDP exceeded 9 per cent and the acceleration in growth rate is the big achievement of economic reforms. With this higher GDP growth India has become the second highest growth rate country in the world, next only to China.

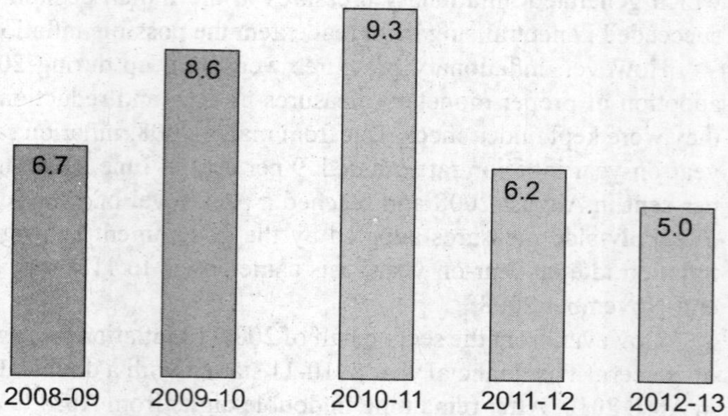

Fig. 5.1. *Revised Estimates for India's GDP Growth Rate, 2008-09-2012-13 (in percentage)*

This higher growth rate has been driven mostly by higher domestic investment which in 2007-08 was estimated to be 37.7 per cent of GDP_{mp}. This higher investment has been substantially financed by domestic saving which was estimated at 36.4% of GDP in 2007-08. In bringing about this higher growth, privatisation and liberalisation of the Indian economy which were undertaken under the economic reforms started in 1991 have played an important role. With these reforms India became one of the fastest growing economy of the world. However, it may noted that as a result of world financial crisis (2008-09) which started due to defaults in sub-prime housing loans in the US and spread to all other countries also hit the Indian economy. This adversely hit our exports and also investment in the Indian economy. Therefore, growth rate in GDP fell to 6.7 per cent in 2008-09 but it again went up to 8.6 per cent in 2009-10 and 9.3% in 2010-11. **However, *there has been slowdown in overall GDP growth rate after 2010-11. India's growth rate fell to 6.2 per cent in 2011-12, to 5.0 per cent in 2012-13 and is estimated at 5.3 per cent in 2013-14 (see Table 5.2 and Figure 5.1).***

It is worth noting that ***services sector*** in India, like that in most developed countries, is the dominant sector in determining economic growth. The compound annual growth of the services sector was on an average 9 per cent for the period 2004, – 05 to 2011-12 and far exceeded the GDP growth of the industrial and agricultural sectors. In 2011-12 and 2012-13 in tune with the general slowdown in the Indian economy, the growth rate of the services sector also declined. The slowdown in growth rate of the services sector in 2011-12 and 2012-13 from the double digit growth of the previous six years contributed significantly to the slowdown in the overall growth of the Indian economy. While some slowdown in growth of services sector can be attributed to the lower growth in agricultural and industrial activities, given the backward and forward linkages with the services, lower demand from the rest of the world has also played a part.

Rate of Unemployment. The NSS Survey 1999-2000 found that unemployment in 1999-2000 increased as compared to that found in NSS 1993-94. It will be seen from Table 5.3 that *all rates of unemployment, namely,* usual status, current weekly status and current daily status, (through which

Table 5.3 : Unemployment Rates : Alternative Measures

Unemployment Rates	Usual Principal Status	Current Weekly Status	Current Daily Status
All India			
1993-94	2.56	3.6	6.0
1999-2000	2.81	4.4	7.3
2004-05	3.06	4.4	8.3
2009-10	2.5	–	6.6
2011-12	2.7	–	5.6
Rural			
1993-94	1.80	3.0	5.6
1999-2000	1.96	3.9	7.2
2004-05	2.5	4.0	8.3
2009-10	2.1	3.3	6.8
2011-12	-	-	-
Urban			
1993-94	5.21	3.0	5.6
1999-2000	5.23	3.9	7.2
2004-05	5.3	4.4	8.3
2009-10	3.7	4.2	6.6
2011-12	-	-	-

Source : Planning Commission, *Tenth Five Year Plan* and GOI, *Economic Survey* 2006-07 and 2007-08.

incidence of unemployment is measured in India) increased in 1999-2000 as compared to those in 1993-94. Further, in the 61st Round (2004-05), the three rates of unemployment further increased in both the rural and urban areas. On current daily status basis in 2004-05 on an average 8.3 per cent persons both in rural and urban areas were found to be unemployed on a day. For All India (both rural and urban) unemployment rate on current daily status basis rose to 8.3 per cent in 2004-05.

This was quite a high rate of unemployment which posed a serious threat to the stability of the Indian society. This high rate of unemployment was only to be expected. The chief drawback of New Economic Policy is that it involves the use of labour-saving modern technology and the competition from the imported products faced by the domestic industries and public sector disinvestment on a large scale. The use of capital-intensive technology not only displaces labour already employed but also lowers the growth of employment from the new investment and capital accumulation.

However, according to 66th round of NSS for the year 2009-10 unemployment on daily status basis has fallen to 6.8% in rural areas and 5.8% in urban areas. For whole India, daily status unemployment fell to 6.6 in 2009-10 per cent from 8.3% in 2004-05 (see Table 5.3). However, doubts were expressed about this fall in unemployment in 2009-10 by many economists including Prof. Amartya Sen. The government decided to go in for a special unemployment survey in 2011-12. According to this latest data India's employment rate has declined to 38.6% of population in 2011-12 of labour force from 39.2% in 2009-10. In 2004-05 the employment rate was 42% of population. As a result of this unemployment rate on usual status basis rose to 2.7% in 2011-12 from 2.5% in 2009-10. The number of unemployed on usual principal and subsidiary status basis rose to 10.8 million in January 2012 from 9.8 million in January 2010. The special unemployment survey data 2011-12 reveals that only 2.7 million new jobs were created in the five years between 2004-05 and 2009-10 – sharply lower than the 60 million jobs created in the previous five years. However, according to unemployment survey 2011-12, 14 million new jobs were added in the two years between 2009-10 and 2011-12, nearly five times the jobs added in the previous five years. This is perhaps due to starting of special employment scheme known as MGNREG scheme started in 2009 and also because of higher agriculutral growth of 6.6 per cent in 2010-11 and 3.6 per cent in 2011-12. Surprisingly, unemployment rate on the current daily status basis has also gone down significantly in 2 years period from 6.6% in 2009-10 to 5.6% between July 2011 and June 2012 when the the special employment survey was conducted. This indicates more persons were fully-employed, that is, their under-employment sharply declined due to the starting of MGREG scheme. Further, this also seems to be the result of fall in labour force participation rate.

Besides, due to the greater role assigned to the private sector, big business houses, foreign capital (MNCs) the already existing inequalities of income and wealth will further increase. This is against the objective of social justice which in the past was the cherished goal of the Indian planning.

Problem of Poverty. An important consequence of economic reforms is that there has been slowdown in reduction of poverty ratio in the post-reform period despite a much higher growth rate of GDP. On the basis of uniform recall period (URP), percentage of population below the poverty line fell from 36 per cent to 1993-94 to 27.5 per cent in 2004-05 which amounts to 0.74 per cent annual average reduction in poverty. This is much less than the reduction in poverty ratio in pre-reform period when percentage of population below the poverty line declined from 51.3 per cent in 1977-78 to 38.9 per cent in 1987-88 which works out to be 1.2 per cent average annual fall in poverty ratio in these ten years.

However, the estimates of poverty in India has become a highly controversial issue. An expert committee under the chairmanship of Late Prof. Suresh Tendulkar examined the problem of estimation of poverty in India. Tendulkar Committee suggested moving away from calorie intake as the defining parameter for poverty line to a more comprehensive method of *using per capita expenditure on basic needs such as food, clothing and services like helath and education.* On the basis of Tendulkar Committee recommendations it was estimated that 29.8 per cent of the population of India was poor in 2009-10 (66th Round NSS) compared to 37.2 per cent in 2004-05 (Note that poverty line in 2009-10 was fixed at ₹ 22.4 per capita daily consumption expenditure in rural areas and ₹ 28.65 per capita in urban areas). The 68th round of National Sample Survey 2011-12 report reveals that there has

Table 5.4. Poverty in India : Rcent Estimates of Head Count Ratio (%)

	2004-05	2009-10	2011-12
All India	37.2	29.8	21.9
Rural	41.8	33.8	24.5
Urban	25.7	16.5	13.7

been not much decline in pvoerty rate in the urban areas in the two years (2010-12) where industrial reforms have been largely made under the new economic policy adopted since 1991. We present the poverty estimates based on Tendulkar Committee recommendations for three years 2004-05, 2009-10 and 2011-12. On the basis of Tendulkar Committee methodology Planning Commission estimated that poverty came down from 37.2 per cent in 2004-05 to 21.9 per cent in 2011-12. This is based on the poverty line adjusted for price rise between 2004-05 and 2011-12. In 2011-12, poverty line is fixed at ₹ 27.20 per person per day in rural areas and ₹ 33.4 per person per day in urban area. **On this basis, in absolute number of people living below the poverty line declined from around 408 million in 2004-05 to 270 million in 2011-12, that is, about 138 million persons were lifted out of poverty in the seven-year period. Moreover, from the decline in All Indian poverty ratio from 37.2 per cent in 2004-05 to 21.9 per cent in 2011-12, it has been concluded that poverty in these seven years declined at the rate of 2.2 per cent per annum in these seven years as against 0.74 per cent per annum between 1993-94 and 2004-05**

However, these poverty estimates have been criticised on the ground that they have been made on the basis of lower poverty line of daily expenditure per person of ₹ 27.20 for rural areas and ₹ 33.4 for urban areas. The critics have pointed out that, given the high prices of foodgrains a person cannot possibly live on ₹ 27.20 in rural areas and ₹ 33.4 in urban areas. Fixing such a low daily expenditure per person for defining poor is making a cruel joke of the poor people. Besides, it has been alleged that UPA government has made a deliberate effort to keep the number of poor people low to show a big achievement of UPA government. In this context it may be noted that according to World Bank which on the basis of poverty line of $ 1.25 per day (on purchasing poverty basis) estimated that 33 per cent of India's population was living below the poverty line.

The second controversial point is whether it is rapid economic growth or greater expenditure on social welfare schemes such as MGNREGS that has brought about such a drastic reduction in poverty.

Thus it cannot said with certainty that higher rate of economic growth under the economic reforms with its privatisation, liberalisation and globalisation have resulted in slowdown in the rate of decline in poverty ratio.

Volatility in Exchange Rate and Economic Stability

Another adverse consequence of liberalisation and globalisation is the creation of volatility in foreign exchange rate of rupee which has adversely affected the Indian economy. Under the policy of globalisation of economic reforms we allowed free movements of capital flows into and out of India and switched over to the market determined exchange rate and made the rupee convertible. From 2003-04 onwards there were large capital inflows into the Indian economy, mainly through portfolio investment by FIIs which caused appreciation of Indian rupee whose value rose from above ₹ 46 to a dollar in 2002-03 and to ₹ 44.27 at the end of March 2006 and further to ₹ 39.4 to a US dollar in mid-Nov. 2007. This appreciation of rupee adversely affected our exports. Besides, large inflows of dollars got converted into rupees which caused rapid increase in money supply generating inflationary pressures in the Indian economy. Further large capital inflows, especially portfolio investment by FIIs in the Indian stock market, artificially caused high rise in price of shares of Indian companies.

In 2008-09 the opposite happened when due to liquidity crunch in the banking system in the US caused by sub-prime housing loans by American banks and mortgage failures, FIIs started selling shares of the Indian companies held by them and making net capital outflows from India. This led to depreciation of Indian rupee. The value of rupee which was about ₹ 40 to a US dollar in January 2008 depreciated to a low of ₹ 50 per US $ in the second week of November 2008 but again appreciated to ₹ 45 per US $ in 2009-10 (average of the year). India is at present under flexible exchange rate system under which exchange rate is determined by demand and supply forees. India has experienced high volatility in capital flows which have been the dominant factor in inducing volatility in the exchange rate of the rupee against the US dollar. The exchange rate appreciated when there were large capital inflows and depreciated when there were capital outflows. Given the stated policy of the Reserve Bank to prevent excessive volatility in exchange rate, it has intervened in the foreign exchange market to buy or sell dollars as the case may be to prevent excessive appreciation or depreciation in exchange rate.

A biggest depreciation of rupee vs US dollar occurred in the month of June to August 2013 when rupee which was around ₹ 56 to a US dollar in the beginning of June 2013, fell to around 60 to a US dollar in the third and fourth week of June 2013 that is, about 7 per cent depreciation in a single month. This sharp depreciation of Indian rupee was triggered by the announcement by Mr. Bermanke, the Governor of Federal Reserve of the US that it will taper the quantitative easing from the fourth quarter of the year 2013 as the US economy had been revived. This spread a panic in the world capital and foreign exchange markets as under the quantitative easing policy capital outflows were taking place from the US to the emerging economies. Under the *quantitative easing* policy the Federal Reserve was buying bonds of $ 85 billion every month and thus pumping money in the US economy to revive it. In the second week of June 2013, the Governor of the Reserve Bank announced that it will reduce the purchases of bonds from $ 85 billion to $ 65 billion per month as the US economy had revived. This caused reversal of capital flows from the Indian economy. In less than a month over $ 57 billion was withdrawn from the Indian debt and stock markets. This resulted in crash in Indian stock market and led to the increase in demand for US dollars resulting in the rapid depreciation of the Indian rupee. This sharp depreciation of rupee has serious consequences for the Indian economy. Not only will it make our imports costlier and fuel another round of inflation, it will also restrain the RBI from pushing through interest rate cuts urgently needed for kick-starting investment and boosting economic growth.

It follows from above that globalisation with liberalisation of capital flows and market determined exchange rate and convertibility of rupee has caused a lot of volatility in exchange rate and is therefore not without risks and dangers. Therefore, one should proceed with caution in liberalising capital flows and capital convertibility of the rupee.

Critical Evaluation of New Economic Policy and Economic Reforms

The supporters of new economic policy and economic reforms who argued for diluting the role of public sector or Government as it does not ensure efficiency in production laid great stress on '*Government failures*' for promoting economic growth. They however turn a blind eye to the *market failures*. To quote an eminent American economist Dr. Joseph Stiglitz[1], who has won Nobel Prize for Economics in recent years, "*Market failures are a fact of life, as are government failures. New liberal ideologies assume perfect markets, perfect information, and a host of other things which even the best performing market economies cannot satisfy*". He therefore forcefully argues for a *balanced approach to government* and *markets* recognising that both are important and complementary".[2] This means both public sector and private sectors should play a complementary role in bringing about economic growth. Due to market failures we cannot rely on private sector alone to bring about sustained economic growth and adequate expansion in employment opportunities and for eliminating poverty.

It is not being argued here that we should go back to '*license-permit Raj*". What we are stating is that (1) markets need to be regulated effectively by the Government if the objective of growth with equity is to be realised. Stock market scam of 1992 prompted by Harshad Mehta and the stock market scam of 2001 engineered by Ketan Parikh are shining examples of the absence of effective regualtion of the market by the Government playing havoc with the economy. Again, UTI fiasco of July 2001 suspending the sale and re-purchase of US-64 units showed that activities of mutual funds must be effectively regulated and not left to the free working of markets.

That there is need for regulating the market economy and intervention by the Government to revive it has been clearly evident from the financial crisis that gripped the world economy in 2007-09. This financial crisis originated from the defaults of sub-prime housing loans given by the American banks but due to the integrated nature of world economy today engulfed the whole world. This financial crisis seriously affected the American banking system with some American banks going bankrupt. The collapse of the American banking system created liquidity crunch for the corporate sector affecting investment and creating conditions of recession in the American economy. Due to the integrated nature of the world economy, the American financial crisis not only affected the corporate sector in the US but also created global meltdown involving not only European countries but also Asian economies (including the Indian economy).

To bail out the American banks, the President Bush came out with 700 billion US dollars plan to help them solve the liquidity problem and restore investors confidence so that the American economy could be revived. This means that now a lesson has been tearnt that the market economy is not self-correcting and as emphasized by J.M. Keynes in the early thirties that in situation of recession the Government has to intervené in the economy through expansionary fiscal and monetary measures

1. Joseph E. Stiglitz, p.84
2. *Ibid*, p. 84

to overcome recession.

Thus the recent global financial crisis (2007-09) has demonstrated that markets are not self-correcting, do not allocate resources efficiently and serve public interest well. The financial crisis that emanated from the US had the roots in massive allocation of resources to housing. When the prices of houses fell sharply, households defaulted in making payments of loan instalments. As a result, millions of families who could not afford them were forced out of their homes. Thus this was great failures of market which led to the financial crisis in the US and spread to other countries of the world.

Since the integration of Indian economy with the world economy as the result of economic reforms aimed at liberalisation of trade and capital flows, the global financial crisis spilled over into the Indian economy as well. The Indian stock market crashed causing crores of losses to the investors. This greatly affected investors' confidence. The shares of banks had been affected most and as a result the capital outflows by FIIs from India not only affected share prices but also caused liquidity problem for the banks and the corporate firms as FIIs converted rupees into dollars which they sent back to meet the liquidity requirements of their present companies. This liquidity crunch for the banks and corporate sector adversely affected the investment environment in the Indian economy. To bail out the banking system and stock market, RBI over different phases reduced cash reserve ratio from 9 per cent to 6.5 per cent and thereby infused ₹ 14,000 crores liquidity into the market to prevent much slowdown in India's economic growth.

The upshot of the argument is that market economy is not self correcting and therefore there is need for effective regualtion and intervention by the Government to ensure not only the stability of the economy but also to sustain the growth momention of the Indian economy.

Apart from regulation of markets and private sector what is needed in the context of the Indian economy is the *paramount role of Government in stepping up public sector investment in infrastructure* if sustained rate of higher growth rate on sustained basis is to be achieved. Government role is also crucial for *adequate investment in social sectors such as education, health care and poverty alleviation programmes* which are generally neglected by the private sector. For the purpose of poverty alleviation, undertaking of rural public works to utilise not only accumulated food stocks but also to generate employment opportunities for the poor and unemployed is of paramount importance for which the Government should increase its expenditure. For the purpose of investment in infrastructure and social sectors (education and health care) and expenditure on employment schemes for the poor the Government should not hesitate to incur moderate fiscal deficit. In this way if there is a moderate increase in fiscal deficit, it should not be considered undesirable. We should not follow unthinkingly IMF inspired policy of reducing fiscal deficit under all circumstances.

In our view reduction in fiscal deficit should not be elevated to a *dogma*. What is relevant is that Government *should spend its borrowing for investment purposes*, especially infrastructure and on development of human capital – education and health care. What is needed is that Government should not borrow for consumption purposes. Prof. Amartya Sen rightly writes that "*the success of liberalisation and closer integration with the world economy* may be severely impaired by India's *backwardness in basic education, elementary health care, gender inequality and limitations of land reforms*. While Manmohan Singh did initiate the correction of governmental *over-activity* in some fields, the need to correct the governmental *under-activity* in other areas has not really been addressed."[3] Further, referring to the higher growth rate in some East and South East countries which have achieved high growth rate with considerable equality he writes, "These countries all share some conditions that are particularly favourable to widespread participation of the population

3. Amartya Sen, Theory and Practice of Development, in *India's Economic Reforms and Development, Essays for Manmohan Singh*, by Isher Judge Ahluwalia and I.M.D. Little(ed) Oxford University Press, 1998, p. 83.

in economic change. *The relevant features include high rates of literacy, a fair degree of female empowerment, and quite radical land reforms.* Can we expect in India results similar to those that the more socially egalitrian countreis have achieved, given that half the Indian population (and two-thirds of the women) are still illiterate, that female empowerment is very little achieved in most parts of India, that credit is very hard to secure by the rural poor, and that land reforms remain only partially and unevenly implemented ? Should we not have expected more in the direction of breaking the terrible neglect of these concerns, on which the basic capabilities of the Indian masses depend ?"[4]

Commenting on the supporters of policies of free market, liberalisation and Washington Consensus Stiglitz writes that these policies "worked badly for developing countries. They were told to stop intervening in agriculture thereby exposing their farmers to devasting competition from the United States and Europe. Their farmers might have been able to compete with American and European farmers *but they could not compete with US and European Union subsidies.* Not surprisingly, investment in agriculture in developing countries faded and food gap widened"[5]. As a result, according to him, policies of neo-liberalism will lead to a large rise in poverty. The policies of free

4. *Ibid*
5. Joseph Stiglitz, The End of New Liberalism, *Economic Times,* 2009
6. *Ibid*

PART II

ANALYSIS OF NATIONAL INCOME AND EMPLOYMENT

- Circular Flow of Income and National Income Accounting
- Determination of National Income : Two Sector Keynesian Model
- Determination of National Income : Three Sector and Four Sector Models
- Consumption Function
- Keynes' Theory of Investment Multiplier
- Investment Demand and Accelerator Theory
- Analysis of Employeemnt and Unemployment

CHAPTER 6

Circular Flow of Income and National Income Accounting

Meaning of National Income

The labour and capital of a country acting on its natural resources produce annually a certain amount of goods and services. This is called national income of the country. *National income of a country can be defined as the total market value of all final goods and services produced in the economy in a year*. Two things must be noted in regard to this meaning of national income. First, it measures the market value of annual output. In other words, national income is a *monetary measure*. This is because there is no other way of adding up the different sorts of goods and services except with their money prices. But in order to know accurately the changes in physical output, the figure for national income is adjusted for price changes. Secondly, for calculating national income accurately all goods and services produced in any given year must be counted only once, and not more than once. Most of the goods go through a series of production stages before reaching a market. As a result, parts or components of many goods are bought and sold many times. Hence, in order to avoid counting several times the parts of goods that are sold and resold, national income only includes the market value of all *final goods* and ignores the transactions involving *intermediate goods*.

The above way of explaining national income is only one way of interpreting it. In fact, the concept of national income has three interpretations. It represents a total value of production (as explained above), it represents a receipts total, and it represents an expenditure total. It is an obvious fact that every expenditure is at the same time a receipt. In other words, amount spent is equal to amount received. But if goods and services are valued at their market prices, we have three-fold identity, namely, that the value received equals the value paid equals the value of goods and services produced and sold.

To explain the above idea let us take an economy where there are only two agents: households and firms. Firms are required to produce goods. To produce them, they require services of factors of production. Factors of production are paid the rewards for their contribution to the production of goods. Thus incomes of these factors arise in the course of production. The sales value of net production must equal the sum total of payments made by the firms to the factors of production in the course of production. The sales value of net production must equal the sum total of payments made by the firms to the factors of production in the form of wages, rents, interest and profits. These incomes in turn become the sources of expenditure. Thus income flows from the firms to the households in exchange for productive services. This income again returns to the firms when expenditure is made by the households on the goods produced by the firms.

From above it follows that: *National Income = National Product = National Expenditure*. In other words, there are three measures of national income of a country.

(*a*) the sum of values of all final goods and services produced.

(*b*) the sum of all incomes, in cash and kind, accruing to factors of production in a year; and

(*c*) the sum of consumers' expenditure, net investment expenditure and government expenditure on goods and services.

Sum of all income, sum of values of all final production, and sum of all expenditures will be the same, but the significance of each arises from the fact that they reflect the three basic activities of the nation's economy, viz., production, distribution and expenditure.

CIRCULAR FLOW OF INCOME

The modern economy is a monetary economy. In the modern economy, money is used in the process of exchange. Money has facilitated the process of exchange and has removed the difficulties of the barter system. Thus money acts as a medium of exchange. The households supply the economic resources or factors to the productive firms and receive in return the payments in terms of money. In is thus clear that, in the monetary economy, there will be flows of money corresponding to the flows of economic resources and the flows of goods and services. But each money flow is in opposite direction to the real flow.

Circular Income Flow in a Two Sector Economy

Real flows of resources, goods and services have been shown in Fig. 6.1. In the upper loop of this figure, the resources such as land, capital and entrepreneurial ability flow from households to business firms as indicated by the arrow mark. In opposite direction to this, money flows from business firms to the households as factor payments such as wages, rent, interest and profits. In the lower part of the figure, money flows from households to firms as consumption expenditure made by the households on the goods and services services produced by the firms, while the flow of goods and services is in

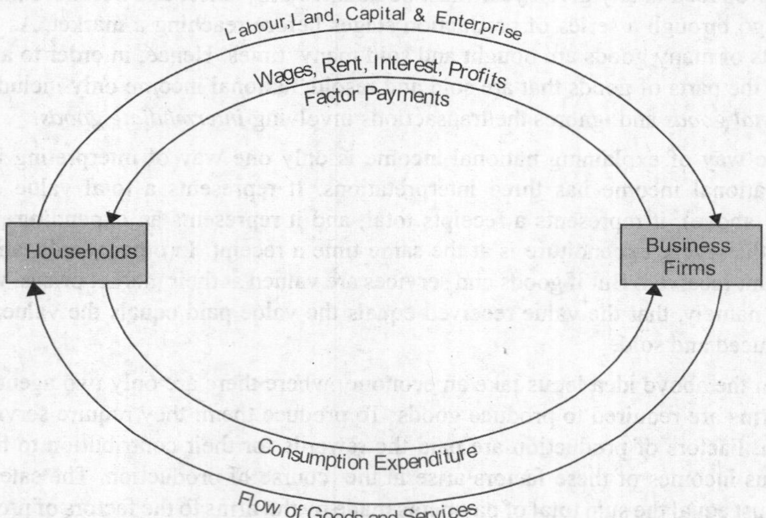

Fig. 6.1. *Circular Flow of Income in a Simple Two Sector Economy*

opposite direction from business firms to households. Thus we see that money flows from business firms to households as factor payments and then it flows from households to firms. Thus there is, in fact, *a circular flow of money or income*. This circular flow of money will continue indefinitely week by week and year by year. This is how the economy functions. It may, however, be pointed out that this flow of money income will not always remain the same in volume. In other words, the flow of money income will not always continue at a constant level. In year of depression, the circular flow of money income will contract, *i.e.*, will become lesser in volume, and in years of prosperity it will expand, *i.e.*, will become greater in volume. This is so because the flow of money is a measure of national income and will, therefore, change with changes in the national income. In year of depression, when national income is low, the volume of the flow of money will be small and in years of prosperity when the level of national income is quite high, the flow of money will be large.

In order to make our analysis simple and to explain the central issues involved, we take many assumptions. In the first place, we assume that neither the households save from their incomes, nor the firms save from their profits. We further assume that the government does not play any part in the national economy. In other words, the government does not receive any money from the people by way of taxes, nor does the government spend any money on the goods and services produced by the firms or on the resources and services supplied by the households. Thirdly, we assume that the economy neither imports goods and services, nor exports anything. In other words, in our above analysis we have not taken into account the role of foreign trade. In fact we have explained above the flow of money that occurs in the functioning of a closed economy with no savings and no role of government.

Circular Income Flow with Saving and Investment

In our above analysis of the circular flow of income we have assumed that all income which the households receive, they spend it on consumer goods and services. A result, circular flow of money speeding and income remains undiminished. We will now explain if households save a part of their income, how their savings will affect money flows in the economy. When households save, their expenditure on goods and services will decline to that extent and as a result money flow to the business firms will contract. With reduced money receipts, firms will hire fewer workers (or lay off some workers) or reduce the factor payments they make to the suppliers of factors such as workers. This will lead to the fall in total incomes of the households. Thus, savings reduce the flow of money expenditure to the business firms and will cause a fall in economy's total income. *Economists therefore call savings a leakage from the money expenditure flow.*

But savings by households need not lead to reduced aggregate spending and income if they find their way back into flow of expenditure. In free market economies there exists a set of institutions such as banks, insurance companies, financial houses, stock markets where households deposit their savings. All these institutions together are called financial institutions or financial market. We assume that all the savings of households come in the financial market. We further assume that there are no inter-households borrowings.

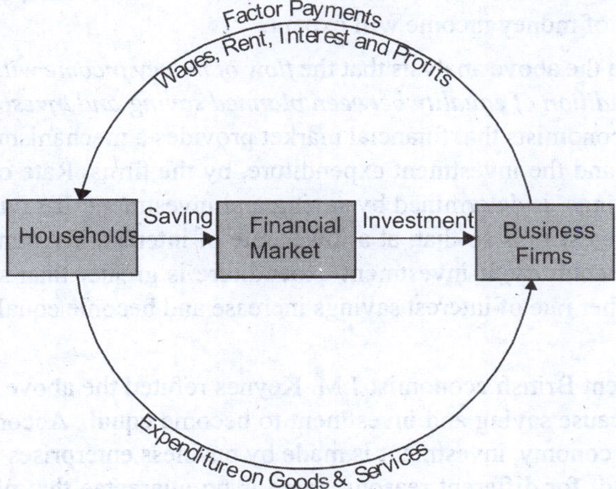

Fig. 6.2. *Circular Money Flow with Saving and Investment*

It is business firms who borrow from the financial market for investment in capital goods such as machines, factories, tools and instruments, trucks. Firms spend on investment in order to expand their productive capacity in future. Thus, through investment expenditure by borrowing the savings of the households deposited in financial market, are again brought into the expenditure stream and as a result total flow of spending does not decrease. Circular money flow with saving and investment is illustrated in Fig. 6.2 where in the middle part a box representing financial market is drawn. Money flow of savings is shown from the households towards the financial market. Then flow of investment expenditure is shown as borrowing by business firms from the financial market[1].

Condition for the Constancy of Circular Income Flow

Now the question arises what is the condition for the flow of money income to continue at a steady level so that it makes possible the production and subsequent flow of a given volume of goods and services at constant prices. To explain this we have to introduce saving and investment in the analysis of circular flow of income. As mentioned above, saving a part of income means it is not spent on consumer goods and services. In other words, saving *is withdrawal of some money from the income flow*. On the other hand, investment means some money is spent on buying new capital goods to expand production capacity. In other words, *investment is injection of some money in circular flow of income*. For the circular flow of income to continue unabated, the withdrawal of money from the income stream by way of saving must equal injection of money by way of investment expenditure. Therefore, planned savings must be equal to planned investment if the constant money income flow in an economy is to be obtained. Now, what will happen if planned investment expenditure falls short of the planned savings? As a result of fall in planned investment expenditure, income, output and employment will fall and therefore the flow of money will contract. If the equality between planned savings and planned investment is disturbed by increase in savings, then the immediate effect will be that the stocks of goods lying in the shelves of the shops will increase (as some of the goods will not be sold due to the fall in consumption *i.e.,* increase in savings). Owing to the deficiency of demand for goods and the accumulation of stocks, retailers will place small orders with the wholesalers. Consequently, smaller amount of goods will be produced and therefore fewer capital goods like machinery will be indeed with the result that fixed investment will tend to fall. Thus the ultimate effect of either the fall in planned investment or the increase in planned savings is the same, namely, the fall in income, output, employment and prices with the result that the flow of money will contract.

On the other hand, if the equality between planned savings and planned investment is disturbed by the increase in investment demand, the result will be increase in income, output and employment. Consequently, the flow of money income will expant.

It is thus clear from the above analysis that the *flow of money income will continue at a constant level only when the condition of equality between planned saving and investment is satisfied.* It was believed by classical economists that financial market provides a mechanism which coordinates the savings of households and the investment expenditure, by the firms. Rate of interest, which is the price for the use of savings, is determined by saving and investment. If savings exceed investment expenditure, rate of interest falls so that, at a lower rate of interest, investment increases and both become equal. On the contrary, if investment expenditure is greater than savings, rate of interest will rise so that at a higher rate of interest savings increase and become equal to planned investment expenditure.

However, an eminent British economist J.M. Keynes refuted the above argument that changes in rate of interest will cause saving and investment to become equal. According to him, since in a free market capitalist economy, investment is made by business enterprises and savings are mostly done by households and for different reasons, there is no guarantee that planned investment will be equal to planned savings and thus fluctuations in income, output and employment are inevitable. As a result, circular flow of income does not continue at a steady level in a free-enterprise capital-

1. It may be noted that business firms also save when they do not distribute among shareholders all the profits made by them and keep the undistributed profits as reserves. We are ignoring them in our money flow analysis as firms themselves use their savings for buying machinery and making other investment expenditure.

ist economy unless certain corrective and preventive steps are taken by the government to maintain stability in the economy.

Saving-Investment Identity in National Income Accounts in a Two Sector Economy

Despite the fact that people who save are different from the business firms which primarily invest, in national income accounts savings are identical or always equal to investment in a simple two sector economy having no roles of Government and foreign trade. This is a basic identity in national income accounts which needs to be carefully understood. Of course, in our above analysis of circular flow of income, we explained that planned investment by business firms can differ from savings by household. But in that analysis we referred to *planned or intended* investment and savings which often differ and affect the flow of national income. However, in national income accounts we are concerned with *actual saving* and *actual investment*. It is these actual or realised saving and investment that are identical in national income accounts. We can prove their identity in the following way.

In a simple economy which has neither government, nor foreign trade, the value of *output produced* which we denote by Y is equal to the value of *output sold*. Since the value of output sold in a simple two sector economy is equal to the sum of consumption expenditure and investment expenditure we have

$$Y \equiv C + I \quad \ldots (i)$$

where Y = Value of aggregate output, C = Consumption expenditure and I = Investment expenditure.

A pertinent question which arises here is what happens to the unsold output. The unsold output leads to the *increase in the inventories of goods* and in national income accounting increase in inventories of goods is treated as a part of actual investment. This may be considered as the firms selling the goods to themselves to add to their inventories. Thus, gross national product (GNP) produced is used either for consumption or for investment.

Now, look at the gross national product or income in the simple economy from the viewpoint of its allocation between consumption and saving. Since national income (which is equal to GNP) can be either consumed or saved,[2]. We have

$$Y \equiv C + S \quad \ldots (ii)$$

From the identities (*i*) and (*ii*) we get

$$C + I \equiv Y \equiv C + S \quad \ldots (iii)$$

The left hand side of the identity (*iii*), namely $C + I = Y$ shows the components of aggregate demand (that is, aggregate expenditure on goods and services produced) and the right-hand side of the identitiy (*iii*) namely $Y = C + S$ shows the allocation of national income to either consumption or saving. Thus, the identity (*iii*) shows that the value of output produced or sold is equal to the total income received. It is income received that is spent on goods and services produced.

Now subtracting the consumption (C) from both sides of the identity (*iii*) we have

$$I \equiv Y \equiv S$$

or

$$I = S$$

Thus, in ***our two sector simple economy with neither government, nor foreign trade, investment is identically equal to saving.***

---

2. Note that decisions about saving are made both by households and business firms. In national income accounts they are generally put together and referred to as private sector savings.

Circulr Income Flow in a Three Sector Economy with Government

In our above analysis of money flow, we have ignored the existence of government for the sake of making our circular flow model simple. This is quite unrealistic because government absorbs a good part of the incomes earned by households. Government affects the economy in a number of ways. Here we will concentrate on its taxing, spending and borrowing roles. Government purchases goods and services just as households and firms do. Government expenditure takes many forms including spending on capital goods and infrastructure (highways, power, communication), on defence goods, and on education and public health and so on. These add to the money flows which are shown in Fig. 6.3 where a box representing Government has been drawn. It will be seen that government purchases of goods and services from firms and households are shown as flow of money spending on goods and services.

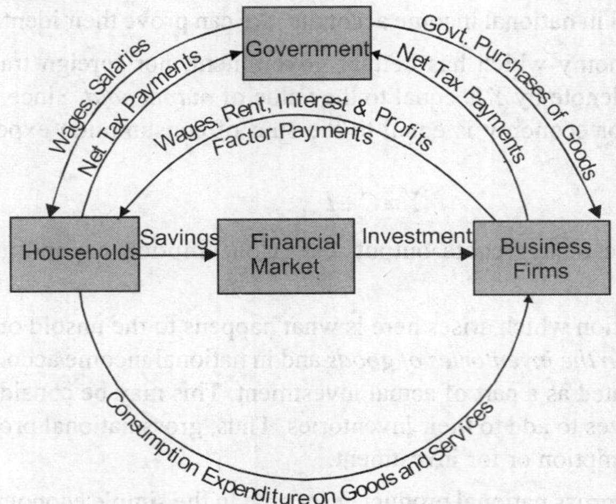

Fig. 6.3. *Circular Income Flow Model with Government*

Government expenditure may be financed through taxes, out of assets or by borrowing. The money flow from households and business firms to the government is labelled as tax payments in Fig. 6.3 This money flow includes all the tax payments made by households less transfer payments received from the Government. Transfer payments are treated as negative tax payments.

Another method of financing Government expenditure is borrowing from the financial market. This can be represented by the money flow from the financial market to the Government and is labelled as Government borrowing (To avoid confusion we have not drawn this money flow from financial market to the Government). Government borrowing increases the demand for credit which causes rate of interest to rise. The government borrowing through its effect on the rate of interest affects the behaviour of firms and households. Business firms consider the interest rate as cost of borrowing and the rise in the interest rate as a result of borrowing by the Government lowers private investment. However, households who view the rate of interest as return on savings feel encouraged to save more.

It follows from above that the inclusion of the Government sector significantly affects the overall economic situation. Total expenditure flow in the economy is now the sum of consumption expenditure (denoted by C), investment expenditure (I) and Government expenditure (denoted by G). Thus

$$\text{Total expenditure } (E) = C + I + G \qquad \ldots (i)$$

Total income (Y) received is allocated to consumption (C), savings (S) and taxes (T). Thus

$$Y = C + S + T \qquad \ldots (ii)$$

Since expenditure(E) made must be equal to the income received (Y), from equations (i) and (ii) above we have

$$C + I + G = C + S + T \quad \text{.. (iii)}$$

Since C occurs on both sides of the equation (*iii*) and will therefore be cancelled out, we have

$$I + G = S + T \quad \text{.. (iv)}$$

By rearranging we obtain

$$G - T = S - I \quad \text{.. (v)}$$

Equation (*v*) is very significant as it depicts what would be the consequences if government budget is not balanced, that is, if Government expenditure (G) is greater than the tax revenue (T), that is, $G > T$, the government will have a deficit budget. To finance the deficit budget, the Government will borrow from the financial market. For this purpose, then private investment by business firms must be less than the savings of the households. Thus ***Government borrowing reduces private investment in the economy. In other words, Government borrowing crowds out private investment.***

Money Income Flows in the Four Sector Open Economy : Adding Foreign Sector

We now turn to explain the money flows that are generated in an open economy, that is, economy which have trade relations with foreign countries. Thus, the inclusion of the foreign sector will reveal to us the interaction of the domestic economy with foreign countries. Foreigners interact with the domestic firms and households through exports and imports of goods and services as well as through borrowing and lending operations through financial market. Goods and services produced within the domestic territory which are sold to the foreigners are called exports.

On the other hand, purchases of foreign-made goods and services by domestic households are called imports. Figure 6.4 illustrates additional money flows that occur in the open economy when exports and imports also exist in the economy. In our analysis, we assume it is only the business firms of the domestic economy that interact with foreign countries and therefore export and import goods and services. A flow of money spending on imports have been shown to be occurring from the domestic business firms to the foreign countries (*i.e.*, rest of the world) . On the contrary, flow of money expenditure on exports of a domestic economy has been shown to be taking place from foreign countries to the business firms of the domestic economy. If exports are equal to the imports, then there exists a balance of trade. Generally, exports and imports are not equal to each other. If value of exports exceeds the value of imports, *trade surplus* occurs. On the other hand if value of imports exceeds value of exports of a country, *trade deficit* occurs.

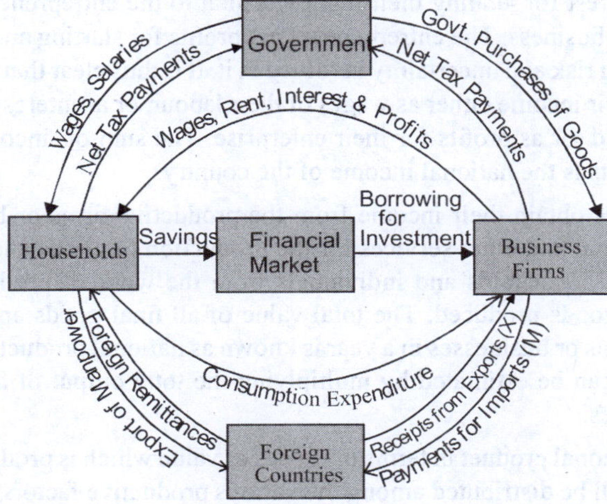

Fig. 6.4. *Circular Flow of Income in an Open Economy with Government and Foreign Sector*

In the open economy there is interaction between countries not only through exports and imports of goods and services but also through borrowing and lending funds or what is also called financial market. These days financial markets around the world have become well integrated. When there is a trade surplus in the economy, that is, when exports (X) exceed imports (M), *net capital inflow* will take place. By net capital inflow we mean foreigners will borrow from domestic savers to finance their purchases of domestic exports. In this way as a result of net capital inflow domestic savers will lend to foreigners, that is, acquire foreign financial assets.

On the contrary, in case of import surplus, that is, when imports are greater than exports, trade deficit will occur. Therefore, in case of trade deficit, domestic consumer households and business firms will borrow from abroad to finance their excess of imports over exports. As a result, foreigners will acquire domestic financial assets.

From the circular flows that occur in the open economy the national income must be measured by aggregate expenditure that includes net exports, that is, $X–M$ where X represents exports and M represents imports. Imports must be subtracted from the total expenditure on foreign produced goods and services to get the value of net exports. Thus, in the open economy

$$\text{National Income} = C + I + G + NX$$

where NX represents net exports, $X–M$.

Since national income can be either consumed, saved or paid as taxes to the Government we have

$$C + I + G + NX = C + S + T$$

NATIONAL INCOME AND NATIONAL PRODUCT

The sum of all incomes of the people of a country is called national income. This national income is greatly related to the national product. In fact in a two sector economy without the Government and its imposition of indirect taxes and grant of subsidies and also assuming no depreciation national income and national product are one and the same thing. The incomes which different people of the society get are obtained by them for their contribution of labour, land, capital and entrepreneurial services to the national production. Hence the income which the labourers get are wages for the productive services which labourers lend to the various firms which undertake the work of production. Similarly, the owners of land get income as rent because of their contribution of land to the productive firms; the capitalists get interest for lending their money capital to the entrepreneurs for undertaking any work of production or business. The entrepreneurs get profits for starting and organising the work of production and bearing risk and uncertainty involved in it. It is thus clear that the different individuals of a country obtain their income either as wages of their labour, or as interest on their money capital, or as rent for their land, or as profits for their enterprise. The sum of incomes obtained as wages, rent, interest and profits is the national income of the country.

Various households obtain their income from the productive firms or businesses which utilise their labour, land, capital and other services for the production of goods and services. The incomes earned by the various households and individuals from the work of production are in fact costs of production of the goods produced. The total value of all final goods and services produced by various productive firms or businesses in a year is known as national product. Therefore, the national product of a country can be estimated by multiplying the total output of final goods and services with their market prices.

Hence the total national product in terms of rupees or value which is produced by various productive firms in a year, will be distributed among the various productive factors which have contributed to its production. Therefore, out of this national production (in value terms) wages will be paid to those households which have sold their labour to the productive firms. Out of this total value of the national product, land owners would get rent for the contribution of the services of land and capitalists would get interest for lending money capital to the productive firms. After the payment of wages, rent, interest, what is left is the profits of the entrepreneurs who set up productive firms, organise their work and bear risk and uncertainty and because of these services they get profits. It is thus clear the national product (value of total output of final goods and services in a year of a country) is distributed among wages, rents, interests and profits. As we have stated above, the sum of total wages, total interest, total rents and total profits is national income. Hence national product will be equal to he national income. The above conclusion that in a two-sector economy national inocme equals national product can be expressed in the form of the following equation.

$$\pi = \frac{275}{250} \times 100 = \frac{25}{250} \times 100 = 10\%$$

From the above analysis it is evident that national income and national product are one and the same thing. Professor J.R. Hicks rightly writes, "*The value of the net social product of the community and the sum of the incomes of its members are exactly equal. The net social product and the social income are one and the same thing.*"[3]

It needs to be emphasised that *the above conclusion regarding equality of national product and national income is valid only in our simple two sector eocnomy where we have assumed no depreciation funds are kept and also no role of Government (and therefore no indirect taxes collected by it and no subsidies granted by it)*. In case of a real economy, firms keep a part of some value created as depreciation allowance which therefore do not become a part of the income of the factors. When role of Government is brought into our analysis, a part of the value of output is taken away by the Government as indirect taxes and therefore the incomes of factor owners are reduced to that extent. Thus, only in the absence of depreciation funds and net indirect taxes, national product will be equal to national income. In our simple economy we assume away these depreciation funds and net indiret taxes levied by the Government on business firms to emphasise the point that national income does not come out of thin air, it is in fact generated by the production of goods and services. Therefore, growth in national income can be achieved by the increase in production of goods and services.

CONCEPTS OF NATIONAL INCOME

There are various concepts of national income which we study below one by one.

Gross National Product (GNP)

This is the basic national accounting measure of the total output or aggregate supply of goods and services. *Gross National Product is defined as the total market value of all final goods and services produced in a year in a country*. Two things must be noted in regard to gross national product. First, it measures the market value of annual output. In other words, GNP is a *monetary meacure*. There is no other way of adding up the different sorts of goods and services produced in a year except in terms of their money prices. But in order to know accurately the changes in physical output, the figure for gross national product is adjusted for price changes.

Secondly, for calculating gross national product accurately, all goods and services produced in any given year must be counted once, and not more than once. Most of the goods go through a series of production stages before reaching a market. As a result, parts or components of many goods are bought and sold many times. Hence to avoid counting several times the parts of goods that are sold

3. J.R. Hicks, *The Social Framework*.

and resold, gross national product includes the market value of only final goods and ignores transactions involving intermediate goods.

Final Goods and Intermediate Goods. What do we mean by *final goods*? Final goods are those goods which are purchased for final use and not for resale or further processing. Intermediate goods, on the other hand, are those goods which are purchased for further processing or for resale. The sale of intermediate goods is excluded from gross national product. Why? Because the value of final goods includes the value of all intermediate goods used in their production. The inclusion of intermediate goods would involve double counting and will therefore give an exaggerated estimate of gross national product. An example will clarify this point. Suppose in our economy only two things are being produced, raw cotton worth ₹ 1000 and cotton cloth worth ₹ 2000. Now what will be the measure of gross national product? For finding it, if we add up the sales value of cloth and cotton, there is clearly an element of *double counting* in the sense that we have added the value of cotton *twice*—one as the sales value of cotton and secondly when we added to it the value of cloth. Actually, the value of cloth includes also the value of cotton which having been accounted for already should not be added second time.

Further, it is worth noting that Gross National Product (GNP) includes only *currently produced* goods and services in a year. It is a *flow measure* of output of goods and services per time period, say in a year. In it are only goods and services produced in a particular year are included. Market transactions involving goods produced in previous periods such as old houses, cars, factories built earlier are not included in GNP of the current year. Similarly, purchase and sale of assets such as stock and bonds do not involve current production of goods and are therefore excluded from GNP of the year.

Lastly, Gross National Product (GNP) refers to the value of goods and services currently produced by *normal residents of a country*. These residents may be national or non-national companies. Thus, many foreign companies have set up plants in India. They are owned by non-nationals but work to produce goods and services within the domestic territory of India and generate incomes for the Indian people employed in them. These foreign companies can only send back to their own countries profits earned by them.

Gross national product has the following components :

1. Value of *final consumer goods and services* produced in a year and consumed by two households which is denoted by to *consumption* (*C*) by households.
2. Value of *new capital goods produced and addition to the inventories of goods* such as raw materials, unfinished goods and consumer goods produced but not sold during a year. This is called *Gross Private Investment* (*I*).
3. Value of output of General Government which is taken to be equal to the value of *purchases of goods and services by the Government* which we denote by *G*.
4. Net Exports (X_n) which is equal to value of goods *exported* minus the value of goods *imported* (*M*).
5. Net Factor Income from Abroad which we will explain below

Net Factor Income From Absoad. Now, what does net factor income from abroad stand for? The sum of factor incomes such as wages and salaries (*i.e.*, compensation of employees), rent, interest and profits generated within the domestic territory of a country in a year is called domestic factor income. It includes factor incomes generated both by residents and non-residents working in the domestic territory of a country. For example, non-residents (*i.e.*, foreigners) work in the domestic territory of India and earn wages and salary. Thus, foreign individuals and companies from the USA, Great Britain and other countries have acquired property such as factories, offices, buildings, places and have also acquired financial assets such as bonds and shares of Indian companies. This generates incomes in the form of rent and interest to them. In addition to this, foreign residents—individuals and companies—have set up industrial plants and factories producing goods and services from which they earn profits.

On the other hand, Indians go abroad and work in the territories of other countries and earn wages and salaries. Likewise, some Indian individuals and corporate companies have acquired assets such as buildings, factories, commercial space, and have also invested in bonds, bank deposits of foreign countries and thus receive rent and interest. Some Indian companies have set up factories abroad and earn profits.

Now, the *net factor income from abroad is the difference between factor income received from abroad by normal residents of India for rendering factor services in other countries on the one hand and the factor incomes paid to the foreign residents for factor services rendered by them in the domestic territory of India on the other.*

Net factor income earned from abroad have therofore the following three components:

1. *Net* compensation of employees.
2. *Net* income from property *i.e.*, rent, interest and income from entrepreneurship (that is, profits and dividends).
3. *Net* retained earnings of the resident companies working in foreign countries.

(Note that '*Net*' in the above means the difference between the relevant income of normal residents earned from abroad and the same type of incomes paid to non-residents working in the domestic territory of a country)

Gross Domestic Product (GDP)

Another important concept of national income is gross domestic product (GDP). *Gross domestic product is the money value of all final goods and services produced by normal residents as well as non-residents working in the domestic territory of a country but does not include net factor income earned from abroad.* Thus difference between gross domestic product (GDP) and gross national product (GNP) at market prices arises due to the existence of '*net factor income from abroad*'. Gross domestic product does not include net factor income from abroad, whereas gross national product

GNP_{MP}	GDP_{MP}	NDP_{MP}	NDP_{FC}
Net factor income from abroad			
Gross Private Investment (I)	Gross Private Investment	Less Depreciation Net Private Investment	Less Net Indirect Taxes
Net Exports (Xn)	Net Exports	Net Exports	Wages + Profits + Interest + Rent
Government Purchases (G)	Government Purchases	Government Purchases	
Consumption Expenditure (C)	Consumption Expenditure	Consumption Expenditure	

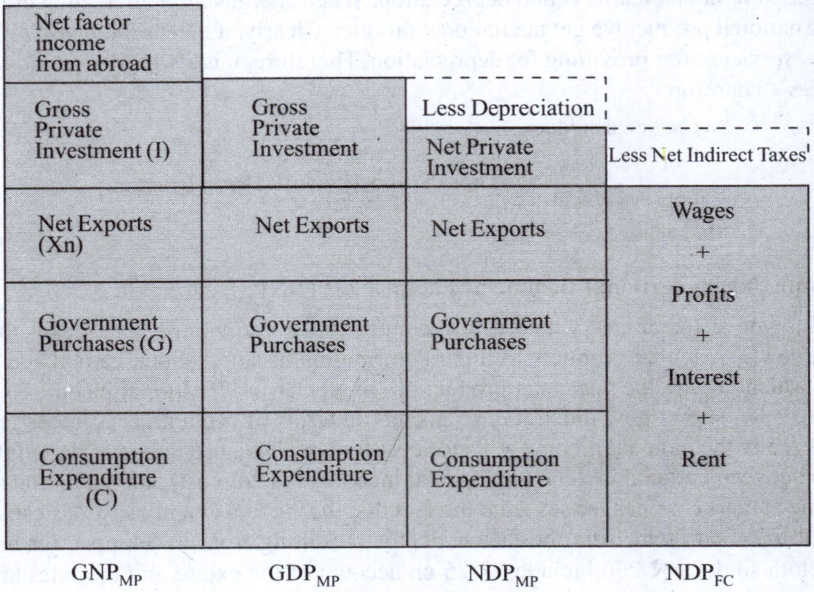

Fig. 6.5. *Various Concepts of National Product*

includes it. Therefore,

Gross Domestic Product (at market prices) or

$GDP_{MP} = GNP_{MP}$ -- net factor income from abroad

or $GNP_{MP} = GDP_{MP}$ + net factor income from abroad

It should however be noted that net factor income from abroad should not be confused with income from *net exports* which are a part of both gross national product (GNP) and gross domestic product (GDP). Net exports equal total exports minus imports. Gross exports are the total value of domestically produced goods and services sold to foriegn buyers in a year and are therefore a part of Gross Domestic Product (GDP) and not a factor income from abroad. On the other hand, imports are the value of imported goods and services pruchased by the domestic buyers. Therefore, imports do not form a part of GDP or GNP. In national income accounting, we subtract the value of imports from the value of exports to arrive at net exports which are a part of GDP and therefore also of GNP. Thus, earnings from net exports are quite distinct from net factor income from abroad.

Thus, we can obtain Gross Domestic Product (GDP) by adding up the first four items of Gross National Product listed above. Thus

$$GDP = C + I + G + X_n$$

$$\text{where } X_n = (X - M)$$

We have graphically depicted GDP by second bar in Figure 2.

GNP GDP NDP_{MP} NDP_{FC}

(Note: *By adding Net Factor Income from Abroad to* NDP_{MP} and NDP_{FC} *we get* NNP_{MP} *and* NNP_{FC} respectively).

Net National Product (NNP) or National Income at Market Prices

The second important concept of national income is that of net national product (NNP). In the production of gross national product of a year, we consume or use up some fixed capital *i.e.*, equipment, machinery, etc. The capital goods, like machinery, wear out or fall in value as a result of its consumption or use in the production process. This consumption of fixed capital or fall in the value of fixed capital due to wear and tear is called depreciation. When charges for depreciation are deducted from the gross national product we get net national product. Clearly, it means the *market value of all final goods and services* after providing for depreciation. Therefore, it is also called '*national income at market prices*'. Therefore,

Net National Product or National Income at Market Prices } = Gross National Product - Depreciation

National Income (NI) or National Income at Factor Cost (NNP_{FC})

National Income at factor cost which is also simply called *national income* means the sum of all incomes earned by resource suppliers for their contribution of land, labour, capital and entrepreneurial ability which go into the year's net production. In other words, national income (or national income at factor cost) shows how much it costs society in terms of economic resources to produce net output. It is really the national income at factor cost for which we use the term National Income. The difference between national income (or national income at factor cost) and net national product (national income at market prices) arises from the fact that *indirect taxes* and *subsidies* cause market prices of output to be different from the factor incomes resulting from it. Suppose for instance, a metre of mill cloth sold for ₹ 200 includes ₹ 25 on account of the excise and the sales tax. In this case while the market price of the cloth is ₹ 200 a metre, the factors engaged in its production and distribution would receive ₹ 175 a metre. The value of cloth at factor cost would thus be equal to its value at market price less the indirect taxes on it. On the other hand, a subsidy causes the market price to be less than the factor cost. Suppose handloom cloth is subsidised at the rate of ₹ 10 per metre and it sells at ₹ 90 per metre. Then while the consumer pays ₹ 90 per metre, the factors engaged in the production and distribution of such cloth will receive ₹ 100 per metre (₹ 90 + 10 = ₹ 100). The value of handloom cloth at factor cost would thus be equal to its market price plus the subsidies paid on it. It follows, therefore, that the national income (or national income at factor cost) is equal to net national product minus indirect taxes plus subsidies.

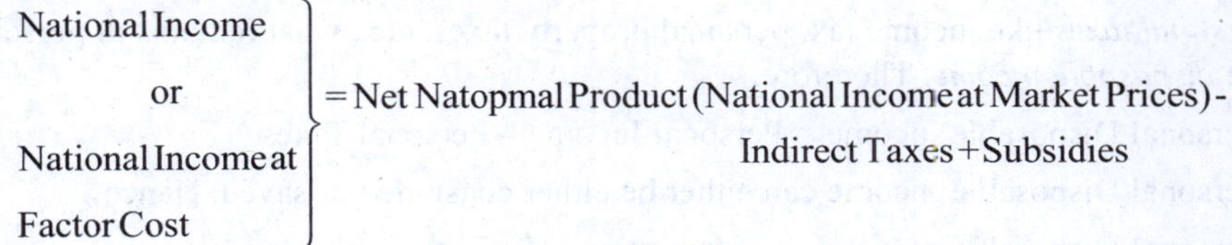

Net of indirect taxes and subsidies is called Net Indirect Taxes. Therefore,

National Income = Net National Product – Net Indirect Taxes

Personal Income (PI)

Personal Income is the sum of all incomes actually received by all individuals or households during a given year. National income, that is, total incomes earned and personal income, that is, total incomes received must be different because some incomes which are earned such as social security contributions, corporate income taxes and undistributed corporate profits are not actually received by households, and conversely, some incomes which are received like transfer payments are not currently earned (examples of transfer payments are old-age pensions, unemployment compensation, relief payments, interest payments on the public debt, etc.). Obviously, in moving from national income as an indicator of income earned to personal income as an indicator of income actually received, we must subtract from national income those three types of income which are earned but not received and add those incomes which are received but currently not earned. Therefore,

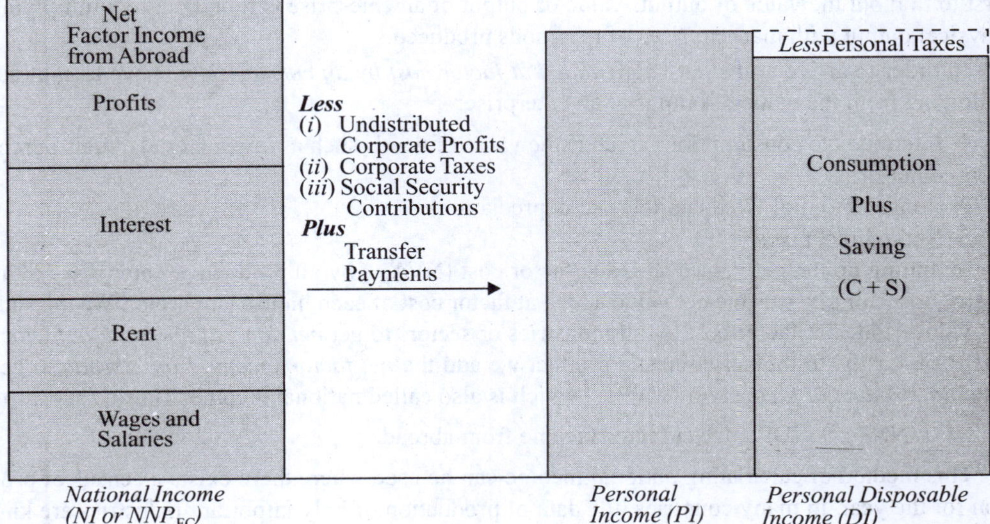

Fig. 6.6. *From National Income to Disposable Income*

Personal Income = National Income — Social Security Contributions — Corporate Income Taxes —Undistributed Corporate Profits + Transfer Payments.

Personal Disposable Income (PDI)

Even whole of the incomes which are actually received by the people are not available to them for consumption. This is because governments levy some personal taxes such as income tax, personal property taxes. Therefore, after a part of personal income is paid to government in the form of *personal taxes* like income tax, personal property taxes, etc., what remains of personal income is called *disposable income*. Therefore,

Personal Disposable Income = Personal Income – Personal Taxes.

Personal Disposable Income can either be either consumed or saved. Hence,

Personal Disposable Income = Consumption + Saving.

How do we get personal income and disposable income from national income is illustrated in Figure 6.6.

MEASUREMENT OF NATIONAL INCOME

Since factor *incomes* arise from the production of goods and services, and since incomes are spent on goods and services produced, three alternative methods of measuring national income are possible.

1. Value Added Method.

This is also called *output method or production method*. In this method the contribution of each enterprise to the generation of flow of goods and services is measured. Under this method, the economy is divided into different industrial sectors such as agriculture, fishing, mining, construction, manufacturing, trade and commerce, transport, communication and other services. Then, the net value added at factor cost (NVA_{FC}) by each productive enterprise as well as by each industry or sector is estimated. Measuring net value added at factor cost (NVA_{FC}) by each industry requires first to find out the value of output. Value of output of an enterprise is found out by multiplying the physical output with market prices of the goods produced.

In order to arrive at the *net value added at factor cost by an enterprise* we have to subtract the following from the value of output of an enterprise:

1. Intermediate consumption which is the value of goods such as raw materials, fuels purchased from other firms
2. Consumption of fixed capital (*i.e.*, depreciation)
3. Net indirect taxes.

Summing up the net values added at factor cost (NVA_{FC}) by all productive enterprises of an industry or sector gives us the net value added at factor cost of each industry or sector. We then add up net values added at factor cost by all industries or sectors to get *net domestic product at factor cost* (*NDP_{FC}*). Lastly, to the net domestic product we add the *net factor income from abroad* to get *net national product at factor cost* (*NNP_{FC}*) which is also called national income. Thus,

NI or $NNP_{FC} = NDP_{FC}$ + Net factor income from abroad

This method of calculating national income can be used where there exists a census of production for the year. In many countries, the data of production of only important industries are known. Hence this method is employed along with other methods to arrive at the national income. The one great advantage of this method is that it reveals the relative importance of the different sectors of the economy by showing their respective contributions to the national income.

Precautions. The following precautions should be taken while measuring national income of a country through value added method:

1. *Imputed rent values* of self-occupied houses should be included in the value of output. Though these payments are not made to others, their values can be easily estimated from prevailing values in the market.
2. Sale and purchase of *second-hand goods* should not be included in measuring value of output of a year because their values were counted in the year of output of the year of their production. Of course, commission or brokerage earned in their sale and purchase has to be included because this is a new service rendered in the current year.
3. *Value of production for self-consumption* are be counted while measuring national income. In this method, the production for self-consumption should be valued at the prevailing market prices.
4. *Value of services of housewives* are not included because it is not easy to find out correctly the value of their services.
5. Value of intermediate goods *must not* be counted while measuring value added because this will amount to double counting.

2. Income Method

This method approaches national income from distribution side. In other words, this method measures national income at the phase of distribution and appears as income paid and or received by individuals of the country. Thus, under this method, *national income is obtained by summing up of the incomes of all individuals of a country*. Individuals earn incomes by contributing their own services and the services of their property such as land and capital to the national production. Therefore, national income is calculated by adding up the rent of land, wages and salaries of employees, interest on capital, profits of entrepreneurs (including undistributed corporate profits) and incomes of self-employed people. This method of estimating national income has the great advantage of indicating the distribution of national income among different income groups such as landlords, owners of capital, workers, entrepreneurs. Measurement of national income through income method involves the following main steps:

1. Like the value added method, the first step in income method is also to *identify* the productive enterprises and then *classify* them into various industrial sectors such as agriculture, fishing, forestry, manufacturing, transport, trade and commerce, banking, etc.

2. The second step is to classify *the factor payments*. The factor payments are classified into the following groups:

1. *Compensation of employees* which includes wages and salaries, employers' contribution to social security schemes.
2. *Rent and also royalty*, if any.
3. *Interest.*
4. *Profits*: Profits are divided into three sub-groups:
   (*i*) Dividends
   (*ii*) Undistributed profits
   (*iii*) Corporate income tax

5. *Mixed income of the self-employed*: In India as in other developing countries there is fifth category of factor income which is termed as *mixed income of self-employed.* In India a good number of people are engaged in household industries, in family farms and other unorganised enterprises. Because of self-employment nature of the business it is difficult to separate wages for the work done by the self-employed from the surplus or profits made by them. Therefore, the incomes earned by them are mix of wages, rent, interest and profit and are, therefore, called *mixed income of the self-employed.*

3. The third step is to *measure factor payments*. Income paid out by each enterprise can be

estimated by gathering information about the number of units of each factor employed and the income paid out to each unit of every factor. Price paid out to each factor multiplied by the number of units of each factor employed would give us the factor's income.

4. The *adding up of factor payments* by all enterprises belonging to an industrial sector would give us the incomes paid out to various factors by a *particular* industrial sector.

5. By summing up the incomes paid out by *all industrial sectors* we will obtain domestic factor income which is also called net domestic product at factor cost (NDP_{FC}).

6. Finally, by adding net factor income earned from abroad to domestic factor income or NDP_{FC} we get net national product at factor cost (NNP_{FC}) which is also called *national income*.

Income approach to measurement of national income is shown through bar diagrams in Figure 6.7

			Net Indirect Taxes
	Net Factor Income from abroad	Consumption of Fixed Capital	Consumption of Fixed Capital
Dividends		Dividends	
Undistributed Profits	Profits	Undistributed Profits	
Corporate Income Tax		Corporate Income Tax	
Interest	Interest	Interest	Interest
Rent	Rent	Rent	Rent
Mixed Income of Self-employed	Mixed Income of Self-employed	Mixed income of Self-employed	Mixed Income of Self-employed
Compensation of Employees	Compensation of Employees	Compensation of Employees	Compensation of Employees
NDP_{FC}	**NNP_{FC}**	**GDP_{FC}**	**GDP_{MP}**

Figure 6.7. *Income Approach to National Income*

Precautions. While estimating national income through income method the following precautions should be taken:

1. *Transfer payments* are not included in estimating national income through this method.

2. *Imputed rent* of self-occupied houses are included in national income as these houses provide services to those who occupy them and its value can be easily estimated from the market value data.

3. *Illegal money* such as *hawala money, money earned through smuggling* etc. are not included as they cannot be easily estimated.

4. *Windfall gains* such as prizes won, lotteries are also not included.

5. Corporate profit tax (that is, tax on income of the companies) should not be separately included as it has already been included as a part of profits.

6. *Death duties, gift tax, wealth tax, tax on lotteries*, etc., are paid from past savings or wealth and not from current income. Therefore, they should not be treated as a part of national income of a year.

7. The receipts from the *sale of second-hand goods* should not be treated as a part of national income. This is because the sale of second-hand goods does not create new flows goods and services in the current year.

8. Income equal to the *value of production used for self-consumption* should be estimated and included in the measure of national income.

Expenditure Method

Expenditure method arrives at national income by adding up all expenditures made on goods and services during a year. Income can be spent either on consumer goods or capital goods. Again, expenditure can be made by private individuals and households or by government and business enterprises. Further, people of foreign countries spend on the goods and services which a country exports to them. Similarly, people of a country spend on imports of goods and services from other countries. We add up the following types of expenditure by households, government and by productive enterprises to obtain national income.

1. Expenditure on consumer goods and services by individuals and households. This is called *final private consumption expenditure*, and is denoted by C.
2. Government's expenditure on goods and services to satisfy collective wants. This is called *government's final consumption expenditure*, and is denoted by G.
3. The expenditure by productive enterprises on capital goods and inventories or stocks. This is called *gross domestic capital formation*, or gross domestic investment and is denoted by I or GDCF. Gross domestic capital formation is divided into two parts:
   (*i*) Gross fixed capital formation
   (*ii*) Addition to the stocks or inventories of goods
4. The expenditure made by foreigners on goods and services of a country exported to other countries which are called exports and are denoted by *X*. We deduct from exports (*X*) the expenditure by people, enterprises and government of a country on imports (*M*) of goods and services from other countries. That is, we have to estimate net exports (that is, exports –imports) or (*X*—*M*).

Thus, we add up the above four types of expenditure to get final expenditure on gross domestic product at market prices (GDP_{MP}). Thus,

GDP_{MP} = Private final consumption expenditure + Government's final consumption expenditure + Gross domestic capital formation + Exports — Imports or

$$GDP_{MP} = C + G + I + (X - M)$$
$$= C + G + I + Xn$$

On deducting consumption of fixed capital (*i.e.*, depreciation) from gross domestic product at market prices (GDP_{MP}) we get net domestic product at market prices (NDP_{MP}).

In this method, we then subtract net indirect taxes (that is, indirect taxes – subsidies) to arrive at net domestic product at factor cost (NDP_{FC}),

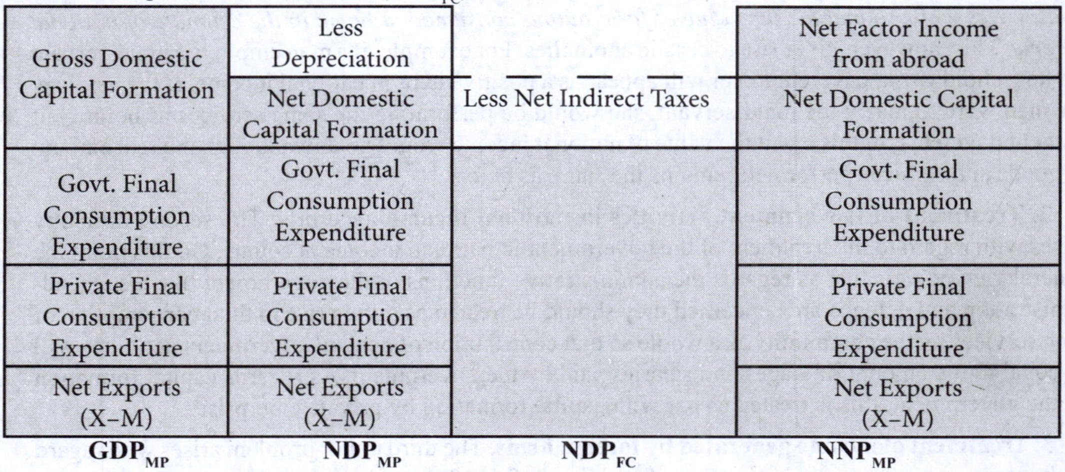

Gross Domestic Capital Formation	Less Depreciation		Net Factor Income from abroad
	Net Domestic Capital Formation	Less Net Indirect Taxes	Net Domestic Capital Formation
Govt. Final Consumption Expenditure	Govt. Final Consumption Expenditure		Govt. Final Consumption Expenditure
Private Final Consumption Expenditure	Private Final Consumption Expenditure		Private Final Consumption Expenditure
Net Exports (X–M)	Net Exports (X–M)		Net Exports (X–M)
GDP_{MP}	NDP_{MP}	NDP_{FC}	NNP_{MP}

Fig. 6.8. *Expenditure Approach to National Income Concepts*

Lastly, we add 'net factor income from abroad' to obtain net national product at factor cost (NNP_{FC}), which is called national income. Thus,

$NNP_{FC} = GDP_{MP}$ – Consumption of Fixed capital - Net Indirect taxes + Net Factor Income from Abroad.

Expenditure approach to national income is shown through bar diagram in Figure 6.8.

(**Note:** To any concept of the domestic product, if we add '*Net Income from Abroad*' we will get corresponding National Product)

Precautions. While estimating Gross Domestic Product through expenditure method or measuring final expenditure on Gross National Product, the following precautions should be taken:

1. *Second-hand goods*: The expenditure made on second-hand goods should not be included because this does not contribute to the current year production of goods and services.

2. *Purchase of shares and bonds*. Expenditure on purchase of old shares and bonds from other people and from business enterprises should not be included while estimating Gross Domestic Product through expenditure method. This is because bonds and shares are mere financial claims and do not represent expenditure on currently produced goods and services.

3. *Expenditure on transfer payments* by government such as unemployment benefits, old-age pension should also not be included because no goods or productive services are produced in exchange by the recipients of these payments.

4. *Expenditure on intermediate goods* such as fertilisers and seeds by the farmers and wool, cotton and yarn by manufacturers of garments should also be excluded. This is because we have to avoid double counting. Therefore, for estimating Gross Domestic Product we have to include only *expenditure on final goods* and services.

Difficulties in the Measurement of National Income

There are many difficulties in measuring national income of a country accurately. The difficulties involved are both conceptual and statistical in nature. Some of these difficulties or problems involved in the measurement of national income are enumerated below.

1. **Treatment of non-monetary transactions.** The first problem relates to the *treatment of non-monetary transactions* such as the services of housewives to the members of their families and farm output consumed at home. On this point, the general agreement is *to exclude the services of housewives while to include the value of farm output consumed at home in the estimate of national income*. This, however, gives rise to certain anomalies. For example, if a man employs a maid-servant for household work, payment to her will appear as a positive item in national income. If the next day the man were to marry the maid-servant, she would be performing the same services as before but without payments. In this event the value of national income would go down though the real amount of goods and services performed remains the same as before.

2. **Treatment of Government activities in national income accounts.** The second difficulty arises with regard to the treatment of the government in national income accounts. On this point the general viewpoint is that as regards the administrative functions of the government like justice, administration and defence are concerned they should be treated as giving rise to final consumption of such services by the community as a whole so that contribution of general government activities will be equal to the amount of wages and salaries paid by the government. As regards capital formation by the government, this is treated as par with capital formation by private enterprises.

3. **Treatment of income generated by foreign firms.** The third major problem arises with regard to the treatment of income arising out of activities of the foreign firms in a country. Should their

income form a part of the national income of the country in which they are located or should it belong to the national income of the country owning the firms? On this point, the IMF viewpoint which is generally accepted is that production and income arising from a foreign enterprise should be ascribed to the country in which production takes place. However, profits earned by foreign companies are credited to the parent country.

Difficulties of Measuring National Income in India

In developing countries like India, we face some special difficulties in estimating national income. Some of these difficulties are given below:

1. A great difficulty in estimating national income in the developing countries like India arises because of the *prevalence of non-monetised transactions in such countries* so that a considerable part of the output does not come into the market at all. Agriculture still being largely in the nature of subsistence farming in these countries, a major part of output is consumed at the farm itself. The national statistician, therefore, has to face the problem of finding a suitable measure of value for this part of national output.

2. Because of illiteracy in India most producers have no idea of the quantity and value of their output and do not follow the practice of keeping regular accounts. This makes the task of getting reliable information from a large number of petty producers all the more difficult.

3. Because of underdevelopment, *occupational specialisation is still incomplete*, so that there is a lack of differentiation in economic functioning. An individual may receive income partly from farm ownership, partly from manual work in industry in the slack season, etc. This makes the task of estimating national income very difficult.

4. Another difficulty in measuring national income in India as in other developing countries arises because *production, both agricultural and industrial, is unorganised* and scattered in these countries. This does not admit of easy calculation. In India, agriculture, cottage industries and indigenous banking are some of the production sectors which are unorganised and scattered. An assessment of output produced by self-employed agriculturists, small producers and owners of household enterprises in the unorganised sectors requires an element of guess work which makes the figure for national income unreliable.

5. The greatest difficulty in the measurement of national income in India is general *lack of adequate statistical data*. Inadequacy, non-availability and unreliability of statistics is a great handicap in measuring national income in these countries. As stated above, statistical information regarding agriculture and allied occupations, and household enterprises is not available. Even the statistical information regarding the enterprises in the organised sector is sketchy and unreliable. There is no accurate information available regarding consumption, investment expenditure and savings of either rural or urban population.

QUESTION FOR REVIEW

1. Explain the circular flow of income in an economy. What does it measure ?
2. Describe the circular flow of income in a two-sector economy with households and business firms. What determines the magnitude of circular flow of income and expenditure ?
3. What is meant by saving and investment ? How do they affect circular flow of income in a free market economy ?
4. Despite the fact that motives to save are different from the motives of business men to invest, in national income accounts savings are always equal to investment.
5. How does the addition of Government in a two sector economy affect circular flow of income? If Government's budget is deficit, how will it affect circular flow of income ?

6. Show with a circular income flow model of a two sector economy that national product equals national income.
7. In a three sector economy with firms, households and Government show with a circular income flow model that the sum of private investment and Government expenditure equals the sum of saving and taxes.
8. What is meant by withdrawals and injections ? How do they affect the size of circular flow of income and expenditure in an economy ?
9. If investment by business firms falls short of savings, how will it affect the circular flow of income ?
10. How will circular income flow in an economy be affected if a country has foreign trade transactions?
11. In a four sector open economy, explain with a circular income flow model show that the sum of investment, Government expenditure and net exports must equal the sum of savings and taxes.
12. Explain how in an open economy foreign capital flows are related to domestic saving and investment.
13. What is menat by Gross Domestic Product (GDP) ? How is it measured through expenditure method ?
14. Distinguish between the following
    (*a*) Net National Product at Market Prices (NNP_{MP}) and National Income
    (*b*) Intermediate Goods and Final Goods
    (*c*) Nominal National Inocme and Real National Income
    (*d*) Government expenditure on goods and services and transfer payments
15. What is meant by '*Net Value Added*'? How is national income of a country measured through value added method.

CHAPTER 7

Determination of National Income : Keynes's Two Sector Model

Keynes's Income-Expenditure Approach

We have explained in the previous chapter how the level of employment is determined in an advanced capitalist economy. We explained there Keynesian theory with special reference to the determination of employment. It is worth noting here that the Keynesian theory is relevant in the context of the short run only since the stock of capital, techniques of production, efficiency of labour, the size of population, forms of business organisation have been assumed to remain constant in this theory. Further in his model of income determination *Keynes assumed that price level in the economy remains unchanged.* Therefore, in the Keynesian theory which deals with the short run, the level of income of the country will change as a result of changes in the level of labour employment. Thus, in an a free market economy in the short run, when capital stock and technology remain unchanged, income is a function of labour employment. In fact, both income and employment go together. The higher the level of employment, the higher the level of income. As level of employment is determined by aggregate demand and aggregate supply, the level of income is also determined by aggregate demand and aggregate supply. In this chapter, we shall explain how the equilibrium level of national income is determined through Keynes's income-expenditure analysis. This analysis explains determination of national income by relating income (output) to aggregate expenditure on goods and services. The, aggregate expenditure shows aggregate demand for goods and services. Keynesian theory of income determination can be explained by assuming two sectors in the economy, namely, households and business firms Keynes focussed on this simply two sector model of determination of national income and derived conclusions regarding policy formulation from this basic model. Analysis of determination of national income can be extended to incorporate Government and foreign trade. We start with the analysis of determination of national income by *taking a simple two-sector economy with a fixed price level.* The two sectors are consumption demand by households and investment demand by entrepreneurs.

Aggregate Expenditure

Aggregate expenditure is the total expenditure which at given fixed prices all households and business firms want to make on goods and services in a period at various levels of national income. In Keynes's original model *aggregate expenditure is* in fact *aggregate demand at given prices.* In a two-sector closed economy, aggregate expenditure or aggregate demand consists of two components: First, there is consumption demand, and secondly, there is a demand for capital goods, which is called investment demand. Thus, by aggregate expenditure we mean how much expenditure the households and the entrepreneurs are willing to make on consumption and investment. Therefore,

Aggregate Expenditure = Consumption Demand + Investment Demand

$$AE = C + I$$

where AE stands for aggregate demand, C for consumption demand and I for investment demand. Note that aggregate demand implies aggregate expenditure (AE), consumption demand (C) implies consumption expenditure and investment demand (I) implies investment expenditure. Thus

$$AE = C + I$$

Consumption Demand. As for consumption demand, it depends upon the propensity to consume of the community and the level of national income. Given the propensity to consume, as income increases, consumption demand will also increase. In other words, given the propensity to consume, consumption demand is a function of income. Consumption function can take several forms. The most common form of short-run consumption function is

$$C = a + bY$$

where a is the intercept term of the function and represents *autonomous consumption* whereas *b* represents the slope of the consumption function.

Consider Fig. 7.1 in which national income is measured along the *X*-axis and consumption demand (*C*) is shown on the Y-axis. In this figure, a straight line *OZ* which makes 45° angle with the *X*-axis has been drawn. This straight line *OZ* with 45° angle with the *X*-axis represents the *reference income line* to measure the difference between consumption and level of income. This is also often called *income line.* This 45° line represents national income in money terms. In fact, national product and income are the same things. In this figure a curve *C* has also been drawn which represents consumption function, $C = a + by$ of the community. This curve of consumption function slopes upward from left to right, which shows that as income increases the amount of consumption demand also increases. As income line *OZ* makes 45° angle with the *X*-axis, the *gap between the consumption function curve C and the income line OZ represents the saving of the community*. The reason for this is that a part of the income is consumed and a part is saved, *i.e.*, National Income = Consumption + Saving. This is also written as $Y = C + S$, where *y* represents income, *C* consumption and *S* saving. It will be seen from Fig. 7.1 that the gap between the consumption function curve *C* and the income line *OZ* goes on increasing as income increases. In other words, the amount of saving or saving gap increases as income increases.

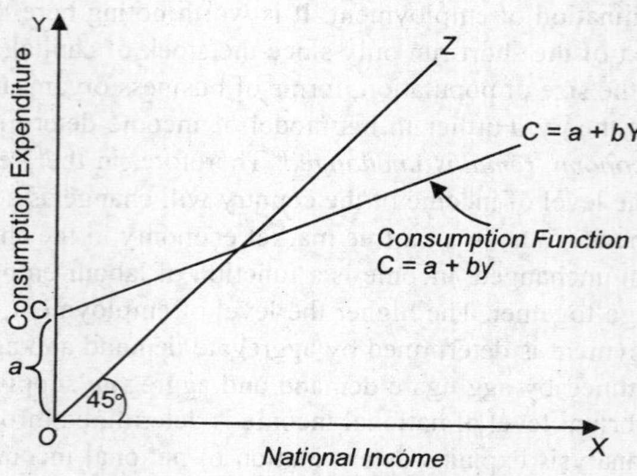

Fig. 7.1. *Consumption Function*

It is worth mentioning that in the short-run consumption function does not change. This is because the propensity to consume, that is, the whole consumption function curve *C* depends upon the tastes, perferences, the income distribution in the soceity, the population level, wealth of the people etc., which do not undergo much change in the short run. The implication of the stability of consumption function is that the consumption demand is primarely determined by the level of current national income.

However, through changes in monetary policy and fiscal policy by the Government the consumption function can be shifted. For example, when rate of interest, an instrument of monetary policy, is reduced, the people borrow more for durable consumer goods such as cars, airconditioners, houses and with this at a given level of income consumption demand increases causing upward shift in the consumption function curve. Similarly, when income tax, an instrument of fiscal policy, is reduced disposable income of the households increases and as a result at a given level of national income (GDP), consumption demand increases leading to the upward shift in consumption function.

Investment Demand. The other component of the aggr gate demand is investment which is a crucial factor in the determination of equilibrium le el of national income. Investment demand depends upon two factors; (1) marginal efficiency of capital and (2) rate of interest. Of these two factors, rate of interest is comparatively stable and uoes not frequently change in the short run. Therefore, the fluctuations in the level of investment demand chiefly depend upon the changes in the marginal efficiency of capital. *The marginal efficiency of capital means the expeted rate of profit which the business* *community hopes to get from the investment in capital assets.* Marginal efficiency of capital depends upon the replacement cost of the capital goods on the one hand, and profit expectations of enterprenuers on the other. Profit expectations are more important because they often change even in the short run and cause fluctuations in investment. If the level of national income and employment is desired to be raised in a free market capitalist economy, then steps should be taken which will raise the expectations of the enterpreneurs (i.e., business firms) regarding profit-earning from investment.

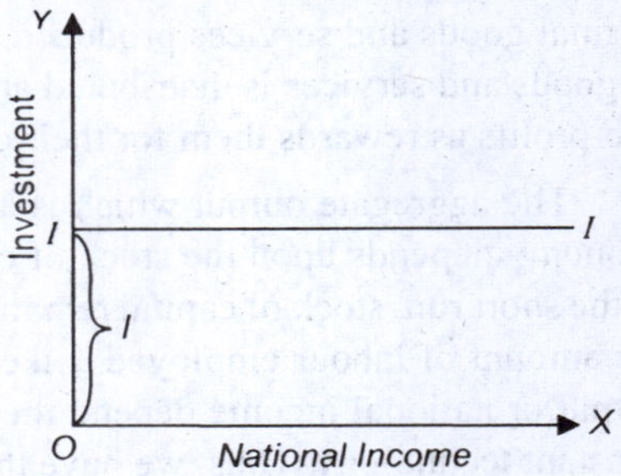

Fig. 7.2. *Autonomous Investment*

In any particular year, there will be a given level of investment demand which, as seen above, is determined by marginal efficiency of capital and a given rate of interest. However, in Keynes's theory investment being determined by marginal efficiency of capital and rate of interest does not depend on the level of income. Thus, in Keynesian theory of income determination, investment does not vary with change in income. In other words, in *Keynes's directly income-expenditure analysis investment is treated as autonomous of income, that is, investment does not change with a change in the level of income.* This type of investment is shown in Figure 7.2. This is the assumption which Keynes made and in this chapter we will also do likewise. In actual practice when the level of income rises, the demand for goods will also rise and this will favourably affect the expectations of the entrepreneurs regarding making of profits. Rise in the profit expectations will raise the marginal efficiency of capital which in turn will increase the level of investment. But it is quite clear that investment demand does not directly depend upon income; it is only affected indirectly by changes in income. Therefore, in our Figure 7.3 we have taken a given amount of investment demand independent of the level of income and added it to upward sloping consumption function curve to get aggregate expenditure curve $C + I$. The distance between the C curve and the $C + I$ curve is parallel to the C curve throughout which indicates that the level of investment is constant and does not change with the change in income. It may however be noted that with either a change in the rate of interest or in marginal efficiency of capital investment will change. Therefore, in income-expenditure diagram as shown in Fig. 7.3, *a different new amount of investment* of will have to be taken.

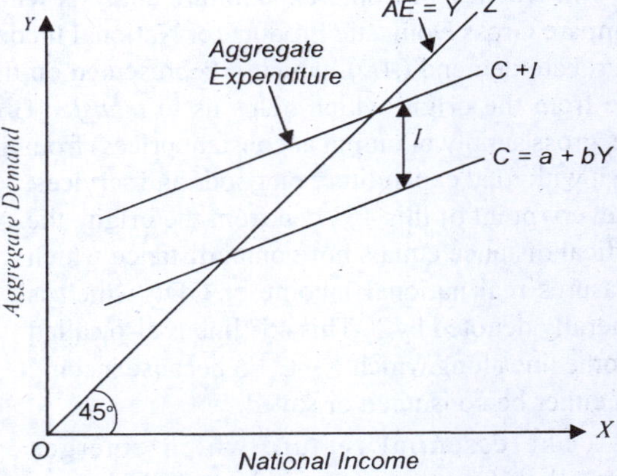

Fig. 7.3. *Aggregate Expenditure Curve of a Two Sector Economy*

Aggregate Output

As mentioned above, in the short run the level of national income and employment in a free-market economy depends upon the equilibrium between aggregate expenditure and aggregate output. We have also explained above the various components of aggregate expenditure on goods and services. We now run to explain the aggregate supply and factors on which it depends. It is important to note again that Keynes in his analysis assumed that prices and wages remain constant in the short run.

In an economy with out any role of Government, national income *means the total money value of final goods and services produced in an economy in a year.* There are two important constituents of aggregate output.

1. the supply or output of final consumer goods and services in a year; and

2. the output of capital goods in a year which are also called producer goods because they help in producing further goods. *Net addition to the stock of capital goods in a year is called investment*.

National income is the same thing as national product as both represents the value of output of final goods and services produced. In fact, aggregate supply or money value of national product of goods and services is distributed among the various factors of production as wages, rent, interest and profits as rewards them for their contribution to the national product.

The aggregate output which is also sometimes referred to as aggregate supply of goods of an economy depends upon the stock of capital, the amount of labour used and the state of technology. In the short run, stock of capital remains constant and therefore output can be increased by increasing the amount of labour employed. Like the classical economists Keynes also thought that aggregate output or national income depend the short-run production function with a given capital stock and constant technology. Thus, we have the following production function in the short run.

$$Y = (N, \bar{K}, \bar{T})$$

where Y is national output, $\bar{K}$ is the constant amount of capital stock, $\bar{T}$ is the constant state of technology and N is the labour employed which is a variable factor.

It may be noted that the amount of production which a given amount of labour can produce depends upon the given stock of capital and state of technology. The higher the level of technology, more can be produced with the help of given resources. Since J.M. Keynes in the nineteen thirties and we at present are concerned with the determination of income and employment *in the short run*, the stock of capital and the state of technology are assumed to be constant. For similar reasons, size of population is also assumed to be constant. However, the amount of labour employed out of this given size of population can vary depending upon the demand for labour.

45° Line as Aggregate Supply Curve of Output (With Fixed Price Level)

In Keynes's income-expenditure analysis with which we are presently concerned we need to compare Gross Domestic Product (or National Income) with aggregate expenditure (AE), also called aggregate demand (AD), which is represented on the vertical axis. For this purpose we draw a 45° line from the origin which helps us to *transfer* Gross Domestic Product or real National Income (i.e. gross supply of output at constant prices) from the horizontal axis to the vertical axis for comparing it with total expenditure on goods and services. At every point of this 45° line from the origin, the vertical distance equals horizontal distance which measures real national income or GDP which is generally denoted by Y. This 45° line is also called income line along which $Y = C + S$ because income can either be consumed or saved.

The essential feature which emerges from all this is that more output will be produced and supplied at the given price level in response to increase in aggregate demand or expenditure. In other words, whatever the aggregate demand, more output of goods will be produced and supplied at the same price before full-employment of resources is reached. This type of aggregate supply curve has been shown by 45° OZ line drawn against the X and Y axes in Fig. 7.4 where along the X-axis real national income (GDP) and along the Y-axis aggregate supply of output are measured. However, as noted above, aggregate output and real national income (GDP) are identical.

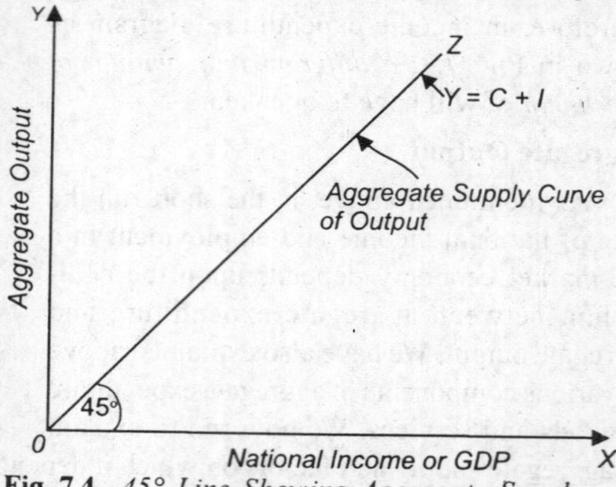

Fig. 7.4. *45° Line Showing Aggregate Supply Curve of Output.*

It follows from above that 45° line shows two things. First, it shows *varying* levels of aggregate production or the supply of goods (both consumer and capital goods) that will be offered for sale at the given price level at various levels of aggregate expenditure. This shows that up to the level of full-employment of resources *any amount* of aggregate supply of output will be forthcoming at the given price level depending on the aggregate demand or expenditures. The greater the aggregate demand or expenditure, the greater the aggregate supply of output at the given price level. Secondly, it represents national income. In fact, as you would have read in national income accounting, national product and national income are the same things.

Equilibrium Level of National Income

Now, we shall explain how through the intersection of aggregate demand and aggregate supply curves the equilibrium level of national income is determined in Keynes's two sector model. $C + I$ curve represents the aggregate expenditure and 45° OZ line represents aggregate supply of output.

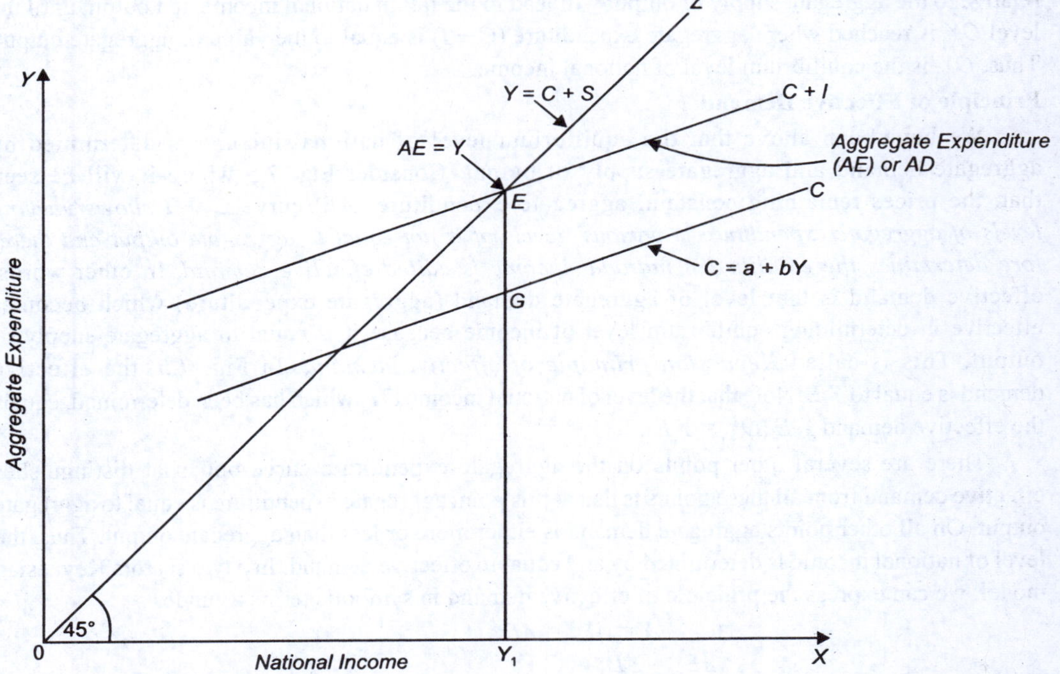

Fig. 7.5. *Determination of National Income : Basic Keynesian Two Sector Model*

Normally the goods and services are produced by firms when they think they can sell them in the market. There will be equilibrium in the goods market when total output of goods and services produced will be equal to the total demand for output. Aggregate demand for them is represented by aggregate expenditure. In equilbrium aggregate expenditure (which is denoted by AE) must equal aggregate output (GDP). Since aggregate output or GDP equals national income (Y) we have the following condition for equilibrium.

$$AE = GDP = Y$$

It will be seen in Fig. 7.5 that aggregate expenditure curve (AE) or $C + I$ curve intersects 45° line at point E which satisfies the equilibrium condition. That is, a point E which corresponds to the income level OY_1, aggregate expenditure is equal to aggregate output. Therefore, E is the equilibrium point and OY_1 represents the equilibrium level of national income. Now, income cannot be in equilibrium at levels smaller than OY_1, since aggregate expenditure exceeds aggregate supply of output as $C + I$ curve which depicts aggregate expenditure of output lies above 45° line. This excess demand will be met by the firms selling goods from their stocks or inventories of goods kept by them. This leads to the decline in inventoires of goods below the desired levels. This unintended fall in inventories will induce the firms to expand their output of goods and services to meet the extra demand for them and keep their inventories of goods at the desired levels. Thus when at a given level of national income, aggregate expenditure (*i.e.*, aggregate demand) exceeds aggregate output, national income will increase. With this increase in national income or output, employment of labour will also rise to produce the increment in output. This process of expansion in output under the pressure of excess demand will continue till national income OY_1 is reached.

On the contrary, the equilibrium level of national income cannot be greater than OY_1 because at any level greater than OY_1 aggregate expenditure or demand $(C + I)$ falls short of aggregate output. This will cause the increase in inventoires of goods with the firms beyond the desired levels. To this situation of the unintended increase in inventories of goods, the firms will respond by cutting down production to keep their inventories at the desired levels. Thus, deficiency in aggregate demand relative to the aggregate supply of output will lead to the fall in national income and output until the level OY_1 is reached where aggregate expenditure $(C + I)$ is equal to the value of aggregate output. Thus, OY_1 is the equilibrium level of national income.

Principle of Effective Demand

We have seen above that the equilibrium level of national income is determined by aggregate demand and aggregate supply of output. Consider Fig. 7.5 where it will be seen that, the prices remaining constant, aggregate expenditure (*AE*) curve *C* + *I shows varying levels of aggregate expenditure at various levels of is not equal to aggregate output and therefore determines the equilibrium national income is called effective demand.* In other words, effective demand is that level of aggregate demand (aggregate expenditure) which becomes effective in determining equilibrium level of income because it is equal to aggregate supply of output. This is called *Keynesian principle of effective demand.* In Fig. 7.5, the effective demand is equal to Y_1E. Note that the level of national income OY_1 which has been determined, equals the effective demand Y_1E $(OY_1 = Y_1E)$.

There are several other points on the aggregate expenditure curve but what distinguishes effective demand from all these points is that at this point aggregate expenditure is equal to aggregate output. On all other points aggregate demand is either more or less than aggregate output. Thus, the level of national income is determined by and equal to effective demand. In a two sectors Keynesian model, we can express the principle of effective demand in symbolic terms as under :

$$Y = AE^* = AD^*$$

$$AE^* = AD^* = C + I$$

$$Y = AD^* = C + I$$

where Y = National Income

AD^* = Effective demand

C = Consumption demand

I = Investment

Note that *star mark* on *AE* or *AD* shows the aggregate demand which becomes effective.

Importance. It is thus clear that national income and employment in the short run are determined by effective demand or in other words, effective expenditure. The higher the level of effective demand, the greater the levels of national income and employment and vice-versa. *Unemployment is due to deficiency of effective demand and the basic remedy to remove this unemployment is to raise the level of effective demand.* Due to their belief in Say's law and in quick adjustment of wages and prices to balance between demand and supply the classical economists believed that effective demand was always large enough to ensure full-employment. But Keynes proved that it was not so and that is why the problem of involuntary unemployment was common in the free-market capitalist economies.

Equilibrium is not Necessary Established at Full-Employment Level.

The most important contention of J.M. Keynes in his now famous work "General Theory of Employment, Interest and Money" was that in a capitalist economy it is not necessary that the equilibrium level of income is established at the level of full-employment. This view of Keynes was quite contrary to the views of the classical economists who believed that the economy always tended towards full-employment. Keynes refuted this important idea of the classical economics. To understand the Keynesian viewpoint consider Fig. 7.6. Suppose the full-employment level of labour corresponds to the level of national income equal to OY_F. Thus OY_F represents the level of income at which there is full-employment in the economy. But, as seen above, the equilibrium level of income

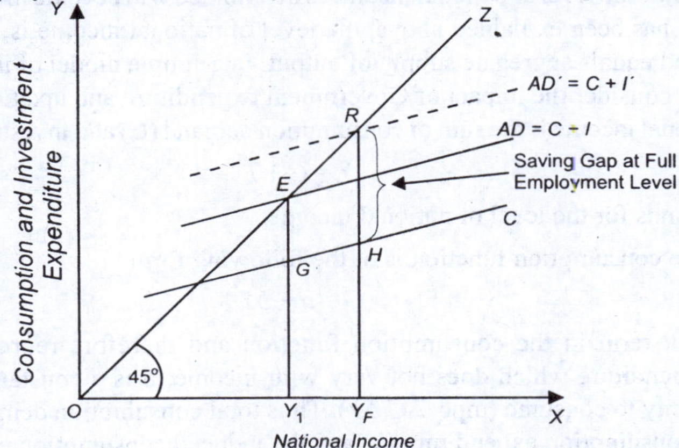

Fig. 7.6. *Under-employment Equilibrium due to Insufficiency of Investment Expenditure*

is not established at OY_F but at OY_1 at which some number of labour will be unemployed. Thus equilibrium at OY_1 is known as *under-employment equilibrium*. It is worth noting that in the situation depicted in Fig. 7.6 the equilibrium level of national income will be established at full-employment level only when investment demand is sufficiently large to fill the saving gap between income and consumption at the full-employment level of income OY_F. It will be seen from Fig. 7.6, that corresponding to the full-employment level of income OY_F, *RH* is the saving of the community. Therefore, if the equilibrium is to be established at OY_F level, then investment demand must be equal to level of saving *RH* at full employment level of income Y_F. But the prevailing investment demand is only equal to *EG* which is less than *RH*. With *RH* as the level of investment and the *C* curve as the level of propensity to consume, *C* + *I* curve intersects the 45° aggregate output curve *OZ* at point *R* and therefore determines equilibrium level of income equal to OY_F at which labour will be fully employed.

But there is not guarantee that the investment demand will be equal to the saving gap corresponding to full-employment level of income. There are various reasons for this. First, the people who save are not necessary those who make investment; while it is the general public which save but only few people constituting the entrepreneurial class undertakes investment. Secondly, the factors which determine saving are quite different from those which determine investment. While the people save for providing for the education, marriages of their children and also for contingency purposes such as diseases and unemployment periods. They also save in order to acquire durable goods such as houses, gold and jewellery. They also save to accumulate sufficient funds for their old age. But the level of investment depends upon marginal efficiency of capital and rate of interest in the short run and on the level of population, technological progress in the long run. Therefore, it is not essential that investment should be equal to the amount of savings by the people at full-employment level. If due to the adverse changes in the profit expectations of the entrepreneurs, level of investment falls, the equilibrium level of national income will also decline.

It is also worth noting that if aggregate expenditure increases beyond the $C + I'$ in Fig. 7.6 it will mean that the economy is spending and demanding more than it can produce. The result of this will be rise in prices of the commodities. In other words, if the investment demand in any year is higher than *HR*, then the inflationary process will start. In this situation, national income will rise beyond OY_F only in money terms but not in real terms.

DETERMINATION OF EQUILIBRIUM LEVEL OF NATIONAL INCOME: ALGEBRAIC ANALYSIS

A study of how the level of national income is determined will become more clear by using simple mathematics. As has been explained above, the level of national income is in equilibrium at which aggregate demand equals aggregate supply of output. In a simple model of income determination in which we do not consider the impact of Government expenditure and taxation and also exports and imports, the national income is the sum of consumption demand (*C*) and investment demand (I), that is,

$$Y = C + I$$

where *Y* stands for the level of national income.

Suppose the consumption function is of the following form :

$$C = a + bY$$

a is the intercept term in the consumption function and therefore represents the autonomous consumption expenditure which does not very with income. b is a constant which represents the marginal propensity to consume (mpc $\Delta C/\Delta Y$). Thus total consumption demand is equal to the sum of autonomous consumption expenditure (*a*) and the induced consumption expenditure (*bY*).

Now suppose that investment demand equals I_a. This investment I_a is autonomous because this does not depend on income. Thus, we get the following three equations for the determination of the equilibrium level of national income.

$$Y = C + I \qquad ...(i)$$

$$C = a + bY \qquad ...(ii)$$

$$I = I_a \qquad ...(iii)$$

Substituting the values of *C* and *I* in equation (*i*) we have

$$Y = a + bY + Ia \qquad ...(iv)$$

$$Y - bY = a + Ia$$

$$Y(1 - b) = a + Ia$$

$$Y = \frac{1}{1-b}(a + I_a) \qquad ...(v)$$

The equation (*v*) shows the equilibrium level of national income when aggregated expenditure equals aggregate supply of output. *The equation (v) reveals that autonomous consumption and autonomous investment ($a + I_a$) generates so much expenditure or aggregate demand which is equal to the income generated by the production of goods and services.* From the equation (*v*) it also follows that the equilibrium level of national income can be known from multiplying the elements of autonomous expenditure (that is, $a + I_a$) by the term $\frac{1}{1-b}$ which is equal to the value of multiplier.

Further, it also follows that equilibrium level of income is higher, the greater the marginal propensity to consume (*i.e. b*) and autonomous consumption (*a*) and autonomous investment (*Ia*)

Illustrations of Equilibrium Level of Income with Numerical Examples

A few numerical examples will make it clear how the equilibrium level of national income is determined.

Problem 1. *Suppose in an economy, autonomous investment (I) is ₹ 600 crores and the following consumption function is given :*

$$C = 200 + 0.8Y$$

Given the above, find out the equilibrium level of income.

Solution. The equilibrium level of income is

$$Y = C + I$$

$$C = 200 + 0.8Y \quad \ldots (i)$$

$$I = 600$$

Putting the values of C and I in the equilibrium (i) we have

$$Y = 200 + 0.8Y + 600$$

$$(Y - 0.8Y) = 200 + 600$$

$$Y(1 - 0.8) = 800$$

or $$Y = \frac{800}{0.2} = \frac{800}{\frac{2}{10}} = \text{₹ } \mathbf{4000.}$$

Alternative Method. In our algebraic analysis of equilibrium level of national income we have derived the following condition for equilibrium level of national income.

$$Y = \frac{1}{1-b}(a + I_a)$$

where $\frac{1}{1-b}$ is investment multiplier and b is marginal propensity to consume α is the intercept term in the consumption function. The above condition can also be used to determine the equilibrium level of national income. Marginal propensity to consume (b) in the given problem is 0.8 and the intercept term a equals 200. Using this alternative method we have

$$Y = \frac{1}{1-b}(1 + I_a)$$

Substituting the value of b, a and I_a we have

$$Y = \frac{1}{1-08}(200 + 600)$$

$$Y = \frac{1}{0.2}(800) = 5(800)$$

$$= 4000 \text{ crore}$$

Problem 2. *Suppose the consumption function of an economy is C = 0.8 Y. Planned investment by entrepreneurs for a year is ₹ 500 crores. Find out what will be the equilibrium level of income.*

Solution.

$$Y = C + I$$

$$C = 0.8Y$$

$$I = \text{₹ } 500 \text{ crores}$$

Substituting the values of C and I in (i) we have

$$Y = 0.8Y + 500$$

$$Y - 0.8Y = 500$$

$$Y(1 - 0.8) = 500$$

$$0.2Y = 500$$

$$Y = 500 \times \frac{10}{2} = \text{₹ } 2500 \text{ crore.}$$

Alternative Method.

$$Y = \frac{1}{1-b}(a + I_a)\ b \text{ in the given problem is 0.8 and a = 0}$$

Thus, $$Y = \frac{1}{1-0.8}\ (500) = 2500 \text{ crore}$$

Problem 3. *For an economy following consumption function is given :*

$$C = 60 + 0.75\ Y.$$

(*a*) *If investment in a year is ₹ 35 crores what will be the equilibrium level of income or output ?*

(*b*) *If full-employment level of income (i.e. level of potential output) is ₹ 460 crores what investment is required to be undertaken to ensure equilibrium at full-employment.*

Solution : (*a*)

$$Y = C + I$$
$$Y = 60 + 0.75Y + 35$$
$$Y - 0.75Y = 60 + 35 = 95$$
$$Y(1 - 0.75) = 95$$
$$0.25Y = 95$$
$$Y = 95 \times \frac{100}{25} = 380$$

(*b*) To ensure full-employment equilibrium, investment should be equal to the saving gap at full-employment income. With the given full-employment income equal to ₹ 460,

Let Y_F stand for full-employment income, C_F for consumption at full employment income level and S_F for saving at full employment inocme level. Thus,

$$S_F = Y_F - C_F = Y_F - (60 + 0.75Y_F)$$
$$= 460 - 60 - (0.75 \times 460)$$
$$= 400 - 345 = 55$$

Thus, investment required for full-employment equilibrium is ₹ 55 crore.

Problem 4. *Suppose the consumption of an economy is given by*

$$C = 20 + 0.6Y$$

The following investment function is given :

$$I = 10 + 02\ Y$$

What will be the equilibrium level of national income ?

Solution. Note that in this problem, investment varies with income. However, this will not change our method of determining equilibrium level of income.

$$Y = C + I \qquad \ldots (i)$$
$$C = 20 + 0.6Y$$
$$I = 10 + 0.2Y$$

Substituting the values of C and I in (i) we have

$$Y = 20 + 0.6Y + 10 + 0.2Y$$
$$Y = 30 + 0.8Y$$
$$Y - 0.8Y = 30$$
$$Y(1 - 0.8Y) = 30$$
$$0.2Y = 30$$
$$Y = 30 \times \frac{10}{2} = 150$$

Thus, we find that the equilibrium level of income to be equal to 150.

National Income and Employment

In our above analysis we have explained the determination of level of national income. Now, how in Keynes's model of determination of level of employment in the economy is related to the determination of national income. In fact, the levels of national income and employment are determined jointly. It will be appropriate if we now explain their determination jointly by aggregate demand and supply. It is worth nothing that, in Keynesian theory, employment is a function of income. Relation between income and labour employment is given by short-run production function showing diminishing returns to labour. This short-run production function can be stated as under :

$$Y = f(N, \bar{K}, \bar{T})$$

According to the above function, given the capital stock and technology, the greater the level of national output (i.e. income or *Y*), the greater will be the number of workers (*N*) employed. As explained above in detail that, according to Keynesian theory, levels of national income and employment are determined by aggregate effective demand. In a closed economy with no intervention by the government, aggregate demand consists of consumption demand and investment demand. According to Keynes, consumption function is stable in the short run and it is investment demand which is highly volatile in the short run as it depends on profit expectations of business men. Equilibrium at full employment level of income is determined when investment expenditure fills the saving gap at full employment level of national income. Consider Fig. 7.7 where in Panel (b) determination of national income is shown through intersection of aggregate demand and aggregate supply curves. According to Keynes, equilibrium at full-employment level of income OY_F will be determined if planned investment expenditure by entrepreneurs is equal to saving *HT* at full-employment level of national income OY_F. Total expenditure (i.e., aggregate demand) and output produced are both equal to *OQ* corresponding to equilibrium point *H*, ($OQ = OY_F$). In the left-side Panel (a) where production function curve *TP* has been drawn , we have measured employment of labour on the X-axis and aggregate output (i.e., national income) on the *Y*-axis. It will be seen from this left-side panel (a) that aggregate output *OQ* is produced by employing ON_F amount of labour. We assume that ON_F represents full employment of labour, that is, all workers who want to work at the prevailing wage

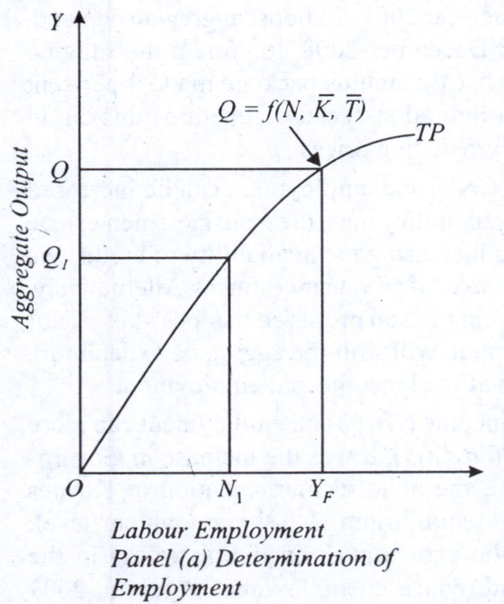

Labour Employment
Panel (a) Determination of Employment

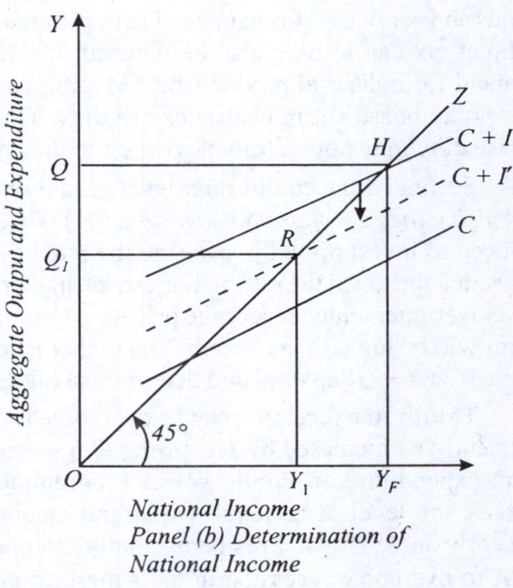

National Income
Panel (b) Determination of National Income

Fig. 7.7. *The Emergence of Involuntary Unemployment.*

rate are getting employment. With this full employment of labour, national income equal to OY_F is being generated ($OY_F = OQ$).

Now, Keynes argued that if somehow or the other profit expectations of entrepreneurs become dim, this would cause a fall in the expected rate of return resulting in reduction in investment expenditure. With the fall in investment expenditure, aggregate demand curve shifts downward to the dotted position $C + I'$ which intersects 45° line OZ at point R. As a result, new equilibrium level of national income OY_1 is determined ($OY_1 = OQ_1$).

It will be seen from left side panel (a) that aggregate output (i.e., national income) OQ_1 is produced by employing ON_1 amount of labour. Thus, as a result of fall in aggregate demand, N_1N_F number of workers are rendered unemployed. N_1N_F workers will be involuntarily unemployed.

According to Keynes, there is no any mechanism which should ensure that this involuntary unemployment will be automatically eliminated. There is therefore need for intervention by the government.

Anti-Recessionary Policy : Shifting Aggregate Expenditure Curve Upward

Now, an important question is what measures can be adopted to overcome recession or involuntary unemployment which comes into existence as a result of deficiency of aggregate demand brought about by a fall in investment.

From our above analysis it is clear that increase in equilibrium level of national income can be brought about by increases in any components of aggregate demand, namely, consumption demand (C), private investment demand (I), Government expenditure (G), and net exports (NX). In order to increase national income through upward shift in the consumption function, *the Government can reduce personal income taxes*. In 1964, the reduction in income tax by John Kennedy Government in USA was quite successful in boosting consumption demand and thereby raising aggregate output. As a result, more income and employment were generated. The rate of unemployment sharply declined and the American economy was lifted out of depression. Recently, in 2002 and again in early 2008, the President George W. Bush made a significant cut of 3.5 billion dollars in income tax to revive the American economy. He refunded a good amount of income tax collected from the people in these years. The cut in direct taxes increases the disposable income of the people which tends to raise their consumption demand. However, there is a limitation of cut in direct taxes for raising aggregate demand because a part of the increase in disposbale income can be saved rather than being spent on goods and services. This happened in the United States in the year 2008. To boost aggregate demand, indirect tax can also be also be reduced. In India also, in December 2008, to correct the sagging demand for industrial products the Government under the fiscal stimulus package made 4 per cent across the board cut in central excise duty. This too has a limitation because benefit of this cut in excise duty may not be fully passed on to the consumers by reducing prices.

Secondly, the equilibrium level of national income (GNP) and employment can be increased by *raising the rate of private investment* (I). Through monetary policy measures businessmen can be induced to invest more by lowering the rate of interest and increasing the availability of credit. We know that the lower the rate of interest, the higher will be the level of private investment. Alternatively, the Government may encourage private investment by reducing tax on profits so that post-tax rate of profit will be higher than before. The higher level of investment will shift the aggregate expenditure curve ($C + I + G$) upward and determine a higher level of national income and employment.

Thirdly, the recession can be overcome and national income (GNP) and employment can more efficiently be increased by *increasing Government expenditure* (G). It was the increase in Government expenditure on Public Works Programme which was the main recommendation of Keynes to raise the level of national output and income to restore equilibrium at full-employment level. Recently in 1993-94, President Clinton stepped up public expenditure on public works in the USA to overcome recession in the American economy and reduce unemployment. Again in 2009 president Obama planned to give a fiscal stimulus of over $ 800 billion the major part of which was the increase in Government expenditure to raise aggregate demand to overcome recession in the American Economy. In India also fiscal stimulus packages were announced in 2008-09 under which government expenditure, especially on infrastruture projects, was increased to revive slowing Indian economy.

Lastly, the *expansion in positive net exports* (*NX*) will also cause an increase in equilibrium level of national income and employment. Exports can be promoted through tax concession on profits earned through exports as well as making credit available on lower interest rate for purpose of exporting goods. Another common measure adopted to promote exports is the depreciation of national currency. Depreciation makes the exports cheaper and imports costlier which raise net exports (*NX*). However, when there is global recession depreciation of its currency by each country will offset the effect of others.

It follows from above that a mix of fiscal and monetary policy measures are adopted to increase in aggregate expenditure and demand and thereby to lift the economy out of recession.

DETERMINATION OF NATIONAL INCOME: SAVING-INVESTMENT APPROACH

We have seen how equilibrium level of national income is determined by the interaction of aggregate demand and aggregate supply. The equilibrium level of national income is established at the point where aggregate demand equals aggregate supply. But there is an alternative method for the explanation of the determination of national income. This alternative method explains the determination of national income directly by intended saving and investment.

Look at the Fig. 7.5 again. In this figure, at the equilibrium level of national income OY_1, saving and investment are equal to *GE*. Given the aggregate demand curve $C + I$, the amount of saving at income greater than OY_1 exceeds investment and for income less than OY_1 investment exceeds saving. It is obvious that intended saving and investment are equal only at the equilibrium level of national income and when intended saving and investment are not equal, national income will not be in equilibrium. Let us see why it is so and how national income is determined by intended saving and investment.

When at a certain level of national income, intended investment by the entrepreneurs is more than intended saving by the people, this would mean that aggregate expenditure is greater than aggregate supply of output. This will lead to the decline in inventories below the desired level. This would induce the firms to increase production, raising the level of income and employment. The result will be that national output will be increased on account of which national income will go up. Further, when at any level of income, investment is less than saving. It means that aggregate demand is less than aggregate supply. As a result, the entrepreneurs will not be able to sell their entire output at given prices. The result will be that output will be reduced which will result in the reduction of national income.

Thus, when, at any level of national income, investment demand of the entrepreneurs is less than the intended savings of the people, the national income will decrease. It will come down to the level at which investment spending is just equal to the planned savings by the community. But, when at any level of national income, intended investment demand on the part of the enterpreneurs is equal to intended savings of the people, it means that aggregate demand is equal to the total output or aggregate supply and therefore the national income will be equilibrium. Hence, equilibrium level of national income will be determined at the level at which the amount of intended investment by the enterpreneurs is equal to the amount of intended savings by the people.

We can explain the determination of national income through saving and investment in another way. *Saving represents withdrawal of some money from the income stream. On the other hand, investment represents injection of money into the income stream*. Now, if intended investment is greater than intended saving, it means that more money has been put into the income stream than has been taken out of it. As a result, income stream, *i.e.*, flow of national income would expand. On the contrary, if investment is less than intended saving, it means that less amount of money has been put into the income stream than has been taken out of it. The result would be that national income would decrease. But when investment is just equal to saving, it would mean that as much money has been put into the income stream as has been taken out of it. The result will be that the national income will neither increase nor decrease, *i.e.*, it will be in equilibrium. It is thus clear that the equilibrium level of national income will be determined at the level at which the intended investment is equal to intended saving.

The determination of national income by investment and saving is illustrated in Fig. 7.8. In this figure, national income is shown along the *X*-axis. *SS* is the saving curve which shows intended saving at different levels of income, *II* curve shows investment demand *i.e.*, intended investment. The *II* investment curve has been drawn parallel to the *X*-axis. This is done on the assumption that in any year the enterpreneurs intend to invest a certain amount of money. This implies that we assume that investment is independent of change in income, that is, investment does not change with income.

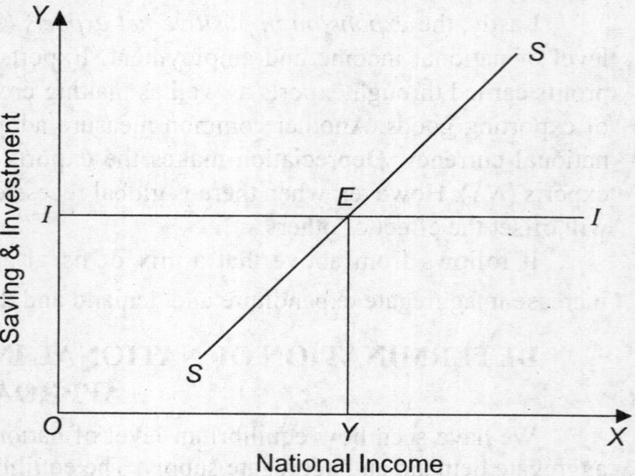

Fig. 7.8. *Determination of National Income*

The saving curve *SS* and the investment curve *II* intersect each other at *E*. That is, the intended investment and intended saving are equal at the *OY* level of income. Hence, *OY* is the equilibrium level of income. It will be seen from the Fig. 7.8 that at the level of income less than *OY*, the amount of intended investment is more than intended savings. As a result, income will increase. On the contrary, at the level of income a greater than *OY*, the amount of intended investment is less than the intended savings with the result that income will decrease. The decrease in income will continue until it becomes equal to *OY*. At the level of *OY* income, intended investment and intended saving are equal, so that there is neither the tendency for income to increase, nor to decrease. Hence, national income *OY* is determined. It is thus clear that national income is determined by the investment and saving.

Synthesis between the Two Approaches

The determination of national income has been explained above by two methods. The equilibrium level of national income is determined where two conditions are fulfilled :

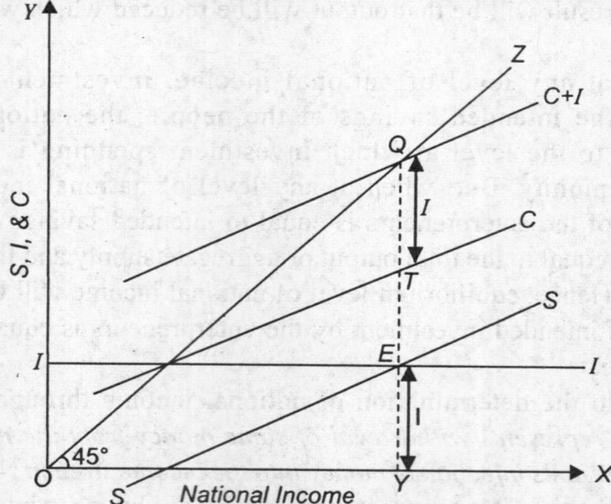

Fig. 7.9. *Synthesis between Income-Expenditure and Saving-Investment Approaches*

(*i*) *Aggregate Expenditure or Demand = Aggregate Supply of output*, and

(*ii*) *Intended Investment = Intended Savings.*

As has been explained above, the equality between aggregate expenditure and aggregate supply of output and equality between intended investment and intended saving in reality mean the same thing. This is illustrated in Fig. 7.9. It will be seen in this figure that aggregate demand curve *C* + *I* intersects aggregate supply curve *OZ* at point *Q* and thereby determines national income equal to *OY*. In the lower part of this diagram we have draw intended savings curve *SS* and intended investment curve *II*. It is worthwhile to note that saving curve *SS* has been derived from the consumption function curve *C* and measures the gap between income and consumption at various levels of income. Further, investment curve *II* drawn in the lower part of the figure represents the difference between consumption function curve *C* and aggregate demand curve *C* + *I*. This difference is the amount of intended investment assumed in this figure. We thus see that both saving and investment curves drawn in the lower part are embedded in the upper part showing aggregate demand and aggregate supply. It is because of this that intended saving and intended investment curves also determine the same level of national income *OY* which is determined through the equality of aggregate demand (*C* + *I*) and aggregate supply.

Saving-Investment Approach : Algebraic Analysis

That the level of national income is determined by the equality of planned saving and planned investment can be derived from the equilibrium condition explained above that level of income is equal to effective demand.

That is,

$$Y = AD^* \qquad \ldots (i)$$

Where AD^* represents effective aggregate demand or expenditure

Now in our simple economy, effective aggregate demand (AD^*) is equal to the sum of consumption expenditure and investment expenditure. Thus

$$AD^* = C + I$$

or
$$Y = C + I \qquad \ldots (ii)$$

Now
$$C = Y - S$$

Substituting $Y - S$ for C in equation (*ii*) we have

$$Y = Y - S + I$$

$$Y - Y + S = I$$

or
$$S = I \qquad \ldots (iii)$$

Thus, we reach at the alternative condition of equlibrium of national income, namely, planned (intended) saving be equal to planned (intended) investment.

We can further extend saving – investment approach to show the determination of national income as a multiple of autonomous factors. Since investment is treated as autonomous of national income, its amount is taken to be a fixed amount determined *exogenously*. Therefore we have

$$I = \overline{I}$$

Saving function as derived from the consumption function ($C = a + by$) can be written as**

$$S = -a + (1 - b)\,Y$$

In equilibrium

$$\overline{I} = -a + (1-b)Y$$

$$(1-b)Y = \overline{I} + a$$

$$Y = \frac{1}{1-b}(\overline{I} + a) \qquad \ldots (iv)$$

where $\frac{1}{1-b}$ is the value of multiplier and b = marginal propensity to consume and therefore $1 - b$ = marginal propensity to save. The equation (*iv*) describes the same condition which we at derived earlier. Note that a in equation (*iv*) is autonomous consumption which is intercept term in the consumption function.

Numerical Problem on Saving-Investment Approach

Problem 5. *Suppose the level of autonomous investment in an economy is 200 crores. The following saving function is given :*

$$S = -80 + 0.25\,Y$$

Find the equilibrium level of income.

Solution. According to the saving-investment approach, the level of income is in equilibrium at which

$$S = I \quad \text{... (i)}$$

Given, $S = -80 + 0.25Y$, and

$I =$ ₹ 200 crores

Substituting the values of S and I in the equilibrium equation we have

$$-80 + 0.25Y = 200$$

$$0.25Y = 200 + 80 = 280$$

$$Y = 280 \times \frac{100}{25} = 1120 \text{ crores}$$

Note that we can also use the equation (iv) derived above to obtain the equilibrium level of national income. Thus $Y = \frac{1}{1-b} = (I + a)$

Now, $b = 1 - 0.25 = 0.75$, $a = 80$ and $I = 200$

Thus $Y = \frac{1}{1-05} = (200 + 80)$

$$= \frac{1}{0.25} \times 280 = 1120 \text{ crores.}$$

Problem 6. *Given the saving function $S = -10 + 0.2Y$ and autonomous investment, $I =$ ₹ 50 crore.*

(*i*) *Find the equilibrium level of income.*

(*ii*) *Find the level of consumption*

(*iii*) *If investment increases permanently by ₹ 5 crores, what will be the new levels of income and consumption.*

Ans. (*i*) According to saving-investment approach, equilibrium level of national income is determined by equality between planned saving and investment. Thus,

$$S = I \quad \text{...(i)}$$

$$-10 + 0.2Y = 50$$

$$0.2\,Y = 50 + 10 = 60$$

$$Y = 60 \times \frac{10}{2} = 300$$

(*ii*)

$$C = Y - S \quad \text{...(ii)}$$

$$S = -10 + 0.2Y$$

$$S\ S = -10 + \frac{2}{10} \times 300 = 50$$

Substituting the value of income and saving(*s*) in equation (*ii*), we have

$$C = 300 - 50 = 250$$

(*iii*) With the increase in investment by ₹ 5 crores, the new investment will become equal to ₹ 55 crores.

$$S = I$$
$$-10 + 0.2Y = 55$$
$$0.2Y = 55 + 10 = 65$$
$$Y = 65 \times \frac{10}{2} = 325$$

Thus, new level of income = ₹ 325 crores.

Now, saving $= -10 + 0.2Y$

$$= -10 + \frac{2}{10} \times 325$$
$$= -10 + 65 = 55$$

Consumption (C) $= Y - S$

$$= 325 - 55$$
$$= 270$$

QUESTIONS FOR REVIEW

1. Explain how equilibrium level of national income is determined by level of effective demand in a simple two-sector Keynesian model. Is this equilibrium necessarily established at full employment level ?
2. Explain the equilibrium of national income by consumption and investment. When will the equilibrium be established at full-employment ?
3. (*i*) Saving and Investment are *always equal*.
   (*ii*) Saving and Investment are *equal only in equilibrium*.
   How would you reconcile the above two statments ?
4. Explain Keynes' income-expenditure approach to the determination of national income. Why can this equilibrium be reached below full-employment level of output ?
5. Define planned (desired) saving and planned (desired) investment. Explain how equilibrium level of national income is determined by planned saving and planned investment. Why is this equilibrium not always attained at full-employment level ?
6. What do you understand by the equilibrium level of national income. Explain that both saving–investment approach and aggregate demand–aggregate supply approach yeild the same level of equilibrium.
7. In a three sectors economy with firms, households and Government show that aggregate demand will equal aggregate supply only at the level of output and income at which savings and taxes equal Government expenditure and planned investment.
8. Explain the Keynesian concept of aggregate demand. How is the Keynesian aggregate demand function different from the classical demand function.
9. The following consumption function of an economy is given :
   $C = 40 + 0.8Y$ where Y is national income
   If the planned level of investment in a year equals ₹ 75 crore what will be the equilibrium level of national income and consumption ?
10. On the basis of Keynes's model of income determination what measures would you suggest to overcome recession in the Indian economy
11. What fiscal stimulus measures can be adopted to overcome recession in the economy ? Which, according to Keynes, fiscal policy or monetary policy is more effective for getting the economy out of recession ?
12. What according to Keynes, according to Keynes is the cause of recession or depression in the economy ? What measures can be adopted to overcome recession in the economy.
13. The following consumption function of an economy is given :
    $C = 40 + 0.8Y$ where Y is national income
    If planned level of investment in a year equals ₹ 75 crore, what will be the equilibrium level of income and *consumption*.
    (**Hint**. After finding the equilibrium level of income by putting $Y = C + I$. Then equilibrium level of consumption can be obtained by substituting Y in the given consumption function).

APPENDIX TO CHAPTER 7

Keynes's Complete Macroeconomic Model : Integrating Goods Market with Money Market

Linking Goods Market with Money Market

As explained in the previous chapter classical economists thought that supply of money only determines the price level and nominal variables and has no effect on the real variables of the economy such as level of real income (output) and employment. However, in Keynes's theory money plays an important role in determination of real income and employment. In fact *Keynes brought about integration between money market and goods market.* Keynes was able to do so because he explained that rate of interest is determined by demand for money (which he called liquidity preference) and supply of money, that is, through market equilibrium, while classical economists thought that rate interest was determined by saving and investment, that is, through capital market equilibrium. It is the rate of interest which is crucial channel through which money market is linked with goods market Changes in money supply by monetary policy can bring about changes is rate of interest which determines investment. And, according to Keynes, it is investment which plays a crucial real in determining level of real income and employment. For example, increase in the supply of money will lower the rate of interest. Since investment depends on the rate of interest and marginal efficiency of capital, at the lower rate of interest more investment will be undertaken. The higher investment will lead to the greater level of real national income and employment. In fact, Keynesian analysis brings out that monetary policy can play significant role in influencing the real variables and controlling business cycles.

However, Keynes pointed out that *effect of increase in money supply depends on interest elasticity of demand for money (i.e. liquidity preference curve) and interest sensitivity of investment demand.* The greater the elasticity of demand for money, and lower the elasticity of investment demand curve, the smaller will be the effect of changes in money supply on national income and employment. Though during the period of great depression (1929 – 33), Keynes pointed out that demand for money was highly elastic and therefore he argued that effect of monetary policy would not be enough to lift the economy out of depression and therefore he emphasised that along with monetary policy expansionary fiscal policy should be adopted to raise aggregate demand and thereby to increase the levels of real income and employment. However, according to him, in *normal times*, monetary policy is quite effective in determining real income and employment.

Empirical evidence after Keynes has revealed that even during recessions demand for money is not absolutely interest-elastic and also investment demand is fairly interest-elastic. Therefore, the modern Keynesian economists emphasise the roles of both monetary and fiscal policies to achieve economic stability.

Keynes's Complete Macroeconomic Model

In Fig. 7A.1 we have graphically depicted Keynes's complete macroeconomic model that shows how Keynes integrates money market and real goods market. In Panel (c) in Fig. 7A.1 money market equilibrium is shown. Given the money supply equal to M_0 money supply curve MS_0 intersects money demand curve *LP* at rate of interest r_0. It will be seen from panel (*d*) that at rate of interest r_0, investment is I_0. Then in panel (*b*) with the consumption function curve C and investment equal to I_0, aggregate demand curve is $C + I_0$ which intersects the 45° income line *OZ* at point *E* and determines level of real national income equal to Y_0. Panel (*a*) of the figure shows that Y_0 level of national income generates N_0 level of labour employment.

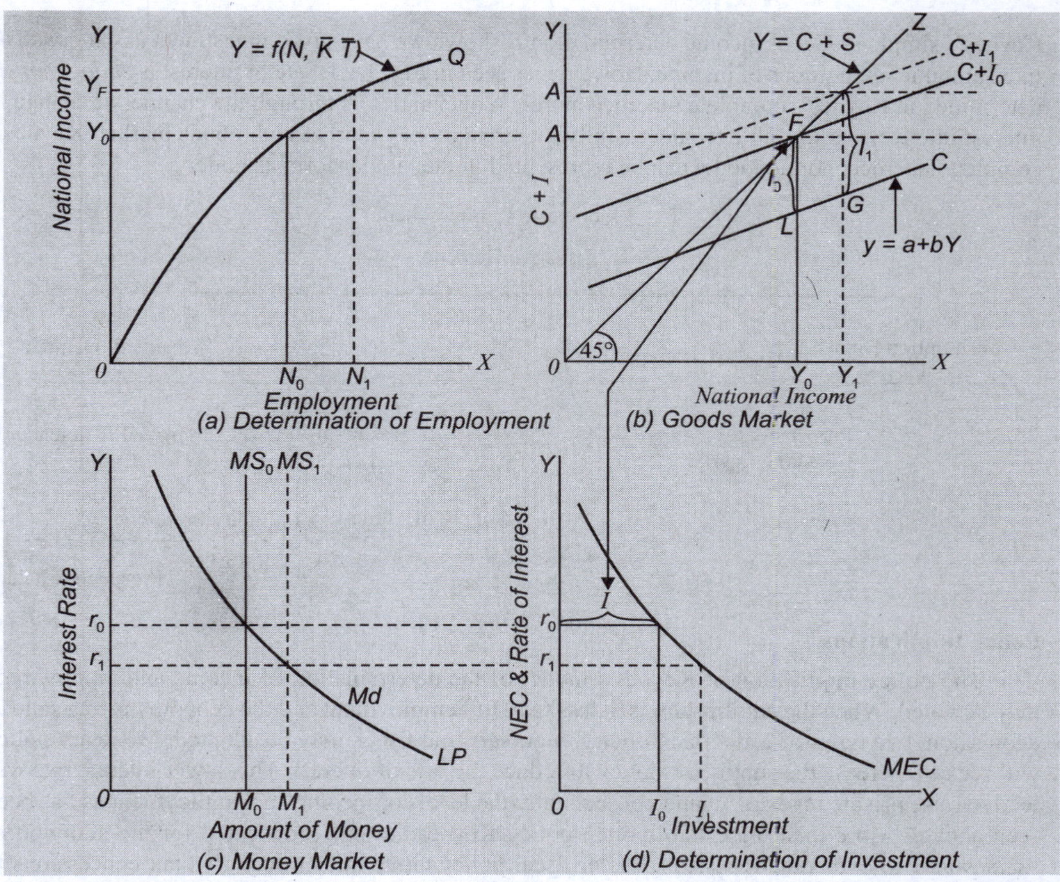

Fig. 7A.1. *The Keynes's Complete Macroeconomic Model : Integrating Money Market with Goods Market*

Now suppose that there is increase in money supply from M_0 to M_1 which causes shifts in money supply curve from MS_0 to MS_1. As a result, rate of interest falls from r_0 to r_1 Panal (*d*) Fig. 7A.1 shows that at a lower interest rate r_1 investment increase from I_0 to I_1. With this increase in investment (ΔI), aggregate demand curve shifts above to the position $C + I_1$. With this increase in aggregate demand, level of real national income increases from Y_0 to Y_1. Corresponding to this increase in real national income the level of labour employment in Panel (*a*) rises from ON_0 to ON_1.

It is evident from above that Keynes succeeded in integrating money market with goods market and with this he showed that money supply plays an important role in determining real variables such as real investment (*i.e.* addition to the stock of capital), real national output and employment.

It follows from above that liquidity preference, money supply, rate of interest, consumption function and investment are crucial elements in Keynes's model which determine level of income and employment. Figure 7A.1 also shows how changes in rate of interest through their effect on investment shifts aggregate expenditure (aggregate demand) curve and thereby affect level of income and employment. For example, if money supply is increased from M_0 to M_1, it will be seen from Panel (*c*) that rate of interest falls from r_0 to r_1. In Panel (*d*) at lower rate interest r_1, investment .increases to I_1, Now, it will be seen Panel from (*b*) that with higher investment I_1 aggregate expenditure curve shifts upward to $C + I_1$ (dotted). With this new expenditure curve ($C + I_1$) equilibrium level of national income increase to Y_1 which causes labour employment to rise from N_0 to N_1. The increase in money supply has led to the increase in real income and employment. In Chapter 7 in Fig. 7.5 where

Keynes's simple model of income determination is shown we have taken investment as *exogenously* fixed amount autonomous of income. However, as seen in Fig. 7A.1, rate of interest is *endogenously* determined in Keynes's complete macroeconomic model and it is through the channel of change in interest rate Keynes was able to successfully integrate money market with goods market Keynes's complete macroeconomic model can be represented in the tabular form as under :

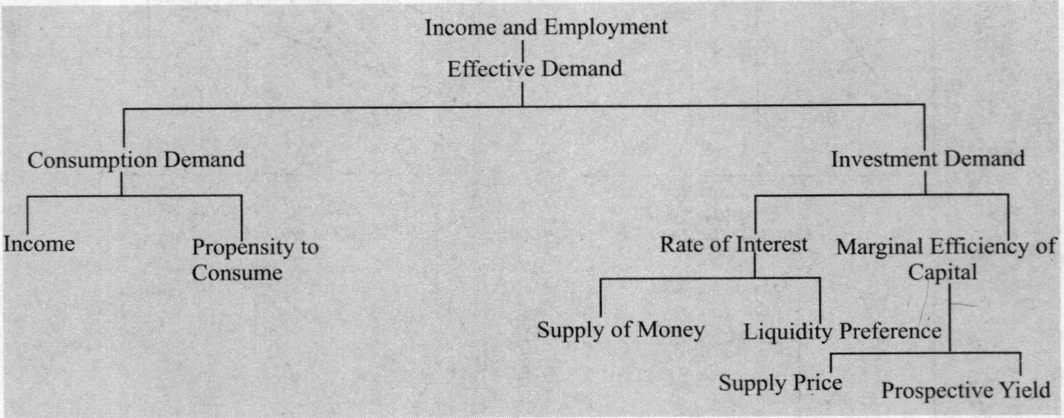

Policy Implications

The policy implication of Keynes's model of the determination of income and employment may be noted. When the equilibrium is at less than full employment and the economy is in a state of depression, two types of economic policies, monetary and fiscal, may be adopted. Monetary policy will seek to increase the supply of money to reduce the rate of interest. This lower interest rate will tend to raise private investment and consequently the levels of income and employment as has been seen above. More than the cheap money policy Keynes strongly advocated for the adoption of *fiscal policy* to overcome recession. Under fiscal policy Government may give tax concessions to the private sector so that their profit may rise resulting in the upward shift in the marginal efficiency of capital (MEC) curve. This will raise the amount of private investment and will help in raising national income and employment. Besides, Keynes emphasized that under fiscal policy Government may itself increase its expenditure on Public Works which will increase income and employment not only directly but also indirectly through the working of multiplier.

EXERCISES

1. Explain how Keynes links money market with goods market. What are its policy implications ?
2. Show how changes in interest rate affect aggregate demand and level of income and employment. Does the decrease in rate of interest by the Central Bank of a country work effectively to overcome recession in an economy ?
3. In Keynes's macroeconomic model money is not neutral and affects the magnitudes of real

CHAPTER 8

Determination of National Income : Three Sector And Four Sector Models

Introduction

We carry our analysis of determination of national income further in this chapter. Having explained the Keynesian two sector model of determination of national income in the previous chapter, we will explain in this chapter the determination of national income in the three sector and four sector models. The three sector model incorporates the role of government with its expenditure and taxation in the determination of national income. In the a four sector model we add the foreign trade in our analysis of determination of national income and discuss how exports and imports affect national income of a country.

DETERMINATION OF NATIONAL INCOME : THREE SECTOR MODEL

Government Expenditure and National Income

In our analysis of two sector model we have explained how the equilibrium level of national income is determined by the consumption function and autonomous investment demand. In our analysis we did not take into account the role of Government expenditure in the determination of national income. However, in all economies today including the free-market capitalist economies such as those of U.S.A., Britain, Japan, the Government expenditure on goods and services plays an important role in the determination of national income and therefore it should also be included in the analysis of income determination. It is important to note here that the magnitude of Government expenditure on such things as highways, public parks, education, health services is governed by the consideration of promoting social welfare, employment and growth in the economy and does not depend on the level of income of the economy. Therefore, in the simple Keynesian model of income determination, the Government expenditure is treated as *autonomous expenditure*. We further assume for the moment that Government spends on goods and services but imposes no taxes. We denote Government expenditure by G. Thus in the three sector economy when we take into account the income generating effects of Government expenditure, we get the following equation for the equilibrium level of national income.

$$Y = C + I + G$$

where Y is national income or output and $C + I + G$ represents the level of aggregate demand including Government expenditure, G.

Since consumption function $C = a + bY$ where b stands for marginal propensity to consume and a for autonomous consumption expenditure, we can rewrite the equilibrium level of national income as under :

$$\begin{aligned} Y &= a + bY + I + G \\ Y - bY &= a + I + G \\ Y(1-b) &= a + I + G \\ &\bar{K}\,(a + I + G) \end{aligned}$$

Thus it is clear that the *equilibrium level of income (when impact of Government expenditure is also considered) is equal to the sum of three types of fixed autonomous expenditure*, namely, autonomous consumption, autonomous investment and Government expenditure ($a + I + G$) multiplied by mous consumption, autonomous investment and Government expenditure $(a + I + G)$ multiplied by the value of the multiplier $[1/(1-b)]$.

Graphic Illustration

The impact of Government expenditure on goods and services on the equilibrium level of national income is illustrated in Fig. 8.1. C is the consumption function curve to which we have added the autonomous investment equal to I. On top of the consumption demand C and investment demand I, we have added the Government expenditure on goods and services (G) to get the aggregate expenditure (or aggregate demand) curve $C + I + G$. With this, the equilibrium national income OY_2 is determined at the level at which the aggregate expenditure curve $(C + I + G)$ interests the 45° line, that is, aggregate expenditure $(C + I + G)$ equals aggregate supply of output. The reason for the determination of equilibrium level of income at OY_2 when Government expenditure is included in the aggregate expenditure curve is the same as stated earlier. It will be observed from Fig. 8.1 that at a level of national income less than OY_2 aggregate expenditure $C + I + G$ exceeds aggregate supply. This implies unintended decline in the inventories of goods with the firms which will induce them to expand the level of aggregate output to the level OY_2. On the contrary, at the level of national income greater than OY_2, the aggregate expenditure is less than aggregate supply of output. This deficiency of demand for goods will cause unintended accumulation of inventories. The firms would respond to this by cutting back production of goods which will lead to the reduction of national income to OY_2.

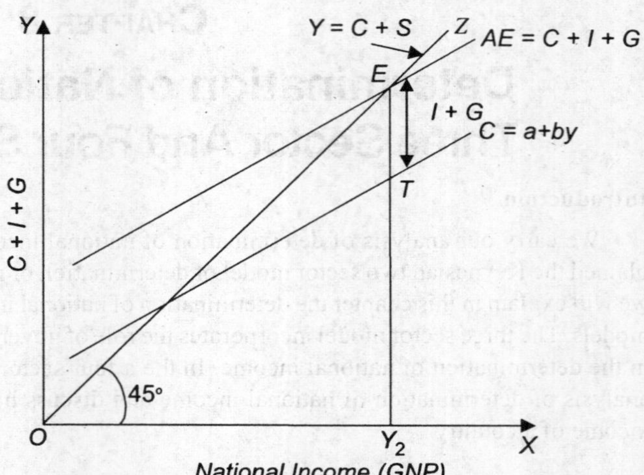

Fig. 8.1. *Government Expenditure and National Income*

It is important to note that in the presence of Government expenditure, national income is determined at the level at which the saving gap is equal to the sum of private investment and Government expenditure $(I + G)$. It will be seen from Fig. 8.1 that at OY_2 equilibrium level of national income (GNP), the saving gap is TE which is equal investment and government expenditure. It may be further noted that just as investment expenditure has a multiplier effect on increase in income Government expenditure too has a multiplier effect.

Government Expenditure, Budget Deficit and Capital Market

We have explained above how the government expenditure affects the product market by bringing about increase in aggregate demand. Now, an important question is how the Government expenditure is financed. Imposition of taxes is an important way of financing Government expenditure. But taxes reduce aggregate demand in the product market by lowering disposable income of the community and thereby causing a decline in its consumption expenditure. Therefore, if Government expenditure equals tax revenue collected $(G = T)$, then Government has a balanced budget and much of the expansionary effect of government expenditure is offset by taxes levied. If Government increases its expenditure without raising taxes, (*i.e.* $G > T$), then it has a *budget deficit* which has a large expansionary effect on the product market and, as seen above, leads to increase in national income (*GDP*). This deficit budget is often financed by borrowing from the public. But borrowing by the Government to finance its deficit affects the capital market. This is because borrowing by the Government will compete with private investors for the savings of the public. As a result of borrowing by the Government from the market, less saving is available for private investment. When the

Government runs a deficit, private saving has two uses (1) to finance private investment and (2) to finance Government budget deficit which is met by borrowing from the public. Equilibrium in the capital market occurs when private saving is equal to private investment plus budget deficit, $G-T$, (i.e. Government borrowing).

Thus, in equilibrium in the capital market

$$S_p = I + (G - T)$$

where *Sp* stands for private saving, *I* for private investment, and $(G - T)$ stands for budget deficit (*i.e.* Government borrowing). How budget deficit or Government borrowing reduces or crowds out private investment is illustrated through Figure 8.2 where to begin with vertical saving curve S_0 intersects the downward-sloping investment curve *II* at point E_0 and determines real interest rate r_0 at which private investment equal to I_0 takes place. Now, as a result of Government borrowing to finance its budget deficit $(G - T)$ saving available for private investment falls and the national saving curve shifts to the left[1] to the new position S_1. Note that when Government borrows to finance budget deficit, Government is said to dissave and therefore in this case Government or public saving is negative $(G-T=-S_g)$. Note further that national saving = private saving and Government saving $(S=S_p+S_g)$. That is why when Government borrows (*i.e.* dissave), national saving curve shifts to the left to S_1. The capital market is now in equilibrium at point E_1 and rate of interest rises to r_1. At this higher interest rate r_1, private investment falls to I_1. Thus, borrowing by the Government to finance its budget deficit has led to crowding out of private investment. As mentional above, a part of private saving is used to finance private investment and a part to finance budget deficit of the Government.

It is worth noting that when Government expenditure is fully matched by increase in taxes (*i.e.* $G = T$) we have a balanced budget but it will still have a expansionary effect on national income, though, as shall be explained below, the multiplier effect of a balanced budget is equal to one. However, since in case of balanced budget increase in Government expenditure is matched by increase in taxes which reduces disposable income $Y_d = Y - T$. And reduction in disposable income (Y_d) leads to decrease in both consumption and saving $(Y_d = C + S)$. This decrease in private saving will cause rate of interest to rise and thereby crowds out private investment.

Further, when the Government has a *budget surplus* (i.e. $T > G$), it has a *positive saving* which will lead to the increase in national saving and make more funds available for private sector to borrow. This will cause real rate of interest to fall. As a result, higher private investment will occur in case of surplus budget.

It is worth noting that *in our above analysis Government expenditure has been treated as consumption expenditure on goods and services purchased to satisfy collective wants*. However, this is strictly true in case of a purely free-market economy such as that of the US where the Government is not a major investor. But in case of India's mixed economy the Government is an important investor and a good part of its borrowing is used for investment purposes, especially for investment in infrastructure projects such as power, transport, highways, roads, ports etc. Such Government borrowing for investment purposes cannot be

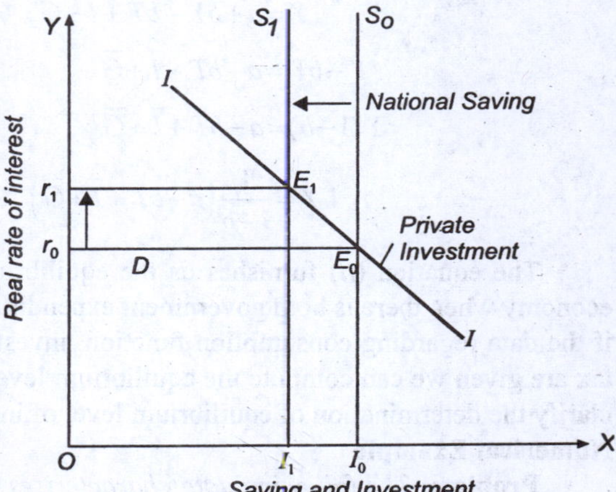

Fig. 8.2. *Effect of Budget Deficit and Government Borrowing on Capital Market*

1. Note that budget deficit and borrowing by the Government is also viewed as Government dissaving

considered as consumption expenditure or *dissaving*. Therefore, it has a large expansionary effect on national income with a usual multiplier effect. Viewed as such Government borrowing for investment, especially for infrastructure projects in developing countries, may *crowd in* private investment rather than *crowding it out*. This is so because lack of adequate infrastructure hinders private investment.

DETERMINATION OF NATIONAL INCOME WITH GOVERNMENT EXPENDITURE AND A LUMP SUM TAX

Now in a three sector model we analyse the impact of Government expenditure when to finance this expenditure the government levies a lump sum tax. Note that a lump sum tax does not vary with income. In this case if government expenditure equals revenue from lump-sum tax, its budget will be in *balance*. On the other hand, if government expenditure exceeds tax revenue, there will be a *deficit budget*. Further, if tax revenue is more than its expenditure, government will have a *surplus budget*. We are here concerned with the impact of government expenditure and taxation on the determination of national income.

Let us assume the government follows a balanced budget policy in which case government expenditure equals tax revenue from lump sum tax. Let us assume that there are no *transfer payments* made by the government. Three sector model with the above specifications can be developed as follows :

$$Y = AD = C + \overline{I} + \overline{G}$$

or
$$Y = C + \overline{I} + \overline{G} \qquad ...(i)$$

Now, consumption function can be stated as :

$$C = a + bY_d$$

Where a is constant autonomous consumption expenditure, Y_d is disposable income. In this three sector model with lump sum tax and no transfer payments, consumption function can be written as

$$C = a + b\,(Y - T)$$

where T = lump sum tax

or
$$C = a + bY - bT$$

Substituting the value of C in income equation (*i*) we have

$$Y = a + bY - bT + \overline{I} + \overline{G}$$

$$Y - bY = a - bT - \overline{I} + \overline{G}$$

$$Y(1-b) = a - bT + \overline{I} + \overline{G}$$

$$Y = \frac{1}{1-b}\left(a - bT + \overline{I} + \overline{G}\right) \qquad ...(ii)$$

The equation (*ii*) furnishes us the equilibrium level of national income in the three sector economy when there is both government expenditure and lump sum tax. Therefore, for an economy if the data regarding consumption function, investment, Government expenditure and lump sump tax are given we can compute the equilibrium level of national income. A numerical example will clarify the determination of equilibrium level of income in this case.

Numerical Example

Problem. *The following data characterises the macroeconomic conditions of a hypothetical economy*

$$C = 50 + 0.8\,Y_d$$
$$I = 100$$
$$G = T = 75$$

where C, I, and Y_d are consumption, investment and disposable income respectively. Calculate equilibrium income of the economy. What is the value of multiplier?

Solution: Note that since $G = T$, budget of the Government is balanced.

$$Y = C + I + G$$

$$C = a + bY_d = a + b(Y - T)$$

Substituting the values of C, I and G we have :

$$Y = 50 + 0.8\,(Y - 75) + 100 + 75$$

$$= 50 + 0.8Y - 60 + 100 + 75$$

$$Y = 165 + 0.8Y$$

$$Y - 0.8Y = 165$$

$$Y(1 - 0.8) = 165$$

$$0.2\,Y = 165$$

$$Y = 165 \times \frac{10}{2} = 825$$

Thus, equilibrium level of income is 825.

Since in the present problem $G = T$, budget is a balanced one

Value of balanced budget multiplier $= \dfrac{1}{1-b} + \dfrac{-b}{1-b}$

where b represents marginal propensity to consume. In the given consumption function,

$$b = 0.8$$

∴ Value of balanced budget multiplier $= \dfrac{1}{1-0.8} + \dfrac{-0.8}{1-0.8} = \dfrac{1}{0.2} - \dfrac{0.8}{0.2}$

$$= 5 - 4 = 1$$

DETERMINATION OF NATIONAL INCOME IN THE THREE SECTOR ECONOMY WITH LUMP SUM TAX AND TRANSFER PAYMENTS

We have explained above the determination of national income in the three sector economy when government expenditure is financed by imposition of lump sum tax. We now extend our model to include transfer payments and see how they affect determination of national income. *Transfer payments are payments to the people by the government for which it receives no service or goods in return from them.* Transfer payments are made by the government to promote social welfare. Unemployment allowance, poverty relief grants, social security contributions, old age pension are some important examples of transfer payments. Transfer payments are antithesis of tax. Whereas tax reduces disposable income of the people, transfer payments increase their disposable income.

Transfer payments may be autonomous of tax or they may be financed by imposition of a lump sum tax. If, like the government expenditure on goods and services, transfer payments are financed through tax, then transfer payments become a part of government expenditure (G) and imposition of additional tax to finance transfer payments become a part of total lump sum tax (T) which reduces disposable income. Therefore, in this case when transfer payments are financed through additional taxes, the analysis of income determination is similar to the model of income determination with government expenditure and lump sum tax explained above. However, the inclusion of transfer payments which are of autonomous type makes the analysis of income determination somewhat different. We describe it below.

Since transfer payments increase the disposable income of the people, they will increase their consumption expenditure depending on their propensity to consume. Thus

$$C = a + bY_d$$

$$Y_d = Y - T + TR$$

where T is lump sum tax and TR is transfer payments

$$C=a+b(Y-T+TR)$$

$$\therefore \quad Y=C+I+G$$

$$=a+b(Y-T+TR)+I+G$$

$$Y=a+bY-bT+bTR+I+G$$

$$Y-bY=a-bT+bTR+I+G$$

$$Y(1-b)=a-bT+bTR+I+G$$

$$Y=\frac{1}{1-b}(a-bT+bTR+I+G) \qquad \text{... (ii)}$$

Government Expenditure Multiplier and Transfer Payments Multiplier

It is important to note that the multiplier of government expenditure on goods and services is different from transfer payments multiplier. This is because whereas Government expenditure on goods and services raises aggregate demand directly by its full amount, the transfer payments raises consumption demand by bTR, that is, *less than the full amount* depending on the marginal propensity to consume. Let us illustrate it by using income equation (*ii*). Suppose government expenditure increases by ΔG. Then, increased income is

$$Y+\Delta Y=\frac{1}{1-b}(a-bT+bTR+I+G+\Delta G) \qquad \text{...(iii)}$$

Subtracting equation (*ii*) from equation (*iii*) we have

$$\Delta Y=\frac{1}{1-b}(\Delta G)$$

or

$$\frac{\Delta Y}{\Delta G}=\frac{1}{1-b}$$

Thus, Government expenditure multiplier, $\frac{\Delta Y}{\Delta G}=\frac{1}{1-b}$.

where b is marginal propensity to consume.

If instead of increasing government expenditure on goods and services, government increases transfer payments by ΔTR we will get the following income equation

$$Y+\Delta Y=\frac{1}{1-b}(a-bT+bTR+b\Delta TR+I+G) \qquad \text{... (iv)}$$

Subtracting equation (*ii*) from equation (*iv*) we have

$$\Delta Y=\frac{1}{1-b}b\Delta TR$$

or

$$\frac{\Delta Y}{\Delta TR}=\frac{b}{1-b}$$

Thus, transfer payments multiplier, $\frac{\Delta Y}{\Delta TR}=\frac{b}{1-b}$

Taking the difference between the Government expenditure multiplier and transfer payments multiplier we have

$$\frac{1}{1-b}-\frac{b}{1-b}=\frac{1-b}{1-b}=1$$

Numerical Example

Problem. *Suppose the structural model of an economy is given below :*

$$C = 100 + 0.75 Y_d$$
$$I = 200$$
$$G = T = 100$$
$$TR = 50$$

where G is government expenditure on goods and services, T is lump sum tax and TR are transfer payments

(1) *Find the equilibrium level of income*

(2) *Calculate Government expenditure multiplier and transfer payments multiplier. What is the difference between the two ?*

(3) *If full-employment level of income is 1600 crores, how much government expenditure be increased to attain full employment ?*

Solution :

$$Y = C + I + G$$
$$= a + bY_d + I + G$$

Disposable income $Y_d = Y - T + TR$

Therefore, $Y = a + b(Y - T + TR) + I + G$

Substituting the values of various parameters and variables we have

$$Y = 100 + 0.75\,(\,Y - 100 + 50) + 200 + 100$$
$$= 100 + 0.75Y - 75 + 37.5 + 200 + 100$$
$$Y - 0.75Y = 100 - 75 + 37.5 + 200 + 100$$
$$Y(1 - 0.75) = 362.5$$
$$0.25\,Y = 362.5$$
$$Y = 362.5 \times \frac{100}{25} = 1450$$

Thus, equilibrium income is 1450 crores

(2) Government expenditure multiplier (G_m) $= \dfrac{1}{1-b} = \dfrac{1}{1-0.75} = \dfrac{1}{0.25}$

$$= 4$$

Transfer payments multiplier (TR_m) $= \dfrac{b}{1-b} = \dfrac{0.75}{1-0.75} = \dfrac{0.75}{0.25}$

$$= 3$$

The difference between G_m and TR_m is $4 - 3 = 1$

(3) The equilibrium income of ₹ 1450 crore, falls short of full-employment income of 1600 crores by 1600 – 1450 = 150 crore. Increase in government expenditure (ΔG) required to achieve full-employment income is given by

$$\Delta Y = G_m \times \Delta G$$

or $\Delta G = \dfrac{\Delta Y}{G_m}$ (G_m is government expenditure multiplier)

$$= \frac{150}{4} = 37.5 \text{ crores}$$

THREE SECTOR MODEL FURTHER EXTENDED

In our above analysis of determination of equilibrium national income in a three sector economy we have assumed autonomous constant investment, apart from consumption function of households and Government expenditure on goods and services and transfer payments. In the further extension of the model we also include *proportional income tax*, that is, a tax levied as a proportion of income. Proportional income tax is therefore expressed as tY where t is the rate or proportion of income which is payable as a tax. In a real economy proportional income tax may be imposed along with any lump sum tax. Thus, the total tax (T) can be expressed as

$$T = \overline{T} + tY$$

where $\overline{T}$ = constant autonomous lump-sum tax

t = rate or proportion of income tax

Y = Income

Equilibrium income, $Y = C + I + G$ ...(*i*)

where $C = a + bY_d$

$$= a + b(Y - \overline{T} - tY + TR)$$

Substituting the consumption function in equation (*i*) for equilibrium income we have

$$Y = a + b(Y - \overline{T} - tY + TR) + I + G$$

$$= a + bY - b\overline{T} - btY + bTR + I + G$$

$$Y - bY + btY = a - b\overline{T} + bTR + I + G$$

$$Y(1 - b + bt) = a - b\overline{T} + bTR + I + G$$

$$Y = \frac{1}{1 - b + bt}\left(a - b\overline{T} + bTR + I + G\right) \quad ...(ii)$$

Note that $\frac{1}{1 - b + bt}$ represents tax multiplier when tax is a proportion of income.

Tax multiplier can also be expressed as $\frac{1}{1 - b(1 - t)}$.

Numerical Problem. *For a closed economy, the following* data is given

Consumption,	C	=	$50 + 0.8Y_d$
Investment,	I	=	70
Government expenditure,	G	=	200
Transfer payments,	TR	=	100
Rate of Income Tax,	t	=	0.2

(a) *Write the reduced form of equation for equilibrium income*

(b) *Find out equilibrium income*

(c) *What is the value of tax multiplier*

Solution :

(a) Reduced form of the equation for equilibrium income is

$$Y = \frac{1}{1 - b + bt}(a + bTR + I + G)$$

(b) Substituting the values of parameters in the above equation for equilibrium income we have

$$Y = \frac{1}{1 - 0.8 + 0.8 \times 0.2}(50 + 0.8 \times 100 + 70 + 200)$$

$$= \frac{1}{1 - 0.64}(50 + 80 + 70 + 200)$$

$$= \frac{1}{0.36}(400)$$

$$=400\times\frac{100}{36}=1111$$

Thus, the equilibrium income is 1111

$$\text{Tax multiplier} = \frac{1}{\quad}=\frac{1}{.8+0.8\times0.2}$$

$$=\frac{1}{1-0.64}=\frac{1}{0.36}$$

$$=\frac{100}{36}=2.77$$

THE LUMPSUM TAX MULTIPLIER

We have explained the multiplier effect of change in Government expenditure on goods and services and of change in transfer payments (*TR*) on the equilibrium level of income. We will now explain the multiplier effect of *change in tax*. Reduction in taxes has often been used by the policy makers to increase aggregate demand of the economy and thereby to lift the economy out of recession. For example, in 1964 John F Kennedy, the president of the United States made a substantial cut in personal and corporate taxes to stimulate expenditure on consumption and investment to bring about expansion in income and employment in the economy. This policy of cut in taxes to revive the American economy had a grand success. There was a large growth in Gross Domestic Product (GDP) of the United States in 1964 and 1965. There was a substantial fall in unemployment as a result of the policy of cut in taxes.

Recently when George Bush was elected president in 2001 the American economy found itself in the grip of recession. He also made a drastic cut in income tax to stimulate aggregate demand so as to overcome recession. Again this policy of tax cut was greatly successful and the American economy recovered in 2003-04.

The change in lump sum income tax and proportional income tax affect equilibrium income differently, but both have a multiplier effect on equilibrium income. We have already explained the effect of lump-sum income tax and proportional income tax on the equilibrium level of income. We are now concerned with analysing the effect of change in lump sum tax and proportional income tax. For the sake of simplicity and convenience we explain the multiplier effect of lump sum income tax. Note that while a cut in tax will have a positive effect on equilibrium income, increase in tax will reduce equilibrium income.

Suppose the government *increases lump-sum income tax* by ΔT we are interested to know its multiplier effect on income. As found above, in the three sector economy with Government expenditure and lump-sum tax :

$$Y=\frac{1}{1-b}(a-bT+I+G) \qquad \text{... (1)}$$

where T is lump sum income tax. Now, a decrease in lump-sum income tax by ΔT will cause a change in income (that is, ΔY). Increase in tax will reduce the disposable income and therefore the consumption demand. As a result of increase in tax, consumption demand will decrease by the change in tax times the marginal propensity consume, that is, $\Delta Y = b\Delta T$. Let us incorporate change in the tax (ΔT) in the three sector equation (1) for equilibrium income and see how much change in income (ΔY) it brings about. Thus

$$Y+\Delta Y=\frac{1}{1-b}[a-b(T+\Delta T)+I+G]$$

$$Y+\Delta Y=\frac{1}{1-b}(a-bT-b\Delta T+I+G) \qquad \text{... (2)}$$

Now subtracting equation (1) from equation (2) we have

$$\Delta Y = \frac{1}{1-b}(-b\,\Delta T)$$

Dividing both sides by ΔT we have

$$\frac{\Delta Y}{\Delta T} = \frac{-b}{1-b} \qquad ...(3)$$

$\frac{\Delta Y}{\Delta T}$ is the expression for tax multiplier. It will be seen that increase in tax by ΔT will *reduce* equilibrium income by a multiple. For example, if marginal propensity to consume is 0.75, then the tax multiplier is

$$\frac{\Delta Y}{\Delta T} = \frac{-b}{1-b} = \frac{-0.75}{1-0.75} = \frac{-0.75}{0.25} = -3$$

This means that increase in tax by Re. 1 will cause a decline in equilibrium income by 3.

Note that we can similarly prove that a *cut in tax* will *raise* the equilibrium income through the tax multiplier. Therefore, in case of *reduction in lump sum income tax*, the tax multiplier is

$$\frac{\Delta Y}{\Delta T} = \frac{b}{1-b}$$

With 0.75 as marginal propensity to consume, tax multiplier of cut in tax is,

$$\frac{\Delta Y}{\Delta T} = \frac{0.75}{1-0.75} = \frac{0.75}{0.25} = 3.$$

BALANCED BUDGET MULTIPLIER

We now analyse the impact of balanced budget of the government. In case of a balanced budget, the government's expenditure is equal to its tax revenue, that is, $G = T$ and therefore when the government increases its expenditure by ΔG, then it also raises taxes to get more tax revenue (ΔT) so that $\Delta T = \Delta G$. The effect of a balanced budget on the equilibrium income is described by the *balanced budget multiplier* which is also called *balanced budget theorem*. According to this, the *balanced budget multiplier is always equal to one.* We prove it below by assuming a lump sum tax.

In order to analyse the effect of a balanced budget multiplier, we reproduce below the equation for equilibrium income for a three sector economy.

$$Y = \frac{1}{1-b}(a - b\overline{T} + I + G) \qquad ...(1)$$

where $\overline{T}$ is constant lump sum tax levied by the government.

Let us incorporate increase in government expenditure (ΔG) fully financed by additional lump sum tax (ΔT), that is, $\Delta G = \Delta T$. By doing so we get

$$Y + \Delta Y = \frac{1}{1-b}\left[a - b(\overline{T} + \Delta T) + I + G + \Delta G\right] \qquad ...(2)$$

Subtracting equation (1) from equation (2) we have

$$\Delta Y = \frac{1}{1-b}(-b\Delta T + \Delta G)$$

Since in a balanced budget, $\Delta T = \Delta G$

$$\Delta Y = \frac{1}{1-b}(-b\Delta G + \Delta G)$$

$$\Delta Y(1-b)=\Delta G(1-b)$$

or $$\Delta Y=\Delta G \quad ...(3)$$

Dividing both sides of the above equation by ΔG we have

$$\frac{\Delta Y}{\Delta G}=\frac{\Delta G}{\Delta G}=1$$

Thus, balanced budget multiplier is equal to one. This implies that when $\Delta G=\Delta T$ and budget is therefore balanced, national income increases by the same amount as the increase in government expenditure.

Alternative Proof

That the balanced budget multiplier is equal to one can be proved in an alternative way. Balance budget multiplier is the sum of government expenditure multiplier and lump sum tax multiplier.

Government expenditure multiplier $(G_m)=\frac{1}{1-b}$

Lump-sum tax multiplier $(T_m)=\frac{-b}{1-b}$

Balanced budget multiplier $=G_m+T_m$

$$=\frac{1}{1-b}+\frac{-b}{1-b}$$

$$=\frac{1-b}{1-b}=1$$

Thus, the balanced budget multiplier is equal to one.

NUMERICAL EXAMPLES

Problem. ***Suppose we have an economy characterised by the following functions :***

$$C=100+0.8\,Y_d$$
$$\bar{I}=100$$
$$\bar{G}=100$$
$$\bar{T}=100$$

(Figures are in crores)

(a) Find the equilibrium level of income.

(b) How much increase in income will take place if government expenditure on goods and services increases by ₹ 60 crores.

(c) Find the tax multiplier and balanced budget multiplier

(d) Find the equilibrium level of national income if $T=\bar{T}+tY=100+0.25Y$

Solution :

(*a*) Equilibrium $Y=C+\bar{I}+\bar{G}$

$$Y=a+bY_d+\bar{I}+\bar{G}$$

Therefore, $$Y=a+b(Y-\bar{T})+\bar{I}+\bar{G}$$

Substituting the values of *a*, *b*, $\bar{T}$, $\bar{I}$ and $\bar{G}$ we have

$$Y=100+0.8\,(Y-100)+100+100$$
$$=100+0.8Y-80+100+100$$

$$Y-0.8Y=220$$

$$Y(1-0.8)=220$$

$$0.2Y = 220$$

$$Y = 220 \times \frac{10}{2} = 1100$$

(*b*) Government expenditure multiplier (G_m) = $\frac{1}{1-b} = \frac{1}{1-0.8} = 5$

Increase in national income if government expenditure increases by 60 crores.

$$\Delta Y = G_m . \Delta G$$

$$= 5 \times 60 = 300$$

(*c*) Tax multiplier, $T_m = \frac{-b}{1-b} = \frac{-0.8}{1-0.8} = \frac{-0.8}{0.2}$

$$= -4$$

Balanced Budget Multiplier = $G_m + T_m$

$$= 5 + (-4)$$

$$= 1$$

(*d*) The equilibrium level of national income when $T = 100 + 0.25Y$

$$Y = \frac{1}{1-b+bt}\left(a - b\overline{T} + \overline{I} + \overline{G}\right)$$

$$= \frac{1}{1-0.8+0.2}(100 - 0.80 \times 100 + 100 + 100)$$

$$= \frac{1}{1-0.6}(100 - 80 + 100 + 100)$$

$$= \frac{1}{0.4}(220)$$

$$= 2.5\ (220) = 550$$

DETERMINATION OF NATIONAL INCOME IN AN OPEN ECONOMY: FOUR SECTOR MODEL

In modern times economies of different countries are integrated with each other though some are more integrated than others. An open economy is one which has not only trade relations with other countries but has financial capital flows between it and other economies of the world. It is because of such openness and integration of the economies of the world that recent financial crisis that occurred in the United States in 2007 has significantly affected other economies (including that of India) causing global meltdown through its affect on trade and capital flows. Under capital flows, funds flow from one country to another. Foreign trade of goods and services affect product market and influences the determination of national income of a country as net exports (*i.e.* exports–imports) is a part of aggregate demand for output produced by an economy. On the other hand, capital flows in an open economy provide funds for financing domestic investment or for financing government budget deficits or for financing current account deficit. If the demand for funds in an economy exceeds domestic national saving, the private sector and Government of an open economy can get them from abroad either through borrowing or direct or portfolio investment by foreign investors. We start with the analysis of impact of inclusion of foreign trade on the determination of national income of a country.

Foreign Trade and National Income in an Open Economy

In the four sector model of determination of national income, we add the foreign trade sector to the three sectors, namely, households, firms, and Government. Foreign trade, that is, volume of exports and imports of a country also affects the level of national income of a country. We now extend the Keynesian model of determination of national income by including the effect of exports and imports of a country on the generation of income. For example, the exports of India represent the foreign demand and generates income for the Indian people. On the other hand, imports represent the demand for foreign goods by the Indians and generate incomes for the people of other countries. Therefore, imports tend to reduce the domestic aggregate expenditure. It therefore follows that national income will depend on the net exports, that is, exports minus imports $(X-M)$ where X stands for exports and M for imports. The exports and imports of a country depend to a great extent on the level of economic activity (that is, the level of output and income of the country). Thus, when the growth of industrial output in India is rapid, it will generate greater demand for imported materials. On the other hand, the higher industrial growth would also cause our exports to rise provided there is demand for our goods abroad. However, in the Keynesian model of income determination, exports and imports are considered as autonomous, that is, independent of income, being determined outside the model. Further, as mentioned above, the increase or decrease in aggregate expenditure or demand due to exports and imports depends on the net exports, that is, $X-M$ which we may write as NX. If the net exports are positive, there will be addition to the aggregate demand or expenditure of a country. On the other hand, if the net exports are negative, there will be decrease in aggregate expenditure.

When we include net exports (X_n) in our analysis we get the following equation for the equilibrium level of income.

$$Y = C + I + G + (X - M)$$

where $$C = a + b(Y - T)$$

$$Y = a + bY - bT + I + G + NX$$

or $$Y(1-b) = a - bT + I + G + NX$$

$$Y = \frac{1}{1-b}(a - bT + I + G + NX)$$

Thus, the equilibrium level of income is the sum of all fixed autonomous expenditures (i.e., $a - bT + I + G + X_n$) times the value of multiplier $[1/1 - b]$. It is worth noting that in the four sector model, national income is determined at the level at which saving gap between consumption and income is equal to the sum of investment, Government expenditure and net exports. (that is, $I + G + Z_n$)

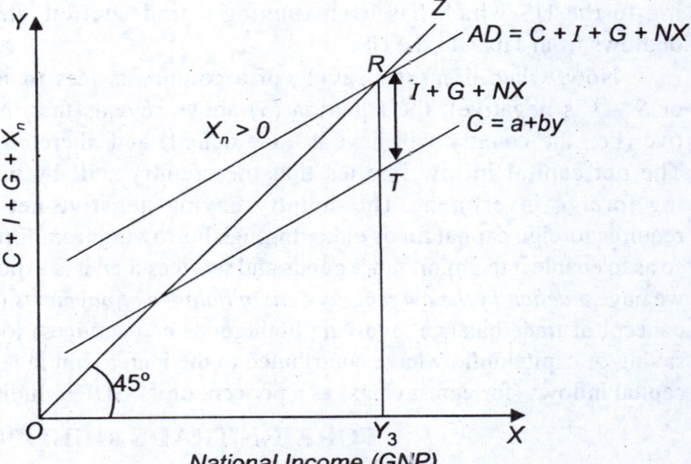

Fig. 8.3. *Determination of National Income with Foreign Trade : Four Sector Model*

Graphic Illustration. In Fig. 8.3, we have depicted the determination of national income when there are positive net exports (that is, when exports exceed imports, $X - M > 0$. To obtain the aggregate demand curve incorporating the positive net exports (NX) we add the $I + G + NX$ to the consumption function curve C to get the higher aggregate demand curve $C + I + G + NX$ which intersects the 45° line at point R and determines a level of income OY_3. If the net exports NX were negative, that is, imports exceed exports, $X - M < 0$, the aggregate demand curve incorporating net exports would lie at a lower level than $C + I + G$ curve and determine a lower level of income.

Trade Balance (Net Exports) and International Capital Flows

In an open economy as in the closed economy product markets and capital markets are closely related. To know this relationship let us consider the equilibrium level of national income in an open economy which is :

$$Y = C + I + G + (X - M) \quad \ldots \text{(i)}$$

where $X - M$ are net exports (NX)

Therefore, rearranging the above equation and writing NX for $X - M$ we have

$$Y - C - G = I + NX \quad \ldots (1)$$

Now $Y–C–G$ represents national saving[1] which we represent by S.

Writting S for national saving ($Y–C–G$) in equation (2) we have

$$S = I + NX \quad \ldots (2)$$

or

$$S - I = NX \quad \ldots (3)$$

From equation (3) it is evident that difference between domestic saving and domestic investment ($S - I$) equals net exports (NX). *Since difference between domestic saving and investment ($S - I$) represents capital flows*, equation (3) reveals that capital flows between an economy and the foreign ones are related to net exports (NX) which are also called *trade balance*. If for a country domestic saving exceeds domestic investment ($S > I$), then the country would have *positive net capital outflows* which means residents of the country would be lending or investing abroad more than the foreigners would be lending or investing in the country concerned. The equation (3) above shows that these *positive net capital outflows* imply that they will be equal to *positive net exports* (NX), that is, the country will be exporting more than it will be importing. Foreigners will need financial loans to buy that country's more goods and services than they are exporting to it. This has been the relationship with Japan and the US. Japan has a trade surplus (i.e. positive net exports) with the US and to enable the US to buy more Japanese goods than Japan is importing from it, it has been lending to the US which has been running a trade deficit, that is, there has been net capital outflows from Japan to the US.

Now, when domestic saving of a country is less than the domestic investment ($S < I$ or $S - I$ is negative), the equation (3) above reveals that the net exports (NX) will be negative (i.e., the country will have a trade deficit) and, therefore, there will be *net capital inflow*. The net capital inflow implies that the country will be borrowing from abroad or receiving foreign investment. The country having negative net exports or deficit trade balance requires foreign capital funds either through borrowing from foreigners or foreign direct investment so as to enable it to import more goods and services than it is exporting to them. For example, in India we have a *deficit in the current account of balance of payments* (which has the same meaning as the concept of trade balance involving both goods and services) for several years now so that foriegn saving or capital inflow have contributed to the increase in investment in India though the share of capital inflows (foriegn savings) as a per cent of its GDP in India is relatively small.

FOREIGN TRADE MULTIPLIER

So far in our analysis of four sector model of income determination we have assumed that both exports and imports are constant autonomous items, that is, independent of income. In our later chapters concerning the external sector we shall explain in detail what are the factors that determine exports and imports of a country. In the model of income determination while exports are regarded as constant autonomous factor *determined exogenously* (that is, $X = \overline{X}$), imports are treated as function of two variables, namely, (1) autonomous imports (*i.e.* independent of income), and (2) level of income. Thus, import function used in the model can be written as

$$M = \overline{M} + mY$$

1. Note that national saving $Y - C - G$ is the sum of private saving ($Y - T - C$) and Government saving ($T - G$). Thus $Y - T - C + T - G = Y - C - G$.

where $\overline{M}$ represents autonomous imports, mY represents imports dependent on level of income (Y) and m is marginal propensity to import. Given the marginal propensity to import (m), as income increases, mY will increase.

By incorporating the above import function we can derive the complete four sector model of income determination as follows

$$Y = C + I + G + (X - M) \quad \ldots(i)$$

where $C = a + b(Y - T)$

and $M = \overline{M} + mY$

Substituting the consumption function and import function in the income equation ... (i) we have

$$Y = a + b(Y - T) + I + G + \left[X - \left(\overline{M} + mY\right)\right]$$

$$= a + bY - bT + I + G + X - \overline{M} - mY$$

$$Y - bY + mY = a - bT + I + G + X - \overline{M}$$

$$Y(1 - b + m) = a - bT + I + G + X - \overline{M}$$

$$Y = \frac{1}{1 - b + m}(a - bT + I + G + Y - \overline{M})$$

where the term $\frac{1}{1-b+m}$ is known as ***foreign trade multiplier*** whose value is determined by marginal propensity to consume (b) and marginal propensity to import (m). Note that change in any autonomous factor of the model such as X, G, I, a, $\overline{M}$ will cause a change in national income by the value of multiplier $\frac{1}{1-b+m}$ times the change in the amount of the factor. Thus, if exports increase by ΔX. the national income will increase by

$$\Delta Y = \frac{1}{1 - b + m}.\Delta X$$

Incorporating Proportional Income Tax in the Four Sector Model

If in the above four sector model of income determination proportional income tax is incorporated, then only the term of foreign trade multiplier will change, the other terms of the model remaining the same. Thus, if income tax is of form $T = \overline{T} + tY$ where T is constant lump sum, t is the proportion of income that is taken as tax. With incorporation of proporational income tax, the value of foreign trade multiplier becomes :

$$= \frac{1}{1 - b(1 - t) + m}$$

or

$$= \frac{1}{1 - b + bt + m}$$

where t is the proportional income tax rate.

With this proportional income tax, the above equilibrium income equation can be written as

$$Y = \frac{1}{1 - b(1 - t) + m}\left(a - bT + I + G + X - \overline{M}\right)$$

NUMERICAL PROBLEMS

Problem 1. *An economy is characterised by the following equations:*

C (Consumption) = $60 + 0.9Y_d$

I (Investment)	=	10
G (Government expenditure)	=	10
T (Tax)	=	0
X (Exports)	=	20
M (Imports)	=	$10 + 0.05\,Y$

(a) *What is the equilibrium income?*
(b) *Calculate trade balance.*
(c) *What is the value of foreign trade multiplier.*

Solution : (*a*) ***National Income***

$$Y = C + I + G + NX$$
$$= (60 + 0.9\,Y_d) + 10 + 10 + 20 - (10 + 0.05Y)$$
$$= 60 + 0.9\,(Y - T) + 10 + 10 + 20 - 10 - 0.05Y$$
$$= 60 + 0.9Y - 0 + 30 - 0.05Y$$
$$Y = 90 + .85Y$$
$$Y - 0.85Y = 90$$
$$0.15Y = 90$$
$$Y = 90 \times \frac{100}{15} = 600$$

(*b*) ***Trade Balance*** $= X - M$
$$= 20 - (10 + 0.05Y)$$

Substituting the value of *Y* we have

Trade balance $= 20 - \left(10 + \frac{5}{100} \times 600\right)$
$$= 20 - 10 - 30$$
$$= -20$$

Trade balance is in deficit.

(*c*) ***Value of foreign trade multiplier*** $= \frac{1}{1 - b + m}$

Where *b* is marginal propensity to consume, and *m* is marginal propensity to import.

$$\text{Foreign trade multiplier} = \frac{1}{1 - 0.9 + 0.05}$$
$$= \frac{1}{1 - 0.85} = \frac{1}{0.15}$$
$$= \frac{100}{15} = 6.66$$

Problem 2. *Behavioural and structural equations of an economy are given below :*

$$C = 100 + b(Y - 50 - tY)$$
$$I = 50$$
$$G = 50$$
$$X = 10$$
$$M = 5 + 0.1Y$$

The marginal propensity to consume (b) is equal to 0.8 and proportional income tax rate, t = 0.25.

(*a*) *Find the equilibrium national income*
(*b*) *Find foreign trade multiplier*
(*c*) *Find equilibrium value of imports*
(*d*) *If equilibrium national income falls short of full-employment income by Rs. 50, how much government should increase its expenditure to attain full-employment.*

Solution :

(*a*) Reduced form of the equation for equilibrium income is

$$Y=\frac{1}{1-b(1-t)+m}(a-bT+I+G+X-\bar{M})$$

Substituting the values of the variables and parameters we have

$$Y=\frac{1}{1-0.8(1-0.25)+0.1}(100-50\times0.8+50+50+10-5)$$

$$Y=\frac{1}{1-0.8+0.2+0.1}(100-40+50+50+10-5)$$

$$=\frac{1}{0.5}(165)$$

$$=2\ (165)=330$$

(*b*) Foreign trade multiplier

$$=\frac{1}{1-b(1-t)+tm}$$

$$=\frac{1}{1-0.8(1-0.25)+0.1}$$

$$=\frac{1}{1-0.8+0.2+0.1}$$

$$=\frac{1}{0.5}=2$$

(*c*) Equilibrium value of imports can be obtained by substituting the equilibrium income (330) in the import function. Thus

$$M=5+0.1Y$$
$$=5+0.1\times330$$
$$=38$$

(*d*) Required increase in Government expenditure to attain Rs. 50 increase in income can be obtained as under

$$\Delta Y=\text{Foreign Trade multiplier}\times\Delta G$$
$$\Delta Y=2\times\Delta G$$

Or

$$\Delta G=\frac{\Delta Y}{2}$$

$$=\frac{50}{2}=25$$

ECONOMIC POLICY IMPLICATIONS OF KEYNESIAN ANALYSIS OF NATIONAL INCOME

Keynesian analysis of determination of national income is highly relevant and of great practical use in the formulation of economic policy to overcome recession or depression in the economy and also to solve the problem of inflation in the economy. A free market economy often faces the problem of recession or slowdown in the economic activtity at sometimes and to contend with the problem of severe inflation at other times.

From our above analysis it is clear that changes in equilibrium level of national income can be brought about by changes in any component of aggregate demand, namely, consumption demand

(C), private investment demand (I), Government expenditure (G), and net exports (X_n). In order to increase national income through upward shift in the consumption function, the Government can reduce personal income taxes. In 1964, the reduction in income tax by John Kennedy Government in USA was quite successful in boosting consumption demand and thereby raising aggregate output. As a result, more income and employment were generated. The rate of unemployment sharply declined and the American economy was lifted out of depression. Recently in 2002, the President George W. Bush made a cut of 3.5 billion dollars in income tax to revive the American economy. This also proved quite successful. Again in 2007-08 the American President made a drastic cut in income tax to increase demand for getting the US economy out of recession which was caused by financial crisis brought about by defaults in payment by the people of sub-prime housing loans. In India too government cut excise duties and service tax under fiscal stimulus package to prevent sharp slowdown of the Indian economy.

Secondly, the equilibrium level of national income (GNP) and employment can be increased by raising the rate of private investment (I). Businessmen can be induced to invest more by lowering the rate of interest and increasing the availability of credit. We know that lower the rate of interest, the higher will be the level of private investment. Alternatively, the Government may encourage private investment by reducing tax on profits so that post-tax rate of profit is higher than before. The higher level of investment will shift the aggregate demand curve ($C + I + G$) upward and determine a higher level of national income and employment.

Thirdly, the national income (GNP) and employment can be increased by increasing Government expenditure on goods and services (G). It was the increase in Government expenditure on Public Works Programme which was the main recommendation of J.M. Keynes to raise the level of national output and income to restore equilibrium at full-employment level. Recently in 1993-94, President Clinton stepped up public expenditure on public works in the USA to overcome recession in the American economy and reduce unemployment. This too proved to be quite successful and in 1994-95 American economy registered a recovery and unemployment declined.

Lastly, the expansion in *positive net exports* (NX) will also cause an increase in equilibrium level of national income and employment. On the contrary, *if the country's trade balance becomes deficit, that is, if imports exceeds exports* (*i.e.*, $X < M$ or $NX_n < 0$), *this will adversely effect the equilibrium level of national income.*

Lastly, inflation is generally caused by excess of aggregate demand over aggregate supply of output at the current level of prices. Keynes explained how when aggregate demand exceeds aggregate supply at full-employment level of income, *inflationary gap* emerges which causes general price level to rise. Both the appropriate fiscal and monetary policies can be adopted to check inflation through lowering of aggregate demand. The government can reduce its expenditure and increase taxes so as to reduce aggregate demand. The RBI can also adopt *tight monetary policy* wherein it can raise rates of interest cash reserve ratio (CRR) to restrict the credit supply.

Thus we see that Keynesian analysis of determination of national income is highly important for formulation of fiscal and monetary policies to solve the economic problems of recession and inflation.

QUESTIONS FOR REVIEW

1. How does Government expenditure on goods and services affect level of national income ? Has it a multiplier effect ? What is the value of government expenditure multiplier.
2. Show that with Government expenditure in a three sector economy (households, firms and Government) equilibrium of national income is established at the level where sum of investment and Government expenditure ($I + G$) is equal to the amount of saving.
3. Show how the increase in Government expenditure without raising taxes (i.e. incurring budget deficit) affects national income, real rate of interest and private investment. Illustrate diagrammatically.

4. It is often asserted that borrowing to finance budget deficit crowds out private investment. Do you agree ? Explain.
5. Show what will be the effect of cut in government expenditure without reduction in taxes (creating budget surplus in this way) affect equilibrium national income, real rate of interest and private investment in the economy.
[Hints. A cut in government expenditure without reducing taxes leads to increase in public saving (i.e. $T-G$ increases). This causes a shift in national saving curve to the right and leads to the fall in rate of interest and increase in private investment.
6. Show how does a cut in taxes without being balanced by cut in government expenditure affect real interest rate and investment.
7. What is effect of a balanced budget (i.e. increasing government expenditure matched by increase in equal amount of taxes) on national income, real interest rate and investment
8. Explain how balanced budget has an expansionary effect. What is value of balanced budget multiplier ? Explain.
9. How does cut in direct taxes lead to increase in national income ? What is the size of lump-sum tax multiplier ?
10. Assuming full-employment in an economy balanced budget increase in taxes and Government expenditure will reduce consumption and investment and raise the real interest rate ? Explain.
11. Assuming full-employment prevails in an economy, increased government expenditure matched by taxes crowds out private investment.
12. When the government runs a budget deficit, how capital market is affected ?
13. What are the components of aggregate expenditure in an open economy. With Government spending on goods and services show that equilibrium level of national income in an open economy is established at the level at which $I + G + NX$ equals saving.
14. Explain foreign trade multiplier (the open economy multiplier). What is its value ? Why is it smaller than closed economy expenditure multiplier ?
15. You are given the following information about an economy.

Consumption function	C = 80 + 0.8Y
Investment function	I = 80
Government fspending	G = 60
Net Taxes	T = 60
Exports	X = 20
Imports	M = 0.2Yd

(i) What is the current account balance for this economy
(ii) What is the value of the open economy multiplier ?
(Note : Since in this question no data of 'invisibles' are given current account balance equals trade balance).
16. You are given the following information about an economy :
Consumption function, C = 1000 + 0.5 (Y – T)
Investment, I = ₹ 2,000 crores, Government expenditure = ₹ 1,000 crores
Taxes = ₹1,000 crores
(*i*) Find the equilibrium level of GDP without taxes.
(*ii*) Find the equilibrium level of GDP with taxes.
(*iii*) Use your answers in (i) and (ii) above to calculate the tax multiplier.
(*iv*) Explain the working of the tax multiplier
[Hints. Find the equilibrium level of GDP (i.e. national income Y), first by taking T = 0 and then find the equilibrium GDP i.e., (Y) by taking T = 1000. Then, tax multiplier $\frac{\Delta Y}{\Delta T}$ is equal to $\frac{-b}{1-b}$. Note that ΔT = 1000.)
17. Explain the relationship between the trade deficit and the inflow of foreign capital.
18. International flow of capital to finance investment and international flow of goods and services are two sides of the same coin. Explain.

CHAPTER 9

Consumption Function

Behavioural Foundations

In the previous chapter we have explained how the level of national income is determined. In the present chapter and the succeeding ones we shall study the various behavioural factors which determine the levels of national income and employment. As we have seen, given the aggregate supply, the level of income or employment is determined by the level of aggregate demand; the greater the aggregate demand, the greater the level of income and employment and vice versa. Keynes was not interested in the factors determining the aggregate supply since he was concerned with the short run and utilisation of the existing productive capacity. We will also not explain in detail the factors which determine the aggregate supply and will confine ourselves to explaining the determinants of aggregate demand. Aggregate demand consists of two parts—consumption demand and investment demand. In this chapter we will explain the consumption demand and the factors on which it depends and how it changes over a period of time. The investment demand will be explained in a later chapter. Consumption demand depends upon the level of income and the propensity to consume. We shall explain below the meaning of the consumption function and the factors on which it depends.

THE CONCEPT OF CONSUMPTION FUNCTION

As the demand for a good depends upon its price, similarly consumption of a community depends upon the level of income. In other words, consumption is a function of income. *The consumption function relates the amount of consumption to the level of income.* When the income of a community rises, consumption also rises. How much consumption rises in response to a given increase in income depends upon the marginal propensity to consume. It should be borne in mind that the consumption function is the whole schedule which describes the amounts of consumption at various levels of income. We give in Table 9.1 such a schedule of consumption function.

Consumption function should be carefully distinguished from the *amount of consumption.* By consumption function is meant the whole schedule which shows consumption at various levels of income, whereas amount of consumption means the amount consumed at a *specific* level of income. The schedule described above reflects the consumption function of a community *i.e.,* it indicates how the consumption changes in response to the change in income. In the consumption schedule given in Table 9.1 it will be seen that at the level of income equal to ₹ 1200 crores, the amount of consumption is ₹ 1090 crores. As the national income increases to ₹ 1500 crores, the amount of consumption rises to ₹ 1300 crore, consumption function remaining the same. Thus, with a given consumption function, amount of consumption is different at different levels of income.

The above schedule of consumption function reveals an important fact that when income rises, consumption also rises but not as much as the income. This fact about consumption function was emphasised by Keynes, who first of all evolved the concept of consumption function. The reason why consumption rises less than income is that a part of the increment in income is saved. Therefore, we see that when income increases from ₹ 1000 crores to ₹ 1100 crores, the amount of consumption rises from ₹ 950 crores to 1020 crores. Thus, with the increase in income by ₹ 100 crores, consumption rises by ₹ 70 crores; the remaining ₹ 30 crores are saved. Similarly, when income rises from ₹ 1100 crores to ₹ 1200 crores, the amount of consumption increases from ₹ 1020 crores to ₹ 1090 crores.

Table 9.1. Linear Consumption Function

Income (₹ *in crores*)	*Consumption* (₹ *in crores*)	*Average Propensity to* Consume $\left(\frac{C}{Y}\right)$	Marginal Propensity to Consume $\left(\frac{\Delta C}{\Delta Y}\right)$
1000	950	$\frac{950}{1000} = 0.950$	—
1100	1020	$\frac{1020}{1100} = 0.927$	$\frac{70}{100} = .70$
1200	1090	$\frac{1090}{1200} = 0.908$	$\frac{70}{100} = .70$
1300	1160	$\frac{1160}{1300} = 0.892$	$\frac{70}{100} = .70$
1400	1230	$\frac{1230}{1400} = 0.878$	$\frac{70}{100} = .70$
1500	1300	$\frac{1300}{1500} = 0.867$	$\frac{70}{100} = .70$
1600	1370	$\frac{1370}{1600} = 0.856$	$\frac{70}{100} = .70$

Here also, as a result of increase in income by ₹ 100, the amount of consumption has risen by ₹ 70 crores and the remaining ₹ 30 crores have been saved. The same applies to further increases in income and consumption. We shall see later that Keynes based his theory of multiplier on the proposition that consumption increases less than the increase in income and this theory of multiplier occupies an important place in macroeconomics.

Consumption demand depends on income and propensity to consume. Propensity to consume depends on various factors such as price level, interest rate, stock of wealth and several subjective factors. Since Keynes was concerned with short-run consumption function he assumed price level, interest rate, stock of wealth etc. constant in his theory of consumption. Thus with these factors being assumed constant in the short run, *Keynesian consumption function considers consumption as a function of income*. Thus

$$C = f(Y)$$

In a specific form, Keynesian function can be written as:

$$C = a + bY$$

where a and b are constants. While a is intercept term of the consumption function, b stands for the slope of the consumption function and therefore represents marginal propensity to consume.

Keynesian consumption function has been depicted by *CC* curve in Fig. 9.1 in which along the *X*-axis national income is measured and along the *Y*-axis the amount of consumption is measured. In Figure 9.1 a line *OZ* making 45° angle with the *X*-axis has been drawn. Because line *OZ* makes 45° angle with the *X*-axis every point on it is equidistant from both the *X*-axis and *Y*-axis. Therefore, if consumption function curve coincides with 45° line *OZ* it would imply that the amount of consumption is equal to the income at every level of income. In this case, with the increase in income, consumption would also increase by the same amount. As has been said above, in actual practice consumption increases less than the increase in income. Therefore, in actual practice the curve depicting the consumption function will deviate from the 45° line. If we represent the above consumption schedule by a curve, we would get the propensity to consume curve such as *CC* in Fig. 9.1.

It is evident from this figure that the consumption function curve *CC* deviates from the 45° line *OZ*. At lower levels of income, the consumption function curve *CC* lies above the *OZ* line, signifying that at these lower levels of income consumption is greater than the income. It is so because at lower levels of income, a nation may draw upon its accumulated savings to maintain its consumption standard or it may borrow from others. As income increases, consumption also increases and at the income level OY_0, consumption is equal to income. Beyond this, with the increase in income, consumption increases but less than the increase in income and therefore, consumption function curve *CC* lies below the 45° line *OZ* beyond Y_0. An important point to be noted here is that beyond the level of income OY_0, the gap between consumption and income is widening. The difference between consumption and income represents savings. Therefore, *with the increase in income, saving gap widens* and, as we shall see later, this has a significant implication in macroeconomics.

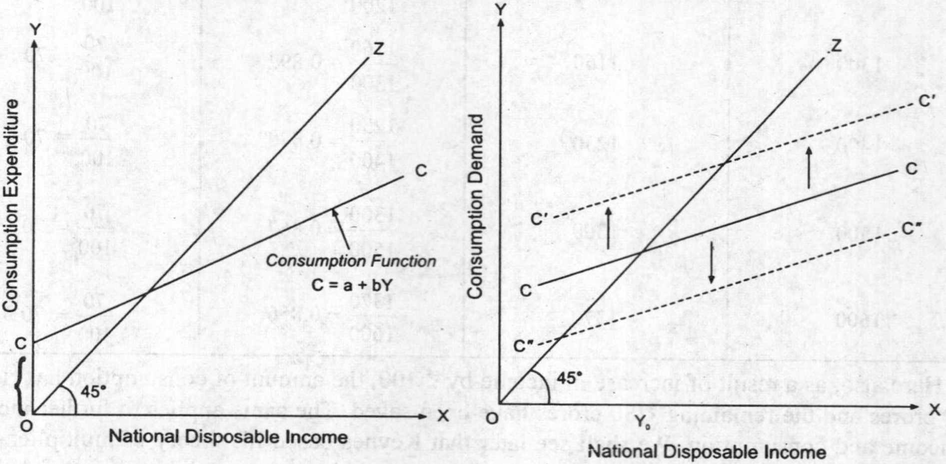

Fig. 9.1. *Keynesian Linear Consumption Function* **Fig. 9.2.** *Shift in Consumption Function*

It is useful to point out here that when the consumption function of a community changes, the whole consumption function curve changes or shifts. When propensity to consume increases, it means that at various levels of income more is consumed than before. Therefore, as a result of increase in propensity to consume of the community, the whole consumption function curve shifts upward as has been shown by the upper curve *C'C'* in Fig. 9.2. On the contrary, when the propensity to consume of the community decreases, the whole consumption function curve shifts downward signifying that at various levels of income, less is consumed than before.

AVERAGE AND MARGINAL PROPENSITY TO CONSUME

There are two important concepts of propensity to consume, the one being average propensity to consume and the other marginal propensity to consume. They should be carefully distinguished, for they are equal in some cases but different in others. Consider Table 9.1, where we have calculated the average and marginal propensity to consume in columns 3 and 4. As seen above, consumption changes as income changes. Now, how much consumption changes in response to a given change in income depends upon the average and marginal propensity to consume. Thus, propensity to consume of a community can be known by the average and marginal propensity to consume. *Average propensity to consume is the ratio of the amount of consumption to total income.* Therefore, average propensity to consume is calculated by dividing the amount of consumption by the total income. Thus,

$$APC = \frac{C}{Y}, \text{ where}$$

APC stands for average propensity to consume,

C for amount of consumption, and

Y for the level of income.

In Table 9.1 it will be seen that at the level of income ₹ 1000 crores, consumption expenditure is equal to ₹ 950 crores. Therefore, average propensity to consume is here equal to $\frac{950}{1000} = 0.95$. When the income rises to ₹ 1100 crores, consumption increases to ₹ 1020 crores. Therefore, the average propensity to consume will be $\frac{1020}{1100} = 0.927$. In this schedule of consumption function, the average propensity to consume falls with the increase in income. Keynesian consumption function *CC* is shown in Fig. 9.3. Average propensity to consume at a point on the consumption function curve can be obtained by measuring the slope of the ray from the origin to that point. For example, at income level OY_1, corresponding point on the consumption function curve is *A*. Therefore, at OY_1 income level, average propensity to consume (*APC*) is the slope of the ray *OA*. Similarly, at income level OY_2, average propensity to consume is given by the slope of the ray *OB*. It will be observed from Fig. 9.3 that slope of *OB* is less than that of *OA*. Therefore, average propensity to consume at income level OY_2 is less than that at income level OY_1. In other words, average propensity to consume has declined with the increase in disposable income.

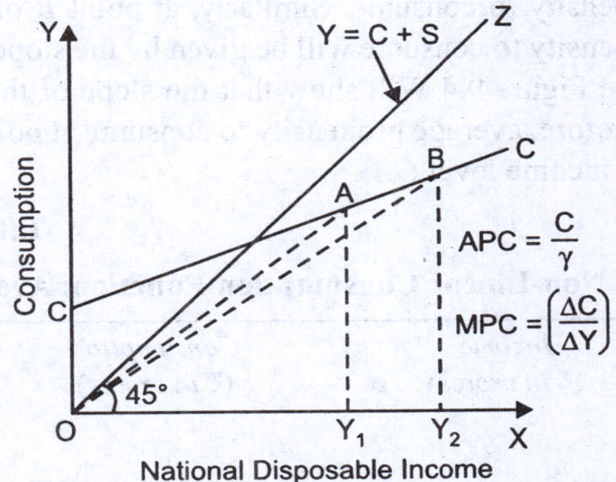

Fig. 9.3. *Keynes's Consumption Function: Declining Average Propensity to Consume*

NON-LINEAR CONSUMPTION FUNCTION : DECLINING AVERAGE AND MARGINAL PROPENSITY TO CONSUME

In the consumption function depicted in Fig. 9.3, though average propensity to consume $\left(\frac{C}{Y}\right)$ declines, marginal propensity to consume which equals $\frac{\Delta C}{\Delta Y}$ remains constant since consumption function curve *CC is a straight line and therefore its slope* $\left(\frac{\Delta C}{\Delta Y}\right)$ *is constant.*

But it is not necessary that marginal propensity to consume should be the same at all levels of income. We have constructed in Table 9.2 another schedule of consumption function in which marginal propensity to consume declines with the increase in income.

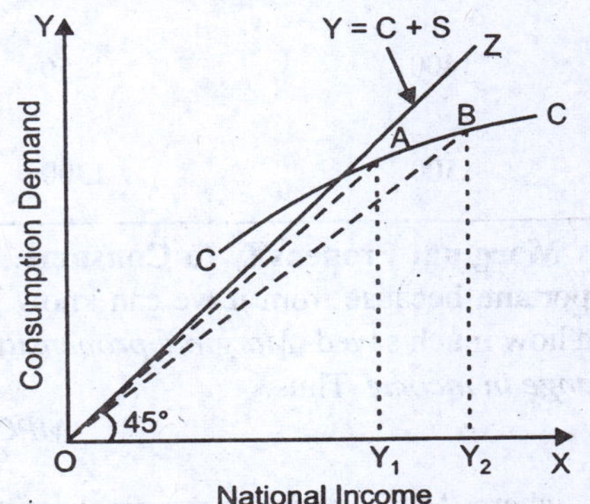

Fig. 9.4. *Non-Linear Consumption Function: Declining Average Propensity to Consume*

It will be seen from Table 9.2 that when the level of income increases from ₹ 1000 crores to 1100 crores, consumption increases from 950 crores to 1040 crores, that, is by ₹ 90 crores. Therefore marginal propensity to consume is 0.9 and when income rises from 1400 crores to ₹ 1500 crores, consumption increases by ₹ 50 crores from ₹ 1250 crores to 1300 crores. Therefore, marginal propensity to consume has declined to 0.5. When with the increase in income marginal propensity to consume declines, then the curve of consumption function is not a straight line but is convex from above as shown in Fig. 9.4. In this case of non-linear consumption function average propensity to consume will also decline. At any point on the propensity to consume curve *CC* we can find out average propensity to consume by joining that point with the point of origin by a straight line whose slope will measure the average propensity to consume. In Fig. 9.4, if we have to find out average propensity to consume at point *A* on the consumption function curve *CC*, we connect point *A* with the origin by a straight line. Now, the slope of the line *OA i.e.*, $AY_1|OY_1$ will measure the average propensity to consume. Similarly, at point *B* of the given consumption function *CC*, the average propensity to consume will be given by the slope of the line *OB* which is equal to BY_2/OY_2. A glance at the Figure 9.4 Will show that the slope of the line *OB* is smaller than the slope of the line *OA*. Therefore, average propensity to consume at point *B* or at income level OY_2 is less than that at point *A* or income level OA_1.

Table 9.2

Non-Linear Consumption Function: Average and Marginal Propensity to Consume

Income (*₹ in crores*)	*Consumption* (*₹ in crores*)	*Average Propensity to Consume* $\frac{C}{Y}$	*Marginal Propensity to Consume* $\frac{\Delta C}{\Delta Y}$
1000	950	$\frac{950}{100} = 0.950$	–
1100	1040	$\frac{1040}{1100} = 0.945$	$\frac{90}{100} = 0.9$
1200	1120	$\frac{1120}{1200} = 0.933$	$\frac{80}{100} = 0.8$
1300	1190	$\frac{1190}{1300} = 0.915$	$\frac{70}{100} = 0.7$
1400	1250	$\frac{1250}{1400} = 0.893$	$\frac{60}{100} = 0.6$
1500	1300	$\frac{1300}{1500} = 0.866$	$\frac{50}{100} = 0.5$

Marginal Propensity to Consume. The concept of marginal propensity to consume is very important, because from it we can know how much part of the increment in income is consumed and how much saved. *Marginal propensity to consume is the ratio of change in consumption to the change in income.* Thus:

$$MPC = \frac{\Delta C}{\Delta Y}$$

where, *MPC* stands for marginal propensity to consume,

ΔC for change in consumption, and

ΔY for change in income.

Marginal propensity to consume needs to be carefully distinguished from average propensity to consume. *Whereas average propensity to consume is the ratio of total consumption to total income, i.e.,* $\frac{C}{Y}$, *the marginal propensity to consume is the ratio of change in consumption to the change in income, i.e.* $\frac{\Delta C}{\Delta Y}$.

The concept of marginal propensity to consume can be easily understood with the aid of Table 9.2 in column 4 of which we have calculated the marginal propensity to consume at various levels of income. In this schedule when income rises from ₹ 1000 crores to ₹ 1100 crores, the consumption increases from ₹ 950 crores to ₹ 1040 crores. Here the increment in income is ₹ 100 crores but the increment in consumption is ₹ 90 crores. Therefore, marginal propensity to consume which is $\frac{\Delta C}{\Delta Y}$ is here equal to $\frac{90}{100}$ or 0.9. Similarly, when national income rises to ₹ 1200 crores and as a result consumption increases from ₹ 1040 crores to ₹ 1120 crores, the marginal propensity to consume is now equal to $\frac{80}{100}$ or 0.8. In Table 9.2, it will be seen that marginal propensity to consume declines as the income rises. It is worth noting that when with the increase in income average propensity to consume declines, marginal propensity to consume is less than average propensity to consume. This is in accordance with the usual relationship between the average and marginal quantities. This is evident from Table 9.2.

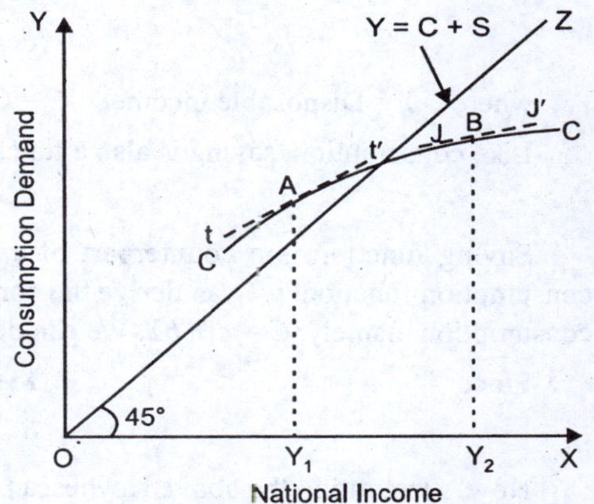

Fig. 9.5. *Non-Linear Consumption Function: Declining Marginal Propensity to Consume*

Marginal propensity to consume can be estimated by drawing the tangent at a point on the consumption function. Consider Fig. 9.5 where curve *CC* depicting the consumption function has been drawn. Marginal propensity to consume at point *A* on this will be equal to the slope of the tangent *tt'* drawn at this point. Similarly, marginal propensity to consume at point *B* on it is given by the slope of the tangent *JJ'* drawn at this point. It will be seen that slope of the tangent *JJ'* is less than the slope of the tangent *tt'*. Therefore, marginal propensity to consume at point *B* on the consumption function *CC* in Fig. 9.5 is smaller than the marginal propensity to consume at point *A* on this consumption function. Thus, marginal propensity to consume is declining with the increases in income in the non-linear consumption function curve *CC* in Fig. 9.5. Thus when marginal propensity to consume declines with the increase in income, consumption function is non-linear whose slope declines as income rises. Non-linear consumption function is shown in Fig. 9.5 where the slope of the propensity to consume curve *CC* declines as income increases. In Fig. 9.1 and Fig. 9.3 propensity to consume curve is a straight line *i.e.*, the slope of the consumption function curve remains constant. Therefore, marginal propensity to consume which is given by the slope of the consumption function curve remains constant in Fig. 9.1 and 9.3.

It is worth noting that marginal propensity to consume is neither zero nor equal to one. It has been found by empirical studies *that marginal propensity to consume varies between zero and unity.* If the marginal propensity to consume was zero, then the whole of the increment in income would have been saved and the consumption function curve would have a horizontal shape. As we have seen before, this is not so realistic. On the other hand, if the marginal propensity to consume was equal to unity, then the whole of the increment in income would be consumed and in that case consumption function curve would have coincided with 45° line.

SAVING FUNCTION

As mentioned above, consumption increases as income increases but less than the rise in income. We will now explain what happens to saving when income increases. Saving is defined as the part of income which is not consumed because disposable income is either consumed or saved.

Thus,

$$Y = C + S$$
$$S = Y - C$$

where Y = Disposable income, C = Consumption, and S = Saving

Like consumption, saving is also a function of income. Thus, saving function can be written as

$$S = f(Y)$$

Saving function is a counterpart of a consumption function, Therefore, given a particular consumption function, we can derive the corresponding saving function. Let us take the Keynesian consumption, namely, $C = a + bY$. We can derive saving function corresponding to it.

Since

$$Y = C + S$$
$$S = Y - C \quad ...(i)$$

Now, substituting the above Keynesean function for C in (i) we have

$$S = Y - (a + bY)$$
$$= Y - a - bY$$
$$= -a + Y - bY$$
$$= -a + (1 - b)\,Y \quad ...(ii)$$

Note that $(1 - b)$ in the above saving function in (ii) is the value of marginal propensity to save where b is the value of marginal propensity to consume. Let us give a numerical example. Suppose the following consumption function is given.

$$C = 150 + 0.80\,Y$$
$$S = Y - C$$

Substituting the given consumption function for C we have

$$S = Y - 150 - 0.80\,Y$$
$$= -150 + Y - 0.80\,Y$$
$$= -150 + (1 - 0.80)\,Y$$
$$= -150 + 0.20\,Y$$

Note that 0.20 represents marginal propensity to save. It also follows from above that the sum of marginal propensity to consume and marginal propensity to save is equal to one ($MPC + MPS = 1$). It is important to distinguish between average propensity to save and marginal propensity to save.

Average Propensity to Save. An important relationship between income and saving is described by the concept of average propensity to save. (APS). Average propensity to save is the proportion of disposable income that is saved (*i.e.,* not consumed). Mathematically

$$APS = \frac{Savings}{Disposable\ Income} = \frac{S}{y}$$

Like the average propensity to consume (APC) average propensity to save also generally varies as income increases. As seen above, average propensity to consume (APC) falls as income increases. This implies that average propensity to save will increase as income rises.

Let us derive an important relationship between average propensity to consume and average propensity to save. Restating below the relation that income is either consumed or saved:

$$C + S = Y$$

Dividing both sides by disposable income *Y* we have

$$\frac{C}{Y} + \frac{S}{Y} = \frac{Y}{Y} = 1$$

Since $\frac{C}{Y}$ is average propensity to consume

and $\frac{S}{Y}$ is average propensity to save, we have

$$APC + APS = 1$$

or $$APS = 1 - APC$$

This means, for example, that if a society consumes 75 per cent of its disposable income, that is, $APC = 0.75$, then it will save 25 per cent of its disposable income or its average propensity to save (*APS*) will be 0.25 ($1 - 0.75 = 0.25$).

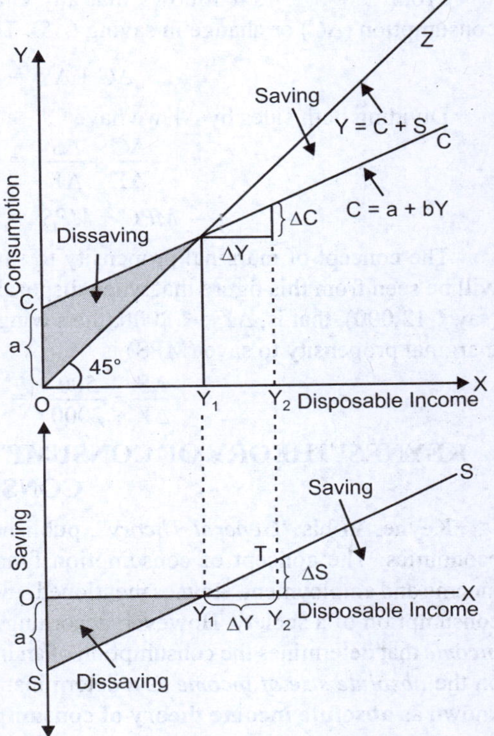

Fig. 9.6. *Saving Function derived from Consumption Function*

In Fig. 9.6 we have drawn the saving curve *SS* in the panel at the bottom. The saving curve *SS* shows the gap between consumption curve *CC* and the income curve *OZ* in the upper panel of Fig. 9.6. It will be seen that up to income level OY_1, consumption exceeds income, that is, there is dissaving. Beyond income level OY_1, there is positive saving. It is worth mentioning that as average propensity to consume (*APC*) falls with the increase in income in the upper panel, average propensity to save rises as income increases. Thus in Fig. 9.6 with the increase in income not only the absolute amount of saving increases, the average propensity to save also increases.

Marginal Propensity to Save (*MPS*). Whereas average propensity to save indicates the proportion of income that is saved, marginal propensity to save represents how much of the additional disposable income is devoted to saving. The marginal propensity to save is therefore change in savings induced by a change in the disposable income.

Thus,

$$MPS = \frac{\Delta S}{\Delta Y}$$

For example, if disposable income increases from ₹ 10,000 to ₹ 12,000 and this causes planned savings to increase by ₹ 500 crores, marginal propensity to save is:

$$MPS = \frac{500}{2000} = \frac{1}{4} = 0.25$$

Since the additional income is either consumed or saved, *the sum of marginal propensity to consume and marginal propensity to save is equal to one.*

$$MPC + MPS = 1$$

This can be mathematically proved as under

From $C + S = Y$, it follows that any change in income (ΔY) must induce either change in consumption (ΔC) or change in saving (ΔS). Thus.

$$\Delta C + \Delta S = \Delta Y$$

Dividing both sides by ΔY we have

$$\frac{\Delta C}{\Delta Y} + \frac{\Delta S}{\Delta Y} = \frac{\Delta Y}{\Delta Y} = 1$$

$$MPC + MPS = 1$$

The concept of marginal propensity to save is graphically shown at the bottom of Fig. 9.6. It will be seen from this figure that when disposable income increases from OY_1 (say ₹ 10,000) to OY_2 (say ₹ 12,000), that is, $\Delta Y =$ ₹ 2000, the saving increases by Y_2T, (₹ 500), that is, ΔS is ₹ 500. Thus marginal propensity to save (MPS) is

$$\frac{\Delta S}{\Delta Y} = \frac{500}{2000} = \frac{1}{4} = 0.25$$

KEYNES' THEORY OF CONSUMPTION AND PSYCHOLOGICAL LAW OF CONSUMPTION

Keynes in his "*General Theory*", published in 1936, laid the foundations of modern macro-economics. The concept of consumption function plays an important role in Keynes' theory of income and employment. Keynes mentioned several subjective and objective factors which determine consumption of a society. However, according to Keynes, of all the factors it is the *current level of income* that determines the consumption of an individual and also of society. Since Keynes laid stress on the *absolute size of income* as a determinant of consumption, his theory of consumption is also known as **absolute income theory of consumption.**

Keynes's Psychological Law of Consumption

Further, Keynes put forward a **psychological law of consumption**, according to which, as income increases consumption increases but not by as much as the increase in income. In other words, marginal propensity to consume is less than one.

$$1 > \frac{\Delta C}{\Delta Y} > 0$$

While Keynes recognized that many subjective and objective factors including interest rate and wealth influenced the level of consumption expenditure, he emphasised that it is the current level of income on which the consumption spending of an individual and the society depends. To quote him: "*The amount of aggregate consumption depends mainly on the amount of aggregate income. The fundamental psychological law, upon which we are entitled to depend with great confidence both a priori from our knowledge of human nature and from the detailed facts of experience is that men (and women, too) are disposed, as a rule and on an average to increase their consumption as their income increases, but not by as much as the increase in their income.*"[1]

In the above statement about consumption behaviour, Keynes makes three points. First, he suggests that consumption expenditure depends mainly on absolute income of the current period, that is, consumption is a positive function of the absolute level of current income. The more income in a period one has, the more is likely to be his consumption expenditure in that period. In other words, in any period the rich people tend to consume more than the poor people do. Secondly, Keynes points out that consumption expenditure does not have a proportional relationship with income. According to him, as the income increases, a smaller proportion of income is consumed. The proportion of consumption to income is called average propensity to consume (*APC*). Thus, Keynes argues that average propensity to consume (*APC*) falls as income increases.

1. J.M. Keynes, *The General Theory of Employment, Interest and Money,* (New York : Harcourt), First Edition, 1936 p. 96.

The Keynes' consumption function can be expressed in the following form:

$$C = a + bY_d$$

where C is consumption expenditure and Y_d is the real disposable income which equals gross national income minus taxes. a and b are constants, where a is the intercept term, that is, the amount of consumption expenditure at zero level of income. Thus, a is *autonomous consumption.* The parameter b is the *marginal propensity to consume (MPC) which measures the increase in consumption spending in response to per unit increase in disposable income.* Thus

$$MPC = \frac{\Delta C}{\Delta Y}$$

It is evident from Fig. 9.1 and 9.3 the behaviour of consumption expenditure as perceived by Keynes implies that marginal propensity to consume (*MPC*) which is measured by the slope of consumption function curve *CC* at a point is less than average propensity to consume (*APC*) which is measured by the slope of the line joining a point on the consumption function curve *CC* to the origin (that is, $MPC < APC$). This is because as *income rises consumption does not increase proportionately and as income falls consumption does not fall proportionately as people seek to protect their earlier consumption standards.* This can be seen from Fig. 9.3 the slope of consumption function curve *CC′* measuring *MPC* and the slopes of lines *OA* and *OB* which give the *APC* $\left(i.e., \frac{C}{Y}\right)$ at points *A* and *B* respectively are falling whereas slope of the linear consumption function *CC′* remains constant.

In Fig. 9.3 we have shown a linear consumption function with an intercept term. In this form of linear consumption function, though marginal propensity to consume ($\Delta C/\Delta Y$) is constant, average propensity to consume (C/Y) is declining with the increase in income as indicated by the slopes of the lines *OA* and *OB* at levels of income Y_1 and Y_2 respectively. The straight line *OB* drawn from the origin indicating average propensity to consume at higher income level Y_2 has a relatively less slope than the straight line *OA* drawn from the origin to point *A* at lower income level Y_1. *The decline in average propensity to consume as the income increases implies that the proportion of income that is saved increases with the increase in national income of the country.* This result also follows from the studies of family budgets of various families at different income levels. The fraction of income spent on consumption by the rich families is lower than that of the poor families. In other words, *the rich families save a higher proportion of their income as compared to the poor families.*

The assumption of diminishing average propensity to consume is a significant part of Keynesian theory of income and employment. This implies that as income increases, a progressively larger proportion of national income would be saved. Therefore, to achieve and maintain equilibrium at full-employment level of income, increasing proportion of national income is needed to be invested. If sufficient investment opportunities are not available, the economy would then run into trouble and in that case it would not be possible to maintain full-employment because aggregate demand will fall short of full-employment output. On the basis of this increasing proportion of saving with the increase in income and, consequently, the emergence of the problem of demand deficiency, some Keynesian economists based the theory of *secular stagnation* on the declining propensity to consume.

IMPORTANT FEATURES OF KEYNES' CONSUMPTION FUNCTION

In macroeconomics, Keynes's consumption function plays a highly important role. Therefore, it is essential to state its important features. The following are the important features of Keynes's consumption function:

1. First, *absolute level of current income is the important factor that determines consumption* of the community. Increase in national income causes an increase in consumption. On the other hand, classical economists thought that it was rate of interest that primarily determined saving and consumption of the community. A rise in rate of interest induces the people to save more and thus to

reduce their level of consumption. According to Keynes, though rate of interest is one of the factors that determine consumption of the community, he did not consider it a very important determinant of it. By considering level of current income as the most important factor determining consumption and saving, Keynes made a significant contribution to the macroeconomic theory.

2. The second important feature of Keynes' consumption function is that *marginal propensity to consume is less than one* but greater than zero ($0 < MPC < 1$). As has been explained above, the feature of Keynes's consumption function that marginal propensity to consume is less than one is known as Keynes's Psychological Law of Consumption. According to this law, as income increases, consumption increases but not as much as the increase in income. We will explain in a later chapter that Keynes's theory of multiplier is based on the marginal propensity to consume being less than one but greater than zero.

3. In Keynes' *consumption function, namely,* $C = a + bY$, *as income increases, average propensity to consume (APC) falls.* Keynes was of the view that rich people relatively save a higher proportion of their income so that at higher levels of income average propensity to consume (*APC*), that is, proportion of total consumption to national income falls as national income rises.

4. Another important feature of consumption function as put forward by Keynes is that it *remains stable in the short run.* Consumption function, according to Keynes, depends on various institutional factors such as distribution of income and wealth and psychological factors such as willingness to save. Since there cannot be much changes in these institutional and psychological factors, consumption function remains stable in the short run, that is, it does not shift upward or downward. Therefore, Keynes in his theory explains the determination of income and employment in the short run by considering that the consumption function is stable.

DETERMINANTS OF PROPENSITY TO CONSUME

The important question is on what factors does the propensity to consume of a community depend. In other words, what are the factors that determine the level and position of the propensity to consume or the consumption function. Keynes divided the factors determining the propensity to consume into two groups: the first group of factors was called by him as subjective factors and the second group was named by him as objective factors. We shall explain below in detail these subjective and objective factors which affect the consumption function of a community.

Subjective Factors

Among the subjective factors are included those factors which induce and prompt people to save some part of their income. First, people save because they want to provide for unforeseen contingencies, such as illness, unemployment, accidents, etc. Secondly, people are induced to save because they want to provide for the expected future needs such as education of the children, marriages of their children, etc. Thirdly, several people wish to save from their current incomes so that they may be able to use accumulated savings for investment which will increase their future income. Investments will bring them more income in the form of more profits and interest. Fourthly, people are motivated to save so that they can accumulate large wealth which will increase their social status. With increased wealth they would think themselves to be economically more independent and they could buy many things with more wealth. Further, many individuals also save so that they can use them for speculative purposes and other business projects. Besides, several people are prompted to save for the sake of leaving a good fortune for their heirs and children. Lastly, many people save because of their miserly instinct and habits. The accumulation of more wealth gives them a great psychic satisfaction.

The above subjective factors increase the propensity to save and therefore reduce the propensity to consume. These subjective factors play a crucial rule in determining the level and shape of the consumption function. However, Keynes pointed out and rightly so that some subjective factors raise the propensity to consume. The desire for ostentation generally leads to greater consumption expenditure. People have a natural instant to imitate others' consumption habits. As pointed out by Duesenberry, people in lower and middle income ranges imitate the consumption standards of the higher income groups and this increases their propensity to consume. This has been called *demonstration effect* which is a great subjective or psychological force that works in raising the propensity to consume.

Subjective factors also lead the business firms to save much or little from their incomes. Many of the subjective factors which influence the savings of the firms are the following : (1) *Enterprise*—Many business industrial firms desire to save a part of their current income so that they can make investment in new enterprises and carry out expansion in the future. Business firms generally save a good part of their income for their further expansion. (2) *Liquidity*—Business firms also are induced to save so that they can face contingencies in the future. If they have good amount of liquid wealth in their hands, they would be able to meet the emergent situations more successfully. More cautious and farsighted firms will save more than others on this count. (3) *Successful Management*—Many managers of the business firms are motivated to save more because they want to prove themselves successful managers. With the investment of the saved money, the income of a firm increases and their managers are regarded as successful. (4) *Financial Prudence*—Business firms desire to save for making up the depreciation in plant and machinery. Since after some years business firms have to replace their plant and machinery, if a good part of their current income is not saved, it would not be possible for them to replace plant and machinery. If the firms put aside a greater part of their income for depreciation or replacement purposes, they would pay lower dividends to the shareholders and this will generally lower the propensity to consume of a community. On the other hand, if the firms keep a relatively small amount for depreciation, they will pay larger amounts as dividends to the shareholders and this will generally increase the propensity to consume of the community. *Lastly*, firms also want to save because they have to repay their debts.

Objective Factors

Keynes mentioned the following six types of objective factors which influence the consumption function:

(1) Changes in the General Price Level: Real Balance Effect. The general price level is an important factor which influences the consumption of a community. When the general price level increases or, in other words, when inflation occurs, the consumption function shifts downward. This is because the rise in the general price level, real value (that is, purchasing power) of people's money balances and financial assets with fixed monetary values declines. This causes a downward shift in the consumption function. This is called *real balance effect*. Similarly, when the general price level falls, real value of money balances and financial assets increase. This will induce people to consume relatively more out of their current income. This will cause an upward shift in the consumption function.

(2) Fiscal Policy. Fiscal policy of the Government, especially taxation policy, affects the propensity to consume of the country. By levying excise duties, sales tax, the Government can cut down the consumption and thereby increase savings of the community. Likewise, when the Government reduces taxes, consumption of the people increases and this raises the propensity to consume. Rationing and price control by the Government also affects the propensity to consume, as was witnessed during the Second World War. In the modern times, pursuing of the welfare state policy by the Government under which progressive taxes have been levied on the rich people and the revenue obtained from them have been spent to provide many social security benefits and amenities to the poor people, has tended to raise the consumption function.

(3) Rate of Interest. Rate of interest also affects the propensity to consume and save. It is generally believed that higher rate of interest induces the people to save more and this results in reducing their propensity to consume. But this is not true in the case of all the people. Some individuals are of such a type who want a certain fixed income in the future. And when the rate of interest rises these individuals consume more and save less because with higher rate of interest they can obtain the given fixed income with lesser savings. Therefore, when the rate of interest rises such individuals save less than before. Thus, it cannot be said with certainty whether with the changes in the rate of interest the propensity to consume of the whole community will change or not.

(4) Stock of Wealth. The stock of wealth owned by the households in the economy is also an important factor that determines propensity to consume. In wealth we include not only real assets such as land, houses, automobiles but also financial assets such as cash balances, saving and fixed deposits with banks, stocks and bonds possessed by households. The greater the amount of wealth accumulated by households in the economy, the greater is generally the propensity to consume (*i.e.,* the greater the amount of consumption out of any level of current income). The important motive of the people to save is to accumulate wealth. Generally speaking, the greater the wealth which people have accumulated, the weaker is the incentive to save further. In other words, the other things remaining the same the increase in wealth generally causes an upward shift in the consumption function and decrease is wealth causes a downward shift in the consumption function.

An important example which is often cited to emphasise the importance of wealth as a determinant of consumption is the stock market crash of 1929 in England (*i.e.,* drastic fall in share prices) which substantially reduced the financial wealth of the households overnight resulting in shifting the consumption function downward.

(5) Credit Conditions and Consumer Indebtedness. The availability of easy credit causes an increase in consumption and shifts the consumption function upward. It is now a common experience in India that in recent years lowering of lending interest rates by Indian banks on loans for houses, cars, computers and other durable consumer goods has greatly increased the consumption of the people and shifted consumption function upward. On the other hand, tightening of credit produces an opposite effect, that is, causes a downward shift in the consumption function, Furthermore, the recent increase in facilities of Credit Cards by banks and their acceptance by sellers of consumer goods have also worked to shift the consumption function upward in India.

Similarly, the level of consumer indebtedness also greatly affects the propensity to consume of the people. If the households are heavily indebted, say 25 to 30 per cent of their current income, they are committed to save (*i.e.,* consume less) to that extent so that they are able to pay their instalments of previous credit taken. Thus, the greater the degree of indebtedness of households in the economy, the higher will be the consumption function curve and *vice versa.*

(6) Income Distribution. Lastly, distribution of income in a society also determines the level of consumption function. If national income is more unequally distributed, the lower will be the propensity to consume. This is because propensity to consume of the rich is relatively less as compared to that of the poor. Therefore, if inequalities in income distribution increase, this reduces the consumption out of any given level of national income and thus causes a downward shift in the consumption function.

(7) Windfall Gains and Losses. Windfall gains and losses also affect the propensity to consume. When the prices of the shares go up, the shareholders begin to think themselves better off and this raises their consumption. On the other hand, when the prices of the shares go down, the shareholders have to suffer sudden losses and they begin to think themselves relatively poorer than before. This induces them to reduce their consumption. We thus see that the windfall gains and losses affect the propensity to consume.

(8) Change in Expectations. Changes in the expectations of the people also influence the propensity to consume. When people expect that war will break out in the near future and they expect prices to go up, then they will try to spend more on goods so as to meet the needs of the immediate future. This raises the consumption function in the current period. On the other hand, when people expect the prices to fall they reduce their current consumption so that they should spend more when the prices actually fall.

We have explained above various subjective and objective factors which taken together determine the consumption function of a community. It is worth noting that propensity to consume does not generally change in the short run, because it depends more on psychological and institutional factors which change only in the long run. *The institutional factors which determine the distribution of income in the society are important forces determining the consumption function.* And these institutional factors do not change in the short run. Therefore, Keynes was of the view that consumption function remains stable in the short run.

LIFE CYCLE AND PERMANENT CONSUMPTION THEORIES

Since Keynes propounded his theory of consumption there have been significant developments in this field and some alternative theories of consumption have been put forward. However, all these post-Keynesian theories of consumption relate consumption to some form of income. First, J.S. Duesenberry expressed the view that consumption expenditure of the individuals depends not on their *absolute incomes* but on their *relative income* with respect to other individuals. Therefore, his theory is also called *'Relative Income Theory of Consumption'*. Second, Modigliani and Ando put forward a theory of consumption known as *"Life Cycle Theory of Consumption"* according to which, individuals plan their consumption profile for their whole life–time. Further, a famous American economist Milton Friedman advanced a theory known as *'Permanent Income Hynothesis'* according to which consumption of individuals depends on their *permanent* income rather than their *current income*. We explain below briefly these post-Keynesion theories of consumption.

Life-Cycle Theory of Consumption

In Keynes's theory of consumption function, consumption expenditure in a period depends mainly on *current income*. After Keynes some economists such as Franco Modigliani and Milton Friedman pointed out that individuals while making their consumption decisions take into account not only the current income which was emphasised by Keynes but also the income they expect to receive in the future. Therefore, the consumption theories of Franco Modigliani and Milton Friedman, both are Nobel Laureates, have been called *Future-Oriented Consumption Theories* by Joseph Stiglitz.[2] Consumption theory put forward by Modigliani is called *Life-Cycle Theory of Consumption*[3] as he emphasises that in deciding about consumption out of income in the working years of their life they attempt to save for the post-retirement period. Their motive for doing so is to smoothen or even their consumption in their entire life span. That is, they save from the income of working period of their life so that they will not have to cut down consumption level after they retire.

The life-cycle theory assumes that an individual in early years of life earns no income and is maintained by his parents or other relatives. In the middle period of his life he works and earns income. Though in the middle period of his life he spends a good deal on consumption of his own and his family members, on balance he earns more than he consumes and therefore saves a part of his income. *His motive of saving is to accumulate assets or wealth, which yields him enough income so as to maintain satisfactory standard of consumption in later years of his life after he retires.*

Thus in the final stage of his life cycle when the individual has retired from work his earnings from work is very little or nil while he spends a good deal on his consumption; it is income from his past savings or accumulated assets that enables him to maintain satisfactory standard of consumption over his whole life cycle.

---

2. See J. Stiglitz, *Economics*, 2002, p. 634
3. Ando A. Franco Modigliani, The Life Cycle Hypothesis of Saving : Aggregate Implications and Tests, *American Economic Review*, March 1963, pp. 55-84.

Permanent Consumption Theory

Like Modigliani, Milton Friedman[4] also thinks that expectations about future income affect current consumption in a period. He points out that people save in good years so that they have not to curtail consumption in bad years. In other words, in Friedman's view, consumption of individuals or households depends on *permanent income* in contrast to *current income* level as emphasised by Keynes. *By Permanent income he means average long-run income.* Therefore, Friedman's theory is known as *permanent Consumption Hypothesis*. According to this view, *temporary changes* in income such as bonus received in a year, or large capital gains received due to rise in prices of shares or real estate do not have much effect on consumption as the permanent changes in income, that is, changes in long-run average income. According to Friedman, temporary or transitory changes in income will have little effect on consumption while permanent changes in income will have large effect on consumption. Thus, according to Friedman's permanent consumption theory, if households could predict their future income level, they will adjust their consumption levels according to their permanent average long-run income.

Thus, according to Friedman, income of an individual consists of permanent income and transitory income.

$$Y = Y_p + y_t$$

$$C = C_p + C_t$$

where Y stands for income, Y_t for transitory income, C for consumption, C_P for permanent consumption and C_t for transitory consumption.

It is worth emphasizing that, according to Friedman, *permanent income should be viewed as earnings both by human and non-human capital of the individual.* By income from human capital he means earnings made from labour and by income from non-human capital is the earnings from physical assets held by him.

Thus, Friedman is of the view that both income and consumption of an individual should be divided into two parts—*permanent and transitory*. Permanent income is the part of income that an individual expects to go on receiving over time in future. On the other hand, *transitory income occurs accidently or by chance*. These transitory incomes may occur due to bad purchases of commodities or assets which yield him losses which therefore represents negative income or they be the result of favourable chance purchases (for example, purchases of certain shares or winning of lotteries) which therefore yield positive income.

Corresponding to the concept of permanent income there is a notion of permanent consumption. *Permanent consumption is the consumption expenditure which an individual expects he will be making over long time in future. The crucial point which Friedman makes is that permanent consumption of individuals depend on permanent income rather than current income as believed by J.M. Keynes.* Besides, according to Friedman, permanent income is *very much a reflection of the capital value or wealth* and this wealth consists of capital value of principal assets possessed by an individual and his *human capital* (i.e. his earning ability depending on the knowledge and skills possessed). According to Friedman, *consumption is proportional to permanent* income Thus,

$$C = kY_p$$

where k represents the proportion of permanent income that is consumed in the current period. This proportion depends on rate of interest (i), desire to accumulate wealth (w) and individual desire for immediate or current consumption. Friedman's consumption theory is summed up in the following equation.

$$C_p = k(i, w, u)Y_p$$

where k is the proportion of permanent income (Y_p) that is spent on permanent consumption. This

4. Milton Friedman, A *Theory of Consumption*, Princeton University Press, 1957.

proportion depends on rate of interest (i), the ratio of non-human (i.e. physical) wealth to income (w) and the preference of individuals for inmediate or current consumption as against his willingness to accumulate assets or wealth (u). According to Friedman, higher rate of interest would induce people to save more and thus reduce his consumption expenditure. Besides, proportion of individual's consumption to their permanent income depends to a great deal on the assets or wealth of an individual, that is, w in the above function. The greater the wealth or assets of an individual, the higher his consumption expenditure. Lastly, the proportion (k) of consumption expenditure to permanent income depends on individual's desire for immediate or current consumption as against his willingness to add to his wealth or assets.

Milton Friedman emphasises that consumption of individuals is affected by changes in individuals' wealth which is a stock variable in contrast to the current income which is a flow variable. Friedman's permanent consumption theory suggests that individuals' consumption depends on how well-off they are and that is better measured by their wealth. Individuals' wealth changes when the value of their assets such as prices of stock shares and real estate change. When their prices rise, people enjoy capital gains which make them wealthier and as a result their consumption out of a given income rises. With this the consumption functions curve shifts above. Commenting on the future-oriented theories of consumption and saving of Modigliani and Friedman, Joseph Stiglitz writes, *"Both Modigliani and Friedman stressed that individuals generally try to stabilise their consumption using savings to smooth consumption so that it does not fluctuate dramatically from year to year. They also stressed that individuals will be forward-looking, basing current consumption decisions on their expectations about future income"*[5].

Implications. There are three important implications of the above two future-oriented theories of consumption and saving. First, important implication is that *changes in expectations about future income* affect the current consumption of individuals even though their current income has not changed. Consider the case when an economy is currently experiencing recession, as has been the case in 2008-09 afflicted by global financial crisis and global meltdown, people became quite pessimistic about their future income prospects which led them to curtail consumption and save more even though their current income did not change. This causes the consumption function curve to shift downward.

Another implication is that *one-time or temporary changes in income will cause only a small change in consumption.* Suppose a person has a windfall gain of ₹ 10 lakhs in a year due to his winning a lottery. Given his marginal propensity to consume equal to 0.8, the Keynesian consumption function predicts that his consumption will increase by ₹ 8 lakhs and the remaining ₹ 2 lakhs will be saved by him in that year. On the other hand, the future-oriented theories of Modigliani and Friedman predict that the consumption of extra income gained by the lottery winner during a year *will be spread over his lifetime or over a long period of time*. Similarly, a more important case from the viewpoint of economic policy is the *temporary reduction in the direct tax* at the time of recession by the government to boost consumption demand as had been done by the US government in 2007-08 and 2008-09 to fight recession. The above two future-oriented theories predict that contrary to the prediction of the Keynesian model the temporary reduction in direct taxes will be much less effective in boosting consumption demand as due to uncertain economic prospects much of the income gained through temporary tax reduction will be saved. The evidence from the US shows this has in fact been the case.

The third related implication of the future-oriented theories is that since changes in income that individuals expect to be only temporary will have only small effect on consumption spending, marginal propensity to consume will be lower and the multiplier effect of such changes in income (such as increase in disposable income brought about by reduction in taxes) will be smaller.

To conclude, leaving aside the cases of temporary changes in income and the concern of the forward-looking people to ensure same consumption standard in the future, *the Keynesian theory of consumption is right in visualising that individuals' consumption spending is more dependent on*

5. Stiglitiz, *op. cit*., p.634

current income. To quote Stiglitz, "The permanent income and life-cycle saving hypotheses contain large elements of truth. Families do save for their retirement and they do smooth their consumption between good years and bad. Even so, *households spending appear to be more depended on current income than either future-oriented theory would saggest*"[6]

CONSUMPTION FUNCTION PUZZLE : KEYNES' CONSUMPTION FUNCTION AND KUZNETS' FINDINGS

Empirical studies of long-term time series data of the US economy for the period 1869-1938 made by the noted American economist Kuznets estimated a consumption function which contradicts Keynes' consumption function which was found to be correct on the basis of cross-section studies of household budget data and short-term time series data. *This contradiction between Kuznet empirical findings and Keynes' consumption function has been called consumption function puzzle.* Efforts have been made by several economists to resolve this puzzle and new theories of consumption function have been put forward to resolve the conflict between Keynes' consumption function and Kuznets' findings. These alternative theories of consumption function will be discussed in the next chapter.

To compare the Keynes' and Kuznets' consumption functions, it will be useful to write them in algebraic form and graphically represent them. Keynes's consumption function can be algebraically written as below:

$$C = a + bY \qquad ...(1)$$

where a is a positive intercept term which is also called *autonomous consumption* as it does not vary with income. The constant a shows that even when income is zero, a certain consumption is present. This is possible when in any year a community can live either on its past savings or borrow from other communities. Keynes' consumption function is shown in Fig. 9.7.

Secondly, b in the consumption function represents marginal propensity to consume $\left(\frac{\Delta C}{\Delta Y}\right)$. The above mentioned Keynes's consumption function ($C = a + bY$) shows that average propensity to consume $\left(\frac{C}{Y}\right)$ falls as income increases. This can be known by comparing slopes of the rays OA and OB at income levels Y_1 and Y_2 respectively in Fig. 9.7.

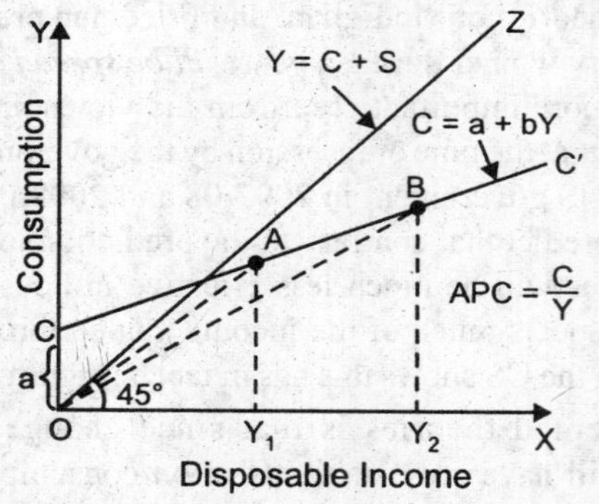

Fig. 9.7. *Keynes' Consumption Function: Declining Average Propensity to Consume and Constant MPC*

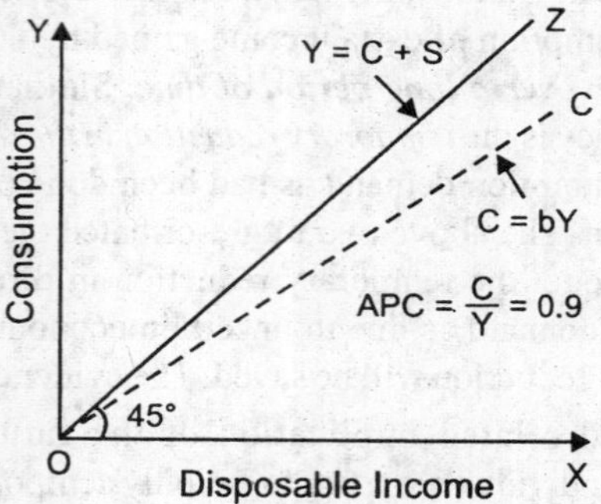

Fig. 9.8. *Kuznets' Consumption Function.*

6. Stiglitiz, *op. cit.*, p.634

Kuznets' Consumption Function

On the other hand, Kuznets found that consumption function is of the following form:

$$C = bY \quad ...(2)$$

In Kuznets' consumption function there is no intercept term (that is, autonomous consumption). This is shown in Fig. 9.8 where it will be seen that Kuznet' consumption function curve starts from the origin and is very near to 45° line depicting that the propensity to consume *(b)* is very high. From his empirical study Kuznets estimated that average propensity to consume was nearly 0.9. Besides, by dividing the entire period (1869-1933) into three overlaping 30 years sub-periods Kuznets found that the proportion of consumption to income (that is, average propensity to consume) was nearly the same and equal to about 0.87 in all the three sub-periods. Thus Kuznets concluded that there was no tendency for the average propensity to consume to decline as disposable income rises. Thus, rounding off Kuznets estimated propensity to consume is equal to 0.9. His consumption function presented in equation (2) can be rewritten as

$$C = 0.9 \quad ...(3)$$

From the above discussion it follows that implication of Keynes' consumption function ($C = a + bY$) and Kuznets' consumption function ($C = bY$) are different. *Whereas in Keynes' consumption function APC falls as income rises, in Kuznets' consumption function it remains constant over a long period.* Further, the value of marginal propensity to consume which is less than one is much higher in Kuznets' function as compared to that of Keynes. The reconciliation between two types of consumption functions has been made by some economists by pointing out that whereas Keynes' function is short-run consumption function, *'Kuznets' function is concerned with long run and is referred to as long-run consumption function.* In the long run, short run consumption function curve shifts above and therefore in the long run consumption function, propensity to consume, is higher as compared to that in the short run. *Further, Friedman's permanent Income Hypothesis and Modigliani's Life Cycle Hypothesis* have also tried to reconcile the two functions by referring to the short-run and long-run consumption behaviour of the people. We will discuss these consumption hypothesis in the appendix.

IMPORTANCE OF KEYNSIAN CONSUMPTION FUNCTION

The concept of consumption function put forward by Keynes is greatly important both in theory and actual practice. To remove unemployment and to control economic fluctuations in the economy, it is very essential to adopt a proper macroeconomic policy. In the formation of such a policy, understanding of the concept to propensity of consume is very essential. Therefore. Prof. A.H. Hansen has remarked that "*consumption function is epoch-making contribution of Keynes to economic theory*". We shall explain below some of the theoretical and practical importance of this consumption function.

(1) The concept of consumption function helps us to invalidate Say's law of classical economics. In fact, Keynes relied on his consumption function for proving the invalidity of Say's law. According to Say's law, every supply creates its own demand and therefore there is no problem of deficiency of aggregate demand. Therefore, general overproduction and unemployment in the economy is not possible because adequate amount of aggregate demand is ever present. Now, according to the Keynesian consumption function, when income increases consumption increases less than the increase in income and therefore saving gap emerges between income and consumption. This saving gap implies that all output produced may not be sold and the problem of deficiency of demand will arise unless this saving gap is matched by an equal amount of investment demand. There is no guarantee that the saving done will be automatically invested or, in other words, it is not necessary that investment demand will be equal to the saving gap. Thus, the contention of the Say's law that every supply creates its equal demand is not valid. No doubt, every supply or production creates income equal to the output produced. But since all income is not consumed and there is no guarantee that investment will be equal to the saving so emerged, Say's law is proved invalid. When investment is less than the saving gap corresponding to full-employment level of income, the aggregate demand is not sufficient to provide full-employment to the people and other resources. Thus, the problem of deficiency of effective demand and hence general unemployment and overproduction arises in a free enterprise capitalist economy.

(2) The concept of propensity to consume is also important because **it brings out crucial significance of investment demand for determination of the level of income and employment** in a capitalist economy. From the concept of propensity to consume we know that consumption increases less than the increase in income and as a result gap emerges between income and consumption. To maintain a certain given level of income and employment, gap between income and consumption at that level must be bridged by investment expenditure otherwise it will not be possible to maintain that level of income and employment because aggregate demand would not be large enough. This indicates the crucial importance of the investment demand in the determination of income and employment. To prevent the establishment of underemployment equilibrium in the economy or, in other words, for achieving full-employment equilibrium, investment demand must be equal to the saving gap at the level of full-employment. Keynes also showed that consumption function remains stable in the short run and therefore economic fluctuations in a capitalist economy are largely due to the fluctuations in investment demand. Thus from the concept of propensity to consume it follows that investment demand is vitally important in determining the level of income and employment. If it were possible to raise the propensity to consume in the short run, then without raising investment, we could have raised the level of income and employment. Since propensity to consume at a given level of income generally remains stable, we have to increase investment for achieving full employment in the economy.

(3) Another crucial importance of the concept of propensity to consume is that from it **we derive the theory of multiplier which has great practical importance in the formulation of macro-economic policy,** especially of public works in times of depression. As we shall study in the next chapter, the magnitude of multiplier is equal to the reciprocal of one minus marginal propensity to consume $\left(K = \dfrac{1}{1 - MPC}\right)$, where K stands for multiplier and MPC for marginal propensity to consume. According to this concept of multiplier, when investment increases, income, output and employment increase by a multiple amount, depending upon the size of the multiplier. Income increases manifold than the original investment because of the nature of consumption function. When some investment in some projects is undertaken, it leads to the increase in income of those employed in the projects but the process does not stop here. The increases in income are further spent on consumption and this leads to further increase in income and so the chain of increases in income and consumption continues and the ultimate increase in income and employment is multiple of the original increment in investment. If the marginal propensity to consume were equal to zero, then all increments in income brought about by additional investment would have been saved and therefore multiplier process would not have worked. Since the marginal propensity to consume is greater than zero, the increase in net investment has a multiplier effect on income, output and employment. Thus, the effect of investment on income depends on the size of the multiplier which depends on the value of the marginal propensity to consume. The greater the marginal propensity to consume, the greater the size of the multiplier.

(4) From the concept of consumption function, we can also explain ***why there is a tendency for the marginal efficiency of capital to decline.*** The declining tendency of the marginal efficiency of capital is due to the nature of the consumption function. Two features of consumption function are important. First, the marginal propensity to consume is less than one which implies that as income increases, consumption increases less than this. Secondly, consumption function is stable in the short run *i.e.,* it does not shift much in the short run. As we know that the level of investment is a crucial factor in the determination of income and employment, fluctuations in the levels of income and employment depend primarily on the fluctuations in investment. The investment demand in the short run is determined by the rate of interest on the one hand and marginal efficiency of capital on the other. Since the rate of interest is relatively sticky, it is the marginal efficiency of capital which greatly affects the level of investment in the short run. Marginal efficiency of capital is nothing but the expected rate of profit on investment in the future. Thus, the marginal efficiency of capital is determined by the expectations of the entrepreneurs regarding the earning of profits from capital assets in the future. But entrepreneurs tend to base their expectations largely on existing facts expecting that the current situation will continue in the future also unless there are definite and concrete signs to the contrary.

The most important fact in the current situation which affects the entrepreneur's expectations regarding profit prospects and thereby the marginal efficiency of capital is the level of current consumption. Thus we see that in the Keynesian scheme of things level of investment ultimately depends upon the level of current consumption. Since marginal propensity to consume is less than one and also the consumption function is stable in the short run, when income increases, consumption does not increase proportionately. As a result, the aggregate demand becomes deficient and the marginal efficiency of capital declines. The decline in the marginal efficiency of capital adversely affects investment which stops rising, As a result, the growth process stops and economic recession occurs. The limited possibilities of increasing investment in the mature capitalist economies are partly due to the constancy of consumption function and declining average propensity to consume which causes the marginal efficiency of capital to decline.

It evident from above that consumption function plays an important role in the determination of income and employment in a free market economy.

QUESTIONS FOR REVIEW

1. What is consumption function ? Explain the objective and subjective factors which determine consumption expenditure in the economy. What are three forms of consumption function ? How do *APC* and *MPC* behave in these forms of consumption function ? Which form of the consumption function seems to be realistic ?
2. Explain Keynes' Psychological Law of Consumption. Explain its importance in the determination of income and employment in the economy.
3. Explain and graphically represent Keynesian consumption function $C = a + bY$. How do marginal propensity to consume (*MPC*) and average propensity to consume (*APC*) change with increase in income in this consumption function ?
4. What is consumption function ? Explain the factors that cause shift in the consumption function.
5. Distinguish between Keynes' consumption function and Kuznets' consumption function. How have these two consumption functions been reconciled ?

6. What is consumption function puzzle ? How has it been resolved ?
7. What is consumption function ? Explain its importance in the theory of determination of income and employment
8. (*a*) What is a saving function ? Derive a saving function from the consumption function, $C = a + bY$

   (*b*) Show that the sum of *APC* and *APS* is equal to one .
9. "Consumption function is an epoch-making contribution to the tools of economic analysis analogous to but even more important than Marshall's discovery of the demand function" (Hansen) Discuss.
10. Why does the *APC* differ from *MPC* ? What factors other than income are likely to be most important in determining consumption ?
11. Given the data of the disposable income (Y_d) and amount of consumption at the initial level of income (₹ 100). Assuming that marginal propensity to consume is 50 per cent to complete the Table and draw the graphs of consumption and saving functions.

Y_d	C	S	APC	MPC	APS	MPS
₹ 100	150					
200						
300						
400						
500						
600						

12. Explain life-cycle theory of consumption and saving. What are its implications for consumer's behaviour regarding reduction in income tax at times of recession for boosting consumption demand ?
13. Explain Friedman's permanent consumption hypothesis. How does it differ from Keynes' consumption function theory ?
14. Explain the importance of Keynsian consumption function. How does it (1) help to refute Say's law of classical economists, (2) show the importance of investment in determining level of income and employment, (3) enables us to derive the theory of multiplier and, (4) explains the tendency of marginal efficiency of capital

CHAPTER 10

Keynes' Theory of Investment Multiplier

THE CONCEPT OF INVESTMENT MULTIPLIER

The theory of multiplier occupies an important place in the modern theory of income and employment. The concept of multiplier was first of all developed by F.A. Kahn in the early 1930s. But Keynes later further refined it. F.A. Kahn developed the concept of multiplier with reference to the increase in employment, direct as well as indirect, as a result of initial increase in investment and employment. Keynes, however, propounded the concept of multiplier with reference to the increase in total income, direct as well as indirect, as a result of original increase in investment and income. Therefore, whereas Kahn's multiplier is known as *'employment multiplier'*, Keynes' multiplier is known as *investment* or *income multiplier.* The essence of multiplier is that total increase in income, output or employment is manifold the original increase in investment. For example, if investment equal to ₹ 100 crores is made, then the income will not rise by ₹ 100 crores only but a multiple of it. If as a result of the investment of ₹ 100 crores, the national income increases by ₹ 300 crores, multiplier is equal to 3. If as a result of investment of ₹ 100 crores, total national income increases by ₹ 400 crores, multiplier is 4. The multiplier is, therefore, the ratio of increment in income to the increment in investment. If ΔI stands for increment in investment and ΔY stands for the resultant increase in income, then multiplier is equal to the ratio of increment in income (ΔY) to the increment in investment (ΔI). Therefore $k = \dfrac{\Delta Y}{\Delta I}$ where k stands for multiplier.

Now, the question is why the increase in income is many times more than the initial increase in investment. It is easy to explain this. Suppose Government undertakes investment expenditure equal to ₹ 100 crores on some public works, say, the construction of rural roads. For this Government will pay wages to the labourers engaged, prices for the materials to the suppliers and remunerations to other factors who make contribution to the work of road-building. The total cost will amount to ₹ 100 crores. This will increase incomes of the people equal to ₹ 100 crores. But this is not all. The people who receive ₹ 100 crores will spend a good part of them on consumer goods. Suppose marginal propensity to consume of the people is 4/5 or 80%. Then out of ₹ 100 crores they will spend ₹ 80 crores on consumer goods, which would increase incomes of those people who supply consumer goods equal to ₹ 80 crores. But those who receive these ₹ 80 crores will also in turn spend these incomes, depending upon their marginal propensity to consume. If their marginal propensity to consume is also 4/5, then they will spend ₹ 64 crores on consumer goods. Thus, this will further increase incomes of some other people equal to ₹ 64 crores. In this way, the chain of consumption expenditure would continue and the income of the people will go on increasing. But every additional increase in income will be progressively less since a part of the income received will be saved. Thus, we see that the income will not increase by only ₹ 100 crores, which was initially invested in the construction of roads, but by many times more.

Derivation of Investment Multiplier

How much increase in national income will take place as a result of an initial increase in investment can be expressed in the following mathematical form:

Increase in income Or $\Delta Y = 100 + 100 \times 4/5 + 100(4/5)^2 + 100(4/5)^3 + 100(4/5)^4 ...$

$$= 100[1 + (4/5) + (4/5)^2 + (4/5)^3 + (4/5)^4...]$$

But the above series is one of geometric progression. Therefore, increase in income,

$$(\Delta Y) = 100 \frac{1}{1-4/5} \quad ...(i)$$

$$= 100 \times \frac{1}{1/5}$$

$$= 100 \times 5$$

$$= 500$$

It is thus clear that if the marginal propensity to consume is 4/5, the investment of ₹ 100 crores leads to the increase in the national income by ₹ 500 crores. Therefore, multiplier here is equal to 5. We can express this in a general formula. If ΔY stands for increase in income, ΔI stands for increase in investment and *MPC* for marginal propensity to consume, we can write the equation (*i*) above as follows:

$$\Delta Y = \Delta I \frac{1}{1-MPC}$$

$$\frac{\Delta Y}{\Delta I} = \frac{1}{1-MPC}$$

$\frac{\Delta Y}{\Delta I}$ measures the size of the multiplier. Therefore,

$$\text{Size of multiplier or } k = \frac{1}{1-MPC} \quad ...(ii)$$

It is clear from above that the size of multiplier depends upon the marginal propensity to consume of the community. The multiplier is the reciprocal of one minus marginal propensity to consume. However, we can express multiplier in a simpler form. As we know that saving is equal to income minus consumption, one minus marginal propensity to consume will be equal to marginal propensity to save, that is, $1 - MPC = MPS$. Therefore, multiplier is equal to $\frac{1}{1-MPC} = \frac{1}{MPS}$.

Algebraic Derivation of Multiplier

The multiplier can be derived algebraically as follows:

Writing the equation for the equilibrium level of income we have

$$Y = C + I \quad ...(1)$$

As in the multiplier analysis we are concerned with changes in income induced by changes in investment, rewriting the equation (1) in terms of changes in the variables we have

$$\Delta Y = \Delta C + \Delta I \quad ...(2)$$

In the simple Keynesian model of income determination, change in investment is considered to be autonomous or independent of changes in income while changes in consumption are function of changes in income.

In the consumption function,

$$C = a + bY$$

where a is a constant term, b is marginal propensity to consume which is also assumed to remain constant. Therefore, change in consumption can occur only if there is change in income. Thus

$$\Delta C = b\Delta Y \qquad ...(3)$$

Substituting (3) into (2) we have

$$\Delta Y = b\Delta Y + \Delta I$$

$$\Delta Y - b\Delta Y = \Delta I$$

$$\Delta Y(1-b) = \Delta I$$

$$\Delta Y = \frac{1}{1-b}\Delta I$$

$$\frac{\Delta Y}{\Delta I} = \frac{1}{1-b}$$

As b stands for marginal propensity to consume,

$$\frac{\Delta Y}{\Delta I} = \frac{1}{1-MPC} = \frac{1}{MPS}$$

This is the same formula of multiplier as obtained earlier. Note that the value of multiplier $\frac{\Delta Y}{\Delta I}$ will remain constant as long as marginal propensity to consume remains the same.

The Size or Value of Investment Multiplier

The multiplier tells us how much increase in income occurs when *autonomous investment* increases by ₹ 1, that is, investment multiplier is $\frac{\Delta Y}{\Delta I}$ and its value is equal to $\frac{1}{1-b}$ where b stands for marginal propensity to consume (*MPC*). Thus, multiplier $= \frac{\Delta Y}{\Delta I} = \frac{1}{1-b}$. Further, since $1 - b$ equals marginal propensity to save (*MPS*) the value of investment multiplier is equal to $\frac{1}{1-b} = \frac{1}{s}$ where s stands for marginal propensity to save. In other words, the size of multiplier is equal to $\frac{1}{1-MPC} = \frac{1}{MPS}$. Thus, the value of multiplier can be obtained if we know either the value of *MPC* or *MPS*.

Now, higher the marginal propensity to consume (b) (or the lower the value of marginal propensity to save (s), the greater the value of multiplier. For example, if marginal propensity to consume (b) is 0.8, investment multiplier is

$$\frac{\Delta Y}{\Delta I} = \frac{1}{1-08} = \frac{1}{0.2} = 1\times\frac{10}{2} = 5$$

If *MPC* or $b = 0.75$, multiplier is

$$= \frac{\Delta Y}{\Delta I} = \frac{1}{1-0.75} = \frac{1}{0.25} = \frac{100}{25} = 4$$

As mentioned above, the size or value of multiplier can be calculated using either the value of marginal propensity to consume (*MPC*) or the value of marginal property to save (*MPS* or s). In fact, the value of multiplier is the reciprocal of marginal propensity to save $\left(\frac{\Delta Y}{\Delta I} = \frac{1}{MPS} \text{ or } \frac{1}{s}\right)$. When marginal propensity to consume is 0.8, marginal propensity to save will be $1 - 0.8 = 0.2$. The multiplier will be $\frac{1}{0.2}$ or $\frac{1}{2/10}$ = 5. Likewise if marginal propensity to consume (b) is 0.75, marginal propensity to save will be 1 – 0.75 = 0.25 and multiplier will be $\frac{1}{0.25} = \frac{1}{25/100} = 4$.

Given the size of multiplier we can find out the increase in income (ΔY) resulting from a certain increase in investment (ΔI) by using the multiplier relationship. Thus

$$\frac{\Delta Y}{\Delta I} = \frac{1}{1-b}$$

$$\Delta Y = \Delta I . \frac{1}{1-b}$$

If marginal propensity to consume is equal to 0.8, with the increase in investment by ₹ 100 crores the increase in income will be:

$$\frac{\Delta Y}{\Delta I} = \frac{1}{1-b}$$

$$\Delta Y = \Delta I \times \frac{1}{1-b} = 100 \times \frac{1}{1-0.8}$$

$$100 \times \frac{1}{0.2} = 100 \times 5 = 500$$

Two Limiting Cases of the Value of Multiplier. There are two limiting cases of the multiplier. One limiting case occurs when the marginal propensity to consume is equal to one, that is, when the whole of the increment in income is consumed and nothing is saved. In this case, the size of multiplier will be equal to infinity, that is, a small increase in investment will bring about a very large increase in income and employment so that full employment is reached and even the process goes beyond that. "In such circumstances, the Government would need to employ only one road builder to raise income indefinitely, causing first full employment and then a limitless spiral of inflation."[1] However, this is unlikely to occur since marginal propensity to consume in the real world is less than one. The other limiting case occurs when marginal propensity to consume is equal to zero, that is, when nothing out of the increment in income is consumed, and the whole increment in income is saved. In this case, the value of the multiplier will be equal to one. That is, in this case, the increment in income will be equal to the original increase in investment and not a multiple of it. But in actual practice the marginal propensity to consume is less than one but more than zero $\left(1 > \frac{\Delta C}{\Delta Y} > 0\right)$. Therefore, *the value of the multiplier is greater than one but less than infinity.*

Working of Multiplier and its Assumptions

In our above explanation of multiplier, we have made many simplifying assumptions. First, we have assumed that the *marginal propensity to consume remains constant throughout* as the income increases in various rounds of consumption expenditure. However, the marginal propensity to consume may differ in various rounds of consumption expenditure. But this constancy of marginal propensity to consume is a realistic assumption, since all available empirical evidence shows that marginal propensity to consume is very stable in the short run. Secondly, we have assumed that there is a net increase in investment in a period and no further indirect effects on investment in that period occur or if they occur they have been taken into account so that there is a given net increase in investment. Further, we have assumed that *there is no any time-lag* between the increase in investment and the

1. Stonier and Hague, *A Textbook of Economic Theory,* 4th edition, 1972.

resultant increment in income. That is, increment in income takes place instantaneously as a result of increment in investment. J.M. Keynes ignored the time-lag in the process of income generation and therefore his multiplier is also called *instantaneous multiplier.* In recent years, the importance of time-lag has been recognised and concept of dynamic multiplier has been developed on that basis.

Another important assumption in the theory of multiplier is that *excess capacity exists in the consumer goods industries* so that when the demand for them increases, more amounts of consumer goods can be produced to meet this demand. If there is no excess capacity in consumer goods industries, the increase in demand as a result of some original increase in investment will bring about rise in prices rather than increases in real income, output and employment. As we shall see later, Keynes' multiplier was evolved in the context of advanced capitalist economies which were in grip of depression and in times of depression and there did exist excess capacity in the consumer goods industries due to lack of aggregate demand. The Keynesian multiplier effect is very small in developing countries like India since there is not much excess capacity in consumer goods industries.

In our above analysis of the multiplier process we have taken a closed economy, that is, we have not taken into account imports and exports. If ours were an open economy, then a part of the increment in consumption expenditure would have been made on imports of goods from abroad. This would have caused increment in income in foreign countries rather than within the country. This will reduce the value of the multiplier. *Imports are important leakage from the multiplier process* and we have ignored them in our above analysis for the purpose of simplicity.

It is worth noting that multiplier not only works in money terms but also in real terms. In other words, multiple increment in income as a result of a given net increase in investment does not only take place in money terms but also in terms of real output, that is, in terms of goods and services. When incomes increase as a result of investment and these increments in income are spent on consumer goods, the output of consumer goods is increased to meet the extra demand brought about by increased incomes. Therefore, real income or output increases by the same amount as the increment in money incomes, since *the prices of goods have been assumed to be constant.* Of course, we have assumed, as has been mentioned above, that there exists excess productive capacity in the consumer goods industries so that when the demand for consumer goods increases, their production can be easily increased to meet this demand. However, if due to some bottlenecks output of goods cannot be increased in response to increasing demand, prices will rise and as a result the real multiplier effect will be small.

Diagrammatic Representation of Multiplier

We have already explained that the level of national income is determined by the equilibrium between aggregate demand and aggregate supply. In other words, the level of national income is fixed at the level where $C + I$ curve intersects the 45° income curve. With such a diagram we can explain the multiplier. The multiplier is illustrated in Fig. 10.1. In this figure C represents marginal propensity to consume. Marginal propensity to consume has been here assumed to be equal to $\frac{1}{2}$ *i.e.,* 0.5. Therefore, the slope of the curve C of marginal propensity to consume curve C has been

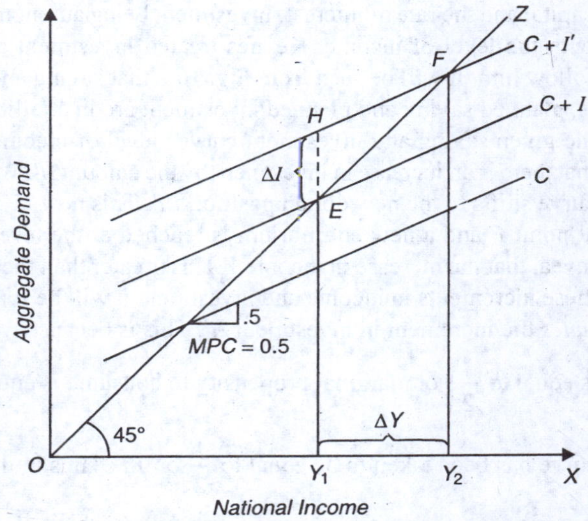

Fig. 10.1. *Keynes' Income Multiplier*

taken to be equal to 0.5. $C + I$ represents aggregate demand curve. It will be seen from Fig. 10.1 that the aggregate demand curve $C + I$ which intersects the 45° line at point E so that the level of income equal to OY_1 is determined. If investment increases by the amount EH we can then find out how much increment in income occur as a result of this. As a consequence of increase in investment by EH, the aggregate demand curve shifted upward to the new position $C + I'$. This new aggregate demand curve $C + I'$ intersects income line at point F so that the equilibrium level of income increases to OY. As a result of net increase in investment equal to EH, the income has increased by Y_1Y_2. It is seen from the figure that Y_1Y_2 is greater than EH. On measuring it will be found that Y_1Y_2 is *twice* the length of EH. This is as it is expected because the market propensity to consume is here equal to $\frac{1}{2}$ and therefore the size of multiplier will be equal to 2.

The multiplier can be illustrated through savings investment diagram also. In a previous chapter we explained the determination of national income also through savings investment diagram. Therefore, the multiplier can also be explained with the help of savings investment diagram, as has been shown in Fig. 10.2. In this figure SS is the saving curve indicating that as the level of income increases, the community plans to save more. II is the investment curve showing the level of investment planned to be undertaken by the investors in the community. The investment has been taken to be a constant amount and autonomous of changes in income. This investment level OI has been determined by the marginal efficiency of capital and the rate of interest. Investment being autonomous of income means that it does not change with the level of income. Keynes treated investment as autonomous of income and we will here follow him. It will be seen from Fig. 10.2 that saving and investment curves intersect at point E, that is, planned saving and planned investment are in equilibrium at the level of income OY_1. Thus, with the given saving and investment curves level of income equal to OY_1 is determined. Now suppose that there is an increase in investment by the amount II'. With this increase in investment, the investment curve shifts to the new dotted position $I'I'$. This new investment curve $I'I$ intersects the saving curve at point F and a new equilibrium is reached at the level of income OY_2. A glance at Fig. 10.2 will reveal that the increase in income Y_1Y_2 is greater than the increase in investment by II''. On measuring these increments in income and investment it will be found that the increment in income $Y_1 Y_2$ is *two times* the increment in investment II'. This is because we have here assumed that propensity to save is equal to $\frac{1}{2}\left(\text{or marginal propensity to consume is equal to } \frac{1}{2}\right)$. Therefore, the slope of the saving curve has been taken to be equal to $\frac{1}{2}$ or 0.5. Thus in this case multiplier is equal to 2.

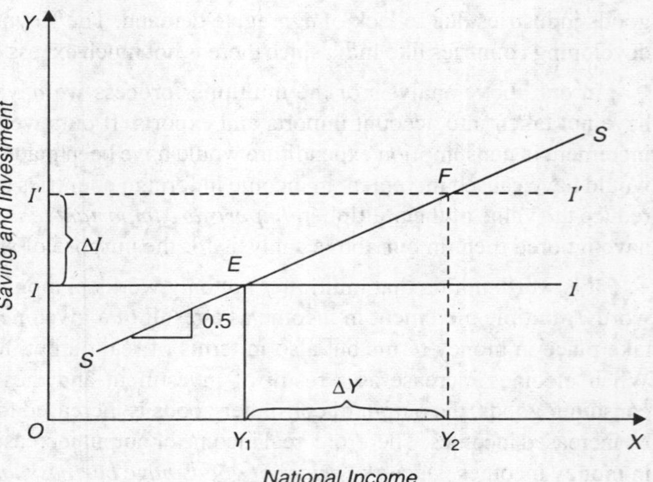

Fig. 10.2. *Multiplier Explained with the Aid of Savings-Investment Diagram*

$$\text{Multiplier} = \frac{\Delta Y}{\Delta I} = \frac{Y_1 Y_2}{II'} = \frac{1}{MPS} = 2$$

Since marginal propensity to save is here equal to $\frac{1}{2}$, the multiplier on the basis of our above formula, namely, $k = \frac{1}{MPS}$ will be equal to 2.

LEAKAGES IN THE MULTIPLIER PROCESS

We have seen above that as a result of increase in investment, the level of income increases by a multiple of it. In our above analysis, saving is a leakage in the multiplier process. Had there been no saving and as a result marginal propensity to consume were equal to 1, the multiplier would have been equal to infinity. In that case as a result of some initial increase in investment, income would go on rising indefinitely. Since marginal propensity to consume is actually less than one, some saving does take place. Therefore, multiplier in actual practice is less than infinity. But besides saving, there are other leakages in the process of income generation which reduce the size of the multiplier. Therefore, the increase in income as a result of some increase in investment will be less than warranted by the size of the multiplier measured by the given marginal propensity to consume. We explain below the various leakages that occur in the income stream and reduce the size of multiplier in the real world.

Paying off debts. The first leakage in the multiplier process occurs in the form of payment of debts by the people, especially by businessmen. In the real world, all income received by the people as a result of some increase in investment is not consumed. A part of the increment in income is used for paying back the debts which the people have taken from moneylenders, banks or other financial institutions. The incomes used for paying back the debts do not get spent on consumer goods and services and therefore leak away from the income stream. This reduces the size of the multiplier. Of course, when incomes received by the moneylenders, banks or institutions are again lent back to the people, they come back to the income stream and enhance the size of multiplier. But this may or may not happen.

Holding of idle cash balances. If the people hold a part of their increment in income as idle cash balances and do not use it for consumption, they also constitute leakage in the multiplier process. As we have seen, people keep part of their income for satisfying their precautionary and speculative motives, money kept for such purposes is not consumed and therefore does not appear in the successive rounds of consumption expenditure and therefore reduces the increments in total income and output.

Imports. In our above analysis of the working of the multiplier process we have taken the example of a closed economy, that is, an economy with no foreign trade. If it is an open economy as is usually the case, then a part of increment in income will also be spent on the imports of consumer goods. The proportion of increments in income spent on the imports of consumer goods will generate income in other countries and will not help in raising income and output in the domestic economy. Therefore, imports constitute another important leakage in the multiplier process. Suppose marginal propensity to save of an open economy is $\frac{1}{4}$, *i.e.*, marginal propensity to consume is $\frac{3}{4}$. Suppose further that marginal propensity to import is $\frac{1}{4}$, the size of the multiplier without imports will be equal to 4 but the size of the multiplier with the marginal propensity to import equal to $\frac{1}{4}$ and the marginal propensity to consume equal to $\frac{3}{4}$ will be smaller.

$$\text{Multiplier in an Open Economy} = \frac{1}{1-(MPC - MPI)} = \frac{1}{1 - MPC + MPI}$$

where *MFC* stands for marginal propensity to consume and *MPI* for marginal propensity to import.

In our example quoted above, where marginal propensity to consume is equal to $\frac{3}{4}$ and marginal propensity to import is equal to $\frac{1}{4}$, the multiplier is:

$$k = \frac{1}{1-\left(\frac{3}{4}-\frac{1}{4}\right)} = \frac{1}{\frac{1}{2}} = 2$$

We, therefore, see that the size of multiplier instead of being equal to 4, as it would have been in the case of a closed economy, is equal to 2 in the open economy with $\frac{1}{4}$ as the marginal propensity to import.

Taxation. Taxation is another important leakage in the multiplier process. The increments in income which the people receive as a result of increase in investment are also in part used for payment of taxes. Therefore, the money used for payment of taxes does not appear in the successive rounds of consumption expenditure in the multiplier process, and the multiplier is reduced to that extent. However, if the money raised through taxation is spent by the Government, the leakage through taxation will be offset by the increase in Government expenditure. But it is not necessary that all the money raised through taxation is spent by the Government as it happens when Government makes a surplus budget. No doubt, if the Government expenditure increases by an amount equal to the taxation, it would not have any adverse effect on the increases in income and investment and in this way there would be no leakage in the multiplier process.

Increase in Prices. Price inflation constitutes another important leakage in the working of the multiplier process in real terms. As we have noted above, the multiplier works in real terms only when as a result of increase in money income and aggregate demand, output of consumer goods is also increased. When output of consumer goods cannot be easily increased, a part of the increases in the money income and aggregate demand raises prices of the goods rather than their output. Therefore, the multiplier is reduced to the extent of price inflation. In developing countries like India the extra incomes and demand are mostly spent on foodgrains whose output cannot be increased so easily. Therefore, the increments in demand raise the prices of goods to a greater extent than the increase in their output. Besides, in developing countries like India, there is not much excess capacity in many consumer goods industries, especially in agriculture and other wage-goods industries. Therefore, when income and demand increase as a result of increase in investment, it generally raises the prices of these goods rather than their output and therefore weakens the working of the multiplier in real terms. Thus, it was often asserted in the past that Keynesian theory of multiplier was not very much relevant to the conditions of developing countries like India.[2] However, we shall discuss later that this old view about the working of Keynes' multiplier is not fully correct.

The above various leakages reduce the multiplier effect of the investment undertaken. If these leakages are plugged, the effect of change in investment on income and employment would be greater.

Multiplier with Changes in Price Level

In our above analysis of multiplier with aggregate demand curve, it is assumed that price level remains constant and the firms are willing to supply more output at a given price. How much national income or GNP increases as a result of any autonomous expenditure such as government expenditure, investment expenditure, net exports is determined by a shift in aggregate demand curve by the size of simple Keynesian multiplier when price level is fixed. This implies a horizontal short-run supply curve. However, as studied above, short-run aggregate supply curve slopes upward as the firms are willing to supply additional output in the short run only at a higher price level. With short-run aggregate supply curve sloping upward, a rightward shift in aggregate demand curve raises new equilibrium GNP level not equal to the horizontal shift in the aggregate demand curve but less than it. Consequently, the size of multiplier is smaller than that of simple Keynesian multiplier with a given fixed price level. This is because a part of expansionary effect of GNP of the increase in autonomous government expenditure is offset by rise in the price level.

---

2. See, V.K.R.V. Rao, Investment, Income and the Multiplier in an Underdeveloped Economy printed in A.N. Agarwala and S.P. Singh (edited), *The Economics of Underdevelopment,* Oxford, 1958.

The multiplier effect in case of upward sloping curve is shown in Fig. 10.3. To begin with, in the top panel of Fig. 10.3 aggregate expenditure curve AE_0 intersects 45° line at point B and determines Y_0 equilibrium level of GNP. In the panel at the bottom of Fig. 10.3 the corresponding aggregate demand curve AD_0 and the short-run aggregate supply curve SAS intersect at B' at the above determined GNP level Y_0. Now suppose autonomous investment expenditure (which is independent of changes in price level) increases by ΔI. As a result, aggregate expenditure curve AE shifts upward to AE_1 and determines new equilibrium GNP level equal to Y_2. In the lower panel (*b*), due to the upward shift in aggregate expenditure curve, aggregate demand curve shifts rightward from AD to AD_1. The horizontal shift in the aggregate demand curve *at a given price level* is determined by the increase in aggregate expenditure multiplied by the simple Keynesian multiplier at the given fixed price level

($B'H$ or $\Delta Y = \Delta I \dfrac{1}{1 - MPC}$)

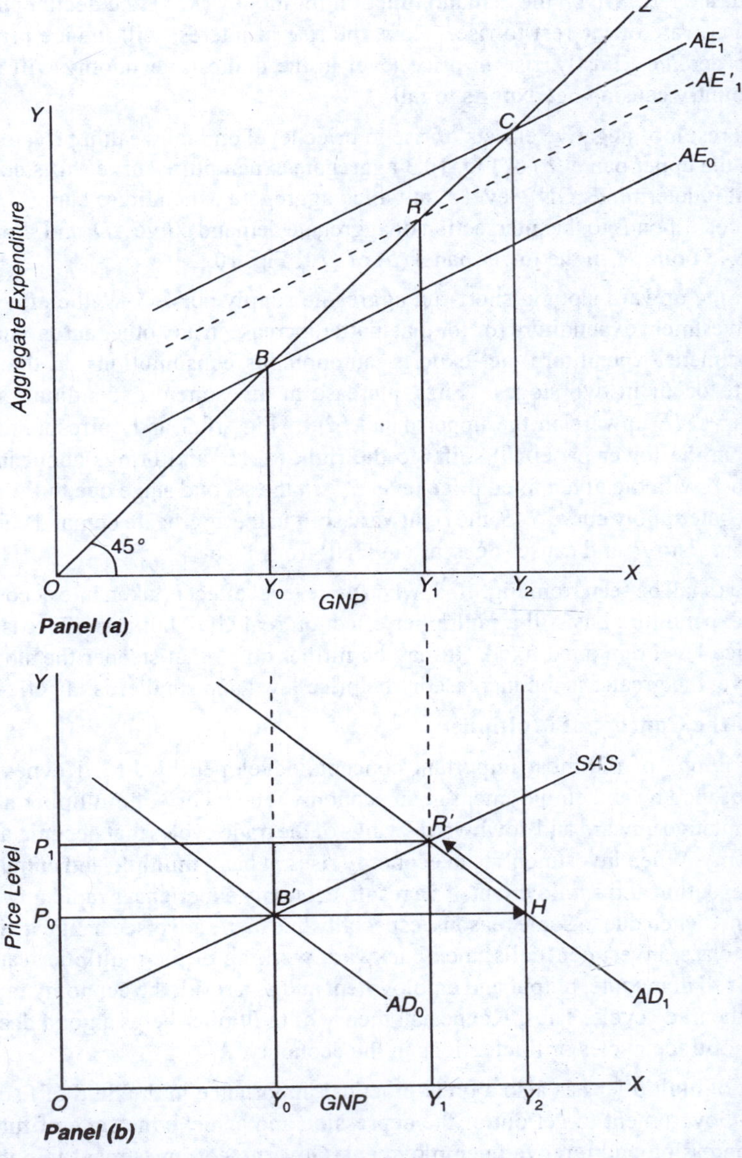

Fig. 10.3. *Multiplier Effect with Changes in Price Level*

But given the upward sloping short-run aggregate supply curve *SAS* with new aggregate demand curve AD_1, price level does not remain fixed. As will be seen from the lower panel (*b*) of Fig. 10.3, the aggregate demand curve AD_1 intersects the short-run aggregate supply curve *SAS* at point *R′* and as a result price level rises to P_1.

Now, with this rise in price level to P_1, aggregate expenditure curve in the upper panel (*a*) will not remain unaffected but will shift downward. This fall in aggregate expenditure curve is due to the adverse effects on wealth or real balances, interest rate and net exports. Much of wealth is held in the form of bank deposits, bonds and shares of companies and other assets. With the rise in price level, *real value or purchasing power* of wealth possessed by the people declines. This induces them to spend less. As a result, consumption expenditure declines due to this wealth effect. Secondly, the rise in price level reduces the *supply of real money balances* (M^s/P) that causes a shift in money supply curve to the left. Given the demand function for money (M^d), the decline in the real money supply will cause rate of interest to rise. Now, the rise in interest will induce private investment expenditure to decline. Lastly, rise in price level in the domestic economy will adversely affect exports of a country causing net exports to fall.

Thus, as a result of negative effects of rise in price level on real wealth, private investment and net exports, in the upper panel (*a*) of Fig. 10.3 aggregate expenditure curve shifts downward to AE_1' (dotted) so that it determines GNP level Y_1 at which aggregate expenditure curve AE_1 intersects 45° line. This also corresponds to the intersection of aggregate demand curve AD_1 and short-run aggregate supply curve *SAS* point *R′* in the lower panel (*b*) of *Q* 1. Fig. 10.3.

Thus with the upward sloping short-run aggregate supply curve *SAS*, the effect of increase in autonomous investment expenditure (or for that matter increase in any other autonomous expenditure such as Government expenditure, net exports, autonomous consumption) on the GNP level can be visualised to occur in two stages. First, increase in investment expenditure shifts aggregate expenditure curve *AE* upward in the upper panel (*a*) of Fig. 10.3 and correspondingly aggregate demand curve in the lower panel (*b*) shifts to the right to AD_1 and brings about increase in GNP level from Y_0 to Y_2 with the given fixed price level P_1. In the second stage due to the upward sloping short-run aggregate supply curve *SAS*, the rightward shift in the aggregate demand curve causes price level to rise from P_0 to P_1 and causes decrease in GNP from Y_2 to Y_1.

However, as shall be seen from Fig. 10.3, when price level effect is taken into account, the increase in investment expenditure has still a multiplier effect on real GDP but this effect is smaller than it would be if price level remained fixed. It may be further noted that steeper the slope of the short-run supply curve, the greater is the increase in the price level and smaller is the effect on real GNP.

Importance of the Concept of Multiplier

Multiplier is one of the most important concepts developed by J.M. Keynes to explain the determination of income and employment in an economy. The theory of multiplier has been used to explain the cumulative upward and downward swings of the trade cycles that occur in a free-enterprise capitalist economy. When investment in an economy rises, it has a multiple and cumulative effect on national income, output and employment. As a result, economy experiences rapid upward movement. On the other hand, when due to some reasons, especially due to the adverse change in the expectations of the business class, investment falls, then backward working of the multiplier causes a multiple and cumulative fall in income, output and employment and as a result the economy rapidly moves on downswing of the trade cycle. Thus, Keynesian theory of multiplier helps a good deal in explaining the movements of trade cycles or fluctuations in the economy.

The theory of multiplier has also a great practical importance in the field of fiscal policy to be pursued by the Government to get out of the depression and achieve the state of full employment. To get rid of depression and remove unemployment, Government investment in public works was recommended even before Keynes. But it was thought that the increase in income will be limited to the amount of investment undertaken in these public works. But the importance of public works is enhanced when it is realised that the total effect on income, output and employment as a result of some initial investment has a multiplier effect. Thus, Keynes recommended Government investment in public works to solve the problem of depression and unemployment.

The public investment in public works such as road building, construction of hospitals, schools, irrigation facilities will raise aggregate demand by a multiple amount. The multiple increase in income and demand will also encourage the increase in private investment. Thus, the deficiency in private investment which leads to the state of depression and underemployment equilibrium will now be made up and a state of full employment will be restored. If the multiplier had not worked, the income and demand would have risen as a result of some public investment but not as much as they rise with the multiplier effect. Inspired by the Keynesian theory of multiplier, expansionary fiscal policy of increase in Government expenditure and reduction in income tax have been adopted by President John Kennedy and President George W. Bush in the United States of America to remove involuntary unemployment and depression. This had a great success in removing unemployment and depression and therefore, Keynesian theory of multiplier was vindicated and as a result people's belif in it increased.

Numerical Problems on Multiplier

Problem 1. *Suppose the level of autonomous investment in an economy is ₹ 200 crores and consumption function of the economy is :*

$$C = 80 + 0.75Y$$

(*a*) *What will be the equilibrium level of income?*

(*b*) *What will be the increase in national income if investment increases by ₹ 25 crores.*

Solution. (*a*) For equilibrium level of income,

$$Y = C + I \quad ...(1)$$

where

$$C = 80 + 0.75$$

$$I = 200 \text{ crores}$$

Substituting the values of C and I in (1) we have

$$Y = 80 + 0.75\text{K} + 200$$

$$(Y - 0.75Y) = 80 + 200 = 280$$

$$0.25\,Y = 280$$

$$Y = 280 \times \frac{100}{25} = 1120$$

Equilibrium level of income is therefore equal to 1120 crores.

(*b*) How much increase in income will occur as a result of increase in investment by ₹ 25 crores depends on the size of multiplier. The size of multipler is determined by the value of marginal propensity to consume. In the given consumption function ($C = 80 + 0.75Y$) marginal propensity to consume is equal to 0.75 or $\frac{3}{4}$. Thus,

$$\text{multiplier} = \frac{1}{1 - MPC} = \frac{1}{1 - \frac{3}{4}} = 4$$

Thus, with increase in investment by ₹ 25 crores, national income will rise by 25 × 4 = 100 crores.

Problem 2. *Suppose in a country investment increases by ₹ 100 crore and consumption is given by C = 10 + 0.6Y (where C = consumption and Y = income). How much increase will there take place in income ?*

Solution.

Multiplier, $$k = \frac{\Delta Y}{\Delta I}$$

or $$\Delta Y = k.\Delta I \quad ...(1)$$

Now, multiplier, $$k = \frac{1}{1 - MPC}$$

In the given consumption, $MPC = 0.6$

$$k = \frac{1}{1-0.6} = \frac{1}{0.4} = \frac{1}{\frac{4}{10}} = \frac{1}{\frac{2}{5}} = 2.5$$

Substituting the value of $k = 2.5$ and ΔI = ₹ 100 in (1) above, we have

$$\Delta Y = 2.5 \times 100 = 250$$

Thus increase in investment by ₹ 100 crore will cause income to rise by ₹ 250 crore.

Problem 3. *What increase in investment needed to raise income by ₹ 4,000 crores, if MPC is 0.75 ? How much will there be increase in consumption and saving due to this increase in income?*

Solution. How much increase in investment is required to raise income by ₹ 4,000 crores depends on the value of multiplier and the size of multiplier (*k*) depends on the marginal propensity to consume (*MPC*). Thus,

$$\text{Multiplier } (k) = \frac{1}{1 - MPC} = \frac{1}{1-0.75} = \frac{1}{0.25} = 4$$

Now, $$k = \frac{\Delta Y}{\Delta I}$$

or $$\Delta I = \frac{\Delta Y}{k} \quad ...(i)$$

Substituting the value of ΔY and k in (*i*), we have

$$\Delta I = \frac{4000}{4} = 1000$$

Thus, investment should rise by ₹ 1,000 crore to achieve ₹ 4,000 crorore increase in income.

THE PARADOX OF THRIFT

An interesting paradox arises when all people in a society try to save more but in fact they are unable to do so. The multiplier theory of Keynes helps a good deal in explaining this paradox. According to this paradox of thrift, the attempt by the people as a whole to save more for hard times such as impending period of recession or unemployment may not materialise and in their bid to save more the s ociety infact may not only end up with the same savings (or, even lower savings) but also in the process cause their consumption or standard of living to decline. Thrift (*i.e.*, the desire to save more) is considered to be a virtue in most of the societies and it is regarded as an act of prudence on the part of individuals to save for a rainy day. According to a proverb, "a penny saved is a penny earned". Further, according to classical economists, savings determine investment which plays a crucial role in accelerating the rate of economic growth. However, the paradox of thrift shows that the efforts to save more, especially in times of depression, may actually deepen the economic crisis and cause output to fall and unemployment to increase. It goes to the credit of Keynes that with his multiplier theory he was able to resolve the paradox of thrift. Keynesian explanation of paradox of thrift has been shown in Fig. 10.4.

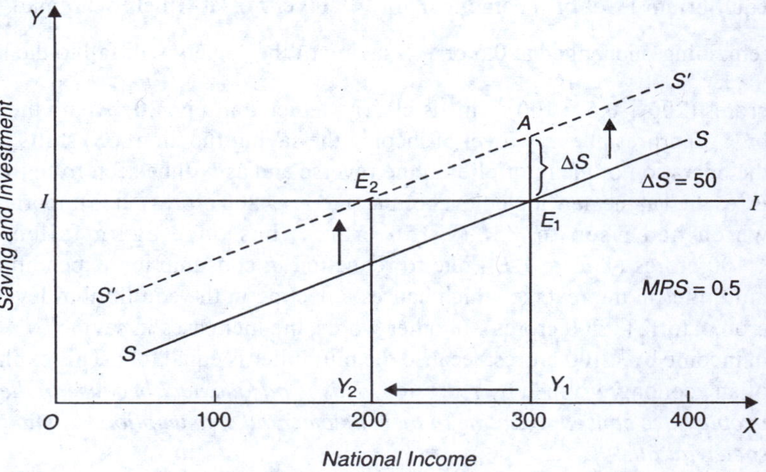

Fig. 10.4. *The Paradox of Thrift*

According to the Keynesian theory, the saying "penny saved is penny earned" is quite inappropriate for the economy as a whole when it is working at underemployment equilibrium, that is, when there prevails recession or depression. Keynes has showed that if *all* people in a society decide to save more, they may actually fail to do so but nevertheless reduce their consumption. This is because, according to Keynes, the effort to save more by all in a society will lower the aggregate demand for goods and services resulting in a drop in the level of national income. At the lower level of national income, the savings fall to the original level but consumption will be less than before which implies that the people would become worse off.

Consider Fig. 10.4, where *SS* is the saving curve with a slope equal to 0.5, and *II* is the planned investment curve. It will be seen that saving and investment curves intersect at point E_1 and determine level of income equal to Y_1 or ₹ 300 crores. Now suppose that expecting hard times ahead all people try to save more by the amount of ₹50 crores which would cause an autonomous downward shift in the consumption function. This downward shift in the consumption function brings about an upward shift by ₹ 50 crores or E_1A in the saving function curve to *S′S′*. This new saving function curve *S′S′* cuts the planned investment curve *II* at point E_2 according to which new equilibrium level of income falls to Y_2 or ₹ 200 crores. It is important to note that level of income does not drop only by the amount (E_1A or ₹ 50 crores), that is, by the extent of reduction in consumption due to more saving but by a multiple of it. With marginal propensity to save (*MPS*) being equal to 0.5 or $\frac{1}{2}$, the value of multiplier would be $1/MPS = 1\frac{1}{2} = 2$. Further, the decline in consumption due to more saving would cause the multiplier to work in reverse, that is, the multiplier would operate to reduce the level of consumption and income by a magnified amount. The decline in consumption expenditure of the people by ₹ 50 crores in the first instance due to more saving by them implies that the producers and sellers of goods and services will find their income to fall by ₹ 50 crores. But the reverse process will not stop here. Given the marginal propensity to consume being equal to 0.5 or $\frac{1}{2}$, the producers/sellers of goods and services in turn would spend ₹ 25 crores less when they find their income has fallen by ₹ 50 crores. It will be observed from Fig. 10.4 that this process of reduction of the level of income will continue till the new saving is equal to investment at the lower level of income Y_2 (₹ 200 crores), that is, the level of income has declined by ₹ 100 crores (50 × 2) from its initial equilibrium level of income Y_1 of ₹ 300 crores. Thus the attempt by all people to save more has led to the decline in the equilibrium level of income to Y_2 or ₹ 200 crores at which, with marginal propensity to consume remaining unchanged at 0.5 or $\frac{1}{2}$, saving of the society will fall to the initial level of Y_1E or ₹ 100 crores (200 × 0.5 = 100). This is clearly depicted in Fig. 10.4. With the decrease in planned saving by ₹ 50 crores at every level of income the saving function (*SS*) shifts upward. This sets in motion the operation of the multiplier in the reverse and as will be seen from the 10.4, the new equilibrium is reached at the new lower level of income Y_2 (₹ 200 crores). It is important to observe that the saving which had risen to Y_1A (₹ 150 crores) has once again fallen to the original level of ₹ 100 crores ($Y_2E_2 = Y_1E_1$) due to reduction in consumption expenditure inducing the working of multiplier in the reverse which causes a decline in the equilibrium level of income from Y_1 (₹ 300 crores) to Y_2 (₹ 200 crores). In other words, the incr eases in saving by ₹ 50 crores has led to the fall in income by ₹ 100 crores because the multiplier is equal to 2. This explains the paradoxical feature of an economy gripped by recession. *This is paradoxical because in their attempt to save more the people have caused a decline in their income and consumption with no increase in the saving of the society at all.*

In our analysis we have assumed that the planned investment is fixed, that is, determined outside the model. In other words, the investment has been assumed to be *autonomous of income,* that is, it does not vary with income.

Can We Avert the Paradox of Thrift?

Paradox of thrift holds good when a free market economy is in the grip of recession or depression and investment demand is inadequate due to lack of profit opportunities. However, it has been pointed out by some economists that paradox of thrift can be averted if the extra savings that the people do for a rainy day are somehow channeled into additional investment through financial markets. Indeed, the classical economists argued that the increase in the supply of savings would lead to the fall in the rate of interest which would induce increase in planned investment. If this happens, then in our saving-investment diagram the investment curve *II* would shift up to *I′I′* and as will be seen from Fig. 10.5 the new equilibrium level of income may not fall and therefore the paradox of thrift is averted.

In Fig. 10.5, initially the saving curve (S_1S_1) and investment curve (*II*) intersect at point E_1 and determine Y_1 level of income. Now, if the people of the society expecting difficult times ahead,\ desire to save E_1A more. If these extra savings, for reasons mentioned above, result in more investment, the investment curve will shift to *I′I′*, the new equilibrium will be at point *A* corresponding to the original level of income Y_1. In this way the paradox of thrift has been averted.

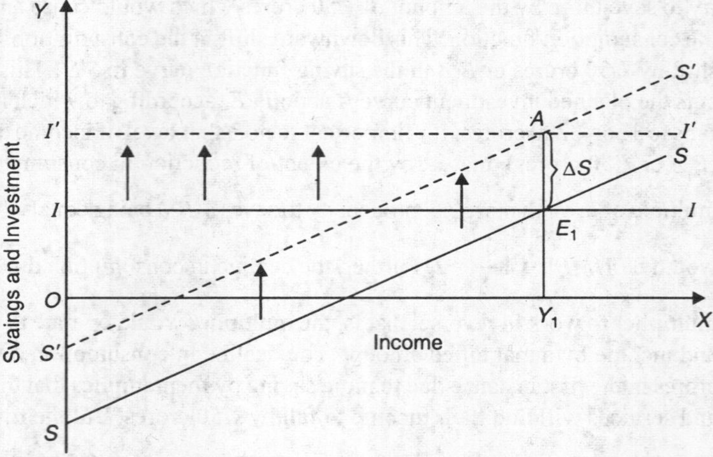

Fig. 10.5. *The situation when paradox of thrift does not hold.*

However, according to the modern economists, especially the followers of Keynes, the empirical evidence does not support the above argument of averting the paradox of thrift. This is because at times of recession or depression, the prospective yields from investment are so small that no possible reduction in the rate of interest will induce sufficient increase in investment. Thus, according to them, in a free-market and private enterprise economy without Government intervention paradox of thrift cannot be averted. Of course, if the Government intervenes as it does even in the present-day predominantly private enterprise economies of the USA and Great Britain, it can mobilise the extra savings of the people and invest them in some worthwhile projects and thus prevent aggregate demand and income from falling. This can happen because the Government undertakes investment because it is not motivated by profit motive but by the considerations of promoting social interest and economic growth. It is because of this that the role of the Government has greatly increased for overcoming recession in the capitalist countries.

THE KEYNESIAN EXPLANATION OF GREAT DEPRESSION: THE IMPACT OF MULTIPLIER

During the 1930s the capitalist economies experienced severe depression which caused widespread involuntary unemployment, substantial loss of output and income and crushing hunger and poverty among the working classes. As explained earlier, the classical economists attributed this unemployment and depression to the higher wage rates maintained by the trade unions and the Government. However, this explanation did not prove to be valid. It was English economist J.M. Keynes who radically departed from the classical thought and put forward the view that it was the large decline in investment that caused the depression and substantial increase in involuntary unemployment. According to Keynes, the investment was highly volatile and it was a drastic decline in it due to the pressimistic expectations of the entrepreneurs about the prospective profits from investment that brought about a decline in aggregate demand (expenditure) which through working of the multiplier in the reverse caused a magnified fall in income (output) and employment. For example, during the first four years (1929-33) of depression in the USA the unemployment which was only 3.2 per cent in 1929 soared to 25 per cent in 1933, that is, one out of four in the labour force in the United States became unemployed. The level of national income dropped from $ 315 billion in 1929 to $ 222 billion in 1933 at 1972 prices, a decline of $ 93 billion in just four years. According to Keynes, this was caused by a drastic fall in investment from $ 56 billion in 1929 to $ 8.5 billion in 1993.

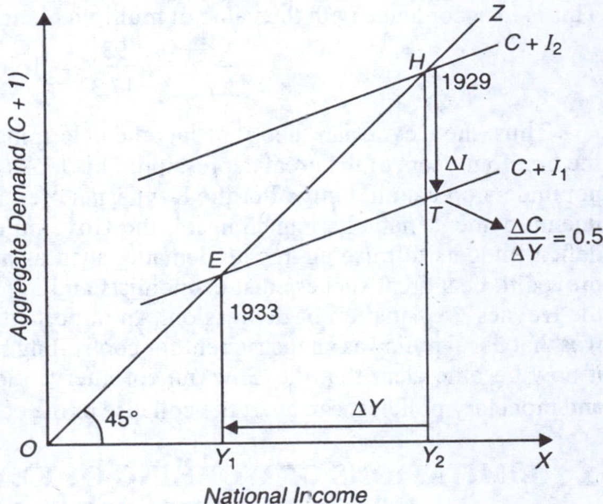

Fig. 10.6. *Depression of 1930s Caused by a Decline in Investment and Working of Multiplier in Reverse*

The huge decline in national income and the emergence of unemployment in the USA, UK and other industrialised capitalist countries during the period of depression is graphically shown in Fig. 10.6. It is assumed that to begin with, say in 1929, the aggregate demand curve $C + I_2$ intersects 45° line at point H and determines equilibrium level of income at full-employment or potential output level OY_1. The sharp decline in investment by the amount *HT* due to the fall in profitability of investment following a crash in stock markets in 1929 and other unfavourable events caused a downward shift in the aggregate demand curve to $C + I_1$ (where $I_1 < I_2$). This new aggregate demand curve $C + I_1$ intersects the 45° line at point *E* and accordingly determines equilibrium level of income OY_1 which is much lower than full-employment level OY_F and thus represents a state of depression with a large unemployment of workers. *The important point made by Keynes was that income would not fall merely equal to the decline in investment but by a multiple of it.* In fact, during the depression period of 1930s, it actually happened so and is evident from Table 10.1. It will be seen from Figure 10.6 that the decline in national income $Y_F Y_1$ is not equal to the fall in investment by *HT* by out by a multiple of it. $Y_F Y_1$ is twice that of *HT*. As explained above, this is due to the working of multiplier in the reverse. Further note that after taking into all leakages in the multiplier process it has been assumed that marginal propensity to consume is equal to 0.5 which yields the value of multiplier 1/1-*MPC* = 1/1-1/2 = 2, This is why fall in income by $Y_F Y_1$ is twice the decline in investment by *HT*.

Now, the historical record of this period about the various components of aggregate demand of the US economy shows that changes in net exports and Government expenditure were quite small and they mostly offset each other during the period 1929-33. The drastic drop in private investment appears to be the basic reason for the huge fall in aggregate demand or spending. The private investment which was $ 56 billion in 1920 fell to only $8.5 billion in 1933 in the U.S.A., the decline

Table 10.1. Impact of Multiplier on National Income and Unemployment during Depression

(in billion US $)

	1929	**1933**	**Change**
Investment	56	8.5	47.5
National Income	315	222	93
Unemployment (% of labour force)	3.2	25	21.8

of $ 47.5 billion in four years. But, as has been explained by Keynes, the decrease in aggregate expenditure was not merely equal to $ 47.5 billion, but by a multiple amount due to the operation of the multiplier in the reverse. It has been estimated that taking into account all leakages in the multiplier process, the value of the multiplier was around 2 during the period. Therefore, as a result of sharp decline in investment by $ 47.5 billion and consequently operation of the multiplier in the reverse there was a fall in the induced consumption expenditure. Thus, as a result of the sharp drop in private investment and resultant fall in induced consumption due to working of multiplier caused much bigger decrease ($ 93 billion) in the level of aggregate effective demand, income and output. This is in accordance with the value of multiplier being equal to around 2. Multiplier is here equal to

$$\frac{\Delta Y}{\Delta I} = \frac{93}{47.3} = 1.96$$

Thus, the Keynesian theory of income determination provides a fairly accurate explanation of the first four years of the great depression. This looks rather simple but during the early 1930s it was not understood at all. Only after the Keynesian prescription to ward off depression and involuntary unemployment, namely, launching by the Government public works programme financed by the deficit budgets to raise aggregate demand, such as adopted under New Deal Policy in the U.S.A. proved to be a great success that economists and intellectuals were convinced about the validity of the Keynes' explanation of depression. An important result of the success of the Keynesian model was that fiscal policy as an instrument for controlling business cycles came into prominence. Further, it now became clear that the Government intervention, through the adoption of appropriate fiscal and monetary policies, can avert the collapse of the economy such as that happened during 1929-33.

LIMITATIONS OF WORKING OF KEYNESIAN MULTIPLIER IN THE DEVELOPING COUNTRIES

The Old View

In the early fifties an eminent Indian economist Dr. V.K. R.V. Rao[3] and some others explained

3. Dr. V.K.R. V. Rao, Investment, Income and Multiplier in an Under developed Economy, *Indian Economic Review,* February 1952.

that in developing countries like India Keynesian multiplier did not work in real terms, that is, does not operate to increase income and employment by a multiple of the initial increase in investment. He claimed that the concept of investment multiplier was valid in the context of the situation of depression in the industrialised developed economies of the UK and the USA where there existed a lot of excess productive capacity and a larger number of open involuntary unemployment. He argued that in such a situation of a depressed economy there was a high elasticity of supply of output to changes in demand for them. Therefore, in the developed capitalist economies ridden with depression increase in investment leading to successive rounds of consumption expenditure raises aggregate demand. Due to the existence of large excess capacity and involuntary unemployment under conditions of depression aggregate supply of outputs highly elastic, increase in aggregate demand brings about increase in real income, output and employment which is a multiple of original increase in investment.

On the other hand, they claimed that in underdeveloped countries there was little excess capacity in consumer goods industries and therefore supply of output was inelastic. Therefore, when there is injection of investment, and as a result through successive rounds of the operation of multiplier, aggregate demand for consumer goods increases, it results mainly in rise in money income brought about through rise in prices and not an increase in real national income.

The second condition, according to Dr. Rao and his followers, for the working of multiplier in raising national income and employment was that the supply of raw materials, financial capital must be sufficiently elastic so that when aggregate demand increases as a result of multiplier effect of increase in investment the supply of output could be increased adequately to meet this higher demand for goods and services. They argued that in underdeveloped countries like India due to under developed nature of their economies, there was acute scarcity of raw materials, other intermediate goods such as steel, cement and financial capital which put great obstacles for the working of multiplier in real terms.

The third condition required for the working of multiplier in real terms was that there should be involuntary open unemployment so that when aggregate demand for goods increases as a consequence of new investment, the adequate supply of workers must be forthcoming to be employed in the production processes of various industries. They argued this condition too was not fulfilled in the under developed countries where there existed disguised unemployment, especially in the agricultural sector. The disguisedly unemployed workers who are supported by joint family system could not be easily shifted to be employed in the industries for expansion of output to achieve the multiplier effect.

Lastly, it was pointed out that the under developed countries like India had predominantly agricultural economies and income elasticity of demand for foodgrains was very high in these economies. In view of this when increase in investment leads to the rise in money incomes of the people, a large part is spent on foodgrains. But the supply of agricultural products is inelastic because their production is subject to uncertain natural factors like monsoon and climate and further there was lack of irrigation facilities, improved seeds, fertilizers etc. Hence it was difficult to increase agricultural production in response to the increase in demand through the multiplier effect of increase in investment.

It follows from above that the Keynesian assumptions for the working of multiplier in real terms, namely (a) the supply of output of goods is elastic due to the existence of large excess capacity, (b) the supply of raw materials and other intermediate goods can be adequately increased, (c) there exist involuntarily unemployed workers searching for work and, (d) sufficiently elastic agricultural output. In view of the earlier economists these assumptions for realising the multiplier effect in terms of rise in real income and employment were not valid in case of under developed countries. Therefore, according to them, Keynesian multiplier did not operate in real terms in under developed countries and actually leads to the rise in price or inflationary conditions in them.

The Modern View

We have explained above the views of some eminent Indian economists, such Dr. V.K.R.V. Rao, Dr. A.K. Dass Gupta, expressed during the early fifties regarding non-operation of the Keynesian multiplier in the under developed countries. But the situation in the present-day developing countries has substantially changed in the last 60 years. There has been a lot of economic growth and structural transformation in the Indian economy during the last half a century so that supply conditions today have become significantly elastic. So in the present state of the Indian economy and also of some other developing economies, it cannot be said that Keynesian multiplier is not applicable in real terms in them. However, it may be noted that even in the fifties and early sixties the view that Keynesian multiplier did not work in the under developed countries did not go entirely unchallenged. Thus commenting on Dr. Rao's article, Dr. K.N. Raj remarked that "Discarding the Keynesian thesis as altogether inoperative in under developed countries is really throwing the baby away with the bath water".[4] Similarly, Dr. D.R. Khatkhate wrote, "In conclusion we may state that the multiplier can operate in an under developed economy when it is associated with a carefully designed pattern of investment. The theory that the multiplier works in a backward economy only with reference to the money income is based on static assumptions and is, therefore, not correct"[5]. Likewise, Dr. Ashok Mathur writes: "Our main objection against the view that Keynesian multiplier does not operate in the under developed countries is that it views the operation of multiplier process in a completely static setting and as a purely short-period concept, whereas the very rationale of economic development is long-run dynamic change. Once we relax these two restrictive assumptions, the essential content of the Keynesian multiplier, that is, increase of investment results in an increase in output which is much in excess of the original outlay on investment, holds true in case of the developing as much as in the developed economies"[6].

At present, in the beginning of the new millennium as a result of economic growth both in the industrial and agricultural sectors the Indian economy has a widely diversified structure and supply of output has become quite elastic, at least in the industrial sector. Besides, at times there is a lot of excess or unutilised capacity in several industries in India due to the deficiency of aggregate demand. The potential for increasing raw materials and intermediate products such as cement, steel and fertilizers has significantly increased to meet the rising demand for them.

If there is injection of investment it will result in manifold increase in output or real income and employment through the working of the multiplier. If the injection of new investment package is quite diversified and balanced, as is generally planned in our Five Year Plans, the investment and growth in several industries simultaneously will create not only additional demand for each other as was visualised by Nurkse[7] but will also create productive capacities in them which will ultimately over a period of result in multiple increase in output and employment.

It is worth noting that in India today there is not only a lot of preexisting excess production capacity in the Indian industries but new investment every year also creates additional production capacity which with some time-lag will result in increase in real income or output, if adequate aggregate demand is forthcoming for its utilisation. Harrod-Domar in their famous dynamic growth models emphasised that investment not only creates demand but also new productive capacity[8].

4. Dr. K.N. Raj, "Dr. Rao on Investment, Income and the Multiplier in an Under developed Economy–a comment", *Indian Economic Review*, p. 1952.
5. D.R. Khatkhate, "The Multiplier Process in Developing Economies", *Indian Economic Journal,* Oct. 1954.
6. Ashok Mathur, "On Throwing the Baby Away with the Bath Water", *Indian Economic Journal,* April-June; 1965.
7. Ragnar Nurkse, *Problems of Capital Formation in Underdeveloped Countries,*
8. See E. Domar, "Capital Expansion, Rate of Growth and Employment", *Economic*, Vol. 14, 1946 and R.E. Harrod, "Towards a Dynamic Economics," Macmillan & Co. London, 1948.

Thus, if we look at increment in investment from the viewpoint of dynamics of development and take a longer time horizon, multiplier effect of new investment in the developing countries can become a reality. It is true that increase in money incomes and demand may tend to occur ahead of the increase in real income but subject to some time-lag between investment and consequent increase in production capacity, the latter would tend to catch up with the former. The significant point to note is that investment not only creates demand but it also creates production capacity. Ultimately there is no reason as to why multiplier effect of new investment on real income or output may not materialise, though the actual period required for realisation of the multiplier effect depends on various time-lags in the process of income generation and capacity creation. The wider the range to industries over which initial investment is undertaken, the greater will be the multiplier effect. This is because monetary demand or expenditure generated by investment in any one industry would be easily met by the increase in production capacity in a variety of industries. In this way increase in demand resulting from investment would not lead to rise in prices but will cause real output to rise.

Agriculture and Multiplier. As mentioned above, the argument for non-operation of multiplier in underdeveloped countries was also partly based on the inelastic nature of supply of agricultural output especially foodgrains as it was pointed out that a large part of monetary demand or money incomes generated by investment would be spent on foodgrains. Inability to meet the rise in demand for foodgrains would cause rise in price level or inflation in the economy rather than increase in real output. It may be pointed out that thanks to the spread of green revolution technology expansion in irrigation facilities in various states of India, foodgrain production can be adequately increased in response to rising demand for foodgrains.

Furthermore, it was asserted by Dr. Rao, the existence of disguised unemployment in underdeveloped countries instead of Keynesian type involuntary open unemployment also prevented the working of multiplier in real terms. In the Indian economy today there are a large number of involuntarily unemployed workers crying out for employment. So this argument for failure of multiplier to work in real terms no longer holds good in the present economic situation.

Conclusion

To conclude, in the present economic situation of the Indian economy with a lot of excess production capacity in several consumer goods industries and a large potential for expanding agricultural production, increase in investment would produce a real multiplier effect on increasing real income and output without causing inflationary pressures in the economy. Multiplier effect of new investment can be further increased, if investment package is quite diversified covering a large number of industries (including agriculture) so that monetary demand and income generated by any one industry can be adequately met by increase in output capacity in other industries. Further, even when there is no preexisting excess capacity in the industries increase in investment leads to the increase in demand for consumption goods which in turn causes further rise on investment to meet that consumption demand. The effect of increase in consumption demand on expansion in investment is generally referred to as *accelerator.* Indeed, the combined working of multiplier and acceleration, which is called *super-multiplier,* leading to manifold increase in output can take place in the growth process in the developing countries like India[9].

QUESTIONS FOR REVIEW

1. What is investment multiplier ? How is it related to marginal propensity to consume ? [**Hints :** Keynes' investment multiplier is also called Income multiplier.]
2. What is income multiplier ? Find out the value of multiplier given the following : *(a)* $MPC = 0.80$, *(b)* $MPC = 0.75$, *(c)* $MPS = 0.20$, *(d)* $MPS = 0.50$.

9. See V.N. Pandit, "Macroeconomic Characteristics of the Indian Economy", in Prabhat Patnaik, ed., *Macro-economics,* Oxford University Press, p. 205.

3. Explain the concept of investment multiplier or marginal propensity to save is 0.1. What is the value of multiplier ?
4. Discuss the Keynesian theory of investment multiplier. What are possible leakages in the multiplier mechanism ?
5. "Keynesian investment multiplier does not operate in the developing countries like India." Do you agree ? Discuss.
6. "Multiplier does not work in real terms in developing countries". *(Dr. V.K.R.V Rao)* What prevents the multiplier to work in real terms in India ?
7. Even though marginal propensity to consume is quite high in LDCs, an increase in government expenditure may have little expansionary effect. Discuss
8. (*a*) Explain the concept of multiplier. How does it work ?
   (*b*) What increase in investment is needed to raise income by ₹ 5,000 crores, if MPC is 0.8 ? How much will there be increase in consumption and saving due to this increase in income ?
9. What is paradox of thrift ? How would you explain it ?
10. "If all people in a society decide to save more, they may actually fail to do so, but nevertheless reduce their consumption.". Explain.

CHAPTER 11

Investment Demand and Accelerator Theory

Introduction

Levels of national income and employment in the short run depend upon the level of aggregate demand. The aggregate demand consists of two constituents—consumption demand and investment demand. In the previous chapter we have studied the consumption function and the various factors which determine it. In the present chapter we shall discuss the factors which determine the investment demand or inducement to invest. Since consumption function is more or less stable in the short run, investment demand is of crucial importance in the determination of income and employment. The greater the level of investment, the greater the level of income and employment. According to Keynes, the equilibrium of a capitalist economy is generally not established at the level of full employment, primarily because investment demand is insufficient to fill up the saving gap corresponding to the level of full employment. Therefore, underemployment equilibrium, on which Keynes laid a great stress, is due to the lack of investment demand as compared to the amount of saving at full-employment level of income, there emerges an *inflationary gap* in the economy which brings about the rise in general price level. We thus see that investment demand plays a vital role in the determination of national income, employment and prices in the country.

Meaning of Investment

It is useful to make the meaning of investment clear. When a person buys shares, bonds or debentures of a public limited company from the market, it is generally said that he has made investment. But this is not the real investment which determines income and employment in the country and with which we are here concerned. Buying of existing shares and bonds by an individual is merely a financial investment. When one individual purchases the shares or bonds, some other one would sell them. Thus, the purchase and sale of the shares merely represents the change in the ownership of assets which already exists rather than the creation of new capital assets. It is the new addition to the stock of physical capital such as plant, machines, trucks, new factories and so on that creates income and employment. Therefore, *by real investment we mean the addition to the stock of physical capital*. Thus, in economics, investment means the new expenditure incurred on addition of capital goods such as machines, buildings, equipment, tools, etc. The addition to the stock of physical capital, *i.e.,* net investment raises the level of aggregate demand which brings about addition to the level of income and employment in the economy. Keynes and many other economists also include the increase in the *inventories* of consumer goods in the capital of the country and therefore in the investment.

TYPES OF INVESTMENT

Distinction must be drawn between the following three types of investment:

1. Business fixed investment
2. Residential investment
3. Inventory investment

We explain below their meanings and the factors which determine them.

Business Fixed Investment

Business fixed investment means investment in the machines, tools and equipment that businessmen buy for use in further production of goods and services. The stock of these machines or plant equipment etc. represents fixed capital. The term 'fixed' in it implies that expenditure made on the machines, equipment etc. continues to be used for production for a relatively long time. This is in contrast to inventory investment whose components will be either used shortly for production or sold shortly to others for further production.

Business fixed investment is important in two respects. First, business fixed investment is an important component of aggregate demand and therefore plays a significant role in the determination of natural income and employment. Business fixed investment is a volatile component of aggregate demand and, as Keynes emphasized, fluctuation in levels of fixed business investment is responsible for business cycles in a free market economy.

As we shall explain in detail later in this chapter Keynes put forward a theory of investment which states that business fixed investment is determined by *expected rate of profit* (which he calls *marginal efficiency of capital*) and rate of interest. Since rate of interest in the short run is relatively sticky, it is changes in expectations about earning profits in future that cause fluctuations in business fixed investment.

According to the neoclassical theory, business fixed investment is determined by the marginal product of capital on one hand and user's cost of capital on the other. The user's cost of capital merely depends on the price of capital goods, the interest rate and the depreciation rate. According to the neoclassical model, if marginal product of capital exceeds user's cost of capital, firms will find it profitable to undertake fixed investment. In this model, rate of interest, which is an important component of the user cost of capital, and taxation of profits play an important role in the determination of business fixed investment. The neoclassical theory will be discussed in detail later in this chapter.

Residential Investment

Residential investment refers to the expenditure which people make on constructing or buying new houses or dwelling apartments for the purpose of living or renting out to others. Residential investment varies from 3 per cent to 5 per cent of GDP in various countries. Two important features of residential investment are worth noting. First, since the average life of a housing unit is of 40 to 50 years, the stock of existing housing units at a point of time is very large as compared to the new residential investment in a year (*i.e.,* flow of residential investment). Second, there is well developed resale market for housing units so that people who construct or own them can sell them in this secondary market.

Residential investment depends on price of existing housing units. The higher the price of existing units, the higher will be investment in constructing and buying new housing units. The price of housing units is determined by demand for housing units which slopes downward and the supply of existing units which is a fixed quantity and its supply curve is therefore vertical straight line.

In the long run demand for housing is determined by rate of population growth and formation of new households. The higher rate of population growth will lead to the increase in demand for housing units. The tendency towards two-member households has led to greater demand for housing units. Income is another important factor determining demand for houses and therefore greater residential investment. Since level of income over time fluctuates a good deal, there is strong cyclical pattern of investment in residential construction.

Finally, interest is another important factor that determines demand for dwelling units. Most houses, especially in cities, are purchased by borrowing funds from banks for a long time, say 20 to 25 years. Generally, the houses purchased are mortgaged with banks or other financial institutions who provide funds for this purpose. The individuals who purchase houses on mortgage borrowing pay monthly installment of original sum borrowed plus interest. Therefore demand for housing units is highly sensitive to changes in rate of interest. Therefore, monetary policy has a substantial effect on residential investment.

Inventory Investment

Firms hold inventories of raw materials, semi-finished goods to be processed into final goods. The firms also hold inventories of finished goods to be sold shortly. The *change in the inventories* or stocks of these goods with the firms is called inventory investment. Now, why do firms hold inventories? The first motive of holding inventories is *smoothing of the level of production.* The firms experience temporary booms and busts in sales of their output. Instead of adjusting their production each time to match the changes in sales of the product they find cheaper to produce goods *at a steady rate.* With this steady rate of production when sales are low, the firms will be producing more than they are selling and therefore in these periods they will hold the extra goods produced as inventories. On the other hand, when sales are high with a steady rate of production, they will be producing less than they sell. In such periods to meet the market demand for goods, they will take out goods from inventories to meet the demand.

The second reason for holding inventories is that *it is less costly* for a firm to buy inputs such as raw materials *less frequently in large quantities* to produce goods and therefore it is required to hold inventories of raw materials and other intermediate products. Buying small quantities of the materials more frequently to produce goods is a more costly affair.

The third reason for holding inventories by the firms is to avoid '*running out of stock' possibilities* when their sales of goods are high and therefore it is profitable to sell at that time. This requires them to hold inventories of goods.

Determinants of Inventory Investment. The inventories of raw materials and goods depend on the level of output which a firm plans to produce. An important model that explains the inventories of raw materials and goods is the *accelerator model.* Though the accelerator model applies to all types of investment, it applies best in case of inventory investment. According to the accelerator model, the firms hold the total stock of inventories of raw materials and goods that is proportional to their level of output. When manufacturing firms' level of output is high, they require to keep more inventories of materials and of goods in process of being converted into finished products. When the economy is booming, retail firms would like to hold more inventories so that the goods they are selling may not go out of stock and their customers go away disappointed. Thus, if N stands for the stock of inventories and Y for level of output, then

$$N = \beta Y$$

where β is proportion of output (Y) that the firms want to hold as inventories.

Now, since inventory investment (I) means the change in stock of inventories, it can be written as follows :

$$I_n = \Delta N = \beta \Delta Y$$

The accelerator model predicts that given the parameter β when output of firms increases, inventory investment will increase and when output falis, the inventory investment by firms will decline. In fact, when output of goods falls due to slackening of demand, the firms will allow the inventories to run down which implies negative inventory investment.

The empirical macroeconomic studies made in United States indicated that for every dollar increase in GDP, there is 0.20 of inventory investment. That is, value of β in the accelerator model is 0.2. In quantitative terms, the accelerator model of inventory investment can be written as

$$I_n = 0.2\,\Delta Y$$

Autonomous Investment and Induced Investment

After Keynes two types of investments have been distinguished. One is *autonomous investment* and the second is *induced investment*. By autonomous investment we mean the investment which does not change with the changes in the income level and is therefore independent of income. Keynes thought that the level of investment depends upon marginal efficiency of capital and the rate of interest. He thought changes in income level will not affect investment. This view of Keynes is based upon his preoccupation with short-run problem. He was of the opinion that changes in income level will affect investment only in the long run. Therefore, considering it as the short-run problem he treated investment as independent of the changes in the income level. In fact the distinction between autonomous investment and induced investment has been made by post-Keynesian economists. *Autonomous investment refers to the investment which does not depend upon changes in the income level.* This autonomous investment generally takes place in houses, roads, public undertakings and in other types of economic infrastructure such as power, transport and communication. This *autonomous investment depends more on population growth and technical progress than on the level of income.* Most of the investment undertaken by Government is of the autonomous nature. The investment undertaken by Government in various development projects to accelerate economic growth of the country is of autonomous type. The autonomous investment is depicted in Fig. 11.1 where it will be seen that whatever the level of national income, investment remains the same at I_a. Therefore the autonomous investment curve is a horizontal straight line.

On the other hand, induced investment is that investment which is affected by the changes in the

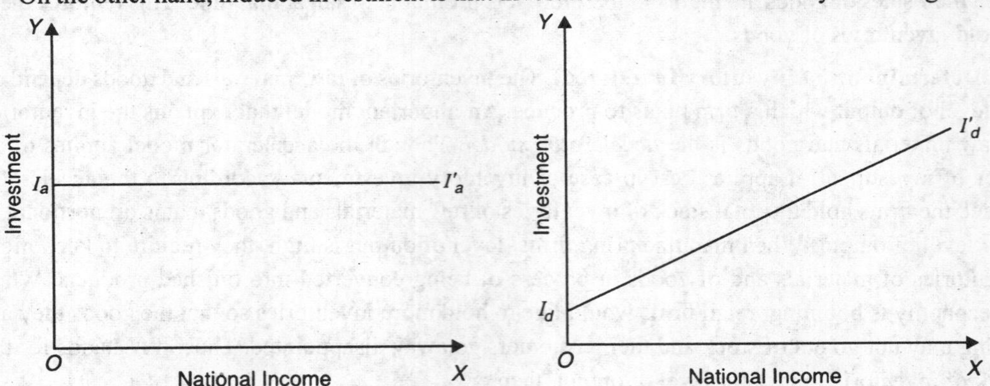

Fig. 11.1. *Autonomous Investment* **Fig. 11.2.** *Induced Investment*

level of income. The greater the level of income, the larger will be the consumption of the community. In order to produce more consumer goods, more investment has to be made in capital goods so that greater output of consumer goods becomes possible. Keynes regarded rate of interest as a factor determining induced investment but the empirical evidence gathered so far suggests that induced investment depends more on income than on the rate of interest. Induced investment is shown in Fig. 11.2 where it will be seen that with the increase in national income, induced investment is increasing. Increase in national income implies that demand for output of goods and services increases. To produce greater output, more capital goods are required to produce them. To have more capital goods more investment has to be undertaken. This induced investment is undertaken both in fixed capital assets and in inventories. The essence of induced investment is that greater income and therefore greater aggregate demand affects the level of investment in the economy. The induced investment underlines the concept of the principle of accelerator, which is highly useful in explaining the occurrence of trade cycles.

DETERMINANTS OF INVESTMENT

Inducement to invest or investment demand depends upon two factors: (1) expected rate of profits to which Keynes gives the name *Marginal Efficiency of Capital,* and. (2) the rate of interest. It can be easily shown that investment is determined by expected rate of profit and the rate of interest. A person having an amount of savings has two alternatives before him. Either he should invest his savings in machines, factories, etc., or he can lend his savings to others on a certain rate of interest. If investment undertaken in machines or factories is expected to fetch 25% rate of profit, while the current rate of interest is only 15%, then it is obvious that the person would invest his savings in machinery or factory.

Rate of Interest

It follows from above, if investment is to be profitable then the expected rate of profit must not be less than the current market rate of interest. If the expected rate of profit is greater than the market rate of interest, new investment will take place. If an entrepreneur does not invest his own savings but has to borrow from others, then it becomes much clear that the expected rate of profit from investment in any capital asset must not be less than the rate of interest he has to pay. For instance, if an entrepreneur borrows funds from others at 15% rate of interest, then the investment proposed to be undertaken will actually be undertaken only if the expected rate of profit from it is more than 15 per cent. We thus see that investment depends upon marginal efficiency of capital on the one hand and the rate of interest on the other. Investment will be undertaken in any given form of capital asset till the expected rate of profit or marginal efficiency of capital falls to the level of the current market rate of interest. The equilibrium of the entrepreneur is established at the level of investment where expected rate of profit or marginal efficiency of capital is equal to the current rate of interest. Therefore, the theory of investment is also based upon the assumption that the entrepreneur tries to maximize his profits.

We will read in the theory of interest that, according to Keynes, rate of interest is determined by liquidity preference and the supply of money. Given the supply of money, the greater the liquidity preference, the greater the rate of interest. Given the liquidity preference curve, the greater the supply of money, the lower will be the rate of interest. We explain below in detail the concept of marginal efficiency of capital and describe the factors on which it depends.

Marginal Efficiency of Capital

Of the two determinants of inducement to invest, marginal efficiency of capital or expected rate of profit is of comparatively greater importance than the rate of interest. This is because rate of interest does not change much in the short run; it is more or less sticky. But changes in the expectations of profits greatly affect the marginal efficiency of capital and make it very much unstable and volatile. As a result of changes in marginal efficiency of capital, investment demand is greatly affected which causes aggregate demand to fluctuate very much. The changes in aggregate demand bring about economic fluctuations which are generally known as trade cycles. When profit expectations of businessmen are good, large investment is undertaken which causes aggregate demand to rise and bring about conditions of boom and prosperity in the economy. On the other hand, when expectations regarding profits are adverse, the rate of investment falls which causes decline in aggregate demand and brings about depression, unemployment and excess productive capacity in the economy. Thus, the changes in the marginal efficiency of capital play a crucial role in causing changes in the investment level and economic activity.

As has been pointed out above, the concept of marginal efficiency of capital refers to the rate of profit expected to be made from investment in certain capital assets. The rate of profit expected from an extra unit of a capital asset is known as marginal efficiency of capital. Now, the question is how the marginal efficiency of capital is measured. Suppose an entrepreneur invests money in a certain machinery, how will he estimate the expected rate of profit from it? To estimate the marginal efficiency of capital, the entrepreneur will first take into consideration how much price he has to pay for the particular capital asset. The price which he has to pay for the particular capital asset is called its *supply price* or *cost of capital.* The second thing which he will consider is that how much yield he expects to obtain from investment from that particular capital asset. A capital asset continues to produce goods and yield income over a long period of time. Therefore, an entrepreneur has to estimate the prospective yield from a capital asset over his whole life period. Thus, the supply price and the prospective yields of a capital asset determine the marginal efficiency of capital. By deducting the supply price from the prospective yield during whole life of a capital asset the entrepreneur can estimate the expected rate of profit or marginal efficiency of capital. Keynes has defined the marginal efficiency of capital in the following words: "I define the marginal efficiency of capital as being equal to that rate of discount which would make the present value of the series of annuities given by the returns expected from the capital asset during its life just equal to its supply price." Thus, according to Keynes, marginal efficiency of capital is the rate of discount which renders the prospective yields from a capital asset over its whole life period equal to the supply price of that asset. Therefore, we can obtain the marginal efficiency of capital in the following way:

$$\text{Supply Price} = \text{Discounted Prospective Yields}$$

$$C = \frac{R_1}{1+r} + \frac{R_2}{(1+r)^2} + \frac{R_3}{(1+r)^3} \cdots\cdots + \frac{R_n}{(1+r)^n}$$

In the above formula, C stands for Supply Price or Replacement Cost and R_1, R_2, R_3, .. R_n etc., represent the annual prospective yields from the capital asset, r is that rate of discount which renders the annual prospective yields equal to the supply price of the capital asset. Thus, r represents the expected rate of profit or marginal efficiency of capital.

The measurement of marginal efficiency of capital can be illustrated by an arithmetical example. Suppose it costs 3000 rupees to invest in a certain machinery and the life of the machinery is two years, that is, after two years it becomes quite useless, having no value. Suppose further that in the first year the machinery is expected to yield income of ₹ 1100 and in the second year ₹ 2420. By substituting these values in the above formula, we can calculate the value of r, that is, the marginal efficiency of capital.

$$\text{Supply Price} = \text{Discounted Prospective Yields}$$

$$C = \frac{R_1}{(1+r)} + \frac{R_2}{(1+r)^2}$$

$$3000 = \frac{1{,}100}{1+r} + \frac{2{,}420}{(1+r)^2}$$

On calculating the value of r in the above equation it is found to be equal to 10. In other words, marginal efficiency of capital is here equal to 10 per cent. If we put the value of r, that is, 10 in the above equation, we obtain the following:

$$3{,}000 = \frac{1{,}100}{1.10} + \frac{2{,}420}{(1+10)^2}$$

$$= 1{,}000 + 2{,}000 = 3{,}000$$

Marginal Efficiency of Capital in General. We have explained above the marginal efficiency of a *particular type* of capital asset. But we also require to know the marginal efficiency of capital *in general.* It is the marginal efficiency of capital in general that will indicate the scope for investment opportunities at a particular time in any economy, *At a particular time in an economy the marginal efficiency of that particular capital asset which yields the greatest rate of profit, is called the marginal efficiency of capital in general.* In other words, marginal efficiency of capital in general is the greatest

of all the marginal efficiencies of various types of capital assets which could be produced but have not yet been produced. Thus, marginal efficiency of capital in general represents the highest expected rate of return to the community from an extra unit of a capital asset which yields the maximum profit which could be produced.

Keeping in view the existing stock of a capital asset, we can always calculate the marginal efficiency of any particular capital asset. The marginal efficiency of capital will vary when more is invested in a given particular capital asset. In any given period of time marginal efficiency of capital from every type of capital asset will decline as more investment is undertaken in it. In other words, marginal efficiency of a particular type of capital asset will be sloping downward as the stock of capital increases. The main reason for the decline in marginal efficiency of capital with the increase in investment in it is that the prospective yields from capital asset fall as more units are installed and used for production of a good. Prospective yields decline because when more quantity of a good is produced with the greater amount of a capital asset prices of goods decline. The second reason for the decline in the marginal efficiency of capital is that the supply price of the capital asset may rise because the increase in demand for it will bring about increase in its cost of production.

Rate of Interest and Investment Demand Curve

We have explained above how the marginal efficiency of capital is estimated. We can represent diminishing marginal efficiency of capital in general by a curve which will slope downward. This has been done in Fig. 11.3 in which along the *X-axis* investment in capital assets is measured and along the *Y*-axis marginal efficiency of capital in general is shown. It will be seen from Fig. 11.3 that when investment in capital asset is equal to OI_1, marginal efficiency of capital is i_1. When the investment is increased to OI_2, marginal efficiency of capital falls to i_2. Likewise, when investment rises to OI_3, marginal efficiency of capital further diminishes to i_3.

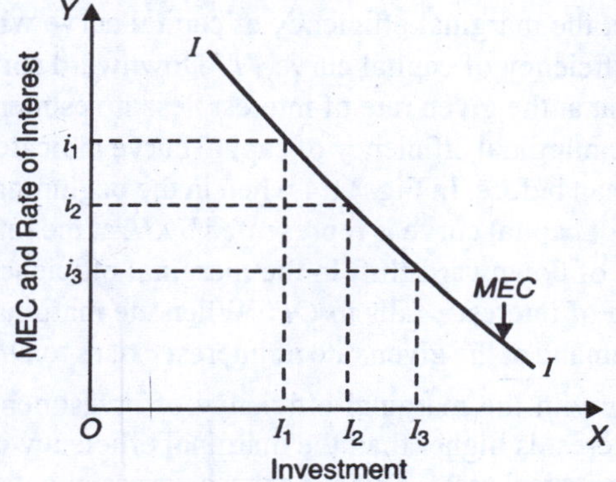

Fig. 11.3. *Investment Demand Curve*

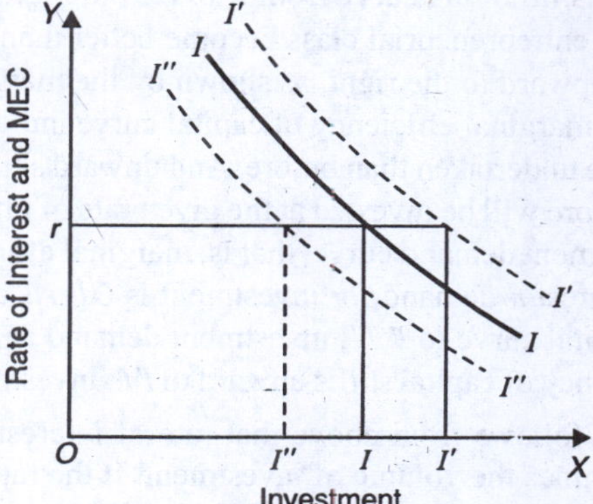

Fig. 11.4. *Shifts in Investment Demand Curve due to Changes in Marginal Efficiency of Capital*

We have seen above that inducement to invest depends upon the marginal efficiency of capital and the rate of interest. With the given particular rate of interest and given the curve of marginal efficiency of capital in general we can show what will be the equilibrium level of investment in the economy. If in Fig. 11.3 along the *Y*-axis, rate of interest is also shown, then level of investment can be easily determined. The equilibrium level of investment will be established at the point where marginal efficiency of capital becomes equal to the given current rate of interest. Thus, if the rate of interest is i_1 then OI_1 investment will be undertaken since at OI_1 level of investment marginal efficiency of capital is equal to the rate of interest i_1. If the rate of interest falls to i_2, investment in the capital assets will rise to OI_2 since at OI_2 level of investment the new rate of interest i_2 is equal to the marginal efficiency of capital. Thus, we see that the curve of marginal efficiency of capital in general shows the demand for investment or inducement to invest at various rates of interest. Hence marginal efficiency of capital curve represents the investment demand curve. This investment demand curve shows how much investment will be undertaken by the entrepreneurs at various rates of interest. If the investment demand curve is less elastic, then investment demand will not increase much with the fall in the rate of interest. But if the investment demand curve or marginal efficiency of capital curve is very much elastic, then the changes in the rate of interest will bring about large changes in investment demand.

Profit Expectations and Shift in Investment Demand Curve

We have studied above that the marginal efficiency of capital depends upon the supply price of capital on the one hand and prospective yields on the other. It is important to note here that the prospective yields are greatly affected by the expectations of the entrepreneurial class regarding profit making. These expectations generally change very frequently. Indeed, it is the profit expectations of the entrepreneur which determine the level of investment. When the expectations of the entrepreneur regarding profit making become dim, the marginal efficiency of capital declines and as a result demand for investment falls. The occurrence of depression is mainly due to the pessimistic expectations of the entrepreneurial class regarding profit making. On the contrary, when the expectations of the entrepreneurs regarding profit opportunities increase, their inducement to invest rises. As a result of the increase in investment, aggregate demand in the economy increases and levels of income and employment increase. We thus see that profit expectations of entrepreneurs greatly affect investment demand and consequently the level of income and employment.

It should be carefully noted that when the expectations regarding profit-earning change, the whole curve of the marginal efficiency of capital will shift. If profit expectations fall, the marginal efficiency of capital curve, that is, investment demand curve will shift downward to left, as shown by the shift of the curve from *II* to *I″I″* in Fig. 11.4. On the other hand, when the profit expectations of the entrepreneurial class become better than before, the marginal efficiency of capital curve will shift upward to the right, as shown by the marginal efficiency of capital curve *I′I′*. Downward shift in the marginal efficiency of capital curve indicates that at the given rate of interest, less investment will be undertaken than before. And upward shift in the marginal efficiency of capital curve indicates that more will be invested at the given rate of interest than before. In Fig. 11.4 when in the beginning, investment demand curve, that is, marginal efficiency of capital curve is represented by *II*, at the rate of interest *r*, demand for investment is *OI*, As a result of downward shift in the marginal efficiency of capital curve to *I″I″*, investment demand at the rate of interest *r* falls to *OI″*. When the marginal efficiency of capital shifts upward to *I′I′*, investment demand at the given rate of interest *r* rises to *OI′*.

It follows from above that rate of interest, along with the marginal efficiency of investment, determines the volume of investment. If the rate of interest is higher than the marginal efficiency of investment, it will not be profitable to invest in a new physical asset. This is because we assume that the aim of the individual investor is to maximise his money profits. Two courses of action are open to an investor: either he can use his money to buy additional physical assets, *i.e.,* he can invest in the Keynesian sense of the term, or else he can lend his money to others at a certain rate of interest. Now, if marginal efficiency of investment is lower than the current rate of interest, it is more profitable to lend one's money rather than use it for investing in new capital assets. On the other hand, if marginal efficiency of investment is higher than the rate of interest, it is better to invest more. At the point where marginal efficiency of investment equals the current rate of interest, we have the equilibrium level of the rate of investment.

It follows, therefore, that the rate of investment also depends on the rate of interest. If it is interest-elastic, a low rate of interest tends to stimulate investment. But it may fail to do so, if marginal efficiency of investment is already lower than the rate of interest (as may well happen during a depression). Of the two determinants of the rate of investment, marginal efficiency of investment is more volatile than the rate of interest.

The rate of interest is usually 'sticky' in the short run, while marginal efficiency of investment can fluctuate from one extreme to another. If there is a divergence between the two, usually the marginal efficiency of investment will adjust to the rate of interest. If, for example, the marginal efficiency of investment is 20 per cent, while the current rate of interest is 12 per cent, forces will be set in motion so as to bring the former to the level of the latter. In such a situation, there will be more investment because marginal efficiency of investment is greater than the rate of interest, and with the increase in investment, marginal efficiency of investment will fall. At the point where it is just reduced to the level of the current rate of interest, further investment will cease.

FACTORS CAUSING SHIFT IN INVESTMENT DEMAND CURVE

Investment is highly volatile and fluctuates greatly. It is fluctuations in investment that is mainly responsible for fluctuations in aggregate demand. We have seen above that investment demand depends on rate of interest and marginal efficiency of capital, that is, expected rate of profit in investment. Now, an important question is what are the factors that determine marginal efficiency of capital which determines investment demand. There are several factors which cause shift in the marginal efficiency of investment curve and bring about change in investment demand. We discuss these factors below:

1. Business Expectations and Animal Spirits. The Keynes theory gives importance to profit expectations of businessmen for determining marginal efficiency of capital in the economy. It is worth mentioning here the concept of **animal spirits** of Keynes. Keynes pointed out that it was not possible to make accurate calculations about the future profitability of investment. He believed that the *swings of optimism and pessimism of the business class* were more important driving forces in the stock market that determine investment. It is these swings of optimism and pessimism about future profitability of investment which he referred to as *animal spirits*. According to Keynes, it is these animal spirits more than the economic *fundamentals* that determine investment by business firms.

However, marginal efficiency of investment by a business firm depends to a large extent on the demand it anticipates for its product. For the economy as a whole the marginal efficiency of investment (*i.e.*, expected net return on investment) depends significantly on the consumption expenditure of households on the products produced in the economy. As studied above in this chapter, apart from income, consumption expenditure on goods and services depends on several factors such as propensity to save of the people, price level, rate of interest, stock of wealth, taxation policy of the government. Changes in these factors would cause a change in consumption of households and demand for the products. As a result, expected rate of return on investment *i.e. MEI* will change.

Marginal efficiency of investment which depends on prospective yields from investment in capital goods which are used in the production of certain products depends on expected demand for these products. The prospective yields also depend on expected monetary and fiscal policies of the government and stock market situation etc. Changes in them will change the marginal efficiency of investment and result in shift in investment demand curve.

In what follows we first analyses the factors that cause changes in marginal efficiency of capital which bring about a shift in the investment demand curve.

2. Technology and Innovations. In the recent years advances in technology and introduction of new products and processes have been important determinants of investment. The introduction of new improved technology and new products makes it necessary to build new plants or install new capital equipment. This stimulates investment in new capital goods. An important recent example of this is the introduction of micro-computers for use in various fields of industries and services. This has spurred new investment in computers and other related equipments. Another important recent example is the introduction of mobile cellular telephones which has boosted investment in telecommunications by business class.

In addition to the above, advances in technology and new inventions *make investment more productive.* Increase in productivity of capital causes the firms to invest more at a given rate of interest. As a result, curve of marginal efficiency of capital shifts to the right.

3. User Cost of Capital. The user cost of capital also greatly influences the rate of return on capital. The user cost of capital depends on the real rate of interest, rate of depreciation, corporate income taxes, investment tax credit, if any. The lower the real rate of interest, lower corporate income taxes, higher investment tax credit, the lower will be the user cost of capital which will increase the rate of return on capital and stimulate investment. On the other hand, the higher the real rate of interest, the higher corporate income tax will discourage investment and shift the curve of marginal efficiency of capital to the left. It may be noted that real rate of interest is the nominal rate of interest minus expected rate of inflation.

4. Availability of Credit. Besides cost of credit, availability of credit also determines investment in the economy. Investment is financed in three ways : (1) Borrowing from the banks and other financial institutions, (2) raising resources through issue of equity capital, that is, selling shares in the stock market, and (3) internal savings of the companies (*i.e.,* retained earnings of the companies). If the Central Bank of a country follows tight monetary policy [*i.e.,* higher bank rate, the higher cash reserve ratio (*CRR*)], credit availability for investment will be less which will decourage private investment. If the Central bank adopts expansionary or easy monetary policy, credit availability from banks increases which is likely to encourage investment.

5. Fiscal Policy. Fiscal policy of the Government, especially expenditure and taxation policy of it, can work in two ways. If Government increases investment and finances it by borrowing from the open market, this will raise the rate of interest which will crowd out private investment. However, if expansionary monetary policy is adopted simultaneously, rate of interest will not rise and therefore crowding out effect will not occur. But there are beneficial effects of expansionary fiscal policy of the Government as well. Increase in Government expenditure, say on infrastructure such as power, communication, highways, roads, will raise the incomes of the people which will through the multiplier effect cause a significant increase in aggregate demand for goods produced by the private sector and raise the profit expectations of business firms. This will encourage private investment. Many Indian economists believe that increase in Government expenditure, especially if it is made on infrastructure projects, *crowds in* private investment rather than *crowds it out.*

ACCELERATOR THEORY OF INVESTMENT

We have explained in a previous chapter the Keynesian concept of multiplier which states that as the investment increases, income increases by a multiple amount. On the other hand, there is a concept of accelerator which was not taken into account by Keynes which has become popular after Keynes, especially in the discussions of theories of trade cycles and economic growth. The acceleration principle describes the effect quite opposite to that of multiplier. According to this, *when income or consumption increases, investment will increase by a multiple amount.* When income and therefore consumption of the people increases, the greater amount of the commodities will have to be produced. This will require more capital to produce them if the already given stock of capital is fully used. Since in this case, investment is induced by changes in income or consumption, this is known as *induced investment.* The accelerator is the numerical value of the relation between the increase in investment resulting from an increase in income. The net induced investment will be positive if national income increases and induced investment may fall to zero if the national income or output remains constant.

To produce a given amount of output, it requires a certain amount of capital. If Y_t output is required to be produced and v is capital-output ratio, the required amount of capital to produce Y_t output will be given by the following equation:

$$K_t = vY_t \qquad ...(i)$$

where K_t stands for the stock of capital,

Y_t for the level of output or income, and

v for capital-output ratio.

This capital-output ratio v is equal to $\frac{K}{Y}$ and in the theory of accelerator this capital-output ratio is assumed to be constant. Therefore, under the assumption of constant capital-output ratio, changes in output are made possible by changes in the stock of capital. Thus, when income is Y_t then required stock of capital $K_t = vY_t$. When output or income is equal to Y_{t-1}, then required stock of capital will be $K_{t-1} = vY_{t-1}$.

It is clear from above that when income increases from Y_{t-1} in period t–1 to Y_t in period, t, then the stock of capital will increase from K_{t-1} to K_t. As seen above, K_{t-1} is equal to vY_{t-1} and K_t is equal to vY_t Hence, the increase in the stock of capital in period t is given by the following equation:

$$K_t - K_{t-1} = vY_t - vY_{t-1}$$

$$K_t - K_{t-1} = v(Y_t - Y_{t-1}) \qquad ...(ii)$$

Since increase in the stock of capital in a year $(K_t - K_{t-1})$ represents investment in that year, the above equation (*ii*) can be written as below:

$$I_1 = V(y_t - y_{t-1}) \qquad ...(iii)$$

Equation (*iii*) reveals that as a result of increase in income in any year t from a previous year $t - 1$, increase in investment will be v times more than the increase in income. Hence, it is v, *i.e.*, capital-output ratio, which represents the magnitude of the accelerator. If the capital-output ratio is equal to 3, then as a result of a certain increase in income, investment will increase three times more, *i.e.*, accelerator here will be equal to 3.

It thus follows that *investment is a function of change in income.* If income or output increases over time, that is, when Y_t is greater than Y_{t-1} then investment will be positive. If income declines, that is, Y_t is less than Y_{t-1} then disinvestment will take place. And if the income remains constant, that is, $Y_t = Y_{t-1}$ the investment will be equal to zero.

An arithmetical example will make clear the working of the accelerator. This has been represented in the accompanying table. We have made the following assumptions in making this table:

(*i*) Capital-output ratio remains constant and is equal to 3.

(*ii*) The depreciation that takes place in the stock of capital is equal to one-fifth of the stock existing in the *previous year.* Therefore, one-fifth of the stock of capital is to be replaced every year.

In the Table 11.1, it is supposed that in period t–1 and several periods before it, output or income is equal to ₹ 500. Given that the capital-output ratio is equal to 3, then to produce ₹ 500 worth of output, ₹ 1,500 worth of capital will be required. [$K = vY$; $1500 = 3(500)$] which is written in column (3). Since depreciation of capital occurred in period t–1, it will be one-fifth of the stock of capital existing in the previous period (which is also ₹ 1,500). Therefore, replacement investment in period t–1 will be equal to ₹ 300. Since as compared to the previous period, there is no change in output in period t–1, the net investment in period t–1 will be equal to zero. As a result, the gross investment in period t–1 will be equal to ₹ 300.

Table 11.1. Explanation of the Accelerator

Period	Output (income)	Required Stock of Capital	Investment: Capital Replacement	Investment: Net Investment	Investment: Gross Investment
(1)	(2)	(3)	(4)	(4)	(6)
$t-1$	500	1,500	300	0	300
t	510	1,530	300	30	330
$t+1$	525	1,575	306	45	351
$t+2$	550	1,650	315	75	390
$t+3$	575	1,725	330	75	405
$t+4$	575	1,725	345	0	345
$t+5$	560	1,680	345	–45	300
$t+6$	550	1,650	336	– 30	306
$t+7$	500	1,500	330	– 150	180
$t+8$	400	1,200	300	–300	0
$t+9$	400	1,200	240	0	240

Now suppose that production in the period t rises to ₹ 510 crores as a result of increase in Government expenditure or autonomous investment. To produce output worth ₹ 510 crores, total capital worth ₹ 1530 is required [$K_t = vY_t$ $1530 = 3(510)$] which is written in column (3). Thus, as a result of increase in output (income) by ₹ 10, net investment has increased by ₹ 30, that is, 1530 – 1500 = 30 which means that accelerator is here equal to 3. In period t the depreciation equation equal to l/5th of the capital stock of period t–1 will occur, that is, capital depreciation of ₹ 300 (1/5 × 1500 = 300) will occur in period t. Therefore, capital replacement investment in period t will be equal to ₹ 300. Thus, gross investment in period t will be equal to 30 + 300 = 330. In this way, if output (or income) increases by ₹ 15 in period $t+1$, ₹ 25 in period $t+2$, and also ₹ 25 in period $t+3$, the net investment will increase by three times the increment in output (or income), that is, net investment will increase by ₹ 45 in period $t+1$, ₹ 75 in period $t+2$ and also ₹ 75 in period $t+3$. It will be further observed from Table 11.1 that when output falls in period $t+5$ by ₹ 15, the net investment will decline by 3 times of it, that is, equal to ₹ 45. Likewise, from changes in output in different periods we can find out net investment that will take place in any period and with the capital replacement investment we can obtain the gross investment that will occur in any period.

A glance at columns 2, 5 and 6 will show that with a change in output, investment will increase by a multiple of it. This shows that acceleration principle is a powerful destabilising force working in the economy. If the accelerator is the only force at work, then we shall have too much of instability in the economy—more than is actually found. In real life, we find that there are limits to instability, both in the upward as well as the downward direction, so that fluctuations in economic activity or what are called business cycles must have a peak as well as a bottom.

Criticism of the Accelerator Theory

The principle of acceleration has come in for a good deal of criticism in recent years. For example, it has been pointed out by Kaldor that we cannot assume a constant value of the accelerator throughout the trade cycle, that is, it is not true that an increase in output or income by an amount must always give rise to a multiple increase in investment. This is because, if already, some machines are lying idle, we shall try to use them before rushing in for new equipment. Also, if expectation of entrepreneurs is that the rise in demand brought about by increase in income or output is only a temporary one, they will try to meet it by overworking the existing machinery rather than installing a new plant. Thus, *in the theory of accelerator it has been assumed that there is no excess capacity existing in consumer goods industries.* In other words, it has been assumed that no machines are lying idle and no extra shift working is possible. If there had been excess capacity and extra shift working was possible, the supply of goods could be increased with the existing equipment and the accelerator would not come into play.

Further, in the acceleration principle it *has also been assumed that in the capital goods industries, there exists surplus productive capacity.* If there is no excess capacity in the machine-making industries, increased demand for machines caused by the requirement for additional output would not lead to increase in the supply of machines. In the absence of supply of machines, investment cannot increase in the short run. It is thus assumed in the accelerator theory that the machine-making industry is capable of increasing its output for the time being at least. The supply can be increased by reducing stocks of finished machines, by working extra shifts, and so on. But stocks cannot be reduced below zero and working double shifts or adoption of other experiments is found to be expensive. Only when the demand has increased permanently, will the entrepreneurs find it worthwhile to increase investment in machine-making industries.

The size of the accelerator does not remain constant over time. Its value will be affected by the businessmen's calculation regarding the profitability of installing new plants to make more machines on the basis of their probable working life. It is also assumed that the demand for machines will remain stable in future, although the increase in demand has suddenly cropped up.

However, in spite of the above limitations of acceleration principle, it points out an important force which causes economic fluctuations in the economy. Economists like Samuelson, Hicks and Dusenberry have shown how accelerator combined with multiplier provides an adequate and satisfactory theory of business cycles that occur in free market economies.

THE NEOCLASSICAL THEORY OF INVESTMENT

After Keynes a neoclassical theory of investment has been developed to explain investment behaviour with regard to fixed business investment. This theory is called neoclassical theory of investment behaviour because it is based on the neoclassical theory of optimal capital accumulation which is determined by relative prices of factors of production.[1] It may be recalled that fixed business investment refers to the purchase of machines, construction of new factories, warehouses, office buildings etc. by businessmen. The neoclassical theory of investment throws new light on the causes of fluctuations in investment which are responsible for occurrence of business cycles in a free market economy. The neoclassical theory explains that at a particular time how much capital stock a firm desires to achieve. Further, according to this theory, *rate of investment is determined by the speed with which* firms adjust their capital stocks towards the desired level. Because it takes time to build and install new machines, construct new factories, warehouses etc., the firms cannot immediately achieve the desired level of capital stock. Therefore, the firms have to decide with what rate or speed per period it makes adjustment in their stock of capital to attain the desired level of capital stock.

Firms use capital along with labour to produce goods and services for sale in the market. In deciding about the amounts of labour and capital to be used for production the firms are guided by not only the prices of these factors but also the contributions they make to the production and revenue of the firms. According to this neoclassical theory, investment, that is, addition to the stock of capital in an economy is determined by *marginal product of capital* (*MPK*) and *user cost of capital* which is also called *real rental cost of capital.* Marginal product of capital (*MPK*) measures the addition to the production by using an additional unit of capital, labour and technology remaining constant. Due to the operation of the law of diminishing returns, marginal product of capital declines as more units of capital are used for production, the other factors being held constant. The user cost of capital

1. See D. W. Jorgenson, Theory of Corporate Investment Behaviour, American Economic Review, Sept 1968 and D. W. Jorgenson and C.D. Siebert, Optimal Capital Accumulation and Corporate Investment Behaviour, Theory of Political Economy, Nov–Dec. 1968.

will be explained in detail later, but it essentially stands for the rental for capital a firm owns or gets it on rent basis and measures the opportunity cost of the funds spent on production or purchase of a capital equipment.

The firms try to maximise profits or maximise the present value. Therefore, as long as the value of marginal product of capital (which are in fact marginal receipts or benefits it gets from the use of capital in production) exceeds the rental or user cost capital, it will be profitable for the firm to add to its stock of capital. It will be maximising its profits when it has achieved the stock of capital at which marginal product of capital (MPK) equals user cost of capital. We can derive the desired stock of capital by using the neoclassical production function which is popularly known as Cobb-Douglas production function. The Cobb-Douglas production function can be written as under :

$$Y = A K^{\alpha} L^{1-\alpha}$$

where Y stands for output, K for capital, L for labour and A is a parameter that measures the level of technology and α is a parameter that measures capital's share of output.

Marginal product of capital can be obtained by differentiating the production function with respect to labour. Thus,

$$MPK = \frac{\partial Y}{\partial K} = \alpha A K^{\alpha-1} L^{1-\alpha}$$

$$MPK = \frac{\alpha A K^{\alpha} L^{1-\alpha}}{K} = \frac{\alpha Y}{K}$$

Thus, $$MPK = \frac{\alpha Y}{K} \qquad ...(1)$$

Let r is the price or user cost of capital and p is the price of output. To maximise profits, a firm will equate the marginal product of capital to the real rental price (*i.e.* user cost) of capital $\left(\frac{r}{p}\right)$.

Thus

$$\alpha \frac{Y}{K} = \frac{r}{p}$$

or $$K = \alpha \frac{p}{r} Y$$

Thus, the desired stock of capital can be written as

$$K^* = \alpha \frac{p}{r} Y_t \qquad ...(2)$$

The equation (2) shows that the desired stock of capital (K^*) depends on the size of output (Y_1), real cost of capital $\left(\frac{r}{p}\right)$. The equation (2) reveals that the higher the rental cost of capital (r), the lower will be the desired capital stock by the firm and vice versa. The equation (2) further reveals that the greater the expected output (Y_t) the greater the desired capital stock. It may be noted that while in accelerator theory the changes in the stock of capital depends on the changes in output in neoclassical theory, the desired stock of capital depends not only on the planned output (Y_t) but also on the ratio of rental price of capital to price of output $\left(\frac{r}{p}\right)$. As shall be explained later in detail, the rental or user cost of capital is determined by the price of capital goods, rate of interest, rate of depreciation and expected rate of inflation and the various features of tax system such as corporate tax rate, investment tax break etc.

The determination of the desired stock of capital is illustrated in Fig. 11.5 where on the *X*-axis we measure capital stock and on the *Y*-axis we measure *MPK* and rental cost of capital. As long as the marginal product of capital (*MPK*) is greater than the rental price or user cost of capital, it pays the firm to add to its stock of capital. It will be seen from Fig. 11.5 that marginal product of capital is diminishing as there is increase in the stock of capital. Thus the firm will continue adding to the stock of capital (*i.e.* continue making investment) until the marginal product of capital (*MPK*) is equal to the rental price of capital. If the rental price of capital is r_0, the firm continues investing until the capital stock K^*_0 is reached. K^*_0 is the desired capital stock, given the rental price of capital equal to r_0 and for the given level of output (*i.e. GDP*) equal to, say, Y_1). It will be further seen from Fig. 11.5 that at the lower rental price of capital r_1, the firm's desired capital stock will increase to K^*_1.

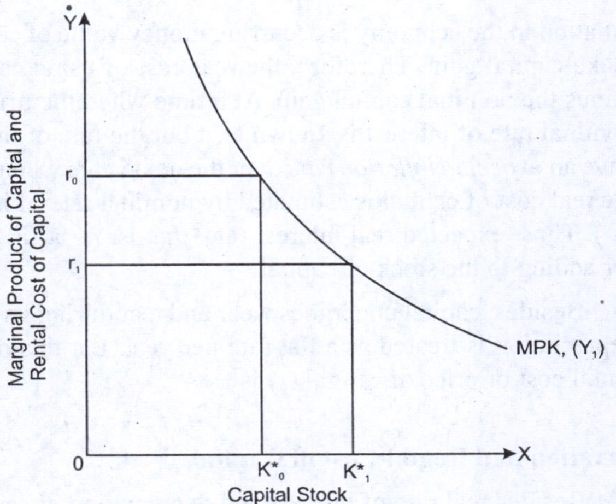

Fig. 11.5. *The Determination of Desired Stock of Capital*

Expected Output and Desired Capital Stock

The equation (2) shows that desired capital stock depends on the level of output (Y_t). But this output level which determines the desired stock of capital is not the current output level but the expected output level for some future period in which capital stock will be used for production. For some investment projects, future time for which output is planned may be few weeks or months away but for investment projects concerning power and steel future output level is planned many years ahead. However, current output level affects the expectations of future output level. As the equation (2) above reveals that desired capital stock depends on the level of output, and in case of the economy as a whole, on the level of national income (*GDP*). When the level of output or national income is expected to increase the whole curve of marginal product of capital (*MPK*) will shift to the right as shown in Fig. 11.6. With this increase in the level of national product rrom Y_0 to Y_1, at the given rental cost of capital r_0, the desired capital stock increases from K_0 to K_1

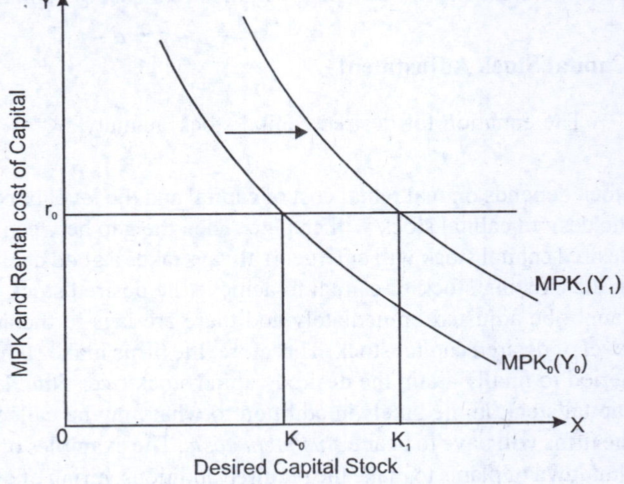

Fig. 11.6. *Desired Capital Stock and the Level of National Product*

Rental Cost of Capital. Since the desired capital stock and change in it depends on the rental cost of capital, it is important to know how rental cost of capital is estimated. If a firm finances its investment (that is, purchase of new capital goods) by borrowing, then rate of interest on the funds borrowed for investment purpose is an important element of rental cost of capital. However, when inflation in the economy is occurring money value of capital rises over time, and as a result the firms make capital gain. Therefore, the real cost of using capital over a year is money interest payment minus the nominal capital gain. At a time when the firm has to decide to undertake investment, the nominal rate of interest is known to it but the rate of inflation is unknown. At the best, the firm can have an *expected inflation rate* over the next years when it has to decide about investment. Therefore, the real cost of capital is estimated by nominal rate of interest adjusted for expected rate of inflation (π^e). Thus, expected real interest rate, that is, $i - \pi^e$ is taken to be the real cost of borrowing funds for adding to the stock of capital.

Besides, capital undergoes wear and tear during its use for production in a year. Conventionally, depreciation is treated as a flat rate per year. Let this depreciation is d per cent per year. Thus, the rental cost or price of capital (r) is

$$r = i - \pi^e + d \qquad ...(3)$$

Taxation and Rental Cost of Capital

Besides real rate of interest and depreciation, taxes levied by the government also affect rental cost of capital. The corporation tax which is the tax on profits of the public limited companies and investment tax break or development rebate are the two important tax elements which influence the rental cost of capital. Corporation tax is generally believed as a proportion, say, of the profits of the companies. The greater the corporation income tax the higher the rental cost of capital. The tax system of various countries also provides for investment tax credit to promote investment and development. Under investment tax credit scheme, the firms are allowed a certain rebate, say, 10 per cent of their investment expenditure, on the tax payable.

Thus investment tax break reduces the rental cost of capital. If t_c represents the percent tax rebate on investment expenditure per year, then real cost of capital can be expressed as under:

$$r = i - \pi + d - t_c.$$

Capital Stock Adjustment

The equation for desired capital stock, namely, $K^* = \alpha \frac{P}{r} Y_t$ shows that the desired capital stock depends on real rental cost of capital and the level of output (Y_t). When these variables change, the desired capital stock will change. Then the gap between the existing actual capital stock and the desired capital stock will emerge. It always takes a good deal of time for the firms to make adjustment in the existing stock of capital to achieve the desired stock of capital. In other words, capital stock cannot be adjusted immediately and there are lags in the adjustment of actual capital stock to the level of desired capital stock. Therefore, the firms make some adjustment in the capital stock in each period to finally attain the desired capital stock over time. If the firms attempt to adjust their actual capital stock immediately,in addition to what may be called the *direct cost* of investment projects, the firms will have to bear *adjustment costs*. The examples of adjustment costs are costs of temporary shutdown of plants to make the required additions, hiring of overtime labour, especially skilled labour, to complete the required construction work in a short period and costs incurred due to disruption of production. In view of these adjustment costs, it is optimal for the firms to make adjustment in the capital stock gradually over time to achieve the level of desired capital stock.

It may be noted that addition to the existing capital stock in each period is called investment. Thus, investing (I_t) in a period can be written as

$$I_t = K_t - K_{t-1}$$

Flexible Accelerator Model. There are a number of hypotheses about the speed at which firms attempt to make adjustment in capital stock over time. An important such hypothesis is called **flexible accelerator model**. According to this model, firms plan to invest, that is, add to the stock of capital per period to make only partial adjustment to fill up the gap between the desired capital stock and the existing capital stock. However, according to this flexible accelerator model, *the greater the gap between the current capital stock and the desired capital stock, the larger the firm's rate of investment per period.*

Thus, according to the flexible accelerator model, to make partial adjustment in each period the firms decide to undertake investment is each period, which is a fraction, say λ, of the total gap between the existing capital stock and the desired capital stock in each period. Let the capital stock at the end of the last period be denoted by K_{t-1}, then the gap between the desired capital stock and the existing capital stock is $K^* - K_{t-1}$. Only fraction λ of the gap $(K^* - K_{t-1})$ will be filled in each period to eventually attain the desired capital stock over time. Thus when the firm adds a fraction λ of the gap, $K^* - K_{t-1}$ to the capital stock existing at the end of the last period (K_{t-1}), the capital stock at the end of the current period (K_t) will be

$$K_t = K_{t-1} + \lambda (K^* - K_{t-1}) \qquad \text{...(4)}$$

Rearranging the equation (4) we have

$$K_t - K_{t-1} = K_{t-1} + \lambda (K^* - K_{t-1})$$

The addition to the capital stock during a period, that is, $K_t - K_{t-1}$ measures the rate of net investment. Therefore, rewriting the equation (4) we have

$$I_t = K_t - K_{t-1} = \lambda (K^* - K_{t-1}) \qquad \text{...(5)}$$

The equation (5) shows the partial and gradual adjustment of capital stock through investment in each period to reach the desired stock of capital over time. Only a part of the desired change in the capital stock is filled in each period by investment. Since in this flexible accelerator model investment in a given period is the result of changes in expected income or output during a number of previous periods, it shows a slower response of investment to changes in current period. This implies that investment will be less volatile in the short run than is the case with the simple accelerator model which visualises the response of investment to changes in current income wholly in one period. Empirical evidence corroborates the results of the flexible accelerator model as investment though volatile is not actually as volatile as simple accelerator model predicts.

The flexible accelerator model can also be modified to allow for changes in the speed with which investment is carried out (that is, the change in fraction λ is in fact the choice variable for the firm which is affected by such factors as the availability of credit, rate of interest, corporate tax rate, investment tax credit etc. For example, if rate of interest is lower, more investment will be undertaken to fill the gap between the desired capital stock and the existing capital stock than would be the case if rate of interest is higher. Thus flexible accelerator model is quite consistent with the Keynesian theory that investment is negatively related to the rate of interest.

Graphic illustration of Capital Stock Adjustment

Capital stock adjustment through investment over time is illustrated in Figure 11.7 where along the horizontal axis we have shown the time and along the vertical axis we measure the capital stock. In the beginning of the period 1, the capital stock is K_1 and suppose the desired capital stock of the firm is K^*. Thus $K^* - K_1$ is the gap between the desired capital stock and the existing capital stock. Suppose the speed of capital stock adjustment is, $\lambda = 0.5$. This implies that in each period one half of the desired capital stock and the existing capital stock is filled. Thus, in period t_1, the existing stock in the beginning of the period of K_1 and given $\lambda = 0.5$, the firm will add to the stock of capital, that is,undertake investment equal to $0.5 (K^* - K_1) = I_1$ in period t_1. Now in period t_2, the existing stock of capital will be K_2 and given $\lambda = 0.5$, the firm will undertake investment of $0.5(K^* - K_2) = I_2$ as shown by the shaded rectangle. It will be seen from Figure 11.7 that investment I_2 in period t_2 is less than investment I_1 in period t_1. This is because as net investment or addition to capital stock is made in period t_1 the gap between desired capital stock and the current capital stock is reduced and therefore the additional adjustment in capital stock in period t_2 becomes less in absolute terms.

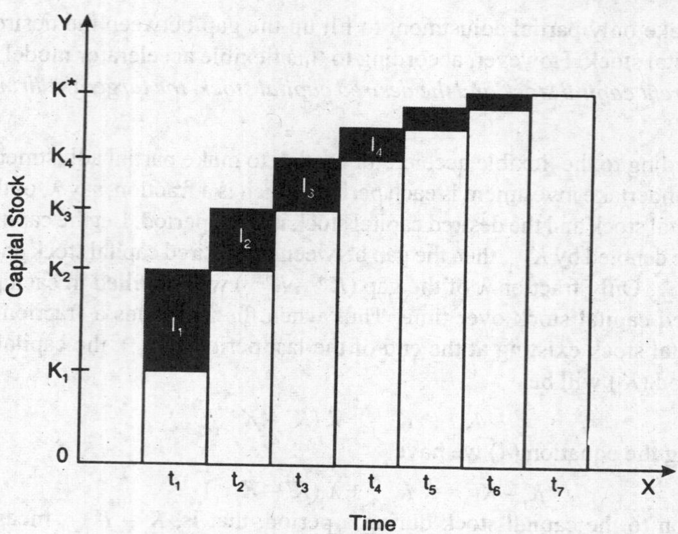

Fig. 11.7. *Adjustment of Capital Stock and Investment*

Similarly, capital stock is adjusted through additional net investments in the next periods, in each period one-half (*i.e.*, 0.5) of the remaining gap is filled until period t_7 when almost the whole gap between the desired capital stock and the existing capital stock is completely closed. It may be noted that the higher λ is, the faster the gap is filled.

In equation (5) we have derived an investment function that shows that investment depends on the desired capital stock K^* and the existing capital stock K_{t-1}. Any factor that raises the desired capital stock will increase the rate of investment. Accordingly, increase in expected output and a reduction in rental cost of capital will cause increase in investment. As seen above, rental cost of capital depends on nominal rate of interest, expected rate of inflation, corporate income tax, the investment tax credit which are important variables that determine the rental cost of capital will also affect investment in the economy.

To conclude our discussion of business fixed investment we have derived the neoclassical investment function of the following form:

$$I_{n,t} = F(Y^e, i_t, d, \pi^e, t_c, K_{t-1}) \qquad ...(6)$$

This shows that net investment depends on expected level of output (Y^e), the various elements of rental or user cost of capital such as nominal interest rate i_t, expected rate of inflation (π^e), corporate income tax including investment tax credit, and the existing stock of capital. Given the existing stock of capital, an increase in expected output (Y^e), expected rate of inflation (π^e) and the investment tax credit will all increase investment. On the other hand, increase in nominal rate of interest (i_t) and the corporate income tax will cause net investment to decline.

The Neoclassical Theory of Investment : Role of Fiscal and Monetary Policies

Now it is important to explain that the neoclassical theory of investment suggests what types of fiscal and monetary policies can promote investment. In our Keynesian analysis of fiscal policy we found that increase in government spending or cut in personal taxes will increase aggregate demand and national income and this will have favourable effect on marginal efficiency of capital which will tend to increase investment. However, this high government spending and low personal tax policy also adversely affects investment because the increase in aggregate demand caused by it would raise the interest rate and *crowd out* private investment. This crowding out effect of high government expenditure and low personal tax policy tends to offset its favourable effect on investment *via,* increase in aggregate demand.

The neoclassical theory explained above suggests that if expansionary fiscal policy (that is, high government spending and low personal tax policy) is combined with a tax policy such as a greater investment tax credit will promote private investment. As seen above, the investment tax credit is a sort of subsidy on investment and lowers the rental cost of capital. As a result, the crowding out effect of expansionary fiscal policy via increase in nominal interest can be avoided. Besides, making adjustment in the rate of investment tax credit, it can be used as an alternative instrument to monetary policy as a means of stabilising investment demand to achieve price stability as both investment tax credit and monetary policy work through change in the rental cost of capital.

In addition to above, the expansionary fiscal policy raises the level of income and expected output of the firms and will therefore raise the level of desired capital stock and hence stimulate investment. (Recall that $K^* = \alpha \frac{p}{r} . Y_t$).

This beneficial effect of expansionary fiscal policy "may be quantitatively more important than any negative effect of a fiscal policy induced increase in interest rates. Which effect dominates depends on the importance of output growth versus the cost of capital as determinants of investment."[2]

However, as regards corporation tax, increase in it is likely to adversely affect rental cost of capital and will therefore discourage investment. On the other hand, reduction in corporation tax will increase profitability of investment through reduction in the rental or user cost of capital.

As regards monetary policy, it affects investment demand through its effect on real rate of interest. The neoclassical theory does not suggest any different monetary policy than that visualised in Keynesian and monetarist macroeconomic theories. In neoclassical theory, expansionary monetary policy lowers interest rate which would reduce rental cost of capital and will increase the desired capital stock. Thus expansionary monetary policy stimulates private investment.

TOBIN'S Q THEORY OF INVESTMENT

Many economists believe that fluctuations in stock market do not reflect the true state of fundamentals of the firms and the economy. Influenced by exogenous factors, even when the fundamentals of the firms or the economy are quite strong stock market prices fall sharply lowering the market value of the capital installed by the firms which discourage more investment by them. Therefore, many consider stock market movements as poor economic indicators. In India we have seen in recent years that stock market is highly volatile and movements in it have been determined not by India's own economic fundamentals but by factors originating abroad such as financial crisis of the US in 2008-09, Eurozone crisis occurring in 2010-2012, who wins the presidential election in the US etc. Of course global happening such US financial crisis and Eurozone debt problem may affect India's exports, but stock market movements in India have been out of all proportions to their effects on Indian firms and give wrong signals about the state of fundamentals of the Indian economy.

However, *in the world today we cannot ignore the link* between the stock market and corporate firms and therefore the economy as a whole as much of investment is made by the corporate firms and this is affected by stock market prices. A noted American economist, James Tobin, put forward a view that links fluctuations in stock market with fluctuations in investment. It should be noted that the *stock* refers to the *total market value of share capital* of a corporate firm which is owned by its shareholders. The shareholders of a firm get return in the form of annual dividends as well as capital gains arising from the rise in prices of shares of a firm. The shares of a corporate firm are traded in the stock market. When the prices of shares of a firm rise, the value of the capital installed by the firm will increase. This will induce the firm to add to its stock of capital installed and thus make more

2. Richard T. Froyen. *Macroeconomics; Theories and Policy, 6th ed.*, Pearson Education, 2001, pp. 299 – 300.

investment. The increase in the market value of capital of firms influences incentive to invest more by the firms. *James Tobin in his q-theory of investment put forward the view that the firms base their investment decision on the estimate of the value the stock market places on the firms' assets or capital installed relative to the cost of replacing them.* It may be noted that share prices of firms tend to be high when firms offer good opportunities for profitable investment because profitable opportunities determine the future incomes of the shareholders of the firms. Tobin writes its q-ratio as under:

$$q = \frac{\textit{Market Value of Firm's Capital Stock}}{\textit{Replacement Cost of the Capital Stock}}$$

The market value of installed capital of firms is determined by the prices of their shares in the stock market while the replacement cost of the installed capital is the cost that will be incurred if the capital assets of the firms have to be produced and procured if they were produced in the current period.

Tobin argued that investments by the firms depend on whether q is greater or less than one. When q-ratio is greater than one, it implies that the stock market places a higher value on firm's installed capital than its replacement cost. This provides incentive to the firms to add to its installed capital stock. That is, the firm will make more investment. On the other hand, if *q-ratio* of a firm is less than one, this implies that the stock market values its stock of capital assets less than its replacement cost. This will discourage managers of a firm to replace its capital assets as they wear out. Thus, according to Tobin, it is q-ratio of a firm as to whether its value is greater or less than one that determines investment by a firm.

Tobin's q-theory of investment has been shown to be closely related to neoclassical theory of investment. *It is noteworthy that Tobin's q depends on both current and future economic profits earned from installed capital.* According to neoclassical theory of investment, if marginal product of capital (MP_K) is greater than the cost of capital, the firm will be making profits on their installed capital. These profits will induce others to own shares of the firm. As a result, the market value of the stock of installed capital by the firm will rise. This means higher value of q-ratio of the firm which will provide incentive to the firm to invest more by producing or buying more capital assets. Likewise, if the marginal product of capital (MP_K) is less than the cost of installed capital of the firms, the firms will be having *losses on* their stock of capital assets. This will reduce the market value of its installed capital and thus lowering the value of q.

Merits of Tobin's q-ratio as a measure of inducement to invest, as mentioned above, is that it reflects both the current and future profitability of capital assets of the firm. For example, if government in its annual budget reduces the corporate income tax beginning next year, this will result in larger expected profits after tax for the firms. These larger expected profits will raise the value of the existing capital of the firm and therefore induce the firms to install more capital, that is, make more investment Mankiw therefore writes, *"Tobin's q-theory of investment emphasises that investment decisions depend not only on current policies but also on policies expected to prevail in the near future"*

INVESTMENT BEHAVIOUR IN DEVELOPING COUNTRIES

Keynesian economics is relevant to the developing countries with regard to its analysis of investment behaviour as distinct from the classical analysis. Classical economists did not distinguish between decision to save and decision to invest. According to them, decisions regarding saving and investment were coterminus. *Keynes distinguished between decision to invest and save and argued that it was investment that determined saving and not the other way round.* According to him, when investment goes up, income will increase through the operation of multiplier and at a higher level of income more will be saved.

An important contribution made by Keynes to the theory of investment refers to the role of *business expectations* in determining investment. According to him, the rate of investment is determined by rate of interest on the one hand and marginal efficiency of capital on the other. Marginal efficiency of capital refers to the expected rate of return on investment. The marginal efficiency of capital depends on the state of business expectations regarding future prospective yields from the investment made in the current period.

When businessmen become pessimistic about future prospective yields, the marginal efficiency of capital declines which adversely affects investment. This investment behaviour as visualised by Keynes is as much relevant to the investment in the modern sector of the developing countries as to the industrialised developed economies. Given this investment behaviour, "*it is then no longer sufficient that the community's propensity to save should be stimulated.* We also need to ensure that investment climate is suitably improved".[3] In building up favourable investment climate business expectations have to be influenced through appropriate fiscal and monetary measures adopted by the Government. Writing about investment behaviour in the contemporary countries, Prof. Chakravarty further writes, "*Given the present state of technical knowledge, there is much greater use of fixed capital in industrial processes. Since decisions to invest in fixed capital imply commitment of resources to a prolonged and uncertain future, the question of time and uncertainty becomes crucial. At this stage we have to introduce the problem of expectations which bring us into the domain of Keynes' theory.*"[4]

In may be noted that the periodic slowdown in private investment, which is an important factor causing slowdown in industrial growth, can be explained by the decline in private investment in new shares and physical capital assets in terms of ***'animal spirits'***, a term used by Keynes to refer to the waves of pessimistic expectations of investors. Due to political and economic uncertainty as well as due to uncertainty about the ability of the Government to pursue certain crucial economic reforms, there is lack of investors' confidence which prevents them from investing in new shares and physical capital assets. Even in India in recent years, 2012-13 and 2013-14, fall in private investment that has resulted in slowdown in economic growth is, according to Dr. Manmohan Singh, is due to animal spirits, that is, pessimistic expectations of investors or loss of investor confidence about future profitability of their investment. He has therefore, laid stress on reviving the animal spirits in order to increase private investment to accelerate the rate of economic growth in India.

Portfolio Choice by Investors in India

Another important element of Keynesian analysis which is relevant to the developing countries is related to Portfolio choice. Since classical economists were concerned with the economy where there existed a commodity money and credit played no role in it, they were not concerned with portfolio choice. In the modern exchange economy even in developing countries like India credit plays a crucial role and portfolio choice by the investors, at least among the types of assets, namely, bonds and shares, physical capital assets and money balances (for example, in the form of bank deposits), must be made. In the developing countries the situation may arise when due to high capital costs and low prospective yields expected from them the investors may not be induced to invest in physical assets and new bonds or shares of companies and instead opt for keeping their savings in the form of money balances (for example, in time deposits of banks).

It is important to note that in recent years (1977-2003) such a Keynesian type situation prevailed in the Indian economy where investment in shares and physical capital assets by households declined and instead investment in bank deposits greatly increased.[5] Economic Survey of Government of India for the year 1998-99 made a special mention of such a change in the portfolio choice by the households. Thus, it wrote, "*The uncertainty combined with performance of stock markets since the boom of 1994 and lack of trust in issuing companies and market intermediaries has also led to a shift of retail investors from riskier investment into safe havens like bank deposits and post office savings*"[6]. The same behaviour was witnessed in 2008-09 when following the global financial crisis, the decline in prices of corporate shares and mutual funds people switched over to investment in fixed deposits of banks.

3. Sukhamoy, Chakravarty, 'Keynes, Classics and Developing Countries', printed in his *Selected Economic Essays,* Oxford University Press, 1993
4. *Ibid.*
5. See Annual Reports of RBI for Years 1996, 1997, 1998, 1999 and 2000.
6. Government of India, *Economic Survey* 1998-99, p. 6.

The portfolio choice also caused stagnation of investment in the years 1996-2003, which, as seen above, cannot be explained in terms of classical economics. In fact, the followers of classical economists think that relative shortage of physical capital in the developing countries, rate of return on investment must be high, which, as seen above, is contrary to what has been actually observed. This clearly brings out the correctness of Keynes' fundamental insight into the determination of investment and portfolio choice. To quote Prof. Chakravarty again, "*We can easily imagine situations where people try to shy away from investing in physical assets, the rate of return and the rate of interest is such as to give an edge to holding savings in the form of cash balances. The resulting situation will be of Keynesian type.*"[7] Elaborating on it further he writes that "*Uncertaintes surrounding physical investment decisions are often much larger in developing countries and the cost of making a wrong decision is often quite high in a market which is very often quite small and slowly growing*".

It is clear from above that with regard to portfolio choice Keynes' insight was quite significant and is relevant to the behaviour of investors both in the developed and developing countries.

MONETARY AND FISCAL POLICY MEASURES AND INVESTMENT

Both monetary and fiscal policy measures affect investment. In what follows we first analyse the effect of discretionary monetary policy and then of discretionary fiscal policy.

Monetary Policy and Investment

As explained above, interest rate measures the cost of capital and along with marginal efficiency of capital (*i.e.* expected rate of return on investment) determines the level of investment. It is primarily through its *effect on interest rate* that monetary policy affects investment decisions. Besides interest rate, investment also depends on the *availability of funds or credit*, especially from the banks. The easy monetary policy which aims at lowering interest rate and increasing the availability of credit will lead to more investment. It may be noted that under easy monetary policy the Central Bank lowers the bank rate and cash reserve ratio. The Reserve Bank of India often uses changes in *repo rate*, which is the interest rate at which banks borrow funds for a short period from RBI, to influence private investment. The lowering of bank rate or *repo rate* sends a signal to the banks to reduce their lending rates. The lowering of cash reserve ratio (CRR) leads to the more liquidity or extra cash reserves with banks. This not only increases the availability of more credit for investment by businessmen but also puts downward pressure on lending interest rates as a result of increase in the supply of lendable funds with the banks. In India, Reserve Bank of India often lowers a *repo rate* to ensure lowering of lending rates by banks and thereby to stimulate private investment. At a lower interest rate, given the schedule of marginal efficiency of capital, more investment will be undertaken by business firms. The Central Bank can also undertake open market operations to increase availability of bank credit for investment. For this purpose it buys government securities from the banks and pays rupee funds to them. This raises money supply in the economy which not only makes more funds available for lending to businessmen but also tends to lower interest rates.

Keynes and his early followers believed that monetary policy is not very effective for increasing private investment. This view was based on the assumption that during the period of depression rate of interest was already very low and at this low interest rate there is *liquidity trap* in the demand curve for money. Under these conditions, they thought the expansion in money supply by the banks will not lower interest rate. Besides, they believed that investment demand is relatively inelastic so that even lowering of interest rate will not cause much increase in investment. However, later empirical evidence shows that at generally prevailing rates of interest demand for money is quite elastic (that is , liquidity trap does not exist at the generally prevailing interest rates). As a result, expansionary monetary policy lowers interest rate and thereby stimulates private investment. Besides, later empirical evidence also

7. Sukhamoy Chakravarty, 'Keynes, Classics and Developing Countries', printed in his *Selected Economic Writings*, Oxford University press, 1993.

shows that investment demand schedule is quite elastic and therefore lowering of interest rate and more availability of funds lead to more investment. Therefore, the modern Keynesians have veered round to the view that discretionary monetary policy can be effective in raising private investment to get rid of recession in the economy and to promote economic growth.

One modification in our above analysis of the impact of monetary policy on investment which is required is the incorporation of distinction between nominal interest rate and real interest rate. As explained earlier, it is the real interest rate that is relevant for investment decisions. Therefore, monetary policy must affect the real interest rate if it has to stimulate private investment. However, it is worth noting that in both the Keynesian and monetarist theories expected inflation depends primarily on the inflation prevailing in the recent past and further that it changes slowly over time. Under these conditions changes in monetary rate of interest will mean changes in real interest rate for all practical purposes. In view of this, our above analysis of the effect of monetary policy on investment remains unchanged.

Fiscal Policy and Investment

We now turn to explain the effect of fiscal policy on investment. It is generally believed that there is *adverse effect* of expansionary fiscal policy on private investment. According to this view, though increase in government spending financed by borrowing would bring about increases in aggregate demand for goods and services, it would raise interest rate. Borrowing by the government would raise the demand for funds or money in the market which, given the supply of money, would cause interest rate to rise. The higher interest rate would lower private investment. Thus, it is asserted that expansionary fiscal policy *crowds out private investment*. Another route through which adverse effect of expansionary fiscal policy is brought out is that the increase in aggregate demand as a result of expansionary fiscal policy in terms of either increase in government expenditure or cut in taxes would raise aggregate demand and lead to increase in national income. However, the increase in national income would bring about increase in transactions demand for money which, given the supply of money, would cause interest rate to rise and lower private investment. The reduction or crowding out of private investment would offset a part of the initial expansionary effect on aggregate demand brought about by increase in government expenditure or reduction in taxation. If investment demand is highly elastic, the decrease in private investment resulting from the rise in interest rate may be quite substantial.

However, in view of the present author even if there is significant crowding-out effect on private investment of expansionary fiscal policy, it can be avoided if as a part of expansionary fiscal policy, policy of providing *investment tax credit* to the business firms is adopted. Under investment tax credit policy, a reduction from business income or profits equal to a certain percentage of investment made is allowed. As this lowers the tax liability of the firm, policy of investment tax credit stimulates investment and consequently there is not any *net adverse effect* of expansionary fiscal policy on private investment.

Further, in our view, the crowding-out effect of expansionary fiscal policy has been exaggerated by the critics of Keynes. As a matter of fact when government raises its expenditure or cuts personal income tax, aggregate demand for goods and services increases which raises expectations of increased sales and revenue of the business firms. This improves profitability or marginal efficiency of investment. This is more valid at times of depression when private investment declines due to lack of demand for goods and services. Thus when expected profitability or marginal efficiency of capital rises due to increase in aggregate demand resulting from expansionary fiscal policy, investment demand curve shifts to the right and businessmen invest more at any given rate of interest. This can more than offset any adverse effect on private investment due to rise in interest.

Further, according to *investment theory based on acceleration principle* investment depends on expected changes in output or national income. Thus, even in the absence of investment tax credit expansionary fiscal policy that increases national output or national income through its beneficial effect on aggregate demand will stimulate private investment through accelerator principle.

In the context of developing country like India the expansionary fiscal policy even when increased government expenditure is financed by borrowing can have beneficial effect on private investment, especially when the economy is experiencing recession or slowdown in economic growth. If in such a situation the government increases its expenditure and spends money on infrastructure projects, it will have a favourable effect on private investment as the latter is often constrained by lack of adequate infrastructure facilities. Besides, when manufacturing industries in developing countries experience recessionary conditions due to sluggish demand, as happened in India during the period 1997 to 2002, and again in 2008-09, increase in public expenditure will lead to increase in aggregate demand through its multiplier effect and thereby improve the demand conditions for increase in private investment.

It follows from above that it is not necessarily true that expansionary fiscal policy crowds out private investment. The expansion in public expenditure can have a beneficial effect on private investment.

QUESTIONS FOR REVIEW

1. What do you understand by investment function ? Explain the factors that influence the level of investment in the economy.
2. Distinguish between autonomous investment and induced investment. Explain the factors that determine the level of investment in the economy
3. What is meant by marginal efficiency of capital ? How is it calculated ? What are the factors that determine marginal efficiency of capital in the economy ?
4. What is marginal efficiency of investment ? What role do expectations of entrepreneurs play in determining marginal efficiency of investment or capital ?
5. How do changes in the rate of interest influence the decision to invest ? Is investment interest elastic ?
6. What is the accelerator theory of investment ? Is it a good representation of investment behaviour ?
7. Critically examine the view that investment spending depends on the changes in the level of output.
8. "Consumption and investment are complementary during deflation, but competitive at full employment." Discuss.
9. The accelerator principle becomes inoperative during periods of excess capacity. Explain.
10. Discuss the view that investment spending depends on change in the level of income.
11. Define marginal efficiency of capital. How does it determine the volume of investment ?
12. Distinguish between marginal efficiency of capital (MEC) and marginal efficiency of investment (MEI). Given marginal efficiency of capital (MEC), how would the stock of capital get adjusted when there is a fall in the rate of interest ?
13. Explain the factors that lead to the discrepancy between the actual and desired stock of capital?

14. Given the saving function $S = -10 + 0.2Y$ and autonomous investment $I =$ ₹ 50 crores

(*i*) Find the level of consumption

(*ii*) If investment decreases permanently by ₹ 5 crore, what is the new level of consumptions ?

[Hints:

$$I_{t1} = V(Y_t - Y_{t-1})$$

$$C = Y - S$$

Given $S = -10 + 0.2Y\ldots$

$$C = Y - (-10 + 0.2Y)$$

$$= Y + 10 - 0.2Y \qquad \ldots(i)$$

Now, in equilibrium $S = I$

$$I = 50$$

$$-10 + 0.2Y = 50$$

$$0.2Y = 60$$

$$Y = 60 \times \frac{10}{2} = 300$$

Now substituting the value of Y in (*i*) we have

$$C = 300 + 10 - 0.2 \times 300$$

$$= 310 - 60 = 250$$

15. Explain how Keynes' theory of investment is relevant to explain investment behaviour in India

16. What is meant by investment portfolio choice ? How will you explain the observed portfolio choice by investors in India ?

CHAPTER 12

Analysis of Employment and Unemployment

Introduction

In the last few chapters we have explained how the equilibrium level of income is determined. When the economy is in equilibrium at less than full-employment level of output, unemployment comes into existence. There are several types of unemployment depending upon the different factors which cause it. Further, the nature and causes of unemployment in developing countries like India are different from those of developed countries. One of the frequent causes of labour unrest in modern societies, both developed and developing, is unemployment among workers and the insecurity of employment. The spectre of unemployment constantly haunts the working classes. Full employment has therefore become the goal of all countries. In what follows we will explain the various types of unemployment and their causes. We shall also explain the concept of full employment and what policies should be pursued to eliminate unemployment and achieve full employment.

Meaning of Unemployment. Technically speaking, *unemployment is defined as a state of affairs when in a country there are a large number of able-bodied persons of working age who are willing to work but cannot find work at the current wage levels.* People who are either unfit for work for physical or mental reasons, or don't want to work, *e.g., sadhus*, are excluded from the category of the unemployed.

Mere engagement in some productive occupation does not necessarily mean absence of unemployment. People, who are only partially employed or are engaged in inferior jobs, though they can do better jobs, are not adequately employed. It is called a state of *underemployment* which is equally bad for the prosperity of a country. Under capitalism, it seems some amount of unemployment is inevitable. The best that can be done is to keep the number of the unemployed as low as possible.

TYPES OF UNEMPLOYMENT

There are three main types of unemployment: (1) frictional unemployment, (2) structural unemployment, and (3) cyclical unemployment. In order to understand the concept of full employment the difference between these types of unemployment needs to be grasped.

Frictional Unemployment

There is always some minimum amount of unemployment that prevails in the economy among workers who have voluntarily quit their previous jobs and are searching for new better jobs or looking for employment for the first time. They are said to be *between jobs*. They are not able to get jobs immediately because of frictions such as lack of market information about availability of jobs and lack of perfect mobility on the part of workers. The distinguishing feature of frictionally unemployed persons is that the number of job vacancies equal to them are available in the economy. They remain unemployed for a relatively short period of time before they are able to get new jobs. This is because some time is required for job searchers to have information about the availability of jobs. When presently fractionally unemployed persons get jobs, the new frictionally unemployed persons come into existence and thus there is always some frictional unemployment prevailing in the economy due to imperfections or lack of market information about the availability of jobs. Since frictionally unemployed are those who have either quit their old jobs voluntarily and are looking for better jobs or those who have entered into the labour force *for the first time* and searching for jobs according to their acquired skills or those who had re-entered the labour force for some time, for example, after having children, the frictional unemployment is considered as voluntary unemployment.

Structural Unemployment

Structural unemployment is another type of unemployment which always exists to some extent in a growing economy. Structural unemployment which refers to the mismatch between the unemployed persons and the demand for specific types of workers for employment occurs because whereas demand for one kind of labour is expanding, the demand for another kind of labour is declining either due to the changes in the structure (*i.e.*, composition) of demand for the industrial products or due to the changes in technology that take place in an economy. *The distinguishing feature of structural unemployment is that the unemployed workers lack skills required by the expanding industries.* Structural unemployment also occurs because of the mismatch between the location of job vacancies of the expanding industries and the present location of the unemployed workers.

Let us give an example of structural unemployment. In a growing economy techniques of production are constantly changing with the result that people are likely to lose their jobs when these are replaced by newer and more efficient techniques. The unemployment created in this way is structural unemployment and is inevitable consequence of technological progress. These structurally unemployed persons will need to acquire new skills and training before they will be absorbed in the new technologically superior jobs. Take another example, when computerisation of banks, offices occurred in India recently some workers were rendered unemployed. But computerisation created new job opportunities. On being given training in computer operations some of them again got jobs. But for some time they remain unemployed. Further, due to changes in demand for some goods, the output of industries producing them declines rendering some people unemployed. On the other hand, in those industries the demand for whose products are increasing, new jobs are created and unemployed workers are absorbed in them but before getting jobs in the expanding industries they remain unemployed.

Structural unemployment tends to last much longer than frictional unemployment because more time is required for people to get new training or acquire new skills or to move to new locations of expanding industries. Structural unemployment is more serious than frictional unemployment. This is because frictionally unemployed are likely to get jobs in a relatively short period of time as job vacancies exist for them. On the other hand, structurally unemployed have no immediate job prospects as they have to get training or acquire new skills required for the jobs available. The structurally unemployed persons can be expected to get only low paying unskilled types of jobs in the immediate future. Some accept such jobs while others prefer to remain unemployed and go on searching for better jobs which match their skills.

Natural Rate of Unemployment

It may be noted that frictional and structural types of unemployment together constitute what is called *natural rate of unemployment* which may be of the order of 4 to 5 per cent of labour force in free market economies. Thus, natural rate of unemployment arises due to labour market frictions and structural changes in a free market economy. Note that even when there is natural rate of unemployment, labour market is in equilibrium. In the late nineties, natural rate of unemployment was estimated to be 5.2 per cent of labour force in the United States. In 2003 actual unemployment rate rose to 6.2 per cent in the United States. This higher than natural rate of unemployment is due to recessionary conditions prevailing in the American economy. *Full employment is said to prevail despite the existence of natural rate of unemployment which is unavoidable in a changing economy.*

Cyclical Unemployment.

It is unemployment due to deficiency of effective demand. It is also called cyclical '*Keynesian unemployment*'. Advanced capitalist countries have been suffering from time to time from this type of unemployment. This type of unemployment greatly increases during periods of recession or depression. Since recession or depression is one phase of the business cycles that generally occur in the industrialised developed economies, this type of unemployment is called cyclical unemployment. This type of unemployment is due to the fact that the total effective demand of the community is not sufficient to absorb the entire production of goods that can be produced with the available stock of capital. In a private enterprise economy, production takes place in response to the profit motive. When businessmen cannot sell their entire output, their profit expectations are not fulfilled so that their reaction in the next period is to reduce their output. The factors of production earn their incomes because of their participation in the process of production and when entrepreneurs decide to reduce their production, some factors of production become unemployed. Since employment is the major source of income for a great majority of the people, a fall in employment signifies a fall in their incomes also.

The deficiency of aggregate demand as an explanation of involuntary unemployment in the industrially advanced countries is associated with the name of J.M. Keynes. Classical and neo classicial economists often denied the very existence of the problem. In the view of classical economists, a freely competitive capitalist economy could never suffer from a deficiency of aggregate effective demand. This belief of Classical economists was based on Say's Law of Markets according to which '*supply creates its own demand*'. This law advanced by J.B. Say (a French economist) and accepted by many other Classical economists in support of their contention was that there could never be a problem of general over-production and that if there was any unemployment it was because of hindrances placed in the working of the freely competitive price system by artificial monopolistic action on the part of trade unions, employers or the government.

The Concept of Full Employment

The above analysis of the types of unemployment requires us to make the concept of full employment clear. Full employment may be defined as the situation wherein all those who are willing and able to work at prevailing wage rates are in fact employed for the work in which they are trained. Two things must be noted in regard to this definition. First, full employment does not mean that everyone is employed. Some people like children, old men and physically or mentally handicapped people are not able to work. There can be no question of their being employed. In fact these people are not included in the labour force of the country. Full employment will exist in spite of their not working. Secondly, some people called 'idle rich' though able to work are not willing to work because they get enough unearned incomes to live on. These people are also not included in the labour force of the country.

From above it follows that *the unemployed people are those who are involuntarily idle. They are able and willing to work but the economy does not provide them jobs*.

Another important qualification to the above definition is worth noting. It is that, at any given time, there is bound to be some frictional and structural unemployment owing to labour-saving technological improvements or a change in consumer tastes for the product of some individual industries, some workers are in the process of voluntarily changing jobs. Some time may elapse before they get a new job after leaving the old one and, therefore, they remain temporarily unemployed. Similarly, some amount of seasonal unemployment is also inevitable. Experience indicates that the total amount of frictional and structural unemployment may amount to 4 to 5 per cent of the labour force.

Thus, *full employment is said to exist in the economy even if there is prevailing some amount of frictional and structural unemployment in the economy.* If the number of unemployed is greater than frictional and structural unemployment, only then we shall say that full employment does not prevail. Keynesian full employment is, by definition, the maximum level of employment that private enterprise countries can attain without experiencing strong inflationary pressure. But for purposes of practical policy it is-necessary to reduce the concept to quantitative terms. It should be possible to say when employment is less than full so that remedial action is called for. The concept, as defined above, raises two quantitative problems, namely, how to determine (1) the number of workers who at the ruling wage rates wish to be employed, and (2) the inevitable minimum amount of frictional and structural unemployment. The first, in turn, depends upon (*a*) the number of people able and willing to work for wages and (*b*) the average number of hours of work which each of them wants to be employed. The number of wage-employment seekers depends upon the following: the size of the population of working age, the persons who, having sufficient unearned incomes, choose to remain idle; the number of persons who, being in command of the requisite means of production, are self-employed; and the prevailing wage rates and other incentives provided. Normally, apart from the size of the population of working age, these factors are likely to be more or less stable over short periods. For instance, the span of life which comes within the working age, while subject to variation as a result of changes in the period of schooling or in the normal age for retirement consequent on changes in health standards and longevity, is likely to remain unchanged in the short period.

Again, since most workers have no large unearned incomes or accumulated savings, they are compelled to try to remain continuously in employment. They cannot, therefore, throw their labour power in the market or withhold it therefrom in some unpredictable manner. Accordingly, the number who choose to remain idle is unlikely to vary much in any short period. And so on. Moreover, even when some of these factors change somewhat, the net quantitative effect may not be important. *Higher wages, for instance, may induce some of the older workers to postpone their retirement while these may impel some of the married women workers, now that their husbands are better off, to relinquish their jobs. The net effect of a rise in wages will not, therefore, be quantitatively important.*[1] *The same applies to other actors.* The size of the population of working age too, though not invariant, is measurable as it changes according to definite trends. It follows that the number of wage-seeking population can be determined with a great measure of accuracy. And since the average number of hours of work which each wage-employment seeker wants to put in is likely to be more or less stable in any short period, *the total amount of wage-employment sought* is quite precisely measurable.

Similar observations may be made regarding the permissible allowance for structural and frictional unemployment. It varies from year to year in accordance with the magnitude of the structural shifts in demand and production that together with immobility of labour and lack of adequate information about the availability and locations of new jobs cause structural and frictional unemployment. It may, therefore, be better defined as a range rather than as a precise figure. Since normally structural shifts in demand and production are unlikely to be violent or spasmodic and since in industrialised countries the incidence of frictional unemployment is bound to be quite low, the allowance for frictional and structural unemployment needs to be very small. A US study has suggested that this allowance need not be beyond a range of 4 to 5 per cent of the available labour force.

The possibility of measuring the size of the available labour force and the inevitable minimum of frictional and structural unemployment makes full employment a determinate quantity. For effective implementation of full-employment policy many countries fix a full-employment target expressed in terms of the permissible range of frictional and structural unemployment. Unemployment in excess of the fixed target would indicate a lapse from full employment calling for a remedial action.

1. Pigou, A.C., *Lapses from Full Employment,* 1945, p. 45.

KEYNES' THEORY OF EMPLOYMENT

In the early thirties of the 20th century when the capitalist countries suffered from severe depression and involuntary unemployment, J.M. Keynes put forward a theory of employment. Keynes' theory of employment provides a reasonably good explanation of what determines level of employment in a free market economy and what causes involuntary unemployment in it. According to Keynes, level of employment is determined by aggregate demand and aggregate supply. When aggregate demand is not sufficient to buy the aggregate supply of output at full-employment level of resources, the problem of demand deficiently arises which causes a fall in level of output and employment. As explained earlier, Classical economists denied the very existence of involuntary unemployment as they believed in Say's Law of Markets according to which *every supply output creates its demand* and therefore output will be expanded to the extent when all resources including labour are fully employed. Besides, they thought if at any time unemployment in the economy occurs, wages and prices will change in a way that employment expands and involuntary unemployment is eliminated. Thus, according to the Classical economists, wage-price flexibility ensures automatic corrections of forces to restore full employment. But classical theory collapsed in 1929-33 when severe depression took place in the Western industrialised countries and rate of involuntary unemployment shot up to around 25 per cent of labour force in the United States.

Besides, there was a drastic decline in Gross National Product (GNP) which fell from 315 billion dollars in 1929 to 222 billion dollars in 1933, that is, national income declined by 30 per cent during these four years period. This reflects a dismal picture of the American economy during the period of Great Depression. In England as well as in other European countries also such a grave situation of severe recession and huge unemployment prevailed during this period. Before 1929-33 and even after it, recessions have occurred in these economies but they have not been as severe as that took place during 1929-33.

Classical economists had no valid explanation of such a severe depression and large-scale cyclical unemployment of labour. A.C. Pigou and other economists of his view attributed this situation to the high wage rates kept by trade unions and Government. Pigou, therefore, suggested all-round cut in wages to increase employment and to remove depression and unemployment. However, this solution of the problem was neither logically sound nor practical to be implemented. Keynes challenged this view of the classical economists and put forward a different explanation of depression and cyclical unemployment which was accepted by many as logical and correct. He explained his viewpoint in his now noted work, '*General Theory of Employment, Interest, and Money*'. He not only gave a sound and valid explanation of depression and its associated problem of cyclical unemployment but also suggested effective policy measures to cure them.

According to Keynes, it is true that supply does create demand for goods and services because various factors of production earn their incomes in the process of production by helping to create additional supply of output. When factors of production are employed to produce goods, they get their reward in the form of wages, rents, interest and profit. But from this it does not follow that the entire supply of national output will always be demanded by them. The incomes of the factors of production are necessarily equal to the value added in the productive process, but it does not mean that the entire income will be automatically spent on goods and services created in a given time period. A part of income will be saved so that this part of income is not available to create demand for goods and services. Unless investors are willing to invest to an equivalent extent of intended savings, the total effective demand which consists of demand for consumer goods and producer goods ($C + I$) will not be sufficient to absorb the entire available supply of output. And if it happens, then producers will not be able to sell their entire output, their profits will fall and they will cut their production and this will create unemployment.

In a given period, consumers are planning to spend a given part of their income and save the rest. Similarly, entrepreneurs are planning to invest in factories, machines, etc., to a given extent. The total effective demand is the sum of the consumption and the investment demand. Savers are saving for different reasons than the investors whose investment is determined by different factors and in a completely free market economy there is no mechanism to ensure that what savers are planning to save is just equal to what investors are planning to invest. If there is any discrepancy between planned saving and investment, output, income and employment will change to correct this discrepancy. If planned investment is greater than planned saving, the current output will not be sufficient to meet the emerging demand and hence income, output and employment will increase and vice versa. Thus, we see that the basic weakness of Say's law arises because of lack of any agency to ensure automatically that intended investments are just equal to intended savings. Since savings and investments are undertaken by different persons and for different reasons a discrepancy between the two is bound to arise and when it arises the necessary mechanism to correct it is through changes in the volume of employment and income.

What Causes Depression or Cyclical Unemployment ?

According to Keynes, the cause of depression and cyclical unemployment in the industrialised capitalist countries was a sharp decline in private investment due to the adverse business expectations about profit making. There was a wave of pessimism prevailing among investors. The decline in private investment due to fall in marginal efficiency of capital (that is, expected rate of return) caused a fall in aggregate demand and resulted in less than full-employment equilibrium. Consequently, level of output and employment fell drastically and involuntary unemployment came to prevail on a large scale. The involuntary unemployment that prevails in times of recession/depression is called cyclical unemployment and, as we have seen above, according to Keynes, it is due to deficiency of aggregate demand.

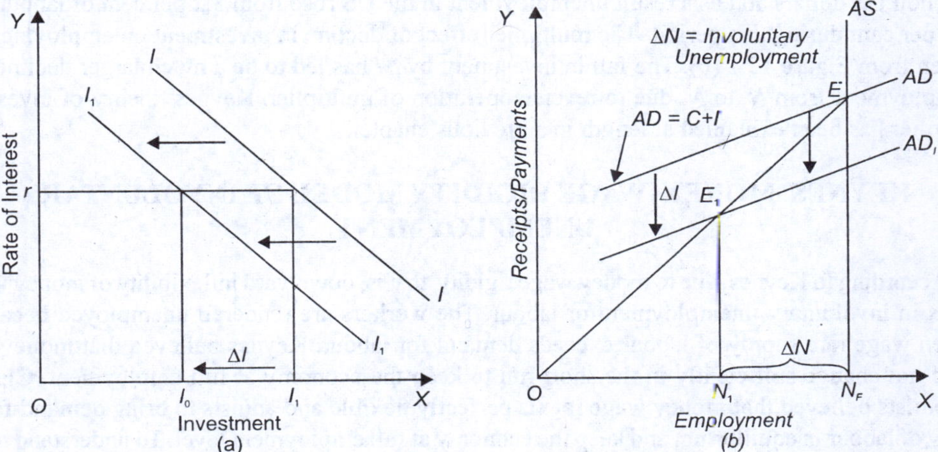

Fig. 12.1. *What causes Depression and Cyclical Unemployment: Keynes' Explanation*

Large fluctuations in investment, according to Keynes, is due to the uncertain basis of profit expectations on which investment decisions are made. To quote him, "*We have to admit that our basis of knowledge for estimating the yield ten years hence of a railway, a copper mine, a textile factory, the goodwill of a patent medicine ... amounts to little and sometimes to nothing.*"[2] In view of this uncertainty of future. Keynes stressed that investment decisions were greatly influenced by how optimistic or pessimistic investors feel. He used the term *animal spirits* to describe these pessimistic or optimistic

2. J.M. Keynes, *The General Theory of Employment, Interest and Money*, pp. 149-150

expectations of the investors about profit earning from investment projects. The term animal spirits implies that there may be no good or intelligent basis for expectations on which investors base their decisions. Thus involuntary unemployment emerges due to fall in aggregate demand. Therefore, the cause of depression or cyclical involuntary unemployment is the deficiency of aggregate demand.

It will be useful to explain through a diagram how a fall in investment causes a decline in level of output and employment and results in cyclical unemployment. This is illustrated in Figure 12.1. It will be seen from Figure 12.1 (*a*) that due to adverse profit expectations or pessimism of investors, investment demand curve shifts to the left from *II* to I_1I_1. With this it will be seen that investment falls from I_1 to I_0 at a given rate of interest. This fall in investment demand by I_1I_0 causes a downward shift in the aggregate demand curve from *AD* to AD_1 [See Figure 12.1(*b*)] As a result, the equilibrium between aggregate demand and aggregate supply which was initially at full employment level N_F (which corresponds to point *E* where the two curves intersect) falls to the new equilibrium level of employment ON_1. Thus involuntary unemployment equal to N_FN_1 or ΔN emerges due to fall in aggregate demand. Therefore, the *cause of Keynesian cyclical unemployment is deficiency of aggregate demand.* It should also be noted that the decline in the level of employment following the fall in investment and aggregate demand also results in decrease in GNP or national income of a country. The emergence of large-scale unemployment and drastic decline in level of output and national income represents a situation of depression.

It is also important to note that with the help of his theory of investment multiplier Keynes showed that the fall in the level of employment and income is not merely due to the decline in investment but by a multiple of it due to the inverse working of multiplier. In fact during the period of recession in the early 1930s, it, happened so in the advanced capitalist countries such as the US. In the US between 1929 and 1933 the fall in investment was 47.5 billion US dollars whereas national income declined from 315 billion US dollars to 222 billion US dollars during the same period that is, a fall by 93 billion US dollars and as a result unemployment in the US rose from 3.2 per cent of labour force to 25 per cent during this period. The multiplier effect of decline in investment on employment can be seen from Figure 12.1 (*b*). The fall in investment by ΔI has led to be a much larger decline (ΔN) in employment from N_F to N_1 due to reverse operation of multiplier. Keynes' theory of investment multiplier has been explained at length in a previous chapter.

KEYNES' MONEY–WAGE RIGIDITY MODEL OF INVOLUNTARY UNEMPLOYMENT

According to Keynes, due to money wage rigidity, that is, downward inflexibility of money wages, results in involuntary unemployment of labour. The workers are rendered unemployed because at a given wage rate supply of labour exceeds demand for labour. Keynes believed that money wage would not change sufficiently in the short run to keep the economy at full employment. Classical economists believed that money wage rate is perfectly flexible and adjusts to bring demand for and supply of labour in equilibrium and keep the economy at full employment level. To understand money wage rigidity which results in unemployment we have to examine why labour market does not clear through reduction in money wages, Keynes gave three reasons for the stickiness of money wage rate. It may be noted that stickiness or rigidity of money wage implies that money wage rate will not quickly change, especially in the downward direction to keep equilibrium at full employment level.

Causes of Money Wage Rigidity

1. **Money Illusion.** The first reason why firms fail to cut wages despite an excess supply of labour is that workers will resist any move for cut in money wages though they might accept fall in real wages brought about by rise in prices of commodities. Keynes attributed this to money illusion on the part of the workers. *By money illusion it is meant that workers fail to realise that value of money, that is, its purchasing power in terms of commodities,*

changes when prices rise. They regard money such as a rupee as something which has a stable value or purchasing power, that a rupee is a rupee and a dollar is a dollar with fixed real purchasing power. Therefore, while they would strongly oppose and resist any cut in money wages, they would not resist much if their real wages are reduced through rise in prices of commodities with money wages remaining constant. Thus Keynes wrote, "*Whilst workers will usually resist a reduction of money wages, it is not their practice to withdraw their labour whenever there is a rise in the price of wage goods*"

There are two reasons for existence of money illusion:

(*i*) First reason for the existence of money illusion is that workers of a firm or industry think that though rise in prices reduce their real wages, but that this rise in prices equally affects workers in other industries so that their relative wages as compared to those employed in other industries remain the same. Therefore, workers who are more concerned with their relative position with other workers will strongly resist the cut in their money wages, while they will not oppose so strongly their cut in real wages through rise in the general price level.

(*ii*) The second reason for strong resistance to cut in money wages is that the workers blame their own employers for this, whereas they think that a cut in real wages through rise in prices in general is the outcome of the working of general economic forces over which strikes in an industry would have little effect. However, it does not necessarily mean that trade unions remain silent spectators if they feel that changes in Government policy adversely affects their economic interests.

From the above two reasons given for money illusion it follows that if additional employment can be created by lowering real wages, it is more practical to do so *through bringing about rise in general price level rather than by cutting money wages.*

2. **Wage Fixation Through Contracts.** In most of the free market economies such as those of USA and Great Britain, wages are fixed by the firms through contracts made with the workers for a year or two. There is little possibility of changing money wages fixed through contracts when the situation of either surplus labour or shortage emerges. For workers organised into trade unions wages are even rigid. Through collective bargaining by trade unions with the employers wage scales are fixed for 3 to 4 years by contract. Money wages cannot be changed when either surplus or shortage of labour emerges during the period of the contract. Trade unions of workers never accept wage cuts even if some of union workers remain unemployed. Thus the sticky or rigid money wages lead to the existence of involuntary unemployment. This means that labour market does not clear in the short run.

3. **Minimum Wage Laws.** Another reason for money wage rigidity or, what is also called money wage stickiness, is the intervention by the Government in fixing minimum wages below which employers are not permitted to pay wages to the workers.

4. **Efficiency Wages.** Another factor which accounts for money wage rigidity is that employers themselves are not interested in lowering wages as high wages make workers more efficient and productive. The adverse effect of lower wages on workers' efficiency may explain the unwillingness on the part of employers to cut money wages despite the excess supply of or unemployment of workers at higher money wages.

We have explained above the practical difficulties pointed out by Keynes and his followers which are faced by firms in reducing wages and which therefore explain money wage rigidity or stickiness. The sticky or rigid money wages above the equilibrium level cause unemployment of labour.

Price Flexibility and Money Wage Rigidity : Keynes' View of Involuntary Unemployment

In Keynes' contractual view of labour market, it is assumed that whereas prices are free to vary, the money wage is fixed. It is important to note that Keynesians do not believe that money wage rate is completely fixed or sticky. What they actually mean by sticky wages is that money wages do not fall quickly to bring demand for and supply of labour in equilibrium at full employment. In their view money wages are very slow to adjust sufficiently to ensure full employment of labour when there is a decline in aggregate demand resulting in lowering of prices of products. As a consequence, involuntary unemployment comes into existence. It may be further noted that Keynes was particularly concerned with downward rigidity of money wages at which the demand for labour exceeds the supply of labour and consequently unemployment or excess supply of labour emerges. It is important to note that Keynes accepted the classical theory of labour demand according to which firms demand labour up to the point at which real wage rate (that is, money wage rate divided by the price level or, W/P) is equal to the marginal product of labour. At a higher real wage rate, less amount of labour will be demanded and, at a lower real wage rate, more labour will be demanded or employed. In other words, demand curve of labour is downward sloping. Keynes' theory of involuntary unemployment based on price flexibility and money wage rigidity is depicted in Figure 12.2.

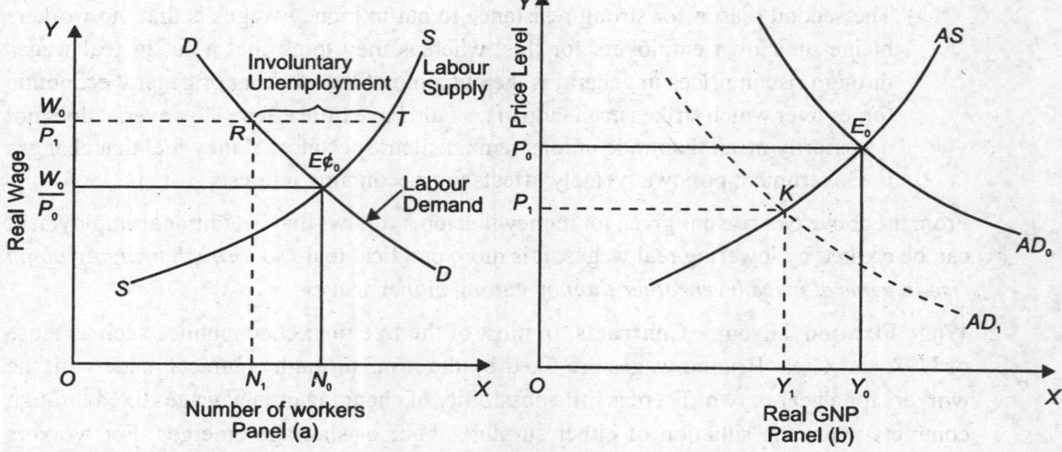

Fig. 12.2. *Keynes' Rigid Money Wage and Flexible Price Model: The Emergence of Involuntary Unemployment*

In panel (*b*) of Figure. 12.2 short-run aggregate supply curve *AS* and aggregate demand curve AD_0 have been drawn and through their interaction determine price level P_0 and the level of real *GNP* equal to Y_0.* It is important to note that short-run aggregate supply curve *AS* has been drawn with a given fixed money wage rate, say W_0. In panel (*a*) of Figure 12.2 the level of labour employment N_0 shows the number of jobs when the economy is producing Y_0 level of national output in panel (b) corresponding to the equilibrium between aggregate supply *AS* and aggregate demand AD_0 at price level P_0, with a fixed money wage and the level of *GNP* equal to Y_0. The labour market must be in equilibrium at point E_0 or at real wage rate W_0/P_0 at which N_0 workers are demanded and employed. All those who are willing to get jobs at the real wage rate W_0/P_0 are in fact demanded and employed. Thus, equilibrium at E_0 or at level of employment N_0 represents full-employment equilibrium.

---

* Students should note that concepts of aggregate demand curve (*AD*) and aggregate supply curve (*AS*) used in this Figure 12.2 are different from those used earlier in this chapter. Aggregate demand curve drawn in this Figure 12.2, means the total expenditure on goods and services which households, firms and Government are willing to make at various price levels. These concepts of aggregate demand and aggregate supply curves will be explained in a separate chapter.

Now consider again panel (*b*) of Figure 12.2. Suppose due to fall in marginal efficiency of capital there is reduction in investment demand which along with its multiplier effect causes a leftward shift in the aggregate demand curve *AD*. Since Keynes believed that with a fixed money wage rate aggregate supply curve *AS* is given and remains unchanged, it will be seen from panel (*b*) of Figure 12.2 that new aggregate demand curve AD_1 and the fixed aggregate supply curve *AS* intersect at point *K* determining new equilibrium lower price P_1 and smaller real *GNP* equal to Y_1. Keynes asserted that the economy would remain stuck at point *K* with less than full-employment level of output Y_1 and lower price level P_1. Now, a glance at panel (*a*) of Figure 12.2 shows that with fixed money image W_0 and lower price level P_1 ($P_1 < P_0$), the real wage rate rises to W_0/P_1. It will be seen from panel (*a*) of Figure 12.2 that at this higher real wage rate W_0/P_1, the smaller amount of labour N_1 will be demanded and employed by all firms in the economy. However, at this higher wage rate W_0/P_1 (with money wage rate fixed at W_0), *RT* number of workers are rendered unemployed. It is in this way that Keynes explained that with money wage rate remaining fixed at the level W_0 and with flexible prices, the fall in aggregate demand results in persistent involuntary unemployment. Thus, by explaining the emergence of persistent involuntary unemployment Keynes made a fundamental departure from the classical view of a free market economy which denied the existence of involuntary unemployment except for a short time.

EXPLAINING GREAT DEPRESSION (1929-33) : MONETARIST VIEW

We have explained above Keynes' view that great depression of 1929-33 was caused by fall in investment due to the drastic fall in the profit expectations of business class. The decline in investment, according to him, caused aggregate demand to fall which along with the reverse working of multiplier caused conditions of depression (*i.e.* high rate of unemployment, substantial decrease in GNP and fall in prices) Keynes and his followers emphasise the role of fiscal policy (increase in Government expenditure and cut in taxation) to stimulate investment. They downplayed the role of monetary policy and in fact pointed out that monetary policy in the thirties during the depression period proved to be unimportant and ineffective. As a matter of fact, they asserted that monetary policy was tried during the depression period to revive the economy but miserably failed. At times of depression, according to them, businessmen are in the grip of pessimism about future profitability of investment and more money made available through easy and liberal monetary policy would not be effective in reviving the economy. It was in this context that some Keynesian economists remarked that '*money does not matter*' and also referred to the policy of making more credit available for investment by businesses 'you can bring horse to water but cannot make it drink'. Thus Keynesian view prevailed during the forties and fifties almost unchallenged.

Keynes' view was attacked by Milton Friedman, a Nobel Laureate in economics, in the middle of sixties. Friedman and Schwartz in their important work '*A Monetary History of the United States*' written in 1963 quoted statistical evidence from the United States, and argued that "a re-examination of of the Great Depression of the 1930s demonstrated that, contrary to general belief, it had been a tragic testament to the great power of monetary policy, not to its impotence"[3] They pointed out drastic decline in the quantity of money was made by Federal Reserve System (the Central Bank of the USA) from 1929 to 1933 which was responsible for severe depression in the American economy. They argued that the failure of the Federal Reserve System to prevent bank failures and the drastic decrease in money supply during 1930-1933 increased the intensity of depression. To quote them, "The US Federal Reserve System could have prevented the *decline of one-third* in the quantity of money that occurred from 1929 to 1933. Had it done so, the evidence indicated, the depression would have been far milder and briefer"[4].

3. Friedman and Schwartz, *Monetary History of the United States*, 1963, p. 300.
4. *Op. cit.*, p. 300

We thus see that Freidman and other monetarists emphasise monetary policy in causing depression. In fact, they go to the other extreme view '*money alone matters*'. However, in our view in recent recession during 2000-2003, the Federal Reserve System made successive cuts in rate of interest more than 7 times to revive the American economy without any success. For stimulating investment and growth, it cut the bank rate to 1 per cent, the lowest in the last 50 years, but failed in its objective to overcome recession. Even in India, Reserve Bank also lowered the bank rate several times during 1998—2003 and reduced it to 6 per cent the lowest in forty years—to bring about industrial recovery but seems to have failed. In the case of the USA, the signs of recovery in the first quarter of 2003-04 seems to have been the result of drastic reduction in taxation to the extent of 3.5 billion dollars and huge increase in defence expenditure for war in Iraq. Both of these are fiscal policies suggested by Keynesians that seems to have worked to start a recovery in the American economy.

To conclude, in the view of present author the truth lies in between the two extreme views of Keynes and Friedman. Therefore, modern economists give importance to both fiscal and monetary policies for influencing investment and growth in GNP. Both can be complements to each other Furthermore, profit expectations of entrepreneurs and cost and availability of credit play a significant role in determining national income, employment and price level in the economy.

POLICY IMPLICATIONS OF KEYNES' THEORY OF EMPLOYMENT AND INCOME

Keynes' theory has important policy implications for raising the level of employment and income in the economy. When the equilibrium of the economy is at less than full-employment level and as a consequence there is depression or recession in the economy and with it huge unemployment of labour prevails. According to Keynes, this occurs due to lack of aggregate effective demand. There are two types of policies which may be adopted to overcome this situation of recession and unemployment. They are (1) monetary policy and (2) fiscal policy. Under monetary policy, through expansion in money supply rate of interest can be lowered which will encourage private investment. With the increase in private investment, aggregate demand will increase (that is, aggregate demand curve will shift upward) which will raise the equilibrium level of employment. As a result, the economy will be lifted out of recessionary conditions and unemployment will be removed.

However, Keynes had serious doubts about the effectiveness of monetary policy. He was of the view that in times of depression rate of interest is already very low and at this liquidity preference curve of the community (that is, the curve of demand for money to hold) is *absolutely elastic, that is, it is of horizontal shape*. Therefore, in this situation when money supply is increased, rate of interest will not fall. Thus, with no fall in the rate of interest, private investment will not pick up further.

Importance of Fiscal Policy

In view of ineffectiveness of monetary policy, Keynes laid stress on the role of fiscal policy in curing recession/depression and removing involuntary unemployment. Under the fiscal policy, a major measure is the *increase in expenditure by the Government on several types of public works* in times of depression. The increase in Government expenditure will cause an upward shift in the aggregate demand curve. This increase in aggregate demand will bring about increase in employment and output. If the increase in Government expenditure and as a result rise in aggregate demand is sufficient, it will help in achieving equilibrium at full-employment level. As a result, depression and involuntary unemployment will be eliminated. It is worth noting that in this regard Keynes put forward a theory of multiplier which strengthened the case for raising Government expenditure on public works in times of depression or when large-scale unemployment prevailed in the economy. We shall discuss the theory of multiplier at length in later chapter. Briefly, theory of multiplier implies that increase in Government expenditure will raise aggregate demand and therefore output and employment not by the amount of increase in Government expenditure but by a multiple of it.

Another important measure of fiscal policy to raise employment and output is the *reduction in taxes*. When rates of personal taxes such as income tax are reduced, disposable income of the people increases which brings about rise in their demand for consumption. The rise in consumption demand pushes up aggregate demand curve and helps in removing recession and unemployment. It may be noted that on the recommendations of Keynesian economists American President John Kennedy made a drastic cut in income taxes in 1964. This had a great success as output and employment in the USA increased significantly and, as a result, recession and unemployment were removed. Cut in personal taxes to boost aggregate demand has also been applied in later years in the USA as well as in Great Britain. Recently in 2003, the then President of the USA Geoge W. Bush has made a 3.5 billion cut in taxes to revive the American economy.

In the end, it is important to note that modern economists though agree with Keynes' view about the effectiveness of fiscal policy in curing recession, they do not share Keynes' view about the ineffectiveness of monetary policy. It may however be noted that, according to the modern Keynesians and others, liquidity preference curve of the community is fairly elastic even in times of recession which implies that expansion in money supply will cause a decline in interest rate and will therefore stimulate private investment. Further, according to them, investment demand curve is also fairly elastic which implies that fall in interest rate will have significant impact on private investment. Thus, according to modern economists, both monetary and fiscal policies are important instruments whereby aggregate demand of the economy can be changed. We shall discuss in detail the roles of monetary and fiscal policies for attaining economic stabilisation in later chapters.

NATURE AND CAUSES OF UNEMPLOYMENT IN DEVELOPING COUNTRIES

Basic Explanation : Lack of Capital and other Productive Assets

As stated above, Keynesian theory is mainly concerned with cyclical unemployment which emerges in the developed capitalist countries, specially in times of depression due to the fall in aggregate demand. During the period 1929-33, the developed capitalist economies suffered from severve depression which caused huge magnitude of unemployment. Keynes analysed this cyclical type of unemployment and asserted that it was caused by deficiency of aggregate demand. *The nature of unemployment in developing countries is quite different; rather than being cyclical it is of chronic and long-term nature*. It is now almost universally recognised that the chronic unemployment and underemployment in less developed countries are not due to the lack of aggregate effective demand which, according to J.M. Keynes, was responsible for unemployment in developed countries in times of depression. Rather it is stated to be due to the lack of land, capital and other complementary resources in relation to the total population and labour force. In the phenomenon examined by Keynes, not only labour force but also capital equipment were unemployed due to the deficiency of aggregate effective demand. In other words, in the Keynesian scheme, both the labour force and capital equipment were crying out for full employment which could be achieved by raising the level of aggregate monetary expenditure. Thus, according to Joan Robinson: "Keynes' theory has little to say, directly, to the underdeveloped countries, for it was framed entirely in the context of an advanced industrial economy, with highly developed financial institutions and a sophisticated business class. The unemployment that concerned Keynes was accompanied by underutilisation of capacity already in existence. It had resulted from a fall in effective demand. The unemployment of underdeveloped economies arises because capacity and effective demand never have been great enough"[5].

The existence of unemployment due to lack of capital or other cooperating factors was an important question which was discussed by Marx in the context of advanced industrialised countries. Therefore such unemployment has often been called *Marxian unemployment*[6] as distinguished from

5. Joan Robinson, *Economic Philosphy*, p. 119.
6. See Joan Robinson, *An Essay on Marxian Economics*.

Keynesian unemployment which is caused by the deficiency of aggregate demand. According to Marx, the number of workers employed by the capitalists depends upon the amount of capital in existence, and there is, what he called, "reserve army of unemployed labour" because there is inadequate capital to employ all the available labour. If A stands for the total amount of available labour, N for the amount of labour-employment which is necessary to work with the existing stock of capital at its normal capacity, then $A–N$ is the reserve army of unemployed labour.[7]

Thus, the standard explanation for the existence of labour surplus or unemployment and under-employment in less developing countries like India is that as compared with the magnitude of population and labour force there is limited availability of capital or complementary resources which include land, factories, machines, tools and implements–the means with which labóur produces. Now, if the population grows faster than the stock of capital of a country, the entire addition to the labour force cannot be absorbed in productive employment because not enough instruments of production would be there to employ them. Since in less developed countries, the stock of capital has not been growing at a rate fast enough to keep pace with the growth of population, the ability to offer productive employment is very limited. This has resulted in surplus labour which is manifested in the existence of huge magnitude of underemployment or disguised unemployment and open unemployment in both the rural and urban areas.

Capital as the major bottleneck to growth of employment was made popular by Harrod-Domar model of economic growth in which capital accumulation plays a pivotal role and according to which rate of growth of output depends upon the proportion of national income saved, divided by the capital-output ratio ($g = s/v$, where g stands for growth rate, s for the proportion of income saved and v for the capital-output ratio). This model assumes capital coefficients (*i.e.,* capital-output ratio and capital-labour ratio) to remain constant. With constant capital-output and capital-labour ratios, the more the capital, the more will be both output and employment. Therefore, when adapted to the less developed countries, this model suggests that the *rate of growth of output and therefore of employment is determined by the growth of capital stock.*[8]

Wage Goods Constraint and Unemployment in Developing Countries

It is worth mentioning a dissenting view regarding the cause of unemployment and under-employment in developing countries. This dissenting view had been put forward by Prof. P.R. Brahmananda and C.N. Vakil of Bombay University. According to them, the basic cause of unemployment in developing countries is the deficiency of the availability of essential consumer goods, often called *wage goods.* They point out that when the unemployed people or disguisedly unemployed people who are withdrawn from agriculture are engaged in some public works, they will have to be supplied with wage-goods so that employed labourers can subsist. If the wage-goods are not sufficiently available, their employment in capital-creation works cannot be sustained. Given the real wage rate, a particular number of people can be employed in the economy, depending upon the supply of wage-goods in the economy. Now, the total quantity of wage-goods required to employ all the disguised unemployed workers in agriculture, according to them, would exceed the actual available supply of wage-goods even when the release of wage-goods by the withdrawal of disguised unemployed is taken into account. Thus, according to Prof. Brahmananda and Vakil, there exists a *wage-goods* gap which is the fundamental cause of unemployment in labour-surplus developing countries

7. It may also be noted that, according to Marx, accumulation of industrial capital, that is, establishment of large-scale factories and machines displaces labour engaged in handicrafts or artisan activities because the latter would not be able to withstand the competiton from the former. Marx believed that the accumulation of industrial capital could never proceed fast enough to create employment for all who were displaced by the new machines. Therefore, Marxian unemployment has also been referred to as "technological unemployment".
8. C.N. Vakil and P.R. Brahmananda, *Planning for an Expanding Economy*. Vora and Co., 1956, pp. 111-112.

A prominent Indian economist, Prof. A.K. Sen, has also emphasised the supply of wage-goods in determining employment in developing countries. According to Prof. Sen, the quantum of wage employment in the economy depends on the total supply of wage-goods on the one hand and the real wage-rate on the other. If E represents the quantum of employment, M represents the supply of wage-goods and W, the real wage-rate, then the employment which can be provided will be given by the following equation.[9]

$$E = \frac{M}{W}$$

It is thus evident from Sen's above equation that if the supply of wage-goods (M) is less than the required supply to provide all labour force, then all workers cannot be fully employed, which will result in the emergence of unemployment. Thus, to generate enough employment and solve the problem of unemployment and underemployment, the wage-goods industries, especially agriculture, must be accorded a high priority in the strategy of economic development.

Most of the unemployment in underdeveloped countries is of a different nature from that in advanced and developed countries. A major part of unemployment in present-day developed countries is of cyclical nature which is due to *deficiency of aggregate effective demand.* But most of the unemployment in developing countries is not cyclical. Thus, in developing countries, there is not much Keynesion type short-term unemployment. Instead, it is a chronic problem.

Causes of Unemployment in the Indian Economy

We have explained above the two *basic* explanations of unemployment and underemployment prevailing in the developing countries. We now explain below in some detail the various causes which account for unemployment and underemployment that still prevails in the developing countries.

1. Lack of the Stock of Physical Capital. The major cause of unemployment and underemployment in underdeveloped countries like India is *the deficiency of the stock of capital* in relation to the needs of the growing labour force. In the modern world, man by himself can hardly produce anything. Even the primitive man needed some elementary tools like the bow and arrow to engage in hunting for the earning of his livelihood. With the growth of technology and specialisation, he needs much more capital with which to engage in the productive activity. If he is an agriculturist, he needs a piece of land and also a plough, a pair of oxen, seeds and some foodgrains and other necessities of life to sustain himself during the period of sowing to the reaping of the harvest. In the industrial sector, he needs factories to work in and machines to work with. All these aids to production belong to the community's stock of capital. Now, if the working force grows faster than the stock of capital of a country, the entire addition of labour force cannot be absorbed in productive employment because not enough instruments of production would be there to employ them. The resulting unemployment is known as the *long-term* or *chronic unemployment.*

A nation's stock of capital can be enlarged by increased investment which, in the absence of any unutilised resources, requires additional saving on the part of the community. The concern of the classical economists was to ensure that the rate of capital formation was kept sufficiently high so that employment opportunities were successively enlarged to absorb the additions to the working force of a country as a result of population growth. This is also the problem that the developing countries like India are facing today. In recent times, the labour force in India has been growing at more than 2 per cent per year, yet our rate of investment expressed as a percentage of our stock of capital has not been growing at a fast enough rate so as to keep pace with the growth of population. As a result, the country's ability to offer productive employment to the new entrants in the labour market has been severely limited. This manifests itself in two things: first, the prevalence of large-scale open unemployment in the urban areas as evidenced by the statistics of employment exchanges; second, it manifests itself in the form of open unemployment in the rural areas as well as disguised unemployment in agriculture.

9. Amartya Sen, *Technology and Employment,* Oxford University Press.

2. Use of Capital-Intensive Techniques. An important factor responsible for slow growth of employment has been the use of capital-intensive techniques of production, even in consumer goods industries where alternative labour-intensive techniques are available. Even before 1991, under the Industrial Policy Resolution 1956, the development of consumer goods industries was left open for the private sector. However, private sector prefers to invest in highly capital-intensive plants and equipment on the basis of technology developed in labour-scarce western countries. It is argued by them that the alternative labour-intensive techniques have low productivity and low surplus-generating capacity. However, the important reason for the use of capital-intensive techniques has been the availability of cheap capital. Even firms in modern small industry sector which were expected to generate large employment opportunities have also tended to use capital-intensive techniques of production. Thus, Prof. J.C. Sandesara states, "*The availability of cheap capital has tended to encourage the modern small-scale industries sector to over-capitalise and use more capital-intensive methods of production and thus reduce employment potential*".[10]

In agriculture, reckless mechanisation of various agricultural operations despite the existence of surplus labour has reduced the employment-augmenting effect of new high-yielding technology involving the use of HYV seeds, fertilisers and pesticides. This has prevented the generation of enough employment opportunities in rural areas.

Now, a pertinent question is why capital-intensive techniques are used in industries despite the condition of labour abundance in the economy. First reason is the *relatively low price of capital*. Relatively low price of capital has been caused by (*a*) lower rate of interest, (*b*) liberal depreciation allowance on capital investment permitted in the taxation system of the country, (*c*) relatively cheap capital equipment imported from abroad. Second, higher wages of labour in the organised sector relative to their productivity under pressure from trade unions. Thirdly, rigid labour laws also discourage the employment of labour. It is difficult to retrench labour even when it is not required in case an industrial unit becomes sick and proposes to close down or exit. Fourthly, Research and Development (R & D) activity has not been adequately directed to discover and identify labour-intensive appropriate techniques to be used in industries which, though labour-intensive, have also reasonably good productivity.

3. Inequitable Distribution of Land. Another cause of unemployment prevailing in the developing countries like India is inequitable distribution of land so that many agricultural households have *no adequate access to land* which is an important asset for agricultural production and employment. Sub-division of land holdings under the pressure of rapid population growth since 1951 has further reduced access to land for several agricultural households. As a result many persons who were self-employed in agriculture have become landless agricultural labourers who suffer from acute unemployment and underemployment.

4. Rigid Protective Labour Legislation. Another reason for the slow growth of employment in the organised sector has been the existence of unduly rigid protective labour legislation which makes it very difficult to retrench a worker who has been employed for 240 days. Labour legislation is so much rigid that it is even difficult to close down the unit and quit the industry. Thus, this excessively protective labour legislation induces private entrepreneurs to prefer the maximum use of capital in place of labour.

5. Neglect of the Role of Agriculture in Employment Generation. An important factor responsible for slow growth of employment opportunities is the neglect of agriculture for generating employment opportunities. The general perception, as existed in the first three five year plans in India (1951-65) as well as in the theoretical models of growth for dualistic economies such as Lewis' "*Economic Development with Unlimited Supplies of Labour*" was that agriculture already contained

10. J C. Sandesara, *Small-scale Enterprises in Industrial Development. The Indian Experience* (1998), Sage Publications, Delhi.

surplus labour and it was required to withdraw this surplus labour from agriculture and employ them in the modern industrial sector. By the mid-sixties it was realised that not to speak of employing new entrants to the labour force year after year, the modern industrial sector could not absorb productivity even a fraction of the then existing unemployed persons in the foreseeable feature.

Agriculture though containing surplus labour can generate employment opportunities if proper strategy for its development is adopted. For instance, the empirical evidence shows that on an irrigated hectare of land the number of manhours employed is almost twice that on the unirrigated hectare. Irrigation requires more labour input for watering the fields, but also since output per hectare on irrigated land is much higher, more labour is used for harvesting and threshing the crop. Besides, irrigation makes the adoption of double cropping possible which greatly raises the employment potential of agriculture.

It is worth noting that new agricultural technology, commonly called green revolution technology, involving the use of HYV (High Yielding Varieties) seeds, greater use of fertilisers and pesticides along with water is highty labour absorptive. What is equally important, this new green revolution technology is *size-neutal*, that is, it can be equally well adopted by small farmers. Further, HYV seeds are of short duration type, that is, they mature in a short time so that they make multiple cropping more feasible. The use of double or multiple cropping greatly enhances the opportunities of employment generation in agriculture. The experience of Punjab, Haryana and Western U.P. is a shining example of large employment generation in agriculture. What is needed for the generation of large employment opportunities in agriculture is that the new green revolution technology should be widely diffused and adopted in the backward and lagging agricultural regions in India.

6. Lack of Infrastructure. We have explained above lack of physical capital with which labour is equipped for productive employment as the cause of unemployment prevailing in the developing countries like India. By capital we generally mean machines, plant and equipment, factory buildings etc. But a similar factor responsible for huge unemployment prevailing in these countries is lack of infrastructure such as roads, power, telecommunications, highways, irrigation facilities in agriculture. Inadequate availability of infrastructure is a great obstacle for the generation of opportunities for productive employment.

It follows from above that unemployment and underemployment prevailing in India and other developing countries is *not cyclical Keynesian type of unemployment caused by decline in aggregate demand.* Unemployment and underemployment in India are caused by more basic structural factors such as lack of capital, use of capital-intensive technologies, lack of access to land for agricultural household, lack of infrastructure, rapial growth of population resulting in large annual increments in labour force year after year. Unemployment in India, as in other developing countries, manifests itself in the following forms :

MEASUREMENT OF UNEMPLOYMENT IN THE INDIAN ECONOMY

The surplus labour in a developing economy such as ours manifests itself in (*a*) open unemployment, (*b*) underemployment and (*c*) disguised unemployment. Therefore, a realistic assessment of the magnitude of surplus labour that exists in the Indian economy should contain information about all these three forms of unemployment. However, the measurement of unemployment in an economy such as ours where self-employment is predominant and the bulk of productive activity is carried on within household enterprises is a different task. A slight difference in the definitions and criteria adopted to measure unemployment often makes enormous change in its magnitude. For example, late Professor Raj Krishna suggested the following four criteria to measure unemployment :

(*a*) *Time Criterion*: This refers to identifying those persons as unemployed who have no gainful work for less than some normal standard of hours in a week or less than a certain normal standard of days in a month or a year.

(*b*) *Willingness Criterion*: This calls a person unemployed when he is either seeking or is available for work at the prevailing wage rate.

(*c*) *Income Criterion*: This considers those persons unemployed or underemployed who have income (or expenditure) less than a certain '*poverty norm*' generally fixed on the basis of minimum calories required for subsistence.

(*d*) *Productivity Criterion*: This considers those persons as unemployed or underemployed who may be working but they have less than some normal standard of productivity.[11]

Thus, a change from time and willingness criteria to productivity criterion changes the estimate of rural unemployment for the year 1972-73 from 8.21 per cent of rural labour force (on daily status basis) to 33.7 per cent.[12]

Note that both willingness and time criteria have been used in India in the various rounds of National Sample Survey to measure unemployment in the economy. Productivity criterion has been used by Ashok Mathur, Shakuntala Mehra, Ashok Rudra and Amartya Sen to measure the extent of disguised unemployment in the Indian agriculture. Further, using household expenditure data from earlier rounds of NSS, Dandekar-Rath in their study of "*Poverty in India*" adopted income criterion to measure the magnitude of unemployment in the Indian economy.

Measurement of Unemployment in India : Dantwala Committee Approach

Let us now first discuss the approaches to measure open unemployment and underemployment in India. On the basis of time and willingness criteria open unemployment and underemployment have been estimated using the following three approaches which were recommended by an expert committee headed by Prof. M.L. Dantwala:

(*i*) **Usual Status Approach.** This approach records only those persons as unemployed who had no gainful work for a *major time* during the 365 days preceding the date of survey and are seeking or are available for work. Thus, the estimates of unemployment obtained on the basis of usual status approach are expected to capture long-term open unemployment.

(*ii*) **Weekly Status Approach.** In this approach current activity status relating to the week preceding the date of survey is recorded and those persons are classified as unemployed who did not *have gainful work even for an hour on any day in the preceding week* and were seeking or were available for work. The persons who may be employed on usual status approach may however become intermittently unemployed during some seasons or parts of the year. Thus, unlike the usual status approach, *weekly status approach would capture not only open chronic unemployment but also seasonal unemployment*. Besides, this approach provides weekly average rate of unemployment.

(*iii*) **Daily Status Approach.** As noted above, the weekly status approach records a person employed *even if he works only for an hour on any day of the whole week*. It is thus clear that the weekly status approach would tend to underestimate unemployment in the economy because it does not appear to be proper to treat all those who have been unemployed for the whole

11. Likewise, Prof. Amartya Sen has distinguished between *income aspect, production aspect* and *recognition aspect* of employment and defined unemployment accordingly. While his concept of unemployment based on 'production aspect' is the same as productivity criterion, his recognition concept of unemployment differs from "willingness criterion" only in that he calls all those persons as unemployed who are seeking work regardless of whether or not they already have some job. His income concept of unemployment, however, conceptually differs from the 'income criterion' in that it is "*concerned with that part of one's income which is received on condition that one works*'" rather than earning of minimum income required for subsistence.

12. 33.7 per cent of labour force was Sen's estimate of rural unemployment for the year 1972-73 on the basis of his productivity criterion.

week except an hour as employed. Indeed, the demand for labour in farming and non-farming households often fluctuates over a small period within a week. Hence the need for the use of daily status approach to measure the magnitude of unemployment and underemployment in India.

In the daily status approach current activity status of a person with regard to whether employed or unemployed or outside labour force is recorded *for each day in reference week*. Further, for estimating employment and unemployment, *half-day has been adopted as a unit of measurement*. A person who works for 4 hours or more up to 8 hours on a day is recorded as employed for the full day and one who works for an hour or more but less than 4 hours on a day is recorded as employed for half-day. Accordingly, persons having no gainful work even for one hour on a day are described as unemployed for full day provided that they are either seeking or are available for work.

Thus, the daily status approach would capture not only the unemployed days of those persons who are usually unemployed but also the unemployed days of those who are recorded as employed on weekly status basis. Hence daily status concept of unemployment is more inclusive than those of usual status and weekly status approaches and would yield an average number of unemployed person-days per day in the year indicating the magnitude of both open unemployment and underemployment. They are also referred to as *person-years unemployed* so as to distinguish them from persons unemployed.[13]

The estimates of unemployment on the basis of above three approaches are presented in Table 12.1. It may be observed from this table that according to NSS 1999-2000 round, 2.8 per cent of labour force were unemployed on usual status basis and 4.4 per cent of labour force were unemployed on weekly status basis and 7.3 per cent of labour force on current daily status (CDS) basis. In 2004-05 (60th Round) unemployment rate further increased. On current weekly status basis, unemployment rate went up to 4.6 per cent in the rural areas and 6.4 per cent in the urban areas and 3.08 for India as a whole. On current daily status basis, in 2004-05 rate of unemployment rose to 8.2 per cent in rural areas and to 8.3 per cent in the urban areas and 8.2 per cent in case of All India. In absolute numbers, Planning Commission estimated unemployment to be of the order of 35 million persons on current daily status basis in April 2002 in the beginning of the 10th Plan. On the basis of 60th round, number of persons unemployed on the current daily status basis rose to 34.7 millions in 2004-05 till 2004-2005. However, according to 66th round of National Sample Survey (NSS) for the year 2009-2010, current daily status (CDS) unemployment rate as per cent of labour declined to 6.8 in rural areas and to 5.8 in urban areas giving us unemployment rate as 6.6% of labour force for whole India. However, in our view this is the result of special employment guarantee scheme, MGNREGA, started in 2007-08 under which people are employed in more construction activities for a short period of time and does not represent the *stable growth* of employment opportunities.

Table 12.1. Magnitude of Unemployment in the Indian Economy (% of Labour Force)

Approach	1972-73	1977-78	1983	1987-88	1993-94	1999-2000	2004-05	2009-10	2011-12
Usual Principal Status	1.61	4.23	2.77	3.77	2.58	2.8	3.1	2.5	2.7
Current Weekly Status	4.32	4.48	4.51	4.80	3.6	4.4	4.4	3.6	–
Current Daily Status	8.35	8.18	8.28	6.09	6.0	7.3	8.3	6.6	5.6

Source: Planning Commission, *Eighth Five Year Plan* 1992-97, Vol. I, p. 134 and *Tenth Five Year Plan*.

As compared to 1993-94, *all rates of unemployment* (*usual status, weekly status and daily status*) increased in 2004-05. This clearly shows that economic reforms initiated since 1991 led to the worsening of unemployment situation in the Indian economy.

Note that, contrary to what could be expected, weekly status unemployment is not much greater than that of the usual status approach. This is for two reasons. First, a person to be identified as

13. See CSO, *National Sample Survey,* 32nd round (1977-78), Report No. 298, p. 20

unemployed on weekly status approach has to pass through a severe test, namely, he did not work even for only an hour in the whole reference week. Now, in an economy where there is predominance of self-employed households engaged in family-based enterprises, it is quite easy for a person to have worked for an hour in a week even during the lean periods of the year and therefore get registered as employed rather than unemployed. Secondly, during the slack seasons of the year some persons, mainly women, withdraw themselves from the workforce. Therefore, instead of being counted as unemployed, they are treated as 'outside labour force', for they generally report as 'not available for work'. As a result, whereas weekly status employment estimates are relatively greater than that of usual status, their unemployment estimates are not much higher.

Further, it is noteworthy that both the usual and weekly status approaches reveal a rather small magnitude of surplus labour. This is because, as mentioned above, *both these approaches measure open unemployment in the country*. However, in India with predominance of self-employed households and absence of social security system to support the people, they can hardly afford to remain absolutely unemployed. The new hands that are added to the labour force every year as a result of increasing population do not remain openly unemployed; they share employment and work with others so that there is more of underemployment and disguised unemployment rather than open unemployment.

Thus, quite expectedly, the daily status approach which seeks to capture both open unemployment and underemployment reveals that quite a large magnitude of surplus labour exists in India. It will be seen from Table 12.1 that around 9 per cent of labour force were found unemployed in 2004 on daily status basis. It has been estimated that the magnitude of daily status unemployment increased to about 40 million person-years in April 2004.

However, even the daily status approach does not fully measure the magnitude of surplus labour in the Indian economy. Evidently, this also would have a tendency to under-record unemployment as it considered a person working for only 4 hours (1/2 of the standard day) as fully employed and a person who worked for an hour (1/8th of the standard day) as employed for half-day. In fact, as an alternative, hourly status approach measuring employment and unemployment in terms of manhours would be probably more appropriate.

Further, the daily status approach (or even the alternative hourly approach), like the usual and weekly status approach, cannot fully capture disguised unemployment of those persons whose intensity of work and consequently productivity is very low even though they are employed for a long time. In India, as in other labour-surplus developing countries, people are generally found to be working longer hours and larger number of days than one is really required to do the given work by stretching or spreading the work. Therefore, *for the proper assessment of the magnitude of surplus labour that currently exists in the Indian economy, unemployment on the basis of daily/hourly status ought to be supplemented by a measure of disguised unemployment based on a norm of productivity or work intensity.*

Despite the above limitations it is clear that daily status unemployment is a relatively better measure of the magnitude of surplus labour as it covers open unemployment as well as a good amount of underemployment.

A good number of unemployment in a labour-surplus country such as India manifests itself in the form of disguised unemployment, especially in the agricultural sector. It is a common knowledge that with minor changes in organisation and with the existing techniques, our agriculture can be looked after by a much smaller number of workers and they can be withdrawn from agriculture without reduction of agricultural output if alternative employment opportunities are available. Since employment opportunities in the non-agricultural sector have not been growing rapidly, the new entrants to the workforce are compelled to remain in agriculture and perpetuate the phenomenon of *disguised unemployment which means that people are engaged in occupations where their marginal productivity is zero (if not negative) and that a shift to alternative occupations will improve their marginal productivity and add to national income of the country.*

The basic solution to the problem of this sort is the faster rate of capital formation so as to enlarge employment opportunities. For this purpose, every possible encouragement should be given to savings and their productive utilisation in increasing the rate of investment. In the developing countries investment incentives for the private sector are very low and the Government can assist in the process of capital formation directly as well as indirectly. Through a fiscal policy which encourages savings and investment and an easy monetary policy it can do much to encourage investors. The Government itself can participate in the process of capital formation by undertaking such development activities which do not attract the private investors. Therefore, the Government has got to assume a special role in speeding up the rate of economic development. The other line of attack has got to be on the rate of population growth. If population grows at a rapid rate then, to maintain the people even at their existing levels, large amounts of capital are needed which could otherwise have been used to raise the amount of capital available per man and hence to raise the living standards at a faster rate. Apart from accumulation of capital (*i.e.,* machines, factory buildings, tools and equipment), we should increase investment in physical infrastructure such as roads, transport, ports, power, highways, irrigation facilities to generate opportunities for productive employment. Further, by adopting suitable fiscal and monetary policies we should discourage the use of capital-intensive techniques. Lastly, land reforms initiated in the earlier periods of planning should be effectively implemented to ensure access to land for agricultural households.

In Chapter 2 we explained the various measures that can be adopted to solve the acute problem of unemployment prevailing in the Indian economy. In what follows we critically examine the chief strategies of employment that have been put forward from time to time.

VARIOUS DEVELOPMENT STRATEGIES FOR EMPLOYMENT GENERATION IN DEVELOPING COUNTRIES

In what follows we shall critically examine some well-known strategies of development, especially from the point of view of whether they provide an adequate answer to the problem of surplus labour in India. Their critical evaluation will enable us to bring out the various policy measures which need to be adopted for designing an appropriate development strategy to ameliorate the problem of unemployment and underemployment in India. It is important to note that a development strategy for promoting the growth of employment is based on a particular diagnosis and explanation of the problem of surplus labour. As an explanation of unemployment and from the viewpoint of generation of new employment opportunities, the various employment strategies and approaches have been proposed from time to time by different economists. The first important approach to unemployment and employment is what can be called **industrialisation-led strategy of development.** Some economists, prominent among whom are Nurkse, Lewis, Eckaus, Robinson, Mahalanobis, Hirschman, Fie-Rains and Jorgenson, attribute unemployment in the developing countries to the lack of industrialisation and therefore suggest stepping up the rate of investment or capital formation for the expansion of modern industrial sector in which to absorb surplus labour.

On the other hand, Vakil and Brahmananda laid stress on wage-goods gap as a cause of unemployment and put forward a development strategy which assigned a high priority to wage-goods industries (especially agriculture) in the allocation of investment resources so as to increase the supply of wage-goods which would enable us to generate more employment opportunities. Another group of economists led by Schumacher[14], Myrdal[15] and Singer holds the use of capital-intensive technology in the large-scale industries responsible for the prevailing unemployment in developing countries. This approach leads to the adoption of labour-intensive techniques as an essential part of the development strategy to create more employment for labour. Finally, some economists, more

14. E.F. Schumacher, *Small is Beautiful*, Bord Briggs, London.
15. Gunnar Myrdal, *Asian Drama; An Enquiry into the Poverty of Nations,* Penguin Books, New York, 1968.

prominently Dandekar and Rath, J.P. Lewis, B.S. Minhas, have proposed undertaking of rural public works on a large scale as a solution to the problem of unemployment and poverty. According to them, adequate employment opportunities cannot be generated, at least in the short run, through any emphasis on particular technological aspects or the pattern of investment within the agricultural and industrial sectors. Hence the argument for undertaking rural public works to generate employment opportunities. In what follows, we shall examine these various strategies of development for productive absorption of surplus labour.

Industrialisation-Led Strategy of Development and Employment

Influenced by the growth experience of the western developed countries, the several developing countries adopted industrialisation-led strategy of development for absorbing surplus labour in productive employment in the modern industrial sector. An essential feature of this approach is that ***it seeks to generate more employment opportunities by achieving a higher rate of industrial growth through accelerating investment or capital formation in it.***

Besides, this approach regards labour and capital as complementary inputs. In the developing countries the stock of capital and modern industries have not been growing at a rate fast enough to keep pace with the growth of population. As a result, the whole of current labour force cannot be absorbed in productive employment because not enough capital is available to employ them. Thus this approach attributes the existence of unemployment and underemployment in developing countries to the lack of capital relative to the magnitude of labour force. A variety of growth models and development strategies come under this approach, all of these, though differing in some other aspects, lay stress on the importance of capital accumulation for generation of employment opportunities. We shall explain below some of the models of this growth-led approach towards employment that fall in this category.

(*a*) **Industrialisation-led Strategy: Harrod-Domar Model.** According to Harrod-Domar model[16] the rate of growth of output depends upon the ratio of total investment to national income divided by the capital-output ratio, *i.e.*,

$$G = \frac{1}{v}$$

where G = rate of growth of output

I = rate of investment (defined as ratio of national income)

v = capital-output ratio

Harrod-Domar model assumes capital-output and capital-labour ratios to remain constant which can happen if there is no technological progress. Thus, in the absence of technological progress, increase in capital would imply increase in both output and employment. Therefore, Harrod-Domor model suggests that the rate of growth of both output and employment is determined by the growth of capital stock. Thus, according to this model, solution to the problem of unemployment lies in sufficient increase in the rate of investment or capital accumulation. However, this model does not distinguish between capital formation in industry and agriculture.

(*b*) **Lewis and Fei-Ranis Models of Growth.** In their growth models for a dualistic economy with surplus labour, Lewis[17] and Fei-Ranis[18] also regard capital as the crucial factor for the expansion

16. Harrod-Domar Model was originally developed to explain the conditions for steady growth in developed industrialised countries but with slight extension this model has been extensively used in economic planning of less developed countries to explain of growth the both output and employment.
17. Harrod-Domar Model was originally developed to explain the conditions for steady growth in developed industrialised countries but with slight extension this model has been extensively used in economic planning of less developed countries to explain the problem of growth of both output and employment. See. Arthur Lewis, Economic Development with Unlimited Supply of Labour, *Manchester School*, Vol. 22, 1954. 22, 1954.
18. J.C.H. Fei, G. Ranis, *Development of the Labour Surplus Economy, Theory and Policy*, Irwin, Homewood, 1964.

of employment in the modern industrial sector. While their models suggest that rate of growth of employment depends upon the rate of capital accumulation and economic growth, it differs from Harrod-Domar model in the sense that they draw distinction between the two sectors of a less developed economy: (1) the subsistence agricultural sector which is characterised by surplus labour, low producitivity and self-employment; and (2) the modern industrial sector which is characterised by wage employment and high productivity.

These dual economy growth models emphasize transfer of surplus labour from the subsistence agricultural sector to the modern industrial sector. And this *transfer of labour and expansion of employment opportunities in the modern industrial sector is determined by the rate of capital accumulation*. Therefore rate of capital accumulation and economic growth in the modern industrial sector increases over a number of years it would withdraw all the disguised unemployed labour from agriculture.

(*c*) **Mahalanobis Heavy Industry Development Strategy and Employment.** This growth model which formed the basis of development strategy adopted in India's Second and Third Plans also laid a great stress on the rate of capital accumulation for determining the rate of growth of employment, especially in the industrial sector. According to Mahalanobis, unemployment of labour is caused by the lack of capital stock. To employ a person in productive work, he needs to be equipped with adequate capital. Therefore, in order to generate more opportunities of productive employment more capital has to be accumulated. Given a closed economy, the rate of capital formation, according to him, depends on the capacity of the economy to produce capital goods. With this premise he showed that in order to achieve a high rate of economic growth, it is necessary to accord a high priority to basic heavy industries producing capital goods in the development strategy of a plan. It is worthwhile to mention that in Mahalanobis' opinion it is necessary to allocate relatively greater resources to basic heavy industries to achieve not only the objective of rapid economic growth but also of expanding opportunities for productive employment. With this, the stock of basic goods like steel, machinery, fertilizers, should be sufficiently increased to eliminate unemployment.[19]

It may be noted that Mahalanobis later realised that basic heavy industries, though important for determining the long-term growth of employment, will themselves not create adequate employment opportunities in the short run. In response to the need to create enough employment opportunities *in the short run*, he extended his model to four sectors wherein he kept the basic heavy industries sector intact but divided the consumption goods sector into three sub-sectors, namely: (1) factory enterprises sector, (2) household and small-scale sector, and (3) services sector.

It was the household and small-scale sector in his four-sector model which being labour-intensive was expected to create a good amount of employment opportunities. However, his four-sector model did not represent any essential change over his two-sector model inasmuch as it maintained the emphasis on basic heavy industries. Moreover, since adequate resources were not provided for the household and small-scale industries, nor was any effort made to improve their productivity so that they could successfully compete with the large-scale industries, they recorded a low growth rate in output and employment.

A Critical Appraisal of Industrialisation-Led Strategy of Employment

Industrialisation-led strategy of employment rightly lays stress on the importance of capital goods for generating employment. Without some capital goods such as tools, implements, machinery and equipment, it is hard to generate productive employment in both the large-scale and small-scale industries. Likewise, capital inputs such as irrigation facilities, fertilizers, etc., play a crucial role for the productive absorption of labour in agriculture. Above all, shortage of infrastructure such as steel, power, cement and transport facilities serves as an important bottleneck for the expansion of

19. P.C. Mahalanobis, "The Approach of Operational Research to Planning in India", *Sankhya*, Vol. 16, 1955.

output and employment in both industry and agriculture. Therefore, expansion in their supply would promote the growth of output and employment in the economy.

However, *industrialisation-led strategy did not sufficiently recognize the importance of wage-goods constraint for generation of employment opportunities*. Thus, at a time when fixed capital goods alone were thought to be necessary, Vakil and Brahmananda[20] made a valuable contribution by highlighting the importance of wage-goods for expansion of employment opportunities. But the assertion that the increase in the supply of wage goods alone is both a necessary and sufficient condition for creation of employment sounds quite unrealistic.[21] It is not a right approach to think of capital goods versus wage-goods. Indeed, increase in the supply of both is needed to solve the problem of unemployment. The availability of wage-goods serves as a constraint for generating wage-employment for without them the demand of the newly employed persons for wage-goods would not be met. But if opportunities for productive employment are to be generated in the very first instance either in industry or in agriculture, labour needs to be provided with some capital goods.

It is worthwhile to note that growth of the modern industrial sector was expected to absorb not only the openly unemployed but also the disguised unemployed persons from agriculture. However, the actual experience belies the hopes of generating sufficient employment opportunities through industrial growth. For instance, an annual average rate of growth of around 7 per cent achieved by the industrial sector in India during the last four decades and a very high increase in the rate of net capial formation (from 5.5 per cent in 1950-51 to 25 per cent of national income in 1995-96) has not been able to solve the problem of unemployment and underemployment in India. It is thus clear that not much employment opportunities can be generated directly through growth of modern industrial sector even with high rate of increase in its output.[22]

A serious drawback of strategies of employment generation through industrial growth is that *they have ignored the possibilities of absorbing labour productively in agriculture*. These strategies regarded agriculture merely as the source of labour supply to the expanding industries. Even in growth models of Lewis and Fei-Ranis of a labour-surplus dual economy, both surplus labour and dualism have been sought to be eliminated by way of shifting labour from agriculture to the modern industrial sector.[23] But there is ample scope for absorbing labour in the Indian agriculture provided proper agricultural policies are adopted. India employs much less labour per hectare than other countries like Japan.[24] A good amount of labour can be productively absorbed in the Indian agriculture through rapid growth of its output by increasing cropping intensity and irrigation facilities and through the adoption of new high yielding technology. Reckless mechanisation, that is, use of labour-displacing agricultural machines such as tractors, combine harvestors, is to be avoided if more employment opportunities are to be created in agriculture.

---

20. C.N. Vakil and P.R. Brahmananda, *Planning for an Expanding Economy*, Vohra & Co., Bombay, 1986.
21. It may believed that Brahmananda later modified his wage-woods strategy by incorporating in what he calls "*Integrated Wage-Goods Complex*" which includes not only the wage-goods but also the capital goods required for the production of wage-goods. But the role of intermediate capital goods such as steel, cement, coal and power required for the production of wage-goods and also for investment sector has not been recognised by him even in his '*Extended Wage-Goods Strategy*'.
22. Note that the growth of modern industrial sector generates few employment opportunities is also corroborated by the experience of Latin American countries such as Brazil, Argentina, Mexico, Columbia, Peru, Venezuela which have achieved annual rate of industrial growth ranging from 7.6 per cent to 10 per cent during the last few decades and still they face the mounting problem of surplus labour.
23. It is important to note that Lewis and Fei-Ranis have emphasised the importance of agricultural development in the growth process of a labour-surplus economy, but they have envisaged such a pattern of agricultural development which ensures more and more agricultural output for less and less use of labour input.
24. In the middle 1950s, labour input per hectare of net sown area was 530 working mandays in Japan, as against only 137 in West Bengal.

Finally, most of the growth strategies described above focussed on industrial growth for employment generation and *ignored the importance of institutional reforms, especially in agriculture, for promoting the expansion of employment opportunities*. Land reforms in agriculture such as redistribution of land and changes in the tenancy system can play an important role in increasing employment opportunities for landless labourers, small and marginal farmers and share-croppers. There exist large inequalities in land ownership in India with the result that whereas a large number of rural households have either insufficient or no land to provide them adequate employment and income, a few families, on the other hand, own such a large amount of land that they cannot manage it efficiently. Consequently, there is underutilisation of land and irrigation potential. Further, it is generally believed that employment per hectare and cropping intensity are higher on small farms as compared to those on large farms. This may be taken to imply that redistribution of land through imposition and effective implementation of ceiling on land holdings will bring about increase in employment opportunities in agriculture.

To sum up, agriculture contains immense employment potential provided proper strategy for its development involving technological and institutional changes is adopted. This has, however, been ignored by the maintsteam of the growth-oriented strategies of employment.

WAGE-GOODS STRATEGY OF EMPLOYMENT

Industrialisation-led strategy of development explained above neglects the constraint of wage-goods availability on employment generation.[25] In their criticism of the development strategy of Second and Third Five Year Plans, Vakil and Brahmananda advanced what is known as wage-goods strategy of development. According to them, unemployment and disguised unemployment in less developed countries are due to the deficiency of the supply of wage-goods. They argued that the magnitude of employment in less developed countries was determined by the available amount of wage-goods. This is because whenever employment for new men is created, say, in rural public works, it cannot be sustained unless adequate amount of wage-goods, especially foodgrains, is available. Of course, when people are openly or disguisedly unemployed, they would be consuming some foodgrains. But in that situation their consumption would be very low because their budget would not allow them to consume more. Therefore, when they are given wage employment, their effective demand for wage-goods will tend to increase. Hence, given the reasonable real wage rate (in terms of wage-goods) we can calculate the total amount of wage-goods required to obtain full employment. They call the difference between the required magnitude of wage-goods and the actually available supply of wage-goods as the '*wage-goods gap*'.[26] Open and disguised unemployment in less developed countries like India, according to them, is due to the existence of this wage-goods gap. The level of full employment can be attained only when this wage-goods gap is bridged by expanding the capacity to produce wage-goods.

We thus see that whereas in Mahalanobis' approach to growth and employment "the entire emphasis was on the role of fixed capital, Vakil and Brahmanand's entire emphasis was on the role

25. Some of the models of industrialisation-led growth do take into account the wage-goods constraint and provide for it. Thus, Nurkse thought that withdrawal of disguised unemployed will leave behind enough foodgrains to be mopped up for feeding the transferred people. Likewise, Lewis and Fei-Ranis also provide for the transfer of food from agriculture to feed the workers employed in expanding modern industrial sector. But the agricultural growth to make available sufficient quantities of foodgrains does not constitute the main thrust of the development designs of Nurkse, Lewis Fei-Rains, for the leading sector in their development models is the modern industrial sector.
26. That the availability of wage-goods is an important constraint on the growth of employment opportunities was first brought out by Ricardo (1815). In classical economics, wage-goods or wage-funds have been treated as working capital as compared to fixed capital which consists of machines and equipment. Thus, importance given by Vakil and Brahmananda to wage-goods for the generation of employment opportunities is merely a revival of Ricardian thought.

of wage-goods as capital."[27] It may be noted that in his later works Brahmananda has modified his strategy in that he now assigns a high priority to what he calls '*Integrated Wage-Goods Complex*' which includes not only wage-goods but also capital goods which are used for the production of wage-goods. Since they consider the supply of wage-goods as the most important determinant of employment in less developed economies, Vakil and Brahmananda proposed a development strategy which assigned the top priority to wage-goods industries, especially agriculture, in the pattern of investment. That is why they severely criticized the development strategy adopted in India's Second and Third Plans which gave high priority to basic heavy industries producing fixed capital goods.

It may be noted that like Nurkse, Vakil and Brahmananda believe that disguised unemployment in developing countries contains saving potential (in the form of wage-goods) for capital accumulation. By withdrawing the disguised unemployed from agriculture, some amount of wage- goods would be released for providing wage employment in the investment sector. But, unlike Nurkse, they think that the surplus of wage-goods so released will not be sufficient to provide employment to all the potentially available labour force. Therefore, they emphasised the expansion of the capacity to produce wage goods and for that purpose advanced a development strategy which envisaged greater allocation of investible resources to agriculture and other wage goods industries.

It is also worth-mentioning that Prof. Amartya Sen winner of Noble Prize in Economics in 1998 who has been a follower of capital-formation approach to employment in his earlier works has explained in his recent study made for ILO "*Employment, Technology and Development*" that a crucial bottleneck in the way of expanding opportunities for wage employment in the less developed countries arises from the deficiency of wage-goods supply. He points out that it is not the lack of demand as visualised in various studies based in input-output models of employment but the availability of sufficient wage-goods which prevents the generation of adequate amount of wage employment. Therefore, Prof. Amartya Sen has argued that to solve the problem of unemployment and underemployment, in the investment strategy wage goods industries, especially agriculture, must be accorded a high priority.

A Critical Evaluation of Wage-Goods Strategy

The assertion by Vakil and Brahmanada that the growth in employment solely and exclusively depends upon the supply of wage-goods and that the capital goods (that is, heavy industry products) play no important role in the creation of employment opportunities is open to question. Under adequate organisation and entrepreneurial ability as well as optimum institutional reforms, two important bottlenecks, namely, capital goods bottleneck and wage-goods bottleneck, are faced in creating opportunities for productive employment. For expansion in productive employment both these bottlenecks have to be overcome and to emphasise the breaking of one bottleneck, while making no attempt to tackle the other, is an unrealistic approach to the employment problem. Wage-goods are required to meet the demands of the newly employed people, but if some people are to be employed in productive activities in the very first instance, they are required to be equipped with some capital goods. Further, for the production of wage-goods themselves, capital goods are required. That is, labour is to be equipped with capital goods to produce wage-goods. Professor Dantwala rightly points our that, "*It is a mistake to consider capital goods and wage-goods as exclusive and unrelated categories. Anyone who studies the composition of inputs needed for transformation of traditional agriculture should be able to appreciate the inter-connection between the two.*"

Thus, development strategy for rapid expansion of employment has to be such as will envisage the increase in production of both wage-goods and capital goods. Thus, to talk of wage-goods versus capital goods is a false issue and an unrealistic approach to the problem of employment since both are needed to generate employment; capital goods are required to make the employment productive and wage-goods are needed to feed the workers provided with new employment, that is, to sustain

27. Bhagwati and Chakravarty, *Indian Economic Analysis*, (1971), p. 14.

their employment. To say this, however, does not imply that all capital goods industries should be necessarily developed at home and given higher priority in the allocation of resources. Which specific capital goods should be produced at home and which imported from abroad should be decided on the basis of resource endowments and comparative advantage conceived in the dynamic context.

EMPLOYMENT STRATEGY OF USING LABOUR-INTENSIVE TECHNOLOGY

An important school of thought led by Schumacher, Singer and Myrdal attribute the mounting problem of unemployment and underemployment in the developing countries to the use of capital-intensive technology. It has been observed that while industrial output in developing countries has increased at a reasonably good rate, growth of employment has lagged far behind. And this is said to be due to the use of capital-intensive technology. Thus, according to this school of thought, the creation of meagre amount of employment opportunities due to the use of capital-intensive technology on the one hand and the growth of population at an alarming rate on the other has resulted in the huge magnitude of surplus labour.

It is worthwhile to note here that the modern industries using capital-intensive technology not only create few new opportunities of employment but also destroy employment in the traditional household industries. This unfavourable impact of modern sector on the traditional employment is what Myrdal calls *backwash effect*. According to this school of thought, modern manufacturing enterprises using capital-intensive technology produce goods on a mass scale which drive out the products of traditional household industries from the market. As a result, a good number of people engaged in these household industries are displaced.[28] They add to either open or disguised unemployment in agriculture.

In this context, **labour migration model of Todaro** has often been invoked, especially by Singer, to explain the mounting problem of urban unemployment in developing countries. According to Todaro[29], decision of rural workers to migrate to urban areas rests on the level of wage rate and the expectations of getting employment in the modern urban sector. A few employment opportunities at relatively higher wage levels created by capital-intensive technology in the modern urban sector attract many more rural workers than it is possible for this to absorb. This results in enormous increase in urban unemployment and underemployment.

Of course, Galenson-Leibenstein, M. Dobb, Amartya Sen have pointed out that *the use of capital-intensive techniques would generate more surplus resources which would be ploughed back into further investment and it would result in greater growth of employment than is possible through labour-intensive techniques*. But this has not been borne out by empirical evidence. For instance, estimates of saving and investment in India reveal that contributions of the public and the private corporate sectors to the domestic savings have not only been too small but have also recorded slow growth in the last four decades in spite of the fact that capital-intensive technology has been used in them. On the contrary, it is the savings of the household sector (consisting of households and unicorporated enterprises) which often use labour-intensive technology that have greatly increased. This raises doubts about the argument that capital-intensive techniques necessarily generate more surplus and therefore greater growth of employment.

There is another important aspect of the use of capital-intensive technology which is worth mentioning. The *use of capital-intensive techniques creates high profit-wage ratio and thereby accentuates inequalities of income*. These income inequalities create demand pattern oriented

28. In his famous study of the Industrial Evolution in India, D.R. Gadgil, "*Industrial Evolution in Recent Times*", clearly brought out the decline of handicraft and displacement labour employed in them as a result of the growth of modern large-scale industries in India.
29. Michael, P. Todaro, "Income Expectations, Rural-Urban Migration and Employment in Africa", *International Labour Review*, Nov. 1971.

towards luxuries which are again produced by the use of capital-intensive techniques. This limits the size of market for labour-intensive goods consumed by the working classes. Thus, the use of capital-intensive techniques gives rise to a vicious circle with causes slow growth not only of direct employment but also of indirect employment through its effects on the pattern of demand.

Why in Developing Countries Capital-Intensive Technology is Used? Now, a pertinent question is why have the developing countries been using capital-intensive technology despite the fact that surplus labour prevails in them? There are two views about this. First, the alternative technology which though efficient but labour-intensive is generally not available. The available technology is the capital-intensive technology that was developed in the Western countries to suit their factor endowments. The Western technology is quite inappropriate for the developing countries which suffer from surplus of labour and shortage of capital. Now, given the technology imported from the Western countries, there is not much possibility of substitution of capital for labour. In view of this, Schumacher and Singer advocate for the development of what has been called *intermediate or appropriate technology*. Appropriate technology for the developing countries is that which though efficient should be labour-intensive so that it conforms to their factor endowments.

According to Schumacher, the development of appropriate technologies does not imply the discovery of altogether new principles of science and technology. What is required is the application of basic principles of modern science and technology to evolve the appropriate production techniques. These appropriate production techniques may be obtained by scaling down the advanced techniques by adapting them so as to make them more labour-intensive, or by scaling up handicrafts technique with the introduction of new tools and simple machines and thus improving economic efficiencies of these techniques while maintaining their labour intensity.

On the other hand, several other scholars such as Ranis, Blaug, Layard and Woodhall, Little, Scott and Scitovsky are of the view that the slow growth of employment opportunities in the industrial sector is not due so much to the lack of flexibility in the production function but to the **distortions in factor prices**.[30] Due to the various concessions and subsidies provided in taxation structure by the Government such as liberal investment or development rebate, policy of low interest rate and over-valued foreign exchange rate have caused the price of capital to be very low relative to its scarcity. On the other hand, the prevailing wage rates are too high for a labour-surplus economy due to the strong bargaining power of the trade unions in the organised sector. According to them, these distortions in factor prices induce the adoption of capital-intensive techniques in industries with the consequence that less labour is employed. In order to promote the use of more labour-intensive techniques, it is therefore imperative that all distortions in factor prices be corrected.

By emphasising the use of labour-intensive technology in developing countries, this strategy has brought into sharp focus the question of appropriate technological choices. In a labour-surplus economy the importance of the use of appropriate technology which is labour absorptive and at the same time quite efficient can hardly be denied. However, appropriate technologies for various manufacturing industries just do not exist and a good deal of more research and development (R & D) would have to be undertaken before appropriate techniques are evolved for several industries. Of course, to encourage the development and use of appropriate techniques the various factor price distortions ought to be removed. Whereas, in view of the prevailing price situation, wage rates of industrial workers do not seem to be high, the effective price of capital is low. Therefore, the various concessions and rebates in taxes on various types of capital investment be drastically reduced and the lending rates of interest charged by banks and other financial institutions be raised so as to curb the tendency to substitute capital for labour.

30. Eckaus in his famous work "*Factor-Proportions Problem in Underdeveloped Countries*" showed that either factor-price disequilibrium or limited possibilities of substituting labour for capital can result in unemployment in less developed economies. Blaug, Layard and Woodhall in their study on educated unemployment have held high wage rates responsible for educated unemployment in India.

As for technological choices in agriculture, it may be noted that new high-yielding technology represented by a package of high-yielding varieties, fertilizers and pesticides is quite appropriate for a labour-surplus economy such as ours, for it not only raises yield per hectare substantially but is also labour-absorptive.

STRATEGY OF DIRECT ATTACK ON UNEMPLOYMENT : EMPLOYMENT GENERATION THROUGH RURAL PUBLIC WORKS

This approach seeks solution to the unemployment problem not through emphasising any particular pattern of resource allocation or technological choice but through special employment schemes, especially rural public works. This approach regards the regular growth process as being incapable of alleviating the problem of unemployment and underemployment in the foreseeable future. This approach of employment generation through rural public works has been combined with food for work programme. Those workers who are employed on rural public works are paid in the form of foodgrains as their remuneration. However, a part of remuneration may be paid in money form. In the UPA Government's Common Minimum Programme (CMP), food for work programme is an important element of strategy for employment generation. The launching of rural works programme on a large scale has been especially advanced by Dandekar and Rath[31] to solve the problem of mass poverty, which they maintain is mainly caused by unemployment and underemployment. Rural public works also constituted the main thrust of the recommendations of the Bhagwati Committee on Unemployment in India to tackle the problem of mass rural poverty and unemployment. Further, the scheme of rural public works as a major source of employment generation in rural areas has also been strongly recommended by J.P. Lewis,[32] K.N. Raj, M.L. Dantwala, and Raj Krishna. Besides, B.S. Minhas[33] also suggests massive rural works programme in his "integrated programme of compulsory consolidation and land development."[34]

Employment generation through Rural Public Works was undertaken in 1977-78 on a regular basis under the '*Food for Work Programme*' during the regime of Janata Government and was later adopted as a part of the Sixth Five Year Plan (1978-83). Under this scheme a major part of wages is paid in terms of foodgrains. The constraint of wage-goods (*i.e.*, foodgrains) which stood in the way of implementation of earlier schemes of rural public works did not then exist. At present rural public works programme has been continued under the scheme called 'National Rural Employment Guarantee Scheme'. This programme intended to provide supplementary employment opportunities to the rural poor seeking work. Projects relating to soil and water conservation, irrigation, flood protection and drainage, field channels in irrigation command areas, construction and improvement of village tanks and ponds, school and dispensary buildings, improvements of village environment, hygiene and sanitation have been undertaken under this programme.

There can be hardly any two opinions that rural public works can be helpful in providing employment to the rural poor, especially the landless labourers and marginal farmers who remain without gainful work for a large number of days in a year. At the same time the programme can be used to build durable community assets which would promote rural development. Further, by providing alternative avenues of wage employment the rural works programme can ensure reasonable wages to the agricultural workers. But the view that these rural public works should serve as a substitute for employment generation through a proper development strategy as was conceived by

31. Dandekar, V.M. and Rath, N., *Poverty in India*, Indian School of Political Economy, Poona, 1971.
32. Lewis J.P., "The Public Works Approach to Low End Poverty Problem, *Journal of Development Planning*, Vol. 5.
33. Minhas,–B.S., "Rural Poverty, Land Redistribution and Development Strategy", *Indian Economic Review*, Vol. 5, 1970.
34. In the strategy proposed by Minhas the scheme of rural public works is to be used for developing land and water resources after consolidation of land has been accomplished.

Dandekar and Rath and some others is open to question. For, being construction activities, rural public works are, at best, an interim or short-run solution of the problem of unemployment and leave the question unanswered as to how the growing number of workforce will be productively employed in the long run. The lasting and long-term solution to the problem of unemployment and underemployment lies in framing a development strategy that involves technological and institutional changes which are appropriate for labour-surplus conditions of the Indian economy. However, the rural public works have an important role to play in an employment-oriented strategy. As stated above, with the scheme of rural public works we can build up durable assets or infrastructural facilities. Now, these assets or facilities will help in creating more employment opportunities in agriculture and rural industries in future. To fulfil this purpose, rural public works need to be integrated with the overall strategy of rural development rather than being formulated and implemented in isolation of it.

QUESTIONS FOR REVIEW

1. Explain Keynes' theory of employment. How does it differ from classical theory ?
2. In what respects do the Classical and Keynesian theories of employment differ ? Spell out the reasons for underemployment equilibrium in the Keynesian model.
3. Explain how, according to Keynes, involuntary unemployment is caused by lack of effective demand. How is the money wage rigidity responsible for the emergence of involuntary unemployment ?
4. The logical starting point of Keynes' theory of employment is the principle of effective demand. Explain.
5. What do you understand by the term 'money illusion' in the Keynesian theory of employment? Is wage-price rigidity a consequence of money illusion?
6. Explain why wage-price flexibility cannot ensure full employment in the economy.
7. Define effective demand. How does it determine level of employment in a country ?
8. What is meant by involuntary unemployment ? Explain Keynes' theory of involuntary unemployment.
9. Explain the following types of employment. What factors are responsible for their existence?
   1. Frictional Unemployment
   2. Structural Unemployment
   3. Cyclical Unemployment
10. Explain the concept of full employment. Is it consistent with the existence of natural unemployment ? Explain the measures that can be adopted to achieve it.
11. What is natural rate of unemployment ? How do the unemployment benefits affect it ?
12. What is full employment ? Discuss with the help of diagram the different wags of attaining equilibrium level of unemployment
13. Distinguish between fiscal policy and monetary policy. How is monetary policy helpful in generation of employment opportunities in the economy ?
14. What is meant by disguised unemployment ? How can the problem of disguised unemployment in developing countries be solved ?
15. Discuss the nature of unemployment in developing countries like India. Explain the limitations of Keynesian policy prescription, namely, deficit financing to increase aggregate demand, to solve the problem of unemployment.

16. Discuss the causes of unemployment and underemployment in developing countries like India. What policy measures would you suggest to solve the unemployment problem in these countries?
17. How is unemployment measured in India ? Distinguish between usual status, weekly status and daily status unemployment. Comment on the recent changes in them.
18. Critically examine industrialisation-led strategy of development for employment generation in labour-surplus developing countries like India.
19. Critically examine Mahalanobis' heavy industry growth strategy from the viewpoint of solving the unemployment problem in India.
20. Explain wage-goods strategy of employment. On what grounds it has been criticized?
21. Unemployment in India is mainly caused by the use of highly capital-intensive technology in industries. Explain why capital-intensive technology is used in Indian industries despite the fact India is a labour-surplus country.
22. Critically examine to what extent rural public works schemes such as MGNREG scheme recently launched in India is a viable strategy for generating stable employment opportunities.

PART — III

BUSINESS CYCLES AND ECONOMIC STABILISATION

- Analysis of Business Cycles
- Economic Stabilisation : Fiscal Policy

CHAPTER 13

Analysis of Business Cycles

Introduction

Many free enterprise capitalist countries such as USA and Great Britain have registered rapid economic growth during the last two centuries. But economic growth in these countries has not followed steady and smooth upward trend. There has been a long-run upward trend in Gross National Product (GNP), but periodically there have been large short-run fluctuations in economic activity, that is, changes in output, income, employment and prices around this long-term trend. The period of high income, output and employment has been called the period of *expansion, upswing or prosperity,* and the period of low income, output and employment has been described as *contraction, recession, downswing or depression.* The economic history of the free market capitalist countries has shown that the period of economic prosperity or expansion alternates with the period of contraction or recession. *These alternating periods of expansion and contraction in economic activity has been* called business cycles. They are also known as trade cycles. J.M. Keynes writes, "A trade cycle is composed of periods of good trade characterised by rising prices and low unemployment percentages with periods of bad trade characterised by falling prices and high unemployment percentages."[1]

A noteworthy feature about these fluctuations in economic activity is that they are recurrent and have been occurring periodically in a more or less regular fashion. Therefore, these fluctuations have been called business cycles. It may be noted that calling these fluctuations as 'cycles' means they are periodic and occur regularly, though perfect regularity has not been observed. The duration of a business cycle has not been of the same length; it has varied from a minimum of two years to a maximum of ten to twelve years, though in the past it was often assumed that fluctuations of output and other economic indicators around the trend showed repetitive and regular pattern of alternating periods of expansion and contraction. However, actually there has been no clear evidence of very regular cycles of the same definite duration. Some business cycles have been very short lasting for only two to three years, while others have lasted for several years. Further, in some cycles there have been large swings away from trend and in others these swings have been of moderate nature.

A significant point worth noting about business cycles is that they have been very costly in the economic sense of the word. During a period of recession or depression many workers lose their jobs and as a result large-scale unemployment, which causes loss of output that could have been produced with full employment of resources, come to prevail in the economy. Besides, during depression many businessmen go bankrupt and suffer huge losses. Depression causes a lot of human sufferings and lowers the levels of living of the people. Fluctuations in economic activity creates a lot of uncertainty in the economy which causes anxiety to the individuals about their future income and employment opportunities and involve a great risk for long-run investment in projects. Who does not remember the great havoc caused by the great depression of the early thirties of the present century? Even boom when it is accompanied by inflation has its social costs. Inflation erodes the real incomes of the people and makes life miserable for the poor people. Inflation distorts allocation of resources by drawing away scarce resources from productive uses to unproductive ones. Inflation redistributes income in favour of the richer sections and also when inflation rate is high, it impedes economic

1. J.M. Keynes, *The General Theory of Employment, Interest and Money*, 1936.

growth. About the harmful effects of the business cycles Crowther writes, "On the one hand, there is the misery and shame of unemployment with all the individual poverty and social disturbances that it may create. On the other hand, there is the loss of wealth represented by so much wasted and idle labour and capital."[2]

Phases of Business Cycles

Business cycles have shown distinct phases the study of which is useful to understand their underlying causes. These phases have been called by different names by different economists. Generally, the following phases of business cycles have been distinguished :

1. Expansion (Boom, Upswing or Prosperity)
2. Peak (upper turning point)
3. Contraction (Downswing, Recession or Depression)
4. Trough (lower turning point)

The four phases of business cycles have been shown in Fig. 13.1 where we start from trough or depression when the level of economic activity *i.e.*, level of production and employment is at the

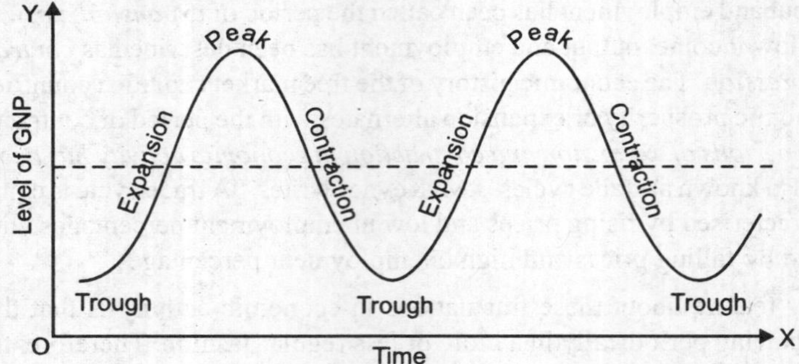

Fig. 13.1. *Four Phases of Business Cycles without Growth Trend*

lowest level. With the revival of economic activity the economy moves into the expansion phase, but due to the causes explained below, the expansion cannot continue indefinitely, and after reaching peak, contraction or downswing starts. When the contraction gathers momentum, we have a depression. The downswing continues till the lowest turning point which is also called trough is reached.

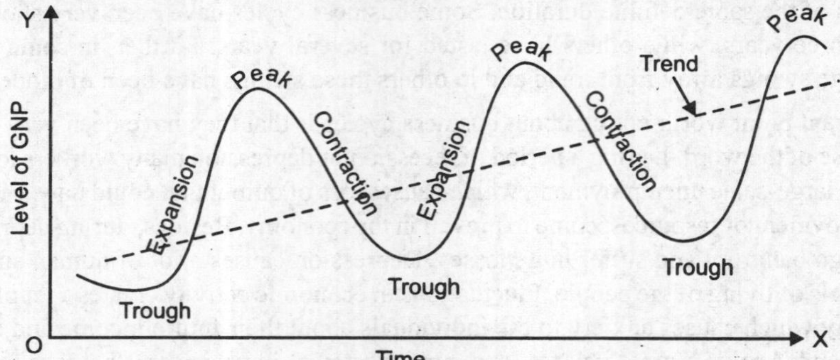

Fig. 13.2. *Cycles with Trend* (*i.e., Growth*)

In this way cycle is complete. However, after remaining at the trough for some time the economy revives and again the new cycle starts. Haberler in his important work[3] on business cycles has named

2. G. Crowther, *An Outline of Money*, (London 1952), p. 192.
3. See G. Haberler, *Prosperity and Depression, A Theoretical Analysis of Cyclical Movements*, Harward University Press, 1960.

the four phases of business cycles as (1) Upswing, (2) Upper turning point, (3) Downswing, and (4) Lower turning point.

There are two types of patterns of cyclic changes. One pattern is shown in Fig. 13.1 where fluctuations occur around a stable equilibrium position as shown by the horizontal line. It is a case of dynamic stability which depicts change but without growth or trend. The second pattern of cyclical fluctuations is shown in Fig. 13.2 where cyclical changes in economic activity take place around a growth path (*i.e.,* rising trend). J.R. Hicks in his model of business cycles explains such a pattern of fluctuations with long-run rising trend in economic activity by imposing factors such as autonomous investment due to population growth and technological progress causing economic growth on the otherwise stationary state. We briefly explain below various phases of business cycles.

Expansion and Prosperity. In its expansion phase, both output and employment increase till we have full employment of resources and production is at the highest possible level with the given productive resources. There is no involuntary unemployment and whatever unemployment prevails is only of frictional and structural types. Thus, when expansion gathers momentum and we have prosperity, the gap between potential GNP and actual GNP is zero, that is, the level of production is at the maximum production level. A good amount of net investment is occurring and demand for durable consumer goods is also high. Prices also generally rise during the expansion phase but due to high level of economic activity people enjoy a high standard of living.

Then something may occur, whether banks start reducing credit or profit expectations change adversely and businessmen become pessimistic about future state of the economy that brings an end to the expansion or prosperity phase. As shall be explained below, economists differ regarding the possible causes of the end of prosperity and start of downswing in economic activity. Monetarists have argued that contraction in bank credit may cause downswing. Keynes has argued that sudden collapse of expected rate of profit (which he calls marginal efficiency of capital, MEC) caused by adverse changes in expectations of entrepreneurs lowers investment in the economy. This fall in investment, according to him, causes downswing in economic activity.

Contraction and Depression. As stated above, expansion or prosperity is followed by contraction or depression. During contraction, not only there is a fall in GNP but also level of employment is reduced. As a result, involuntary unemployment appears on a large scale. Investment also decreases causing further fall in consumption of goods and services. At times of contraction or depression prices also generally fall due to fall in aggregate demand. A significant feature of depression phase is the fall in rate of interest. With lower rate of interest people's demand for money holdings increases. There is a lot of excess capacity as industries producing capital goods and consumer goods work much below their capacity due to lack of demand. Capital goods and durable consumer goods industries are especially hit hard during depression. Depression, it may be noted, occurs when there is a severe contraction or recession of economic activities. The depression of 1929-33 is still remembered because of its great intensity which caused a lot of human suffering.

Trough and Revival. There is a limit to which level of economic activity can fall. The lowest level of economic activity, generally called trough, lasts for some time. Capital stock is allowed to depreciate without replacement. The progress in technology makes the existing capital stock obsolete. If the banking system starts expanding credit or there is a spurt in investment activity due to the emergence of scarcity of capital as a result of non-replacement of depreciated capital and also because of new technology coming into existence requiring new types of machines and other capital goods. The stimulation of investment brings about the revival or recovery of the economy. The recovery is the turning point from depression into expansion. As investment rises, this causes induced increase in consumption. As a result industries start producing more and excess capacity is now put into full use due to the revival of aggregate demand. Employment of labour increases and rate of unemployment falls. With this the cycle is complete.

Features of Business Cycles

Though different business cycles differ in duration and intensity, they have some common features which we explain below:

1. Business cycles occur *periodically*. Though they do not show same regularity, they have some distinct phases such as expansion, peak, contraction or depression and trough. Further the duration of cycles varies a good deal from minimum of two years to a maximum of ten to twelve years.
2. Secondly, business cycles are *synchronic*. That is, they do not cause changes in any single industry or sector but are of all-embracing character. For example, depression or contraction occur simultaneously in all industries or sectors of the economy. Recession passes from one industry to another and chain reaction continues till the whole economy is in the grip of recession. Similar process is at work in the expansion phase, prosperity spreads through various linkages of input-output relations or demand relations between various industries. and sectors.
3. Thirdly, it has been observed that fluctuations occur not only in level of production but also simultaneously in other variables such as employment, investment, consumption, rate of interest and price level.
4. Another important feature of business cycles is that investment and consumption of durable consumer goods such as cars, houses, refrigerators are affected most by the cyclical fluctuations. As stressed by J.M. Keynes, investment is greatly volatile and unstable as it depends on profit expectations of private entrepreneurs. These expectations of entrepreneurs change quite often making investment quite unstable. Since *consumption of durable consumer goods* can be deferred, it also fluctuates greatly during the course of business cycles.
5. An important feature of business cycles is that consumption of *non-durable goods and services* does not vary much during different phases of business cycles. Past data of business cycles reveal that households maintain a great stability in consumption of non-durable goods.
6. The immediate impact of depression and expansion is on the *inventories of goods*. When depression sets in, the inventories start accumulating beyond the desired level. This leads to cut in production of goods. On the contrary, when recovery starts, the inventories go below the desired level. This encourages businessmen to place more orders for goods whose production picks up and stimulates investment in capital goods.
7. Another important feature of business cycles is that *profits fluctuate more than any other type of income.* The occurrence of business cycles causes a lot of uncertainty for businessmen and makes it difficult to forecast the economic conditions. During the depression period profits may even become negative and many businesses go bankrupt. In a free market economy profits are justified on the ground that they are necessary payments if the entrepreneurs are to be induced to bear uncertainty.
8. Lastly, business cycles are *international in character*. That is, once started in one country they spread to other countries through trade relations between them. For example, if there is a recession in the USA, which is a large importer of goods from other countries, it will cause a fall in demand for imports from other countries whose exports would be adversely affected causing recession in them too. Depression of 1930s in USA and Great Britain engulfed the entire capital world.

THEORIES OF BUSINESS CYCLES

We have explained above the various phases and common features of business cycles. Now, an important question is what causes business cycles. Several theories of business cycles have been propounded from time to time. Each of these theories spells out the factors which cause business cycles. Before explaining the modern theories of business cycles we first explain below the *earlier* theories of business cycles as they too contain important elements whose study is essential for proper understanding of the causes of business cycles.

Sun-Spot Theory

This is perhaps the oldest theory of business cycles. Sun-spot theory was developed in 1875 by Stanley Jevons. Sun-spots are storms on the surface of the sun caused by violent nuclear explosions there. Jevons argued that sun-spots affected weather on the earth. Since economies in the olden world were heavily dependent on agriculture, changes in climatic conditions due to sun-spots produced fluctuations in agricultural output. Changes in agricultural output through its demand and input-output relations affect industry. Thus, swings in agricultural output spread throughout the economy.

Other earlier economists also focused on changes in climatic or weather conditions in addition to those caused by sun-spots. According to them, weather cycles cause fluctuations in agricultural output which in turn cause instability in the whole economy. Even today weather is considered important in a country like India where agriculture is still important. In the years when due to lack of monsoon there are drought in the Indian agriculture, it affects the income of farmers and therefore reduces demand for the products of industries. This causes industrial recession. Even in USA in the year 1988 a severe drought in the farm belt drove up the food prices around the world. It may be further noted that higher food prices reduce income available to be spent on industrial goods.

Critical Appraisal. Though the theories of business cycles which emphasise climatic conditions for business cycles contain an element of truth about fluctuations in economic activity, especially in the developing counties like India where agriculture still remains important, they do not offer an adequate explanation of business cycles. Therefore, much reliance is not placed on these theories by modern economists. Nobody can say with certainty about the nature of these sun-spots and the degree to which they affect rain. There is no doubt that climate affects agricultural production. But the climate theory does not adequately explain periodicity of the trade cycle. If there was truth in the climatic theories, the trade cycles may be pronounced in agricultural countries and almost disappear when the country becomes completely industrialised. But this is not the case. Highly industrialised countries are much more subject to business cycles than agricultural countries which are affected more by famines rather than business cycles. Hence variations in climate do not offer complete explanation of business cycles.

Hawtrey's Monetary Theory of Business Cycles

An old monetary theory of business cycles was put forward by Hawtrey.[4] *His monetary theory of business cycles relates to the economy which is under gold standard.* It will be remembered that economy is said be under gold standard when either money in circulation consists of gold coins or when paper notes are fully backed by gold reserves in the banking system. According to Hawtrey, increases in the quantity of money raises the availability of bank credit for investment. Thus, increasing the supply of credit expansion in money supply causes rate of interest to fall. The lower rate of interest induces businessmen to borrow more for investment in capital goods and also for investment in keeping more inventories of goods. Thus, Hawtrey argues that lower rate of interest will lead to the expansion of goods and services as a result of more investment in capital goods and inventories. Higher output, income and employment caused by more investment induces more spending on consumer goods. Thus, as a result of more investment made possible by increased supply of bank

4. R.G. Hawtrey, *Good and Bad Trade*, Constable and Co., London, 1913.

credit economy moves into the expansion phase. The process of expansion continues for some time. Increases in aggregate demand brought about by more investment also causes prices to rise. Rising prices lead to the increase in output in two ways. First, when prices begin to rise, businessmen think they would rise further which induces them to invest more and produce more because prospects of making profits increase with the rise in prices. Secondly, the rising prices reduce the real value of idle money balances with the people which induces them to spend more on goods and services. In this way rising prices sustain expansion for some time.

However, according to Hawtrey, the expansion process must end. He argued that rise in incomes during the expansion phase induces more expenditure on domestically produced goods as well as on imports of foreign goods. He further assumes that domestic output and income expand faster than foreign output. As a result, **imports of a country increase more than its exports causing *trade deficit* with other countries. If exchange rate remains fixed, trade deficit means there will be *outflow of gold* to settle its balance of payments deficit.** Since the country is on gold standard, outflow of gold will cause reduction in money supply in the economy. The decrease in money supply will reduce the availability of bank credit. Reduction in the supply of bank credit will cause the rate of interest to rise. Rising interest rate will reduce investment in physical capital goods. Reduction in investment will cause the process of contraction to set in. As a result of reduced order for inventories, producers will cut production which will lower income and consumption of goods and services. In this state of reduced demand for goods and services, prices of goods will fall. Once the prices begin to fall businessmen begin to expect that they will fall further. In response to it traders will cut order of goods still causing further fall in output. The fall in prices also causes real value of money balances to rise which induces people to hold larger money holdings with them. In this way contraction process gathers momentum as demand for goods starts declining faster and with this economy plunges into depression.

But after a lapse of some time depression will also come to an end and the economy will start to recover. This happens because in the contraction process imports fall drastically due to decrease in income and consumption of households, whereas exports do not fall much. **As a result, *trade surplus* emerges which causes *inflow of gold.* The inflow of gold would lead to the expansion of money supply and consequently availability of bank credit for investment will increase.** With this, the economy will recover from depression and move into the expansion phase. Thus, the cycle is complete. The process, according to Hawtrey, will go on being repeated regularly.

Critical Appraisal. Hawtrey maintains that the economy under gold standard and fixed exchange rate system makes his model of business cycles self-generating as there is built-in tendency for the money supply to change with the emergence of trade deficit and trade surplus which cause movements of gold between countries and affect money supply in them. Changes in money supply influence economic activity in a cyclical fashion. However, Hawtrey's monetary theory does not apply to the present-day economies which have abandoned gold standard in 1930s. However, Hawtrey's theory still retains its importance because it shows how changes in money supply affect economic activity through changes in price level and rate of interest. In modern monetary theories of trade cycles this relation between money supply and rate of interest plays an important role in determining the level of economic activity.

Under-Consumption Theory

Under-consumption theory of business cycles is a very old one which dates back to the 1930s. Malthus and Sismodi criticised Say's Law which states '*supply creates its own demand*' and argued that consumption of goods and services could be too small to generate sufficient demand for goods and services produced. They attribute over-production of goods to lack of consumption demand for them. This over-production causes piling up of inventories of goods which results in recession.

Under-consumption theory as propounded by Sismodi and Hobson was not a theory of recurring business cycles. They made an attempt to explain how a free enterprise economy could enter a long-run economic slowdown. A crucial aspect of Sismodi and Hobson's under-consumption theory is the distinction they made between the rich and the poor. According to them, the rich sections in the society receive a large part of their income from returns on financial assets and real property owned by them. Further, they assume that the rich have a large propensity to save, that is, they save a relatively large proportion of their income and, therefore, consume a relatively smaller proportion of their income. On the other hand, less well-off people in a society obtain most of their income from work, that is, wages from labour and have a lower propensity to save. Therefore, these less well-off people spend a relatively less proportion of their income on consumer goods and services. In their theory, they further assume that during the expansion process, the incomes of the rich people increase relatively more than the wage-income. Thus, during the expansion phase, income distribution changes in favour of the rich with the result that average propensity to save falls, that is, in the expansion process saving increases and therefore consumption demand declines.[5]

According to Sismodi and Hobson, increase in saving during the expansion phase leads to more investment expenditure on capital goods and after some time-lag, the greater stock of capital goods enables the economy to produce more consumer goods and services. But since society's propensity to consume continues to fall, consumption demand is not enough to absorb the increased production of consumer goods. In this way, lack of demand for consumer goods or what is called under-consumption emerges in the economy which halts the expansion of the economy. Further, since supply or production of goods increases relatively more as compared to the consumption demand for them, the prices fall. Prices continue falling and go even below the average cost of production bringing losses to the business firms. Thus, when under-consumption appears, production of goods becomes unprofitable. Firms cut their production resulting in recession or contraction in economic activity.

Karl Marx and Under-Consumption. It is worth mentioning that Karl Marx, the philosopher of scientific socialism, had also predicted the collapse of the capitalist system due to the emergence of under-consumption. He predicted that capitalism would move periodically through expansion and contraction with each peak higher than its previous peak and each crash (*i.e.,* depression) deeper than the last. Ultimately, according to Marx, in a state of acute depression when the cup of misery of working class is full, they will overthrow the capitalist class which exploits them and in this way the new era of socialism or communism would come into existence.

Like other under-consumption theorists, Marx argues that driving force behind business cycles is ever increasing income inequalities and concentration of wealth and economic power in the hands of the few capitalists who own the means of production. As a result, the poor workers lack income to purchase goods produced by the capitalist class resulting in under-consumption or over-production. With the capitalist producers lacking market for their goods, capitalist economy plunges into depression. Then the search for ways of opening of new markets is started. Even wars between capitalist countries take place to capture other countries to find new markets for their products. With the discovery of new methods of production of finding new markets, the economy recovers from depression and the new upswing starts.

Critical Appraisal. The view that income inequalities increase with growth or expansion of the economy and further that this causes recession or stagnation is widely accepted. Therefore, even many modern economists suggest that if growth is to be sustained (that is, if recession or stagnation is to be avoided), then consumption demand must be increasing sufficiently to absorb the increasing production of goods. For this, deliberate efforts should be made to reduce inequalities in income distribution. Further, under-consumption theory rightly states that income redistribution schemes will reduce the amplitude of business cycles.

Besides, the suggested behaviour of average propensity to save and consume of the property

5. J.A. Hobson, *The Economics of Unemployment*, London: Allen & Unwin Ltd., 1922.

owners and wage earners in this theory have been found to be consistent with the observed phenomena. Even in the theory of economic development the difference in average propensity to save (APS) of the property owners and workers has been widely used.

It is clear from above that under-consumption theory contains some important elements, especially the emergence of the lack of consumption demand as the cause of recession but it is regarded as too simple. There are many features other than growing income inequalities which are responsible for causing recession or trade cycles. Although under-consumption theory concentrates on a significant variable, it leaves too much unexplained.

Hayek's Over-Investment Theory of Business Cycles

It has been observed that over time investment varies more than that of total output of final goods and services and consumption. This has led economists to investigate the causes of variation in investment and how it is responsible for business cycles. Two versions of over-investment theory have been put forward. One theory offered by Hayek emphasises monetary forces in causing fluctuations in investment. The second version of over-investment theory has been developed by Knut Wickshell which emphasises spurts of investment brought about by innovation. We explain below both these versions of over-investment theory. It is worth noting that in both the versions of this theory distinction between natural rate of interest and money rate of interest plays an important role. Natural rate of interest is defined as the rate at which saving equals investment and this equilibrium interest rate reflects marginal revenue product of capital or rate of return on capital. On the other hand, money rate of interest is the rate at which banks give loans to the businessmen.

Hayek's Monetary Version of Over-Investment Theory. Hayek[6] suggests that it is monetary forces which cause fluctuations in investment which are prime cause of business cycles. In this respect *Hayek's theory is similar to Hawtrey's monetary theory except that it does not involve inflow and outflow of gold causing changes in money supply in the economy.*

To begin with, let us assume that the economy is in recession and businessmen's demand for bank credit is therefore very low. Thus, lower demand for bank credit in times of recession pushes down the money rate of interest below the natural rate. This means that businessmen will be able to borrow funds, that is, bank credit at a rate of interest which is below the expected rate of return in investment projects. This induces them to invest more by undertaking new investment projects. In this way, investment expenditure on new capital goods increases. This causes investment to exceed saving by the amount of newly created bank credit. With the spurt in investment expenditure, the expansion of the economy begins. Increase in investment causes income and employment to rise which induces more consumption expenditure. As a result, production of consumer goods increases. According to Hawtrey, the competition between capital goods and consumer goods industries for scarce resources causes their prices to rise which in turn pushes up the prices of goods and services.

But this process of expansion cannot go on indefinitely because the excess reserves with the banks come to an end which force the banks not to give further loans for investment, while demand for bank credit goes on increasing. Thus, the inelastic supply of credit from the banks and mounting demand for it cause the money rate of interest to go above the natural rate of interest. This makes further investment unprofitable. But at this point of time there has been over-investment in the sense that savings fall short of what is required to finance the desired investment. When no more bank credit is available for investment, there is decline in investment which causes both income and consumption to fall and in this way expansion comes to an end and the economy experiences downswing in economic activity.

6. F.A. Hayek, *Monetary Theory and Trade Cycles*, New York, Harcourt Brace, 1933 and also *Profits, Interest and Investment*, London, Routledge, 1935.

However, after a lapse of some time the fall in demand for bank credit lowers the money rate of interest which goes below the natural rate of interest. This again gives boost to investment activity and as a result recession ends. In this way alternating periods of expansion and contraction occur periodically.

Wicksell's Over-Investment Theory. Over-investment theory developed by Wicksell[7] is of non-monetary type. Instead of focusing on monetary factors it attributes cyclical fluctuations to spurts of investment caused by new innovations introduced by entrepreneurs themselves. The introduction of new innovations or opening of new markets makes some investment projects profitable by either reducing cost or raising demand for the products. The expansion in investment is made possible because of the availability of bank credit at a lower money rate of interest. The expansion in economic activity ceases when investment exceeds saving. Again it may be noted that there is over-investment because the level of saving is insufficient to finance the desired level of investment. The end of investment expenditure causes the economy to go into recession. However, another set of innovations occurs or more new markets are found which stimulates investment. Thus, when investment picks up as a result of new innovations, the economy revives and moves into the expansion phase once again.

Appraisal. Though the over-investment theory does not offer an adequate explanation of business cycles, it contains an important element that fluctuations in investment are the prime cause of business cycles. However, it does not offer a valid explanation as to why changes in investment take place quite often. Many exponents of this theory point to the behaviour of banking system that causes diverges between money rate of interest and natural rate of interest. However, as Keynes later on emphasised, investment fluctuates quite often because of changes in profit expectations of entrepreneurs which depends on several economic and political factors operating in the economy. Thus, the theory fails to offer adequate explanation of business cycles.

KEYNES' THEORY OF BUSINESS CYCLES

J.M. Keynes in his seminal work '*General Theory of Employment, Interest and Money*' made an important contribution to the analysis of the causes of business cycles. According to Keynes theory, in the short run, the level of income, output or employment is determined by the level of aggregate effective demand. In a free private enterprise, the entrepreneurs will produce that much of goods as can be sold profitably. Now, if the aggregate demand is large, that is, if the expenditure on goods and services is large, the entrepreneurs will be able to sell profitably a large quantity of goods and therefore they will produce more. In order to produce more they will employ a larger amount of resources, both men and materials. In short, a higher level of aggregate demand will result in greater output, income and employment. On the other hand, if the level of aggregate demand is low, smaller amount of goods and services can be sold profitably. This means that the total quantity of national output produced will be small. And a small output can be produced with a small amount of resources. As a result, there will be unemployment of resources, both labour and capital. Hence, *the changes in the level of aggregate effective demand will bring about fluctuations in the level of income, output and employment.* Thus, according to Keynes, the fluctuations in economic activity are due to the fluctuations in aggregate effective demand. Fall in aggregate effective demand will create the conditions of recession or depression. If the aggregate demand is increasing, economic expansion will take place.

Now the question arises : What causes fluctuations in aggregate demand? The aggregate demand is composed of demand for consumption goods and demand for investment goods. Thus aggregate demand depends on the total expenditure of the consumers on consumption goods and entrepreneurs on investment goods. Propensity to consume being more or less stable in the short run, fluctuations in aggregate demand depend primarily upon the fluctuations in investment demand. Keynes shows

7. Knut Wicksell, *Interest and Prices,* London: Macmillan, 1936.

that the fundamental cause of fluctuations in aggregate demand and hence in fluctuations in economic activity is the fluctuations in investment demand. *Investment demand is very unstable and volatile and brings about business cycles in the economy.*

Let us start from the phase of economic expansion to explain Keynes' theory of business cycles. We first explain how in Keynesian theory expansion comes to end and recession or depression sets in. During an economic expansion two factors eventually work to cause investment to fall. First, during the expansion phase increase in demand for capital goods due to large-scale investment activity leads to the rise in prices of capital goods due to rising marginal cost of their production. Higher prices of capital goods raise the cost of investment projects and thereby reduce marginal efficiency of capital (that is, expected rate of return). Secondly, as income rises during expansion phase, the demand for money increases which raises interest rate. Higher interest rate makes some potential projects unprofitable. Thus, fall in marginal efficiency of capital on the one hand and rise in interest rate on the other cause decline in investment demand. Declining trend of investment, according to Keynes, raises doubts about the *prospective yield on capital goods* which is more important factor determining marginal efficiency of capital than cost of investment projects and rate of interest. When among businessmen pessimism sets in about future profitability of investment projects stock prices tumble. The crash in stock prices worsens the situation and causes investment to fall even more. Besides, fall in prices of shares reduces wealth of households. Wealth, according to Keynes, is an important factor determining consumption. Thus, the decline in stock prices reduces autonomous consumption demand of households. With the fall in both investment and consumption demand aggregate demand declines which results in accumulation of unintended inventories with the firms. This induces the firms to cut production of goods.

It follows from above that besides the rise in cost of capital goods and rise in rate of interest towards the end of the expansion phase, it is the fall in expected prospective yield that reduces the marginal efficiency of capital and causes investment demand to fall. This induces a wave of pessimistic expectations among businessmen and speculators. These pessimistic expectations cause stock prices to tumble which work like adding fuel to the fire. They cause a further fall in the marginal efficiency of capital. *The turning point from expansion to contraction is thus caused by a sudden collapse in marginal efficiency of capital.* In terms of graph, a sudden fall in the marginal efficiency of capital causes leftward shift in the investment demand curve, for example from I_0I_0 to I_1I_1 in Figure 13.3 resulting in decline in investment from I_0* to I_1* at the given rate of interest. Note that decrease in investment does not automatically decrease in rate of interest to offset the fall in the marginal efficiency of capital.

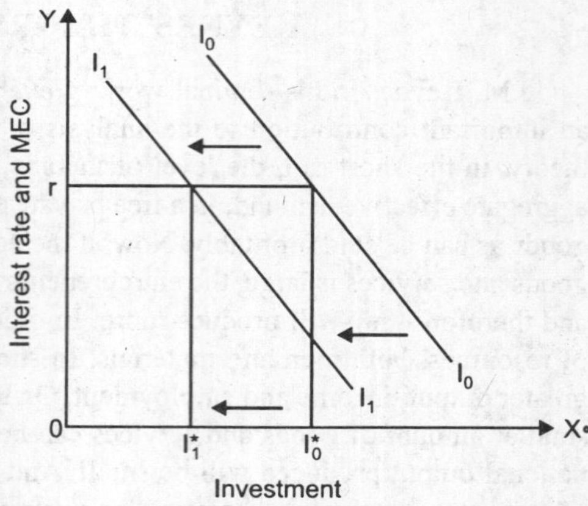

Fig. 13.3. *A Decline in Investment Expenditure due to Fall in Marginal Efficiency of Capital*

However, an additional factor that makes Keynes' business cycle theory potent is the working of multiplier which was an important discovery of J.M. Keynes. According to Keynes, a decrease in investment expenditure causes a decline in income which in turn reduces consumption expenditure. The reduction in consumption expenditure further reduces income and this process of reduction in income continues further. The total fall in income (ΔY) due to an initial decline in investment (ΔI) will be equal to $\Delta I \times \dfrac{1}{1-MPC}$ where $\dfrac{1}{1-MPC}$ is the value of multiplier. If marginal propensity to consume is 0.75, the multiplier will be equal to 4. Thus, a decline in investment by 100 crores will lead to the decline in income by 400 crores. Note that multiplier here works in reverse. Thus, the multiplier process magnifies the effect of decline in investment expenditure on aggregate demand and income and further deepens the depression. As income and output are falling rapidly under the multiplier effect, the employment also goes tumbling down. Thus, the Keynes theory of income multiplier plays a significant role in causing magnified changes in income, output and employment following a reduction in investment.

It is important to note that, in Keynes' views, wages and prices are not flexible enough to offset the decline in investment expenditure and thereby restore full employment. This is in sharp contrast to the classical theory where changes in wages and prices ensure continuous full employment. In Keynes' model wages and prices are "sticky" downward which implies that though wages and prices do not remain constant but when demand falls wages and prices will fall but not sufficient to restore full employment in the economy.

Since wage and price flexibility does not ensure the recovery of the economy out of the state of depression, Keynes thinks that marginal efficiency of capital must rise to stimulate investment. During depression investment falls to a very low level, capital stock begins to wear out and requires replacement. Further, some existing capital equipment become technologically obsolete and have to be abandoned. This generates demand for replacement investment. A long period of time is necessary for existing capital to depreciate because most capital goods are durable as well as irreversible. By durability of capital goods we mean that they last for a long time and by irreversibility we mean that they cannot be used for purposes other than those for which they are meant.

Thus, just as the collapse of marginal efficiency of capital is the main cause of the upper turning point, similarly the lower turning point, *i.e.,* change from recession to recovery, is due to the revival of the marginal efficiency of capital, that is, expected rate of profit. Restoration of business confidence is the most important, yet the most difficult factor to achieve. Even if the rate of interest is reduced, the investment will not increase. This is because of the fact that in the absence of confidence the profitability of investment may remain so low that no practicable reduction in the rate of interest will stimulate investment. The interval which will elapse between the upper turning point and the start of recovery is conditioned by two factors: (*i*) the time necessary for wearing out of durable capital assets, and (*ii*) the time required to absorb the excess stocks of goods left over from the boom. Just as the expected rate of profit was pushed down by the growing abundance of capital during the period of boom, similarly as the stocks of capital goods are depleted and there grows a scarcity of capital goods, then the expected rate of profit rises thereby inducing the businessmen to invest more. When the level of investment increases, income increases by a magnified amount due to the multiplier effect. So the cumulative process starts upward.

Thus, over time as depreciation of capital stock occurs without replacement and also some existing capital equipment become technologically obsolete, the size of capital stock declines. New investment must be undertaken even to produce reduced depression level of output. Thus with the emergence of scarcity of capital, marginal efficiency of capital rises which boosts investment. Once investment increases, it induces further rise in income and consumption demand through the multiplier process. Now, the multiplier works to magnify the effect of increase in investment on raising aggregate demand. The mood of businessmen changes from pessimism to optimism which drives up stock prices. All these factors work to lift the economy out of depression and puts it on the road to prosperity.

However, it is noteworthy that the recovery process from depression takes a very long time. Keynes argued that Government should not wait for long for the natural recovery to occur. This is because persistence of depression creates a lot of human sufferings. He, therefore, advocated for the active intervention by the Government to raise aggregate demand through fiscal policy, that is, stepping up its expenditure or reducing taxes. Thus, he argued for the adoption of policy of deficit budget to boost aggregate demand so that economy is lifted out of depression.

It may be noted that Keynes' business cycle theory is self-generating. In it the economy passes through a long phase of expansion. But eventually some forces automatically work, for example, the growing abundance of capital stock, which reduces marginal efficiency of capital. Pessimisin overtakes businessmen. This causes reduction in investment which is responsible for bringing about downswing in the economy. The idea that it is the fluctuations in investment that bring about the fluctuations in the level of economic activity is an important contribution made by Keynes. Of course, even before Keynes, it was believed that the fluctuations in the investment demand have something to do with the business cycles, but a systematic exposition was lacking. Keynes propounded a definite relationship between a change in investment and the resulting change in income and employment. This relationship is embodied in his famous theory of multiplier.

The Critical Appraisal of Keynes' Theory

J.M. Keynes has made three important contributions to the business cycle theory. First, it is fluctuations in investment that cause changes in aggregate demand which brings about changes in economic activity (*i.e.,* income, output, and employment). Secondly, fluctuations in investment demand are caused by changes in expectations of businessmen regarding making of profits (that is, marginal efficiency of capital). Thirdly, Keynes put forward an important theory of multiplier which tells us how changes in investment bring about magnified changes in the level of income and employment.

But the Keynesian theory of multiplier alone does not offer a full and satisfactory explanation of the trade cycles. A basic feature of the trade cycle is its cumulative character both on the upswing as well as on the downswing, *i.e.,* once economic activity starts rising or falling, it gathers momentum and for a time feeds on itself. Thus, what we have to explain is the cumulative character of economic fluctuations. The theory of multiplier alone does not prove adequate for this task. For example, suppose that investment rises by 100 rupees and that the magnitude of multiplier is 4. From the theory of multiplier we know that national income will rise by 400 and if multiplier is the only force at work, that will be the end of the matter, with the economy reaching a new stable equilibrium at a higher level of national income. But in real life this is not likely to be so, for a rise in income produced by a given rise in investment will have further repercussions in the economy. This reaction is described *in the principle of the accelerator*. According to the principle of acceleration, a change in national income will tend to induce changes in the rate of investment. *While multiplier refers to the change in income as a result of change in investment, the acceleration principle describes the relationship between a change in investment as a result of change in income.*

In the above example, when income has risen by 400 rupees, people's spending power has risen by an equivalent amount. This will induce them to spend more on goods and services. When the demand for goods rises, initially this will be met by overworking the existing plant and machinery. All this leads to an increase in profits with the result that businessmen will be induced to expand their productive capacity and will instal new plants, *i.e.,* they will invest more than before. Thus, *a rise in income leads to a further induced increase in investment.* The accelerator describes this relation between an increase in income and the resulting increase in investment. Thus, Samuelson combined the accelerator principle with the multiplier and showed that the interaction between the two can bring about cyclical fluctuations in economic activity.

SAMUELSON'S MODEL OF BUSINESS CYCLES : INTERACTION BETWEEN MULTIPLIER AND ACCELERATOR

We have briefly explained above that Keynes made an important contribution to the understanding of the cyclical fluctuations by pointing out that it is the ups and downs in investment demand, depending as it is on the profit expectations of the entrepreneurs, that causes changes in aggregate demand which affect the levels of income, output and employment. Further, by putting forward the theory of multiplier, Keynes has shown how the effect of increase and decrease in investment on output and employment gets magnified when multiplier is working during either the upswing or downswing of a business cycle. However, Keynes did not explain the cyclical and cumulative nature of the fluctuations in economic activity. This is because Keynes did not give any importance to the accelerator in his explanation of business cycles. Samuelson in his seminal paper[8] convincingly showed that it is the interaction between the multiplier and accelerator that gives rise to cyclical fluctuations in economic activity. The multiplier alone cannot adequately explain the cyclical and cumulative nature of the economic fluctuations. An autonomous increase in the level of investment raises income by a magnified amount depending upon the value of the multiplier. This increase in income further induces the increases in investment through the acceleration effect. The increase in income brings about increase in aggregate demand for goods and services. To produce more goods we require more capital goods for which extra investment is undertaken. Thus the relationship between investment and income is one of mutual interaction; investment affects income which in turn affects investment demand and in this process income and employment fluctuate in a cyclical manner.

We have shown below in Fig. 13.4 how income and output will increase by even larger amount when accelerator is combined with the Keynesian multiplier.

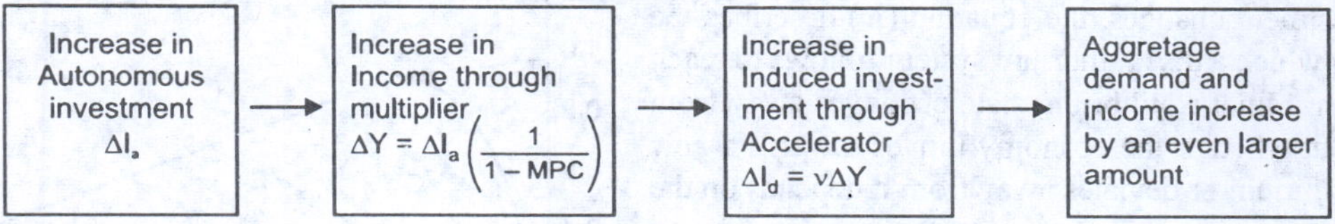

Fig. 13.4. *Combining Accelerator with Keynesian Multiplier*

where ΔI_a = Increase in autonomous investment

ΔY = Increase in Income.

$\frac{1}{1-MPC}$ = Size of multiplier where MPC = Marginal propensity to consume.

ΔI_d = Increase in induced investment

v = Size of accelerator.

Fluctuations in investment are the main cause of instability in a free private enterprise economy. This instability further increases due to the interaction of the multiplier and accelerator. The changes in any component of aggregate demand produce a multiplier effect whose magnitude depends upon the marginal propensity to consume. When consumption, income and output increase under the influence of multiplier effect, they induce further changes in investment and the extent of this induced investment in capital goods industries depends on the capital-output ratio, that is, the interaction between the multiplier and accelerator without any external shocks can give rise to the business cycles whose pattern differs depending upon the magnitudes of the marginal propensity to consume and capital-output ratio. The model of interaction between multiplier and accelerator can be mathematically represented as under:

$$Y_1 = C_1 + I_t \quad ...(i)$$

$$C_t = C_a + c\,(Y_{t-1}) \quad ...(ii)$$

$$I_t = I_a + v\,(Y_{t-1} - Y_{t-2}) \quad ...(iii)$$

where Y_t, C_t, it stand for income, consumption and investment respectively for a period t, C_a stands for autonomous consumption, I_a for autonomous investment, c for marginal propensity to consume and v for the capital-output ratio or accelerator.

8. Samuelson, P.A., "Interaction Between the Multiplier Analysis and the Principle of Acceleration" in *Review of Economic Statistics*, May 1939, p. 751.

From the above equations it is evident that consumption in a period t is a function of income of the previous period Y_{t-1}. That is, one period lag has been assumed for income to determine the consumption of a period. As regards induced investment in period t, it is taken to be the function of the change in income in the previous period. This means that there is two periods gap for changes in income to determine induced investment. In the equation (*iii*) above, induced investment equals $v(Y_{t-1} - Y_{t-2})$ or $v(\Delta Y_{t-1})$. Substituting equations (*ii*) and (*iii*) in equation (*i*) we have the following income equation which states how changes in income are dependent on the values of marginal propensity to consume (c) and capital-output ratio v(*i.e.,* accelerator).

$$Y_t = C_a + c(Y_{t-1}) + I_a + v(Y_{t-1} - Y_{t-2}) \qquad ...(iv)$$

In static equilibrium, the level of income determined will be:

$$Y = Ca + cY + I$$

This is due to the fact that in static equilibrium, given the data of the determining factors, the equilibrium level of income remains uncharged, that is, in this case, $Y_t = Y_{t-1} = Y_{t-2} = Y_{t-n}$ so that period lags have no influence at all and accelerator is reduced to zero. Thus, in a dynamic state when autonomous investment changes, the equation (*iv*) describes the path which a disequilibrium system follows to reach either a final equilibrium state or moves away from it. But whether the economy moves towards a new equilibrium or deviates away from it depends on the values of marginal propensity to consume (c) and capital-output ratio v (*i.e.,* accelerator).

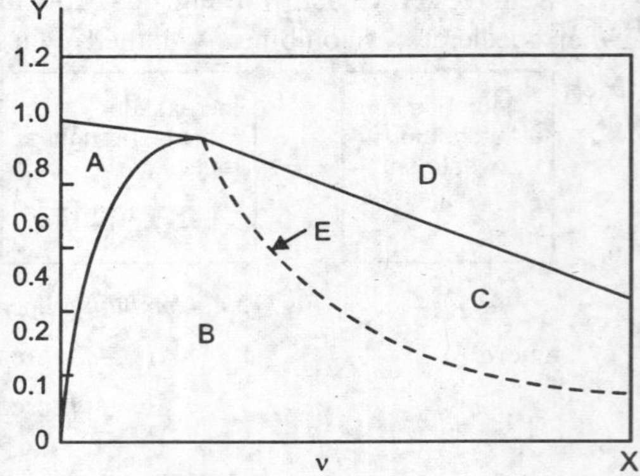

Fig. 13.5. *Combinations of c & v*

By taking different combinations of the values of marginal propensity to consume (c) and capital-output ratio (v), Samuelson has described different paths which the economy will follow. The various combinations of the values of marginal propensity to consume and capital-output ratio (which respectively determine the magnitudes of multiplier and accelerator) are shown in Fig. 13.5. The five paths or patterns of movements which the economic activity (as measured by gross national product or income) can have depending upon various combinations of the values of marginal propensity to consume (c) and capital-output ratio (v) are depicted in Fig. 13.6. When the combinations of the value of marginal propensity to consume (c) and capital-output ratio (v) lie within the region marked *A*, with a change in autonomous investment, the gross national product or income moves upward or downward at a decreasing rate and finally reaches a new equilibrium as is shown in panel (*a*) of Fig. 13.6. If the values of c and v are such that they lie within the region *B*, the change in autonomous investment or autonomous consumption will generate fluctuations in income which follow the pattern of a series of damped cycles whose amplitudes go on declining until the cycles disappear as is shown in panel (*b*) of Fig. 13.6.

The region *C* in Fig. 13.5 represents the combinations of c and v which are relatively high as compared to the region *B* and determine such values of multiplier and accelerator that bring about explosive cycles, that is, the fluctuations of income with successively greater and greater amplitude. The situation is depicted in panel (*c*) of Fig. 13.6 which shows that the system tends to explode and diverges greatly from the equilibrium level. The region *D* in Fig. 13.5 provides the combinations of c and v which cause income to move upward or downward at an increasing rate which has somehow to be restrained if the cyclical movements are to occur. This is depicted in panel (*d*) of Fig. 13.6. Like the values of multiplier and accelerator of region *C*, their values in region *D* cause the system to explode and diverge from the equilibrium state by an increasing amount.

In a special case when values of *c* and *v* (and therefore the magnitudes of multiplier and accelerator) lie in region *E* of Fig. 13.5 they produce fluctuations in income of *constant amplitude* as is shown in panel (*e*) of Fig. 13.6.

It follows from above that region *A* and *B* are alike, they after a disturbance caused by a change in autonomous investment or consumption finally bring about stable equilibrium in the system. On the other hand, the values of *c* and *v* and therefore the magnitudes of multiplier and accelerator of region *C* and *D* resemble each other but are such that they cause great instability in the system as both of these values cause successively greater divergence from the equilibrium level and the system tends to explode. The case of region *E* lies in between the two as the combinations of values of *c* and *v* in it are such that cause cyclical movements of income which neither move toward nor away from the equilibrium.

It is worth noting that all the above five cases do not give rise to cyclical fluctuations or business cycles. *It is only combinations of c and v lying in regions B, C and E that produce business cycles.* The values of accelerator and multiplier in the region *A* are such that with a disturbance caused by a change in autonomous investment or autonomous consumption, the economic activity (as measured by the level of income or Gross National Product) moves smoothly from an initial equilibrium to a new equilibrium with no cyclical fluctuations or oscillations. On the other hand, the values of *c* and *v* (and therefore of multiplier and accelerator) of the region *B* produce cyclical fluctuations which are of the type of *damped oscillations* that tend to disappear over time, that is, the amplitude of the cycles shrinks to zero over a period of time. However, this contradicts the historical experience which reveals that there is no tendency for the cyclical movements to disappear or die out over time. However, it is worth noting that the case *B* explains the impact of a single disturbance on income and employment. For example, the effect of a one time increase in autonomous investment goes on diminishing over time if no other disturbance takes place. However, in reality, further disturbances such as technological advances, innovations, natural disasters and man-made disasters such as security scam in India in 1991-92 do take place quite frequently and at random intervals and in a way they provide shocks to the system.[9] Thus, *the values of c and v of region B can generate cyclical fluctuations over time without dying out if the above-mentioned disturbances are occurring frequently at random.* This

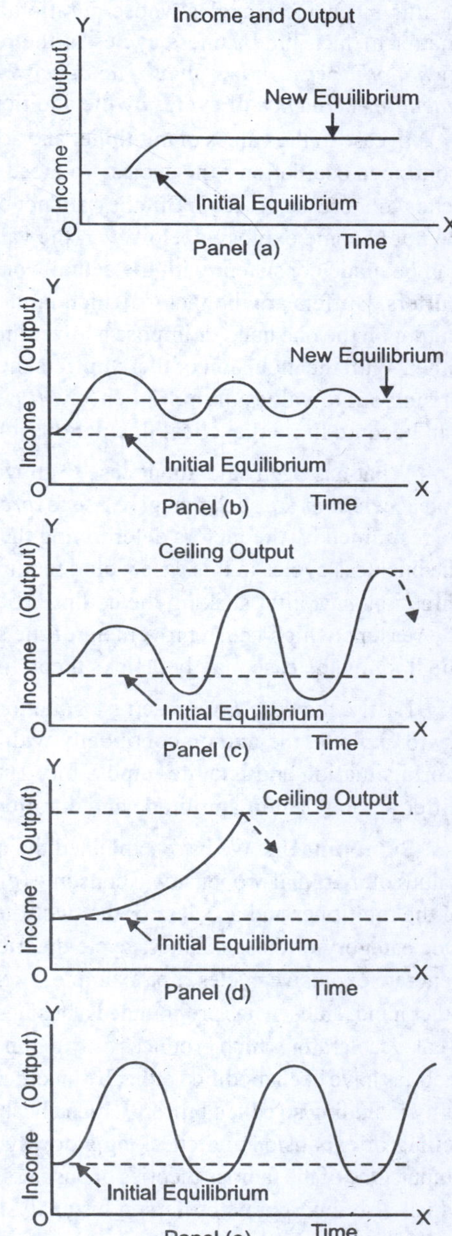

Fig. 13.6. *Interaction between Multiplier and Accelerator: Different Patterns of Income (Output) Movements for Various Values of c and v*

9. The concept of erratic shocks has been put forward by a Nobel Prize winner in economics *R.* Frisch, "Propagation Problems and Impulse Problems in Dynamic Economics" in *Economic Essays in Honour of Gustav Cassel*. Allen and Unwin, 1993, pp. 171-205.

results in business cycles whose duration and amplitude are quite irregular and not uniform. As a matter of fact, the business cycles in the real world also reveal such irregular pattern. To sum up, "*what otherwise shows up as a tendency for the cycle to disappear in case B may be converted into unending sequence* of cycles by the addition of randomly disturbed erratic shock system."[10]

In case of the values of multiplier and accelerator falling within the region *C*, though they generate continued oscillations, the cycles produced by them tend to become 'explosive' (*i.e.,* their amplitude tends to increase greatly). But they are not consistent with the real world situation where oscillations do not become explosive. However, the values of multiplier and accelerator falling within region *C* can be made consistent with the actual world situation by incorporating in the analysis the so called buffers. Buffers are the factors which impose upper limit or ceiling on the expansion of income and output on the one hand or impose a lower limit or floor on the contraction of output and income on the other. With the inclusion of these buffers the otherwise explosive upward and downward fluctuations arising out of values of multiplier (or *MPC*) and accelerator (or capital-output ratio) of the region *C* can become limited cyclical fluctuations, characteristic of the real world situation.

What has been said about case *C* above also applies to region *D* where the values of multiplier and accelerator are such that give rise to *directly explosive upward or downward movement* which can be restrained by the factors determining the ceiling and floor. However, the adequate explanation of the business cycles in this case would require the reasons why the system starts moving in the reverse direction, say, after striking the ceiling. Hicks in his famous theory of the business cycles provides the reasons which cause movement of the system in the reverse direction after it hits the ceiling or the floor as the case may be. Hicks theory of business cycles will be explained below at length.

Lastly, the case *E* represents a situation where the business cycles neither try to disappear, nor try to explode, they go on continually with a *constant amplitude*. This however contradicts the real world situation and is quite impossible. This is because in the real world situation, business cycles differ a good deal in amplitude and duration.

Summing Up. We have explained the interaction of multiplier and accelerator in case of various values of marginal propensity to consume (c) and capital-output ratio (v). On the basis of the interaction of the multiplier and accelerator the two categories of business cycle theories have been put forward. One category of these business cycle theories assumes the values of multiplier and accelerator which generate explosive cycles. For example, Hicks' theory of business cycles falls in this category. On the other hand, Hansen has propounded a business cycle theory based on the interaction of multiplier with a weak accelerator which produces only damped oscillations. Further, as indicated above, the interaction theories have been modified either by incorporating in the analysis erratic shocks or random disturbances or by including so called buffers which check the upward movement of income and output by imposing ceiling of expansion and checking a downward movement by imposing a floor on the contraction of output. One of the famous theories of business cycles based on the interaction of multiplier and accelerator which also incorporate buffers in his analysis of fluctuations is that put forward by the noted English economist J.R. Hicks. We discuss below his theory of business cycles in detail.

A Numerical Example of the Interaction of the Multiplier and Accelerator

How the interaction between the multiplier and accelerator gives rise to the cyclical movements in economic activity (as measured by income or output) will become clear from Table 13.1. In formulating this table we have assumed that marginal propensity to consume (c) being equal to 2/3 or 0.66 and capital-output ratio (v) or accelerator being equal to 2. Further, one period time-lag has been assumed which implies that an increase in income in a period induces the increase in consumption in the next period. It is assumed that initially in period $t + 1$, autonomous investment is of ₹ 10 crores.

10. Shapiro Edward, *Macroeconomic Analysis*, Fourth Edition, 1978, p. 378.

Table 13.1. A Multiplier-Acceleration Interaction Model

Period	*Autonomous Investment*	*Induced Consumption* (c = 2/3)	*Induced Investment* (v = 2)	*Change in Income from the Base Period t*
1	2	3	4	5
	₹ in Crores	₹ in Crores	₹ in Crores	₹ in Crores
t	0	0	0	0
$t + 1$	10	0	0	10
$t + 2$	10	6.7	13.4	30.1
$t + 3$	10	20.0	26.6	56.6
$t + 4$	10	37.8	35.6	83.4
$t + 5$	10	55.6	35.6	101.2
$t + 6$	10	67.6	23.8	101.2
$t + 7$	10	67.6	0.2	67.8
$t + 8$	10	51.8	−10.0	51.8
$t + 9$	10	34.6	−10.0	33.8
$t + 10$	10	23.0	−10.0	23.0
$t + 11$	10	15.4	−10.0	15.4
$t + 12$	10	10.2	− 10.0	10.2
$t + 13$	10	6.8	− 6.8	10.0
$t + 14$	10	6.6	+0.2	16.8

In period $t + 3$, with autonomous investment being maintained constant at ₹ 10 crores, the deviation of total income in the period $t + 3$ as compared to the base period will be equal to 10 + 20 + 26.6 = ₹ 56.6 crores. Similarly, the changes in induced consumption and induced investment and hence in income brought about by the initial increase in autonomous investment of ₹ 10 crores which is maintained throughout, can be found out. It will be seen from column 5 of Table 13.1 that there are large fluctuations in income. Under the influence of the interaction between the multiplier and accelerator, the income increases up to the period $t + 6$. In other words, period up to $t + 6$ represents the expansion phase or upswing of the business cycle. Therefore, the period $t + 6$ is the upper turning point of the business cycle beyond which the contraction phase or downswing of the business cycle begins. It will be further observed that beyond the period $t + 13$, income again starts rising, that is, *recovery from the depression begins*. Thus, $t + 13$ represents the lower turning point of the business cycle. In this way we see that the interaction between the multiplier and accelerator can give rise to the cyclical movements of the economic activity and its various phases. It is worth mentioning that we have taken particular values of marginal propensity to consume (which determine the size of the multiplier) and capital-output ratio (which determines the size of the accelerator). The other values of multiplier and accelerator that have been explained above would give rise to the different patterns of fluctuations.

HICKS' THEORY OF BUSINESS CYCLES

Hicks[11] put forward a complete theory of business cycles based on the interaction between the multiplier and accelerator by choosing certain values of marginal propensity to consume (c) and capital-output ratio (v) which he thinks are representative of the real world situation. According to Hicks, the values of marginal propensity to consume and capital-output ratio fall in either region C or D of Fig. 13.7. As seen above, in case values of these parameters lie in the region C, they produce cyclical

11. Hicks, J.R., A *Contribution to the Theory of Trade Cycles*, Oxford University Press, p. 50.

movements (*i.e.*, oscillations) whose amplitude increases over time and if they fall in region *D*1 they produce an *explosive upward movement* of income or output without oscillations. To explain business cycles of the real world which do not tend to explode, Hicks has incorporated in his analysis the role of buffers. On the one hand, *he introduces output ceiling* when all the given resources are fully employed and prevent income and output to go beyond it, and, on the other hand, he visualises a *floor or the lower* limit below which income and output cannot go because some autonomous investment is always taking place.

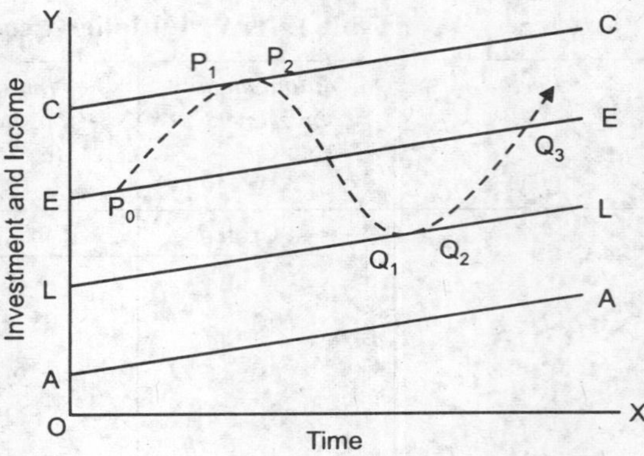

Fig. 13.7. *Hicks' Model of Business Cycles*

Another important features of Hicks' theory is that business cycles in the economy occur in the background of economic growth (*i.e.*, the rising trend of real income of output over time). In other words, cyclical fluctuations in real output of goods and services take place *above and below this rising line of trend* or growth of income and output. Thus in his theory he explains business cycles along with an equilibrium rate of growth. In Hicks' theory of long-run equilibrium growth that is determined by rate of increase of autonomous investment over time and, therefore, long-run equilibrium growth of income is determined by the autonomous investment and the magnitudes of multiplier and accelerator. Hicks assumes that autonomous investment, depending as it is on technological progress, innovations and population growth, grows at a constant rate. With further assumptions of stable multiplier and accelerator, equilibrium income will grow at the same rate as autonomous investment. It follows therefore that the failure of actual output to increase along the equilibrium growth path, sometimes to move above it and sometimes to move below it, determines the business cycles.

Hicks' theory of business cycles has been explained with the help of Fig. 13.7. In this figure, *AA* line represents autonomous investment. Autonomous investment is that investment which is not induced by changes in income and is made by entrepreneur as a result of technological progress or innovations or population growth. Hicks assumes that autonomous investment grows annually at a constant rate given by the slope of the line *AA*. Given the marginal propensity to consume, the simple multiplier is determined. Then the magnitude of multiplier and autonomous investment together determine the equilibrium path of income shown by the line *LL*. Hicks calls this the floor line as this sets the lower limits below which income (output) cannot fall because of a given rate of growth of autonomous investment and the given size of the multiplier. But induced investment has not yet been taken into account. If national income grows from one year to the next, as it would move along the line *LL*, there is some amount of induced investment via accelerator. The line *EE* shows the equilibrium growth path of national income determined by autonomous investment and the combined effect of the multiplier and accelerator. *FF* is the full employment ceiling. It is a line that shows the maximum national output at any period of time when all the available resources of the economy are fully employed. Given the constant growth of autonomous investment, the magnitude of multiplier and the induced investment determined by the accelerator, the economy will be moving along the *equilibrium growth* path line *EE*. Thus starting from point *E*, the economy will be in equilibrium moving along the path *EE* determined by the combined effect of multiplier and accelerator and the growing level of the autonomous investment.

Suppose when the economy reaches point P_0 along the path *EE*, there is an *external shock*—say an outburst of investment due to certain innovation or jump in governmental investment. When the economy experiences such an outburst of autonomous investment it pushes the economy above the equilibrium growth path *EE* after point P_0. The rise in autonomous investment due to external shock *causes national income to increase at a greater rate than that shown* by the slope of *EE*. This greater increase in national income will cause further increase in induced investment through acceleration effect. This increase in induced investment causes national income to increase by a magnified amount through multiplier. So under the combined effect of multiplier and accelerator, national income or output will rapidly expand along the path from P_0 to P_1. Movement from P_0 to P_1 represents the upswing or expansion phase of the business cycle. But this expansion must stop at P_1 because this is the full employment output ceiling. The limited human and material resources of the economy do not permit a greater expansion of national income than shown by the ceiling line *CC*. Therefore, when point P_1 is reached the rapid growth of national income must come to an end. Prof. Hicks assumes that the full employment ceiling grows at the same rate as autonomous investment. Therefore, *CC* slopes gently unlike the very steep slope of the line from P_0 to P_1. When point P_1 is reached the economy must grow at the same rate as the usual growth in autonomous investment.

For a short time the economy may crawl along the full employment ceiling *CC*. But because national income has ceased to increase at the rapid rate, the induced investment via accelerator falls off to the level consistent with the modest rate of growth determined by the constant rate of growth of autonomous investment. But the economy cannot crawl along its full employment ceiling for a long time. The sharp decline in growth of income and consumption when the economy strikes the ceiling causes a sharp decline in induced investment. Thus with the sharp decline in induced investment when national income and hence consumption ceases to increase rapidly, the contraction in the level of the income and business actually must begin. Once the downswing starts, the accelerator works in the reverse direction. That is, since the change in income is now negative the inducement to invest must begin to decrease. Thus there is slackening off at point P_2 and national income starts moving toward equilibrium growth path *EE*. This movement from P_2 downward therefore represents the downswing or contraction phase of the business cycle. In this downswing investment falls off rapidly and therefore multiplier works in the reverse direction. The fall in national income and output resulting from the sharp fall in induced investment will not stop on touching the level *EE* but will go further down. The economy must consequently move all the way down from point P_2 to point Q_1. But at point Q_1 the floor has been reached.

Whereas the upswing was limited by the output ceiling set by the full employment of available resources, in the downswing the national income cannot fall below the level of output represented by the floor. This is because the floor level is determined by simple multiplier and autonomous investment growing at constant rate, while during the downswing after a point accelerator ceases to operate. It may be noted that during downswing the limit to negative investment (disinvestment) and therefore the limit to the contraction of output is set by the depreciation of capital stock. There is no way for the businessmen to make disinvestment at a desired rate higher than the depreciation. When during downswing such conditions arise, accelerator becomes inoperative. After hitting the floor the economy may for some time crawl along the floor through the path Q_1 to Q_2. In doing so, there is some growth in the level of national income. This rate of growth as before induces investment and both the multiplier and accelerator come into operation and the economy will move towards Q_3 and the full employment ceiling *CC*. This is how the upswing of cyclical movement again starts.

Critical Appraisal of Hicks' Theory

But Hicks' theory of trade cycles is not without critics. A major weakness of Hicks' theory, according to Kaldor, is that it is based on the principle of acceleration in its rigid form.[12] If the rigid form of acceleration principle is not valid, then the interaction of the multiplier and accelerator which

12. See Kaldor N., "Hicks on the Trade Cycles" in *Economic Journal*, Dec. 1951, pp. 833-478.

is the crucial concept of the Hicksian theory of trade cycles is not valid. Thus Duesenberry writes, "The basic concept of multiplier-accelerator interaction is important one but we cannot really accept to explain observed cycles by a mechanical application of that concept."[13] and, according to him, Hicks in his business cycle theory actually tries to do so.

It may be noted that Kaldor puts forward a theory of business cycles which does not make use of the rigid or strict form of the acceleration principle. In his trade cycle theory Kaldor provides for investment being *directly related* to the level of income and *inversely related* to the stock of capital. Thus Kaldor's approach which is also supported by Goodwin abandons the rigid and inflexible relation of investment to changes in income (output) as implied by the rigid acceleration principle [*i.e.*, $I_t = I_a + v\,(Y_{t-1} - Y_{t-2})$] and instead has used the following form of the investment function

$$I_t = I_a + gY_{t-1} - jK_t$$

where I_t stands for investment in period t, I_a for autonomous investment, Y_{t-1} for income in the previous period, K_t for the stock of capital, and g and j are constants.

A look at the above investment function used by Kaldor will reveal that investment is directly related to the income and inversely related to the stock of capital. Thus in Kaldor-Goodwin investment function, the increase in income, the capital stock remaining constant, will cause an increase in investment which will enlarge the stock of capital. On the other hand, according to this new investment function, if capital stock increases, output or income remaining constant, investment will fall due to its being negatively related to capital stock. Thus, Kaldor-Goodwin approach to investment while gives up the rigid acceleration principle but still retains the basic idea of investment related to income because in this approach investment will cause the capital stock to expand towards the stock of capital as desired for the production of output of the preceding year.

However, despite the shortcomings of Hicks' theory of business cycles, this is a valuable contribution to the theory of business cycles. Even its critics such as Kaldor though indicating some of its weaknesses acknowledge its merit. Thus Kaldor writes that "Hicks' theory of trade cycles provides us many brilliant and original pieces of analysis". Duesenberry considers it as an "ingenious piece of work'.

QUESTIONS FOR REVIEW

1. Explain briefly characteristics of a trade cycle.
2. Explain briefly the different phases of business cycle.
3. Explain Hawtrey's Monetary Theory of Business Cycle. Show that his model of business cycles is self-generating.
4. What is meant by under-consumption? What factors, according to Karl Marx, are responsible for it ? How does under-consumption cause trade cycles in the economy ?
5. Critically examine Hayek's over-investment theory of business cycles. Compare it with Wicksell's over-investment theory of business cycle.
6. Explain Keynes' contribution to business cycle theory. Is his theory a sufficient explanation of business cycles ?
7. What is accelerator? What role does it play in explaining business cycles in the economy?
8. Explain how interaction of multiplier and accelerator explains cyclical fluctuations in the economy.
9. Critically examine Hicks' model of trade cycles. What determines floor and ceiling in his model ?

13. Duesenberry, J.S., "Hicks on the Trend and Cycles" in *Quarterly Journal of Economics,* August 1950, pp. 464-76.

CHAPTER 14

Economic Stabilisation : Fiscal Policy

Introduction: Macroeconomic Policy and Stabilisation

The economy does not always work smoothly. There often occur fluctuations in the level of economic activity. At times the economy finds itself in the grip of recession when levels of national income, output and employment are far below their full potential levels. During recession, there is a lot of idle or unutilised productive capacity, that is, available machines and factories are not working to their full capacity. As a result, unemployment of labour increases along with the existence of excess capital stock. On the other hand, at times the economy is '*overheated*' which means inflation (*i.e.,* rising prices) occurs in the economy. Thus, in a free market economy there is a lot of economic instability. The classical economists believed that an automatic mechanism works to restore stability in the economy; recession would cure itself and inflation will be automatically controlled. However, the empirical evidence during the 1930s when severe depression took place in the Western capitalist economies and also the evidence of post-Second World II period amply shows that no such automatic mechanism works to bring about stability in the economy. That is why Keynes argued for intervention by the Government to cure depression and inflation by adopting appropriate tools of macroeconomic policy. *The two important tools of macroeconomic policy are fiscal policy and monetary policy.* According to Keynes, monetary policy was ineffective to lift the economy out of depression. He emphasized the role of fiscal policy as an effective tool of stabilising the economy. However, in view of the modern economists both fiscal and monetary policies play a useful role in stabilising the economy. In the present chapter we shall dwell upon the role of fiscal policy for stabilising the economy and will discuss the role of monetary policy in bringing about stabilisation in the next chapter.

Goals of Macroeconomic Policy

Stabilising the economy at a higher level of employment and national output is not the only goal of macroeconomic policy. Ensuring price stability is its another goal. Both inflation (that is, rising prices) and deflation (that is, falling prices) have bad economic consequences. It is therefore desirable to achieve price stability. Similarly, every nation wants to raise the level of living of its people which can be attained through bringing about economic growth which in turn depends on raising the rates of saving and investment and accumulating capital. Macroeconomic policies can play a useful role in raising the rate of saving and investment and therefore ensure rapid economic growth. Thus, three important goals or objectives of macroeconomic policy (both fiscal and monetary) are as follows:

1. Economic stability at a high level of output and employment.
2. Price stability.
3. Economic growth.

In the present chapter we shall confine ourselves to the discussion of the role of fiscal policy in achieving economic stability at full employment level and in controlling inflation and deflation and thus attaining price stability. The role of monetary policy for encouraging economic growth will be discussed at length in a later chapter.

DISCRETIONARY FISCAL POLICY FOR STABILISATION

Fiscal policy is an important instrument to stabilise the economy, that is, to overcome recession and control inflation in the economy. Fiscal policy is of two kinds: *Discretionary fiscal policy and Non-discretionary fiscal policy of automatic stabilisers.* By discretionary policy we mean deliberate change in the Government expenditure and taxes to influence the level of national output and prices. Fiscal policy generally aims at managing aggregate demand for goods and services. On the other hand, non-discretionary fiscal policy of automatic stabilisers is a built-in tax or expenditure mechanism that automatically increases aggregate demand when recession occurs and reduces aggregate demand when there is inflation in the economy without any special deliberate actions on the part of the Government. In this section we shall confine ourselves to the discussion of discretionary fiscal policy.

At the time of recession the Government increases its expenditure or cuts down taxes or adopts a combination of both. On the other hand, to control inflation the Government cuts down its expenditure or raises taxes. In other words, *to cure recession expansionary fiscal policy and to control inflation contractionary fiscal policy is adopted.* It is worth mentioning that fiscal policy aims at changing aggregate demand by suitable changes in Government spending and taxes. Thus, *fiscal policy is mainly a policy of demand management.* It should be further noted that when the Government adopts expansionary fiscal policy to cure recession, it raises its expenditure without raising taxes or cuts down taxes without changing expenditure or increases expenditure and cuts down taxes as well. With the adoption of any of these types of expansionary fiscal policy Government's budget will have a deficit. Thus expansionary fiscal policy to cure recession and unemployment is a deficit budget policy. If, on the other hand, to control inflation, Government reduces its expenditure or increases taxes or adopts a combination of the two, it will be planning for a budget surplus. *Thus policy of budget surplus, or at least reducing budget deficit is adopted to remedy inflation.* In what follows we will discuss fiscal policy first to cure recession and then to control inflation.

Fiscal Policy to Cure Recession

As we know, the recession in an economy occurs when aggregate demand decreases due to a fall in private investment. Private investment may fall when businessmen become highly pessimistic about making profits in future, resulting in decline in marginal efficiency of investment. As a result of fall in private investment expenditure, aggregate demand curve shifts down creating a *deflationary or recessionary gap.* It is the task of fiscal policy to close this gap by increasing Government expenditure, or reducing taxes. Thus there are two fiscal methods to get the economy out of recession:

(*a*) Increase in Government expenditure

(*b*) Reduction of taxes.

We discuss below both these methods.

(*a*) **Increase in Government Expenditure to Cure Recession.** For a discretionary fiscal policy to cure depression, the increase in Government expenditure is an important tool. Government may increase expenditure by starting public works, such as building roads, dams, ports, telecommunication links, irrigation works, electrification of new areas etc. For undertaking all these public works, Government buys various types of goods and materials and employs workers. The effect of this increase in expenditure is both direct and indirect. The direct effect is the increase in incomes of those who sell materials and supply labour for these projects. The output of these public works also goes up together with the increase in incomes. Not only that, Keynes showed that increase in Government expenditure also has an *indirect effect* in the form of the working of a multiplier. Those who get more incomes spend them further on consumer goods depending on their marginal propensity to consume. As during the period of recession there exists *excess capacity* in the consumer goods industries, the increase in demand for them brings about expansion in their output which further generates employment and incomes for the unemployed workers and so the new incomes are spent and res-pent further and the process of multiplier goes on working till it exhausts itself.

How large should be the increase in expenditure so that equilibrium is established at full employment or potential level of output? This depends on the magnitude of GNP gap caused by deflationary gap on the one hand and the size of multiplier on the other. It may be recalled that the size of the multiplier depends on the marginal propensity to consume. The impact of increase in Government expenditure in a recessionary condition is illustrated in Fig. 14.1. Suppose to begin with the economy is operating at full-employment or potential level of output Y_F with aggregate demand curve $C + I_2 + G_2$ intersecting 45° line at point E_2. Now, due to some adverse happening (say, due to the crash in the stock market), investor's expectations of making profits from investment projects become dim causing a decline in investment. With the decline in investment, say, equal to E_2B, aggregate demand curve will shift down to the new position $C + I_1 + G_1$ which will bring the economy to the new equilibrium position at point E_1 and thereby determine Y_1 level of output or income. The fall in output will create involuntary unemployment of labour and also excess capacity (*i.e.,* idle capital stock) will come to exist in the economy. Thus emergence of deflationary gap equal to E_2B and the reverse working of the multiplier has brought about conditions of recession in the economy. It will be observed from Fig. 14.1 that, to overcome recession if the Government increases its expenditure by E_1H, the aggregate demand curve will shift upward to original position $C + I_2 + G_2$ and as a result the equilibrium level of income will increase to the full-employment or potential level of output *YF* and in this way the economy would be lifted out of depression. Note that the increase (ΔY) in national income or output by Y_1Y_F is not only equal to the increase in Government expenditure by ΔG or E_1H but a multiple of it depending on the marginal propensity to consume. Thus, increase in national income is equal to $\Delta G \times \frac{1}{1-MPC}$ where $\frac{1}{1-MPC}$ is the value of multiplier.

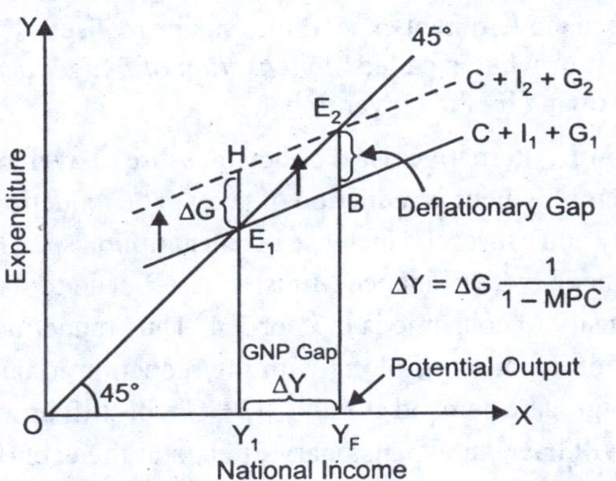

Fig. 14.1. *Increase in Government Expenditure to Cure Recession*

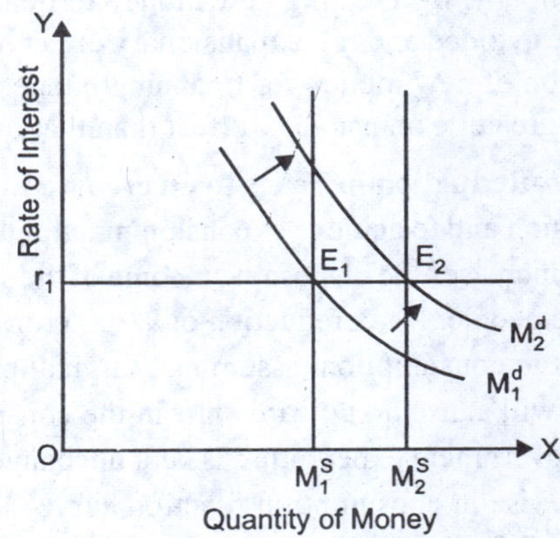

Fig. 14.2. *Accomodative Expansion in Money Supply by the Central Bank to Keep the Rate of Interest Unchanged*

It may also be further noted that increase in Government expenditure without raising taxes (and therefore the policy of deficit budgeting) will fully succeed in curing recession if rate of interest remains unchanged. With the increase in Government expenditure and resultant increase in output and employment demand for money for transaction purposes is likely to increase as is shown in Fig. 14.2 where demand for money curve shifts to right from M_1^d to M_2^d as a result of increase in transaction demand for money. Money supply remaining constant, with increase in demand for money rate of interest is likely to rise which will adversely affect the private investment. The decline in private investment will tend to offset the expansionary effect of rise in Government expenditure. Therefore, if fiscal policy of increase in Government expenditure (or of deficit budgeting) is to succeed in overcoming recession, the Central Bank of the country should also pursue accomodative expansionary monetary policy and take steps to increase the money supply so that increase in Government expenditure does not lead to the rise in rate of interest. It will be noticed from Fig. 14.2 that if money supply is increased from M_1^S to M_2^S, the rate of interest does not rise despite the increase in demand for money. With rate of interest remaining unchanged, private investment will not be adversely affected and increase in Government expenditure will have full effect on raising national income and employment.

Financing Increase in Government Expenditures and Budget Deficit

An important question is how to finance the increase in Government expenditure which is undertaken to cure recession. This increase in Government expenditure must not be financed by raising taxes because rise in taxes would reduce disposable incomes and consumers' demand for goods. As a matter of fact, rise in taxes would offset the expansionary effect of rise in Government spending. Therefore, proper discretionary fiscal policy at times of recession is to have the budget deficit if expansionary effect is to be realised.

Borrowing. One way to finance budget deficit is to borrow from the public by selling interest-bearing bonds to them. However, there is a problem in adopting borrowing as a method of financing budget deficit. When the Government borrows from the public in the money market, it will be competing with businessmen who also borrow for private investment. The Government borrowing will raise the demand for loanable funds which in a free market economy, if rate of interest is not administered by the Central Bank, will drive up the rate of interest. We know the rise in rate of interest will reduce or crowd out some private investment expenditure and interest-sensitive consumer spending for durable goods.

Creation of New Money. The more effective way of financing budget deficit is the creation of new money. By creating new money to finance the deficit, the crowding out of private investment can be avoided and full expansionary effect of rise in Government expenditure can be realised. Thus, creation of new money for financing budget deficit or what is called *monetisation of budget deficit* has a greater expansionary effect than that of borrowing by the Government.

(*b*)**Reduction in Taxes to Overcome Recession.** Alternative fiscal policy measure to overcome recession and to achieve expansion in output and employment is reduction of taxes. The reduction in taxes increases the disposable income of the society and causes the increase in consumption spending by the people. If tax reduction of ₹ 200 crores is made by the Finance Minister, it will lead to ₹ 150 crores in consumption, assuming marginal propensity to consume is 0.75 or 3/4. Thus reduction in taxes will cause an upward shift in the consumption function. If along with the reduction in taxes, the Government expenditure is kept unchanged, aggregate demand curve $C + I + G$ will shift upward due to rise in consumption function curve. This will have an expansionary effect and the economy will be lifted out of recession, and national income and employment will increase and as a result unemployment will be reduced. Note that reduction in taxes, with Government expenditure remaining constant, will also result in budget deficit which will have to be financed either by borrowing or creation of new money.

It is worth noting that *reduction in taxes has only an indirect effect on expansion and output* through causing a rise in consumption function. But, like the increase in government expenditure, the increase in consumption achieved through reduction in taxes will have a multiplier effect on increasing income, output and employment. As we have shown in a previous chapter, the increase in income due to *tax multiplier,* as it is called, is given by

$$\text{Tax multiplier} = \Delta T \times \frac{MPC}{1 - MPC}$$

The effect of reduction in taxes in curing recession and in causing expansion in income and output can be graphically shown by a figure such as Fig. 14.1. In case of reduction in taxes, instead of increase in Government expenditure G, it is increase in consumption C which will cause upward shift in the aggregate demand curve $(C + I + G)$ and will result in, through the working of multiplier, a higher level of equilibrium national income.

There are some instances in the history of the capitalist world, especially U.S.A, when taxes were reduced to stimulate the economy. In 1964, President Kennedy reduced personal and business taxes by about $12 billion to give a boost to the American economy when there was high unemployment and lower capacity utilisation in the American economy. This tax cut was quite successful in reducing unemployment substantially and expanding national income through full utilisation of excess capacity. Again, over the period 1981-84, President Reagan made a very large tax reduction to get out of recession and to achieve expansion in national income to reduce unemployment. There is some debate whether President Reagan's tax cut alone had positive effect on national income as some economists attribute the recovery in that period to the monetary expansion that took place. However, tax reduction by President Reagan did play a significant role for bringing about the recovery.

Fiscal Policy Option: Increase in Government Expenditure or Reduction in Taxes

Is it better to use Government expenditure or changes in taxes to stabilise the economy at full employment and potential level of output. The answer depends to a great extent upon one's view regarding the role of public sector. Those who think that public sector should play a significant role in the economy to meet various failures of a free market system will recommend the increase in Government expenditure during recession on public works to achieve expansion in output and employment. On the other hand, those economists who think that public sector is inefficient and involves waste of scarce resources would advocate for reduction in taxes to stimulate the economy.

The choice between tax reduction and increase in Government expenditure depends on the basis of another factor, namely, the magnitude of the effect of expenditure multiplier and tax multiplier. The value of tax multiplier is less than the Government expenditure multiplier. Ignoring the signs of the multipliers, it should be noted that whereas expenditure multiplier is equal to $\frac{1}{1-MPC}$, the tax multiplier equals $\frac{MPC}{1-MPC}$ or $MPC \times \frac{1}{1-MPC}$ which is less than $\frac{1}{1-MPC}$. Suppose marginal propensity to consume is 0.75 or 3/4 so that value of expenditure multiplier is 4. Increase in Government expenditure by ₹ 100 crores will raise national output by ₹ 400 crores. On the other hand, reduction in taxes by ₹ 100 crores will increase income and output by $100 \times \frac{MPC}{1-MPC} = 100 \times \frac{3/4}{1-3/4} =$ ₹ 300 crores. Thus, the effect of reduction in taxes by an equal amount as the increase in Government expenditure has a smaller impact on national income than that of increase in Government expenditure. This difference in the effects of the two methods of expanding output has implications for the size of the Government deficit. If we want to achieve expansion in income by the same amount, we need to cut taxes by more than we would need to increase Government expenditure because the size of the tax multiplier is less than that of expenditure multiplier. In other words, in case we adopt the policy of tax reduction, to achieve expansion by a given amount the budget deficit planned will have to be much greater.

However, the size of expenditure multiplier relative to the size of the tax multiplier is not the sole deciding factor for the choice of a policy option. For example, reduction in taxes is greatly welcomed by the people as it directly increases their disposable incomes. Further, it is individual or households who themselves decide how to spend their extra disposable income made possible by a tax cut, while in case of increase in expenditure the Government decides how to spend it.

Fiscal Policy to Control Inflation

When due to large increases in consumption demand by the households or investment expenditure by the entrepreneurs, or bigger budget deficit caused by too large an increase in Government expenditure, aggregate demand increases beyond what the economy can potentially produce by fully employing its given resources, it gives rise to the situation of *excess demand* which results in inflationary pressures in the economy. This inflationary situation can also arise if too large an increase in money supply in the economy occurs. In these circumstances *inflationary gap* occurs which tends to bring about rise in prices. If successful steps to check the emergence of excees demand or close the inflationary gap are not taken, the economy will experience a period of inflation or rising prices. For the last some decades, problem of demand-pull inflation has been faced by both the developed and developing countries of the world.[1] An alternative way of looking at inflation is to view it from the angle of business cycles. After recovery from recession, when during upswing an economy finds itself in conditions of boom and becomes overheated prices start rising rapidly. Under such circumstances *anticyclical fiscal policy* calls for reduction in aggregate demand. Thus, *fiscal policy measures to control inflation are* (1) *reducing Government expenditure and* (2) *increasing taxes.* If in the beginning the *Government is having balanced budget,* then increasing taxes while keeping Government expenditure constant will yield budget surplus. The creation of budget surplus will cause downward shift in the aggregate demand curve and will therefore help in easing pressure on prices. If there is a balanced budget to begin with and the Government reduces its expenditure, say on defence, subsidies, transfer payments, while keeping taxes constant, this will also create budget surplus and result in removing excess demand in the economy.

It is important to mention that in the developing countries like India, the main factor responsible for inflationary pressures is *heavy budget deficit* of the Government for the last several years resulting in excess demand conditions. Rate of inflation can be reduced not necessarily by planning for budget surplus which is in fact impracticable but by *trying to take steps to reduce budget deficits.* It has been estimated that the aim should be to reduce fiscal deficit[2] to 3 per cent of GNP to achieve price stability in the Indian economy.

How the reduction in Government expenditure will help in checking inflation is shown in Fig. 14.3. It will be seen from this figure that an aggregate demand curve $C + I + G_1$ intersects 45° line at point E and determines equilibrium national income at full-employment level of income Y_F. However, if due to excessive Government expenditure and a large budget deficit, the aggregate demand curve shifts upward to $C + I + G_2$, this will determine Y_2 level of income which is greater than full employment or potential output level Y_F. Since output cannot increase beyond Y_F, income will rise only in money terms through rise in prices, real income or output remaining unchanged. To put it in other words, while the economy does not have labour, capital and other resources sufficient to produce Y_2 level of income or output, the households, businessmen and Government are demanding Y_2 level of output. This excess demand pushes up the price level so that level of only nominal income increases, real income or output remaining constant. It is thus clear that with the increase in aggregate demand beyond the full-employment level of output to $C + I + G_2$ causes excess demand equal to EA to emerge in the economy. It is this excess demand EA relative to full-employment output Y_F which causes the price level to rise and thus creates inflationary situation in the economy. This excess demand EA at full-employment level has therefore been called inflationary gap. *The task of fiscal policy is to close this inflationary gap by reducing Government expenditure or raising taxes.* With equilibrium

1. It is worth noting that in the mid-nineties in the developed countries inflation has become very moderate which is currently at the rate of about 4 per cent per annum.
2. There is some difference in the meaning of budget deficit and fiscal deficit. However, we shall not go into this issue and will be treating them to be of the same meaning.

at point *H* and nominal income equal to Y_2, if Government expenditure equal to *HB* (which is equal to inflationary gap *AE*) is reduced, aggregate demand curve will shift downward to $C + I + G_1$ which will restore the equilibrium at the full-employment level Y_F. The reduction in Government expenditure equal to *HB* through the operation of multiplier will result in a multiple decline in the level of national income or output. It will be seen from Fig. 14.3 that the decrease in Government expenditure by *HB* has led to a much bigger decline in output by Y_2Y_F. Ideally Government expenditure should cut down its expenditure on non-development or unproductive heads such as defence, unnecessary subsidies. It may however be noted that in India to control inflation the Government has been reducing capital expenditure which is mainly of development nature and has therefore been validly criticised.

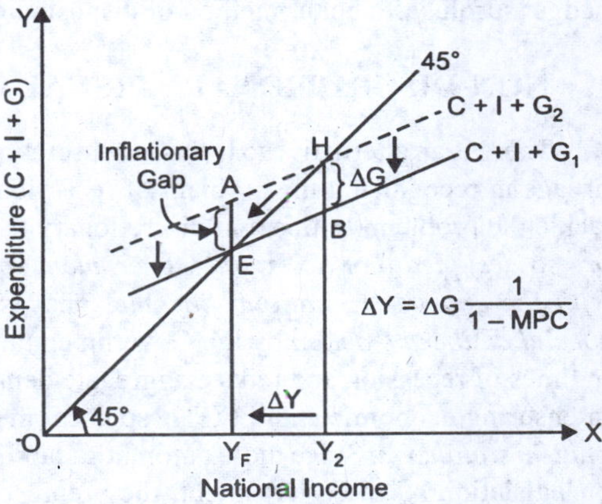

Fig. 14.3. *Reducing Expenditure to Check Inflation.*

Raising Taxes to Control Inflation. *As an alternative to reduction in Government expenditure, the taxes can be increased to reduce aggregate demand.* For this purpose especially personal direct taxes such as income tax, wealth tax, corporate tax can be raised. The hike in taxes reduces the disposable incomes of the people and thereby forces them to reduce their consumption demand. Note that in Fig. 14.3 as a result of hike in personal taxes it is the decrease in consumption-demand (*C*) component which will cause the aggregate demand curve $C + I + G_2$ to shift downward. Since, as shown above, the magnitude of tax multiplier is smaller than the expenditure multiplier, the tax revenue will be raised by a greater amount to achieve contraction in national income by Y_2Y_F.

Disposing of Budget Surplus. As have seen above, to control demand-pull inflation, the Government either reduces its expenditure or raises taxes to lower aggregate demand for goods and services. Reduction in expenditure or hike in taxes results in decrease in budget deficits (if occurring before such steps) or in the emergence of budget surplus if the Government was having balanced budget prior to the adoption of anti-inflationary fiscal policy measures. Let us assume that anti-inflationary fiscal policy results in budget surplus. Anti-inflationary impact of budget surplus depends to a good extent on how the Government disposes of this budget surplus. There are two ways in which budget surplus can be disposed of: (1) reducing or retiring public debt and (2) impounding public debt.

We examine below the anti-inflationary effects of these two ways of disposing of the budget surplus.

1. **Retiring Public Debt.** The budget surplus created by anti-inflationary policy can be used by the Government to pay back the outstanding debt. However, using budget surplus for retiring public debt will weaken its anti-inflationary effect. In paying off the debt held by the public, the Government will be returning the money to the public which it has collected through taxes. Further, this will also add to the money supply with the public. The general public will spend a part of the money so received which will raise consumption demand. Besides, retiring of public debt will result in the expansion of money supply in the money market which will tend to lower the rate of interest. The lower rate of interest will stimulate consumption and investment demand while anti-inflationary policy requires that they should be reduced.

2. **Impounding of Public Debt.** To realise a large anti-inflationary effect of budget surplus it is desirable to impound the surplus fund. The impounding surplus funds means that they should be kept idle. Thus by impounding the budget surplus, the Government shall be withdrawing some income

or purchasing power from the income-expenditure stream and thus will not create any inflationary pressures to offset the deflationary impact of the budget surplus. To conclude, the impounding of budget surplus is a better method of disposing of budget surplus than of paying off public debt.

NON-DISCRETIONARY FISCAL POLICY: AUTOMATIC STABILIZERS

There is an alternative to the use of discretionary fiscal policy which generally involves problems of lags in recognising the problem of recession or inflation and lag of taking appropriate action to tackle the problem. In this non-discretionary fiscal policy, *the tax structure and expenditure pattern are so designed that taxes and Government spending vary automatically in appropriate direction with the changes in national income.* That is, these taxes and expenditure pattern *without any special deliberate action* by the Government and Parliament automatically raise aggregate demand in times of recession and reduce aggregate demand in times of boom and inflation and thereby help in ensuring economic stability. These fiscal measures are therefore called *automatic stabilizers or built-in stabilizers.* Since these automatic stabilizers do not require any fresh deliberate policy action or legislation by the government, they represent non-discretionary fiscal policy. Built-in stability of tax revenue and Government expenditure of transfer payments and subsidies is created because they vary with national income. These taxes and expenditure automatically bring about appropriate changes in aggregate demand and reduce the impact of recession and inflation that might occur in an economy at some time. This means that because of the existence of these automatic or built-in stabilizers recession and inflation will be shorter and less intense than otherwise would be the case. Important automatic fiscal stabilizers are personal income taxes, corporate income taxes, transfer payments such as unemployment compensation, welfare benefits, corporate dividends.

We discuss below these taxes, revenue from which varies directly with the change in national income.

Personal Income Taxes. The tax rate structure is so designed that revenue from these taxes directly varies with income. Moreover, personal income taxes have progressive rates; the higher rates are charged from the upper income brackets. As a result, when national income increases during expansion and inflation, increasing percentage of the people's income are paid to the Government. Thus, through causing a decline in their disposable income these taxes automatically reduce people's consumption and therefore aggregate demand. This decline in aggregate demand because of imposition of progressive personal income taxes tends to check inflation from becoming more severe. On the other hand, when national income declines at times of recession, the tax revenue declines as well which prevents aggregate demand from falling by the same proportion as the decline in income.

Corporate Income Taxes. Companies, or corporations as they are called now, also pay a percentage of their profits as tax to the Government. Like personal income taxes, corporate income tax rate is also generally higher at higher levels of corporate profits. As recession and inflation affect corporate taxes greatly, they have a powerful stabilizing effect on aggregate demand; the revenue from them rises greatly during inflation and boom which tends to reduce aggregate demand, and revenue from them falls greatly during recession which tends to offset the decline in aggregate demand.

Transfer Payments: Unemployment Compensation and Welfare Benefits. When there is recession and as a result unemployment increases, the Government has to spend more on compensation for unemployment and other welfare programmes such as food stamps, rent subsidies, subsidies to farmers. This hike in Government expenditure tends to make recession shortlived and less intense. On the other hand, when at times of boom and inflation national income increases and therefore unemployment falls, the Government curtails its programme of social benefits which results in lowering Government expenditure. The smaller spending by the Government helps to control inflation.

Corporate Dividend Policy. With economic fluctuations, corporate profits also rise and fall. However, corporations do not so quickly increase or reduce dividends in tune with fluctuations in profits and follow a *fairly stable dividend policy.* This permits the individuals to spend more during recession and spend less than would have been the case if dividends were lowered in time of recession and raised in conditions of boom and inflation. Thus, fairly stable dividends tend to cushion a recession and curb inflation by stabilizing consumption expenditure.

Conclusion

It follows from above that automatic stabilizers reduce the intensity of business fluctuations, that is, both recession and inflation. However, the automatic or built-in stabilizers cannot alone correct the recession and inflation significantly. According to an estimate made for the U.S.A., automatic stabilizers have been able to reduce fluctuations in national income only by one-third. Therefore, the role of discretionary fiscal policy, namely, deliberate and explicit changes in tax rates and amount of Government expenditure, are required to cure recession and curb inflation.

CROWDING-OUT EFFECT AND EFFECTIVENESS OF FISCAL POLICY

The critics of Keynesian theory have pointed out that expansionary effect of fiscal policy is not as much as Keynesian economists suggest. In the Keynesian theory it is asserted that when Government increases its expenditure without raising taxes or when it reduces taxes without changing expenditure, it will have a large expansionary effect on national income. In other words, deficit budget would lead to the large increase in aggregate demand and thereby help to expand national output and income. However, it has been pointed that the above analysis of effect of expansionary fiscal policy of budget deficit ignores the effect of increase in Government expenditure or budget deficit on private investment. It has been argued that increase in Government expenditure or creation of budget deficit adversely affects private investment which offsets to a good extent the expansionary effect of budget deficit. This adverse effect comes about as increase in Government expenditure or reduction in taxes causes rate of interest to go up. There are two ways in which rise in rate of interest is explained. First, within the framework of Keynesian theory increase in Government expenditure leads to the rise in national output which raises the transactions demand for money. Given the supply of money in the economy, the increase in transactions demand for money will cause the rate of interest to go up. Secondly, in order to finance its budget deficit the Government will borrow funds from the market. This will raise the demand for loanable funds which will bring about rise in the rate of interest.

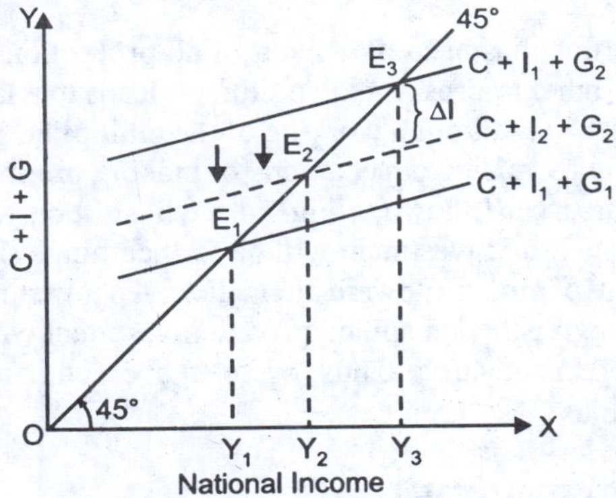

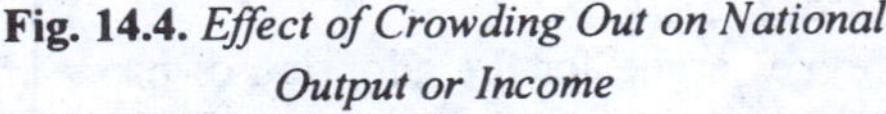
Fig. 14.4. *Effect of Crowding Out on National Output or Income*

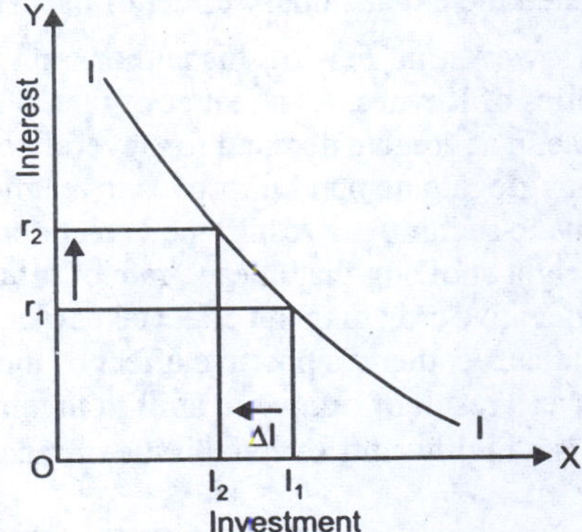

Fig. 14.5. *Crowding Out of Private Investment*

Whatever the mechanism, the budget deficit or increase in Government expenditure to achieve expansion in national income and output will cause the rate of interest to go up. The rise in the rate of interest will discourage private investment. As we know from the theory of investment, at a higher rate of interest, private investment declines. Thus, *increase in Government expenditure or fiscal policy of budget deficit crowds out private investment.* This fall in private investment as a result of the rise in rate of interest will offset or cancel out a part of the expansionary effect of increase in Government expenditure. The magnitude of this crowding out effect depends on the elasticity of the investment demand. If investment demand is more elastic, the decrease in private investment consequent to the rise in rate of interest will be quite substantial and will greatly offset the expansionary effect of the increase in Government expenditure. On the contrary, if investment demand is relatively inelastic, the rise in rate of interest will lead to only a small decline in private investment and therefore crowding out effect will be relatively small.

It, therefore, follows that the magnitude of crowding out weakens the effectiveness of fiscal policy. The crowding out effect of expansionary fiscal policy and its effect on national output and employment is graphically shown in Figs. 14.4. and 14.5. To begin with the economy is in equilibrium at Y_1 level of income where aggregate demand curve $C+I_1+G_1$ intersects the 45° line and determines Y_1 level of income. Let us assume that this is much below the potential or full-employment level of output. Suppose in order to raise the level of national income and output, the Government raises its expenditure from G_1 to G_2 so that the aggregate demand curve shifts upward to the new position $C+I_1+G_2$ which intersects the 45° line at point E_3. With increase in Government expenditure national income will rise by ΔG × multiplier, that is, by $\Delta G \times \left(\frac{1}{1-MPC}\right)$. In the absence of crowding out effect, national income will rise to Y_3. This change in national income, ΔY or by Y_1Y_3 is equal to the increase in Government expenditure (G) times the value of multiplier $\frac{1}{1-MPC}$. However, as explained above, the increase in Government expenditure or the creation of budget deficit causes the rate of interest to rise, say from r_1 to r_2 (See Figure 14.5). It will be seen from Fig. 14.5 that with the rise in interest from r_1 to r_2, private investment decreases from I_1 to I_2. Now, with the decline in private investment expenditure, aggregate demand curve in Fig. 14.4 shifts below to the new lower position $C+I_2+G_2$ (dotted) and as a result new equilibrium is reached at Y_2 level of income. Thus, net result of increase in Government expenditure (ΔG) and crowding out of private investment equal to I_1I_2 or ΔI is the expansion in national income equal to only Y_1Y_2 which is relatively very small as compared to the rise in income by Y_1Y_3 in the absence of crowding out effect. Thus, the crowding out effect has weakened the expansionary effect of fiscal policy.

However, in view of this author crowding out effect has been blown out of all proportions by the critics of Keynes. As a matter of fact, when Government raises its expenditure, it leads to a large increase in aggregate demand for several goods and services through working of the multiplier. This rising aggregate demand improves investment climate by raising expectations of making profits by the private sector. As a result, the investment demand curve *II* shown in Fig. 14.5 will shift outward to the right showing that at each rate of interest more private investment will be forthcoming. Thus, while negative crowding out effect takes place as a result of moving upward along the given investment demand curve, there is positive effect of increase in aggregate demand on private investment which occurs as a result of rightward shift in the investment demand curve. Thus, we see that crowding out effect is a highly controversial issue of macroeconomics.

QUESTIONS FOR REVIEW

1. What is meant by fiscal policy? Why did Keynes argue for the adoption of proper fiscal policy as an instrument of demand management to get out of depression.
2. Explain the various objectives of fiscal policy in the advanced developed economies.

3. Explain the role of fiscal policy in overcoming recession and in achieving economic stability at full-employment level.
4. What are automatic stabilisers? Explain their role in stabilisation of the economy.
5. What is meant by discretionary fiscal policy? How does it differ from the fiscal policy of automatic stabilizers? Explain the effectiveness of discretionary fiscal policy in curing recession and attaining equilibrium at full employment level.
6. Expansionary fiscal policy and expansionary monetary policy are complementary with each other.
7. What is effective demand ? How will it change if the Government covers its entire expenditure by (a) raising tax or (b) printing more currency.
8. Explain fiscal policy measures to control inflation. How far do you think they can be effective?
9. In an inflationary situation, the task of fiscal policy is to close the inflationary gap by reducing government expenditure or raising taxes. Discuss.
10. What is meant by crowding out effect ? Show how the expansionary effect of fiscal policy is reduced by the crowding out effect.
11. Increase in government expenditure, especially financed by borrowing from the open market, crowds out private investment. Discuss.
12. How does mechanism of crowding out of private investment work? Does it always occur ? Explain.
13. How is private investment affected if increase in Government spending is financed by sale of Government bonds ? Do you think borrowing from the Central Bank to finance budget deficit is preferable if desired expansionary effect is to be realised ?
14. Explain how through fiscal policy measures inflation can be controlled.
15. To overcome recession whether increase in government expenditure or reduction in direct taxes would have greater expansionary effect. Explain.

PART — IV

ANALYSIS OF MONETARY SECTOR

- Demand for Money
- Supply of Money and its Determinants
- Money Market Equilibrium
- Monetary Policy for Economic Stabilisation
- Monetary Policy of Reserve Bank of India : Growth with Stability

CHAPTER 15

Demand for Money

Introduction

Why people have demand for money to hold is an important issue in macroeconomics. The level of demand for money not only determines the rate of interest but also prices and national income of the economy. *Classical economists considered money as simply a means of payment or medium of exchange*. In the classical model, people therefore demand money in order to make payments for their purchase of goods and services. In other words, they want to keep money for transaction purposes. *On the other hand, J.M. Keynes laid stress on the store of value function of money*. According to him, money is an asset and people want to hold it so as to take advantage of changes in the price of this asset, that is, the rate of interest. Therefore, Keynes emphasised another motive for holding money which he called speculative motive. As will be explained in detail below, under speculative motive people demand to hold money balances to take advantages from the future changes in the rate of interest, or what means the same thing, from the future changes in bond prices.

An essential point to be noted about people's demand for money is that what people want is not *nominal* money holdings but *real money balances* (This is also referred to as simply *real balances*). This means that people are interested in the purchasing power of their money holdings, that is, the value of money balances in terms of goods and services which they could buy. Thus, people would not be interested in merely nominal money holdings irrespective of the price level, that is, the number of rupee notes and bank deposits. If with the doubling of price level, nominal money holdings are also doubled, their *real money balances* would remain the same. If people are merely concerned with nominal money holdings irrespective of the price level, they are said to suffer from *money illusion*.

The demand for money has been a subject of lively debate in economics. Interest in the study of demand for money has been due to the important role that monetary demand plays in the determination of the price level, interest and income. Till recently there were three approaches to demand for money, namely, transactions approach of Fisher, Cash-balance approach of Cambridge economists, Marshall and Pigou and Keynes theory of demand for money. However, in recent years Baumol, Tobin and Friedman have put forward new theories of demand for money. We critically examine below all these theories of demand for money.

FISHER'S TRANSACTIONS APPROACH TO DEMAND FOR MONEY

In his theory of demand for money Fisher[1] and other classical economists laid stress on the medium of exchange function of money, that is, money as a means of buying goods and services. All transactions involving purchase of goods, services, raw materials, assets require payment of money as value of the transaction made. If accounting identity, namely value paid must equal value received is to occur, value of goods, services and assets sold must be equal to the value of money paid for them. Thus, in any given period, the value of all goods, services or assets sold must equal to the number of transactions T made multiplied by the average price of these transactions. Thus, the total value of transactions made is equal to PT.

1. Irving Fisher, *Purchasing Power of Money,* Macmillan, 1911.

On the other hand, because value paid is identically equal to the value of money flow used for buying goods, services and assets, the value of money flow is equal to the nominal quantity of money supply M multiplied by the average number of times the quantity of money in circulation is used or exchanged for transaction purposes. The average number of times a unit of money is used for transactions of goods, services and assets is called *transactions velocity of circulation* and is denoted by V.

Symbolically, Fisher's equation of exchange is written as under :

$$MV = PT \qquad ...(1)$$

where
M = the quantity of money in circulation
V = transactions velocity of circulation
P = Average price
T = the total number of transactions.

The above equation (1) is an identity, that is true by definition. However by taking some assumptions about the variables V and T, Fisher transformed the above identity into a theory of demand for money.

According to Fisher, the nominal quantity of money M is fixed by the Central Bank of a country (note that Reserve Bank of India is the Central Bank of India) and is therefore treated as an exogenous variable which is assumed to be a given quantity in a particular period of time. Further, the number of transactions in a period is a function of national income; the greater the national income, the larger the number of transactions required to be made. Further, since Fisher assumed that full employment of resources prevailed in the economy, the level of national income is determined by the amount of the fully employed resources. Thus, with the assumption of full employment of resources, the volume of transactions T is fixed in the short run.

But most important assumption which makes Fisher's equation of exchange as a theory of demand for money is that velocity of circulation (V) remains constant and is independent of M, P and T. This is because he thought that *velocity of circulation of money (V) is determined by institutional and technological factors involved in the transactions process*. Since these institutional and technological factors do not vary much in the short run, the transactions velocity of circulation of money (V) was assumed to be constant.

As we know that for money market to be in equilibrium, nominal quantity of money supply must be equal to the nominal quantity of money demand. In other words, for money market to be in equilibrium

$$M_s = M_d$$

where M_s is fixed by the Central Bank of a country.

With the above assumptions, Fisher's equation of exchange in (1) above can be rewritten as

$$M_d = \frac{PT}{V}$$

or

$$M_d = \frac{1}{V}.PT \qquad ...(2)$$

Thus, according to Fisher's transactions approach, demand for money depends on the following three factors:

(1) the number of transactions (T)

(2) the average price of transactions (P)

(3) the transaction velocity of circulation of money

It has been pointed out that Fisher's transactions approach represents some kind of a mechanical relation between demand for money (M_d) and the total value of transactions (PT). Thus Prof. Suraj Bhan Gupta says that in Fisher's approach the relation between demand for money M_d and the value of transactions (PT) "*betrays some kind of a mechanical relation between it (i.e. PT) and M_d as PT represents the total amount of work to be done by money as a medium of exchange. This makes demand for money (M_d) a technical requirement and not a behavioural function*"[2].

In Fisher's transactions approach to demand for money some serious problems are faced when it is used for empirical research. First, in Fisher's transactions approach, not only transactions involving current production of goods and services are included but also those which arise in sales and purchase of capital assets such as securities, shares, land etc. Due to frequent changes in the values of these capital assets, it is not appropriate to assume that T will remain constant even if Y is taken to be constant due to full-employment assumption.

The second problem which is faced in Fisher's approach is that it is difficult to define and determine a general price level that covers not only goods and services currently produced but also capital assets just mentioned above.

The Cambridge Cash Balance Theory of Demand for Money

Cambridge Cash Balance theory of demand for money was put forward by Cambridge economists, Marshall and Pigou[3]. This Cash Balance theory of demand for money differs from Fisher's transactions approach in that it *places emphasis on the function of money as a store of value or wealth* instead of Fisher's emphasis on the use of money as a medium of exchange. It is worth noting that the exchange function of money eliminates the need to barter and solves the problem of double coincidence of wants faced in the barter system. On the other hand, the function of money as a store of value lays stress on holding money as a general purchasing power by individuals over a period of time between the sale of a good or service and subsequent purchase of a good or service at a later date. Marshall and Pigou focussed their analysis on the factors that determine individual demand for holding cash balances. Although they recognised that current interest rate, wealth owned by the individuals, expectations of future prices and future rate of interest determine the demand for money, they however believed that changes in these factors remain constant or they are proportional to changes in individuals' income. Thus, they put forward a view that individual's demand for cash balances (*i.e.* nominal money balances) is proportional to the nominal income (*i.e.* money income). Thus, according to their approach, aggregate demand for money can be expressed as

$$M_d = kPY$$

where

Y = real national income

P = average price level of currently produced goods and services

PY = nominal income

k = proportion of nominal income (PY) that people want to hold as cash balances

Cambridge Cash balance approach to demand for money is illustrated in Fig. 15.1 where on the X-axis we measure nominal national income (PY) and on the Y-axis the demand for money (M_d). It will be seen from Fig. 15.1 that *demand for money (M_d) in this Cambridge Cash Balance Approach is a linear function of nominal income*. The slope of the function is equal to k, that is, $k = \frac{M_d}{P_y}$. Thus

2. S.B. Gupta, *Monetary Economics, Theory, Policy and Institutions*, 4th edition. 1997, p. 183.
3. A.C. Pigou, "Value of Money", *Quarterly Journal of Economics*, Vol. 32, 1917, pp. 38-65.

important feature of Cash balance approach is that *it makes the demand for money as function of money income alone.* A merit of this formulation is that it makes the relation between demand for money and income as behavioural in sharp contrast to Fisher's approach in which demand for money was related to total transactions in a mechanical manner.

Although, as mentioned above, Cambridge economists recognised the role of other factors such as rate of interest, wealth as the factors which play a part in the determination of demand for money but these factors were not systematically and formally incorporated into their analysis of demand for money. In their approach, these other factors determine the proportionality factor *k*, that is, the proportion of money income that people want to hold in the form of money, *i.e.* cash balances. It was J.M. Keynes who later emphasised the role of these other factors such as rate of interest, expectations regarding future interest rate and prices and formally incorporated them explicitly in his analysis of demand for money. Thus, Glahe rightly writes, "Cambridge approach is conceptually richer than the transactions approach, the former is incomplete because it does not formally incorporate the influence of economic variables just mentioned on the demand for cash balances... John Maynard Keynes first attempted to eliminate this shortcoming."[4]

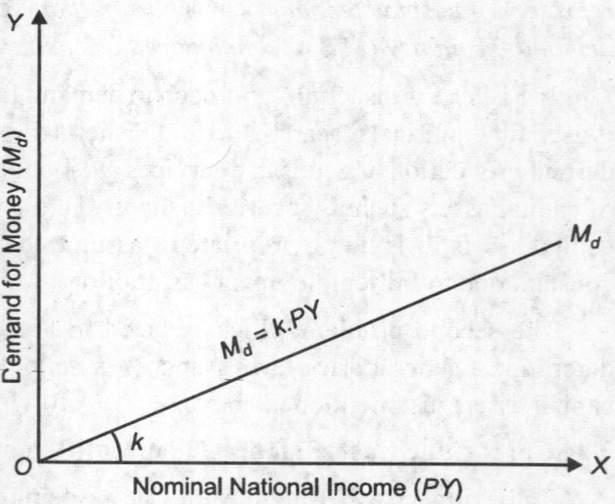

Fig. 15.1. *Demand for Money : Cambridge Cash Balance Approach.*

Another *important feature of Cambridge demand for money function is that the demand for money is proportional function of nominal income* ($M_d = kPY$). Thus, it is proportional function of both price level (P) and real income (Y). This implies two things. First, income elasticity of demand for money is unity and, secondly, price elasticity of demand for money is also equal to unity so that any change in the price level causes equal proportionate change in the demand for money.

Criticism. It has been pointed out by critics that other influences such as rate of interest, wealth, expectations regarding future prices have not been formally introduced into the Cambridge theory of the demand for cash balances. These other influences remain in the background of the theory. "It was left to Keynes, another Cambridge economist, to highlight the influence of the rate of interest on the demand for money and change the course of monetary theory."[5]

Another criticism levelled against this theory is that income elasticity of demand for money may well be different from unity. Cambridge economists did not provide any theoretical reason for its being equal to unity. Nor is there any empirical evidence supporting unitary income elasticity of demand for money. Besides, price elasticity of demand is also not necessarily equal to unity. In fact, changes in the price level may cause non-proportional changes in the demand for money. However, these criticisms are against the mathematical formulation of cash balance approach, namely, $M_d = kPY$. They do not deny the important relation between demand for money and the level of income. Empirical studies conducted so far point to a strong evidence that there is a significant and firm relation between demand for money and level of income.

---

4. Fred R. Glahe, *Macroeconomics: Theory and Policy*, 2nd Edition, 1977, Harcourt, p. 164.
5 S.B. Gupta, *op. cit.*, p. 184.

KEYNES' THEORY OF DEMAND FOR MONEY

In his well-known book[6], Keynes propounded a theory of demand for money which occupies an important place in his monetary theory.

It is also worth noting that for demand for money to hold Keynes used the term what he called *liquidity preference*. How much of his income or resources will a person hold in the form of ready money (cash or non-interest-paying bank deposits) and how much will he part with or lend depends upon what Keynes calls his "*liquidity preference*." Liquidity preference means the *demand for money to hold* or the desire of the public to hold cash.

Demand for Money or Motives for Liquidity Preference : Keynes' Theory

Liquidity preference of a particular individual depends upon several considerations. The question is: Why should the people hold their resources liquid or in the form of ready money when they can get interest by lending money or buying bonds? The desire for liquidity arises because of three motives : (*i*) the transactions motive, (*ii*) the precautionary motive, and (*iii*) the speculative motive.

The Transactions Demand for Money. The transactions motive relates to the demand for money or the need for money balances for the current transactions of individuals and business firms. Individuals hold cash in order "to bridge the interval between the receipt of income and its expenditure". In other words, people hold money or cash balances for transaction purposes, because receipt of money and payments do not coincide. Most of the people receive their incomes weekly or monthly while the expenditure goes on day by day. A certain amount of ready money, therefore, is kept in hand to make current payments. This amount will depend upon the size of the individual's income, the interval at which the income is received and the methods of payments prevailing in the society.

The businessmen and the entrepreneurs also have to keep a proportion of their resources in money form in order to meet daily needs of various kinds. They need money all the time in order to pay for raw materials and transport, to pay wages and salaries and to meet all other current expenses incurred by any business firm. It is clear that the amount of money held under this business motive will depend to a very large extent on the turnover (*i.e.*, the volume of trade of the firm in question). The larger the turnover, the larger, in general, will be the amount of money needed to cover current expenses. It is worth noting that money demand for transactions motive arises primarily because of the use of money as a medium of exchange (*i.e.* means of payment).

Since the transactions demand for money arises because individuals have to incur expenditure on goods and services during the receipt of income and its use of payment for goods and services, money held for this motive depends upon the level of income of an individual. A poor man will hold less money for transactions motive as he spends less because of his small income. On the other hand, a rich man will tend to hold more money for transactions motive as his expenditure will be relatively greater.

The demand for money is a demand for *real* cash balances because people hold money for the purpose of buying goods and services. The higher the price level, the more money balances a person has to hold in order to purchase a given quantity of goods. If the price level doubles, then the individual has to keep twice the amount of money balances in order to be able to buy the same quantity of goods. Thus the demand for money balances is demand for *real* rather than *nominal* balances.

According to Keynes, the transactions demand for money depends only on the real income and is not influenced by the rate of interest. However, in recent years, it has been observed empirically and also according to the theories of Tobin and Baumol transactions demand for money also depends on the rate of interest. This can be explained in terms of *opportunity cost* of money holdings. Holding one's asset in the form of money balances has an opportunity cost. The cost of holding money

6. J.M. Keynes, *General Theory of Employment, Interest and Money*, Macmillan, 1936

balances is the interest that is foregone by holding money balances rather than other assets. The higher the interest rate, the greater the opportunity cost of holding money rather than non-money assets. Individuals and business firms economise on their holding of money balances by carefully managing their money balances through transfer of money into bonds or short-term income yielding non-money assets. Thus, at higher interest rates, individuals and business firms will keep less money holdings at each level of income.

Precautionary Demand for Money. Precautionary motive for holding money refers to the desire of the people to hold cash balances for unforeseen contingencies. People hold a certain amount of money to provide for the danger of unemployment, sickness, accidents, and the other uncertain perils. The amount of money demanded for this motive will depend on the psychology of the individual and the conditions in which he lives.

Speculative Demand for Money. The speculative motive of the people relates to the desire to hold one's resources in liquid form in order to take advantage of market movements regarding the future changes in the rate of interest (or bond prices). The notion of holding money for speculative motive was a new and revolutionary Keynesian idea. Money held under the speculative motive serves as a store of value as money held under the precautionary motive does. But it is a store of money meant for a different purpose. The cash held under this motive is used to make speculative gains by dealing in bonds[7] whose prices fluctuate. If bond prices are expected to rise which, in other words, means that the rate of interest is expected to fall, businessmen will buy bonds to sell when their prices actually rise. If, however, bond prices are expected to fall, *i.e.*, the rate of interest is expected to rise, businessmen will sell bonds to avoid capital losses. Nothing is certain in the dynamic world, where guesses about the future course of events are made on precarious basis, businessmen keep cash to speculate on the probable future changes in bond prices (or the rate of interest) with a view to making profits.

Given the expectations about the changes in the rate of interest in future, less money will be held under the speculative motive at a *higher current* rate of interest and more money will be held under this motive at a *lower current* rate of interest. The reason for this inverse correlation between money held for speculative motive and the prevailing rate of interest is that at a lower rate of interest less is lost by not lending money or investing it, that is, by holding on to money, while at a higher current rate of interest holders of cash balance would lose more by not lending or investing.

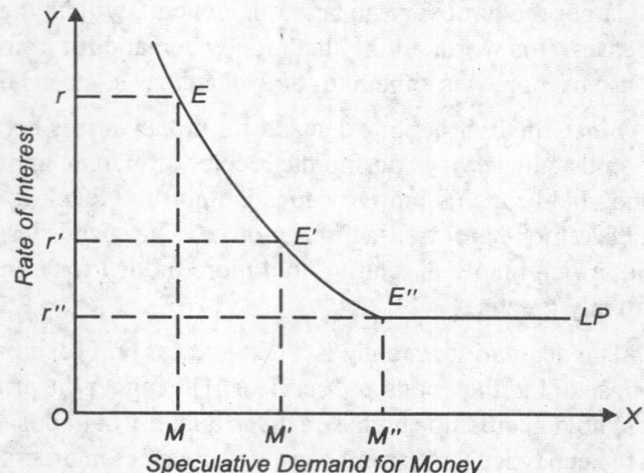

Fig. 15.2. *Liquidity Preference Curve and Liquidity Trap.*

Thus the demand for money under speculative motive is a function of the current rate of interest, increasing as the interest rate falls and decreasing as the interest rate rises. Thus, demand for money under this motive is a decreasing function of the rate of interest. This is shown in Fig. 15.2. Along *X*-axis we represent the speculative demand for money and along the *Y*-axis the current rate of interest The liquidity preference curve *LP* is downward sloping towards the right signifying that the higher the rate of interest, the lower the demand for money for speculative

7. All securities and other such papers which yield a fixed and known rate of interest over a period of time are known as bonds.

motive, and vice versa. Thus at the high current rate of interest *Or*, a very small amount *OM* is held for speculative motive. This is because at a high current rate of interest more money would have been lent out or used for buying bonds and therefore less money would be kept as inactive balances. If the rate of interest falls to *Or'*, then a greater amount of money *OM'* is held under speculative motive. With the further fall in the rate of interest to *Or'*, money held under speculative motive increases to *OM*.

Liquidity Trap. It will be seen from Fig. 15.2 that the liquidity preference curve *LP* becomes quite flat *i.e.*, perfectly elastic at a very low rate of interest; it is horizontal line beyond point *E''* towards the right. This perfectly elastic portion of liquidity preference curve indicates the position of *absolute liquidity* preference of the people. That is, at a very low rate of interest people will hold with them as inactive balances any amount of money they come to have. This portion of liquidity preference curve with absolute liquidity preference is called *liquidity trap* by the economists because expansion in money supply gets trapped in the sphere of liquidity trap and therefore cannot affect rate of interest and therefore the level of investment. According to Keynes, it is because of the existence of liquidity trap that monetary policy becomes ineffective to tide over economic depression.

But the demand for money to satisfy the speculative motive does not depend so much upon what the current rate of interest is, as on expectations about changes in the rate of interest. If there is a change in the expectations regarding the future rate of interest, the whole curve of demand for money or liquidity pref rence for speculative motive will change accordingly. Thus, if the public on balance expect the rate of interest to be higher (*i.e.*, bond prices to be lower) in the future than had been previously supposed, the speculative demand for money will increase and the whole liquidity preference curve for speculative motive will shift upward.

Aggregate Demand for Money : Keynes' View

If the total demand of money is represented by M_d we may refer to that part of M held for transactions and precautionary motive as M_1 and to that part held for the speculative motive as M_2. Thus $M_d = M_1 + M_2$. According to Keynes, the money held under the transactions and precautionary motives, *i.e.*, M_1, is completely interest-inelastic unless the interest rate is very high. The amount of money held as M_1, that is, for transactions and precautionary motives, is mainly a function of the size of income and business transactions together with the contingencies growing out of the conduct of personal and business affairs. We can write this in a functional form as follows:

$$M_1 = L_1(Y) \quad \text{...}(i)$$

where Y stands for income, L_1 for demand function, and M_1 for money demanded or held under the transactions and precautionary motives. The above function implies that money held under the transactions and precautionary motives is a function of income.

On the other hand, according to Keynes, money demanded for speculative motive, *i.e.*, M_2, as explained above, is primarily a function of the rate of interest. This can be written as:

$$M_2 = L_2(r) \quad \text{...}(ii)$$

where r stands for the rate of interest, L_2 for demand function for speculative motive.

Since total demand of money $M_d = M_1 + M_2$, we get from (*i*) and (*ii*) above

$$M_d = L_1(Y) + L_2(r)$$

Thus, according to Keynes' theory of total demand for money is an *additive demand function* with two separate components. The one component, $L_1(Y)$ represents the transactions demand for money arising out of transactions and precautionary motives is an increasing function of the level of money income. The second component of the demand for money, that is, $L_2(r)$ represents the speculative demand for money, which depends upon rate of interest, is a decreasing function of the rate of interest.

Critique of Keynes' Theory

By introducing speculative demand for money, Keynes made a significant departure from the classical theory of money demand which emphasized only the transactions demand for money. However, as seen above, Keynes' theory of speculative demand for money has been challenged. The main drawback of Keynes' speculative demand for money is that *it visualises that people hold their assets in either all money or all bonds*. This seems quite unrealistic as individuals hold their financial wealth in some combination of both money and bonds. This gave rise to portfolio approach to demand for money put forward by Tobin, Baumol and Friedman. The portfolio of wealth consists of money, interest-bearing bonds, shares, physical assets etc. Further, while according to Keynes' theory, demand for money for transaction purposes is insensitive to interest rate, the modern theories of money demand put forward by Baumol and Tobin show that money held for transaction purposes is interest elastic. We will discuss in the next chapter the post-Keynesian theories of demand for money put forward by Tobin, Baumol and Friedman.

Further, Keynes' *additive form* of demand for money function, namely, $M_d = L_1(Y) + L_2(r)$ has now been rejected by the modern economists. It has been pointed out that *money represents a single asset*, and not the several ones. There may be more than one motive to hold money but the same units of money can serve several motives. Therefore, the demand for money cannot be divided into two or more different departments independent of each other.

Further, as has been argued by Tobin and Baumol, the transactions demand for money also depends upon the rate of interest. Others have explained that speculative demand for money is an increasing function of the total assets or wealth. If income is taken as a proxy for total wealth then even speculative demand for money will depend upon the size of income, apart from the rate of interest. In view of all these arguments, the Keynesian total demand for money function is written in the following modified form

$$M_d = L(Y, r)$$

where it is conceived that demand for money function (M_d) is increasing function of the level of income, it is a decreasing function of the rate of interest. The presentation of the demand for money function in the above revised and modified form, $M_d = L(Y, r)$ has been a highly significant development in monetary theory.

TOBIN'S PORTFOLIO APPROACH TO DEMAND FOR MONEY

American economist James Tobin, in his important contribution, explained that rational behaviour on the part of the individuals is that they should keep a portfolio of assets which consists of both bonds and money. In his analysis he makes a valid assumption that people prefer more wealth to less. According to him, an investor is faced with a problem of what proportion of his portfolio of financial assets he should keep in the form of money (which earns no interest) and interest-bearing bonds. The portfolio of individuals may also consist of more risky assets such as shares. According to Tobin, *faced with various safe and risky assets, individuals diversify their portfolio by holding a balanced combination of safe and risky assets*[8]. He points out that individual's behaviour shows *risk aversion*. That is, they prefer less risk to more risk at a given rate of return. In Keynes' analysis an individual holds his wealth in either all money or all bonds depending upon his estimate of the future rate of interest. But, according to Tobin, individuals are uncertain about future rate of interest. If a wealth holder chooses to hold a greater proportion of risky assets such as bonds in his portfolio, he will be earning a high average return but will bear a higher degree of risk. Tobin argues that a risk averter will not opt for such a portfolio with all risky bonds or a greater proportion of them.

8. James Tobin, "Liquidity Preference as Behaviour Towards Risk", *Review of Economic Studies,* Vol. 25 (1958).

On the other hand, a person who, in his portfolio of wealth, holds only safe and riskless assets such as money (in the form of currency and demand deposits in banks) he will be taking almost zero risk but will also be having no return and as a result there will be no growth of his wealth. Therefore, people generally prefer a mixed diversified portfolio of money, bonds and shares, with each person opting for a little different balance between riskiness and return.

It is important to note that a person will be unwilling to hold all risky assets such as bonds unless he obtains a higher average return on them. In view of the desire of individuals to have both safety and reasonable return, they strike a balance between them and hold a mixed and balanced portfolio consisting of money (which is a safe and riskless asset) and risky assets such as bonds and shares though this balance or mix varies between various individuals depending on their attitude towards risk and hence their trade-off between risk and return.

Tobin's Liquidity Preference Function

Tobin derived his liquidity preference function depicting relationship between rate of interest and demand for money (that is, preference for holding wealth in money form which is a safe and "riskless" asset[9]. He argues that with the increase in the rate of interest (*i.e.* rate of return on bonds), wealth holders will be generally attracted to hold a greater fraction of their wealth in bonds and thus reduce their holding of money. That is, at a higher rate of interest, their demand for holding money (*i.e.*, liquidity) will be less and therefore they will hold more bonds in their portfolio. On the other hand, at a lower rate of interest they will hold more money and less bonds in their portfolio. This means, like Keynes' speculative demand for money, in Tobin's portfolio approach demand function for money as an asset (*i.e.* his liquidity preference function curve) slopes downwards as is shown in Fig. 15.3, where on the horizontal axis asset demand for money is shown. This downward-sloping liquidity preference function curve shows that the asset demand for money in the portfolio increases as the rate of interest on bonds falls. In this way Tobin derives the aggregate liquidity preference curve by determining the effects of changes in interest rate on the asset demand for money in the portfolio of individuals. Tobin's liquidity preference theory has been found to be true by the empirical studies conducted to measure interest elasticity of the demand for money. As shown by Tobin through his portfolio approach, these empirical studies reveal that aggregate liquidity preference curve is negatively sloped. This means that most of the people in the economy have liquidity preference function similar to the one shown by curve M_d in Fig. 15.3.

Evaluation

Tobin's approach has done away with the limitation of Keynes' theory of liquidity preference for speculative motive, namely, individuals hold their wealth in *either all money or all bonds*. Thus, Tobin's approach, according to which individuals simultaneously hold both money and bonds but in different proportion at different rates of interest, yields a *continuous* liquidity preference curve. Further, Tobin's analysis of simultaneous holding of money and bonds is not based on the erroneous Keynes' assumption that interest rate will move only in one direction but on a simple fact that individuals do not know with certainty which

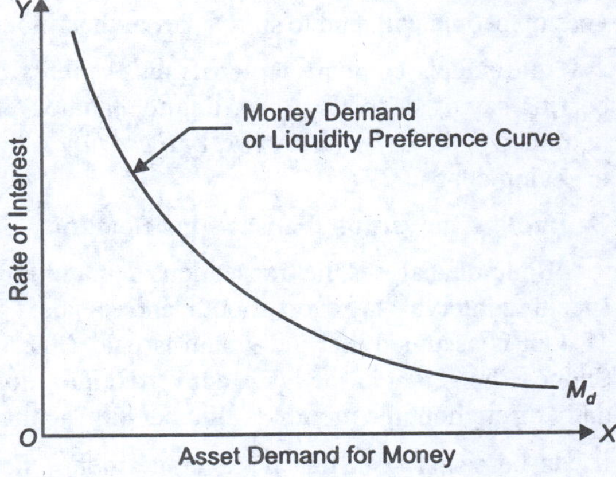

Fig. 15.3. *Tobin's Liquidity Preference Curve.*

9. Note that riskless is written in quotes because strictly speaking even money defined as currency and demand deposits is also not completely riskless in view of the frequent changes in prices of commodities. If inflation occurs, it reduces the value of money and thus inflicts a capital loss on its holders.

way the interest rate will change. It is worth mentioning that Tobin's portfolio approach, according to which liquidity preference (*i.e.* demand for money) is determined by the individual attitude towards risk, can be extended to the problem of asset choice when there are several alternative assets, not just two, of money and bonds.

BAUMOL'S INVENTORY APPROACH TO TRANSACTIONS DEMAND FOR MONEY

Instead of Keynes' speculative demand for money, Baumol concentrated on transactions demand for money and put forward a new approach to explain it. Baumol explains the transactions demand for money from the viewpoint of the inventory control or inventory management similar to the inventory management of goods and materials by business firms. As businessmen keep inventories of goods and materials to facilitate transactions or exchange in the context of changes in demand for them, Baumol asserts that individuals also hold *inventory of money* because this facilitates transactions (*i.e.* purchases) of goods and services.[10]

In view of the cost incurred on holding inventories of goods there is need for keeping *optimal inventory* of goods to reduce cost. Similarly, individuals have to keep *optimum inventory of money* for transactions purposes. Individuals also incur cost when they hold inventories of money for transaction purposes. They incur cost on these inventories as *they have to forgo interest which they could have earned if they had kept their wealth in saving deposits or fixed deposits or invested in bonds*. This interest income forgone is the cost of holding money for transaction purposes. In this way *Baumol and Tobin emphasised that transaction demand for money is not independent of the rate of interest.*

It may be noted that by money we mean currency and demand deposits which are quite safe and riskless but carry no interest. On the other hand, bonds yield interest or return but are risky and may involve capital loss if wealth holders invest in them. However, saving deposits in banks, according to Baumol, are quite free from risk and also yield some interest. Therefore, Baumol asks the question why an individual holds money (*i.e.* currency and demand deposits) instead of keeping his wealth in saving deposits which are quite safe and earn some interest as well. According to him, it is for convenience and capability of it being easily used for transactions of goods that people hold money with them in preference to the saving deposits. Unlike Keynes both *Baumol and Tobin argue that transactions demand for money depends on the rate of interest*. People hold money for transaction purposes "*to bridge the gap between the receipt of income and its spending*."[11] As interest rate on saving deposits goes up people will tend to shift a part of their money holdings to the interest-bearing saving deposits.

Individuals compare the costs and benefits of funds in the form of money with the interest-bearing saving deposits. According to Baumol, the cost which people incur when they hold funds in money is the *opportunity cost of these funds*, that is, interest income forgone by not putting them in saving deposits.

Baumol's Analysis of Transactions Demand

Baumol analyses the transactions demand for money of an individual who receives income at a specified interval, say every month, and spends it gradually at a steady rate. This is illustrated in Fig. 15.4. It is assumed that individual is paid ₹ 12000 salary cheque on the first day of each month. Suppose he gets it cashed (*i.e.* converted into money) on the very first day and gradually spends it daily throughout the month. (₹ 400 per day) so that at the end of the month he is left with no money. It can be easily seen that his average money holding in the month will be ₹ $\frac{12000}{2}$ = ₹ 6,000

10. See James Tobin, "The Interest Elasticity of Transactions Demand for Cash," *Review of Economics and Statistics*, Vol. 38 (1956).
11. W.J. Baumol, "The Transactions Demand for Cash: An Inventory Theoretic Approach", *Quarterly Journal of Economics*, Vol. 66 (Nov. 1952).

(before 15th of a month he will be having more than ₹ 6,000 and after 15th day he will have less than ₹ 6,000). Average holding of money equal to ₹ 6,000 has been shown by the dotted line. Now, the question arises whether it is the optimal strategy of managing money or what is called optimal cash management. The simple answer is no. This is because the individual is losing interest which he could have earned if he had deposited some funds in interest-bearing saving deposits instead of withdrawing all his salary in cash on the first day. He can manage his money balances so as to earn some interest income as well. Suppose, instead of withdrawing his entire salary on the first day of a month, he withdraws only half of it (*i.e.* ₹ 6,000) in cash and deposits the remaining amount of ₹ 6,000 in saving account which gives him interest of 5 per cent, his expenditure per day remaining constant at ₹ 400. This is illustrated in Fig. 15.5. It will be seen that his money holdings of ₹ 6,000 will be reduced to zero at the end of the 15th day of each month. Now, he can withdraw ₹ 6,000 on the morning of 16th of each month and then spends it gradually, at a steady rate of 400 per day for the next 15 days of a month. This is a better method of managing funds as he will be earning interest on ₹ 6,000 for 15 days in each month. Average money holdings in this money management scheme is ₹ $\frac{6000}{2} = 3000$.

Likewise, the individual may decide to withdraw ₹ 4,000 (*i.e.*, 1/3rd of his salary) on the first day of each month and deposits ₹ 8,000 in the saving deposits. His ₹ 4,000 will be reduced to zero, as he spends his money on transactions (that is, buying of goods and services), at the end of the 10th day and on the morning of 11th of each month he again withdraws ₹ 4,000 to spend on goods and services till the end of the 20th day and on 21st day of the month he again withdraws ₹ 4,000 to spend steadily till the end of the month. In this scheme on an average he will be holding ₹ $\frac{4000}{2} = 2000$ and will be investing remaining funds in saving deposits and earn interest on them. Thus, in this scheme he will be earning more interest income.

Now, which scheme will he decide to adopt? It may be noted that investing in saving deposits and then withdrawing cash from it to meet the transactions demand involves cost also. Cost on brokerage fee is incurred when one invests in interest-bearing bonds and sells them. Even in case of saving deposits, the asset which we are taking for illustration, one has to spend on transportation costs for making extra trips to the bank for withdrawing money from the Savings Account. Besides, one has to spend time in the waiting line in the bank to withdraw cash each time from the saving deposits. Thus, the greater the number of times an individual makes trips to the bank for withdrawing money, the greater the broker's fee he will incur. If he withdraws more cash, he will be avoiding

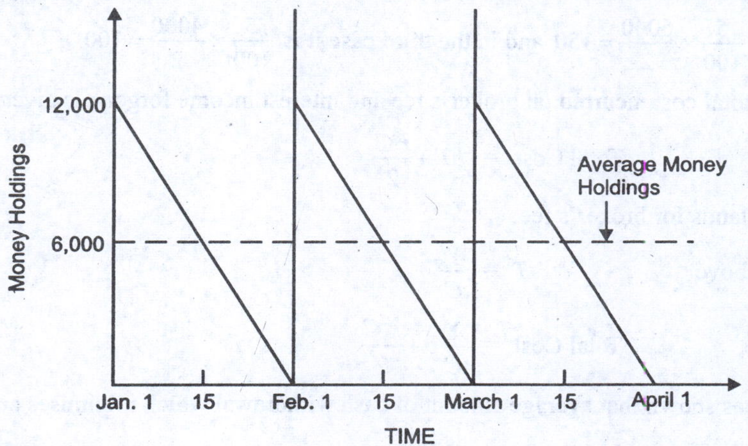

Fig. 15.4. *Stream of Cash Payments and Transactions Demand for Money.*

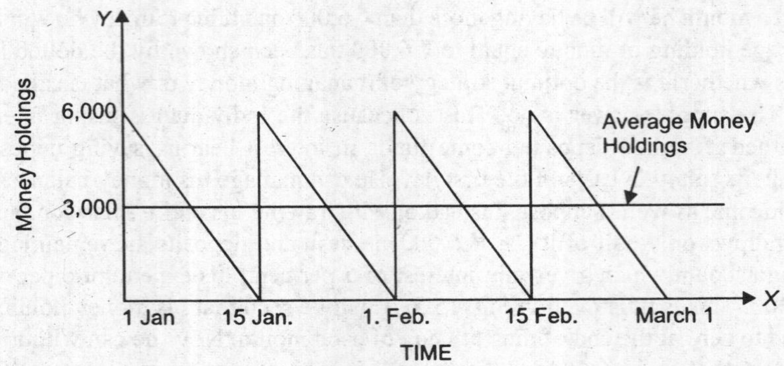

Fig. 15.5. *Transactions Demand for Money and Stream of Cash Payments.*

some costs on account of brokerage fee. Thus, individual faces a *trade-off problem*; the greater the amount of pay cheque he withdraws in cash, less the cost on account of broker's fee but the greater the opportunity cost of forgoing interest income. The problem is therefore to determine an optimum amount of money to hold. Baumol has shown that *optimal amount of money holding is determined by minimising the cost of interest income forgone and broker's fee.* Let us elaborate it further.

Let the size of the pay cheque (*i.e.* salary) be denoted by *Y*, the average amount of the cash he withdraws each time the individual goes to the bank by *C*, the number of times he goes to the bank to withdraw cash by *T*, broker's fee which he has to bear each time he makes a trip to the bank by *b*. In the first scheme of money management when he gets his whole pay-cheque cashed on the first day of every month he incurs broker's fee only once since he makes only a single trip to the bank. Thus *T* in our first case is equal to one $T = \frac{Y}{C} = \frac{12000}{12000} = 1$ because in this case $C = Y$. In the second case $T = \frac{12000}{6000} = 2$ and in the third case $T = \frac{12000}{4000} = 3$.

Interest income lost by holding money is the average amount of money holding multiplied by the interest rate. As seen above, average money held is one half of cash withdrawn each time $\left(i.e, \frac{C}{2}\right)$. Thus, interest income lost in the first case is $\frac{rC}{2} = \frac{5}{100} \times \frac{1200}{2} =$ ₹ 300, in the second case interest lost $= r.\frac{C}{2} = \frac{5}{100} \times \frac{6000}{2} = 150$ and in the third case it is $\frac{5}{100} \times \frac{4000}{2} = 100$.

Thus the total cost incurred on broker's fee and interest income forgone is given by

$$\text{Total Cost} = bT + \frac{r.C}{2}$$

where *b* stands for broker's fee.

As seen above $$T = \frac{Y}{C}$$

Therefore, $$\text{Total Cost} = \frac{Y}{C}b + \frac{r.C}{2}$$

Baumol has shown that average amount of cash withdrawal which minimises cost is given by

$$C = \sqrt{\frac{2bY}{r}}$$

This means that average *amount of cash withdrawal which minimises cost is the square root of the two times broker's fee multiplied by the size of individual's income (Y) and divided by the interest rate*. This is generally referred to as *Square Root Rule*. For this rule, it follows that a higher broker's fee will raise the money holdings as it will discourage the individuals to make more trips to the bank. On the other hand, a higher interest rate will induce them to reduce their money holdings for transaction purposes as they will be induced to keep more funds in saving deposits to earn higher interest income. That is, at a higher rate of interest transactions demand for money holdings will decline.

As we have studied earlier, Keynes thought that transactions demand for money was independent of rate of interest. According to him, transactions demand for money depends on the level of income. However, Baumol and Tobin have shown that transactions demand for money is sensitive to rate of interest. As explained above, *interest represents the opportunity cost of holding money instead of bonds, saving and fixed deposits*. The higher the rate of interest, the greater the opportunity cost of holding money (*i.e.* the greater the interest income forgone for holding money for transactions). Therefore, *at a higher rate of interest people will try to economise the use of money and will demand less money for transactions*. At a lower interest rate on bonds, saving and fixed deposits, the opportunity cost of holding money will be less which will prompt people to hold more money for transactions. Therefore, according to Baumol and Tobin, transactions demand curve for money slopes downward as shown in Fig. 15.6. At higher interest rates, bonds, savings and fixed deposits are more attractive relative to money holding for transactions. Therefore, at higher interest rates people tend to hold less money for transaction purposes. On the other hand, when the rates of interest are low, opportunity cost of holding money will be less and, as a consequence, people will hold more money for transactions. Therefore, the curve of transactions demand for money slopes downward.

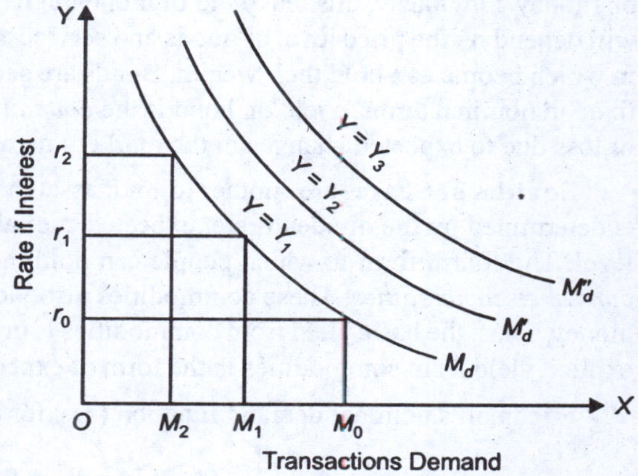

Fig. 15.6. *Transactions Demand for Money : Baumol-Tobin Approach.*

It will be observed from the square root rule given above that transactions demand for money varies directly with the income (*Y*) of the individuals. Therefore, the higher the level of income, the greater the transactions demand for money at a given rate of interest. In Fig. 15.6. the three transactions demand curves for money M_d, M_d' and M_d'', for three different income levels, Y_1, Y_2, Y_3 are shown. It will be known from the square root rule that optimum money holding for transactions will increase less than proportionately to the increase in income. Thus, transactions demand for money, according to Baumol and Tobin, is function of both rate of interest and the level of income.

$$M_{td} = f(r, Y)$$

where M_{td} stands for transactions demand for money, *r* for rate of interest and *Y* for the level of income.

FRIEDMAN'S THEORY OF DEMAND FOR MONEY

A noted monetarist economist Friedman put forward demand for money function which plays an important role in his restatement of the quantity theory of money and prices. In this section we shall be concerned with Friedman's money demand function and will explain in a later chapter money which shows how the changes in money supply affect the price level in the economy. *Friedman believes that money demand function is most important stable function of macroeconomics. He treats money as one type of asset in which wealth holders can keep a part of their wealth.* Business firms view money as a capital good or a factor of production which they combine with the services of other productive assets or labour to produce goods and services. Thus, according to Friedman, individuals hold money for the services it provides to them. It may be noted that the service rendered by money is that it serves as a general purchasing power so that it can be conveniently used for buying goods and services. *His approach to demand for money does not consider any motives for holding money,* nor does it distinguish between speculative and transactions demand for money. Friedman considers the demand for money merely as an application of a general theory of demand for capital assets.

Like other capital assets, money also yields return and provides services. He analyses the various factors that determine the demand for money and from this analysis derives demand for money function. Note that the value of goods and services which money can buy represents the real yield on money. Obviously, this real yield of money in terms of goods and services which it can purchase will depend on the price level of goods and services. Besides money, *bonds* are another type of asset in which people can hold their wealth. Bonds are securities which yield a stream of interest income, fixed in nominal terms. Yield on bond is the *coupon rate of interest* and also anticipated capital gain or loss due to expected changes in the market rate of interest.

Equities or Shares are another form of asset in which wealth can be held. The yield from equity is determined by the dividend rate, expected capital gain or loss and expected changes in the price level. The fourth form in which people can hold their wealth is the *stock of producer and durable consumer commodities*. These commodities also yield a stream of income but in kind rather than in money. Thus, the basic yield from commodities is implicit one. However, Friedman also considers an explicit yield from commodities in the form of expected rate of change in their price per unit of time.

Friedman's nominal demand function (M_d) for money can be written as

$$M_d = f\left(W, h, r_m, r_b, r_e, P, \frac{\Delta P}{P}, U\right)$$

As demand for real money balances is nominal demand for money divided by the price level, demand for real money balances can be written as

$$\frac{M_d}{P} = f\left(W, h, r_m, r_b, r_e, \frac{\Delta P}{P}, U\right)$$

where M_d stands for *nominal* demand for money and $\frac{M_d}{P}$ for demand for real money balances, W stands for wealth of the individuals, h for the proportion of human wealth to the total wealth held by the individuals, r_m for rate of return or interest on money, r_b for rate of interest on bonds, r_e for rate of return on equities, P for the price level, $\frac{\Delta P}{P}$ for the change in price level (*i.e.* rate of inflation), and U for the institutional factors.

1. **Wealth** (*W*): The major factor determining the demand for money is the wealth of the individual (*W*). In wealth Friedman includes not only *non-human wealth* such as bonds, shares, money which yield various rates of return but also *human wealth* or *human capital*. By human wealth Friedman means the value of an individual's present and future earnings. Whereas non-human wealth can be easily converted into money, that is, can be made liquid. Such substitution of human wealth is not easily possible. Thus human wealth represents illiquid component of wealth and, therefore, the proportion of human wealth to the non-human wealth has been included in the demand for money function as an independent variable.

Individual's demand for money directly depends on his total wealth. Indeed, the total wealth of an individual represents an upper limit of holding money by an individual and is similar to the budget constraint of the consumer in the theory of demand. The greater the wealth of an individual, the more money he will demand for transactions and other purposes. As a country becomes richer, its demand for money for transaction and other purposes will increase. Since as compared to non-human wealth, human wealth is much less liquid, Friedman has argued that as the proportion of human wealth in the total wealth increases, there will be a greater demand for money to make up for the illiquidity of human wealth.

2. Rates of Interest or Return (r_m, r_b, r_e). Friedman considers three rates of interest, namely, r_m, r_b and r_e which determine the demand for money. r_m is the own rate of interest on money. Note that money kept in the form of currency and demand deposits does not earn any interest. But money held as saving deposits and fixed deposits earns certain rates of interest and it is this rate of interest which is designated by r_m in the money demand function. Given the other rates of interest or return, the higher the own rate of interest, the greater the demand for money.

In deciding how large a part of his wealth to hold in the form of money the individual will compare the rate of interest on money with rates of interest (or return) on bonds and other assets. As mentioned earlier, *the opportunity cost of holding money is the interest or return given up by not holding these other forms of assets*. As rates of return on bond (r_b) and equities (r_e) rise, the opportunity cost of holding money will increase which will reduce the demand for money holdings. Thus, the *demand for money is negatively related to the rate of interest (or return) on bonds, equities and other such non-money assets*.

3. **Price Level (P).** Price level also determines the demand for money balances. A higher price level means people will require a larger *nominal money balance* in order to do the same amount of transactions, that is, to purchase the same amount of goods and services. *If income (Y) is used as proxy for wealth (W) which, as stated above, is the most important determinant of demand for money, then nominal income is given by Y.P* which becomes a crucial determinant of demand for money. Here Y stands for real income (*i.e.* in terms of goods and services) and P for price level. As the price level goes up, the demand for money will rise and, on the other hand, if price level falls, the demand for money will decline. As a matter of fact, people adjust the nominal money balances (M) to achieve their desired level of real money balances $\left(\frac{M}{P}\right)$.

4. **The Expected Rate of Inflation $\left(\frac{\Delta P}{P}\right)$.** If people expect a higher rate of inflation, they will reduce their demand for money holdings. This is because inflation reduces the value of their money balances in terms of its power to purchase goods and services. If the rate of inflation exceeds the nominal rate of interest, there will be negative rate of return on money. Therefore, when people expect a higher rate of inflation they will tend to convert their money holdings into goods or other assets which are not affected by inflation.

On the other hand, if people expect a fall in the price level, their demand for money holdings will increase.

5. **Institutional Factors (U).** Institutional factors such as mode of wage payments and bill payments also affect the demand for money. Several other factors which influence the overall economic environment affect the demand for money. For example, if recession or war is anticipated, the demand for money balances will increase. Besides, instability in capital markets, which erodes the confidence of the people in making profits from investment in bonds and equity shares, will also raise the demand for money. Even political instability in the country influences the demand for money. To account for these institutional factors Friedman includes the variable U in his demand for money function.

Simplifying Friedman's Demand for Money Function

A major problem faced in using Friedman's demand for money function has been that due to the non-existence of reliable data about the value of wealth (W), it is difficult to estimate the demand for money. To overcome this difficulty Friedman suggested that since the *present value of* wealth or $W = \frac{Y_P}{r}$ (where Y_p is the permanent income and r is the rate of interest on money.), permanent income Y_p can be used as a proxy variable for wealth. Incorporating this in Friedman's demand for money function we have

$$M_d = \left(Y_p, h, r_m, r_b, r_e \frac{\Delta P}{P}, U\right)$$

If we assume that no price change is anticipated and institutional factors such as h and U remain fixed in the short run and also all the three rates of interest return are clubbed into one, Friedman's demand for money function is simplified to

$$M_d = f(Y_p r)$$

QUESTIONS FOR REVIEW

1. Explain Tobin's Portfolio Approach to demand for money. Why, according to Tobin, asset demand for money increases as the rate of interest on bonds falls ?
2. How does Tobin's approach to liquidity preference differ from Keynes' liquidity preference function ?
3. How does Baumol-Tobin model explain that the transactions demand for money is a function of interest rate and level of income ?
4. Explain why the transactions demand for money depends not only on the level of income but also on the rate of interest.
5. Explain Friedman's theory of demand for money. How does it differ from Keynes' theory of demand for money ?
6. What, according to Friedman, are the main factors that determine demand for money. How do the stock of wealth and rate of interest influence the demand for money ?
7. State and explain Friedman's Quantity Theory of demand for money. Friedman thinks that his theory is closely related to Cambridge version of quantity theory of money while Don Patinkin holds that Friedman provides us a most elegant and sophisticated statement of Keynesian theory of demand for money. Discuss.

CHAPTER 16

Supply of Money and Its Determinants

Money supply plays a crucial role in the determination of price level and interest rate. In the present chapter we shall explain what determines the money supply in an economy. In economic analysis it is generally presumed that money supply is determined by the policy of Central Bank of a country and the Government. However, this is not fully correct as in the determination of money supply, besides Central Bank and Government, the public and commercial banks also play an important role. There are various measures of money supply depending upon which types of deposits of banks and other financial institutions are included in it. We will explain various measures of money supply later in this chapter.

Importance of Money Supply

Growth of money supply is an important factor not only for acceleration of the process of economic development but also for the achievement of price stability in the economy. What constitutes the money supply and what factors cause variation and growth in money supply will be explained in the present chapter. There must be controlled expansion of money supply if the objective of development with stability is to be achieved. A healthy growth of an economy requires that there should be neither inflation nor deflation. Inflation is the greatest headache of a developing economy. A mild inflation arising out of the creation of money by deficit financing may stimulate investment by raising profit expectations and extracting forced savings. But a runaway inflation is highly detrimental to economic growth. The developing economies have to face the problem of inadequacy of resources in initial stages of development and it can make up this deficiency by deficit financing. But it has to be kept strictly within safe limits. Thus, increase in money supply affects vitally the rate of economic growth. In fact, it is now regarded as a legitimate instrument of economic growth. Kept within proper limits it can accelerate economic growth but exceeding of the limits will retard it. Thus, management of money supply is essential in the interest of steady economic growth.

THE CONCEPT OF MONEY SUPPLY AND ITS MEASUREMENT

By money supply we mean the total stock of monetary media of exchange available to a society for use in connection with the economic activity of the country. According to the standard concept of money supply, it is composed of the following two elements:

1. Currency with the public,
2. Demand deposits with the public.

Before explaining these two components of money supply two things must be noted with regard to the money supply in the economy. First, the money supply refers to the total sum of money available to the public in the economy *at a point of time*. That is, money supply is a *stock concept* in sharp contrast to the national income which is a flow representing the value of goods and services produced *per unit of time*, usually taken as a year. Secondly, money supply always refers to the amount of money *held by the public*. In the term public are included households, firms and institutions other than banks and the government. The rationale behind considering money supply as held by the public is to separate the producers of money from those who use money to fulfil their various types of demand for money.

Since the Government and the banks produce or create money for the use by the public, the money (cash reserves) held by them are not used for transaction and speculative purposes and are excluded from the standard measures of money supply. This *separation of producers of money from the users of money is important from the viewpoint of both monetary theory and policy.*[1]

Let us explain the two components of money supply at some length.

Currency with the Public

In order to arrive at the total currency with the public in India we add the following items:

1. Currency notes in circulation issued by the Reserve Bank of India.
2. The number of rupee notes and coins in circulation.
3. Small coins in circulation.

It is worth noting that *cash reserves* with the banks has to be deducted from the value of the above three items of currency in order to arrive at the total currency with the public. This is because cash reserves with the banks must remain with them and cannot therefore be used for making payments for goods or by any commercial bank's transactions. It may further be noted that these days paper currency issued by Reserve Bank of India (RBI) are not fully backed by the reserves of gold and silver, nor it is considered necessary to do so. Full backing of paper currency by reserves of gold prevailed in the past when gold standard or silver standard type of monetary system existed. According to the modern economic thinking the magnitude of currency issued should be determined by the monetary needs of the economy and not by the available reserves of gold and silver. As mentioned in the last chapter, as in other developed countries, since 1957 Reserve Bank of India follows Minimum Reserve System of issuing currency. Under this system, minimum reserves of ₹ 200 crores of gold and other approved securities (such as dollars, pound sterling, etc.) have to be kept and against this any amount of currency can be issued depending on the monetary requirements of the economy.

As stated earlier, RBI is not bound to convert notes into equal value of gold or silver. In the present times currency is inconvertible. The word written on the note, say 100 rupee notes and signed by the governor of RBI that 'I promise to pay the bearer a sum of 100 rupees' is only a legacy of the past and does not imply its convertibility into gold or silver. Another important thing to note is that paper currency or coins are *fiat money*, which means that currency notes and metallic coins serve as money on the bases of the *fiat* (*i.e.* order) of the Government. In other words, on the authority of the Government no one can refuse to accept them in payment for the transaction made. That is why they are called *legal tender*.

Demand Deposits with the Public

The other important component of money supply are demand deposits of the public with the banks. These demand deposits held by the public are also called *bank money* or *deposit money*. Deposits with the banks are broadly divided into two types: demand deposits and time deposits. Demand deposits in the banks are those deposits which can be withdrawn by drawing cheques on them. Through cheques these deposits can be transferred to others for making payments from whom goods and services have been purchased. Thus, cheques make these demand deposits as a medium of exchange and therefore make them to serve as money. It may be noted that demand deposits are *fiduciary money proper*. Fiduciary money is one which functions as money on the basis of *trust of* the persons who make payment rather than on the basis of the authority of Government. Thus, despite the fact that demand deposits and cheques through which they are operated are not legal tender, they function as money on the basis of the trust commanded by those who draw cheques on them. They are money as they are generally acceptable as medium of payment.

---

1. S. B. Gupta, *Monetary Economics : Institutions, Theory and Policy*, S. Chand & Co., New Delhi, 3rd Edition, 1997, p. 272.

Bank deposits are created when people deposit currency with them. But far more important is that banks themselves create deposits when they give advances to businessmen and others. On the basis of small cash reserves of currency, they are able to create a much larger amount of demand deposits through a system called *fractional reserve system* which will be explained later in detail.

In the developed countries such as USA and Great Britain deposit money accounted for over 80 per cent of the total money supply, currency being a relatively small part of it. This is because banking system has greatly developed there and also people have developed banking habits. On the other hand, in the developing countries banking has not developed sufficiently and also people have not acquired banking habits and they prefer to make transactions in currency. However in India after 50 years of independence and economic development the proportion of bank deposits in the money supply has risen to about 50 per cent.

FOUR MEASURES OF MONEY SUPPLY

Several definitions of money supply have been given and therefore various measures of money supply based on them have been estimated. First, different components of money supply have been distinguished on the basis of the different functions that money performs. For example, demand deposits, credit card and currency are used by the people primarily as a medium of exchange for buying goods and services and making other transactions. Obviously, they are money because they are used as a medium of exchange and are generally referred to as M_1. Another measure of money supply is M_3 which includes both M_1 and time deposits held by the public in the banks. Time deposits are money that people hold as store of value.

The main reason why money supply is classified into various measures on the basis of its functions is that effective predictions can be made about the likely effects on the economy of changes in the different components of money supply. For example, if M_1 is increasing fastly it can be reasonably expected that pepole are planning to make a large number of transactions. On the other hand, if time-deposits component of money supply measure M_3 which serves as a store of value is increasing rapidly, it can be validly concluded that people are planning to save more and accordingly consume less. Therefore, it is believed that for monetary analysis and policy formulation, a single measure of money supply is not only inadequate but may be misleading too. Hence various measures of money supply are prepared to meet the needs of monetary analysis and policy formulation.

Recently in India as well as in some developed countries, four concepts of money supply have been distinguished. The definition of money supply given above represents a narrow measure of money supply and is generally described as M_1. From April 1977, the Reserve Bank of India has adopted four concepts of money supply in its analysis of the quantum of and variations in money supply. These four concepts of measures of money supply are explained below.

Money Supply M1 or Narrow Money. This is the narrow measure of money supply and is composed of the following items:

$$M1 = C + DD + OD$$

where C = Currency with the public

DD = Demand deposits with the public in the commercial and cooperative banks.

OD = Other deposits held by the public with Reserve Bank of India.

The money supply is the most liquid measure of money supply as the money included in it can be easily used as a medium of exchange, that is, as a means of making payments for transactions.

Currency with the public (C) in the above measure of money supply consists of the following:

(*i*) Notes in circulation.

(*ii*) Circulation of rupee coins as well as small coins

(*iii*) Cash reserves on hand with all banks.

Note that in measuring demand deposits with the public in the banks (*i.e., DD*), inter-bank deposits, that is, deposits held by a bank in other banks, are excluded from this measure.

In the other deposits with Reserve Bank of India (*i.e., OD*) deposits held by the Central and State Governments and a few others such as RBI Employees Pension and Provident Funds are excluded. However, these other deposits of Reserve Bank of India include the following items:

(*i*) Deposits of Institutions such as UTI, IDBI, IFCI, NABARD etc.

(*ii*) Demand deposits of foreign Central Banks and Foreign Governments.

(*iii*) Demand deposits of IMF and World Bank.

It may be noted that other deposits of Reserve Bank of India constitute a very small proportion (less than one per cent).

Money Supply *M2*. *M2* is a broader concept of money supply in India than *M*1. In addition to the three items of *M*1, the concept of money supply M_2 includes savings deposits with the post office savings banks. Thus,

$$M2 = M1 + \text{Savings deposits with the post office savings banks.}$$

The reason why money supply *M2* has been distinguished from *M*1 is that saving deposits with post office savings banks are not as liquid as demand deposits with commercial and cooperative banks as they are not chequable accounts. However, saving deposits with post offices are more liquid than time deposits with the banks.

Money Supply *M3* or Broad Money. *M3* is a broad concept of money supply. In addition to the items of money supply included in measure *M*1, in money supply *M3* time deposits with the banks are also included. Thus

$$M3 = M1 + \text{Time Deposits with the banks.}$$

It is generally thought that time deposits serve as store of value and represent savings of the people and are not liquid as they cannot be withdrawn through drawing cheque on them. However, since loans from the banks can be easily obtained against these time deposits, they can be used if found necessary for transaction purposes in this way. Further, they can be withdrawn at any time by forgoing some interest earned on them.

It may be noted that recently *M3* has become a popular measure of money supply. The working group on monetary reforms under the chairmanship of late Prof. Sukhamoy Chakravarty recommended its use for monetary planning of the economy and setting target of the growth of money supply in terms of *M3*. Therefore, recently RBI in its analysis of growth of money supply and its effects on the economy has shifted to the use of *M3* measure of money supply. In the terminology of money supply employed by the Reserve Bank of India till April 1977, this *M3* was called *Aggregate Monetary Resources* (AMR).

Money Supply M4. The measure *M4* of money supply includes not only all the items of *M3* described above but also the total deposits with the post office savings organisation. However, this excludes contributions made by the public to the national saving certificates. Thus,

$M4 = M3 +$ *Total Deposits with Post Office Savings Organisation.*

Let us summarise the four concepts of money supply as used by Reserve Bank of India in the following tabular form:

Money Supply

*M*1	*M*2	*M*3	*ML*1
=	=	=	=
Currency (*C*)	*M*1	*M*1	*M*3
+	+	+	+
Demand Deposits (*D*) + Other Deposits of RBI (*DD*)	Savings Deposits with Post Office Savings Banks	Time Deposits with the Banks	Total Deposits of Post Office Savings Organisation (excluding NSC)

DETERMINANTS OF MONEY SUPPLY

In order to explain the determinants of money supply in an economy we shall use M_1 concept of money supply which is the most fundamental concept of money supply. We shall denote it simply by M rather than M_1. As seen above, this concept of money supply is composed of currency held by the public (C_p) and demand deposits with the banks (D). Thus

$$M = C_p + D \qquad ...(1)$$

where
M = Total money supply with the public
C_p = Currency with the public
D = Demand deposits held by the public

The two important determinants of money supply as described in equation (1) are (*a*) the amounts of high-powered money which is also called *Reserve Money* by the Reserve Bank of India and (*b*) the size of money multiplier. We explain below the role of these two factors in the determination of money supply in the economy.

1. **High-Powered Money (*H*).** The high-powered money which we denote by H consists of the currency (notes and coins) issued by the Government and the Reserve Bank of India. A part of the currency issued is held by the public, which we designate as C_p and a part is held by the banks as reserves which we designate as R. A part of these currency reserves of the banks is held by them in their own cash vaults and a part is deposited in the Reserve Bank of India in the Reserve Accounts which banks hold with RBI. Accordingly, the high-powered money can be obtained as sum of currency held by the public and the part held by the banks as reserves. Thus

$$H = C_p + R \qquad ...(2)$$

where
H = the amount of high-powered money
C_p = Currency held by the public
R = Cash Reserves of currency with the banks.

It is worth noting that Reserve Bank of India and Government are *producers of the high-powered money* and the commercial banks do not have any role in producing this high-powered money (H). However, commercial banks are *producers of demand deposits* which are also used as money like currency. But for producing demand deposits or credit, banks have to keep with themselves cash *reserves of currency* which have been denoted by R in equation (2) above. Since these cash reserves with the banks serve as a basis for the multiple creation of demand deposits which constitute an important part of total money supply in the economy, it provides high-poweredness to the currency issued by Reserve Bank and Government. A glance at equations (1) and (2) above will reveal that the difference in the two equations, one describing the total money supply and the other high-powered money, is that whereas in the former, demand deposits (D) are added to the currency held by the public, in the latter it is cash reserves (R) of the banks that are added to the currency held by the public. In fact, it is against these cash reserves (R) that banks are able to create a multiple expansion of credit or demand deposits due to which there is large expansion in money supply in the economy.

The theory of determination of money supply is based on the supply of and demand for high-powered money. Some economists therefore call it '*The H Theory of Money Supply*'[2]. However, it is more popularly called '*Money-multiplier Theory of Money Supply*' because it explains the determination of money supply as a certain multiple of the high-powered money. How the high-powered money (H) is related to the total money supply is graphically depicted in Fig. 16.1. *The base of this figure shows the supply of high-powered money (H), while the top of the figure shows the total stock of money supply.* It will be seen that the total stock of money supply (that is, the top) is determined by a multiple of the high-powered money (H). It will be further seen that whereas currency held by the public (C_p) uses the same amount of high-powered money, that is, there is one-to-one relationship between currency held by the public and the money supply. In sharp contrast to this, bank deposits (D) are a multiple of the cash reserves (R) of the banks which are part of the supply of high-powered money. That is, one rupee of high-powered money kept as bank reserves gives rise to much more amount of demand deposits. Thus, the relationship between money supply and the high-powered money is determined by the money multiplier. The money multiplier which we denote by m is the ratio of total money supply (M) to the stock of high-powered money, that is, $m = \frac{M}{H}$. The size of money multiplier depends on the preference of the public to hold currency relative to deposits, (that is, ratio of currency to deposits which we denote by K) and banks' desired cash reserves ratio to deposits which we call r. We explain below the precise multiplier relationship between high-powered money and the total stock of money supply.

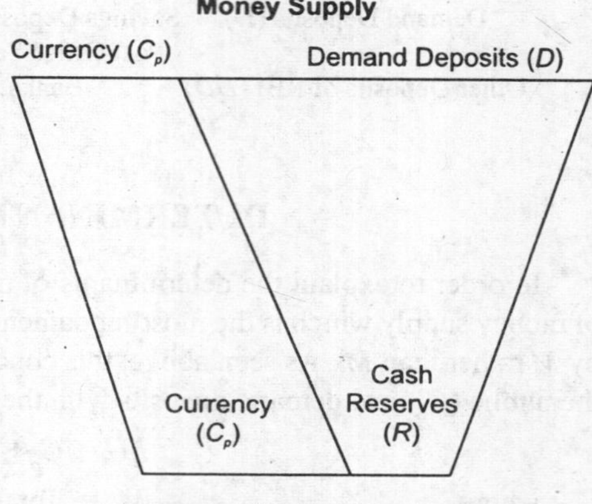

Fig. 16.1. *The High-Powered Money and the Stock of Total Money Supply*

It follows from above that if there is increase in currency held by the public which is a part of the high-powered money with demand deposits remaining unchanged, there will be a direct increase in the money supply in the economy because this constitutes a part of the money supply. If instead currency reserves held by the banks increase, this will not change the money supply immediately but will set in motion a process of multiple creation of demand deposits of the public in the banks. Although banks use these currency reserves held by the public which constitutes a part of the high-powered money to give more loans to the businessmen and thus create demand deposits, they do not affect either the amount of currency or the composition of high-powered money. The *amount of high-powered money is fixed by RBI by its past actions. Thus, changes in high-powered money are the result of decisions of Reserve Bank of India or the Government which owns and controls it.*

2. **Money Multiplier.** As stated above, money multiplier is the degree to which money supply is expanded as a result of the increase in high-powered money. Thus

$$m = \frac{M}{H}$$

2. See S.B. Gupta, *Monetary Economics: Institutions, Theory and Policy*, 3rd Edition, 1992, S. Chand & Co., New Delhi

Rearranging we have, $M = H.m$ ...(3)

Thus money supply is determined by the size of money multiplier (m) and the amount of high-powered money (H). If we know the value of money multiplier we can predict how much money will change when there is a change in the amount of high-powered money. As mentioned above, change in the high-powered money is decided and controlled by Reserve Bank of India, the money multiplier determines the extent to which decision by RBI regarding the change in high-powered money will bring about change in the total money supply in the economy.

Size of Money Multiplier

Now, an important question is what determines the size of money multiplier. It is the cash or currency reserve ratio r of the banks (which determines deposit multiplier) and currency-deposit ratio of the public (which we denote by k) which together determines size of money multiplier. We derive below the expression for the size of multiplier.

From equation (1) above, we know that total money supply (M) consists of currency with the public (C_p) and demand deposits with the banks. Thus

$$M = C_p + D \quad ...(1)$$

The public hold the amount of currency in a certain ratio of demand deposits with the banks. Let this currency-deposit ratio be devoted by k,

$$C_p = kD$$

Substituting kD for C_p in equation (1) we have

$$M = kD + D = (k+1)D \quad ...(2)$$

Now take equation which defines high-powered money (H) as

$$H = C_p + R \quad ...(3)$$

where R represents cash or currency reserves which banks keep as a certain ratio of their deposits and is called cash-reserve ratio and is denoted by r. Thus

$$R = rD$$

Now substituting rD for R and kD for C_p in equation (3) we have

$$H = kD + rD$$

$$H = (k+r)\,D \quad ...(4)$$

Now, money multiplier is ratio of total money supply to the high-powered money, therefore we divide equation (1) by equation (4), to get the value of multiplier, which we denote by m. Thus

$$m = \frac{M}{H} = \frac{(k+1)D}{(k+r)D} = \frac{k+1}{k+r}$$

or, $$\text{Money multiplier} = \frac{M}{H} = \frac{1+k}{r+k}$$

or, $$M = H \cdot \frac{1+k}{r+k} \quad ...(5)$$

where r = Cash-reserve ratio of the banks

k = Currency-deposit ratio of the public.

where H is the high-powered money and $\frac{1+k}{r+k}$ is money multiplier

From above it follows that money supply in the economy is determined by the following :

1. H, that is, the amount of high-powered money, which is also called reserve money
2. r, that is, *cash reserve ratio* of banks (*i.e.*, ratio of currency reserves to deposits of the banks).

This cash reserve ratio of banks determines the magnitude of deposit multiplier.

3. k, that is, *currency-deposit ratio of the public.*

From the equation (4) expressing the determinants of money supply, it follows that *money supply will increase* :

1. When the supply of high-powered money (*i.e.*, reserve money) H increases;
2. When the currency-deposit ratio (k)[3] of the public decreases; and
3. When the cash or currency reserves-deposit ratio of the banks (r) falls.

Cash Reserve Ratio of the Banks and the Deposit Multiplier. In a later chapter we will see that because of *fractional reserve system*, with a small increase in cash reserves with the banks, they are able to create a multiple increase in total demand deposits which are an important part of money supply. The ratio of change in total deposits to a change in reserves is called the *deposit multiplier* which depends on cash reserve ratio. The value of deposit multiplier is the reciprocal of cash reserve ratio, $\left(d_m = \frac{1}{r}\right)$ where d_m stands for deposit multiplier. If cash reserve ratio is 10 per cent of deposits, then $d_m = \frac{1}{0.10} = 10$. Thus deposit multiplier of 10 shows that for every ₹ 100 increase in cash reserves with the banks, there will be expansion in demand deposits of the banks by ₹ 1000 assuming that no leakage of cash to the public occurs during the process of deposit expansion by the banks.

Currency-Deposit Ratio of the Public and Money Multiplier. However, in the real world, with the increase in reserves of the banks, demand deposits and money supply do not increase to the full extent of deposit multiplier. This is for two reasons. First, the public does not hold all its money balances in the form of demand deposits with the banks. When as a result of increase in cash reserves, banks start increasing demand deposits, the people may also like to have some more currency with them as money balances. This means during the process of creation of demand deposits by banks, some currency is leaked out from the banks to the people. This drainage of currency to the people in the real world reduces the magnitude of expansion of demand deposit and therefore the size of money multiplier. Suppose the cash reserve ratio is 10 per cent and cash or currency of ₹ 100 is deposited in bank A. The bank A will lend out ₹ 90 and therefore create demand deposits of ₹ 90 and so the process will continue as the borrowers use these deposits for payment through cheques to others who deposit them in another bank B. However, if borrower of bank A withdraws ₹ 10 in cash from the bank and issues cheques of the remaining borrowed amount of ₹ 80, then bank B will have only ₹ 80 as new deposits instead of ₹ 90 which it would have if cash of ₹ 10 was not withdrawn by the borrower. With these new deposits of ₹ 80, bank B will create demand deposits of ₹ 72, that is, it will lend out ₹ 72 and keep ₹ 8 as reserves with it $\left(80 \times \frac{10}{100} = 8\right)$. The drainage of currency may occur during all the subsequent stages of deposit expansion in the banking system. The greater the leakage of currency, the lower will be the money multiplier. We thus see that the currency-deposit ratio, which we denote by k, is an important determinant of the actual value of money multiplier.

---

3. It will be noticed that in the equation $M = H\frac{1+k}{r+k}$ k appears both in the numerator and denominator. While in the numerator k is added to unity, in the denominator it is added to fraction. Mathematically, it means that a fall in k will affect the denominator relatively more than the numerator. Therefore, with fall in k, the value of multiplier term $\frac{1+k}{r+k}$, will increase. Thus, with *decrease* in k, the money supply will *increase* and *vice versa*.

It is important to note that deposit multiplier works both ways, positively when cash reserves with banks increase, and negatively when the cash reserves with the banks decline. That is, when there is a decrease in currency reserves with the banks, there will be multiple contraction in demand deposits with the banks.

Excess Reserves. In the explanation of the expansion of demand deposits or deposit multiplier we have assumed that banks do not keep currency reserves in excess of the required cash reserve ratio. The ratio r in the deposit multiplier is the *required cash reserve ratio* fixed by Reserve Bank of India. However, banks may like to keep with themselves some excess reserves, the amount of which depends on the extent of liquidity (*i.e.* availability of cash with them) and profitability of making investment and rate of interest on loans advanced to business firms. Therefore, the *desired reserve ratio* is greater than the statutory minimum required reserve ratio. Obviously, the holding of excess reserves by the banks also reduces the value of deposit multiplier.

Conclusion

Theory of determination of money supply explains how a given supply of high-powered money (which is also called *monetary base or reserve money*) leads to multiple expansion in money supply through the working of money multiplier. We have seen above how a small increase in reserves of currency with the banks leads to a multiple expansion in demand deposits by the banks through the process of deposit multiplier and thus causes growth of money supply in the economy. Deposit multiplier measures how much increase in demand deposits (or money supply) occurs as a result of a given increase in cash or currency, reserves with the banks depending on the required cash reserve ratio (r) if there are no cash drainage from the banking system. But in the real world drainage of currency does take place which reduces the extent of expansion of money supply following the increase in cash reserves with the banks. Therefore, *the deposit multiplier exaggerates the actual increase in money supply from a given increase in cash reserves with the banks*. In contrast, money multiplier takes into account these leakages of currency from the banking system and therefore measures actual increase in money supply when the cash reserves with the banks increase. *The money multiplier can be defined as increase in money supply for every rupee increase in cash reserves (or high-powered money), drainage of currency having been taken into account. Therefore, money multiplier is less than the deposit multiplier*.

It is worth noting that rapid growth in money supply in India has been due to the increase in high-powered money H, or what is also called Reserve Money (Lastly Reserve Bank of India, the money multiplier remaining almost constant.

The money supply in a country can be changed by Reserve Bank of India by undertaking open market operations, changing minimum required currency reserve-deposit ratio, and by varying the bank rate. The main source of growth in money supply in India is creation of credit by RBI for Government for financing its budget deficit and thus creating high-powered money. Further, though the required currency reserve-deposit ratio of banks can be easily varied by RBI, the actual currency reserve-deposit ratio cannot be so easily varied as reserves maintained by banks not only depend on minimum required cash reserve ratio but also on their willingness to hold excess reserves.

Lastly[4], an important noteworthy point is that though money multiplier does not show much variation in the long run, it can change significantly in the short run causing large variations in money supply. This unpredictable variation in money multiplier in the short run affecting money supply in the economy prevents the Central Bank of a country from controlling exactly and precisely the money supply in the economy.

4. Note that Reserve Bank of India calls the high-powered money as *Reserve Money* (RM).

FACTORS DETERMINING MONEY SUPPLY : RBI'S ANALYSIS

In its analysis of factors determining money supply in India and sources of variation in it, Reserve Bank of India does not follow any explicit theory of money supply such as money multiplier theory explained above. It provides only purely *accounting or ex-post analysis* of variations in money supply and the factors or sources causing these variations. Although Reserve Bank provides figures of the high-powered money in its analysis, it virtually clubs high-powered money with the ordinary money to calculate the total money supply in the country and therefore does not give due importance to the high-powered money as an important factor causing variation in money supply in the economy. Further, Reserve Bank also does not lay emphasis on the two behavioural ratios, namely, desired currency-deposit ratio (k) of the public and desired cash reserve ratio (r) of the banks, as determinants of money supply, though it provides *ex-post* or realised figures of these ratios. We explain below Reserve Bank's analysis of sources of variation in money supply.

Reserve Bank of India classifies factors determining money supply into the following categories:

(*a*) Government borrowing from the banking system;

(*b*) Borrowing of the private or commercial sector from the banking system;

(*c*) Changes in net foreign assets held by the Reserve Bank of India caused by changes in balance of payments position; and

(*d*) Government's currency liabilities to the public.

(*a*) Bank Credit to the Government. When the Government expenditure exceeds government revenue and there is deficit in government's budget, then it resorts to borrowing from the Reserve Bank of India which creates new currency notes for the purpose. This creation of new currency for financing the deficit of the Central Government Budget is known as *monetisation of deficit*. It was previously called deficit financing. Monetisation of deficit is an important source of change in money supply in the economy. It may be noted here that since 1995, a good part of budget deficit is financed through open market operations by RBI by selling Government securities to the banks. This is done to neutralise the monetary impact of large accumulation of net foreign exchange assets with RBI caused by *capital inflows* on a large scale. Therefore, there has been a decline in RBI's credit to the Government in the last about 10 years.

The Government also borrows from the ordinary commercial banks. When banks lend money to the Government, they create credit. For instance, for purchase of foodgrains by the Food Corporation of India, the banks gives a large amount of loan to the Government. The creation of deposits by the banks when they create credit for the Government leads to the increase in money supply in the economy.

(*b*) Bank Credit to the Commercial or Private Sector. The private sector also borrows from the banking system when its own resources are less than its total expenditure. This also adds to the money supply with the public because when banks lend, they create credit. This also affects the money supply in the same manner as the Government borrowing from the banking system. There is, however, an important difference. Whereas Government can borrow more or less compulsorily from Reserve Bank of India, the private sector cannot do so from the commercial banks.

(*c*) Changes in Net Foreign Exchange Assets. Changes in the foreign exchange assets held by the Reserve Bank can also bring about a change in the money supply. The change in the net foreign assets may be caused by balance of payment situation. Suppose the balance of payments is adverse or unfavourable and therefore available foreign exchange is less than the country needs to pay for its imports, both visible and invisible. In order to meet this adverse balance of trade the country will have to dispose of some of its foreign exchange assets. If there is a net adverse balance of payments, rupees would flow into the Reserve Bank which pays out foreign exchange. This would have the effect of reducing the *Reserve Money* (*i.e.* the high-powered money) in India and the contraction of the money supply with the public. Opposite result would follow when there is a net surplus in the balance of payments of a country.

It follows from above that a deficit in the balance of payments on current account decreases the supply of rupee currency (that is, high-powered or reserve money) in the economy and thereby causes contraction in money supply with the public. On the contrary, a surplus in the balance of payments will increase the foreign exchange assets and thereby will lead to the expansion in reserve money and money supply in the economy. It may also be noted that apart from balance of payments on current account foreign exchange reserves or assets may also come through either foreign aid or deposits in Indian banks by NRI or foreign direct investment made by foreign companies in India. For example, in recent years there has been a large-scale inflow of foreign exchange through investment made by foreign companies and NRI deposits in India. As a result, our foreign exchange reserves have substantially gone up, which have resulted in the issue and expansion of rupee currency in circulation. In August 2004 foreign exchange reserves has risen to US $ 119 billion. But RBI has *neutralised its monetary impact* by mopping up liquidity of the banks through open market operations by selling them Government securities. This is called *sterilisation* of inflows of foreign exchange. Further, to deal with the problem of excess liquidity of the Indian banks caused by the rise in foreign exchange reserves, and with a view to check rise in inflation rate Reserve Bank of India has in April 2004 entered into an agreement with the Central Government to sterilise the monetary impact of these reserves. With this agreement, *Market Stabilisation* Scheme (MSS) has been started. Under this scheme the Central Government has issued Market Stabilisation Bonds. These bonds were sold by RBI to commercial banks to mop up excess liquidity of ₹ 60,000 crore in 2004-05. But these ₹ 60,000 crore were kept apart in special deposits with RBI and were not meant to be used by the Government.

It should be noted that if the foreign exchange reserves are used to import goods in short supply, it will help in lowering inflation rate for two reasons. First, this will reduce rupee currency in circulation which will cause reduction in money supply in the economy. Contraction in money supply will help in controlling inflation through reducing aggregate demand. Secondly, the imports of goods will increase aggregate supply of goods in the economy which will tend to lower prices.

(*d*) **Government's Currency Liabilities to the Public.** Changes in money supply in the economy are also brought about by Government's currency liabilities to the public. Coins and one-rupee notes represent Government's currency liabilities to the public. On 31st March 2004-05, there were outstanding balances of Government currency liabilities of ₹ 7291 crores as compared to ₹ 7071 crores on March 31, 2003. If Government's currency liabilities increase, the money supply also increases.

BUDGET DEFICIT AND MONEY SUPPLY

A budget deficit is also an important source of expansion of money supply in the economy. There are two possible links between budget deficit and growth in money supply. First, when following an expansionary fiscal policy the government raises its expenditure without financed by extra taxation and thereby causing a budget deficit, it will tend to raise interest rate. This happens when budget deficit is financed through borrowing from the market. As a result, demand for money or loanable funds increases which, given the supply of money, causes interest rate to rise. Rise in interest rate tends to reduce or crowd out private investment. If the Central Bank is following the policy of a fixed interest rate target, when the government resorts to borrowing to finance the budget deficit, then to prevent the rise in interest rate the Central Bank will take steps to increase the money supply in the economy.

The second link between budget deficit and expansion in money supply is direct. This occurs when the Central Bank itself purchases government securities when the government resorts to borrowing.[5] The Central Bank is said to *monetise* budget deficit when it purchases government securities as it prints new notes for the purpose and gives it to the government for meeting public expenditure. In some countries such as the US, Federal Reserve (which is the Central Bank of the USA) enjoys a good deal of independence from the Treasury (*i.e.,* the Government) and voluntarily decides when and how much to purchase government securities to finance its budget deficit.

Central Bank's Dilemma

The Central Bank of a country faces a dilemma in deciding whether or not to monetise budget deficit. If the Central Bank does not monetise budget deficit to meet its increased expenditure, the government will borrow from the market and in the absence of any accommodating monetary policy this will tend to raise interest rate and thereby *reduce or crowd out private investment.* Referring to the policy of Federal Reserve of the United States, Dornbusch, Fischer and Startz write, "There is accordingly a temptation for the Federal Reserve to prevent crowding out by buying government securities thereby increasing the money supply and hence allows an expansion in income without a rise in interest rates"[6].

But the policy of monetisation of budget deficit by the Central Bank involves a risk. If the economy is working near-full employment level, that is, at near-full production capacity, monetisation of budget deficit will cause inflation in the economy. However, if the economy is in the grip of a severe depression, the risk of causing inflation through monetisation of budget deficit and consequent growth in money supply is not much there.

It follows from above that in any particular case the Central Bank, if it enjoys freedom from the Government, has to judge whether it should adopt accommodatory monetary policy to achieve its goal of *interest-targeting* or *allow fiscal expansion through monetisation of budget deficit accompanied by the tight monetary policy to check inflation.* It is the latter course of action that was adopted by Reserve Bank of India before 1995 when government's fiscal deficit was high and a good part of it was monetised by it.

MONEY SUPPLY AND THE OPEN ECONOMY

The transactions of an open economy also affect the growth of money supply in it. In the open economy there is free flow of goods and services through trade with foreign countries. Besides, in the open economy there are flows of capital between countries. The impact of transactions of an open economy on the money supply can be better understood from national income identity of an open economy. National income of the open economy is written as

$$Y = C + I + G + NX \qquad ...(1)$$

or

$$NX = Y - (C + I + G) \qquad ...(2)$$

where NX stands for net exports or trade balance. In the trade balance if we also include exports and imports of services (*i.e.,* invisibles), then NX can be taken as current account balance.

The current account balance (NX) can be either positive or negative. If in equation (2) above aggregate expenditure ($C + I + G$) exceeds national output (Y), current account balance or NX will be negative, that is, imports will be greater than exports. In other words, there will be deficit in current account of the balance of payments. On the other hand, if aggregate expenditure is less than national income [$(C + I + G) < Y$], there will be surplus in the current account balance of payments. This implies that our exports will be greater than imports.

Now, if in a year there is deficit in current account, that is, NX is negative, it means our demand

5. It is important to note that when government borrows from the market, it does so through sale of its securities (*i.e.* bonds).
6. Dornbusch, Fischer, and Startz, *op. cit.* 9th edition, 2004, p.275.

for foreign exchange, say, the US dollars, for imports of goods and services will exceed the supply of foreign exchange. This situation is depicted in Fig. 16.2 where the curve *DD* represents demand curve for foreign exchange (US $) and *SS* is the supply curve of foreign exchange (US $) at exchange rate (₹ per US dollar) and *OR* and *LK* represent deficit in current account.

If the economy is under flexible exchange rate regime and the Central Bank of the country does not intervene at all, the exchange rate will change to *OR*′ and as a result deficit in current account balance will be eliminated and equilibrium restored at the new exchange rate. If there is such a situation, there is no impact on the money supply. However, if the Central Bank wants to maintain the exchange rate at *OR*, then current account deficit equal to *LK* has to be met. If there are no capital inflows, then to maintain the exchange rate at *OR*, the Central Bank of the country has to supply foreign exchange equal to *LK* out of the reserves held by it. But when the Central Bank (RBI in case of India) pays out foreign exchange from its reserves, *it will receive money (i.e., rupees in India)* from *importers of goods and services in return for foreign exchange paid to them to meet the deficit*. Thus some money (say Indian rupees) will flow into the Central Bank and thus withdrawn from circulation. As a result of Central Bank intervention to meet the current account deficit and to maintain the exchange rate money supply in the economy decreases. It is important to note that the Central Bank of the country cannot go on supplying foreign exchange reserves, year after year, for a long time because foreign exchange assets with the Central Bank are available in limited amount.

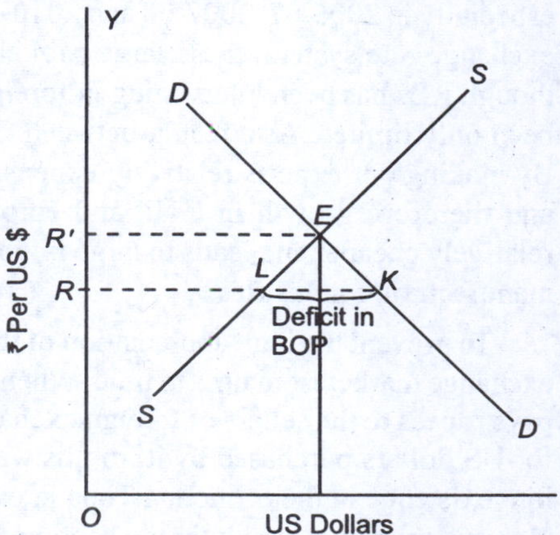

Fig. 16.2. *Deficit in Balance of Payments and Foreign Exchange Market*

The above analysis of contraction in money supply as a result of use of foreign exchange reserves to meet the current account deficit is based on two assumptions. First, it is assumed that there are no capital flows to meet the deficit in current account balance. Second, it is assumed the exchange rate is not allowed to change as a result of inbalance between demand and supply of foreign exchange due to current account deficit.

Capital Inflows. However, if there are sufficient net capital inflows accruing from the capital account of the balance of payments, then deficit in current account (*i.e.*, negative *NX*) can be met by these capital inflows. In this case there will be no impact of deficit in current account balance of payments on money supply in the economy.

Now take the opposite case of surplus in current account balance (*i.e.*, when *NX* is positive). This implies that the supply of foreign exchange exceeds demand for it. In the absence of capital out-flows this excess supply of foreign exchange will have to by purchased by the Central Bank if exchange rate is to be maintained. The Central Bank (RBI) will print new notes to pay for the purchase of foreign exchange. This will lead to the increase in money supply in the economy. However, if exchange rate is allowed to change, as is the case under flexible exchange rate system, the exchange rate will adjust to bring supply and demand for foreign exchange in equilibrium.

Overall Balance of Payments and Capital Inflows

When in an open economy with flexible exchange rate regime there is *deficit in overall balance of payments* (*i.e.*, on both current and capital accounts), it means that capital inflows are insufficient to bridge the gap in the balance of payments, then, in case of India, this has to be met with use of foreign exchange reserves by the Reserve Bank of India. When Reserve Bank of India pays foreign exchange (*e.g.* US $) to finance the deficit in overall balance of payments, it gets rupees in return. Thus rupee currency flows into the RBI. As a result, money supply (rupee currency) in the economy will decline. However, as explained above, under flexible rate system, if RBI does not intervene, the deficit in overall balance of payments will cause rupee to depreciate.

Now suppose there is *surplus in overall balance of payment* as capital inflows exceed the deficit in current account. The large capital inflows can occur due to heavy foreign direct investment (FDI) and portfolio investment by foreign institutional investors (FII) as it happened in some years in India, especially in 2006-07, 2007-08 and 2010-11. In the absence of intervention by RBI under the flexible exchange rate system, these large capital inflows will cause appreciation of Indian Rupee. In fact, though RBI has been intervening in foreign exchange market from time to time, its intervention has been only limited. As a result, between Oct. 2006 and Oct 2007, rupee appreciated by 15 per cent. By making our exports relatively expensive the appreciation of rupee adversely affects our exports and therefore growth in GNP and employment. Besides, appreciation of rupee makes imports relatively cheaper and leads to large imports of goods and materials and thereby harms our domestic manufacturing industries.

To prevent the high appreciation of the Indian Rupee RBI purchases US dollars from the foreign exchange market from time to time. When RBI purchases dollars from the foreign exchange market, it pays rupees to the sellers of foreign exchange. To do so more rupee currency is printed by RBI to pay for US dollars purchased by it. In this way more rupee currency (*i.e.,* high-powered money) comes into existence in the economy. Thus intervention by RBI to prevent appreciation of rupee results in increase in money supply in the economy.

The effect of large capital inflows and its effect on appreciation of currency and money supply in the Indian economy is illustrated in Fig. 16.3 where exchange rate of rupee for US dollars (₹ per US $) is measured on the *Y*-axis and number of US dollars are measured on the *X*-axis. Initially the

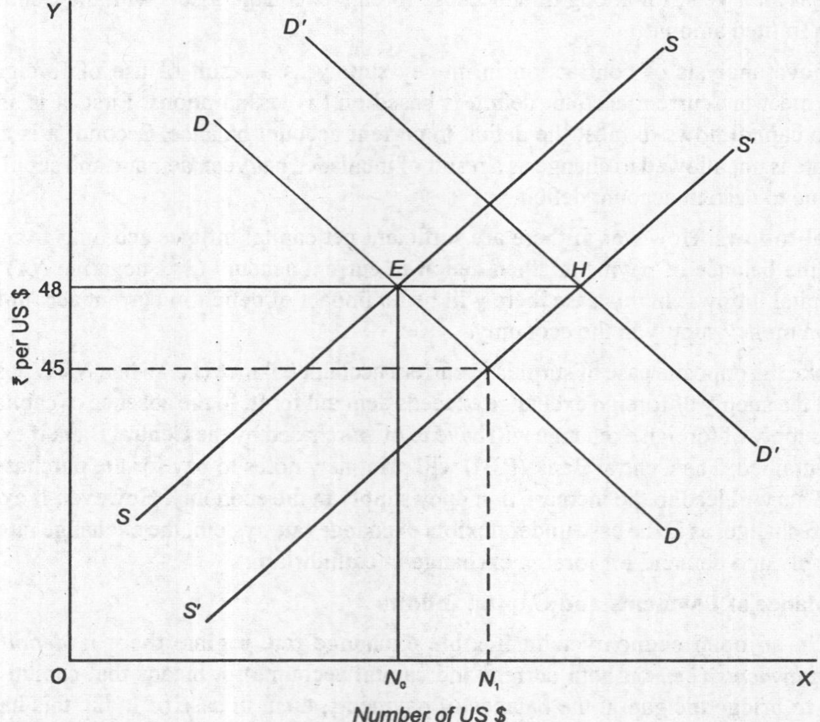

Fig. 16.3. *Capital Inflows and Appreciation of Rupee*

equilibrium between demand for and supply of dollars in the Indian foreign exchange market determines equilibrium exchange rate equal to ₹ 48 per US \$. As a result of large capital inflows supply curve of US dollars shifts to the right to *S'S'*. With this, at the existing exchange rate of ₹ 48 per US dollar, *EH* is the increase in capital inflows. Now, under a variable exchange rate regime as it exists today, if exchange rate is allowed to adjust freely, rupee will rise to ₹ 45 per US dollar. If Reserve Bank wants to manage it and tries to maintain it at ₹ 48 per US dollar, it will have to buy US dollars equal to *EH* from the market. By buying US dollars equal to *EH,* RBI will cause the demand curve for US dollars to shift to the right to the new position *D'D'* and the new equilibrium is established at point *H* which corresponds to ₹ 48 per US dollar.

But for buying US dollars equal to *EH*, RBI will have to print new rupee currency to pay for US dollars. Thus more high-power money (*i.e.*, rupee currency) would come into circulation in the Indian economy. Thus RBI did not intervene sufficiently to prevent the appreciation of rupee between Oct. 2006 and Oct. 2007. This is because such intervention leads to the increase in money supply that is likely to cause inflation in the Indian economy. Therefore, RBI intervened only to a small degree and let the rupee appreciate to some extent.

On the other hand, in 2011 the RBI faced the opposite problem when after August 2011, there was net *large capital outflow* from India due to uncertainty caused by European debt crisis and economic slowdown in the US. The FIIs started selling Indian equity and bonds and converting rupee into US dollars. This led to the increase in demand for dollars resulting in appreciation of US dollar and *depreciation of Indian rupee*. The value of rupee which was around ₹ 44 to a US dollar in the first week of September 2011 depreciated to around ₹ 53 in the second week of December 2011. This depreciation of rupee will make our imports constlier which will tend to raise inflation if not matched by fall in international commodity prices. To prevent sharp depreciation of rupee the RBI intervened in the foreign exchange market by selling dollars in the market. Again its intervention was only limited. In fact, the RBI has no fixed target for maintaining exchange rate of rupee at any level and instead its policy is to *allow exchange rate of rupee to fluctuate within a band. In fact, RBI faces a dilemma which we discuss below.*

RBI Dilemma : External Balance and Internal Balance

RBI faces a dilemma because if it does not intervene in the face of large capital inflows rupee will appreciate much which will adversely affect our exports and therefore growth of GNP and employment in our economy. On the other hand, if it intervenes and purchases enough US dollars from the market to prevent any appreciation of rupee, it will cause large increase in money supply that would cause higher rate of inflation. A major objective of RBI is to control inflation. Therefore, RBI has to strike a balance between the two alternatives. It has been intervening in the foreign exchange market to prevent large appreciation of rupee. But it cannot buy inflows of foreign exchange indiscriminately as it leads to higher inflation. RBI has also resorted to *sterilization* of increase in money supply by selling government securities to the banks and thereby getting back the money issued by it. But there is limit to this sterilization operation as it has not unlimited amount of government securities to sell them to the banks. Hence the dilemma faced by it. We explain the sterilization operations by RBI later.

It follows from above that the two objectives of external balance and internal balance clash with each other. External balance occurs when balance of payments is in equilibrium or close to it. When external balance does not exist the Central Bank will either go on losing foreign exchange reserves which it cannot do so for long or it will be gaining foreign exchange reserves which also poses a problem as it leads to increase in money supply and causes inflationary pressures in the economy.

On the other hand, internal balance exists when the economy is in equilibrium at full employment or full productive capacity level without any inflationary pressures. Thus, to ensure internal balance requires that money supply should not be allowed to increase much. Since the two require different types of policy measure by the Central Bank, they clash with each other. Hence, the dilemma faced by the Central Bank.

Sterilization by the Central Bank

Sterilization provides a way out of the problem of clash between the goals of external balance and internal balance. *Sterilization refers to the action by the Central Bank of a country to offset or cancel the impact of its foreign exchange market intervention on the money supply through open market operations.* The sterilization measures can be used both to offset the reduction in money supply when in case of current account deficit the Central Bank of the country sells foreign exchange in the market and also when the Central Bank offsets the effect of increase in money supply when it buys foreign exchange from the market in case of surplus in balance of payments or when large capital inflows are coming into the economy.

Let us first explain sterilisation operation by the Central Bank in case of deficit in current account of the balance of payments. As seen above, the deficit in current account balance requires the Central Bank to sell foreign exchange from its reserves to prevent the depreciation of domestic currency (that is, to maintain the exchange rate constant). The sale of foreign exchange in foreign exchange market by the Central Bank causes money supply in the economy to decrease that has deflationary effect on the economy. To avoid this adverse effect, the Central Bank buys government securities (*i.e.,* bonds) through open market operations. When it does so the Central Bank prints domestic currency to pay for the bonds it purchases. In this way money supply in the economy increases which offsets the decrease in money supply brought about by the Central Bank when it sells foreign exchange to prevent the depreciation of the domestic currency. Thus, provided it has enough foreign exchange assets, with sterilization operations by the Central Bank *persistent* deficit in balance of payments is possible because it *insulates* the money supply changes in the domestic economy from the Central Bank intervention in the foreign exchange market.

Sterilization Operations in Case of Surplus in Balance of Payments or Large Capital Inflows

Now, we take up the opposite case when there is surplus in balance of payments or when large capital inflows are taking place. This situation requires that Central Bank intervenes in the foreign exchange market and buys foreign exchange inflows from the market to maintain the foreign exchange rate or to prevent the appreciation of domestic currency. As mentioned above, in the two years (2006-08) due to large net capital inflows in the Indian economy there was quite a large appreciation of the Indian rupee against US dollar that produced undesirable effects. Therefore, Reserve Bank intervened in the foreign exchange market by buying US dollars to prevent too much appreciation of the Indian rupee. The purchase of foreign exchange (US dollars) from the foreign exchange market by the Reserve Bank led to the increase in money supply in the Indian economy that caused inflationary pressures. To sterilize the effect of this increase in money supply RBI undertook open market operations by *selling* government securities to the banks which paid rupees to it. In this way some rupee currency had been withdrawn from the economy. In this way inflationary pressures created by the original increase in money supply through intervention in foreign exchange market have been offset.

QUESTIONS FOR REVIEW

1. Explain the concept of money supply. What are the factors responsible for rapid increase in money supply?
2. Explain how supply of money depends upon the high-powered money, the currency deposit ratio and cash reserve ratio.
3. Discuss the various measures of money supply adopted by RBI. How are these official measures of money supply different from the traditional money supply ?
4. What are the measures of money supply used by the Reserve Bank of India ? What is their respective purpose ?
5. Explain RBI's measures of money supply in India. What factors can cause changes in measures of supply of money ?

6. Account for the rapid growth of money supply in the Indian economy.
7. Explain what factors can lead to the increase in money supply in the economy ?
8. What is money multiplier? What determines its size? Show how the money multiplier determines money supply in the economy.
9. Show how budget deficit affects money supply in the economy. Is monetisation of budget deficit always inflationary?
10. Explain how current account deficit (CAD) in the absence of capital inflow influences money supply in the open economy.
11. Explain how surplus in overall balance of payments affect money supply in the economy.
12. Explain the effect of large capital inflows on the money supply in an open economy.
13. What is meant by **Sterilisation** by the Central Bank of a country? How is it used to offset the impact of current account deficit on the economy in the absence of capital inflows?
14. What is meant by external balance and internal balance? Show the dilemma the Central Bank of a country faces when it tries to achieve them.

CHAPTER 17

Money Market Equilibrium

Introduction

We have explained in the previous chapters the factors which determine supply of money and demand for money. In the previous chapter we have discussed various theories of demand for money. In this chapter we will explain how money market equilibrium comes about. *Money market is in equilibrium when at a rate of interest demand for and supply of money are equal.* It is worth noting that in the money market people increase or decrease the money they hold by selling short-term bonds that carry a fixed rate of interest. These bonds may be of corporate companies, generally called corporate bonds or debentures or may be securities of government, which are called treasury bills.

Money as a Financial Asset

The wealth of a household and a business firm consists of tangible assets such as a house, commercial property and the value of financial assets. Financial assets include (1) *stocks*, that is, equity shares of corporate firms (*i.e.* public limited companies), (2) *bonds* which carry a fixed rate of interest and (3) *money*. *Money is a financial asset*. We have seen in a previous chapter as to why people demand money. It is important to note that money is different from income or wealth. In macroeconomics demand for money has a narrower meaning. *Demand for money is a part of wealth of the people which they want* to hold in the form of money rather than other assets. What part of their wealth people want to hold in the form of money determines the demand for money to hold.

Transactions and Speculative Demand for Money

In the previous chapter we have explained the various theories of demand for money. Broadly speaking, people demand money for two purposes : (1) Transactions demand for money and (2) Speculative demand for money. When the number of transactions in the economy increases, demand for money increases. The most important factor determining the volume of transactions is the level of national income or aggregate output. In a modern economy most goods are produced in the various stages of production. Money is required to buy raw materials for production, to make payment of wages to labour and so forth. A larger stock of money is therefore required to undertake more transactions.

As explained in the previous chapter, a society keeps a certain proportion of national income in the form of money to carry out various transactions. The greater the level of national income, the higher the demand for money, given the proportion of income which a society keeps in the form of money. Thus

$$M_T^d = kY \quad \text{...}(i)$$

where M_T^d stands for transaction demand for money, Y is the level of national income and k is the proportion of national income which is kept in the form of money. The constant proportion k does not have to be unity because one unit of money is used more than once for exchanging goods and services produced. The number of times a unit of money is used for buying goods and services is called *income velocity of money*. Thus, $V = \frac{Y}{M}$ where V stands for income velocity of money. It is worth noting that low income velocity of money implies that demand for money is a higher fraction of income. This indicates that individuals and business organisations keep their money stock for a longer period of time with themselves or in demand deposits with the banks and do not *quickly* use their money holdings for transaction purposes.

On the other hand, a high income velocity of money implies that demand for money is a smaller fraction of income. This means that individuals and firms quickly use their money stock for purposes of buying goods and services and do not keep it for a longer period with them or in their banks.

Speculative Demand for Money. Keynes in his book '*The General Theory*' emphasised that individuals demand money to hold for speculative purpose. Money demand for speculative purpose means that individuals want to hold money to take advantages of the 'changes in future rate of interest, that is, changes in bond prices'. At any given time households or individuals want to keep a certain portfolio of assets consisting of both real and financial assets. When people decide how much money to hold with them for speculative purposes, they make a *portfolio choice*. At a time some people would like to hold more money and therefore will sell bonds or other assets. Some people may like to hold more bonds or other assets in their portfolio and to achieve this they would withdraw money from demand deposits to buy the bonds and other assets.

Cost of Holding Money and Portfolio Choice

The money held by the people in their wallets or in demand deposits with the banks do not earn any interest[1]. Instead of holding money in their wallets or demand deposits, they can buy government bonds or corporate bonds and earn higher nominal rate of interest. The cost of holding money as an asset arises from the fact that money earns no interest or very low interest. Thus, *interest rate on government or corporate bonds is the opportunity cost of holding money*. The assets other than money such as government bonds or corporate bonds earn higher rate of return. But keeping money and other assets in investment portfolio have advantages and disadvantages. The advantage of holding money as an asset is that it can be easily and quickly used to purchase goods and services. Its disadvantage, as mentioned just above, is that it earns no interest or very low interest. On the other hand, other assets such as bonds cannot be directly or quickly used for transaction purposes and when they are sold to convert them into money for being used for these purposes, they involve costs such as brokerage fees apart from time and efforts involved in their sale.

Deciding about how much money to hold as an asset is deciding about a portfolio choice. This portfolio choice depends on individuals' assessment of advantages and disadvantages of holding money as an asset as compared to other financial assets. At a given interest rate on bonds, an individual or household decides about an investment portfolio after weighing their advantages and costs. If rate of interest on bonds rises, bonds would become more attractive than money. In this case, the holding of money will decline and that of bonds will increase in the portfolio.

Demand for Money and Interest Rate

It is evident from above analysis that demand for money as an asset, that is, for speculative purposes depends on rate of interest on bonds, which is the opportunity cost of holding money. If rate of interest is higher, the people would demand less money to hold for speculative purposes. This is because at a higher rate of interest they would go in for holding more bonds or other financial assets in their investment portfolio. On the other bond, at a lower rate of interest on bonds, they would demand more money to hold.

Thus, demand for money to hold for speculative purposes, that is, as an asset is negatively related to rate of interest. Therefore, demand curve for money for speculative purposes slopes downward. This indicates that at a higher rate of interest, less money is held as an asset and at a lower interest rate, more money is held as an asset. Demand for money to hold for speculative purposes is drawn as M^d_{sp} in Figure 17.1.

1. Demand deposits may earn very low interest rate.

Mathematically, we can express the demand for money to hold for speculative purposes as follows:

$$M^d_{sp} = f(i) = hi \qquad ...(ii)$$

where h is the sensitivity of money demand to hold as an asset to changes in rate of interest (i).

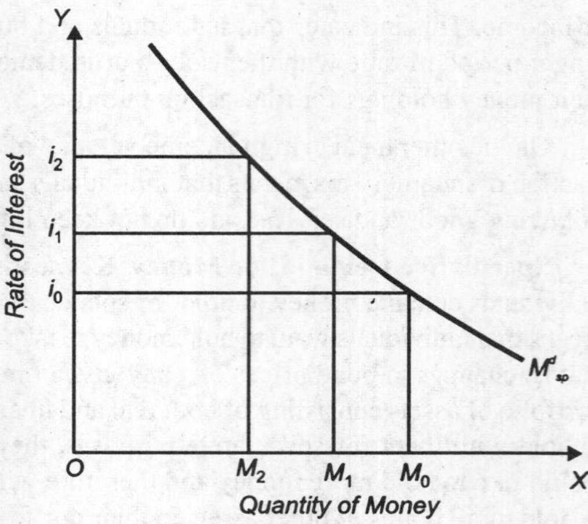

Fig. 17.1. *Demand for Money and Rate of Interest.*

Total Demand for Money. Demand for money to hold comes from transactions and speculative purposes[2]. Therefore, total demand for money to hold depends on level of income and rate of interest. Thus, by adding demand for money equations (i) and (ii) we have

$$M^d = M^d_T + M^d_{sp}$$

$$M^d = kY - hi \qquad ...(iii)$$

Two things are worth noting in the money demand equation (iii). First, demand for money to hold depends on level of income and rate of interest. The higher the income (Y), the greater will be demand for money. Secondly, demand for money is negatively related to rate of interest (i). At a given level of income, the higher the rate of interest, the lower will be demand for money. In Figure 17.2 total demand for money curve M_{d1} has been drawn at the given level of income Y_1.

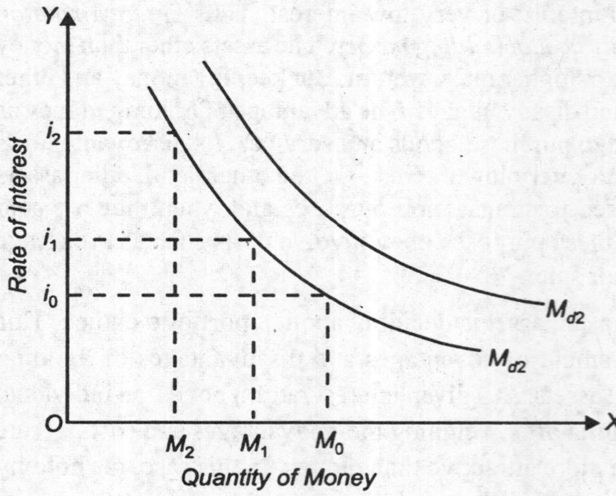

Fig. 17.2. *Demand for Money, Rate for Interest and Level of Income.*

As with the increase in income, demand for money for transaction purposes increases at all rates of interest, the rise in level of national income will cause a shift of M_d curve to the right. At the given level of income Y_1, if rate of interest rises we move up the money demand curve M_{d1} indicating that quantity of money demanded will decrease, and if rate of interest falls, the quantity of money demanded will increase.

The Demand for Money in a Two-Asset Economy : Portfolio Choice

In order to explain the demand for money and interest rate determination, Kenyes assumed a simplified economy where there are two assets which people can keep in their portfolio balance. These two assets are : (1) money in the form of currency and demand deposits in the banks which earn no interest and (2) long term bonds. It is important to note that rate of interest and bond prices are inversely related. When bond prices go up, rate of interest rises and vice versa. The demand for money by the people depends upon how they decide to balance their portfolio between money and bonds. This decision about the portfolio balance can be influenced by two factors.

---

2. For simplicity sake we include demand for money for precautionary motive in the transaction motive for holding money.

First, the higher the level of nominal income in a two asset-economy, people would want to hold more money in their portfolio balance. This is because of transactions motive according to which at the higher level of nominal income, purchases by the people of goods and services in their daily life will be relatively larger which require more money to be kept for transaction purposes.

Second, the higher the nominal rate of interest, the lower the demand for money for speculative motive. This, is firstly, because a higher nominal rate of interest implies a higher opportunity cost for holding money. At a higher rate of interest holders of money can earn more incomes by holding bonds instead of money. Secondly, if the current rate of interest is higher than what is expected in the future, the people would like to hold more bonds and less money in their portfolio. On the other hand, if the current rate of interest is low (in other words, if the bond prices are currently high), the people will be reluctant to hold larger quantity of bonds and instead they could hold more money in their portfolio for the fear that bond prices would fall in the future causing capital losses to them.

It follows from above that quantity of money demanded increases with the fall in the rate of interest or with the increase in level of nominal income. At a given level of nominal income, we can draw a money demand curve showing the quantity of money demanded at various rates of interest. As demand for money is inversely related to the rate of interest, the money demand curve at a given level of income, say Y_1, will be downward-sloping as is shown by the curve Md_1 in Figure 17.2. When the level of money income increases, suppose from Y_1 to Y_2, the curve of demand for money shifts upward to the new position M_{d2}.

The Supply of Money

Money is an important factor which is used as a medium of exchange for undertaking transactions and for holding as an asset. Money can perform these functions if it is kept scarce, that is, supply of money at a given point of time is fixed and over time it is increased at a limited rate. Therefore, the Central Bank of a country (in case of India, Reserve Bank of India) is given the right to control the supply of money in the economy. The money supply is fixed by the policy actions of the Central Bank of the country, Through open market operations changes in cost reserve ratio (CRR) cf banks Central Bank of a country can influence the creation of bank credit which constitutes an important part of the money supply of the country. Besides, the extent to which the Central Bank of the country absorbs foreign exchange reserves, also affects the supply of money in the economy. When the Reserve Bank of India buys more foreign exchange from the market, it issues new money to make payments for purchase of foreign exchange from the market. However, it is assumed that money supply does not vary with either level of income or rate of interest[3] unless Reserve Bank decides to change it. In Fig. 17.3 we have therefore drawn a vertical supply curve

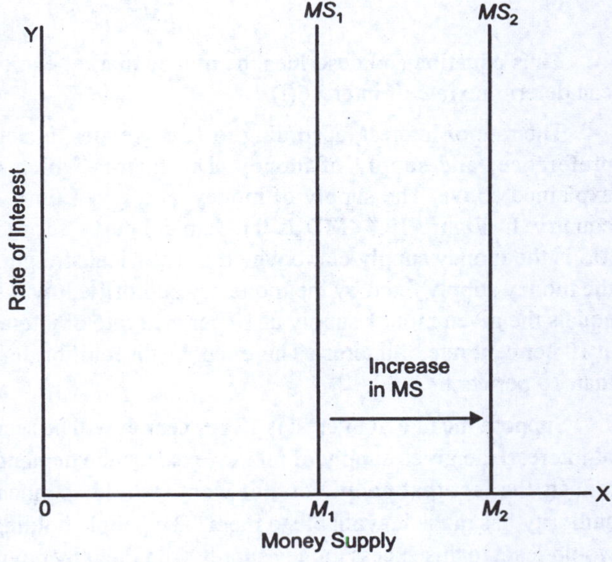

Fig. 17.3. *Money supply is independent of rate of interest.*

3. It may be noted that rate of interest can influence the decisions of banks to create credit and can therefore affect *to some extent* the money supply in the economy. We however assume that interest induced changes in money supply are undone by Reserve Bank of India by taking appropriate policy measures.

of money with measuring interest rate on the *Y*-axis. If the Central Bank of the country decides to increase money supply and fixes it at M_2, money supply curve shifts to the right as shown in Figure 17.3. On the other hand, if the Central Bank decides to reduce the money supply in the economy, money supply curve will shift to the left.

MONEY MARKET EQUILIBRIUM : DETERMINATION OF RATE OF INTEREST

Once the Central Bank of a country fixes the money supply in the economy, households and business firms can make individual decisions regarding how much money to hold. But the *total money supply will be unaffected* by their decisions to hold more or less money to fulfil transaction and speculative purposes. *Money market is in equilibrium at a rate of interest when demand for money is equal to the fixed money supply.* Thus money market is in equilibrium when

$$MS = MD$$

As explained above, money demand (*MD*) is determined by the level of income and rate of interest. Assuming that money demand is a linear function, we can write it as

$$MD = kY - hi$$

Thus, money market is in equilibrium when

$$MS = kY - hi$$

or

$$i = \frac{1}{h}(kY - MS) \qquad ...(iv)$$

Thus equation (*iv*) describes the money market equilibrium. Given the level of income (*Y*), we can determine rate of interest (*i*).

The rate of interest, according to J.M. Keynes, is determined by demand for money (liquidity preference) and supply of money. The factors which determine demand for money has been explained above. The supply of money, at a given time, is fixed by the monetary authority of the country. In Figure 17.4 MD is the demand curve for money at a given level of nominal income. *MS* is the money supply curve which is a vertical straight line showing that 200 crores of rupees is the money supply fixed by the monetary authority. It will be seen that quantity demanded of money equals the given money supply at 10 per cent rate of interest. So the money market is in equilibrium at 10 per cent rate of interest. There will be disequilibrium if rate of interest is either higher or lower than 10 per cent.

Suppose the rate of interest is 12 per cent. It will be seen from Figure 17.4 that at 12 per cent rate of interest, the given supply of money exceeds the demand for money. The excess supply of money reflects the fact that people do not want to hold as much money in their portfolio as the monetary authority has made it available to them. The people holding assets in the present two-asset economy would react to this excess money supply with them by buying bonds and thus replace some of money in their portfolios with bonds. Since the *total money supply* at a given moment remains fixed, it cannot be reduced by buying bonds by individuals. But the bond-buying spree would lead to the rise in prices of bonds. The rise in bond prices means the fall in the rate of interest. As will be seen from Figure 17.4, with the fall in the interest rate from 12 per cent to 10 per cent, quantity demand of money has increased to be once again equal to the given supply of money and the excess supply of money is entirely eliminated and money market equilibrium is restored.

On the other hand, if the rate of interest is lower than the equilibrium rate of 10 per cent, say it is 8 per cent, then as will be seen from Figure 17.4 there will emerge *excess demand for money*. As a reaction to this excess demand for money, people would like to sell bonds in order to obtain a greater quantity of money for holding at the lower rate of interest. The stock of money remaining fixed, the attempt by the people to hold more money balances at a rate of interest lower than the equilibrium level through sale of bonds will only cause the bond prices to fall. The fall in bond prices implies the rise in the rate of interest. Thus, the process started as a reaction to the excess demand for money at an interest rate below the equilibrium level will end up with the rise in the interest rate to the equilibrium level.

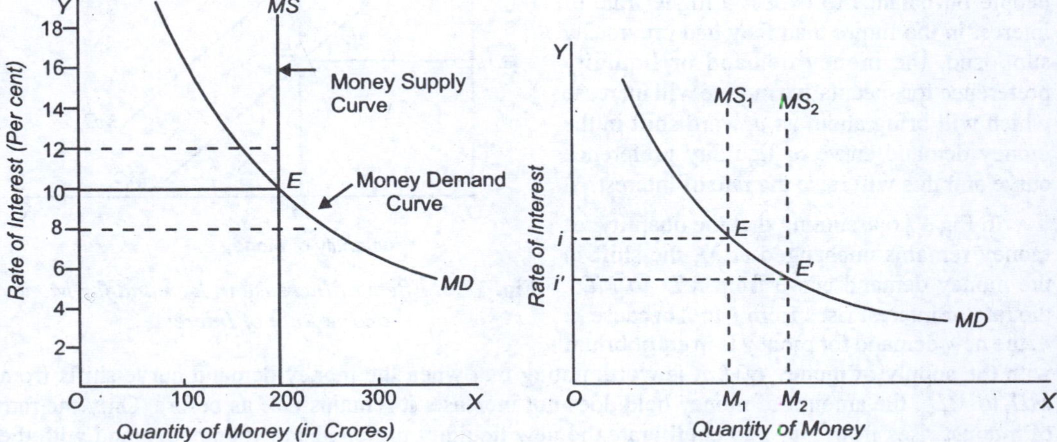

Fig. 17.4. *Money Market Equilibrium.*

Fig. 17.5. *Effect of Increase in Money Supply on the Rate of Interest.*

Effect of an Increase in the Money Supply

Let us now examine the effect of increase in money supply on the rate of interest. In Fig. 17.5, *MD* is the demand for money for satisfying various motives. To begin with, OM_1 is the quantity of money available. Rate of interest will be determined where the demand for money is in balance or equal to the fixed supply of money OM_1. It is clear from Fig. 17.5 that demand for money is equal to OM_1 quantity of money at *i* rate of interest. Hence *i* is the equilibrium rate of interest. Assuming no change in expectations and nominal income, an increase in the quantity of money (through buying securities by the Central Bank of the country from the open market) will lower the rate of interest. In Fig. 17.5, when the quantity of money increases from OM_1 to OM_2 the rate of interest falls from *i* to *i'* because the new quantity of money OM_2 is in balance with the demand for money at *i'* rate of interest. In this case we move down on the curve. Thus, given the money demand curve or curve of liquidity preference, an increase in the supply of money brings down the rate of interest.

Let us see how increase in money supply leads to the fall in the rate of interest. With initial equilibrium at *i*, when the money supply is expanded from M_1 to M_2, there emerges excess supply of money at the initial *i* rate of interest. The people would react to this excess quantity of money supplied by buying bonds. As a result, the bond prices will go up which implies that the rate of interest will decline. This is how the increase in money supply leads to the fall in rate of interest.

Effect of Increase in Money Demand

The position of money demand curve depends upon two factors: (1) the level of nominal income, and (2) the expectations about the changes in bond prices in the future which implies changes in rate of interest in future. As has been explained above, a money demand curve is drawn by assuming a certain level of nominal income. With the increase in nominal income, money demand for transactions motive increases causing an upward shift in the money demand curve.

Shift in money demand curve (or what Keynes called liquidity preference curve) can also be caused by changes in the expectations of the people regarding changes in bond prices or movements in the rate of interest in the future. If some changes in events lead the people on balance to expect a higher rate of interest in the future than they had previously supposed, the money demand or liquidity preference for speculative motive will increase which will bring about an upward shift in the money demand curve or liquidity preference curve and this will raise the rate of interest.

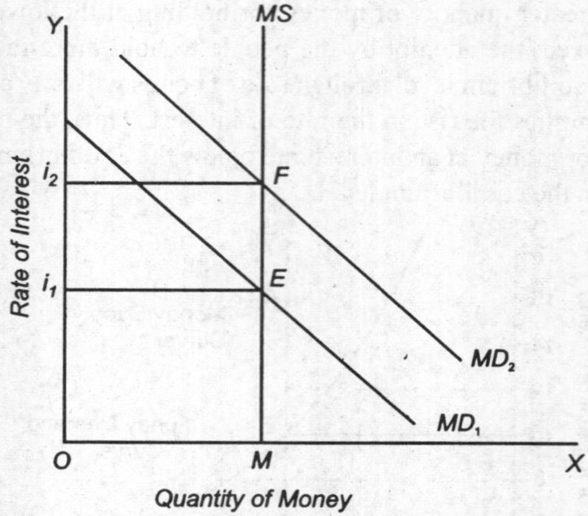

Fig. 17.6. *Effect of Increase in Demand for Money on the Rate of Interest.*

In Fig 17.6 assuming that the quantity of money remains unchanged at *M*, the shift in the money demand curve from MD_1 to MD_2, the rate of interest rises from i_1 to i_2 because *at* i_2, the new demand for money is in equilibrium with the supply of money *OM*. It is worth noting that when the money demand curve shifts from MD_1 to MD_2, the amount of money held does not increase; it remains *OM* as before. Only the rate of interest rises from i_1 to i_2 to equilibrate the new liquidity preference or money demand with the available quantity of money *OM*.

Critical Appraisal

Thus we see that *Keynes explained interest in terms of purely monetary forces and not in terms of real forces like productivity of capital and thrift which formed the foundation stones of both classical and loanable fund theories.* According to him, demand for money for speculative motive together with the supply of money determines the rate of interest. He agreed that the marginal revenue product of capital tends to become equal to the rate of interest but the rate of interest is not determined by marginal revenue product of capital. Moreover, according to him, interest is not a reward for saving or thriftiness or waiting but for parting with liquidity. Keynes asserted that it is not the rate of interest which equalises saving with investment. But this equality is brought about through changes in the level of income.

According to Keynes, rate of interest is determined by liquidity preference (*i.e.* demand for money) and supply of money. However, as we have seen, liquidity preference, especially demand for money for transactions motive, depends on level of income. Now, when income increases, liquidity preference curve (that is, money demand curve) will shift to the right and, given the supply of money, new equilibrium rate of interest will be obtained. Thus, at different levels of income there will be different money demand curves. As a result, at different levels of income, there will be different equilibrium rates of interest. Thus, we cannot know the rate of interest unless we know the liquidity preference curve, and also we cannot know the liquidity preference curve unless we know the level of income. According to different levels of income, there will be different demand curves for money and therefore different rates of interest, given the supply of money. In this way we can derive *LM* curve which indicates various combinations of interest rate and income at which money market is in equilibrium. We will explain in detail in a later chapter the derivation of *LM* curve.

Thus, Keynes' analysis at the most helps us to obtain *LM* curve which shows what will be the rate of interest at different levels of income and not any unique or particular rate of interest. Thus, the Keynesian theory, like the classical theory, is indeterminate. "In the Keynesian case the supply and demand for money curves cannot give the rate of interest unless we already know the income level, in the classical case the demand and supply schedules for saving offer no solution until the income is known. Precisely the same is true of loanable funds theory. Keynes' criticism of the classical and lonable funds theories applies equally to his new theory[4].

NUMERICAL PROBLEMS

Problem 1. *The following demand for money function is given :*

$$M_d = 0.6Y - 75i$$

where income Y is in crores of rupees, and interest rate i is in percentage.

(*a*) *Calculate the demand for money when income is 4000 crores and the interest is 5 per cent.*

(*b*) *Given that level of income remains equal to ₹ 4000 crores, (i) if rate of interest falls to 2 per cent, how will it affect demand for money ? (ii) if rate of interest rises to 8 per cent, what will be demand for money ?*

Solution :

(*a*) $M_d = 0.6Y - 75i$

Substituting the values of Y and i we have

$$M_d = 0.6 \times 4000 - 75 \times 5$$
$$= 2400 - 375$$
$$= 2025$$

(*b*) When the rate of interest is 2 per cent

$$M_d = 0.6 \times 400 - 75 \times 2$$
$$= 2400 - 150 = 2250$$

Thus, at a lower interest rate demand for money to hold is more.

(*c*) When rate of interest is 8 per cent,

$$M_d = 0.6 \times 400 - 75 \times 8$$
$$= 2400 - 600$$
$$= 1800$$

Thus, at a higher rate of interest, people demand less money to hold.

Problem 2. *For an economy, the following money-demand function is given :*

$$M_d = 0.5Y - 60i$$

If the Central Bank of the country has set money supply equal to ₹ 1520 crores, find out the rate of interest when money market is in equilibrium. Assume the level of income is ₹ 4000 crores.

Solution :

For money market to be in equilibrium

$$M_d = M_s$$
$$0.5Y - 60\,i = 1520$$

Given that $Y = 4000$ crores, then

$$0.5 \times 4000 - 60\,i = 1520$$
$$2000 - 60i = 1520$$
$$60i = 2000 - 1520$$

4. A. H. Hansen, *Guide to Keynes*. p. 141

$$60\,i = 480$$

$$i = \frac{480}{60} = 8 \text{ per cent}$$

Problem 3. *Given the following money demand function of an economy*

$$MD = 0.5Y - 60i$$

Suppose income of the economy is ₹ 4000 crore and the Central Bank has fixed money supply equal to ₹ 1520 crores. If at a time interest equal to 5 per cent per annum prevails, will the money market be in equilibrium? How interest rate will change if it is not the equilibrium interest rate.

Solution :

Money market is in equilibrium when

$$MD = MS$$

Demand for money $MD = 0.5Y - 60i$

Given that interest $i = 5$ per cent and income is ₹ 4000 crores

$$MD = 0.5 \times 4000 - 60 \times 5$$

$$= 2000 - 300$$

$$= 1700 \text{ crores}$$

$1700 > 1520$. Thus, given money supply of ₹ 1520 crores. at 5 per cent rate of interest, demand for money exceeds supply of money. This excess demand for money will lead to rise in interest to the level where money demand equals the given money supply.

QUESTIONS FOR REVIEW

1. What is meant by money market equilibrium ? How is rate of interest determined by equilibrium in the money market ?
2. Distinguish between transaction demand for money and speculative demand for money. On what factors do they depend ?
3. Money is an asset. Explain. Why do people hold money when it earns no rate of interest ?
4. What is the cost of holding money ? If bond prices rise, how will it affect cost of holding money ?
5. Explain how demand for money is related to interest rate and real income of the economy.
6. Suppose that Reserve Bank of India increases money supply. Show the effects of this action on the rate of interest.
7. Consider the following money demand function:

   $Md = 0.6Y - 120\,r$

   where Y is income and r is rate of interest.

   Suppose that supply of money is 1440 and income is 4000. What will be the equilibrium rate of interest ?
8. Critically examine Keynes' theory of determination of rate of interest. Is it indeterminate ?
9. Rate of interest is a purely monetary phenomenon. Do you agree with Keynes' that real factors such as saving and investment do not play any role in determination of rate of interest ?

CHAPTER 18

Instruments of Monetary Policy and Economic Stabilisation

Introduction

Monetary policy is another important instrument with which objectives of macroeconomic policy can be achieved. *Monetary policy is concerned with the measures taken to regulate the supply of money, the cost and availability of credit in the economy*. It is worth noting that it is the Central Bank of a country which formulates and implements the monetary policy in a country. In some countries such as India the Central Bank (the Reserve Bank is the Central Bank of India) works on behalf of the Government but enjoys some independence in its decision making. However, in some countries such as the USA, the Central Bank (*i.e.*, Federal Reserve Bank System) enjoys an independent status and pursues its independent policy. Like the fiscal policy the *broad objectives of monetary policy are to establish equilibrium at full-employment level of output, to ensure price stability and to promote economic growth of the economy.* Monetary policy is concerned with changing the supply of money stock and rate of interest for the purpose of stabilizing the economy at full-employment or potential output level by influencing the level of aggregate demand. More specifically, at times of recession monetary policy involves the adoption of some monetary tools which tend to increase the money supply and lower interest rates so as to stimulate aggregate demand in the economy. On the other hand, at times of inflation, monetary policy seeks to contract the aggregate spending by tightening the money supply or raising the rate of interest.

It may however be noted that in a developing country such as India, in addition to achieving economic stability by controlling inflation and deflation, monetary policy has also to promote and encourage economic growth both in the industrial and agricultural sectors of the economy. Thus, in the context of developing countries the following three are the important goals or objectives of monetary policy:

(1) to ensure economic stability at full-employment or potential level of output;
(2) to achieve price stability by controlling inflation and deflation; and
(3) to promote and encourage economic growth in the economy.
(4) to ensure exchange rate stability

In line with the above goals of monetary policy it has often been asserted by Governors of Reserve Bank of India that *growth with price stability is the goal of monetary policy of the Reserve Bank of India*. The various objectives of the Reserve Bank of India will be discussed in detail in the next chapter. The role of monetary policy in achieving economic stability at a higher level of output and employment will be discussed below and its role in promoting economic growth in developing country with special reference to India will be explained and critically examined at length in the next chapter. Let us discuss the various instruments of monetary policy in some detail

INSTRUMENTS OR TOOLS OF MONETARY POLICY

The central bank of a country has the responsibility of controlling the volume and direction of credit in the country. Bank credit has become these days an important constituent of the money supply in the country. The volume and direction of bank credit has, therefore, an important bearing on the level of economic activity. Excessive credit will tend to generate inflationary pressures in the economy, while deficiency of credit supply may tend to cause depression or deflation. Lack of the availability of cheap credit may also hinder economic development of a country. At times of depression, there is a need to expand credit and at times of boom there is need to contract credit. For promoting economic development, expansion of cheap credit (credit at low rates of interest) is desirable. In order to prevent booms and depressions (*i.e.,* to maintain economic stability) and to promote economic growth, central bank seeks to control credit in accordance with the needs of the situation:

Broadly speaking, there are two types of methods of controlling credit.

(1) **Quantitative or General Methods.** These instruments seek to change the total quantity of credit in general. These are three in number: (*i*) *changing the bank rate and repo rate* (*ii*) *undertaking open market operaions*; (*iii*) *changing the cash reserve ratio.*

(2) **Qualitative or Selective Control Methods.** These tools aim at changing the volume of a specific type of credit. In other words, the selective control methods affect the use of credit for particular purposes.

We discuss below these methods in detail.

Bank Rate Policy

Bank rate is the minimum rate at which the central bank of a country provides loans to the commercial banks of the country. Bank rate is also called *discount rate* because in the earlier days central bank used to provide finance to the commercial banks by rediscounting bills of exchange. Through changes in the bank rate, the central bank can influence the creation of credit by the commercial banks. Bank credit these days is an important component of the supply of money in the economy. Changes in money supply affect aggregate demand and thereby output and prices. For instance, when the central bank raises the bank rate, the cost of borrowings by the commercial banks from the central bank would rise. This would discourage the commercial banks to borrow from the central bank . Further, when the bank rate is raised, the commercial banks also raise their lending rates. When the lending rates of interest charged by the commercial banks are higher, businessmen and industrialists would feel discouraged to borrow from commercial banks. This would tend to contract bank credit and hence would result in the reduction of money supply in the economy. The reduction in the supply of money would reduce aggregate demand or money expenditure. This would reduce prices and check inflation in the economy. Thus when the economy is gripped by inflation or rising prices, the bank rate is generally raised to contract credit creation by the banks.

On the other hand, when there is recession or depression in the economy, the bank rate is lowered to overcome it. A fall in the bank rate will cause the reduction in lending interest rates of the commercial banks. With credit or loans from banks becoming cheaper, businessmen would borrow more from the commercial banks for investment and other purposes. This would lead to the increase in aggregate demand for goods and services and help in overcoming recession and bringing about recovery of the economy.

If a country permits the free flow of funds in and out of the country, then the changes in the bank rate will also have an effect on the external flows. For instance, as said above, when the bank rate is raised all interest rates in the market would also generally rise. With the rise in the deposit rates of interest of the banks, funds from outside would be attracted to the banks of the country. Further, with the rise in deposit rates, outflow of funds from the banks to the other countries would be prevented. Therefore, these effects on the capital flows of the rise in bank rate will have a favourable effect on the balance of payments of the country as it will help to meet the current account deficit of the country. At present in India we are facing a huge current account deficit in our balance of payments as our import bill of crudes oil, petroleum products and gold have gone up while our exports have slowed down.

Capital outflows create a lot of problems. When foreign capital is withdrawn from our debt and equity markets, not only our stock market crashes but also they raise the demand for US dollars to send abroad. As a result of increase in demand for dollars, the exchange rate of rupee per US dollar falls, that is, Indian rupee depreciates. Depreciation of a currency is generally considered as desirable as it tends to raise exports and reduce imports. However, because our demand for imports is inelastic, the prices rise as a result of depreciation, but the volume of imports remain unaffected. The rise in prices of imports therefore contributes to inflation in the economy and worsens it further. To prevent this rate of interest must be kept high

It is important to note that the *changes in bank rate affect the credit creation by banks through altering the cost of credit.* Changes in the cost of credit affect borrowings by the commercial banks from the central bank and also affect the demand for credit by businessmen from the commercial banks.

Repo Rate in India. However, changes in bank rate as a tool of monetary policy in India has been quite limited. Before 1991, bank rate remained unchanged at 10 per cent in the whole decade of 1981-1991. This was because prior to 1991, interest rates charged by banks were administered by the Reserve Bank and therefore could not be used as a reference rate by the banks for the purpose of fixing their lending rates. In the post-reform period from July 1991, to control inflationary pressures in the Indian economy bank rate was raised from 10 per cent to 11 per cent. However, since then bank rate has been rarely used. This is for two reasons. The bank rate is meant **for a longer intermediate period for regulating interest rates charged by the banks** from their customers and thereby influences the cost of credit. However, in the Indian context what was needed was to regulate liquidity of the banks for a very short period, even on daily basis. Second even now when lending rates of interest have been freed from control by RBI, there **is not much refinance** being made available at the bank rate and therefore the banks can ignore it as a reference in setting their own lending rates.

However, the need for influencing the lending rates of banks and liquidity of the Indian banks was very much needed. Therefore, for this purpose in 1997 RBI introduced under its **liquidity adjustment facility,** a rate of interest called **repo rate.** Under *repo rate system* bank could get overnight short term loans from the RBI to meet their needs of liquidity if they arise. Through repo system RBI buys securities from the banks and thereby provide loans to them. the rate of interest at which the RBI lends overnight funds to the banks against securities is called *repo ratio.* Repo rate is short-run interest rate and bank rate is the long-term interest rate at which banks could borrow from the RBI. The introduction of repo rate helps the Reserve Bank to increase the liquidity of the banks by purchasing from them Government securities and meeting their needs for liquidity when they arise. There is also ***reverse repo mechanism*** in which the banks park their surplus funds with the RBI on which they earn interest. *The interest rate which RBI pays to the banks for the funds they keep with it for the short term under this scheme is called reverse repo rate.* Through reverse repo system, the RBI mops up liquidity from the banking system.

Repo refers to agreement for a transaction between RBI and banks through which RBI supplies funds immediately against Government securities and simultaneously banks agree to repurchase the same or similar securities after a specified time which may be one day to 14 days. Through *reverse repo,* RBI mops up liquidity from the banking system by selling them securities when it finds that there is excess liquidity in the system which may create inflationary pressures. Under the repo agreement banks can get short-term loans from RBI against the securities to meet the needs of liquidity when they arise. Thus, Repo and Reverse Repo operations are useful tool of short-run liquidity management by RBI. Repo and Reverse Repo operations should not be confused with open market operations as the latter involve sale and purchase sale and purchase of Government securities in the market for a longer intermediate period and not for one day or few days. Besides, on Repo and Reverse Repo rates of interest are fixed by RBI white in open market operations rate of interest varies and depends on demand and supply conditions of funds.

As a tool of monetary policy when Reserve Bank of India wants to check inflation, **it raises the repo rate.** When the commercial banks find that borrowing from the RBI has become costly and if they have not much excess reserves with them they will raise their lending rates. At higher lending rates businessmen will be discouraged for taking loans from the banks to finance their investment projects. Likewise, persons who want loans for building or purchasing houses and cars will also be discouraged to get loans from the banks. This will result in contraction of credit which will tend to lower aggregate demand and thereby help in controlling inflation.

On the other hand, when there are recessionary conditions in the economy, the RBI lowers the repo rate. With fall in the repo rate the banks can borrow from the banks at lower short term rate of interest. In turn they lower their lending rates to businessmen for investment and to the consumers who seek home loans and car loans. This raises investment and consumption demand which through the operation of multiplier helps to raise the level of income and employment. As a result, the economy is lifted out of recession. Such a situation prevailed in India in 2007-09 when following the global financial crisis resulted in the decline of our exports landing the Indian economy into recession. Them RBI lowered its repo rate from 9 per cent to 4.5 per cent during a period from Oct. 2008 to March 2009. This helped to raise investment and consumption demand which led to recovery of the Indian economy in 2009-10 and 2010-11.

Limitations of Bank Rate and Repo Rate Policy

Bank rate policy does not have always the desired effect on investment, output and prices. There are certain conditions which must be met for the successful working of the bank rate policy. These conditions are:

(1) All other rates should follow the bank rate in its movement so that bank credit should expand or contract as desired. This will not happen if the commercial banks have considerable reserves of their own at their disposal and, therefore, their dependence on borrowed funds from the central bank may be very less. Further, for the changes in the bank rate to cause changes in all other interest rates in the market, a well-organised money market is needed. If well-organised money market does not exist as is the case in India where indigenous bankers contribute a good part of the money market, changes in the bank rate would not be followed by the appropriate changes in all rates.

(2) The second important condition for the successful working of the bank rate policy is the responsiveness of businessmen to the changes in the lending rates of interest. If businessmen and investors reduce their borrowings when the bank rate and hence the lending rates of commercial banks are raised, and increase their borrowings for investment when the bank rate and lending rates of the banks are reduced, the changes in the bank rate will have the effect, predicted in the bank rate theory. However, empirical studies conducted recently have shown that rate of interest does not exercise a strong influence on borrowings for investment and other purposes. When there is inflationary situation in the economy, the rate of interest will have to be raised very high in order to have desirable effects. Similarly, the response of investment to the fall in the rate of interest is never vigorous. Demand by businessmen for credit for investment purposes from the banks depends on the economic situation prevailing in the economy. When the economy is gripped by severe depression and consequently prospects for making profits are bleak, businessmen would be reluctant to borrow for investment even though the lending rates of interest have been lowered considerably to induce them to borrow. It has been aptly remarked that *'you can bring the horse to water but you cannot make it drink'*.

The present belief is that bank rate policy will play only a subsidiary role in the monetary control. The bank rate or repo rate at the best could check a boom and inflation but could not bring about a recovery if the country was suffering from recession or depression. Thus it has much greater potential effectiveness if it is desired to arrest credit expansion than when it is sought to stimulate credit. But used in conjunction with other instruments it can still play a useful role. The bank rate and repo rate have the value as a signal. If the traditions are that a signal must be obeyed, the bank rate and repo rate policy *can fulfil its purpose since it will be in keeping with respectable conduct.*

Open Market Operations

Open market operations are another important instrument of credit control, especially in the developed countries. The term open market operations means the purchase and sale of securities by the central bank of the country. The theory of open market operations is like this: The sale of securities by the central bank leads to the contraction of credit and the purchase thereof to credit expansion. When the central bank sells securities in the open market, it receives payment in the form of a cheque on one of commercial banks. If the purchaser is a bank, the cheque is drawn against the purchasing bank. In both cases the result is the same. The cash balance of the bank in question, which it keeps with the central bank, is to that extent reduced. With the reduction of its cash, the commercial bank has to reduce its lending. Thus, credit contracts. When the central bank purchases securities, it pays through cheques drawn on itself. This increases the cash balance of the commercial banks and enables them to expand credit. *'Take care of the legal tender money and credit will take care of itself'* is the maxim.

The open market operations method is sometimes adopted to make the bank rate or repo rate policy effective. If the member-banks do not raise lending rates following the rise in the bank rate due to surplus funds available with them, the central bank can withdraw such surplus funds by the sale of securities and thus compel the member-banks to raise their rates. Scarcity of funds in the market compels the banks directly or indirectly to borrow from the central bank through rediscounting of bills. If the bank rate or repo rate is high, the market rate of interest cannot remain low.

It may be noted that to check inflation the RBI sells government securities to the banks through open market operations and receive in return cash from them. This reduces the cash reserves with the banks and thus reducing their liquidity. This causes contraction of credit which help in fighting inflation.

On the other hand, when RBI faces recessionary problem in the economy it will seek to expand credit or money supply in the economy. This can be done through open market operations by buying securities from the open market. With this purchase of securities from the market the RBI pays cash funds to the banks and thus raise their cash reserves or liquidity. Against this increase in cash reserves, banks are able to create credit or bank deposits through providing loans by a multiple of the increase in their cash reserves depending on the value of deposit multiplier.

Limitations of the Open Market Operations. It is obvious that this method will succeed only if certain conditions are satisfied. The limitations are discussed below:

(1) According to the theory of open market operations, when the central bank purchases securities, the cash reserves of the member-banks will be increased and, conversely, the cash reserves will be decreased when the central bank sells securities. This, however, may not happen. The sale of securities may be offset by return of notes from circulation and hoards. The purchase of securities, on the other hand, may be accompanied by a withdrawal of notes for increased currency requirements or for hoarding. In both the cases, therefore, the cash reserves of the member-banks may remain unaffected.

(2) But even if the cash reserves of the member-banks are increased or decreased, the banks may not expand or contract credit accordingly. The percentage of cash to credit is not rigidly fixed and can vary within quite wide limits. The banks will expand and contract credit according to the prevailing economic and political circumstances and not merely with reference to their cash reserves.

(3) The third condition is that when the commercial bank's cash balances increase, the demand for loans and advances should increase too and vice versa. This may not happen. Owing to economic or political uncertainty, even cheap money rate may not attract borrowers. Conversely when trade is good and prospects of profits bright, entrepreneurs would borrow even at high rates of interest.

(4) Finally, the circulation of bank credit should have a constant velocity. But the velocity of bank deposits is rarely constant. It increases in periods of rising business activity and decreases in periods of depression. Thus, a policy of contracting credit may be neutralised by increased velocity of circulation, and vice versa.

Open market operations as an instrument of credit control have proved to be quite successful in regulating the availability of credit in developed countries. This is for two reasons. First, when the central bank purchases or buys securities, the reserves of the commercial banks automatically expand or contract. The changes in the reserves of the banks directly affect their capacity to lend. Unlike in the case of instrument of bank rate, the success of the market operations does not depend on the attitude or responsiveness of the commercial banks; their capacity to provide credit is affected automatically. Secondly, the open market operations can be managed in a way that the cash reserves of the banks increase or decrease to the desired extent.

Since for the success of market operations it is necessary that there should be broad and active market in short and long-term government securities, and such markets exist only in the U.S.A. and Great Britain and other developed countries, this method of credit control has been most effectively used in these countries.

Open market operations which did not play a significant role as an instrument of credit control in India in the past has now become an important tool and are being used extensively by RBI. This is because market for Government securities in India has now become quite wide and there is excess liquidity in the banking system. General public do not buy more than a fraction of government securities. It is generally banks and other financial institutions that buy or sell government securities. When there is excess liquidity in the banking system, banks are willingly invest in Government securities more than the statutory limits.

Changing the Cash Reserve Ratio (CRR)

Another method to vary the quantity of credit is to change the cash reserve ratio. By law, banks have to keep a certain amount of cash money with themselves as reserves against the deposits. If the legal minimum cash reserve ratio, for example, is 10%, the bank will have to keep ₹ 2,000 as reserves against the deposits of ₹ 20,000. The central bank of a country has the authority to vary the cash reserve ratio. If now the central bank increases the cash reserve ratio from 10% to 20%, then the reserves of ₹ 2,000 could support only deposits of ₹ 10,000 and therefore the banks having reserves of ₹ 2,000 will have to reduce their deposits from ₹ 20,000 to ₹ 10,000. That means the contraction of credit.

On the other hand, if the central bank reduces the cash reserve ratio from 20% to 10%, then the reserves of ₹ 2,000 could support the deposits of ₹ 20,000. Therefore, the banks having reserves of ₹ 2,000 can increase their deposits, *i.e.*, expand credit to ₹ 20,000. To sum up, increase in the legal cash reserve ratio leads to the contraction of credit and decrease in the legal reserve ratio leads to the expansion of credit. *An increase in the legal cash reserve ratio will succeed in contracting credit only when banks have no excess reserves.* If banks are holding excess reserves, the increase in the legal reserve ratio will not bring about the contraction of credit. On the other hand, the reduction in the cash reserve ratio will have the desired effect of expanding credit only if the borrowers respond favourably. As a result of reduction in the cash reserve ratio, the availability to lend by the banks increases and the banks tend to make more credit available to borrowers, or to make it available at lower rates. Now, if the borrowers for one reason or another do not respond favourably, *i.e.*, are not prepared to borrow, credit will not be expanded.

Reserve Bank of India has often used this monetary tool to influence the availability of bank credit depending the conditions prevailing in the Indian economy. For example, when there was recessionary conditions in the Indian economy following the global financial crises in 2007-09, RBI over several stages sharply reduced the cash reserve ratio (CRR) to overcome recession and bring about recovery. With the reduction in cash reserve ratio, a lot of cash reserves were released for the banks which was used by the banks to provide more loans to businessmen for investment purposes and to individuals for buying houses, cars and scooters, This led to the increase a in aggregate demand in the economy which helped in recovery of the Indian economy.

On the other hand, when during 2011-12 and 2012-13, a serious problem of inflation (*i.e.*, rise in general price level) prevailed in the Indian economy, Reserve Bank of Indian raised the cash reserve ratio (CRR). As a result, banks had to keep more cash reserves with the RBI resulting in decline in the credit availability of the banks. This helped to curtail consumption and investment demand in the economy due to lack of credit. This increase in cash-reserve ratio for the banks helped a lot in reducing aggregate demand in the economy and bringing about fall in the WPI inflation rate to around 5 per cent in April 2013.

Selective Credit Controls

The methods of credit control described above are known as quantitative or general methods as they are meant to control the availability of credit in general. Thus, bank rate policy, open market operations and variations in cash reserves ratio expand or contract the availability of credit for all purposes. On the other hand, selective credit controls are meant to regulate the flow of credit for particular or specific purposes. Whereas, the general credit controls seek to regulate the total available quantity of credit (through changes in the high powered money) and the cost of credit, the selective credit control seek to change the distribution or allocation of credit between its various uses. The selective credit controls have both the positive and negative aspects. In its positive aspect, measures are taken to stimulate the greater flow greater flow of credit to some particular sectors considered as important. Thus in India, agriculture, small and marginal farmers, small artisans, small-scale industries are the priority sectors to which greater flow of bank credit has been sought to be encouraged by the Reserve Bank of India. In its negative aspect, several measures are taken to restrict the credit flowing into some specific activities or sectors which are regarded as undesirable or harmful from the social point of view. The selective credit controls generally used are:

(1) Changes in the minimum margin for lending by banks against the stocks of specific goods kept or against other types of securities.

(2) The fixation of maximum limit or ceiling on advances to individual borrowers against stocks of particular sensitive commodities.

(3) The fixation of minimum discriminatory rates of interest chargeable on credit for particular purposes.

(4) Prohibition of the discounting of bills of exchange involving sale of sensitive commodities.

The selective credit controls originated in U.S.A. to regulate the flow of bank credit to the stock market (*i.e.*, the market for shares). They were also used to restrict the volume of credit available for purchasing durable consumer goods during the period of the Second War. However, in India, the selective credit controls are being used by the Reserve Bank to prevent speculative hoarding of commodities so as to check the rise in prices of these commodities. The selective credit controls in India are being used in the case of foodgrains, oilseeds, vegetable oils, cotton, sugar, gur and khandsari.

Though, all the above techniques of selective credit control are used, in India it is the first technique, namely, the changes in the minimum margin against stocks of commodities or other securities that has been mostly used. It may be noted that the central bank of a country has the power to vary the minimum margin requirements against the security of stocks of commodities. While lending advances to businessmen, the commercial banks leave a margin of the value of stock kept as security to be financed by the businessmen from their own sources and lend funds to them equal to the remaining amount of the value of the stock. This minimum requirement of the value of the stock left to be financed by the borrowers themselves is known as margin. Suppose the margin fixed for a stock of particular commodity is 60 per cent. In this case the businessmen can borrow up to the value of 40 per cent of the stock of that commodity while the 60 per cent of the value of stock will be financed by the businessmen themselves. Now, if the bank raises the margin to 70 per cent, then businessmen can borrow from the bank to the extent of 30 per cent of the value of the stock of that commodity. This will lead to the contraction of credit for holding the stock of the commodity by the businessmen. If the businessmen are not able to finance the holding of 10 per cent extra stock of the commodity, they will be forced to sell that in the market and thus raising market supply of the commodity. This will lower the prices of the commodity, other things remaining the same.

In developed countries, the selective credit controls are generally used to prevent excessive speculation in share market. In the share market, the buyers purchase a good amount of shares by making a small payment and the remaining value of shares are paid by brokers through borrowing from the banks against the shares thus purchased. When the central bank raises the margin, the buyers of shares have to pay a larger sum of money for the shares purchased and as a result bank credit contracts and the speculative activity in the stock market is discouraged.

We shall explain how the above various tools can be used for formulating a proper monetary policy to influence levels of aggregate output, employment and prices in the economy. In times of recession or depression, *expansionary monetary policy* or what is also *called easy money policy* is adopted which raises aggregate demand and thus stimulates the economy. On the other hand, in times of inflation and excessive expansion, *contractionary monetary policy* or what is also called *tight money policy* is adopted to control inflation and achieve price stability through reducing aggregate demand in the economy. We discuss below both these policies.

EXPANSIONARY MONETARY POLICY TO CURE RECESSION OR DEPRESSION

When the economy is faced with recession or involuntary cyclical unemployment, which comes about due to fall in aggregate demand, the central bank intervenes to cure such a situation. Central Bank takes steps to expand the money supply in the economy and/or lower the rate of interest with a view to increase the aggregate demand which will help in stimulating the economy. The following three monetary policy measures are adopted as a part of an expansionary monetary policy to cure recession and to establish the equilibrium of national income at full-employment level of output.

1. The central bank undertakes open market operations and *buys securities in the open market.* Buying of securities by the central bank from the public, chiefly from commercial banks will lead to an increase in reserves of the banks or amount of currency with the general public. With greater reserves, commercial banks can issue more credit to the investors and businessmen for undertaking more investment. More private investment will cause aggregate demand curve to shift upward. Thus buying of securities will have an expansionary effect.
2. The Central Bank *may lower the bank rate or (what is also called discount rate,)* or repo rate which are the rate of interest charged by the central bank a of country on its loans to commercial banks. At a lower bank rate, the commercial banks will be induced to borrow more from the central bank and will be able to issue more credit at the lower rate of interest to businessmen and investors. This will not only make credit cheaper but also increase the availability of credit or money supply in the economy. The expansion in credit or money supply will increase the investment demand which will tend to raise aggregate output and income.
3. Thirdly, the *central bank may reduce the Cash Reserve Ratio (CRR) to be kept by the commercial banks*. In countries like India, this is a more effective and direct way of expanding credit and increasing money supply in the economy by the central bank. With lower reserve requirements, a large amount of funds is released for providing loans to businessmen and investors. As a

result, credit expands and investment increases in the economy which has an expansionary effect on output and employment. In April 1996, when *Reserve Bank* lowered the CRR from 14 per cent to 13 per cent, it was estimated that this would release funds equal to ₹ 5,000 crores for the banks and thereby would significantly increase their lending capacity.

Similar to the Cash Reserve Ratio (CRR), in India there is another monetary instrument, namely, *Statutory Liquidity Ratio* (SLR) used by the Reserve Bank to change the lending capacity and therefore credit availability in the economy. As explained in a previous chapter, according to Statutory Liquidity Ratio, in addition to the Cash Reserve Ratio (CRR) banks have to keep a certain minimum proportion of their deposits in the form of some specified liquid assets such as Government securities. To increase the lendable resources of the banks, Reserve Bank can lower this Statutory Liquidity Ratio (SLR). Thus, when Reserve Bank of India lowers statutory liquidity ratio (SLR), the credit availability for the private sector will increase.

It may be noted that the use of all the above tools of monetary policy leads to an increase in reserves or liquid resources with the banks. Such reserves are the basis on which banks expand their credit by lending, the increase in reserves raises the money supply in the economy, Thus, *appropriate monetary policy at times of recession or depression can increase the availability of credit and also lower the cost of credit.* This leads to more private investment spending which has an expansionary effect on the economy.

How Expansionary Monetary Policy Works : Keynesian View

Now, it is important to understand how expansionary monetary policy works to cause increase in output and employment and thus help the economy to recover from recession. In the Keynes' theory rate of interest is determined by the demand for and supply of money. According to Keynesian theory, expansion in money supply causes the rate of interest to fall. And this fall in the rate of interest will encourage businessmen to borrow more for investment spending. As is well known, *rate of interest is the opportunity cost of funds invested for purchasing capital goods*. As rate of interest falls, it becomes profitable to invest more in producing or buying capital goods. Thus, fall in the rate of interest raises the investment expenditure which is an important component of aggregate demand. The increase in aggregate demand causes expansion in aggregate output, national income and employment. How, according to Keynesian view, expansion in money supply can help to cure recession is illustrated in Fig. 18.1. In panel (*a*) of Fig. 18.1 it will be seen that when as a result of some measures taken by the central bank, the money supply increases from M_1 to M_2, the rate of interest falls from r_1 to r_2. It will be seen from panel (*b*) that with this fall in rate of interest, investment increases from I_1 to I_2. Now, in panel (*c*), it is shown how the increase in investment expenditure from I_1 to I_2 shifts the aggregate demand curve $(C + I_1 + G)$ upward so that the new aggregate demand curve $C + I_2 + G$ intersects the 40° line at point E_2 and thus establishes equilibrium at full-employment output level Y_F. It may be noted that with the given increase in investment how much aggregate output or national income will increase depends on the size of income multiplier which is determined by marginal propensity to consume. The greater the size of multiplier, the greater the impact of increment in investment on expansion of output and income.

From above, it is clear that monetary policy can play an important role in stimulating the economy and ensuring stability at full-employment level. But it is worth mentioning that there are several weak links in the full chain of increase in money supply achieving a significant expansion in economic activity. In fact, *Keynes himself was of the view that in times of depression, monetary policy would be ineffective in reviving the economy and therefore he laid stress on the adoption of fiscal policy to overcome depression.*

The first weak link in the above argument of expansionary monetary policy relates to the elasticity of *money-demand* (*i.e., liquidity preference*) *curve* M^d in panel (*a*) of Fig. 18.1. As shall be explained at length below, if demand for money curve M^d is nearly flat (*i.e.*, highly elastic), the increase in money supply by the central bank will not greatly affect the rate of interest and consequently further steps of significant expansion in investment and aggregate demand will not be realized. Besides, even if money demand curve is elastic and, therefore, expansion of money supply lowers the rate of interest significantly, the investment may not rise much. This is because if the investment demand curve is steep or inelastic, that is, investment is not sensitive to the changes in rate of interest, the fall in the rate of interest will fail to cause any significant increase in investment. As a result, aggregate demand curve will not change much and expansionary effect on output and employment will not be realized.

Further, the effect of increase in investment on output and employment depends on the size of multiplier. If there are several leakages in the multiplier process, even increase in investment may not

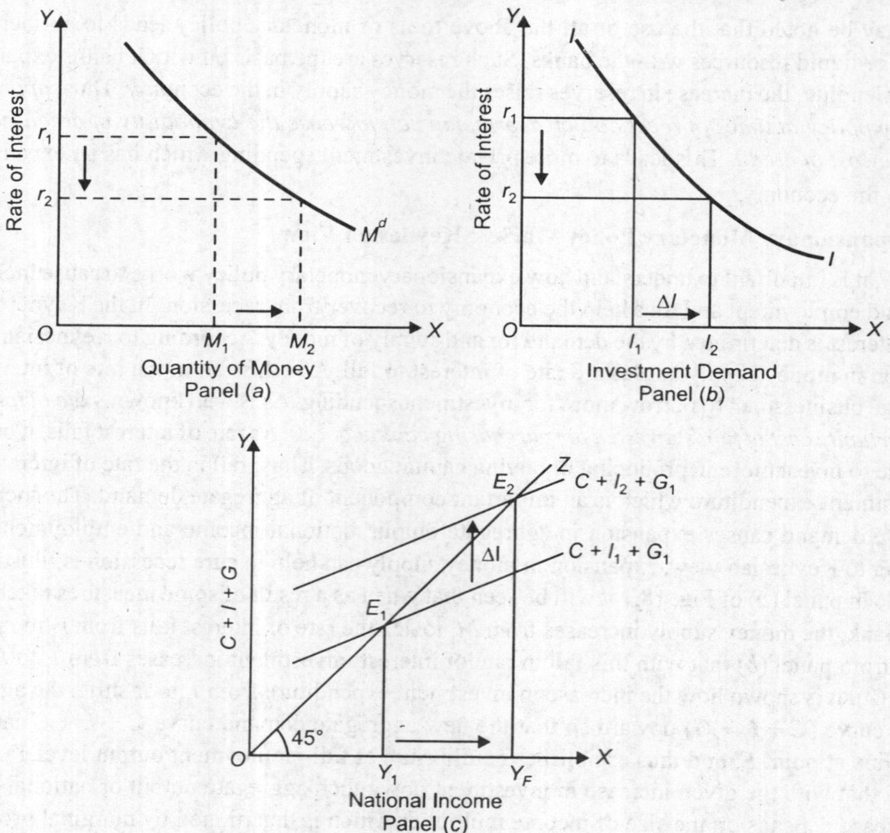

Fig. 18.1. *How Expansionary Monetary Policy Works : Keynesian View*

bring about much change in output and employment. Thus, because of several weak links in the process or chain of expansion in money supply bringing about expansion, Keynes remarked that *there are many a slip between the cup and the lip*. Therefore, for all these reasons (especially because of the liquidity trap in the demand for money curve at lower rates of interest), Keynes was of the view that monetary policy is not an effective instrument in bringing about revival of the economy from the depressed state.

It may however be noted that modern Keynesians do not share the pessimistic view of the effectiveness of monetary policy. They think that liquidity preference curve is not flat and further that investment demand is fairly sensitive to the changes in the rates of interest. Therefore, *modern Keynesians equally advocate for the adoption of discretionary monetary policy as for the discretionary fiscal policy to get rid of recession.*

TIGHT MONETARY POLICY TO CONTROL INFLATION

When aggregate demand rises sharply due to large consumption and investment expenditure or more importantly, due to the large increase in Government expenditure relative to its revenue resulting in huge budget deficits, a demand-pull inflation occurs in the economy. Besides, when there is too much creation of money for one reason or the other, it generates inflationary pressures in the economy. To check the demand-pull inflation which has been a major problem in India and several other countries in recent years, the adoption of *contractionary* monetary policy which is popularly called tight monetary policy is called for. Note that tight or restrictive money policy is one which reduces the availability of credit and also rises its cost. The following monetary measures which constitute tight money policy are generally adopted to control inflation :

1. *The Central Bank sells the Government securities to the banks, other depository institutions and the general public through open market operations.* This action will reduce the reserves with the banks and liquid funds with the general public. With less reserves with the banks, their lending capacity will be reduced. Therefore, they will have to reduce their demand deposits by refraining from giving new loans as old loans are paid back. As a result, money supply in the economy will shrink.
2. *The bank rate may also be raised which will discourage the banks to take loans from the central bank.* This will tend to reduce their liquidity and also induce them to raise their own lending rates. Thus this will reduce the availability of credit and also raise its cost. This will lead to the reduction in investment spending and help in reducing inflationary pressures.

   It may be noted that in India changes in bank rate have not been generally used to bring stability in the economy. It is the instruments of repo rate and reverse rate changes that have often used to fight inflation and recessionary situation. *Repo rate is the interest rate at which Reserve Bank of India lends funds to the commercial banks for a short period of time. To control inflation repo rate is raised.* Hike in repo rate raises the cost of funds for the banks which, if they do not have excess reserves or enough liquidity, would raise their lending rates. The rise in lending rates of banks which will raise the borrowing costs for businessmen will lead to the reduction in demand for bank credit and thus lower investment and consumption demand. The opposite happens when to fight recession the RBI lowers repo rate and thus reducing lending rate for the banks.
3. The most important anti-inflationary measure is the *raising of statutory Cash Reserve Ratio (CRR).* Rise in cash reserve ratio (CRR) reduces cash reserves of banks. To meet the new higher reserve requirements, banks will reduce their lending, that is, credit availability. This will have a direct effect on the contraction of money supply in the economy and help in controlling demand pull inflation. Besides Cash Reserve Ratio (CRR), the Statutory Liquidity Ratio (SLR) can also be increased through which excess reserves of the banks are mopped up resulting in contraction in credit.
4. Fourthly, an important anti-inflationary measure is the use of qualitative credit control, namely, *raising of minimum margins for obtaining loans from banks against the stocks of sensitive commodities* such as foodgrains, oilseeds, cotton, sugar, vegetable oil. As a result of this measure, businessmen themselves will have to finance to a greater extent the holding of inventories of goods and will be able to get less credit from banks. This selective credit control has been extensively used in India to control inflationary pressures.

How the Tight Monetary Policy Works : Keynesian View

It is important to understand how tight monetary policy works to check inflation. As explained above, tight monetary policy seeks to reduce the money supply through contraction of credit in the economy and also raising the cost of credit, that is, lending rates of interest. The reduction in money supply itself raises the rate of interest. The higher interest rate reduces investment spending which results in lowering of aggregate demand curve $(C + I + G)$. The decrease in aggregate demand tends to restrain demand pull inflation. How tight money policy helps in checking inflation is graphically shown in Fig. 18.2. Let us assume that full-employment level of national income is Y_F as depicted in panel (*c*) of Fig. 18.2. Now, if due to a large budget deficit and excessive creation of money supply, aggregate demand curve shifts to $C + I_2 + G_2$; inflationary gap of E_1H comes to exist at full-employment level. That is, the sum of consumption expenditure, private investment spending and Government expenditure exceeds the full-employment level of output by E_1H. This creates a demand-pull inflation causing rise in prices. Though with aggregate demand curve $C + I_2 + G_2$ equilibrium reaches at point E_2 and as a result national income increases but only in money terms ; real income or output level remaining constant at OY_F.

Now, it will be seen from panel (*a*) that if tight money policy succeeds in reducing money supply from M_2 to M_1 the rate of interest will rise from r_1 to r_2. Panel (*b*) of Fig. 18.2 shows that at a higher interest rate r_2, private investment falls from I_2 to I_1. This reduction in investment expenditure shifts aggregate demand curve $C + I_2 + G_2$ downward to $C + I_1 + G_1$ and in this way inflationary gap is closed and equilibrium at full-employment output level Y_F is once again established. In our figure it has been assumed that contraction of money supply from M_2 to M_1 and as a result rise in rate of interest from r_1 to r_2 is sufficient to reduce investment expenditure equal to $I_2 - I_1$ which is equal to inflationary gap and in this way macroeconomic equilibrium without any inflationary pressure is established at output level Y_F.

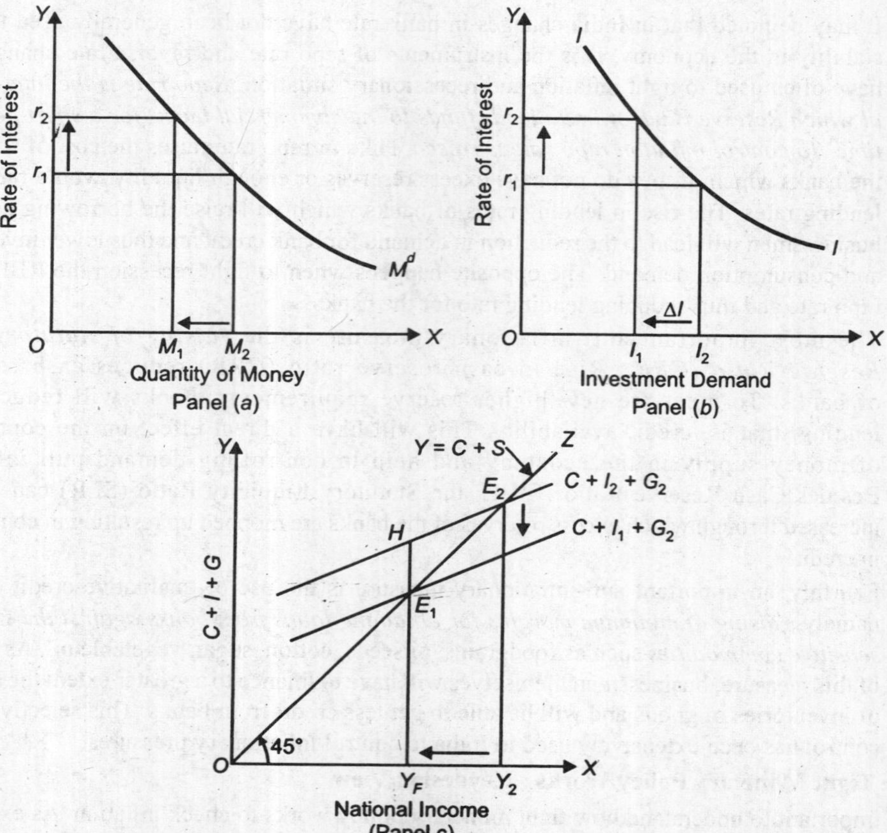

Fig. 18.2. *How Anti-inflationary Monetary Policy Works : Keynesian View*

It should be further remembered that in our analysis of the successful working of the tight monetary policy it is assumed that demand for money curve (*i.e.*, liquidity preference curve) is fairly steep so as to push up the rate of interest from r_1 to r_2 and further that investment demand curve *II* in panel (*b*) of Fig. 18.2 is fairly elastic so that rise in rate of interest from r_1 to r_2 is sufficient to reduce investment by $I_2 - I_1$ or ΔI. If these conditions regarding the slopes of the money demand curve and investment demand curve represent the real world situation, then tight monetary policy will succeed in controlling inflation and ensuring price stability.

To sum up, Keynesian view of how expansionary and contractionary (tight) monetary policies work to achieve the twin goals of price stability and equilibrium at full-employment level of output is shown in the accompanying box.

Monetary Policy : Keynesian View

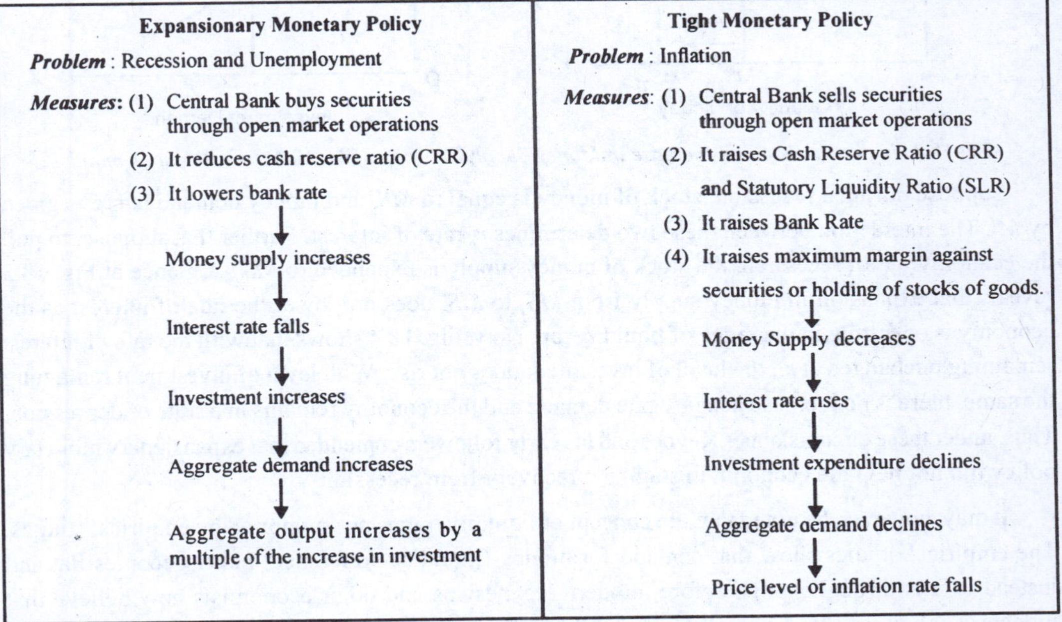

Liquidity Trap and Ineffectiveness of Monetary Policy

Keynes and his early followers doubted the effectiveness of monetary policy in pulling the economy out of depression. They therefore emphasized the role of fiscal policy for fighting severe recession. According to Keynes and his followers, during severe recession people have a high elastic demand for money at low rates of interest. At low rate of interest banks hold on to whatever money reserves they happen to get and the people in general also hold on to whatever money they spare. According to Keynes, demand for money or what he calls liquidity preference is determined mainly by transactions and speculative motives. Whereas transactions demand for money is determined by the level of national income, the speculative demand for money depends on the expectations regarding future rates of interest. During depression, current rate of interest may fall so low that most of the people expect the interest rate to rise in future and therefore they hold on to their money for the present. This makes the demand for money absolutely elastic at a low rate of interest as is shown in Fig. 18.3. It will be seen from Fig. 18.3 that at the low rate of interest r_0 demand curve for money M^d is absolutely elastic showing people demand or hold on to all the increases in money supply beyond MS_1 for speculative purposes and not invest in bonds. Under these circumstances the economy is said to have fallen in a liquidity trap. A liquidity trap occurs when under conditions of depression the economy finds itself in a situation where people hold all the increments in the stock of money so that demand for money becomes absolutely elastic and therefore money demand curve M^d takes a horizontal shape.

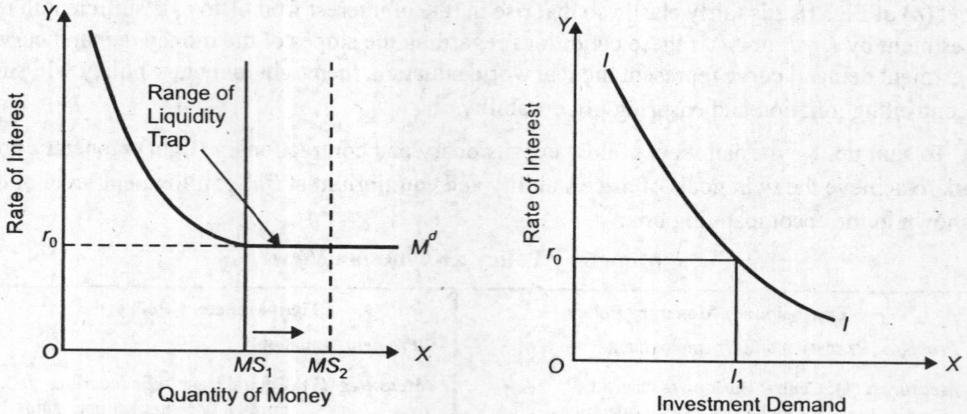

Fig.18.3. *Liquidity Trap and Increase in Money Supply* **Fig. 18.4.** *Investment Demand*

Suppose during a recession, stock of money is equal to MS_1 and money demand curve is given by M^d. The interaction between these two determines r_0 rate of interest. Further that suppose, to pull the economy out of recession, the stock of money supply is expanded to MS_2. A glance at Fig. 18.3 reveals that expansion in money supply from MS_1 to MS_2 does not lower the rate of interest as the economy is operating in the range of liquidity tap. Now, Fig. 18.4 shows that with the rate of interest remaining unchanged at r_0, the level of investment does not rise. With level of investment remaining the same, there is no increase in aggregate demand and the economy remains in a state of depression. Thus, under these circumstances Keynes and his early followers contended that expansionary monetary policy did not help the economy in staging a recovery from recession.

It may, however, he noted that the concept of liquidity trap is not supported by empirical studies. The empirical studies show that demand for money (liquidity preference) never becomes flat and instead it falls throughout. Therefore, modern Keynesians and other economists now believe that monetary policy can play a useful role in stabilising the economy at full-employment level. However, as shall be discussed below, it is the *monetarists* led by Friedman who do not favour discretionary monetary policy to check cyclical instability.

MONETARY POLICY : MONETARIST VIEW

Though most of the modern economists regard both fiscal and monetary policies as important tools for stabilising the economy, there is a group of economists known as *monetarists* led by Friedman who think that changes in money supply are the key determinants in the level of economic activity and the price level. They contend that demand curve for money is quite steep and the investment demand curve is quite elastic so that when there is a change in money supply, it significantly affects the investment demand and therefore the equilibrium level of nominal income.

However, surprisingly enough, the most monetarists do not advocate the use of discretionary monetary policy, namely, an expansionary or easy money policy, to lift the economy out of recession and tight monetary policy to check inflationary boom and thereby correct the `downs' and `ups' of the business cycles. In fact, Friedman, *the chief exponent of monetarism, contends that, historically, far from stabilising the economy, discretionary changes in money supply or rates of interest have a destabilising effect on the economy.* On the basis of his study of monetary history of United States, he contends that faulty decisions regarding changes in money supply, made by the monetary authorities, are responsible for a lot of instability that prevailed during the period of his study. Thus, according to monetarists, *it is not the presence of certain inherent destabilising factors in a free-market economy but the monetary mismanagement* by the discretionary monetary policies which is the root cause of economic instability that has been existing in the free market economies.

Sources of Monetary Mismanagement

According to monetarists, there are two important sources of monetary mismanagement: (1) *variable time lags* concerning the effect of money supply on the nominal income and (2) *treating interest rate as the target of monetary policy* for influencing investment demand for stabilising the economy. We examine below both these sources of monetary mismanagement.

1. Variable Time Lags. First, there is a problem of variable long time-lags that occur for changes in money supply to bring about desirable effect on nominal income. From his empirical studies Friedman concludes that it takes six months to two years for the changes in money supply to produce a significant effect on nominal income. Monetarists argue that since it is extremely difficult to know the time-lag involved in a specific monetary policy measure adopted to tackle the problem, it is impossible to determine *when* a particular policy measure should be taken and *which policy measure*, expansionary or tight, is suitable under the given situation. In fact, according to the monetarists, in view of the uncertainty about the exact duration of time-lags involved, the use of discretionary monetary policy to stabilise the economy may backfire and further intensify the cyclical instability. For example, if expansionary monetary policy is adopted because the various economic indicators show the situation of mild recession, then, due to the time-lags involved, say six to eight months, for the policy to yield results, the economic situation might change and become reverse during that period and become one of mild inflationary situation. Expansionary monetary policy which produces the effect after 6 to 8 months may, therefore, actually intensify the inflationary situation.

2. Interest Rate as a Wrong Target Variable. The second source of money mismanagement is the wrong target variable chosen by the monetary authorities. Monetarists have asserted that monetary authorities have tried to control the interest rates to stabilise the economy. It has been argued that Central Bank cannot simultaneously stabilise both the interest rate and money supply. By controlling the interest rate it has actually destabilised the economy. For example, if the economy is recovering from recession and is presently approaching full employment with aggregate demand, output, employment and prices all registering a rise, the transactions demand for money will increase. This increase in transactions demand for money will cause the rate of interest to rise. But if the monetary authorities have chosen to stabilise the interest rate, they would adopt tight monetary policy to prevent the interest rate from going up. But the tight money supply to check the rate of interest from rising will lower the aggregate demand when the economy is recovering from recession, and will again cause the recessionary situation. Thus an attempt by the Central Bank to stabilise the interest rate will make the economy unstable. Similarly, when the economy is going into recession, it will result in lowering aggregate output and prices. This fall in aggregate output and prices will cause a decline in the transactions demand for money. And the decrease in transactions demand will lead to the fall in interest rate. To prevent this fall in interest rate, if money supply is increased, it will generate inflationary pressures in the economy. Thus, steps taken to stabilise the interest rate cause instability in the economy rather than removing it.

Monetary Rule : Monetary Policy Prescription

From the above analysis it follows that monetarists are not in favour of stabilising the interest rate, they advocate for the *adoption of a rule rather than pursuing discretionary monetary policy* to stabilise the economy. They prescribe a *rule for the growth of the money supply* to achieve economic growth with stability. According to the monetary rule suggested by Friedman, *money supply should be allowed to grow at the rate equal to the rate of growth of output*. If the economy is expected to grow annually at the rate of 3, 4 or 5 per cent, money supply should also grow at this rate. The growth of output of an economy will absorb the extra money supply created as per this rule, without generating inflationary or recessionary conditions, and will thus ensure stability in the economy. To quote Ritter and Silber, "Such a rule would eliminate the major cause of instability in the economy—the capricious and unpredictable impact of counter cyclical monetary policy. As long as the money supply grows at a constant rate each year, be it 3, 4 or 5 per cent, any decline into recession will be temporary. The liquidity provided by a constantly growing money supply will cause the aggregate demand to expand. Similarly, if the supply of money does not rise at more than average rate, any inflationary increase in spending will burn itself out for lack of fuel."[1]

Monetary rule has been criticised by the Keynesian economists. They have argued that monetary rule will have a destabilising effect. Given that the velocity of money (V) is unstable or variable, increase in money supply (M), according to this rule, may not ensure growth of aggregate demand (which, according to monetarist theory, is equal to MV) equal to the rate of growth of output in a year which is difficult to predict. Thus, money supply increase may sometimes exceed the growth of output and sometimes fall short of it and as a result may cause sometimes demand-pull inflation and sometimes necessary conditions. Thus, according to Keynesian economists, policy of monetary rule does not guarantee economic stability and it may itself create economic instability.

QUESTIONS FOR REVIEW

1. What is meant by monetary policy ? Briefly explain the instruments of monetary policy.
2. Explain the objectives of monetary policy.
3. Explain monetary policy measures that should be adopted for curing recession (or depression) and reviving the economy. How does expansionary monetary policy work ? How does Keynesian view in this regard differ from the monetarist view ?
4. What are the factors that determine the effectiveness of monetary policy in reviving the economy from recession? Why Keynes thought that monetary policy was ineffective in reviving the economy from depression ?
5. What is liquidity trap ? How does it make the expansionary monetary policy ineffective in reviving the economy from recession ?
6. Explain the main instruments of monetary policy that can be adopted to control inflation in the economy.
7. Explain the mechanism through which tight monetary policy works to check inflation. Illustrate diagrammatically.

---

1. L.S. Riter and W.L. Silber, Money, 5th ed., Basic Books publishers, 1984, pp. 141-142.

8. Discretionary monetary policy can play an important role in stabilising the economy at full employment. Discuss.

9. Explain the views of Friedman and his follower modern monetarists regarding monetary policy as a tool of economic stabilisation. In this connection also comment on the monetarist view that interest rate is a wrong target variable of proper monetary policy.

10. What is meant by 'time-lags' ? How do they affect the efficiency of monetary policy to stabilise the economy?

11. What are the instruments of monetary policy ? Explain the role of changes in bank rate and open market operations in controlling trade cycles.

12. What is cash reserve ratio ? How a reduction in cash reserve ratio by RBI has a multiplier effect on aggregate demand ?

13. What are open market operation ? How do the open market purchase of government securities by the RBI help to revive the economy from recession.

CHAPTER 19

Monetary Policy of Reserve Bank of India : Economic Growth with Stability

Introduction

Monetary policy is concerned with the measures taken to regulate the supply of money, the cost and availability of credit in the economy. Further, it also deals with the distribution of credit between uses and users and also with both the lending and borrowing rates of interest of the banks. In developed countries the monetary policy has been usefully used for overcoming depression and inflation as an anti-cyclical policy. However, in developing countries it has to play a significant role in promoting economic growth. As Prof. R. Prebisch writes, "The time has come to formulate a monetary policy which meets the requirements of economic development, which fits into its framework perfectly." Further, along with encouraging economic growth, the monetary policy has also to ensure price stability, because the excessive inflation not only has adverse distribution effect but hinders economic development also.

It is important to understand the distinction between *objectives* or *goals*, *targets* and *instruments* of monetary policy. Whereas goals of monetary policy refer to its objectives which, as mentioned above, may be price stability, full employment or economic growth, *targets refer to the variables such as supply of money or bank credit, interest rates which are sought to be changed through the instruments of monetary policy so as to attain these objectives*. The various instruments of monetary policy are changes in the supply of currency, variations in bank rates and other interest rates, open market operations, selective credit controls, and variations in reserve requirements. We have explained these instruments in detail in a previous chapter. We shall first explain below the objectives or goals of monetary policy in a developing economy with special reference to those adopted by Reserve Bank of India. After having explained the objectives we shall explain role of monetary policy in promoting economic growth with stability in a developing country like India. In the end we will explain monetary policy of reserve Bank of India in different periods of planned development, especially soft-interest and liberal credit policy adopted by Reserve Bank of India since 1996.

OBJECTIVES OF MONETARY POLICY OF RESERVE BANK

Before explaining in detail the monetary measures undertaken by RBI to regulate credit and growth of money supply, it is important to explain the objectives of monetary policy pursued by RBI in formulation of its policy. Since monetary policy is one instrument of economic policy, its objectives cannot be different from those of overall economic policy. The three important objectives of monetary policy are:

1. ensuring *price stability,* that is, containing inflation.
2. to encourage *economic growth.*
3. to ensure *stability of exchange rate of the rupee,* that is, exchange rate of rupee with the US dollar, pound sterling and other foreign currencies.

Let us explain below these objectives in some detail.

Price Stability or Control of Inflation

It may be noted that each instrument of economic policy is better suited to achieve a particular objective. Monetary policy is better suited to the achievement of price stability, that is, containing inflation. To quote C. Rangarajan, a former Governor of Reserve Bank of India, "Faced with multiple objectives that are equally relevant and desirable, there is always the problem of assigning to each instrument the most appropriate target or objective. Of the various objectives, *price stability is perhaps the one that can be pursued most effectively by monetary policy.* In a developing country like ours, acceleration of investment activity in the context of supply shocks in the agricultural sector tends to be accompanied by pressures on prices and, therefore, monetary policy has much to contribute in the short-run management."[1]

Thus, achieving price stability has remained the dominant objective of monetary policy of Reserve Bank of India. It may however be noted that price stability does not mean absolutely no change in price at all. In a developing economy like ours where structural changes take place during the process of economic growth some changes in relative prices do occur that generally put upward pressure on prices. Therefore, some changes in price level or, in other words, a certain rate of inflation is inevitable in a developing economy. Thus, *price stability means reasonable rate of inflation.* A high degree of inflation has adverse effects on the economy. First, *inflation raises the cost of living of the people and hurts the poor* most. Therefore, inflation has been described as enemy No. 1 of the poor. Inflation sends many people below the poverty line. Secondly, *inflation makes exports costlier and, therefore, discourages them*. On the other hand, due to higher prices at home people are induced to import goods to a large extent. Thus, inflation has an adverse effect on the balance of payments. Thirdly, when due to a higher rate of inflation *value of money is rapidly falling, people do not have much incentives to save*. This lowers the rate of saving on which investment and economic growth depend. Fourthly, a high rate of inflation *encourages people to invest in the unproductive assets* such as gold, jewellery, real estate etc.

An expert committee on monetary reforms headed by Late Prof. S. Chakravarty suggested 4 per cent rate of inflation as a reasonable rate of inflation and recommended that monetary policy by RBI should be so formulated that ensures that rate of inflation does not exceed 4 per cent per annum. Emphasising the importance of price stability from the viewpoint of India's balance of payments, Prof. Rangarajan writes, "*The increasing openness of the economy, the need to service external debt and the necessity to improve the share of our exports in a highly competitive external environment require that the domestic price level not be allowed to rise unduly, particularly since our major trading partners have had notable success in recent years in achieving price stability.*[2]

Economic Growth

Promoting economic growth is another important objective of the monetary policy. In the past Reserve Bank has often been criticised that it pursued the objective of controlling inflation and achieving price stability and neglected the objective of promoting economic growth. Monetary policy can promote economic growth through ensuring adequate availability of credit and lower cost of credit. There are two types of credit requirements of businesses. First, they have to finance their requirements of working capital and for importing needed raw materials and machines from abroad. Secondly, they need credit for financing investment in projects for building fixed capital. Easy availability of credit at low interest rate stimulates investment and thereby quickens economic growth.

However, during the periods of high inflation, Reserve Bank followed a tight monetary policy under which Cash Reserve Ratio (CRR) and Statutory Liquidity Ratio (SLR) were raised to restrict

1. C. Rangarajan, "*Issues in Monetary Management*" printed in *Indian Economy* : Essays on Money and Finance, 1998, p. 6.
2. *Op. cit.*, p. 7.

the availability of credit for private sector. Besides, by raising bank rate and repo rate at which banks borrow from Reserve Bank of India lending rates of interest of banks were kept at high levels which discouraged private investment. This tight monetary policy worked against promoting growth. However, in the opinion of Prof. Rangarajan, *there is no conflict between the objectives of price stability and growth.* Price stability, according to him, is a means to ensure economic growth. To quote him, "*It is price stability which provides the appropriate environment under which growth can occur and social justice can be ensured.*" However, in our opinion, this may be true in the long run but in the short run there exists *trade off between growth and inflation.* To ensure higher economic growth the adequate expansion of money supply and greater availability of credit at a lower rate of interest is needed. But large expansion in money supply and bank credit leads to the increase in aggregate demand which tends to cause a higher rate of inflation. This raises the issue of what is *acceptable trade off between growth and inflation, that is, what rate of inflation is acceptable to promote growth through appropriate monetary policy.*

Expert Committee on monetary policy headed by Late Prof. Chakravarty suggested a target of 4 per cent as "the acceptable rise in prices". According to it, the growth of money supply and availability of credit should be so regulated that rate of inflation does not exceed 4 per cent per annum. However, C. Rangarajan, former Governor of Reserve Bank, fixed a higher target, namely, 5 to 6 per cent rate of inflation in the context of objective of achieving 6 to 7 per cent rate of economic growth. To quote him, "*keeping the price and growth objectives in view the money supply growth should be so regulated that inflation rate comes down, eventually to 5 to 6 per cent. That indeed must be the goal of monetary policy.*"[3]

It may be noted that in the context of the openness of the economy and floating exchange rate system, as is the case of the Indian economy today, the objective of achieving higher rate of economic growth through monetary measures may also conflict with objective of exchange rate stability, that is, value of rupee in terms of the US dollar and other foreign currencies. Whereas prevention of the depreciation of rupee requires tightening of monetary policy, that is raising of interest rate, reducing liquidity of the banking system so that banks restrict their credit supply, the promotion of growth objective requires lower lending rates of interest and greater availability of credit for encouraging private investment. It is this dilemma of conflicting objectives of supporting higher economic growth or achieving price stability through control of inflation by RBI which is being presently faced in India (2012-13 and 2013-14).

Exchange Rate Stability

Until 1991, India followed fixed exchange rate system and only occasionally devalued the rupee with the permission of IMF. The policies of floating exchange rate and increasing openness and globalisation of the Indian economy, adopted since 1991, have made the exchange rate of rupee quite volatile. The changes in capital inflows and capital outflows and changes in demand for and supply of foreign exchange, particularly US dollar, arising from the imports and exports cause great fluctuations in the foreign exchange rate of rupee. In order to prevent large depreciation and appreciation of foreign exchange rate Reserve Bank has to take suitable monetary measures to ensure foreign exchange rate stability. Owing to the fixed exchange rate system prior to 1991 the concern about foreign exchange rate had not played a significant role in the formulation of monetary policy.

Today, the exchange rate of rupee is determined by demand for and supply of foreign exchange (say, US dollar). When there is mismatch between demand for and supply of foreign exchange, external value of rupee changes. For instance, from August 2011 to December 2011 depreciation

3. C. Rangarajan, "*The Changing Context of Monetary Policy*". Address at 31st Convocation of the Indian Statistical Institute, March 31, 1997.

of rupee as against US dollar had been caused by the increase in demand for dollars from (1) the corporate sector for financing their imports, (2) Foreign Institutional Investors (FII) who wanted to take out their dollars from India (*i.e.,* capital outflow) to the US risen and (3) increase in demand for US dollar by the Indian banks on the instructions of the public sector undertakings for financing necessary imports from abroad. Since export earnings and capital inflows which determine the supply of dollars had not risen adequately, mismatch between dollars and supply of dollars had arisen causing the depreciation of rupee as against the US dollar.

Thus when there is large current account deficit (CAD) that exceeds comfortable level (which in Indian situation is estimated at 2.5 per cent of GDP as it can be financed by normal capital inflows), it tends to depreciate the Indian rupee. In 2011-12 there was current account deficit (CAD) of 4.2 per cent and for 2012-13 it is expected that current account deficit (CAD) will be around 5 per cent of GDP. This is too high current account deficit which is putting downward pressure on the exchange rate of rupee. The depreciation of rupee raises the costs of imports which adds to the inflationary pressures in the Indian economy. Therefore, reducing current account deficit (CAD) to the comfortable level is not only essential for exchange rate stability but also for controlling inflation and achieving price stability. According to D. Subbarao, the present Governor of RBI, the widening of current account deficit in India during the last two years (2011-12 and 2012-13) has emerged as a major constraint on easing of monetary policy as causing lower lending interest rates and large availability of funds with banks will lead to more imports which will add to the current account deficit.

To arrest the fall in value of rupee Reserve Bank raises the bank rate and repo rate and thus send signals to the banks to raise their lending rates. It also raises cash reserve ratio (CRR) to reduce the liquidity in the banking system and thus reducing lendable resources of the banks. Thus, through rise in the cost of credit and reduction in the availability of credit, borrowing from the banks are discouraged which is expected to reduce the demand for dollars. The higher interest rates in India would also discourage foreign institutional investors and Indian corporates to invest abroad. This will also work to reduce the demand for dollars which will prevent the fall in the value of the rupee.

Alternatively, to prevent the depreciation of the rupee, Reserve Bank can release more dollars from its foreign exchange reserves. The release of more dollars by Reserve Bank will increase the supply of US dollars in the foreign exchange market and will therefore tend to correct the mismatch between demand for and supply of the US dollars. This will help in stabilising the exchange rate of the rupee.

It is clear from above that in the context of flexible exchange rate system, Reserve Bank has to intervene frequently to achieve stability of exchange rate at a reasonable level.

ROLE OF MONETARY POLICY FOR PROMOTING ECONOMIC GROWTH

Economic growth implies the expansion in productive capacity or capital stock in the economy so that increases in real national output or income are attained. As is well known, economic growth can be speeded up by accelerating the rate of savings and investment in the economy. This requires the following steps:

(*a*) Increase in the aggregate rate of savings in the economy,

(*b*) Mobilisation of these savings so that they are made available for the purpose of investment and production,

(*c*) Increase in the rate of investment,

(*d*) allocation of investment funds for productive purposes and priority sectors of the economy.

Proper monetary policy can help in producing favourable effects on the above requirements of economic growth. We explain below the appropriate monetary policy to promote growth in developing countries.

(a) Monetary Policy and Savings

Several monetary measures can be adopted to raise the aggregate rate of saving. First, a high interest rate policy can promote savings. In the fifties and sixties of the 20th Century it was widely believed that interest rate reflected the price of capital and since capital was scarce in developing countries, the real interest rates should be kept at higher levels to promote saving so that capital accumulation is speeded up. However, this argument in favour of higher real interest rates in developing countries was based upon the belief or assumption that *savings were positively elastic or sensitive to the interest rate.*

It is worthwhile to mention an opposite view point regarding interest rate policy which has gained large support in recent years. According to this view (emphasised by Keynes in his monetary theory), rate of interest represents the cost of investment, and lower the rate of interest, the greater will be inducement to invest. However, Keynes was of the view that investment was not much sensitive or elastic to lower rate of interest Dr. K.N.Raj argued that *since investment is an important factor determining economic growth in developing countries, it should be promoted by lowering the interest rates*. However, this is not fully correct. This is because whereas inducement to invest may be promoted by lowering the interest rates the adequate amount of savings or resources needed to finance larger investment may not be forthcoming at lower interest rates. Further, a low interest rate policy in developing countries like India is likely to promote more investment in inventories and luxury consumer goods such as cars, airconditioners, luxury houses rather than that in fixed capital goods.

In our view therefore in a developing economy *a reasonably positive real interest rate policy* should be pursued to provide incentives for more savings so that large sources are made available for investment in fixed capital stock. If monetary policy in a developing country is to promote economic growth it must aim at raising the rate of saving. It may be recalled that *real rate of interest is nominal rate of interest minus rate of inflation.* In our view real rate of interest should not be allowed to fall below 5 per cent per annum, if it is to provide reasonable rate of return on savings. Actually for past some years in India, rate of interest on bank deposits (which are main assets in which people keep their savings) is negative. For three years fixed deposits rate of interest is around 9 per cent or even 8.5 per cent in some banks, whereas rate of inflation as measured by consumer price index (CPI) has been around 10 per cent in past some years. (It was 9.52 per cent y-on-year basis in Aug. 2013). This means real rate of interest which people are getting is negative, that is, keeping money in banks fixed deposits is eating into your savings. It is not surprising that people are prompted to invest their savings in gold and jewellery, real estate which are socially unproductive assets. Therefore, with the rise in rate of inflation nominal rate of interest should also be raised to keep incentives for saving intact. It may be noted that in recent years (2011-12 and 2012-13) in India low deposit rates offered to the public by banks have prompted the people to invest their savings in unproductive assets such as gold, jewellery, real estate, accumulation of inventories. *This led to the fall in financial saving* required for productive investment. This has led the Finance Minister, Mr. Chidambaram, in his budget for 2013-14 to announce issuing of **inflation-indexed bonds** on which nominal interest rate will automatically rise with the increase in inflation rate.

Besides, the monetary policy can play a strategic role in increasing national savings by promoting the expansion of banking facilities and other financial intermediaries in India, especially in their rural areas. With more bank branches in under-banked and under-developed regions, the people who consume away their surplus incomes, will be induced to save them in the form of bank deposits which are quite safe as a store of value. The commercial banking encourages thrift or propensity to save by offering a return on savings in the form of interest rate on bank deposits. It also induces more savings by providing outlets for mutual funds which can be equity linked and other saving schemes for fruitful investment of the savings by the people who would have otherwise put them to unproductive or wasteful uses such as buying land, real estate, gold and jewellery. But to tap and raise savings sufficiently and to prevent its unproductive use banks and other financial institutions need to be numerous and dispersed throughout the economy in both the urban and rural areas. Speaking from the development experience of various countries. Prof. Lewis, a development economist, has emphasised that the volume of savings depends partly upon how widespread banking and other financial institutions are. To quote him, "*if the saving institutions are placed under the individual's nose, people save more than if the nearest saving institutions is some distance away.*"[4]

Thus growth in saving in the form of bank deposits will be greater, if a reasonable real rate of interest policy is pursued. Similarly, with the expansion of other financial institutions, the people will feel induced to save more for buying financial assets. It is generally agreed that the rapid expansion of banking facilities after the nationalisation of major commercial banks in 1969 promoted by the Reserve Bank of India has contributed considerably to the growth of aggregate savings. While the aggregate saving rate increased from 16.5 per cent in 1969-70 to 22.7 per cent in 1982-83, bank deposits which accounted for 8.7 per cent of total domestic savings in 1969-70, accounted for 22.5 per cent of these savings in 1982-83. The number of commercial banks offices increased from 8,262 in July 1969 to 44,521 in 1984 and to 62,350 in 1995. Although it is difficult to establish a precise quantitative relationship between expansion of bank branches and savings in the form of bank deposits, its significant contribution to the promotion of savings cannot be denied. Therefore, the future branch expansion policy must fully take into account the untapped saving potential of under-banked and under-developed regions.

It may be noted that in order to facilitate mobilisation of an increasing proportion of savings by the banking system it is essential to maintain a reasonable price stability. Dr. Manmohan Singh, when he was Governor of Reserve Bank of India, pointed out, "*It is only under conditions of reasonable price stability that people will have less attraction for savings in the form of physical assets such as gold, real estate and excessive accumulation of inventories.*" Further, if banks are to mobilise adequate amount of savings in the form of bank deposits, interest rates on bank deposits must remain positive in real terms. That is, the nominal rate of interest should be maintained at a higher level than the rate of inflation. If through excessive rise in prices, real rate of interest becomes negative, people will be discouraged to save.

2. Monetary Policy and Investment.

Monetary policy has an important role to play in boosting up the level of investment by making available savings or resources mobilised by banks for purposes of investment and production. The banks fulfil this task by offering bank credit for investment to business and industry.

If the private sector plays an important role in the development process, as it does in India after economic reforms undertaken since 1991, monetary policy has also to ensure that the need for bank credit for investment and production in the private sector are fully met. The banks must provide adequate bank credit to meet at least essential working capital requirements of industry and agriculture. Both large-scale and medium industries require funds for investment in fixed capital, working capital and for maintaining inventories. Subject to appropriate norms fixed for inventory holdings, the credit needs of the private sector should be met if existing capacities in the private sector are to be fully used and also more productive capacity is to be built up. In India banks have been asked by the Reserve Bank of India to give specific percentage of loans at concessional rates of interest to some priority sectors such as agriculture and small and medium enterprises.

Cost of Credit. It may be noted that Keynesian theory of monetary policy emphasises that the effect of a change in the supply of money on the level of production and investment operates through the changes in the rate of interest. The increase in the supply of money by the monetary authority will cause the market rate of interest to fall. At lower rate of interest, the entrepreneurs will be induced to invest more. Accordingly, Keynesian monetary theory has been described as "*cost of credit*" theory.

4. Arthur Lewis, *Theory of Economic Growth*, George Allen and Unwin, 1960.

However, Keynes himself and several economists after him believed that this effect of changes in money supply on investment which operates through rate of interest is not very vigorous. It has been asserted that investment in fixed capital is interest inelastic. That is why Keynes did not have much faith in the effectiveness of monetary policy and instead emphasised the role of fiscal policy in influencing the level of economic activity. However, it is now generally believed by the economists that since interest is an important cost of investment, *investment demand is fairly interest elastic*. Therefore, to promote investment, the easy monetary policy should be adopted. It may be noted that in the post-was reform period from 1996 to 2003 easy or low interest rate policy adopted to promote private investment so as to revive the industrial sector whose growth slowed down from 1996-97 to 2002-03. Following the soft-interest rate policy of Reserve Bank of India prime lending rates of interest of commercial banks which varied between 15 and 16 per cent prior to 1996, were reduced over a period of time to 9 to 10 per cent in 2003. Again when in September 2008 global financial crisis occurred as a result of bust of housing bubble in the US, there was worldwide (including India) economic slowdown, Reserve Bank of India in October 2008 reduced its repo interest rate from 9 per cent in July 2008 to 7 per cent in October 2008 and further to 4.75 per cent on March 4, 2009, to promote private investment so as to prevent sharp economic slowdown in India.

However, the soft interest rate policy does not always, especially during recession, achieve much success in stimulating private investment. This is because when there are sluggish demand conditions, the existing fixed capital is underutilised, it is not profitable to make more investment for expanding fixed capital stock, private enterprises are therefore not willing to make further investment despite lower interest rates. It is for such economic conditions that it has been said that '*you can bring the horse to water but you cannot make it drink*'. However, in normal circumstances cheap interest rate policy promotes private investment and therefore helps to achieve higher economic growth.

Availability of Credit. It is noteworthy that in the recent times monetary theory emphasises the **credit-availability effect on investment** of the changes in the supply of money. According to this, an increase in the supply of money causing expansion in the reserve money with the banks directly enlarges the availability of bank credit for investment purposes and thereby raises the level of investment in the economy. On the contrary, contraction in money supply, will directly reduce the availability of credit and hence tend to decrease investment in the economy.

Further, in this context it is noteworthy that in developing countries, Government or public investment plays a crucial role in the development of their economies. Therefore, monetary policy requires to promote not only private investment but also public investment by making available adequate amount of credit for it.

Monetary Policy and Public Investment. Let us first explain the promotion of the public investment through monetary policy. Monetary policy has to ensure that the banking system contributes to the financing of the planned public investment. For this a good part of bank deposits mobilised by the banks should be invested in Government and other approved securities so that the government should be able to finance its planned investment, especially in infrastructure. At present in India, there is lack of infrastructure such as power, roads, highways, ports, irrigation facilities which is obstructing economic growth. Besides, when industry faces demand recession, public investment is an ideal tool to develop infrastructure and to increase the demand for industrial products through the operation of multiplier. This will stimulate private investment. Therefore, in our view, policy of raising public investment will *crowd in* private investment rather than *crowding it out*. In India a new technique of monetary policy has been designed to secure larger resources from the banking system for financing public investment. This technique has been described as *Statutory Liquidity Ratio* (SLR). According to this, *in addition to cash reserve requirements* banks in India are required to keep a minimum proportion of its total demand and time deposits in the form of specified liquid assets. And the most important specified liquid asset for this purposes is the investment in Government and other securities. To raise the lendable resources of the banks, cash reserve ratio of the banks must be kept at low level.

3. Allocation of Investment Funds : Credit Rating

Mobilisation of savings alone would not do. Proper canalisation of these into suitable directions of investment is or perhaps more important than mobilisation itself. The monetary policy should restrict the growth of wasteful lines of investment which are inimical to economic growth. It should be able to direct investment in productive channels. In this regard, the monetary policy has to play a selective or qualitative role in so far as it is possible through its operations to *discriminate between productive and unproductive outlays. It should give a fillip to the former and stint* the growth of the latter. Further, it has to be designed as to influence the specific sectors and industries which are most significant to affect the growth of the economy. In fact, the particularised application of credit can greatly activise the process of economic growth. Therefore, it is necessary to operate the *selective credit rationing with a view to influence the pattern of investment*. However, in the gamut of monetary policy, there are selective credit control measures of both general and specific nature. In the general category are included measures such as voluntary credit restriction and moral suasion. In the category of specific measures there exist measures to control credit institutions.

For the purpose of regulating the individual credit institutions, the method of varying the reserve requirements is quite effective. On the other hand, in order to divert the financial resources into desired channels, the method of **credit rationing** should be used by the Central Bank. This may be done by fixation of a ceiling on the aggregate portfolio of the commercial banks, thereby making it incumbent that loans and advances do not exceed the fixed ceiling. Alternatively, it may be done by directly allocating funds that can be granted and used. Besides, policies such as the selective rediscount policy, prior deposit requirement policy and the fixation of deposit requirement policy can also be adopted to achieve similar goals. However, it may be pointed out that the potency of credit planning depends upon the extent of the area over which it operates. The developing economies must strive for an extension of credit planning over wider areas.

Credit control measures such as noted above promote growth by directing the stream of domestic savings into the desired lines of investment. Measures such as lengthening the periods of repayment, lowering of margin requirements, providing rediscounting facilities at rates below the bank rate, provision of special loans by commercial banks to be used for specific purposes or the setting up of special Investment institutions such as Industrial Development Bank can provide the required inducement to channelise savings in the desired directions. In the indirect sense, these measures may prove conducive to growth in two ways. Firstly, the qualitative credit control measures prevent the savings from being wasted in unproductive channels. Through their application it becomes possible to deny or discourage certain lines of investment that are inimical to the growth of the economy. However, the extent to which such measures can help providing resources for investment in the desired directions depends on the extent to which the flow of credit towards the undesirable channels can prevented.

Secondly, such measures may go a long way in galvanising the process of growth by restraining inflation and its adverse effects. When inflationary tendencies set in, generally the bank advances to businessmen tend to rise. In this way certain undesirable and unproductive enterprises may grow and flourish. For instance, activities such as speculative demand for building up inventories, accumulation of precious metals for purchase of foreign exchange and real estate get a fillip. Growth of these and such other unproductive activities can be held in check by raising the margin requirements for the blackballed collaterals. Further, the monetary authority can fix a ceiling by holding the loans and advances of the value of the collateral. Thus, it *serves the dual purpose of curbing inflation and protecting certain essential productive forms of investment from being restricted.*

In the context of the planned development of the underdeveloped countries, the use of methods of selective credit controls and credit rationing are not only necessary but also essential. They greatly widen the horizons of development along predetermined and desired directions. They are not only helpful in preventing inflation but also *act as a positive means of directing the process of economic development on the desired lines*. Furthermore, the policy of selective credit controls is especially suited to the needs of underdeveloped countries where the orthodox monetary techniques have limited applicability. As it is, the structure of these economies is not very conducive to the general methods of credit control.

The huge investment expenditure made by the government in the public sector in its endeavour to accelerate the process of growth is not amenable to control by the monetary authority. The monetary authority is, in fact, subversive to the wishes of the government in the matter of providing resources for development. Further, in order to help government borrowings, the bank rate policy of the Reserve Bank tends to become more or less inflexible. Besides, for the sake of supporting government loans, the institutions such as SEBI (Stock Exchange Board of India) is also required to stabilise the securities market.

MONETARY POLICY OF RESERVE BANK OF INDIA

Monetary Policy is an important instrument of economic policy to achieve multiple objectives. Like all central banks in the developing countries, Reserve Bank of India has been playing both a *regulatory and promotional* (*i.e.,* developmental) roles in achieving social objectives. Monetary policy of Reserve Bank has been changing from time to time depending on the prevailing economic situation and circumstances. It is important to note that changes in monetary policy, unlike in case of fiscal policy, can be made at any time during a year. It needs to be emphasised that *monetary policy acts through influencing the availability and cost of credit and growth of money supply in the economy.* The effectiveness of monetary policy depends on the institutional framework available for transmitting impulses released by the monetary policy of the central bank.

In its developmental or promotional role, RBI adopted measures to deepen and widen the financial system to promote saving and investment in the Indian economy. RBI was instrumental in the setting up *apex* institutions for ensuring provision of agricultural credit, providing *term finance* to industries and adequate credit for export.

Monetary Policy during the Pre-Reforms Period (1972–1991): Tight Monetary Policy

It is worth noting that prior to 1991 monetary policy in India has been framed in response to *fiscal policy* of the Government. Fiscal Policy in India during the seventies and eighties had been such that large fiscal deficits were incurred. A good part of fiscal deficit was monetised, that is, financed by borrowing from Reserve Bank which created money against treasury bills issued by the Government. This resulted in a very large increase in Reserve Bank credit to the Government which caused rapid growth in money supply. This highlights the close link between the fiscal policy and monetary policy and further that there is a need for coordination between two policies. Monetary policy adopted in the seventies and eighties was concerned mainly with the task of *neutralising inflationary impact* of the growing budget deficits by continually mopping up large increases in *reserve money* (which in economic theory is also called *high-powered money*). The instruments used were changes brought about mainly in Cash Reserve Ratio (CRR) and Statutory Liquidity Ratio (SLR) which were quite often raised during seventies to offset the effect of budget deficits and consequently increase in reserve money.

Given the fully administered nature of interest rates during most part of this period, the excess liquidity in the banking system was mopped up by raising the cash reserve ratio to the legally maximum limit, namely, 25 per cent. Besides, since rates of interest on Government securities were much below the open market rates, excess liquidity from the banking system could not be withdrawn through open market operations. Further, in view of the below market rates of interest, banks and other financial institutions could not be induced to invest in Government securities to meet the borrowing requirements of the Government. Statutory Liquidity Ratio (SLR) had therefore to be progressively raised to meet the borrowing needs of the Government and eventually it was increased to the maximum limit of 38.5 per cent. To quote C. Rangarajan, a former Governor of Reserve Bank of India. "*Until the overall reform process was initiated in 1991, the basic goal of monetary policy was to neutralise the impact of the fiscal deficits*. . . . Monetary management took the form of compensatory increases in the cash reserve ratio (CRR) for banks, controls on growth of commercial credit (mainly to the enterprises sector) and adjustments of administered interest rates. The fixation of CRR and SLR at their maximum levels *crowded out* credit for the commercial sector. Thus, even when money supply was growing at a rapid rate, private sector could not get the needed credit for financing industry and trade."[5]

The banks were compelled to fund most of the large fiscal deficit at below the market rates of interest as they had to meet the high and rising SLR imposed on them by Reserve Bank of India. This is because rates of interest on Government securities were kept at lower levels than the prevailing market rates of interest.

Thus, Y.V. Reddy, the present Governor of Reserve Bank commenting on the monetary policy of Pre-reform period prior to 1991 writes, "given the command and controlled nature of the Indian economy, the RBI had to resort to direct instruments like interest rate regulation, selective credit control and Cash Reserve Rate (CRR) as major monetary instruments. *These instruments were used to neutralise the monetary impact of the Government's budgetary operations*."

On the recommendation of S. Chakravarty Committee report, in the late eighties and early nineties the rates of interest on Government securities were raised close to the market levels. This had two implications. First, with market rates of interest on Government securities, Reserve Bank could now undertake open market operations. Secondly, with higher interest rates on Government securities banks and other financial institutions could now be induced voluntarily to invest more in Government securities. Accordingly, statutory liquidity ratio (SLR) was reduced below its maximum statutory level.

RECENT MONETARY POLICY STANCE OF RESERVE BANK OF INDIA

The major thrust of the Reserve Bank of India throughout has been to promote growth of the economy without inflation. The changes in domestic economy affect economic growth, price stability, and financial stability in the Indian economy. These changes pose serious challenges in the conduct of monetary policy. Depending on the particular situation facing the Indian economy at a particular time, RBI has been changing its monetary policy stance from time to time. RBI formulates its monetary policy on its estimates of economic growth and its target rate of inflation. Targets for growth of money supply and credit expansion by commercial banks are fixed keeping in view the twin objectives of facilitating growth keeping inflation under control.

RBI Dilemma : Inflation vs Growth

RBI often finds itself in a dilemma as it often faces the problem of trade-off between inflation and growth. To control inflation tightening of monetary policy (that is, high interest rate and high cash reserve ratio (CRR) are required. But this tightening of monetary policy discourages investment and hurts economic growth. Therefore, when inflation is very high the RBI is prepared to sacrifice some growth to curb inflation. On the other hand, when to promote growth RBI follows expansionary or easy monetary policy, namely, lowering of interest rate and cash reserve ratio (CRR) it leads to increase in aggregate demand and causes inflationary pressures. Therefore, RBI has to adopt a monetary policy that balances its concerns for controlling inflation on the one hand and promoting growth on the other though in actual practice doing such balancing act is a difficult task. We discuss below monetary policy adopted by the RBI since 2006-07. During the last many years RBI has been changing its monetary policy stance depending on the prevailing economic situation and keeping

5. C. Rangarajan, *op. cit.*

in view its concern for controlling inflation and facilitating growth. Targets for growth of monetary policy and credit expansion are set so as to achieve growth with price stability.

Monetary Policy of RBI Since 2008-09

Beginning from March 2008 there was spurt in inflation rate which became serious as year-on-year inflation rate reached 9 per cent in June 2008, and then reached the two digit level of 10 to 11 per cent in July 2008 and reached the alarming figure of around 13 per cent in mid-August 2008 and then it came down to 11.8 per cent and 11.4 per cent in Oct. 2008 and further to 10.8 per cent and 8.4 per cent in Nov. 2008. In order to tackle this inflation RBI raised the cash reserve ratio (CRR) to a high level of 9 per cent and repo rate also to 9 per cent as shown in Table 19A.1. It is these tight monetary measures that reduced liquidity in the banking system and growth of credit and money supply was brought down. The year-on-year inflation rate fell from peak of 12.6 per cent in Sept. 2008 to 11.4 per cent in Oct. 2008. Due to fall in international commodity prices and decline in price of crude oil from $ 147 per barral to $ 50 per barrel in Nov. 2008 inflation rate further came down to 8.4 per cent in end-Nov. 2008.

Reversal of Monetary Policy from Oct. 2008

In the mean time world financial crisis assumed alarming proportion. Foreign Institutional Investors (FII) started selling shares in capital market in India and repatriating dollars. This not only caused depreciation of Indian rupee and stock market crash but also created liquidity crunch in the banking system which restricted credit flow for investment purposes. To solve this liquidity problem and restore investors' confidence RBI reversed its monetary policy. In the first week of Oct. 2008, it reduced cash reserve ratio from 9 per cent to 7.5 per cent and repo rate from 9 per cent to 7.5 per cent. Such a large reduction in cash reverse ratio increased the liquidity in the banking system and it was expected to increase availability of credit for investment. Lowering of repo rate was expected to lower lending rates of interest and thus to ensure cheap credit for investment. Reduction in cash reserve ratio from 9 per cent to 7.5 per infused liquidity in the banking system to the turne of Rs. 1,25,000 crores. With these measures it was hoped that slowdown in rate of economic growth would be prevented. It was further expected that due to fall in international commodity prices and sharp decline in price of crude oil along with the improved supply of agricultural commodities would help in containing inflation. With inflation well under control, to give further boost to investment by increasing availability of credit, RBI further infused liquidity in the banking system by lowering cash reserve ratio (CRR) from 7.5 to 5.5 per cent in Oct. 31, 2008. Besides on Dec. 6, 2008 it further cut key interest rates signalling a further movement towards soft interest rate regime. To ensure that banks should reduce their landing rates it lowered its repo rate i.e. short-term lending rate for borrowing by banks from 7.5 per cent to 6.5 per cent on Dec. 6, 2008. Besides it cut *reverse repo rate* (i.e., the overnight rate at which banks park their surplus funds with RBI) from 6 per cent to 5 per cent. This was meant to encourage banks to give credit to private enterprises rather than keep liquid funds with RBI.

Table 19.1: Monetary Policy Changes from the Second Half of 2008-09 to the First Half of 2009-10

Date	Repo Rate	Reverse Repo Rate	Cash Reserve Ratio (CRR)
August 30, 2008	9.0	6.0	9.0
October 3, 2008	7.5	6.0	7.5
October 31, 2008	—	—	5.5
December 6, 2008	6.5	5	—
January 2, 2009	5.5	4	5.0
March 4, 2009	5.0	3.5	5.0
April 21, 2009	4.75	3.25	5.0

Source GOI, *Economic Survey,* 2008-09 and 2009-10.

However, the above monetary measures taken during October-December 2008 did not have desired effects. The creation of credit for businesses and consumers remained subdued. In the beginning of 2009, there was a distinct evidence of further slowdown of the Indian economy as a consequence of global financial crisis and global meltdown. RBI cut its forecast for GDP growth rate of the Indian economy for 2008-09 to 7 per cent from 7.5 to 8 per cent. Though many banks had lowered their lending rates of interest, the others had yet to do so.

The US Federal Reserve had reduced its Federal Fund rate to almost zero to revive the American economy. The Central Banks of countries such as the UK, Germany, Euro area and Japan too lowered their benchmark interest rates to overcome recession.

In the environment of sluggish exports and drop in manufacturing output in the third quarter (Oct.–Dec. 2008) of 2008-09, Reserve Bank of India on January 2, 2009, further reduced its three key policy rates, namely, cash reserve ratio (CRR), repo rate and reverse repo rate in an attempt to allow banks to cut lending interest rates further. RBI reduced its cash reserve ratio from 5.5 per cent to 5 per cent. With this it injected additional liquidity of ₹ 20,000 crores in the Indian financial system bringing the total infusion of liquidity in the banking system to over ₹ 300,000 crore since Sept. 2008 to revive the growth of credit for businesses for investment and for consumers buying houses and automobiles. On January 2, 2009 repo rate was reduced from 6.5 per cent to 5.5 per cent and on March 4, 2009 this was further cut to 5 per cent. This was expected to reduce further lending rates by banks and thus making credit cheaper for business and for those taking housing and auto loans. Reverse repo rate was also reduced from 5 per cent to 4 per cent on January 2, 2009 and further to 3.5 per cent on March 4, 2009 which was expected to discourage banks for parking their surplus funds with RBI and instead lend them to business for productive purposes.

Monetary Policy Stance During the First Half of 2009-10

The monetary policy in 2008-09 had to address the emerging economic situation, wherein the position in the second half of the year was substantially different from the first half. The policy had to contend with the spill-over effects of the global financial crisis on the country's growth path. The liquidity situation had improved significantly towards the end of 2008-09 in the wake of measures taken by the RBI. For the year 2009-10, RBI had envisaged a macroeconomic scenario with the real GDP growth at 6.0 per cent and WPI inflation to be around 4.0 per cent by end-March 2010. Taking into account the need to respond to sluggish economic growth witnessed lately, the RBI envisaged growth in money supply (M3) for 2009-10 at 17.0 per cent in April 2009 which was later (July 28) raised to 18 per cent as an indicative projection. Consistent with this, the growth in aggregate deposits of scheduled commercial banks has been projected to grow at 18.0 per cent and non-food credit by 20.0 per cent in 2009-10 as against 17 per cent in 2008-09. The Annual Policy Statement for 2009-10 was announced on April 21, 2009. In it marginal reductions in the key rates were announced. The salient points of Annual Monetary Policy Announcement of April 21, 2009 and Quarterly Review of July 28, 2009 while, the bank rate was retained unchanged at 6.0 per cent. Besides the repo rate under the liquidity adjustment facility (LAF) was reduced by 25 basis points from 5.0 per cent to 4.75 per cent with immediate effect from April 21. In the Annual Policy Statement for 2009-10 the cash reserve ratio (CRR) of scheduled banks was retained unchanged at 5.0 per cent of net demand and time liabilities (NDTL).

In first quarterly review (July 28, 2009), the wholesale price inflation was expected to rise to 5 per cent by the end of March 2010, which would make it imperative for the RBI to start tightening monetary policy. The RBI felt overall macroeconomic scenario continued to be uncertain, although stimulus measures were expected to boost demand in 2009-10 and ensure economic growth and boost private sector investment. *"The task for the Reserve Bank is to maintain the accommodative monetary stance till demand conditions further improve and the credit flow takes hold, but to be ready with a roadmap to reverse the expansionary stance quickly and effectively thereafter,*" said RBI Governor, D. Subbarao. Thus, in its Quarterly Review (28 July 2009) RBI visualised *monetary tightening* (*i.e.* revising repo rate, reverse repo rate of interest and cash reserve ratio (CRR) upward) when inflation was expected to rise after Sept. 2009. Exact timing of monetary tightening was said to depend on the situation of inflation.

Evaluation of Easy Monetary Policy of 2008-09 and First Half of 2009-10

With the adoption of above measures by the RBI, banks lowered their lending rates but not to the extent by which the RBI reduced their short-term interest rate, that is, repo rate and the extent to which the cash reserve ratio was lowered to increase the liquidity of the banks. As a result of monetary policy measures adopted, bank credit during 2008-09 increased by 17.3 per cent as against 22.3 per cent in 2007-08. It was the public sector banks which issued more credit, private sector banks and foreign banks lagged far behind. Even this modest achievement RBI was not only able to contain inflation as measured by WPI but also along with the expansionary fiscal policy helped to achieve 6.7 per cent growth of GDP in 2008-09. However, as a result of RBI's measures banks were saddled with huge liquid resources as **credit off-take** remained subdued reflecting moderation in demand for credit. To keep their profitability the banks invested in government securities, mutual funds and were also keeping their surplus funds in reverse repo window of Liquidity Adjustment Facility (LAF) of RBI. The usual response of the banks in such a high liquidity condition is to cut lending rates of interest so that private firms borrow more for investment and other purposes. One limitation that banks faced in reducing their lending rates was because they had raised deposits at higher interest rates to meet the demand for credit in the high growth period of first half of financial year 2008-09 and before. These high interest rates on deposits came in the way of cutting lending rates to stimulate investment demand. However, *banks reduced their deposit rates and also reduced their lending rates sufficiently* and with the increase in their liquidity position more credit was made available for private sector. However, off-take of credit was relatively very poor and as a result banks were flush with the liquidity.

In India easy monetary policy adopted from Oct. 2008 to the first half of 2009-10 along with the Government's fiscal stimulus had been successful to boost credit growth and to prevent slowdown in economic growth. This is despite the fact due to global meltdown, stock market crashed and sluggish demand conditions businessmen were quite pessimistic about future profitable investment opportunities. But large reduction in repo rate (i.e., the interest rate at which RBI lends to the banks), lowering of cash reserve ratio which increased the liquidity of the banks by ₹ 3,88,000 crore overcame the reluctance and risk aversion of banks for lending money for investment and consumption of durable goods such as, housing, cars, etc. The reduction in excise duties and service tax under the fiscal stimulus packages by the governments helped to increase the demand for goods and services. With aggregate demand in the economy increased India was successful in preventing preventing large reduction in rate of economic growth. Thus, while the US, European countries and a number of developing countries were experiencing recession, India achieved 6.7 per growth in GDP in 2008-09 and 8.6 per cent in 2009-10.

TIGHTENING OF MONETARY POLICY STANCE IN THE SECOND HALF OF 2009-10

In the later half of 2009-10 there was a significant improvement in the economic situation. While recovery of the Indian economy gained momentum with overall growth in GDP estimated to rise to 7.5 per cent and manufacturing growth rising to over 11 per cent. However, despite this higher growth rate, problem of inflation worsened during the second half of 2009-10. While inflation as measured by WP1 on year-on-year basis went up to 8 per cent in Jan. 2010, food inflation rose to about 18 per cent and it was feared that food inflation would soon spill over to general inflation. It was widely felt that to tackle the problem of inflation in the third Quarter Review of monetary policy of 2009-10, RBI would tighten its monetary policy. However, some believed that tightening of monetary policy, especially raising of interest rates (*i.e.*, repo rate and reverse repo rate) by RBI would adversely affect economic growth and retard the recovery process. Thus, to tackle inflation it was not easy to exit the expansionary monetary policy without hurting economic growth.

Even in its second quarterly review of its monetary policy in Oct. 2009 RBI signalled that the situation required to shift its stance from "*management of crisis*" to "*management of recovery*" and hinted at tightening its monetary policy if inflation became worse. Even then (in Oct. 2009) in its policy review RBI shut all windows for refinance by it and also raised statutory liquidity ratio (SLR) from 24 per cent to 25 per cent so that liquidity with the banks be reduced. One per cent hike in statutory liquidity ratio for the banks meant that banks' holding of more Government bonds and less money in the banks' kitty for providing-loans to the private commercial sector. But this measure proved quite ineffective because banks had already invested about 28 per cent of their deposits in Government bonds. This means raising of statutory liquidity ratio (SLR) from 24 to 25 per cent could not have any effect on liquidity. Similarly, withdrawal of refinance facilities for non-banking financial companies, housing finance firms, mutual funds and exporters and for swapping banks foreign exchange liabilities hardly made any difference because these were rarely used.

Hike in Cash Reserve Ratio (CRR) in January 2010. To check inflationary expectations in its third quarterly review of its credit policy in January 29, 2010, RBI raised cash reserve ratio (CRR) from 5 per cent to 5.75 per cent. In doing so RBI sucked out ₹ 36000 crore from the banking system. However, in its Jan. 29 review of the policy, contrary to the expectations, it kept its key interest rates, namely, repo rate, reverse repo rate and bank rate unchanged. RBI refrained from raising its short-term interest rates as it thought such a policy action would deal a below to the economic recovery by adversely affecting private investment demand and consumption expenditure whose increase was necessary to keep the growth momentum. It pointed out that till Oct. 2009, growth was primarily driven by Government's fiscal stimulus but since then private consumption and private demand had started picking up and therefore dependence on Government's fiscal stimulus for keeping growth momentum had declined. It further emphasised that Government must begin the process of fiscal consolidation (*i.e.* reduce fiscal deficit by withdrawing cuts in taxes and reduce its expenditure.

In its view RBI thought withdrawal of liquidity from the banking system through hike in CRR would be enough to curtial inflationary expectations without having any adverse effect on economic growth. "In its interview, defending the hike in CRR while keeping interest rate unchanged D. Subbarao says, "*The recovery is not broad based and we need to encourage more investments in supply before the output gap gets closed. So, it's important that we support the recovery process in order to control inflationary pressures from the demand side.* Also, on growth-inflation trade-off, it's important to recognize that even as there is some trade-off in the short term, if you look slightly beyond the short term, inflation will anyway continue. So we had to take into account inflation concerns and growth considerations. *We expect that the CRR hike will anchor inflationary expectations without hurting growth impulses*."

As a matter of fact RBI could not completely reverse its policy of monetary accomodation as long as Government did not reduce its borrowing from the market. In 2009-10 to meet its large fiscal deficit of 6.8% of GDP. Government had to borrow heavily from the market (mainly banks). Such Government borrowing required enough liquid funds with the banks so as to lend them to the Government. Therefore, the RBI urged upon the Government to return to the path of fiscal consolidation so as to make it easier for the RBI to take strong anti-inflationary measures such as hike in repo rate of interest. On Jan. 29, 2010 statement as a policy measure 75 bps hike in CRR was considered as a more potent instrument than a combination of a 50 bps hike in CRR and 25 bps rise in repo rate that legal cash reserves kept in RBI by the banks do not earn any interest rate. Therefore, a very high increase in CRR would compel the banks to keep their liquid funds at zero rate of interest instead of earning 3.5 per cent interest by keeping funds under reverse repo window. This implies that without raising repo rate, through steep hike in CRR, RBI was able to raise the cost of money lending for the banks who were expected to raise their lending rates sooner or later. When in the end of first week of March general inflation shop up to 9.89 per cent year-on-year basis RBI raised its repo rate and reverse rupee rate by 25 bps. *Therefore, in middle of March 2010 RBI raised repo rate from 4.75 per cent to 5 per cent and reverse repo rate from 3.25 per cent to 3.50 per cent. In our view it was "too little and too late a measure" to control inflation.*

RBI found that credit during 2009-10 was not high, it was actually around 15 per cent till January 2010 against the earlier projection of 18 per cent by the RBI. It was therefore felt that large hike in repo interest rate would slowdown the growth of credit for productive and investment purposes and adversely affect the recovery process. In view of the poor credit off-take till Jan. 2010, it even lowered its target of credit expansion from 18 per cent to 16 per cent. It even found that money supply growth of 16.5 per cent till Jan. 2010 was modest. Thus RBI found that growth of bank credit and money supply expansion was very modest and could not be held responsible for inflation which as measured by WPI on year-on-year basis reached 7.31 per cent by end of Dec. 2009 and was estimated to rise to 8.5 per cent by middle of Jan. 2010. However, even in first week of March inflation, based on WPI, shot up to 9.89 per cent. Food inflation was very high at around 18 per cent in Feb. 2010. But RBI emphasized that food inflation was due to supply-side factors and not due to excessive increase in aggregate demand. Further, according to it food inflation was spilling over to general inflation.

Thus RBI maintained that hike in repo interest rate would lead to immediate increase in lending rates by the banks and would further slowdown credit growth and adversely affect the recovery process and economic growth. Thus keeping the repo interest rate and bank rate unchanged even in its. Third Quarterly Review of its policy for 2009-10 RBI in Jan. 28, 2010 showed that it continued *to maintain a positive pro-growth stance*. Even in its credit policy review in Oct. 2009, RBI noted that growth was primarily driven by fiscal stimulus (*i.e.* increase in public expenditure and cuts in taxes) by the Government but after Oct. 2009, private consumption and private demand had picked up to ensure growth. Therefore, RBI Governor urged upon the Government to begin the process of fiscal consolidation so that excessive borrowing by it from the market be reduced.

Lastly, RBI noted inflation in India, especially food inflation during 2009-10, *was so far primarily due to supply-side factors as failure of adequate monsoons caused drought conditions in many parts of the country in 2009-10* and rate of agricultural growth was negative (– 0.2 per cent). It pointed out that monetary policy of higher interest rates and reduction in liquidity helped to check demand-pull inflation and was not appropriate to tackle inflation driven by supply-side factors. In fact the main *emphasis of latest credit policy of RBI was that it was moving from a mode of crisis management to that of handling the recovery process.*

Comments

The inflationary situation again emerged in 2010. Inflation which was initially food driven was late getting generalised. Though RBI substantially raised cash reserve ratio (CRR) by 75 bps and it sucked out mere 36000 crore from the system whereas the size of reverse repo operations indicated that liquidity in the banks was of the order of around ₹ 80,000 crore at that time. Therefore, after the rise in CRR by RBI, there still remained a large amount of liquidity in the banking system. In view of the ample liquidity with the banks, it was unlikely that they would raise their lending rates to curtail demand for credit. By keeping its key interest rates at relatively low levels and not taking enough measures to reduce surplus liquidity in the system it *served* to promote private investment to strengthen the recovery process and to achieve higher growth. For anti-inflationary measures it urged the Government to reduce fiscal deficit and cut its fiscal stimulus. In fact, the Governor of the RBI in its credit policy announcement emphasised that to exit expansionary monetary policy to tackle inflation without hurting growth was a very difficult task in the then prevailing complex situation.

Monetary Policy Stance During 2010-11 : Further Tightening of Monetary Policy.

The accommodative expansionary monetary policy which was purused starting mid-Sept. 2008 instilled confidence in investors and producers and reduced the adverse impact of global financial crisis on the Indian Economy. As a result, the Indian economy started recovering ahead of most other economies. However, when in the second half of 2009-10, food inflation rose with the risk of it raising inflationary expectations, the RBI started *exit* from the expansionary monetary policy beginning from Oct. 2009. However, its anti-inflationary policy in the second half of 2009-10 merely consisted in giving warning that it would tighten its monetary policy if serious inflation problem emerged for its policy was not to hurt economic growth by raising its short-term rates, namely, repo rate and reverse repo rate and increasing cash reserve ratio (CRR). It is only in the end of the FY 2009-10 in the months of February and March 2010 that it raised CRR by 25 bps from 5.50 to 5.75 (see Table 19.2) to suck out some liquidity from money market and also raised by 25 bps repo rate from 4.75 to 5 per cent and reverse repo rate from 3.50 to 3.75 per cent to control inflation. Thus in 2009-10 only half -hearted monetary measures were taken by the RBI to control inflation. This was explained by pointing out that inflation then was driven by supply-side factors and monetary policy was inappropriate for fighting inflation driven by supply-side shocks.

The monetary policy stance in the Annual Policy Statement for the year 2010-11 announced on April 20, 2010 was guided by the following considerations.

1. The need to move in a calibrated manner in the direction of normalising the monetary policy instruments to control inflation without hurting growth.
2. The need to ensure that demand-side inflation did not become entrenched.

Table 19.2. Movements in Key Policy Rates in 2010 and 2011

Effective Since	Repo Rate	Reverse Repo Rate	Cash Reserve Ratio (CRR)
April 21, 2009	4.75 (– 0.25)	3.25 (– 0.25)	5.0
Feb. 13, 2010	4.75	3.25	5.50 (+ 0.50)
Feb. 27, 2010	4.75	3.25	5.75 (+ 0.25)
March 19, 2010	5.00 (+ 0.25)	3.50 (+ 0.25)	5.75
April 20, 2010	5.25 (+ 0.25)	3.75 (+ 0.25)	5.75
April 24, 2010	5.25	3.75	6.00 (+ 0.25)
July 2, 2010	5.50 (+ 0.25)	4.00 (+ 0.25)	6.0
July 27, 2010	5.75 (+ 0.25)	4.50 + 0.50	6.0
Sep. 16, 2010	6.00 (+0.25)	5.00 (0.50)	6.0
Nov. 2, 2010	6.25 (+ 0.25)	5.25 (+ 0.25)	6.0
Jan. 25, 2011	6.50 (+ 0.25)	5.50 (+ 0.25)	6.0
March 17, 2011	6.75 (+ 0.25)	5.75 (+ 0.25)	6.0
May 17, 2011	7.25 (+ 0.50)	6.25 (+ 0.50)	6.0
June 16, 2011	7.50 (+ 0.25)	6.50 (+ 0.25)	6.0
July 26, 2011	8.00 (+ 0.50)	7.0 (+ 0.50)	6.0

3. The need to balance the monetary policy objective of controlling inflation by absorbing liquidity while ensuring that credit was available to both the Government and the private sector.

Significant developments took place subsequent to the announcement of the monetary policy in April 2010. Though recovery of economic growth was consolidating, problem of inflation worsened. The upward revision in administered fuel prices on June 25, 2010 also influenced inflation in the subsequent months. In the First Quarterly Review on July 2, 2010, the RBI raised repo rate and reverse repo rate under LAF by 25 bps each. As will be seen from Table 19A.2, on July 2, 2010 repo rate was raised from 5.25 to 5.50 per and reverse repo rate was raised from 3.75 per cent of per cent to 4 per cent while cash reserve ratio was kept unchanged at 6 per cent. Again on July 27, 2010 due to further rise in WPI inflation rate, repo rate was further raised to 5.75 per cent and reverse repo rate was increased from 4 per cent to 4.50 per cent. Besides, on July 27, 2010, in its First Quarter Review

(July 2010) the RBI revised upward its projections for real GDP growth for the year 2010-11 to 8.5 per cent and raised its projection for WPI inflation for March 2011 to 6.0 per cent. The monetary policy action during 2010-11 was intended to moderate inflation by reining in demand pressures and inflationary expectations and to maintain financial conditions conducive to sustained growth.

With worsening of inflation, the RBI, in its *Mid-Quarterly Review* on Sept. 16, 2010, further increased the repo rate under LAF by 25 basis points from 5.75 per cent to 6 per cent and the reverse repo rate by 50 bps from 4.5 per cent to 5.0 per cent, keeping cash reserve ratio unchanged.

Monetary Policy Stance in 2011-12: Continuation of Tight Monetary Policy

In its Annual Monetary Policy for 2011-12 the Reserve Bank announced on May 3, 2011 aggressive monetary measures to control inflation. The inflation which was previously confined to food inflation became quite generalised in the preceding three months. The RBI move was guided by the fact that headline WP inflation which stood at 9 per cent in March 2011 was expected to remain at an elevated level and might even get worse during the year due to some risk factors that were working to raise it. The Reserve Bank which in its earlier policy measures during 2010-11 was avoiding to hurt growth, for the first time it pointed out that it was necessary to check inflation even by sacrificing some growth in the short run so as to achieve *sustained growth in the medium term*. According to the Annual Monetary Policy statement, *inflation is inimical to sustained growth as it harms growth by creating uncertainty*". It further states that current elevated rates of inflation pose significant risks to future growth. Bring them down therefore even at the cost of some growth in the short run should take precedence.

To control inflation the Reserve Bank raised the rate at which it lends to the banks by 50 bps from 6.75% to 7.25 per cent and reverse Repo rate, the rate at which banks park their surplus funds with it from 5.75% to 6.25 per cent on May 3, with effect from May 17, 2011. For the first time in 19 years it raised saving bank rate from 3.5 per cent to 4 per cent, cash reserve ratio (CRR) and statuary liquidity ratio were left unchanged. It lowered its estimate of rate of growth of the Indian economy from 8.6 per cent for the year 2011-12 to 8 per cent. Besides, it estimated that inflation would be moderated to 6% with an upward bias by the end of March 2012 while it would remain high till September 2011. In view of hike in repo rate the target for credit growth during the year 2011-12 was fixed at 19 per cent.

Since in May 2011 banks were working under tight liquidity conditions, the monetary transmission mechanism of the hike in repo rate was thought to be effective and the banks were expected to pass on the increase in cost of funds resulting from hike in repo rate to constomers. As a result, cost of auto-loans and house loans which are highly interest-sensitive was expected to go up. As a result, credit for purchase of automobiles and houses would decline.

The *RBI expressed doubts whether the government would be able to meet its fiscal deficit target of 4.5%* of gross domestic product for the year 2011-12 with many assumptions getting thrown into the winds. "Critical assumption that petroleum and fertiliser subsidies would be capped is bound to be seriously tested at prevailing high crude oil prices," said Subbarao. Even though adjustment of administered retail prices of petroleum products may add to inflation in the short run, the Reserve Bank believes this needs to be done as soon as possible. Otherwise, the consequent increase in fiscal deficit will counter the moderating trend in aggregate demand." To ensure more credit flow to industry, the RBI barred banks from investing more than 10% of their net worth in liquid schemes of mutual funds.

Justification for Aggressive Credit Policy in 2011. Justifying the very aggressive credit policy in 2011, Dr. D. Subbarao pointed out that as compared to the last year the conditions in 2011 were changed. The last year the domestic economy was facing uncertainty and inflation was more due to high food inflation and supply-side factors. This year the economy is on firm footing and inflation has spread from food to non-food manufactured products and has been generalised and demand-side pressures have been working to bring it about. He further emphasised that the aim of our strategy this year, now in 2011, is to check inflation by restraining demand and force the conditions for sustained growth by bringing environment of price stability. *The baby step approach was good for last year's growth-inflation dynamics. The dynamics have changed now and we have hiked more than we have done so far*.

Explaining the causes of persistent inflation despite increasing repo interest rate several times in the last year and projections of inflation of the RBI going wrong he said that there were *a series of unexpected supply shocks such as vegetable crisis and adjustment in coal prices and escalating demand pressures which made our projections go off track*. Producers were able to pass on higher input prices to consumers due to demand pressures. The aim of the RBI is to attain sustained growth in the environment of low inflation.

RBI indicated some risks that may lead to more inflationary pressures than anticipated. First, if monsoon is not normal, then food supply may not keep pace with the growth of demand. Second, food inflation may lead to increase in wages which would cause cost-push inflation. Third, subsidy bill of the Government may increase due to higher oil prices causing larger fiscal deficit which would add to demand pressure.

The RBI again laid stress that Government must check its fiscal deficit which is important for the success of monetary policy in controlling inflation. The Government should stick to its fiscal deficit targets against the backdrop of rising global crude oil prices and other commodity prices. The RBI wanted the Government to raise domestic retail prices of petroleum products to cut expenditure on subsidies in order to fight inflation, Dr. D. Subbarao, the Governor of RBI says "*Even though adjustments of administered retail prices of petroleum products may add to inflation in the short run, the Reserve Bank believes that this needs to be done as soon as possible. Otherwise, the consequent increase in the fiscal deficit will counter the moderating trend in aggregate demand.*"

Mid-Quarterly Review (15 June 2011). Since the announcement of Annual Monetary Policy on May 3, 2011, macroeconomic environment underwent a change and a high inflation rate (9.06% year on year basis) prevailed in May 2011, despite raising interest rate by it earlier. Further **core inflation** (*i.e.*, inflation other than food and fuel) hardened at 8.71 per cent at May 2011 compared to 7.93% in April 2011. Thus the main worry for the Central Bank was non-food manufactured products. Accordingly, to check inflation it increased the repo rate under liquidity adjustment facility by another 25 bps *from 7.25 per cent to 7.5 per cent* on May 2011. Similarly, in tandem with repo rate reverse repo rate was raised to 6.5 per cent and marginal standing facility (MSF) rate to 8.5%.

The RBI said that inflation persisted at an uncomfortable level and headline inflation rate then understated the inflationary pressures because the then domestic fuel prices had yet to reflect the global crude oil prices. While at that time the government had raised patrol prices sharply but delayed the decision to increase diesel, kerosene and cooking gas prices. It was felt that increased diesel prices would cause high inflationary pressures as it would raise transportation costs that would lead to rise in product prices through cascading effect.

The industry associations called for a halt or pause in interest rate increases as, according to them, demand for industrial products was slowing. One industrialist pointed out, *"For infrastructure companies looking for a debt instrument, this hike will come as a death sentence."* Though industrial production slowed in the preceding two quarters the RBI was of the view that slowdown was not particularly sharp or severe.

Continuing with Anti-Inflationary Stance : First Quarterly Review of Monetary Policy 2011-12 on July 26, 2011

In its first quarterly review of its credit policy on July 26, 2011, Reserve Bank of India raised its repo and reverse repo rates by 50 basis points each. Accordingly, it raised repo rate from 7.5 per cent to 8 per cent and reverse repo rate from 6.5 per cent to 7 per cent with immediate effect. In its credit policy review cash reserve ratio (CRR) and statuary liquidity ratio (SLR) were remained unchanged. This was in sharp contrast to small 25 bps hike each time in these interest rates in previous reviews of its monetary policy ten times since March 2010. Through these large hike in the interest rates, Reserve Bank sought to give strong signals to the market and industry that this time it is determined to check inflation and anchor inflationary expectations. As a matter of fact, in its previous reviews hike in interest rate by 25 bps each time for ten reviews since March 2010, failed to check inflation. The inflation rate based on WPI in June 2011 was found to be 9.44% which was likely to be revised to 10% when the rise in oil prices made in June 2010 was fully reflected in WPI. This inflation rate was more than that estimated by RBI. In its new macroeconomic assessment it made a forecast that inflation rate will fall to 7% by March 2012 against its earlier forecast of 6%. In fact the earlier small hike in policy rates popularly called baby steps did not produce the desired effect of reining in inflation as they were quite on expected lines and were factored in by the business class while adjusting the prices of their products.

Against this large rise in interest rate by RBI it was argued by the critics of RBI that it would hurt economic growth as this would discourage investment by raising the cost of funding the investment projects. By raising the cost of borrowing it was expected to affect adversely the growth of interest-sensitive sectors such as automobiles, houses, (*i.e.,* real estate) etc.

RBI in this 11th time hike in interest rates rightly thought that *infaltion was going to remain at an elevated level in the short run and therefore substantial hike in interest rate was called for to moderate inflation.* Some sacrifice in growth in the short term was necessary to control inflation if 8 per cent sustained growth in GDP was to be achieved in the medium term.

RBI pointed out that even with these relatively high rise in interest rates, inflation rate in India could still rise further if world commodity prices, especially of oil, do not soften fast enough, if debt crisis in Europe and the US squeeze the dollar flows that finances our imports and further if food prices spurt on a week monsoon during 2010-11 and, lastly, if fiscal deficit of the Government is not reduced to ease demand pressure. The *Reserve Bank made a strong case that in the absence of complementary policy measures such as reduction in fiscal deficit by cutting government expenditure, especially on subsidies which have outlived their utility, and make a shift in its expenditure toward investment in infrastructure and agriculture so as to overcome supply-side bottlenecks to ease supply-side pressures it was difficult to control inflation.*

A Critical Evaluation of Tight Monetary Policy to Fight Inflation

The Reserve Bank raised its overnight repo interest rate at which it lends to the banks 11 times since March 2010 till July 2011 through a series of baby steps, i.e. raising it each time by 0.25% except on two occasions when it increased it by 0.50 per cent. By doing so it raised the cost of borrowing through which it sought to limit the growth of bank credit. It kept the cash reserve ratio (CRR) unchanged at 6 per cent and therefore the *availability of credit* had not been affected.

The hikes in repo rate lowered the demand for credit for interest-sensitive sectors such as automobiles, houses (real estate) and other durable consumer goods. As a result, growth in consumption demand slowed down. But investment demand by the corporate sector had not been affected and credit had been made available to them. Therefore, the growth of bank credit has only marginally declined. However, a relatively large reduction in bank credit is essential to bring inflation under control. Inflation which from the later half of 2009-10 began with food inflation became generalised in 2010-11 and 2011-12 and spread to non-food manufactured products. The series of 11 hikes in interest rates (repo and reverse repo rates) till July 26, 2011 failed to check WPI inflation rate. Headline inflation (i.e., WPI inflation) rate rose to 9.44 per cent year-on-year basis in June 2011 and to 10 per cent in Sept. 2011 making life tough for the people. Inflation rate will further rise if global commodity prices, particularly oil do not soften fast enough; if debt crisis in Europe and America reduce the capital flows that finance our imports; if food prices spurt in the later half of 2011 due to below normal monsoon in 2011 (as is now expected); and if fiscal deficit increases. All these events will tend to raise inflationary pressures in the economy. The RBI's projected target of inflation of 5.5 percent in WPI inflation (which had been raised to 7 per cent) by March 2011 went wrong and actually stood at 9 per cent. Now, despite its several hikes in repo rate WPI inflation in Sept. 2011 went up to 10 per cent. Despite hike in repo rate to 8 per cent in Oct. 2011 and then to 8.5 per cent in Nov. 2011, inflation rate remained at an elevated level. It was estimated at 9.72 per cent year-on year basis in Oct. 2011 and at 9.11 per cent in November 2011. Due to the sharp decline in food inflation headline WPI inflation came down to 7.47% in 2011.

It is worth noting that even after latest hike in repo rate to 8 per cent on July 26, 2011, it was still below 9 per cent that prevailed prior to global financial crisis which started affecting India in September 2008. The private corporate sector and their supporters raise hue and cry when hike in repo interest rate is made on the ground that it would discourage investment and growth. However, they ignore the fact that despite 11 times hike in interest till July 2011 since March 2010, fixed deposit rates of banks for 1 year to 2 years duration were around 6 to 8 per cent in different banks and therefore with around 10 per cent rate of WPI inflation in Oct. 2011, *real rate* of interest for savers, was still in *negative* territory. That is, monetary policy still favoured the borrowers and investors at the cost of savers, especially the persons with fixed incomes and those who live on their past savings while inflation continue unabated. This is not only unjust but will discourage savings which finance investment. Already, due to negative real interest rates on bank deposits people had started investing their savings in gold, jewellery, real estate which are unproductive investment. As a result, there has been diversion of bank deposits to these unproductive types of investment and currency holding by the people.

Further, as stressed by the Reserve Bank of India in its monetary policy review of July 26, 2011 that tight monetary policy alone will not succeed in controlling inflation, the government must also contribute to it by fiscal consolidation by preventing wasteful Government expenditure and targeting subsidies to the really needy people so as to check the excess demand in the system. The Government can also help in controlling inflation if it steps up its *investment in infrastructure and agriculture so as to remove supply-side bottlenecks that feed inflation.*

In our view RBI's monetary policy had not been very effective in controlling inflation because government was incurring high fiscal deficit which led to the increase in inflationary pressures in the Indian economy. Besides, global situation regarding high oil prices also contributed to the inflationary pressures in the Indian economy. These high prices could not be passed on to the consumers which added to the subsidy bill of the government which contributed to the high **fiscal deficit** of the government. Besides, inflation was partly driven by supply-side factors and therefore tight monetary policy could not be able to check it, while it discouraged growth. Further, RBI in its conduct of tight monetary policy there could not successfully resolve the problem of inflation-growth trade-off. It sent confused signals regarding controlling inflation but at the same time supporting growth.

It needs to be emphasized that in a growing economy though in the short run there is trade-off between inflation and growth, in the long run there is no trade-off between them. This is because *investment has a dual effect, demand effect and capacity effect*. In the short run investment leads to the increase in aggregate demand and causes increases in inflation. This should be tackled through supply management by the government. But its effect on increase in productive capacity materialises in the long run and therefore leads to the increase in aggregate supply of goods in the economy and therefore counters the inflationary tendency in the economy. Monetary policy should be so conducted that while high interest rates should be pursued to discourage demand, especially of gold, automobiles, real estate, luxury consumer durable goods, whose demand is interest-elastic, at the same time they should promote investment in productive sectors of the economy which augments aggregate supply in the long run by making adequate funds available for them.

In 2011-2012 throughout inflation persisted at an elevated level. It was only in its First Quarterly Review in July 2011 that RBI talked of *sacrificing some growth in the short run to achieve price stability for the sake of sustained growth in the long run.* However, at that time inflation was getting out of hand because not only the demand pressure on non-food manufactured products increased but also because of higher food inflation resulted in increases in wages which gave rise to cost-push inflation as well. *By then inflation was being driven by both the demand-side and supply-side factors and became quite generalised by spreading to non-food manufactured products.* Such inflation cannot be bought under control merely by tightening monetary policy but proper fiscial policy aimed at fiscal consolidation through reduction in Government wasteful expenditure was also needed to tackle it. Besides, demand management through appropriate monetary and fiscal policies, efforts should be made to augment supply of those goods which are in great demand by raising their production and lowering cost of production through increasing productivity. To ensure that shortage of some goods should not emerge, efforts and investment should be so directed that supply must match demand, if price stability is to be achieved.

Monetary Policy Changes in 2012-13

During the financial year, 2012-13 growth has slowed markedly, even as inflation remained above the Reserve Bank's comfort level. Monetary Policy responded to this evolving growth-inflation dynamics through calibrated easing. After lowering the cash reserve ratio (CRR) by 125 basis points (bps) during Q4 of 2011-12, the Reserve Bank made a reduction in its repo rate by 50 bps in April 2012. Even as elevated inflation and the twin deficits severely restricted the room for further easing of the policy rate since April 2012, subsequent measures were directed towards ensuring adequate liquidity to facilitate a turnaround in credit deployment to productive sectors for supporting growth. As part of liquidity management measures, the CRR was reduced in two stages : first on Jan. 28, 2012 from 6 per cent to 5.50 per cent and then on March 3, 2012 to 4.75 per cent to ease monetary and liquidity conditions. Also, the statutory liquidity ratio (SLR) of scheduled commercial banks (SCBs) was reduced from 24 per cent since May 2012 to 23 per cent in August 2012 to improve the credit conditions facing the private sector (Table 19A.3).

Table 19.3. Movements in Key Policy Variables During 2011-12

(Percent)

Effective since	Repo Rate		Reverse Repo Rate		Cash Reserve Ratio*		Statutory Liquidity Ratio*	
1	2		3		4		5	
May 3, 2011	7.25	(+0.50)	6.25	(+0.50)	6.00		24	
June 16, 2011	7.50	(+0.25)	6.50	(+0.25)	6.00		24	
July 26, 2011	8.00	(+0.50)	7.00	(+0.50)	6.00		24	
September 16, 2011	8.25	(+0.25)	7.25	(+0.25)	6.00		24	
October 25, 2011	8.50	(+0.25)	7.50	(+0.25)	6.00		24	
January 28, 2012	8.50		7.50		5.50	(–0.50)	24	
February 13, 2012	8.50		7.50		5.50		24	
March 10, 2012	8.50		7.50		4.75	(–0.75)	24	
April 17, 2012	8.00	(–0.50)	7.00	(–0.50)	4.75		24	
June 18, 2012	8.00		7.00		4.75		24	
August 11, 2012	8.00		7.00		4.75		23	(–1.00)
September 22, 2012	8.00		7.00		4.50	(–0.25)	23	
November 3, 2012	8.00		7.00		4.25	(–0.25)	23	

Figures in parentheses indicate changes in policy rates/ratios.

* : Per cent of Net Demand and Time Liabilities.

Furthermore, apart from supplying liquidity through daily liquidity adjustment facility (LAF), the Reserve Bank made active use of the auctions under outright open market operations (OMOs) and injected primary liquidity of about ₹ 1.1 trillion coupled with liquidity injection of around ₹ 229 billion through anonymous trading platform (NDS-OM) in 2012-13 upto January-end 2013. The judicious use of the two sets of instruments, *i.e.,* keeping the policy rate unchanged since April 2012 and proactive liquidity easing measures conferred dual benefits that were evident as inflation gradually declined from its peak and credit off-take showed signs of improvements during most of November and December 2012. Inflation, however, continued remain above the Reserve Bank's level.

Global economic and financial conditions continued to deteriorate during this period and with a sharper reduction in domestic growth, the growth-inflation trade-off needed a revisit. In the assessment of the Reserve Bank of India, keeping in view the inflation in the country, further reduction in policy rates at this juncture (during September 2012 to 28 January 2013) could accentuate inflationary pressures rather than supporting growth. Further, since the risk to inflation was also arising from the high fiscal deficit, uncertainty in international prices of crude oil and structural imbalances in demand-supply of food (particularly protein foods), a cautious monetary policy stand was preferred by the RBI. However, the actions taken by the Government since September, particularly with regard to the *increase in the administered prices of diesel, fixing cap on the use of* LPG, *announcement of fiscal road map with clear medium term fiscal deficit targets and initiatives to improve investor perception* had created a favourable environment and had signalled a shift towards investment and capacity addition. Some of the inflationary pressures from excess demand was expected to be alleviated by these government measures the RBI would have room for more accommodative monetary policy.

The slowdown of economic activity was also getting reflected through a moderation in money supply and bank credit growth. While liquidity conditions continued to remain manageable, a widening of the gap between deposit and credit growth combined with a seasonal pick-up in credit demand are likely to keep up the pressure on liquidity. Policy actions in terms of reduction in CRR and SLR in the recent months had been supportive and tended to pre-empt a prospective tightening of liquidity conditions and reinforce the growth stimulus.

RBI Adopts Growth-Supporting Monetary Policy in the Third Quarter of 2012-13

Reserve Bank of India in its third quarterly review on July 29, 2012, cut its key policy rates, repo rate and cash reserve ratio (CRR) by 25 basis points each to revive the growth momentum. After holding the repo rate constant for nine months, RBI on Jan. 29, 2013, cut it from 8 per cent to 7.75 per cent. Along with it RBI also cut cash reserve ratio (CRR) from 4.25 to 4 per cent. This cut in CRR was estimated to release ₹ 18,000 crore for the bank to lend. The simultaneous cut in repo rate and cash reserve ratio was to ensure effective transmission of monetary policy to low lending rates by bank so as to promote investment and growth.

RBI justified its relaxation of monetary policy on the basis of three considerations. The first was, according to it, inflation had moderated, both headline wholesale inflation and core inflation (*i.e.,* non-food manufacturing inflation). Further, RBI thought that momentum of inflation was coming down. The second factor related to the deceleration of growth. The growth in the first quarter of 2012-13 was 5.4 per cent and in the second quarter was 5.3 per cent. The deceleration of economic growth, according to it, was not just due to fall in investment but also of net exports and consumption demand. The third consideration that weighed with RBI was liquidity, which was quite tight over the last few months.

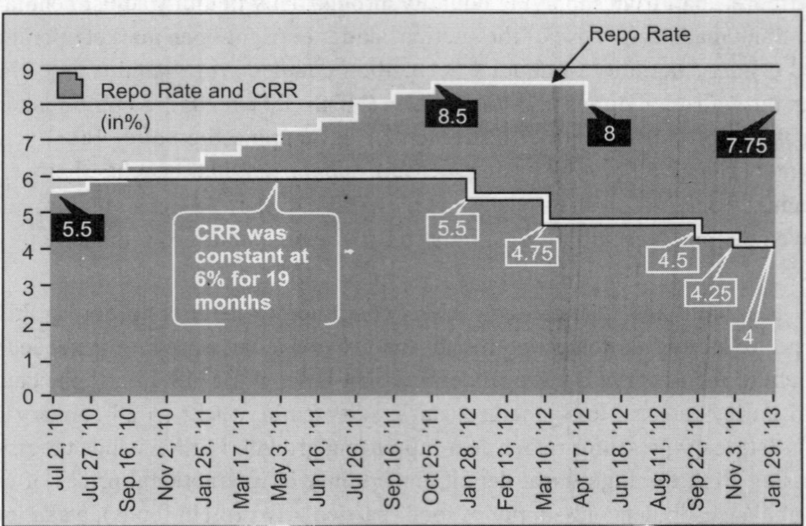

Fig. 19.1. *Movements in Key Policy Rates*

The daily drawings at the liquidity adjustment facility in the month of January 2013 averaged ₹ 90,000 crore despite RBI pumping in ₹ 82,000 crore through CRR cut and open market operations. This suggested that there was a structural liquidity deficit and that prompted the CRR decision in addition to the rate action.

To give a furher push to economic growth, RBI further lowered repo rate by 0.25 per cent from 8 to 7.75 per cent on 29, January 29, 2013 and on March 19, 2013, repo rate was further reduced to 7.50 per cent.

Risk Factors to Growth

There are five risk factors to economic grwoth that IBI indicated. The first risk factor related to twin deficits : risk arising from *high current account deficit* (CAD) and *large fiscal deficit;* the second risk was from global outlook, implications of which were for financing our current account deficit (CAD); the third risk factor related to the *inflation outlook:* even as demand pressures has ebbed, sustained reduction in inflation would have to come from vigorous supply response; the fourth risk factor was *about investment*, which was very important because the key to stimulating growth was a vigorous and sustained revival in investment; finally RBI also mentioned the *bank asset quality.* Banks and indeed the RBI were quite understandably concerned about the high level of bad loans but it was also concerned that the high bad loans should not cut into the flow of credit to productive sectors of the economy. RBI pointed out that decline in inflation provided some room for relaxation of monetary policy to give greater emphasis to growth risk.

Risk of Inflation. However, RBI pointed out that despite the recent decline in inflation there were upside risks to inflation in future. The first risk was about food inflation. Both in WPI and CPI, the share of food inflation had been high and that could put upward pressure on inflationary expectations and there would be pressure and obligation on monetary policy to respond to entrenched inflationary expectations. The second risk came from the monthly diesel price increases. This was a good thing for long-term inflation management but in the short term it would put inflationary pressures and thereby have implications for inflationary expectations.

The third risk to inflation related to *global crude prices.* They had plateaued in the last couple of months. Crude oil prices, going forward, will depend on economic, financial and geo-political factors. As far as the RBI was concerned, crude oil price also depended on the exchange rate movement.

The fourth risk factor to inflation is *suppressed inflation*. The RBI expected that coal prices would be adjusted later this year, perhaps in April. There will be a consequent adjustment in electricity prices. Hence, some of the suppressed inflation would come out and that would exert inflationary pressure.

Finally, there was the *pressure from wages*. Rural wages continued to go up. What was of concern was that this increase was not accompanied with commensurate improvement in productivity.

Risk of Current Account Deficit

By far the biggest risk, according to RBI, for inflation and for macroeconomic management was the CAD in the context of slowing growth and high fiscal deficit. For the first half of FY 2013, CAD was 4.7 per cent of GDP, Third quarter trade numbers were quite disturbing for which CAD was estimated at 6.7 per cent of GDP. It was a problem because it had implications for financing the CAD and for our exchange rate stability.

Caution for Future Monetary Policy

RBI in its third quarterly review of the year 2012-13 cautioned that if inflation and current account deficit did not improve as expected by it, then the scope for further easing of monetary policy would be limited.

Annual Monetary Policy Statement 2013-14.

In its annual monetary policy announced on May 3, 2013, RBI *further eased its monetary* policy by lowering its repo rate from 7.5% to 7.25 per cent to revive slowing of economic growth but cash reserve ratio (CRR) kept unchanged at 4 per cent. This was prompted by a fall in global commodity prices and drop in WPI-based inflation rate to 5.96 per cent in March 2013, though it was higher than the target inflation rate of RBI. This reduction in repo rate to 7.25 per cent rate of RBI in annual policy statement for 2013-14 came with the warning that the risk of rise in inflation rate left *little space* for further monetary easing. It is fourth time since March 2012 that the RBI lowered to repo rate to reduce borrowing costs to spur GDP growth, estimated to have slumped to 5 per cent in the year ended 31st March 2013, the slowest rate in a decade. Before May 3, 2013, RBI lowered its repo rate by 50 bps pounds in April 2012 and then by 25 bps each in January 2013 and March 13, 2013 (Note that 100 bps = 1 per cent). But both the banks and the industrial sectors expected that cash reserve ratio will be reduced as well by 0.25 per cent to ease the presently tight liquidity conditions. However, RBI announced its plan to adjust liquidity through open market operations (that is, through buying of bonds i.e., government securities from the banks). The governor of RBI repeated his earlier viewpoint that monetary policy action by itself cannot revive growth. It needs to be supplemented by efforts towards easing supply bottlenecks by the government, improving governance and stepping up public investment along with continuing efforts to achieve fiscal consolidation.

Representatives of banks expressed the view that the chance of transmission of cut in repo rate to lending rates cuts is very little in the immediate future. However, we agree with RBI governor that there is always time lag between the rate cut by it and reduction in lending rates by banks that takes place in the next 3-6 months, not just the result of May 3 – cut in repo rate but all the cuts over the last nine months.

Table 19.4. Movements in Key Policy Variables, 2013

Effective Since	Repot Rate	Reverse Repo Rate	Cash Reserve Ratio	Statutory Liquidity Ratio
January 29, 2013	7.75 (–0.25)	6.75 (–0.25)	4.25	23
February 9, 2013	7.75	6.75	4.00 (0.25)	23
March 19, 2013	7.50 (–0.25)	6.50 (–0.25)	4.00	23
May 3, 2013	7.25 (–0.25)	6.25 (–0.25)	4.00	23
July 15, 2013	7.25	6.25	4.00	23
July 30, 2013	7.25	6.25	4.00	23

On inflation the RBI's key concern was that the threats might come from demand–supply imbalances (in food and infrastructure segments), the correction in administrated prices (of diesel and coal) and pressures from increases in minimum support prices of agricultural commodities. Considering the demand-supply balance, the outlook for global commodity prices and the forecast of a normal monsoon, the wholesale price index (WPI) based-inflation rate, according to the RBI estimates, may be around 5.5 per cent (annual average) for the year 2013-14 compared to the actual 7.3 per cent (annual average) for the year 2012-13.

Table 19.5. Key Policy Rates Estimates by RBI

	2012-13	2013-14
GDP Growth Rate	5 %	5.7 %
WPI Inflate Rate (Annual average)	7.3 %	5.5 %
Money Supply (M_3) Growth	13.3%	13%
Credit Growth	14%	15%
Deposit Growth Rate	14.3%	14%

The RBI projected GDP growth for 2013-14 at 5.7 per cent which was later revised to 5.5% lower than 6.1 to 6.7 per cent made by the government. According to the RBI, the outlook for the industrial activity remains subdued, with the pipe line of new investment drying up and the existing projects stalled by bottlenecks and implementation gaps.

A snapshot of how the RBI expects key markers to perform in the current year 2013-14 compared to 2012-13 is given above in the Table 19.5.

Credit Policy Review, July 30, 2013

In its review of credit policy on July 30, 2013 the RBI *kept key lending rates (i.e., repo rate, bank rate) unchanged* to prop up a depreciating rupee. Thus Reserve Bank put its focus firmly on managing the rupee's slide as it considered it as a greater worry than spurring investment despite a crippling industrial slowdown. In the previous weeks prior to July 30, 2013, it had taken a string of measures to curb speculation in the foreign exchange market and to prop up the rupee which had hit a record level of ₹ 61.25 to a dollar on July 8, 2013. In July 30, 2013 review of credit policy, RBI retained the repo rate at 7.25 per cent and cash reserve ratio (CRR) at 4 per cent. It was expected that RBI would reduce repo rate which would have lowered the borrowing costs of banks prompting them in turn to lower their lending rates of interest which would have spurred investment and industrial growth. But lowering of lending interest rate would have led to borrow more for imports and speculation in foreign exchange causing increase in demand for dollars. The increase in demand for dollars would have adversely affected current account deficit and further weaken the rupee. Besides, further depreciation or weakening of rupee would have increased the cost of imports and fueled inflation. Therefore, containing rupee volatility (the value of rupee had fallen by around 12 per cent then since May, 2013) was a bigger worry at that point and this forced the RBI to keep interest rate at a relatively high level. RBI however pointed out that in order to stimulate investment and economic activity it had made 1.25 percentage points reduction in repo rate since April 2012. But it thought further reduction in repo rate would adversely affect the value of rupee and inflation.

The RBI's targeted confortable level of inflation is 5% to be attained by March 2014. The large current account deficit, well above the sustainable level of 2.5% of GDP for three years in a row, according to it, is a formidable structural risk factor. It has brought the external payments situation under increased stress, reflecting large current account deficit (CAD), rising external indebtedness and sharply depreciating rupee.

Restrictions by RBI on Aug. 14, 2013 to Prevent Depreciation of Rupee

In a move that seemed like a return of the pre-1991 controlled economy era the RBI on August 14, 2013 imposed a series of foreign exchange restrictions in its fight to stablise the rupee whose value was falling rapidly. These restrictions are the following :

The companies will now have to seek RBI permission if they want to invest overseas any amount beyond 100% of their *net worth* (which includes reserves and profit). Earlier this limit was 400% of the *net worth* of the companies. However, investment in oil and gas exploration and those by Navratna PSUs have been exempted from this new rule. It may be noted that Indian firms had invested abroad over $7 billion in 2012-13. It is expected that this restriction on Indian companies for investing their net worth abroad will save a lot of foreign exchange and help in reducing current account deficit and shore up the rupee.

These controls on foreign exchange outflow could affect Indian companies overseas mergers and acquisitions (M8A) plans. Further, the reduced limit would also apply to remittances abroad under the overseas direct investment scheme by Indian companies for setting up incorporated entities outside India in the energy and natural resources sectors.

The limit on *foreign exchange* that an individual can carry abroad was lowered to $75000 annually from the existing $ 200,000. Besides, the use of this liberalised remittance scheme for individuals for buying property overseas will now not be permitted. Obviously this will effect the Indian families to buy property overseas. However, this will benefit the Indian economy as this restriction will reduce dollar outflows from India and help in stabilising the value of rupee. It may be noted that during the last financial year 2012-13 $ 1.2 billion dollar outflows were made under this route known as liberalised Remittance Scheme.

RBI and the Finance Minister clarified that the above measures to cutb outflows of foreign exchange were only temporary. When the value of rupee is stabilised these measures will be reversed.

Incentivising US dollar Deposits by NRI

To incentivise inflows of dollars into the Indian banks the RBI exempted fresh deposits of US dollar by overseas Indians from reserve requirements of the banks. Currently 4 per cent of their demand and time deposits banks have to keep them as reserves with the Reserve bank on which they earn no interest. Besides, RBI also *raised the ceiling on foreign currency non-resident (bank) deposits to 400 basis points (100 basis points is equal to 1 per cent)* above the benchmark Libor (i.e. London interbank offered rates) from 300 basis points earlier for deposits maturing between 3 years and 5 years. Further, the interest rates that banks can offer on non-resident deposits have been delinked from the domestic rupee deposit rates. Earlier, banks had to keep their rates on non-resident (external) rupee deposits lower or at par with the rates offered on domestic rupee deposits.

Ban on Gold. RBI also banned imports of gold coin and medallations and tightened the links between gold imports and gold coins. This would also tend to reduce the outflows of dollars from India.

Sale of Bonds for ₹ 22000 crore every week. Another measure to check volatility in the rupee, the Reserve Bank of India on August 14, 2013 announced that it would auction ₹ 22000 crore of government bonds every monday *to suck out liquidity* of the banking system. This sales of bonds every week by the government would limit little room for traders to speculate on the rupee as less funds would be available for this purpose from the banks.

RELATION BETWEEN MONETARY POLICY AND FISCAL POLICY

Monetary policy in a planned economy of India cannot be framed independently of fiscal policy as achieving growth with price stability are the objectives of both these policies. In India the Reserve Bank of India has often adopted accomodative monetary policy to Government's fiscal policy. Prior to 1991 when economic reforms were initiated the basic goal of monetary policy was to neutralise the impact of large fiscal deficits of the Government. To boost public sector investment for accelating economic growth there was large increase in Government expenditure under various Five Year plans which was financed by borrowing by the Government and deficit financing (i.e., monetatisation of budget deficit). Both Government borrowing from the market and deficit financing leads to the increase in aggregate demand and have therefore potential for causing inflation. Therefore, to ensure adequate funds to meet the borrowing requirements of the Government the statuary liquidity ratio (SLR) of the banks was raised to the maximum limit of 38.5 per cent. That is, banks were to buy government securities to this extent.

Besides, to check inflation, cash reserve ratio (CRR) of banks was raised to a high level of 15 per cent. The high cash reserve leaves less funds with the banks to lend to the private commercial sector. In this way large expansion of credit for private sector was prevented. To quote C. Rangarajan the former Governor of the Reserve Bank of India, *"Until the overall reforms process was initiated in 1991 the basic goal of monetary management took the form of compensatory increase in the cash reserve ratio (CRR) for banks, controls on the growth of commercial credit (mainly to the private enterprises sector) and adjustments of administered interest rates.* The fixation of CRR and SLR at their maximum levels crowded out credit for the commercial sector. Thus, even when money supply was growing at a rapid rate, private sector could not get the needed credit for financing industry and trade". Explaining the monetary policy adopted prior to reform process of 1991, Dr. Y.V. Reddy, also a former Governor of the Reserve Bank of India writes, *"given the command and controlled nature of the Indian economy, the RBI had to resort to direct instruments like interest rate regulation selective credit control and cash Reserve Ratio (CRR) as major policy instruments. These instruments were used to neutralise the monetary impact of the Government's budgetary operations*".

In the recent post-reform years, mainly, 2008-09 accomodative nature of monetary policy to the Government's fiscal policy may be noted. In October 2008, a severe global financial crisis gripped the world economy following from the bankruptsy of Lehman's brothers in the US. This affected the growth of our exports and also led to the capital outflows from the Indian economy leading to the depreciation of the Indian economy and crash in Indian stock market. As a result, industrial and overall growth of the Indian economy started declining. To check the economic slowdown the Government increased its expenditure, especially on infrastructure projects, and cut indirect taxes such as excise duty service tax to boost private sector investment and expenditure. To supplement and accommodate Government expansionary policy, the Reserve Bank reversed its earlier tight monetary policy in October 2008 and to boost private sector investment it reduced its repo rate from 9 per cent in July 2008 to 7.5 per cent in Oct. 2008 and further to 4.75 per cent in March 2009. Similarly, RBI reduced cash reserve ratio (CRR) from 9 per cent in July 2008 to 6.5 per cent in Oct. 2008 and further to 5 per cent in March 2009 to make more funds available with banks to buy Government securities for financing sits borrowing and also to the private sector for expanding investment.

Thus, the RBI's monetary policy has been accomodatory in the sense that it provided support to Government's fiscal stimulus package to promote investment and growth. When in the later half of 2009-10 inflation rate again started rising the RBI began the process of withdrawing from the accommodative monetary policy stance in Oct. 2009 and started tightening its monetary policy to fight inflation.

QUESTIONS FOR REVIEW

1. Discuss the objectives of monetary policy in a developing economy.
2. What is meant by price stability ? "Of the various objectives price stability is perhaps the one that can be pursued most effectively by monetary policy" (C. Rangarajan). Discuss.
3. "The objective of achieving price stability through monetary policy clashes with its objective of economic growth". Do you agree ? Discuss.
4. "Both the large depreciation and appreciation of rupee is bad" Explain the measures that have been taken by RBI from time to time to ensure exchange rate stability.
5. Explain the role of monetary policy to promote economic growth in the economy.
6. Explain the role of monetary policy in promoting saving and investment in developing countries.
7. Explain the role of monetary policy in ensuring price stability in a developing economy. What tools of monetary have been used by Reserve Bank to control inflation in the Indian economy and with what success ?
8. Explain monetary policy of Reserve Bank of India before 1996. Was it targeted only at controlling inflation in the Indian economy ?
9. From Oct. 2008 to Jan. 2009 Reserve Bank of India followed easy monetary policy to promote private investment and revive the Indian economy from recession. Explain what monetary steps it had taken in this direction and how far they succeeded in raising investment.
10. What are repo rate and reverse repo rate ? How are they used to regulate liquidity in the Indian economy ?
11. Monetary policy faces the ticklish problem of trade-off between inflation and growth. Has RBI successfully tackled this problem since 1996 ? Explain.
12. To get rid of recession, monetary policy is ineffective and fiscal policy can be successfully used to revive the economy. In the light of this Keynes's view, comment on the success of policies adopted in the US and India to tackle recession/slowdown during 2007-09.
13. Explain the tight monetary policy adopted by the Reserve Bank of India from the second half of 2009-10. Discuss why it failed to control inflation.
14. Despite raising repo rate 13 times from Jan. 2010 to Nov. 2011, by the Reserve Bank of India, inflation remained at the elevated level of above 9 per cent year-on-year basis. Discuss why this dear monetary policy failed to check inflaton.
15. Explain '*growth as inflation*' dilemma faced by the Reserve Bank of India in the conduct of its tight monetary policy.

PART – V

INTEGRATION OF COMMODITY AND MONEY MARKETS AND ANALYSIS OF INFLATION AND UNEMPLOYMENT

- The IS-LM Curve Model : The Integration of Commodity and Money Markets
- Inflation and Unemployment : Phillips Curve
- Analysis of Inflation and Hyperinflation: Causes, Effects and Control

CHAPTER 20

The IS-LM Curve Model

THE GOODS MARKET AND MONEY MARKET : LINKS BETWEEN THEM

Keynes in his analysis of national income explains that national income is determined at the level where aggregate demand (*i.e.,* aggregate expenditure) for consumption and investment goods ($C + I$) equals aggregate output. In other words, in Keynes' simple model the level of national income is shown to be determined by the *goods market equilibrium*. In this simple analysis of equilibrium in the goods market Keynes considers investment to be determined by the rate of interest along with the marginal efficiency of capital and is shown to be independent of the level of national income. The rate of interest, according to Keynes, is determined by money market equilibrium by the demand for and supply of money. In this Keynes' model, changes in rate of interest either due to change in money supply or change in demand for money will affect the determination of national income and output in the goods market through causing changes in the level of investment. In this way changes in money market equilibrium influence the determination of national income and output in the goods market. However, there is apparently one flaw in the Keynesian analysis which has been pointed out by some economists and has been a subject of a good deal of controversy. It has been asserted that in the Keynesian model whereas the changes in rate of interest in the money market affect investment and therefore the level of income and output in the goods market, *there is seemingly no inverse influence of changes in goods market i.e., (investment and income)* on the money market equilibrium.

It has been shown by J.R. Hicks and others that with greater insights into the Keynesian theory one finds that the changes in income caused by changes in investment or propensity to consume in the goods market also influence the determination of interest in the money market. According to him, the level of income which depends on the investment and consumption demand determines the transactions demand for money which affects the rate of interest. Hicks, Hansen, Lerner and Johnson have put forward a complete and integrated model based on the Keynesian framework wherein the variables such as investment, national income, rate of interest, demand for and supply of money are inter-related and mutually interdependent and can be represented by the two curves called the *IS* and *LM* curves. This extended Keynesian model is therefore known as *IS-LM* curve model. In this model they have shown how the level of national income and rate of interest are jointly determined by the simultaneous equilibrium in the two interdependent goods and money markets. Now, this *IS-LM* curve model has become a standard tool of macroeconomics and the effects of monetary and fiscal policies are discussed using this *IS* and *LM* curves model.

GOODS MARKET EQUILIBRIUM : THE DERIVATION OF THE *IS* CURVE

The *IS-LM* curve model emphasises the interaction between the goods and money markets. The goods market is in equilibrium when aggregate demand is equal to income. The aggregate demand is determined by consumption demand and investment demand. In the Keynesian model of goods market equilibrium we also now introduce the rate of interest as an important determinant of investment. With this introduction of interest as a determinant of investment, the latter now becomes an endogenous variable in the model. When the rate of interest falls the level of investment increases and vice versa. Thus, changes in the rate of interest affect aggregate demand or aggregate expenditure by causing changes in the investment demand. When the rate of interest falls, it lowers the cost of investment projects and thereby raises the profitability of investment. The businessmen will therefore undertake greater investment at a lower rate of interest. The increase in investment demand will bring about increase in aggregate demand which in turn will raise the equilibrium level of income. *In the derivation of the IS curve we seek to find out the equilibrium level of national income as determined by the equilibrium in goods market by a level of investment determined by a given rate of interest. Thus IS curve relates different equilibrium levels of national income with various rates of interest.* As explained above, with a fall in the rate of interest, the planned investment will increase which will cause an upward shift in aggregate demand function ($C + I$) resulting in goods market equilibrium at a higher level of national income.

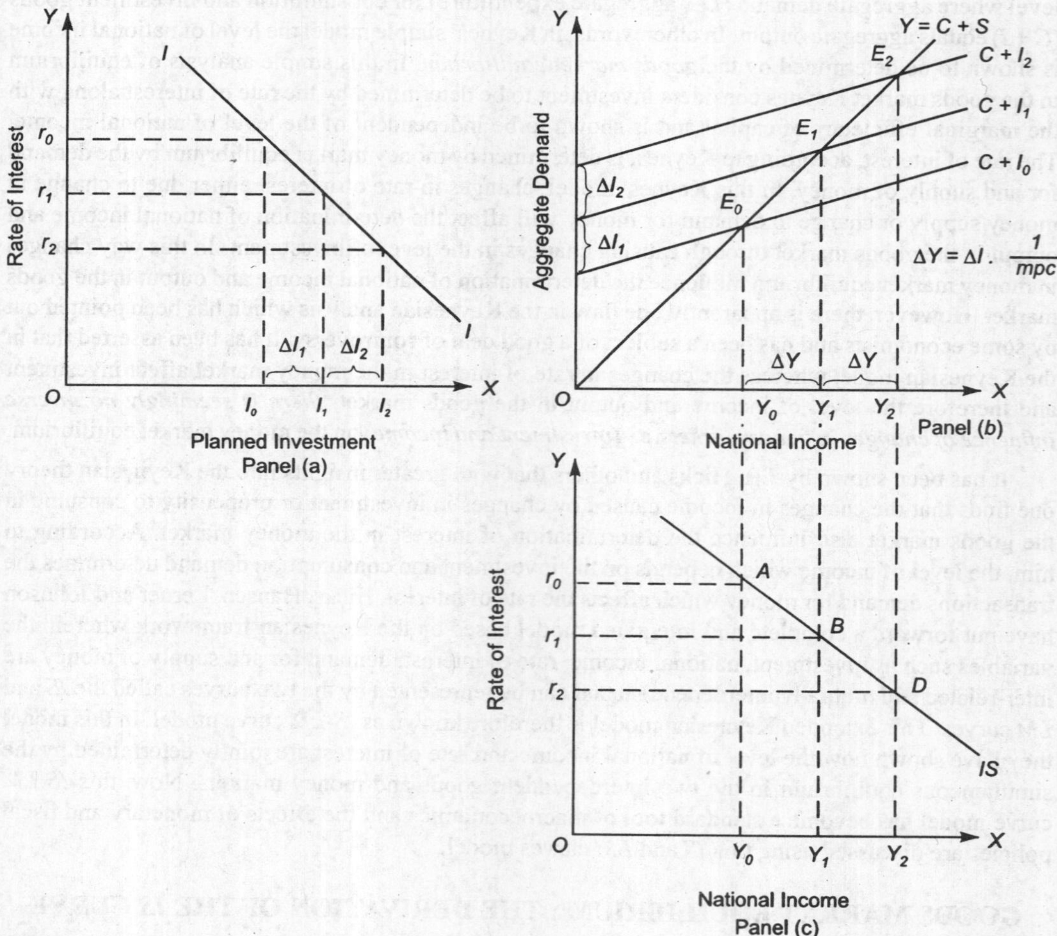

Fig. 20.1. *Derivation of IS Curve : Linking Rate of Interest with National Income through Investment and Aggregate Demand*

The lower the rate of interest, the higher will be the equilibrium level of national income. Thus, the *IS* curve is the locus of those combinations of rate of interest and the level of national income at *which goods market is in equilibrium*. How the *IS* curve is derived is illustrated in Fig. 20.1. In panel (*a*) of Fig. 20.1 the relationship between rate of interest and planned investment is depicted by the investment demand curve *II*. It will be seen from panel (*a*) that at rate of interest Or_0 the planned investment is equal to OI_0. With OI_0 as the amount of planned investment, the aggregate demand curve is $C + I_0$ which, as will be seen in panel (*b*) of Fig. 20.1 equals aggregate output at OY_0 level of national income. Therefore, in the panel (*c*) at the bottom of the Fig. 20.1, against rate of interest Or_0, level of income equal to OY_0 has been plotted. Now, if the rate of interest falls to Or_1, the planned investment by businessmen increases from OI_0 to OI_1 [see panel (*a*)]. With this increase in planned investment, the aggregate demand curve shifts upward to the new position $C + I1$ in panel (*b*), and the goods market is in equilibrium at OY_1 level of national income. Thus, in panel (c) at the bottom of Fig. 20.1 the level of national income OY_1 is plotted against the rate of interest, Or_1. With further lowering of the rate of interest to Or_2, the planned investment increases to OI_2 [see panel (*a*)]. With this further rise in planned investment the aggregate demand curve in panel (*b*) shifts upward to the new position $C + I_2$ corresponding to which goods market is in equilibrium at OY_2 level of income. Therefore, in panel (*c*) the equilibrium income OY_2 is shown against the interest rate Or_2. By joining points *A*, *B*, *D* representing various interest-income combinations at which goods market is in equilibrium we obtain the *IS* curve. It will be observed from Fig. 20.1 that the *IS* curve is downward sloping (*i.e.*, has a negative slope) which implies that when rate of interest declines, the equilibrium level of national income increases.

Why does *IS* Curve Slope Downward?

What accounts for the downward-sloping nature of the *IS* curve. As seen above, the decline in the rate of interest brings about an increase in the planned investment expenditure. The increase in investment spending causes the aggregate demand curve to shift upward and therefore leads to the increase in the equilibrium level of national income. Thus, a lower rate of interest is associated with a higher level of national income and vice versa. This makes the *IS* curve, which relates the level of income with the rate of interest, to slope downward.

Steepness of the IS curve depends on (1) *the elasticity of the investment demand curve, and* (2) *the size of the multiplier*. The elasticity of investment demand signifies the degree of responsiveness of investment spending to the changes in the rate of interest. Suppose the investment demand is highly elastic or responsive to the changes in the rate of interest, then a given fall in the rate of interest will cause a large increase in investment demand which in turn will produce a large upward shift in the aggregate demand curve. A large upward shift in the aggregate demand curve will bring about a large expansion in the level of national income. Thus when investment demand is more elastic to the changes in the rate of interest, the investment demand curve will be relatively flat (or less steep). Similarly, when investment demand is not very sensitive or elastic to the changes in the rate of interest, the *IS* curve will be relatively more steep.

The steepness of the *IS* curve also depends on the magnitude of the multiplier. As has been explained in a previous chapter, the value of multiplier depends on the marginal propensity to consume (*mpc*). It may be noted that the higher the marginal propensity to consume, the aggregate demand curve ($C + I$) will be more steep and the magnitude of multiplier will be large. In case of a higher marginal propensity to consume (*mpc*) and therefore a higher value of multiplier, a given increment in investment demand caused by a given fall in the rate of interest will help to bring about a greater increase in equilibrium level of income. Thus, the higher the value of multiplier, the greater will be the rise in equilibrium income produced by a given fall in the rate of interest and this makes the *IS* curve flatter. On the other hand, the smaller the value of multiplier due to lower marginal propensity to consume, the smaller will be the increase in equilibrium level of income following a given increment in investment caused by a given fall in the rate of interest. Thus, in case of smaller size of multiplier the *IS* curve will be more steep.

Shift in *IS* Curve

It is important to understand what determines the position of the *IS* curve and what causes shifts in it. It is the level of autonomous expenditure which determines the position of the *IS* curve and changes in the autonomous expenditure cause a shift in it. *By autonomous expenditure we mean the expenditure, be it investment expenditure, the Government spending or consumption expenditure, which does not depend on the level of income and the rate of interest.* The government expenditure is an important type of autonomous expenditure. Note that the Government expenditure, which is determined by several factors as well as by the policies of the Government, does not depend on the level of income and the rate of interest. Similarly, some consumption expenditure has to be made if individuals have to survive even by borrowing from others or by spending their savings made in the past year. Such consumption expenditure is a sort of autonomous expenditure and changes in it do not depend on the changes in income and rate of interest. Further, autonomous changes in investment can also occur.

In the goods market equilibrium of the simple Keynesian model the investment expenditure is treated as autonomous or independent of the level of income and therefore does not vary as the level of income increases. However, in the complete Keynesian model, the investment spending is thought to be determined by the rate of interest along with marginal efficiency of investment. Following this complete Keynesian model, in the derivation of the *IS* curve we consider the level of investment and changes in it as determined by the rate of interest along with marginal efficiency of capital. However, there can be changes in investment spending autonomous or independent of the changes in rate of interest and the level of income. For instance, growing population requires more investment in house construction, school buildings, roads, etc., which does not depend on changes in level of income or rate of interest. Further, autonomous changes in investment spending can also take place when new innovations come about, that is, when there is progress in technology and new machines, equipment, tools etc., have to be built embodying the new technology. Besides, Government expenditure is also of autonomous type as it does not depend on income and rate of interest in the economy. As is well known, government increases its expenditure for the purpose of promoting social welfare and accelerating economic growth. Increase in Government expenditure will cause a rightward shift in the *IS* curve.

MONEY MARKET EQUILIBRIUM : DERIVATION OF *LM* CURVE

Derivation of the *LM* Curve

The *LM* curve can be derived from the Keynesian theory from its analysis of money market equilibrium. According to Keynes, demand for money to hold depends upon transactions motive and speculative motive. It is the money held for transactions motive which is a function of income. The greater the level of income, the greater the amount of money held for transactions motive and therefore higher the level of money demand curve.

The demand for money depends on the level of income because they have to finance their expenditure, that is, their transactions of buying goods and services. The demand for money also depends on the rate of interest which is the cost of holding money. This is because by holding money rather than lending it and buying other financial assets, one has to forgo interest.

Thus demand for money (M^d) can be expressed as:

$$M^d = L(Y, r)$$

where M^d stands for demand for money, Y for real income and r for rate of interest. Thus, we can draw a family of money demand curves at various levels of income. Now, the intersection of these various money demand curves corresponding to different income levels with the supply curve of money fixed by the monetary authority would gives us the *LM* curve. The *LM* curve relates the level of income with the rate of interest which is determined by money-market equilibrium corresponding to different levels of demand for money. The *LM* curve tells what the various rates of interest will be (given the quantity of money and the family of demand curves for money) at different levels of income. But the money demand curve or what Keynes calls the liquidity preference curve alone cannot tell us what exactly the rate of interest will be. In Fig. 20.2 (*a*) and (*b*) we have derived the *LM* curve from a family of demand curves for money. As income increases, money demand curve shifts outward and therefore the rate of interest which equates supply of money with demand for money rises. In Fig. 20.2 (*b*) we measure income on the *X*-axis and plot the income level corresponding to the various interest rates determined at those income levels through money market equilibrium by the equality of demand for and the supply of money in Fig. 20.2 (*a*).

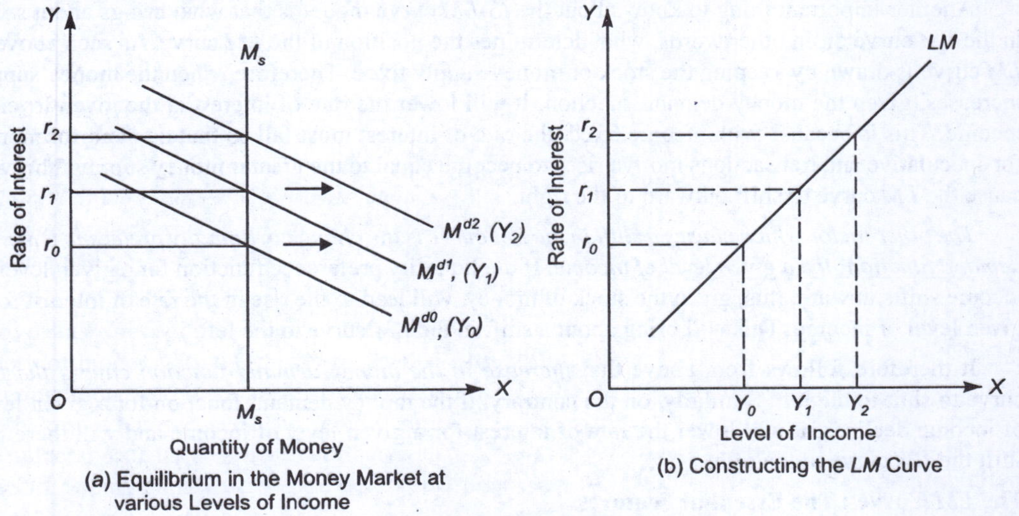

Fig. 20.2. *Derivation of LM Curve*

Slope of *LM* Curve

It will be noticed from Fig. 20.2 (*b*) that the *LM* curve slopes upward to the right. This is because with higher levels of income, demand curve for money (M^d) is higher and consequently the money-market equilibrium, that is, the equality of the given money supply with money demand curve occurs at a higher rate of interest. This implies that rate of interest varies directly with income. It is important to know the factors on which the slope of the *LM* curve depends. There are two factors on which the slope of the *LM* curve depends. First, *the responsiveness of demand for money (i.e., liquidity preference) to the changes in income*. As the income increases, say from Y_0 to Y_1, the demand curve for money shifts from M^d_0 to M^d_1, that is, with an increase in income, demand for money would increase for being held for transactions motive, M^d or $L_1 = f(Y)$. This extra demand for money would disturb the money market equilibrium and for the equilibrium to be restored the rate of interest will rise to the level where the given money supply curve intersects the new demand curve corresponding to the higher income level. It is worth noting that in the new equilibrium position, with the given stock of money supply, money held under the transactions motive will increase whereas the money held for speculative motive will decline. The greater the extent to which demand for money for transactions motive increases with the increase in income, the greater the decline in the supply of money available for speculative motive and, given the demand for money for speculative motive, the higher the rise in the rate of interest and consequently the steeper the *LM* curve. $r = f(M_2, L_2)$ where r is the rate of interest, M_2 is the stock of money available for speculative motive and L_2 is the money demand or liquidity preference function for speculative motive.

The second factor which determines the slope of the *LM* curve is the *elasticity or responsiveness of demand for money (i.e., liquidity preference for speculative motive) to the changes in rate of interest*. The lower the elasticity of liquidity preference for speculative motive with respect to the changes in the rate of interest, the steeper will be the *LM* curve. On the other hand, if the elasticity of liquidity preference (money demand function) to the changes in the rate of interest is high, the *LM* curve will be flatter or less steep.

Shifts in the *LM* Curve

Another important thing to know about the *IS-LM* curve model is that what brings about shifts in the *LM* curve or, in other words, what determines the position of the *LM* curve. As seen above, a *LM* curve is drawn by keeping the stock or money supply fixed. Therefore, when the money supply increases, given the money demand function, it will lower the rate of interest at the given level of income. This is because with income fixed, the rate of interest must fall so that demand for money for speculative and transactions motive rises to become equal to the greater money supply. This will cause the *LM* curve to shift outward to the right.

The other factor which causes a shift in the LM curve is the change in liquidity preference (money demand function) for a given level of income. If the liquidity preference function for a given level of income shifts upward, this, given the stock of money, will lead to the rise in the rate of interest for a given level of income. This will bring about a shift in the *LM* curve to the left.

It therefore follows from above that *increase in the money demand function causes the LM* curve to shfit to the left. Similarly, on the contrary, if the money demand function for a given level of income declines, it will lower the rate of interest for a given level of income and will therefore shift the *LM* curve to the right.

The *LM* Curve : The Essential Features

From our analysis of the *LM* curve, we arrive at its following essential features:

1. The *LM* curve is a schedule that describes the combinations of rate of interest and level of income *at which money market is in equilibrium*.
2. The *LM* curve slopes upward to the right.
3. The *LM* curve is flatter if the interest elasticity of demand for money is high. On the contrary, the *LM* curve is steep if the interest elasticity demand for money is low.
4. The *LM* curve shifts to the right when the stock of money supply is increased and it shifts to the left if the stock of money supply is reduced.
5. The *LM* curve shifts to the left if there is an increase in the money demand function which raises the quantity of money demanded at the given interest rate and income level. On the other hand, the *LM* curve shifts to the right if there is a decrease in the money demand function which lowers the amount of money demanded at given levels of interest rate and income.

SIMULTANEOUS EQUILIBRIUM OF THE GOODS MARKET AND MONEY MARKET

The *IS* and the *LM* curves relate the two variables: (*a*) income and (*b*) the rate of interest. Income and the rate of interest are therefore determined together at the point of intersection of these two curves, *i.e.*, *E* in Fig. 20.3. The equilibrium rate of interest thus determined is Or_2 and the level of income determined is OY_2. At this point income and the rate of interest stand in relation to each other such that (1) the goods market is in equilibrium, that is, the aggregate demand equals the level of aggregate output, and (2) the demand for money is in equilibrium with the supply of money (*i.e.*, the desired amount of money is equal to the actual supply of money). It should be noted that *LM* curve has been drawn by keeping the supply of money fixed.

Thus, the *IS-LM* curve model is based on: (1) the investment-demand function, (2) the consumption function, (3) the money demand function, and (4) the quantity of money. *We see, therefore, that according to the IS-LM curve model both the real factors, namely, saving and investment, productivity of capital and propensity to consume and save, and the monetary factors, that is, the demand for money (liquidity preference) and supply of money play a part in the joint determination of the rate of interest and the level of income. Any change in these factors will cause a shift in IS or LM curve and will therefore change the equilibrium levels of the rate of interest and income.*

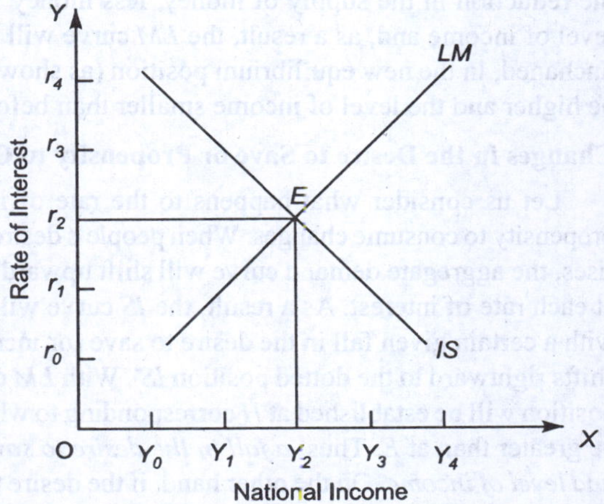

Fig. 20.3. *The IS and LM Curves Combined: The Integration of Commodity and Money Markets and Joint Determination of Interest Rate and Income Level*

The *IS-LM* curve model explained above has succeeded in integrating the theory of money with the theory of income determination. And by doing so, as we shall see below, it has succeeded in synthesising the monerary and fiscal policies. Further, with the *IS-LM* curve analysis, we are better able to explain the effect of changes in certain important economic variables such as desire to save; the supply of money, investment, demand for money on the rate of interest and level of income.

Effect of Changes in Supply of Money on the Rate of Interest and Income Level

Let us first consider what will happen if the supply of money is increased by the action of the Central Bank. Given the liquidity preference schedule, with the increase in the supply of money, more money will be available for speculative motive at a given level of income which will cause the interest rate to fall. As a result, the *LM* curve will shift to the right. With this rightward shift in the *LM* curve, in the new equilibrium position, rate of interest will be lower and the level of income greater than before. This is shown in Fig. 20.4 where with a given supply of money, *LM* and *IS* curves intersect

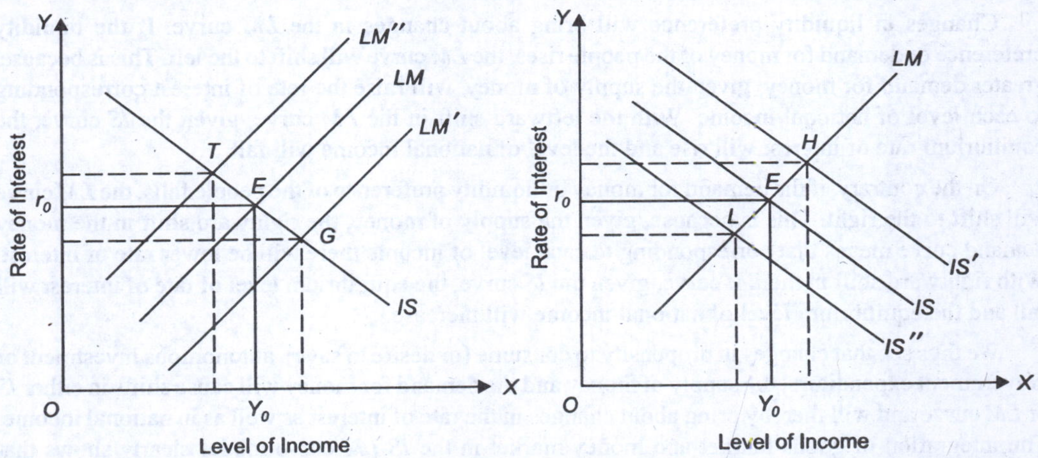

Fig. 20.4. *Impact of Changes in Supply of Money*

Fig. 20.5. *Impact of Changes in Propensity to Save*

at point *E*. With the increase in the supply of money, *LM* curve shifts to the right to the position *LM′*, and with *IS* schedule remaining unchanged, new equilibrium is at point *G* corresponding to which rate of interest is lower and level of income greater than at *E*. Now, suppose that instead of increasing the supply of money, Central Bank of the country takes steps to reduce the supply of money. With the reduction in the supply of money, less money will be available for speculative motive at each level of income and, as a result, the *LM* curve will shift to the left of *E*, and the *IS* curve remaining unchaned, in the new equilibrium position (as shown by point *T* in Fig. 20.4) the rate of interest will be higher and the level of income smaller than before.

Changes in the Desire to Save or Propensity to Consume

Let us consider what happens to the rate of interest when desire to save or, in other words, propensity to consume changes. When people's desire to save falls, that is, when propensity to consume rises, the aggregate demand curve will shift upward and, therefore, level of national income will rise at each rate of interest. As a result, the *IS* curve will shift outward to the right. In Fig. 20.5 suppose with a certain given fall in the desire to save (or increase in the propensity to consume), the *IS* curve shifts rightward to the dotted position *IS'*. With *LM* curve remaining unchanged, the new equilibrium position will be established at *H* corresponding to which rate of interest as well as level of income will be greater than at *E*. Thus, *a fall in the desire to save has led to the increase in both rate of interest and level of income*. On the other hand, if the desire to save rises, that is, if the propensity to consume falls, aggregate demand curve will shift downward which will cause the level of national income to fall for each rate of interest and as a result the *IS* curve will shift to the left. With this, and *LM* curve remaining unchanged, the new equilibrium position will be reached to the left of *E*, say at point *L* (as shown in Fig. 20.5) corresponding to which both rate of interest and level of national income will be smaller than at *E*.

Changes in Autonomous Investment and Government Expenditure

Changes in autonomous investment and Government expenditure will also shift the *IS* curve. If either there is increase in autonomous private investment or Government steps up its expenditure, aggregate demand for goods will increase and this will bring about increase in national income through the multiplier process. This will shift *IS* schedule to the right, and given the *LM* curve, the rate of interest as well as the level of income will rise. On the contrary, if somehow private investment expenditure falls or the Government reduces its expenditure, the *IS* curve will shift to the left and, given the *LM* curve, both the rate of interest and the level of income will fall.

Changes in Demand for Money or Liquidity Preference

Changes in liquidity preference will bring about changes in the *LM* curve. If the liquidity preference or demand for money of the people rises, the *LM* curve will shift to the left. This is because, greater demand for money, given the supply of money, will raise the rate of interest corresponding to each level of national income. With the leftward shift in the *LM* curve, given the *IS* curve, the equilibrium rate of interest will rise and the level of national income will fall.

On the contrary, if the demand for money or liquidity preference of the people falls, the *LM* curve will shift to the right. This is because, given the supply of money, the rightward shift in the money demand curve means that corresponding to each level of income there will be lower rate of interest. With rightward shift in the *LM* curve, given the *IS* curve, the equilibrium level of rate of interest will fall and the equilibrium level of national income will increase.

We thus see that changes in propensity to consume (or desire to save), autonomous investment or Government expenditure, the supply of money and the demand for money will cause shifts in either *IS* or *LM* curve and will thereby bring about changes in the rate of interest as well as in national income. The integration of goods market and money market in the *IS-LM* curve model clearly shows that Government can influence the economic activity or the level of national income through monetary and fiscal measures. Through adopting an appropriate monetary policy (*i.e.*, changing the supply of money) the Government can shift the *LM* curve and through pursuing an appropriate fiscal policy (expenditure and taxation policy) the Government can shift the *IS* curve. Thus both monetary and fiscal policies can play a useful role in regulating the level of economic activity in the country.

A Critique of the *IS-LM* Curve Model

The *IS-LM* curve model makes a significant advance in explaining the simultaneous determination of the rate of interest and the level of national income. It represents a more general, inclusive and realistic approach to the determination of interest rate and level of income. Further, the *IS-LM* model succeeds in integrating and synthesising fiscal with monetary policies, and theory of income determination with the theory of money. But the *IS-LM* curve model is not without limitations. Firstly, it is based on the assumption that the rate of interest is quite flexible, that is, free to vary and not rigidly fixed by the Central Bank of a country. If the rate of interest is quite inflexible, then the appropriate adjustment explained above will not take place. Secondly, the model is also based upon the *assumption that investment is interest-elastic*, that is, investment varies with the rate of interest. If investment is interest-inelastic, then the *IS-LM* curve model breaks down since the required adjustments do not occur. Thirdly, Don Patinkin[1] and Milton Friedman have cirticised the *IS-LM* curve model as being too artificial and over-simplified. In their view, division of the economy into two sectors – monetary and real – is artificial and unrealistic. According to them, monetary and real sectors are quite interwoven and act and react on each other. Further, Patinkin has pointed out that the *IS-LM* curve model has ignored the possibility of changes in the price level of commodities. According to him, the various economic variables such as supply of money, propensity to consume or save, investment and the demand for money not only influence the rate of interest and the level of national income but also the prices of commodities and services. Patinkin has suggested a more integrated and general equilibrium approach which involves the simultaneous determination of not only the rate of interest and the level of income but also of the prices of commodities and services.

IS-LM CURVE MODEL : EXPLAINING ROLES OF FISCAL AND MONETARY POLICIES

With the help of *IS-LM* curve model we can explain how the *intervention by the Government* with proper fiscal and monetary policies can influence the level of economic activity, that is, income

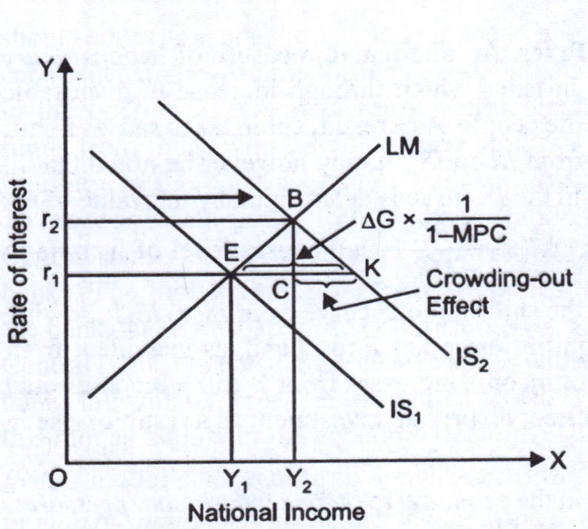

Fig. 20.6. *Expansionary Fiscal Policy : Impact of Increase in Government Expenditure on Interest Rate and Income*

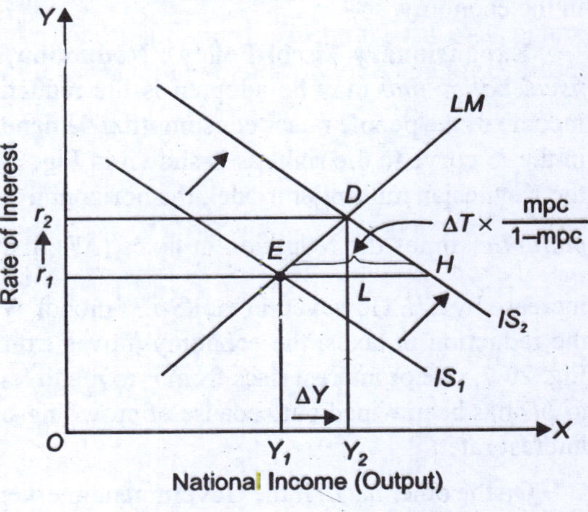

Fig. 20.7. *Expansionary Fiscal Policy: Effect of Cut in Taxes*

and employment level. We explain below the impact of changes in fiscal and monetary policy on the economy in the *IS-LM* model.

1. Don Patinkin, *Money, Interest and Prices*, Harper and Row, 1965.

Effect of Fiscal Policy

Let us first explain how *IS-LM* model shows the effect of expansionary fiscal policy of increase in Government expenditure on level of national income. This is illustrated in Fig. 20.6. As explained above, increase in Government expenditure which is of autonomous nature raises aggregate demand for goods and services and thereby causes an outward shift in *IS* curve, as is shown in Fig. 20.6 where increase in Government expenditure leads to the shift in *IS* curve from IS_1 to IS_2. Note that the horizontal distance between the two *IS* curves is equal to the increase in government expenditure times the government expenditure multiplier, that is, $\Delta G \times \frac{1}{1-MPC}$ which shows the increase in national income equal to the horizontal distance *EK* that occurs in Keynes' multiplier model. However, in *IS-LM* model actual increase in national income is not equal to *EK* caused by the working of Keynesian multiplier. This is because with the rightward shift in *IS* curve rate of interest also rises which causes reduction in private investment. It will be seen from Fig. 20.6 that, with the *LM* curve remaining unchanged, the new IS_2 curve intersects *LM* curve at point *B*. Thus, in *IS-LM* model with the increase in Government expenditure (ΔG), the equilibrium moves from point *E* to *B* and with this the rate of interest rises from r_1 to r_2 and income level from Y_1 to Y_2. Income equal to *CK* has been wiped out because of rise in interest causing a decline in private investment. Thus *CK* represents ***crowding-out effect*** of increase in government expenditure Thus, *IS-LM* model shows that expanoinary fiscal policy of increase in Government expenditure raises both the level of income and rate of interest.

It is worth noting that in the *IS-LM* model increase in national income by Y_1Y_2 in Fig. 20.6 is less than *EK* which would occur in Keynes' model. This is because Keynes in his simple multiplier model assumes that investment is fixed and autonomous, whereas *IS-LM* model takes into account the fall in private investment due to the rise in interest rate that takes place with the increase in Government expenditure. That is, *increase in Government expenditure crowds out some private investment.*

Likewise, it can be illustrated that the reduction in Government expenditure will cause a leftward shift in the *IS* curve, and given the *LM* curve unchanged, will lead to the fall in both rate of interest and level of income. It should be noted that Government often cuts expenditure to control inflation in the economy.

Expansionary Fiscal Policy : Reduction in Taxes. An alternative measure of *expansionary fiscal policy that* may be adopted is the reduction in taxes which through increase in disposable income of the people raises consumption demand of the people. As a result, cut in taxes causes a shift in the *IS* curve to the right as is shown in Fig. 20.7 from IS_1 to IS_2. It may however be noted that in the Keynesian multiplier model, the horizontal shift in the *IS* curve is determined by the value of *tax multiplier* times the reduction in taxes (ΔT), that is, $\Delta T \times \frac{MPC}{1-MPC}$ and causes level of income to increase by *EH*. However, in the *IS-LM* model, with the shift of the *IS* curve from IS_1 to IS_2 following the reduction in taxes, the economy moves from equilibrium point *E* to *D* and, as is evident from Fig. 20.7, rate of interest rises from r_1 to r_2 and level of income increases from Y_1 to Y_2. Income equal to *LH* has been wiped out because of crowding-out effect on private investment as a result of rise in interest rate.

On the other hand, if the Government intervenes in the economy to *reduce inflationary pressures, it will raise the rates of personal taxes to reduce disposable income of the people. Rise in personal taxes will lead to the decrease in aggregate demand.* Decrease in aggregate demand will help in controlling inflation. This case can also be shown by *IS-LM* curve model.

Role of Monetary Policy to Ensure Economic Stability : Explained through *IS-IM* Curve Model

Through making appropriate changes in monetary policy the Government can influence the level of economic activity. Monetary policy may also be expansionary or contractionary depending on the prevailing economic situation. *IS-LM* model can be used to show the effect of expansionary and tight monetary policies. As has been explained above, a change in money supply causes a shift in the *LM* curve; expansion in money supply shifts it to the right and decrease in money supply shifts it to the left.

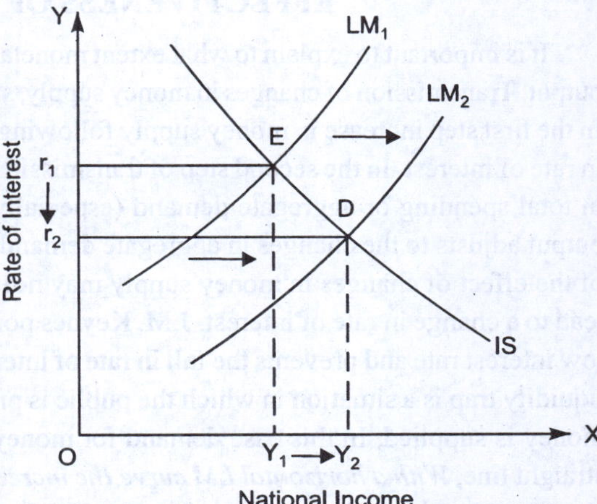

Fig. 20.8. *Effect of Expansion in Money Supply on Interest Rate and Income*

Suppose the economy is in grip of recession, the Government (through its Central Bank) adopts the expansionary monetary policy to lift the economy out of recession. Thus, it takes measures to increase the money supply in the economy. The increase in money supply, state of liquidity preference or demand for money remaining unchanged, will lead to the fall in rate of interest. At a lower interest there will be more investment by businessmen. More investment will cause aggregate demand and income to rise. This implies that with expansion in money supply *LM* curve will shift to the right as is shown in Fig. 20.8. As a result, the economy will move from equilibrium point *E* to *D* and with this the rate of interest will fall from r_1 to r_2 and national income will increase from Y_1 to Y_2. Thus, *IS-LM* model shows that expansion in money supply lowers interest rate and raises income. We have also indicated what is called *monetary transmission mechanism*, that is, how *IS-LM* curve model shows the expansion in money supply leads to the increase in aggregate demand for goods and services. We have thus seen that increase in money supply lowers the rate of interest which then stimulates more investment demand. Increase in investment demand through multiplier process leads to a greater increase in aggregate demand and national income.

If the economy suffers from inflation, the Government will like to check it. Then its Central Bank should adopt tight or contractionary monetary policy. To control inflation the Central Bank of a country can reduce money supply through open market operations by selling bonds or government securities in the open market and in return gets currency funds from those who buy the bonds. In this way liquidity in the banking system can be reduced. To reduce money supply for fighting inflation, the Central Bank can also raise cash reserve ratio of the banks. The higher cash reserve ratio implies that the banks have to keep more cash reserve with the Central Bank. As a result, the cash reserves with the banks fall which force them to contract credit. With this money supply in the economy declines. Thus, *IS-LM* model can be used to show *that reduction in money supply will cause a leftward shift in LM curve and will lead to the rise in interest rate and fall in the level of income*. The rise in interest rate which will cause reduction in investment demand and consumption demand and help in controlling inflation. This is shown in Fig. 20.9.

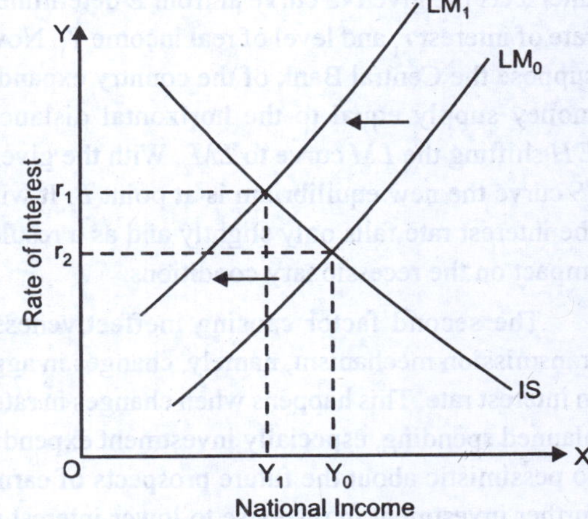

Fig. 20.9. *Contractionary Monetary Policy to Fight Inflation*

EFFECTIVENESS OF MONETARY POLICY

It is important to explain to what extent monetary policy is effective in influencing level of national output. Transmission of changes in money supply, say through open market operations, runs as follows, In the first step increase in money supply following the expansionary monetary policy leads to the fall in rate of interest. In the second step of transmission mechanism, fall in rate of interest causes increase in total spending or aggregate demand (especially, investment expenditure). Finally, the aggregate output adjusts to the changes in aggregate demand. However, some linkages in transmission process of the effect of changes in money supply may not work. First, the change in money supply may not lead to a change in rate of interest. J.M. Keynes pointed out that the *liquidity trap* may occur at a very low interest rate and prevents the fall in rate of interest following the expansion in money supply. The liquidity trap is a situation in which the public is prepared at a given rate of interest to hold whatever money is supplied, In this case demand for money is perfectly elastic and *LM* curve is a horizontal straight line, *With a horizontal LM curve, the increase in money supply does not cause a shift in it and therefore does not affect the rate of interest.*[2] With rate of interest remaining unaffected, the expansion in money supply, say through open market operations, will not affect the aggregate spending (both consumption and investment demand). With no change in aggregate demand on spending, the level of national output will remain unchanged. Thus in the *situation of liquidity trap "monetary policy carried out through open market operations is powerless to affect the interest rate."*

The effect of increase in money supply on aggregate output in case of horizontal *LM* curve is a bit complicated to show diagrammatically through *IS-LM* curve model. However, the ineffective -ness of monetary policy in case of the liquidity trap situation can be easily understood if we take the case of relatively flat *LM* curve (which can be considered as proxy for completely horizontal *LM* curve) caused by liquidity trap. This is depicted in Fig. 20.10. where a relatively flat LM_1 curve intersects the given *IS* curve at front *E* determines rate of interest r_1 and level of real income Y_1. Now suppose the Central Bank of the country expands money supply equal to the horizontal distance *EH* shifting the *LM* curve to LM_2. With the given *IS* curve the new equilibrium is at point *B*. It will be seen from the new equilibrium at point *B* that the interest rate falls only slightly and as a result real national income hardly increases to have any impact on the recessionary conditions.

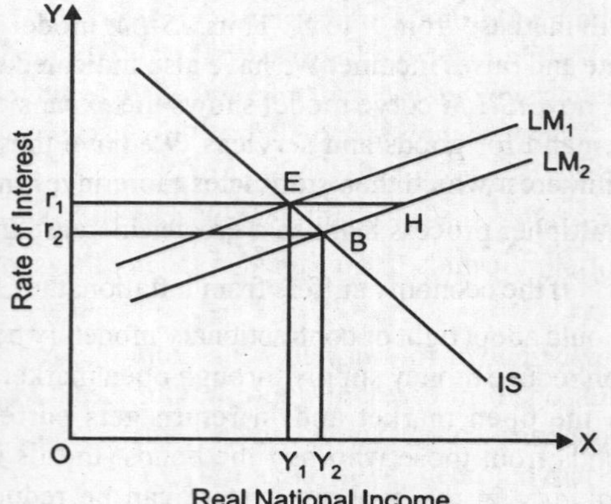

Fig. 20.10: *Flat LM Curve implies that monetary policy is not much effective*

The second factor causing ineffectiveness of monetary policy occurs in the third step of transmission mechanism, namely, changes in aggregate spending or demand in response to changes in interest rate. This happens when changes in rate of interest have insignificant effect on autonomous planned spending, especially investment expenditure. This situation occurs when business firms are so pessimistic about the future prospects of earning profits that they are reluctant to undertake any further investment in response to lower interest rate. As a result, increase in money supply causing lower interest rates does not lead to the increase in real national income. Under these circumstances of unresponsiveness of investment to changes in interest rate the *IS* curve is a vertical straight line as

2. See Dornbusch, Fischer and Startz, *op.cit.* p.245

shown in Figure 20.11 where with the increase in money supply (ΔM) equal to E_1H does not raise real national income which is 'stuck' at Y_1 level

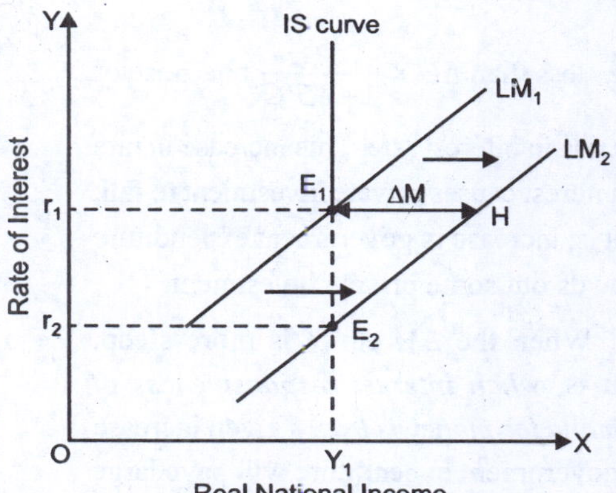

Fig. 20.11. *Zero interest responsiveness of investment spending (i.e.,vertical IS curve) implies expansionary monetary policy is ineffective in raising national income.*

Banks' Reluctance to Lend. The third case when monetary policy has only limited effect on investment spending and therefore on real national income occurs when banks are reluctant to increase lending for investment in response to lower interest rate. This happened in the US in 1991 and then in 2008-09 and 2009-10, when global financial crisis occurred. This situation also seems to have occurred in India in 2008-09 following the global financial crisis. In this case when the Central Bank of the US expanded money supply leading to lower interest rate, banks were reluctant to increase lending for the fear that lending might create bad loans with little possibility of being paid back. In the US banks had made bad loans relating to real estate *i.e.,* housing. Instead of lending for private spending and investment, banks purchased government securities such as treasury bills which are quite safe investment for banks. If due to risk aversion banks do not lend for private investment, the link in transmission mechanism that involves more private investment in response to lower interest rate breaks down to give boost to real national income. In India too, when in 2008-09 the Reserve Bank of India lowered its repo rate and cash reserve ratio (CRR) for the banks, they were not much enthusiastic for lending to private firms for fear of default by them in repaying the loans. Therefore, to earn some return on their excess cash reserves due to easy monetary policy, some banks opted for investing in government securities beyond what was required under statutory liquidity ratio (SLR). However, both in the US in 1991 and 2008-09 and in India in 2008-09 ***larger cuts in interest rate and expansion in money supply*** did bring about boost in lending for private investment and consumption for buying durable consumer goods leading to the recovery in the economies. In this context, it is worth mentioning the policy of '*quantitative easing*' (*QE*) which the Federal Reserve of the US is pursuing to revive the American economy under the leadership of its governor Ben Bernanke. Under the policy of quantitative easing the Federal Reserve has been continuously buying government securities since 2010 and pumping into the American economy more money, that is, the US dollars, on a large scale keeping zero rate of interest. This unconventional monetary policy of quantitative casing ultimately seems to have worked in raising the levels of output and employment in the US and thus achieving recovery of the US economy in 2013 with rate of unemployment falling to 7.6 per cent compared to 10 per cent in the year 2009.

EFFECTIVENESS OF FISCAL POLICY

We have seen above how the changes in fiscal policy shift the *IS* curve. Recall that the *IS* curve describes equilibrium in the goods market. We have explained that *IS* curve slopes downward because as the rate of interest falls investment spending increases causing rise in aggregate demand that leads to the increase in real national income (*i.e., GDP*). Expansionary fiscal policy may be either in the form of increase in government expenditure or cut in taxes. In both these forms of fiscal stimulus, the *IS* curve shifts to the right. In our previous Fig. 20.6 of *IS-LM* curve model we have explained that given the normal upward sloping *LM* curve increase in government expenditure leads to increase in output or real national income less than that under Keynesian government expenditure multiplier (*i.e.*, less than $\Delta G \times \frac{1}{1-MPC}$) because of the rise in interest rate. This increase in rate of interest causes private investment to fall, that is, increase in government expenditure crowds out some private investment.

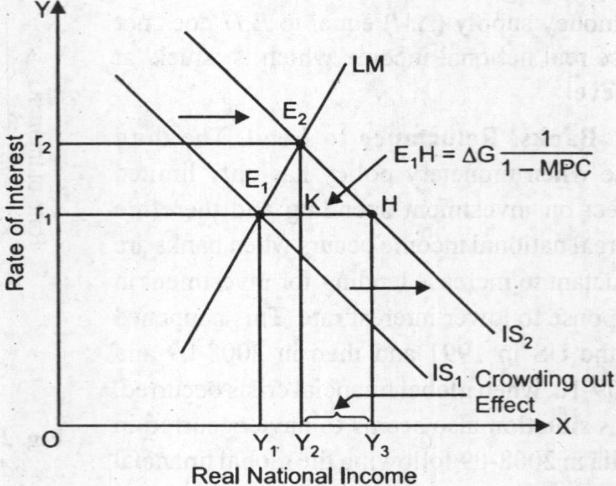

Fig. 20.12. *Large crowding-out effect in case of steep LM curve and as a result, increase in government expenditure causes only a small increase in real national income.*

When the *LM* curve is more steep, that is, *when interest responsiveness of demand for money is less*, a given increase in government expenditure will have large crowding-out effect as shown in Fig. 20.12. Initially, the *IS* and *LM* curves intersect at point E_1 and determine Y_1 national income and r_1 rate of interest of (The given *LM* curve is relatively steep). Now suppose under the expansionary fiscal policy the government increases its expenditure so that there is a shift in the IS_1 curve to the right to IS_2. This new IS_2 curve intersects the given steep *LM* curve at point E_2 and, as will be seen from Figure 20.12, rate of interest rises to r_2 and the real national income increases from Y_1 to Y_2. A larger income equal to Y_2Y_3 or *KH* has been wiped out due to crowding-out effect of rise in interest rate on investment. To conclude, in case of lower interest-responsiveness of demand for money expansionary fiscal policy is not very effective in bringing about a sufficient increase in real national income.

Horizontal *LM* Curve. Note that contrary to Figure 20.12 where due to steep upward-sloping *LM* curve, increase in government expenditure on national income has less than full Keynesian multiplier effect on the equilibrium level of national income due to large crowding-out effect of rise in rate of interest, there is no crowding-out effect when there is *infinite interest responsiveness* of demand for money and the *LM* curve is horizontal which occurs *when the economy is in the liquidity trap.*

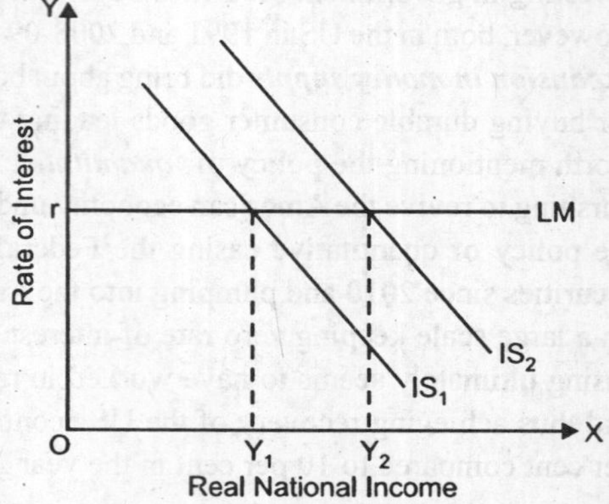

Fig. 20.13. *With a horizontal LM curve when there is no crowding out effect, expansionary fiscal policy has maximum effect on natural income.*

In this case of horizontal *LM* curve shown in Fig. 20.13 increase in the government expenditure causing a shift in the *IS* curve to the right to IS_2 position. As will be seen from Figure 20.13, rate of interest of remains fixed and as a result there is no crowding out effect and the national income increases by the full multiplier effect of increase in government expenditure, that is by $\Delta G \frac{1}{1-MPC}$. It may however be noted that the horizontal *LM* curve depicting liquidity trap in the demand for money in which case there is no crowding out effect of fiscal stimulus is an extreme case that may occur when there is severe depression in the economy.

The Classical Case of Zero Interest-responsiveness of Demand for Money and Crowding-Out Effect

Expansionary fiscal policy, that is, increase in government expenditure or cut in taxes has no effect on the level of real income when the *LM curve is vertical, that is, interest-responsiveness of demand for money is zero.* This is a classical case where fiscal stimulus provided by increase in government spending increases only the interest rate which crowds out private investment equal to the increase in government expenditure times the multiplier, that is, $\Delta G \times \frac{1}{1-MPC}$. As a result, level of national income remains unaffected, Thus, with a vertical *LM* curve (*i.e.*, zero interest -responsiveness of demand for money), there is *full or complete crowding out.* This is shown in Fig. 20.14 where a vertical *LM* curve is drawn at the level of national income Y_1. Initially, the IS_1 curve intersects the vertical *LM* curve so that in equilibrium rate of interest is r_1 and real national income is Y_1. Now suppose the government adopts expansionary fiscal policy and increases its expenditure shifting the *IS* curve to IS_2. However, the new equilibrium between IS_2 curve and the given vertical *LM* curve is at point E_2. In this new equilibrium situation rate of interest has risen from r_1 to r_2, the level of real national income remains unchanged at Y_1. *This means rise in interest rate has completely wiped out the expansionary effect on the level of real national income by crowding out private investment.* In this case crowding-out of private investment equals the increase in government expenditure times its multiplier (i.e. $\Delta G \times \frac{1}{1-MPC}$) and therefore leaves real national income unaffected. Numerous historical episodes show that the crowding-out effect is neither complete or full, nor is it non-existent, it is only partial as shown in the Figure 20.6 depending upon the degree of steepness of *LM* curve. Whether crowding out is zero, complete or partial depends on the interest-responsiveness of demand for money, that is, slope of the *LM* curve.

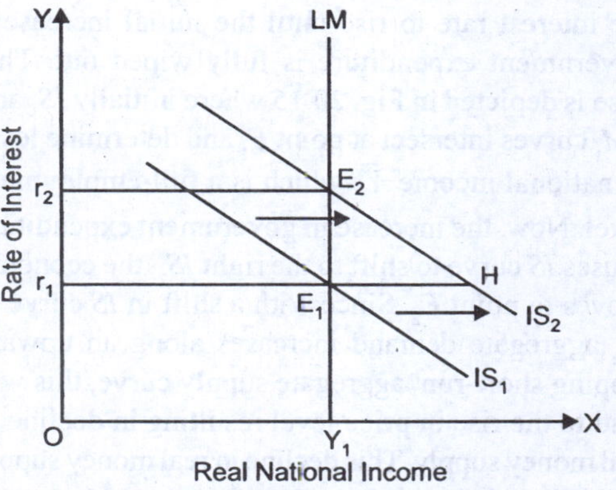

Fig. 20.14. *Full Crowding-Out of Fiscal Stimulus: The Classical Case*

The Importance of Crowding-Out Effect Expansionary Fiscal Policy

We have seen above that the increase in real national income (*i.e.*, multiplier effect) as a result of expansionary fiscal policy (*e.g.*, increase in government expenditure) depends on interest elasticity of demand for money (that is, shope of *LM* curve). Three points are worth considering about the effect of fiscal stimulus on real national income. First, *in our analysis of IS-LM curves model, we have assumed that prices remain constant and the existing level of aggregate output (i.e., real national income) is below the full-employment level.* In this situation there is a scope for increase in output or real national income and therefore when the government expands its expenditure causing increase in aggregate demand, the firms increase their output and employment. In this case the magnitude of fiscal multiplier is quite large.

However, in a fully employed economy crowding out of fiscal stimulus occurs through a different route. When there is full employment in the economy, increase in aggregate demand leads to the rise in price level as the economy moves up along an upward-sloping short-run aggregate supply curve. Now, the rise in price level, nominal money supply remaining constant, reduces the real money supply, that is, $\frac{M}{p}$ decreases. The reduction in money supply shifts the *LM* curve to the left raising the interest rate to rise until the initial increase in aggregate demand as a result of expansion in government expenditure is fully wiped out. This case is depicted in Fig. 20.15 where initially IS_1 and LM_1 curves intersect at point E_1 and determine level of national income $\overline{Y}$ which is a full-employment level. Now, the increase in government expenditure causes *IS* curve to shift to the right IS_2, the economy moves to point E_2. Since with a shift in *IS* curve to IS_2 aggregate demand increases along an upward sloping short-run aggregate supply curve, this will lead to the rise in price level resulting in decline in real money supply. This decline in real money supply will bring about a leftward shift in the *LM* curve to the left to LM_2 position and *raise the interest rate to* r_2 so that the initial increase in national income is fully crowded out. As a result, expansionary fiscal policy fails to raise level of real national income and has therefore zero multiplier effect.

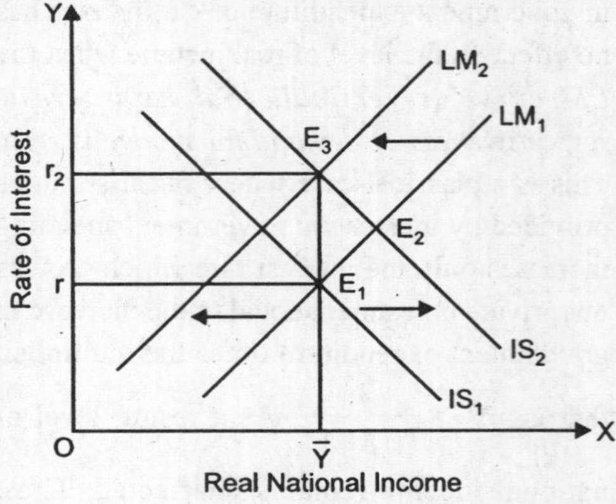

Fig. 20.15. *Full Crowding-Out of Fiscal Stimulus in Case of Existing Full Employment of Resources*

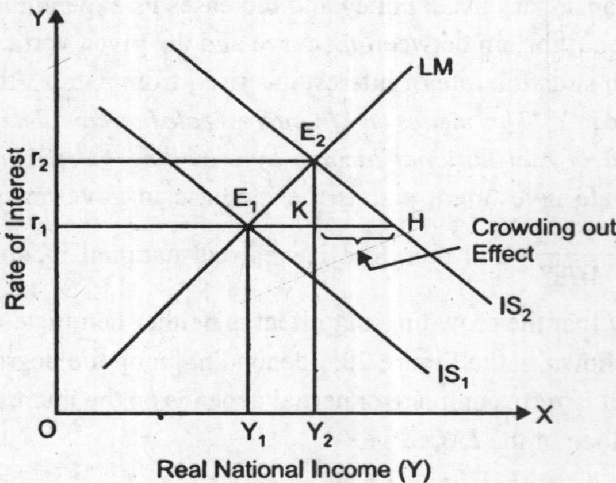

Fig. 20.16. *In case of unemployment of resources, there is partial crowding out and expansionary fiscal policy has some multiplier effect*

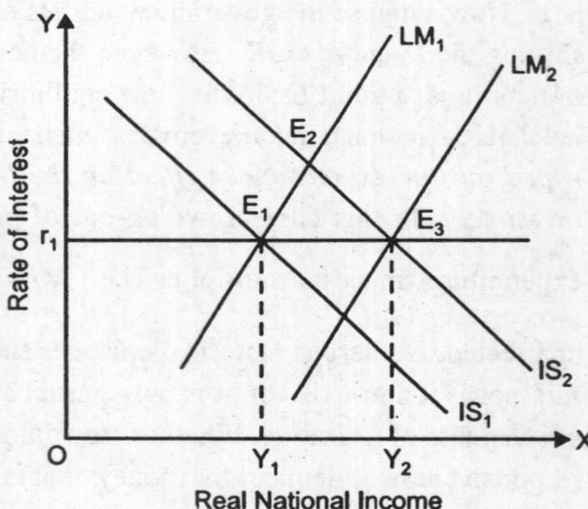

Fig. 20.17. *Monetary Accommodation of Expansionary Fiscal Policy*

The second case occurs when there is unemployment of resources in the economy and the *LM* curve slopes upward to the right. In this case fiscal stimulus through increase in government expenditure will raise interest rate but level of real national income will also increase. *Due to unemployment resources, there will not be much increase in price level when aggregate demand increases*. As a result, *crowding-effect of fiscal stimulus is only partial,* and there is net increase in national income. Therefore, in this case there is some multiplier effect of expansionary fiscal policy though it is less than the Keynesian multiplier effect (*i.e.,* $\Delta G.\frac{1}{1-MPC}$). This case is depicted in Fig. 20.16 where initially IS_1 and *LM* curves intersect at point E_1. Expansionary fiscal policy with its multiplier effect shifts *IS* curve to IS_2 equal to the horizontal distance E_1H. With the given *LM* curve and the new IS_2 curve the new equilibrium is reached at point E_2 and, as will be seen from the Figure 20.16, the national income increases from Y_1 to Y_2, the income equal to *KH* has been wiped out due to crowding-out effect of rise in interest rate from r_1 to r_2.

However, there is further effect of expansionary fiscal policy. With the net increase in national income from Y_1 to Y_2 resulting from the shift in *IS* curve from IS_1 to IS_2 the *level of saving* will increase. This increase in saving enables the economy to finance a large budget deficit with smaller amount of government borrowing which would ensure interest rate will not rise much and as a result crowding-out effect of expansionary fiscal policy on private investment will be smaller.

Monetary Accommodation. The third case occurs when there is unemployment in the economy so that there is possibility of increases in output as a result of increase in aggregate demand. In this case interest rate need not rise when there is increase in government spending shifting *IS* curve to the right but at the same time the Central Bank of the country raises the money supply to prevent the rise in interest as a result of increase is government spending. This is called monetary accommodation by the Central Bank. Thus, *"Monetary policy is accommodating when in the course of fiscal expansion, the money supply is increased to prevent interest rates from rising"*[3]. In this case of sufficient monetary accommodation, rate of interest does not rise, and therefore there is no crowding-out effect on private investments, the expansionary fiscal policy brings about increase in national income equal to increase in government expenditure times the Keynesian multiplier (*i.e.*, $\Delta G \times \frac{1}{1-MPC}$). This case of monetary accommodation of fiscal expansion is depicted in Fig. 20.17 in which it will be seen that initially equilibrium is at point E_1 where IS_1 and LM_1 curves intersect determine Y_1 level of income and r_1 rate of interest Now, fiscal stimulus by the government shifts the *IS* curve to IS_2 and given the LM_1 curve, equilibrium will be at point E_2 where rate of interest rises to r_2 which would crowd out private investment. To prevent this crowding out, the Central Bank adopts the monetary accommodation policy and for this it increases money supply sufficiently so that *LM* curve shifts to the right to LM_2 which intersects IS_2 curve at point E_3 so that interest remains at the initial level r_1 and income increases to Y_2. Thus the increase in income equal to $E_1 E_3$ or $Y_1 Y_2$ that occurs equals the increase in government expenditure times the Keynesian multiplier (*i.e.*, $\Delta G. \frac{1}{1-MPC}$); crowding out having been eliminated by expansion in money supply by the Central Bank.

It may be noted that in 2008-09 and 2009-10 when due to global financial crisis, India faced the problem of large slowdown of the economy, the Indian government adopted fiscal stimulus measures such as raising its expenditure through borrowing on a large scale from the market and cut rates of many indirect taxes to prevent sharp slowdown of the Indian economy, the Reserve Bank of India adopted accommodative monetary policy so that rate of interest does not rise To this end, the RBI greatly reduced its repo rate (the ratio at which it lends to the commercial banks) and also lowered the cash reserve ratio (*CRR*) of the banks so that more finds are available with them to lend to the business firms for investment and consumption purposes, such as housing loans, car loans at lower rate of interest. This policy succeeded and India achieved 6.7 per cent growth in the crisis year 2008-09 and 8.6 per cent in 2009-10.

IS – LM MODEL : ALGEBRAIC ANALYSIS

In the foregoing analysis we have explained the *IS-LM* curve model with graphs. In this section we make algebraic analysis of *IS-LM* curves model. We first derive the equations for *IS* and *LM* curves and then combine them to show how level of national income and rate of interest are jointly determined through the simultaneous equilibrium of goods and money markets. This algebraic analysis of *IS-LM* model provides additional insights into how fiscal and monetary policy instruments affect national income and rate of interest.

The Derivation of *IS* Curve : Algebraic Method.

The *IS* curve is derived from goods market equilibrium. The *IS* curve shows the combinations of levels of income and interest at which goods market is in equilibrium, that is, at which aggregate

3. Dornbusch, Fischer, and Startz, *Macroeconomics*, Tata MacGraw-Hill, 8th edition, p. 253

demand equals income. Aggregate demand, as explained earlier, consists of consumption demand, investment demand, government expenditure on goods and services and net exports. Consumption demand is function of disposable income. Disposable income is level of income minus taxes ($Y_d = Y - T$) where Y_d stands for disposable income and T for taxes. However, in a two-sector model where we do not incorporate taxation by the government, $Y_d = Y$.

Investment depends on rate of interest. With a given level of income, a higher rate of interest reduces investment demand and a lower rate of interest leads to more investment, that is, investment is negatively related to rate of interest. Thus,

$$I = \bar{I} - di$$

Therefore, we have the following equation for aggregate demand (*AD*)

$$AD = C + I + G + NX \quad \text{...(1)}$$

where $C = a + bY$ (Consumption function)

$I = \bar{I} - di$ (Investment function)

where $\bar{I}$ is autonomous investment, that is, independent of income and rate of interest

G is government expenditure on goods and services and NX is net exports, that is, exports–imports.

Product market is in equilibrium when

$$Y = AD = C(Y) + I(i) + G + NX \quad \text{...(2)}$$

or

$$Y = (a + bY) + (\bar{I} - di) + G + NX$$

$$Y - bY = a + \bar{I} - di + G + NX$$

$$Y(1 - b) = a + \bar{I} - di + G + NX$$

$$Y = \frac{1}{1-b}(a + \bar{I} + G + NX) - \frac{di}{1-b} \quad \text{...(3)}$$

The above equation (3) describes *IS* curve. Terms in the brackets are all autonomous expenditure and are independent of both income and rate of interest. If we denote all these autonomous items by $\bar{A}$, then equation (3) for *IS* can be written as

$$Y = \frac{1}{1-b}(\bar{A}) - \frac{1}{1-b}(di)$$

or

$$Y = \frac{1}{1-b}(\bar{A} - di) \quad \text{...(4)}$$

$\frac{1}{1-b}$ is the income multiplier and b is marginal propensity to consume. Given the value of autonomous expenditure, we can obtain value of Y at different rates of interest to draw an *IS* curve. It is worth noting that the value of autonomous ($\bar{A}$) determines the intercept of the *IS* curve, d in the term di in equation (3) shows the sensitivity of investment to the changes in rate of interest and determines the slope of *IS* curve. Since fall in interest rate increases investment spending, it will raise aggregate demand and thus the equilibrium level of income. Besides, the slope of the *IS* curve depends on the size of income multiplier.

NUMERICAL PROBLEMS ON *IS* CURVE : TWO-SECTOR MODEL

Problem 1. The following equations describe an economy :

$C = 10 + 0.5\,Y$ (Consumption function)

$I = 190 - 20\,i$ (Investment function)

Derive the equations for IS curve and represent it graphically

Solution :

IS curve describes the equation for product market equilibrium at various combinations of level of income and rate of interest.

$$Y = AD = C + I$$

Thus,

$$Y = 10 + 0.5Y + 190 - 20i$$

$$Y - 0.5Y = 200 - 20i$$

$$Y(1 - 0.5) = 200 - 20i$$

$$\frac{1}{2}Y = 200 - 20i$$

$$Y = 400 - 40i$$

Thus, *IS* curve is : $Y = 400 - 40i$

Alternative Method

Alternative way to get *IS* curve is to directly use *IS* curve equation and fill in it the values of various parameters and variables.

The equation for *IS* curve is given by:

$$Y = \frac{1}{1-b}(\overline{A} - di)$$

where $\overline{A} = a + \overline{I}$ (*i.e.* the sum of autonomous consumption (a) and investment expenditure ($\overline{I}$), b is marginal propensity to consume, d is sensitivity of investment to changes in rate of interest. Y and i are level of income and rate of interest respectively.

Substituting the values of various parameters we have the following *IS* equation :

$$Y = \frac{1}{1-0.5}[(10+190) - 20i]$$

$$= \frac{1}{0.5}(200 - 20i)$$

$$= 400 - 40i$$

or equation for *IS* curve : $Y = 400 - 40i$

Graphic Representation : We can represent the *IS* equation graphically by taking some values of interest and calculate the level of income using the *IS* equation.

Suppose rate of interest is 5 per cent. Substituting this value of interest in *IS* equation we have

$$Y = 40 - 40i$$

$$= 40 - 40 \times 5$$

$$= 400 - 200 = 200$$

Thus, at 5 per cent rate of interest level of income is 200,

Now, suppose rate of interest is 2, then the level of income,

$$Y = 400 - 40 \times 2$$

$$= 400 - 80 = 320$$

At 2 per cent rate of interest, level of income is 320.

We have now two combinations of interest and income. We can plot these and obtain *IS* curve. This is done in Figure 20.18.

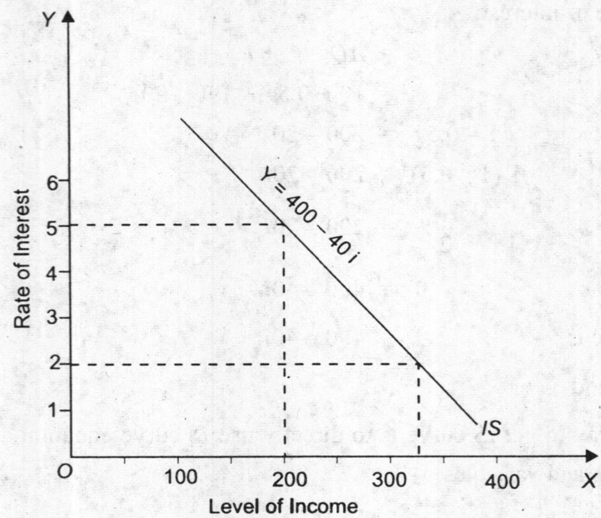

Fig. 20.18. *Graphic Representation of IS Curve*

IS Curve : Three-Sector Model with Taxation and Transfer Payments

In the last section we have derived the *IS* curve taking government expenditure G on goods and services without considering taxation and transfer payments by it. In fact the concept of consumption function conceives consumption as a function of disposable income and is therefore written as

$$C = a + bY_D \qquad ...(1)$$

Now, disposable income Y^D is obtained from deducting tax and adding transfer payments by the government. Thus

$$Y_D = Y - T + R$$

where T is tax revenue and R is the transfer payments by the government. Whereas a tax reduces disposable income, transfer payment raises it.

Further, whereas transfer payments are assumed as lump sum amount, tax can be lump sum tax or levied as proportion of income. If we assume proportionate income tax, then,

$$T = tY$$

where t is the proportion of income which is taken away by way of tax. ...(2)

Let us derive *IS* equation incorporating proportionate income tax and lump sum transfer payments.

$$Y = AD = C + I + G + NX$$

$$Y = a + bY_D + I + G + NX$$

$$= a + b(Y - tY + R) + \overline{I} - di + G + NX$$

$$= a + bY - btY + bR + \overline{I} - di + G + NX$$

$$= a + b(1-t)Y + bR + \overline{I} - di + G + NX$$

$$Y = \overline{A} + b(1-t)Y - di \qquad ...(3)$$

where $\overline{A} = a + bR + \overline{I} + G + NX$

Rearranging equation (3) we have

$$Y - b(1-t)Y = \bar{A} - di$$

or

$$Y[1 - b(1-t)] = \bar{A} - di$$

$$Y = \frac{1}{1-b(1-t)}(\vec{A} - di) \quad ...(4)$$

where $\frac{1}{1-b(1-t)}$ is the value of multiplier in case of proportionate income tax. Equation (4) represents *IS* curve in case of proportionate income tax.

It may be noted in the context of *IS* equations (3) and (4) that a change in autonomous spending $(\bar{A})$ as a result of any of its components will cause a shift in IS curve.

Numerical Problems on The *IS* Curve : Three-Sector Model (With Taxation)

Problem 1. The following equations describe an economy

$$C = 100 + 0.75\,Y_d$$

$$I = 50 - 25i$$

$$T = G = 50$$

where C is aggregate consumption, Y_d is disposable income, I is aggregate investment, T is taxes, G is government purchases and i is the interest rate. Derive the *IS* curve for the economy.

Solution. $Y = C + I + G$

Now, $C = 100 + 0.75\,Y_d = 100 + 0.75\,(Y - T)$

$$C = 100 + 0.75\,(Y - 50)$$

$$I = 50 - 25\,i$$

$$G = 50$$

$$T = 50$$

$$Y = 100 + 0.75\,(Y - 50) + 50 - 25i + 50$$

$$Y = 200 + 0.75\,Y - 0.75 \times 50 - 25i$$

$$Y - 0.75Y = 200 - 37.5 - 25i$$

$$Y(1 - 0.75) = 162.5 - 25i$$

$$\frac{1}{4}Y = 162.5 - 25i$$

$$Y = 650 - 100\,i$$

IS equation is : $Y = 650 - 100\,i$

DERIVATION OF *LM* CURVE : ALGEBRAIC ANALYSIS

Having derived algebraically equation for *IS* curve we now turn to the derivation of equation for *LM* curve. It will be recalled that *LM* curve is a curve that shows combinations of interest rates and levels of income at which money market is in equilibrium, that is, at which demand for money equals supply of money. We explain the derivation of *LM* curve in two steps. First, we show how money demand depends on interest rate and level of income. It is worth noting that in their demand for money people care more about the purchasing power of money, that is, people's demand is for *real money balances* rather than nominal money balances. Real money balances are given by $\frac{M}{P}$ where M stands for nominal money demand and P for price level.

The demand for real money balances depends on the level of real income and interest rate. Thus $M_d = L(Y, i)$. As explained earlier, demand for real money balances increases with the rise in level of income and decreases with rise in rate of interest. Let us assume that money demand function is linear. Then

$$L(Y, i) = kY - hi \qquad k, h > 0 \qquad \text{...(5)}$$

Parameter k represents how much demand for real money balances increases when level of income rises. Parameter h represents how much demand for real money balances decreases when rate of interest rises. The equilibrium in the money market is established where demand for real money balances equals supply of real money balances and is given by

$$\frac{M}{P} = kY - hi \qquad \text{...(6)}$$

Money supply (M) is set by the central bank of a country and we assume it to remain constant for a period. Besides, we assume the price level (P) to remain constant.

Solving the equation (6) for interest rate we have

$$i = \frac{1}{h}\left(kY - \frac{M}{P}\right) \qquad \text{...(7)}$$

The above equation (7) describes the equation for *LM* curve. To be precise it gives us the equilibrium interest rate for any given value of level of income (Y) and real money balances. In drawing *LM* curve, real money balances are assumed to be constant. Thus *LM* curve describes money market equilibrium for different values of income and rate of interest, given a fixed value of real money balances $\left(\frac{M}{P}\right)$. Thus, given the real money balances $\left(\frac{M}{P}\right)$, we can obtain a rate of interest for different values of income.

Let us state some conclusions about *LM* curve as given by equation (7). First, since in equation (7) for *LM* curve, the coefficient (k) of income (Y) is positive, *LM* curve will slope upward. That is, higher income requires higher interest rate for money market to be in equilibrium, given the supply of real money balances. Second, since the coefficient of real money balances is negative, the expansion in real money balances will cause a shift in the *LM* curve to the right, and decrease in the real money balances will shift *LM* curve to the left.

From the coefficient of income k/h, we can know whether *LM* curve is steep or flat. If demand for money is not much sensitive to level of income, then k will be small. Therefore, in case of small k (*i.e.* low sensitivity of interest with respect to changes in income), small change in interest rate is required to offset a small increase in money demand caused by a given *increase in income.*

NUMERICAL PROBLEMS

Problem 1. *Given the following data about the monetary sector of the economy* :

$$M_d = 0.4Y - 80\,i$$

$$Ms = 1200 \text{ crores.}$$

where M_d is demand for money, Y is level of income, i is rate of interest and M_s is the supply of money

1. *Derive the equation for LM function*

2. *Give the economic interpretation of the LM curve. Draw LM curve from the above data*

Solution :

For money market to be in equilibrium

$$M_d = M_s$$

$$0.4\,Y - 80\,i = 1200$$

$$80\,i = 0.4\,Y - 1200$$

$$i = \frac{0.4Y}{80} - \frac{1200}{80}$$

$$i = \frac{1}{200}Y - 15$$

Thus we get the following *LM* function :

$$i = \frac{1}{200}Y - 15 \qquad ...(i)$$

Alternatively, *LM* equation or function can also be stated as:

$$Y = 200\,i + 3000 \qquad ...(ii)$$

LM curve means what would be rate of interest when money market is in equilibrium, given the level of income. Thus, if level of national income is ₹ 4000 crores, then using *LM* equation (*i*) we have

$$i = \frac{1}{200} \times 4000 - 15$$

$$= 20 - 15 = 5\%$$

Thus, at income of ₹ 4000 crores, rate of interest will be 5 per cent when money market is in equilibrium.

Now, if level of income is ₹ 4400 crores, equilibrium rate of interest will be

$$i = \frac{1}{200}Y - 15$$

$$= \frac{1}{200} \times 4400 - 15$$

$$= 22 - 15 = 7\%$$

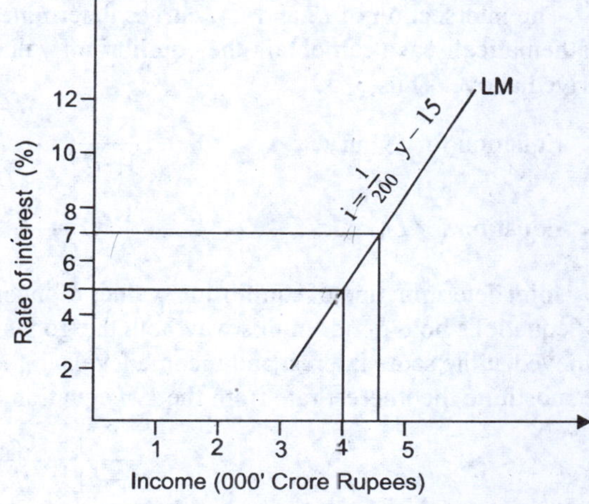

Fig. 20.19. *Drawing LM Curve*

With two combinations of interest rate and income level when money market is in equilibrium we can draw *LM* curve as shown in 20.19.

Problem 2. *The following data is given for the monetary sector of the economy.*

Transaction demand for money, $M_t = 0.5Y$. *Speculative demand for money,* $M_{sp} = 105 - 1500\,i$

Money supply $M_s = 150$

Derive *LM equation from the above data*

Solution. Total demand function for money can be obtained by adding up the transactions demand for money (M_t) and speculative demand for money (M_{sp}). Thus

$$M_d = M_t + M_{sp}$$

$$M_d = 0.5Y + 105 - 1500\,i$$

In money market equilibrium

$$M_d = M_s$$
$$0.5Y + 105 - 1500i = 150$$
$$1500\,i = 0.5Y + 105 - 150$$
$$i = \frac{0.5Y}{1500} - \frac{45}{1500}$$
$$= \frac{1}{3000}Y - \frac{3}{100}$$

Thus, *LM* equation is :

$$i = \frac{1}{3000}Y - \frac{3}{100}$$

Alternatively, *LM* equation can be written as

$$Y = 3000i + \frac{3}{100} \times 3000$$
$$Y = 3000\,i + 90$$

IS – LM MODEL : ALGEBRAIC ANALYSIS

(Joint Equilibrium of Income and Interest Rate)

The intersection of *IS* and *LM* curves determines joint equilibrium of income and interest rate. Mathematically, we can obtain the equilibrium values by using the equations of *IS* and *LM* curves derived above. Thus,

Equation for *IS* curve : $$Y = \frac{1}{1-b}(\bar{A} - di) \quad ...(i)$$

Equation for *LM* curve: $$i = \frac{1}{h}(kY - \frac{M}{p}) \quad ...(ii)$$

Joint determination of equilibrium values of income and interest rate requires that both the *IS* and *LM* equations hold good. In this way both the goods market and money market equilibrium will be achieved at the same interest and income levels in the two markets. To find such equilibrium values we substitute the interest rate from the *LM* equation (*ii*) into the *IS* equation (*i*). Doing so we have

$$Y = \frac{1}{1-b}\left[\bar{A} - \frac{d}{h}(kY - \frac{M}{P})\right]$$

$$Y = \frac{1}{1-b}\left[\bar{A} - \frac{d}{h}(kY) + \frac{d}{h}\left(\frac{M}{P}\right)\right] \quad ...(iii)$$

The equation shows that the equilibrium level of income depends on exogenously given autonomous variables $(\bar{A})$ such as autonomous consumption, autonomous investment, government expenditure on goods and services, and the real money supply $\left(\frac{M}{P}\right)$ and further on the size of multiplier $\left(\frac{1}{1-b}\right)$. It will be noticed from equation (*iii*) that higher the autonomous expenditure, the higher the level of equilibrium income. Further, the greater the real money supply, the higher the level of national income.

NUMERICAL PROBLEMS ON *IS-LM* MODEL

Problem – 1. *For an economy the following functions are given* :

$$C = 100 + 0.8\,y$$
$$S = -100 + 0.2\,y$$
$$I = 120 - 5\,i$$
$$M^s = 120$$
$$M^d = 0.2y - 5i$$

Find out (1) IS equation, (2) LM equation, (3) equilibrium level of income and interest rate

Solution :

IS curve : $$Y = \left[\frac{1}{1-b}(a+\bar{I}) - di\right]$$

where $b = MPC$, a and $\bar{I}$ are autonomous consumption and autonomous investment respectively, d is sensitivity of investment demand to changes in rate of interest (i).

Substituting the values of various parameters we have

$$Y = \frac{1}{1-0.8}[(100+120)-5i]$$
$$= \frac{1}{0.2}=(220-5i)$$
$$Y = 5(220-5i)$$
$$Y = 1100 - 25i$$

Thus *IS* curve is :

$$Y = 1100 - 25i \qquad \text{...(i)}$$

Derivation of *LM* Equation :

For money market equilibrium

$$M^d = M^S$$
$$0.2Y - 5i = 120$$
$$5i = 0.2Y - 120$$
$$i = \frac{0.2}{5}Y - 24$$

LM curve is :

$$i = \frac{0.2}{5}Y - 24 \qquad \text{...(ii)}$$

Substituting the value of i in the *IS* equation (i) we have

$$Y = 1000 - 25\left(\frac{0.2}{5}Y - 24\right)$$
$$= 1100 - (1Y - 600)$$
$$Y = 1100 - Y + 600$$
$$2Y = 1700$$
$$Y = \frac{1700}{2} = 850$$

Thus the equilibrium level of income is 850. To obtain the equilibrium rate of interest we substitute the value of Y in *LM* equation (*iii*) obtained above we have

$$i = \frac{0.2}{5}(850) - 24$$

$$= \frac{1}{25}(850) - 24$$

$$= 34 - 24 = 10$$

Thus equilibrium rate of interest is 10 per cent.

Problem 2

Consider the following economy :

$$C = 100 + 0.8\, Y_d$$

$$I = 50 - 25i$$

$$G = T = 50$$

$$\frac{M^s}{P} = 200$$

$$M^d = Y - 25i$$

1. *Calculate the IS and LM curves.*
2. *Calculate the equilibrium levels of output and interest.*

Solution :

$$Y = C + I + G$$

Substituting the values of C, I and G we have

$$Y = 100 + 0.8\, Y_d + 50 - 25\, i + 50$$

$$Y = 100 + 0.8\, (Y - T) + 50 - 25i + 50$$

or

$$Y = 100 + 0.8\, (Y - 50) + 50 - 25\, i + 50$$

$$Y = 200 + 0.8Y - 40 - 25i$$

$$= 160 + 0.8Y - 25i$$

$$(Y - 0.8Y) = 160 - 25i$$

$$Y(1 - 0.8) = 160 - 25i$$

$$0.2Y = 160 - 25i$$

$$Y = 800 - 125i$$

IS curve is :

$$Y = 800 - 125i \qquad \text{...(i)}$$

Money Market Equilibrium : Money market is in equilibrium when $M^d = \frac{M^s}{P}$

Thus, in equilibrium

$$M^d = \frac{M^S}{P}$$

$$Y - 25i = 200$$

$$Y = 200 + 25i$$

Thus, *LM* curve is :

$$Y = 200 + 25i \qquad \text{...(iii)}$$

Since in equilibrium *IS* and *LM* curves intersect (or *IS* = *LM*) we have

$$200 + 25i = 800 - 125i$$

$$150\,i = 800 - 200 = 600$$

$$i = \frac{600}{150} = 4$$

Thus equilibrium rate of interest is 4%.

Substituting the value of i in *IS* equation (i) we have :

$$Y = 800 - 125 \times 4$$

$$= 800 - 400 = 400$$

Thus, the equilibrium rate of interest is 4 per cent and equilibrium level of income is 200

Problem 3. *Consider an economy with the following features*

Consumption, $C = 100 + 0.9\,Y_d$

Income tax, $t = \frac{1}{3}Y$

Investment, $I = 600 - 30i$

Government expenditure, $G = 300$

Transaction demand money for $M_d = 0.4Y$

Speculative demand for money, $M_2 = -50i$

Nominal money supply $\bar{M} = 1040$

Price level $= 2$

(where Y_d *stands for disposable income, and i for rate of interest)*

Derive the IS and LM equations and fund out the equilibrium levels of income and rate of interest.

Solution :

(i) Obtaining *IS* equation :

$$Y = C + I + G$$

$$= 100 + 0.9\,Y_d + 600 - 30i + 100$$

$$= 100 + 0.9\left(Y - \frac{1}{3}Y\right) + 600 - 30i + 300$$

$$= 1000 + 0.9y - 0.3y - 30i$$

$$Y - 0.9y + 0.3Y = 1000 - 30i$$

$$Y(1 - 0.9 + 0.3) = 1000 - 30i$$

$$0.4Y = 1000 - 30i$$

$$Y = 1000 \times \frac{10}{4} - \left(30 \times \frac{10}{4}\right)i$$

$$= 2500 - 75i$$

Thus *IS* equation is : $Y = 2500 - 75i$ ...(i)

(i) Obtaining *LM* equation :

For money market equilibrium :

$$M^d = M^S$$

$$M^d = M_1 + M_2$$

$$= 0.4y - 50i$$

Real money supply $M^S = \frac{\bar{M}}{P} = \frac{1040}{2} = 520$

Therefore, $0.4Y - 50i = 520$

$$0.4Y = 520 + 50i$$

$$Y = 520 \times \frac{10}{4} + (50 \times \frac{10}{4})i$$

$$= 1300 + 125i$$

LM function is : 1300 + 125*i*

In equilibrium $IS = LM$

$$2500 - 75i = 1300 + 125i \quad ...(ii)$$

$$125i + 75i = 2500 - 1300$$

$$200i = 1200$$

Therefore, interest, $i = \frac{1200}{200} = 6\%$

Substituting the value of $i = 6$ in *IS* equation we have

$$Y = 2500 - 75 \times 6$$

$$= 2500 - 450$$

$$= 2050$$

Thus, equilibrium income is 2050 and equilibrium interest is 6 %.

Problem 4 (Four-Sector Model) : The major macro aggregates for an economy are given as follows :

Consumption, $C = 60 + 0.8Y_d$ (Y_d is disposable income)

Investment $I = 100 - 5i$

% Interest rate $i = 6$

Government expenditure, $G = 76$

Lump sum Tax, $T = 15$

Transfer payments, $TR = 60$

Exports $X = 70$

Imports $M = 12 + 0.2Y$

1. *Derive the IS curve using the above data*
2. *Calculate equilibrium level of income*
3. *Calculate foreign trade multiplier*

Solution :

$$Y = C + I + G + X - M \quad ...(i)$$

and $Y_d = Y - T + TR$

Substituting the values of variables in equation (i) we have

$$Y = 60 + 0.8\,(Y - 15 + 60) + 100 - 5i + 76 + 70 - (12 + 0.2Y)$$

$$= 60 + 0.8Y + 0.8X\,45 + 100 + 76 + 70 - 12 - 0.2Y - 5i$$

$$Y - 0.8Y + 0.2Y = (60 + 36 + 100 + 76 + 58) - 5i$$

$$Y(1-0.8+0.2)\,Y = 330-5i$$

$$0.4Y = 330-5i$$

or $$\frac{2}{5}Y = 330-5i$$

$$Y = 330\times\frac{5}{2}-\frac{5}{2}\times 5i$$

$$Y = 825-12.5i$$

(*i*) Equation for *IS* curve is : $Y = 825-12.5i$

(*ii*) Equilibrium level of income when rate of interest is 6 per cent

$$Y = 825-12.5\times 6$$
$$= 825-75 = 750$$

(*iii*) Foreign trade multiplier $\frac{1}{1-b+m}$

where $b = MPC = 0.8$

m = marginal propensity to import = 0.2

Thus, foreign trade multiplier $\frac{1}{1-0.8+0.2}=\frac{1}{0.4}=\frac{5}{2}=2.5$

Problem 5. *The following data are given for an economy*

Consumption :	$C = 40+0.75y$
Investment :	$I = 140-10i$
Government expenditure :	$G = 100$
Lump sum tax	$T = 80$
Money demand,	$M^d = 0.2\,Y-5i$
Money supply,	$M^S = 85$

(i. is % interest rate; other figures in ₹ crores)

(*a*) *Find out the equilibrium income, Y and interest rate i*

(*b*) *Suppose the government increases its expenditure on education and health services by ₹ 65 crores? what would be its effect on equilibrium income and rate of interest.*

Solution. In order to obtain equilibrium income, we have to find out first the equations for *IS* and *LM* curves.

$$Y = C+I+G$$

where $C = 40+0.75\,Y_d$ and $I = 140-10i$ and $G = 100$

Therefore,
$$Y = 40+0.75\,Y_d+140-10i+100$$
$$= 40+0.75\,(Y-80)+140-10i+100$$
$$= 40+0.75Y-60+140-10i+100$$

$$Y-0.75\,Y = 220-10i$$

$$0.25\,Y = 220-10i$$

$$\frac{1}{4}Y = 220-10i$$

$$Y = 880-40i$$

Thus *IS* equation : $Y = 880-40i$ ...(*i*)

To obtain *LM* function, we equate demand for money with supply of money.

$$M^d = M^s$$
$$0.2Y - 5i = 85$$
$$5i = 0.2Y - 85$$
$$i = \frac{0.2}{5}Y - 17$$

Thus, *LM* function is

$$i = 0.04\,Y - 17 \qquad ...(ii)$$

Substituting the value of *i* in the *IS* function equation (*i*) we have

$$Y = 880 - 40\,(0.04\,Y - 17)$$
$$= 880 - 1.6Y + 680$$
$$Y + 1.6Y = 880 + 680$$
$$2.6Y = 1560$$
$$Y = 1560 \times \frac{10}{26} = 600$$

Thus, equilibrium level of national income is 600 crores

Substituting the value of 600 for *Y* in *IS* equation (*i*) we have

$$600 = 880 - 40i$$
$$40i = 880 - 600 = 280$$
$$i = \frac{280}{40} = 7$$

The equilibrium rate of interest is 7 per cent.

(b) With the increase in Government expenditure by ₹ 65 crores

New Income, $Y' = C + I + G + \Delta G$

$$Y' = 40 + 0.75\,(Y' - 80) + 140 - 10i + 100 + 65$$
$$= 40 + 0.75Y' - 60 + 140 - 10i + 100 + 65$$
$$Y' - 0.75\,Y' = 285 - 10i$$
$$Y'(1 - 0.75) = 285 - 10i$$
$$\frac{1}{4}Y' = 285 - 10i$$
$$Y' = 1140 - 40i$$

New equation for *IS* curve is = $Y' = 1140 - 40i$

Substituting the value of *i* from *LM* function equation (*ii*) we have

$$Y' = 1140 - 40(0.04\,Y' - 17)$$
$$Y' = 1140 - 1.6Y' + 680$$

---

* The students can check this with the general equation for *IS* curve, that is, $Y = \frac{1}{1-b+m}(\bar{A} - di)$ where A is the sum of autonomous factors, that is, $\bar{A} = a + bTR - bT + \bar{I} + \bar{G} + \bar{X} - \bar{M}$ and $\frac{1}{1-b+m}$ is foreign trade multiplier

$$Y' + 1.6Y' = 1820$$
$$Y'(1 + 1.6) = 1820$$
$$2.6Y' = 1820$$
$$Y = 1820 \times \frac{10}{26} = 700$$

Now, substituting the value of Y in the LM equation (*ii*) we have

New interest $\quad i = 0.04\,(700) - 17$
$$= 28.00 - 17 = 11$$
$$= 11$$

Thus, the new equilibrium income is 700 crores and interest rate is 11 per cent

Problem 6

An economy shows the following features :

Consumption, $\quad C = 50 + 0.9\,(Y - T)$

Tax Revenue, $\quad T = 100$

Investment, $\quad I = 150 - 5i$

Government expenditure, $\quad G = 100$

Money demand, $\quad L = 0.2\,Y - 10\,i$

Real money supply $\quad \frac{M}{P} = 100$

Exports, $\quad X = 20$

Imports, $\quad M = 10 + 0.1\,Y$

where Y = income, i = rate of interest (figures in ₹ crores).

(*a*) *Obtain the IS and lM equations of the economy*

(*b*) *Find out equilibrium income and rate of interest atom*

(*c*) *Find the balance of trade*

Solution :

Let us first obtain the IS equation

$$Y = C + I + G + (X{-}M)$$
$$= 50 + 0.9\,(Y - 100) + 150 - 5i + 100 + 20 - (10 + 0.1Y)$$
$$= 50 + 0.9Y - 90 + 150 - 5i + 100 + 20 - 10 - 0.\,1Y$$
$$Y - 0.9\,Y + 0.1Y = 50 - 90 + 150 - 5i + 100 + 20 - 10$$
$$Y(1{-}0.9 + 0.1) = 220 - 5\,i$$
$$0.2Y = 220 - 5\,i$$
$$Y = 220 \times 5 - 25i$$
$$Y = 1100 - 25i \qquad ...(i)$$

In money market equilibrium :

$$M^d = M^s$$
$$0.2Y - 10i = 100$$
$$0.2Y = 100 + 10\,i$$

LM Equation is : $Y = 500 + 50\,i$

$$\text{In equilibrium } IS = LM$$
$$1100 - 25i = 500 + 50i$$
$$75i = 600$$
$$i = \frac{600}{75} = 8\%$$

Substituting the value of $i = 8$ in *IS* equation (*i*) we have

$$Y = 1100 - 25i = 1100 - 25 \times 8 = 1100 - 200 = 900$$

Balance of Trade (BOT) = $X - M$

$$X = 20$$
$$\text{Imports, } M = 10 \times 0.1Y$$
$$\text{As found above } Y = 900$$
$$\text{Imports, } M = 10 + 0.1 \times 900$$
$$= 10 + 90 = 100$$
$$\text{BOT} = 20 - 100 = -80$$

Trade Deficit $= 80$

Alternative Method : Using Straightaway the *IS* equation

$$Y = \frac{1}{1-b+m}(\overline{A} - di)$$

where $\overline{A} = a - bT + \overline{I} + G + \overline{X} - \overline{M}$

$$Y = \frac{1}{1-0.9+0.1}[(50-90+150+100+20-10)-5i]$$
$$= \frac{1}{0.2}(220-5i)$$
$$= 5(220 - 5i)$$
$$Y = 1100 - 25i$$

QUESTIONS FOR REVIEW

1. What is *IS* curve ? How is it derived from goods market equilibrium ?
2. Define *IS* curve. What are the factors that determine the slope or steepness of *IS* curve ?
3. What is *LM* curve ? How is it derived from money market equilibrium ? On what factors do its slope and position depend ?
4. How do the product and money markets interact to determine the short-run equilibrium level of national income and the rate of interest ?
5. Using *IS-LM* model analyse the impact of an increase in money supply on the equilibrium level of income and rate of interest.
6. Using *IS-LM* model, show that fiscal policy is more effective at low rate of interest and low level of income, while monetary policy is more effective when the levels of income and rate of interest are high.
7. Explain how far expansionary monetary policy is effective in increasing the level of national income in each of the three ranges of *LM* curve. In which range is fiscal policy most effective?

8. Using *IS-LM* curve model analyse the impact of an increase in the money supply on the equilibrium level of national income and the rate of interest.
9. What do the *IS* and *LM* curves signify ? Under what conditions would the *IS-LM* model be unstable?
10. What is crowding out effect of Government's fiscal policy ? Is it very significant ? What role does interest elasticity of investment play in determining the slope of *IS* curve ?
11. Explain and show graphically how product market is in equilibrium along *IS* curve.
12. Explain *IS* and *LM* curves. What is the role of these two curves in simultaneous determination of equilibrium rate of interest and level of income ?
13. (*a*) Derive *IS* curve for an economy. What are the factors which determine slope of the *IS* curve ?

    (*b*) Show how *IS* curve will change as a result of increase in Government expenditure.
14. Why does *IS* curve slope downward ? How is *IS* curve related to investment multiplier in the Keynesian Income theory ? What are the factors which cause a shift in *IS* curve ?
15. Discuss the features of *IS* and *LM* curves. Is the equilibrium between *IS* and *LM* curves always stable ?
16. How is *LM* curve derived from money market equilibrium ? Why does *LM* curve slope upward ? How will *LM* curve shift with increase in money supply in the economy ?
17. Explain with the aid of *IS-LM* curves role of monetary policy for stabilisation of the economy.
18. Explain with the help of *IS-LM* curve model, role of fiscal policy in overcoming recession in the economy.

CHAPTER 21

Inflation and Unemployment : Phillips Curve and Rational Expectations Theory

Introduction

In the simple Keynesian model of an economy, the aggregate supply curve (with variable price level) is of inverse *L*-shape, that is, it is a horizontal straight line up to the full-employment level of output and beyond that it becomes horizontal. This means that during recession or depression when the economy is having a good deal of excess capacity and large-scale unemployment of labour and idle capital stock, the aggregate supply curve is perfectly elastic. When full-employment level of output is reached, aggregate supply curve becomes perfectly inelastic. With this shape of aggregate supply curve assumed in the simple Keynesian model, increase in aggregate demand before the level of full employment causes increase in the level of real national output and employment with price level remaining unchanged. That is, no cost has to be incurred in the form of rise in the price level (*i.e.,* inflation rate) for raising the level of output and reducing unemployment. In the Keynesian model, once the full-employment level of output is reached and aggregate supply curve becomes vertical, further increase in aggregate demand caused by the expansionary fiscal and monetary policies will only raise the price level in the economy. That is, in this simple Keynesian model, inflation occurs in the economy only after full-employment level of output has been attained. Thus, *in the simple Keynesian model with inverse L-shaped aggregate supply curve there is no trade-off or clash between inflation and unemployment.*

INFLATION-UNEMPLOYMENT TRADE-OFF: PHILLIPS CURVE

However, the actual empirical evidence did not fit well in the above simple Keynesian macro model. A noted British economist, A.W. Phillips,[1] published an article in 1958 based on his good deal of research using historical data from the U.K. for about 100 years in which he arrived at the conclusion that *there in fact existed an inverse relationship between rate of unemployment and rate of inflation.* This inverse relation implies a trade-off, that is, for reducing unemployment, price in the form of a higher rate of inflation has to be paid, and for reducing the rate of inflation, price in terms of a higher rate of unemployment has to be borne. On graphically fitting a curve to the historical data Phillips obtained a downward sloping curve exhibiting the inverse relation between rate of inflation and the rate of unemployment and this curve is now named after his name as *Phillips Curve.* This Phillips curve is shown in Fig. 21.1 where along the horizontal axis the rate of unemployment and along the vertical axis the rate of inflation is measured. It will be seen that when rate of inflation is 10 per cent, the unemployment rate is 3 per cent, and when rate of inflation is reduced to 5 per cent per annum, say by pursuing contractionary fiscal policy and thereby reducing aggregate demand, the rate of unemployment increases to 8 per cent of labour force. The actual Phillips curve drawn from the data of sixties (1961-69) for the United States also shows the inverse relation between unemployment rate and rate of inflation (see Fig. 21.2). Such empirical data pertaining to the fifties and sixties for

1. A.W. Phillips, "Relation between Unemployment and Rate of Change in Money Wages in the United Kingdom, 1861-1957." *Economic* 25 (Nov. 1958), pp. 283-299.

other developed countries seemed to confirm the Phillips curve concept. On the basis of this, many economists came to believe that there existed a *stable Phillips curve* which depicted a predictable

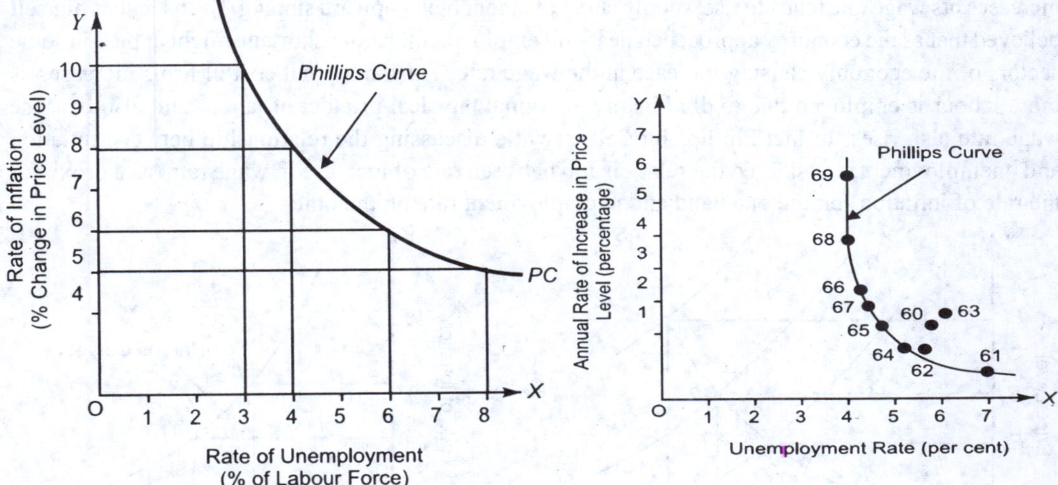

Fig. 21.1. *Phillips Curve Showing Negative Relationship between Rates of Inflation and Unemployment*

Fig. 21.2. *Phillips Curve in the Sixties of the United States*

inverse relation between inflation and unemployment. Further, on the basis of a *stable Phillips curve* for a country, they emphasised the trade-off that confronts the economic policy makers. This trade-off presents a dilemma for the policy makers; should they choose a higher rate of inflation with lower unemployment or a higher rate of unemployment with a low inflation rate? In what follows we first explain the rationale underlying the Phillips curve, that is, how the inverse relationship between inflation and unemployment can be theoretically explained. We will further explain why this concept of stable Phillips curve depicting inverse relation between inflation and unemployment broke down during seventies and early eighties. During seventies a strange phenomenon was witnessed in the USA and Britain when there existed *a high rate of inflation side by side with high unemployment rate*. This was contrary to both Phillips curve concept and the simple Keynesian model. This simultaneous existence of both high rate of inflation and high unemployment rate (or low level of real national product) during the seventies and early eighties has been described as *stagflation* which has been explained in the previous chapter.

Explanation of Phillips Curve

Let us first provide an explanation for the Phillips curve. Both Keynesians and Monetarists agreed to the existence of the Phillips curve. The explanation of Phillips curve by the Keynesian economists is quite simple and is graphically illustrated in Fig. 21.3. It may be noted that Keynesian economists assume the upward-sloping aggregate supply curve. In fact, Keynes himself recognised that the curve *AS* is upward sloping in intermediate range, that is, as the economy approaches near-full employment level, the aggregate supply curve slopes upward. According to Keynesian economists, aggregate supply curve is upward sloping for two reasons. First, as output is increased by the firms in the economy, diminishing returns to variable factors, especially to labour, occur or accure resulting in fall in marginal physical product (MPP_L) of labour. With money wage rate (W) as given and fixed, the fall in the marginal physical product of labour causes the rise in the marginal cost (MC) of production $\left(\text{Note that } MC = \dfrac{W}{MPP_L}\right)$. With the fall in the MPP of labour, wage rate remaining constant, the term $\dfrac{W}{MPP_L}$ measuring marginal cost (MC) will rise.

The second reason for the marginal cost to go up is the rise in the wage rate as employment and output are increased. When under pressure of aggregate demand for output, demand for labour increases, its wage rate tends to rise, supply curve of labour being upward sloping. Even Keynes himself believed that as the economy approached near-full employment, labour shortage might appear in some sectors of the economy causing increase in the wage rate. Thus, marginal cost of firms increases as more labour is employed due to diminishing marginal physical product of labour and also because wage rate also rises. In fact Phillips himself, sswhile discussing the relationship between inflation and unemployment, considered the relationship between rate of increase in wage rate (as a proxy for the rate of inflation) on the one hand and unemployment rate on the other.

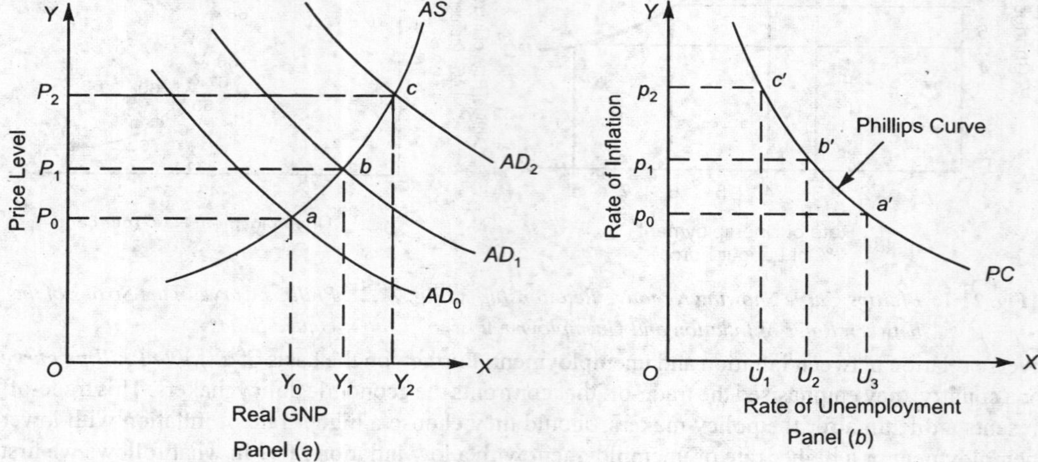

Fig. 21.3. *Keynesian Explanation of Phillips Curve*

Now, it will be seen from panel (*a*) of Fig. 21.3 that with the initial aggregate demand curve AD_0 and the given aggregate supply curve *AS*, the price level P_0 and output level Y_0 are determined. Now, suppose the aggregate demand curve increases from AD_0 to AD_1, it will be seen that price level rises to P_1 and aggregate national output increases from Y_0 to Y_1. Note that increase in aggregate national product means increase in employment of labour and therefore reduction in unemployment rate. Thus the rise in the price level from P_0 to P_1 (*i.e.*, occurrence of inflation) results in lowering of unemployment rate showing inverse relation between the two. Further, if aggregate demand increases to AD_2, the price level further rises to P_2 and national output increases to Y_2 which will further lower the rate of unemployment. The greater the rate at which aggregate demand increases, the higher will be the rate of inflation which will cause greater increase in aggregate output and employment resulting in much lower rate of unemployment. Thus, *a higher rate of increase in aggregate demand and consequently a higher rate of rise in price level is associated with the lower rate of unemployment and vice versa.* This is what is represented by Phillips curve. Consider panel (*b*) of Fig. 21.3 where point *a*′ on the downward sloping Phillips curve *PC* corresponds to point *a* of panel (*a*) of Fig. 21.3. In panel (*b*) of the Fig. 21.3 we have shown the rate of unemployment equal to U_3 corresponding to the price level P_0 of panel (*a*). When the aggregate demand shifts to AD_1, there is a certain rate of inflation and price level rises to P_1 and aggregate output expands to Y_1. As seen above, this increase in aggregate output leads to the increase in employment of labour bringing about decline in unemployment rate. Suppose the rate of rise in the price level (*i.e.*, the rate of inflation) when it increases from P_0 to P_1 in panel (*a*) following the increase in aggregate demand is greater than the rate of rise in the price level of the previous period, we obtain a lower rate of unemployment U_2 than before corresponding to a higher inflation rate p_1 in the Phillips curve *PC* in panel (*b*). With a still higher rate of inflation, say p_2, when price level rises from P_1 to P_2 in panel (*a*) following the increase in aggregate demand to

AD_2, we have a further lower rate of unemployment equal to U_1 in panel (*b*) corresponding to point *c*′ on the Phillips curve *PC*. This gives us a downward-sloping Phillips curve *PC*.

It is clear from above that through increase in aggregate demand and upward-sloping aggregate supply curve, Keynesians were able to explain the downward-sloping Phillips curve showing the negative relation between rates of inflation and unemployment.

Collapse of Phillips Curve (1971-91)

During the sixties Phillips curve became an important concept of macroeconomic analysis. The stable relationship described by it suggested that policy makers could have a lower rate of unemployment if they could bear with a higher rate of inflation. On the contrary, they could achieve a low rate of inflation only if they were prepared to reconcile with a higher rate of unemployment. But a stable Phillips curve could not hold good during the seventies and eighties, especially in the United States. Therefore, experience in the two decades (1971-91) has prompted some economists to say that the stable Phillips curve has disappeared. Figure 21.4 shows data regarding the behaviour of inflation and unemployment during the seventies and eighties in the United States which do not conform to a stable Phillips curve. *In these two decades we have periods when rates of both inflation and unemployment increased (that is, a high rate of inflation was associated with a high unemployment rate, which shows the absence of trade-off.* We have shown the data of inflation rate and unemployment in case of the United States in Fig. 21.4. From the data it appears that instead of remaining stable, the Phillips curve shifted to the right in the seventies and early eighties and to the left during the late eighties. (see Fig. 21.4).

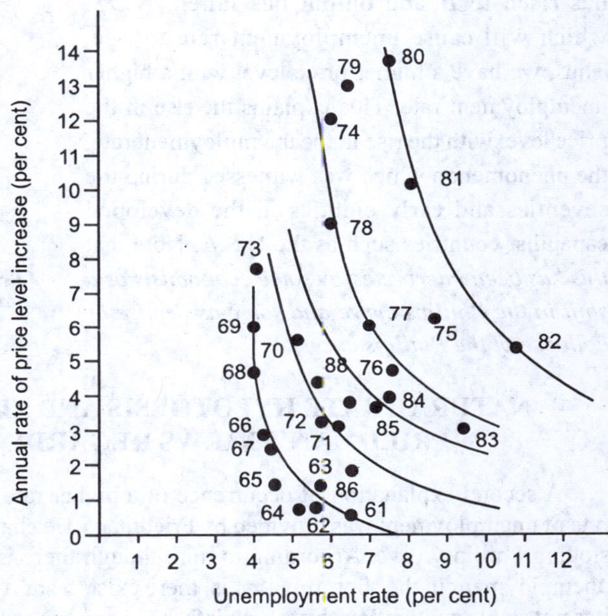

Fig. 21.4. *Shift in Phillips Curve : United States*

Causes of Shift in Phillips Curve

Now, what could be the cause of shift in the Phillips curve? There are two explanations for this. First, according to Keynesians, the occurrence of higher inflation rate along with the increase in unemployment rate witnessed during the seventies and early eighties was due to the *adverse supply shocks* in the form of fourfold increase in the prices of oil and petroleum products delivered to the American economy first in 1973-74 and then again in 1979-80. Consider Fig. 21.5 where AD_0 and AS_0 are in equilibrium at point *E* and determine price level OP_0 and aggregate national output OY_0. The hike in price of oil by *OPEC*, the cartel of oil producing Middle East countries brought about a rise in the cost of production of several commodities for the production of which oil was used as an energy input. Further, the oil price hike also raised the transportation costs of all commodities. The increase in cost of production and transportation of commodities caused a shift in the aggregate supply curve upward to the left. This is generally described as adverse supply shock which raised the unit cost at each level of output. It will be seen from Fig. 21.5 that due to this adverse supply shock aggregate supply curve has shifted to the left to the new position AS_1 which intersects the given aggregate demand curve AD_0 at point H. At the new equilibrium point H, price level has risen to P_1 and output has fallen to OY_1 which will cause unemployment rate to rise. Thus, we have a higher price level with a higher unemployment rate. This explains the rise in the price level with the rise in the unemployment rate, the phenomenon which was witnessed during the seventies and early eighties in the developed capatalist countries such as the U.S.A. Note that *this has been interpreted by some economists as a shift in the Phillips curve and some as demise or collapse of the Phillips curve.*

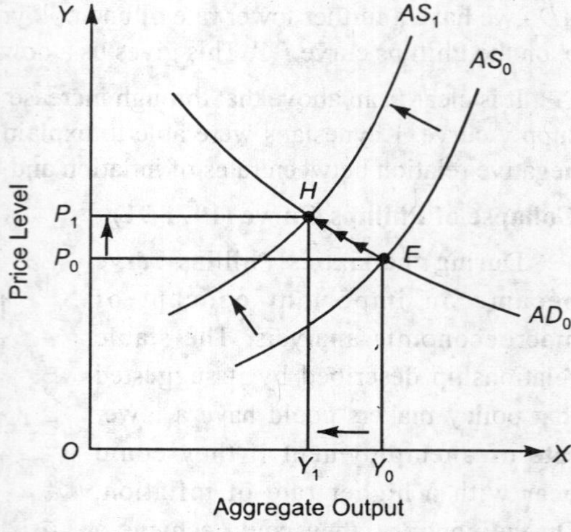

Fig. 21.5. *Adverse Supply Shock Giving Rise to Stagflation and Break down of Phillips Curve*

NATURAL RATE HYPOTHESIS AND ADAPTIVE EXPECTATIONS: FRIEDMAN'S VIEWS REGARDING PHILLIPS CURVE

A second explanation of occurrence of a higher rate of inflation simultaneously with a higher rate of unemployment was provided by Friedman.[2] He challenged the concept of a *stable* downward-sloping Phillips curve. According to him, though there is a trade-off between rate of inflation and unemployment in the short run, that is, there exists a short-run downward sloping Phillips curve, but it is not stable and it often shifts both leftward or rightward. He argued that there is no long-run stable trade-off between rates of inflation and unemployment. His view is that the economy is stable in the long run at the natural rate of unemployment and therefore *the long-run Phillips curve is a vertical straight line.* He argues that misguided Keynesian expansionary fiscal and monetary policies based on the wrong assumption that a *stable* Phillips curve exists only result in increasing rate of inflation.

Natural Rate of Unemployment. It is necessary to explain the concept of natural rate of unemployment on which the concept of long-run Phillips curve is based. *The natural rate of unemployment is the rate at which in the labour market the current number of unemployed is equal to the number of jobs available.* These unemployed workers are unemployed for the frictional and structural reasons, though the equivalent number of jobs are available for them. For instance, the fresh entrants may spend a good deal of time in searching for the jobs before they are able to find work. Further, some industries may be registering a decline in their production rendering some workers unemployed, while others may be growing creating new jobs for workers. But the unemployed workers may have to be provided new training and skills before they are deployed in the newly created jobs in the growing industries. It is these frictional and structural unemployments that constitute the natural rate of unemployment. Since the equivalent number of jobs are available for them, full employment is said to prevail even in the presence of this natural rate of unemployment. It is presently believed that 4 to 5 per cent rate of unemployment represents a natural rate of unemployment in the developed countries.

Theory of Adaptive Expectations and Natural Rate Hypothesis

Another important thing to understand from Friedman's explanation of shift in the short-run

2. Milton Friedman, "Inflation and Unemployment," *Journal of Political Economy*, 1977.

Phillips curve is that expectations about the future rate of inflation play an important role in it. Friedman put forward *a theory of adaptive expectations* according to which people form their expectations on the basis of previous and present rate of inflation, and change or adapt their expectations only when the actual inflation turns out to be different from their expected rate. According to this Friedman's theory of adaptive expectations, there may be a trade-off between rates of inflation and unemployment in the short run, but there is no such trade-off in the long run.

The view of Friedman and his follower monetarists is illustrated in Figure 21.6. To begin with SPC_1 is the short-run Phillips curve and the economy is at point A_0, on it corresponding to the natural rate of unemployment equal to 5 per cent of labour force. The location of this point A_0 on the short-run Phillips curve depends on the level of aggregate demand. Further, we assume that the economy is currently experiencing a rate of inflation equal to 5%. The other assumption we make is that nominal wages have been set on the expectations that 5 per cent rate of inflation will continue in the future.

Now, suppose for some reasons the government adopts expansionary fiscal and monetary policies to raise aggregate demand. The consequent increase in aggregate demand will cause the rate of inflation to rise, say to seven per cent. Given the level of money wage rate which was fixed on the basis that the 5 per cent rate of inflation would continue to occur, the higher price level than expected would raise the profits of the firms which will induce the firms to increase their output and employ more labour. As a result of the increase in aggregate demand resulting in a higher rate of inflation and more output and employment, the economy will move to point A_1 on the short-run Phillips curve SPC_1 in Figure 21.6, where unemployment has decreased to 3.5 per cent while inflation rate has risen to 7%. It may be noted from Figure 21.6 that in moving from point A_0 to A_1, on SPC_1 the economy accepts a higher rate of inflation at the cost of achieving a lower rate of unemployment. Thus, this is in conformity with the concept of Phillips curve explained earlier. However, the advocates of natural rate theory interpret it in a slightly different way. They think that lower rate of unemployment achieved is only a temporary phenomenon. They think *when the actual rate of inflation exceeds the one that is expected, unemployment rate will fall below the natural rate only in the short run. In the long run, the natural rate of unemployment will be restored.*

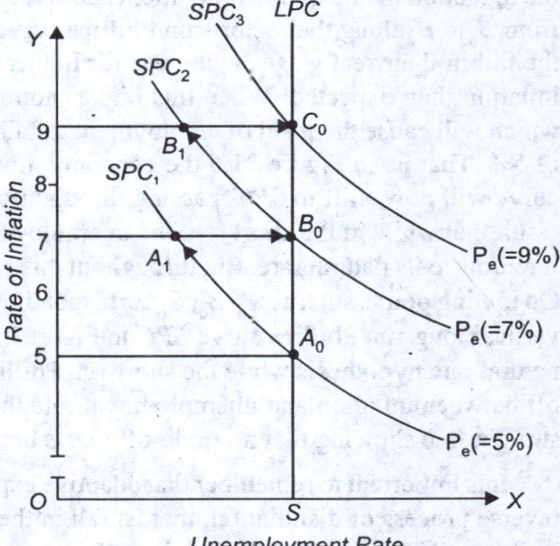

Fig. 21.6. *Shift in Short-Run Phillips Curve and Long-Run Phillips Curve*

Long-Run Phillips Curve and Adaptive Expectations

This brings us to the concept of long-run Phillips curve, which Friedman and other natural rate theorists have put forward. According to them, the economy will not remain in a stable equilibrium position at A_1. This is because the workers will realise that due to the higher rate of inflation than the expected one, their real wages and incomes have fallen. The workers will therefore demand higher nominal wages to restore their real income. But as nominal wages rise to compensate for the higher rate of inflation than expected, profits of business firms will fall to their earlier levels. This reduction in their profit implies that the original motivation that prompted them to expand output and increase employment resulting in lower unemployment rate will no longer be there. Consequently, they will reduce employment till the unemployment rate rises to the natural level of 5%. That is, with the increase is nominal wages in Figure 21.6 the economy will move from A_1 to B_0, at a higher inflation rate of 7%. It may be noted that the higher level of aggregate demand which generated inflation rate of 7% and caused the economy to shift from A_0 to A_1 still persits.

Further, at point B_0, and with the actual present rate of inflation equal to 7 per cent, the workers will now expect this 7 per cent inflation rate to conitnue in future. As a result, the short-run Phillips curve *SPC* shifts upward from SPC_1 to SPC_2. It therefore follows, according to Friedman and other natural rate theorists, that the movement along a Phillips curve *SPC* is only a temporary or short-run pheonomenon. In the long when nominal wages are fully adjusted to the changes in the inflation rate and consequently unemployment rate comes back to its natural level, a new short-run Phillips curve is formed at the higher expected rate of inflation.

However, the above process of reduction in unemployment rate and then its returning to the natural level may continue further. The Government may misjudge the situation and think that 7 per cent rate of inflation is too high and adopt expansionary fiscal and monetary policies to increase aggregate demand and thereby to expand the level of employment. With the new increase in aggregate demand, the price level will rise further with nominal wages lagging behind in the short-run. As a result, profits of business firms will increase and they will expand output and employment causing the reduction in rate of unemployment and rise in the inflation rate. With this, the economy will move from B_0 to B_1 along their short-run Phillips curve SPC_2. After some time, the workers will recognise the fall in their real wages and press for higher normal wages to compensate for the higher rate of inflation than expected. When this higher nominal wages are granted, the business profits decline which will cause the level of employment to fall and unemployment rate to return to the natural rate of 5%. That is, in Figure 21.6 the economy moves from point B_1 to C_0. The new short-run Phillips curve will now shift to SPC_2 passing through point C_0. The process may be repeated again with the result that while in the short run, the unemployment rate falls below the natural rate, in the long run it returns to its natural rate. But throughout this process the inflation rate continuously goes on rising. On joining points such as A_0, B_0, C_0 corresponding to the given natural rate of unemployment we get a vertical long-run Phillips curve *LPC* in Figure 21.6. Thus, in the adaptive expectations theory of the natural rate hypothesis while the short-run Phillips curve is downward sloping indicating that trade-off between inflation and unemployment rate the short run, the long run Phillips curve is a vertical straight line showing that no trade-off exists between inflation and unemployment in the long run.

It is important to remember that adaptive expectations theory has also been applied to explain the reverse process of disinflation, that is, fall in the rate of inflation as well as inflation itself. Suppose in Figure 21.6 the economy is originally at point C_0 with 9% rate of inflation. Now, if a decline in aggregate demand occurs, say as a result of contraction of money supply by the Central Bank of a country, this will reduce inflation rate below the 9 per cent expected rate. As a result, profits of business firms will decline because the prices will be falling more rapidly than wages. The decline in profits will cause the firms to reduce employment and consequently unemployment rate will rise. Eventually, firms and workers will adjust their expectations and the unemployment rate will return to the natural rate. The process will be repeated and the economy in the long run will slide down along the vertical long-run Phillips curve showing falling rate of inflation at the given natural rate of unemployment.

It follows from above that according to adaptive expectations theory any rate of inflation can occur in the long run with the natural rate of unemployment.

LONG-RUNG PHILLIPS CURVE: RATIONAL EXPECTATIONS THEORY

In the end we explain the viewpoint about inflation and unemployment put forward by Rational Expectations Theory which is the cornerstone of recently developed macroeconomic theory, popularly called *new classical macroeconomics*. As explained above, Friedman's adaptive expectations theory assumes that nominal wages lag behind changes in the price level. This lag in the adjustment of nominal wages to the price level brings about rise in business profits which induces the firms to expand output and employment in the short run and leads to the reduction in unemployment rate below the natural rate. According to the rational expectations theory, which is another version of natural unemployment rate theory, there is no lag in the adjustment of nominal wages consequent to the rise in price level. The advocates of this theory further argue that nominal wages are *quickly* adjusted to any expected changes in the price level so that there does not exist Phillips curve showing trade-off between rates of inflation and unemployment. According to them, as a result of increase in aggregate demand, there is no reduction in unemployment rate. The rate of inflation resulting from increase in aggregate demand is *fully and correctly anticipated* by workers and business firms and get completely and quickly incorporated into the wage agreements resulting in higher prices of products. Thus, it is the price level that rises, the level of real output and employment remaining unchanged at the natural level. Hence, aggregate supply curve according to the rational expectations theory is a vertical straight line at the full-employment level.

Rational expectations theory rests on two basic elements. First, according to it, workers and producers being quite rational have a correct understanding of the economy and therefore correctly anticipate the effects of the Government's economic policies using all the available relevant information. On the basis of these anticipations of the effects of economic events and Government's policies they take correct decisions to promote their own interests.

The second premise of rational expectations theory is that, like the classical economists, *it assumes that all product and factor markets are highly* competitive. As a result, wages and product prices are highly flexible and therefore can quickly change upward and downward. Indeed, the rational expectations theory considers that new information is quickly assimilated (*i.e.*, taken into account) in the demand and supply curves of markets so that new equilibrium prices immediately adjust to the new economic events and policies, be it a new technological change or a supply shock such as a drought or act of OPEC oil cartel or change in Government's monetary and fiscal policies.

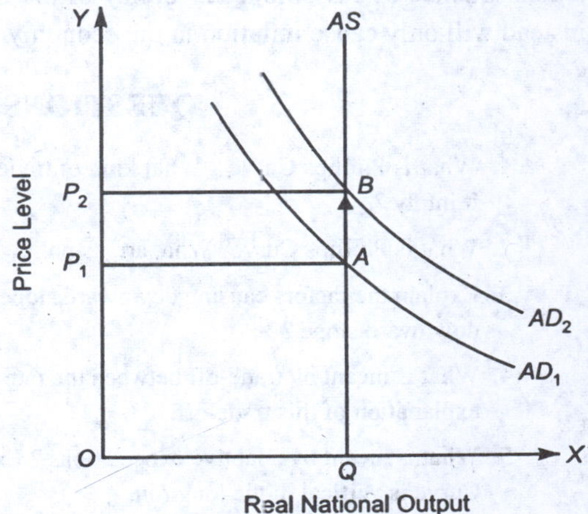

Fig. 21.7. *Inflation and Output : Rational Expectations Theory*

Figure 21.7 illustrates the standpoint of rational expectations theory about the relation between inflation and unemployment. In this *OQ* is the level of real national output corresponding to the full employment of labour (with a given natural rate of unemployment). *AS* is aggregate supply curve at *OQ* level of real national output. To begin with, AD_1 is the aggregate demand curve which intersects the aggregate supply curve *AS* at point *A* and determines price level equal to P_1. Suppose Government adopts an expansionary monetary policy to increase output and employment. As a consequence, aggregate demand curve shifts upward to the new position AD_2. According to rational expectations theory, people (*i.e.*, workers, businessmen, consumers, lenders) will correctly anticipate that this expansionary policy will cause inflation in the economy and they would take prompt measures to protect themselves against this inflation. Accordingly, workers would press for higher wages and get it granted, businessmen would raise the prices of their products, lenders would hike their rates of interest. All these increases would take place immediately. It is thus clear that the increase in aggregate demand (*i.e.*, aggregate expenditure) brought about by expansionary monetary policy will cause the price level to rise to P_2. Thus, the increase in aggregate demand or expenditure will be fully reflected in higher wages, higher interest rates and higher product prices, all of which will rise in proportion to the anticipated rate of inflation. Consequently, the levels of real national product and employment, wage rate, interest rate, levels of investment and consumption would remain unchanged. This can be easily understood with the help of monetarist equation of exchange $P = \frac{MV}{Q}$. Expansionary monetary policy leads to the increase in money supply M. As a result, aggregate expenditure, which in quantity theory, is equal to MV increases. (Note that V is the velocity of circulation of money which remains stable). But people's anticipations or expectations of inflation cause an increase in P in equal proportion to the expansion in MV. This means that despite the increase in MV, real output Q and the level of employment will remain unchanged.

It is clear from above that people's anticipations or expectations of inflation and acting upon them in their decision making when expansionary monetary policy is adopted frustrate or nullify the intended effect (that is, increase in real output and employment) of Government's monetary policy. In other words, according to the rational expectations theory, the intended effect of expansionary monetary policy on investment, real output and employment does not materialise. As seen above, in Fig. 21.7 it is due to the anticipation of inflation by the people and quick upward adjustments made in wages, interest etc., by them that the price level instantly rises from P_1 to P_2, the level of output Q remaining constant. That is why, according to the rational expectations theory, aggregate supply curve is a vertical straight line. The vertical aggregate supply curve means that there is no trade-off between inflation and unemployment, that is, downward-sloping Phillips curve does not exist. Thus, according to rational expectations theory, the increase in aggregate demand or expenditure as a consequence of easy monetary policy of the Government will fail to reduce unemployment and instead will only cause inflation in the economy.

QUESTIONS FOR REVIEW

1. What is Phillips Curve ? What kind of trade-off between unemployment rate and inflation rate does it imply ?
2. What is Phillips Curve? What are its policy implications ?
3. Explain the factors causing downward slope of Phillips Curve. What is the policy significance of the downward slope ?
4. What is meant by trade-off between the rate of inflation and unemployment ? Explain the Keynesian explanation of this trade-off.
5. What is meant by adaptive expectations ? Explain how with their help Friedman proves that Phillips Curve is vertical in the long run.
6. What effect do expectations regarding rate of inflation have on the short-run Phillips curve ? Can this help to explain stagflation ?
7. What is meant by rational expectations ? How does rational expectations theory show that aggregate supply curve is a vertical straight line and that there is no trade-off between rate of inflation and rate of unemployment.

CHAPTER 22

Aggregate Demand and Aggregate Supply with Flexible Price Level (AD-AS Model)

Before analysing the causes of inflation we need to explain aggregate demand-aggregate supply model with flexible price level. Keynes in his income-expenditure analysis of income and employment assumed that price level remained constant. Concerned as he was with the unemployment problem of the economy under the grip of depression characterised by demand deficiency and excess capacity in the economy he validly assumed the price level to remain constant. But during the Second World War and after, the problem of inflation, that is, continuous rise in general price level, was faced by many capitalist advanced countries. During this period Keynes himself explained inflation in terms of his *inflationary gap* which arises due to excess demand when the economy is working at its full capacity with full employment of workers. Behind his analysis of inflation were aggregate demand and aggregate supply with flexible price level though he did not explicitly use the concepts of aggregate demand and aggregate supply curves with flexible price level. After Keynes it is with the concepts of aggregate demand and aggregate supply curves with flexible price level that inflation has been explained. It is therefore useful to explain these concepts before analysing the problem of inflation.

Aggregate Demand (AD)

Let us first explain aggregate demand. ***Aggregate demand*** *is the total desired quantity of goods and services that are bought by consumer households, private investors, government and foreigners at each possible price level, other things being held constant.* Thus aggregate demand is not any quantity demanded at a particular price level but is a schedule of total cutput demanded at various price levels and is represented by a curve. Thus aggregate demand has four components: consumption demand, private investment demand, Government purchases of goods and services and net exports. *Thus, aggregate demand curve depicts the total output of goods and services which households, firms, and Government are willing to buy at each possible price level.*

Thus aggregate demand curve shows the relationship between the total quantity demanded of goods and services and general price level. It is worth noting that aggregate demand curve (*AD*) differs from the ordinary demand curve of an individual commodity with which we are concerned in microeconomics though both slope downward to the right. In case of a demand curve of an individual commodity when price of a commodity rises, it will tend to be substituted by other commodities which are its close substitutes resulting in fall in the quantity demanded of the commodity at a higher price. Thus, the slope of demand curve of an individual commodity depends mainly on the possibility of substitution between the commodities. On the other hand, as we shall

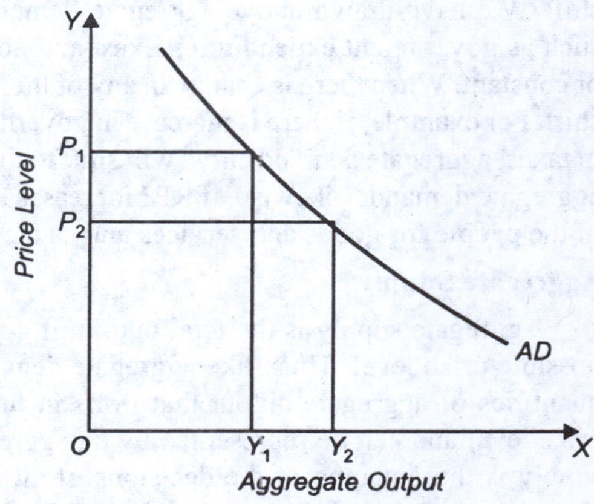

Fig. 22.1. *Aggregate Demand Curve with Varying Price Level*

see below, the slope of aggregate demand curve depends on factors totally different from those that cause demand curve of an individual commodity to slope downward. We have drawn an *AD* curve in Figure 22.1 where on the horizontal axis we measure level of aggregate output and on the vertical axis we measure the general price level. As will be seen from Figure 22.1, aggregate demand curve *AD* slopes downward to the right.

It is important to note that the *AD-AS* model is unlike that of market demand-supply model of microeconomic theory. When we consider demand and supply in a particular market, say for cotton cloth, rise in its price will cause increase in its quantity supplied but in doing so resources will be withdrawn from other goods. Such reallocation of resources between products and consequently rise in output of one product and fall in that of the other is not considered in macroeconomics where we are concerned with determination of aggregate output and total employment of resources in the economy as a whole. Similarly, in macroeconomic model of aggregate demand and aggregate supply we study the determination of general price level which does not explain the relative prices of various products.

We explain below in detail the concepts of aggregate demand (*AD*) and aggregate supply (*AS*) curves and their likely shape and factors determining them. We will also discuss some important controversial issues of macroeconomics with this *AD-AS* model.

Why does Aggregate Demand Curve Slope Downward ? Like the demand curve for an individual commodity, aggregate demand curve slopes downward but for different reasons. There are three factors responsible for downward-sloping aggregate demand curve. First, as the general price level falls, the *real value or purchasing power of money balances and monetary assets* with the public increases. This makes the people feel better off or richer which induces them to increase their consumption which is an important component of aggregate demand. This is called *real balance effect*. Second, with the fall in general price level, transactions demand for money falls which causes *interest rate to fall*. At a lower interest rate investment demand increases which also operates to bring about rise in aggregate demand at a lower general price level. This is called *interest rate effect*.

Thirdly, the fall in general price level makes exports of a country relatively cheaper leading to an increase in export demand for domestic goods produced in the economy. Besides, due to cheaper domestic goods as a result of fall in general price level, the people buy domestic goods instead of imported ones which reduces imports of a country. This causes *net exports* of the country to rise and leads to the increase in aggregate demand at a lower price level. This is known as *foreign trade effect*.

Shifts in Aggregate Demand Curve. Now, which factors cause aggregate demand curve to shift? We have drawn above aggregate demand curve *AD* in Fig. 22.1 keeping non-price factors such as government expenditure, taxes, autonomous investment, money supply as remaining fixed or constant. When there is change in any of these non-price factors, aggregate demand curve *AD* will shift. For example, if there is increase in government expenditure without being matched by increase in taxes, aggregate demand curve will shift to the right indicating that at each price there will be more aggregate demand. Likewise, if RBI increases money supply in the economy, this will raise demand of the people for goods and services and cause a shift in aggregate demand curve to the right.

Aggregate Supply

Aggregate supply is the total output of goods and services that firms want to produce at each possible price level. Thus, like aggregate demand, aggregate supply is the whole schedule of total quantities of aggregate output that firms in the economy are willing to produce at each possible price level and can be represented by an aggregate supply curve. It is worth noting that aggregate supply is the outcome of the decisions of all producers in the economy to hire workers and buy other inputs for production of goods and services for selling them to consumers, other producers, government as well as for exporting them to other countries. It may be noted while drawing aggregate supply curve that depicts relationship been quantities of aggregate output that are produced for sale in the market by the firms in the economy at various price levels, all other factors that affect aggregate supply being held constant.

There is a lot of disagreement among economists about the shape of aggregate supply curve. The classical economists assumed that there normally prevailed full-employment of resources in the economy. According to them, if at any time there is deviation from this full-employment level, the wages, interest and prices quickly and automatically adjust and change to restore equilibrium at the full-employment level. Thus, in the classical theory, the aggregate supply curve of output is

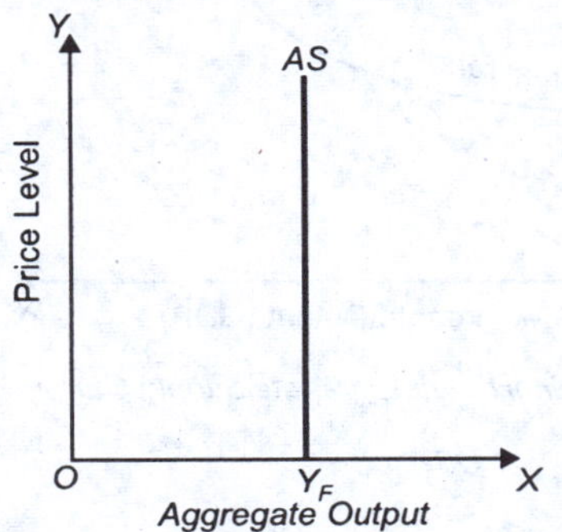

Fig. 22.2. *Aggregate Supply Curve : Classical View*

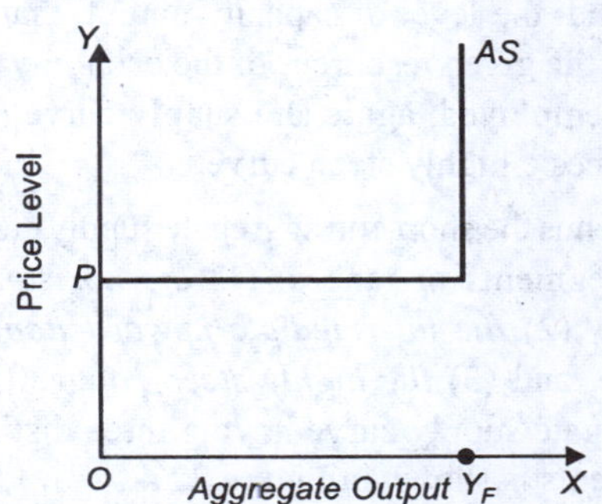

Fig. 22.3. *Keynes' Original Aggregate Supply Curve*

perfectly inelastic (*i.e.* a vertical straight line) at the output level corresponding to full-employment level of resources. This aggregate supply curve relating aggregate supply with price level of the classical theory of income and employment is shown in Figure 22.2 by a vertical *AS* curve.

On the other hand, Keynes considered the situation of economic depression when the economy was operating before the level of full employment of resources. He further believed that in such a situation money wage rates were sticky *i.e.* remained constant. He further assumed that average and margined products of labour remain constant when more of it is employed following the increase in aggregate demand. With these assumptions, more aggregate output is produced and supplied at the given price level in response to increase in aggregate demand. But when full employment of labour and capital stock is attained and aggregate demand further increases, aggregate supply curve being unable to increase any more, it is the price level that will rise in response to the increase in aggregate demand Keynes' aggregate supply curve depicting the relationship between price level and the aggregate production (supply) during the period of depression and involuntary unemployment when there is a lot of excess capacity in the economy is shown in Figure 22.3 where it will be seen that aggregate supply is a horizontal straight line (*i.e.* perfectly elastic) up to full-employment output Y_F showing thereby that more is produced and supplied at the same price level *OP* but corresponding to full-employment level point Y_F it becomes vertical.

It may however be noted that Keynes recognised that as the aggregate supply approaches close to the full-employment level, the cost of output per unit tends to rise due to the rise in wage rate and also due to diminishing returns to extra factors employed. But, according to Keynes, the rise in price at full-employment level before full employment or less than capacity output will not be much.

It is evident from above that shape of aggregate supply curve has been a highly controversial issue. However, there is now a general consensus among modern economists that when the economy is working substantially below capacity, that is, at times of depression or severe recession, more can be produced without much rise in marginal cost of production and therefore the aggregate supply curve is nearly flat. This first range is therefore called *horizontal range*. With the given stock of capital (*i.e.* plant and equipment) when output is expanded beyond this range the diminishing returns and rising marginal costs occur which ultimately cause the aggregate supply curve to slope upward gently. Thus there is a part of gently rising short-run aggregate supply curve which represents *intermediate range* of short-run aggregate supply curve. But as the firms in the economy approach near their capacity output, their marginal costs sharply rise which causes sharply rising aggregate supply curve. Beyond the level of capacity output, that is, when the given resources of the economy are fully employed, aggregate supply curve (*AS* becomes a highly steep curve.

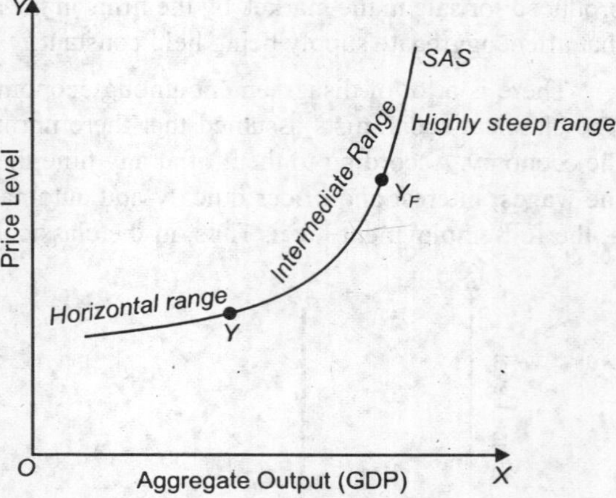

Fig. 22.4. *Short-run Aggregate Supply Curve with Three Ranges*

Thus the short-run aggregate supply curve has segments or ranges: (1) *the horizontal range,* (2) *the intermediate upward-sloping range*, and (3) *the highly steep range.* This aggregate supply curve having three distinct segments is shown in Figure 22.4.

Shifts in Short-Run Aggregate Supply Curve

In explaining the upward-sloping nature of short-run aggregate supply we stated that aggregate supply curve depicts the relationship between price level and aggregate output (*i.e.*, real GDP), *other factors* such as wages, input prices, technology and indirect taxes that determine aggregate supply being held constant. Now, it is the *changes* in these other determining factors that cause a *shift* in the aggregate supply curve. We explain below the factors that cause a shift in aggregate supply curve.

Changes in Wage Rate. Change in wage rate of workers is an important factor that causes a shift in short-run aggregate supply curve. For example, when wage rate of workers increases, it causes a leftward shift in short-run aggregate supply curve. This is because increase in wages raises cost per unit of output. With a given price of output, higher wage rate means profit per unit of output will decline. As production becomes less profitable, it is likely that the firms will cut back on production and supply less output. Now when wage rate of workers increases, it causes a leftward shift in short-run aggregate supply curve as shown in Fig. 22.5.

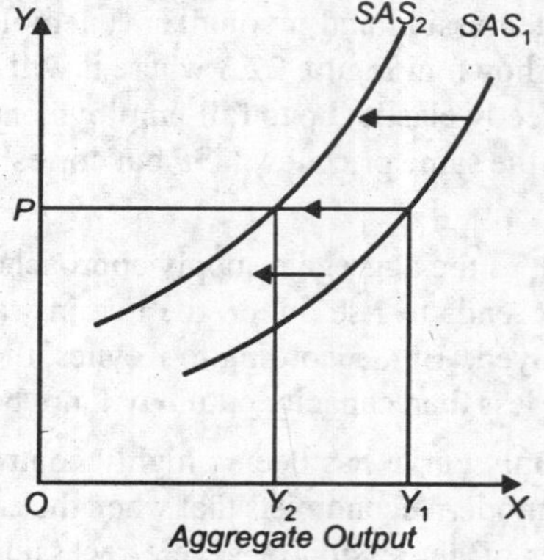

Fig. 22.5. *Leftward Shift in Aggregate Supply Curve*

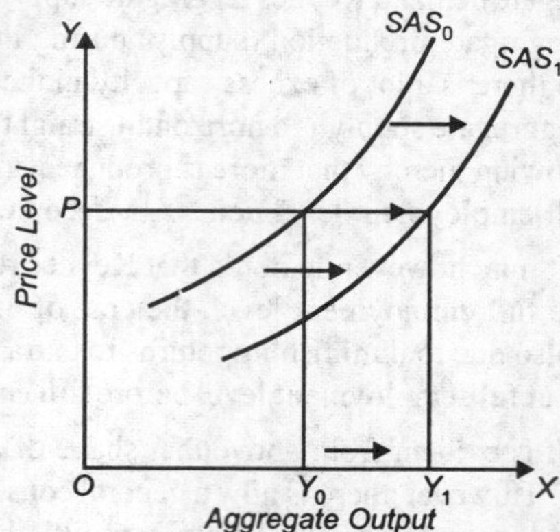

Fig. 22.6. *Rightward Shift in Aggregate Supply Curve*

Prices of Inputs. Changes in prices of other inputs such as energy (for example, crude oil) and raw materials also bring about a shift in short-run aggregate supply curve. It is well known that increase in price of crude oil by OPEC in 1973 and again in 1979 affected aggregate supply by raising cost per unit of production. This caused a leftward shift in short-run aggregate supply curve as shown in Fig. 22.5 This *leftward shift* in the aggregate supply curve implies that at any given price level less output is supplied than before.

On the other hand, when price of crude oil falls as has happened at several occasions in the past, aggregate supply curve shifts to the right as is shown in Fig. 22.6 indicating that at any given price level more output will be produced and supplied than before.

Change in Technology. The change in technology is another important factor that causes a shift in aggregate supply curve. When there is improvement in technology, productivity of factors rises causing a fall in the unit cost of production. This brings about a rightward shift in aggregate supply curve showing that at any given price level more will be produced and supplied than before.

Business Taxes and Subsidies. Increase in rates of business taxes such as excise duty, sales tax, customs duties raise per unit cost of production just as rise in wage rate. (Note that tax is considered as cost of production as it raises the supply price of output.) Thus, by levying business taxes or increasing their rates causes a leftward shift in the aggregate supply curve. On the other hand, lowering of taxes as happened during the recent global slowdown (2007-09), caused by bursting of sub-prime housing loans bubble in United States, will cause a shift in the aggregate supply curve to the right. Provision of subsidies on products of various industries also causes a shift in the aggregate supply curve to the right.

Available Supply of Resources. Lastly, a very important factor determining the position of aggregate supply curve is the available quantity of resources. When the available supplies of resources such as labour and capital increase, the short-run aggregate supply curve will shift to the right. As labour force grows and supply of capital is increased through investment, the short-run aggregate supply curve will shift to the right implying that more output will be produced for sale at any given price level.

LONG-RUN AGGREGATE SUPPLY CURVE

In our above analysis we have explained the short-run aggregate supply curve with a variable price level. In the modern macroeconomic analysis the distinction is drawn between the long-run and short-run aggregate supply curve. Since classical economists who were concerned with determination of national income and employment in the long run, they considered the long-run aggregate supply. The long-run aggregate supply is determined by three real factors such as availability of labour, the quantity of capital stock and the state of technology. In the long run price level is variable and the aggregate supply curve is vertical. On the other hand, Keynes considered the short-run aggregate supply which is perfectly elastic at the fixed price level in the period of depression. However, in the modern or new Keynsian macroeconomics short-run aggregate supply curve slopes upward. Further, this short-run aggregate supply fluctuates over the course of a business cycle, that is, in different phases of the business cycle. The level of employment fluctuates around full-employment level and GDP fluctuates around the potential GDP. Note *that the quantity of real GDP when there is full employment of labour or, in other words, when unemployment is at its natural rate is known as potential GDP*. Potential GDP depends on the given labour force and capital stock when they are fully employed or used, given the state of technology. We explain below in detail the concept of long-run aggregate supply and short-run aggregate supply.

Long-run Aggregate Supply

The long-run aggregate supply of output or real GDP depends on three factors: (1) the quantity of available labour, (2) the stock of capital and (3) the state of technology. The aggregate production function which describes the influence of these three factors is written as :

$$Y = F(L, K, T)$$

where Y is the quantity of aggregate output or real GDP, L is the quantity of labour, K is the stock of capital and T is the state of technology. At any given time, the stock of capital and state of technology are given and fixed. Though at any time population of a country is fixed but the quantity of labour is variable; it depends on the preferences between work and leisure of the people on the one hand and the decisions of the firms about the demand for labour on the other. People supply labour only if wage rate which is reward for their work effort is sufficient to overcome their preference for leisure. The higher the wage rate, the greater is the quantity of labour supplied. On the other hand, the firms demand labour if it is profitable to use it for production. The lower the wage rate, which is the cost of labour, the greater is the quantity of labour used. The equilibrium wage rate and the quantity of labour employed are determined by labour market equilibrium. The labour market is in equilibrium at the wage rate at which the quantity of labour demanded equals the quantity of labour supplied. *At this equilibrium wage rate, all those who are willing to supply their labour are is fact demanded and employed. Therefore, at this equilibrium wage rate, full employment of labour is said to prevail.*

However, even at full employment, there are always some workers searching for jobs and some firms are looking for workers to offer them employment. This is because of two factors, frictional and structural. Every week some workers leave their old jobs and search for new better jobs more suited to their skills and ability. But due to lack of information, it takes time to find the new jobs even though these are available. This represents what is called *frictional unemployment*. Second, every week or month some industries are declining due to technological changes in technology or preferences of the people for goods while others are expanding. In this case while some people are laid off from the declining industries but some time is required before they acquire new skills and training needed for employment in the expanding industries. Therefore, for some time they remain unemployed though job vacancies for them exist. This second type of unemployment is called *structural unemployment*.

Thus, at any time some frictional and structural unemployment inevitably exist in a free market economy. Therefore, in modern macroeconomics, the amount of frictional and structural unemployment is called the *natural rate of unemployment*. Around 4 to 5 per cent of labour force in the developed free-market economies represents the natural rate of unemployment. And full employment is said to exist in spite of the existence of frictional and structural unemployment. As mentioned above, the quantity of real GDP produced and supplied when there is full employment (that is, when there exists only natural rate of unemployment) is called potential GDP. It may be noted again that potential GDP depends on full employment of labour, the full use of the existing stock of capital and the available technology.

The long-run aggregate supply describes the relationship between the quantity of real GDP and the price level in the long run when real GDP equals potential GDP. The long-run aggregate supply curve is a vertical line (at potential GDP level as shown by *LAS* in Figure 22.7. The long-run aggregate supply is vertical because potential GDP does not vary with price level, that is, it is independent of the price level. The reason for the independence of potential GDP from the price level is that the movement along the long-run aggregate supply curve involves not only the change in price level of goods but also prices of factor inputs such as wages of labour etc. For example, when there is 5 per cent decrease in the prices of goods and services, this is matched by the same (*i.e.* 5 per cent) decline in wage rate and other factor

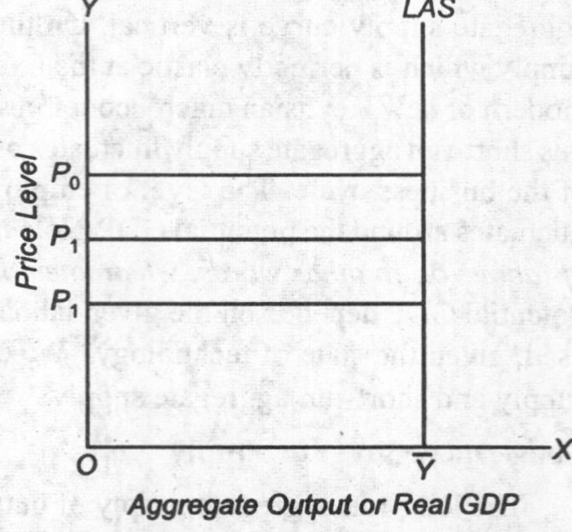

Fig. 22.7. *Long Run Aggregate Supply Curve*

prices so that relative prices and real wage rate remain unchanged. This explains why it is profitable to produce the same quantity of real GDP at lower price level of goods and services. When price level of goods and services falls, the cost also falls as wage rate and other factor prices fall by the same percentage. Therefore, aggregate supply of output (*i.e.* real GDP) in the long run also remains constant at potential GDP level.

It is evident from above that long-run aggregate supply curve is the same as the classical aggregate supply curve.

Changes in Long-Run Aggregate Supply Curve

We have seen above that long-run aggregate supply curve is a vertical straight line at the level of potential GDP. Changes in price level bring about a movement along the long-run aggregate supply, but the quantity of aggregate supply remains fixed at the level of potential GDP. It is changes in potential GDP that causes a shift in the long-run aggregate supply curve. The following factors cause a change in potential GDP resulting in a shift in the long-run aggregate supply curve:

1. The change in the full-employment quantity of labour.
2. Change in the stock of capital.
3. Progress in technology.

Increase in Labour Force

Labour is an important resource of production. Over time, given the capital stock and the state of technology potential GDP will increase as full-employment quantity of labour force increases. Therefore, the increase in the full-employment quantity of labour force causes a shift in the long-run aggregate supply curve to the right as shown in Figure 22.8. It may be noted that changes in labour employment over the business cycle cause fluctuations in real GDP. But these changes in real GDP that take place over the business cycle are not changes in potential GDP. As mentioned above, changes in potential GDP occur due to changes in labour force and stock of capital, and improvement in technology.

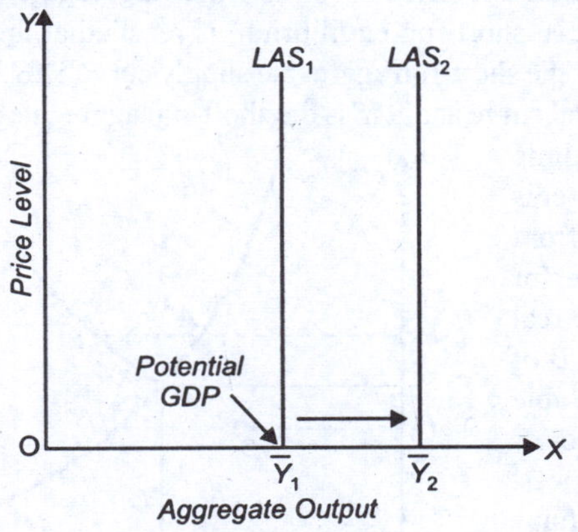

Fig. 22.8. *Increase in labour force, capital stock and progress in technology increases potential GDP and shifts LAS curve to the right.*

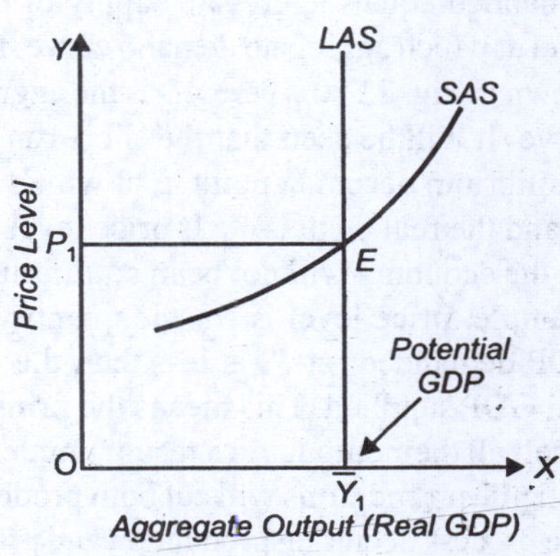

Fig. 22.9. *Short-run Aggregate Supply Curve*

Growth in the Stock of Capital. The stock of capital in an economy determines the productive capacity of the economy. The larger the stock of capital in the economy, the more productive is the labour force of the economy and the greater is its potential GDP. The higher per capita output and potential GDP of the American economy as compared to those of the Indian economy are mainly due to the greater stock of capital in the United States. Note that in the capital stock the modern economists include not only physical capital but also human capital. Human capital means the acquired skills, education and training of the workers. Like the increase in labour force, growth in capital stock also brings about increase in potential GDP and causes a shift in the long-run aggregate supply curve (LAS) to the right.

Progress in Technology. Progress in technology enables firms to produce more from the given resources. Empirical research studies have shown that technological progress is by far the most important source of increase in GDP over the past two centuries. It is due to advances in technology that a modern worker, both in industry and agriculture, produces many times more output than the worker in the olden times. Thus, even with the fixed quantities of labour and capital, progress in technology raises potential GDP and causes shift in the long-run aggregate supply curve to the right.

We have shown long-run aggregate supply curve *LAS* and short-run aggregate supply curve together in Fig. 22.9. It will be seen that short-run aggregate supply curve at potential GDP level and beyond potential GDP level $\overline{Y}_1$, it becomes highly steep.

DETERMINATION OF GDP AND PRICE LEVEL : *AS-AD* MODEL

Having explained the concepts of aggregate demand and aggregate supply with variable price level, now we shall explain how macroeconomic equilibrium is reached between the aggregate supply and aggregate demand to determine the amount of real GDP and the price level. As there is difference between the long-run and the short run aggregate supply curves, the long-run equilibrium differs from the short-run macroeconomic equilibrium. While long-run equilibrium is the state towards which the economy is moving, short-run equilibrium is the actual state of the economy in the short run as it fluctuates around potential GDP. The purpose of *AS-AD* model is to explain how the changes in various factors, fiscal and monetary policies bring about changes in real GDP and the general price level, that is, inflation. We explain below both the short-run and long-run macroeconomic equilibrium.

Short-run Macroeconomic Equilibrium

Short-run macroeconomic equilibrium occurs at the price level at which aggregate output demanded equals aggregate supply of output. That is, short-run equilibrium is reached at the price level at which aggregate demand curve *AD* intersects the short-run aggregate supply curve *SAS*. This is shown in Fig. 22.10 where *AD* is the aggregate demand curve and *SAS* is the short-run aggregate supply curve. It will be seen that the short-run macroeconomic equilibrium occurs at point *E* at which the price level is P_0 and the real GDP is Y_0. If price level is different from P_0, the economy will not be in equilibrium. Suppose, for example, price level is P_2, the quantity P_2A of the real GDP demanded at P_2 is less than the quantity P_2B of real GDP supplied. This means the firms will not be able to sell all their output. As a result, unintended inventories well pile up and firms will cut both production and prices. The process of cutting production and prices will continue until the equilibrium price level P_0 is reached and real GDP produced and sold is Y_0.

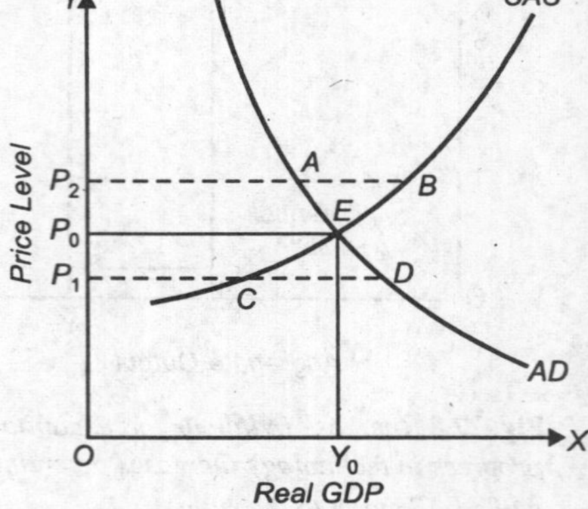

Fig. 22.10. *Short-run Macroeconomic Equilibrium : Joint Determination of GDP and Price Level*

Now suppose that price level is P_1. It will be seen from Fig. 22.10 that at price level P_1 the quantity of aggregate output demanded (P_1D) exceeds the aggregate supply (P_1C). Thus at the price level P_1, the people will not be able to get all the goods and resources they want to buy. As a result, inventories of goods with the firms will decrease below the desired level. This will induce firms to increase production and raise prices. The production and price level will rise until price level P_0 is reached and real GDP produced is Y_0 which meets the demands of the people fully at the price level P_0. Thus, the price level P_0 and real GDP equal to Y_0 represent the short-run macroeconomic equilibrium.

It is worthwhile to note that in the short run the money wage rate is fixed. *It does not adjust to bring macro-equilibrium at full-employment level of real GDP.* Thus, in the short run macro-equilibrium can be attained with real *GDP* less than or greater than potential GDP (*i.e.* the level of GDP at which there is full employment of labour) depending on the level of aggregate demand. It is only in the long run when money wage rate adjusts that equilibrium is restored at potential GDP.

It is worth noting that, as Keynes emphasized, the equilibrium between aggregate demand and aggregate supply may not necessarily be at full-employment level. Besides, when the economy is working at the level of full productive capacity, the increase in aggregate demand will lead to inflation in the economy.

Shift in Short-run Aggregate Supply Curve and Stagflation

Let us now turn to examine the effect of changes in aggregate supply, aggregate demand remaining constant. With the advent of *supply-side economics and new classical macroeconomics* embodying rational expectations in recent years economists are increasingly concerned with shifts in aggregate supply curve. Important factors that cause a shift in supply are changes in factor-prices and availability of resources, change in productivity and expectations about future inflation. Institutional factors such as Government regulations that affect resource use efficiency also cause shift in aggregate supply curve.

An important cause of shift in aggregate supply curve is the *rise in prices of resources such as large increase in oil price by OPEC* in 1973-74 and again in 1979-80. The rise in oil prices causes the aggregate supply curve to shift to the left as shown in Figure 22.11 where due to the higher per unit resource cost aggregate supply curve has shifted leftward from SAS_0 to SAS_1. The aggregate demand curve *AD* remaining constant, with the leftward shift in aggregate supply curve from AS_0 to AS_1, leads to the new macroeconomic equilibrium being established at *T*, at which price level is higher and aggregate output smaller than before.

The emergence of rise in price level or inflation due to the leftward shift in aggregate supply curve is called cost-push inflation. There is an important difference between demand-pull inflation cost-push inflation. *Whereas in case of demand-pull inflation, price rises along with rise in GDP, in case of cost-push inflation price level rises but GDP declines.*

Thus, in Fig. 22.11 leftward shift in the *SAS* curve leads to rise in the price level from P_0 to P_1, while national output falls from Y_0 to Y_1. ***When both inflation and recession occur simultaneously, economists call this situation as stagflation***. We thus see that increase in costs or resource prices are both inflationary and recessionary.

It may be noted that stagflation is also said to occur when instead of absolute fall in aggregate output there is *slowdown in economic growth rate* when inflation rate remains steadily high and also unemployment levels are quite high. It is evident from above that stagflation occurs as a result of supply shock, that is, rise in price of essential inputs such as crude oil which causes a shift in the short-run aggregate supply curve to the left. Given the aggregate demand curve, the new equilibrium is reached at a higher price level (*i.e.,* inflation) and at the same time reduced aggregate output (*i.e.,* GDP) which generates unemployment in the economy.

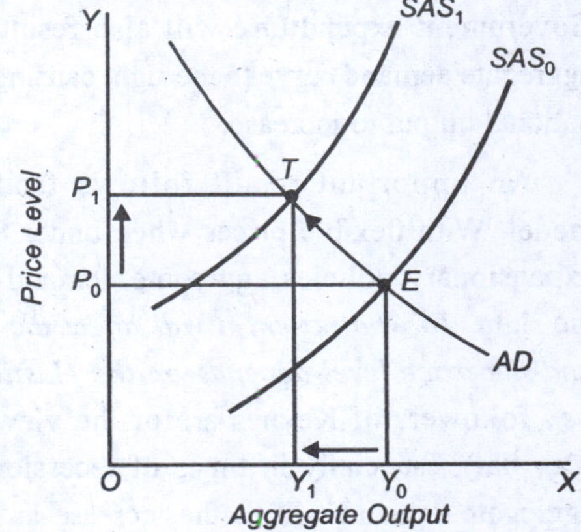

Fig. 22.11. *Emergence of stagflation due to leftward shift in aggregate supply curve*

We have explained above stagflation as a result of sharp rise in price of crude oil effected by restriction of oil output by collusive agreement of OPEC. In India stagflation can arise when there is decline in agricultural output due to failure of monsoon. The decline in agricultural output causes *food inflation* which in turn leads to rise in wages of workers which causes a shift in the short-run aggregate supply curve to the left. Besides, drastic decline in agricultural output also leads to the rise in prices of raw materials provided by agricultural sector to industries. The rise in raw material prices for industries shifts aggregate supply curve to the left causing both inflation and reduction in output.

Solution. To solve the problem of stagflation is a difficult task. In the seventies when the problem of stagflation was first faced efforts were made to solve it through demand management policies. However, when to reduce inflation, steps were taken to reduce aggregate demand by cutting expenditure, the result was decline in aggregate output which further worsened the unemployment problem. On the other hand, when to reduce unemployment attempt was made to increase aggregate expenditure through expansionary fiscal and monetary policies, the result was acceleration in inflation.

The proper solution of stagflation is to shift the short-run aggregate supply curve to the right by reducing cost through raising productivity levels. The productivity in both industry and agriculture can be raised through technological improvements and more capital accumulation. Besides, rightward shift in short-run aggregate supply can be made by reducing indirect taxes such as excise duties, sales tax, customs duties not only on final products but also on essential inputs used in the production of commodities.

Role of Fiscal and Monetary Policies in Keynesian, Monetarist and Classical Models

With this aggregate demand-aggregate supply model, popularly known as *AD-AS* model, we can explain the effects of fiscal and monetary policies on aggregate output (*i.e., GNP*) and price level in the economy. For example, if Government steps up its expenditure without increasing taxes, this will cause aggregate demand curve *AD* to shift to the right and thereby will lead to the increase in Gross National Product (*i.e.,* National Income) and the price level as is illustrated in Figure 22.12. Likewise, expansion in money supply, increase in private investment, or reduction in taxes without reducing Government expenditure will also result in shift in the aggregate demand curve to the right causing price level and national output to increase.

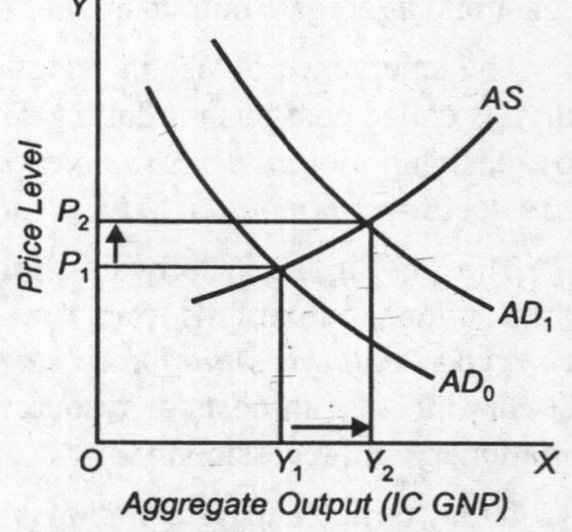

Fig. 22.12. *Keynesian View: Expansionary Fiscal and Monetary Policies in times of recession lead to more increase in GNP and less rise to price level.*

An important result follows from this *AD–AS* model. With flexible prices when under the influence of expansionary policies aggregate demand curve shifts to the right. *To what extent it will affect the national output and the price level depends on the elasticity of aggregate supply curve.* Keynesian economists *i.e.,* followers of Keynes are of the view that the aggregate supply curve is relatively elastic (*i.e.,* flat), especially in times of recession, and therefore most of the response to expansion in aggregate demand will be the increase in output rather than rise in the price level as is shown in

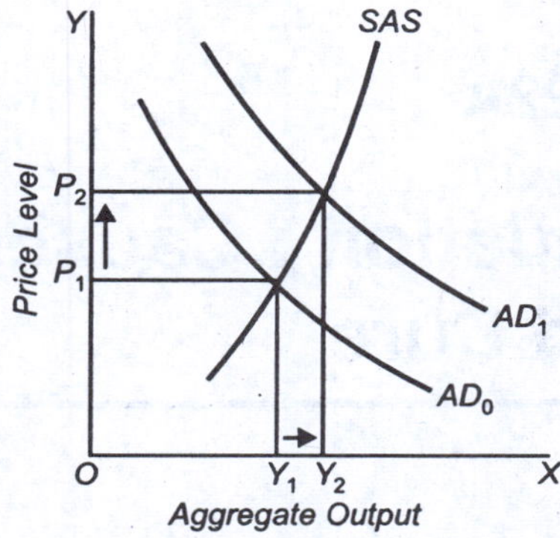

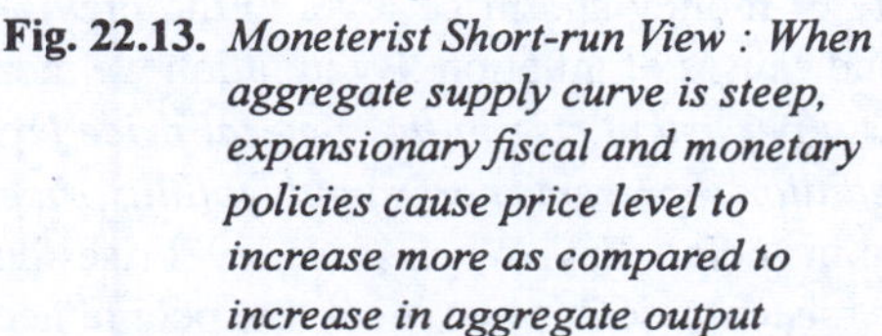

Fig. 22.13. *Moneterist Short-run View : When aggregate supply curve is steep, expansionary fiscal and monetary policies cause price level to increase more as compared to increase in aggregate output*

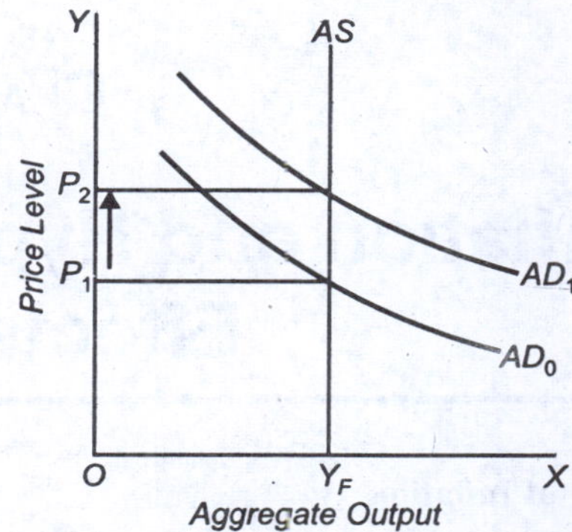

Fig. 22.14. *Classical View : With full employment of resources aggregate supply curve is vertical straight line and an increase in aggregate demand will cause price level to rise without change in aggregate output*

Figure 22.12. On the other hand, moneterists think that the supply curve is *steep as is shown* in Fig. 22.13 and in this case the expansionary fiscal and monetary policies causing outward shift in *AD* curve will bring about rise in price more than the increase in output. In the extreme case of *perfectly elastic aggregate supply curve* which Keynes assumed in his analysis of depression increase in aggregate demand will not affect the price level and its full effect will be to raise the level of GDP.

Lastly, when the economy is operating at the level of capacity output (*i.e.,* full employment level) as the classical economists assumed, increase in aggregate demand in this case will lead only to higher price level or inflation in the economy without affecting aggregate output (national income). The view of classical economists is illustrated in Figure 22.14 where aggregate supply curve *AS* is a vertical straight line at the full-employment level of output OY_F. It will be seen from this figure that when as a result of expansionary fiscal and monetary policies aggregate demand curve shifts outward to the right from AD_0 to AD_1, price level rises from P_1 to P_2 whereas aggregate output remains constant at OY_F level.

QUESTIONS FOR REVIEW

1. Briefly explain *AS-AD* model of determination of national product. With this model explain the impact of (1) increase in aggregate demand and (2) decrease in aggregate supply on price level and aggregate output.
2. Draw the aggregate demand curve (with price flexibility). Why does it slope downward? Show the effect of an increase in nominal money stock on aggregate demand curve.
3. Compare the Keynesian and Classical aggregate supply curve. Briefly explain their policy implications.
4. What is stagflation? Explain with *AS-AD* model what can cause stagflation.
5. Distinguish between short-run aggregate supply and long-run aggregate supply. What are the factors that cause shift in them?

CHAPTER 22A

Inflation and Hyperinflation : Causes, Effects and Cure

Meaning of Inflation

Having discussed the relationship between quantity of money and price level in the previous chapter, we are now in a position to explain the nature and causes of inflation. By inflation we mean *a general rise in prices*. To be more correct, *inflation is a persistent rise in the general price level rather than a once-for-all rise in it*. On the other hand, *deflation represents persistently falling prices*. Inflation or persistently rising prices is a major problem in India today. When price level rises due to inflation the value of money falls. When there is a persistent rise in price level, the people need more and more money to buy goods and services. To enable the people to meet their daily needs of consumption of goods and services when their prices are rising, their incomes must rise if they have to maintain their standard of living. For government employees, their dearners allowance is increased. Wages and salaries employed in the organised private sector are also raised, though after some time-lag. But people with fixed incomes and those who are self-employed are unable to raise their prices and suffer a lot due to inflation. The poor suffer the most from persistent rise in prices, especially of foodgrains and other essential items. Rate of inflation during the seventies and eighties was very high as compared to the rates of inflation experienced earlier during previous periods. In India, in recent years, 2010-11, 2011-12 and 2012-13, rate of inflation as measured by consumer price index (CPI) has been in double digit figures. Prior to Jan. 2013, even WPI inflation was quite high which compelled Reserve Bank of India to adopt tight monetary policy.

Causes of Inflation

Let us understand how the inflation originates or what causes it. Depending upon the specific causes, three types of inflation have been distinguished: (1) *Demand-pull inflation*, (2) *Cost-push inflation*, and (3) *Structuralist inflation.* An important cause of demand-pull inflation is the excessive growth of money supply in the economy. We will explain this cause of inflation in the *Monetarist Theory of Inflation.* We will explain and discuss below these three types of inflation.

DEMAND-PULL INFLATION

This represents a situation where the basic factor at work is the increase in aggregate demand for output either from the households or the entrepreneurs or government organised. The result is that the pressure of demand is such that it cannot be met by the currently available supply of output. If, for example, in a situation of full employment, the government expenditure or private investment goes up, this is bound to generate an inflationary pressure in the economy. Keynes explained that inflation arises when there occurs an *inflationary gap* in the economy which comes to exist when aggregate demand for goods and services exceeds aggregate supply at full-employment level of output. Basically, inflation is caused by a situation whereby the pressure of aggregate demand for goods and services exceeds the available supply of output (both being counted at the prices ruling at the beginning of a period). In such a situation, the rise in price level is the natural consequence.

Now, this imbalance between aggregate demand and supply may be the result of more than one force at work. As we know, aggregate demand is the sum of consumers' spending on consumer goods and services, government spending on goods and services and net investment being contemplated by the entrepreneurs. *When aggregate demand for all purposes—consumption, investment and government, expenditure—exceeds the supply of goods at current prices, there is a rise in price level. Since inflation is a continuous increase in the price level, not a one time rise in it, sustained inflation requires continuous increase in aggregate demand.* In the modern macroeconomics, inflation is explained with *AD-AS* model. Inflation can be explained by increase in aggregate demand (called "***demand shock***") or decrease in aggregate supply or rise in cost of production generally called "***supply shock***". Demand-pull inflation occurs when there is upward shift in aggregate demand when supply shocks are absent.

As stated above, demand-pull inflation occurs when there is increase in any component of aggregate demand, namely, consumption demand by households, investment by business firms, increase in government expenditure unmatched by increase in taxes (that is, deficit spending by the government financed by either creation of new money by the central bank or borrowing by the government from the market). To illustrate the cause of demand-pull inflation, let us assume the government adopts expansionary fiscal policy under which it increases its expenditure without levying extra taxes to finance its increased expenditure by borrowing from the Reserve Bank of India.

To illustrate the above point, let us assume that the government adopts expansionary fiscal policy under which it increases its expenditure on education, health, defence and finances this extra expenditure by borrowing from Reserve Bank of India which prints new notes for this purpose. This will lead to increase in aggregate demand ($C + I + G$). If aggregate supply of output does not increase or increases by a relatively less amount in the short run, this will cause demand-supply imbalances which will lead to demand-pull inflation in the economy, that is, general rise in price level.

Similarly, an inflationary process will be initiated if business firms anticipating the opportunities of making profits decide to invest more and to finance the new investment projects by borrowing from the banks being unable to get sufficient funds through savings out of profits and savings invested by the public in them. This new investment by the firms leads to the increase in aggregate demand for goods and services. However, inflation will occur by this new investment if aggregate supply of output does not increase adequately in the short run to match the increase in aggregate demand. Therefore, *demand-pull inflation generally occurs when the economy is already working at full-employment level of resources or what is now generally called when there is natural rate of unemployment*. This is because if aggregate demand increases beyond the full-employment level of output, output of goods cannot be increased adequately without much increase in cost. Note that in developing countries such as India, there are difficulties of measuring employment, unemployment and full employment. Therefore in the Indian context, instead of full-employment level of output, we use ***full capacity output of the economy beyond which supply of output cannot be increased***

It is important to note that Keynes in his booklet *How to Pay for the War* published during the Second World War explained inflation in terms of excess demand for goods relative to the aggregate supply of their output. His notion of the *inflationary gap* which he put forward in his booklet represented excess of aggregate demand over full-employment output. This inflationary gap, according to him, leads to the rise in prices. Thus, Keynes explained inflation in terms of demand-pull forces. Therefore, the theory of demand-pull inflation is associated with the name of Keynes. Since beyond full-employment level of aggregate supply output cannot increase in response to increase in demand, this results in rise in prices under the pressure of excess demand. Aggregate supply curve, according to him, is vertical at full-employment level.

Demand-pull inflation is shown in Figure 22A.1. In the modern macroeconomics distinction is drawn between *long-run aggregate supply curve (LAS) and short-run aggregate supply curve* (*SAS*). The long-run aggregate supply curve (*LAS*) is a *vertical line drawn at the full-employment level* (*i.e.* at natural rate of unemployment) or in the Indian context *full-capacity output level.* This full-employment level or full-capacity output is also called ***potential output.*** The short-run aggregate supply curve SAS_0 slopes upward to the right which shows more supply of output is forthcoming at a higher price and *is drawn with a constant wage rate.* This short-run aggregate supply curve (*SAS*) slopes upward because with the increase in employment of labour, diminishing returns to labour occur which raises marginal cost of production. This short-run aggregate supply curve slopes upward to the right even beyond full-employment or potential level of output. This is because, as explained earlier, even at full-employment level, some unemployment occurs due to frictional and structural factors and therefore beyond full-employment level, employment of labour can increase with reduction in natural unemployment under the pressure of aggregate demand. It will be seen from Figure 22A.1 that short-run aggregate supply curve SAS_0 cuts long-run aggregate supply curve *LAS* at point E_0. To begin with, aggregate demand curve AD_0 intersects both short-run aggregate suply curve SAS_0 and long-run aggregate supply curve (*LAS*) at point E_0 and this shows that at point E_0 there is long-run equilibrium at potential or full-employment GDP level $\overline{Y}$ and at price level P_0.

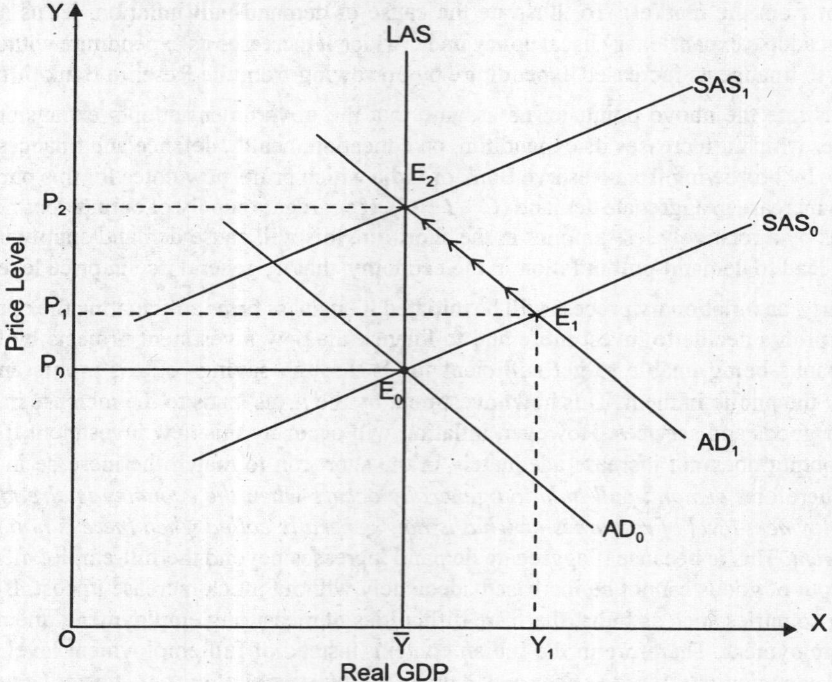

Fig. 22A.1. *Demand-Pull Inflation*

Now suppose without increasing taxes government increases its expenditure on goods and services and finances it by borrowing from the Reserve Bank which in turn prints money for this purpose. As a result of increase in government expenditure, aggregate demand curve shifts to the right to AD_1 which intersects the short-run aggregate supply curve SAS_0 at point E_1 and as a result price level rises to P_1 and real *GDP* to Y_1. It needs to be emphasized that price level has risen as a result of rightward shift in aggregate demand curve to AD_1 because aggregate supply has not increased to the extent of increase in aggregate demand and thereby creating demand-supply imbalances. If short-run aggregate curve had been horizontal line through point E_0, the aggregate supply would have increased by an equal amount to the increase in aggregate demand when aggregate demand curve shifts to right to AD_1. Thus, *the price level has risen because aggregate demand has increased relatively more than the aggregate supply, that is, due to demand-supply imbalances.*

However, the response to the initial increase in aggregate demand to AD_1 does not stop at point E_1. It may be recalled that in drawing short-run aggregate supply curve wage rate of labour is kept constant. Now, the rightward shift in aggregate demand curve to AD_1 has caused the price level to rise from P_0 to P_1 and real gross domestic output (GDP) has risen to Y_1. This rise in price level, the wage rate remaining constant, would cause decline in workers' real wage rate, $\frac{W}{P_1} < \frac{W}{P_0}$ where $P_1 > P_0$. When workers realise that their real wage has fallen as a result of increase in aggregate demand causing rise in price level, they will demand higher wages in their negotiations with their employers which are likely to be conceded to. Further, as pointed out above, equilibrium to the right of potential GDP level $\overline{Y}$ implies that unemployment has fallen below the natural rate of unemployment and will cause shortage of labour which implies wage rate will rise. When wages are raised by the firms short-run aggregate supply curve will shift upward and this process of shifting short-run aggregate supply curve upward will continue until it reaches SAS_1 which cuts the new aggregate demand curve AD_1 at point E_2 that lies at the long-run supply curve *LAS* and as a result price level further rises to P_2. Equilibrium between aggregate demand and aggregate supply with price as P_2 and at point E_2 on the long-run average supply curve *LAC* the wage rate has risen by E_0E_2 equal to the rise in price level by P_0P_2. Thus, real wage has been restored at the level prior to increase in aggregate demand from AD_0 to AD_1. Note that equilibrium and wage rate at point E_1 on the short-run average supply curve will move to point E_2 at the long-run average supply curve not with a single jump but through various steps of wage adjustment and upward shifting of short-run aggregate supply curve. That is why we depicted this movement from point E_1 to point E_2 on the *LAS* through *various* arrows. Note that not only there is shifting upward of short-run average supply curve to restore previous level of real wage rate but also real GDP has returned to potential or full-employment GDP level $\overline{Y}$.

Demand-Pull Inflation Process to Cause Continuous Rise in Price Level

We have explained above the process of demand-pull inflation when for a given increase in aggregate demand, *price level has eventually gone up to price level* P_2 and wages have risen enough to restore the real wage to its previous full-employment level. But, as noted above, *inflation is a continuous increase in the price level and not a one-time jump in the price level in response to a given increase in aggregate demand.* For sustained or persistent inflation to take place the continuous increase in aggregate demand must occur. In our example aggregate demand can persistently increase if a government has a large persistent budget deficit that it finances by borrowing from the Central Bank or alternatively borrowing from the market year after year. Besides, continuous increase in aggregate demand can occur if quantity of money is persistently increased by the Central Bank of the country. In these two cases aggregate demand increases year after year causing price level to rise persistently. This continuous rise in price level is shown in Fig. 22A.2 in which we have assumed that government runs the budget deficit year after year and finances it by borrowing from the Central Bank (that is, government sells its bonds to the Central Bank which prints new money to pay for these bonds).

As a result, aggregate demand increases year after year bringing about continuous rise in price level. Initially, the equilibrium is at point E_0 at which an aggregate demand curve AD_0 intersects long-run aggregate supply curve (*LAS*) as well as short-run aggregate supply curve SAS_0. Now suppose that increase in government expenditure financed by borrowing from the Central Bank shifts aggregate demand curve to AD_1 which intersects the short-run aggregate supply curve SAS_0 at point E_1 raising the price level to P_1. As explained above, with rise in price level to P_1 real wages of labour will fall and they will demand higher wages. As a result of rise in wage rate over a number of stages or steps short-run aggregate supply curve (*SAS*) shifts to the left till it intersects the new aggregate demand curve AD_1 at point E_2 that lies at the long-run aggregate supply curve (*LAS*). With this equal rise in price level and wage rate, real wage rate of workers is restored.

Now suppose next year the government again incurs a budget deficit and finances its further increase in expenditure by borrowing more from the Central Bank. With this aggregate demand curve shifts to the right to AD_2 and cuts the short-run aggregate supply curve SAS_1 at E_3 and causes price level to rise further to P_3 as shown in Fig. 22A.2. The rise in price level will cause the fall in real wage rate of workers who will demand increase in their money wage rate further. When higher money wage rate is conceded to, short-run aggregate supply curve will start shifting to the left and the process will eventually end when short-run aggregate supply curve has shifted to the position SAS_2 which intersects aggregate demand curve AD_2 at point E_4 at which price level has risen to P_4 and with that real wage rate of workers is restored at full-employment level with potential GDP equal to $\overline{Y}$. If government further increases its expenditure next year and finances it by borrowing from the Central Bank, price level will further rise. In this way there is continuous inflation triggered by increase in government expenditure and the operation of wage price spiral under the pressure of increase in aggregate demand. In Fig. 22A.2 we *have traced the rise in price level through arrows as aggregate demand increases and short-run aggregate supply curve shifts to the right as a result of increase in money wage rate.*

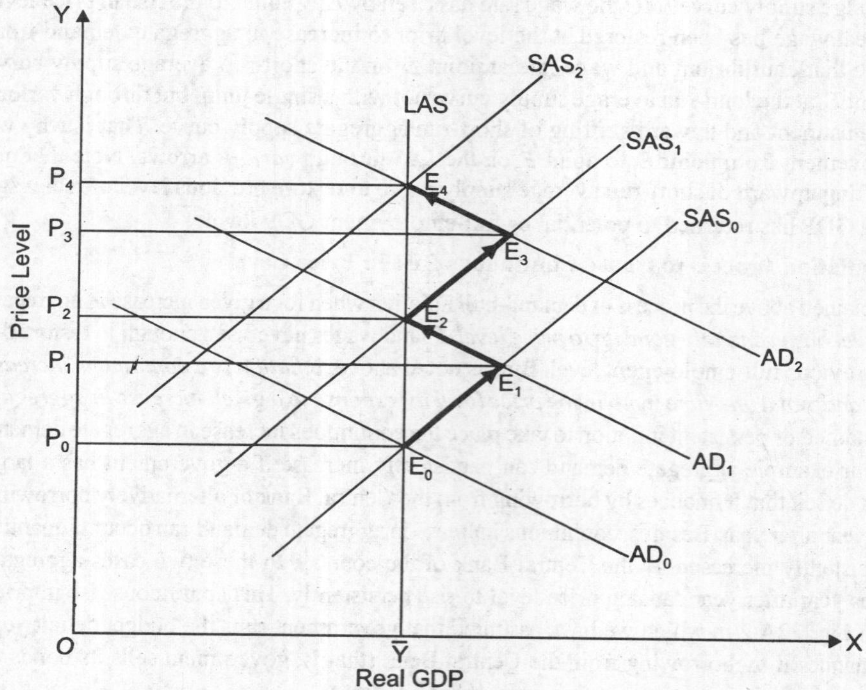

Fig. 22A.2. *Demand-Pull Inflation Process : Persistent Increase in Price Level*

Inflationary Expectations

Inflationary expectations are an important cause of inflation. The expectations of future prices play a significant role in decision-making by firms regarding price and output. If a firm expects that its rival firms will raise their prices, it may also raise its own price in anticipation. Suppose inflation has been occurring at a rate of 8 per cent per annum in the past, a firm will expect this inflation rate to continue in future too and therefore it will raise its price by 8 per cent. If every firm expects that other firms will raise their prices by 8 per cent, every one will raise its prices by 8 per cent. As a result, inflation rate of about 8 per cent will occur. This is how inflationary expectations cause inflation. Elaborating on this, Case and Fair write, "*Expectations can lead to an inertia that makes it difficult to stop an inflationary spiral. If prices have been rising and if people's expectations are adaptive, that is, if they form their expectations on the basis of past pricing behaviour – that firms may continue raising prices even if demand is slowing.*"[1] Therefore, to check inflation, steps should be taken to break the inflationary expectations.

COST-PUSH INFLATION

We can visualise situations where even though there is no increase in aggregate demand, prices may still rise. This may happen if there is initial increase in costs *independent of any increase in aggregate demand.* The four main autonomous increases in costs which generate cost-push inflation have been suggested:

1. *Oil Price Shock*
2. *Farm Price Shock*
3. *Import Price Shock*
4. *Wage-Push Inflation*

Cost-Push inflation is also called *supply-side inflation.*

1. **Oil Price Shock.** In the seventies the supply shocks causing increase in marginal cost of production became more prominent in bringing about cost-push inflation. During the seventies, *rise in prices of energy inputs* (hike in crude oil price made by OPEC resulting in rise in prices of petroleum products). The sharp rise in world oil prices during 1973-75 and again in 1979-80 produced significant supply shocks resulting in cost-push inflation.

   The sharp rise in the price of oil leads to inflation in all oil-importing countries. The rise in oil price also occurred in 1990, 1999-2000 and again in 2003-08 which resulted in rise in rate of inflation in oil-importing countries such as India. In recent years, there have been a good deal of fluctuations in oil prices; in some periods they go up and in some others they go down. It may be noted that rise in oil prices not only gives rise to the increase in inflation, but also adversely affects the balance of payments raising current account deficit of the oil-importing countries such as India.

2. **Farm Price Shock.** Cost-push inflation can also come about from increase in prices of other raw materials, especially farm products, in economies such as that of India where they are of greater importance. In India when monsoon is not adequate or come very late or when weather conditions are quite unfavourable, they reduce the supply of agricultural products and raise their prices. These farm products are raw materials for various industries such as sugar industry, other agro-processing industries, cotton textile industry, jute industry and as a result when prices of farm products rise they lead to rise in prices of goods which use the farm products as raw materials. This is farm price shock causing cost-push inflation. Even rise in food prices or what is called *food inflation* is caused by supply-side factors such as inadequate rainfall or untimely monsoon and other adverse weather conditions and inadequate availability of fertilizers which lead to reduction in output of food grains is the example of cost-push or supply-side inflation.

3. **Import Price Shock.** These days currencies of most countries of the world are *flexible*, that is, determined by demand for and supply of a currency and they can appreciate or depreciate every month in terms of the US dollar. For example, when the Indian rupee depreciates, more rupees are required to buy one US dollar and therefore in terms of rupees, imports become costlier. The Indians who import raw materials for industries such as petroleum products, coal, machines and other equipment, oilseeds, fertilizers, Indian consumers who imports gold, cars and other final products have to pay higher prices in

1. Karl E. Case, and Race C. Fair, *Principles of Economics*, Pearson Education, 6th Edition, 2002,

terms of rupees when Indian rupee depreciates against US dollar. This raises the cost of production of the producers who in turn raise the prices of final products produced by them. *This inflation is the result of import price shock.* Thus depreciation of rupee causes cost-push inflation. For example, in the month of June 2013, there was sharp depreciation of the Indian rupee. The value of rupee fell by about 9.5 per cent in this single month from about ₹ 56 to a US dollar in the first week of June 2013 to around ₹ 61 to a dollar in the last week of June 2013.

4. **Wage Push Inflation.** It has been suggested that the growth of powerful trade unions is responsible for the spread of inflation, especially in the industrialized countries. When trade unions push for higher wages which are not justifiable either on grounds of a prior rise in productivity or of cost of living they produce a cost-push effect. The employers in a situation of high demand and employment are more agreeable to concede to these wage claims because they hope to pass on these rises in costs to the consumers in the form of hike in prices. If this happens we have cost-push inflation. It may be noted that as a result of cost-push effect of higher wages, short-run aggregate supply curve of output shifts to the left and, given the aggregate demand curve, results in higher price of output.

Cost-Push Inflation Spiral

Let us consider Figure 22A.3 where to begin with aggregate demand curve AD_0 and short-run aggregate supply curve SAS_0 intersect at point E_0 and determine price level P_0 and output level Y_0. Further suppose that Y_0 is the full-capacity (*i.e.*, full-employment) level of output and therefore long-run aggregate supply curve *LAS* is vertical at Y_0 level of output. Suppose there is increase in oil prices which causes shifts in short-run aggregate supply curve to the left from SAS_0 to SAS_1. As a result, price level rises to P_1 but output falls from Y_0 to Y_1. With decline in output unemployment will also increase. *Thus cost-push inflation not only causes rise in price level (or inflation) but also brings about fall in GDP level. The rise in price level or inflation and simultaneously fall in GDP level is called* ***stagflation****. Thus cost-push inflation* ***results in stagflation***.

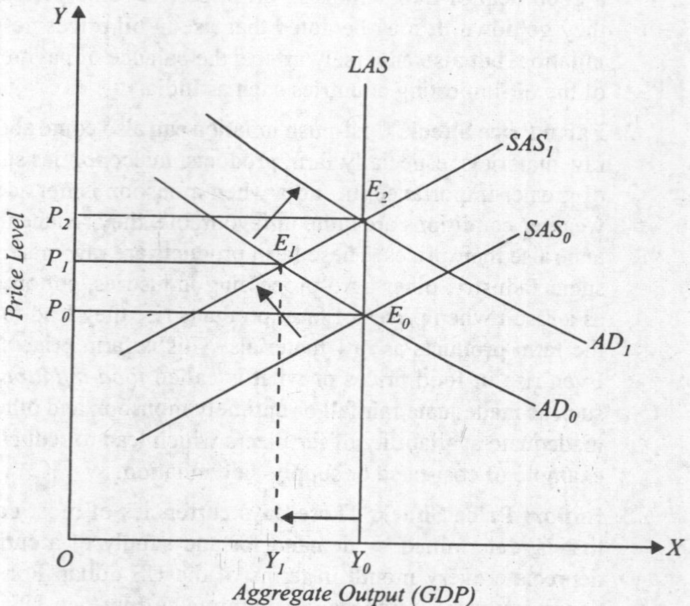

Fig. 22A.3. *Cost-Push Inflation*

When the real GDP decreases as a result of cost-push inflation in the first stage, the unemployment will also rise. When unemployment emerges there is a huge hue and cry by the workers who are rendered unemployed. In such a situation either the Central Bank will respond by increasing the money supply to raise aggregate demand or the government will *increase its expenditure to provide fiscal stimulus to aggregate demand.* As a result of either of these responses, aggregate demand curve shifts to the right from AD_0 to AD_1. With this, the economy moves from equilibrium position E_1 to the equilibrium position E_2. As will be seen from Fig. 22A.3, as a result of this increase in aggregate demand while real GDP has returned to the potential GDP level Y_0, price level has further risen to P_2(that is, more inflation will occur). But the inflationary process of cost-push inflation will not stop at equilibrium point E_2. If there is further rise in any of the cost-push factors such as rise in oil price, increase in price of farm output, import price shock or wage rate increase takes place short-run aggregate supply curve *SAS* will shift further to the left of SAS_1 and intersects the aggregate demand curve AD_1 to the left of the long-run aggregate supply curve *LAS* causing further rise in price level or inflation above P_2 and fall in GDP from the potential level Y_0 *resulting again in unemployment of workers*. To restore full employment and raise GDP to the potential level Y_0, the Central Bank will further increase the money supply or the government will further increase its expenditure. As a result, aggregate demand curve will again shift to the right of AD_1. With this, *GDP* level will be back at the potential level Y_0 and full employment of workers will be restored but price level or inflation will further rise. In this way cost-push inflation spiral will work to cause sustained or persistent inflation.

Many economists think inflation in the economy is generally caused by the interaction of the demand pull-and cost-push factors. The inflation may be started in the first instance either by cost-push factors or by demand-pull factors, both work and interact to cause sustained inflation over time. Thus, according to Machlup, "There cannot be a thing as cost-push inflation because without an increase in purchasing power and demand, cost increases will lead to unemployment and depression, not to inflation".[2] Likewise, Cairncross writes, "*There is no need to pretend that demand and cost inflation do not interact or that excess demand does not aggrevate wage inflation, of course it does.*"[3]

MONETARIST THEORY OF INFLATION

We have explained above the Keynesian theory of demand-pull inflation. It is important to note that both the original quantity theorists and *the modern monetarists, prominent among whom is Milton Friedman, also explain inflation in terms of excess demand for goods and services*. But there is an important difference between the monetarist view of demand-pull inflation and the Keynesian view of it. Keynes explained inflation as arising out of real sector forces. In his model of inflation excess demand comes into being as a result of *autonomous* increase in expenditure on investment or consumption, or increase in government expenditure on goods and services, that is, the increase in aggregate expenditure or demand occurs independent of any increase in the supply of money.

On the other hand, monetarists explain the emergence of excess demand and the resultant rise in prices on account of the increase in money supply in the economy. To quote Friedman, "*Inflation is always and everywhere a monetary phenomenon........ and can be produced only by a more rapid increase in the quantity of money than in output*".[4]

Friedman holds that when money supply is increased in the economy, then there emerges an excess supply of real money balances with the public over the demand for money. This disturbs the equilibrium. In order to restore the equilibrium, the public will reduce the money balances by increasing expenditure on goods and services. Thus, according to Friedman and other modern quantity theorists, the excess supply of real monetary balances results in the increase in aggregate demand for goods and services. If there is no proportionate increase in output, then extra money supply leads to excess demand for goods and services. This causes inflation or rise in prices. The whole argument can be presented in the following scheme:

$$M^S > kPY \rightarrow AD\uparrow \rightarrow P\uparrow \qquad ...(1)$$

2. Fritz Machlup, "Another View of Cost-Push and Demand-Pull Inflation" in *Review of Economics and Statistics*, Vol. 42, 1960.
3. Alec Cairncross, *Inflation Growth and International Trade*, George Allen and Unwin, 1975.
4. See N.G. Mankiw, *Principles of Economics*, Second Edition, p. 6.41

where M^S stands for quantity of money and P for the price level. Therefore, $\frac{M^S}{P}$ represents real cash balances. Y stands for national income and k for the ratio of income which people want to keep in cash balances. Hence kPY represents demand for cash balances (*i.e.*, demand for money), AD represents aggregate demand for or aggregate expenditure on goods and services which is composed of consumption demand (C) and investment demand (I).

In the above scheme it will be seen that when the supply of money (M^S) is increased, it creates excess supply of real cash balances. This is expressed by $M^S > kPY$. This excess supply of real money balances leads to (→) the rise (↑) in aggregate demand (AD). Then increase (↑) in aggregate demand (AD) leads to (→) the rise (↑) in prices (P).

Friedman's monetarist theory of inflation can be better explained with quantity equation $\left(P = \frac{MV}{Y} = \frac{M}{Y} \cdot \frac{1}{k}\right)$ written in percentage form which is written as below taking V or k as constant

$$\frac{\Delta P}{P} = \frac{\Delta M^S}{M^S} - \frac{\Delta Y}{Y} \qquad ...(2)$$

where $\frac{\Delta P}{P}$ is the rate of inflation, $\frac{\Delta M^S}{M^S}$ is the rate of growth of money supply and $\frac{\Delta Y}{Y}$ is the rate of growth of output. Thus, according to equation (2), rate of inflation $\left(\frac{\Delta P}{P}\right)$ is determined by growth of money supply $\left(\frac{\Delta M^S}{M}\right)$ and rate of growth of output $\left(\frac{\Delta Y}{Y}\right)$, with velocity of circulation (V) or k remaining constant. Friedman and other monetarists claim that *inflation* is predominantly a monetary phenomenon which implies that changes in velocity and output are small.

It thus follows that when money supply increases, it causes disturbance in the equilibrium, that is, $M^S > kPY$. According to Friedman and other monetarists, the reaction of the people would be to spend the excess money supply on goods and services so as to bring money supply in equilibrium with the demand for money. This leads to the increase in aggregate demand or expenditure on goods and services which, k remaining constant, will lead to the increase in *nominal* national income (PY). They further argue that the real national income or aggregate output (*i.e.*, Y in the demand for money function stated above) remains stable at full-employment level in the long run due to the flexibility of wages. Therefore, according to Friedman and his followers (modern monetarists), in the long run, the increase in nominal national income (PY) brought about by the expansion in money supply and resultant increase in aggregate demand will cause a proportional increase in the price level.

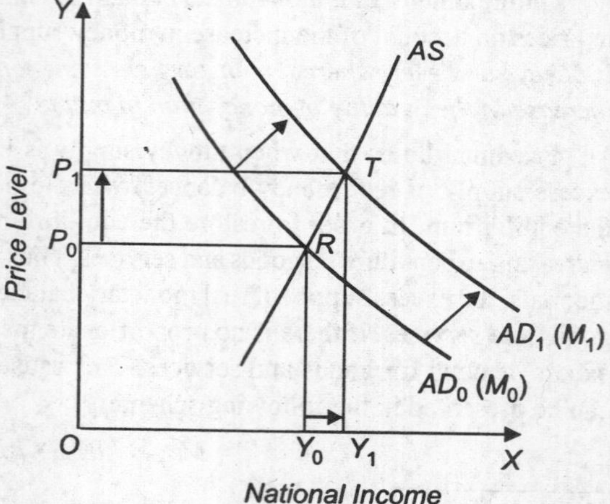

Fig. 22A.4. *The effect of expansion in money supply in the short run is split up into price rise and increase in Real National Income: Friedman's Monetarist Approach.*

However, in the short run, like Keynesians, they believe that the economy may be working at less than full employment, that is, in the short run there may prevail excess capacity and unemployment of labour so that expansion in money supply and consequent increase in nominal income partly induces expansion in real income (Y) and partly results in rise in the price level as shown in Fig. 22A.4. To what extent price level increases depends upon the elasticity of supply or aggregate output in the short run. It will be seen from Fig. 22A.4 that effect of increase in money supply from M_0 to M_1 and resultant increase in aggregate demand curve for goods and services from AD_0 to AD_1 is split up into the rise in price level (from P_0 to P_1) and the increase in real income or aggregate output (from Y_0 to Y_1).

It should be noted that Friedman and other modern quantity theorists believe that in the short run full employment of labour and other resources may not prevail due to recessionary conditions and, therefore, they admit the possibilities of increase in output. But they emphasise that in the short run when the growth in money supply is greater than the growth in output, the result is excess demand for goods and services which causes rise in prices or demand-pull inflation.

It follows from above that both Friedman and Keynesians explain inflation in terms of excess demand for goods and services. Whereas Keynesians explain the emergence of excess demand due to the increase in *autonomous expenditure,* independent of any increase in money supply. Friedman explains that inflation is caused by *proportionately greater increase in money supply than the increase in aggregate output.* In both views inflation is of demand-pull variety.

Money and Sustained Inflation

Many economists believe in the monetarist view of inflation. Increase in money shifts the aggregate demand curve to the right and if the economy is operating at full capacity (*i.e.,* along the vertical part of the aggregate supply curve), the upward shift in aggregate demand curve will cause price level to rise. A big drawback of this approach is that it assumes that supply of output does not increase sufficiently to counter this effect of expansion in money supply on aggregate demand. In this context there is a need to distinguish between a *one-time increase* in the price level and *sustained inflation* which occurs when the general price level continues to rise over a long period of time. It is generally believed by most of the economists that whatever be the initial cause of inflation (demand-pull, cost-push or inflationary expectations), for the price level to continue rising, period after period, it must be *accommodated* by expansion in money supply. *Sustained inflation is therefore considered as a purely monetary phenomenon.* It is not possible for the price level to continue rising if the money supply remains constant. The increase in money supply continues shifting the aggregate demand curve to the right; if aggregate supply does not increase sufficiently to match the increase in aggregate demand, price level will continue rising.

Sustained inflation can be better understood when Government increases its expenditure without raising taxes. This leads to the increase in aggregate demand which, *aggregate supply remaining constant,* will cause a rise in price level. It is important to know what happens when the price level rises. The higher price level raises the demand for money to rise for transaction purposes. With supply of money remaining constant, the greater demand for money causes interest rate to rise. The rise in interest rate *crowds out* private investment. If the Central Bank of a country wants to prevent the fall in the private investment, it will expand the money supply to keep the interest constant. But this expansion in money supply through its effect on aggregate demand will cause the price level to rise further if increase in more supply of output is not possible. This further rise in price level will again cause greater demand for money leading to higher interest rate. And the Central Bank, if it is committed to keep the interest rate constant so that private investment does not decline, will further expand the money supply which will cause further inflation. This process could lead to *hyperinflation* which represents *a rapid* and *continuous rise in price level,* period after period. The historical experience shows this hyperinflation in some countries when the Central Bank or Government of these countries kept pumping in more and more money either to finance its persistent budget deficit of the government year after year or to prevent the interest rate to rise. However, as mentioned above, hyperinflation disrupts the payment system and people's loss of credibility of the currency. This leads to a deep crisis in the economy. If hyperinflation is to be avoided, then the process of rapid expansion in money supply must be halted.

STRUCTURALIST THEORY OF INFLATION

Structuralist theory, another important theory of inflation, is also known as *structural theory of inflation* and explains inflation in the developing countries in a slightly different way. The structuralists argue that increase in investment expenditure and the expansion of money supply to finance it are the only proximate and not the ultimate factors responsible for inflation in the developing countries. According to them, one should go deeper into the question as to why aggregate output, especially of foodgrains, has not been increasing sufficiently in the developing countries to match the increase in demand brought about by the increase in investment expenditure and money supply. Further, they argue why investment expenditure has not been fully financed by voluntary savings and as a result excessive deficit financing has been done.[5]

Structuralist theory of inflation has been put forward as an explanation of inflation in the developing countries especially of Latin America. The well-known economists, Myrdal and Streeten[6], who have proposed this theory have analysed inflation in these developing countries in terms of structural features of their economies. Recently Kirkpatrick and Nixon have generalised this structural theory of inflation as an explanation of inflation prevailing in all developing countries.[7]

Myrdal and Streeten have argued that it is not correct to apply the highly aggregative demand-supply model for explaining inflation in the developing countries. According to them, there is a lack of balanced integrated structure in them where substitution possibilities between consumption and production and inter-sectoral flows of resources between different sectors of the economy are not quite smooth and quick so that inflation in them cannot be reasonably explained in terms of aggregate demand and aggregate supply. In this connection it is noteworthy that Prof. V.N. Pandit of Delhi School of Economics has also felt the need for distinguishing price behaviour in the Indian agricultural sector from that in the manufacturing sector.[8]

Thus, it has been argued by the exponents of structuralist theory of inflation that economies of the developing countries of Latin America and India are structurally underdeveloped as well as highly fragmented due to the existence of market imperfections and structural rigidities of various types. The result of these structural imbalances and rigidities is that whereas in some sectors of these developing countries we find shortages of supply relative to demand, in others underutilisation of resources and excess capacity exist due to lack of demand. According to structuralists, these structural features of the developing countries make the aggregate demand-supply model of inflation inapplicable to them. They therefore argue for analysing disaggregative and sectoral demand-supply imbalances to explain inflation in the developing countries. They mention various sectoral constraints or bottlenecks which generate the sectoral imbalances and lead to rise in prices. Therefore, to explain the origin and propagation of inflation in the developing countries, the forces which generate these bottlenecks or imbalances of various types in the process of economic development need to be analysed. A study of these bottlenecks is therefore essential for explaining inflation in the developing countries. These bottlenecks are of three types : (1) Agricultural bottlenecks which make supply of agricultural products inelastic, (2) resources constraint or Government budget constraint, and (3) foreign exchange bottleneck. Let us explain briefly how these structural bottlenecks cause inflation in the developing countries.

---

5. G.Myrdal, *Asian Drama, An Enquiry into the Poverty of Nations,* 1968, Penguin Books.
6. P. Streeten, *The Frontiers of Development Studies*, 1972, London, MacMillan.
7. C. Kirkpatrick and F. Nixon, "Inflation and Stabilisation Policy in LDC's" in N. Gemmel (ed.), *Surveys in Development Economics,* 1987, Basil, Blackwell.
8. See V.N. Pandit, "An Analysis of Inflation in India, 1950-75," *Indian Economic Review,* Vol. 22, 1978

Agricultural Bottlenecks. The first and foremost bottlenecks faced by the developing countries relate to agriculture and they prevent supply of food grains to increase adequately. Of special mention of the structural factors are disparities in land ownership, defective land tenure system which act as disincentives for raising agricultural production in response to increasing demand for them arising from increase in people's incomes, growth in population and urbanisation. Besides, use of backward agricultural technology also hampers agricultural growth. Thus, in order to control inflation, these bottlenecks have to be removed so that agricultural output grows rapidly to meet the increasing demand for it in the process of economic development.

Resources Gap or Government's Budget Constraint. Another important bottleneck mentioned by structuralists relates to the lack of resources for financing economic development. In the developing countries planned efforts are being made by the Government to industrialise their economies. This requires large resources to finance public sector investment in various industries. For example, in India, huge amount of resources were used for investment in basic heavy industries started in the public sector. But socio-economic and political structure of these countries is such that it is not possible for the Government to raise enough resources through taxation, borrowing from the public, surplus generation in the public sector enterprises for investment in the projects of economic development. Revenue raising from taxation has been relatively very small due to low tax base, large scale tax evasion, inefficient and corrupt tax administration. Consequently, the government has been forced to resort to excessive deficit financing (that is, creation of new currency) which has caused excessive growth in money supply relative to increase in output year after year and has therefore resulted in inflation in the developing countries. Though rapid growth of money supply is the proximate cause of inflation, it is not the proper and adequate explanation of inflation in these economies. For proper explanation of inflation one should go deeper and enquire into the operation of structural forces which have caused excessive growth in money supply in these developing economies. Besides, resources gap in the private sector due to inadequate voluntary savings and underdevelopment of the capital market have led to their larger borrowings from the banking system which has created excessive bank credit for it. This has greatly countributed to the growth of money supply in the developing countries and has caused rise in prices. Thus, Kirkpatrick and Nixon write, "The increase in the supply of money was a permissive factor which allowed the inflationary spiral to manifest itself and become cumulative—it was a system of the structural rigidities which give rise to the inflationary pressures rather than the cause of inflation itself."[9]

Foreign Exchange Bottleneck. The other important bottleneck which the developing countries have to encounter is the shortage of foreign exchange for financing needed imports for development. In the developing countries ambitious programme of industrialisation is being undertaken. Industrialisation requires heavy imports of capital goods, essential raw materials and in some cases, as in India, even food grains have been imported. Besides, imports of oil on a large scale are being made. On account of all these imports, import expenditure of the developing countries has been rapidly increasing. On the other hand, due to lack of export surplus, restrictions imposed by the developing countries, relatively low competitiveness of exports, the growth of exports of the developed countries has been sluggish. As a result of sluggish exports and mounting imports, the developing countries have been facing balance of payment difficulties and shortage of foreign exchange which at times has assumed crisis proportions. This has affected the price level in two ways. First, due to foreign exchange shortage domestic availability of goods in short supply could not be increased which led to the rise in their prices. Secondly, in Latin American countries as well as in India and Pakistan, to solve the problem of foreign exchange shortage through encouraging exports and reducing imports devaluation in the national currencies had to be made. But this devaluation caused rise in prices of imported goods and materials which further raised the prices of other goods as well due to cascading effect. This brought about cost-push inflation in their economies.

---

9. *Op. cit.*

Physical Infrastructural Bottlenecks. Further, the structuralists point out various *bottlenecks* such as lack of infrastructural facilities, *i.e.*, lack of power, transport and fuel which stands in the way of adequate growth in output. At present in India, there is acute shortage of these infrastructural inputs which are hampering growth of output. Sluggish growth of output on the one hand, and excessive growth of money supply on the other have caused what is now called *stagflation*, that is inflation which exists along with stagnation or slow economic growth.

According to the structuralist school of thought, the *above bottlenecks and constraints are rooted in the social, political and economic structure of these countries*. Therefore, in its view a broad-based strategy of development which aims to bring about social, institutional and structural changes in these economies is needed to bring about economic growth without inflation. Further, many structuralists argue for giving higher priority to agriculture in the strategy of development if price stability is to be ensured. Thus, we see that structuralist view is greatly relevant for explaining inflation in the developing countries and for the adoption of measures to control it. Let us further elaborate the causes of inflation in the developing countries.

THE SOCIAL COSTS AND EFFECTS OF INFLATION

Having discussed the so called inflation fallacy we proceed to explain in detail the social cost and effects of inflation. Apart from reducing the purchasing power of people's incomes, inflation inflicts some other costs on the society. To explain such costs of inflation it is necessary to distinguish between anticipated inflation and unanticipated (*i.e.,* unexpected) inflation. As noted above, in case of anticipated inflation, the expected rise in price level is taken into account while making economic transactions, for example, in negotiating wage rate of labour etc.

Costs of Anticipated Inflation

Suppose in an economy there has been annual inflation rate of 5 per cent for a long time in the past and everybody expects that this 5 per cent rate of inflation will continue in the future too. In such a case all contracts made by the people such as loan agreements with borrowers, wage contracts with labour, property lease contracts will provide for 5 per cent annual rise in rates of interest, wages, rent to compensate for inflation of that order. That is, in any contract in which passage of time is involved 5 per cent rate of inflation will be taken into account and rates will be agreed to rise per period equal to the anticipated rate of inflation. If rates of interest, wages, rent etc are agreed to rise at the anticipated rate of inflation, then there will be no cost of inflation except the following two types of costs – shoe-leather costs and menu costs which are not very high. We explain below both these types of costs.

1. **Shoe-leather Costs.** This type of cost occurs because on account of inflation cost of holding money in the form of currency (*i.e.,* notes and coins) rises with the increase in inflation rate. Such cost arises because no interest is paid on holding currency, while money kept in deposits with the bank or used for keeping bonds earns interest. When inflation rate rises, the nominal interest rate on bank deposits rises, the interest lost by holding currency by the people therefore increases. In order to reduce the cost of holding currency people will tend to reduce their holdings of currency for transaction purposes. Accordingly, at a time people will hold less currency with them and keep as long as possible greater amount of money in bank deposits that yield interest. Therefore, rather than withdrawing a large amount of currency from banks at a time, they will withdraw less money which is sufficient for meeting daily expenses for a few days, say for a week. But for doing so the people will make more trips to withdraw cash. More trips to a bank in a month involves greater cost to the people. These costs have to be incurred on spending on petrol if car is used for making trips, more wear and tear of car, the time spent for making a trip. These costs of making more trips to

the bank for withdrawing currency is metaphorically called *shoe-leather costs* of inflation, as walking to banks more often one's shoes wear out more rapidly and one has to spend money on new shoes more often.

2. **Menu Costs.** The second type of anticipated inflation is menu costs, a term derived from a restaurant's cost of printing a new menu. Menu costs arise because high inflation requires them to change their listed prices more often. Changing prices is somewhat more expensive because the firms have to print new catalogues listing new prices and distribute them among their customers. They have even to incur expenditure on advertisements to inform the public about their new prices.
3. **Macroeconomic Inefficiency in Resource Allocation.** A third cost of inflation arises because firms having menu costs change their prices quite infrequently. Given the reluctance to change prices frequently, the higher the rate of inflation, the greater the variability in relative prices of a firm. Suppose a firm issues a new catalogue listing prices of its products once in a year, say in the month of January of every year. If during the year inflation occurs, there will be change in the relative prices of a firm to the general price level. If inflation rate of one per cent per month takes place in a year the firm's relative prices to the general price level will *fall* by 12 per cent by the end of the year. As a result, his sales will tend to be lower in the early part of the year (when its prices are relatively high) and higher in the later part of the year (when its prices are relatively low). Thus when due to inflation relative prices of a firm vary during a year as compared to the overall price level, it causes distortion in production and therefore leads to microeconomic inefficiencies in resource allocation.[10]
4. **Inconvenience of Living.** Lastly, another social cost of inflation is the *inconvenience of living* in a world with a changing price level. Money is the yardstick with which we measure the value of transactions. When inflation is taking place the value of money changes and as a result it becomes difficult to correctly estimate the value of transactions in real terms every time a transaction is made during a year. The rising price level makes it difficult to make optimal decisions about saving and investment and thus do the rational financial planning covering a long period of time. To quote Mankiw, "A dollar saved today and invested at a fixed nominal interest rate will yield a fixed dollar amount in the future. Yet the real value of that dollar amount – which will determine the retiree's living standard – depends on the future price level. *Deciding how much to save would be much simpler* if people could count on the price level in 30 years being similar to its level today."[11]

Conclusion. Taking account of all costs of anticipated inflation one finds that the cost of anticipated inflation are quite small or trivial and if these alone are considered, it is then surprising why inflation is a matter of serious concern for the policy makers and politicians. In our opinion the above view of costs of inflation does not consider the true cost of inflation which, as mentioned above, refers to the reduction in purchasing power or real incomes of the people which lowers their standard of living. Besides, there is ample cross-country evidence that *high rates of inflation lead to low rate of sustained economic growth.*[12]

It may be further noted that in the above analysis of cost of inflation it is assumed that there is only small to moderate inflation rate, say a single digit rate of inflation occurs so that it does not disrupt the payment system. With such a low to moderate inflation, costs of inflation are small. The

---

10. Mankiw, *op. cit.*, p. 98.
11. Stanley Fishcher, "Macroeconomic Factors in Economic Growth", *Journal of Monetary Economics*, Dec. 1993.
12. See D. Felix, "Profit Inflation and Industrial Growth, *Quarterly Journal of Economics*, August 1956, pp. 441-63 and E.J. Hamilton, "Prices as a Factor in Business Growth", *Journal of Economic History*, December 1952, pp. 325-49.

hyperinflation has more harmful effect as it disrupts the payment system which leads to the collapse of the economy.

Cost of Unanticipated Inflation

Unanticipated inflation has a more substantial and harmful effect as compared to the cost of anticipated inflation rate. The significant effect of unanticipated inflation is that it *arbitrarily re-distributes wealth* among individuals. Consider the value of assets fixed in nominal terms. Between 1995 and 2006, price level in India rose by about 100 per cent. This implies that those who held *claims on assets fixed in nominal terms in 1996*, their real value in terms of purchasing power would have declined significantly. Thus, a person who bought government bond of 10 years maturity with a face value of ₹ 1000 bearing 8 per cent nominal interest rate in 1996 will find that ₹ 1000 he gets back in 2006 has far less value than when he purchased the bond in 1996.

Similarly, unanticipated inflation harms the individuals, who retire on pensions fixed in rupee terms. After some years of inflation, the real value or purchasing power of the fixed nominal pension will greatly decline and will therefore reduce his standard of living in his old age. Thus inflation hurts individuals with fixed pensions. Workers and the private firms often agree on fixed nominal pension payable to the workers after retirement. Workers are greatly harmed when inflation is higher than anticipated. Likewise, higher than anticipates a inflation rate hurts the creditors who give loans to the others and get back the principal amount after the stipulated period. Thus *inflation redistributes wealth in favour of debtors*.

Bad Effects of Inflation on Long-term Economic Growth : An Important Social Cost of Inflation

An important social cost of inflation, especially in developing countries, is its bad effect on long-run economic growth. Some economists have argued that inflation of a creeping or mild variety has a tonic effect on the long-run economic growth. In their support they give the example of today's industrialised countries in the Eighteenth and Nineteenth Centuries when the rate of growth of output had been more rapid during long periods of inflation witnessed in these countries. The driving force in the process of economic growth, according to them, has been *high profit margins* created by inflation. They argue that wages lag behind the rise in general price level and thus creating higher profit margins for businessmen and industrialists. This tends to increase the profit share in national income. The businessmen and industrialists who receive profits as income belong to the upper income brackets whose propensity to save is higher as compared to the workers. As a result, savings go up which ensures higher rate of investment. With greater rate of investment more accumulation of capital is made possible. More rapid capital accumulation generates a higher rate of long-run economic growth.

Looking at the problem from an alternative angle, with wages lagging behind rise in prices, inflation causes a large shift of resources away from the production of consumer goods for the wage earners to the production of capital goods. The higher rate of expansion in capital stock raises the growth of productive capacity of the economy and productivity of labour. This generates rapid economic growth.

However, it is now widely recognised that, far from encouraging savings and generating higher rate of economic growth, inflation slows down the rate of capital accumulation. There are several reasons responsible for this. First, as seen above, when due to rapid inflation value of money is declining, people will not like to keep money with themselves and will, therefore, be eager to spend it before its value goes down heavily. This raises their consumption demand and therefore lowers their saving. Besides, people find that the rapid inflation will erode the real value of their savings. This discourages them to save. Thus, *inflation or rapid rise in prices serves as a disincentive to save.* Further, as a consequence of the rise in prices, a relatively greater part of the income of the people is spent on consumption to maintain their level of living and therefore little is left to be saved. Thus, not only does inflation reduce the willingness to save, it also slashes their ability to save.

Secondly, *inflation or rising prices lead to unproductive form of investment* in gold, jewellery, real estate, construction of houses etc. These unproductive forms of wealth do not add to the productive capacity of the economy and are quite useless from the viewpoint of economic growth. Thus, inflation may lead to more investment but much of this is of unproductive type. In this way economic surplus is frittered away in unproductive investment.

Thirdly, a highly undesirable consequence of inflation, especially in developing countries, is that *it accentuates the problem of poverty in these countries*. It is often said inflation is enemy number one of the poor people. Due to rising prices poor people are not able to meet their basic needs and maintain minimum subsistence level of consumption. Thus inflation sends many people to live below the poverty line with the result that the number of people living below the poverty line increases. Besides, due to inflation, consumption of a large number of poor people is reduced much below what may be regarded as *productive consumption*, that is, essential consumption required to maintain health and productive efficiency. In India, rapid inflation in recent years is as much responsible for the mounting number of people below the poverty line as the lack of employment opportunities.

Fourthly, *inflation adversely affects balance of payments* and thereby hampers economic growth, especially in the developing countries. When prices of domestic goods rise due to inflation, they cannot compete abroad and as a consequence exports of a country are discouraged. On the other hand, when domestic prices rise relatively to prices of foreign goods, imports of foreign goods increase. Thus, falling exports and rising imports create disequilibrium in the balance of payments which may, in the long run, result in a foreign exchange crisis. The shortage of foreign exchange prevents the country to import even essential materials and capital goods needed for industrial growth of the economy. The Indian experience during 1988-92 when foreign exchange reserves declined to abysmally low level and created an economic crisis in the country, shows the validity of this argument.

There is no agreement among economists whether or not moderate or mild inflation encourages saving and therefore ensures higher rate of capital accumulation and economic growth. However, there is complete unanimity that a rapid inflation discourages saving and hinders economic growth. However, barring the special case of hyperinflation, whether or not saving is encouraged by inflation depends on whether there exists *wage lag*. While there is sufficient evidence in the industrialised countries such as the U.S.A., Great Britain, France etc., about the existence of wage lag in the period *before World War II*, in the period after this there is no solid evidence of it. In the present wages quickly catch up with the rising prices. Indeed, there is evidence in some developed countries that the share of profits in national income has declined and that of wages has gone up during the post-World War II period. Therefore, "To the extent that rate of long-run economic growth depends on the rate of capital accumulation, *a major basis for the conclusion that inflation promotes rapid economic growth is undermined given that wages no longer lag during inflation as they apparently did in time of past*."[13]

However, it may be noted that in the developing countries like India where labour is mostly unorganised and trade unions of labour are not strong and further there is a lack of information which causes wages lagging behind prices during periods of inflation. This itself will cause greater proportion of national income going to profits and other business incomes which should ensure higher saving rate. However, in India, businessmen are prone to make unproductive investment in speculative activities, gold, jewellery, real estate and palatial houses whose prices rise rapidly during periods of inflation. Such kind of investment is not only counter-productive and anti-growth but is repugnant to social justice as it further accentuates inequalities in the distribution of income and wealth.

It follows from above that rising prices as a goal of monetary policy are full of disastrous consequences for the economy and the people and therefore cannot be recommended as a desirable

13. E. Shapiro, *Macroeconomic Analysis*, Harcourt, Fourth Edition, 1978, p. 443 (*Italics added*)

goal for the economic policy. Rising prices often get out of hand and hyperinflation might set in which will shake the confidence of the people in the monetary and fiscal system of the country.

FURTHER BAD EFFECTS OF INFLATION

Inflation is a very unpopular happening in an economy. Opinion surveys conduted in India, the U.S.A. and other countries reveal that inflation is the most important concern of the people as it badly affects their standard of living. The political fortunes of many political leaders (Prime Ministers and Presidents) and Governments in India and abroad have been determined by how far they have succeeded in tackling the problem of inflation. So much so that some American presidential candidates called '*inflation as enemy number one*'. Same is the case in India where inflation is the most hotly debated issue during the general elections for Parliament and Assemblies. A high rate of inflation makes the life of the poor very miserable. It is, therefore, described as anti-poor. It redistributes income and wealth in favour of some and greatly harms others. By making the rich richer and the poor poorer, it militates against social justice. Besides, inflation lowers national output and employment and impedes long-run economic growth, especially in developing countries like India. We shall discuss below all these effects of inflation.

Anticipated and Unanticipated Inflation

The difference between anticipated inflation and unanticipated inflation is of crucial importance as the effects of inflation, especially its redistributive effect, depend on whether it is anticipated or not. If rate of inflation is anticipated, then people take steps to make suitable adjustments in their contracts to avoid the adverse effects which inflation could bring to them. For example, if a worker correctly anticipates the rate of inflation in a particular year to be equal to 10 per cent and if his present wage rate is ₹5000 per month, he can enter into contract with the employer that to compensate for the 10 per cent rise in prices his money wage per month next year be raised by 10 per cent so that next year he gets ₹ 5500 per month. In this way he has been able to prevent the erosion of his real income with the automatic revision of his money wage depending on the anticipated rate of inflation.

Take another example. You lend ₹ 10,000 to a person at a rate of 10 per cent per annum. After a year you will receive ₹ 11,000. But if it is anticipated that during the year there will be 8 per cent rate of inflation, then 8 per cent of your income will be offset by the rise in prices that would occur so that you will get only 2 *per cent real rate of interest*. Therefore, in order to receive 10 per cent real rate of interest, in view of 8 per cent anticipated inflation rate you must demand 18 per cent nominal rate of interest.

On the other hand, effects of unanticipated inflation are unavoidable because in this case you do not know what would be the rise in the price level. That is, unanticipated inflation catches you by surprise. In what follows we shall examine the *effects of unanticipated inflation*. The effects of inflation can be divided into three categories:

Inflation Erodes Real Incomes of the People

To examine the effect of inflation it is important to note the difference between money income and real income. It is the change in the general price level that creates the crucial difference between the two. Money income or what is also called nominal income means the income such as wages, interest, rent *received in terms of rupees*. On the other hand, *real income* implies the amount of goods and services which you can buy. In other words, real income means the purchasing power of your income. If your money or nominal income increases at a lower rate than the rate of rise in the general price level (*i.e.*, the rate of inflation), you will be able to buy less goods and services, that is, your real income will decline. Real income will rise only if nominal income rises faster than the rate of inflation. For illustration, take the case of workers who enter into contract with their employer at an agreed wage rate of ₹ 5000 per month for the period, say 5 years. Now, suppose the rate of inflation is 10 per cent per annum. This means after a year, with money wage rate of ₹ 5,000 workers will be able to buy less goods and services. That is, their real income will decrease and therefore their standard of living will fall.

Take another example. Suppose you deposit your saving of ₹100 in a saving account which carries 5 per cent rate of interest. After a year you will receive ₹ 105. However, if during that year rate of inflation has been 12 per cent, you will be a loser in real terms. In fact your real interest-income will be negative as, with 12 per cent rate of inflation, ₹ 105 after a year will buy less goods and services than what you can purchase with ₹ 100 today.

The above two examples clearly show that inflation reduces the purchasing power of money and thereby adversely affects real income of the people.

Effect on Distribution of Income and Wealth

An important effect of inflation is that it redistributes income and wealth in favour of some at the cost of others. Inflation adversely affects those who receive relatively fixed incomes and benefits businessmen, producers, traders and others who enjoy flexible incomes. Inflation brings windfall profits for the producers and traders. Thus, all do not lose as a result of inflation, rather some gain from it. We examine below how inflation redistributes income and wealth and thereby harms some people and benefits others.

Creditors and Debtors. Unanticipated inflation harms creditors and benefits debtors and in this way redistributes income in favour of the latter. As explained above, value of money declines due to inflation. For creditors (including financial institutions such as banks and insurance companies) who enter into agreement with the borrowers to provide loans at fixed nominal rate of interest, the real value of money in terms of goods and services which they will receive at the end of the period would be much less if during the period prices rise sharply. Thus, the debtors or borrowers gain because they would return the loan-money when its real value has declined greatly due to the unexpected rapid rate of inflation.

Fixed Income Groups. Those who get fixed incomes and pensioners stand to lose from inflation. Workers and salaried people who earn fixed wages and salaries are hit hard by unanticipated inflation. These people often enter into contract with the employers regarding wages or salaries fixed in nominal terms. When inflation occurs, the purchasing power of their nominal incomes falls greatly causing a decline in their levels of living. Thus, when inflation persists for some years there are demands for revision of wages and salaries. It may be mentioned that now-a-days workers and other salaried people get dearness allowances to compensate them for the rise in cost of living due to inflation. However, these dearness allowances do not fully neutralise the rise in price level and therefore they also demand revision of wages and pay scales.

Businessmen : Producers and Traders. Businessmen, that is, entrepreneurs and traders, stand to gain by inflation. During periods of inflation, the prices of goods produced by entrepreneurs rise relatively faster than the cost of production because wages lag behind the rise in prices of goods. Consequently, *inflation increases the profits of businessmen*. The value of the inventories or stocks of goods and materials kept by the entrepreneurs and traders increases due to rise in prices of goods which brings about an increase in their profits.

Wealth Holders of Cash, Bonds and Debentures. Inflation also adversely affects wealth holders who hold their wealth in the form of cash money, demand deposits, saving and fixed deposits and interest-bearing bonds and debentures. These wealth holders are severely hurt by inflation as inflation reduces the real value of their wealth. Saving and demand deposits, bonds and debentures represent assets whose value is fixed in terms of money. The rise in prices reduces the purchasing power of these fixed-value money assets such as saving and time deposits, bonds and debentures which bear a fixed nominal rate of interest.

Inflation, therefore, reduces the real rate of interest earned by them. Consequently, it has been observed that during periods of rapid inflation people try to convert their holdings of money and near money into goods and physical property so as to avoid the loss due to inflation. It may also be noted that if inflation is anticipated and all expect equal rates of inflation the nominal rates of interest are adjusted upward so as to obtain targeted real rate of interest. Thus, if creditors want real rate of interest equal to 10 per cent and anticipate rate of inflation is equal to 8 per cent, they will try to have nominal rate of interest fixed at 18 per cent. This is known as **Fischer effect** *which states that market or nominal rate of interest is equal to the real rate of interest (based on productivity of capital and rate of time preference) plus the anticipated rate of inflation*. Thus nominal rate of inflation includes what is called *inflation premium* to prevent the erosion of purchasing power due to inflation.

Loss of Economic Efficiency

It is generally believed that inflation causes misallocation of resources and therefore results in loss of economic efficiency. Inflation causes distortions in prices which misallocate resources and result in inefficiency. This distortion in prices occurs because, as a result of inflation, all prices do not rise to the same extent so that there are changes in relative prices. It may be noted that price distortions occur when prices deviate from right prices as determined by costs and demand conditions. An important example of price distortion caused by inflation is the *change in real rate of interest* which is the price for the use of money. As explained above, real rate of interest is money rate of interest minus the rate of inflation. Currency and demand deposits generally do not earn any interest, that is, money rate of interest on currency and demand deposits is zero. However, when there is inflation, say at the rate of 12 per cent per annum, the real rate of interest on currency and bank deposits will become negative. This is price distortion which causes people to unload their stocks of currency and demand deposits in times of rapid inflation and buy other assets. This leads to economic inefficiency as people have to spend real resources for trying to economise the use of currency or, in other words, to reduce their holdings of currency and demand deposits. For example, they have to go to banks more often to withdraw their money holdings. They use up their shoes and such other things in going to banks too often and also spend a good deal of their valuable time. In times of inflation, in their bid to economise the use of currency, the business firms also spend some resources for proper management of their cash funds.

Another important price distortion caused by inflation is in respect of taxes. In a progressive income tax structure people will have to pay higher rates of taxes as their money income increases as a result of inflation. As money incomes of the people increase due to inflation, the average rate of tax automatically rises as they are pushed into higher income tax slabs. This is generally called inflation *tax*. As a result of this inflation their rewards for work or other factor services go below what is justified by the real productivity of their work or other factor services. This causes misallocation of labour and other factors which create economic inefficiency and unnecessary loss of output. It is due to this adverse effect of taxes on resources allocation that in some countries taxes are also indexed, that is, adjusted in tune with the rise in general price level so that inflation induced distortion be avoided.

HYPERINFLATION AND ECONOMIC CRISIS

When inflation is extremely rapid, it is called hyperinflation. *A hyperinflation is generally defined as inflation at the rate of 50 per cent or more per month*. Some economists, prominent among them R. Dornbusch, have defined *hyperinflation as rise in price level at the rate of 1000 per cent in a year*.[14] There are several examples of hyperinflation that occurred in European countries after World Wars I and II. The most important episode of hyperinflation took place in Germany between Aug. 1922 and Nov. 1923. German inflation occurred at the rate of 322 per cent per month during this period and in the final months rate of inflation in Germany reached the highly extreme rate of 32000

---

14. See R. Dornbusch, et. al., "Extreme Inflation, Dynamics and Stabilisation", *Brookings Paper on Economic Activity,* 1977.

per cent per month.[15] It may be noted that German hyperinflation was caused by deficit financing by the government (*i.e.*, creation of new money) to finance the budget deficit during World War I when it had to pay massive reparations it had to pay to Britain and France. Argentina, Brazil, Peru and Poland all suffered from inflation rate of 1000 per cent per year for one or more years in late 1980 or 1990. The effect of hyperinflation on national output and employment turns out to be devastating. *Thus hyperinflation is generally caused when Government issues too much currency which greatly adds to the money supply in the economy.*

However, some economists are of the view that even mild or moderate inflation may ultimately lead to hyperinflation. They argue that when prices go on creeping upward for some time, people start expecting that prices will rise further and value of money will depreciate. In order to protect themselves from the fall in the purchasing power of money in the future, they try to spend money now. That is, they try to beat the anticipated price increases. This raises the aggregate demand for goods in the present. Businessmen too increase their purchases of capital goods and build up larger than normal inventories if they anticipate rise in prices. Thus, inflationary expectations raise the pressure on prices and in this way inflation feeds on itself. Further, the rise in prices and the cost of living under the influence of rising aggregate demand prompts the workers and their unions to demand higher wages to compensate them for the rise in the prices. During the periods of boom these demands of the workers for hike in wages are generally conceded. But rise in labour costs due to higher wages are recovered by business firms from the consumers by raising the prices of their products. This increase in prices gives rise to demand for further increases in wages resulting in still higher costs. Thus, *cumulative wage-price inflationary spiral starts operating which may culminate in hyperinflation.*

The major reason for hyperinflation is rapid growth of money supply as a result of financing budget deficits through creation of new money. During wars government expenditure increases more than the revenue. But hyperinflation does not occur during the war period as controls are imposed on prices during the war period and therefore inflation remains suppressed. When controls are lifted after the war, hyperinflation takes places as a consequence of excessive deficit financing and monetary growth during the war period.

Some economists attribute hyperinflation to the *accommodation of adverse supply shocks* that may take place as a result of rise in wage rates or rise in oil prices, as these supply shocks cause inflation on the one hand and unemployment or fall in GDP on the other. To increase employment opportunities to get rid of unemployment, the government or its Central Bank increases the supply of money to raise aggregate demand. This higher aggregate demand succeeds in eliminating unemployment but generate still higher inflation. This gives rise to *wage-price spiral* under which every time when the price level rises, money wages are raised to restore real wages. This process goes on and ultimately ends in hyperinflation.

The Cost of Hyperinflation

The cost of hyperinflation is much greater than the cost of moderate inflation. For example, when prices are rising at an extremely high rate, the incentives to minimise holding of currency become quite strong that result in enormous *shoe-leather costs*. In the situation of hyperinflation workers are paid much more frequently, even on daily basis and people rush out to spend their wages on goods (or to convert their currency in some other form such as a foreign currency or into gold and silver) before the prices rise even more. The greater time and energy are spent in getting rid of currency as soon as possible. Thus hyperinflation involves lot of wastes of resources and leads to disruption of production.

15. Robert J. Gordon, *Macroeconomics,* 12th edition, 2012, p. 14

Hyperinflation not only has disruptive redistributive effect, it also brings about economic crisis and may even cause collapse of the economic system. Hyperinflation encourages speculative activity on the part of people and businessmen who shy away from productive activities, as they find it highly profitable to hoard both finished goods and materials on the basis of expectations of further rise in prices. But such hoardings of goods and materials restrict the supply and availability of goods and tend to intensify the inflationary pressures in the economy. Instead of making productive investment, people and businesses tend to invest in unproductive assets such as gold and jewellery, real estate, houses etc., as a means of protecting themselves from inflation.

In the extreme when as a result of issuing too much money supply to finance government deficit or working of wage-price spiral, inflation becomes extremely rapid or what economists called hyperinflation, normal working of the economy collapses. In this situation, "prices are so rapidly rising and consequently purchasing power of money is so much dwindling that businessmen do not know what to charge for their products and consumers do not know what to pay. Resource suppliers will want to be paid with actual output rather than with rapidly depreciating money. Creditors will avoid debtors to escape the repayment of debts with cheap money. Money becomes virtually worthless and ceases to do its job as a measure of value and a medium of exchange. The economy may be literally thrown into a state of barter. Production and exchange grind towards a halt and the net result is economic, social and political chaos."[16]

Such grim and gloomy situation created by hyperinflation did occur in Germany during 1920s and in Hungary and Japan in the forties. At that time, money depreciated so much that for some time barter system came to prevail and after some time, the new currency had to be issued. It is therefore desirable that appropriate anti-inflationary measures be taken so that inflation should not go out of control and get transformed into hyperinflation.

Measures to End Hyperinflation

It is important to note that all hyperinflation episodes lasted for one to 2 years. The governments succeeded in controlling them through the adoption of proper *stabilisation policy*. The stabilisation measures adopted were the following:

1. The most important measure was to reduce sharply budget deficit *by cutting down government expenditure and subsidies and raising more resources through taxes*. This resulted in slowdown in growth of money and helped in controlling inflation.

2. The Central Bank made creditable announcement that it would not automatically monetise the budget deficits of the government. The government on their part also assured that they would finance its expenditure through taxes and would not resort to deficit financing. Once the people were convinced about the commitments by the Central Bank and the government they did not rush to spend the money income they earned and kept it with them to spend when needed. This helped to curb inflationary expectations.

As suggested by some economists, to control hyperinflation some type of control on wages often called **incomes policy** was needed. This visualised reducing the frequency of wages-indexation or agreement among firms and labour unions not to raise wages until hyperinflation was brought under control. Besides, this also involved commitments by the firms not to raise their profit margins. However, the experience of several countries which succeeded in ending hyperinflation suggests that, "stopping hyperinflation is a complex and difficult task. Much depends on the credibility of the government, that is, public belief that budget deficit and monetary growth are really going to stop. It may take several dramatic actions all at once to achieve credibility."[17]

16. Robert J. Gordon, *op. cit.* p.337
17. Robert Gordon, *op. cit.*, P. 337

MEASURES TO CONTROL DEMAND-PULL INFLATION

As has been explained above, inflation occurs due to the emergence of excess demand for goods and services relative to their supply of output at the prevailing prices. Inflation of this type is called *demand-pull inflation.* Various fiscal and monetary measures can be adopted to check this inflation. We discuss below the efficacy of the various policy measures to check demand-pull inflation which is caused by excess aggregate demand.

1. Fiscal Policy: Reducing Fiscal Deficit

The budget deals with how a Government raises its revenue and spends it. If the total revenue raised by the Government through taxation, fees, surpluses from public undertakings is less than the expenditure it incurs on buying goods and services to meet its requirements of defence, civil administration and various welfare and developmental activities, there emerges a fiscal deficit. It may be noted here that the budget of the government has two parts: (1) *Revenue Budget*, (2) *Capital Budget*. In the revenue budget on the receipts side revenue raised through taxes, interests, fees, surpluses from public undertakings are given and on the expenditure side consumption expenditure by the government on goods and services required to meet the needs of defence, civil administration, education and health services, subsidies on food, fertilizers and exports, and interest payments on the loans taken by it in the previous years are important items. In the capital budget, the main items of receipts are market borrowings by the government from the banks and other financial institutions, foreign aid, small savings (*i.e.*, Provident Fund, National Savings Schemes etc.). The important items of expenditure in the capital budget are defence, funding of public enterprises for developmental purposes, especially those relating to infrastructure projects and loans to States and Union territories.

Fiscal deficit can be financed in two ways. First, borrowing by the government from the central bank (RBI in case of India) against its own securities. This leads to the creation of more money supply and therefore gives rise to inflationary pressures in the economy. Some years ago, this was called *deficit financing* which was held to be the main cause of demand-pull inflation in India. Now, we call it *monetisation of fiscal deficit.* However, in recent years *fiscal deficit in India is financed mainly through borrowing by the Government through sale of its bonds which are generally purchased by banks, insurance companies, mutual funds and corporate firms*. The increase in government expenditure made possible by borrowing without being matched by extra taxation causes aggregate demand to increase. The net increase in Government expenditure leads to multiple increase in aggregate demand through *Government expenditure* multiplier.

In the opinion of many economists, the expansion in aggregate expenditure caused by fiscal deficit leads to the excess aggregate demand and inflationary pressures in the economy, especially when aggregate supply of output is inelastic. To some extent increase in aggregate demand may not generate demand-pull inflation because if the aggregate output increases, especially of essential consumer goods such as food grains, cloth, the extra demand arising out of increase in expenditure would be matched by extra supply of output.

But when increase in expenditure occurs and the economy is already utilising its production capacity fully or working near to it, this leads to demand-pull inflation. Therefore, to tackle the problem of demand-pull inflation fiscal deficit should be reduced. In its recommendation for India, IMF has suggested that fiscal deficit must be reduced to 3 per cent of GDP if inflation has to be kept under check.

To reduce fiscal deficit the Government can mobilise more resources through taxes, both direct and indirect. In India there is a lot of scope for raising resources through taxation. In both personal and corporate income taxes, there are a large number of unnecessary exemptions which lower the effective rate of income tax. Thus it has been found that though there is 33 per cent tax on corporate income but because of several exemptions which have outlived their utility, effective rate of corporate income tax in India is only about 24 per cent. Thus withdrawal of these exemptions can lead to significant increase in revenue of the Government. Besides improving efficiency of tax-collecting administration tax evasion which occurs on a large scale in India and generates a lot of black money can *yield* large revenue for the Government. On the other hand, it can reduce fiscal deficit by curtailing its wasteful and inessential expenditure, especially subsidies to the non-poor people. In India, it is often argued that there is a large scope for pruning down non-plan expenditure on defence, police and general administration and on subsidies being provided on food, fertilizers and fuel oil. Though it is easy to suggest cutting down of Government expenditure, it is difficult to implement it in practice. However, in our view, there is a large-scale inefficiency in resource use and also a lot of corruption involved in spending by the Government which can be curtailed to a good extent. Thus, both by greater resource mobilisation on the one hand and pruning down of wasteful and inessential Government expenditure on the other, the fiscal deficit can be reduced. This will help in controlling inflation.

2. Monetary Policy to Control Inflation : Monetary Tightening

Monetary policy refers to the adoption of suitable policy regarding *interest rate* and the *availability of credit*. Monetary policy is an important measure for reducing aggregate demand to control inflation. As an instrument of demand management, monetary policy can work in two ways. First, it can affect the *cost of credit* and second, it can influence the *credit availability* for private business firms. Let us first consider the cost of credit. The higher the rate of interest, the greater the cost of borrowing from the banks by the business firms. As anti-inflationary measure, the rate of interest has to be raised to discourage businessmen to borrow more so that less bank credit is created. The cheap credit policy (*i.e.*, lower interest rates) is recommended on the ground that lower rate of interest will promote more private investment which is an important factor determining economic growth. Keeping in view this consideration, cheap money policy was adopted in India up to 1972 and accordingly bank rate was kept low.

The dear money policy (that is, *higher interest rate policy*) has been often used in India to curb the inflationary pressures in the Indian economy. In India, bank rate has not been generally used to check inflation. Instruments like *repo rate* and *reverse repo rate* have often been used to manage aggregate demand. Repo rate is the interest rate at which Reserve Bank of India lends funds to the commercial banks *for a short period.* To curb inflation *repo rate* is raised. Hike in repo rate raises the cost of funds for the banks which will, if they do not have excess reserves, raise their *lending rates*. The higher lending rates will lower the demand for bank credit for investment and for purchases of cars (auto loans) and housing (housing loans). Under these circumstances to mobilise funds banks raise their deposit rates. The higher rate of interest on savings and fixed deposits will induce more savings by the households and help in cutting down aggregate consumption expenditure. Besides, higher rates of interest will discourage more investment in inventories and consumer durables and will help in reducing aggregate demand.

However, rise in repo rate will lead to the decline in credit growth if ***monetary transmission mechanism*** works. This will happen only if banks are short of liquid funds. If the banks have excess liquid reserves with them they would not raise their lending rates when the RBI raises repo rate. Therefore, for monetary transmission mechanism to work liquidity with the banks must be curtailed. This can be done by the RBI by raising cash reserve ratio (CRR) and by *open market operation* through sale of Government securities.

It is noteworthy that a recent monetary theory emphasizes that it is the changes in the ***credit availability*** rather than ***cost of credit*** (*i.e.*, rate of interest) that is a more effective instrument of regulating aggregate demand. There are several methods by which credit availability can be reduced. Firstly, it is through *open market operations* that the central bank of a country can reduce the availability of credit in the economy. Under open market operations, the Reserve Bank sells Government securities. Those, especially banks, who buy these securities will make payment for them in terms of cash reserves. With their reduced cash reserves, their capacity to lend money to the business firms will be curtailed. This will tend to reduce the supply of credit or loanable funds by the banks which in turn would tend to reduce aggregate demand.

However, in the past in India open market operations did not play a significant role as an instrument of credit control to fight against inflationary situation. This was because market for Government securities was narrow as well as captive. However, with financial reforms this is no more the situation. At present RBI often uses open market operations to influence liquidity of the banking system. General public do not buy more than a fraction of Government securities. It is the institutions such as commercial banks, LIC, GIC and Provident Funds which are required by law to invest a certain proportion of their funds in buying Government securities. The RBI can reduce the liquidity with the banks by selling Government securities to them through open market operations.

In India, it is the ***Cash Reserve Ratio*** **(*CRR*)** which can be effectively used to curb inflation. By law banks have to keep a certain proportion of cash money as reserves against their demand and time deposits. This is called cash reserve ratio. To reduce liquidity with the banks and thereby to contract credit availability Reserve Bank can raise this ratio. In recent years to squeeze credit for checking inflation, cash reserve ratio in India has been raised from time to time.

Statutory Liquidity Ratio **(SLR).** Another instrument with Reserve Bank of India for affecting credit availability is the statutory liquidity ratio. In addition to *CRR*, banks have to keep a certain minimum proportion of their deposits in the form of specified liquid assets. And the most important specified liquid asset for this purpose is the Government securities. To mop up extra liquid assets with banks which may lead to undue expansion in credit availability for the business class, the Reserve Bank has often raised statutory liquidity ratio.

Limitations of Tight Monetary Policy

However, tight monetary policy for controlling inflation is not without its limitations. First, monetary transmission mechanism may be weak and raising of short-term interest rates by the RBI may not actually lead to the restriction of bank credit. First, the banks may have surplus liquidity (*i.e.,* cash reserves) with them and therefore they may not follow tight monetary policy and raise their lending rates. As a result, supply of credit by banks will not be restricted. Secondly, if the economic environment is such that boom conditions prevail in the economy and aggregate demand for products is quite high, demand for credit may not be much affected by higher lending rates. As emphasized by J.M. Keynes, investment is determined more by marginal efficiency of capital (that is, expected rate of return) rather than rate of interest. Thirdly, at present in India corporate firms are more easily able to borrow from foreign capital markets (*i.e.,* external commercial borrowing, ECB) especially when rates of interest in the US, European zone and Japan are extremely low. Therefore, unless this debt-capital inflow (*i.e.,* ECB) is checked RBI's monetary policy may not be effective to check the supply of credit to control inflation in the economy.

Thirdly, when the stock market prices are rising and aggregate demand is quite high, the corporate sector is able to raise funds itself more easily from the capital market. This will also offset the impact of tight monetary policy of the RBI to control inflation. Fourthly, if adequate internal funds are available with the corporate firms as a result of *retained profit earnings* by the companies they can use them to finance their expansion plans and thereby add to the aggregate expenditure or demand. This will also nullify the tight monetary policy of the RBI to curb inflation.

It may be noted that in recent years to control inflation the Reserve Bank of India raised its *repo rate* 13 times from March 2010 to Nov. 2011 (from 4.75% in March 2010 to 8.50% in Nov. 2011) but inflation as measured by the WPI remained at an elevated level. It was estimated at 10 per cent (YoY) in September 2011, 9.73% in Oct. 2011 and 9.11 per cent in Nov. 2011. After Nov. 2011, WPI inflation declined because of dip in food inflation due partly to the base effect and partly due to easing of supply position of some food articles. Thus tight monetary policy failed to check inflation despite 3.75 percentage points increase in repo rate. The RBI explained failure of its tight monetary policy to curb inflation by blaming the *large fiscal deficit* of the Government in 2011-12. Due to large fiscal deficit, aggregate demand was increasing which was feeding inflation in the Indian economy. According to the RBI, unless fiscal deficit is brought down by the Government, tight monetary policy alone will not succeed in checking inflation. Besides, the RBI *blamed supply-side factors* responsible for food inflation which has contributed to overall rise in WPI inflation.

Lastly, if inflation in the economy has originated from the **supply-side factors**, for example, if production of food grains and other essential food articles such as milk, vegetables, fruits etc. in a year declines or does not increase adequately to meet the growing demand for them due to certain supply-side bottlenecks, this will cause the demand-supply imbalances leading to the rise in inflation. Such supply-side inflation cannot be checked by raising interest rates under the tight monetary policy. This happened in 2009-10 when due to the shortage of monsoon rainfall, drop in agricultural production was expected, inflationary pressures emerged in the Indian economy raising food-inflation to around 20 per cent in December 2009. This food inflation continued to prevail at double digit level till November 2010. Tight monetary policy which is aimed at management of aggregate demand rather than augmentation of supply is ineffective in tackling this supply-side inflation as in case of food inflation in 2010. Likewise, in 2010-11 and 2011-12 *shortage of protein-based food* products such as pulses, milk, fruits and vegetables, eggs, meat and fish, contributed a good deal to the persistence of food inflation. It is only after Oct. 2011 when there was a drop in food-inflation, that headline WPI inflation also declined. Similarly, supply-side inflation arises when prices of petroleum products rise which is passed on to the domestic consumers and cannot be tackled with use of tight monetary policy. In addition to fuel, if output growth in *core industries* such as steel, cement, coal declined as they did during 2011-12 in India, they create supply-side bottlenecks in various industries leading to supply-side inflation.

Now to control food inflation what is required is to take long-term measures to augment supply of food grains and other food articles by raising agricultural productivity by undertaking appropriate technological changes and land-reform measures. In the short run to control food inflation what is needed is to release food stocks through public distribution system (PDS) which should be properly monitored to check black market. Besides, to control rise in food prices in the short run release of food stocks for sale in the open market should be made. However, this pre supposes enough food stocks with the Government. Further, to check food-inflation, food grains, pulses, oil seeds and other feed articles in short supply can be imported.

It may however be noted that when inflationary expectations arise as a result of emergence of shortage of supply of some essential commodities there is tendency on the part of traders to hoard stocks of goods in short supply for speculative purposes. To discourage such speculative hoarding of goods in short supply monetary policy of high interest rates can be helpful. Besides, as explained above, selective credit controls of monetary policy can also be used to check excessive hoarding.

QUESTIONS FOR REVIEW

1. Define demand-pull inflation. How is it caused by the Central Bank insistence on keeping the market rate of interest low so as to stimulate investment?

2. What are the main factors that cause cost-push inflation ? Suggest measures to control cost-push inflation.

3. Distinguish between demand-pull inflation and cost-push inflation. How are they often intertwined ?
4. Inflation may originate because of cost-push but it cannot be sustained for long unless it is supported by demand-pull inflation.
5. Critically examme monetarist theory of inflation.
6. What is stagflation ? Explain how cost-push inflation leads to stagflation.
7. An inflationary process may begin on the supply side but it will not continue for long unless there is increase in demand. Discuss.
8. Distinguish between demand-pull and cost-push inflation. How can demand-pull inflation be controlled?
9. Inflation is always and everywhere a purely monetary phenomenon. Critically examine.
10. Define inflation. Explain its effects on (*a*) creditors and deletors (*b*) persons of fixed income group.
11. Explain the effects of inflation on economic growth and distribution of income.
12. How does inflation distort the pattern of production and distribution in an economy?
13. Define inflation. What measures would you suggest to control it?
14. What are the main causes of inflation in India? Which policies of government have helped to check rise in prices ?
15. What is *inflation fallacy* with regard to cost of inflation ? How far is it valid ? Discuss.
16. Explain the social cost of (*a*) anticipated inflation and (*b*) unanticipated inflation.
17. How does inflation adversely affect long-term economic growth of a country?
18. What is hyperinflation ? How does it lead to economic crisis ?

PART VI

INTERNATIONAL BUSINESS ENVIRONMENT

- International Trade : Comparative Cost and Hecksher Ohlin Theories
- National Income and Foreign Trade : ForeignTrade Multiplier
- International Linkages and Mundell-Fleming Model
- Foreign Trade Policy : Free Trade vs. Protection
- India's Foreign Trade Policy : Import-substitution Vs. Export Orientation
- Foreign Exchange Rate
- International Organisations : IMF and World Bank
- Balance of Payments
- Foreign Investment and Multinational Corporations
- India and the World Economy : Globalisation
- WTO and India

Chapter 23

INTERNATIONAL TRADE : COMPARATIVE COST AND HECKSHER-OHLIN THEORIES

Introduction

In one of our previous chapters we discussed personal specialisation or division of labour. We also discussed the great part which personal specialisation plays in the functioning of the modern economic organisation. Equally important are the roles of the regional and international specialisation. *Regional specialisation means that various regions or areas in a country specialise themselves in the production of different products. International specialisation means that different countries of the world specialise in producing different goods.* Factors which determine regional specialisation are more or less the same as those which determine international specialisation. A country which produces surplus of a good, *i.e.*, produces more than its requirements, will export it to other countries in exchange for the surplus products of those countries.

In the modern world, there is mutual interdependence of the various national economies. Today it is hard to find the example of a closed economy. All economies of the world have become open. But the degree of openness varies from one country to another. Thus, *in the modern world no country is completely self-sufficient.* Self-sufficiency, in the sense used here, means the proportion of the goods and services consumed to their total output produced within a country. But the degree of self-sufficiency varies from one country to another.

The Theory of Absolute Advantage

The theory of absolute advantage was put forward by Adam Smith who argued that different countries enjoyed absolute advantage in the production of some goods which formed the basis of trade between the countries. Consider Table 23.1 where man-hours required to produce a unit of wheat or cloth in the U.S.A. and India are given.

Table 23.1 : Man-hours required to produce one unit of wheat and cloth

	U.S.A.	*India*
Wheat	3	10
Cloth	6	4

It will be seen from the above table that to produce one unit of wheat in the U.S.A. 3 man-hours and in India 10 man-hours are required. On the other hand, to produce one unit of cloth, in the U.S.A. 6 man-hours and in India 4 man-hours are required. Thus the U.S.A. can produce wheat more efficiently (that is, at a lower cost), while India can produce cloth more efficiently. To put it in other words, while the U.S.A. has an *absolute advantage in the production of wheat, India has an absolute advantage in the production of cloth.* Adam Smith showed that the two countries would benefit and world output will increase if the two countries specialise in the production of goods in which they have absolute advantage and trade with each other. How such specialisation and trade would lead to gain in output and would be mutually beneficial for the two countries is shown in Table 23.2

Table 23.2. Gain in output when labour resources are transferred

	U.S.A	*India*	*World Output*
Gain in Wheat	+ 2 Wheat	–1Wheat	+ 1 Wheat
Gain Cloth	– 1 cloth	+ 2.5 Cloth	+ 1.5 Cloth

Suppose to specialise in the production of Wheat, the U.S.A. withdraws 6 man-hours from the production of cloth and devote them to the production of wheat, it will lose 1 unit of cloth and gain 2 units of wheat. Similarly, to specialise in the production of cloth if India withdraws 10 hours of labour from wheat and use them for the production of cloth, it will lose one unit of wheat but gain 2.5 units of cloth. In this way, transfer of labour resources to the goods in which they have absolute advantage, will result in the net gain of one unit of wheat and 2.5 units of cloth. The gain in output can be distributed between the two countries through voluntary exchange.

It is also clear from above that without any increase in productive resources international division of labour and trade leads to the expansion in world output and wealth. *According to Adam Smith, given perfect competition in the industries and free trade between the countries, it is the market forces that would ensure specialisation and trade on the lines of absolute advantage.*

THEORY OF COMPARATIVE COSTS OR COMPARATIVE ADVANTAGE

The fundamental cause of international specialisation and hence international trade is the difference in costs of production. It is the relative differences in costs which determine the products to be produced by different countries. Considering climatic conditions, availability of mineral and other resources and differences in costs arising from them, every country seems to be better suited for the production of certain articles rather than for others. A country tends to specialise in the *production of those goods for which it has got relative or comparative advantage.* A country can produce numerous goods. But it will not produce all of them since it will simply not be paying to do so. It will be much better if after comparing the costs of the various articles that it can produce, it selects those in which the comparative costs are lower or in which it enjoys relative advantage. It will be to the advantage of each country as well as of the world as a whole that each country specialises in the production of those commodities for which it has comparative advantage. In this way the productive resources of the country and of the whole world will be optimally utilised.

The theory of comparative costs is simply an application of the principle of division of labour to different countries. An individual can do a number of jobs but he cannot do them all alike. Take the case of a doctor. Undoubtedly, he can do the dispensing work better than his dispenser. But still he employs a dispenser, and he himself specialises in examining the patients. He knows that the time which he will spend in dispensing can be more remuneratively employed by examining patients. The work of dispensing can be done by a low-paid person, while he can earn much more as a doctor.

Similarly, a professor may be able to teach his own son who is reading in a lower class much better than any school teacher. But if the hour that he devotes to the teaching of his son is devoted to coaching of a student for the degree examination, he will get much more payment than he has to pay a tutor whom he may employ for coaching his son. This specialisation is very gainful. This is the application of the theory of comparative costs to the case of individuals. Each individual compares the cost and the income of the various jobs that he could take up and of these he selects that one which is most profitable.

Now, let us see how this principle applies to international specialisation. The fundamental cause as to why international specialisation occurs is the differences in costs, which result from the differences in the availability of the amount and the quality of resources, the prices of these resources or factors and the method of their use. Considering the differences in costs of producing different goods, every country seems to be better suited for the production of certain goods rather than the others. *A country tends to specialise in the production of those goods in which it has got comparative advantage or lower comparative cost.* A country can produce many goods. But it will not produce all of them since it will simply not be paying to do so. It will be much better if after comparing the costs of the various goods which it can produce it selects those in which the comparative costs are lower or in which it enjoys comparative advantage. It will be to the advantage of each country as well as of the world as a whole that each country specialises in the production of those commodities for which it has comparative advantage. In this way the productive resources of the country will be optimally utilised. It is worth mentioning that *specialisation necessitates trade or exchange of goods with other countries*. Under specialisation, a H country will import a good it does not produce and exports the good in which it specialises. The advantage of having a country specialise in the production of the good which it can produce more efficiently and exporting some of it in exchange for the imports of the good it can produce relatively less efficiently is that such specialisation increases the total supply of goods. In this way both countries are able to increase their level of consumption beyond what is possible in the absence of specialisation.

Let us take two countries U.S.A. and India and two goods, wheat and cloth. We shall explain what would be the basis of trade between these two countries and how the two would gain from specialising and trading with each other on the basis of comparative advantage or comparative cost. In order to simplify our analysis, we make the following assumptions :—

1. There are no transport costs between the two countries.
2. Conditions of perfect competition prevail in both countries.
3. Labour is the only resource of production and prices of products are equal to their relative labour costs.
4. There is free trade between the countries.

Specialisation and Trade with Comparative Advantage

When each country has an absolute advantage over the other in the production of a commodity, the gain from specialisation and trading between countries is quite obvious. However, a pertinent question is if the U.S.A. can produce both the commodities wheat and cloth more efficiently than India, would she gain from specialisation and trading with India. In fact, it was this question which was raised by David Ricardo, a classical economist, who put forward the theory of comparative costs (advantage) as an explanation of the potential gain from international trade.

Let us illustrate the theory of comparative cost (or comparative advantage) with a numerical example. Taking two countries, two commodities model as used by Ricardo we give in table 23.3 *labour requirements per unit of cloth and wheat in the U.S.A. and India.*

Table 23.3. Man-hours Required to Produce One Unit of Wheat and Cloth

	Wheat	*Cloth*	*Domestic Exchange Ratio between Wheat and Cloth*
U.S.A.	3	6	1 Wheat = 0.5 Cloth
India	12	9	1 Wheat = 1.33 Cloth

It will be seen from Table 23.3 that U.S.A. is more efficient (or has absolute advantage) in the production of both wheat and cloth. To produce one unit of wheat the U.S.A. requires 3 man-hours, while India requires 12 man-hours. In case of cloth, to produce one unit of it 6 hours of labour are needed in the USA, while 9 hours are needed in India. It is thus evident that the U.S.A. is more efficient in the production of both the commodities as it produces them at a lower labour cost than India. That is, U.S.A. has an absolute advantage in the production of both the commodities. However, Ricardo argued that the two countries can still gain from specialising and trading between them if they produce according to their comparative advantage. It will be seen from above table that the U.S.A. is four times more efficient in the production of wheat as compared to India, while its efficiency in the production of cloth is 1.5 times greater than India. Thus, while U.S.A. has absolute advantage in the production of both wheat and cloth, it has a *comparative advantage* in the production of wheat. On the other hand, India is less efficient in the production of both wheat and cloth, its inefficiency is comparatively less in cloth. *India is said to have comparative advantage in the production of cloth*. Both the countries will be better off if the U.S.A. specialises in the production of wheat and exports it to India for import of cloth and India specialises in the production of cloth and exports it to the U.S.A. and import wheat from it.

It might appear that the U.S.A. which can produce both wheat and cloth more efficiently than India has nothing to gain by trading with India which is comparatively inefficient in the production of both wheat and cloth. Even though the U.S.A. is more efficient in the production of both wheat and cloth, she will still gain by having specialisation and trading with India. Let us see how the two countries will gain if they specialise and trade on the lines of comparative advantage. In the absence of trade between the U.S.A. and India, depending on their labour costs one unit of wheat will be exchanged for 0.5 units of cloth in the U.S.A. and 1.33 units of cloth in India. When the U.S.A. and India specialise in wheat and cloth respectively and trade takes place between them, the U.S.A. will gain if it has to give less than can get more than 0.5 units of cloth from India for one unit of wheat and India will gain if it 1.33 units of cloth to the U.S.A. for import of one unit of wheat. Hence any exchange ratio between 0.5 and 1.33 units of cloth against one unit of wheat represents a gain for both the countries. The actual exchange rate settled between them will be determined by the *reciprocal demand* of the two countries for wheat and cloth.

Now, the question is what will be the source of gain from specialisation in the present case. The answer to this is that whereas the U.S.A. has an absolute advantage in the production of both wheat and cloth, its *margin of advantage* is greater in case of wheat as compared to cloth. Likewise, although India has absolute disadvantage in the production of both wheat and cloth, the extent of its disadvantage is less in case of cloth. Thus, with increases U.S.A. specialising in the production of wheat and India in cloth, through reallocation of labour between wheat and cloth, the total production will increase. How does the total joint output of the two countries increases if U.S.A. specialises in wheat for which it has comparative advantage and India in cloth for which it enjoys comparative advantage ? We show below in Table 23.4 the gain in wheat output that occurs when U.S.A. shifts its labour resources by reducing the production of cloth by one unit and India shifts its labour to cloth by reducing the production of wheat by one unit (the above data of man-hours cost of wheat and cloth are used).

Table 23.4. Gain in Output Resulting From Shift of Labour

	U.S.A.	*India*	*World output*
Wheat	+ 2 Wheat	– 1 Wheat	+ 1 Wheat
Cloth	– 1 Cloth	+ 1.33 cloth	+ 0.33 Cloth

It will be seen from Table 23.3 and 23.4 that if U.S.A. reduces the production of cloth by one unit 6 man-hours of labour will be released and if these are used for the production of wheat it will gain 2 units of wheat production. On the other hand, if India reduces production of one unit of wheat, 12 hours of labour will be released which on using for cloth production will result in gain of 1.33 units of cloth. It will be seen from Table 23.4 that total world output (*i.e.* joint output of the two countries) will rise by 1 unit of wheat and 0.33 units of cloth as a result of the above shift of man-hours to the products of their comparative advantage.

Thus, specialisation, according to the comparative advantage, would lead to the increase in production of both wheat and cloth and the two countries would gain from trading with each other by exporting the goods in which they speicalise.

COMPARATIVE COST THEORY : OPPORTUNITY COST APPROACH

Comparative cost theory explained above is based upon labour theory of value. But this labour theory of value has been abandoned by the modern economists. However, comparative cost theory is still believed to be valid and important basis of international trade. The labour theory of value does not hold good because the wages of labour are not brought to equality throughout the country. Further, labour is not homogeneous and the wages of different non-competing groups do not tend to be equal at least in the short run. Another serious objection against labour theory of value has been that goods are not produced by labour alone but by various combinations of different factors of production, land, labour and capital. Therefore, to compare the values of the two commodities by taking into account only their labour content would give a wrong view of the relative values because one commodity may require more capital than labour, another may require more land than labour. Therefore, variable proportions of factors used in the production of different commodities make the labour theory of value inapplicable in determining comparative cost of commodities. Therefore, a noted economist Haberler has explained comparative cost doctrine in terms of opportunity costs. As explained in an earlier chapter, the opportunity cost of a commodity, say wheat, is amount of another commodity, say cloth, which a country has to give up to produce an additional unit of wheat. Thus opportunity cost measures the ratio of marginal costs of the two commodities. In the explanation of comparative cost theory, the concept of opportunity cost is generally illustrated through production possibility curve.

Constant Opportunity Costs

We shall first explain the case when opportunity costs of the commodities in each country have been assumed to be constant. Suppose, with given resources, India can produce 20 kgs. of wheat or 40 meters of cloth, whereas with the same resources, the U.S.A. can produce 60 kgs of wheat and 80 metres of cloth. This is given in the Table 23.5.

Table 23.5 : Production Possibilities in U.S.A. and India

Country	*Wheat*		*Cloth*
U.S.A	60 kgs	or	80 Metres
India	20 Kgs	or	40 Metres

From these production possibilities, it follows that U.S.A. is more efficient in the production of both wheat and cloth. However, in case of wheat its efficiency is three times greater and in case of cloth two times greater as compared to India. From these prodution possibilities we can calculate the opportunity cost of wheat and cloth in the two countries. In U.S.A. opportunity cost of 60 kg. of wheat is 80 metres of cloth, that is, 1 kg. of wheat has opportunity cost of 80/60 or 1.33 metres of cloth. Likewise, 80 metres of cloth in U.S.A. has the opportunity cost of 60 kg. of wheat, that is, 1

Table 23.6. Opportunity Costs of Wheat and Cloth in U.S.A. & India

Country	*Wheat*	*Cloth*
U.S.A.	1.33 metres of cloth	0.75 kg of wheat
India	2.00 metres of cloth	0.50 kg of wheat

metre of cloth has the opportunity cost of 0.75 kg. of wheat in U.S.A. In India one kg. of wheat has the opportunity cost of 2 metres of cloth and one metre of cloth has 0.50 kg. of wheat. In Table 23.6 opportunity costs of the two countries are given.

It is evident from the above table that in U.S.A. opportunity cost of wheat is less than that of India, while in India opportunity cost of cloth is less than that of U.S.A. *These opportunity costs reflect comparative advantage.* Thus, it would be to the advantage of U.S.A. to specialise in the production of wheat and of India in the production of cloth.

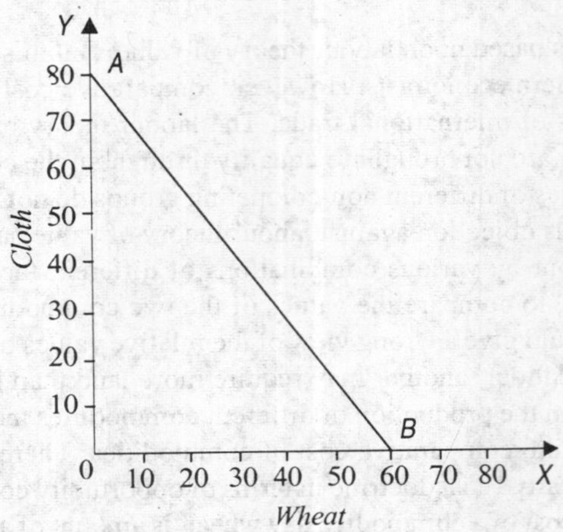

Fig. 23.1. *Opportunity Cost of U.S.A.*

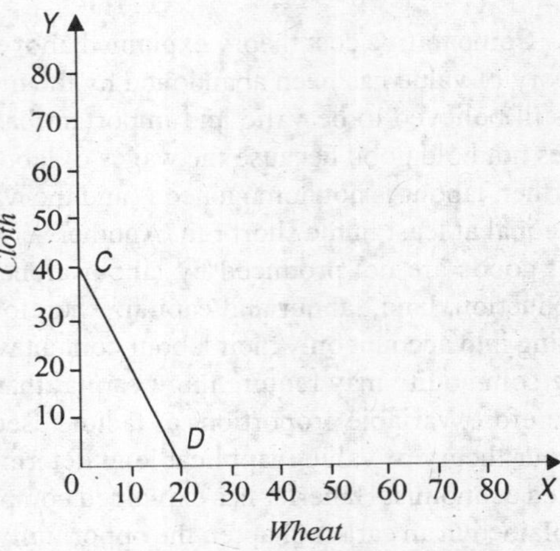

Fig. 23.2. *Opportunity Cost of India*

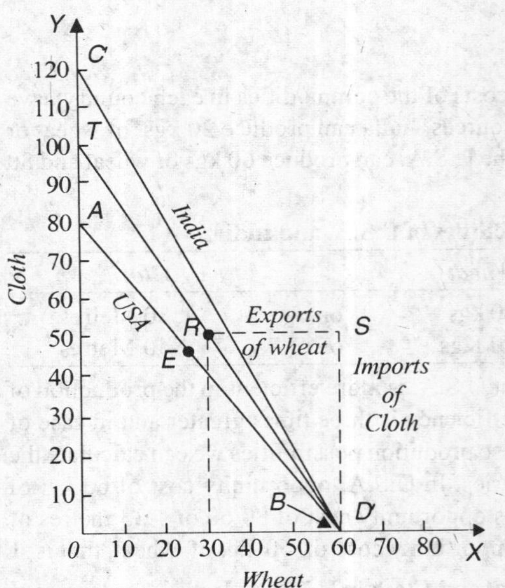

Fig. 23.3. *Comparative Cost Theory : Constant Opportunity Costs*

Production possibilities between wheat and cloth of U.S.A. has been show in Fig. 23.1 where on the *X*-axis wheat and on the *Y*-axis cloth have been measured, Now, line *AB* represents the production possibility curve in India between wheat and cloth. As constant costs are assumed, a straight line production possibility curve has been drawn. Similarly, in Fig. 23.2 production possibility curve between wheat and cloth of India is *CD*. In order to explain the comparative cost theory and the gain from trade we have to superimpose the production possibility curve of one country over that of the other. It will be seen from the slopes of the production possibility curves of the two countries that while India can produce cloth at the lower comparative cost, the U.S.A.can produce wheat at a comparatively cheaper cost. Therefore, it would be advantageous for India and U.S.A. to specialise in cloth and wheat respectively. This can be shown by superimposing the opportunity cost curve *CD* of India over the opportunity cost of U.S.A., in such a way that point *D* is joined with point *B* of U.S.A. This has been shown in Figure 23.3 the product possibility. Now, suppose that before trade U.S.A. is producing and consuming at point *E* on her production possibility curve *AB*. The slope of the production possibility curve *AB* shows the comparative cost ratio of the two commodities in U.S.A. If U.S.A. can trade with another country, say India, at a different price-ratio than this, it will then gain from the trade. It will be seen from Fig. 23.3

that the product possibility curve *AB* of U.S.A. lies India's production possibility curve *C'D'*. The terms of trade which will be settled between the two will lie between the production possibility curve *C'D'* of India and the production possibility curve *AB* of *U.S.A.* Suppose, *D'T'* is the terms of trade line showing the price ratio settled between the two countries. Since U.S.A. has a comparative advantage in the production of wheat it will specialise in wheat and would produce *OB* or 60 units of wheat, whereas India has comparative advantage in the production of cloth and will specialise in cloth production. After trade the equilibrium of U.S.A. would lie at some point on the terms of the trade line *D'T*, depending upon its demand for goods. Suppose *R* is such point on the terms of trade line *D'T*. Thus U.S.A. would now get the combination of the goods indicated by point *R* for its consumption while it would be producing only wheat. It will be seen From Fig. 23.3 that U.S.A. would gain from specialisation and trade as point *R* lies at a higher level than point *E*. At point *R*, U.S.A. would be consuming more of both wheat and cloth than at point *E* which is the position before trade. At point *R*, U.S.A. would be exporting *RS* amount of wheat and would be getting in return for it *SD'* amount of cloth from India. Similarly, it can be shown that India will also gain from specialising in cloth and exchanging it for wheat with U.S.A.

It may be noted that in case of constant opportunity costs, there is complete specialisation, that is, of the two goods a country produces only one commodity, that is, either wheat or cloth after specialisation and trade.

Comparative Cost Theory : Increasing Opportunity Costs

In the above analysis of opportunity cost version of the comparative cost theory we have assumed that opportunity costs are constant. The constancy of opportunity costs implies that the various resources are equally suitable for the production of each of the two goods. However, this does not represent the real situation, where all resources do not produce equally well both of the two commodities. Some resources may be equally suitable for the production of both wheat and cloth but all resources are not of this kind. Resources such as land, villagers trained for the art of agriculture, are more suited for the production of wheat. On the other hand, resources such as spindles, looms, technicians are suitable for producing cloth. When resources are not equally efficient in the production of the two commodites we may have the situation of increasing costs. In case of increaisng opportunity costs, the production possibility curve instead of being a straight line is concave to the origin, as shown in Figure 23.4. This indicates as we shift resources from the production of wheat to the production of cloth, marginal opportunity cost of cloth (that is, the amount of wheat forgone for a unit of cloth) goes on increasing and vice versa.

Under conditions of increasing opportunity costs, the production possibility curve is not identical with a price curve as in case of constant opportunity costs. The domestic price-ratio (that is, the rate of which two goods would be exchanged in the absence of trade) are not determined by the production possibility curve alone. Instead, this domestic exchange rate is determined by the production possibilities (i.e. supply or cost conditions) and the demand for the goods. In the equilibrium situation, the two goods would be produced in such quantities where :

$$MRT_{CW} = \frac{P_C}{P_W}$$

where

MRT_{CW} stands for marginal rate of transformation between the two goods
P_C denotes price of cloth
P_W denotes price of wheat.

In Figure 23.4 suppose the price-ratio line between wheat and cloth, as determined by demand and supply conditions, is *pp'*. The production equilibrium in the absence of trade will be reached at point R where the price line is tangent to the production possibility curve so that the marginal rate of transformation between the two goods is equal to the price ratio between them.

Now, if foreign trade possibilities are such that price of cloth is relatively more in foreign market than at home, it would be advantageous for the country to enter into trade and increase the production of cloth and reduce that of wheat. Suppose the price-ratio line in the foreign market (or what is also called *terms of trade* line) is given by the price line *tt* in Figure 23.4. It will be seen from this figure that slope of the price-ratio line *tt* indicates higher price for cloth and lower one for wheat as compared to domestic price-ratio line *pp'* since according to *tt* more wheat can be obtained for a given amount of cloth.

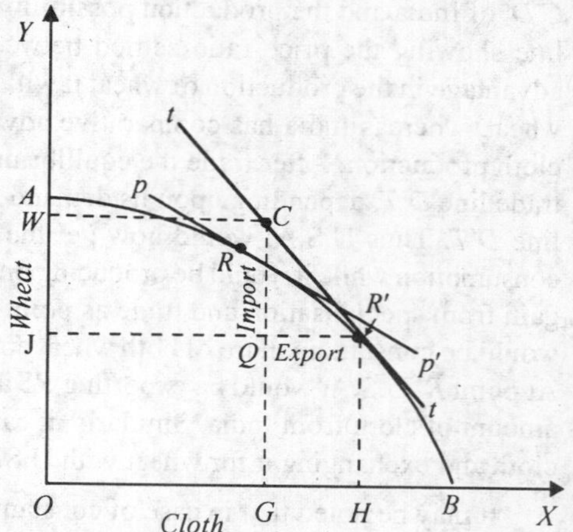

Fig.23.4. *Comparative Cost Theory : Increasing Opportunity Costs.*

Given these trade possibilities, it would be advantageous for India to increase the production of cloth. (or so to say specialise in cloth) by shifting to it some resources from wheat. With price-ratio (or terms of trade) line *tt*, India would be in equilibrium at point *R'* where its production possibilities curve *AB* is tangent to the terms of trade line *tt*. However, the consumption of two goods in a country depends on the tastes or demand pattern for the goods. In the modern international trade theory, tastes or demand for goods in a country are shown through the medium of community indifference curves, the use of which we are avoiding at this stage. It will suffice to mention here that consumption of the two goods in India would take place at a certain point on the terms of trade line *tt* to the left of point *R*, say at point *C*. Of course, this consumption point *C* would be determined by the demand conditions in India. With production at *R'* and consumption at *C* in India after it enters into trade with U.S.A. it follows that India would produce *OH*(= *JR'*) of cloth, *OJ* (or *HR'*) of wheat, and would consume *OG* (or *WC*) of cloth and *OW* (= *GC*) of wheat. Further India will export *QR'* of cloth and import *QC* of wheat. It is evident from Figure 23.4 *that trade has enabled India to consume more of both cloth and wheat than it could produce at home with its own production possibilities*.

It is noteworthy that unlike in case of constant opportunity costs, in case of increasing opportunity costs, specialisation is not likely to be complete. This is because of the occurrence of diminishing returns or increasing costs as the production of one commodity is stepped up at the expense of the other commodity. When production of cloth is expanded productive resources less suited to the production of cloth are drawn into that industry. This raises per unit cost of cloth. On the other hand, as more factors of production are drawn from wheat for allocating them to the production of cloth, per unit cost of wheat falls. The opposite will happen in the trading partner who will increase the production of wheat and reduce that of cloth by shifting resources out of the latter into the former. Cost ratios in the two countries may become equal *before* either country completely specialises in the production of a single commodity.

The law of comparative costs when freed from the labour theory of value and expressed in terms of opportunity costs is still believed to be true by the modern economists. In a two-commodity world when one country can produce both of them at a lower cost than another, it will pay to it to specialise in the production of a commodity which it can produce at comparatively lower cost and import the other commodity for which it has a comparatively higher costs. It gains from trade as it is able to get a higher price for the commodity in which it specialises because of its relatively lower cost of production and also because it pays a relatively lower price for the commodity for which its efficiency is relatively not so high.

CRITICAL APPRAISAL OF COMPARATIVE COST THEORY

Theory of comparative cost which is the important doctrine of classical economics is still valid and widely acclaimed as the correct explanation of international trade. Most of the criticisms that have been leveled against this doctrine relate to the Ricardian version of comparative cost theory based on labour-theory of value. Haberler and others broke away from this labour-cost version and reformulated the comparative cost theory in terms of opportunity costs which takes into consideration all factors. The basic contention of the theory that a country will specialise in the production of a commodity and export it for which it has a lower comparative cost and import a commodity which can be produced at a lower comparative cost by others, is based on a sound logic. The theory correctly explains the gain from trade accruing to the participating countries if they specialise according to their comparative costs. These merits of the theory have led Professor Samuelson to remark, "If theories, like girls, could win beauty contents, comparative advantage would certainly rate high in that it is an elegantly logical structure."[1] He further writes, "the theory of comparative advantage has in it a most important glimpse of truth.... A nation that neglects comparative advantage may have to pay a heavy price in terms of living standards and potential rates of growth"[2] Despite the sound logical structure and vivid explanation of gains from trade, the comparative cost theory, especially the Ricardian version based on labour theory of value has been criticized. The following criticisms have been levelled against this theory :–

1. In the first place, Ricardian version of comparative cost theory has been attacked on the ground that being *based on labour theory of value*, it considers only labour cost to measure the comparative costs of various goods. It has been pointed out that labour is not the only factor needed for the production of commodities, other factors such as capital, raw materials, land also contribute to production. Therefore, it is the total money costs incurred on labour as well as other factors that should be considered for assessing comparative costs of various commodities.

Taussig tried to defend Ricardo by pointing out that even if labour theory of value was defective and even if other factors made important contributions to the production of goods, comparative costs could still be based on labour cost alone, if it is assumed that the trading countries are at the same stage of technological development. This is because, he argued that given the same technological development, the proportions in which other factors could be combined with labour would be the same. In view of this he asserted that other factors could be validly ignored and for purpose of comparative costs relative efficiency of labour alone of different countries could be considered. However, Taussig's defense of Ricardian version of comparative cost theory is poor and invalid. The various trading partners are not at the same stage of technological development and therefore the factor proportions used for the production of commodities in different countries are vastly different. Hence, it is quite unrealistic and improper to consider relative efficiency of labour alone.

However, as stated earlier, Haberler rescued the comparative cost theory from labour theory of value and reformulated it in terms of opportunity cost which covers all factors. The opportunity cost version of comparative cost theory has already been explained above.

2. The comparative cost theory explained that different countries would specialise in the production of goods on the basis of comparative costs and that they would gain from trade if they export those goods in which they have comparative advantage and import those goods from abroad in

---

1. P.A. Samuelson, *Economics*, McGrawHill, 8th Edition, 1973.
2. Ibid.

respect of which other countries enjoyed comparative advantage. But it could not provide a satisfactory explanation *of why comparative costs of producing commodities in various countries differ*. Ricardo thought comparative costs of producing commodities in various countries differed due to the differences in efficiency of labour. But this begs the question why labour efficiency is different in various countries.

The credit of providing an adequate and valid answer to this question goes to Heckscher and Ohlin who explained that comparative costs of different commodities in the two countries vary because of the following factors :

1. The various countries differ in respect of factor endowments suited for the production of different commodities.

2. The different commodities require different factor proportions for their production.

Thus Heckscher and Ohlin supplemented the comparative costs theory by providing valid reasons for differences in comparative costs in various countries. We shall explain in detail the Heckscher-Ohlin theory of international trade in the next chapter.

3. Against the Ricardian doctrine of comparative cost it has also been said that it is based on the constant cost of production in the two trading countries. This assumption of constant costs leads them to conclude that different countries would *completely specialise* in the production of a single product on the basis of their comparative costs. Thus, of the two commodities cloth and wheat, if India has a comparative advantage in the production of cloth, it will produce all cloth and no wheat. On the other hand, if U.S.A. has a comparative advantage in the production of wheat, it will produce all wheat and no cloth. But the pattern of international trade shows that this is far from reality. As a matter of fact, a stage comes when it is no longer advantageous for India to import wheat from U.S.A. (because of increasing costs in producing wheat). Further, in the real world it is found that countries do not have complete specialisation. Indeed, a country produces a certain commodity and also imports a part of it.

However, it may be noted that even if the phenomenon of increasing costs is taken into account, foreign trade can still be explained in terms of differences in comparative costs. Only in the situation of increasing costs, countries would not have complete specialisation. As explained earlier, opportunity cost version of comparative costs theory does consider the case of increasing costs.

4. The Ricardian theory of comparative costs, has also been critcized for its not going into the question *what determines the terms of trade* between the countries. Voicing this criticism Elseworth remarks, 'the comparative costs theorem, the way in which Ricardo set up his illustration, tended to obscure the problem of the terms of trade."[3] Ricardian theory of comparative costs explains what commodity a country will export and what commodity it will import but it does not investigate at what rate it will exchange its exports for imports (*i.e.* terms of trade). However, the fixation of terms of trade is a vital issue, for on it a country's share of gains from trade depends.

It is worthwhile to note that J.S. Mill, another noted classical economist, removed this shortcoming of the comparative cost theory by supplementing it with *Reciprocal Demand Theory* which explains the determination of terms of trade. We shall explain Mill's reciprocal demand theory in a later chapter.

5. Ohlin attacked the comparative cost theory for its assumption that *factors of production were perfectly mobile within a country but immobile between countries*. He pointed out that immobility

3. P.T. Elseworth, *The International Economy*.

of factors between countries could not serve as a basis for international trade, since immobility of factors is not peculiar the relations between countries but is also present between different regions of the same country. He further expressed the view that comparative cost doctrine applied not only to international trade but also to inter-regional trade. Indeed, according to him, *international trade is only a special case of inter-regional trade*. He further criticized the classical theory of comparative cost for its emphasis on supply conditions as an explanation of international trade and its neglect of the importance of demand conditions in determining the pattern of international trade. He writes, "The comparative cost reasoning alone explains very little about international trade. It is indeed nothing more than an abbreviated account of the condition of supply"[4] According to him, prices of different goods and their quantities produced and consumed depend on both supply and demand conditions. He therefore, propounded a new theory of international trade based on general equilibrium theory of value.

It may be mentioned here that Ohlin's criticisms do not invalidate comparative cost theory. Indeed, he only refined and modified it. Even in his theory, popularly known as factor-proportions theory of international trade, comparative costs serve as a basis of international trade. His contribution lies in his inquiring into the question why comparative costs of commodities in different countries differ and offering a satisfactory explanation of it in terms of different factor-proportions required for the production of various goods. He further improved the comparative cost theory by incorporating in his analysis the demand aspect as be based his international trade theory on the general equilibrium theory of value.

6. It is alleged that comparative cost theory is *static in character as it is based on fixed supplies of factors of production, the given technology, and the fixed and identical production functions in the trading countries*. Its conclusions cannot therefore be applied in the context of a dynamic economy, especially in the present-day developing countries where resources are being developed, technology is being improved, production functions are undergoing a change. Indeed, structural changes are being brought about in these economies. In view of the changes in factor supplies and technology in developing countries, comparative costs of producing different commodities are also changing. In this dynamic context, a developing economy may have a comparative disadvantage in producing a certain commodity but may attain a comparative advnatage after a certain stage of its development.

Note that this criticism about the static character of the comparatice cost theory does not invalidate it. It only pinpoints the need for reformulating and refining it so as to make it applicable to the dynamic conditions of the developing countries.

Conclusion

To sum up, bereft of the labour theory of value and expressed in terms of opportunity costs comparative cost theory is still a valid explanation of international trade. It highlights the need for removal of artificial restrictions in the form of tariffs and other means on foreign trade so that various countries specialise on the basis of their comparative costs and derive mutual benefits from trade. This theory has been a victim of undue criticisms such as that it assumes the absence of transport costs, the existence of perfect competition and full employment, and further that it considers two commodities, two countries model. These are only simplifying assumptions and do not invalidate its conclusions in a substantial way. Indeed, every theory makes some such simplifying assumptions in order to bring out the economic forces that have an important bearing on the subject under investigation.

---

4. B. Ohlin, *Interregional and International Trade*, p. 586

HECKSCHER – OHLIN'S THEORY OF INTERNATIONAL TRADE

The classical comparative cost theory did not satisfactorily explain why comparative costs of producing various commodities differ as between different countries. The new theory propounded by Heckscher and Ohlin went deeper into the underlying forces which cause differences in comparative costs. They explained that it is differences in factor endowments of different countries and different factor-proportions needed for producing different commodities that account for difference in comparative costs. This new theory is therefore-called Heckscher-Ohlin theory of international trade. Since there is wide agreement among modern economists about the explanation of intenational trade offered by Heckscher and Ohlin this theory is also called *modern theory of international trade*. Further, since this theory is based on general equilibrium analysis of price determination, this is also known as *General Equilibrium Theory of International Trade*.

It is worthwhile to note that, contrary to the viewpoint of classical economists, Ohlin asserts that there does not exist any basic difference between the domestic (inter-regional) trade and international trade. Indeed, according to him, *international trade is only a special case of inter-regional trade*. Thus, Ohlin asserts that it is not the cost of transport which distinguishes international trade from domestic trade, for transport cost is present in the domestic inter-regional trade. Trade because currencies of different countries are related to each other through foreign exchange rates which determine the value or purchasing power of different currencies. Ohlin, therefore, regards different nations as mere regions separated from each other by national frontiers, different languages and customs, etc. But these differences are not such that prevent the occurrence of trade between nations. He, therefore, asserts that general theory of value which can be applied to explain inter-regional trade can also be applied equally well to explain international trade.

According to general equilibrium theory of value, relative prices of commodious are determined by demand for and supply of them. In the long-run equilibrium under conditions of perfect competition, relative prices of commodities, as determined by demand and supply, are equal to average cost of production. The cost of production of a commodity, as is well-known, depends upon the prices paid for the factors of production employed in the production of that commodity. Factor prices in turn determine the incomes of the factor owners and hence the demand for goods. Thus trade is mutual inter-dependence between prices of commodities and prices of factors, and the exchange of goods and factors between between demand for commodities and demand for factors. This is how general equilibrium theory of value explains prices of commodities and factors between different individuals in a region or a country. However, according to Ohlin, the classical analysis presumes it to apply to a single market in a country and ignores the space factor whose intrdocution is crucial for explanation of trade between regions. The factors which explain the trade between different regions also explain the trade between different nations or countries as well.

Heckscher-Ohlin Theorem

According to Ricardo and other classical economists, international trade is based on differences in comparative costs. It is important to note that Heckscher and Ohlin agreed with this fundamental proposition and only elaborated this by explaining the factors which cause differences in comparative costs of commodities between different regions or countries. Ricardo and others who followed him explained differences in comparative costs as arising from differences in skill and efficiency of labour alone. This is not a satisfactory explanation of differences in comparative cots. Ohlin pointed out more significant factors, namely, differences in factor endowments of the nations and difference in factor proportions of producing different commodities, which account for differences in comparative costs and hence from the ultimate basis of inter-regional or international trade. Thus,

Heckscher-Ohlin theory does not contradict and supplant the comparative cost theory but supplements it by offering sufficiently satisfactory explanation of what causes differences in comparative costs. According to Ohlin, the underlying forces behind differences in comparative costs are two-fold :

1. *The different regions or countries have different factor endowments.*
2. *The different goods require different factor-proportions for their production.*

It is a well-known fact that various countries (regions) are differently endowed with productive factors required for production of goods. Some countries posses relatively more capital, some relatively more labour, and some relatively more land. The factor which is relatively abundant in a country will tend to have a lower price and the factor which is relatively scarce will tend to have a higher price. Thus, according to Ohlin, factor endowments and factor prices are intimately associated with each other, Suppose K stands for the availability or supply of capital in a country, L for that of labour and PK for price of capital and PL for the price of labour. Further, take two countries A and B; in country A capital is relatively abundant and labour is relatively scarce. The reverse is the case in country B. Given these factor-endowments, in country A capital will be relatively cheaper. In symbolic terms :

$$\text{Since} \left(\frac{K}{L}\right)_A > \left(\frac{K}{L}\right)_B$$

$$\text{Since} \left(\frac{PK}{PL}\right)_A < \left(\frac{PK}{PL}\right)_B$$

Thus the differences in factor endowments cause differences in factor prices and therefore account for differences in comparative costs of producing different commodities.

Together with the difference in factor-endowments, differences in factor proportions required for the production of different commodities also constitute an important force underlying differences in comparative costs as between different countries. Some commodities are such that their production requires relatively more capital than other factors ; they are therefore called capital-intensive commodities. Still other commodities require relatively more land than capital and labour and are therefore called land-intensive commodities. These differences in factor-productions (or what is also called differences in *factor-intensities*) needed for the production of different commodities account for differences in comparative costs of producing different commodities. The differences in comparative costs of producing different commodities lead to the differences in market prices of different commodities in different countries.

It follows from above that some countries have a comparative advantage in the production of a commodity for which the required factors are found in abundance and comparative disadvantage in the production of a commodity for which the required factors are not available in sufficient quantities. Thus a country A which has a relative abundance of capital and relative scarcity of labour will have a comparative advantage in specialising in the production of capital-intensive commodities and in return will import labour-intensive goods. This is because $\left(\frac{PK}{PL}\right)_A < \left(\frac{PK}{PL}\right)_B$.

On the other hand, a labour-abundant country B with a scarcity of capital will have a comparative advantage in specialising in the production of labour-intensive commodities and export some quantities of them and in exchange for import capital-intensive commodities. This is because in this country $\left(\frac{PL}{PK}\right)_B < \left(\frac{PL}{PK}\right)_A$.

If factor endowments in the two countries are the same and factor-productions used in the production of different commodities do not differe, there will be no differences in relative factor prices $\left[i.e. \left(\frac{PK}{PL}\right)_A = \left(\frac{PK}{PL}\right)_B \right]$ which will mean differences in comparative costs of producing commodities in the two countries will be non-existent. In this situation the countries will not gain from entering into trade with each other.

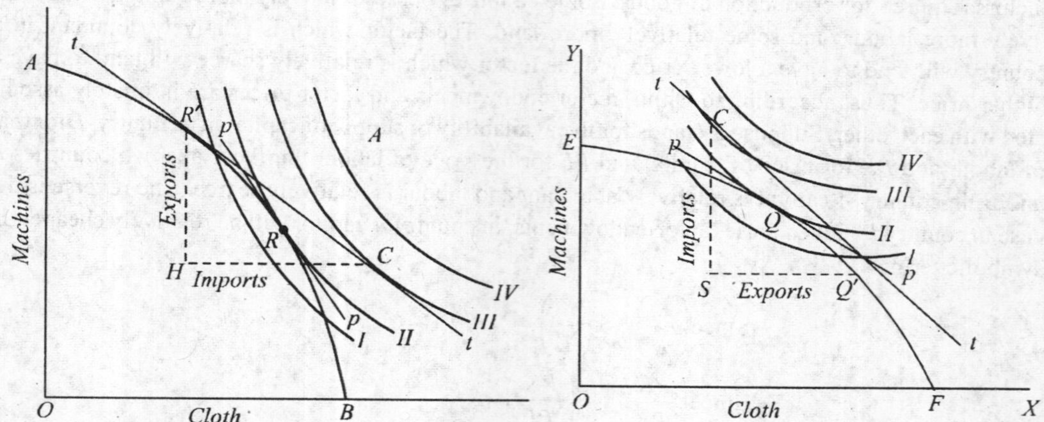

Fig. 23.5. *Exports and Imports of U.S.A.* **Fig. 23.6.** *Exports and Imports of India*

Let us graphically explain the Heckscher-Ohlin theory of international trade. Take two countries U.S.A. and India. Assume that there is a relative abundance of capital and scarcity of labour in U.S.A. and, on the contrary, there is a relative abundance of labour and scarcity of capital in India. (This is the real situation as well). Given these factor endowments we have drawn the production possibility curves (also known as transformation curves) between two commodities, cloth and machines of the two countries, U.S,.A. and India in Fig. 23.5 and 23.6 respectively. Since the two countries have different factor endowments their production possibility curves will differ. As will be seen from Fig. 23.5, the production possibility curve *AB* of U.S.A. shows that given its factor endowments, U.S.A. can produce relatively more of capital-intensive commodity machines and relatively less of labour-intensive commodity cloth. On the contrary, as will be seen from Fig. 23.6 with given factor endowments, India can produce relatively more of labour-intensive commodity cloth and relatively less of capital-intensive commodity machines. In the absence of foreign trade, equilibrium in each country would be determined by the following rule :

$$MRT_{MC} = MRS_{MC} = \frac{PM}{PC}$$

Where MRS_{MC} stands for a marginal rate of transformation of machines into cloth, MRS_{MC} for marginal rate of substitution of machines for cloth and $\frac{PM}{PC}$ for the price ratio between the two commodities.

In the geometric terms, the above rule implies that in the absence of foreign trade the production and consumption in the two countries would take place at the tangency point of the given production possibility curve with the highest possible community indifference curve.

It will be observed from Figure 23.5 that in the absence of trade, U.S.A. will be in equilibrium position with production and consumption at point *R* where its production possibility curve *AB* is tangent to its community indifference curve *II*. The tangent *pp* to the production possibility curve *AB* and the community indifference curve *II* at point *R* indicates the ratio of price of the two commodities (*i.e.* the domestic rate of exchange) before trade in U.S.A.

As regards India, as shown in Figure 23.6 before trade, she will be in equilibrium with production and consumption at point *Q* at which its production possibility curve is tangent to its community indifference curve *II*. Tangent *pp* at point *Q* to its production possibility curve *EF* and the community indifference curve *II* shows the domestic rate of exchange of two commodities before foreign trade.

It will be seen from Figures 23.5 and 23.6 that the price ratio (rate of exchange) of the two commodities in the two countries differs (slopes of tangents *pp* in them vary). It will therefore pay the two countries to enter into trade with each other. Suppose, the terms of trade, that is, the ratio of exchange of goods between the two countries is given by the line *tt*. It will be observed that with terms of trade line *tt*, U.S.A. will be in equilibrium from the view point of production at point *R′* at which the terms of trade line *tt* is tangent to its production possibility curve *AB*. However, its consumption point after trade is *C* which is determined by the tangency of the terms of trade line *tt* with the community indifference curve *III*. It will be seen from Figure 23.5 that in U.S.A. the consumption point *C* after trade lies at a higher indifference curve than before trade indicating the gain from trade it obtains. The consumption point *C* of U.S.A. as compared to its production point *R′* after trade reveals that U.S.A. produces *HR′* more of machines and *HC* less of cloth than it consumes domestically. Thus U.S.A. will export *HR′* of machines and import *HC* of cloth.

As regards India, it is evident from Figure 23.6 that as a result of trade its production point will shift to point *Q′* where its product possibility curve *EF* is tangent to the terms of trade line *tt*. After trade, consumption in India will take place at point *C* at which the terms of trade line *tt* is tangent to its community indifference curve *III*. As a result of trade India has also gained as she has reached a higher community indifference curve. Thus after trade with the production point *Q′* and consumption point *C*, India will produce *SQ′* more of cloth and *SC* less of machines than it consumes at home. Thus India will export *SQ′* of cloth and import *SC* of machines.

It follows from above that due to differences in factor endowments in U.S.A. and India also and due to different factor proportions required for the production of different commodities the basis for trade between the two countries exists and both would gain from trade by specialising in the production of commodities which require factors in respect of which they are well endowed and will import those commodities which need factors which are relatively in scarce supply.

EQUALIZATION OF FACTOR PRICES

As explained above, trade takes place when relative prices of commodities differ between countries due to difference in comparative costs. The volume of trade goes on expanding until the differences in relative prices of commodities (ignoring transport costs) are eliminated. Thus, in the absence of transport costs and tariffs, the effect of trade would be to equalise the relative commodity prices in the trading countries. For instance, in the example given above, as a result of trading between U.S.A. and India under the given conditions, the exports of machines to India by the U.S.A. will lower the prices of machines in India and raise them in U.S.A. This is because before opening up of trade, the price of machines was relatively high in India as compared to that in U.S.A. Now, with the increase in supply of machines in India due to their imports from U.S.A., their prices will fall. On the other hand, prices of machines in U.S.A. will rise due to the reduced supply in the domestic market than before as a result of their exports to India. Thus the prices of machines would tend to rise in U.S.A. and those in India would tend to fall. The flow of trade would continue expanding till the prices of machines in the two countries (in the absence of transport costs and tariffs) would become equal. Likewise, the price of cloth which before trade is lower in India than in U.S.A. would tend to become equal in the two countries following the opening up of trade between them.

Equalisation of Factor Prices

It is important to note that *trade tends to equalise not only commodity prices but also factor prices*. The exports of a product using the abundant factor by a country will cause the demand for that factor to increase and thereby make it relatively less abundant and raise its price. On the other hand, the imports of a product embodying large amounts of relatively scarce factor would make it less scarce and tend to lower its price. Thus changes in factor prices following the trade of commodities between the two countries result in equalisation of factor prices in them.

Let us take an example. As noted above, in U.S.A. capital is relatively abundant and cheap whereas labour is relatively scarce and expensive. On the countrary, in India labour is relatively abundant and cheap whereas capital is scarce and expensive. With these factor endowments it will pay India to export labour-intensive commodity cloth which it can produce at a cheaper price and in exchange to import capital-intensive commodity machines from U.S.A. which it can produce them at a lower price. As a result of this trade, the demand for labour in India would increase and its price would tend to increase. Now, with the imports of labour-intensive commodity cloth by U.S.A. and concentrating its more resources on production of capital-intensive machines, the demand for labour in U.S.A. would decrease and its price would tend to fall. Thus, other things remaining the same, the price of labour in India and U.S.A. would tend to become equal after opening up of trade between the two countries. The same applies to the price of capital. To sum up, *according to Heckscher-Ohlin theory, free trading of commodities between the two countries results in equalisation of factor prices*. If factors were mobile between countries, then the free movement of factors from one country to another would have equalised their prices.

But in actual practice factors lack interregional and international mobility. Therefore, in absence of trade of commodities, factor prices would not tend to the become equal in the different countries. Thus Ohlin argues that what would have been accomplished through free movement of factors between countries is indirectly accomplished through movement of commodities embodying different factor-proportions. Indeed, according to Ohlin, *international trade in commodities serves as a substitute for international mobility of factors*.

It is worthwhile to note that trade would achieve complete factor price equalisation only when some conditions and assumptions are fulfilled. It is also realised that these conditions and assumptions are quite restrictive so that in actual practice differences in factor-prices are not completely eliminated. The conditions and assumptions underlying the factor-price equalisation theorem are :

1. Tastes, that is, demand pattern for commodities, are the same
2. It is the supply conditions of the factors which are different in different countries and no qualitative differences prevail in them. This implies that the level of technological progress is the same in the different countries.
3. Production function of each commodity is the same in the different countries and is of a simple character, that is, it is either capital-intensive, or labour-intensive. In other words, production functions of commodities provides a limited degree of factor substitution.
4. There are no restrictions on trade in the form of tariffs and quotas in the trading countries.
5. There are no transport costs.

6. There exists perfect competition in the commodity market as well as in factor markets in each region or country.

Since in the real world, above conditions are not fulfilled, complete factor price equalisation does not take place. However, this does not invalidate the factor price equalisation theorem. Indeed, every theory is based upon some assumptions. What this theory asserts is that, given the above conditions, factor prices would become equal. To the extent these conditions do not exist, factor prices will remain unequal even after trade takes place between the countries.

Critical Evaluation of Heckscher-Ohlin Theory of International Trade

Heckscher and Ohlin theory has made invaluable contributions to the explanation of international trade. Though this theory accepts comparative costs as the basis of international trade, it makes several improvements in the classical comparative cost theory. First, it rescued the theory of international trade from the grip of labour theory of value and based it on the general equilibrium theory of value according to which both demand and supply conditions determine the prices of goods and factors. Second, Heckscher-Ohlin theory removes the difference between intenational trade and inter-regional trade, for the factors determining the two are the same. Third, a significant improvement is the explanation offered for difference in comparative costs of commodities between trading countries. Ricardo thought that the differences in labour efficiency alone accounted for the differences in comparative costs. According to Heckscher and Ohlin, as seen above, the differences in factor-endowments of the countries and also the differences in factor proportions required for producing various commodities explain differences in comparative costs and hence from the ultimate basis of intenational trade. These reasons advanced by Heckscher and Ohlin for differences in comparative costs of commodities in different countries are considered to be broadly true.

Fourth, as has been pointed out by Prof. Lancaster, Heckscher-Ohlin model provides a satisfactory picture of the future of foreign trade. According to the Ricardian theory, international trade exists because of differences in skill and efficiency of labour alone. This implies that as there is transmission of knowledge between the countries so that they master the techniques and skills of each other, then differences in comparative costs would cease to exist and as a result international trade would come to an end. But this is not likely to occur despite the fact that transmission of knowledge and techniques has greatly increased these days. Heckscher and Ohlin explain that international trade is due to the differences in factor-endowments (*i.e.* differences in supplies of all factors and not only of labour efficiency) and different factor-proportions required for different commodities. Since the factors such as land and other natural resources lack mobility, international trade would not cease to exist even if there is perfect transmission of knowledge between the countries.

Despite the above merits of Heckscher-Ohlin theory, it has some shortcomings which are briefly discussed below :

1. **Leontief Paradox.** In the Heckscher-Ohlin theory it has been assumed that relative factor prices reflect the relative supplies of factors. That is, a factor which is found in abundance in a country will have a lower price and vice versa. This means that in the determination of factor-prices supply outweighs demand. But if demand for factors prevails over supply, then factor prices so determined would not conform to the supplies of factors. Thus, if in a country there is abundance of capital and scarcity of labour in physical terms but there is relatively much greater demand for capital, then the price of capital would be relatively higher to that of labour. Then, under these circumstances, contrary to its factor-endowments, the country many export labour-intensive goods and import capital-intensive goods. Perhaps it is this which lies behind the empirical findings by Leontief that though America is a capital abundant and labour-scarce country, in the structure of its

imports capital-intensive goods are relatively greater whereas in the structure of its exports labour-intensive goods are relatively greater.[5] As this is contrary to the popularly held view, this is known as *Leontief Paradox*.

2. **Difference in Preferences or Demands for Goods.** Against Hecksher-Ohlin theorem, it has also been pointed out that differences in tastes and preferences for goods or, to put it in other words, differences in pattern of demand also give rise to trade between the countries. This is because under differences in demand or preferences for goods, the commodity price-ratios would not conform to the cost-ratios based on factor endowments. Let us take an extreme example. Suppose there are two countries *A* and *B* with same factor-endowments. According to Heckscher-Ohlin theorem, with same factor endowments cost-ratio of producing the two commodities and hence the commodity price ratio would be the same. Hence there is no possibility of trade between the two countries on the basis of Heckscher-Ohlin theorem. However, trade between the two countries is possible if the demand pattern or preferences of the people of the two countries for wheat and rice greatly differ.

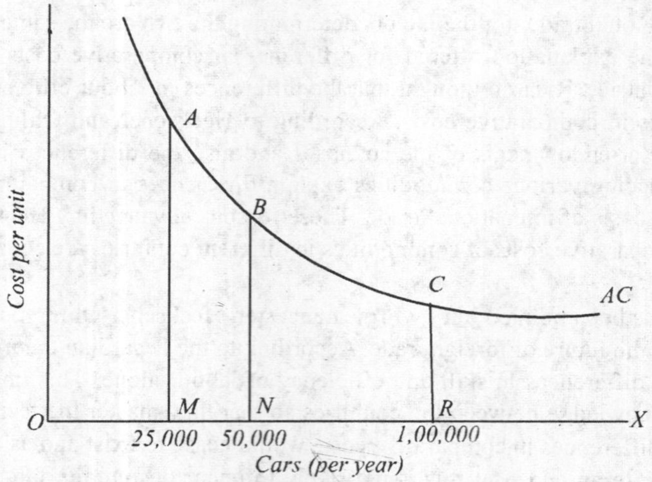

Fig. 23.7. *Economies of Scale as the Basis of Trade*

OTHER EXPLANATIONS OF INTERNATIONAL TRADE

In addition to the defferences in factor endorments causing differences in comparative costs, other explanations of international trade have been offered. They are explained below.

1. Differences in demand or preference pattern for goods.

As noted above, differences in demands for goods by the people of various countries also give rise to trade between countries.

Economies of Scale

In addition to differences in factor endowments, economies of scale also form the basis of trade. Economies of scale means as firms increase their size (scale), cost per unit of output declines. Therefore, the phenomenon of economies of scale is also called decreasing costs. How the economies of scale can form the basis of trade is shown in Figure 23.7. Suppose that Indian firm and the

5. See W.W. Leontief. 'Factor Proportions and Structure of American Trade, *Review of Economic Statistics, 1956*.

US firm has the same cost conditions so that average cost of productions is given by average cost curve *AC* in Fig. 23.7. *AC* curve declines due to economies of scale upto output level of 100,000 cars beyond which it remains constant. Scale of production of 100,000 cars per annum is called *minimum efficient scale.* Cost per unit of 25,000 cars per year is *AM* and of producing 50,000 cars per year is *BN* and of producing 100,000 cars is *CR*. If the demand for cars in both India and the US is 50,000 cars per annum, in both countries cost per unit of cars is the same and therefore no trade will take place between them as due to same cost per car, the same price per car will be set in each country.

Now, suppose the demand for cars in the US increases, say due to increase in incomes of their people, to 100,000 cars per year while the demand for cars in India remains at 50,000 cars per year. The firm in the USA will expand its production and reap the benefits of economies of scale resulting in lower cost per unit to *CR* which will be much less than that in India. This will also result in reduction in prices of car in the US as compared to India. Since cost per car beyond 100,000 cars in the USA remains the same, the US can increase its production to more than 100,000 cars and the extra cars it produces, it can export to India at lower price than that prevailing in India. We thus see economies of scale can form the basis of trade. Note that we have given an hypothetical example to show that economies of scale can be another explanation of trade.

Learning by Doing

In our above analysis, we have assumed that cost per unit of a product varies with the level of output. However, modern economists emphasize that cost per unit may also fall in a country due to the experience gained and accumulated by firms in producing a commodity over time. This is called *learning by doing* which is another explanation of trade. As a country produces a larger quantity of a particular product over time, its workers and managers gain experience in performing particular tasks required for producing a commodity. As a result, cost per unit of the product falls which makes it profitable for a country to export it to other countries. There is ample evidence that such learning by doing does occur and can form a basis of trade. Thus learning curve has important

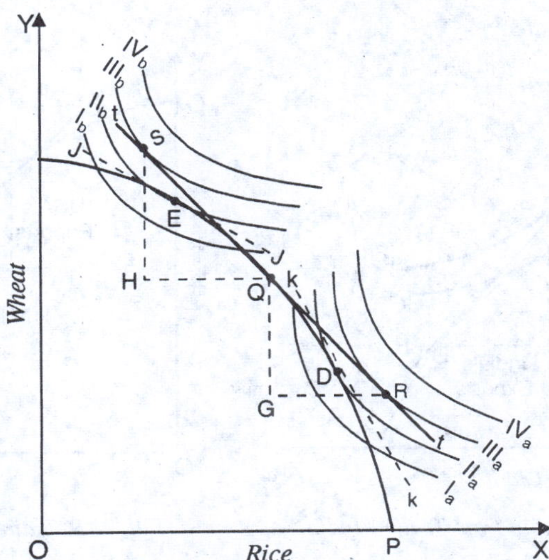

Fig. 23.7(a). *Differences in Consumption Pattern and International Trade*

implications for trade between countries. The country that produces products at a lower cost per unit because it has *learned* to use its labour and capital more efficiently creates a basis for trade.

Note that in this case of learning by doing comparative cost is something that is created. In this case therefore it is not the lower cost per unit because of different resource endowment that causes a country to specialise and trade. Instead, it is specialisation that causes lower cost per unit and accounts for trade.

Differences in Demand Pattern

Suppose people of country A prefer rice to wheat and people of country *B* prefer wheat consumption. With these preferences for wheat and rice we have drawn the community indifference curves of the two countries *A* and *B* in Fig. 23.7(*a*). Since factor-endowments in the two countries are the same, *PP* is the production possibility curve in both of them. In the absence of trade country *A* is in equilibrium at point *D* where its community indifference curve II_a is tangent to the production possibility curve *PP*. *kk* is the commodity price-ratio line determined in country *A*. Country *B* is in equilibrium at point E where its community indifference curve II_b is tangent to the production possibility curve *PP*. *JJ* is the commodity price-ratio determined in country *B*. Thus, due to difference in demand (preferences) for rice and wheat in the two countries different commodity price ratios have come to prevail in the two countries though their factor endowments (and therefore the cost-ratios of the two commodities) are the same. Because of the differences in commodity price ratios the trade is possible and will be mutually beneficial. The opening of trade would equalise commodity prices in the two countries and would therefore change their pattern of production giving rise to exports and imports by the two countries. Let *tt* be the commodity price ratio (*i.e.* terms of trade) that is settled between the two countries. It will be noticed in Fig. 23.7(*a*) that with terms of trade *tt* each country would produce at point *Q*. But the consumption of the two commodities would be different in the countries. After trade whereas country *A*'s consumption would be at *R* where terms of trade line *tt* is tangent to its indifference curve III_a; country B's consumption would be at point *S* on its indifference curve III_b. It is evident that country *A* would be importing *GR* rice and exporting *GQ* wheat, whereas country *B* would be exporting *QH* rice and importing *HS* wheat. It will be further noticed that through trade both have reached at their higher indifference curves

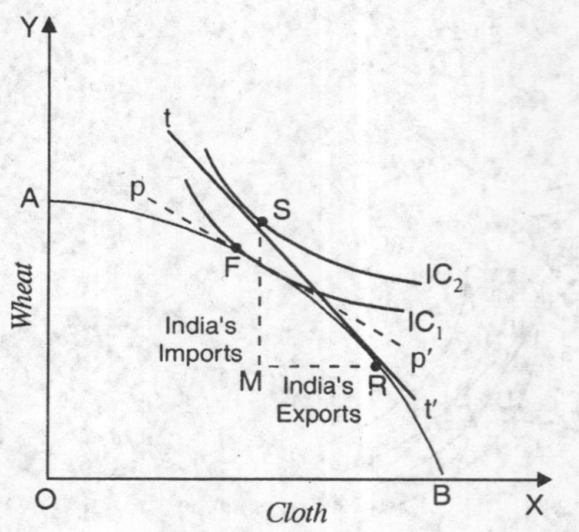

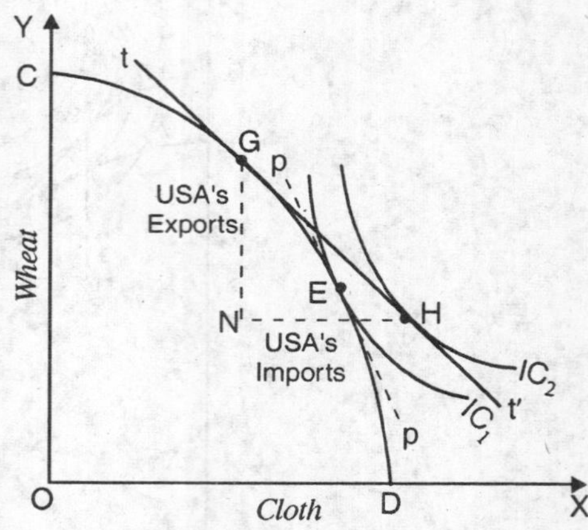

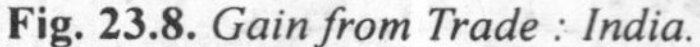

Fig. 23.8. *Gain from Trade : India.* **Fig. 23.9.** *Gain from Trade : U.S.A.*

indicating higher level of welfare than before trade.

GAINS FROM TRADE

Foreign trade confers a good deal of benefits on the trading countries. If different countries specialise on the basis of their comparative costs, it would enable them to make optimum use of their resources and thereby add to their output, income and welfare of their people. Gains from trade are broadly divided into two types :

(*i*) *Static Gains* (*ii*) *Dynamic Gains.*

Static gains from trade refer to the increase in utility or welfare of the people of the trading countries as a result of the optimum utilisation of their given factor-endowments, for they specialise on the basis of their comparative costs. On the other hand, dynamic gains refer to the contributions which foreign trade makes to the overall economic growth of the trading countries. We shall explain below in detail these two types of gains.

Static Gains from Trade

As stated above, static gains from trade are measured by the increase in the utility or level of welfare when there is opening of trade between the countries. Note that in modern economics increase in utility or welfare is measured through indifference curves. When as a result of foreign trade, a country moves from a lower indifference curve to a higher one, it implies that the welfare of the people has increased. Tó show the static gains from trade, let us take an example. Suppose two commodities cloth and wheat are produced in two countries, India and U.S.A., before they enter into trade. Their production possibility and indifference curves are shown in Figures 28.4 and 23.9. It will be seen from Fig. 23.8 that before trade India would be in equilibrium at point F (*i.e.* producing and consuming at point F) where the price line pp' is tangent to both production possibility curve AB and indifference curve IC_1. The slope of the price line pp' shows the price-ratio (or cost ratio) of the two commodities in India. India can gain if international price-ratio (terms of trade) is different from the domestic price-ratio represented by pp'. Suppose the terms of trade settled are such that we get tt as the terms of trade line showing the price ratio at which goods can be exchanged between India and the U.S.A. Now, with tt' as the given terms of trade line (*i.e.* new price-ratio line). India would produce at point R at which the terms of trade line tt is tangent to her production possibility curve. It will be seen from Fig. 23.8 that at point R, India will produce more of cloth in which it has comparative advantage and less of wheat than at F. Though India will produce at point R on his production possibility curve, where the terms of trade line tt is tangent to her production possibility curve AB it will not consume the quantities of wheat and cloth represented by the point R. Given the new price-ratio represented by the terms of trade line tt the consumption of the goods will depend upon the pattern of demand of the country. To incorporate this factor we have drawn social indifference curves IC_1, IC_2 of the country. These social indifference curves represent the demands for the two goods, or, in other words, the scale of preferences between the two goods of the society.

It will be seen from Fig. 23.8 that the terms of trade line tt is tangent to the social indifference curve IC_2 of India at point S. Therefore, after trade India will consume the quantities of cloth and wheat as represented by point S. It is therefore clear that as a result of specialisation and trade India has been able to shift from point F on indifference curve IC_1 to the point S on higher indifference curve IC_2. This is the gain obtained from specialisation and trade and implies that trade enables a country to increase her consumption beyond her production possibility curve. (It will be seen that point S lies beyond the production possibility curve AB of India).

It is also worth noting that when specialisation and trade occur, the quantities of the two goods consumed by a country, will differ from the quantities of the two goods produced by her. In Fig. 23.8 whereas India produces the quantities of two goods represented by point R, it will consume the quantities of the two goods represented by the point S. The difference arises due to exports and imports of goods. In Fig. 23.8, while India will export MR quantity of cloth it will import MS quantity of wheat.

Now consider the position of U.S.A. which is depicted in Fig. 23.9. Given its factor endowments *CD* is the production possibility curve between wheat and cloth of the U.S.A. It is evident from the production possibility curve *CD* that the factor endowments of the USA are more favourable for the production of wheat. It will also be seen from Fig. 23.9 that before trade the U.S.A. will produce and consume at point *E* on her production possibility curve *CD* where the domestic price ratio line *pp* and indifference curve IC_1 are tangent to it. The USA will gain from trade if it can sell at a different price ratio from *pp*. Suppose the terms of trade line is *tt*. With this terms of trade line *tt* the U.S.A. will produce at point *G* on her production possibility curve *CD*. She will now produce more of wheat in which she has comparative advantage and less of cloth than before. On the other hand, given the price ratio as represented by the terms of trade line *tt* the USA will consume the quantities of the two goods given by the point *H* where the terms of trade line is tangent to her indifference curve IC_2. It is therefore clear that the specialisation and consequently trade with India has enabled the U.S.A. to shift from her lower indifference curve IC_1 to her higher indifference curve IC_2. This is the gain which she obtains from trade.

By comparing the production and consumption points of the U.S.A. it will be observed that the U.S.A. will export *NG* amount of wheat and import *NH* amount of cloth.

It is worth remembering that while in case of constant opportunity cost, each country attains complete specialisation, that is, it produces one of the two goods after trade, in case of increasing opportunity cost specialisation is not complete. In case of increasing opportunity cost, a country produces only a relatively large amount of the good in which it has comparative advantage.

DYNAMIC GAINS FROM TRADE : INTERNATIONAL TRADE AND ECONOMIC GROWTH

We have seen above in the discussion of comparative cost theory that specialisation followed by international trade makes it possible for the countries to have more of both commodities than before. This additional production of commodities is the gain which flows from specialisation by different countries in the production of different goods and then trading with each other. Specialisation by different countries in the production of different goods according to their efficiency and resource endowment brings about an increase in the total world production by increasing the level of their productivity. It is this trade that makes possible the division and specialisation of labour on which higher productivity of different countries is so largely based. If the various countries could not exchange the products of their specialised labour, each of them would have to be self-sufficient (*i.e.*, each of them would have to produce all goods it requires, even those which it could not produce efficiently) with the result that their productivity and standard of living will go down. Thus, according to Professor Haberler, "*International division of labour and international trade, which enable every country to specialise and to export those things which it can produce cheaper in exchange for what others can provide at a lower cost, have been and still are one of the basic factors promoting economic well being and increasing national income of every participating country.*"[6]

We thus see that the main gain from specialisation and trade is the increase in national production, income and consumption of the participating countries. But the above explanation of gains from trade in terms of comparative cost theory deals only with *static* gains from trade, that is, the

6. G. Haberler, *International Trade and Economic Development*

gains which accrue to a country from reallocation of a given amount of resources. We shall now discuss, *dynamic gains* from trade, that is gains from trade which accrue to a country in terms of promotion of its economic growth.

Dennis Robertson described foreign trade as "*an engine of growth.*" With greater income and production made possible by specialisation and trade, greater savings and investment become possible and as a result higher rate of economic growth can be achieved. Through promotion of exports, a developing country can earn valuable foreign exchange which it can use for the imports of capital equipment and raw materials which are so essential for economic development. Therefore, Professor Haberler argues that since international trade raises the level of income, it also promotes economic development. He thus remarks : "What is good for the national income and the standard living is, at least potentially, also good for economic development; for the greater the volume of output the greater can be the rate of growth—provided the people individually or collectively have the urge to save and to invest and economically to develop. The higher the level of output, the easier it is to escape the "vicious circle of poverty" and to "take off into self-sustained growth" to use the jargon of modern development theory. Hence, *if trade raises the level of income, it also promotes economic development*[7].

As pointed out above, the importance of and gain from international trade follows from the theory of comparative cost. Specialisation by different countries according to their production efficiency and factor endowments *ensures optimum use and allocation of resources* of the countries. Differences in production possbilities and costs of production of various products between different countries of the world are so great that tremendous gain interms of additional output and income accrues to the world community from in ternational specialisation and trade. For instance, the relative differences in cost of production of industrial products and food and raw materials between developed and developing countries are almost infinite in the sense that either type of these countries cannot produce what they buy from the other.

But the theory of comparative cost is static. it indicates only those gains which accure to the trading countries as a result of the differences in *given cost* of production and *given production possibilities* of various products at *a given point of time.* As pointed out above, besides the static gains indicated by comparative cost theory, international trade bestows very important indirect gains and benefits, which are generally described as *dynamic gains,* upon the participating countries. These dynamic gains also promote economic growth in the participating countries. It is worth noting that both developed and developing countries have obtained benefits from trade. The international trade has contributed a good deal to the economic development of under-developed countries. To quote Professor Haberler again "If we were to estimate the contribution of international trade to economic developent especially of the under-developed countries solely by the static gains from trade in any given year on the usual assumption of *given production capabilities,* we would indeed grossly under-rate the importance of trade. For over and above the direct stastic gains dwelt upon by the traditional theory of comparative cost, trade bestows very important indirect benefits upon the participating countries".[8] Dynamic gains which' accrue to the developing countries from international trade are as follows:

Firstly, through foreign trade, developing countries get material means of production such as capital equipment, machinery and raw materials which are so essential for economic growth of

7. G. Haberler, *Op, cit.* (emphasis added)
8. *Op. cit.*

these countries. There has been rapid technological progress in the developed countries. This advanced and superior technology is incorporated or embodied in various types of capital goods. It is thus clear that developing countries derive tremendous gains from technological progress in the developed countries through the imports of capital goods such as machinery, transport equipment, vehicles, power generation equipment, road building machinery, medicines, chemicals. It is worth mentioning here that the pattern of import trade of the underdeveloped countries has changed in the last several years and now consists of greater quantity of various forms of capital goods and less of textiles.

Secondly, even more important than the importation of capital goods is the transmission of technical know-how, skills, managerial talents., entrepreneurship through foreign trade. When the developing countries come to have trade relationship with the developed countries, they also often import technical know-how, with all their skills, managers, etc., from them. With this they are also able to develop their own technical know-how, managerial and entrepreneurial ability. The growth of technical know-how, skill and managerial ability is an important requisite for economic development of developing countries. Professor Haberler rightly says: "The late-comers and successors in the process of development and industrialization have always had the great advantage that they could learn from the experinces, from the successes as well as from the failures and mistakes of the pioneers and forerunners. . . Today the developing countries 'have a tremendous, constantly growing store of technical know-how to draw from. True, simple adoption of methods, developed for the conditions of the developed countries is often not possible. B_1 adaptation is surely much easier than the first creation. . . . Trade is the most important vehicle for the transmission of technological know-how . . . . Today there are a dozen industrial centres in Europe, the U.S., Canada, and Japan, and Russia which are ready to sell machinery as well as engineering advice and know-how."[9]

QUESTIONS FOR REVIEW

1. Explain how international trade extends a country's consumption possibility beyond its production possibility frontier.
2. Taking an example of two countries, two goods and one factor of production, illustrate the Ricardian theory of comparative advantage.
3. Explain the theory of comparative cost with the opportunity cost approach.
4. In the Ricardian model of trade do you think introduction of trade would lead to complete specialisation. Explain briefly.
5. Distinguish between absolute difference in cost and comparative difference in cost. How does free trade between countries benefit consumers in both countries ?
6. Suppose that labour is the only factor of production and is homogeneous in two countries *A* and *B*, who produce only two goods *X* and *Y*. Country *A* is endowed with 6000 units of labour and country *B* is endowed with 3000 labour units. The labour units required to produce one unit of a good in each country are as follows :

9. Haberler, *Op, cit.*

Labour Units required in

Country	A	Country B
1 unit of X	4	1
1 unit of Y	3	2

Answer the following questions :

(*a*) Which country has absolute advantage over the other in which good/goods ?

(*b*) Which country has comparative advantage over the other in which good/goods ?

(*c*) Is trade possible between *A* and *B* ? What will be the basis of trade ?

(*d*) Before trade, what will be the price of good *X* in terms of good *Y* in country *A* and *B* ?

(*e*) In which price range will international trade be beneficial to both the countries, assuming note transport costs ?

(*f*) Draw the production possibility frontier of country *A* and *B* before and after trade.

[**Hints.** The country *B* has absolute advantage in the production of both goods *X* and *Y* over country *A*. However, country *B* is comparatively more efficient in the production of good *X*, whereas country *A* is relatively less inefficient in the production of *Y*. Thus country *B* has comparative advantage in the production of *X* and the country *A* has comparative advantage in the production of good *Y*.

The comparative advantage is the basis of trade between the two countries).

7. Show that gain from trade arises partly from the opportunity to trade at the international price ratio and partly from the specialisation in the product in which the country has comparative advantage.

8. Identify the conditions that may give rise to trade between two nations. How can two countries simultaneously gain from trade ?

9. (*a*) There are two countries *A* and *B*, each producing two goods *X* and *Y*, with full employment of its resources, country *A* can produce a maximum of 18 units of *X* or 12 units of *Y*; country *B* can produce a maximum of 6 units of *X* or 12 units of Y. In both countries the marginal rates of transformation are constant.

(*i*) If trade is allowed, which countries specialise in which goods ?

(*ii*) In the pre-trade situation, country A produces 9 units of *X* and 6 units of *Y*, and country *B* produces 4 units of *X* and 4 units of *Y*. With trade the international rate of exchange becomes $P_x = P_y$. Calculate the gains from trade for each country.

10. What is the Heckscher-Ohlin theorem of trade ? Clearly state its underlying assumptions.

11. Using the Hecksher-Ohlin model of trade show that free trade is better than no trade. Explain graphically the gains from trade to the countries.

12. Show that under Hechsher-Ohlin framework international trade would normally lead to equalisation of relative factor price.

14. Under what conditions are factor prices equilised by trade between two countries.

14. Two nations A and B have identical production possibility curves. Can trade between them still be beneficial to both ?

OR

Show that in a two country, two commodity two factor world, trade can take place even if factor endowment are different ?

15. "Commodity trade acts as a substitute for international mobility of factors of production in its effect on factor prices" Discuss,
16. What is meant by factor intensity reversed ? Is factor intensity non-reversal a necessary condition for Hechscher-Ohlin model of trade to be valid.
17. What do you understand by factor-intensity reversal ? What are its implications for factor price equalisation ?
18. What are the necessary and sufficient conditions for the factor price equalisation theorem to hold ? Explain
19. Do you agree with the view that difference in factor endownments are neither a necessary nor a sufficient basis for international trade ? Give arguments in support of your answer ?
20. Free trade is better than no trade Discuss.

CHAPTER 24

National Income and Foreign Trade Multiplier : Saving-Investment Approach

Introduction

Keynes explained his investment multiplier in the context of a closed economy where neither exports nor imports of goods occur. Keynesian theory of multiplier has been extended to the open economy where there are flows of goods and capital between a country and others. We have seen in the saving-investment approach that in a closed economy equilibrium level of national income is determined by the equality between intended saving and investment ($S = I$). Now, in the open economy foreign trade, that is, exports and imports of an economy are also to be taken into account as these also influence the determination of national income. Further, like investment expenditure, exports have also a multiplier effect on changes in the national income of a country. The value of *foreign trade multiplier* or what is also called *export multiplier* depends not only on the marginal propensity to save but also on the marginal propensity to import. Therefore, in what follows we shall first explain the concept of the import function and how marginal propensity to import is derived from it. After explaining this we shall proceed to explain how foreign trade multiplier depends on marginal propensity to import and how changes in exports and imports create multiplier effect on changes in the equilibrium level of national income.

The Import Function

In an open economy consumers of a country also spend some income on imported goods. The imports of a country depend on its level of income. The higher the level of income, the prices of imported goods and tastes of consumers remaining the same, the greater will be its imports. *The*

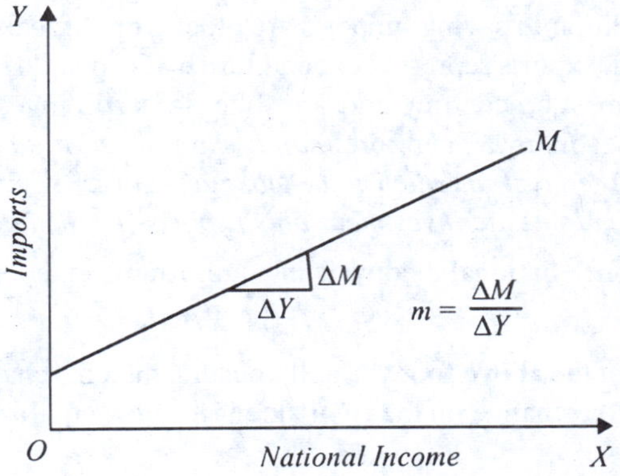

Fig. 24.1. *The Import Function*

relationship between imports and level of income of a country is called the import function and is written as

$$M = f(Y)$$

where M stands for imports and Y for income of a country.

We have shown the import function in Fig. 24.1 where on the X-axis the level of national income and on the Y-axis imports of a country are measured. It will be seen that even at zero national income some imports are undertaken by exporting some capital accumulated in the past or by borrowing from abroad. There are two concepts of propensity to import which should be understood. First, *average propensity to import is defined as* the *proportion or percentage of national income spent on imports*, that is, it is rupee value of imports divided by national income or $\frac{M}{Y}$. Large countries such as the U.S.A., Russia and India have low average propensity to import and small countries such as Great Britain and Holland have high average propensity to import. The average propensity to import in India is between 0.02 and 0.03.

More important concept is the marginal propensity to import. *The marginal propensity to import measures the change in import as a result of increase in national incomes* and is algebraically expressed as $\frac{\Delta M}{\Delta Y}$ where ΔM is the change in value of imports and ΔY is the increase in national income. If imports increase by Rs. 3 when national income rises by Rs. 100, the marginal propensity to import $\left(\frac{\Delta M}{\Delta I}\right)$ will be equal to $3/100 = 0.03$ or 3 per cent. If increase in income by Rs. 100 leads to the increase in imports by Rs. 10, the marginal propensity to imports is $10/100 = 0.1$ or 10 per cent.

The Foreign Trade Multiplier in an Open Economy

In a closed economy equilibrium level of national income is determined at the level where intended saving equals intended investment ($S = I$). Saving represents leakage or *withdrawal* of some money from the income flow, while investment is the *injection* of some money into the income stream. The level of national income is in equilibrium (that is, circular flow of income is constant) when leakage from the income stream in the form of savings is equal to the injection of investment expenditure. In an open economy, the role of foreign trade, that is, exports and imports of a country are also to be considered. Imports by consumers of a country represent the expenditure on imported goods by the residents of the country and leads to the leakage of some income from domestic economy. Therefore, in addition to saving, imports are other from of leakage that occur in an open economy. On the other hand, exports represent expenditure by the people of foreign countries on the goods produced in the domestic economy and are, like domestic investment, injection into the income stream of an open economy. Therefore, *equilibrium level of national income in an open economy is determined at the level at which total leakage, that is, savings plus imports* ($S + M$) *equal total injection, that is, domestic investment plus exports* ($I + X$) *into the income stream.*

Thus, in an open economy, national income is in equilibrium at the level at which

$$S + M = I + X$$

When a change in any of the above four variables occurs, then the change on the left side of the above equation must equal the change on the right side if the new equilibrium is to be achieved.

Hence

$$\Delta S + \Delta M = \Delta I + \Delta X \quad \text{. . . (1)}$$

Now, change in saving, $\Delta S = s.\,\Delta Y$

Where s = marginal propensity to save and

ΔY = change in national income.

Likewise, change in imports, $\Delta M = m.\,\Delta Y$

where m = marginal propensity to import.

Thus, rewriting equation (1) we have

$$s\Delta Y + m.\Delta Y = \Delta I + \Delta X$$

or

$$\Delta Y(s+m) = \Delta I + \Delta X$$

$$\Delta Y = \frac{1}{s+m}(\Delta I + \Delta X) \qquad ...(2)$$

It will be known from equation (2) that change in either investment or exports will cause income to increase by the multiple, $\frac{1}{s+m}$. Thus $\frac{1}{s+m}$ is the foreign trade multiplier which is generally denoted by K_f. Thus, if exports increase by ΔX, the national income will rise by $\Delta X \cdot \frac{1}{s+m}$.

Hence, $K_f = \frac{1}{s+m}$

In Chapter, we found that foreign trade multiplier is equal to $\frac{1}{1-mpc+m}$. Since s = 1– mpc, the value of foreign trade multiplier (K_f) becomes equal to $\frac{1}{s+m}$.

Thus, *foreign trade multiplier is equal to the reciprocal of marginal propensity to save (s) plus marginal propensity to import* (*m*). It is evident that smaller the leaks, that is, smaller the values of marginal propensity to save (*s*) and marginal propensity to import (*m*) the greater the value of foreign trade multiplier. Let us given an example. If $s = 0.2$ and $m = 0.2$, then

Foreign trade mutiplier, $K_f = \frac{1}{0.2+0.2}$

$$= \frac{1}{0.4} \text{ or } 2.5$$

Again, if $s = 0.3$ and $m = 0.2$, then

Foreign trade multiplier $= \frac{1}{0.3+0.2} = \frac{1}{0.5}$

$= 2$

Graphic Representation of Foreign Trade Multiplier

The foreign trade multiplier has been graphically illustrated in Fig. 24.2 where $S + M$ is the saving plus import function curve and X_0 is the export curve which is constant as it has been assumed to be an autonomous variable, that is, independent of the level of income. To simplify our analysis we assume that there is no investment, equilibrium level of national income will therefore be determined by consumption (saving) and exports.

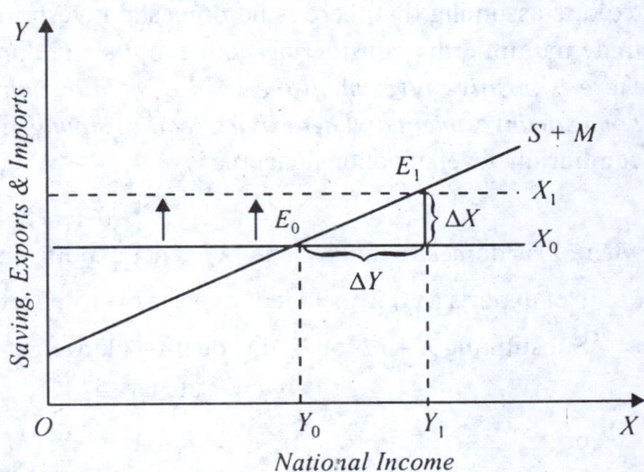

Fig. 24.2. *Foreign Trade Multiplier with No Investment*

Initially, the economy is in equilibrium at level of income Y_0 where $S + M = X_0$, investment being zero. Suppose there is autonomous increase in exports so that export curve shifts upward from X_0 to X_1, It will be seen from Fig. 24.2 that equilibrium income increases to Y_1.

Thus, increase in exports (ΔX) has led to the increase in income (ΔY) equal to $Y_1 - Y_0$ which is much greater than change in exports (ΔX). Theexpression $\frac{\Delta Y}{\Delta X}$ represents the foreign trade multiplier whose value depends on the slope of saving-import function curve $S + M$ which is equal to the reciprocal of the sum of marginal propensity to save and marginal propensity to import $\left(\frac{1}{s+m}\right)$

How the Foreign Trade Multiplier Works ?

The foreign trade multiplier works in the same way as Keynes' investment multiplier. When there is increase in exports, it will cause the increase in income of the exporters and those employed in the export industries. They will save some of the increase in their incomes and will spend a good part of the increases in their incomes on consumer goods, both domestic and imported ones. While savings do not generate further income and represent leakage from the income stream, expenditure on imports leads to the increase in the incomes of the foreign countries from which goods are imported. Thus expenditure on imports also represents a leakage from the income stream as far as domestic economy is concerned. But the increased expenditure on domestic goods as a result of increase in exports will go on increasing incomes in various successive rounds of spending till the multiplier fully works itself out.

It may be noted that increase in exports of a country can occur due to several reasons. There may be change in tastes or demand of the people of foreign countries for goods of a country. To begin with, the exporters may meet the demand for exported goods by selling their inventories and enjoy higher incomes. But in the next periods, they will make efforts to increase the production of exported goods and employ more workers. This will generate new income and employment in the export industries. But the working of multiplier does not stop here. Those employed in export industries will spend a good part of their increased incomes on goods produced by other industries and in this way increases in income, production and employment will spread in the whole of the domestic economy.

The Foreign Trade Multiplier : With both Exports and Domestic Investment

In our foregoing analysis we have explained the multiplier effect of autonomous increase in exports assuming that there is no domestic investment. We will now further elaborate the foreign trade multiplier by considering both exports and domestic investment. *In an open economy when there is positive investment the level of equilibrium in national income is reached when sum of domestic investment and net exports equals saving*. Thus, in an open economy the condition for the equilibrium level of national income is

$$I_d + X_n = S \qquad ...(1)$$

where I_d is domestic investment, X_n is net exports and S is the saving

Net exports (X_n) is the net of exports over imports, that is, $X_n = X - M$

Substituting $X - M$ for X_n in equation (1) we get

$$I_d + (X - M) = S$$

or

$$I_d + X = S + M$$

In the case when there is positive domestic investment the determination of the equilibrium level of national income is graphically shown in Fig. 24.3. The curve I_d represents autonomous domestic investment which remains constant. S is the saving function curve showing that saving is the increasing function of income. Over the domestic investment curve (I_d) we have added the exports (X) of the economy to get $I_d + X$ curve. To the saving function curve we have added the import function curve to obtain the aggregate of saving and import functions curve ($S + M$). It will be observed from Fig. 24.3. That $I_d + X$ equals $S + M$ at point E and thus the equilibrium level of national income Y_0 is determined. Note that at Y_0 level of income saving (S) and domestic investment (I_d) are also equal. Thus, at equilibrium income Y_0 :

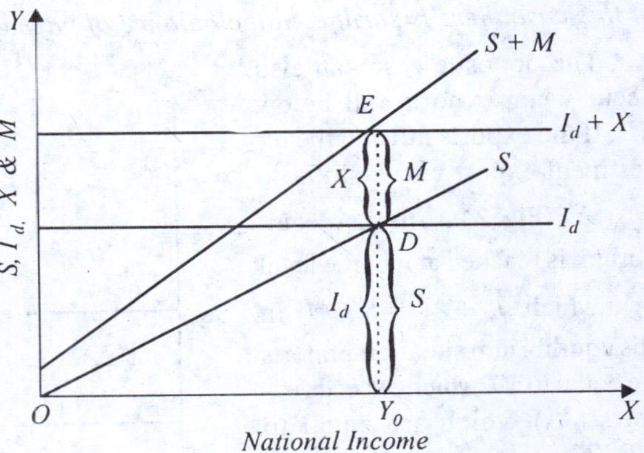

Fig. 24.3. *Foreign Trade Multiplier with Both Exports and Investment*

$$I_d + X = S + M$$

and $$I_d = S$$

Therefore, at Y_0 equilibrium income :

$$X = M$$

The equality of exports (X) with imports (M) implies that there is equilibrium in the *balance on the current account.* However, it is important to note that it is *not necessary* that at equilibrium level of national income exports (X) equal imports (M). This *equilibrium in the current account balance along with equilibrium of saving and domestic investment occurs only when exports are equal to imports at the equilibrium level of income determined by the equality of saving and domestic investment.* In Fig. 24.3. at equilibrium income Y_0 at which saving equals domestic investment, imports are equal to DE. If exports happen to be equal to DE, the equilibrium in the current account balance will also occur. However, this is not necessary because exports may be greater or less than the imports DE.

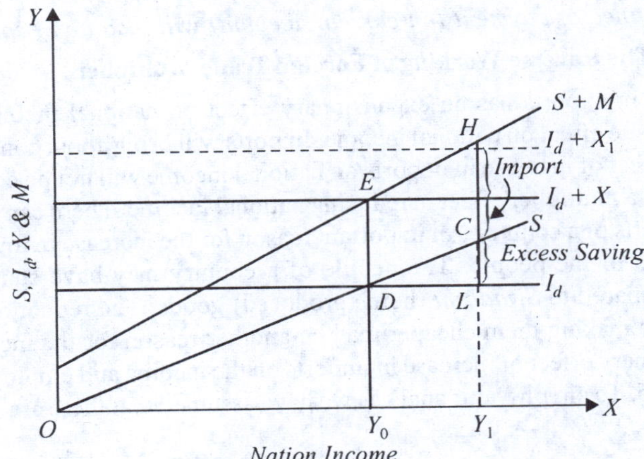

Fig. 24.4. *Equilibrium with Export Surplus*

Suppose autonomous exports increase so that the investment - exports curve shifts above to $I_d + X_1$ as shown in Figure 24.4. This new $I_d + X_1$ curve intersects $S + M$ curve at point H and as a result equilibrium national income Y_1 is determined. It will be seen from Fig. 24.4 that at national income

Y_1 the volume of exports is LH which exceeds the imports CH by LC amount. Note that LC is the amount by which saving exceeds domestic investment. It is this excess of saving over domestic investment that maintain the equation $I_d + X = S + M$ despite exports (X) being not equal to imports (M). Thus, *in this case there is surplus in the balance of payments on current account.*

The opposite case can also occur when exports fall below ED. If the exports fall and the investment-export curve shifts to $I_d + X_2$ (Fig. 24.5), the new equilibrium is reached at income level Y_2 at which $I_d + X_2 = S + M$. In this equilibrium situation imports are equal to VT which exceeds exports (X_2) which are equal to KT. Thus, though the open economy is in equilibrium as $I_d + X_2 = S + M$ at income level Y_2, there exists *import surplus* or deficit in current account balance which again implies that there is *disequilibrium in the balance of payment on the current count.* However, in this case of import surplus(i.e. deficit in current account balance) , domestic investment must exceed domestic saving by an equal amount so as to maintain the equality of $I_d + X$ with $S + M$. This is possible only if a country borrows from abroad to keep investment greater than domestic savings.

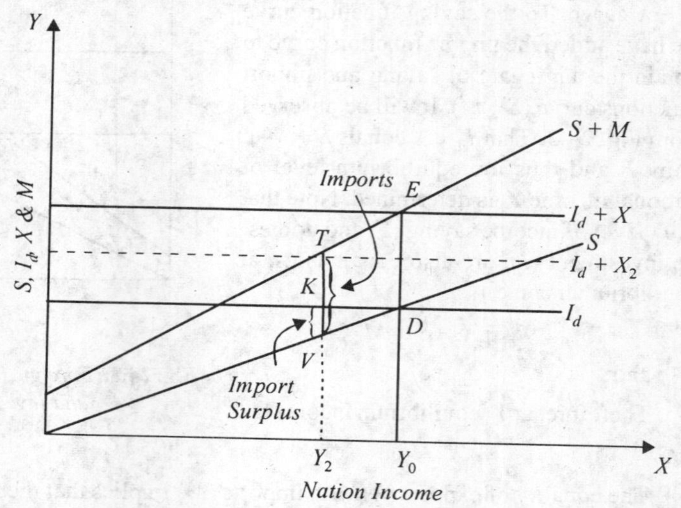

Fig. 24.5. *Equilibrium with Import Surplus*

The above analysis shows that while the *open economy as a whole may be in equilibrium, it is not necessary that balance of payment (on current account) will also be in equilibrium.*

Increase in Imports : The Reverse Working of Foreign Trade Multiplier

Whereas increase in exports has an expansionary effect on national income, the increase in imports will have opposite effect on national income. Imports will bring about contraction in national income. Further, the effect of increase in imports on national income will not be equal to the increase in imports but will have a multiplier effect in reducing national income. There can be several reasons for the increase in imports of a country. An important reason for the increase in imports is the change in tastes or preferences of the people. The people of a country may have started preferring the imported goods as compared to *Swadeshi* (home produced) goods. The reduction in import duties on the imports and thus making them cheaper may be another reason for the increase in imports a country. The contractionary effect of increase in imports on the income and employment in a country is illustrated in Fig. 24.6. To simplify our analysis we have assumed that there are no net savings and investment.

In this Fig. 24.6 the export curve is a horizontal straight line since exports are assumed to be authonomous of changes in national income. The curve M represents the import function curve which slopes upward showing that it changes with national income. The two curves X and M intersect at point E and determine Y_0 equilibrium level of national income. Now suppose that there is increase in imports ($\Delta M = ET$), say due to the change in preferences for foreign goods, and as a result import function curve shifts above to the position M_1, the export curve X remaining unchanged. It will seen from Fig. 24.6 that new import function curve M_1 and export curve X intersect at point E_1 and as result the equilibrium level of income falls to Y_1. Note that reduction in income is greater than the increase in imports; ΔY is much greater than ΔM. This is due to the working of foreign trade multiplier which in the present case works to reduce income. When the consumers buy more foreign goods and less domestically produced goods, the demand for domestically produced goods decreases which result in fall in incomes and employment of those engaged in the domestic industries. These reduced incomes further reduce the expenditure on the purchase of other home-produced goods and so on. The reverse process of contraction of income, production and employment goes on till the multiplier fully works itself out.

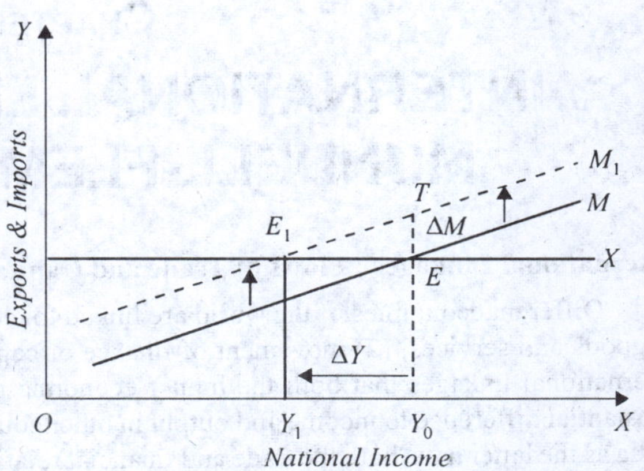

Fig. 24.6. *Reverse Working of Foreign Trade Multiplier*

It is important to note that initial attempt to increase imports has not finally resulted in any increase in imports. Imports Y_0E at the initial equilibrium income Y_0 are equal to imports Y_1E_1 in the new equilibrium at the much lower level of income. This is another paradox which is described as *import paradox*. What has actually happened is that the increase in imports and consequent upward shift in the import function leads to a large contraction in income through the reverse working of foreign trade multiplier so that in the new equilibrium at a much lower income, less is imported. This is generally referred to as income effect. Thus, this *import paradox* is of the same nature as paradox of thrift explained earlier.

QUESTIONS FOR REVIEW

1. What are import function and marginal propensity to import ? How does marginal propensity to import determine the value of foreign trade multiplier ?
2. What do you understand by foreign trade multiplier ? How is it related to marginal propensity to save and import ?
3. In an open economy national income is in equilibrium when the sum of saving and imports equals the sum of domestic investment and exports. Explain and illustrate diagrammatically.
4. What is foreign trade multiplier ? Explain how it works.
5. Explain that in an open economy the equilibrium in the current account balance occurs only when exports are equal to imports at the equilibrium level of national income determined by the equality of planned saving and domestic investment.
6. Suppose in an open economy, imports increase. How will it affect national income ? In this context explain the reverse working of foreign trade multiplier.
7. While the overall open economy may be in equlibrium, it is not necessary that balance of payment (on current account) will also be in equilibrium. Explain.

CHAPTER 25

INTERNATIONAL LINKAGES AND MUNDELL-FLEMING MODEL

International Linkages : Flows of Trade and Capital

Different economies of the world are linked together through two channels: (1) through trade in goods and services; (2) movement of finance or capital across countries. It is because of these international linkages that both the higher economic growth and recession in the U.S.A. make a substantial difference to income and output in other countries such as India, Mexico, Japan and vice versa as the latter have both the trade and financial relations with the former. For example, recession in the United States that reduces the incomes of the American people affects their demand for imported goods and would affect India's exports to the United States. Besides, if the Central Bank of America lowers interest rate below that prevailing in India, this will increase capital outflows from the United States to India as was witnessed during in 2002-03 and 2003-04. Dollar inflows into India will affect the foreign exchange rate of rupee and also the reserves of foreign exchange with Reserve Bank of India. It will be recalled that reserves of foreign exchange with RBI determine the money supply in India.

It is quite evident from above that in this age of globalisation when the economies of the world have been integrated through flows of trade and capital, growth and recession in one economy have world-wide repercussions. International linkages in the area of financial and capital movements have acquired crucial importance in modern times. The households, banks or corporate firms, say of the USA, can hold assets such as government bonds, corporate bonds, equity (i.e. share capital) of companies not only of their own country but also those of foreign countries. In most countries of the world today (India included) there are no restrictions on holding of financial assets such as corporate bonds, equity capital (i.e. corporate shares) and physical assets abroad. As a matter of fact, portfolio managers of the banks or large corporations shop around the world for parking their funds in the assets of the countries which offer them most attractive yields. It is through shifting of their assets by rich households, banks or corporate firms that link financial markets around the world. This mobility of capital or finance to search for better yield around the world affects income and employment, exchange rates and interest rates at home and abroad.

As mentioned above, households, institutional investors, banks and corporate firms search around the world for the highest return (of course, adjusted for risk). As a result, returns or yields in capital markets in various open economies get linked together. For example, if rates of interest or return on equity capital in India rise relatively to those in the USA, the US investors would try to lend or invest their capital in India to take advantage of higher returns. On the other hand, the borrowers would turn to the USA to borrow funds from the US financial markets to take advantage of lower rates of interest.

National Income and Trade Balance in the Open Economy

An important difference between the open economy and the closed economy is that in an open economy, the aggregate expenditure in any year need not be equal to its output of goods and services. This is because a country can spend more than the income it earns from production of goods and services. It can do so by borrowing from abroad. On the contrary, a country can spend less than the value of goods and services it produces because it can lend the difference to foreigners. To understand it fully recall the national income accounting explained in an earlier chapter.

It will be recalled that the economy's gross domestic output (GDP) can be divided into the four components :

$$Y = C + I + G + NX \qquad \text{... (1)}$$

where C stands for consumption expenditure, I for investment, G for government purchases of domestic goods and services and NX for net exports. NX is the difference between expenditure on exports (EX) and expenditure on imports (IM). Thus, net exports (NX) = $EX - IM$. The net exports is also known as belance of trade.

From the national income accounts identity given in equation (1) above we can know the relationship between net exports, gross national product and aggregate domestic expenditure. To do so we rearrange the equation (1) above as under :

$$NX = Y - (C + I + G) \qquad \text{... (2)}$$

where ($C + I + G$) represents aggregate domestic expenditure and Y represents Gross Domestic Product (GDP). The equation (2) shows that if Gross Domestic Product (Y) exceeds aggregate domestic expenditure ($C + I + G$), net exports (NX) are positive, that is, we are exporting more than we are importing. On the other hand, if a country's Gross Domestic Product is less than aggregate domestic expenditure, it will be importing more than it is exporting and therefore its net exports will be negative.

SAVING, INVESTMENT AND INTERNATIONAL FLOWS OF GOODS AND CAPITAL

We have seen that saving and investment play an important role in determining the level of national income and employment in an economy in the short run. Besides, saving and investment are crucial to the long-run economic growth of a country. It is therefore important to know how saving and investment are related to the international flows of goods and capital. This can be shown by rearranging the national income accounts identity. Let us first rewrite the national income identity.

$$Y = C + I + G + NX \qquad \text{... (1)}$$

Rearranging we have

$$Y - C - G = I + NX \qquad \text{... (2)}$$

Since saving is the part of national income (Y) that is left after expenditure on consumption by households and Government purchases of goods and services[1], $Y - C - G$ in (2) above represents saving (S) of the economy. Note that national saving $Y - C - G$ is the sum of private saving which is equal to $Y - T - C$ (where T represents taxes) and public saving which is equal to $T - G$. Thus National Saving = Private Saving + Public Saving

or

$$S = (Y - T - C) + (T - G)$$
$$= Y - C - G$$

writing S for $Y - C - G$ in national income identity in (2) above we have

$$S = I + NX \qquad \text{... (3)}$$

Subtracting I from both sides of equation (3) we have

$$S - I = NX \qquad \text{... (4)}$$

---

1. All Government expenditure on goods and services is treated as consumption expenditure. Though this is strictly true of the capitalist developed economies, it is not true of developing countries like India where Government undertakes a lot of investment expenditure.

The national income accounts identity of the open economy presented in (4) above shows that economy's net exports (*NX*) must always be equal to the difference between saving and domestic investment ($S - I$). This difference between saving and domestic investment represents net capital outflow. The equation (4) above shows that net capital outflow equals net exports. Net capital outflow is also called *net foreign investment* by some economists. Thus the equation (4) indicates that if saving (*S*) exceeds domestic investment (*I*), that is, if net capital outflow is positive, the economy will be lending or investing the excess saving abroad. If, on the other hand, domestic investment in the economy is greater than its saving that is, if capital outflow is negative it means it will be receiving net investment funds from abroad. Thus net capital outflow, that is, the difference between saving and investment of the economy ($S - I$) equals the difference between the amounts the residents of country will be lending or investing abroad and the amount that the foreigners will be lending or investing in that country.

Thus the net capital outflow represents the international flow of funds to finance investment in a country. It follows from above that the difference between national saving and domestic investment, that is, net capital outflows always equals the net exports. It may be noted that *net exports is also called trade balance* because it represents what extent trade in goods and resource of a country departs from the equality of imports and exports. Thus

Net Capital Outflow ($S - I$) = Trade Balance

From our above analysis we arrive at the following conclusions :

(1) If saving exceeds domestic investment ($S > I$) for an economy it follows from above that net exports (*NX*) or trade balance will be positive. In other words, in this case the country will be running a *trade surplus*. This case implies that the residents of the country would be lending or investing abroad.

(2) If saving is less than domestic investment ($S < I$ or $S - I < 0$) of a country, its net exports will be negative, that is, the country will be running a *trade deficit*. In this case there will be capital inflows to finance the extra imports.

(3) Thirdly, if saving equals investment ($S = I$ or $S - I = 0$), the net exports (*NX*) will be zero, that is, the country will have a *balanced trade*.

It follows from the above the identity of national income accounts of an open economy ($S - I = NX$) that the international flows of capital and international flow of goods and services are the two sides of the same coin. It may however be noted that international flows of capital can take many forms. First, foreigners can lend to a country when it has excess of imports over exports. Secondly, the foreign can buy domestic assets such as the American firms buying shares in the Indian Stock Exchange or buying physical assets in India. By buying assets of another country, the foreigners are making investment and providing financial funds to the country.

THE GOODS MARKET AND *IS* CURVE IN THE OPEN ECONOMY

The analysis of determination of national income, employment and rate of interest in open economies is also made in the framework of *IS –LM* model with a few changes. In particular, *IS* curve in the open economy contains a new term of net *exports (NX)*.

An important change in the *IS-LM* model applicable to an open economy is that in it *domestic spending* does not determine level of national income and output. Instead, it is *spending on domestic goods* that determines level of national income and employment in an open economy. A part of

2. It will be interesting to note that for the last three years (2002 – 2003, 2003 – 2004 and 2004 – 2005) India's Gross Saving exceeds Gross Domestic Investment, which means we are lending or investing the excess saving abroad.

spending by domestic residents is done on imports from foreign countries and the rest on domestically produced goods and services. Besides, a part of spending on domestic goods is by foreigners to whom we export goods. Thus, net exports which means exports minus imports together with spending by domestic residents on domestic goods constitute aggregate demand for or spending on domestic goods. Thus, goods market equilibrium in an open economy is represented by the following equation:

$$Y = C + I + G + NX$$

or

$$Y = C + I + G + (X\text{–}M)$$

Where NX or $(X\text{–}M)$ represents next exports. The above equation states that equilibrium level of national income is equal to the sum of consumption demand (C), investment demand (I), government purchases of goods and services (G) and net exports (NX). Consumption expenditure (C) depends on disposable income or Y-T, investment depends negatively on interest rate, G is autonomous government expenditure and net exports, among others, depends on exchange rate (e).

Incorporating the above in the *IS* equation we have the following *IS* curve for an open economy :

$$IS \text{ curve} : Y = C(Y\text{–}T) + I(r) + G + NX(e)$$

Net Exports (*NX*). The term net exports (NX) needs further elaboration. Net exports, as mentioned above, represents the excess of exports over imports, depend on domestic income (Y) which affects spending on imports and therefore net exports. Besides, net exports depend on (1) foreign income (Y_f) which affects foreign demand for our exports and (2) the real exchange rate which we denote by R. Depreciation in real exchange rate will increase our exports and reduce our imports and as a result improves our trade balance as demand shifts from foreign goods to the domestically produced goods. It may be noted that real exchange rate is the ratio of price of goods at home (P) to price of goods abroad (P_f). That is, $R = \dfrac{e.P_f}{P}$ **.** If e is the nominal exchange rate (that is, ratio of prices of domestic and foreign currencies), then the real exchange rate R equals $\dfrac{eP_f}{P}$. Now, depreciation of national currency will lower the prices of its exports and raise the prices of its imports. This will tend to increase exports and reduce imports and thereby tend to improve trade balance. The net exports or trade balance can be represented as under:

$$NX = X - M$$

$$NX = X(Y_f, R) - M(Y,R)$$

$$NX = NX(Y, Y_f, R)$$

It follows from the last equation that net exports depend on (1) domestic income or output (Y), which determines imports; (2) foreign income (Y_f) which determines demand for our exports; and (3) real exchange rate (R) which determines prices of our exports and imports. Three important results follow from the equation for net exports.

1. *A rise in our domestic income, other things remaining the same, will raise our spending on imports and hence adversely affect trade deficit.*

2. *A rise in foreign income, say of the USA, other things remaining the same, will increase our exports and improve our trade balance. As a result, aggregate demand will increase in our country with a favourable effect on our national income, output and employment..*

3. *A depreciation in real exchange rate of our currency will increase our exports and reduce our imports with a favourable effect on national output and employment.*

MACRO-ECONOMIC EQUILIBRIUM IN AN OPEN ECONOMY: IS-LM MODEL

IS – LM curve model involves the determination of national income and rate of interst through joint equilibrium of goods market and money market. Since in an open economy a part of increase in income is spent on imports rather than on domestically produced goods, *IS* curve of an open economy is steeper than that of a closed economy. This means that for a given reduction in interest rate, a smaller increase in output and income is required to restore equilibrium in the goods market.

Besides, as explained above, *IS* curve of the open economy also includes net exports (*NX*) as a component of aggregate demand for goods. The real exchange rate of the national currency, which determines the prices of exports and imports and thereby determine net exports also affects the open economy *IS* curve. Fore example, depreciation of real exchange rate of the national currency which raise exports and lowers imports results in increase in net exports and will therefore cause an outward shift in the *IS* curve to the right. Similarly, increase in foreign income which will raise foreign spending on our goods will lead to the increase in net exports, which is a component of aggregate demand, will also cause a shift in the IS curve to the right.

LM curve which represents money market equilibrium at various rates of interest and level of income is represented by the following equation:

$$\frac{M}{P} = L(r, Y)$$

where $\frac{M}{P}$ stands for supply of real money balances, and $L(r, Y)$ for demand for money which is determined by rate of interest (r) and level of income (Y).

The intersection of open-economy *IS* and *LM* curves determine jointly the income and rate of interest in the open economy. This is shown in Figure 25.1. It will be seen that open economy *IS* and *LM* curves interest at joint *E* and determine Y_0 equilibrium level of income and r equilibrium rate of interest.

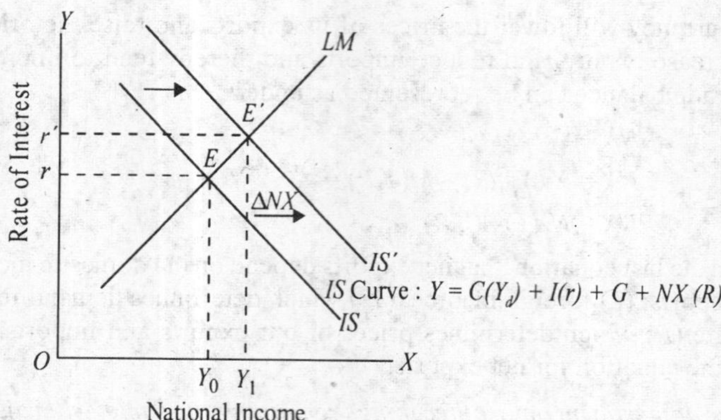

Fig. 25.1. *Determination of Income in the Open Economy through IS and LM Curves*

Impact of Increase in Net Exports (NX). Since equilibrium level of income in the open economy depends on foreign income (Y_f) and real exchange rate (R), changes in foreign income or real exchange rate will affect equilibrium level of income. For example, if foreign income increases, it will raise the foreign spending on domestic goods or, in other words, it will increase our net exports. The increase in net exports (*NX*) will cause a shift of *IS* curve to the right. This is shown in Figure 25.1 where as a result of increase in foreign income, say of the United States, which is our important trade partner. *IS* curve shifts from *IS* to *IS′* With this it will be seen that equilibrium level of income has risen to Y_1 and rate of interest to r'. It should be noted that increase in income also implies increase in output and employment.

On the other hand, if there is recession in foreign economies, as was the case of American economy during 2001-03, it will reduce their imports and thereby reduce foreign demand for our exports. This will cause a leftward shift in the *IS* curve. As a result, our level of income and output will fall. Besides, rate of interest will also decline.

Effect of Depreciation in Exchange Rate

Let us now see how depreciation in real exchange rate of the national currency, say Indian rupee, affects our national income. This can also be explained with the help of Figure 25.1 As explained above, depreciation in exchange rate encourages exports and discourages imports and thereby leads increase in net exports. Since net exports increasese at each level of income, *IS* curve shifts to the right, say to *IS′* in Figure 25.1. Thus, as a result of depreciation in real exchange rate, equilibrium level of income will increase.

Conclusion: In the Table 25.1 given below, we summarise the effects of changes in domestic spending, foreign income and depreciation in real exchange rate on domestic income and net exports. It may be noted that + sign indicates increase and – sign indicates decrease. It will be seen from this table that increase in domestic spending leads to *increase in domestic income and to decrease in net exports*. Increase in domestic spending leads to greater aggregate demand for

Table 25.1. Effects of changes in domestic spending, foreign income and real depreciation on domestic income and net exports

	Increase in Domestic Spending	Increase in Foreign Income	Depreciation in real Exchange Rate
Domestic Income	+	+	+
Net Exports	–	+	+

goods and services and have therefore favourable effect on the level of domestic income. Since a part of increase in domestic spending is made on imports of goods from abroad, it increases imports and, given the exports, will cause a decrease in net exports of the economy.

Increase in foreign income causes an increase in foreign demand for our goods (i.e. exports) which are a component of aggregate demand and has therefore a favourbale effect on the level of domestic income. Likewise, as increase in foreign income leads to more exports and, given the imports, will cause an increase in net exports.

Lastly, as explained above, since depreciation in real exchange rate causes increase in exports and decrease in imports, it leads to increase in net exports. Increase in net exports raises aggregate demand for goods and has, therefore, a favourable effect on domestic income.

THE MUNDELL - FLEMING MODEL

One of the important fact about the world economy today is the high degree of integration or linkage among financial or capital markets. As mentioned above, households, banks or corporations of different countries search around the world for the highest return (of course, adjusted for risk). As a result, returns or yields in capital markets in different countries get linked together. For example, if rates of interest or return on equity capital in India rise relative to those in the USA, the US investors would try to lend or invest their capital in India to take advantage of higher returns. On the other hand, the borrowers would turn to the USA to borrow funds from the US financial markets to take advantage of lower rates of return.

The tendency for the rates of return on capital to become equal in financial markets of different countries as a result of perfect mobility of capital was formalised in a model in the 1960s by

Robert Mundell, now a professor at Columbia University and the Late Marcus Fleming, an economist at the IMF. They assume (1) **a small open economy** (2) ***tax rates are the same everywhere***, (3) *foreign investors do not face political risk (i.e. the fear of nationalism of foreign assets, restrictions of transfer of assets, risk of default by foreign governments)*. Under these conditions and with perfect mobility of capital investors or foreign asset holders would try to invest in the asset in any country that yields the highest return. This would force rates of return on assets to become equal everywhere in the international capital markets because no one would invest at a lower return. It may however be noted that perfect equlisation of returns in different countries is crucially dependent on the twin assumptions of perfect mobility of capital and fixed foreign or world interest rate for an economy. In fact, as mentioned above, Mundell-Fleming model assumes a small open economy which is incapable of influencing world interest rate. Besides, it assumes perfect capital mobility.. "*Capital is perfectly mobile internationally when investors can purchase assets in any country they choose, quickly with low transaction costs, and in unlimited amounts.* When capital is perfectly mobile, asset holders are willing and able to move large amounts of funds across borders in search of the highest return or lowest borrowing costs"[1] The assumption of a small open economy with perfect capital mobility plays an important role in Mundell-Fleming model. The assumption of a small open economy implies that the economy can borrow or lend as much as it likes in world financial markets without affecting rate of interest. Thus, for a small open economy, rate of interest is determined by the world interest rate. Mathematically, we can state this assumption as

$$r = r_f$$

where r stands for domestic interest rate in the economy and r_f is the world rate of interest. It is the perfect mobility of capital that makes domestic interest rate (r) equal to the world interest rate. If due to some event or economic policy domestic interest rate happens to be lower than the world interest rate, the capital outflows would drive the domestic interest rate back to the world interest rate. On the other hand, if some event or policy causes domestic interest to exceed world interest rate, then the capital inflows would bring down the domestic interest rate to the level of world interest rate. Hence the equation $r = r_f$ represents that internationd flow of capital quickly brings the domestic interest rate equal to the world interest rate.

The Mundell-Fleming model, with domestic interest rate determined by the world interest rate, focuses on the role of exchange rate in the determination of national income in the short run. Another important aspect of Mundell-Fleming model is that behaviour of the economy depends on whether it adopts the fixed exchange rate system or flexible exchange rate system. In what follows we first explain below Mundell-Fleming model when the economy operate under the fixed exchange rate system and then analyse the model when the economy has adopted the flexible exchange rate system.

The Mundell-Fleming model of a small open economy with perfect capital mobility can be described by the following equations for *IS* and *IM* curves

IS equation : $Y = C\,(Y - T) + I(r_t) + G + NX(R)$

LM equation : $\dfrac{M}{P} = L\,(r_f,\ Y)$

The *IS* equation describes the goods marks equilibrium and the second *LM* equation describes money market equilibrium. *G* and *T* are the variables determined by fiscal policy, *M* is the monetary policy variable and they are important exogenous variables. The price *P* and world interest rate (r_4) are the other exogenously given variables. The interest rate being given, the intersection of *IS* and

1. R. Dornbusch, S Fischer, R. Startz, *Macroeconomics*, TATA McGRAWHILL, 2002, P.282.

LM curves determine the level of national income at which both the goods market and money market are in equilibrium. Besides, in case of the variable exchange rate system, the equilibrium of the two markets also determine the exchange rate.

However, Mundell – Fleming Model is based on same conditions which do not prevail in the real world. First, there are tax differences among countries which hinder the mobility of capital in response to interest-rate differentials among countries. Secondly, exchange rates between different currencies can change, sometimes considerably, which affect return in dollars on foreign investment. Finally, countries adopt measures to restrict capital outflows or simply default in making payments. These are some of the reasons due to which interest rates in different countries are not equal.

Mundell-Fleming Model of the Small Open Economy with a Fixed Exchange Rate Regime : Impact of Monetary Policy

An important result of the Mundell–Fleming linkage model under fixed exchange rate regime is that a central bank of a country cannot pursue an independent monetary policy. Under perfect mobility, a very small difference in interest rates in different countries would cause infinite capital flows that would bring about changes in balance of payments. These changes in balance of payments will affect exchange rate between different national currencies which would eliminate interest rate differential. Take an example. Suppose Central Bank of a country tightens its monetary policy so as to raise interest rate in the economy. When with the adoption of this policy interst rate rises in the economy, foreigners will shift their investible funds to this country so as to take advantage of the higher interest rate. With a huge inflow of capital, foreign exchange rate of the domestic currency will rise, that is, the currency of the country that adopts a higher interest rate monetary policy will appreciate. This appreciation of the currency will discourage exports and encourage imports which would have an adverse effect on balance of payments. This will force the Central Bank of the country which is committed to maintain the exchange rate at the fixed level to intervene to prevent the appreciation of exchange rate of the national currency.

To prevent the currency from appreciation, the Central Bank will buy the foreign currency, say US dollar. This will lead to the increase in foreign exchange reserves with the Central Bank which will issue more national currency against the increase in foreign exchange reserves. As a result, money supply in the economy will expand causing the rate of interest to fall. Thus, with the perfect mobility of capital and given a fixed exchange rate, domestic interest rate has been pushed back to the initial level. To quote Dornbusch and Fischer again, *"Under fixed exchange rates and perfect capital mobility, a country cannot move out of line with those prevailing in the world market. Any attempt at independent monetary policy leads to capital flows and need to intervene until interest rates are back in line with those in the world market"*[2].

It follows from above that, given a higher degree of capital mobility across countries, interest rates cannot be very much different. The differences in interest rates beyond a point will bring about capital flows across countries that will tend to provide world level yield in all of them.

Expansionary Monetary Policy Under Fixed Exchange Rate and Perfect Capital Mobility. Let us now analyse the effect of monetary expansion under the fixed exchange rate regime using *IS-LM* model. Consider Figure 38.2 where in panel (a) we have drawn the *IS* and *LM* curves as well as the horizontal straight line *BP*. The horizontal line *BL*= 0 at domestic interest rate *i* equal to foreign

2. Dornbusch and Fischer, *op. cit.* p.285

interest rate i_f $(i=i_f)$ shows that the country has neither deficit nor surplus in its balance of payments, that is, its balance of payments is in equilibrium. At any other interest rate

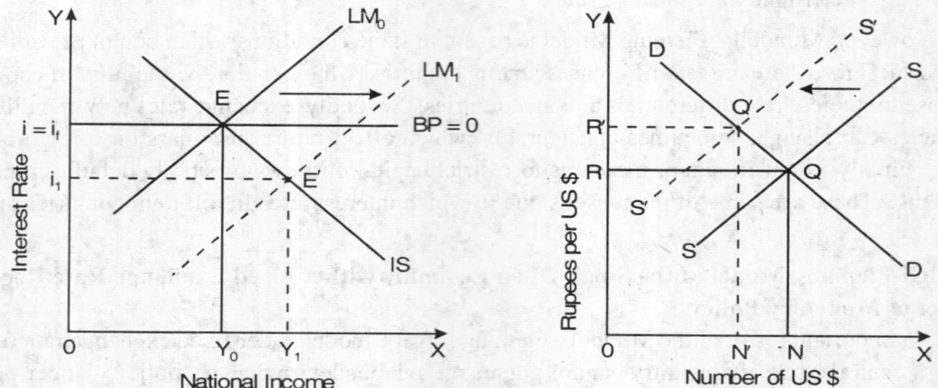

Panel (*a*) IS-LM Model of the Open Economy Panel (*b*) Determination of Foreign Exchange Rate

Fig. 25.2. *Effect of Monetary Expansion Under the Fixed Exchange Regime and Perfect Capital Mobility*

massive capital flows will occur which will cause disequilibrium in the balance of payments and will force the Central Bank to intervene to maintain the exchange rate.

To illustrate this we consider that Government adopts a policy of monetary expansion. Let the economy in panel (a) of Fig. 25.2 is initially at point *E* where the given *IS-LM* curves intersect at *E* which determines domestic rate of interest *i* which is equal to foreign rate of interest i_f. With monetary expansion, *LM* curve shifts to the right and as a result the economy moves to the new equilibrium position *E′* where domestic rate of interest has fallen to i_1. At the new position *E′* economy will have a large deficit in balance of payments which will exert a pressure on the exchange rate of domestic currency to *depreciate*. Determination of foreign exchange rate is shown in panel (*b*) of Fig. 25.2 where initially demand curve *DD* and supply curve *SS* of US dollars determine exchange rate equal to *OR* (*i.e.* number of rupees per US dollar). When as a result of expansion in money supply, LM_1 curve shifts to the right to the new position *LM* and consequently domestic rate of interest falls to i_1 (panel (*a*) of Figure 25.2), there will be large capital outflows. These capital outflows will reduce the supply of US dollars in foreign exchange market and as a result supply curve of US dollars shifts to the left to $S'S'$ (panel (*b*) of Figure 25.2) resulting in the new exchange rate R' (that is, more rupees per US dollar). This means Indian rupee will depreciate. To maintain the exchange rate, the Central Bank of the country will intervene; it will sell foreign currency reserves in the foreign exchange market. The supply of domestic money supply in the economy will therefore decrease. As a result of this reduction in domestic money supply, *LM* curve will shift back to the left [see panel (a) of Fig. 25.2]. This process of contraction in money supply and consequent shifting back of *LM* curve to the left will continue until the initial equilibrium at *E* is reached again. As a matter of fact, with perfect capital mobility, the economy is not likely to reach at the new equilibrium joint *E′*. This is because the response of capital flows is so large and quick that the Central Bank will be forced to reverse quickly the initial expansion in money supply before the new equilibrium at *E′* is reached.

Contraction in Money Supply Under Fixed Exchange Rate System. Conversely, if the Central Bank adopts the policy of contraction in money supply, *LM* curve will shift to the left of the initial equilibrium point *E*. Given the *IS* curve the new equilibrium will be reached at a higher domestic rate of interest as compared to foreign interest rate. This will induce massive capital inflows which will increase the demand for domestic currency and as a result domestic currency will appreciate.

To maintain the exchange rate, the Central Bank will buy the foreign currency and give the domestic currency in exchange. As a result, central bank will be forced to expand the money supply and this monetary expansion will cause shift in *LM* curve to the right so that ultimately the domestic economy returns to the initial equilibrium situation .

Conclusion. From the foregoing analysis of Mundell-Fleming model under the fixed exchange rate regime, it follows that when capital mobility is perfect, interest rates in the home country cannot deviate from those prevailing abroad. It is quite evident from above that *with perfect mobility of capital, under fixed exchange rate regime, monetary policy in a small open economy is quite ineffective to influence the levels of national income (output) and employment.* Any attempt by the central bank of the country to reduce interest rate by expansion in money supply would lead to massive outflows of capital tending to cause depreciation of the home currency. The Central Bank, which is under obligation to maintain the exchange rate at a fixed level, would buy the domestic currency in exchange for foreign currency. This will result in reduction in money supply to its original level with the home economy again attaining equilibrium at the initial level. This shows under fixed exchange rate regime, the *Central bank of a country cannot undertake an independent monetary policy.*

Mundell-Fleming Model : Role of Expansionary Fiscal Policy under Fixed Exchange Rate System

While expansionary monetary policy under fixed rate regime is quite ineffective to affect national income and output, fiscal policy is highly effective, given the perfect mobility of capital. To show this through open economy *IS-LM* model, consider Figure 25.3. Suppose adopting expansionary fiscal policy Government increases its expenditure with money supply remaining unchanged. It will be seen from panel (a) that increase in government expenditure causes shift in the *IS* curve to the right to the new position *IS'*. As will be seen from panell (a) this raises both the interest rate and level of national income (output). The higher domestic rate of interest *as compared to the world interest rate* (i_f) *will cause capital inflows into the economy*. These capital inflows will bring about

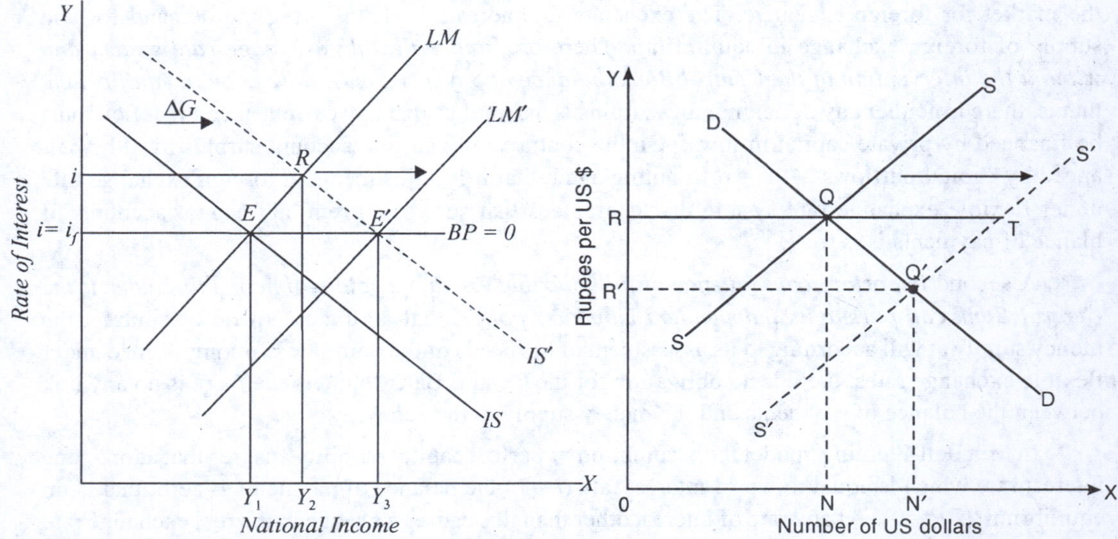

Panel (*a*) : *Determination of National Income and Rate of Interest* Panel (*b*) : *Determination of Foreign Exchange Rate*

Fig. 25.3 *Effect of Expansionery Fiscal Policy in a Small Open Economy under Fixed Exchange Rate*

appreciation in exchange rate of national currency. The determination of foreign exchange rate is illustrated in panel (*b*) of Figure 25.3. It will be observed from panel (*b*) that as a result of capital inflows, supply curve of foreign exchange (*i.e.* US dollars) shifts to the right from *SS* to *S'S'* . The new supply curve *S'S'* of foreign exchange rate intersects the demand curve for foreign exchange at point *Q'* and determines the lower new foreign exchange rate *R'* (rupees per US dollar). This implies that there is appreciation of rupee. To maintain the exchange rate at *R* the Central Bank will have to expand money supply which will cause a shift in *LM* curve to the right and increase national income further. It will be seen from panel (*a*) of Figure 25.3 that money supply is increased so much that *LM* curve shifts to the new position *LM'* and domestic rate of interest falls back to the original level so that it is again equal to the world interest rate ($i=i_f$). Thus, in this case, with endogenous expansion in money supply to maintain the exchange rate, interest rate effectively remains fixed at a given level. Fiscal expansion leads to increase in national income by Y_1Y_3, equal to the Keynesian multiplier effect.

Conclussion

The upshot of the above analysis is that the *commitment to maintain a fixed exchange rate makes the changes in money supply endogenous*. This is because the Central Bank through its intervention has to sell or buy the foreign exchange as the case may be to maintain the exchange rate system at the fixed level. The Central Bank under the fixed exchange rate system with perfect capital mobility *cannot conduct an independent monetary policy* to achieve domestic economic stability. However, *government can use expansionary fiscal policy to raise the level of national income and employment.*

MUNDELL-FLEMING MODEL FOR A SMALL OPEN ECONOMY UNDER FLEXIBLE EXCHANGE RATES

We now use Mundell-Fleming Model to explain how monetary and fiscal policies in a small open economy work when there is completely flexible exchange rate regime and perfect capital mobility. It is assumed that domestic prices remain fixed while exchange rate is fully flexible. It is important to note that under flexible exchange rate regime, the Central Bank does not intervene in the market for foreign exchange. The exchange rate adjusts itself to bring the demand for and supply of foreign exchange in equilibrium. Therefore, *under flexible exchange rate system and without the intervention of the Central Bank, balance of payments must always be in equilibrium*, that is, there is neither any deficit nor any surplus. This implies that any current account deficit must be financed by private capital inflows. On the contrary, any current account surplus must be balanced by capital outflows. It is worth noting again that it is adjustments in foreign exchange rate under flexible exchange rate system that guarantees that sum of current and capital accounts of blance of payments is zero

A second *important consequence of fully flexible exchange rate regime is that under it the Central Bank can pursue its independent monetary policy*, that is, it can expand or contract the money supply at will according to its assessment of the needs of the domestic economy. Since under flexible exchange rates, there is no obligation for the Central Bank to intervene there is no any link between the balance of payments and the money supply in the economy.

In Mundell-Fleming model the assumption of perfect capital mobility ensures that at only one interest rate which is equal to world interest rate ($i = i_f$) the balance of payments is zero, that is, in equilibrium ($BP = 0$). At any rate of interest other than this causes a change in the real exchange rate through its effect on capital flows for the domestic economy. Assuming that domestic and foreign prices of goods (p and p_f) remain constant, decline in the domestic interest rate below the world interest rate (*i.e.* i_f) will cause unlimited capital outflows and bring about depreciation in the exchange rate. As explained above, exchange rate is a determinant of net exports (NX) which in the open economy affects aggregate demand and therefore determines level of open-economy IS curve (IS curve : $Y = (Y, i) + NX(Y, Y_f, R)$ where R stands for real exchange rate and NX for net exports). Now, depreciation in the exchange rate following capital outflows when $i < i_f$ will raises exports and reduce imports and will cause increase in net exports (NX). The increase in net exports will shift the IS curve to the right and therebv affect national income and output.

On the contrary, if $i > i_f$, there will be unlimited capital inflows causing appreciation in the exchange rate which will reduce exports and increase imports and will thus lead to the reduction in net exports (NX). The reduction in net exports (NX) as a result of appreciation in the exchange rate causes a shift in the IS curve to the left and will therefore affect national income and output.

In the small open economy with international linkages in terms of trade of goods and capital flows, our open economy model under flexible exchange rate regime consists of the following three equations.

$$IS \text{ curve} : Y = A(Y, i) + NX(Y, Y_f, R) \quad \ldots (i)$$

$$BP = NX(Y, Y_f, R) + CF(i - i_f) \quad \ldots (ii)$$

$$i = i_f \quad \ldots (iii)$$

where CF stands for capital flows.

With this Mundell-Fleming linkage model of a small open economy under flexible exchange rate regime we explain below the effect on national income (output), interest rate and exchange rate of the following factors and policies.

1. Exogenous increase in exports
2. Fiscal policy
3. Monetary policy

Exogenous Increase in Exports under Flexible Exchange Rate

The effect of exogenous increase in exports, say due to the increase in world demand for our goods, is shown in Figure 25.4 Initially, the economy is in equilibrium at point E with national output equal to Y_0 and interest rate i which is equal to world interest rate i_f ($i = i_f$). When there is exogenous increase in our exports, IS curve shifts to the right to IS'.

Now, new IS' curve interests LM curve at point E' where both goods and money markets clear. It may be noted that at this new equilibrium point, E', national income increases. The increase in national income also induces the rise in equilibrium interest rate above the world interest rate i_f. This higher domestic interest rate will lead to the capital inflows which will exert pressure on the exchange rate. These capitals inflows, as seen above, will cause the domestic currency to appreciate. The appreciation in exchange rate will make our exports relatively expensive and imports cheaper than before. As a result, demand shifts away from domestic goods and as a result net exports (NX) to decline.

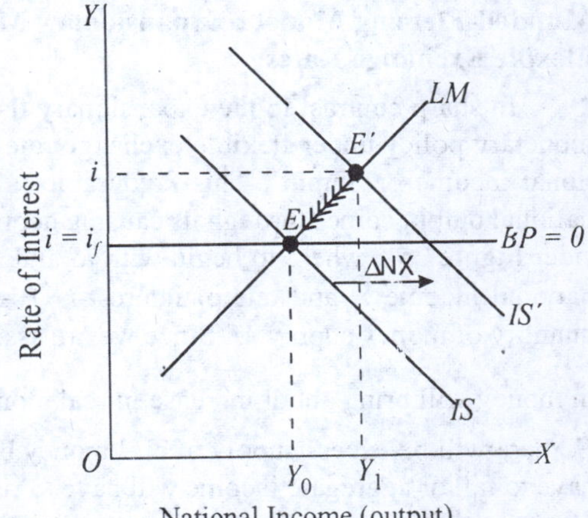

Fig. 25.4. *Effect of Exogenous Increase in Exports*

In Figure 25.4, the appreciation of exchange rate and consequently decline in net exports will cause a shift in the *IS* curve back to the left. The capital inflows will continue and net exports will go on declining as a result of appreciation of domestic currency until *IS* curve shifts back to the original level *IS* and equilibrium level of national income and output is restored at OY_0 level which is consistent with monetary equilibrium at the world rate of interest.

Conclusion. It follows from above that under conditions of perfect capital mobility, increase in exports of a small open economy has no lasting effect on the equilibrium level of national income and output. Increase in net exports (NX) causes interest rate to rise through increase in level of national income. This induces capital inflows which result in appreciation of the exchange rate and reduces net exports. This cancels out the effect on national income of the initial exogenous increase in exports of a country.

Effect of Expansionary Fiscal Policy in a Small Open Economy under Flexible Exchange Rate

We can use the Mundell-Fleming linkage model to analyse the effect of expansionary fiscal policy in a small open economy under flexible exchange rate system. Expansionary fiscal policy has the same effect as that of exogenous increase in exports explained above. Under expansionary fiscal policy either government expenditure is increased or taxes are reduced. This fiscal expansion leads to the increase in aggregate demand and causes a shift in the *IS* curve to the right. This, given the *LM* curve, induces the interest rate to rise and invites capital inflows into the economy. These capital inflows result in appreciation of the exchange rate. This appreciation of the exchange rate induced by higher interest rate leads to reduction in exports and increase in imports. As a result, there is the reduction in net exports which completely offsets the impact of fiscal expansion on national income and output.

We arrive at an important conclusion from our above analysis. *Real disturbances such as exogenous increase in exports or expansion in government expenditure or a tax cut does not affect equilibrium level of income in a small open economy under flexible exchange rate system with perfect capital mobility.* We have seen above that under the fixed exchange rate regime, expansionary fiscal policy in a small open economy is highly effective in increasing the level of national income. However, under flexible exchange rate system with conditions of perfect capital mobility, equilibrium level of aggregate income or output remains unaffected as a result of expansionary fiscal policy. Under flexible exchange rate fiscal expansion causes appreciation of exchange rate which causes exports to decrease and imports to increase and thus leads to a shift in the composition of domestic demand towards foreign goods and away from domestic goods.

Mundell-Fleming Model : Expansionary Monetary Policy in a Small Open Economy under Flexble Exchange Rates

In sharp contrast to the expansionary fiscal policy, in Mundell-Fleming model expansionary monetary policy under flexible exchange rate regime is highly effective in raising the level of national income or output. This favourable affect of expansion in money supply on the level of national output comes through its causing depreciation in exchange rate of domestic currency. Consider Figure 25.5 where to begin with *IS* and *LM* curves interest at point *E* and determine level of national income Y_0 and rate of interest i, $(i = i_f)$. Now, suppose there is increase in the nominal quantity of money supply *M*. Since we are assuming that prices of goods remain constant, increase in money will bring about increase in real money balances, $\frac{M}{P}$. With this at the equilibrium point *E*, there will be excess supply of real money balances. To restore equilibrium, rate of interest will have to fall or aggregate income will have to rise. As a result *LM* curve shifts to the right to the new position *LM′*. The new *LM′* curve interesects the original *IS* curve at new point *E′*. At the new point *E′*, whereas goods and money markets are in equilibrium (at the initial exchange rate), rate of interest has fallen below the world interest rate i_f. This will cause capital outflows from the country.

These capital outflows will reduce the supply of foreign exchange (say *US* dollars) and lead to the depreciation of the domestic currency. The depreciation of domestic currency will make exports of the country relatively cheaper and its imports relatively expensive than before. This will lead to increase in exports and reduction in imports of the country resulting in larger net exports (*NX*). Increase in net exports (*NX*), which is a component of aggregate demand, will cause *IS* curve to shift to the right. The point E' is really not a final equilibrium point as adjustment process is not complete at point *E*. *IS* curve will continue shifting to the right until the joint equilibrium of goods market and money market is established at the rate of interest which is equal to the world interest rate. In Figure 25.5. such equilibrium is reached at point E'' at which new *LM* and *IS* curves interesect and determine rate of interest $i = i_f$. It will be seen from Figure 25.5 that at the new final equilibrium point E'', level of national income (or aggregate output) Y_1 is greater than the initial income Y_0.

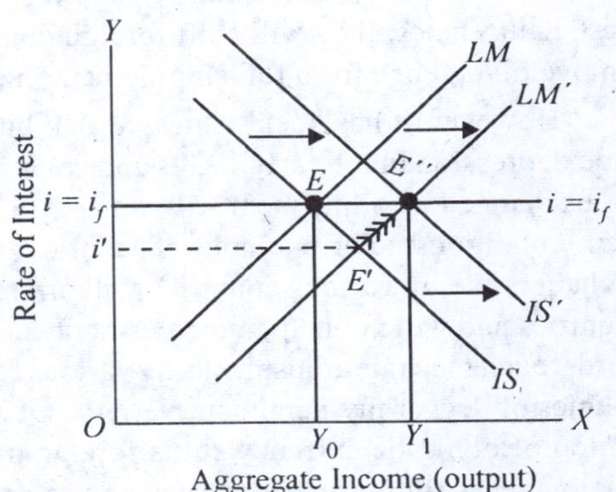

Fig. 25.5. *Mundell Fleming Model : Effect of Expansion in Money Supply on Level of Income or Output in a Small Open Economy under Flexible Exchange Rate System*

Comparison. It is interesting to compare in case of a small open economy the impact of expansion in money supply under flexible rate system with that under fixed exchange rate regine. Under the fixed exchange rate regime the expansionary monetary policy is quite ineffective in raising national income or âggregate output. Any attempt to increase money supply lowers rate of interest below the world interest rate which causes unlimited capital outflows. These capital outflows lead to the reversal of increase in money supply so that finally the equilibrium of the economy is restored at the initial level of income or output.

On the other hand, under flexible exchange rate system where Central Bank does not intervene, increase in money supply, as seen above, is not *reversed* in the foreign exchange market. Capital outflows that take place in the foreign exchange market following the fall in the rate of interest below the world rate of interest leads to depreciation of domestic currency. This depreciation causes exports to increase and imports to decline resulting in increase in net exports (*NX*). Consequently, expansion in income or output actually occurs assuming fixed prices. Thus, ability of the Central Bank to control money supply under flexible exchange rate is an important effect of the flexible exchange rate system.

Beggar Thy Neighbour Policy and Competitive Depreciation

We have seen above expansionary monetary policy causes depreciation of domestic currency and thereby leads to increase is net exports and therefore an increase in income and employment in the economy. Depreciation of domestic currency causes a shift in demand from foreign goods towards domestic goods. As a result, income (or output) and employment abroad decline. That is, one country gains at the expense of the other country. Therefore, expansion in net exports and therefore in income and employment as a result of depreciation has been called *beggar thy-neighbour policy*. That is, increase in output and employment in one country takes place by creating unemployment and loss of output in other countries.

It follows from above that *depreciation in exchange rate is mainly a way of shifting demand from foreign goods towards domestic goods rather than increasing the level of world demand.* Exchange rate adjustment can play an important role in promoting economic stability at full employment level when different countries find themselves in different phases of business cycles. That is, some are in boom phases and experiencing over full employment while others are in recession phase of business cycles. In this case, if the countries experiencing recession depreciate their domestic currencies, they will shift foreign demand to their domestic products. In this way this will remove divergence from full employment in each country.

However, it has been witnessed that business cycles are highly synchronised such as world-wide depression in the early 1930s and consequence of oil shack of 1973 and also recently in 2001-03, exchange rate adjustment will not contribute much towards achieving world-wide full employment conditions. For example, if level of total world demand is deficient, then depreciation in exchange rate by various countries will affect only the distribution of given world demand among countries and will not help in increasing the level of world demand for goods and services. In other words, exchange rate adjustments by various countries experience recessionary conditions are merely policies of beggar thy-neighbour variety. Of course, from the angle of an individual country depreciation of domestic currency shifts foreign demand to itself and is able to increase its output and employment. But, if one country can raise its output and employment by depreciating its currency, others can also do so. This leads to *competitive depreciation by different countries* for attracting world demand for their goods at the expense of others.

CHAPTER 26

Foreign Trade Policy : Free Trade Versus Protection

Introduction

In this chapter we shall discuss foreign trade policy which is a highly important issue in economics. The foreign trade policy is concerned with whether a country should adopt the policy of free trade or of protection. If the policy of protection of domestic industries is adopted, the question which is faced whether protection should be achieved through imposing tariffs on imports or through the fixation of quota or through licensing of imports. The foreign trade policy has been the subject of heated discussion since the time of Adam Smith who advocated for free trade and recommended that tariffs should be removed to avail of the advantages of free trade[1]. Even today, economists are divided over this question of foreign trade policy. Various arguments have been given for and against free trade. If the policy of protection of domestic industries is adopted, the question is whether for this purpose tariffs should be imposed on imports or quantitative restrictions through quota and licensing be applied. In India certain political parties and group have been demanding a policy of '*Swadeshi*' which in essence means that domestic industries should be protected against low-priced imports of goods from abroad, that is, free foreign trade should not be allowed.

Besides Adam Smith, the other famous classical economist David Ricardo in his famous work "*On the Principles of Political Economy and Taxation*" also defended free trade to promote efficiency and productivity in the economy. We have seen in a previous chapter that Adam Smith and the other earlier economists thought that it pays a country to specialise in the production of those goods it can produce more cheaply than any other country and import those goods it can obtain at less cost or price than it would cost to produce them at home. This means they should specialise according to absolute cost advantage. However, Ricardo put forward the 'Theory of Comparative Cost' where he demonstrated that to obtain benefits from trade it is not necessary that countries should produce these goods for which their absolute cost of production is the lowest. He proved that it could pay a country to import a good even though it could produce that good at a lower cost, if its cost is relatively lower in the production of some other good. Ricardo's theory of trade rests on the idea of relative efficiency or comparative cost.

Despite the classical arguments for free trade to promote efficiency and well-being of the people, various countries have been following the protectionist policies which militate against free trade. By imposing heavy tariff duties on imports of goods or fixing quotas of imports they have prevented free trade to take place between countries. Several arguments have been given in favour of protection. In what follows we spell out this free trade vs. protection controversy.

TRADE POLICY : TARIEFS AND QUOTAS

Despite many benefits of free trade, the various countries have put up barriers to trade to protect their domestic industries. A number of instruments are used to protect the domestic industries to free trade but most important are tariffs and quotas. Both tariffs and quotas can be imposed either on imports or exports but they are mostly imposed on imports. Barriers to exports are quite uncommon.

---

1. See Adam Smith, *The Wealth of Nations*, Modern Library Edition.

We briefly explain below these tariff barriers.

1. **Tariffs.** Tariffs are excise duties imposed on imported goods. The objective of imposing tariffs may be either raising revenue for the Government or providing protection to the domestic industries. Therefore, two types of tariffs are distinguished: (1) revenue tariffs, and (2) protective tariffs. *Revenue tariffs* are usually imposed on the imports of those products which are not produced domestically. Rates of revenue tariffs are generally small but yields a good revenue for the Government. For example in USA, tariffs are imposed on tin, coffee and bananas which are not produced in that country. Their obvious purpose is to provide revenue to the Government.

Protective tariff, on the other hand, are imposed to provide protection to the domestic producers from foreign competition. The rates of these tariffs are not so high as to completely prohibit their imports into a country. Rise in prices of their products as a result of imposition of tariffs, foreign producers lose their superior competitive power.

2. Import Quotas

Import quotas are another instrument used to check free trade. Import quotas refer to the maximum quantities of goods which may be permitted to be imported during any period of time. They are also referred to as *quantitative restrictions* on imports. Quotas are more effective method of reducing trade than tariffs. A given commodity may be imported in a relatively large quantity despite high tariffs but low quotas totally stop the imports of a commodity beyond the fixed quota of the commodity. Since international negotiations to reduce trade barriers have tended to focus on tariffs, the various countries have resorted to non-tariff barriers to free trade. We discuss below the effects of tariffs and quotas.

Effects Of a Tariff

Let us now examine the economic effects of tariffs used as a trade barrier to protect domestic industries. We use partial equilibrium approach represented by supply and demand analysis to examine the effects of tariffs. Let us take a product, say computer, in which India has a comparative disadvantage. In Fig. 26.1 we have drawn domestic demand and supply curve D_d and S_d respectively of computers in India. In the absence of foreign trade, domestic price OP_d is determined at which OQ quantity of computers is demanded and sold. Assume now that the Indian economy is now opened to trade with USA which has a comparative advantage in the production of computers. Suppose OP_w represents the world price at which USA sells computers. We assume that when the Indian economy is opened to trade, it can import computers from the USA at this world price OP_w. In other words, free trade price is OP_w. It will be seen from Fig. 26.1 that at free trade OP_w, the domestic demand (or consumption) for computers is OH and the domestic producers are supplying ON quantity. Thus, with free trade out of OH quantity of consumption of computers, domestic production is ON. The quantity NH of computers is being imported.

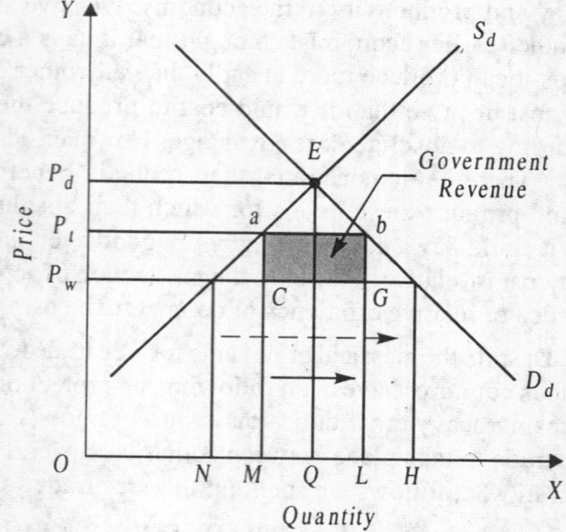

Fig. 26.1. *Economic Effects of a Tariff*

Consumption Effect. Now suppose that in order to protect domestic computer industry India imposes a tariff of P_wP_t per computer. As a result price of computer in India will rise to OP_t. The imposition of tariff and consequently rise in the price of computers in India will have a variety of effects. First, as shall be seen from Fig. 26.1 that at a higher price OP_t, the consumption of computers in India will decline to *OL* computers as the higher price causes buyers of computers to move up the demand curve D_d. This is a *consumption effect* of the tariff. It follows that the Indian consumers of computers have been badly hurt by the imposition of tariff on computers. As a result of tariff, they pay P_wP_t more per computer which they now buy at the higher price. Besides, tariff induces them to buy fewer computers with the result that they reallocate a part of their expenditure to less desired substitute products.

Production Effect. Second, tariff benefits Indian producers of computers as they will now be able to sell their computers at a higher price OP_t instead of free trade price OP_w. Further, at a higher price OP_t, they will produce and supply more computers by moving up the domestic supply curve S_d. It will be seen from Fig. 26.1 that at price OP_t, domestic producers of computers raises domestic production and quantity supplied from *ON* to *OM*. This is the *production effect* of tariff. It should be further noted that the increase in domestic production of computers by *NM* implies that some scarce resources will be bid away from other presumably more efficient industries.

Trade Effect. Third, as a result of imposition of tariff by India, American producers will be hurt. It may be noted that American producers would not get the higher price OP_t as the higher price is due to tariff which will be obtained by the Indian Government. For American producers price of computers will remain at OP_w. Since due to rise in price to OP_t, domestic production increases to *OM* and domestic consumption falls to *OL*, the imports of computers fall from *NH* to *ML*. This is trade effect of tariff.

Revenue Effect. Now, the important effect which is to be examined is whether economic well-being of the nation will increase as a result of imposition of tariff. The answer is in the negative. Of course, the Indian Government will gain from tariff equal to the revenue it collects from tariff. With rise in price by P_wP_t per computer and the import of computers reduced to *ML*, (or *ab*) the total revenue of the Government from tariff will be equal to the shaded area *abGC*. This is the revenue effect of tariff. This revenue from tariff obtained by the Government is "essentially a transfer of income from the consumers to government and does not represent any net change in the nation's well being. The result is that government gains a portion of what consumers lose." [2]

But the effects of tariffs go beyond what has been explained above on the basis of partial equilibrium analysis of demand and supply. As seen above, the imposition of tariff on computers will reduce export earnings of American computer industry–the industry in which it has a comparative advantage. Because of lower exports of computers, the production of computers will be reduced in the USA. This will cause the resources to be shifted from relatively more efficient computer industry to relatively inefficient industries of the USA in which it has a comparative disadvantage. Thus *tariffs cause misallocation of resources*. To conclude in the words of Professors McConnel and Brue, "*specialisation and unfettered world trade based on comparative advantage would lead to the efficient use of world resources and an expansion of the world's real output. The purpose and effect of protective tariffs are to reduce world trade. Therefore, aside from their specific effects upon consumers, foreign and domestic producers, tariffs diminish the world's real output.*[3]

Effects of Quotas

Quotas are quantitative restrictions on the quantity or value of a commodity to be imported in a country during a period. Since quota limits the imports of a commodity, it reduces supply of a

2. Campbell R. McConnell and Stanley L. Brue, *Economics: Principles, Problems and Policies*, 11th edition, McGraw-Hill, New York, 990, p. 784.
3. *Ibid.*, p. 784.

commodity in a country as compared to the case with a free trade. Like tariffs, quotas raise the prices of imported goods and encourage domestic production of those goods. But in case of quotas, the government does not collect any revenue. Quotas may be imposed against imports from all countries or used against the imports of only a few countries.

Economic effects of quota are graphically shown in Fig. 26.2 where *DM* and *SM* are domestic demand and supply curves of a commodity respectively. In the absence of trade, price of the commodity in the country is P_A. Suppose the world price of the product is P_w. Under free trade, at price P_w of the commodity the domestic producers of country will produce OQ_1 quantity but as domestic demand of the product at price P_w is OQ_3, the quantity $Q_1 Q_3$ represents the imports at the world price P_w. Now assume that the Government imposes a quota and fixes the quantity of the product equal to Q_1Q_2 to be imported. With this the total supply of the product in the domestic market will be away from the domestic supply S_M equal to the distance $Q_1 Q_2$. Incorporating the quota equal to $Q_1 Q_2$, we draw a new supply curve S_M + Quota, which lies to the left of the free-trade supply curve S_M. It will be seen from Fig. 26.2 that interaction of the supply curve (S_M + Quota) with the domestic demand curve D_M determines price P_d which is higher than the world price P_w. It will be seen from Fig. 26.2 that difference *AB* between demand and domestic supply at price P_d is exactly equal to the fixed quota of Q_1Q_2 quantity of imports. It is thus dear that, like tariffs, fixation of quota has served to limit trade and raise price. It will therefore have same effects as we have explained in case of tariff. It may however be noted that, unlike tariff, in case of quota Government would not collect any revenue.

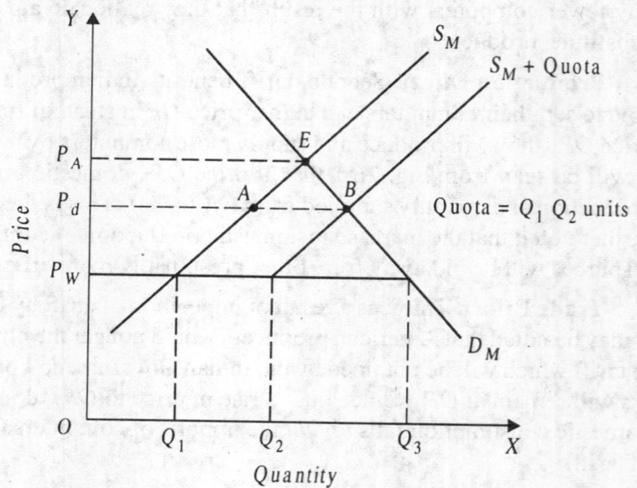

Fig. 26.2. *Effects of Quota*

CASE FOR FREE TRADE

The following arguments have been given in defence of free trade.

1. Gains in Output and Well-being from Specialisation

The case for free trade is fundamentally based on the gain in output and well-being a country obtains from specialising in the production of those goods in which it is relatively more efficient and therefore export a part of them and in exchange gets those goods from other countries in production of which they are comparatively more efficient. Specialisation and trading in this way would achieve a more efficient allocation of resources and a higher level of output and well-being. To quote Prof. Haberler, "International division of labour and international trade which enable every country to specialise and to export those things which it can produce cheaper in exchange for what others can provide at a lower cost, have been and still are one of the basic factors promoting well-being and increasing national income of every participating country"[4]

2. Gains from Economies of Scale

An important gain from trade is that it enables the trading countries to benefit from the economies of scale. If a country does not trade with others, its firms will produce goods to meet the

4. G. Haberler, *International Trade and Economic Growth.*

domestic demand for a product. If domestic demand for a product is small, each of them will produce at a higher cost since they would not be able to enjoy the benefits of the economies of large scale production. Accordingly, the production of goods will be inefficient. Trade allows a country to export goods with the result that level of output of goods in a country will exceed domestic demand within a country. Thus trade expands the market for goods and enables the producers to take advantage of the economies of scale. Adam Smith was the first economist who pointed out that specialisation was limited by the size of the market. Trade makes it possible for the producers to move beyond domestic market into international market and therefore makes it worthwhile to specialise and produce on a large scale and thereby to lower cost per unit.

For example, in a small country such as Ceylon domestic demand would not be sufficient to produce efficiently large luxury cars on a large scale at a lower cost. Their production on a large scale at lower cost requires wider international market for sale of luxury cars.

3. Long-Run Dynamic Gains

Free trade also leads to dynamic gains being obtained from trade. Dynamic gains from trade refer to its stimulation of economic growth. Dennis Robertson described foreign trade as '*an engine of growth*'. The stimulation of growth through foreign trade are apparent from the rapid growth of such economies such as Japan, Taiwan, South Koria, Singapur, Hongkong and China. Free trade promotes economic growth through: (1) raising the rate of saving and investment; (2) import of capital goods, and (3) transfer of technology.

(*i*) *Raising rate of saving and investment.* As mentioned above, increase in national product or real national income of a country obtained through trade above the level that prevails in autarky leads to a higher level of saving. The higher level of saving ensures a higher rate of investment and capital formation which stimulates growth. Hence if trade raises the rate of saving, it also promotes economic growth. The higher rate of saving makes it easier for the developing countries to break 'the vicious circle of proverty' and to "take off into self-sustained growth"[5]

(*ii*) *Import of capital goods.* Besides trade permits a country to import capital goods in exchange for exports of consumer goods or surplus raw materials. and thereby accelerates industrial growth. Imports of capital goods adds to the capital stock in a country and raises its productive capacity more than it would have been possible without trade. Free trade also often enables a country to borrow from other countries to finance import of capital goods.

(*iii*) *Transfer of technology.* If different countries worked in isolation the new technology developed in one country would remain confined locally. Through trade technological progress tends to feed on each other. A technology discovered by one is improved by another and so technology goes on being improved successively. Imagine if every country had to invent a wheel, a steam engine, electricity operating in an isolated manner, how slow would have been the progress in technology. The trade increases international diffusion of technology and in this way transfer of technology from the developed countries to the developing countries have been possible. In the modern times technology developed in one country by a firm is licensed to firms in other countries. Through this process, technology is transferred from country to country. In the absence of trade between countries such transfer of technology would not take place and as a result economic growth would be slower.

4. Promotes Competition and Prevents Monopoly

The case for free trade also rests on the fact that it promotes competition and prevents the emergence of monopolies in the domestic economy. In the absence of trade and therefore without facing any competition from foreign firms, domestic firms tend to become inefficient which causes

5. *Ibid.*

rise in cost per unit of output and therefore higher prices of goods.

When trade is free, increased competition by foreign firms forces domestic firms to adopt measures to increase their efficiency and make efforts to reduce cost by employing lowest-cost production techniques. Free trade also compels them to be innovative and to improve the quality of their products. Further, free trade provides consumers a wide range of products from which to choose. The increase in efficiency and the adoption of improved technology not only lowers prices of products but also contributes to economic growth.

5. Political Gains from Free Trade

Free trade, as explained above, increases well-being or standared of living of the trading countries and this mutual welfare gains from trade make different nations economically dependent on each other. The economic interdependence raises the likelihood of reduced hostility between countries. Economic interdependence provides powerful incentives for peaceful solution of disputes. Trade between economically interdependent countries increases the potential losses from war and thus reduces the likelihood of armed conflict.

Despite the above gains from free trade, countries have put up various barriers to free trade flows. The important barriers to free trade are (1) the imposition of tariffs (i.e., duties on imports of goods), (2) the fixation of import quotas, (3) the licensing of imports. *The reasons for these trade barriers are that different nations want to protect their domestic industries, to increase employment opportunities, to improve their balance of payments and to achieve* other goals. We therefore discuss below the case for protection and then in a later section will examine the impact of trade barriers, especially tariffs on welfare and growth.

CASE FOR PROTECTION

Despite gains from free trade, many arguments have been given against free trade and in favour of protection. By protection we mean in order to safeguard the domestic industries from low-priced imports some barriers against import of foreign goods are imposed. Some arguments given in defence of protection are irrational and invalid, whereas some are valid. We critically examine below various arguments given in favour of protection (*i.e.*, against free foreign trade).

Nationalism

First argument for protection has been that nationalistic feeling or patriotism requires that people of a country should buy products of their domestic industries rather than foreign products. In the USA there has been a campaign '*Be American, buy American*' appealing people to buy American goods instead of imported foreign products. Similarly, in India recent campaign of '*Swadeshi*' appeals to the patriotic feeling of the Indian people that we should protect our indigenous industries and impose barriers on imports of foreign goods or provide subsidies to our industries. However, this argument is misplaced and invalid. Those policy makers who yield to such arguments deny the people of a country the gains from trade such as rise in productive efficiency and greater well-being, stimulus to growth through higher capital formation and spread of superior technology. Thus restrictions imposed on trade in the name of nationalism or *swadeshi* are actually contrary to our national interests because they promote inefficiency and prevents rapid economic growth.

Employment Argument

An important argument for protection is that it will lead to increase in domestic employment or at least preserves present domestic employment. It is often believed that imports of goods from abroad reduce domestic employment. Therefore, if instead of imports we produce those goods at home, employment in the country will increase. Besides, as prices of imported goods are lower, the domestic producers would not be able to compete with them and may be competed out of the market.

This will destroy even present jobs in the domestic industries. It is therefore concluded that protection of domestic industries will lead to their expansion and therefore employment in them will increase.

In our view employment argument for protection is not logical and valid. This argument ignores the adverse effects of protection on our industries. An important economic principle is that exports must pay for imports. If imports are restricted by imposing barriers, the exports cannot remain unaffected. For example, many raw materials and capital goods are imported to be used in industries which export goods. If imports are restricted, exports will therefore fall. This will lead to the decline in employment in export industries which will offset the increase in employment in the import-substituting industries.

Further, when you restrict imports to protect domestic industries so that they should expand, other countries are likely to retaliate and will impose restrictions on our exports which are imported by them. This too will reduce exports and cause reduction in employment in export industries. Thus net effect on employment of restricting imports for providing protection to domestic industries may not be positive.

Infant Industry Argument

A powerful argument given in support of protection, especially in the context of developing countries is infant industries should be provided protection from the competition of low-priced imports of the mature and well-established industries of the developed industrialised countries. Shortly after American Revolution, Alexander Hamilton argued that British industrial supremacy was due to its early start over American infant industries. He pointed out that these infant American industries required temporary protection for some time so that they should grow and achieve production efficiency and economies of scale before they could successfully compete with low-cost British goods. He thus argued that temporary protection of infant American industries was necessary for industrial development of America.

Similarly, the infant industry argument has been advanced for protecting infant industries of the developing countries from competition of the low-cost firms of the industrialised developed countries. Given some time, these infant industries will grow and will be able to benefit from the economies of scale and learn the techniques necessary to lower their cost of production. As a result, over a period of time their cost per unit will go down and will therefore be in a position to compete with the foreign imports. Therefore, for some time they should be protected otherwise they would be destroyed by foreign competition.

However, there are some lacuna in infant industry argument. First, it is assumed that protected infant industries will make efforts to lower cost when provided protection. However, actual experience shows that it is more likely that protected industries lose incentives to become efficient and lower cost. It is said "once an infant, always an infant." Secondly, even if an industry makes efforts to improve productivity and lower cost per unit when it is provided protection, it has been assumed in the argument that the Government is the best judge as to which industries will prove to be capable of competing low-priced foreign goods. It has been asserted in defence of free trade that selection of industries which will acquire competitive strength can be done better by private market mechanism. It is pointed out that when opening up the economy to foreign competition the domestic industries would try to increase their efficiency. As a result, only those industries will survive which are efficient and produce at a lower cost. Therefore, it is argued that it is better if the domestic industries are left to foreign competition and in this way they will have incentives to improve productivity to escape from losses. Only those domestic industries will survive and operate which are efficient and produce at a low cost per unit.

Indian Automobile industry is a shining example of an industry not making any efforts to become efficient even after given protection for more than three decades. Before the setting-up of Maruti Udyog with Japanese collaboration, Indian car industry was fully protected by heavy duties on imports of cars. The two domestic firms producing Ambassador and Fiat cars did not make any efforts to improve their efficiency, nor did they bring out any better models of their cars. It is only after 1991 that following the policy of liberalisation that new foreign firms such as Daewoo of South Korea, General Motors have come in India and producing new models and at relatively low prices. Even Maruti is now trrying to improve its efficiency further and brought out new models of Maruti such as Zen, Esteem.

However, it may be noted that in developing countries the Government is in a better position to protect certain industries such as steel, cement *which lead to an expansion of the infrastructure of the developing economies*. This is because these industries create external economies and the private firms will not be compensated for creating these external benefits.

Anti-dumping Argument

The other important argument for protection is that foreign producers compete unfairly by dumping the goods in another country. Dumping is a form of price discrimination when producers of a country sells goods in another country at lower prices than those charged at home. Of course, consumers in a country in which foreign goods are dumped are beneficiaries, the industries of that country suffer as they are unable to compete with the '*dumped goods*'. Besides, there is more harmful '*predatory dumping*' which implies that foreign firms try to sell goods in other countries even below cost to establish a worldwide monopoly by driving competitors out of the market. Once the local industries are competed out, they raise prices to obtain monopoly profits.

There is a lot of evidence that firms of USA and Japan often indulge in dumping of their goods in other countries to eliminate competition. But, in our view, instead of providing protection to domestic industries through tariffs or non-tariffs barriers, it will be a better policy to enact laws against dumping. Dumping should be prohibited by law declaring it illegal. In India such a law has been enacted but is not being properly implemented.

Correcting Balance of Payments Deficit

Correcting deficit in balance of payments is also mentioned as justification for imposing tariffs to restrict imports or fixing of quotas of imports. This appears to be a valid argument for providing protection. However, in our view the solution for fundamental disequilibrium in the balance of payments lies in the adoption of suitable adjustment in exchange rate, appropriate fiscal and monetary policies to lower domestic prices so as to encourage exports. The deficit in balance of payments can be reduced by ensuring rapid growth in exports of a country.

Redistribution Income

Case for protection has also been built up on the ground that it can be used for making desirable redistribution of income from one section of society to another. Protection makes some people better off, while others worse off. By providing protection to domestic producers their profits can be raised at the expense of consumers who suffer a loss in consumer surplus as protection denies them consumption of low-priced imported goods. That is, protection redistributes income in favour of domestic producers.

Sometimes protection causes transfer of income from some factors to the others. For example, Heckscher-Ohlin Model of international trade shows that trade benefits the abundant factor and harms the scarce factor. It is therefore scarce factor that demands protection by the Government against imports so that its income may not decrease. This implies that the workers, the owners of labour, and capitalists tend to take opposite views with regard to protection. This is however not confirmed by empirical evidence.

In some countries one of the objectives of economic policy is to redistribute income from the rich to the poor. This can be done by imposing high tariffs on imports of goods considered to be luxury items and levying tariffs on exports of those goods which are considered as necessities. Higher import tariffs on luxuries will reduce the incomes of the rich as they would pay taxes to the Government. Similarly, higher taxes on exports of necessities ensure greater supplies of them in the domestic market which would lower their domestic prices and benefit the poor.

It may however be noted that direct taxes such as income tax are considered better methods of redistributing income among various sections of a society than the commercial policy. This is because as we shall see below import tariffs levied for protecting industries cause downweight loss of welfare which are avoided under the direct tax system.

Conclusion

We have critically examined the various arguments in favour of protection. Some of them are valid, other appears to be misplaced. Some people consider trade as a '*zero sum game*', that is, in trading if one gains, the other loses. This has given rise to the doctrine of exploitation. For example, it is believed by some that the developing countries like India are exploited by the developed countries such as the USA, Japan, Britain. That is, the developing countries are net losers in trading with the developed countries. However, in our view, this is wrong thinking. No trade can occur without expectations of gain. India would not have entered into trade relations with USA if it did not expect to gain from it. Trade occurs between two countries if it benefits both the trading partners, the developed and the developing countries. Therefore, in our view world trade should be promoted by lifting barriers put up by various countries based on wrong notions about effects of free trade. Some countries such as USA and Japan have resorted to protectionist measures as a retaliation against foreign countries who restrict imports into their countries. The retaliatory actions of imposing trade barriers have done great harm to the expansion of world trade. New international organisation WTO (World Trade Organisation) which has replaced earlier GATT has been set up. WTO has framed rules which every country should observe so that barriers to trade be removed and world trade be promoted without doing any injustice to the member countries. It may be noted that retaliatory activities of restricting imports from foreign countries generally lead to the depression in the economies of the world as it happened during the worldwide depression of 1930s. The retaliatory activities may cause another global depression.

QUESTIONS FOR REVIEW

1. Explain the gains from free trade for a developing country like India. In view of these gains from free trade, explain why the various countries put up various barriers to trade.

2. Critically examine the case for free trade in respect of developing countries like India.

3. What arguments are given in favour of protection? Do you think protection is right trade strategy for India in the emerging international economic environment ?

4. Critically examine the following arguments in support of protection.

1. Infant industry argument
2. Employment argument
3. Balance of payment argument
4. Promotion of *Swadeshi*

5. Explain the economic effects of tariffs. Compare them with effects of quota.

6. Tariffs cause misallocation of resources. Discuss.

7. The purpose and effect of protective tariffs is to reduce world trade. Discuss.

8. Explain the effects of quota. The fixation of quota for imports of goods reduces trade and raise prices. Examine critically.

CHAPTER 26A

Foreign Trade Policy : Import-Substitution Vs. Export Orientation

Introduction

Trade policy plays an important role in achieving the objectives of rapid economic growth and self-reliance. We have explained in a previous chapter both static and dynamic gains from trade with other country. It is on the basis of these static and dynamic gains of trade that case for free trade or liberalisation of trade was bas been built. When a country specialises on the basis of its comparative cost or production efficiency and export and import accordingly, it enables it to make optimum use and allocation of its resources. As a result, output, income and welfare of its people increase. These gains emanating from trade through improved allocation of given resources of a country are generally described as static gains. Thus, Professor Haberler writes, "International division of labour and international trade which enable every country to specialise and to export those things which it can produce in exchange for what others can provide at a lower cost have been and still are one of the basic factors promoting economic well-being and increasing national income of every participating country"[1].

However, importance of trade is not confined to static gains flowing from improved allocation of the given resources. Foreign trade also promotes economic growth of a country. It is the beneficial effect of trade on economic growth that is described as dynamic gains. D.H. Robertson, described foreign trade as **"an engine of grwoth".** With greate income and production made possible by specialisation and trade, greater servings and investment become possible and as a result higher rate of economic growth can be achieved. Through promotion of exports, a developing country can earn valuable foreign exchange which it can use for imports of capital equipment and raw materials which are so essential for economic growth. To quote Haberler again. "The higher the level of output, the easier it is to escape the 'vicious circle of poverty and to 'take off into self-sustained growth' to use the jargon of modern development theory. Hence, if trade raises the level of income, it also, promotes economic development"[2]. Elaborating how trade promotes growth he emphasises the following factors.

1. Through foreign trade developing countries can get material resources such as capital equipment, machinery and raw materials which are so essential for industrial growth.
2. The developing countries through trade can import and use superior technology which has been invented in advanced developed countries and is embodied in the machines, capital equipment which they import.
3. Foreign trade enables the transmission of technical know how, skills, managerial talents to the developing countries.

India's Trade Policy of Import Substitution

As we began cur planning for development, the two options were open to us with regared to our

1. G. Haberler, *Interuational Trade and Economic Development*
2. G. Haberler, *Op. cit.*

foreign trade policy. First, we should lay stress on export promotion in our strategy of development for accelerating economic growth. The second option was to adopt import-substitution as a major element of our trade policy. Note that the second policy of import-substitution does not emphasise the role of foreign trade for accelerating economic growth. In fact, the policy of import-substitution was adopted in view of the perceived bleak prospects of raising India's exports. When exports could not be increased substantially, we could not pay for imports on a large scale. Therefore, India's strategy of industrialisation was based on substitution of imports rather than export-oriented trade policy. The policy of import-substitution for promoting growth was also thought to be quite feasible in view of India's vast domestic market.

It is clear from above that India adopted the policy of import substitution because of what is now called *export-pessimism*. In fact, in the fifties and sixties export pessimism characterised the thinking of the most development economists. For example, Raul Prebisch postulated that the terms of trade of developing countries have a tendency to deteriorate over time regardless of the policies of developing countries.[3] Prebisch's postulate was based on three grounds. First, demand for primary products which under-developed countries were exporting were income inelastic. Second, technological progress that was taking place in developed countries was of the nature that saved the use of raw materials which underdeveloped countries were exporting. Third, because of the prevailing monopolies in the manufacturing industries of the developed countries, the prices of their manufactured products was relatively higher than the prices of primary and agricultural products whose production and sale were being done under competitive conditions. Thus, according to Prebish, export expansion by developing countries were quite unprofitable.

Similarly, R. Nurkse, another pioneer in development economics believed that for the newly emerging countries like India foreign trade could no longer serve as 'engine of growth'. Nurkse's export pessimism arose from his belief that foriegn market could not absorb imports on a sufficient scale as developing countries accelerated their process of economic growth. In view of this external environment, Nurkse concluded that in order to accelerate growth developing countries should undertake a balanced pattern of investment in a number of different industries so that they can generate mutual demand for each other's product leading to the expansion in size of hone market. To quote Nurkse, "When developing countries face difficulties in exporting both traditional and new exports, import-substitution strategy may be adopted by them as an escape route from stagnation"[8]. Nurkse further writes, "International trade cannot now be an effective engine of 'economic growth' and in the strategy of growth, underdeveloped countries have of necessity to lay emphasis on 'balanced growth' – a coordinated development of local industries in accordance with the growth and structure of domestic demand"[4]

It is interesting to note here that our present Prime Minister Dr. Manmohan singh was perhaps the first economist who challenged this export pessimism of early development economists, especially in the context of India. On the basis of his empirical findings about the export-potential of the Indian economy, he concluded that it was not easy to meet the increase in import requirements in raising the rate of economic growth by any other means but export promotion. Arguing the case for export-orientation of strategy of development he writes, "*whatever the development strategy the function of international trade as a supplier of "material means indispensable for development' is likely to retain its importance for most underdeveloped countries in their quest for higher rates of economic growth...Imports, however, have to be paid for either by current export earnings or by withdrawal from reserves of foreign exchange or by a fresh capital inflows. The withdrawal from reserves is not unlimited process,..capital inflows ultimately lead to higher service charges and*

3. R. Nurkse, *Patterns of Trade and Development,* Wicksell Lectures, 1989,
4. R. Nurkse, *Op. cit.*

repayment obligations. In the long run, therefore, the import capacity of an economy and its ability to utilise the above mentioned benefits of international trade is crucially dependent on its export capaicty.[5]

But Dr. Manmohan Singh not only highlighted the need for export promotion for accelerating economic growth but with his empirical study he demonstrated in India's case that export promotion to meet the growing needs for imports was in fact possible and that the stagnation of India's exports 1951-61 was partly a consequence of faulty Indian economic policies. Commenting on Dr. Manmohan Singh's work. Prof. Amartya Sen writes, "Rapid increase in exports would be impossible if export pessimism prevailing at that time were well-grounded". And Professor himself answers that "with its very careful and painstaking empirical arguments, Dr. Manmohan Singh demostrated that it was not so well grounded after all".[6]

Empirically, the export pessimism of the fifties (post-war period) has been proved to be untrue and unjustified. Word trade in the fifties and sixties grew faster than world income. Several developing countries used export promotion as a means of attaining a fast economic growth. In the early 1960s Japan was the shining example of using export promotion strategy to achieve a fast rate of economic growth, beginning from a state of underdevelopment. Japanese growth experience is often described as **Japanese miracle.** In the later period, other success stories of achieving high growth through outward-looking strategy of development have been of Asian countries of South Korea Taiwan, China, Thailand, Singapur and Honkong. Owing to their rapid economic growth in seventies and eighties they have been called '**Asian Tigers.** It is also worth mentioning that the expansion in exports of developing countries which have used export-promotion as a strategy of growth has not been confined to primary products such as fuel and agricultural products (food, agricultural raw materials). As a matter of fact, there has been significant change in the composition of exports of developing countries towards manufacturers.

It may be noted that the fifties and early sixties free trade was opposed on political grounds also. Fears were expressed that through free trade industrial developed countries would acquire political domination, as happened in case of India. East India company of Britain which came to India for trading acquired political domination. It may however be noted such fears of political domination through trade has now receded in the present political context. In fact, the *protectionist sentiment is now stronger in the developed countries* such as US and EU. There is now huge and cry in USA for protecting American jobs by banning outsourcing of business services (BPO) to India.

The success in export promotion accelerates economic growth in the country. The emergence of Japan and Germany and recently China as major economic powers has shown that their success in export expansion made them economically more independent and strong. On the other hand, developing countries like India which followed import-substitution strategy had to face recurrent balance of payments crises and the persistence of huge external debt problem which made them more dependent on developed countries and international institutions such as IMF and World Bank.

Import-Substitution

As mentioned above, for at least upto 1980, India adopted a trade strategy of import substitution. The choice of this policy was based on export pessimism which led the Indian planners to

---

5. Manmohan Singh, *India's Export Trends and Prospects for Self-sustained Growth*, Oxford : Clarendon Press, 1964 pp. 3-4
6. Amartya Sen, Theory and Practice of Development' published in *India & Economic Reforms and Development* , Essays for Manmohan Singh, Isher Judge Ahluwalia and I.M.D. Little, (ed.) Delhi, Oxford University Press. 28.
7. Jagdish Bhagwati, Export Promoting Trade Strategy. Issues and Evidence, *The World Bank Research Observer*, Vol,3. NO.1.

believe that export earnings of India cannot be increased. The choice of this inward-looking strategy was further strengthened by the vast size of Indian domestic market To implement this trade policy of import-substitution the imports of several commodities into India were banned and quantitative restrictions on some other commodities were imposed. Besides, to give protection to the domestic industries, customs duties were levied on a number of commodities to discourage their imports by raising their prices. The customs duties levied in India on certain commodities were as high as 200 per cent or 150 per cent which were one of the highest in the world. In addition to these. The import-licensing was used so as to regulate the quantities of some essential goods and raw materials that could be imported and accordingly licences for import quotas were issued by the Government. A scheme of import licensing in case of certain commodities was introduced under which imports were permitted to the extent that domestic production fell short of domestic demand. Further, stringent foreign exchange regulations were introduced and foreign exchange was released to the holders of import licences for importing specific commodities.

It may be noted that India's policy of import substitution was indiscriminate and also continued for quite a long period. This is unlike some other countries such as Japan and South Korea which adopted import substitution only for some period of time and that too in case of selected commodities for which they had potential comparative advantage.

Results of Import-Substitution Policy. However, it may be noted that policy of import substitution contributed significantly to industrial growth between 1956-66. But several weaknesses of the policy of import substitution became evident during the course of time. First, the policy makers-underestimated the possibilities of expansion in exports. As in the path-breaking study about the trends in exports, Dr. Manmohan Singh found that a lot of export possibilities was lost due to faulty trade policies. As a result, India's share of world exports declined from about 2 per cent in 1951 to about 0.53 per cent in 1992.

Second, policy of import substitution underestimated the import-intensity of import substitution process itself. Growth of import-substituting industries required large quantities of imports of capital goods machines, raw materials etc. As a consequence, whereas imports increased substantially there was no adequate growth in exports resulting in balance of payment problems. In 1966 we had to devalue the rupee to promote exports and discourage imports in order to solve balance of payments problem. However, 1966 devaluation did not succeed in improving the trade deficit.

It may be noted that deficit in balance of payments which arose mainly due to import-substitution policy forced Indian policy makers to make some changes in attitude towards exports. Accordingly, in the third plan period (1961-66) and the fourth plan period (1969-74) several export promotion measures (including devaluation of 1966) were taken. However, as has been correctly pointed out by C. Rangarajan that "Until the end of 1970s, exports *were primarily regarded as a source of foreign exchange rather than as an efficient means of allocating resources. Import substitution remained the basic premise of the development strategy*".[9]

Since import-substituting industrialisation was pursued regardless of comparative cost considerations, inefficiencies crept into the system resulting in the Indian economy becoming increasingly high-cost economy. This high cost and inefficiency in production was an important reason for poor export performance despite the various incentives and concessions given by the Government for export promotion.

---

8. Manmohan Singh, *op. cit.*
9. C. Rangarajan, *India's Balance of Payments : The Emerging Dimensions*, Gobind Ballabh Pant Lecture, January 1994, (ialics mine)

Export-Promotion Measures in the Eighties

In the early eighties because of the deficits in balance of payments export-promotion meaures "acquired great urgency". A committee headed by P.L. Tandon made a large number of recommendations for export-promotion in January 1991. Promotional measures for exports taken in the eighties are :

1. Incentives scheme to promote exports was launched which provided for imports of raw materials, machinery and capital equipment and accessories against exports. This schemes we called Replenishment (Rep.) Scheme which was later replaced by Exim Scrips.

   Exim scripts. Exim scripts equivalent to the 30 per cent value of their exports were given to the exporters. These exim scripts could be even sold in the market at premium. Exim scripts entitled exporters to import a certain amount of materials and machinery for expanding exports. Thus, **'import-liberalisation for export promotion'** became the focus of trade policy.
2. Fiscal concessions for export promotion were given. The important fiscal concession was the introduction of *'duty drawback scheme'* under which taxes paid on materials used in the manufacture of goods for export were refunded. Besides a good proportion of profits or income earned from exports was exempted from income tax. Further a 5-year tax holiday was provided to the units set up in Special Exporting Zones (SEZ) for financing exports.
3. Liberal credit facilities at concessional rates of interest were given by the commercial banks to exporters.
4. Bilateral Trade Agreements with some countries were made to step up exports.
5. In the later half of eighties the *'exchange entitlement'* scheme was introduced to enable exporters to utilize a part of their foreign exchange earnings for the purpose of market development.
6. **Cash Compensatory Scheme.** A scheme of providing cash assistance to the exporters was started. Under this scheme cash assistance was given to the exporters to compensate them for the taxes paid by them on the imported inputs used by them for the production of exported goods. This was in fact a form of export subsidy paid for providing incentives to the exporters.
7. In the later half of eighties quota system in case of several commodities was replaced by tariffs. This liberalised imports further on the one hand and provided revenue to Government on the other.

It is evident from above that in the eighties, especially in the later half of eighties, a more liberal trade policy was adopted to promote exports on the one hand and to provide for imports of capital goods and technology so as to enable India to obtain benefits from international trade. It needs to be emphasised that liberalisation of trade policy in the eighties was in view of the mounting deficits in balance of payments as a consequence of pure import substitution policy followed earlier. In 1981 IMF had also advised India to use export promotion and not export restrictions as the strategy for reducing deficit in balance of payments.

INDIA'S TRADE POLICY SINCE 1991 : IMPORT LIBERALISATION AND EXPORT ORIENTATION : A GENERAL REVIEW

There was a severe economic crisis in 1991. This economic crisis had its root in persistent deficits in balance of payments in the last several years. Gulf war of 1990 added to the problem as it resulted in shooting up of oil prices which required enhanced spending in terms of foreign exchange. By March 1991, current account deficit in balance of payments reached a record level of about 10 billion US dollars or over 3 per cent of our GDP. Exports were declining. Foreign borrowing in last several years raised the ratio of short-term debit to foreign exchange reserves to an extremely high level of 146.5 per cent. Foreign debit reserve ratio rose to a peak of 35.5 per cent. As result, our foreign exchange reserves dwindled to a merge amount which was hardly adequate to meet only a few weeks imports. A default on payments for the first time in our history became a distinct possibility in June 1991. Foreign capital was flying from India. No one was willing to lend us any more.

The severe economic crisis of 1991 forced us to make drastic reforms in trade policy. Fortunately, Dr. Manmohan Singh was appointed as Finance Minister. Since then many far-reaching reforms in trade policy have been undertaken. Though some liberalisation of trade policy was undertaken in the eighties, a truly liberalised trade policy was adopted from 1991 onward.

The liberalisation of trade policy in India is characterised by two important features :

1. Import liberalisation and
2. Export-orientation of trade policy.

This new trade policy has accelerated India's transition to a globally oriented economy by stimulating exports and facilitating imports of essential inputs and capital goods. The steps were taken to promote exports by removing anti export bias in the earlier policy. This policy of import liberalisation and export-orientation was in fact the policy that was recommended by IMF and World Bank the solve the balance of payments problem facing the developing countries and to accelerate rate of economic growth. We explain below this trade policy in some detail.

Import Liberalisation

The first important reform in India's trade policy has been the elimination of quantitative restrictions in a phased manner on most of intermediate and capital goods since 1991. Secondly, prior to 1991 imports were regulated by means of positive list of freely importable items. Instead, since 1992 as a part of trade policy reforms only a *short negative list of imports* is subject to regulations by Government. Other goods can be imported, subject of course on payment of duty.

Abolition of Licensing. Prior to 1991 a large number of goods was subject to import-licencing restrictions. Now, most of the items of imports have been put on Open General Licence (OGL). That is, for their imports prior approval or license from any authority is not required. Thus, License - Permit Raj regarding imports has been done away with.

Tariff Reduction. An important step towards import liberalisation has been reduction in import-duties to eliminate protection given to domestic industries from foreign competition. The maximum import duty which was as high as around 150 per cent was reduced to 110 per cent in 1992-93. This was further reduced to 85 per cent in 1993-94, to 65 per cent in 1994-95 and to 50 per cent in 1950-96 Now, in 2004-05 average customs duty has been reduced to 20 per cent only.

Empirical evidence shows reduction in protection increases efficiency and productivity in the domestic industries as it exposes them to foreign competition.

Liberalisation of imports of gold and Silver. Another significant import liberalisation has been that imports of gold and silver have been liberalised. This has helped in printing smuggling of these metals.

Critique of Import Liberalisation

It may be noted that fears were expressed about import liberalisation both by certain politicians and economists, especially with leftist leanings. They contended that import liberalisation would kill domestic industries as they would not be able to compete with the cheap foreign products. This would lead to closure of a large number of industrial units, especially small scale industries, Besides, they claimed that the large-scale imports would require substantial foreign exchange resources. Thus, according to them import liberalisation would worsen the balance of payments problem rather than solving it. Even a reputed economist. Dr. Bimal Jalan, a former Governor of Reserve Bank of India, expressed reservations about the policy of import liberalisation and pointed out that it would be highly risky for the Indian economy. Writing in 1991, he says, "given the balance of payments constraints operating now, and the financing operations currently available, import-liberalisation as strategy does not seem to be feasible option over the next few years. This pragmatic view is not dependent on the theoretical validity (or otherwise) of the liberalisation argument. By implication, import liberalisation would have the effect of raising, even in the short sun, the ratio of import to GDP. This may not be undesirable in itself, but it would require larger inflows of external capital in the next few years and this is not available *on appropriate terms*. Past experience shows that further commercial borrowing to finance import liberalisation ...would also be undesirable, given the high level of external debt. In this situation, import liberalisation would be unduly risky and could lead a repetition of the unfortunate experiences of several other developing countries."[15]

However, as shall be explained later, in actual experience, these fears about import-liberalisation leading to adverse consequences have not proved to be true.

Export-Orientation of Trade Policy

Along with import laberalisation, export-orientation was also given to India's trade policy pursued since 1991. In other words, for the first time greater emphasis was placed on export promotion in our trade policy by *removing anti-export* bias of our earlier policy. Some economists describe it **out-ward looking strategy** was adopted since 1991 in place of inward-looking strategy of import-substraction followed earlier. We explain below the various export-promotion measures taken to give export-orientation to trade policy.

1. **Reduction in customs duties to end anti-export bias.** As mentioned above, prior to 1991 costums duties of India were the highest in the world and were levied to promote import substitution. These very high customs duties provided a high degree of protection to domestic industries. In actual practice, the high degree of protection lowers efficiency and is not conducive to optimum use and allocation of resources In the absence of competition from imported products, the prices of domestic goods were high and this served to induce import substitution but worked against promotion for exports. Since prices of products in international markets were lower, it was not profitable to produce for export. Therefore to remove this anti-export bias and promote the growth of exports, customs duties were reduced and in 2004-05, average rate of customs duties have been reduced to 20 per cent.

Devaluation or Rupee. Another important step to promote exports was devaluation of rupee by 20 per cent in July 1991. Devaluation lowered the prices of our exports and gave an important boost to them. Prior to 1991 rupee currency was overvalued and to ensure growth in exports to make some foreign exchange earning, export subsidy in the form of cash compensatory scheme was provided to exporters. Therefore, along with devaluation cash compensation scheme was withdrawn.

Market Determined Exchange Rate : Convertibility of Rupee. After two years, in 1993, exchange rate of rupee was made market determined, that is, exchange rate of rupee with foreign currencies were left to be determined by demand for and supply of rupee and other currencies. This implies that rupee can appreciate or depreciate in terms of other currencies every day depending on demand and supply conditions. This flexible exchange rate works to some extent to correct disequilibrium in the balance of payments. However, it is worth mentioning that exchange rate though determined by demand for and supply of foreign exchange can be influenced by RBI through buying and selling of dollars or other foreign currencies. Therefore, present exchange rate system is more correctly described as **managed float.**

It may be noted that over a period of time since 1993, exchange rate of rupee has declined, that

10. Bimal Jalan, *India's Economic Crusis: The Way Ahead,* Oxford University Press, *1991.*

is, rupee has depreciated. This has tended to promote exports and discourage imports. In addition to the introduction of market determined exchange rate rupee has been made convertible on current account of balance of payments, that is, importers can now get their rupees converted into dollars and exporters can sell their dollars for rupees at market-determined exchange rate. Thus, convertibility of rupee has facilitated imports and exports and has contributed to the globlisation of the Indian economy.

3. **Leberalisation of control over exports**. Through continuous review and revisions during the last 12 years controls on exports has been liberalised to the extent that now *all goods may be exported without any restriction except the few items* mentioned in the negative list of exports. The items in the negative list of exports are regulated because of strategic considerations, environmental and ecological grounds, essential domestic requirements, employment generation and on account of socio-cultural heritage.

4. **Duty-free import of capital goods for use in production for exports.** A significant export-promoting measure is that capital goods meant to be used for production of exportable products can be imported free of customs duty. There are two windows to fulfil export obligation on FOB (free on board) and NFE (net foreign exchange basis).

5. **Advance licences for imports against exports.** Advance licences which are used to import specified raw materials without payment of any customs duty against confirmed export order and/or letter of credit have been made transferable after export obligation has been fulfilled.

6. **Exemption from tax and credit subsidies.** Profits or incomes from exports are *completely exempt from income taxes*. Besides, exporters are provided preferential access to credit from banks. Concessional rates of interest are charged por pre-ship and post-ship credit to exporters.

7. **The Duty Drawback Scheme.** In this important scheme of providing incentives to exporters customs duty and excise duty paid on inputs which are used for production of exports are reimbursed to exporters.

8. **Incentive to exports of services.** In an attempt to provide massive thrust to export of services EXIM Policy 2003-04 has introduced duty free import facility for the service sector units having a minimum foreign exchange earnings of Rs. 10 lakes. The scheme is likely to provide a major boost to export of services like health care, entertainment, professional services and tourism.

9. Small-scale industries (SSI) reservations have been withdrawn from a large number of items so that a large-scale producers can produce these terms cheaply and export them. Further details of export import policy (EXIM) will be explained at length in the next chapter.

CASE FOR EXPORT ORIENTATION

The export orientation of trade policy (or outward-looking growth strategy) is believed to have many advantages and is regarded as superior to import-substitution policy. We explain some of these advantages below.

First, it has been pointed out that export-oriented trade policy is conducive to *more efficient use and allocation of resources*. Jagdish Bhawati has emphasized the efficiency gain of export promoting trade strategy. He is of view that export orientation and import liberlisation trade strategy will ensure domestic resource allocation closer to efficient production of goods in accordance with comparative cost of a country. According to him, such a trade strategy will not lead to profit-seeking unproductive activities.

An important advantage of export-oriented strategy arises from *economies of scale* which can

11. Jagdish Bhagwati, 'Export-Promoting Trade Strategy : Issues and Evidence'. *The Word Bank Research Observer*. Vol. 3, No. 1

be reaped more effectively. As a result, cost per unit of output rises which will tend to lower prices of export. Lower export prices will help in significant expansion in exports and enable us to earn more foreign exchange. As export demand or market size for a good expands this will lead to economies of scale. With adequate size of market even small-scale and medium enterprises can set up plants of optimum size to enjoy the economies of scale.

Export-oriented trade policy makes substantial contribution to economic growth by *relaxing the foreign exchange constraints.* Export-promoting trade policy places emphasis on industries geared towards earning foreign exchange. This helps to keep the balance of payments in equilibrium. It has been found that import-substitution trade strategy generally causes shortage of foreign exchange and leads to the balance of payments problem, as happened in case of India in 1991. Shortage of foreign exchange and balance of payments problem lower rate of economic growth.

On the other hand, export-oriented trade policy does not have to face the problem of shortage of foreign exchange and is therefore conducive to higher rate of economic growth. Further, a significant merit of export-oriented trade policy is that *it will help to achieve self-reliance, that is, self sustained growth of the Indian economy*. As a matter of fact, import substitution strategy was adopted in India with the belief that through it we will achieve self reliance. But the policy underestimated the import intensity of import-substitution process. Import-substitution strategy substantially increased our import requirements for equipment and raw materials. This necessitated a large amount of foreign exchange which could not be earned sufficiently through exports. Thus, far from helping to do away with foreign assistance import-substitution strategy increased our dependence on foreign capital inflows.

Export-oriented trade policy coupled with liberalised foreign investment will enable us to earn adequate foreign exchange to solve our balance of payments problem and ensure self-sustained economic growth. Above all, several studies have found a highly positive relation between growth of national income and expansion in export. However, as Balassa has promoted out that for relation between export-orientation and economic growth initial conditions matter a lot. These initial conditions include resource endowment, expansion opportunities of trade, stock of technical knowledge. No doubt, these initial condition are important for determining economic growth. However, trade policy is certainly important for providing incentives for expansion of exports for availing of the opportunities thrown up by international trade. This will lead to the optimum use and allocation of material resources which will stimulate economic growth.

FOREIGN TRADE POLICY, 2004-09

Introduction

After every five years Government reviews its export and import policy in view of the changes in international economic situation. The foreign trade policy or what is also called export-import (EXIM) policy relates to promotion of exports and regulation of imports so as note only to overcome trade deficite but also to promote economic growth. UPA-1 Government announced its foreign trade policy for a five year period (2004-09) on August 31, 2004. This new trade policy carries further the process of trade liberalisation. Exemptions and incentives given in the earlier 2002-07, and Mini Exim Policy 2004 have not been changed and new incentives for promotion of exports have been provided. We explain below the various provisions of this new trade policy. Mr. Kamal Nath, our present Commerce Minister claims that the new trade policy was not just Export-Import (EXIM) policy but it goes beyond that. According to him, *new foreign trade policy is an effective instrument of accelerating economic growth and employment generation through exports*. An important feature of new trade policy is that it seeks to eliminate taxes and duties from exports so as to make exports

12. See B. Balassa, 'Outward Orientation C. Bliss, 'Trade and Development in H. Chenery. T.N. Sriniwasan (eds), *Handbook of Development Economics*, Amstred am, North Hollan, 1990.

Table 26.6 : Export Growth & Share in World Exports of Selected Countries

Country	CAGR	Annual % Growth Rate		Share in World Exports %		
	2000-07	2007	2008	2000	2008	Change in Share
China	25.4	25.6	17.3	3.9	9.1	5.1
Hong Kong	7.9	8.7	5.3	3.2	2.3	0.4
Malaysia	8.7	9.6	19.1	1.5	1.3	0.2
Indonesia	8.8	114.7	24.4	1.0	0.9	0.1
Singapore	11.7	10.1	13.0	2.2	2.1	– 0.1
Thailand	12.1	17.0	12.9	1.1	1.1	0.0
India	19.8	20.3	20.7	0.7	1.1	0.4
Brazil	16.5	16.6	23.2	0.9	1.3	0.4
Mexico	7.3	8.6	7.3	2.6	1.8	0.8
Russia	18.9	16.9	44.3	1.7	3.2	1.6
South Korea	12.8	14.1	13.6	2.7	2.7	0.0
Emerging Developing Economies (EDEs)	16.9	14.7	21.1	26.0	38.4	12.4
World	11.7	13.9	14.3	100	100	100

Source : GOI, *Economic Survey*, 2008-09
CAGR : Compound Annual Growth Rate

more competitive. According to it, 'we have to export goods and services and not taxes'. The Duty Exemption Pass Book scheme which allows exporters to claim exemption from excise duties and relief on customs duties has been continued for now, but it will be replaced with an effective scheme in line with WTO commitments.

Foreign Trade Target : Doubling of India's Share in World Trade in Five Years (2004-09)

The new foreign trade policy aims to double India's share of world merchandise trade in the next five years. As shown in Table 26.6 in India's share in World export was just 0.8 per cent as compared to 5.9 per cent of China. Thus China has surged ahead of India in expanding its share of world trade. The new trade policy seeks to raise India's shore in world exports to 1.5 per cent by 2009.In the past the Indian Government had set target of capturing 1 per cent of global exports. So the target of achieving 1.5 per cent share in five years in world exports is a very ambitious target. In absolute term this implies raising India's exports from 61.9 billion US dollars to 195 billion by 2009. This means 21 per cent compound annual growth in exports. This is based on the assumption that world trade will grow at 10 per cent per annum.

Focus on Employment Generation through Export Strategy. In line with the UPA Government's priority to employment goveration foreign trade policy also focuses on employment generation through an appropriate export Strategy. Employment opportunities will increase as a result of expansion of agricultural exports for which new policy provides special incentives. Other sectors identified for employment-generation and export-promotion include handlooms, handicrafts, gems and jewellery, and leather and footwear, apart from services. Non-IT service sectors on which the policy focuses are tourism, health care and education. At present, merchandise exports are valued at over $70 billion, while services contribute more than $50 billion.

Focus on Agro-exports to boost export growth. The new five-year Foreign Trade Policy moots a special package to boost agro-exports by offering fiscal incentives to exporters. It includes launching a special farm produce scheme called Vishesh Krishi Upaj Yojana (VKUY) to promote the export of fruits, vegetables, flowers and minor forest produce and their value-added products and permission for duty-free import of capital goods for installation anywhere in the agri-export zones (AEZs). The procedures for the import of seeds, bulbs, tubers and planting material and the export of plant portion, derivatives and extracts have been liberalised. The measure is expected to help facilitate the production of export-worthy agriculutral products. It will also help boost the export of medicinal plants and herbal products.

Exemption of Exports from Service Tax. A significant measure to promote exports is that exports of all goods and services have been exempted from 10 per cent service tax and 2 per cent cess on it. Export Oriented Units (EOUs) have also been given exemption from service tax in proportion of their exported goods and services. To accelerate services export, the foreign trade policy has also provided sops–in terms of duty free entitlement — to individual service providers (who earn forex of at least Rs. 5 lakh), other service providers (who earn forex of at least Rs. 10 lakh) of 10% of the foreign exchange earned by them.

The foreign trade policy announcement on service tax exemption for all goods and services exported including those from the domestic tariff area (DTA) – will be available on 161 tradable services. This list of all 161 tradable services covered under the General Agreement on Trade in Services (GATS) where such payment of services is received in free forex, according to the policy document. As of now, the announcement is statement of fact because all payments received by Indian service providers in foreign exchange are currently exempt from service tax.

Promoting Exports of Services. Recognising the key role of the service sector in the economy, the foreign trade policy has unveiled the '*Served from India*' scheme to accelerate growth in service exports. The scheme aims at creating a brand instantly recognised and respected world over. The earlier DFEC (Duty Free Entitilement Certificate) scheme has been revamped and recast into the new scheme. Individual service providers who earn foreign exchange of at least Rs. 5 lakh, and other service providers with forex earnings of at least Rs. 10 lakh, will be eligible for a duty credit entitlement of 10 per cent of total forex earned by them.

Apart from setting up the export promotion council, the policy has announced two other major initiatives to boost services exports. The government would promote establishment of a common facility centres for home-based service providers. To boost exports, a new scheme '*Target Plus*' has been introduced. With this exporters who achieve quantum growth would be entitled to substantially higher duty-free credit based on incremental exports .

New Export-Promotion Schemes. In the new foreign trade policy, three new schemes have been introduced and others revamped to boost exports. *No existing export-promotion scheme has been withdrawn.* A new scheme named '*served from India*' has been launched to popularise non-IT services in line with the existing '*Made in India*' scheme to promote export of Indian goods. Similarly, a *Vishesh Krishi Upaj Yojana* has been announced to promote export of fruits, vegetables, flowers, minor forest produce and their value-added products. A '*Target Plus*' scheme has also been announced.

Another new scheme '*Free Trade and Warehousing Zones* (FTWZ) has been introduced to improve trade related infrastructure. Foreign direct investment would be permitted up to 100 per cent in the development and establishment of the zones and their infrastrcutral facilities. Each zone would have a minimum outlay of Rs. 100 crores and five lakh square metres of built-up area. These units will quality for all benefits applicable for special economic zones.

Target Plus Scheme to promote exports. A new scheme call "Target Plus" has been launched to accelerate export growth. Under this scheme special incentives have been provided to all exporters who exceed the normal export target growth of 16% fixed by the commerce ministry for 2004-05. For instance if a firm shows a 25% growth in exports it will get duty free credit totalling 10% of the value of incremental exports. The duty free credit entitlement goes up to 15% of incremental exports if exports grow by 100% during the year. This is expected to provide incentives to exporters to achieve a quantum growth in exports. But past experience has shown that such schemes also get misused widely.

Establishment of Bio-Technology Parks. Taking note of the significance of biotechnology, the new policy has announced the establishment of biotechnology parks, which will get all the facilities of 100 per cent export oriented unit. In this regard sectors with significant export and employment potential in semi-urban and rural areas have been identified.

Restrictions on Imports of Second-Hand Capital Goods Waived. For the first time all capital goods regardless of age are made freely importable without any actual *user condition* or requirement of minimum residual life. Free imports of second hand machinery is expected to bring down the cost of investment and strengthening the forces of industrial restructuring. However free imports does not apply to computer and laptops.

Free Transferability of DFECC (Duty Free Entitlement Credit Certificates). The main improvement in the DFECC scheme is that the portion related to agriculture exports zones is freely transferable. These will make incentive attractive and give push to the AEZs. (Agriculture Export Zones). The DFECC for normal exports, which varies from 5 to 15% of export value depending upon export growth rate, is a non-stater mainly because of the actual user condition and restriction on transferability of the entitlement. Unless the negotiability of the entitlement is improved, the scheme will not take off.

Evaluation of New Foreign Trade Policy, 2004-09

Chambers of Commerce and Industry have welcomed the new foreign trade policy. According to CII president Sunil Kant Munjal, "*The foreign trade policy is forward looking*". It presents schemes to develop exports across all sectors of the economy, sets a target of doubling India's share in global trade and presents a vision of India as a 'gloabl hub' for manufacturing, trading and services". In view of India's increasing integration with the global market, there is a need for a more integrated approach to foreign trade policy. The chamber said it is looking forward to interacting with the Board of Trade which is expected to play a greater role in developing foreign trade related initiatives. FICCI president Y.K Modi said, "This policy not only encompasses the entire export chain but takes cognizance of India's export competitiveness against the background of bilateral and multilateral trade processes that India has entered into."

The chamber has appreciated the commerce minister's statement that Indian exports can be competitive only if the current practice of exporting local taxes is put to an end. The proposed **Service Export Promotion Council** and the '**Served from India**' scheme will help even non-IT services like entertainment, medical tourism, accounting services, financial services to realise their greater potential. Assocham president Mahendra K Sanghi said it is a good idea to set up free trade warehouse zones through which service exports will be encouraged. The duty free import of capital goods for agriculture exporters and permitting 100% FDI in the Free Trade Zones are good measures to boost India's agricultural exports.

According to S.S.H Rehman, chairman, CII tourism council, "We welcome the maintenance of the duty free entitlement scheme of imports of professional equipment and consumables including liquor, amounting to the average of the previous 3 years +earnings in foreign exchange, in respect of hotels. The step of enhancing the entitlement for stand alone restaurants to 20% is also positive. PHDCCI president Ravi Wig said the emphasis on a partnership approach between industry and government for doubling India's merchandise exports in the next five years is a positive step. Further, the thrust on promotion of agri-products would lead to substantial foreign exchange earnings as well as employment generation.

The new foreign trade policy seeks to double India's share of global exports from today's 0.8% to 1.5% in the next five years. To do that, the policy exempts all exports from the new service tax, allows unlimited foreign investment in free trade and warehousing zones, provides incentives fro biotech parks and scrapped restrictions on imports of used capital goods. To boost exports, some imported inputs necessary for exporting industries have been made duty-free. There is a scheme to boost foreign sales of value-added farm products, fruits and flowers. None of this is earthshaking; they're workmanlike ideas which could speed up exports to some extent.

Though services exports are growing at a scorching rate and are expected to continue at this pace for many years, India needs to boost manufacture exports. To do that the entire structure of indirect taxes, which penalises manufacturing, has to be overhauled. Instead of taxing manufactures with a host of Central and State-level taxes like excise, octroi, sales tax and so on, whose fiscal impact cascades into high prices and loss of competitiveness. There is urgent need for replaicng this with a single-rate value-added tax (VAT).

Further, instead of charging different tariff rates for different imports at relatively high rates compared to global standards, the governemnt should shift to a single reasonable tariff rate for all imports. This has two important benefits. First, it will cut out all procedural complications and most of the red tape that goes with trade. It will also minimise the graft, rent-seeking and policing, inevitable in a multiple-rate system. Finally, the key to a competitive economy is its investment regime. There's no reason why India cannot implement a liberal foreign investment policy that allows 100% investment in most sectors, and curbs it in a few areas that are deemed too sensitive for foreign funding. The growth of trade is linked intimately with the health of the economy. History shows that countries with clear, investor-friendly policies do better than those that cripple businesses with red tape and taxes.

In our view the prime driver of exports in a globalising economy has to be *competitiveness* and not promotion. And competitiveness is created by a range of factors, very few of which are in the commerce minister's control. True, promotion of exports is not irrelevant and to that extent, the new thrust given to export of agriculture, handicrafts, leather, gems and jewellery, and services is welcome. However, it is inexplicable that the one sector in which India's export opportunity is going to zoom in the near future, that is textiles, has been virtually ignored, except for some leftover concessions for garments. Besides, in our view the lifting of restrictions on imports of second hand capital goods will have an adverse effect on the domestic capital goods industries.

Annual Supplement (2006) to Foreign Trade Policy

In its annual supplement in April, 2006 to foreign trade policy, 2004-09, the Commerce Minister proposed a series of important trade initiatives to put India's exports on a trajectory of quantum growth and create two million new jobs in the export sector by 2009-10. India's merchandise exports crossed 100 billion US dollars and touched 101 billion US $ in the fiscal year 2005-06, that is, 25 per cent growth on the top of 26 per cent growth achieved last year (2004-05). The target for the current year, 2006-07 is the achieve 20 per cent growth rate in exports. If our exports continue to maintain this 20 per cent or above growth rate, then the export target of 150 billion US dollars in 2008-09 is quite achievable.

In the fiscal year 2005-06, as against the exports of 101 billion US dollars, merchandise imports have been estimated at 140 billion US $ (which includes imports of 43 billion US $ of petroleum oil alone). In this annual supplement to foreign trade policy the two new schemes namely, Focus Product Scheme and Focus Market Scheme have been announced, especially for the objective of creating employment opportunities in semi urban and rural areas. These two schemes will replace the Target Plus Scheme which has been abolished. Some details of these two schemes are :

Focus Product Scheme. Under the focus product scheme a duty-free credit facility at 2.5 per cent of FOB (Free on Board) value of exports will be provided on 50 per cent of the export turnover of notified products such as fish and leather, stationery items, sports goods, toys and handlooms and handicrafts. This will encourage exports and since these products are labour-intensive, their growth will generate a large number of employment opportunities.

Focus Market Scheme. This focus market scheme offers a similar incentive for all products exported to notified countries which may include Africa and Latin America.

It has been estimated that above two schemes would not involve much loss of revenue for the government.

Stimulus to Exports of Gem and Jewelry. In this annual supplement to foreign trade policy, favourable policy measures have been announced that will not only help boost exports by 20-25 per cent but will also pave the way for increased FDI in India. An important policy measure in this regard has been the reduction in value-addition norms of exports of gold and silver which have been brought down from 7 per cent to 4.5 per cent. Increase of gold and silver prices over the past few years had made the present value-addition criteria on exports of gold and silver jewellery unrealistic.

Further, the foreign trade policy has allowed re-import of rejected jewellery subject to refund of duty exemption benefits on inputs only not the duty on entire jewellery. On several occasions exporters used to face the dilemma of unsold jewellery in foreign markets because of changing designs and other such factors. The new initiative well help exporters to overcome this problem as now jewellery export would be possible on consignment basis.

Beside, the permission to export cut and polished precious and semi-precious stones for treatment and subsequent re-import within a period of 120 days has been given. This will enhance the quality of these products and afford higher value in the international market. The idea behind these steps is to prevent India's gems and jewellery business from shifting to Dubai. Boosting the gems and jewellery sector would create more jobs in smaller centres such as Surat.

Boost to Auto Sector. To provide stimulus to the auto sector, foreign trade policy seeks to promote India as an *auto component hub*, import of cars for R & D purposes will be allowed without going the expensive homologation. This will enable import of new model cars for testing components.

The Videsh Krishi Upaj and Gram Yojana (VKUGY). In the new foreign trade policy, the Videsh Krishi Upaj Yojana (VKUY) has been replaced by the Videsh Krishi Upaj and Gram Yojana (VKUGY) under which gram udyog products will also be entitled for a customs duty credit of 5 per cent of free-on-board (FOB) value of exports made after April 2006.

Duty Free Authorisation Scheme. Besides, in the new foreign trade policy a new duty free authorisation scheme has been introduced with effect from May 1, 2006 with combined features of Advance License Scheme (ALS) and Duty Free Replinishment Certificate (DFRC). DFRC scheme has been discontinued with effect from April 30, 2006 while the advance.

Duty Drawback and DEPB Rates. It has been decided to include service tax and fringe benefit tax (FBT) under the export promotion schemes such as Duty Drawback and Duty Entitlement Pass Book Scheme (DEPB) which will be notified later in year 2006 . Revenue loss to the government on this count will be around Rs. 800 crores.

EPCG Scheme Made Flexible. The Export Promotion Capital Goods Scheme which allows import of capital goods at a concessional customs duty of 5 per cent has been made more flexible. In this regard export obligation period has been extended to a maximum of 12 years. These changes would help genuine exporters who were unable to fulfil the export obligation due to changed market conditions.

Evaluation of Annual Foreign Trade Policy (2006)

It has been claimed by the Commerce Minister that the growth of exports at the rate of 26 per cent in 2004-05 and 25 per cent in 2005-06 shows the success of foreign trade policy, 2004-09. As a matter of fact, our exports have grown at more than 20 per cent in the last four years (2002-06). Of course, foreign trade policy to promote exports pursued in the past some years has contributed to such robust growth in exports. However, many other things account for such robust growth in our exports, apart from the trade policy. Macroeconomic stability, gradual elimination of the anti-export bias in our economic policy built up by huge tariff barriers in the past, increasing confidence of

India producers, availability of imported inputs at nearly global prices, availability of relatively cheap finance are some other factors that that have boosted the competitiveness of Indian exports. The ability of Indian goods and services to gain market-share abroad is ultimately a function of the competitiveness of Indian producers.

If momentum of export growth of over 20 per cent per annum is maintained, then India's aim to double its share in global trade from 0.8 per cent to 1.5 per cent by the end of present foreign trade policy period (*i.e.* by 2008-09) appears to be achievable.

For expanding production of goods and services for export, producers need efficient infrastructure, flexible and less restrictive labour laws, and reforms in the complicated tax structure. Thus, in addition to efficient infrastructure Indian exporters urgently need a full fledged goods and service tax and abolition of all cascading, non VAT commodity taxes like Octoi, entry tax and turnover tax if export target of 150 billion US $ by 2008-09 is to be achieved. The more difficult goal is the generation of an additional two million jobs in the export sector.

Trade Policy measures by Government in 2008-09

FOREIGN TRADE POLICY, 2009-14

Against the fall in exports for the last 10 months, (October 2008 to July 2009) the Government announced its foreign trade policy for 2009-14 on August 27, 2009. Due to the global slowdown, some countries have resorted to protectionist measures posing barrier to free trade which has aggrevated the problem for Indian exporters. The Government's short-term goal through this foreign trade was to reverse the declining trend of exports and provide support to the export sectors that have been hit badly by recession in the developed world. The Government does not expect immediate outlook for exports to improve and pegged export growth for the year 2009-10 at 3 per cent. But for 2010-11 it has set the target of 15 per cent growth in exports and an ambitious $ 200 billion target for exports to be achieved by March 2011. In the remaining three years 2011-14 it expected to return to high growth path for exports at 25 per cent per annum. It set the target of doubling our exports of goods and services by March 2014. Its long-term aim is to double India's share of global goods and services exports by 2020, that is from 1.64 per cent in 2008-09 to 3.28 per cent in 2019-20. By and large the new foreign trade policy is similar to the previous one for the period 2004-09 and has the same promotion measures, but with some additional incentives. The main features of new foreign trade policy for 2009-14 are given next page :

Duty free imports for labour-intensive sectors. An import measure of the new foreign trade policy is allowing duty-free imports of capital goods required for the manufacture of export goods as against the existing 3 per cent duty. These labour intensive sectors include engineering, electronics, basic chemicals and pharmaceuticals, apparel and textiles, plastics as will as leather and leather products. This incentive under the Export Promotion Capital Goods (EPCG) scheme will be applicable until-March 31, 2010. Besides, the period of export obligation for importing capital goods free of import duty has been extended to 12 years.

Further, the *other sectors in addition to the above* have also been allowed to import capital goods under EPCG scheme at a concessional duty of 3 per cent. In their case too the period of export obligation has been expended to 12 years. *The objective has been to increase the productivity of the export-industries through technological upgradation by importing required capital goods.* This will help our exporters to increase the share of world exports.

Extension of Duty Entitlement Passbook Scheme (DEPBS). Foreign trade policy for 2009-14 has also extended the Duty Entitlement Passbook Scheme (DEPBS) until December 2010. Under this scheme exporters obtain a refund on a proportion of indirect taxes paid by them. Since this scheme is not WTO compliant alternative scheme is being worked out.

Expansion of Focus Markets Scheme (FMS). As India's existing export markets are reeling under recession, the new foreign trade policy has expanded its Focus Market Scheme (FMS) to 26 more markets, 16 in Latin America and 10 in Africa and IS countries (Common Wealth of Independent States). The new policy has also increased the incentive under this scheme to the exporters from *2.5 per cent to 3 per cent of the value of the exports* if they cater to these markets. Explaining the policy the commerce Minister, Mr. Anand Sharma said, "We cannot remain oblivious to declining demand in the developed world and we need to set in motion strategies and policy measures which will catalyse the growth of exports." At present, exports to Europe, US and Japan amount to 36%, 18% and 16%, respectively, of India's total exports of $ 168 billion in 2008-09. Due to global recession, India's exports have declined by almost 30% in the last 10 months. This forced the government to induce exporters to sell in new markets.

More Incentives and Greater Coverage for Focus Product Scheme (FPS). While the incentive available under the Focus Market Scheme (MS) has been raised from 2.5 to 3 per cent, that under the Focus Products Scheme (FPS) has been raised from 1.25 to 2 per cent. Engineering products such as agricultural machinery, parts of trailers, sewing machines, hand tools, garden tools, musical instruments, clocks and watches and railway locomotives, value-added plastic products, jute and sisal products, technical textiles, green technology products such as wind mills and wind turbines, electrically operated vehicles, project goods, and certain electronic items have been included in Focus Product Scheme (FPS).

Export of products like pharmaceuticals, synthetic textile fabrics, value-added rubber products, value-added plastic goods, textile made-ups, knitted and crocheted fabrics, glass products, certain iron and steel products and certain articles of aluminium would be eligible for FMS if exports are made to 13 identified markets (Algeria, Egypt, Kenya, Nigeria, South Africa, Tanzania, Brazil, Mexico, Ukraine, Vietnam, Cambodia, Australia and New Zealand).

Market-linked FPS benefits have also been extended for export to more new markets for certain products. These products include auto components, motor cars, bicycles and parts, and apparel, among others.

Extension of other Export Booster Schemes. The other booster schemes, which were announced earlier, will also continue under the new foreign trade policy. Some of the such schmes are *2 percentage points interest subvention* on pre-shipment credit and *enhanced insurance coverage through Export* Credit Guarantee Corporation (ECGC). These measures will now continue till March 31, 2010. ECGC provides a range of credit risks insurance cover to exporters against loss in exports of goods and services. It also provides guarantees to banks and financial institutions to enable exporters to obtain better facilities from them.

Incentives to Gems and Jewellery. The $ 27 billion Indian gems and jewellery sector which contributes 13% to India total exprots, has received a host of incentives, including input duty refunds (under duty drawback scheme) on gold jewellery export and setting up of diamond bourses to make the country diamond-trading hub. "It shall be our endevaour to make India an international diamond-trading hub and we plan to establish diamond bourses in the coming years," commerce minister Anand Sharma said unveilling the new Foreign Trade Policy.

The Rs. 80,000 crore diamond cutting & polishing industry that has an 80% global market share has suffered behavily because of the recession in the world's largest diamond markets, the US and Europe. Surat, the diamond city, saw more than 3,000 units shutting down with around 4 lakh workers losing jobs in Gujarat alone.

Relief for Export-oriented Units (EOUs)

EoUs can sell 90% of the output in domestic market instead of 75%. But over a period of 75% of the production has to be exported.

HIGHLIGHT'S OF FOREIGN TRADE POLICY 2009-14

- The foreign trade policy 2009-14 tries to find solutions to the crisis and set the agenda for future.

TARGETS

- Annual export growth of 15% with an annual export target of $200 billion by March 2011
- 2011-14 annual export growth of 25% per annum. Double India's exports of goods and services by 2014.
- Double India's share in global trade by 2020.

MAJOR INITIATIVES

- 26 new markets added under Focus Mkt Scheme, incentives hiked from 2.5% to 3%
- Incentive under Focus product scheme raised to 2% from 1.25% more products included
- EPCG scheme at zero duty introduced
- Duty entitlement passbook (DEPB) scheme extended till December 31, 2010
- 2% interest subvention on pre-shipment credit extended till March 31, 2010
- Duty drawback on gold jewellery exports allowed
- India to promote diamond bourses to make the country an international diamond trading.
- Single-window scheme for export of perishable farm goods
- EOUs allowed to sell products in domestic tariff area to an extent of 90%
- Market-linked Focus Product Scheme introduced for export of identified products to 13 identified markets.

Measures to Reduce Transaction Costs

With a view to boost exports, the government initiated several measures to rationalise procedures and reduce transaction costs in its new foreign trade policy (FIP), announced today. Following the demand of industry, the application and redemption forms under the Export Promotion Capital Goods (EPCG) scheme have been simplified.

The maxium fee charged on authorisation or licence applications on schemes like focus product, focus market, market access initiative and market development assistance, has been slashed to Rs. 1 lakh from Rs. 1.5 lakh (manual applications) and to Rs. 50,000 from Rs. 75,000 (for electronic applications). No fee shall now be charged for granting incentives under the schemes which deals with export incentives of foreign trade policy.

The government has extended the time within which exporters can convert shipping bills from one export scheme to another, from one month to three months. An inter-ministerial committee would also be formed to resolve issues of exporters. In order to reduce transaction costs, dispatch of imported goods directly from the port to the site has been allowed under the Advance Authorisation Scheme for deemed supplies. At present, duty-free imported goods could be taken only to the manufacturing unit of the authorisation holder or its supporting manufacturer.

To facilitate duty-free import of samples by exporters, number of samples or pieces has been increased from the existing 15 to 50. Customs clearance of such samples shall be based on declarations given by the importers with regard to the limit of value and quantity of samples. The government has also allowed disposal of manufacturing wastes, after payment of the excise duty. Besides, automobile firms, which have their own R&D centres, would be allowed free import of petrol and diesel up to 5 kl.

The commerce and industry ministry is also promoting the use of electronic systems with initiatives like electronic data interface (EDI) ports, electronic message exchange between Customs and the Directorate General of Foreign Trade.

Evaluation of Foreign Trade Policy, 2009-14

The various sops and incentives to the exporters in the new foreign trade policy is expected to arrest shrinking exports. The dynamic policy initiatives announced by the Government in the new foreign trade policy towards expansion and diversification of export markets, technological upgrade increased flexibility and procedural simplifications will help our exporters retain market share, and will hopefully reverse the declining trend in our exports. The extension of the DEPB (Duty Entitlement Passbook) scheme, expansion of the focus market scheme (FMS) to 26 new countries, extension of interest subvention and zero duty on capital goods imports under the Export Promotion Credit Guarantee (EPCG) scheme are measures which will help revive exports and protect employment.

The *emphasis on reducing transaction costs* and simplifying trade and tax procedures in the new foreign trade policy would help enhance the competitiveness of Indian exports and would specially benefit small and medium sized exporters. The micro, small and medium enterprises, or MSMEs, are in need of technological upgrade in order to be cost-effective and competitive in international markets. The technological upgradation Scheme, by providing imports of capital goods for certain sectors under EPCG at zero per cent duty will help. The new policy initiatives relating to import of capital goods are, indeed, timely. The EPCG (Export Promotion Capital Goods) scheme has really been benefiting the upgrade and modernisation of India's export manufacturing sector and the new incentive of giving access at zero duty would certainly help the beneficiary sectors such as engineering and electronic products, pharmaceuticals and chemicals, apparels and textiles, leather and leather products. These are sectors where India enjoys a comparative advantage and the zero-duty capital goods import facility should go a long way in speeding up the process of technology upgrade.

The *new foreign trade policy has taken important measures to diversify our export market and offset the inherent disadvantage for our exporters in the emerging markets* of Africa, Latin America, Oceania such as credit risk, higher transaction costs etc through appropriate policy instruments. The policy focuses on the immediate objective of reversing the decline in exports and for that purpose provides support and incentives to the exporters. But in our view, the new foreign trade policy lacks the long-term strategic vision and does not provide any new approach on how India's share of world trade can double by 2020, given the competition that India faces from China which has already raised its share of total world trade to 10 per cent while India's share is still only 1.6 per cent. It would not be easy for our exporters to be weaned off the Western developed countries (where little can be done till demand there revives) by diversifying exports to Africa and Latin America where purchasing power of the people is quite small. In our view Asia itself presents a long opportunity for our exports, Therefore, the bilateral agreements made by our Government with Asean and South Korea are appropriate steps to expand our exports.

To revive exports in the immediate future, the new foreign trade policy has righly increased the incentives under the time tested export-promotion schemes which in the past contributed to export growth and has made an attempt to diversify markets for our exports. But long-term strategy to double our share of world export by 2020 is lacking in our foreign trade policy for 2010-14.

Trade Policy Measures in 2009-10 and 2010-11 to Check Inflation

Trade policy measures taken by the Government and the RBI in 2009-10 and 2010-11 focussed on reviving exports and export-related employment. The Government followed a mix of policy measures including fiscal incentives, institutional changes, procedural rationalisation and enhanced market access to the world and diversification of export markets, improvement in infrastructure related to exports; bringing down transaction costs and providing full refund of all indirect taxes and levies were there major areas of focus.

Some of the trade policy measures to check inflation during 2009-10 and 2010-11 in the country are the following :

1. Import duties reduced to zero for rice, wheat, pulses, edible oils (crude), butter and ghee to 7.8 per cent for refined and hydrogenated oils and vegetable oils.
2. Import of raw sugar allowed at zero duty under open general licence (OGL).
3. Import of white/refined sugar allowed. The facility was extended up to 31 December 2010 without any quantitative,
4. Levy obligation in respect of raw sugar and white/refined sugar removed.
5. Export of basmati rice, edible oils, except coconut oil and forest-based oil and pulses (Kabuli Chana), banned.
6. Minimum export price (MEP) used to regulate exports of onions (at $ 1200 per tonne for Dec. 2010) and Basmati rice ($ 900 PMT) were fixed.
7. Export of onions (all varieties) including Bangalore rose onions and Krishna puram onions, fresh or chilled, frozen, provisionally prepared or dried (but excluding onion-cut and sliced or broken in powder form) *not permitted with effect* from 22 December 2010 and until further orders.
8. Full exemption from basic customs duty provided to onions and shallots with effect from 21st December 2010. Consequently these items are exempt from special duty of 4 per cent and education cess. The exemption is open-ended and does not carry a validity clause prescribing a terminal date, and secondary and higher education cess.

The Important Foreign Trade Policy Measures, 2012-13

Budget Related

1. Imports of equipment for initial setting up or substantial expansion of fertilizer projects fully exempted from basic customs duty of 5 per cent for a period of three years up to 31 March 2015; and basic customs duty on some water- soluble fertilizers and liquid fertilizers other than urea reduced from 7.5 per cent to 5 per cent and from 5 per cent to 2.5 percent.
2. Concessional import duty available for installation of mechanized Handling Systems and Pallet Racking Systems in mandis or warehouses extended for horticultur produce.
3. Full exemption from basic customs duty for coal-mining projects .
4. Basic customs duty on plant and machinery imported for setting up or substantial expansion of iron ore pellet plants or iron are beneficiation plants reduced from 7.5 per cent to 2.5 per cent.
5. Full exemption from basic customs duty of 5 per cent for automatic shuttle-less looms and reduction in basic customs duty on wool waste and wool tops from 15 per cent to 5 per cent.
6. Basic customs duty increased on standard gold bars; gold coins of purity exceeding 99.5 per cent and platinum from 2 per cent to 4 per cent and on non-standard gold from 5 per cent to 10 per cent.

Credit Related

1. In November 2011, the RBI increased the all-in cost ceilings for External Commercial Borrowings (ECBs) increased to 350 basis points (bps) over 6-months Libor/Euro Libor / Euribor for a maturity period between three and five years and 500 bps over 6 Months Libor/Euro Libor/Euribor for a maturity period more than five years. Accordingly, the all-in cost ceiling on trade credits has also been increased to 350 bps over 6-months Libor/ Euro Libor / Euribor until 31 March 2013.

2. With effect from 5 May 2012, banks were allowed to determine their interest rates on export credit in foreign currency with the objective of increasing the availability of funds to exporters.
3. On 18 June 2012, the RBI enhanced the eligible limit of the export credit refinance (ECR) facility for scheduled banks (excluding regional rural banks [RRB]) from 15 per cent of the outstanding export credit eligible for refinance to 50 per cent, with effect from 30 June 2012. The objective was to provide additional liquidity support to banks of over ₹ 300 billion. The rate of interest charged on the ECR facility was retained at the prevailing repo rate under the liquidity adjustment facility (LAF).

   The 2 per cent Interest Subvention Scheme, earlier meant only for handlooms, handicrafts, carpets, and SMEs, was extended on 1 April 2012 to 31 March 2013 for labour-intensive sectors also, viz. toys, sports goods, processed agricultural products, and readymade garments. This was further extended upto 31 March 2014 and 134 tariff lines of engineering goods were also included in the scheme.

Foreign Trade Policy Measures in 2012-13

1. **Incentive on Incremental Exports:** Incentives to be granted on incremental exports made during the period January- March 2013 over the base period January-March 2012. The incentive to be granted to an Importer and Exporter Code (IEC) holder at the rate of 2 per cent on incremental growth of exports made to the USA, Europe, and Asian countries during this particular quarter, i.e. January-March 2013.
2. **Export Promotion Capital Goods (EPCG) Scheme:** Zero Duty EPCG Scheme extended up to 31st March 2013 and its scope enlarged. Export obligation under this scheme to be 25 per cent of the normal export obligation for export of products from north-eastern states and export of specified products through notified Land Customs Stations of the north-eastern region provided additional incentive to the extent of 1 per cent of Free on Board (FOB) value of exports.
3. **Support for Export of Green Technology Products:** To promote exports of 16 identified green technology products, export obligation for manufacturing of these products under the EPCG Scheme reduced to 75 per cent of the normal export obligation.
4. **Support for Infrastructure for the Agriculture Sector :** Status holders exporting products under ITC (HS) Chapter 1 to Chapter 23 (both inclusive) are getting Duty Credit Scrip equivalent to 10 per cent of FOB value of agricultural products so exported. Import of 14 specified equipments had bee notified for setting up of pack- houses besides import of capital goods and equipment for cold storage units, pack-houses, etc.
5. **Incentives for Promoting Investment in Labour-intensive Sectors:** Status holders issued status holders incentive scrip (SHIS) to import capital goods for promoting investment in upgradation of technology of some specified labour- intensive sectors like leather, textile and jute, handicrafts, engineering, plastics and basic chemicals. Up to 10 per cent of the value of these scrips will be allowed to be utilized to import components and spares of capital goods imported
6. **Market and Product Diversification:** Seven new markets have been added to the Focus Market Scheme (FMS) and seven to the Special Focus Market Scheme (Special FMS). Forty-six new items have been added to the Market Linked Focus Product Scheme (MLFPS). The MLFPS has been extended till 31 March 2013 for exports to the USA and EU in respect of items falling under Chapter 61 and Chapter 62. Around 100 new items have been

added to the Focus Product Scheme (FPS) list. Three new items have been added to the Vishesh Krishi and Gram Udyog Yojana (VKGUY). Additional measures announced as trade facilitation measures by widening and deepening of export incentives under chapter 3 of FTP in December, 2012 to be made effective from 01.01.2013. These include addition of 5 new markets to FMS, one new market to Special FMS, 62 new items to MLFPS and 102 new items to FPS.

7. **Simplification of Procedures:** Import under advance authorization (AA) permitted at any of the Electronic Data Interchange (EDI) ports, irrespective of the EDI port in which the AA has been registered. There would be no requirement of Telegraphic Release Advice (TT{A). Export shipments from Delhi and Mumbai through post, courier, or e-Commerce to be entitled for export benefits under the FTP.
8. **New 'e-BRC' Initiative:** A major EDI initiative the 'e-BRC' launched which would herald electronic transmission of foreign exchange realization from the respective banks to the Directorate General of Foreign Trade (DGFT) server on a daily basis. The exporter will not be required to make any request to the bank for issuance of a *bank export and realization certificate (BRC)*.

Exports Policy Changes in 2013-14.

To give boost to exports which contracted by 1.76 per cent in 2012-13 to $ 300.6 billion, the government in its annual exports policy for 2013-14 announced several incentives. These include easier land requirement norms, simpler exit options, cheaper credit and tax breaks for import of machinery. The highlights of the export policy changes for SEZs in 2013-14 are the following :

1. The new rules for SEZs will allow IT firms to claim tax breaks by moving offshore work to such duty-free enclaves. The earlier requirement of minimum 10-heactares for such campses has been done away with

2. IT SEZs can now be set up if the these are spread across at least 100,000 square metres in seven major cities including Mumbai, Delhi and NCR, Chennai, Hyderabad, Bangalore, Pune and Kolkata.

3. For category B cities, IT companies can set up SEZs even in a smaller built-up area of 50,000 square metres and for remaining cities in only 25,000 square metres. IT firms allowed to set up SEZs in campuses as small as 2500 sequare metres.

4. Minimum land area requirement halved to 500 hectares for multipurpose SEZs and to 50 hectares for sector-specific ones.

5. Ownership transfer of SEZ unit sales has been permitted.

6. Export Promotion Capital Goods scheme, which allows exporters to import machinery and capital goods at zero duty, was extended beyond March 2013 and would be applicable to all sectors.

It follows from above the package of export-policy reforms was meant to revive investor incentives for SEZs. It has been realised that SEZs have not realised their full potential.

IT industry body Nasscom welcomed these reforms in export policy and was delighted to note that the government has recognised that IT exports as a key growth driver for India's exports.

QUESTIONS FOR REVIEW

1. What is meant by import-substituion ? Why India adopted import-substitution policy in the early five year plans ?
2. What were the consequences of India's import-substitution policy ?
3. Critically evaluate India's current trade policy of 'import liberalisation for export promotion'?
4. Write a short on export-led strategy of economic grwoth.
5. What is meant by export-orientation ? Give arguments for export-orientation of trade policy.
6. Crtically examine India's Foreign Trade Policy 2009-14. What changes have been made in it in recent years.

CHAPTER 27

India's Foreign Trade

Introduction

No country is self-sufficient in the world today. Therefore, every country has to import goods and to pay for imports it has to export goods to other countries. Ideally, every country should specialise in accordance with its comparative cost. But in addition to comparative costs several other factors including political considerations have played a part in determining the pattern of imports and exports. In the past, to protect domestic industries, many countries had imposed heavy tariffs to restrict imports. However, in recent years the world opinion has become in favour of free trade so that different countries by specialising according to their comparative costs are able to accelerate their economic growth and raise living standards of their people. Therefore, recently World Trade Organisation (WTO) has been set up to promote free trade among nations of the world. As a result of agreements under WTO different countries have reduced their tariffs and removed quantitative restrictions on imports. With these measures, world trade is expected to grow at a more rapid rate than before.

India started its planned development in 1951 with strategy of import substitution and neglected the importance of expansion of export as a means of efficient allocation of resources to ensure higher economic growth. Therefore, the share of India's exports which was about 2 per cent of world trade in 1951 declined to only 0.6 per cent in 1995 but slightly rose to 0.85 in 2001. But the requirements of economic development compelled us to import large quantities of capital goods, raw materials and essential consumer goods. Therefore, over the 60 years of planning period our imports grew rapidly and exceeded our exports with the result that there has been deficit in our trade balance.

Volume of India's Foreign Trade and Trade Balance

In Table 27.1 we have given the value of India's exports and imports and trade balance since 2000-01. It will be seen from the table that value of India's exports increased from 44,560 million US

Table 27.1. India's Exports, Imports and Balance of Trade

(US $ million)

Year	*Exports*	*Imports*	*Trade Balance*
2000-01	44560	50536	–5976
2001-02	43827	51413	–7587
2002-03	52719	61412	–8693
2003-04	63843	78149	–14307
2004-05	83536	111517	–27981
2005-06	103091	149166	–46075
2006-07	126414	185735	–59321
2007-08	163132	251654	–88522
2008-09	185295	303696	–118401
2009-10	178751	288373	–109622
2010-11	251136	369769	–118633
2011-12	304624	489181	–184558
2012-13 (April-Dec.)	214100	361272	–157172

Source: DGCI & S, Kolkata

dollars in 2000-01 to 178751 million US dollars in 2009-10—about 400 times increase in 10 years period. Further, it will be seen that value of imports of India increased from 50536 million US dollars in 2000-01 to 288373 million US dollars in 2009-2010, that is, more than 400 times increase in ten years period. As a result, larger increase in imports as compared to growth in exports, deficit in our trade balance which was 5976 million US dollars in 2000-01 rose to an alarming figure of 109622 million US dollars in 2009-10, and further to 184558 million US dollars in 2011-12.

Composition of India's Exports

One of the important aspects of foreign trade of a country is its commodity structure, that is, its composition. The composition of India's exports has greatly changed over 60 years of planned development. In 2011-12 value of India's exports amounted to 304624 million US dollars, of which agriculture and allied products accounted for 37618 million US dollars, ores and minerals accounted for 8546 million US dollars, manufactured goods contributed 201237 million US dollars, mineral fuels and lubricants accounted for 57015 million US dollars.

Among exports of agriculture and allied products, coffee, tea, oil cakes, tobacco, cashew kernels, spices, fish and fish preparations were major export products. Among ores and minerals, iron was the major article of export. Among the industrial manufactured goods, prominent export products are textile products; readymade garments, jute manufactures, leather and leather products, handicrafts, gems and jewellery, chemical and chemical products, engineering products such as machinery, transport and metal products, iron and steel.

Change in Composition of Exports

Indian exports are broadly classified as *traditional and non-traditional exports*. Jute manufactures, tea, cotton textiles, mineral ores, raw hides and skins, cashewnuts, unmanufactured tobacco and spices have for long been the main export items, so that they are known as India's traditional exports. Recent years have witnessed the emergence of several new export items, which may therefore be called the 'non-traditional' items. Some of such exports such as engineering goods (*i.e.,* machinery transport and metal products, iron and steel & chemicals and chemical products) have, in fact, now become even more important than the traditional items in the country's commodity exports. The rising share of non-traditional items in our export trade is indication of the industrial development of our economy. The substantial rise in the exports of engineering goods and chemical products is the direct outcome of India's industrial development in the last 60 years of economic development.

In Table 27.2 we have given the percentage shares of various export commodities in our exports for the years 2001-02 to 2011-12. It will be seen from this table that share of agriculture and allied products in our exports which was 44.2 per cent in 1960-61 fell to 13.4 per cent in 2001-02 and was about 12.4 per cent in 2011-12. Similarly, the share of primary products (*i.e.,* ores and minerals) which was 8.1 per cent in 1970-71, fell to 2.8 per cent in 2011-12.

Compositional changes in India's export basket have been taking place over the years. While the share of primary products in India's exports fell over the years from 16 per cent in 2000-01, in 2012-13 (April-November) it regained the share of 16 per cent mainly due to the export of agricultural items like rice and guar gum meal. The share of manufacturing exports fell drastically from 78.8 per cent in 2000-1 to 66.1 per cent in 2011-12 and further to 64.5 per cent in 2012-13 (April-November) mainly due to the fall in shares of traditional items like textiles and leather and leather manufactures even though the share of engineering goods and chemicals and related products increased. Share of gems and jewellery fell marginally. Share of petroleum, crude and products exports, which also include refined items, increased from 4.3 per cent in 2000-1 to 18.3 per cent in 2011-12 and to 18.6 per cent in 2012-13 (April-November).

Table 27.2 : Changes in Composition of Indian Exports *(Percentage Share)*

Commodity Group	*2001-02*	*2007-08*	*2008-09*	*2009-10*	*2010-11*	*2011-12*
1. Agriculture and Allied Products	**13.4**	**11.6**	**9.0**	**9.9**	**9.7**	**12.4**
of which :						
1.1 Cereals	2.2	0.5	1.3	2.0	1.3	2.1
1.2 Tea	0.8	0.3	0.3	0.3	0.3	0.3
1.3 Coffee	–	0.3	0.3	0.3	0.3	0.3
1.4 Cashewnuts	0.9	0.3	0.4	0.3	0.2	0.3
1.5 Raw Cotton	Neg.	1.4	1.1	1.3	1.2	1.5
1.6 Marine products	2.8	1.1	1.4	1.1	1.0	1.1
1.7 Spices	–	0.6	0.6	0.8	0.7	0.9
1.8 Oil meals	–	1.2	1.0	1.2	1.0	0.8
1.9 Fruits, Vegetables and Pulses	–	0.5	0.6	6.5	0.6	0.5
2. Ores and Minerals (excluding Coal)	**2.9**	**5.0**	**5.5**	**5.5**	**3.4**	**2.8**
of which :						
2.1 Iron Ore	71.0	3.6	3.1	3.6	1.9	1.5
2.2 Other Ores and Minerals	0.9	1.2	1.3	1.2	0.6	0.6
2.3 Processed minerals	–	–	–		0.9	0.6
3. Manufactured Goods	**76.1**	**64.4**	**67.2**	**63.6**	**69.0**	**66.1**
of which:						
3.1 Readymade Garments		5.4	7.0	5.9	4.6	4.5
3.2 Leather footwear	–	0.7	0.8	0.7	0.6	0.6
3.3 Leather and Leather Manufactures	2.8	1.4	2.4	2.1	1.0	1.0
3.4 Handicrafts	2.5	0.3	0.3	0.3	0.1	0.1
3.5 Gems and Jewellery	**16.7**	**12.1**	**12.6**	**12.1**	**16.1**	**14.7**
3.6 Drugs, Fine Chemicals & Pharmaceuticals	4.7	4.7	4.7	4.7	4.3	4.4
3.7 Engineering Goods*	**14.4**	**17.9**	**19.0**	**18.8**	**19.4**	**19.5**
3.8 Dyes and Coaltar, Chemicals		1.8	1.8	1.7	1.2	1.3
3.9 Cotton, Yarn, Fabrics etc.	–	2.9	3.3	2.9	2.3	2.2
4. Crude and Petroleum Products (incl Coal)	–	**17.8**	**15.0**	**17.8**	**16.8**	**18.7**
5. Others and unclassified items	**2.8**	**1.2**	**3.3**	**3.0**	**0.9**	**0.5**
Total	100.0	100.0	100	100	100	100

*Includes *metal products, machinery and instruments, transport equipment, iron and steel, electronic goods.*

The destination-wise exports of major items to the major trading partners from 2009-10 to 2012-13 (April-November) show great changes in the composition of exports to USA and China. In the case of India's exports to the USA, the share of exports of primary products has increased from 6.8 per cent in 2009-1 0 to 21.3 per cent in 2012-13 (April-November), mainly due to the rise in share of agriculture and allied products, while the share of manufactured goods in India's exports to the USA has fallen from 89.1 per cent to 74.2 per cent during the same period. This decline has been mainly due to the fall in growth rates of exports of textiles and gems and jewellery. In the case of India's exports to China, the share of primary products has fallen from 65.7 per cent in 2009-10 to 38.4 per cent in 2012-13 (April-November) due to the fall in share and growth rate of ores and minerals. The share of manufactures in India's exports to China has increased from 32.2 per cent to 58.0 per cent during this period, mainly due to the rise in share of engineering goods, textiles, and chemicals and related products. In the case of India's exports to the EU, there has been a marginal rise in the share of primary products and petroleum products and a fall in the share of manufactured goods.

The reason for India's export growth in 2012-13 (April-November) *being more negative than in* 2009-10 in the aftermath of the global recession can be seen from India's commodity-country export performance. India's exports to EU and China have been more negative during the recent global slowdown than in 2009-10, while its performance to USA has been better for most of the sectors except gems and jewellery. The performance of India's exports to EU of textiles and readymade garments, gems and jewellery and ores, and to China of manufactures, engineering goods, chemicals, gems and jewellery and ores was worse off in 2012-13 (April-November) compared to 2009-10. India's POL export growth to all major markets also decelerated in 2012-13 (April-November) compared to 2009-10. Thus, *the Euro Zone crisis and the Chinese slowdown have affected India's exports more during the recent slowdown than in 2009-10.*

Export Diversification

In 2011, India had a global export share of 1 per cent or more in 53 out of a total of 99 commodities at the two-digit harmonized system (HS) level. While noticeable changes can be seen in India's market diversification, the same is not the case with its product diversification.

India has been fairly successful in diversifying its export markets from developed countries like the US and Europe to Asia and Africa, which has helped to a great extent in weathering the global crisis of 2008 and the recent global slowdown (Table 27.3). However, in terms of product diversification a lot more needs to be done.

Table 27.3 : Region-wise Share of India's Exports

	2000-1	2005-6	2011-12	2012-13 (Apr.-Nov.)
(1) Europe	25.9	24.2	19.0	18.7
(2) Africa	5.3	6.8	8.1	9.6
(3) America	24.7	20.7	16.4	19.5
(4) Asia	37.4	46.9	50.0	50.4
(5) CIS and Baltics	2.3	1.2	1.0	1.3

***Source* : GOI, Economic Survey 2012-13 (Computed from DGCI & S data).**

We thus see that composition of India's exports has significantly changed during the 60 years of economic development since 1951. Thus, while in the beginning of planning era, raw materials and foodstuffs predominated in the country's exports, now as a result of industrialisation under the Five Year Plans, manufactured articles are the most important class of exports. The commodity composition is now broader and vastly diversified. The country has now *come out of the stage of being an exporter of primary products*. Further, in the pattern of our exports over the six decades of planned development (1951-2010), three main trends can be discerned. *Firstly,* among commodities which are directly or largely based on agricultural production (which still account for the bulk of India's exports), such as jute manufactures, tea, cotton textiles, hides and skins, spices and tobacco on the whole, exports have not improved. The share of traditional exports has been declining. Of the total exports in 1950-51, tea, jute manufactures and cotton manufactures—India's traditional exports—represented 56 per cent. This proportion fell to about 6 per cent in 2009-10. The share of exports of gem and jewellery in India's total export which was just 2.9 per cent in 1970–71 rose to about 16.5 per cent in 2004-05 and in 2009-10 stood at 12.1 per cent. *Thus, India's exports are not now as greatly concentrated on the traditional exports as they used to be.*

Secondly, significant increases have been achieved in the exports of new manufactures like engineering goods, leather and leather manufactures, chemicals and allied products and handicrafts and products like iron ore. The growth of exports have now offset the decline in the traditional exports. The share of exports of engineering products which was hardly 4.5 per cent of total exports in 1960-61 and 12.9% in 1970-71 has improved to about 19 per cent in 2009-2010. Similarly, the share of drugs, fine chemicals and pharmaceuticals which was only 1.9 per cent of total exports in 1970-71 has risen to 4.7 per cent in 2009-10.

The export composition has further seen major changes in the decade (2000-2010) with a 10 percentage point fall in shares of manufactures, a 12.6 percentage point gain in shares of petroleum crude and products, and a 3.3 percentage point fall in shares of primary products. This trend continued during the last three years, i.e. from 2008-09 to the first half of 2010-11, with the share of the major category, i.e. manufactures, stagnating at 68.9 per cent and even falling to 64 per cent in 2009-10; share of primary products (including agricultures) falling to 10 per cent in 2009-10; and share of crude and petroleum products increasing to around 18 per cent in 2009-10. Within manufactures, compared to 2000-01 the share of engineering goods has increased substantially while that of textiles including readymade garments (RMG) has fallen heavily from 23.6 per cent in 2000-01 to 5.9 per cent in 2009-10. The chemicals and related products category has made some gains in share, while leather and leather manufacutres and handicrafts have lost their shares.

COMPOSITION OF INDIA'S IMPORTS

The strategy of import substitution adopted in the major part of planned economic development in India in the last fifty years involved to restrict imports to essential consumer goods, raw materials and capital goods required for domestic production and for expansion of exports. The pattern of India's imports reflects the impact of import-substitution strategy of development followed in India.

Table 27.4 : Commodity Composition of India's Imports

Commodity Group	Percentage share					CAGR	Growth rate*			
	2000-01	2010-11	2011-12	2011-12 (Apr.- Nov.)	2012-13 (Apr.- Nov.)	2000-01 to 2009-10	2010-11	2011-12	2011-12 (Apr. -Nov.)	2012-13 (Apr. -Nov.)
I. Food and allied products, of which	**3.3**	**2.9**	**3.1**	**3.1**	**3.5**	**22.7**	**2.2**	**44.4**	**38.0**	**11.6**
1. Cereals	0.0	0.0	0.0	0.0	0.0	24.3	15.8	–34.2	–46.6	6.8
2. Pulses	0.2	0.4	0.4	0.4	0.4	38.3	–23.1	27.2	11.3	9.2
3. Edible oils	2.6	1.8	2.1	2.1	2.5	17.2	19.0	57.7	55.3	18.0
II. Fuel, of which	**33.5**	**30.9**	**37.4**	**34.3**	**38.0**	**21.0**	**22.4**	**59.7**	**52.3**	**9.8**
4. POL	31.3	28.7	31.7	30.7	34.6	21.0	21.6	46.2	50.6	11.7
III. Fertilizers	**1.3**	**1.9**	**2.4**	**2.3**	**2.2**	**29.0**	**4.8**	**72.1**	**32.2**	**–6.8**
IV. Capital gools, of which	**10.5**	**13.6**	**14.1**	**12.6**	**11.9**	**26.1**	**19.2**	**36.9**	**25.6**	**-6.5**
5. Machinery except electrical & machine tool	5.9	7.0	7.2	6.7	6.3	24.4	24.0	35.8	28.2	–5.8
6. Electrical machinery	1.0	1.0	1.0	1.0	0.9	22.7	25.1	33.1	26.6	–5.5
7. Transport equipment	1.4	3.1	3.0	2.5	2.3	36.4	–0.9	31.8	13.1	–8.3
V. Others, of which	**52.5**	**49.6**	**49.0**	**47.6**	**44.3**	**19.3**	**43.2**	**30.8**	**29.6**	**–7.6**
8. Chemicals	5.9	5.2	5.1	5.0	5.1	19.5	29.6	31.8	24.3	1.1
9. Pearls, precious, semi-precious stones	9.7	9.3	6.1	6.1	4.1	14.0	116.9	–13.3	4.3	–32.3
10. Gold & silver	9.3	11.5	12.6	13.0	10.5	23.0	43.0	44.5	59.2	–20.4
11. Electronic goods	7.0	7.1	7.1	7.0	6.5	21.6	28.4	31.7	22.2	–7.7
Total imports	**100.0**	**100.0**	**100.0**	**100.0**	**100.0**	**21.5**	**28.2**	**32.3**	**36.2**	**–0.8**

***Source*: Computed from DGCI S data.** *** Growth rate in US dollar terms**

***Source*: Economic Survey, 2012-13. CAGR = Compound Annual Growth Rate)**

There have **been some significant compositional changes in India's import basket in recent years.** The share of POL imports increased from 28.7 per cent in 2010-11 to 31.7 per cent in 2011-12 (with a very high growth rate) and 34.6 per cent in 2012-13 (April-November). The share of gold and silver imports increased from 9.3 per cent in 2000-1 to 12.6 per cent in 2011-12 with a high import growth rate of 44.5 per cent. However, in part due to policy measures like raising import duty on gold, from 4 per cent to 6 per cent in Budget for 2012-13 there was a moderation in gold and silver imports in 2012-13 (April-November) with its share falling to 10.5 per cent following a negative growth of –20.4 per cent. The import share of pearls, precious and semi-precious stones also fell sharply in 2011-12 to 6.1 per cent following a negative growth of –13.3 per cent and further to 4.1 per cent in 2012-13 (April-November), with a high negative growth rate of –32.3 per cent. Another important development is related to the share of capital goods imports which increased from 10.5 per cent in 2000-1 to 13.6 per cent in 2010-11 and further to 14.1 per cent in 2011-12, declining thereafter to 11.9 per cent in 2012-13 (April-November) following a negative growth rate of –6.5 per cent. Among capital goods, the import shares of all items of machinery except electrical and machine tools, transport equipment, project goods, and electrical machinery fell, clearly signalling a slowdown in industrial activity. The share of electronic goods, which includes both consumer electronics and capital goods, also fell in 2012-13 (April-November) as is seen from Table 27.4.

India's Import Growth

After recovering in 2010-11 from the previous year's fall, India's merchandise imports increased further to US $ 489.2 billion with a growth of 32.3 per cent in 2011-12. This was due to the increase in growth of petroleum, oil, and lubricant (POL) imports by 46.2 per cent and non-POL imports by 26.7 per cent. POL imports (wtih a share of 31.7 per cent in India's total imports) registered a high growth mainly due to increase in import price of the Indian crude oil import basket by 31.5 per cent in 2011-12 as against 22 per cent in 2010-11.

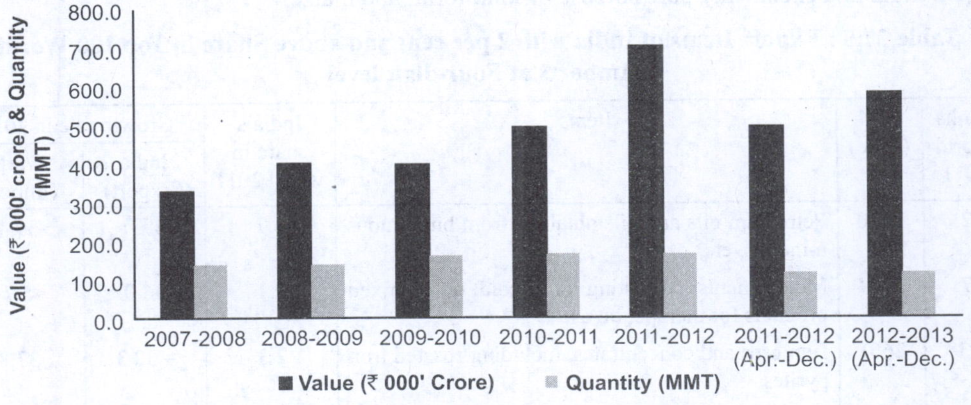

Fig. 27.1. ***POL imports***

(Source: Based on Ministry of Petroleum and Natural Gas data)

POL import volume growth decelerated from 14.9 per cent in 2009-10 to 3.7 per cent in 2010-11 and 3.5 per cent in 2011-12. International oil prices (Brent) which reached a high of US $ 132.47/bbl in July 2008 declined sharply to US $ 40.35/bbl in December 2008, following the global recession. From 2009 onwards, oil price has been increasing with intermittent volatility, reaching US $ 125.33/ bbl in March 2012 and falling marginally with volatility in the following months. Currently Brent oil price is hovering around US $ 110/bbl.

Gold and silver imports (with a share of 12.6 per cent in India's total imports) grew by 44.5 per cent in 2011-12. Gold imports alone accounted from 91.7 per cent of the total imports of gold and silver. In 2011-12, gold imports grew by 38.8 per cent in value and 11.2 per cent in volume terms. Non-POL non-bullion imports increased by 23.3 per cent in 2011-12 compared to 29 per cent in 2010-11.

At US $ 406.9 billion imports in 2012-13 (April-January) registered a growth of 0.01 per cent. During 2012-13 (April-December), POL imports at US $ 125.2 billion grew by 12.8 per cent. Non-POL imports at US $ 239.8 billion declined by 5.1 per cent and gold and silver imports at US $ 39.3 billion declined by 14.7 per cent. Non-POL and non-bullion imports which basically reflect the imports of capital goods needed for industrial activity and imports needed for exports declined by 3.0 per cent.

Export Diversification of India

In 2009, India had a global export share of 1 per cent or more in 48 out of a total of 99 commodities at the two-digit Harmonised System (HS) level, but a significant share of 5 per cent or more in 12 items (Table 27.5). Among these, three items, pearls, precious stones, metals, coins, etc., man-made filaments; and ores, slag, and ash had an increase in global share by 0.5 per cent point or more in 2009 over 2008. Six items, which include silk; carpets and other textile floor coverings; lac, gum, resins, vegetable saps and extracts; cotton; vegetable plaiting materials, vegetable products; and coffee, tea, mate, and spices, *lost global shares in 2009 over 2008*. Noticeable is the near doubling in share of pearls, precious stones, metals, coins, etc., with growth in trading activity, and the fall of nearly 2 percentage points in lac, gums, resins, vegetable saps, and extracts, due to crop failures coupled with competition from substitute products and competing countries. Of the remaining 38 items, 11 lost their shares in 2009 over 2008.

In the top 100 imports of the world at the four-digit HS level in 2011, India has only 6 items in the top 50; it has only 5 items with a share of 5 per cent and above and 18 items with a share of 2 per cent and above (Table 27.5), with 6 new items with high export growth (India) entering the list and 3 going out of the list in 2011 compared to 2010. The new items are medicaments consisting of mixed or unmixed products for therapeutic use; other articles of iron and steel; men's or boys' suits, ensembles; cruise ships, excursion boats, ferry-boats, cargo ships, barges and similar vessels; cane or beet sugar and chemically pure sucrose in solid form; and maize.

Table 27.5 : Export Items of India with 2 per cent and above Share in Top 100 World Imports at Four-digit level

Rank# World 2011	HS4 (code)	Items	India's share in world 2011	Growth rate in 2011	
				India (Export)	World (Import)
2	2710	Petroleum oils and oils obtained from bituminous minerals, etc.	6.7	49.0	39.4
7	3004	Medicaments consisting of mixed or unmixed products for therapeutic use	2.1	36.0	5.7
11	2601	Iron ores and concentrates, including roasted iron pyrites	2.3	– 32.3	37.8
14	7102	Diamonds, whether or not worked, but not mounted or set.	23.8	44.7	14.7
34	7403	Refined copper and copper alloys, unwrought	3.2	– 53.7	12.2
39	8803	Parts of goods of heading no. 88.01 or 88.02.	3.5	45.4	1.2
51	6403	Footwear with outer soles of rubber	3.1	23.0	9.2
52	6204	Women's or girls' suits, ensembles, jackets, blazers, dresses	4.9	34.8	9.2
55	7210	Flat-rolled products of iron or non-alloy steel	2.8	0.8	12.2
56	7113	Articles of jewellery and parts thereof, of precious metal	28.5	83.6	13.4
61	2902	Cyclic hydrocarbons.	4.4	47.8	27.8

68	7326	Other articles of iron or steel.	2.0	97.9	13.9
69	3902	Polymers of propylene or of other olefins, in primary forms.	2.8	46.0	17.3
72	6203	Men's or boys' suits, ensembles, jackets, blazers, trousers, etc.	2.3	31.5	16.4
92	6109	T-shirts, singlets & other vests, knitted or crocheted	6.0	22.1	12.1
97	8901	Cruise ships, excursion boats, ferry-boats, cargo ships, barges, and similar vessels	2.2	40.0	–25.8
99	1701	Cane or beet sugar and chemically pure sucrose, in solid form.	6.0	123.1	20.1
100	1005	Maize	3.4	103.1	34.1

***Source*: GOI, *Economic Survey* 2012-13, Computed from UN Comtrade data extracted on 9 January 2013.**

***Note*: # Rank is in top 100 world imports.**

India has a very high export share in world imports in the case of only two four-digit HS items, jewellery and diamonds. While India can increase its shares further in the other 16 items given in the table, there are many other simple items in the top 100 world imports with high demand where India has developed its competence. Most of the items come under the **three Es, electronic, electrical, and** engineering items and some textiles items. Greater focus on these items could lead to a perceptible increase in India's share of exports in world imports.

Direction of India's Foreign Trade

There has been significant market diversification in India's trade. Region-wise, while India's exports to Europe and America have declined, its exports to Asia and Africa have increased. However, in 2012-13 (April-November), the share of India's exports to the USA increased to 13.5 per cent. Within Asia, while the share of North East Asia (consisting of China, Hong Kong, Japan) and ASEAN (Association of South East Asian Nations) fell from 14.8 per cent and 12.0 per cent in 2011-12 to 13.1 per cent and 10.3 per cent respectively in 2012-13 (April-November), there was a noticeable rise in the share of West Asia-GCC (Gulf Cooperation Council) countries from 14.9 per cent in 2011-12 to 17.7 per cent in 2012-13 (April-November).

In 2012-13 (April-November), compared to 2000-01, the share of India's imports from Europe has declined to 16.7 per cent from 27.6 per cent, while that from Asia has increased substantially to 61.1 per cent from 27.7 per cent. The share of America in India's imports also increased to 11.5 per cent from 7.9 per cent. India's top 15 trading partners have nearly 60 per cent in share in its trade with the top three contributing nearly half of this share. While Iran and UK are out of this top 15 list in 2011-12, Iraq and Kuwait are the new entrants. The musical chairs for the top slot among the top three trading partners seems to be continuing with the USA relegated to third position in 2007-8 from first, UAE relegated to second position from first in 2011-12 by China, and China in turn relegated to second position by the UAE in 2012-13 (April-November). The final word for 2012-13 is not yet out as the USA is inching closer to China with its share increasing by around one percentage point and that of China falling.

At 10 per cent in 2011-12 India's trade deficit as a per cent of GDP is one of the highest in the world. Export-import ratios reflecting the bilateral trade balance show that among its top 15 trading partners, India had bilateral trade surplus with four countries in 2011-12, viz. the UAE, USA, Singapore, and Hong Kong. In 2012-13 (April-November), India's trade balance with the UAE has turned slightly negative while it has improved further with the USA and Hong Kong. Another important trend is the growing trade deficit of India with China and Switzerland, increasing from $ 28 billion and $ 24.1 billion in 2010-11 to $ 39.4 billion and $ 31.3 billion respectively in 2011-12. In 2012-13 (April-November), the export-import ratio with China worsened further to 0.23 from 0.31 in 2011-12.

PERFORMANCE OF FOREIGN TRADE SECTOR

We have explained above the composition of India's exports and imports. The severity of economic crisis of 1991 provided an opportunity to the Government to make far-reaching changes in macroeconomic policy. There was liberalisation of domestic investment by removing direct controls on private sector and adopted fiscal and monetary policies to promote growth. Besides, the New Economic Policy pursued since 1991 also liberalised foreign trade and investment. The growth strategy was made export-oriented. Not only quantitative restrictions on imports have been removed but also customs duties have been drastically reduced. Thus efforts have been made to integrate the Indian economy with the global economy. Rupee was devalued in 1991 and from 1993 exchange rate of rupee was made market-determined. It is, therefore, important to know how India's foreign trade sector has performed in response to these important changes in economic policy framework. The performance of foreign trade since 1991 is shown in Table 27.6 which reveals that after a transition period of 2 years, merchandise exports grew at about 20 per cent a year in dollar terms for three

Table 27.6. The Performance of Foreign Trade Sector

	Annual Percentage Change		*As a percentage of GDP_{MP}*		
Year	Exports	Imports	Trade Balance	Invisibles (net) as%	Current account balance
1990-91	9.0	14.4	–3.0	–0.1	–3.1
1991-92	–1.5	–19.4	–1.0	0.6	–0.3
1992-93	3.8	12.7	–2.3	0.6	–1.7
1993-94	20.0	6.5	–1.5	1.1	–0.4
1994-95	18.4	23.0	–2.8	1.8	–1.0
1995-96	20.8	28.0	–3.1	1.6	–1.7
1996-97	5.3	6.7	–3.8	2.7	–1.2
1997-98	4.6	6.0	–3.8	2.4	–1.4
1998-99	–5.1	2.2	–3.2	2.2	–1.0
1999-2000	10.8	17.2	–4.0	2.9	–1.1
2000-2001	21.1	4.6	–2.7	2.1	–0.6
2001-2002	–1.6	–2.8	–2.4	3.1	+0.7
2002-2003	20.3	19.4	–2.1	3.4	+1.3
2003-2004	21.1	27.3	–2.3	4.6	+2.3
2004-2005	30.8	42.7	– 4.8	4.5	– 0.4
2005-2006	23.4	33.8	– 6.4	5.2	– 1.2
2006-2007	22.6	24.5	–6.8	5.7	–1.0
2007-2008	29.0	35.5	–7.8	6.3	–1.3
2008-2009	13.6	26.7	–12.0	7.8	–2.4
2009-2010	–3.5	–6.0	–8.7	5.9	–2.8
2010-2011	40.5	28.2	7.4	4.6	–2.8
2011-12	21.3	32.3	–10.1	6.0	–4.2
2012-13	–1.8	0.4	–10.8	–	–4.8

Source : Economic Surveys for 2010-11, 2011-12 and 2012-3

Note : 1. Exports and imports are estimated in US dollar values.

2. Trade balance, invisibles and current account balance ratios of GDP are based on rupee equivalents of BOP

successive years during 1993-94 to 1995-96. Then due to slowdown in world trade and recession in the USA which is India's major trade partner, annual growth of exports slowed down from 1996-97 to 1999-2000. However after 2000 up till 2007-08 with the exception of year 2001-02 there was more than 20 per cent annual growth of exports on sustained basis for over eight years (2000 to 2008) and in 2007-08 average annual growth rate of our exports was around 29 per cent.

Despite the sluggish performance of exports from 1996-97 to 1998-99 *deficit* in trade balance remained *below 4 per cent of GDP* (See Col. IV of Table 27.8) due to the equally subdued growth in imports during this period. During the four-year period, 2004-05 to 2007-08, India's imports grew at a much higher rate due to robust industrial growth relative to growth in our exports and as a result deficit in our trade balance greatly increased; as a percentage of GDP it was 4.8 per cent in 2004-05, 6.8 per cent in 2006-07, and 7.8 per cent in 2007-08. Due to global financial crisis and consequent economic slowdown in the US and European countries, the growth rate of our exports fell to 13.6 per cent in 2008-09, whereas imports grew at 26.7 per cent. As a result *deficit* in our trade balance rose to 12 per cent of GDP.

Bolstered by the measures taken by the government to help exports in the aftermath of the world recession of 2008 and also the low base effect, *India's export growth of 40.5 per cent in 2010-11 reached an all time high since Independence.* Though it decelerated in 2011-12 to 21.3 per cent, it was still above 20 per cent and higher than the compound annual growth rate (CAGR) of 20.3 per cent for the period 2004-05 to 2011-12. After registering very high growth of 56.5 per cent in July 2011, export growth started decelerating with a sudden fall to single digits in November 2011 as a result of the emerging global situation and then to negative figures from March 2012. Export growth rate in 2012-13 was negative and equal to – 1.8%. For three months in 2012-13, exports declined YOY by double digits with the largest decline recorded in July 2012 at – 15.1 per cent.

Export growth in dollar terms was negative at –1.8 per cent in 2012-13, compared to 21.3 per cent growth in 2011-12 (full year). In rupee **India's export growth has almost continuously been above world export growth in the 2000s decade and in 2011.** *One issue that has been a topic of debate is whether India's export growth rate is dependent on world growth/trade or exchange rate.* There is a strong correspondence between India's export growth and world export growth (see Figure 27.2). This is clearly visible in 2009 when there was a big dip in both world exports and India's exports. The relationship between changes in real effective exchange rate (REER) and India's export growth is not however as clear-cut as that with world trade.

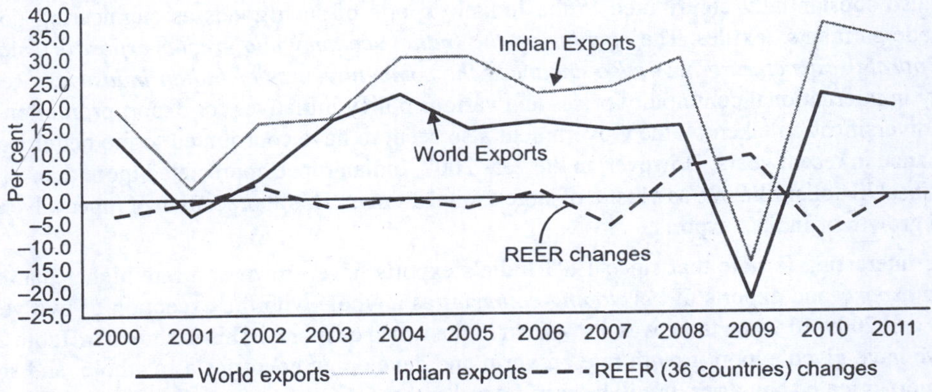

Fig. 27.2. *Growth of exports of World and India and REER changes*

Robust Growth in our Invisibles. An important feature of India's foreign trade is *robust growth of trade in invisibles*, especially after 1994-95, and as a result invisibles (net) as a percentage of GDP has been within the range of 2.2 per cent to 5.2 per cent from 1995-96 to 2005-06 and rose to 5.8 per cent in 2006-07. It is because of high growth in invisibles (net) that current account balance of payments has been *less than 2 per cent of GDP* throughout in 9 years period from 1991-92 to 2000-01 as compared to the deficit of 3.1 per cent in the pre-reform year 1990–91 (See Col. VI of Table 27.8). Further, for the first time after several years due to robust growth in invisibles (net) that there was *surplus* on current account balance for the three successive years, 2001-02 to 2003-04. In the next three years, deficit in current account balance was quite small, 0.4 to 1.2% of GDP_{mp}. Due to global financial crisis and consequent global slowdown the growth of exports fell to 13.6 per cent in 2008-09 and despite good growth in invisibles our current account deficit rose to 2.4 per cent of GDP.

Higher Growth Rate in Exports. India's exports have been witnessing 20 per cent plus growth rate since 2002-03 (except for the years 2008-09, 2009-10 and 2012-13 when there was world-wide slowdown due to global financial crisis) and displaying a tendency of moving to higher growth trajectory. The *increase in volume of exports* is the main contributor to the strengthening of our export performance. Net terms of trade (which is the ratio of prices of exports to the prices of imports) increased on an average by 1.5 per cent during the 1990s have witnessed a continuous decline since 1999-2000. The decline in prices of exports relative to prices of imports was quite significant in the five years (2002-07) and was caused by the resurgence in international crude oil prices. However, the strong growth in *exports in volume terms*, the income terms of trade which measure purchasing power of exports has consistently improved during the nineties and thereafter.

It is worth mentioning that *exports of services* (that is, non-factor commercial services) have been playing a significant role in boosting Indian exports. There was an upward shift in the trend growth of services exports (in US dollar terms) from 7.9 per cent in the first half of the decade in the 1990s to 15.3 per cent during 2000-01 to 2003-04. Software and other miscellaneous services (including professional, technical and business services) have emerged as the main categories in India's exports of services. From a relatively low share of only 10.2 per cent in 1995-96, share of exports of software services in *total exports of services* went up to 49 per cent in 2003-04.

Factors Responsible for High Export Performance from 2002-03 to 2011-12 with the exception of 2009-10

Both external and domestic factors have contributed to the satisfactory performance of exports since 2002-03. The expansion in world trade as a result of *global recovery* has helped the strengthening of Indian exports. Besides, the expansion in *domestic economic activity, especially the manufacturing sector,* also substantially contributed to the Indian exports of such goods as engineering goods, readymade garments, textiles. The *opening up the Indian economy and greater export orientation and corporate restructuring have also enhanced the competitiveness of Indian industries.* Recent recovery in international commodity prices and various policy initiatives for export promotion and market diversification taken by the Government also seem to have contributed to the better export performance in recent years. However, in the year 2007, Indian rupee appreciated more than 11 per cent against US dollar till 2006 as a result of large capital inflows. This appreciation of rupee adversely affected growth of India's exports.

It is interesting to note that since 1995 India's exports have grown at a rate higher than that of *world exports* and exports of *developing countries* as a whole with the exception of two years, 2008-09 and 2009-10 when there was slowdown in the world economy. This is shown in Table 27.9 where we have given export growth rate of world and developing countries as a whole and some other export-oriented countries. It will be seen from this that CAGR (compound annual growth rate) for the years 2000 to 2007 and annual growth rate for the year 2008, rate of growth of exports of India was not only higher than the growth of exports of world and developing countries (with the sole exception of China) but also of the export growth of countries such as Hong Kong, Malaysia,

Singapore, Thailand, Koroa which are called *Asian tigers* who have achieved high growth rates of GDP. For example, in the year 2008 while world exports grew by 15.9 per cent and those of the emerging and developing economies (EDEs) by 25.3 per cent, exports of India grew by about 29.7 per cent. China has been an outstanding export performer for years. However, for the first time in 2005 India's growth in exports surpassed that of China. It will be seen that in last decade (2000-2010), India's export performance is better relative to the world as a whole and the developing countries except that of China.

Dismal Export Performance in 2012-13 and 2013-14

India's exports battered by the drying up of orders for most part of the year 2012-13 and contracted by 1.8 per cent to $300.6 billion in the year. However, the last quarter of the year, January to March 2013, exports showed positive signs and grew by 6.97 per cent in March 2013. Exports in March 2013 stood at $30.8 billion (₹ 1,69,400 crore) compared to $28.8 billion (₹ 1,58,400 crore) in the same month of the previous year.

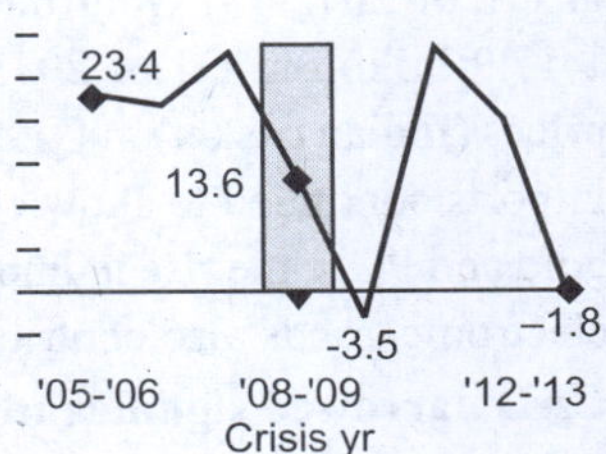

Fig. 27.3. *Export Growth (%).*

Imports dipped by 2.87 per cent to $41.16 billion in March 2013, leaving a trade deficit of $10.31 billion – down from $13.5 billion in March last year. For the entire fiscal 2012-13, however, exports shrank by L8% to $300.6 billion. Export performance started picking up in the last quarter of the year 2012-13. For March it picked by a slightly robust figure as compared to the previous two months. It was expected that this trend would continue and help in consolidating. SR Rao, commerce secretary, said, "If the trend continues, exports should grow by at least 10% in the year 2013-14." Given a very weak performance for major part of the year, 2012-13 it was thought that in the last 3-4 months, we really covered a good deal of ground. It may not be sufficient, but certainly there was progress in exports," he said.

Table 27.7 : India's Merchandise Trade

(US billion)

Item	April- March				April- March			
	2011-12		2012-13 P		2012-13		2013-14	
	Value	Growth	Value	Growth	Value	Growth	Value	Growth
1	2	3	4	5	6	7	8	9
Exports	306.0	21.8	300.6	–1.8	73.5	–4.0	72.5	–1.4
Of which : Oil	56.0	35.1	60.0	7.1	13.0	–15.2	13.2	1.6
Non-oil	249.9	19.2	240.6	–3.7	60.4	–1.2	59.2	–2.0
Gold	6.7	10.9	6.5	–3.3	1.6	–3.1	1.4	–13.6
Non-oil Non-gold	243.2	19.5	234.1	–3.8	58.8	–1.1	57.8	–1.7
Imports	489.3	32.3	491.5	0.4	115.7	–5.7	122.6	6.0
Of which: Oil	155.0	46.2	169.4	9.3	39.4	–0.2	41.9	6.4
Non-oil	334.4	26.7	322.1	–3.7	76.4	–8.3	80.8	5.8
Gold	56.5	39.3	53.8	–4.7	9.2	–42.6	17.9	93.5
Non-oil Non-gold	277.9	24.5	268.3	–3.4	67.1	–0.1	62.9	–6.3
Trade Deficit	–183.4		–190.9		–42.2		–50.2	
Of which: Oil	–98.9		–109.4		–26.3		–28.6	
Non-oil	–84.4		–81.5		–15.9		–21.6	
Non-oil Non-gold	–34.7		–34.2		–8.3		–5.1	

Source : DGCT & S.

Trends in exports and imports in Q1 of 2013-14 suggest a widening of the merchandise trade deficit. *The trade deficit widened from US $ 42.2 billion in Q1 of 2013-14, mainly on account of a sharp increase in gold imports.* Reflecting global demand conditions, exports contracted in May and June 2013 after recording growth for five consecutive months (since December 2012). The engineering goods, gems & jewellery, electronics and iron ore sectors were the main contributors to the decline in exports in Q1 of 2013-14.

In contrast, imports grew by 6.0 per cent in Q1 of 2013-14 as against a decline of 5.7 per cent in Q1 of 2012-13. Gold imports almost doubled from US $9.2 billion in Q1 of 2012-13 to US $ 17.9 billion in Q1 of 2013-14. Notwithstanding a fall of 5.7 per cent in international crude oil prices (Indian basket) in Q1 of 2013-14 (y-o-y), POL imports grew by 6.4 per cent. Non-oil non-gold imports continued to show contraction, reflecting subdued domestic growth conditions. Apart from gold and POL, the rise in imports of pearls, precious & semi-precious stones, non-ferrous metals and electronic goods also contributed to higher imports in Q1 of 2013-14. (See Table 22.7)

CAD narrowed significantly in Q4 of 2012-13

The current account deficit (CAD) moderated sharply to 3.6 per cent of GDP in Q4 of 2012-13 from 6.5 per cent in Q3 (4.4 per cent of GDP in Q4 of 2011-12). This was owing to the narrowing of the merchandise trade deficit underpinned by a pick-up in exports and a decline in imports (BoP basis) in Q4. However, net service exports remained subdued in Q4 of 2012-13. The moderation in net secondary income compared with Q4 of 2011-12 mainly reflected a fall in the net private remittances from abroad. Further, there was a significant outflow on account of income payments, reflecting growing liability-servicing obligations (See Table 27.8).

Table 27.8 : Major Items in the External Sector, 2011-12 and 2012-13

		2011-12	2012-13	2012-13			
		(PR)	(P)	Q1(PR)	Q2(PR)	Q3(PR)	Q4(P)
1		2	3	4	5	6	7
1.	Goods Exports	309.8	306.6	75.0	72.6	74.2	84.8
2.	Goods Imports	499.5	502.2	118.9	120.4	132.6	130.4
3.	Trade Balance (1-2)	–189.7	–195.7	–43.8	–47.8	–58.4	–45.6
4.	Services Exports	140.9	145.7	35.8	35.0	37.1	37.8
5.	Services Imports	76.9	80.8	20.8	18.7	20.4	20.9
6.	Net Services (4-5)	64.0	64.9	15.0	16.3	16.6	17.0
7.	Goods & Services Balances (3+6)	–125.7	–130.7	–28.8	–31.5	–41.7	–28.7
8.	Primary Income (Net)	–16.0	–21.5	–4.9	-5.6	–5.8	–5.2
9.	Secondary Income (Net)	63.5	64.4	16.8	16.1	15.7	15.8
10.	Net Income (8+9)	47.5	42.9	11.9	10.5	9.9	10.6
11.	Current Account Balance (7+10)	–78.2	–87.8	–16.9	–21.0	–31.9	–18.1
12.	Capital Account Balance	–0.1	–0.3	–0.2	–0.2	0.02	0.2
13.	Financial Account Balance	80.7	85.4	16.1	21.0	30.8	17.6
	of which : Change in Reserves	12.8	–3.8	–0.5	0.2	–0.8	–2.7
14.	Errors & Omissions - (11 + 12 + 13)	–2.4	2.7	1.1	0.2	1.1	0.3
Memo : As a ratio to GDP							
15.	Trade Balance	–10.1	–10.6	–10.2	–11.4	–12.0	–9.0
16.	Net Services	3.3	3.5	3.5	3.9	3.4	3.3
17.	Net Income	2.5	2.3	2.8	2.5	2.0	2.1
18.	Current Account Balance	–4.2	–4.8	–4.0	–5.0	–6.5	–3.6
19.	Capital and Financial Account, Net (Excl. changes in reserves)	3.6	4.8	3.8	4.9	6.5	4.0

Note : Total of sub-components may not tally with aggregate due to rounding off. P : Preliminary : PR: Partially Revised.
Source: First quarterly, Report of RBI, July 29, 2013

Despite the moderation in the CAD in Q4, the overall CAD during 2012-13 at 4.8 per cent of GDP was far above the sustainable level (Table 27.8). Trends in trade data suggest that the CAD may remain high in Q1 of 2013-14. However, in subsequent quarters, the CAD is expected to improve, since the import demand for gold is expected to moderate. With the end of the gold super-cycle, the speculative demand for gold is likely to decline. Besides, various measures have been undertaken domestically to curb import demand for gold, that *inter alia* include (*i*) a hike in customs duty to 10 per cent and (*ii*) measures towards rationalisation of gold imports by both nominated agencies and banks.

In particular, on July 22, 2013, all nominated banks/agencies were instructed to ensure that at least one-fifth of every lot of import of gold (in any form/purity) is retained in customs bonded warehouses for the purpose of export and fresh imports of gold is permitted only after 75 per cent of the retained gold is actually exported. This new measure replaced the earlier restrictions on import of gold on consignment basis and opening letters of credit subject to 100 per cent cash margin. To some extent, the recently launched *inflation-linked bonds* was also expected to wean away investors who use gold as a hedge against inflation. If the current recovery in the US and Japan continues, it may help improve India's exports to these destinations. The combined influence of these factors may augur well for India's CAD during 2013-14.

To achieve robust growth in exports we need to diversify our exports market and also make them competitive by raising productivity in the export sector.

India's Export Growth and Share in World Exports

It will also be seen from Table 27.9 that India'a share in world's exports rose from 0.7 per cent in 2000 to 1.7 per cent in 2011 and was estimated at 1.6% in 2012 (Jan.–Oct. 2012).

Table 27.9 : Export growth and share in world export : India and other select countries

	Value (US$ billion)	Export Grwoth rate %				Share in world exports (%)				
		CAGR	Anual							Change in shares
	2011	2000-09	2010	2011	2012 (Jan-Oct.)	2000	2010	2011	2012 (Jan-Oct.)	2011/2000
EDEs	**7400**	**12.3**	**28.8**	**24.9**	**1.8**	**25.4**	**39.2**	**41.0**	**41.7**	**15.6**
of which										
China	1899	19.1	31.3	20.3	7.9	3.9	10.4	10.5	11.2	6.6
Russia	522	12.5	32.0	30.4	3.1	1.7	2.7	2.9	2.9	1.2
Mexico	350	3.6	29.8	17.3	7.0	2.6	2.0	1.9	2.1	–0.7
India	303	16.3	37.3	33.8	–5.1	0.7	1.5	1.7	1.6	1.0
Malaysia	228	5.4	26.2	14.8	–0.6	1.5	1.3	1.3	1.3	–0.3
Brazil	256	12.0	32.0	26.8	–5.2	0.9	1.3	1.4	1.3	0.6
Thailand	226	9.2	28.6	15.9	0.8	1.1	1.3	1.3	1.3	0.2
Indonesia	201	6.9	32.1	26.9	–6.2	1.0	1.0	1.1	1.0	0.1
South Africa	97	8.5	30.7	18.5	–9.8	0.5	0.5	0.5	0.5	0.1
NIAEs*										
Korea, Republic	557	8.6	29.0	19.3	–1.3	2.7	3.1	3.1	3.0	0.4
Hong Kong	429	5.2	22.5	9.9	1.4	3.2	2.6	2.4	2.4	–0.8
Singapore	410	7.8	30.4	16.4	0.3	2.2	2.3	2.3	2.3	0.1
Taiwan	308	3.6	34.8	12.2	NA	2.3	1.8	1.7	NA	–0.6
World	18033	7.7	22.0	19.4	–0.2	100.0	100.0	100.0	100	-

Source : Economic Survey, 2012-13 *where it has been* computed from IMF, International Financial Statistics, January 2013.

Note : * Newly Industrialized Asian Economies, NA : Not Avaialble.

Thus there was 1 per cent increase in 2011 over 2000. Therefore, India presents a success story in case of export performance in the post-reform period. The increase in China's share of world exports between 2000 and 2011 at 6.6 percentage points was slightly less than one-half of the total increase in the share of developing countries over this period. However, China's export growth rate which was 19 per cent in the period 2000-09, while India's exports at around 16.3 per cent during 2009-09. However in 2012-13, India's export growth was negative. The export performance of China is spectacular with is share in world exports increasing by 6.6 percentage points between 2000 and 2011, comprising 42.4 per cent of the total increase in EDEs share over this period, while India's rise in share of 1 percentage point in 2011 over 2000 constitutes only 6.5 per cent of the total increase. However, China's export growth rate at 20.3 percent in 2011 was substantially lower than that of India. India's export growth rate of 33.8 per cent in 2011 over and above the 37.3 per cent growth of 2010 is one of the highest in the world. India's share in world merchandise exports which started rising fast from 2004, reached 1.5 per in 2010 and 1.7 percent in 2011. It declined marginally to 1.6% in 2012 due to its relatively higher negative export growth compared to the negative world export growth. In Contrast China's share in world exports increased to 11.2% in 2012 (January-October) with a positive export growth of 7.9 per cent (See Table 27.9).

India's significant export growth in recent years has (expect the years 2012-13 and 2013-14) has been on account of several favourable external developments and domestic policy initiatives. Improved growth of the world economy and recovery in world trade helped the growth of Indian exports. The opening of the Indian economy and restructuring of corporate sector has increased the competitiveness of Indian industry. Besides, there is a far greater export orientation of domestic industries and corporate sector has been pursuing new growth strategies in response to economic reforms. Expansion of domestic economic activity, especially resurgence of the manufacturing sector, helped in promoting exports. Further, reforms in India's foreign trade policy, continuation of foreign trade promotion measures, market diversification and trade facilitation efforts seem to have paid good dividends. The nominal effective exchange rate (NEER) measuring the value of countries' currency relative to the currencies of principal trading partners is a proximate indicator of its *competitiveness in international trade*. The NEER–5 (base 2000 = 100) which is a five currency export-weighted index depreciated till 2004-05 and after a bout of appreciation in 2005-06 depreciated steadily in 2006-07 till August 2006. This depreciation of rupee helped a good deal in promoting exports. However in year 2007, the Indian rupee appreciated over 11 per cent till October 2007. This adversely affected growth of our exports. Global financial crisis (2007-09) also adversely affected the growth of our exports which registered only 13.6 per cent growth in 2008-09. With global recovery in later half of 2009 and 2010 the growth of Indian exports also picked up.

TRADE IN SERVICES

In recent years, the focus of services trade has shifted away from just facilitating trade in goods since the services sector has emerged as an independent entity in itself with services trade in the four supply modes opening up new opportunities. The integration of telecommunication and computer technology has made virtually all services tradable across borders. Virtually all commercial services are now tradable across borders. The trend towards globalization, reinforced by liberalization policies and the removal of regulatory obstacles, has fuelled steady growth of international investment and trade in services.

World Trade in Services

The US $ 3.35 trillion world export of commercial services was dominated by the developed countires in 2009, with the exception of India and China which were also among the top 12 exporters. As in the case of merchandise trade, India has improved its rank in *commercial services trade*. As per the latest **'International Trade Statistics 2010'** brought out by the WTO in 2009, world export and import growth in services fell to (–) 12 per cent in 2009. The decline was more or less similar in most of the major regions like North America, Europe, and Asia. Import growth in commercial services fell in the US, EU, and Japan and was at (–) 9 per cent, (–) 13 per cent, and (–) 10 per cent, respectively. While India's import growth and export growth of commercial services were at (–) 9 per cent and (–) 15 per cent respectively, those of China were at 0 per cent and (–) 12 per cent respectively. While

India ranks 21st in world merchandise exports in 2009 compared to China which is in first position, in commercial services exports it ranks 12th compared to China at fifth rank.

Table 27.10 : World Exports of Commercial Trade by Major Categories, 2000-09

	Value (US$ billion)	Annual percentage change			
	2009	2000-09	2007	2008	2009
Commercial services	3350	9	20	13	–12
Transport	700	8	20	17	–23
Travel	870	7	15	10	–9
Other commercial services	1780	12	23	12	–9

***Source*: WTO**

The three broad categories of commercial services, namely transport, travel, and other commercial services, witnessed a decline in export growth in 2009 (Table 27.10). Among top exporters/importers of services (with EU-27 taken as a single unit) India ranked among the first five countries in the export of other commercial services, computer and information services, communication services, and personal, cultural and recreational services in 2009/2008 (Table 27.10).

As per the **WTO's International Trade Statistics 2010**, in 2009, all commercial services sectors were affected by the global crisis but not to the same extent. Transport services growth fell mirroring the fall in world trade. Financial services were severely hit due to the turmoil in the financial markets resulting in world exports of financial services declining by 15 per cent in 2009 though they began slowly to recover in the last few months of the year. Europe's financial sector was the most affected by the economic crisis. The EU's exports of financial services plummeted by 19 per cent, to US $ 133 billion in 2009. In the United States, the second largest world exporter of financial services, as well as in Hong Kong, the decline was by 7 per cent. At the start of 2010, there was an upward trend in exports of financial services. Estimates for the first quarter of 2010 indicate recovery across all countries. Construction, the most dynamic sector in 2008, also saw its growth fall sharply. Computer and information services as well as royalties and licence fees were more resilient. World exports of computer and information services decreased by 6 per cent in 2009, after record growth of 23 per cent in 2008. While exports of computer and information services fell by 9 per cent in Europe and by 14 per cent in the CIS, in North America, they stagnated and in Asia, fell by 2 per cent. In 2009, world travel exports fell by 9 per cent, reflecting the worldwide drop in international tourism with tourist arrivals down by 4 per cent. The decline was most pronounced in Europe (-13 per cent), North America (-11 per cent), and the CIS (-22 per cent). Asian economies were less affected with a 3 per cent decline. World tourism started recovering rapidly in 2010 with forecasts from the World Tourism Organization indicating that the number of international tourists will increase by 3.4 per cent in 2010.

In commercial services imports, India moved from 13th position in 2005 and 2008, to 12th position in 2009, with a 2.5 per cent share. The United States, the European Union, China, and Japan are the major importers of services in the world.

World's Commercial Services Trade, 2011 and 2012

Like world merchandise trade, world commercial services trade which was badly hit by the 2008 global crisis, crossed the pre-crisis level in 2011 to reach US $ 4.17 trillion after a gap of two years. The export growth rate of commercial services which was at 11 per cent in 2000-05 and became negative at – 12 per cent in 2009, took a full turn to reach 11 per cent again in 2011. As per the WTO's International Trade Statistics, Europe recovered from its 4 per cent growth of commercial services exports in 2010 to 11 per cent in 2011, while North America maintained the same growth rate of 9 per cent. The Commonwealth of Independent States (CIS) was the most dynamic region followed by South and Central America with 19 per cent and 13 per cent growth respectively in 2010. Asian economies saw their growth rates more than halved to 11 per cent in 2011 from 23 per cent in 2010 due to slower growth in transportation and other commercial services, namely transport, travel, and other commercial services. All the three broad categories of commercial services, namely transport, travel, and other commercial services, registered reasonably good growth in 2011. In 2012, services trade growth decelerated as is evident from the WTO's first quarter to third quarter data for 2012 which shows that export and import growths were zero per cent and 1 per cent in Q2 of 2012 and –2 per cent and –1 per cent in Q3 of 2012 over corresponding period of the previous year. Europe had a very high negative growth of –7 per cent in both exports and imports.

India's Services Trade

India and China are the two important developing countries which are making rapid strides in the services trade sector. However, the pattern of growth of the different services in India differs from that of other countries. While other commercial services is the major category for most of the top services exporters, in the Indian case its share is proportionately higher than in that of others at 77.4 per cent in 2008 compared to 56.5 per cent for the USA, 54.8 per cent for the EU, 45.9 per cent for China, and 60.6 per cent for Japan. Thus this category containing many dynamic services is important for India. The share of travel at 11.5 per cent is relatively lower than in most other countries. The shares of the US and China are more than double that of India. Even in transportation, India's share is less than half that of many leading exporters of services, partly reflecting India's lower volume of merchandise trade and partly the relatively lower participation of India's shipping sector in India's export trade. *Thus the composition of services exports highlights the need to pay special attention to developing shipping and travel services in India.* The composition of India's imports compared to other service trading countries also shows the relatively higher importance of other commercial services particularly in 2009-10.

India's services export growth has been faster than that of merchandise exports with the export of services growing at a CAGR of 23.6 per cent during 2001-02 to 2011-12, while merchandise exports grew at a CAGR of 21.4 per cent during the same period. However, growth in services exports became erratic in the post-global crisis period. Reflecting the impact of uncertainty in the global economy and weak growth in advanced economies, services exports at $ 142.3 billion showed a lower growth of 14.2 per cent in 2011-12 as against 29.8 per cent in the preceding year. Growth in services exports decelerated further to 4.3 per cent during H1 of 2012-13 as against 22.7 per cent during H1 of 2011-12 (Table 27.11)

Table 27.11 : India's Export of Services

Commodity Group	Percentage Share				CAGR	Growth rate[a]			
	2001-02	2011-12	2011-12 (Apr.- Sept.)	2012-13 (Apr.- Sept.)	2001-02 to 2011-12	2010-11	2011-12	2011-12 (Apr.- Sept.)	2012-13 (Apr.- Sept.)
Travel	18.3	13.0	11.9	10.7	19.4	33.2	16.9	21.3	–5.9
Transportation	12.6	12.8	13.3	12.1	23.8	27.4	28.0	37.1	–4.8
Insurance	1.7	1.8	1.8	1.6	24.8	22.3	35.3	39.8	–9.3
GNIE	3.0	0.3	0.4	0.4	–0.8	21.3	–10.7	30.6	7.7
Miscellaneous	64.4	72.0	72.6	75.2	25.0	29.8	11.3	20.2	8.0
Software Services	44.1	43.7	43.3	45.6	23.5	6.8	17.2	21.8	9.8
Non-Software Services	20.3	28.3	29.3	29.6	27.8	83.4	3.3	18.1	5.4
Of which:									
Business Services	3.0	18.2	17.8	21.2	47.9	112.4	7.7	10.6	23.9
Financial services	1.7	4.2	4.3	3.8	35.2	76.2	–8.3	–6.2	–6.9
Communication Services	4.4	1.1	1.1	1.3	7.8	27.2	2.4	1.1	16.5
Total Services Exports	**100.0**	**100.0**	**100.0**	**100.0**	**23.6**	**29.8**	**14.2**	**22.7**	**4.3**

***Source*: GOI, *Economic Survey* 2012-13 where it has been computed from RBI data.**

Notes: [a] Growth rate is based on values in US dollar terms. GNIE = Government not included elsewhere.

Growth moderation in services exports was observed in almost all categories. Miscellaneous services, accounting for nearly 75 per cent of total services exports in H1 of 2012-13, grew by 8 per cent during this period as compared to 20.2 per cent in corresponding period of the previous year. Within miscellaneous services, growth in exports of software services, accounting for nearly 46 per cent of total services exports, was in single digit at 9.8 per cent in H1 of 2012-13 compared to the 21.8 per cent in H1 of 2011-12. Some categories like travel, transport, and insurance services showed a negative growth rate leading to lower growth in overall services exports. For 2012-13, NASSCOM has projected a lower export growth in IT and business process management of 8.4 per cent mainly due to reduced spending on technology by US corporations and continued crisis in Europe. While the challenges facing global economic growth persist, it has been projected that worldwide IT spending will increase by 4.2 per cent in 2013 (from US $ 3.58 trillion in 2012 to US $ 3.73 trillion in 2013) Among non-software services, business services export growth was high at 23.9 per cent in the first half of 2012-13. However, export growth of this category of services has been very erratic in recent years. Communication services export growth in 2012-13 (April-September) was high at 16.5 per cent.

India's Services Imports

India's services imports at US $ 78.2 billion declined by 2.9 per cent in 2011-12, as against an increase of 34.2 per cent in the preceding year. However, imports of services by India resurged in H1 of 2012-13 and grew sharply by 10.3 per cent as compared to a decline of 0.5 per cent in H1 of 2011-12. This rise in import of services was mainly on account of higher imports of software and business services which increased by 89.7 per cent and 22 per cent respectively during H1 of 2012-13 as against a decline of 47.5 per cent and 4.4 per cent respectively in H1 of 2011-12. However, financial services showed a decline of 34.7 per cent as against an increase of 17.7 per cent in H1 of 2011-12, which is perhaps a reflection of the fragile global financial conditions. Similarly, imports of transportation, travel, insurance also recorded a decline in H1 of 2012-13 as against positive growth in H1 of 2011-12 (Table 27.12)

Table 27.12 : India's Export of Services

Commodity Group	Percentage Share				CAGR	Growth rate[a]			
	2001-02	2011-12	2011-12 (Apr.- Sept.)	2012-13 (Apr.- Sept.)	2001-02 to 2011-12	2010-11	2011-12	2011-12 (Apr.- Sept.)	2012-13 (Apr.- Sept.)
Travel	21.8	17.6	19.3	15.2	16.4	18.0	24.8	39.4	–12.9
Transportation	25.1	20.9	21.0	18.9	16.8	16.3	18.0	14.5	–1.0
Insurance	2.0	1.9	2.0	1.4	18.3	8.9	7.0	3.6	–23.3
GNIE	2.0	1.0	1.0	0.8	10.7	56.2	–4.9	9.2	–11.3
Miscellaneous	49.0	58.6	56.7	63.7	21.1	44.6	–14.3	–13.4	23.9
Software Services	4.9	1.6	1.7	2.9	6.5	49.5	–42.8	–47.5	89.7
Non-Software Services	44.2	56.9	55.0	60.8	22.0	44.4	–13.0	–11.7	21.9
Of which:									
Business Services	10.9	34.2	33.8	37.4	33.4	53.4	–3.3	–4.4	22.0
Financial services	9.1	10.2	10.7	6.4	20.2	61.2	6.7	17.7	–34.7
Communication Services	2.7	2.0	2.0	0.6	15.5	–15.0	35.2	42.8	–66.2
Total Services Exports	**100.0**	**100.0**	**100.0**	**100.0**	**18.9**	**34.2**	**–2.9**	**–0.5**	**10.3**

***Source*: Computed from RBI data.**

Notes: [a] Growth rate is based on values in US dollar terms. GNIE = Government not included elsewhere.

Balance of Trade in Services

There is growing concern about a high merchandise trade deficit coupled with inflation derailing the growth momentum. However, *fall in services trade surplus in some years added to the woes on the current account deficit front, instead of acting as a cushion.* Services trade surplus which increased steadily in this decade (2000-2010) to reach US $53.9 billion in

2008-09, fell drastically in the global crisis year of 2009-10 to US $ 35.7 billion. This was caused by the collapse in exports of non-software services, particularly business services, the slow growth of software services, and the rise in import of non-software services, particularly business and financial services. The low service trade surplus situation continued in the first half of 2010-11. This was due to the sudden rise in imports of non-software services, particularly business and financial services which overshadowed the rise in exports of business and financial services. If this situation continues in the second half of this year and coming years, then we have to reconcile to the fact that the hitherto extra cushion provided by the services sector for trade balance will not be available. The impact on growth of the rising import of business and financial services also needs to be evaluated.

Table 27.13 : India's Exports, Imports and Balance of Trade in Services

Billion US dollars

	Exports	Imports	Trade Balance
2000-01	16.3	14.6	1.7
2001-02	17.1	13.8	3.3
2002-03	20.8	17.1	3.6
2003-04	26.9	16.7	10.1
2004-05	43.2	27.8	15.4
2005-06	57.7	34.5	23.2
2006-07	73.8	44.3	29.5
2007-08	90.3	51.5	38.9
2008-09	106.0	52.0	53.9
2009-10	95.8	60.0	35.7
2011-12	–	–	64.1

Source : Computed from RBI data.

Surplus on account of India's services exports has been a cushioning factor for financing a large part of the merchandise trade deficit in recent years. During 2006-07 to 2011-12, surplus in services exports, on average, financed around 38 per cent of merchandise trade deficit. During 2011-12, net surplus on account of services exports at US $ 64.1 billion stood significantly higher than that in 2010-11 and financed 33.8 per cent of trade deficit. During H1 of 2012-13, with slower growth in services exports and rise in services imports, the surplus at US $ 29.6 billion was 2.8 per cent lower than in H1 of 2011-12, financing 32.6 per cent of trade deficit. Going forward, downward risks to export of services persist as global economic conditions remain less conducive.

Policies and Barriers to Trade in Services

In the light of the global recession, some measures were taken to help the services sector. These include extension of sunset clauses for Software Technology Parks of India (STPIs) and export-oriented units (EOUs) up to 2010-11 and doubling of duty free entitlement to hotels under the '*served from India*' scheme. A coordinated and synchronized effort is needed towards the services sector as at present services activities are dispersed and fall within the purview of different departments of the Government. There are also many barriers to trade in services. These include the *State-level licensing* and the '*Buy American*' provisions in the case of business services and IT services in the US; the requirement of the Office of the Comptroller of Currency (OCC) in the US and some State banking supervisors to maintain 'asset pledges' in addition to the paid up capital they maintain in their home country in the case of financial services; the fragmentation of the US insurance market into 56 different jurisdictions and direct discrimination on a number of fronts; restriction in the case of transport and related services and the *recent protectionist policies in the US and other economies that deny market access to other countries*. There is need to negotiate at bilateral and multilateral levels for the removal of the market access barriers to trade in services.

APPENDIX TO CHAPTER 27

Special Economic Zones (SEZs) in India

India recognized early the effectiveness of the export processing zone (EPZ) model in promoting exports, with Asia's first EPZ set up in Kandla in 1965. With a view to overcome the multiplicity of controls and clearances; absence of world-class infrastructure; and an unstable fiscal regime to attract larger foreign investments in India, the Special Economic Zones (SEZs) Policy was announced in April 2000. SEZs in India functioned from 1 November 2000 to 9 February 2006 under the provisions of the Foreign Trade Policy and fiscal incentives were made effective through the provisions of relevant statutes. The SEZ Act 2005, supported by SEZ Rules, came into effect on 10 February 2006, providing for drastic simplification of procedures and for single window clearance on matters relating to Central as well as State Governments. T*he SEZ Rules provide for different minimum land requirements for different classes of SEZs*.

In addition to seven Central Government SEZs and 12 State/private-sector SEZs set up prior to the enactment of the SEZ Act 2005, formal approval has been accorded to 580 proposals out of which 374 SEZs have been notified. The performance of SEZs has been reasonably good despite some criticism.

Performance of SEZ in India

SEZs are becoming increasingly important in India's. The performance of SEZs is mainly examined in three areas, exports, employment, and investment.

Exports: A total of 130 SEZs are already exporting. Out of this 75 are information technology (IT)/IT enabled services (ITES), 16 multi-product and 39 other sector specific SEZs. The total number of units in these SEZs is 3139. The physical exports from the SEZs have increased by 121 per cent to ₹ 2,20271 crore in 2009-10 with a CAGR (compound annual growth rate) of 58.6 per cent during 2003-04 to 2009-10 compared to the CAGR of 19.3 per cent for total merchandise exports of

Table 27A.1: SEZs Exports and India's Total Exports: A Comparison Year

	Exports from SEZs		*Exports from India*		*SEZs Share of Exports in total exports*
	Value (₹ crore)	Growth (%)	Value (₹ crore)	Growth (%)	
2003-04	13,854	39.0	2,93,367		4.7
2004-05	18,314	32.2	3.75,340	27.9	4.9
2005-06	22,840	24.7	4,56,418	21.6	5.0
2006-07	34,615	51.6	5,71,779	25.3	6.1
2007-08	66,638	92.5	6,55,863	14.7	10.2
2008-09	99,689	49.6	8,40,755	28.2	11.9
2009-10	2,20,711	121.4	8,45,534	0.6	26.1
2010-11 (Apr.-Dec.)	2,23,132	–	7,51,633	23.4	29.7

the country for the same period. When the whole world including India was reeling under the effects of the global recession, growth in exports from SEZs was 121 per cent in 2009-10 compared to a paltry 0.6 per cent growth in total exports from India. Exports during the first three quarters of the current year (2010-11) have been to the tune of ₹ 2,23,132 crore. The share of SEZs in India's total exports has increased consistently from 4.7 per cent in 2003-04 to 26.1 per cent in 2009-10 and 29.7 per cent in the first three quarters of 2010-11 (see Table 27A.1).

One of the criticisms SEZs is that exports are mainly from the old SEZs which were formerly free trade zones (FTZs) and no from greenfield SEZs. It is interesting to know that not only have many greenfield SEZs started exporting but also the exports of new SEZs, i.e. SEZs notified under the SEZ Act 2005, have grown rapidly over the years resulting in the highest share of 53.4 per cent for this category in 2009-10 compared to Central Government SEZs and State Government/ private SEZs established prior to the SEZ Act 2005 (see Table 27A.2).

Table 27A.2: Exports from New and Old SEZs

	2005-06	2006-07	2007-08	2008-09	2009-10
Central Govt SEZs					
Value (in ₹ crore)	19,657	25,358	39,275	46,985	58,037
Growth (%)	–	29	54.9	19.6	23.5
Share (%)	86.1	73.3	58.9	47.1	26.3
State Govt/Pvt. SEZs Established prior to SEZ Act, 2005					
Value (in (₹ crore)	3183	9134	22,167	31,640	44,729
Growth (%)	–	187	142.7	42.7	41.4
Share (%)	13.9	26.4	33.3	31.7	20.3
SEZs notified under SEZ Act, 2005					
Value (in ₹ crore)	–	122	5195	21,064	1,17,946
Growth (%)			4518.2	305.5	459.9
Share (%)	–	0.4	7.8	21.1	53.4

Employment: Out of the total employment of 6,44,073 persons in SEZs, an incremental employment of 5,09,369 persons was generated after February 2006 when the SEZ Act came into force. At least double this number obtains indirect employment outside the SEZs as a result of the operations of SEZ units. This is in addition to the employment created by the developer for infrastructure activities.

Investment: The total investment in SEZs till 31 December 2010 is approximately ₹ 195,348 crore including ₹ 1,91,313 crore in the newly notified zones. In SEZs 100 per cent FDI is allowed through automatic route. The Government's role has been more as a facilitator by fast tracking the approvals rather than providing any direct monetary support. SEZs being set up under the SEZ Act 2005 are primarily private investment driven.

Issues Relating to SEZs

Some important issues relating to SEZ are the following :

Direct Tax Code (DTC) Impact : The issue is related to deadlines for profit-linked deductions: As per the DTC, SEZ developers will be allowed profit-linked deductions for all SEZs notified on or before 31 March 2012. Units in SEZs that will commence commercial operations by 31 March 2014 too will be allowed profit-linked exemptions. Developers and units notified after these dates will only have investment-linked exemptions and not proift-linked exemptions. There is concern about these dates among developers and units particularly in the big SEZs with long gestation time.

Goods and Services Tax (GST): As per the GST model being considered, GST will be levied on imports with necessary constitutional amendments. Though full and complete set off would be available on the GST paid on import of goods and services, after the introduction of the GST, tax exemptions, remissions, etc. related to industrial incentives should be converted, if at all needed, into cash refund schemes after collection of tax, so that the GST scheme on the basis of a continuous chain of set-offs is not disturbed. Regarding special Industrial Area Schemes, such exemptions, remissions would continue up to legitimate expiry time both for the Centre and the States. However, any new exemption, remission, or continuation of an earlier one would not be allowed. In such cases, the Central and State Government could provide reimbursement after collecting the GST.

Issue of Power generation and distribution. Another area of concerns is the generation and distribution of power by the SEZ developers/units. While one opinion is that it should be left to the entrepreneur to decide whether he would like to provide power as an infrastructure, as defined in the SEZ Act, or set up a unit to sell power as a good, another view is that power cannot be an infrastructure and can be only a good to be generated and distributed by the unit. It may be worth considering appropriate policy to encourage power generation and distribution.

Coordination issues : The Directors, STP1, have been declared Development Commissioners (DCs) for the IT SEZs under their respective jurisdiction. An STP1 is under administrative control of the Department of Information Technology. Other multi-product and sector-specific SEZs are under the charge of DCs appointed by the Department of Commerce. However a number of issues, for example processing of notification of IT SEZs, coordination with state governments etc, relating to IT SEZs are also looked after by the DCs appointed by the Department of Commerce. This leads to a situation of dual control adversely impacting effective coordination and needs to be resolved.

Disinvestment: The new SEZs have come up mainly in the private sector with no funding from the Government. Now the time has possibly come to see whether some of the established SEZs which are state owned could also be privatized. Disinvestment in these SEZs could not only add to the kitty of the Government and release more money for social-sector development but could also make these SEZs more efficient.

Special Economic Zones Progress.

Since Special Economic Zones (SEZ) Act and Rules were notified in February 2006, formal approvals have been granted for setting up of 579 SEZs, of which 384 have been notified. Of the total employment provided to 9,45,990 persons in SEZs as a whole, that to 8, 11, 286 persons is incremental employment generated after February 2006 when the SEZ Act came into force. This is apart from the million mandays of employment created by the developer for infrastructure activities. While in 2010-11 physical exports from SEZ were worth ₹ 3,15,868 crore, in 2011-12, registering a growth of 15.4 per cent, the total physical exports from SEZs in the first half of the financial year 2012-13 have been to the tune of ₹ 23969 crore approximately, registering a growth of 36 per cent over exports in the corresponding period of the previous year. The total investment in SEZs till 30 September 2012 was ₹ 2,18,795 crore approximately, including ₹ 2,14,760 crore in the newly notified areas. As per the provision of SE2 Act 2005, 100 per cent FDI is allowed in SEZ *through the automatic* route. A total of 160 SEZs are exporting goods and services. Of this 93 are IT/ITES, 17 multiproducts and 50 other sector-specific SEZs. The total number of units in these SEZs is 3308.

CHAPTER 28
Foreign Exchange Rate

In the last chapter we have discussed the balance of payments which describes the transactions of goods and services and movements of financial capital between countries. The value of these transactions depends upon the prices of the currencies of various countries. For example, in India the value of transactions involving balance of payments is measured either in rupee terms or in terms of US dollars. Given the volume of these transactions, their value in rupees or dollars would depend on the rate of exchange of rupee with US dollar.

Foreign Exchange Rate and Foreign Exchange Market

It may be noted that the *foreign exchange is the name given to any foreign currency. Thus US dollars* or *British pounds* are *foreign exchange for India.* Further, the exchange rate is the *price of a country's currency in terms* of another country's currency. Thus, at present (Aug. 30, 2013) one US dollar is exchanged for about 65.70 rupees of India (the spot exchange rate). Thus 65.70 Indian rupees for one US at present dollar is the exchange rate of a dollar in terms of rupees.

Table 35.1 Foreign Exchange Rates of Indian Rupee

(Market Rate in ₹ Per Unit of Foreign Currency)

Foreign Currency	*Exchange rate (on Nov. 27, 2008)*	*Dec. 29, 2011*	*March 5 2013*	*August 30 2013*
US Dollar	49.44	52.71	54.9	65.70
British Pound	75.96	82.41	83.26	101.82
Canadian Dollar	40.35	51.75	53.56	62.36
Euro*	64.24	68.91	71.5	86.87
UAE (*Dhiran*)	13.57	14.35	14.39	17.88
Swedish Kroner		7.57	8.21	9.93
Swiss Francs	–	56.10	57.8	70.69
Japanese 100 Yen	52.89	67.63	58.5	66.92
Australian Dollar	32.09	53.57	56.2	58.48
Singapore Dollar	32.81	40.78	44.0	51.53
New Zeland Dollar	–	40.62	44.6	50.79

*Euro is the Common Currency of European Union consisting of a number of European countries.

In the above table we give the exchange rates of Indian rupee in terms of currencies of some important countries of the world. It will be seen from the above table that there has been a lot of volatility in the exchange rate of rupee. There had been 15 per cent appreciation of Indian rupee vis-a-vis US Dollar between Oct. 2006 and Dec. 2007. Beyond Jan.2008, rupee started depreciating under pressure of capital outflows by FIIs and it fell to ₹ 49.44 to a US dollar on Nov. 27, 2008. From later half of 2009-10 to Aug. 2011, as a result of return of capital flows to India, rupee started appreciating and its value rose to around ₹ 45 to a US dollar at end-Aug. 2011. However, again from Sept. 2011 due to Eurozone sovereign debt crisis there had been large capital outflows by FIIs from India (and other emerging economies) resulting in drastic depreciation of Indian rupee which fell to even ₹ 54 to a US dollar on Dec. 15, 2011. But due to intervention of RBI by way of selling dollars in the foreign exchange market from its foreign exchange reserves, the value of rupee fluctuated within range of ₹ 52 to ₹ 53 to a US dollar between December 16, 2011 and January 13, 2012. It will be seen that Indian rupee depreciated against currencies of all countries in March 5, 2013 except Japan. On March 5, 2013, value of rupee was 54.9 rupees per US dollar.

However, a very large depreciation of rupee has occurred since May 22, 2013. In the month of June 2013, the rupee fell from to around ₹ 56 to a US dollar in the first week of June 2013 to ₹ 60 to a dollar in the end of June 2013 and hit very level of ₹ 61.21 to a dollar on July 8, 2013. The RBI intervened by selling US dollars from its foreign exchange reserves and took steps to discourage the import of gold so as to reduce the demand for dollars. The Finance Minister also raised the duty on gold, first from 6% to 8% and then to 10% to restrict the imports of gold to check further depreciation of rupee. However, despite these measures, depreciation of rupee continued and the value of rupee hit a record of ₹ 68.83 to a US dollar on Aug. 28, 2013. Then with aggressive intervention by the RBI through sale of dollars from its foreign exchange reserves and as a result the value of rupee rose to ₹ 65.70 to a dollar on Aug. 30, 2013. That is, about 18% fall in the value of rupee from early June 2013.

Both domestic and external factors are responsible for this sharp depreciation of rupee since May 2013. The domestic factor responsible for this steep slide of rupee has been the emergence of large current account deficit (CAD) which was estimated at $ 88 billion in 2012-13 (4.8% of GDP of the year) due to sluggish exports and rise in imports causing a net increase in demand for US dollars over their supply. The external factor which triggered the sharp depreciation of rupee was the announcement by the governor of the US Reserve System in May 2013 that since the US economy had recovered, he would start the unwinding of the policy of *quantitative easing* (QE) under which it was purchasing bonds worth $ 85 billion per month from the market to revive the US economy. This triggered capital outflows by FIIs from the emerging economies including India. These capital outflows on a large scale from India contributed to the sharp slide in the exchange rate of rupee.

Floating (Flexible) and Fixed Exchange Rate System

Since exchange rate is a price, its determination can be explained through demand for and supply of currencies. Suppose we consider the transactions between two countries, India and USA. In this case therefore the demand for and supply of dollar is the demand for and supply of foreign exchange from the Indian perspective and the price of a US dollar in terms of Indian rupees or a number of dollars per Indian rupee is the exchange rate. *The system of exchange rate in which the value of a currency is allowed to adjust freely or to float as determined by demand for and supply of foreign exchange is called a flexible exchange system which is also known as floating exchange system.*

On the other hand, if the exchange rate instead of *being determined by demand for and supply of foreign exchange is fixed by the Government, it is called the fixed exchange rate system* which prevailed in the world under an agreement reached at Bretton Woods in New Hampshire in July 1944. It may be noted that under the fixed exchange rate system, exchange rate is not determined by demand for and supply of foreign exchange but is pegged at a certain rate. At the fixed exchange rate, if there is disequilibrium in the balance of payments giving rise to either excess demand or excess supply of foreign exchange, the Central Bank of the country has to buy and sell the required quantities of foreign exchange to eliminate the excess demand or supply.

In 1977 USA decided to float its dollar and switched over to the flexible exchange system resulting in the collapse of Bretton Woods System of fixed exchange rate. Both the floating (flexible) and fixed exchange rate system have ther merits and demerits which will be discussed in a later section.

Appreciation and Depreciation of Currencies

It is important to explain the meanings of the terms, appreciation and depreciation, of currencies which are often mentioned in the discussion of foreign exchange rate. Let us consider the exchange rate of rupee for dollar. Appreciation of a currency is the increase in its value in terms of another foreign currency. Thus, if the value of a rupee in terms of U S dollar increases from ₹ 45.50

to ₹ 44 to a dollar, Indian rupee is said to appreciate. This indicates strengthening of the Indian rupee. Note that when Indian rupee in dollar terms appreciates, the dollar would depreciate. On the other hand, if the value of Indian rupee in terms of US dollars falls, say from ₹ 45.5 to ₹ 46 to a dollar, the Indian rupee is said to depreciate which shows the weakening of Indian rupee. Thus, under a flexible exchange system, the exchange value of a currency frequently appreciates or depreciates depending upon the demand for and supply of a currency.

In a fixed exchange rate system the government has to buy or sell foreign exchange in order to maintain the rate at the controlled level. However, even under the fixed exchange rate system, the value of one's currency can be changed only occasionally. For instance, in June 1966, the value of rupee in terms of US dollar and U.K's, pound sterling was lowered. Again in July 1991 India reduced its value of rupee in terms of dollar by about 20 per cent. Such a one-time lowering of value of its currency in terms of foreign exchange occasionally by a country is called *devaluation* as distinguished from depreciation which can often take place under the influence of changes in demand for and supply of a currency. On the other hand, with a fixed rate exchange system if a country raises the value of its currency in terms of foreign currency, it is called *revaluation.* It should be noted that since March 1993 India has also now made its rupee convertible into a foreign currency and allowed its value to adjust freely depending upon demand and supply forces.

DETERMINATION OF EXCHANGE RATE

We are now in a position to explain how in a flexible exchange rate system the exchange of a currency is determined by demand for and supply of foreign exchange. We assume that there are two countries, India and USA, the exchange rate of their currencies (namely, rupee and dollar) is to be determined. Thus, we explain below how the value of a dollar in terms of rupees (which will conversely indicate the value of a rupee in terms of dollars) is determined.

At present in both USA and India there is floating or flexible exchange regime. Therefore, the value of currency of each country in terms of the other depends upon the demand for and supply of their currencies.

It is in the foreign exchange market that the exchange rate among different currencies is determined. The foreign exchange market is the market in which the currencies of various countries are converted into each other or exchanged for each other. In our case of the determination of exchange rate between US dollar and Indian rupee, the Indians sell rupees to buy US dollars (which is a foreign currency) and the Americans or others holding US dollars will sell dollars in exchange for rupees. It is the demand for and supply of a foreign currency or exchange that will determine the exchange rate between the two.

Demand for Foreign Exchange (US Dollars)

The demand for US dollars comes from the Indian people and firms who need US dollars to pay for the goods and services they want to import from the USA. The greater the imports of goods and services from the USA, the greater the demand for the US dollars by the Indians. Further, the demand for dollars also arises from Indian individuals and firms wanting to purchase assets in the USA, that is, desire to invest in US bonds and equity shares of the American companies or build factories, sales facilities or houses in the USA. The demand for dollars also arises from those who want to give loans or send gifts to some people in the USA. Thus, for whatever reasons the Indian residents need dollars they have to buy them in the foreign exchange market and pay for them with the Indian currency, the rupees. All of these constitute demand for dollars, the foreign exchange.

To sum up, the demand for dollars by the Indians arises due to the following factors:

1. The Indian individuals, firms or Government who import goods from the USA into India.

2. The Indians travelling and studying in the USA would require dollars to meet their travelling and education expenses.

3. The Indians who want to invest in equity shares and bonds of the US companies and other financial instruments.

4. The Indian firms who want to invest directly in building factories, sales facilities, shops in the USA.

An important thing to understand is how the demand curve for a foreign exchange would look like. *When there is a fall in the price of dollar in terms of rupees, that is, when the dollar depreciates, fewer rupees than before would be required to get a dollar.* With this, therefore, a dollar's worth of US goods could be purchased with fewer rupees, that is, the US goods would become cheaper in terms of rupees for Indians. This will induce the Indian individuals and firms to import more from the USA resulting in the increase in quantity demanded of dollars by the Indians. On the other hand, *if the price of US dollar rises, (that is US dollar appreciates) a dollar's worth of US goods would now cost more in terms of rupees making American goods relatively expensive than before.* This will discourage the imports of US goods to India causing a decrease in quantity demanded of dollars for imports.

It therefore follows from above that at a lower price of dollars, the greater quantity of dollars is demanded for imports from the USA and at a higher price of dollar, the smaller quantity of dollars is demanded for imports from the USA by the Indians. This makes the demand curve for dollars downward sloping as shown by the *DD* curve in Fig. 28.1.

Supply of US Dollars (i.e., Foreign Exchange)

What determines the supply of dollars in the foreign exchange market. The individual firms and Government *which export Indian goods to the USA will earn dollars from the American residents who would buy the Indian goods imported into the USA and pay their price in dollars.* Further, the Americans who travel in India and use the services of Indian transport, hotels etc., will also supply dollars to be converted into rupees for meeting these expenses.

Besides, the *American firms and individuals who want to buy assets in India, such as bonds and equity shares of Indian companies or wish to make loans to the Indian individuals and firms will also supply dollars.* There are Indians who are working in the USA and send their earnings in dollars to their relatives and friends. The supply of these dollars by the Indians working in the USA popularly called *remittances from the USA* also add to the supply of dollars. Those holding dollars who have earned them from exports to the USA and the foreign firms and individuals who want to invest in India or those who want to make loans to Indians or the American tourists travelling in India, and remittances from USA by the Indians working there will supply dollars in the foreign exchange market.

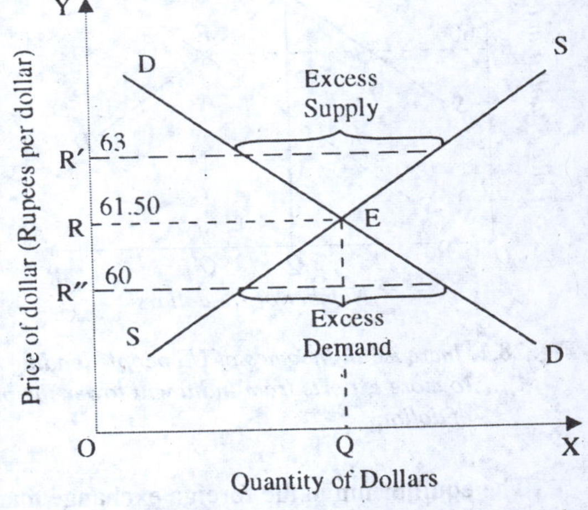

Fig. 28.1. *Determination of Exchange Rate of a Dollar in terms of Rupess*

The supply curve of dollars plotted against the price of dollar in terms of rupees is positively sloping as shown in Fig. 28.1. What accounts for the upward sloping nature of the supply curve of the dollars. At a higher price of dollar in terms of rupees (or, in other words, lower value of the Indian rupee in terms of dollar), 100 rupees worth of Indian goods would be relatively cheaper in terms of dollars. This will tend to boost exports of the Indian goods to the USA at a higher price of dollar and thus ensure more supply of dollars in the foreign exchange markets. On the other hand, if the price of US dollar in terms of rupees falls (i.e. its exchange rate for Indian rupee declines) the 100 rupees worth of Indian goods would become relatively expensive in terms of dollars. This will discourage the exports of Indian goods to the USA and reduce the quantity supplied of dollars in the foreign exchange market.

The Equilibrium Exchange Rate

It will be seen from Figure 28.1 that the equilibrium exchange rate, that is, the equilibrium price of dollar in terms of rupees is equal to *OR* or ₹. 61.50 per dollar at which demand for and supply curve of dollars intersect and therefore the market for dollars is cleared at this rate. At a higher price of dollars *OR′* or ₹ 63, the quantity supplied of dollars exceeds the quantity demanded. With the emergence of excess supply of dollars, its price, that is, the exchange rate will again fall to *OR* or ₹ 61.50. On the other hand, if the rate of exchange is lower than *OR*, say it is *OR″* or ₹ 60 to a dollar, there will emerge the excess demand for dollars. This excess demand of dollars would push up the price of dollars to the level of *OR* or ₹ 61.50 per dollar.

CHANGES IN EXCHANGE RATE

In our analysis of determination of exchange rate through demand and supply of foreign exchange we have assumed that the underlying forces which determine demand for and supply of foreign exchange remain constant. In our foregoing analysis it is only changes in the exchange rate that cause the quantity supplied and demanded of foreign exchange to change and bring about the equilibrium between demand for and supply of foreign exchange.

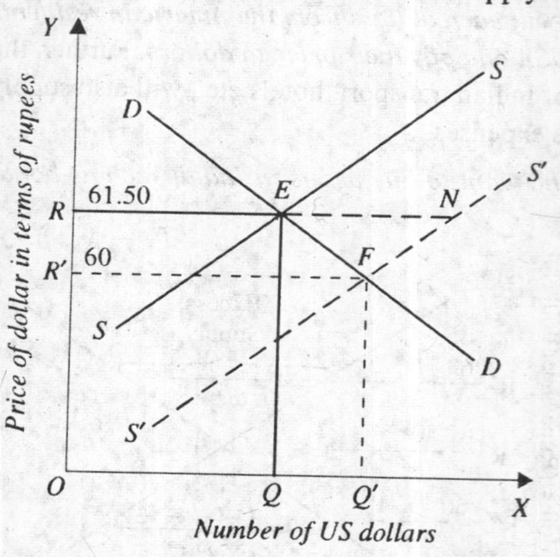

Fig. 28.2. *Increase in Incomes of US people leading to more exports from India will lower the price of dollar.*

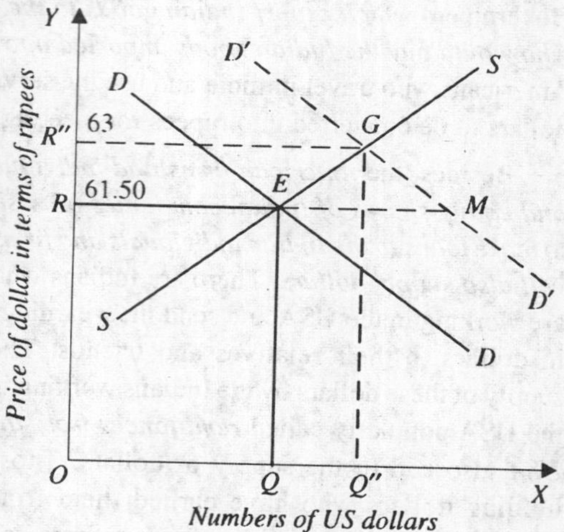

Fig. 28.3. *Increase in the imports from USA by the Indians causes increase in demand for dollars and lowers the price of rupee or raise the price of US dollar.*

The equilibrium in the foreign exchange market will be disturbed if some changes occur in the underlying factors that determine the demand for and supply of foreign exchange. For example, if there is increase in incomes of the American people due to the boom conditions in the US economy, it will affect the equilibrium rate of exchange. The increase in incomes of the people of USA will lead to the increase in demand for imported goods including those of India. Now, with this increase in demand for imported Indian goods, they will spend more dollars on the Indian goods. This will increase the supply of dollars to buy Indian goods in the foreign exchange market causing a rightward shift in the supply curve from *SS* to *S′S′* , as shown in Fig. 28.2. This increase in the supply of dollars in foreign exchange market will lower the price of dollar in terms of rupees from *OR* (₹ 61.50 to a dollar) to *OR′* (₹ 60 to a dollar). This implies that increase in imports by USA from India leading to more exports from India will cause the dollar to depreciate and the Indian rupee to appreciate. It will be seen from Figure 28.2 that with the increase in india's exports to the USA and as a result increase in supply of dollars, supply curve of US dollars shifts to the right to *S′S′* position. With this, at the original price *OR* (or ₹ 61.50 to a dollar) there is excess supply of dollars by *EN* amount which will result in lowering the price of dollar to the level of *OR′* or ₹ 60 to a dollar. This means increase in supply of dollars has led to *the appreciation of rupee* from ₹ 61.50 to a dollar to ₹ 60 to a dollar and depreciation of US dollar.

On the other hand, if due to the increase in incomes of the Indian people causing a rise in demand for American consumer goods or there is pick up of industrial activity in India requiring more imports of materials, machines, equipments and other capital goods from the USA the Indian imports from USA will increase. The increase in imports from USA by India will have to be paid in dollars causing the demand for dollars to increase and as a result demand curve for dollar shifts to the right from *DD* curve to *D′D′* curve (see Fig. 28.3). This will upset the initial equilibrium at price *OR* (₹ 61.50 to a dollar) as with the increase in demand for dollars following the increase in imports from USA there will emerge excess demand for dollars which will push up the price of dollar to *OR′ ′* (₹ 63 to a dollar) so as to bring balance between demand for and supply of dollars (*i.e.*, foreign exchange). Note that rise in price of dollar in terms of rupees implies depreciation of the value of rupee from ₹ 61.50 to ₹ 63 to a dollar.

It will be observed in Fig. 28.3 that as a result of adjustments following the increase in demand for dollars, the price of dollar has risen to *OR″* (₹ 63 to a dollar) and the amount of dollars spent by Indians on imports from the USA increases to *Q″*

FOREIGN EXCHANGE RATE AND BALANCE OF PAYMENTS

It will be understood from above that the various items in the country's balance of payments lie at the back of demand for and supply of a foreign currency. That is why the explanation of determinantion of foreign exchange rate through demand and supply is also called the *Balance of Payments Theory of Foreign Exchange*. The demand for foreign exchange arises from the debit items in the balance of payments, whereas the supply of foreign exchange arises from credit items. The debit items relate to all payments made during a given period by residents of a country to foreigners, and credit items include all payments received during the given period from foreigners by the residents. These payments may be on any account, *e.g.* goods bought and sold, services rendered and received, capital borrowed or lent, and so on.

By way of illustration, if India has a net debit in its balance of payments, its demand for foreign exchange, say, U.S. dollar, must exceed its supply of U.S. dollar with the result that the rupee price of U.S. dollar will go up or, what comes to the same thing, the external value of the rupee must go down in terms of dollar. The rupee becomes cheap in terms of dollar. Conversely, a net credit in India's balance of payments will lead to a fall in the rupee-price of dollar, which means a higher value of the rupee or expensive rupee in terms of US dollar.

When the balance of payments is in deficit, the country will have a weak exchange rate position. There will be increase in the demand for foreign exchange relative to the supply thereof because more payments have to be made than receipt of payments from abroad. In this case there will be decline in the external value of the domestic currency. But the depreciated external value of its currency will stimulate exports and help it to wipe out the deficit.

If a country has a surplus on current account, it is said to have a favourable balance of payments. There are more people abroad who have to make payments to this country. The demand for this country's currency will increase on the part of the holders of foreign currency. The result will be that the external value of the domestic currency will appreciate. This is how the balance of payments affecting demand for foreign exchange and supply of foreign exchange determines the rate of exchange.

The explanation of foreign exchange through demand or what sometimes is called balance of payments theory of exchange rates is superior because (*a*) it is more realistic as the price of foreign currency is seen here as a function of many significant variables and not merely purchasing power expressed in general price level, and (*b*) it clearly shows the possibility of correcting balance of payments disequilibrium through exchange rate adjustment rather than through domestic price deflation as implied by the purchasing power parity.

The chief merit of demand-supply approach to the determination of exchange rate or what is sometimes called balance of payments theory of foreign exchange is that it explains the determination of foreign exchange rate through general demand and supply analysis. Further, important fact brought out by the theory is that not only exports and imports of goods but also other items in the balance of payments such as invisible items, long-term capital movements also play a significant part in determining demand for and supply of foreign exchange and the equilibrium rate of exchange. Thus, this theory puts forward more correct explanation of the determination of foreign exchange rate by visualising foreign exchange as a function of several variables and not just purchasing power representing the general price level. This theory also highlights an important fact that disequilibrium in the balance of payments, if left to the market forces, can be corrected through depreciation or appreciation in exchange rate.

FACTORS AFFECTING EXCHANGE RATE

Having now explained how the exchange rate between different currencies of various countries is determined, we can now explain the factors that are likely to affect the exchange rate between currencies. Changes in all those factors mentioned above which determine the demand for and supply of currencies can influence the exchange rate which will adjust according to the changes that have occurred.

Purchasing Power Parity: The Relative Price Levels

If there are no restrictions imposed on trade by the countries the exchange rate between two national currencies is allowed to adjust freely and with the further assumption that costs of transport of goods between the countries is nil, then the exchange rate between the two currencies will reflect the differences in the price levels in the two countries. This is because with the above-mentioned assumptions if the price of the same good BPL TV set is lower in Britain than in India, then it will pay traders to buy the BPL TV sets in Britain and sell them in India. This will reduce the supply of TV set in Britain pushing up its price there and increase the supply of TV sets in India and thus causing a decline in its price in India. This process would continue till the price differential of the same quality of T.V. sets is eliminated and the same price of TV set prevails in the two countries. Thus, if law of same price holds and each country consumes the same market basket of goods, the exchange rate between the two currencies would be determined by the relative price levels in the two countries. For example, if prices in Britain and India are such that a pair of same quality of shoes costs 5 pound in England and 350 rupees in India, then the exchange rate between rupees and pound would be 1 pound for 70 rupees. If the exchange rate between the two is different from this, it will be possible for the businessmen to make profits in sending pairs of shoes from a country to the other depending on the price levels in the two countries. We therefore conclude that price levels of commodities in the different countries influence the exchange rate between their currencies.

It may however be noted that it is only in the long run and with no restrictions on the trade between the two countries that relative price level in the two countries will be reflected in the exchanges rate.

Rate of Inflation and Exchange Rate

Having shown the effect of relative price levels in the countires on the exchange rate between their currencies, we can now explain how a relatively higher rate of inflation in a country can affect the exchange rate of its currency. Suppose in India a relatively higher rate of inflation prevails than in the USA, how will it affect the exchange rate between the rupee and dollar?

A relatively higher rate of inflation causing rise in prices of the goods in India as compared to those in the USA will make US goods relatively cheapter and the Indian goods expensive. This will serve as incentive for the Indian individuals and firms to increase their imports of goods from USA.

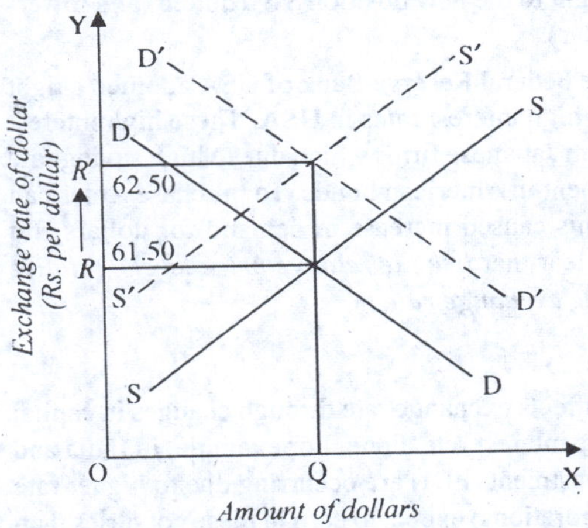

Fig. 28.4. *Effect of a relatively higher rate of inflation on the domestic economy the exchange rate of a country : Rupee depreciates and US dollar appreciates*

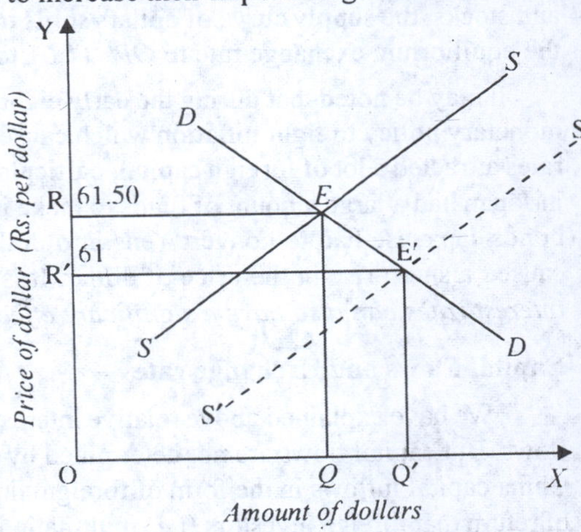

Fig. 28.5. *Effect of a relatively higher rate of interest in India on the exchange rate : Indian Rupee Appreciates*

This will raise the demand for US dollars shifting the demand curve for dollars in the foreign exchange market to the right, as shown in Fig. 28.4 where the demand curve of US dolars is shown to have shifted from *DD* to *D′D′* under the influence of higher rate of inflation in India leading to greater imports by India.

However, at the same time due to higher price level American people will find Indian goods more expensive and as a result will reduce their imports of Indian goods. This will cause á decline in exports of goods from India to the USA, shifting the supply curve of dollars to the left to *S′S′*. Both these effects of a higher price level due to higher rate of inflation in a country, namely, rise in imports of US goods into India and the reduction in Indian exports to the USA will cause the foreign exchange rate of dollar in terms of rupees to rise and the price of Indian rupee in terms of dollar will fall. *Thus, as a result of higher rate of inflation in India, the US dollar will appreciate and the Indian rupee will depreciate* (See Figure 28.4).

Interest Rates and Exchange Rate

Another important factor influencing the exchange rate is the interest rate in a country relative to interest rate of other countries with which it trades its goods. Suppose there are no restrictions imposed by the Governments on the flow of capital funds between the countries. Assume that interest on securities or bonds in USA is 5 per cent whereas it is 8 per cent in India. Thus businessmen, firms, banks etc., with funds to invest would obviously have incentive to buy securities and bonds of India companies. That is, there will be *flight of capital* from the USA or capital inflows into India as the American business corporations, firms, banks etc. will use their funds to purchase high-yielding Indian securities. In order to buy the Indian securities, they will have to convert dollars into rupees, and thus increasing the supply of dollars. Consequently, the supply curve of dollar will shift to the right. This will pull down the foreign exchange rate of dollar in terms of rupees (Conversely, the exchange rate of rupee in terms of dollar will appreciate). Thus, *a relatively higher interest rate in India as compared to the USA would lead to the depreciation of dollar and appreciation of rupee.* This is what actually happened in India in the fiscal years 2003-04, 2004-05 and 2005-06 .

Figure 28.5 illustrates the effect of higher interest rates in India on the dollar-rupee exchange rate. Initially, the demand for and the supply of US dollar are given by the curves *DD* and *SS* respectively. The balance between the two determines *OR* (or ₹ 61.50 to a dollar) as the exchange rate between the two. With the flow of United States funds into India to buy the Indian securities and stocks, the supply curve of dollars shifts to the right to the new position *S′S′* (dotted) and lowers the equilibrium exchange rate to *OR′* (₹ 61 to a dollar).

It may be noted that during the early eighties, the Federal Reserve Bank of USA adopted a tight monetary policy to fight inflation which caused very high interest rates in USA. These high interest rates attracted a lot of foreign capital, particularly from Japanese firms which due to high saving rate in Japan had a large amount of funds to make investment in American bonds. To purchase American bonds Japanese had to convert Yens into dollars. This caused increase in demand for dollars and caused a sharp rise in the price of dollar. It is thus clear that *like the relative price levels, relative interest rates can also have a significant effect on the exchange rate.*

Capital Flows and Exchange rate

We have explained above relative interest rate affects exchange rate through changes in capital flows. But capital flows are not determined by relative interest rate alone. For example, in India and China capital inflows in the form of foreign direct investment (FDI) are occurring due to higher rate of return that foreign investors (*i.e.*, multinational corporations) expect to earn in these countries than in their domestic economies. Besides, capital inflows in India occur when foreign institutional investors (FII) and Non-resident Indians buy in the equity (*i.e.*, share capital) of Indian Companies in Indian stock market. On the other band, when Indian business class invests abroad, capital outflows from India occur. It may be noted that these capital inflows and capital outflows are recorded in the capital account of the balance of payments. On the other hand, trade of goods and services are recorded in the current account of the balance of payments.

We are interested here to show how capital flows affect exchange rate of the currency of a country. This is shown in Figure 28.5 (a) and 28.5 (b) where determination of exchange rate between rupee and US dollar is shown. To begin with in Fig. 28.5 (a), we have drawn demand curve *DD* and supply curves *SS* of US dollar as determined by flows of trade of goods (that is, imports and exports) between the two countries, without any capital flows of taking place between the two countries. These demand and supply curves, *DD* and *SS*, determine equilibrium exchange rate *OR* (or ₹ 61 to a US dollar). Note that at this equilibrium exchange rate, there is equilibrium in the current account balance of payments since we are so far assuming that no capital flows occur.

Now suppose foreign institutional investors (FII) and Non-Resident Indians buy shares of the Indian companies. They will therefore bring dollars and convent them into rupees for buying shares of the Indian companies. These capital inflows will increase the supply of US dollars causing a shift in the supply curve to the right, say to the new position S_1S_1. The new supply curve of dollars S_1S_1

1. We consider invisibles which mainly consist of services as a part of trade balance. Therefore, in our case here, no distinction is drawn between trade balance and current account balance.

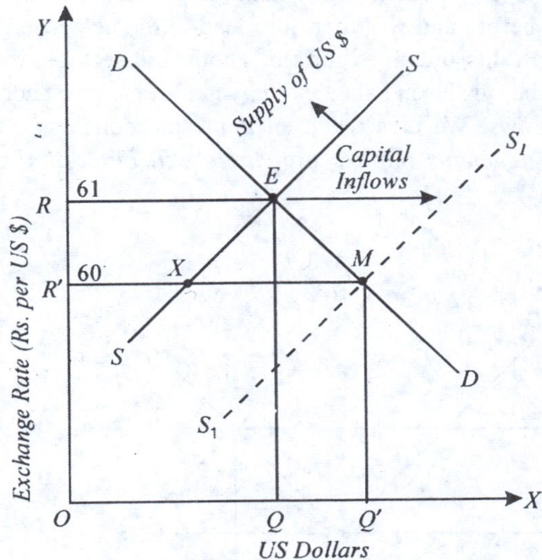

Fig. 28.5(a). *Appreciation of Rupee as a Result of Capital Inflows*

intersects the demand curve *DD* of dollars at point *M* and determine the new exchange rate *OR*' (or ₹ 60 to a dollar). Thus, as a result of capital inflows, the Indian rupee has appreciated (and dollar depreciated). It may be noted that at the new equilibrium exchange rate *OR*' (or ₹ 60 to a dollar), the overall balance of payments (that is, total inflows and outflows of US dollars on account of both trade and capital flows) will be in equilibrium. However, in this situation due to capital inflows as depicted in Fig. 28.5 (*a*), *current account must be in deficit* while the overall balance of payments is in equilibrium. Since as a result of capital inflows the exchange rate of rupee has appreciated, this will cause the total Indian exports of goods and services to decline. Total exports of goods and services at the new exchange rate *OR*' (or ₹ 60 to a dollar) is given by the point *X* on the *original* supply curve of dollars *SS* corresponding to this new exchange rate *OR*'. From Figure 28.5(*a*), it is clear that total exports of goods and services *R'X* are less than the imports of goods and resources *R'M*. Thus there is deficit of *XM* on current account. This deficit on current account is met by surplus in capital inflows of capital account since overall balance of payments balances at the new equilibrium exchange rate. We thus reach an important conclusion that the *deficit in current account implies capital inflows (i.e., foreign investment) of that order occur in the economy in that year, if there are no withdrawal from foreign exchange reserves.*

Capital Outflows. Let us take the opposite case when instead of net capital inflows, there are net apital outflows. For example, the rate of return on investment rises in the USA or interest rate falls in India as compared to that in USA. This will cause capital outflows from India and result in shifting the demand curve of US dollars in foreign exchange market. This is illustrated in Figure 28.5 (b). where demand curve of US dollars *DD* and supply curve *SS* of US dollars determine equilibrium exchange rate *OR* (or ₹ 61 to a dollar) when there are no capital flows. Now suppose that net capital outflows occur due to the factors mentioned above. Capital outflows require that those who want to invest abroad will convert Indian rupees into US dollars to invest in the USA. This will cause an increase in demand for US dollars resulting in a shift of the demand curve for US dollars to the right, say to D_1D_1. The new demand curve for US dollars intersects the given supply curve *SS* of dollars at the new point *T* and determines the exchange rate *OR*" (or ₹ 62 to a dollar), that is, US dollar appreciates and the Indian rupee depreciates. Since the Indian rupee depreciates, the Indian exports of goods and services will increase because depreciation of Indian rupee will make the India goods and services cheaper. In Figure 28.5 (*b*), at the new exchange rate *OR*" (₹ 62 to a dollar) exports of Indian goods and services increase to $R''T$. On the other hand, depreciation of Indian rupee will make the Indian imports costlier than before and will therefore lead to the decrease in imports to $R''M$ at the new exchange rate OR''. With this Indian exports of goods and services exceed its imports by the amount MT. Thus, there will be surplus in balance of payments on current account of India which will be equal to the capital outflows. We thus reach an important conclusion that *surplus on current account of the balance of payments implies that there will be capital outflows of that order.*

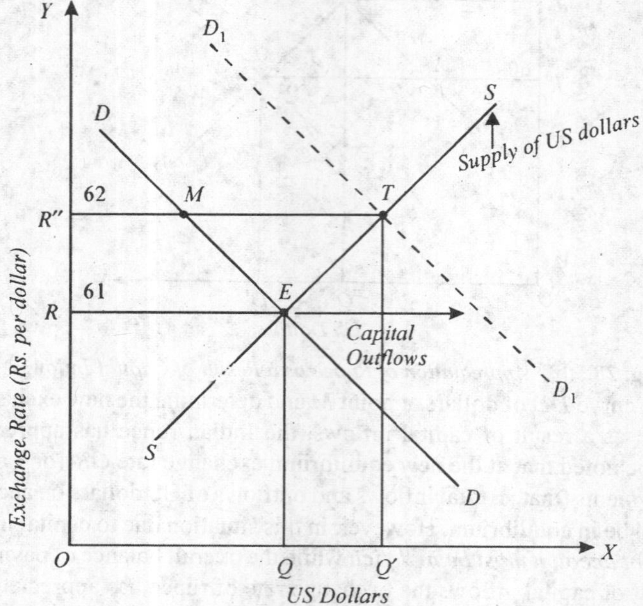

Fig. 28.5(b). *Depreciation of Rupee with Capital Outflows*

PURCHASING POWER PARITY THEORY

No country today is rich enough to have a free gold standard, not even the U.S.A. All countries have now paper currencies and these paper currencies of the various countries are not convertible into gold or other valuable things. Therefore, these days various countries have paper currency standards. The exchange situation is difficult in such cases. In such circumstances the ratio of exchange between the two currencies is determined by their respective purchasing powers.

The purchasing power parity theory was propounded by Professor Gustav Cassel of Sweden. According to this theory, rate of exchange between two countries depends upon the relative purchasing power of their respective currencies. Such will be the rate which equates the two purchasing powers. For example, if a certain assortment of goods can be had for £1 in Britain and a similar assortment with ₹ 80 in India, then it is clear that the purchasing power of £1 in Britain is equal to the purchasing power of ₹ 80 in India. Thus, the rate of exchange, according to purchasing power parity theory, will be £1 = ₹ 80.

Let us take another example. Suppose in the USA one $ purchases a given collection of commodities. In India, same collection of goods cost 60 rupees. Then rate of exchange will tend to be

$1 = 60 rupees.

Now, suppose the price levels in the two countries remain the same but somehow exchange rate moves to $1 = 61 rupees.

This means that one US$ can purchase commodities worth more than 46 rupees. It will pay people to convert dollars into rupees at this rate, (\$1 = ₹ 61), purchase the given collection of commodities in India for 60 rupees and sell them in U.S.A. for one dollar again, making a profit of 1 rupee per dollar worth of transactions. This will create a large demand for rupees in the USA while supply thereof will be less because very few people would export commodities from USA to India. The value of the rupee in terms of the dollar will move up until it will reach \$1 = 60 rupees. At that point, imports from India will not give abnormal profits. \$1 = 60 rupees and is called the purchasing power parity between the two countries.

Thus while the value of the unit of one currency in terms of another currency is determined at any particular time by the market conditions of demand and supply, in the long run the exchange rate is determined by the relative values of the two currencies as indicated by their respective purchasing powers over goods and services. In other words, the rate of exchange tends to rest at the point which expresses equality between the respective purchasing powers of the two currencies. This point is called the purchasing power parity. Thus, under a system of autonomous paper standards the external value of a currency is said to depend ultimately on the domestic purchasing power of that currency relative to that of another currency. In other words, exchange rates, under such a system, tend to be determined by the relative purchasing power parities of different currencies in different countries.

In the above example, if prices in India get doubled, prices in the USA remaining the the same, the value of the rupee will be exactly halved. The new parity will be \$1 = 120 rupees. This is because now 120 rupees will buy the same collection of commodities in India which 60 rupees did before. We suppose that prices in the USA remain as before. But if prices in both countries get doubled, there will be no change in the parity.

In actual practice, however, the parity will be modified by the cost of transporting goods (including duties etc.) from one country to another.

A Critique of Purchasing Power Parity Theory

The purchasing power parity theory has been subject to the following criticisms:

The actual rates of exchange between the two countries very seldom reflect the relative purchasing powers of the two currencies. This may be due to the fact that governments have either controlled prices or controlled exchange rates or imposed restrictions on import and export of goods. Moreover, the theory is true if we consider the purchasing power of the respective currencies in terms of goods which enter into international trade and not the purchasing power of goods in general. But we know that all articles produced in a country do not figure in international trade. Therefore, the rate of exchange cannot reflect the purchasing power of goods in general. For example, in India we may be able to get a dozen shirts washed with ₹ 40, but only 2 shirts with one dollar in the USA. Obviously, the purchasing power of one dollar in the USA is much less than the purchasing power of ₹ 40 in India. This is due to the fact that *dhobis* do not form an article of international trade. If dhobis entered into international trade and freely moved into the U.S.A., then in terms of clothes washed, the purchasing power of ₹ 40 may be equalised with the purchasing power of a dollar.

Further, it is very difficult to measure purchasing power of a currency. It is usually done with the help of index numbers. But we know that the index numbers are not infallible. Among the difficulties connected with index numbers are the following important ones: (*i*) Different types of goods that enter into the calculation of index numbers; (*ii*) Many goods which may enter into domestic trade may not figure in international trade; (*iii*) Internationally traded goods also may not have the same prices in all the markets because of differences in transport costs.

Besides, the theory of purchasing power applies to a stationary world. Actually the world is not static but dynamic. Conditions relating to money and prices, tariffs, etc., constantly go on changing and prevent us from arriving at any stable conclusion about the rates of exchange. The internal prices and the cost of production are constantly changing. Therefore, a new equilibrium between the two currencies is almost daily called for. As Cassel observes, "differences in two countries' economic situation, particularly in regard to transport and customs, may cause the normal exchange rate to deviate to a certain extent from the quotient of the currencies intrinsic purchasing powers." If a country raises its tariffs, the exchange value of its currency will rise but its price level will remain the same.

Besides, many items of balance of payments like insurance and banking transactions and capital movements are very little affected by changes in general price levels. But these items do influence exchange rates by acting upon the supply of and the demand for foreign currencies. The Purchasing Power Parity Theory ignores these influences altogether. Further, the theory, as propounded by Cassel, says that changes in price level bring about changes in exchange rates but changes in exchange rates do not cause any change in prices. This latter part is not true, for exchange movements do exercise some influence on internal prices.

The purchasing power parity theory compares the general price levels in two countries without making any provision for distinction being drawn between the price level of domestic goods and that of the internationally traded goods. The prices of internationally-traded goods will tend to be the same in all countries (transport costs are, of course omitted). Domestic prices on the other hand, will be different in the two countries, even between two areas of the same country.

The purchasing power parity theory assumes that there is a direct link between the purchasing power of currencies and the rate of exchange. But in fact there is no direct relation between the two. Exchange rate can be influenced by many other considerations such as tariffs, speculation and capital movements.

Keynes' Critique. According to Keynes, there are two basic defects in the purchasing power parity theory, namely, (*i*) it does not take into consideration the elasticities of reciprocal demand, and (*ii*) it ignores the influences of capital movements. In Keynes's view, foreign exchange rates are determined not only by the price movements but also by capital movements, the elasticities of reciprocal demand and many other forces affecting the demand for and supply of foreign exchange. "By elasticity of reciprocal demand is meant the responsiveness of one country's demand for another country's exports with respect to price or income." As for price elasticity, generally speaking, greater the proportion of luxuries and semi-luxuries in the exports demanded, the more elastic will be the country's demand for another country's exports. It will also be more elastic, when there is a greater number of alternative markets in which to buy and greater the capacity to produce the effective substitutes for goods imported. As for the income elasticity of demand for imports, changes in demand for goods and services and in the derived demand for foreign exchange is functionally related to the changes in national income. How far is a country's demand for another's exports responsive to a change in national income, will influence the rate of exchange. In other words, it is the character of the propensity to import out of a given income that is supposed to affect the exchange rate independently of international price movements. Technological improvement adding to the productivity of the country and making its goods cheaper and better, tariff changes and exports subsidies affect exchange rates via their influence upon reciprocal demand quite independently of international price movements.

Capital movements, both short-term and long-term, are the other important influences. There is hot money flying from a country so as to make profits or avoid losses on exchange rate fluctuations and there is a 'refugee capital' seeking safety and security abroad. An actual or expected change in the domestic price of a foreign currency may lead to inflow or outflow of 'hot money' causing a further change in the exchange rate without there being price changes in either country. The inflows tend to raise the exchange value of the currency of the capital receiving country and outflows will lower it. Long-term movements of capital also has a similar effect.

In view of the defects pointed out above the purchasing power parity theory does not offer an adequate or satisfactory explanation of fluctuations in the rates of exchange. The determination of the exchange rate depends not only on international price relations but also on many other factors as mentioned above. This leads to a more adequate explanation of the determination of foreign exchange rates through demand for and supply of foreign exchange viz. balance of payments theory. This theory has been explained above.

EFFECTS OF CHANGES IN EXCHANGE RATE (DEPRECIATION OR DEVALUATION)

Under the recent economic reforms in India, not only have we liberalised the industrial sector but have also opened up the economy, made our currency convertible and allowed exchange rate to adjust freely. It is important to understand the full implications of opening up the economy and allowing our currency to 'float'. It is worthwhile to note that under a fixed exchange rate system when citizens of a country spend some of their income on imports, it reduces the value of multiplier because imports, like savings and taxes, serve as a leakage from the circular flow of income. On the other hand, exports, like investment and Government expenditure, raise the aggregate demand for domestically produced goods and services and thereby cause an expansion in output through a multiplier process.

However, under a variable or floating exchange rate system, the effect of imports and exports on real output is highly complicated. First, the volume of imports and exports depends not only on income, price level, interest rate but also on the exchange rates themselves. Thus when due to some factors, foreign exchange rate changes, it will have an effect on the level of GNP and the price level. Further, exchange rates themselves will adjust to the changes in the economy. We discuss below the effects of changes in the exchange rate, especially of depreciations and devaluation of the exchange rate, on exports, imports, national income, balance of payments and the price level in the economy.

Effects of Depreciation (or Devaluation) on Imports, Exports and Real National Income

From our foregoing discussion of determination of exchange rate through demand and supply curves of foreign exchange it follows that when a currency of a country, say Indian rupee, depreciates as a result of demand and supply conditions or is devalued by the Government, the prices of Indian exports in terms of foreign currency (say dollar) will fall. This will cause the increase in quantity demanded of Indian exports. As a result, Indian exports will increase. On the other hand, depreciation or devaluation of Indian rupee will make the imports from foreign countries more expensive in terms of rupees (for example, a dollar's worth of US goods will cost more in terms of the Indian rupee) when the Indian rupee depreciates or is devalued. Thus, higher prices of imports will induce individuals and firms in India to import less and they will make an attempt to substitute domestically produced goods for imports from abroad. Thus, *as a result of depreciation or devaluation and consequently increase in exports and decline in imports, the net aggregate demand for domestically produced goods will increase.* And if level of output, especially industrial output is lower because of demand recession, the increase in net aggregate demand or increase in expenditure on domestic output will cause expansion in output and is therefore likely to increase GNP or real national income. This is illustrated in Fig. 28.6 where as a result of increase in net exports aggregate demand curve shifts to the right. As a result, given the short-run aggregate supply curve the levels of GDP (National income) and price level increases. Thus a *devaluation or depreciation can therefore serve as a stimulus to the economy.*

It will be recalled that in the Keynesian model of determination of real national income (GNP), the effect of net exports, that is, X–M, where X denotes value of exports and M denotes value of imports, is similar to investment in its effect on national income. Both raise national income through a multiplier process. It may be noted here that because of the favourable effect of depreciation or devaluation of currency on exports, imports and real GNP, the countries are tempted at times to intervene in the foreign exchange market, devalue their currency to provide stimulus to their economies. However, if one country devalues its currency to stimulate its economy, the other countries can also do so. Now, when all countries attempt to devalue their currencies, there will be no gain in real income for any of them. Such a situation actually occurred during the early years of Great Depression (1929-33). In their attempt to maintain their exports and protect their level of income and employment, many countries devalued their currencies without bothering about its adverse effects on the economies of the other countries. Such policies of competitive devaluation are generally called "**beggar-neighbour**" policies. Since all followed this beg thy-neighbour policy, no one could maintain their export sales and protect domestic employment and level of economic activity which were badly hurt by the severe depression that gripped their economies.

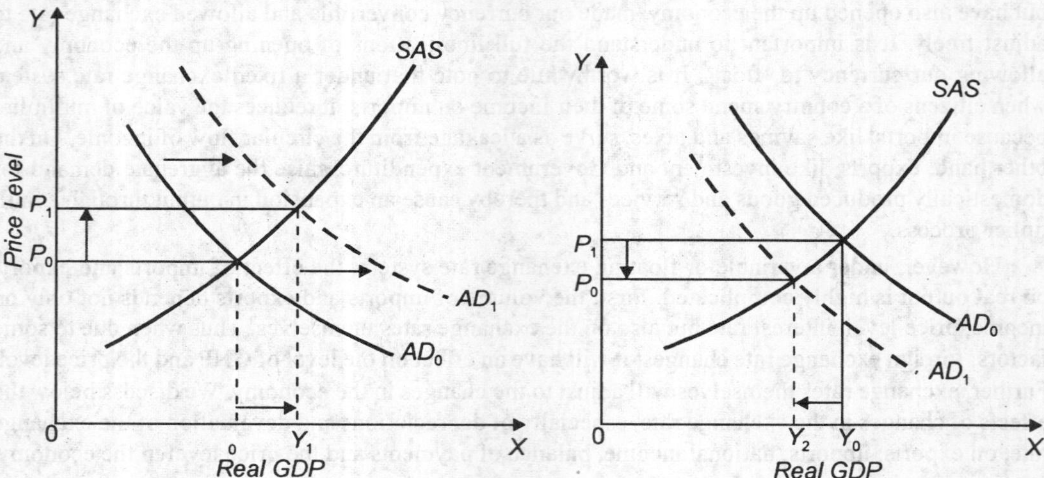

Fig. 28.6. *Depreciation causes net exports to rise which leads to the increase in both GDP and price level.*

Fig. 28.7. *Appreciation of national currency causes fall in net exports and leads to decline in both GDP and price level.*

On the contrary, the appreciation of a national currency will have opposite effect. When the currency of a country appreciates, its exports will become costlier causing a decline in them, whereas its imports will become cheaper resulting in increase in them. As a result net exports of the country will decline leading to the decrease in net exports and will therefore cause leftward shift in the aggregate demand curve *AD* as is shown in Fig. 28.7. This will cause fall in both real GDP and price level.

Devaluation and the Balance of Trade: The J Curve

As explained above lowering of the value of a currency of a country tends to raise its exports by making its goods cheaper for foreigners. On the other hand, devaluation or depreciation makes the imports from abroad expensive in terms of domestic currency (rupees in case of India) and therefore the imports tend to fall. *With exports increasing and imports declining, it is expected that devaluation (depreciation) will reduce a country's trade deficit.* As a matter of fact, in recent years when a country experienced a severe disequilibrium in the balance of trade or balance of payments, it devaluated its currency to raise exports and reduce imports and thus to restore equilibrium in the balance of payments. However, it may be noted that the effect of devaluation or depreciation on balance of trade is ambiguous and quite uncertain because a good deal depends on the price elasticity of exports and imports of a country. For example, if the *price-elasticity of exports* in terms of a foreign currency of a country is less than unity, the value of exports in terms of a foreign currency will fall as increase in physical volume of exports will be more than offset by the depreciation of the currency. On the other hand, if the demand for imports is inelastic; they will not decrease despite devaluation.

Many economists are of the view that devaluation is likely to worsen the balance of trade for the few quarters (probably three to six) after the initial devaluation. However, they think after a time lag, the balance of trade may improve. In fact, a concept called *J. Curve effect* has been put forward. According to this, after the initial depreciation the balance of trade moves according to the shape of the letter *J*. This means that in the first few quarters following devaluation the balance of trade becomes worse and after that it becomes positive and starts improving. This *J*-curve effect is shown in Fig. 28.8 where along the X-axis we measure time, that is, quarters after devaluation and on the Y -axis we measure the balance of trade. If the value of balance of trade is positive, that is, if the balance of trade lies above the zero line and the curve rises the balance of trade improves. If the balance of trade is negative, it will be below the zero line and if the curve slopes down, it implies that balance of trade worsens. It will be seen from Fig. 28.8 that in the first few quarters, the balance of trade remains negative and also deteriorating and then starts improving and ultimately in the long run turns positive.

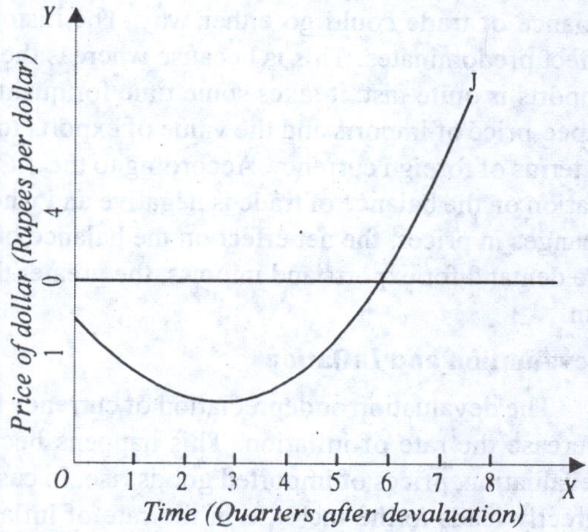

Fig. 28.8. *The Effect of Devaluation on the Balance of Trade : The J curve*

Now, pertinent question arises how the *J*-curve comes about. We will explain this with reference to devaluation (depreciation) of rupee. It may be recalled here that balance of trade is equal to the value of exports minus value of imports. Thus;

Balance of Trade = Value of Exports in Rupees – Value of Imports in Rupees

It may be noted that value of both exports and imports is equal to the volume of exports or imports multiplied by the rupee price of exports and imports respectively. The depreciation (devaluation) of the currency affects both the volume and rupee price of exports and imports. First, depreciation (devaluation) of currency increases the volume of exports and reduces the volume of imports, both of which have a favourable effect on the balance of trade, that is, they will lower the trade deficit or increase the trade surplus. This has been explained above. Secondly, as a result of devaluation, rupee-price of exports is not likely to change much in the short run. The rupee-price of exports depends on the domestic price level and, in the short run, the devaluation (depreciation) of rupee will have only a very small effect on the domestic price level. On the other hand, the rupee-price of imports increases immediately after devaluation. Imports into India from abroad would be more costly because as a result of devaluation a hundred rupee note will buy fewer US dollars and pound sterlings than before. Thus, *a rise in the rupee-price of imports has a negative effect on the balance of trade*, that is, it will tend to increase the trade deficit or reduce the trade surplus.

Price effect and quantity effect of devaluation. An example will make clear the negative effect of depreciation or devaluation on the balance of trade as a result of devaluation or depreciation. Suppose the rupee cost of a particular US machine goes up from ₹ 50,000 to 60,000 following the devaluation of rupee from ₹ 46 per dollar to ₹ 44 per dollar. Thus with the rise in price of a US machine, Indians *will spend more* on a US machine than before. This is a *price effect*. But increase in the price of the US machine will lead to *the decrease in the quantity demanded* of US machines by the Indians. This is the *quantity effect*. Now, the net effect of devaluation on the *value of imports* depends on whether quantity effect is larger than price effect or vice versa. And this depends on the price elasticity of imports. It therefore follows that net effect of devaluation (depreciation) on the balance of trade could go either way. The historical experience shows that initially the negative effect predominates. This is because whereas the effect of devaluation/depreciation on the price of imports is quite fast, it takes some time for quantity of imports to decline in response to the rise in rupee-price of imports and the value of exports to increase in response to the fall in price of exports in terms of foreign currency. According to the *J-Curve Effect*, the initial effect of devaluation/depreciation on the balance of trade is negative and when in the long run imports and exports adjust to the changes in prices, the net effect on the balance of trade becomes positive. The more price elastic is the demand for exports and imports, the greater the improvement in the balance of trade in the long run.

Devaluation and Inflation

The devaluation or depreciation of currency tends to raise the price level in the country and thus increase the rate of inflation. This happens because of two reasons. As a result of depreciation/devaluation, prices of imported goods rise. In case of imports of consumer goods rise in their prices directly leads to the increase in the rate of inflation. In case of imports of capital goods and raw materials, the rise in their import prices will not only directly raise the price level but as they are used as inputs in the production of other goods, rise in their imports prices will also push up the cost of production of these other goods and thus will bring about cost-push inflation.

Second, as explained above, depreciation makes the exports cheaper and therefore more competitive in the world markets. This causes the exports of goods to increase and reduces the supply and availability of goods in the domestic market which tends to raise the domestic price level. Besides, due to higher prices of imported goods, people of a country tend to substitute domestically produced goods for the now more expensive imports. As a result, the aggregate demand or expenditure on domestically produced goods and services will increase causing either expansion in output of goods or rise in their prices or both. However, if the economy is working close to the capacity output, the effect will be more on raising prices of goods.

FIXED EXCHANGE RATE AND THE BRETTON WOODS SYSTEM

Until a few years ago, there was fixed exchange rate system introduced during the last year of the Second World War. This fixed exchange rates system under Bretton Woods System of foreign exchange is known as the Bretton Woods System as a group of economists from the United States and Europe met at the Bretton Woods, a town in New Hampshire to devise this system. According to the agreement made there, an international organisation, called *International Monetary Fund* (IMF) was set up to administer the new fixed exchange rates system. According to the rules framed under the agreement, the USA was to fix a parity or par value for its dollar *in terms of gold*, whereas other countries were required to fix parities for their currencies *in terms of dollars*. Since US dollar was tied to gold, the currencies of other countries with fixed exchange rate with US dollar automatically got pegged (that is, fixed) with a certain gold value. The Government of the USA made a commitment to maintain the convertibility between dollar and gold at a fixed rate, whereas other countries agreed to maintain the convertibility of their currencies with US dollar. The

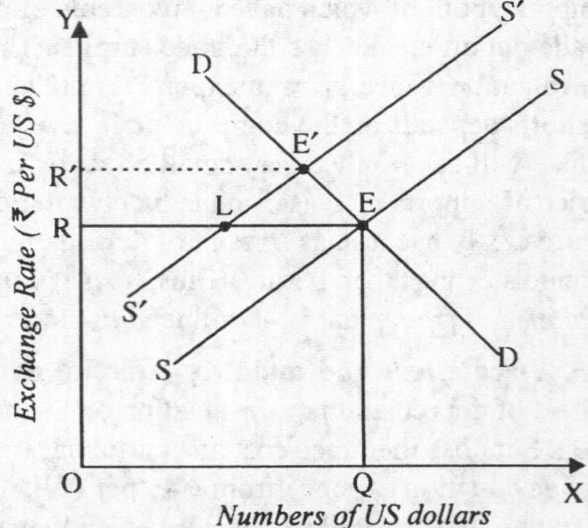

Fig. 28.9. *Government Intervention to Maintain the Exchange Rate at the Fixed Level*

USA fixed $35 per ounce of gold as the convertible rate. The change in these fixed exchange rates (devaluation or revaluation) was to be made with the consent of IMF in case of *fundamental disequilibrium* in the balance of payments. The Bretton Woods agreement did not define the fundamental disequilibrium but in practice it came to mean *chronic and large* deficit in the balance of payments. Therefore, when a country was experiencing a *large and persistent* deficit in balance of payments it was allowed by IMF to devalue its currency to the extent required to improve the balance of payments position. Thus, faced with the serious problem of balance of payments India devalued its rupee by 36.5 per cent in 1966. Again in July 1991, India devalued its rupee by about 20 per cent to tide over the serious foreign exchange crisis which arose due to deficits in balance of payments.

IMF maintains funds or reserves with itself which are contributed by member countries. IMF was given power to give loans to the member countries when they had short-term or temporary deficit in the balance of payments from its reserves. In case of fundamental disequilibrium its function was to advise the countries to devalue their currency to tide over the problem of deficit in balance of payments. The purpose was to achieve a relatively fixed or stable exchange rate system which was required for promotion of world trade.

It may be noted that, under Bretton Woods System, *to maintain the exchange rate at the specified level, the Governments (or their Central Banks) were to keep with themselves reserves of internationally accepted foreign currencies*. Thus gold, which in the previous years served as an international currency was substituted by reserves of foreign currencies that were widely used in international dealings. The US dollar became the important currency in which the reserves were to be kept by the other countries to maintain the exchange rate of their currency. Pound Sterlings, German Marks, Japanese Yen were also kept for this purpose.

To maintain the fixed exchange rate Bretton Woods System required the intervention by the Governments or their Central Banks. How they maintained the exchange value of their currency by using the reserves of foreign currencies is illustrated in Fig. 28.9 where the *demand and supply curves DD and SS of US dollars* are drawn. Along the *X*-axis the quantity of US dollars and on the *Y*-axis, the exchange rate of rupee in terms of US dollar is measured.

Suppose the Government of India is committed to maintain the exchange rate of its currency at *OR* level which is also assumed to be the equilibrium rate as determined by demand for and supply of rupees. Now, suppose due to the recessionary conditions the demand of the USA for Indian exports greatly declines. This will reduce the supply of US dollars causing a shift to the left of the supply curve of dollars to *S′S′*. Now, given the demand curve *DD* of dollars remaining unchanged, at fixed exchange rate *OR*, the quantity supplied of dollars falls to *RL* whereas quantity demanded of dollars continues to be *RE*. As a result, the excess demand for dollars emerges at the fixed exchange rate *OR* and, if left free to the market forces, the equilibrium exchange rate *will rise to OR′ level.* That is, price of US dollar in terms of rupees will appreciate or in other words, the Indian rupee will depreciate. *In order to maintain the exchange rate of rupee in terms of dollar, and to prevent it from depreciating, the Government or Reserve Bank of India must sell dollars from its foreign exchange reserves*. With the sufficient sale of dollars in the market, the supply curve of dollars will shift to the right to the original position *SS* which will restore the exchange rate *OR*. This is how the exchange rates of different countries remained fixed under Bretton Woods system despite the frequent changes in demand for and supply of their currencies.

Collapse of the Bretton Woods System

Fixed exchange rate system under the Bretton Woods arrangement came under heavy pressure during the sixties and it ultimately collapsed in the early seventies. As seen above, under the Bretton Woods System the US dollar became internationally accepted currency in which reserves of the countries were kept for international transactions. Before the Bretton Woods System gold was accepted as international medium of exchange. Under the Bretton Woods System, the US dollar also assumed the role of international currency for three reasons. First, after World War II, the United States emerged as the strongest economy. Secondly, the United States had accumulated a large stock of gold. Thirdly, during 1934 and 1971, the United States had been following the policy of selling and buying gold to other countries at a fixed exchange rate of $35 per ounce. As under the Bretton Woods System, the dollar was converted into gold at a fixed rate (that is, $35 per ounce), it was considered '*as good as gold*'.

Since the World's supply of gold did not increase adequately to meet the requirements of rapidly expanding international trade and finance, the dollar increasingly became the world currency in which international reserves were kept by various countries. But a serious problem arose which caused the demise of Bretton Woods system. The United States had a large and persistent deficit in balance of payments during the fifties and sixties. To meet these deficits, the US used its gold reserves for making payments to other countries, especially Germany and Japan. Obviously, this could not go on for ever because its gold reserves would have eventually run out. In fact, this was the big flaw in the fixed exchange rate system adopted under the Bretton Woods arrangement. Further, as a result of surplus balance of payments with the United States, other countries, especially Germany and Japan, acquired not only gold but also a large quantity of the dollars from the US which were kept as reserves.

With the passage of time reserves of dollars and gold held by other countries increased very much while the reserves of gold with USA declined a great deal, the doubts arose about the ability of the USA to fulfil its commitments of converting dollars into gold at the agreed exchange rate of $35 per ounce. Widespread fears emerged that there would be run on the dollar, that is, countries holding dollars would *en masse* try to exchange dollars for gold. If it had actually happened it would have greatly hurt the international trade and finance. Therefore, in view of the large and persistent deficit in balance of payments, it was decided by the US Government to withdraw convertibility of dollar into gold at the rate of $35 per ounce on August 15, 1971. This brought about the collapse of the Bretton Woods System which was supported by the US commitment to convert dollar into gold at a fixed rate. With this the link between gold and international value of the dollar ended and consequently the *dollar was floated*, that is, permitted its exchanged rate with other currencies to be determined by market forces.

FIXED AND FLEXIBLE EXCHANGE RATES

A study of economic history shows that three different exchange rate systems have been prevailing in the world economy. The first exchange rate system, popularly called *Gold Standard* prevailed over 1879-1934 period with the exception of World War I years. Under the gold standard, currencies of different countries were tied to gold (that is, the value of currency of each country was fixed in terms of a certain quantity of gold). With this the exchange rate between different countries got automatically fixed. Thus, the gold standard represented fixed exchange rate system. As explained above, from the end of World War II to 1971, another fixed exchange rate system, generally known as Bretton Woods System prevailed. Under this the US dollar was tied to a certain quantity of gold and the currencies of other countries were tied to dollar or in some countries directly to gold. However, as seen above, in 1971 due to large and persist deficit in balance of payments of the United States. Bretton Woods system also broke down. Since then, the *flexible* or what is also called *floating exchange rate system* has been existing. But even in this flexible or floating exchange rates the Government (or the Central Bank) of the countries intervenes to keep the international value of their currencies (i.e., exchanges rate) within certain limits. Therefore, even in the post 1971 period, the exchange rate system is not *purely* flexible and has therefore been called **Managed Float System**. We discuss below the merits and demerits of the fixed and flexible exchange rate system.

Merits of Fixed Exchange Rate System

Exchange Rate Stability. In defence of fixed exchange rate system, it has been pointed out that it ensures stability in exchange rate. Exchange rate stability, it is said, is necessary for orderly development of the international economy and rapid growth of world trade. If the exchange rate is unstable or variable, the exporters will not be certain about the price they would receive for the goods to be exported by them; the importers will not be certain about the price and the payments they have to make for their imports. These uncertainties involve risks for exporters and importers. This greatly harms the growth of world trade. Thus, the chief merit of fixed exchange rate system is that it eliminates the possibilities of such uncertainties and associated risks and thereby promotes foreign trade.

It is important to note that for the developing countries a stable or fixed exchange rate system has a special advantage. This is because the developing countries have a large and persistent balance of payment deficits. As a consequence, if the exchange rate is flexible and not fixed, due to these large persistent deficits, the exchange rate or international value of their currencies will be continuously falling. Thus fixed exchange rate system prevents this continuous tendency for the depreciation of their currencies.

Promotes Capital Movements. Another advantage of fixed exchange rate is that it facilitates capital movement by private firms. A stable currency does not involve any uncertainties about capital loss on account of changes in exchange rate. Therefore, fixed exchange rate system would attract foreign capital investments. Foreign private firms would not be interested in making investment in those countries whose currency is not stable. Since foreign investment is an important source of economic growth, the fixed exchange rate system would promote rapid economic growth of the developing countries.

Prevents capital outflow. Further, flexible and unstable exchange rates may at times of difficult economic situation may encourage *flight of capital*, as happened in case of Mexico a few years ago causing a serious balance of payments problem. On the other hand, a stable exchange rate ensures that such capital outflow would not occur.

Prevents Speculation in foreign exchange market. Another important merit of fixed exchange rate system is that it does away with speculation in foreign exchange markets. The advocates of fixed exchange rate system points out that the flexible and unstable exchange rate encourages speculation in foreign exchange market. The operators in foreign exchange market try to take advantage of the fluctuations in exchange rate as freely determined by demand and supply forces. They try to manipulate the exchange rate through their actions of buying and selling foreign exchange and try to obtain speculative gain in this way. Ragnar Nurkse in his study of *International Currency Experience* which he conducted for the period of twenties found that because of speculative activities, flexible exchange rate had a destabilising influence. It caused greater fluctuations than would have been the case otherwise. By eliminating speculation fixed exchange rate system ensures stability in the exchange rate.

Serves as an anchor against inflation. Another important advantage of fixed exchange rate system is that it prevents the Government of the countries from adopting inflationary policies. Generally, Governments have often been tempted to pursue undue expansionary fiscal and monetary policies to lower unemployment and create boom conditions. However, inflation has several bad effects for the economies. It increases inequalities of income and wealth and hurts the poor most. Further, inflation hampers economic growth in the long run. Fixed exchange rate system forces the Governments to achieve price stability by taking effective anti-inflationary measures. This is because in the case of fixed exchange rate, inflation will cause balance of payments deficits and

---

1. B.Soderston, *International Economics*, 2nd edition, Macmillan, 1980, p. 402.

result in loss of international reserves. Therefore, this forces the Government to adopt measures to check inflationary pressures in the economy. To quote B. Soderston, "Fixed exchange rates can serve as an anchor. Inflation will cause balance of payments deficits and losses in reserves. Hence the authorities will have to take counter measures to stop inflation. Fixed exchange rates should therefore impose a discipline on governments and stop them from pursuing inflationary policies which are out of tune with the rest of the world."[1]

Promotes economic integration of the world. It has also been argued in favour of fixed exchange rate system that it is necessary for achieving economic integration of the world community. This is similar to a single common currency in a country which promotes economic integration of a nation in the sense that it facilitates communication, trade and free movement of finance between different regions of a country. It ensures free competition among all producers and consumers of various countries. Similarly, a common currency would promote economic integration of the world. Fixed exchange rate between the currencies of the various countries approximately serves the purpose of a single currency between diferent countries. Thus, fixed exchange rates among different currencies is a necessary condition for the purpose of *forming economic union* between various countries, that is, forming a regional grouping. To enjoy the advantages of economic unity in recent years, there is a proposal for issuing a single currency for European countries to strengthen the economic integration of European countries.

Promotes growth of internal money and capital markets. Another big advantage of the fixed exchange rate system is that it promotes growth of internal money and capital markets. Since flexible exchange rates cause uncertainties about the future exchange rates, individuals, companies and institutions are reluctant to lend to and borrow from the internal money and capital markets.

In view of the above advantages, a fixed exchange rate system prevailed for a long time from 1944 to 1971. As we have seen above that the Bretton Woods aggreement adopted a fixed exchange rate system because of the above mentioned merits, IMF permitted a change in the exchange rate only in case of fundamental disequlibrium in the balance of payments.

Demerits and Problems of Fixed Exchange Rate System

Fixed exchange rate had however a great flaw in that the countries with a large and persistent balance of payments deficits were losing gold and other foreign assets. This could not go on forever as evidently stock of gold and foreign currencies would have run out. That is why the USA abandoned Bretton Woods System which represented fixed exchange rate system. The other countries facing problem of balance of payment deficit found their international reserves dwindling which forced them to devalue their currency. The devaluation has an inflationary potential.

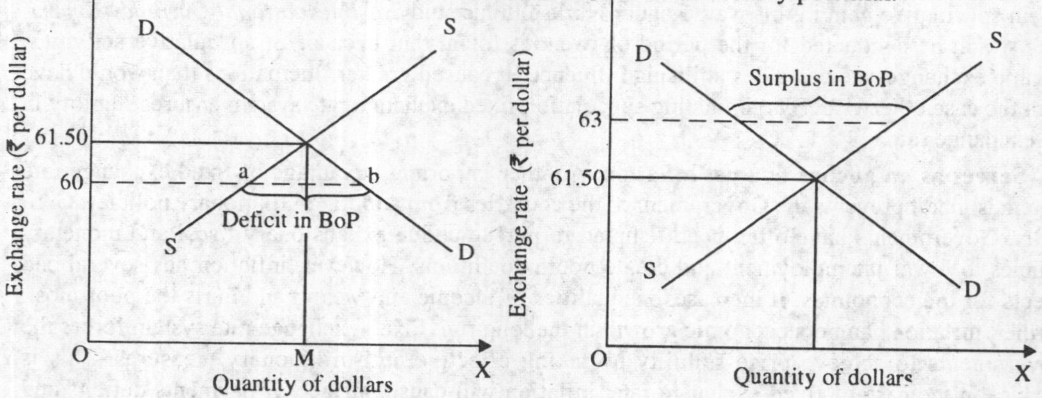

Fig. 28.10. *Overvaluation of a Currency Cuasing Deficit in BoP.*

Fig. 28.11. *Undervaluation of a Currency Leading to the Problem of Surplus in BoP.*

On the other hand, under the fixed exchange rates, the countries with a balance of payments surplus will be providing its national currency and in return it will receive foreign currencies and assets such as US dollar, pounds, gold. The increase in foreign assets would lead to the expansion in money supply which is likely to create inflationary pressures in the economy. But remember an important difference between the countries with balance of payments deficits and the countries having balance of payment surplus. Whereas due to depletion of reserves of gold and foreign currencies, the countries with deficit balance of payments are forced to *devalue* their currency to overcome the deficit, the countries with a balance of payments surplus generally do not *revalue* their currency for the fear that it would discourage exports. Instead, the countries with surplus BoP face the problem of inflation and try to tackle it with other policies.

Another problem with the fixed exchange rate system is that *at what level exchange rate should be fixed*. If the exchange rate of a foreign currency with a national currency is fixed or pegged at the equilibrium level, that is, at the rate at which its quantity demanded equals quantity supplied, no problem arises. However, for the Government it is difficult to find such an equilibrium exchange rate of a foreign currency in terms of the national currency. Further, as underlying conditions change as they do so frequently, the equilibrium exchange rate will also change giving rise to the problems. If the exchange rate of a national currency in terms of the foreign currency, say US dollar, is fixed at a higher level, there will be deficit in the balance of payments (BoP). On the other hand, if the exchange rate of a national currency in terms of US dollar is fixed at a lower than the equilibrium level, there will be surplus in balance of payments (BoP). Consider Fig. 28.10, where demand and supply curves of dollars respectively for India are drawn. ₹ 61.50 to a US dollar is the equilibrium exchange rate. If the Government or Reserve Bank of India fixes the exchange rate at a higher rate, say ₹ 60 to a US dollar as the exchange rate, the quantity demanded of dollars by Indians would exceed the quantity supplied so that there would be deficit in India's balance of payments. This means that at ₹ 60 to a dollar *Indian rupee is overvalued*. As a result, India's stock of foreign exchange (*i.e.*, dollars) and other foreign assets will decline. Sooner or later India will be forced to take policy measures to correct this deficit in BoP. India will have to adopt contractionary fiscal and monetary policies to reduce aggregate expenditure in the economy so that imports decrease or it will impose various restrictions on imports to reduce them. With the reduction in imports through these policy measures demand curve of dollars in Fig. 28.10 will shift to the left and may interested the supply curve *SS* at point *a* to be in equilibrium at the exchange rate of ₹ 60 to a dollar. To reduce persistent deficit in BoP, it may even resort to devaluation if it has a fixed exchange rate system.

Now, consider Fig. 28.11 if the Government fixes the exchange rate of rupee at a lower rate, say ₹ 63 per US dollar, the quantity supplied of dollars by other countries would exceed the quantity demanded by the Indians. As ₹ 63 per US a dollar, the *Indian rupee is under-valued* (or, which is the same thing, *dollar is overvalued* in terms of rupees). Historical experience shows that countries with surplus in BoP have been reluctant to *revalue* their currency (that is, to raise the international value of their currency). Thus, a *surplus in balance of payments also gives rise to a problem*. As a result of this surplus due to under-valuation of the rupee, India will accumulate dollars (*i.e.*, foreign exchange) for which it would pay rupees, the national currency. The new rupee notes would be printed to pay for dollars. Thus, surplus in BoP leads to the expansion in money supply generating inflationary pressures in the Indian economy. To check inflation, the Indian Government might therefore take steps to eliminate the surplus in BoP by encouraging imports or restricting exports. Further, it may try to take steps to neutralise the impact of surplus in BoP on expansion in money supply. For this purpose, it might encourage *capital outflows* (*i.e.*, investment abroad) by private firms or provide concessional financial assistance to other countries.

In view of the above drawbacks and problems the fixed exchange rate system has been given up despite its various advantages explained above.

Merits of Flexible Exchange Rates System

Under the flexible exchange rate system, exchange rate between different currencies, like the prices of commodities are freely determined by market forces, that is, by demand and supply forces. With the change in economic conditions underlying demand and supply, the exchange rate will automatically change without any intervention by the Government. That is why, it is called flexible or variable exchange rate system. It has the following merits.

Problems of undervaluation and overvaluation are avoided. The advocates of flexible exchange rates contend that under it the problems of undervaluation and overvaluation of currencies which are found in the fixed exchange rate system are avoided. Whenever there is deficit in balance of payments implying overvaluation of the national currency under the flexible exchange rates, it will depreciate (that is, its value will fall) which on the one hand will make exports cheaper and thereby encourage them and on the other will make the imports costlier than before which will tend to discourage them. Thus, increase in exports and decline in imports as a result of depreciation will lead to the automatic correction in the balance of payments.

On the other hand, whenever there is surplus in the balance of payments, the exchange rate will appreciate which will tend to reduce exports and raise imports. This again will tend to automatically restore the balance of payments equilibrium. This is how the flexible exchange system works to ensure the equilibrium in the balance of payments. To quote Prof. Soderston, "The same factors which under the fixed rates give rise to deficits and surpluses in the balance of payments would under floating rates make the exchange rate depreciate or appreciate. Thereby equilibrium would be preserved and the Government could be freed from consideration regarding external balance".

Promotes growth of multilateral Trade. The advocates of flexible exchange rates system are strongly of the view that as unlike fixed exchange rates system, this does not create serious and difficult problems, it will ensure rapid growth of multilateral world trade.[2] Further, they point out that promotion of world trade under the flexible exchange rates would not interfere in any way the adoption of policies to achieve domestic economic stability.[3]

Flexible exchange rates does not necessarily show large fluctuations. It has been pointed out in defence of the flexible exchange rates that the problems of undervalued or overvalued currency found under the fixed exchange rate regime are not found in the flexible exchange rate system. Further, it is contended that exchange rates being flexible does not necessarily mean there will be large fluctuations in them. Even under flexible exchange system there need not be large fluctuations in exchange rates. According to them, changes in exchange rates will occur only when economic conditions underlying demand for and supply of foreign currencies change. Further, according to them, random fluctuations around the normal exchange rates would be smoothened out through operations by private speculators. Thus, according to Soderston "if the currency appreciated above its equilibrium value, if its price fell in terms of foreign currency, speculators would buy the currency; and if it depreciated, speculators would sell the currency. Thereby they would smooth out fluctuations and help to keep the exchange rate stable. If the underlying conditions changed, however the price of foreign exchange would also change."

It ensures individual freedom. The system of floating exchange rate is advocated on the basis of philosophy that Government should intervene in the economy as little as possible and the individuals should be left free to pursue their economic interests. It has been noted above, the alternative to floating exchange rates system is the fixed exchange rates which require controls and restrictions which are implemented by experts who generally do not work under effective democratic controls.

2. See Miltion Friedman, 'The Case for flexible Exchange Rate', AEA, *Readings in International Economics*, Vol. XI.
3. *Ibid.*

Generally, they fix the exchange rate out of consideration for other than economic objectives, for example for the purpose of retaining a certain market structure or influencing income distribution.

It frees the Government from problems of balance of payments. A great merit of flexible exchange rates is that it frees the Government from problems of balance of payments. As has been seen above, the fixed exchange rates system leads either to deficit or surplus in balance of payments. Under this system the Government remains preoccupied with the questions of devaluation or revaluation of their currencies. Since floating exchange rates work automatically to restore balance of payments equilibrium, the Government need not pay any attention to the balance of payments. Instead, the Governments can concentrate on solving their domestic problems of economic stability, inflation and unemployment. "Flexible exchange rates should therefore give an increased freedom both to individuals and countries to pursue whatever aims they have for their economic policies."[4]

Demerits of Flexible Exchange Rate System

Flexible exchange rates system is also not without shortcomings. It has been opposed on some important grounds. We briefly explain below some important arguments given against flexible exchange rates.

1. Flexible Exchange Rates Create a Situation of Instability and Uncertainty. An important argument against flexible exchange rates is that too frequent fluctuations in exchange rate under it create uncertainty about the exact amount of receipts and payments in foreign exchange transactions. *This instability hampers foreign trade and capital movements between the countries.* However, Friedman does not accept this charge against flexible exchange rates. He argues that flexible exchange rate is not necessarily an unstable exchange rate. According to him, it is the underlying economic conditions determining foreign trade that often change causing changes in the foreign exchange rate and for this the flexible exchange rates should not be blamed.

2. Dampening Effect on Foreign Trade. Under the flexible exchange rates, the price of foreign exchange or international value of the national currency is quite uncertain. As a result, they are unable to take proper decisions regarding exports and imports of goods. Obviously, this has a dampening effect on the volume and growth of foreign trade. However, Friedman does not agree with this and points out that traders can always protect themselves against risks arising out of the changes in the exchange rate by hedging in the future market.[5] However, Soderston has challenged this view of Friedman and points out that no markets exist today that can protect traders against risks arising out of flexible exchange rates.[6]

It may however be noted that from the empirical evidence since 1971 when exchange rates have been flexible, it does not appear that flexible exchange rates have a dampening effect on the growth of foreign trade. In fact, the growth of world trade since 1971 has been fairly good.

3. Widespread Speculation with a Destabilising Effect. The system of flexible exchange rates has been opposed on the ground that under it there is widespread speculation regarding exchange rates of currencies which has a large destabilising effect on these rates. Friedman, on the other hand, contend that *speculation has a stabilising influence on exchange rates*. However, whether or not speculation has a destablising or stabilising effect is a highly controversial issue in economics which has so far remained unresolved.

4. Provides an inflationary bias to an economy. Another shortcoming of the flexible, exchange rates is that they have an inflationary impact on the economy. It has been pointed out that whenever due to deficit in balance of payments, the currency depreciates, the prices of imports go up. The higher prices of imported materials raise the prices of industrial products and thus generate

4. B. Soderston, *op. cit.*
5. Milton Friedman, *op. cit*
6. B. Soderston, *op. cit.*, p. 303.

cost-push inflation. However, in defence of flexible exchange rates, it has been pointed out that when demand for imports decline due to appreciation of national currency, the *foreign suppliers are compelled to reduce their prices* to protect markets. Through this reduction in prices in the face of declining demand is theoretically possible, it may not happen in actual practice.

To sum up, there are merits and demerits of flexible exchange rate system. Whether a flexible exchange rate systems suits an economy depends on circumstances. It depends on characteristics of the economy which adopts flexible exchange rate system. Further, it may be noted that since 1971 when Bretton Woods System representing the fixed exchange rate system was abandoned, it is not perfectly free flexible exchange rate system that has been adopted. Instead, it is what is called *Managed Float System* that has been prevailing. Under the managed float systém, the exchange rates are flexible, that is, they change as a result of changes in demand and supply of currencies, but the Government or Central Bank intervenes through demand and supply to keep the variations in exchange rate within certain limits so as to ensure stability and certainty of the foreign exchange rates.

CURRENCY CONVERTIBILITY

For the rapid growth of world trade and capital flows between countries convertibility of a currency is desirable. Without free and unrestricted convertibility of currencies into foreign exchange trade and capital flows between countries cannot take place smoothly. Therefore, to achieve higher rate of economic growth and thereby to improve living standards through greater trade and capital flows, the need for convertibility of currencies of different nations has been greatly felt. Under Bretton Woods system fixed exchange rate system was adopted by various countries. In order to maintain the exchange rate of their currencies in terms of dollar or gold various countries imposed several controls over the use of foreign exchange. This required some restrictions on the use of foreign exchange and its allocation among different uses, the currency of a nation was converted into foreign exchange on the basis of officially fixed exchange rate.

When Bretton Woods system collapsed in 1971, the various countries switched over to the floating foreign exchange rate system. Under the floating or flexible exchange rate system, exchange rates between different national currencies are allowed to the determined through market demand for and supply of them. However, various countries still imposed restrictions on the free convertibility of their currencies in view of their difficult balance of payment situation.

Meaning of Currency Covertibility

Let us first explain what is exactly meant by currency convertibility. By convertibility of a currency we mean currency of a country can be freely converted into foreign exchange at *market determined rate of exchange*, that is, exchange rate as determined by demand for and supply of a currency. For example, convertibility of rupee means that those who have foreign exchange (*e.g.* US dollars, Pound Sterlings etc.) can get them converted into rupees and vice-versa at the market determined rate of exchange. Under convertibility of a currency there are authorised dealers of foreign exchange which constitute foreign exchange market. The exporters and others who recieve US dollars, Pound Sterlings etc. can go to these dealers which are generally banks and get their dollars exchanged for rupees at the market determined rates of exchange. Similarly, under currency covertibility, importers and other who require foreign exchange can go to these banks dealing in foreign exchange and get rupees converted into foreign exchange.

Current Account and Capital Account Convertibility of Currency

A currency may be convertible on current account (that is, exports and imports of merchandise and invisibles) only. A currency may be convertible on both current and capital accounts. We have explained above the convertibility of a currency on current account only.

By capital account convertibility we mean that in respect of capital flows, that is, flows of portfolio capital, direct investment flows, flows of borrowed funds and dividends and interest payable on them, a currency is freely convertible into foreign exchange and vice-versa at market determined exchange rate. Thus, by convertibility of rupee on capital account means those who bring in foreign exchange for purchasing stocks, bonds in Indian stock markets or for direct investment in power projects, highways steel plants etc. can get them freely converted into rupees without taking any permission from the government. Likewise, the dividends, capital gains, interest received on purchased stock, equity etc. profits earned on direct investment get the rupees converted into US dollars, Pound Sterlings at market determined exchange rate between these currencies and repatriate them. Since capital convertibility is risky and makes foreign exchange rate more volatile, is introduced only some time after the introduction of convertibility on current account when exchange rate of currency of a country is relatively stable, deficit in balance of payments is well under control and enough foreign exchange reserves are available with the Central Bank.

Convertibility of Indian Rupee

In the seventies and eighties many countries switched over to the free convertibility of their currencies into foreign exchange. By 1990,70 countries of the world had introduced currency convertibility on current account, another 10 countries joined them in 1991.

As a part of new economic reforms initiated in 1991 rupee was made partly convertible from March 1992 under the "*Liberalised Exchange Rate Management*" scheme in which 60 per cent of all receipts on current account (*i.e.* merchandise exports and invisible receipts) could be converted freely into rupees at market determined exchange rate quoted by authorised dealers, while 40 per cent of them was to be surrendered to Reserve Bank of India at the officially fixed exchange rate. These 40 per cent exchange receipts on current account was meant for meeting Government needs for foreign exchange and for financing imports of essential commodities. Thus, partial convertibility of rupee on current account meant a *dual exchange rate system*. This partial convertibility of rupee on current account was adopted so that essential imports could be made available at lower exchange rate to ensure that their prices do not rise much. Further, full convertibility of rupees at that stage was considered to be risky in view of large deficit in balance of payments on current account.

As even after partial convertibility of rupee foreign exchange value of rupee remained stable, *full convertibility on current account* was announced in the budget for 1993-94. From March 1993, rupee was made convertible for *all trade in merchandise*. In March 1994, even indivisibles and remittances from abroad were allowed to be freely convertible into rupees at market determined exchange rate. However, on capital account rupee remained nonconvertible.

Advantages of Currency Convertibility

Convertibility of a currency has several advantages which we discuss briefly :

1. **Encouragement to exports.** An important advantage of currency convertibility is that it encourages exports by increasing their profitability. With convertibility profitablility of exports increases because market foreign exchange rate is higher than the previous officially fixed exchange rate. This implies that from given exports, exporters can get more rupees against foreign exchange (*e.g.* US dollars) earned from exports. Currency convertibility especially encourages those exports which have low import-intensity.

2. **Encouragement to import substitution**. Since free or market determined exchange rate is higher than the previous officially fixed exchange rate, imports become more expensive after convertibility of a currency. This discourages imports and give boost to import substitution.

3. **Incentive to send remittances from abroad.** Thirdly, rupee convertibility provided greater incentives to send remittances of foreign exchange by Indian workers living abroad and by NRI. further, it makes illegal remittance such '*hawala money*' and smuggling of gold less attractive.

4. **A self - balancing mechanism.** Another important merit of currency convertibility lies in its self-balancing mechanism. When balance of payments is in deficit due to over-valued exchange rate, under currency convertibility, the currency of the country depreciates which gives boost to exports by lowering their prices on the one hand and discourages imports by raising their prices on the other. In this way, deficit in balance of payments get automatically corrected without intervention by the Government or its Central bank. The opposite happens when balance of payments is in surplus due to the under-valued exchange rate.

5. **Specialisation in accordance with comparative advantage.** Another merit of currency convertibility ensures production pattern of different traditng countries in accordance with their comparative advantage and resource endowment. It is only when there is currency convertibility that market exchange rate truly reflects the purchasing powers of their currencies which is based on the prices and costs of goods found in different countries. Since prices in comeptitive environment reflect that prices of those goods are lower in which the country has a comaparative advantage, this will encourages exports. On the other hand, a country will tend to import those goods in the production of which it has a comparative disadvantage. Thus, currency convertibility ensures specialisation and international trade on the basis of comparative advantage from which all countries derive benefit.

6. **Integration of World Economy.** Finally, currency convertibility gives boost to the integration of the world economy. As under currency convertibility there is *easy access to foreign exchange*, it greatly helps the growth of trade and capital flows between the countries. The expansion in trade and capital flows between countries will ensure rapid economic growth in the economies of the world. In fact, currency convertibility is said to be a prerequisite for the success of gloabilisation.

Capital Account Convertibility of Rupee

As explained above, under Capital Account Convertibility any Indian or Indian company is entitled to move freely from the Rupee to another currency to convert Indian financial assets into foreign financial assets and back, *at an exchange rate fixed by the foreign exchange market and not by RBI*. In a way, capital account convertibility removes all the restrains on international flows on India's capital account. There is a basic difference between current account convertibility and capital account convertibility. In the case of current account convertibility, it is important to have a transaction – importing and exporting of goods,buying and selling of services, inward or outward remittances, etc. involving payment or receipt of one currency against another currency. *In the case of capital account convertibility, a currency can be converted into any other currency without any transaction.*

The Reserve Bank of India appointed in 1997 the Committee on Capital Account Convertibility with Mr. S.S. Tarapore, former Deputy Governor of RBI as its chairman. Tarapore Committee defined capital account convertibility as the freedom to convert local financial assets with foriegn financial assets and vice-versa at market determined rate of exchange. In simple language, capital account convertibility allows any one to freely move from local currency into foreign currency and back. *The purpose of capital convertibility is to give foreign investors an easy marekt to move in and* move out and to send a strong message that Indian economy was strong enough and that India had sufficient forex reserves to meet any flight of capital from the country to any extent.

The Benefits of Capital Account Convertibility

The Tarapore Committee mentioned the following benefits of capital account convertibility to India.

1.availibility of large funds to supplement domestic resources and thereby promote economic growth.

2. improved access to international financial markets and reduction in cost of capital.

3. incentive for Indians to acquire and hold international securities and assets, and

4. improvement of the financial system in the context of global competition.

Accordingly, the Tarapore Committee recommended the adoption of capital account convertibility. Under the system of capital account convertibility proposed by this committee the following features are worth mentioning :

(a) Indian companies would be allowed to issue foreign currency denominated bonds to local investors to invest in such bonds and deposits, to issue Global Deposit Receipts (GDRs) without approval of the RBI or Government to go in for external commercial borrowings within certain limits, etc.

(b) Indian residents would be permitted to have foreign currency denominated deposits with banks in India, to make financial capital transfers to other countries within certain limits, to take loans from non-relatives and others upto a ceiling of $ 1 million, etc.

(c) Indian banks would be allowed to borrow from overseas markets for short-term and long-term upto certain limits, to invest in overseas money markets, to accept deposits and extend loans denominated in foreign currency. Such facilities would be available to financial institutions and financial intermediaries also.

(d) All-India financial institutions which fulfil certain regulatory and prudential requirements would be allowed to participate in foreign exchange market along with authorised dealers (ADs) who are, at present, banks.In a later stage, certain select NBFCs would also be permitted to act as authorised dealers in foreign exchange market.

(e) Banks and financial institutions would be allowed to operate in domestic and international markets and they would also be allowed to buy and sell gold freely and offer gold denominated deposits and loans.

Preconditions for Capital Account Convertibility

The Tarapore Committee recommended that, before adopting capital account convertibility (CAC), India should fulfil three crucial pre-conditions :

(i) **Fiscal deficit** should be reduced to 3.5 per cent. The Government should also set up a Consolidated Sinking Fund (CSF) to reduce Government debt.

(ii) The Governments should fix the annual inflation target between 3 to 5 per cent. This was called *mandated inflation target* — and give full freedom to RBI to use monetary weapons to achieve the inflation target.

(iii) The Indian financial sector should be strengthened. For this, interest rates should be fully deregulated, gross non-performing assets (NPAs) should be reduced to 5 per cent, the average effective cash reserve ratio (CRR) should be reduced to 3 per cent and weak banks should either be liquidated or be merged with other strong banks.

Apart from these thee essential pre-conditions, the Tarapore Committee also recommended that :

(a) RBI should have a monitoring exchange rate band of 5 per cent around Real Effective Exchange Rate (REER) and should intereven only when the real exchange rate (RER) is outside the band :

(b) The size of the current account deficit should be within manageable limits and the debt service ratio should be gradually reduced from the present 25 per cent to 20 per cent of the export earnings :

(c) To meet import and debt service payments, forex reserves should be adequate and range between $ 22 billion and $ 32 billion; and

(d) The Government should remove all restrictions on the movement of gold.

It was generally agreed that full convertibility of the rupee, both on current account and capital account was a welcome measure and ***is necessary for closer integration of the Indian economy with the global economy***.

The major difficulty with the Tarapore Committee recommendation was that it would like the capital account convertibility to be achieved in a 3 year period – 1998 to 2000. The period was too short and the pre-conditions and the macroeconomic indicators could not be achieved in such short period. Basically, the Committee failed to appreciate the political instability in the country at that time, and the complete absence of political will and vision to carry forward the process of economic reforms and economic liberalisation. The outbreak of Asian financial crisis at this time was also responsobile for shelving the recommendation of Tarapore Committee.

Conclusion

In a speech at RBI on March 18, 2006, Prime Minister Dr. Manmohan Singh stated: "Given the changes that have taken place during the last two decades, there is merit in moving towards fuller capital account convertibility with a transparent framework... I will, therefore, request the Finance Minister and RBI to revisit the subject and come out with a roadmap based on current realities." Promptly, within two days RBI constituted the "**Comittee on Fuller Capital Account Convertibility**" with S.S. Tarapore again as chairman. This Tarapore Committee submitted its report in September 2006 (more commonly called the Second Tarapore Report).

The second Tarapore Committee had drawn up a roadmap for 2011 as the target date for fuller capital convertibility of rupee and mentioned that the conditions were quite favourable. These conditions were

1. Strong fundamentals of the Indian economy
2. A good amount of foreign exchange reserves of $ 165 million that existed in 2006.
3. More liberalised use of foreign exchange already in place.
4. A financial system better geared to deal with external capital flows

The fuller capital convertibility of rupee seemed to be desirable at the end of 2006 when the committee submitted its report. However, economic events, especially global financial crisis of 2007-09, broughly about a sea change in the economic situation. The Indian economy would have been greatly affected by the global financial crisis if we had implemented the recommendations of Tarapore Committee recommendations. We could not have coped with the extent of capital outflows that took place during 2008-09.

Problems

It may be noted that convertibility of currency can give rise to some problems. Firstly, since market determined exchange rate has been generally higher than the previous officially fixed exchange rate, prices of essential imports rise which may generate cost-push inflation in the economy. Secondly, if currency convertibility is not properly managed and monitored, market exchange rate may lead to the *depreciation of domestic currency*. If a currency depreciates heavily, the confidence in it is shaken and no one will accept it in its transactions. As a result, trade and capital flows in the country are adversely affected.

Thirdly, convertibility of a currency sometimes makes it highly volatile. Further, operations by speculators make it more volatile. Further, operations by speculators make it more volatile and unstable. When due to speculative activity, a currency depreciates and confidence in it is shaken there is capital fight from the country as it happened in 1997-98 in case of South East Asian economies such as Thailand, Malaysia, Indonesia, Singapore and South Korea. This adversely affects economic growth of the economy. In the context of heavy depreciation of the currency not only there is capital flight but inflow of capital in the economy is discouraged as due to depreciation of the currency profitability of investment in an economy is adversely affected.

Managed Float System in India

It is important to note that India as most of other countries including USA, Great Britain, France, there is at present flexible or floating exchange rate system. Besides, like other countries India has not adopted a perfectly flexible or floating exchange rate system. The changes in exports and imports, capital outflows and capital inflows bring about a large fluctuations in foreign exchange rate of rupee. It may be noted that large depreciation or appreciation of exchange rate adversely affects the economy, especially its exports and imports. In order to prevent large appreciation and depreciation of Indian rupee, Reserve Bank of India often invervenes to ensure that exchange rate should remain within reasonable limits. When the rupee is depreciating too much, Reserve Bank of India intervenes and sells dollars from its reserves of foreign exchange. This increases the supply of dollars in the market and prevents the depreciation of the rupee.

On the other hand, when rupee is appreciating too much, Reserve Bank of India intervenes and buys dollars from the market. This redcues the supply of dollars in foreign exchange market which prevents the appreciation of exchange rate of rupee. Therefore, through the intervention by Reserve Bank of India, exchange rate of rupee is not allowed to change beyond certain limits. Therefore, such a system that has been adopted by India is not completely flexible or floating exchange rate system. Therefore, it is called *managed float system*.

ANALYSIS OF SOME EXCHANGE RATE CONCEPTS

As the Indian economy gets more integrated with the world economy (that is, has extensive trade and capital flows with the rest of the world), exchange rate of rupee with foreign currencies will play a very important role as it will determine competitiveness of Indian goods and services in the international markets. The rupee has different exchange rates with foreign currencies of its various trade partners. A bilateral exchange rate with a foreign currency, say the US dollar, in nominal terms is not a good exchange rate with which to measure the competitiveness of the rupee. Further, the exchange rate of rupee with a single currency in nominal terms would not measure the differences in changes in prices and costs in the domestic economy as compared to the changes in prices in all the trade partners. To deal with this issue the effective exchange rate (EER) concept is used.

Nominal Exchange Rate (NER). Foreign exchange rate is generally quoted as the number of units of a domestic currency required to purchase one unit of a foreign currency. For example, rupees 40 per US dollar refers to foreign exchange rate of the Indian rupee in terms of US dollar and means that ₹ 40 can buy one US dollar in foreign exchange market. Likewise, there is foreign exchange rate between rupee and the pound sterling, between rupee and the Yen, between rupee and Mark and so on. This exchange rate of rupees per US dollar, or per pound sterling is called *nominal exchange rate* (NER).

Nominal Effective Exchange Rate (NEER). In addition to the nominal exchange rate, the economists often use the concept of nominal effective exchange rate. The nominal *effective exchange rate is the weighted average of nominal exchange rates* where the weights used are the shares of the trading partners in the foreign trade of a country. Suppose the US accounts for 60 per cent of total trade with India, and the United Kingdom accounts for 40 per cent of trade with India, then the nominal effective exchange rate is given by

Nominal Effective exchange rate (NEER) = $(NER_{US}\ W_{US}) + (NER_{UK} \times W_{UK})$

where NER_{US} and NER_{UK} are the nominal exchange rates of the US and UK respectively for the India rupee and W_{US} and W_{UK} are trade shares of the US and UK respectively with India. Suppose the US accounts for 60 per cent in India's trade and NER of the Indian rupee with the US dollar is ₹ 44 while UK accounts for 40 per cent in India's trade and nominal exchange rate of rupee with pound sterling is ₹ 85, the nominal effective exchange rate is

$$\begin{aligned} NEER &= 44 \times 0.6 + 85 \times 0.4 \\ &= 26.4 + 34.0 = 60.4 \end{aligned}$$

Real Exchange Rate. Real exchange rate measures the relative price of the two currencies after adjusting for price levels prevailing within two countries. For example, *real exchange rate between rupee and US dollar is defined as the rupee price of a basket of goods in India relative to a* *dollar price of the same basket of goods in the USA.* Thus real exchange rate is given by

$$RER = NER\left(\frac{P_{US}}{P_{In}}\right)$$

where NER is the nominal exchange rate between the two currencies and P_{US} is the price level in the USA and P_{In} is the price level in India. While the nominal exchange rate measures the rate at which currencies of the two countries are exchanged, real exchange rate measures the rate at which domestic goods can be exchanged for foreign goods. An example will clarify the meaning of real exchange rate. Suppose ₹ 44 are required to buy one US dollar, that is ₹ 44 per US dollar is the nominal exchange rate (NER) between the Indian rupee and the US dollar. If a basket of goods costs ₹ 200 in India and the same basket of goods costs 20 dollars, then real exchange rate (RER) will be

$$RER = (NER)\frac{P_{US}}{P_{In}} = 44 \times \frac{20}{200} = 4.4$$

Thus 4.4 is the real exchange rate of the Indian rupee. This means 4.4 units of Indian goods are needed to buy one unit of US goods. Real exchange rate is used as a measure of *international competitiveness*. A rise in real exchange rate indicates foreign goods (in our example the US goods) have become more expensive relative to domestic goods of a country. This means competitiveness of our goods has increased relative to that of the USA.

Real Effective Exchange Rate (REER). *Real effective exchange rate is the weighted average of real exchange rates with all its trade partners, the shares of different countries in its total trade are used as weights.* Thus, in India 5 countries real effective exchange rate (REER) is prepared and the shares of major trade partners such as the USA, UK, other European countries, Japan with India are used as weights for calculating real effective exchange rate.

Changes in India's Nominal Effective Exchange Rate (NEER) and Real Effective Exchange Rate (REER)

India's NEER (base 2000 = 100) which is composed of 5 foreign currencies namely, US dollar, Euro, Pound sterling and Japanese Yen. This India's NEER depreciated on a yearly basis till 2004-05 to reach a level of 90.75. With a bout of appreciation during April – June 2005, it depreciated thereafter but it again rose during Jan. to Feb. 2006 to 94.06. In 2006-07 it depreciated steadily till Aug. 2006 when it reached a low of 88.05. It once again rose to 91.31 in Nov. 2006. This shows there has been quite a large changes in NEER causing uncertainty about what exchange rate will prevail in future.

As regards the real effective exchange rate (REER), it appreciated to 106.79 in 2005-06. After depreciating to 100.6 in Aug. 2006, it rose to 109.0 in Nov. 2006.

Devaluation and Depreciation of Exchange Rate

An important issue in regard to foreign exchange rate has been at what level it should be fixed or stabilised. Even under Bretton Woods system 1 per cent change in fixed exchange rate on either side the parity value was allowed to be varied. For more than one per cent change in the exchange rate the permission of IMF was necessary to restore equilibrium in the balance of payments. A proposal was mooted to increase this *permissible band* for variation or adjustment to be raised to 10 per cent from the parity value to correct disequilibrium in the balance of payments. However, in 1973 Bretton Woods system of fixed exchange rate collapsed. The US dollar and Pound Sterling were floated, that is, allowed to be determined freely by demand for and supply of these currencies. However, India continued with the fixed exchanger rate system. But instead of based on parity value in terms of gold or the US dollar it determined exchange rate of rupee on the basis of exchange rate movements of a basket of foreign currencies, namely, the pound sterling, US dollar, Yen and Mark.

In 1991 India faced a serious balance of payments crisis with stagnant exports and rising imports, especially of petroleum oil. On the advice of IMF India devalued its rupee in July 1991 to solve the balance of payments problem. It was about 25 per cent devaluation against the currencies of our major trading partners. As a result of this devaluation India's exports increased substantially and also black market in foreign exchange that prevailed before came to end.

In addition to devaluation, ***a dual exchange rate system*** was introduced in 1992. Under the dual exchange rate system there were two rates: (1) the official exchange rate that was controlled and (2) the market rate of exchange which was free to change according to demand and supply conditions. Under this dual exchange rate system 40 per cent of earnings from the exports of goods and services were to be surrendered to RBI through authorised dealers at officially fixed exchange rate. The foreign exchange reserves received in this way was used by RBI for financing preferred imports. The remaining 60 per cent of export earnings in foreign exchange were converted into rupees by the exporters at the market determined exchange rate.

However, in the year 1993-94 the policy of dual exchange rates was dropped and rupee was allowed to float. With this a *unified market determined exchange* rate came to prevail which can change as a result of changes in demand and supply of foreign currencies.

Managed Float System and Implications of RBI Intervention

It is important to note that even with the present flexible exchange rate system in India there is a managed float system because RBI intervenes in foreign exchange market to influence the exchange rate of rupee and keep fluctuations in it within reasonable limits. Thus when rupee in the free market depreciates much and RBI does not want much depreciation, it will sell foreign exchange from its reserves in the foreign exchange market to prevent it from depreciating. On the other hand, when rupee appreciates much against foreign currencies RBI intervenes and buys foreign exchange. This move of RBI prevents rupee from appreciating.

Note that appreciation of rupee as compared to other currencies makes the Indian exports expensive and therefore discourages them. Although RBI does not follow any fixed exchange rate target through sale and purchase of foreign exchange, it aims at preventing large volatility in foreign exchange rate of rupee.

However through sale and purchase of foreign exchange by RBI has implications for maintaining price stability. This is because when RBI buys foreign exchange from the market it issues new money (i.e. rupee currency) to pay for it. This new money comes into circulation in the Indian economy and thus leads to the expansion in money supply. If aggregate supply of goods remains the same or does not increase much, this expansion in money will cause rise in general price level (i.e. inflation) in the economy. To check inflation, RBI can *sterlise* the impact of increase in foreign exchange inflows by selling government securities to the banks. The banks will give cash to RBI against the purchase of these securities. In this way RBI mops up excess liquidity (i.e. cash reserves) of the banks caused by the inflows of foreign exchange. The proceeds of the government securities sold to the banks can be kept by RBI in a separate account which cannot be used by the Government and therefore cannot affect prices. However, there is limit to which the sterlisation can take place.

As noted above, from Aug. 2006 the Indian rupee started appreciating and its exchange rate with US dollar rose to eight year high of ₹ 43 per US on March 28, 2007 and further to ₹ 41.57 on April 23, 2007. In the last four months (Jan-April 2007) RBI did not intervene much to buy foreign exchange from the market and as a result continued inflows of dollars in India resulted in the exchange rate of rupee to appreciate. On Nov. 12, 2007, the exchange rate of rupee per US $ rose to ₹ 39.4. The RBI did not intervene to a large extent in the foreign exchange market and let the rupee appreciate in order to check inflation in the Indian economy. If RBI intervenes in the foreign exchange market to mop up excess US dollars from the market it, as explained above, leads to the increase in money supply in the economy and this causes inflation. Further, appreciation of rupee makes imports cheaper which encourages imports. The increase in imports leads to the rise in aggregate supply of goods which helps in checking inflation.

Changes and Volatility in Foreign Exchange Rate of Rupee

As a result of the above developments, rupee depreciated a good deal from 1991-92 to 2000-03. From ₹ 21 per US dollar in 1990-91 average annual exchange rate was reduced to ₹ 27 in 1991-92 (*i.e.*, about 25 per cent fall in value as a result of devaluation made in July 1991), and it then gradually fell to ₹ 36 in 1997-98 and to ₹ 48 in 2001-02. With effect from 2002-03 under pressure of capital inflows, rupee started appreciating and rose to ₹ 47 per US dollar in 2002-03, to ₹ 44.27 in 2005-06. In 2006-07 and 2007-08, there was large inflows of capital through portfolio investment which led to further appreciation of rupee which rose to 39.4 to a dollar on Nov. 12, 2007 which was ten years high level. In the year 2007 alone there was net capital inflows of 17 billion US dollars through FII which pushed up the value of rupee to a dollar. Then there was a sub-prime housing loan crisis in the United States which created liquidity crisis in America. To meet the requirements of liquidity at home, FIIs started selling shares in the Indian market and as a result capital outflows occurred during 2008 which gathered momentum in the months of September and October 2008 when rupee depreciated rapidly and its value fell to ₹ 48.53 to a US dollar on Oct. 10, 2008 and to ₹ 49.5 for a US dollar in Nov. 2008 (For some days it fell to ₹ 50 for a US dollar). The capital outflows by FIIs not only caused depreciation of rupee but also stock market crash in Oct. 2008 and Nov. 2008 and liquidity crunch in the Indian banking system. To ensure credit needs of industries for investment the RBI intervened in the economy by reducing cash reserve ratio (CRR) form 9 per cent to 6.5% and thereby infused liquidity in the economy to the extent of ₹ 1,40,000 crores and promised to do more if needed.

In the later half of 2011 from September to December 2011, due to uncertainty caused by Eurozone Crisis there has been capital outflows by FIIs from India which caused a sharp depreciation of rupee. Despite some limited intervention by RBI, the value of rupee fell to ₹ 53 to US$ in Mid-December 2011 against ₹ 44 in August 2011, that is ₹ 18 per cent fall in the value of rupee in four months. This is a matter of serious concern as it has raised the costs of imports of crude oil and other commodities and therefore will not only raise inflation in the economy but will also adversely affect of our balance payments. Besides, the weak rupee will discourage foreign investment in India as investors will suffer losses due to the fall in exchange value of the Indian rupee.

DEPRECIATION OF RUPEE IN 2013: CAUSES, EFFECTS AND CURE

From May 22, 2013 the value of Indian rupee was ₹ 55.48 to a US dollar and within fifteen days it fell to ₹ 57.07 to a US dollar and its slide went on as a result of surge in dollar demand from imports and capital outflows by FIIs pulling out the debt market that resulted in fall in value of rupee

Table 28.2. FII Weekly Net Flow (Cr) during May-June 2013

Week	*Equity*	*Debt*	*Total*
Apr 29-May 3	4,328.0	7,549.0	**11,877.0**
May 6-10	4,446.6	3,194.6	**7,641.2**
May 13-17	4,836.9	1067.7	**5,904.6**
May 20-24	5,384.9	–433.6	**4,951.3**
May 27-31	3,335.9	–4939.8	**–1,603.9**
Jun 3-7	1,249.3	–7,185.4	**–5,936.1**
Jun 10-14	–2,520.0	–1,291.4	**–13,811.4**
Jun 17-21	–3,261.3	–3893.3	**–7,154.6**
Jun 24-26	–4,593.8	–7.284.9	**–11,878.7**

to ₹ 60.72 on June 26, 2013, that is, around 6 per cent in single month of June. Though RBI had a foreign exchange reserve of $ 291 billion, it tried to stem the slide of rupee through sale of some US dollars from its foreign exchange reserves but failed to stabilise the exchange rate of rupee because capital outflows gathered momentum as will be seen from the Table 28.2 given abow.

The RBI was selling dollars at ₹ 59.90 to a US dollar but such was the pressure on the rupee by FIIs pulling out capital from the debt and equity markets and demand for dollars by the corporates, oil firms that rupee slipped below ₹ 60 to ₹60.73 to a dollar on June 20, 2013. This made imperative for the RBI to take more tough measures to check the fall in the value of rupee.

Capital Outflows from India and Unwinding of Quantitative Easing. It is worth noting that capital outflows by FIIs were triggered by the announcement by Ben Bernanke, the governor of the US Reserve System, that since the US economy had shown the signs of recovery from recession as shown by the decline in unemployment rate to 7.6 per cent in April 2013, as against its peak level of 10 per cent in December 2010 it would start soon start unwinding of the stimulus in the form of *quantitative easing* (*QE*) that was being pursued by it. At present under the Quantitative Easing Policy (*QE*) the US Reserve System was pumping in 85 billion dollars per month by ***purchasing government and other bonds*** to provide stimulus to the US economy and now it will soon unwind this stimulus in a phased manner and to begin with it will reduce buying of bonds to 65 billion dollars per month. Ben Bernanke's statement immediately prompted FIIs to pull out swiftly from first debt market and then equity market to send dollars to safe haven of the US where they expected to earn higher returns as a result of revival of the US economy. These large capital outflows coupled with the increased demand for dollars by the Indian importers such as oil firms, corporate companies and banks increased pressure on dollars resulting in rupee depreciation despite efforts made by the RBI to stabilize the value of rupee by selling US dollars from its foreign exchange reserves through public sector banks. However, the RBI could not sell sufficient dollars to stem the downward slide of the rupee as it also needed dollars to meet the current account deficit that had reached 6.7 per cent of GDP in December quarter of the year 2012-13 and 4.8 per cent of GDP for the whole year 2012-13.

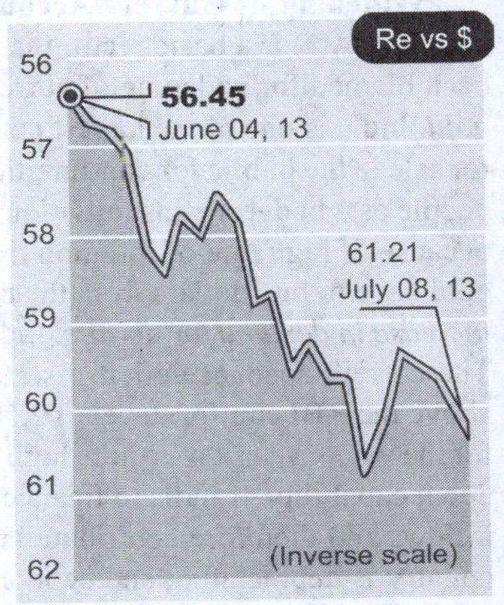

Fig. 28.12. *Downhill Slide of Rupee*

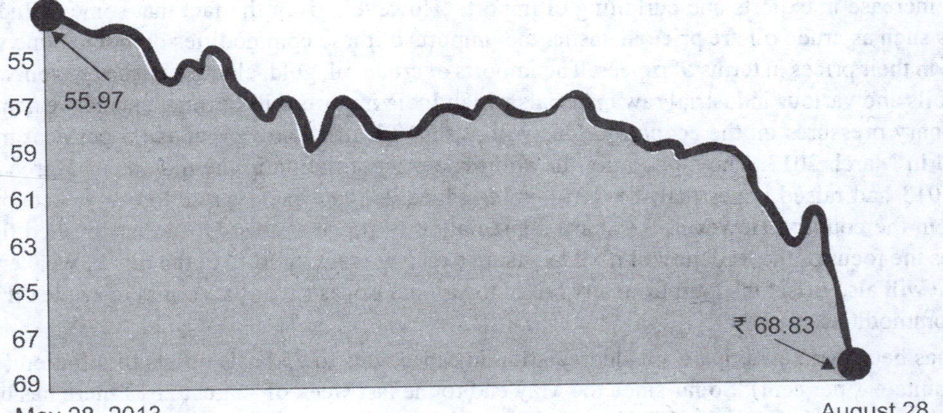

Fig. 28.13. *Rupee Continued on its Downward Slide*

The vicious circle came into operation. The weakening of rupee further hit the debt and equity markets as the worried foreign investors saw their returns from investment in India being eroded who had already pulled out away around $ 6 billion in June 2013 continued this process in July 2013 as well. These outflows of dollars were bound to weaken the rupee further and on July 8, 2013, the rupee fell to a very low level of ₹ 61.21 to a dollar. The RBI which was initially slower in response to fast depreciation of rupee started taking tough measures to stem further slide of rupee. These measures will be explained later. However, the process of depreciation continued despite raising customs duty on imports of gold and imposing various restrictions on outflows of foreign exchange. The value of rupee depreciated to a record low level of ₹ 68.83 on Aug. 28, 2013.

Widening of Current Account Deficit. Besides capital outflows, widening current account deficit (CAD) is a basic factor that is responsible for large depreciation of rupee. Two factors have been blamed for widening of current account deficit (CAD). *One important factor is the import of gold.* India is one of the largest consumers of gold. The gold is demanded for making of jewellery, for sale to the public for consumption. The second reason for import of gold is investment in it by the people as a hedge against inflation and for investment purposes was more in 2012-13 and 2013-14 because of high rate of inflation that prevailed in these years. For imports of gold the importers of gold have to buy dollars from the market. *The crude oil is other major import which causes a large increase in demand for dollars.* India imports crude oil for more than 75 per cent of its requirements. The current account deficit rose to 6.7 per of GDP in December of 2012-13 quarter which was above the RBI comfort level of 2.5%. In the fourth quarter of 2012-13, CAD fell to 3.6 per cent but for the whole year it was quite high at 4.8 per cent. This shattered the confidence of foreign investors about capability of India to finance its current account deficit. This also caused slowdown in capital inflows and therefore contributed to further weakening of rupee. At a time when the currency of a country is depreciating and economic growth is sluggish (the rate of economic growth was 5% in 2012-13, the lowest in a decade), foreign investors were wary of investing in India since every dollar they would bring in India for investment their earnings from it will be eroded by further depreciation of rupee against US dollar when they repatriate their earnings out of India. Thus a sort of vicious circle was set in as the value of rupee falls. FIIs tried to pull out their money and that in turn made the rupee dip further. This can be offset only by stable capital inflows through FDI or longer-term overseas borrowing.

HOW DEPRECIATION OF RUPEE HURTS THE INDIAN ECONOMY

A weak Indian rupee will make imports costlier. Normally, economic theory suggests this should lead to increase in exports and curtailing of imports. However, given the fact that some of India's imports such as crude oil are price inelastic, the imports of these commodities do not decline with the rise in their prices in terms of rupees. The imports of crude oil, gold, electronic goods, iron, coal, edible oils and various industrial raw materials which India imports will become expensive and put inflationary pressures on the economy. This will push WPI inflation back above 5 per cent mark reached in March 2013. The moderation in wholesale price inflation in the months of March and April 2013 had raised hopes that the RBI would reduce its repo interest rate to revive economic growth in the country. However, the sharp depreciation of rupee against US dollar dashed these hopes as the focus of the RBI now shifted to ensure exchange rate stability of the rupee. Weakening of rupee will also offset the gain from any fall in the global prices (in dollar terms) of crude oil and other commodities.

It has been estimated that a 1% depreciation in rupee adds to 15 basis points to inflation (100 basis points = 1 per cent). So far since the May end to the last week of August 2013 there has been around 18 per cent depreciation in value of rupee which means rise in inflation rate will rise by 270 basis points that is, by 2.7 per cent. Given the around 5% rate of inflation in May end, this means inflation in August 2013 will have risen by about 2.7 per cent if there is no lag in adjustment of prices to changes in import cost. Since in practice there is a time lag between rise in import cost and adjustment of prices, inflation will rise to the above estimates, after two or three months.

Besides, rise in import costs of crude oil and fertilizers will raise government expenditure if government does not pass on additional rise in prices to consumers by raising prices of crude oil and fertilizers to consumers. The increase in expenditure on subsidies will lead to the increase in fiscal deficit which is planned to be reduced to 4 per cent in 2014-15.

It follows from above that the weaker rupee will add to inflationary pressures in the economy, widen the fiscal deficit and slowdown the capital inflows.

Depreciation of rupee will not only hurt the Indian economy as a whole but will adversely affect some individual industries and services. First, prices of laptops, tablets, desktops and smart phones would go up by anywhere between 5 and 12 per cent by the end of September 2013 as the imported components of these products have become costlier due to depreciation of rupee. Besides, prices of cars and other automobiles which were raised a few months earlier will go up further if further depreciation of rupee is not checked. Further, due to rise in air fares as a result of depreciation of rupee foreign travels will become expensive which will impact vacation budget in peak summer. Besides, it will hit getting foreign education by the Indians because studying abroad will become more expensive as fees, cost of living and other expenses will increase.

In India the durable consumer goods will become costlier as the prices of their imported components will go up as a result of rupee depreciation. Some companies such as LG, Samsung, Bluestar have already announced a hike in the prices of their products ranging between 2.5 per cent and 7.5 per cent. Other foreign companies will also raise their prices. However, most adverse effect of depreciation will be on prices of fuel (crude oil). Petrol and diesel prices have already been raised substantially. If slide of rupee further continues, there will be still more burden on households. Not only prices of car will go up but prices of its components will also rise. The rise in prices of petrol, diesel and components will raise the running costs of cars. This may reduce the demand for cars. To conclude the impact of depreciation, the WPI inflation that had eased in March and April 2013 will go up due to depreciation. Inflation as measured by consumer price index (CPI) or what is called **retail inflation** which is already around 10 per cent is likely to rise further.

RBI has cautioned about inflation pressures in the economy and is unlikely to ease its monetary policy in near future against the backdrop of challenging economic scenario. The RBI had said in its June 2013 policy review that going forward, inflation outlook would be determined by suppressed inflation being released through revisions of administered prices, including the minimum support prices (MSP) of agricultural product as well as the recent depreciation of the rupee.

Consumer price inflation is still very high at about 10% YOY basis and you can expect further pressure on food prices as well. WPI inflation will definitely go above above 7%.

MEASURES TO STEM THE SLIDE OF RUPEE

When value of a rupee fell to ₹ 61.21 to a dollar on July 8, 2013, the RBI took tough steps to stem the further slide of rupee. Reserve Bank pushed up short-term rates in the money markets which would choke speculators and attract dollars into India. According to these measures, the **RBI has limited its lending of overnight funds to all banks** to **₹ 75,000 crore and for an individual bank overnight lending by it has been restricted to 5% of its deposits. If banks need more funds they** would have to pay higher penal interest rate of **marginal standing facility** (MSF) which too has been raised to 10.25%. As the current overnight borrowing by the banks was to the tune of ' 93000 crore its immediate effect was **raising of cost of overnight borrowing by the banks from the RBI.** This in turn was expected to translate into higher cost of short-term borrowing by the companies which might cross 10 per cent. Besides, the **market which was expecting cut in repo rate of interest in view of the fact that headline WPI inflation rate had fallen below 5 per cent**

in May and June 2013 was now seen as unlikely to happen. It may be noted that market perception of likely tapering off US quantitative easing (*QE*) had triggered outflows of portfolio investment from India, particularly from the debt market.

Second measure that the RBI took was to announce that *it would sell bonds worth 22,000 crore every week*. This would suck out rupee currency from the market thereby reducing liquidity in the market. The higher rate of interest and less liquidity in the banking system was expected to curb speculation in foreign exchange, especially in dollars which was contributing to depreciation of rupee. As a result of this measure bond prices were expected to fall sharply as investors were expecting better returns from them.

Thirdly, in tandem with the above measures **bank rate which is a rate of interest for a long term borrowing was raised by RBI from 8.25% to 10.25%.**

As a result of the above measures it was expected that speculation in dollars would be curbed and there will be rise in the value of the rupee that had sharply depreciated in the last six weeks. Countries with large current account deficits, such as India, have been particularly affected despite their relatively promising economic fundamentals. The exchange rate pressure also evidences that the demand for foreign currency has increased vis-a-vis that of the rupee in part because of the improving domestic liquidity situation.

RBI measures will have wider implications on the economy as cost of funds would go up. But the measures were likely to be relaxed if the rupee stabilizes. Bankers said RBI's observation shows that it is convinced that some of the pressure on the rupee is because of speculation. The main motivation appears to be to make the rupee more attractive vis-a-vis investments in the dollar. The measures will benefit the rupee which will gain as foreign institutional investors see an opportunity to invest in short-term debt. But at the same time this could have longer-term ramifications for the Indian economy.

Since the problem of sharp depreciation of rupee in the months of June and July 2013, the RBI shifted its focus to stabilise the exchange rate of rupee. ***In its 30th July review of credit policy the RBI kept its policy rate unchanged,*** that is, it did not reduce its repo rate of interest. In 30th July review repo rate was retained at 7.25 and CRR at 4%. The RBI thought that lowering of repo interest rate weould offset the impact of its earlier measures aimed at reducing liquidity in the banking system to curb speculation on exchange rate of rupee. However, keeping the repo interest rate at a high level was impeding economic growth and the pro-growth lobby including our Finance Minister

Mr. P. Chidambaram wanted reduction in repo rate of interest to spur economic growth. The RBI governor was of the view that for checking inflation and achieving price stability was its main objective and that lowering of repo rate of interest would give a push to inflation which badly affects the poor. He rightly pointed out that in *the short run some sacrifice of growth is inevitable to achieve price stability*.

To check the weakening of rupee the RBI made limited and subtle intervention by selling dollars through public sector banks from its foreign exchange reserves to reduce volatility of rupee. At time it succeeded in preventing further slide of rupee through sale of dollars from its foreign exchange reserves. As a result of the measures taken by RBI, the value of rupee remained in the range of ₹ 59 to ₹ 60 to a US dollar in June 2013, except on some days the value of rupee fell even below ₹ 61 to a dollar. However, in August 2013, the situation worsened and the value of rupee fell even below ₹ 68 to a dollar. On August 28 the rupee hit its record low of ₹ 68.83 to a US dollar. However, intervention by RBI brought it to around ₹ 65 to a dollar a in a few days time and in a months's time to around ₹ 62 to a dollar.

The other step adopted by RBI is that the exporters who benefit from rupee depreciation have been asked not to hold on to their foreign exchange earnings but bring in their dollar earnings within **nine months** of *shipping or executing orders instead of 12 months*. This would accelerate dollar flows into India and push up the rupee. It is because of sale of dollars by the exporters that leads to increase in the supply of dollars and keeps the exchange rate of rupee within limits though daily fluctuations in the exchange rate of rupee can continue.

Opening Special Window. RBI has also decided to open a special window to sell US dollars for the companies importing crude oil and to the government for importing defence equipment. This would reduce market demand for US dollars and help in checking high volatility in the exchange rate of rupee.

Tightening Gold Imports. Another important measure the RBI has taken to make gold imports for domestic consumption tougher. The RBI has announced that 20% of imports of gold by businessmen must be imported in the form of jewellery. This would reduce imports of gold as only a very small portion of gold imports is exported now in the form of jewellery. If any importer of gold fails to export 20%. of its imports of gold, he would be debarred from importing any more gold. This would have a dual effect. On the one hand, 20% export condition will lower imports of gold and, on the other hand, it would encourage the exports of gold jewellery.

Both the government and the RBI have been targetting gold imports to reduce the current account deficit which is the basic factor responsible for sharp depreciation of rupee. Gold, which accounts for more than half of the deficit, has been at the receiving end of the regulators, with the finance minister P Chidambaram raising import duties to 8% from 6% on August 13, 201. Import duty on gold was further raised to 10 per cent. Further import duty on silver was also raised to 10% as against 6% earlier. Furthermore, RBI had made bank funding tough by insisting on near cash payments for any gold import for local needs.

Of the 970 tonnes of gold imported last year, only 70 tonnes were exported. Now, the industry has to follow the 80 : 20 ratio. The government wants to bring down gold import to 500 tonne and raise exports of gold jewellery to 100 tonnes.

Auction of ₹ 22,000 crore of Government Bonds. As an additional measure to check volatility in the rupee, on August 8, the RBI announced that it would make out-of-turn auction of 22000 crore of government bonds every Monday to suck out liquidity from money market. This would make rupee scarce and therefore would limit the room for traders to speculate on the rupee.

Record Payment of Surplus by RBI as Dividend to the Government. In its board meeting held on August 8 the RBI announced that it would transfer a record surplus of ₹ 33,010 crore to the government soon in 2013-14, an increase of 106% over ₹ 15,010 crore in the previous year. The RBI is owned by the central government and therefore its earnings, which RBI calls dividend of the government, go to the government. The RBI generates its surplus largely from intervention in foreign exchange and money markets. RBI's profits are usually the highest during period of hight volatility in rupee. The transfer of such a huge amount of ₹ 33,010 crore soon will help the government to contain its fiscal deficit to 4.8 per cent of GDP in 2013-14 which will promote confidence of foreign investors so that they invest in India and not pull out funds for investment in the US.

It is evident from above that the foreign exchange rate of rupee is now quite flexible. It changes as market conditions of demand for and supply of foreign exchange change.

QUESTIONS FOR REVIEW

1. What is meant by foreign exchange rate ? How is it determined ?
2. Distinguish between floating exchange rate and fixed exchange rate. What type of exchange rate system has been currently adopted by India ?
3. Explain the factors that cause changes on the exchange rate of a currency. How the exchange rate of rupee in terms of US dollar will be affected if India has a deficit on current account of the balance of payments ?

4. Explain the factors which determine demand for foreign exchange, say US dollars.
5. Explain the factors which determine supply of foreign exchange, say US dollar, for India.
6. Explain the fixed exchange rate system adopted under the Brelton Woods system. Why did it collapse?
7. Explain how a foreign exchange rate is determined. How will the following factors affect foreign exchange rate of rupee ?
   (*a*) Higher rate of inflation in India (*b*) Higher rates of interest in India
8. Critically examine purchasing power parity theory of foreign exchange. What shortcomings of this theory was pointed out by Keynes.
9. What is meant appreciation of Indian rupee? How will it affect exports, imports and level of national income of India.
10. Distinguish betwen depreciation and devaluation. How will devaluation or depreciation will affect balance of trade and the national economy. Explain in this connection the concept of *J-Curve*.
11. What is meant by appreciation of a currency ? What will be the effect of appreciation of rupee against dollar on our balance of trade, foreign exchange reserves and price level in the Indian economy.
12. How is exchange rate determined in open market ? What factors make exchange rate fluctuate ?
13. Explain the merits of a flexible exchange rate system. Discuss why Bretton Woods system had favoured relatively fixed exchange rates.
14. A real depreciation will worsen the trade balance in the short run, but will gradually improve in the long run.
15. How do exchange rate changes help in the trade adjustment process ? Discuss the role of monetary or domestic credit factors.
16. How far under flexible exchange rates can countries pursue their own national montary and fiscal policies without having to worry about the balance of payments ? Is there a need for policy synchronization ?
17. (*a*) What is meant by *Currency Convertibility* ? Distinguish between current account and capital count convertibility of a currency.
    (*b*) What are the advantages of currency convertibility and what problems are faced by making convertibility of a currency.
18. Explain the concepts of Nominal Effective Exchange Rate (NEER) and Real Effective Exchange Rate (REER). What is the importance of distinguishing between them ?
19. What is managed float system ? Why has RBI not intervened to a sufficiently large extent to prevent the appreciation of Indian rupee ?
20. What problem are being faced by India because of excessive dollar inflows (*i.e.*, capital inflows) in the Indian economy ?
21. Distinguish between convertbility of currency on current account and capital account. Why has India not so far gone in for full convertibility on capital account.
22. What is capital account convertbility of a currency ? What are its benefits and problems ? Are the present conditions in India suitable for going in for full capital account convertibility ?

28A

Role of International Organisations : IMF and World Bank

In order to promote cooperation among different nations of the world and to reduce economic tensions and conflicts among them, after the Second World War two important international institutions were set up. Their task is to help member countries to overcome their balance of payments difficulties and provide financial help for reconstruction and development. These two important institutions are: (1) International Monetary Fund, popularly called IMF, (2) Bank for Reconstruction and Development, popularly called World Bank. Besides, a subsidiary of World Bank called International Development Association (IDA) has been set up to provide financial help to the developing countries. We discuss below these international institution and how India has gained from them.

INTERNATIONAL MONETARY FUND (IMF)

The International Monetary Fund, which is briefly called IMF, is one of the twin institutions which were established as a result of discussion among the monetary and financial delegations of the member countries of the United Nations held at Bretton Woods (U.S.A.) in 1944. Its establishment on Ist March, 1947, is a great landmark in the history of international economic relations, particularly in the monetary field.

IMF and its Membership

The funds of the IMF. consist of the subscription of the members, who have been assigned their respective subscription quotas. In 1982, it had 146 members whose total subscribed capital stood at $ 60 billion. Twenty-five per cent of the quota or 10 per cent of the official gold holdings of the member country, whichever is less, is payable in gold—the rest of the quota is to be paid in terms of the member's national currency. Recently, the requirement of gold payment has been done away with.

Under the IMF articles, a member country can purchase foreign currency not exceeding one-fourth of its quota in any 12-month period. The total holdings of foreign currencies by a member country must not, however, exceed 200 per cent of its quota, which means in effect that the upper limit for IMF's short-term assistance is equivalent to the country's quota plus its gold contribution. With effect from January 2, 1970 a system of Special Drawing Rights (SDRs) was set up. The SDRs are designed to supplement the gold and the reserve currencies, *viz.*, the pound and the dollar. The SDRs represent entirely a new form of paper money which will serve like gold or US dollar, and hence are called *Paper Gold.*

Main Functions of IMF

The main functions of the International Monetary Fund are :—

(*i*) *Regulating Rate of Exchange.* Each member-country on joining the Fund has to declare the par value of its currency in terms of gold or U.S. dollers (now in terms of SDRs) is required to maintain this parity. It can, however, change it up to 10 per cent without the IMF's permission. For further changes up to 10 per cent the IMF will have to be consulted which will have to give the acceptance or refusal to the proposed change within 72 hours. Changes beyond 20 per cent can be effected but only with the concurrence of the IMF and only to correct a "*fundamental disequilibrium*" in the balance of payments. The internal policies of the member-countries to restore equilibrium are not to be interfered with by the IMF.

(*ii*) *Assistance for Meeting Balance of Payments Deficit.* When a country suffers from a deficit in its balance of payments on current account, it can obtain from the IMF, in exchange for its own currency, the currency which it needs to pay off its deficit. As already mentioned, there is, however, a limit to the amount which it can thus obtain.

(*iii*) *Rationing Out Scarce Currencies.* Currencies which are in great demand by the member-countries and IMF cannot meet all demands for them are declared as scarce currencies and are rationed by IMF among the countries needing them. The IMF can also increase the supply of such 'scarce' currencies by borrowing or by purchasing them against gold. The member-countries are permitted to impose exchange restrictions in cash of such 'scarce' currencies.

(*iv*) *Elimination of Exchange Restrictions.* IMF has to see that the member-countries do not impose exchange restrictions on current transactions. In view of the abnormal conditions existing after the war. IMF allowed a period of transition extending over 3 years during which the members could remain such restrictions. The period is over and many countries have relaxed their exchange restrictions. However, their complete removal is not likely in the near future.

Leading Mechanism by IMF

The IMF helps its member countries under a number of different programmes.

Stand-by Arrangements. The most widely used way to lend by IMF is stand-by arrangements. Under this arrangement a credit tranche which is equal to 100 per cent of member country's quota is available for lending to it. A member country can borrow from IMF from this credit tranche to meet its balance of payments difficulties. A certain norms regarding government expenditure and money supply targets have to be fulfilled before resources are released, especially in higher credit tranches. It is expected that government of a country borrowing under this arrangement will adopt measures to rectify the balance of payments disequilibrium. Typically, stand-by arrangements last for 12-18 months period. Repayments of loans under this arrangement are made within 3-5 years of each drawing the money from IMF.

Extended Fund Facility (EFF). The Extended Fund Facility was created in 1974 to help the developing countries over longer periods (upto 3 years) than stand-by arrangements (12-18 months). Further, in this facility developing countries can borrow more than their quota. The loans taken under this facility can be paid back over a period of 4-10 years.

Under the extended fund facility, since developing countries can borrow to meet for long-term balance of payments difficulties strigent conditions are to be fulfilled for availing borrowing facility under this scheme. A country borrowing under this programme has to provide every year a detailed statement of measures and policies it has adopted to solve its balance of payments problems. IMF releases resources in instalments *with conditionalities* regarding the particular steps to be taken by the borrowing country, Commenting on this extended fund facility, Thirwall writes that despite the conditionalities "the facility represented an important and significant shift in emphasis from viewing the balance of payments as a stabilisation problem to recognising the balance of payments as a fundamental long-term constraint on growth that cannot be rectified in a short period of time."[1]

Stand-by arrangement and extended fund facility (EFI) are very important methods of finance support by IMF for meeting balance of payments difficulties of developing countries. However in recent years other special facilities provided by IMF are being extensively used by the developing countries to tackle their problem arising from balance of payments. The important special facilities are (1) Poverty Reduction and Growth Facility (PRGF) (2) Supplemental Reserve Facility (SRF), and (3) Contingent Credit Line (CCL). We briefly explain them below.

Poverty Reduction and Growth Facility (PRGF). This was set up in 1999 to provide financial assistance to low income (i.e., developing) countries for reduction of poverty. Prior to this, IMF provided financial assistance to the poor developing countries under a programme known as *Enhanced Structural Adjustment Facility* (ESAF) so that they can undertake structural adjustment reforms. In 1999 it was felt to focus more on poverty reduction in the developing countries. Therefore, in 1999 Enhanced Structural Adjustment Facility was replaced by Poverty Reduction and Growth Facility (PRGF). Assistance under this programme is given by IMF on the basis of Poverty Reduction Strategy Paper prepared by a poor country in cooperation with World Bank and other experts. Interest charged on the loans given by IMF under this programme is only 0.5 per cent per annum. Moreover, the borrowing country can repay the loans taken under this programme in a long period of 10 years.

Supplemental Reserve Facility (SRF). This was set up in 1997 in response to Financial Crisis in East Asia and other developing countries. Under this facility, IMF provides financial assistance to the member countries who are experiencing exceptional balance of payments problems arising from a sudden loss of market confidence in their currencies. Assistance under SRF in not subject to usual quota limits but instead depends on the country's requirements, its ability to repay the loan and policies it adopts to restore confidence. The repayments have to be made within 2.5 years of taking the loan.

Contingent Credit Line (CCL). This facility was established in 199 to deal with the problem of countries who are anticipating a financial crises *that well cause capital outflow on capital account* of balance of payments. It was a precautionary measure to provide assistance to a country to overcome the impending crises on capital account. It may be noted that financial assistance under this facility was avaited only when crises actually occurred. The repayment period for the loan taken is also 2.5 years.

Special Oil Facility. The oil crises of 1973 touched off by the Arab oil producing countries created a most serious balance of payments problem for the developed as well as developing countries. Among the developing countries India was the most severely hit. To aid member-countries, the IMF has started a special fund, from which the member-countries in acute difficulties are helped out. This is called the *special oil facility.*

Benefits to India from International Monetary Fund's Membership

It is good that India joined the IMF. There is no doubt that this membership has been greatly beneficial to India.

(*i*) International regulation by IMF in the field of money has certainly contributed towards *expansion of international trade* and thus prosperity. India has, to that extent, benefitted from these fruitful results.

(*ii*) *Large Financial Assistance.* Not only indirectly but directly also, her membership has been of great advantage. We know how, in the post-partition period, India had serious balance of payments deficits, particularly with the dollar and other hard currency countries. She could not

1. A.P. Thirwall, *Growth and Development*, Pelgrave Macmillan, Seventh Edition, 2003 p 718

possibly reduce her imports, since these consisted of essential foodstuffs, capital equipment and industrial raw materials. Her exports, on the other hand, could not be immediately expanded since under conditions of limited production in the country, increased exports were sure to create serious internal shortages. Under such difficult circumstance, it was the IMF that came to her rescue.

Subsequently, India has been one of the most frequent borrowers from the IMF. From the inception of IMF up to March 31, 1971, India purchased foreign currencies of the value of Rs. 817.5 crores from the IMF, and the same have been fully repaid. Recently, since 1970, the assistance that India, as other member countries of the IMF, can obtain from it has been increased through the setting up of the Special Drawing Rights (SDRs). India had recourse to borrowing from the Fund in the wake of the steep rise in the prices of its imports, food, fuel and fertilisers. A total of Rs. 753.8 crores had been drawn till the end of August 1975, when the second oil facility drawing of Rs. 207 crores took place. In November 1981, India was given a massive loan of about Rs. 5,000 crores to overcome foreign exchange crisis resulting from persistent deficit in balance of payments on current account.

(*iii*) The total figures of borrowings by India from the IMF do not convey the extent of the support that it extended to her. What are of greater significance are the *crucial timings of and special circumstances under which such assistance was availed of.* Such help was forthcoming when the country was faced with critical foreign exchange situations.

(*iv*) *Aid from World Bank and Other International Financial Agencies.* The membership of the IMF has benefited India in yet another important way. India wanted large foreign capital for her various river projects, land reclamation schemes and for the development communications. Since private foreign capital was not forthcoming, the only practicable method of obtaining the necessary capital was to borrow from the International Bank for Reconstruction and Development (*i.e.* World Bank). The membership of the IMF is a necessary condition precedent to the membership of the World Bank. Thus, India's membership of the IMF has entitled her to be a member of the World Bank and its affiliates *viz.*, International Finance Corporation (IFC) and International Development Association (IDA). In fact, in absolute figures though not on per capita basis, India has been the largest borrower from the World Bank group.

The International Finance Corporation (IFC) has made substantial investment in Indian companies engaged in the production of fertilizers, caustic soda, ball and bearings, pumps, etc. A large bulk of the financial assistance obtained by India from World Bank is from the Soft-loan Affiliate, the IDA—loans from it are payable over 50 years, are interest-free; bear only a service-charge of 0.75 per cent per annum.

Since the fiscal year 1975-76 (July-June), the World Bank has been extending **"Third Window"** loans meant to help countries with a per capita income of less than $ 375. India got a substantial share out of the 'Third Window' fund.

(*v*) India has availed of the *services of specialists* of the IMF for the purpose of assessing the state of the Indian economy. Teams of experts have often been coming to India and submitting reports. In this way India has had the benefit of independent scrutiny and advice.

(*vi*) *Contribution to International Monetary Concord.* The important place which India has thus occupied in the international councils in the fields of world trade and finance has been a guarantee that her interests would not suffer. Rather, she can avail of whatever facilities are available from the more fortunate nations. Then, apart from her own gain, by her membership, she is contributing to international concord and co-operation in the monetary and financial fields.

(*vii*) *Provision of Oil Facility.* The balance of payments position of India having gone utterly out of gear on account of the oil price escalation since October 1973, the IMF has started making available oil facility by setting up a special fund for the purpose. According to a report of the IMF,

India is the worst hit among the developing countries of the world. This special aid from IMF is, therefore, of great value to her. In October 1974, India drew Rs. 194 crores from IMF and Rs. 207 crores in August 1975.

In 1981 India succeeded in getting a massive loan of Rs. 5000 crores from IMF to tide over the balance of payments problem faced by it. This was the single largest loan made by IMF to a member country. India prudently used this loan and used only Rs. 3900 crores and surrendered the balance to IMF.

IMF and European Debit Crisis

The IMF has been called upon to bail out several European countries such as Greece, Spain, Itale, Portugal which are faced with severe sovereign debt crisis. The IMF has $ 384 billion in its lending funds which are quite insufficient and limited to finance the needs of European countries' needs. At the same time current economic and political climate in the advanced economies such as the US, Germany makes it highly unlikely that they are in a position to provide additional resources to the IMF.

Tripling IMF resources was part of the G20 leaders' response to the global recession in 2009. As the European debt crisis threatens to spread and further damp the global recovery, the IMF was asked by its steering committee in Oct. 2011 to review whether its resources are sufficient.

According to Christine Lagrade, the present chairman of IMF, the funds credibility and hence effectiveness rests on its perceived capaicty to cope with worst-case scenarios. She further adds that lending capacity "looks comfortable today but pales in comparison with the potential financing needs of vulnerable countries and crisis in the debt-ridden European Countries.

A Critique of the Role of IMF

The role of IMF in providing financial assistance to developing countries for overcoming balance of payments problem and undertaking structural adjustment for promoting economic development has been severely criticised. Besides, the manner in which IMF dealt with financial crisis in East Asian countries in the late nineties has also come under severe attack. In its structural adjustment policies IMF has been guided by the supermacy of the free market in promoting economic growth. Thus, according to Stiglitz, a winner of Nobel Prize in economies. "Over the years since its inception the IMF has changed markedly. Founded on the belief that markets often worked badly, it now champions market supremacy with ideological fervor. Founded on the belief that there is a need for international pressure on countries to have more expansionary economic policies such as increasing expenditures, reducing taxes or lowering interest sates to stimulate economy, today the IMF typically provides funds only if countries engage in policies like cutting deficits or raising interest rates that lead to a contraction of the economy".[2]

The same policy approach has been applied to the vast majority of developing countries as if they all were one homogeneous mass and could be properly treated in the same way. Joseph Stiglitz has severely criticised the functioning of IMF for serving the needs of G-7 (the group of seven developed countries) and has failed to promote global economic stability for which it was set up.

He writes, "A half country after its founding, it is clear that IMF has failed in its mission. It has not done what it was supposed to do... provide funds for countries facing an economic downturn, and in spite of IMF efforts during the past quarter century, *crisis around the world have been more frequent* (and with the exception of the Great Depression, deeper..... Worse, many of the policies that the IMF pushed, in particular *premature capital market liberalisation have contributed to global instability.*"[3]

---

2. Josaph Stiglitz, *Globalisation and its Discontents,* Penguin Books, 2002
3. Op. cit., p.15.

IMF policy of providing financial assistance to the poor developing countries subject to the fulfillment of certain conditions by the latter have come in for severe criticism. These conditionalities refer to the structural adjustment policies, namely, (1) privatisation of public enterprises, (2) Capital market liberalisation, (3) market-based pricing (that is, withdrawal of subsidies granted by the government), (4) liberalisation of foreign trade and investment. If commitments regarding fulfillment of these conditionalities by the developing countries in need of finance were not forthcoming, no financial assistance was provided. In fact, capital market liberalisation proved to be disastrous for many countries because they were not ready and able to deal with the great volatility of capital inflows and outflows. This policy of premature capital-market liberalisation actually resulted in severe *East Asian crisis* in the late nineties. The Fund was undoubtedly shaken by the 1997 East Asian crisis which it does not foresee even though there was a massive build-up of current account deficits and capital had started to flow out of South-East Asia long before the crises hit" The IMF now conceders that liberalising capital and financial markets contributed to the East Asia's crisis of 1990.

As regards market-based pricing which involves elimination of food and fuel subsidies also landed the poor developing countries into trouble. Elimination of subsidies has been resisted by the people in developing countries. So far even in India government has not succeeded very much in this regard. The riots broke out in Indonesia in 1998 when food and fuel subsidies were withdrawn at the instance of the IMF.

Even policy of trade liberalisation has not been entirely successful in attaining its objective of reduction of poverty and unemployment. The issue of trade liberalisation is being hotly debated at WTO sponsored Ministerial Conferences where developed countries of EU (European Union) and the United States are reluctant to eliminate subsidies and reduce tariffs sufficiently which they are providing to protect their agriculture and manufacturing industries. As a result, market access for the products of developing countries is quite limited.

Besides, the result of liberalisation of trade (*i.e.*, heavy reduction of tariffs and removal of quantitative restrictions) by the developing countries resulted in increase in unemployment in them. Commenting on this Stiglitz writes, "It is easy to destroy jobs and this is often the immediate impact of trade liberalisation as inefficient industries close down under pressures from international competition. IMF ideology holds that new more productive jobs will be created as the old, inefficient jobs that have been created behind protectionist walls are eliminated. But this is simply not the case .... It takes capital and *entrepreneurship* to create new jobs and in development countries there is often shortage of them. ... The IMF in many countries has made matters worse because *its austerity programmes often entailed such high interest rates sometimes exceeding 20 per cent*"[5]. In the view of present author the small-scale and medium enterprises in India which employ a large number of workers could not complete with the imported products and also multinational corporations. As a result, many small firms in India closed down. Of course these is higher industrial growth due to the use of highly capital-intensive technologies but unemployment rate has increased in the post-reform period as a result of structural adjustment policies.

To conclude, IMF policy of laying emphasis on elimination of subsidies, liberalisation of trade and capital market privatisation as conditions for providing financial assistance to the developing countries has not led to the solution of the twin problems of poverty and unemployment in the developing countries. In case of many developing countries IMF policies led to economic crises. In recent years there has been realisation on the part of IMF of the improper nature of its policies and therefore some corrections are being made to achieve the goals of rapid global growth, global economic stability and the solutions of the problems of poverty and unemployment in the poor developing countries.

---

4. A.P. Thirwall, op. cit., p. 725.
5. Joseph Stiglitz. op. cit. p.59

WORLD BANK OR INTERNATIONAL BANK FOR RECONSTRUCTION AND DEVELOPMENT (IBRD)

The World Bank bank was established in 1946 as a twin institution with the IMF (International Monetary Fund) as a result of the Bretton Woods Conference. It assists reconstruction and development of the needy countries through long and medium term loans. It pays special attention to the development of under-developed countries. It not only grants loans out of its own funds, but it also assists private foreign investment by guaranteeing or participating in loans and investments made by private investors and coordinates the lending activities of the rich countries at a governmental level. It has thus helped in raising productivity and the living standards in developing countries.

The World Bank advances loans to the developing countries subject to the following conditions.

(*a*) the overall economy of the borrowing country is soundly operated

(*b*) if the overall economic plans would reinforce the basic soundness of economy, and

(*c*) the projects which the bank is asked to finance have been carefully prepared and are economically and financially justified.

In order to obtain IBRD loans it is necessary for a developing country to keep a constantly critical eye on the soundless of its budget structure, on healthy relationship between wages and prices, on the effective utilisation of its available productive resources, on the flow of goods within its borders and the volume and character of its imports and exports; and on all the diverse aspects of national life which reflect the health of its economy. The Bank charter provides that its loans must be for productive purposes and meant to finance foreign exchange requirements of specific projects. Before a loan is granted the merits of the projects to be financed are carefully studied and it is ensured that only the most urgent and useful projects are taken up first. Also, before making or guaranteeing any loan, the Bank must satisfy itself that the borrowing country cannot obtain the loans from private sources at reasonable terms. The Bank makes prudent assessment of the projects to make sure that the loans will be repaid. The broad aim is to help strengthening the economy of the borrowing country and stimulate production activity in general rather than help the production of particular goods. It does not engage in equity financing.

The World Bank has become a part of a broadening stream of financial and technical assistance to the less developed countries. Although now other sources and institutions have also joined in the task which the Bank pioneered with such imagination and purposiveness, it has not detracted from the importance of the part which the Bank is playing in mobilising international assistance to developing countries. However, there is a definite limit to the amounts that the Bank can lend. Its entire subscribed capital is not really available for lending. Additional funds are raised by issuing bonds and here also there is a limit to the total amount that the Bank can raise by issuing bonds. The capacity of the developing countries to absorb capital for really productive purposes also imposes a limit.

The Bank has repeatedly made it clear that the main burden of international finance must fall on private investors or on loans at nominal interest or outright grants by rich countries. It cannot be expected to meet capital requirements of the developing countries in their entirety. There is thus need for other sources or organisations to undertake this all important task. The Bank can render a useful service by providing technical assistance in preparing development plans and by supplying relevant information to the other lenders. Above all, it can serve as a negotiation forum and provide mediation.

The World Bank has given a large financial assistance to India for economic development. Special mention may be made of the assistance World Bank has given to India in the development of infrastructure such as electric power, transport, communication, irrigation projects, steel industry. For a long period, India was the signal largest borrower from the World Bank. At present India is the third largest borrower of funds from the World Bank. Till June, 1999 India got, 172 loans amounting to 26 billion US dollers from World Bank.

The Role of IBRD (World Bank)

Countries with a per capita income of less than $ 5,225 that are not IDA-only borrowers are eligible to borrow from IBRD. Countries with higher per capita incomes may borrow under special circumstances or as part of a graduation strategy. It is important to note, however, that the amount that countries can borrow from IBRD depends on their creditworthiness. Thus, countries may be eligible to borrow but may not have access to IBRD resources because of poor creditworthiness. In addition, IBRD loans outstanding to any individual borrower, irrespective of its creditworthiness, may not exceed $ 13.5 billion.

Seventy-five per cent of poor people who live on less than $1 per day live in countries that received IBRD lending. IBRD borrowers are typically middle-income countries that enjoy some access to private capital markets. Some countries are eligible for IDA lending due to their low per capita incomes, but they are also creditworthy for some IBRD borrowing. These countries are known as *blend borrowers*. Even excluding IBRD loans to the blend countries, a full 25 percent of those who live on less than $1 a day live in countries that are IBRD borrowers. IBRD provides important support for poverty reduction by facilitating access to capital in larger volumes on good terms, with longer maturities, and in a more sustainable manner than the market provides.

IBRD is a AAA-rated financial institution—with some unusual characteristics. Its shareholders are sovereign governments. Its member borrowers have a voice in setting its policies. IBRD loans (and IDA credits) are typically accompanied by nonlending services to ensure more effective use of funds. Also, unlike commercial banks, IBRD is driven by development impact rather than profit maximization.

In the fiscal year 2002 IBRD raised $ 23 billion at medium to long-term maturities in international capital markets. The funding volume in year 2002 was above the $ 17 billion raised in the fiscal year 2001. Borrowings, along with shareholder equity, fund IBRD's loans and investments. Its financial strength is based on the support it receives from its shareholders and on its financial policies and practices, which are designed to maintain a high credit standing in the international markets.

Cofinancing. *Cofinancing describes funds committed by official bilateral partners, multilateral partners, export credit agencies, or private sources to specific Bank-funded projects*. Cofinancing enables the World Bank to increase its resources with additional financing to benefit the recipient country. Financing provided by multiple sources in support of individual projects also allows harmonization of policies and procedures, thus reducing the administrative burden on the recipient country and improving effectiveness. In the fiscal year 2002 IBRD and IDA financing of $ 19.5 billion was supplemented by $ 4.7 billion from such sources.

Trust Funds. A number of industrial countries, a few of a larger developing countries, the private sector, and non-governmental organizations maintain trust funds with the World Bank that can be used to supplement Bank resources for specific agreed-on initiatives. The trust funds available cover areas that facilitate providing grants for high-priority development needs, including technical assistance and advisory services, debt relief, and postconflict transition. In the fiscal year 2002, trust fund assets grew to $ 5.34 billion.

World Bank's Strategy : Stronger Focus on Results

Development experience over the past 50 years has highlighted the importance of focusing on economic and social outcomes. Donors demand that funds provided by their taxpayers achieve results. The citizens of developing countries are impatient to see tangible improvements in their living conditions within a reasonable time frame. Both expect the World Bank and other development agencies to be able to demonstrate the results of joint efforts. Developing more accurate and timely data on social and economic outcomes and conducting independent evaluations of projects and country programs provide a basis for ensuring accountability and, more importantly, learning from experience. Figure 28A.1 shows official development assistance made by various developed countries to World Bank.

The Bank has, in the last few years, significantly increased its focus on monitoring the quality of implementation, sustainability, and development outcomes of the programs it finances. Its monitoring and evaluation systems have been strengthened to more comprehensively capture the poverty impact of its policy and investment lending as well as its advisory services. This will enable it to more closely track its progress toward meeting the Millennium Development Goals (MDG).

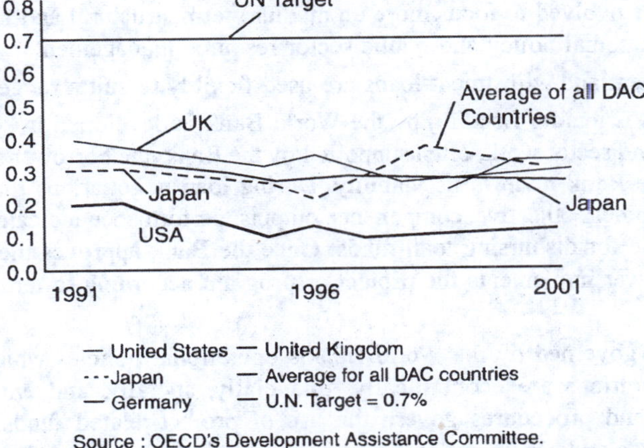

Source : OECD's Development Assistance Committee.

Fig. 28A.1. Net Official Development Assistance as a Percentage of Gross National Income

Evaluation Department indicates continuing improvements with 82 per cent of the projects accounting for 78 per cent of financing are rated as satisfactory.

Financing the Poverty Removal : Efforts by World Bank

The World Bank is a cooperative institution that mobilizes financing by means of outright contributions from the richer member countries for IDA, and by borrowing from the international capital markets for IBRD. It channels these resources for the benefit of the poor in borrowing countries. The clients of IDA are the poorest countries, who usually cannot afford to borrow on commercial terms. IDA offers concessional, no-interest loans (or credits) to the poorest countries, repayable in 35 to 40 years after a 10-year grace period. In the fiscal year 2002 IDA provided $ 8.1 billion in financing for 133 projects in 62 low-income countries.

The clients of IBRD, on the other hand, are generally the middle-income countries and, because of the limitation on IDA resources, some of the larger low-income countries that are deemed creditworthy for borrowing from World Bank. IBRD (World Bank) offers loans at near-market terms but with long maturities. In the fiscal year 2002 IBRD provided loans totaling $ 11.5 billion in support of 96 projects in 40 countries. Poverty reduction is at the core of lending from both IDA and IBRD, through investments that support growth as well as investments in basic public services. In what follows we describes the Bank's lending instruments and the process of loan approval to reduce poverty in the less developed countries.

The Bank offers an array of customized services through IBRD and IDA – including loans, technical assistance, and advice – to its developing and in-transition member countries. It uses two basic types of lending instruments: investment loans and adjustment loans.

Investment Loans. Investment loans provide finance for goods, works, and services in support of economic and social development projects in a broad range of sectors. The nature of the Bank's investment lending has evolved over time. Originally focused on hardware, engineering services, and bricks and mortar, investment lending has come to focus more on institution building, social development, and the public policy infrastructure needed to facilitate private sector activity as the Bank's priorities have changed.

Adjustment Loans. Adjustment loans provide quick-disbursing external financing to support policy and institutional reforms. Adjustment loans were originally designed to provide short-term balance of payments support for macro-economic policy reforms, including reforms in trade policy. Over time they have evolved to focus more on medium-term structural and institutional reforms in the financial sector, social policy and public sector resource management.

Both investment and adjustment loans are used flexibly to suit a range of purposes.

How a Loan is Made. Lending by the World Bank is developed in several phases. On the basis of economic and sector work, often supported by the Bank, the borrower identifies and prepares the project, and the Bank reviews its viability. During loan negotiations the Bank and borrower agree on the development objective, components, outputs, performance indicators, an implementation plan, and a schedule for disbursing loan funds. Once the Bank approves the loan and it becomes effective, the borrower implements the project or program according to terms agreed on with the Bank.

All loans are governed by the World Bank's operational policies which aim to ensure that Bank-financed operations are economically, financially, socially, and environmentally sound. Fiduciary policies and procedures govern the use of project-related funds, particularly for the procurement of goods and services. Safeguard policies help to prevent unintended adverse effects on third parties and the environment. The Bank therefore supervises the implementation of each loan and evaluates its results. Three-fourth of outstanding loans are managed by country directors located away from the Bank's Washington, D.C., headquarters. Nearly 30 per cent of World Bank's staff are based in nearly 100 country offices worldwide.

INTERNATIONAL DEVELOPMENT ASSOCIATION (IDA)

International Development Association (IDA) is another new international financing agency which was set up in 1960 as subsidiary of the World Bank, all members of the World Bank being its members. It has a capital of 1,000 million with three-fourths of it being in cash. The prosperous members like the U.S. and U.K., are expected to make higher contributions. Its financial resources were also strengthened by floating loans and by raising the capital base during the next five years.

The aim of the Association is to provide development finance to less developed countries on terms more flexible than those offered by the World Bank. In the initial stages, it financed more or less the same type of projects as the World Bank such as power generation, heavy industry, transport and thus increasing the total loan assistance for such projects. But later it took up other projects also. All the present projects leading to accelerated industrial development are being given priority over other projects such as those providing social benefits.

The terms of the loan given by IDA are more flexible and less burdensome, the rate of interest varying from project to project. The rate is normally below the bank rate. It thus compares favourably with the loans of the World Bank. It can also give interest-free loans in exceptional cases. The terms of repayment are also flexible. It can be allowed in full in local currency in deserving cases. It is hoped that in course of time the IDA will make a significant contribution towards the economic development of less developed countries. The IDA commenced its operations in November 1960, even in a year it extended development credits totalling $ 137 million to six countries including India which received $ 66 million. The credits are for 50 years and interest-free and there is ten years period of grace for repayment.

The Role of IDA

IDA is the world's largest source of concessional financial assistance for the poorest countries and invests in basic economic and human development projects. *Eligibility for access to IDA resources is governed by two basic criteria: a country's relative poverty (as measured by per capita income) and its lack of creditworthiness.* The operational income cut-off for IDA eligibility in the fiscal year 2002 is a per capita gross national income of $ 885. In order to receive IDA resources, countries must also be pursuing sound policies to promote growth and reduce poverty; IDA assistance is allocated based on annual assessments of countries' policies and institutions. In exceptional circumstances IDA extends eligibility to countries that are above the income cut-off but are not fully creditworthy to borrow from IBRD. Such exceptions have been made for small island economies.

IDA recipient countries face complex challenges in striving for progress toward the MDGs. IDA supports countries in their development efforts by promoting sound policies to secure the basis for economic growth and poverty reduction. Policy priorities include improving the quality of and access to basic education by the poor; strengthening the fight against the spread of communicable diseases, including HIV/AIDS; and building a healthy investment climate. IDA is a leader among development institutions in targeting assistance to countries that pursue sound policies, and it has refined its performance-based allocation system to place an even greater emphasis on good governance.

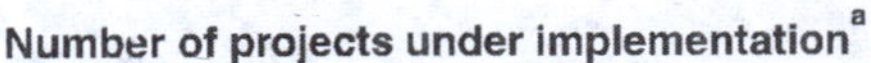

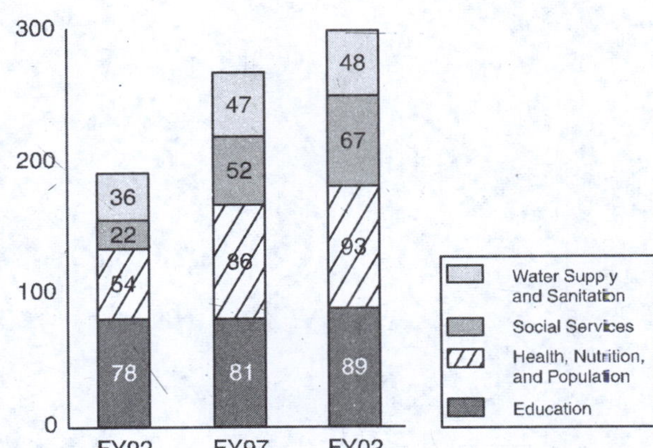

a, includes projects in both IDA-only and blend borrowing countries.

IDA commitment value of ongoing social sector projects

Year 1992: $8.1 billion

Year 1997: $13.2 billion

Year 2002: $13.7 billion

Fig. 28A.2. *IDA's Stepped-Up Effort in the Social Sectors*

IDA's increased efforts on financing expenditure on various types of social sectors such as education, health and nutrition, water supply and sanitation in poor developing countries is illustrated in Figure 28A.2. It financed 297 on going projects in fiscal year 2002 as compared with 190 a decade ago. IDA is financed by a partnership of donors, who meet every three years to decide on the amount of new resources required to fund IDA's future lending programme and to discuss lending policies and priorities.

Fiscal year 2002 marked the last year of the 12th Replenishment of IDA, which funded commitments for fiscal year 2000 through 2002. Special drawing rights (SDRs) of 8.7 billions were provided by donors countries, and SDR 6.6 billion came from internal resources, including repayments of past credits, service charges, and IBRD net income.

Chapter 29
Balance of Payments and Performance of India's External Sector

Balance of Payments Problem

We have explained the concept of balance of payments in Chapter 2 of this book. As explained there, two types of balance of payments, balance of current account and capital account are distinguished. The various items falling in these two types of balance of payments have also been explained there at length. In the present chapter we will explain the concept of equilibrium in the balance of payments and causes of disequilibrium. What measures can be adopted to tackle the problem of disequilibrium in the balance of payments will also be discussed: About 15 years ago in 1991 India had to experience a severe balance of payments crisis . A default on payments, which would have a disastrous consequent for the Indian economy, had become for the first time in our history a serious possibility in June 1991. It was at this time that new Congress Government with Dr. Manmohan Singh as our Finance Minister took several short-term and long-term measures to overcome the balance of payments crisis.

Apart from undertaking verious measures of domestic liberalisation, he took several for-reaching measures relating to balance of payments problem. Rupee was devalued in July 1991 and later in two years's time, foreign exchange rate of rupee was made market-determined and also convertible into foreign currencies. *Anti-export basis* in our economic strategy was removed and accordingly tariffs on imports were reduced. so as to promote competition. In this way costly import-substitution strategy of industrialisation was abandoned. These measures bore fruits and India was successful in solving the balance of payments problem. Our exports started growing at a relatively rapid rate than before. Capital flows and remittances by NRIs increased manifold. Of course for a short time, we got special assistance from IMF and World Bank to fulfil our obligations regarding balance of payments.

The story of what led to the crisis of balance of payments in 1991 and the performance of the external sector of India economy since then will be explained later in this chapter. Before that we explain the various causes of disequilibrium in the balance of payments and the measures that can be taken to restore equilibrium

Balance of Trade and Balance of Payments

Balance of trade and balance of payments are two related terms but they should be carefully distinguished from each other because they do not have exactly the same meaning. *Balance of trade refers to the difference in value of imports and exports of goods only, i.e., visible items only*. Movement of goods between countries is known as visible trade because the movement is open and can be verified by the customs officials.

During a given period of time, the exports and imports of goods or merchandise may be exactly equal, in which case, the balance of payments of trade is said to be balanced. But this is not necessary, for those who export and import are not necessarily the same persons. If the value of exports exceeds the value of imports, the country is said to experience an *export surplus* or a favourable balance of trade. If the value of its imports exceeds the value of its exports, the country is said to have a *deficit or an adverse balance of trade.*

The terms "*favourable*" and "*unfavourable*" are derived from the mercantilist writers of the 18th century. In those days, settlements of the foreign transactions were made in gold. If India had exported ₹ 100 crore worth of goods but had imported ₹ 80 crore worth of goods, India would receive ₹ 20 crores worth of gold from the foreign countries. As gold was regarded as wealth and as the receipts of gold made a country wealthy, the mercantilist writers regarded exports surplus as being favourable to the country.

On the other hand, if India had exported ₹ 100 crores worth of goods, but imported ₹ 150 crores worth of goods, it had to pay ₹ 50 crores in gold to the foreigners. India would be losing gold and would be poorer to that extent. Therefore, an import surplus was regarded by the mercantilist writers as adverse balance. But in these days, the international transactions are not settled in terms of gold. Even then, the terms "*favourable*" and "*unfavourable*" balance of trades have continued to be used till today

Distinction between Current Account and Capital Account

The distinction between the current account and capital account may be noted. The current account deals with payment for *currently produced goods and services*; it includes also interest earned or paid on claims and also gifts and donations. *The capital account, on the other hand, deals with payments of debts and claims*. The current account of the balance of payments affects the level of national income directly. For instance, when India sells its currently produced goods and services to foreign countries, the producers of those goods get income. In other words, current account receipts have the effect of increasing the flow of income in the country. On the other hand, when India imports goods and services from foreign countries and pays for them, money which would have been used to demand goods and services within the country flows out to foreign countries; current account payments to foreigners involve reduction of the flow of income within the country and constitute a leakage. Thus, the current account or trade account of the balance of payments has a direct effect on the level of income in a country. The capital account, however, does not have such a direct effect on the level of income; it influences the volume of assets which a country holds.

Determinants of Balance of Payments

There are several variables which determine balance of payments position of a country. They are (1) national income at home and abroad, (2) exchange rate of national currency, (3) the domestic prices of goods and factors, (4) international oil and commodity prices and (4) demand for and supply of foreign currency. At the back of these variables lie the supply factors, production function, the state of technology, tastes, distribution of income, economic conditions, the state of expectations, etc. If there is a change in any of these variables and there are no appropriate changes in other variables, disequilibrium in balance of payments will occur.

The main cause of disequilibrium in the balance of payments arises from imbalance between exports and imports of goods and services, that is, deficit or surplus in balance of trade. When for one reason or another value of exports of goods and services of a country are smaller than the value of its imports the disequilibrium in balance of payments is likely to occur. The value of exports may be small due to the lack of exportable surplus which in turn results from the low production of goods to be exported or the exports may be small because of the high cost and prices of exportable goods and severe competition in the world markets. The important causes of lower exports are inflation or rising prices in the country or over-valued exchange rate. When there is higher rate inflation in a country resulting in higher prices of exportable goods, its exports are discouraged and imports encouraged . If it is not matched by other items in the balance of payments, disequilibrium will occur.

EQUILIBRIUM IN THE BALANCE OF PAYMENTS

Before we analyse the causes of disequilibrium in the balance of payments, we would like to explain what is meant by equilibrium in the balance of payments. We have noted above that when we add up all the demand for foreign currency and all the sources from which it comes, these two amounts are *necessarily equal* and thus the overall account of the balance of payments necessarily balance or must always be in *equilibrium.*

What then do we mean by when we say that the balance of payments of a country is in equilibrium or disequilibrium. As a matter of fact, when we speak of equilibrium or disequilibrium in the balance of payments we refer to the balance on those parts of the account which do not include the accommodating items such as borrowing from the IMF, use of SDRs, drawing from the reserves of foreign currencies held by the Central Bank, etc. *When excluding these accommodating items there is neither deficit nor surplus in the overall balance of payments, it is said to be in equilibrium. When in this sense, there is either deficit or surplus, the balance of payments is said to be in disequilibrium.* The deficit in balance of payments can be financed by drawings from the IMF, use of SDRs, drawings from the reserves of foreign currencies and loan and aid received from abroad. For example in 2001-02, we added to our foreign exchange reserves to the tune of 11757 million US dollars. However for previous several years India's balance of payment on current account was in deficit. To finance the dificits India borrowed from IMF or from other countries or even resorted to commercial borrowing from abroad. But India's balance of payments for the year 2001-02 was favourable.

Basic Balance of Payments, Autonomous Items and Accommodating Items

However, a more important and popular concept of balance of payments equilibrium has been of *basic balance*. The concept of basic balance is based upon the idea of *autonomous items* in the balance of payments. The autonomous items in the balance of payments are those items which cannot be influenced or changed so easily or quickly by the Government and they are determined by some long-term factors. In this concept of basic balance, besides the items in the current account, *the long-term capital movements* both on private or Government account contained in the capital-account balance of payments are regarded as autonomous. On the other hand, in the capital account *short-term capital movements* such as borrowing from IMF or Central Banks of other countries, drawings from SDR, change in foreign exchange reserves are transitory and of *accommodating nature* and are therefore excluded from the concept of basic balance or of dequilibrium. The recourse has to be made to these accommodating items (also called *compensatory items*) so as to ensure equality between payments and receipts of foreign exchange. Changes in the compensatory items are made so as to offset the surplus or deficit in the autonomous items. Thus," *when autonomous movements cancel out over some appropriate time period and there is no need for compensatory movements, the balance of payments is in equilibrium.*[1] *Note that the equilibrium is a state of balance which can be sustained without intervention by the Government.*

The concept of balance of payments in the sense of basic balance can be represented by the following equation:

$$(X - M) + LTC = 0$$

where X stands for exports including invisible items,

M stands for imports including invisible items,

LTC stands for long-term capital movements.

If $(X - M)$ is positive (*i.e.*, $X > M$), then for balance of payments to be in equilibrium, LTC will be negative and equal to $(X - M)$. This implies that there will be *net capital outflow*. On the other

1. C.P. Kindleberger, *op. cit.*, p. 311.

hand, if $M > X$, then for the balance of payments to be in equilibrium *LTC* must be positive (that is, there will be *net capital inflow* to offset the deficit in the current account).

When the balance of payments of a country is in equilibrium, the demand for the domestic currency is equal to its supply. The demand and supply situation is thus neither favourable nor unfavourable. If the balance of payments moves against a country, adjustments must be made by encouraging exports of goods, services or other forms of exports, or by discouraging imports of all kinds. No country can have a permanently unfavourable balance of payments. Total liabilities and total assets of nations, as of individuals, must balance in the long run.

This does not mean that the balance of payments of a country should be in equilibrium individually with every other country with which she has trade relations. This is not necessary, nor is it the case in the real world. Trade relations are multilateral. India, for instance, may have balance of payments deficit with the United States and surplus with the United Kingdom and/or other countries, but each country, in the long run, cannot receive more value than she has exported to other countries taken together.

Equilibrium in the balance of payments, therefore, is a sign of the soundness of a country's economy. But disequilibrium may arise either for short or for long periods. A continued disequilibrium indicates that the country is heading towards economic and financial bankruptcy. Every country, therefore, must try to maintain balance of payments in equilibrium. To know how this can be done involves the study of the causes of disequilibrium.

CAUSES OF DISEQUILIBRIUM IN THE BALANCE PAYMENTS

There are several variables which join together to constitute equilibrium in the balance of payments position of a country, *viz*., national income at home and abroad, the prices of goods and factors, the supply of money, the rate of interest, etc., all of which determine the exports, imports and demand and supply of foreign currency. At the back of these variables lie the supply factors, production functions, the state of technology, tastes, the distribution of income, the state of anticipations, etc. If there is a change in any of these variables and there are no appropriate changes in other variables, disequilibrium will be the result.

The main cause of the disequilibrium in the balance of payments arises from imbalance between exports and imports of goods and services. When for one reason or another exports of goods and services of a country are smaller than their imports, disequilibrium in the balance of payments is the likely result. Exports may be small due to the lack of exportable surplus which in turn result from low production or the exports may be small because of the high costs and prices of exportable goods and severe competition in the world markets. An important cause of small exports is the inflation or rising prices in the country. When the prices of goods are high in the country, its exports are discouraged and imports encouraged. If it is not matched by other items in the balance of payments, disequilibrium emerges.

Cyclical Disequilibrium. Cyclical disequilibrium is caused by the fluctuations in the economic activity or what are known as trade cycles. During the periods of prosperity, prices of goods fall and incomes of the people go down. These changes in incomes of the people and prices of goods affect exports and imports of goods and thereby influence the balance of payments."If prices rise in prosperity and decline in depression, a country with a price elasticity for imports greater than unity will experience a tendency for a decline in the value of imports in prosperity, while those for which imports price elasticity is less than one will experience a tendency for increase. These tendencies may be overshadowed by the effects of income changes, of course. Conversely, as prices decline in depression, the elastic demand will bring about an increase in imports, the inelastic demand a decrease."[2]

2. C.P. Kindleberger, *op. cit.*, p. 526.

Secular or Long-Run Disequilibrium. *Secular (long-run) disequilibrium in balance of payments occur because of long-run and deep-seated changes in an economy* as it develops from one stage of growth to another. The current account in the balance of payments follows a varying pattern from one stage to another. In the initial stages of development, domestic investment exceeds domestic savings and imports exceed exports. Disequilibrium arises due to lack of sufficient funds available to finance the import surplus, or the import surplus is not covered by available capital from abroad. Then comes a stage of growth when domestic savings tend to exceed domestic investment and export outrun imports. Disequilibrium may result because the long-term capital outflow falls short of the surplus savings or because surplus savings exceed the amount of investment opportunities abroad. At a still later stage of growth domestic savings tend to equal domestic investment and long-term capital movements are , on balance, zero.

Thus we see that a secular disequilibrium will occur when either the long-term capital movements get out of adjustment with deep-seated factors affecting savings and investment, or planned savings and investment change without an offsetting change in the movement of long-term capital. If investment adjusted itself readily to the amount of domestic savings plus foreign capital there could be no tendency for secular disequilibrium.

The balance-of-payments position will be in equilibrium, if the international capital flow falls into line with the requirements of domestic investment minus domestic savings. There is a tendency to secular disequilibrium, because of domestic savings and domestic investment are independent of the foreign capital flow and are of different magnitudes. There is a strong tendency for underdeveloped countries to over-invest and/or undersave. The underdeveloped countries are investing larger than their domestic savings and exports allow them because they are eager to acclerate the rate of economic growth. This tendency to over-invest causes a secular disequilibrium in the balance of payments.

Technological Disequilibrium. *Technological disequilibrium* in the balance of payments is caused by various technological changes. Technological changes involve inventions or innovations of new goods or new techniques of production. These technological changes affect the demand for goods and productive factors which in turn influence the various items in the balance of payments. Each technological change implies a new comparative advantage to which a country adjusts to. The innovation leads to increased exports if it is a new good and export-biased innovation. The innovation may lead to decline in imports if it is import-biased. This will create a disequilibrium. A new equilibrium will require either increased imports or reduced exports.

Structural Disequilibrium. Let us see how the structural type of disequilibrium is caused." *Structural disequilibrium at the goods level* occurs, when a change in demand or supply of exports alters a previously existing equilibrium, or when a change occurs in the basic circumstances under which income is earned or spent abroad, in both cases without the requisite parallel changes elsewhere in the economy."[3]

Suppose demand in foreign countries for Indian handicrafts falls. The resources engaged in the production of these handicrafts must shift to some other line or the country must restrict imports, otherwise the country will experience a structural disequilibrium. A change in supply may also cause a structural disequilibrium. Suppose Indian jute crop falls because of the change in the shift in the crop-pattern, Indian jute exports will fall and a disequilibrium will be created. Apart from goods, a loss of service income may also upset the balance-of-payments position on current account. Besides, the loss of income may arise because foreign investment has proved a failure or it has been confiscated or nationalised, *e.g.* nationalisation of Anglo-Iranian Company in Iran. A war also produces structural changes which may affect not only goods but also factors of production.

3. C.P. Kindleberger, *op. cit.*, p. 526.

A deficit arising from a structural change can be filled by increased production or decreased expenditure, which in turn affect international transactions in increased exports or decreased imports. Actually, it is not so easy because the resources are relatively immobile and expenditure not readily compressible. Under such circumstances, more drastic steps are called for to correct a serious disequilibrium.

"Structural disequilibrium *at the factor level* results from factor prices which fail to reflect accurately factor endowments ... *i.e.*, when factor prices, out or line with factor endowments, distort the structure of production from the allocation of resources which appropriate factor prices would have indicated"[4] If, for instance, the price of labour is too high, it will be used more sparingly and the country will import highly capital-intensive equipment and machinery. This will lead to disequilibrium in the balance of payments on the one hand and unemployment of labour on the other.

Conclusion

We have explained above four types of disequilibria-cyclical, secular and two kinds of structural disequilibria and how they are caused. In each case, the causes manifest themselves through changes in export of goods and services, making one exceed the other.

We have already detailed the various items that enter into the balance of payments. Any cause that leads to a persistently one-sided movement in those items may cause a disequilibrium. For instance, certain causes may lead to falling off in the export of merchandise, imports remaining unaffected or moving in the opposite direction. Falling off in exports may be due to all sorts of causes. Take, for example, the case of exports and imports of goods. Our exports may fall because of decreased production due to seasonal factors or other causes. The demand for our goods in the international market may fall off because of a fall in the purchasing power of consumers of such goods or because of a comparatively high cost of production in India which reduces our competitive strength in the international market. Our exports may become dear to foreigners because of an appreciation of our exchange rate, that is, a rise in the value of the rupee, say from ₹ 42.50 per US dollar to ₹ 40 per US dollar. If we persist in artificially keeping the value of the rupee at a higher level than justified by economic forces, unfavourable balance of trade and payments will tend to persist.

In the same way, disequilibrium may arise due to excessive imports or services neither balanced by exports nor import of capital, etc. Compulsory exports in the form of reparations or indemnities also cause international disequilibrium and obstruct the harmonious trade relations between the countries concerned.

HOW DISEQUILIBRIUM CAN BE CORRECTED

When serious disequilibrium arises in a country's balance of payments, steps must be taken to correct it, if the country's economy is to be kept in a sound condition. Obviously, the causes which are responsible for such a state of affairs must be removed. The 'classical' view of the adjustment mechanism is: "An active or passive balance, accompanied by an inflow or outflow of gold, was formally supposed to result in an expansion or contraction of the domestic money supply; and this expansion or contraction was expected to bring about a rise or fall in the level of domestic costs and prices tending, in the former case, to stimulate imports and discourage exports or, in the latter to discourage imports and stimulate exports. Gold flows, changes in the quantity of money and changes in relative levels thus appeared as the principal factors in the mechanism of adjustments"[5]

But gold standard has been abandoned long ago. These days different countries of the world are under managed currency standard. Therefore gold flows no longer occur to bring the balance of

4. See. C.P. Kindleberger, *International Economics*, 1978.
5. See C.P. Kindleberger, *International Economics*, 1978.

payments into equilibrium. Recent currency experience has, however, led to certain modifications in the classical theory. It is now thought that changes in the flow of income induced by balance of payments serve as an equilibrating factor."The main point is that any active or passive balance of current transaction....tends directly to expand or contract the total flow of money income within a given country... The changes induced by the balance of payments in the flows of income and expenditure affect, in turn, the demand for imported as well as home-produced goods and so react on the balance of payments to bring it into equilibrium".[6]

However, these automatic adjustments or corrections in the balance of payments through either changes in prices of goods and factors or through changes in the incomes do not always work due to the presence of various rigidities and immobilities in the system. When the causes of disequilibrium in the balance of payments are deeper and serious, then the automatic correction via price and income changes does not work at all. Under such circumstance, some concrete measures are required to be taken to restore the equilibrium in the balance of payments. Disequilibrium in the balance of payments may be corrected by the following methods by the Government.

There are four well-known methods of correcting in adverse balance of payments:

1. Trade Policy Measures : Expanding Exports and Restraining Imports

Trade policy measures to improve the balance of payments refer to the measures adopted to promote exports and reduce imports. Exports may be encouraged by reducing or abolishing export duties and lowering the interest rate on credit used for financing exports. Exports are also encouraged by grainting subsidies to manufacturers and exporters. Besides, on export earnings lower income tax can be levied to provide incentives to the exporters to produce and export more goods and services. By imposing lower excise duties, prices of exports can be reduced to make them competitive in the world markets.

On the other hand, imports may be reduced by imposing or raising tariffs (*i.e.*, import duties) on imports of goods. Imports may also be restricted through imposing import quotas, introducing licenses for imports. Imports of some inessential items may be totally prohibited.

Before the economic reforms carried out since 1991. India had been following all the above policy measures to promote exports and restrict imports so as to improve its balance of payments position. But they had not achieved full success in their aim to correct balance of payments disequilibrium. Therefore, India had to face great difficulties with regard to balance of payments. At several occasions it approached IMF to bail it out of the foreign exchange crisis that emerged as a result of huge deficits in the balance of payments. At long last, economic crisis caused by persistent deficits in balance of payments forced India to introduce structural reforms to achieve a long-lasting solution of balance of payments problem.

2. Expenditure-Reducing Policies

The important way to reduce imports and thereby reduce deficit in balance of payments is to adopt monetary and fiscal policies that aim at reducing aggregate expenditure in the economy. The fall in aggregate expenditure or aggregate demand in the economy works to reduce imports and help in solving the balance of payments problem. The two important tools of reducing aggregate expenditure are the use of (1) tight monetary policy and (2) contrationary fiscal policy. We explain them below.

Tight Monetary Policy. Tight monetary is often used to check aggregate expenditure or demand by raising the cost of bank credit and restricting the availability of credit. For this bank rate is raised by the Central Bank of the coutnry which leads to higher lending rates charged by the commercial banks. This discoruages businessmen to borrow for investment.and consumers to

---

6. *Ibid.*

borrow for buying durable cosnumers goods. This therefore leads to the reduction in investment and consumption expenditure. Besides, availability of credit to lend for investment and consumption purposes is reduced by raising the cash reserve ratio (CRR) of the banks and also undertaking of open market operations (selling Government securities in the open market) by the Central Bank of the country. This also tends to lower aggregate expenditure or demand which will helps in reducing imports. But there are limitations of the successful use of monetary policy to check imports, especially in a developing country like India.This is because tight monetary policy adversely affects investment increase in which is necessary for accelerating economic grwoth. If a developing country is experiencing inflation, tight monetary policy is quite effective in curbing inflation by reducing aggregate demnad. This will help in reducing aggregate expenditure and, depending on the income propensity to import, will curtail imports. Besides, tight monetary policy helps to reduce prices or lower the rate of inflation. Lower price level or lower inflation rate will curb the tendency to import, both on the part of businessmen and consumers.

But when a developing country like India is experiencing recession or slowdown in economic growth along with deficits in balance of payments, use of tight monetary policy that reduces aggregate expenditure or demand will not help much as it will adversely affect economic growth and deepen economic recession. Therefore, in a developing country, monetary policy has to be used along with other policies such as a appropriate fiscal policy and trade policy to tackle the problem of disequilibrium in the balance of payments.

Contractionary Fiscal Policy. Appropriate fiscal policy is also an important means of reducing aggregate expenditure. An increase in direct taxes such as income tax will reduce aggregate expenditure. A part of reduction in expenditure may lead to decrease in imports. Increase in indirect taxes such as excise duties and sales tax will also cause reduction in expenditure. The other fiscal policy measure is to reduce Government expenditure, especially unproductive or non-developmental expenditure. The cut in Government expenditure will not only reduce expenditure directly but also indirectly through the operation of multiplier.

It may be noted that if tight monetary and contractionary fiscal policies succeed in lowring aggregate expenditure which causes reduction in prices or lowering the rate of inflation, they will work in two ways to improve the balance of payments. First, fall in doemstic prices or lower rate of inflation will induce people to buy doemstic products rather than imported goods. Second, lower doemstic prices or lower rate of inflation will stimulate exports. Fall in imports and rise in exports will help in reducing deficit in balance of payments.

However, it may be emphasised again that the method of reducing expenditure through contractionary monetary and fiscal policies is not without limitations. If reduction in aggregate demand lowers investment, this will adversely affect economic growth. Thus, correction in balance of payments may be achieved at the expense of economic growth. Further, it is not easy to reduce substantially government expenditure and impose heavy taxes as they are likely to affect incentives to work and invest and invite public protest and opposition. We thus see that correcting the balance of payments through contractionary fiscal policy is not an easy matter.

3. Expenditure - Switching Policies : Devaluation

A significant method which is quite often used to correct fundamental disequilibrium in balance of payments is the use of expenditure-switching policies. Expenditure switching policies work through changes in relative prices. Prices of imports are increased by making domestically produced goods relatively cheaper. Expenditure switching policies may lower the prices of exports which will encourage exports of a country. In this way by changing relative prices, expenditure-switching policies help in correcting disequilibrium in balance of payments.

The important form of expenditure switching policy is the reduction in foreign exchange rate of the national currency, namely, devalaution. By devaluation we mean reducing the value or exchange rate of a national currency with respect to other foreign currencies. It should be remembered that devaluation is made when a country is under fixed exchange rate system and occasionally decides to lower the exchange rate of its currency to improve its balance of payments. Under the Bretton Woods System adopted in 1946, fixed exchange rate system was adopted, but to correct fundamental disequilibrium in the balance of payments, the countries were allowed to make devaluation of their currencies with the permission of IMF. Now, Bretton Woods System has been abandoned and most of the countries of the world have floated their currencies and have thus adopted the system of flexible exchange rates as determined by market forces of demand for and supply of them. However, even in the present flexible exchange rate system, the value of a currency or its exchange rate as determined by demand for and supply of it can fall. *Fall in the value of a currency with respect to foreign currencies as determined by demand and supply conditions is described as depreciation.* If a country permits its currency to *depreciate* without taking effective steps to check it, it will have the same effects as devaluation. Thus, in our analysis we will discuss the effects of fall in value of a currency whether it is brought about through devaluation or depreciation. In July 1991, when India was under Bretton-Woods fixed exchange rate system, it devalued its rupee to the extent of about 20%. (From ₹ 20 per dollar to ₹ 25 per dollar) to correct disequilibrium in the balance of payments.

Now, the question is how devaluation of a currency works to improve balance of payments. As a result of reduction in the exchange rate of a currency with respect to foreign currencies, the prices of goods to be exported fall, whereas prices of imports go up. This encourages exports and discourages imports. With exports so stimulated and imports discouraged, the deficit in the balance of payments will tend to be reduced. Thus policy of devaluation is also refered to as *expenditure switching policy* since as a result of reduction of imports, people of a country switches their expenditure on imports to the domestically produced goods. It may be noted that as a result of the lowering of prices of exports, export earnings will increase if the demand for a country's exports is price elastic (*i.e.*, $e_r > 1$). And also with the rise in prices of imports the value of imports will fall if a country's demand for imports is elastic. If demand of a country for imports is inelastic, its expenditure on imports will rise instead of falling due to higher prices of imports.

Devaluation: Marshall Lerner Condition. It is clear from above that whether devaluation or depreciation will lead to the rise in export earnings and reduction in import expenditure depends on the price elasticity of foreign demand for exports and domestic demand for imports. Marshall and Lerner have developed a condition which states that devaluation will succeed in improving the balance of payments if sum of price elasticity of exports and price elasticity of imports is greater than one. Thus, according to Marshall-Lerner Condition, devaluation improves balance of payments if

$$e_x + e_m > 1$$

where e_x stands for price elasticity of exports

e_m stands for price elasticity of imports

If in case of a country $e_x + e_m < 1$, the devaluation will adversely affect balance of payments position instead of improving it. If $e_x + e_m = 1$, devaluation will leave the disequilibrium in the balance of payments unchanged.

Income-Absorption Approach to Devealuation. Further, for devaluation to be successful in correcting disequilibrium in the balance of payments a country should have sufficient exportable surplus. If a country does not have adequate amount of goods and services to be exported, fall in their prices due to devaluation or depreciation will be of no avail. This can be explained through income-absorption approach put forward by Sidney S Alexander[7]. According to this approach, trade balance is the difference between the total output of goods and services produced in a country and its absorption by it. By absorption of output of goods and services we mean how much of them is used up for consumption and investment in that country. That is, absorption means the sum of consumption and investment expenditure on domestically produced goods and services. Expressing algebraically we have

$$B = Y - A$$

where B = trade balance or exportable surplus
Y = national income or value of output of goods and services produced
A = Absorption or sum of consumption and investment expenditure

It follows from above that if expenditure or absorption is less than national product, it will have positive trade balance or exportable surplus. To create this exportable surplus, expenditure on domestically produced consumer and investment goods should be reduced or national product must be raised sufficiently.

To sum up, it follows from above that *for devaluation or depreciation to be successful in correcting disequilibrium in the balance of payments, the sum of price elasticities of demand for a country's exports and imports should be high (that is, greater than one) and secondly it should have sufficient exportable surplus*. The devaluation will also not be successful in the achievement of its aim if other countries relaliate and make similar devaluation in their currencies and thus competitive devaluation of the exchange rate may start.

After Independence India devalued its currency three times, first in 1949, the second in June 1966 and third in July 1991 to correct the disequilibrium in the balance of payments. The devaluation of June 1966 was not successful for some time to reduce deficit in the balance of payments. This is because the demand for bulk of our traditional exports was not very elastic and also we could not reduce our imports despite their higher prices. However devaluation of July 1991 proved quite successful as after it our exports grew at a rapid rate for some years and growth of imports remained within safe limits.

4. Exchange Control

Finally, there is the method of exchange control. We know that deflation is dangerous; devaluation has a temporary effect and may provoke others also to devalue. Devaluation also hits the prestige of a country. These methods are, therefore, avoided and instead foreign exchange is controlled by the government. Under it, all the exporters are ordered to surrender their foregin exchange to the central bank of a country and it is then rationed out among the licensed importers. None else is allowed to import goods without a licence. The balance of payments is thus rectified by keeping the imports within limits.

After the Second War World a new international institution 'International Monetary Fund (IMF)' was set up for maintaining equilibrium in the balance of payments of member countries for a short term. Member countries borrow from it for a short period to maintain equilibrium in the balance of payments. IMF also advises member countries how to correct fundamental disequilibrium in the balance of Payments when it does arise. It may, however, be mentioned here that no country now needs to be forced into deflation (and so depression) to root out the causes underlying disequilibrium as had to be done under the gold standard. On the contrary, the IMF provides a mechanism by which changes in the rates of foreign exchange can be made in an orderly fashion.

Conclusion. In short, correction of disequilibrium calls for a judicious combination of the following methods:

(*i*) Monetary and fiscal changes affecting income and prices in the country;
(*ii*) Exchange rate adjustment, *i.e.*, devaluation or appreciation of the home currency;

---

7. Sidney S. Alexander, "Effects of Devaluation on Trade Balance", *IMF Staff Papers*, Vol. 11 (April, 1952).

(*iii*) Trade restrictions, *i.e.*, tariffs, quotas, etc.;
(*iv*) Capital movement, *i.e.*, borrowing or lending aborad; and
(*v*) Exchange control.

No reliance can be placed on any single tool. There is room for more than one approach and for more than one device. But the application of the tools depends on the nature of the disequilibrium. There are, we have said, three types of disequilibrium: (1) cyclical disequilibrium, (2) secular disequilibrium, (3) structural disequilibrium (at the goods and the factor level). It is more appropriate that fiscal measures should be used to correct cyclical disequilibrium in the balance of payments. To correct structural disequilibrium adjustment in exchange rate should be avoided. Capital movements are needed to offset deep-seated forces in secular disequilibrium.

The main methods of desirable adjustment are, therefore, monetary and fiscal policies which directly affect income, and exchange depreciation (that is, devaluation) which affects prices in the first instance. Devaluation or depreciation of exchange rate can also have income effect through price effects. Monetary and fiscal policies affect relative prices also.

INDIA'S BALANCE OF PAYMENTS

India's Balance of Payment Crisis, 1991

The crisis of Indian economy of 1991 which led to the liberalisation and other structural reforms in the India economy had roots in balance of payments problem which emerged in acute form in 1990-91. As will be seen from Tabele 29.1 during the later half of eighties (1985-90) average annual current account deficit in balance of payment was 2.2 per cent of GDP and rose to 3.1 per cent of GDP in 1990-91. Gulf war of 1991 added to the balance of payments problem in two ways. First, this war caused sharp rise in prices of crude oil and petroleum products which substantially increased the import bill of the Indian economy. Secondly, inward remitances by the Indian workers working in the Gulf countries which were important source of foreign exchange during the eighties stopped due to war conditions.

But in addition to Gulf war there were many other causes of large deficits on current account balance incurred year after year. In the external sector, an important reason for current account deficit was *over-valued exchange rate* of rupee which made our exports costlier and imports cheaper. This caused sluggish growth in exports, while imports sharply increased. This contributed to current account deficit.

Secondly, our foreign trade policy which was one of import substitution was *biased against exports*. Dr. Manmohan Singh had warned against this much earlier. Dr. Manmohan Singh writes, "*On the one hand*, there *was a wide-spread feeling that not much could be done to increase export earnings in view of the stagnant demand of India's major exports. On the other hand, responsible economists were assuring the country that import-substitution would by itself be able to solve India's balance of payments difficulties .... The result was neglect of exports*"[8]

It is evident from above that export-pessimism prevented Indian Government for adopting aggressive export promoting policies. This was largely responsible for slow growth of Indian exports. The extent of anti-export bias in trade and balance of payments policies can be judged by the fact that in 1985-86 our merchandise exports accounted for only 4.1 per cent of GDP whereas imports formed 7.6 per cent of GDP, that is, 80 per cent higher than that of exports giving rise to trade deficit of 3.5 per cent of GDP which is of a very high order.

For the seventh five-year plan period, 1985-90 the trade deficit averaged 3 per cent of GDP while current account deficit averaged 2.2 per cent of GDP. These large trade and current account deficits during the later half of eighties were *financed by various forms of external borrowing* such

8. Manmohan Singh, *India's Exports Trends and Prospects for Self-Sustained Growth*. Oxford : Clarendon Press, 1964, pp. 377.

as external assistance, commercial borrowing and NRI deposits. Besdies, to meet these current account deficits, foreign exchange reserves were also run down. The large-scale borrwoing led to substantial increase in annual interest payments to be made in addition to paying back the funds borrowed over a time span. As a result of heavy commercial borrowing in the later half of eighties, *debt-service ratio* (*i.e.* ratio of debt service charges to the current receipts of current account balance shaply rose to 35 per cent in 1990-91 (See Table 29.2). This was also responsible for deterioration in deficit in balance of payments.

Since the balance of payments crisis of 1991 several reforms have been undertaken. After *temporary measures* of import compression and a dual exchange rate system to regulate imports, basic reforms in the external sector were undertaken to tackle the balance of payments problem on a long term basis. Even in July 1991, the nominal exchange rate of rupee was devalued to correct the overvaluation of the Indian rupee and thereby to remove anti-export bias. Further, all export subsidies and *most of the quantitative restrications on imports of intermediate and capital goods* were withdrawn in 1991.

Besides, customs duties on imports have been greatly reduced over a period of time. The peak tariff rate on non-agricultural imports which was as high as 355 per cent[1] was reduced to 45 per cent in 1997 and further to 35 per cent in 2002-03, to 20 per cent in January 2004, to 15 per cent in budget for 2005-06, to 12.5 per cent in budget for 2006-07 and in budget for 2007-08 peak tariff rate for all imports was reduced to 10 per cent. This reduction in customs duties has also worked to remove anti-export bias in our foreign trade policy. With lower customs duties the domestic industries get imported raw materials and capital goods at cheaper rates to produce exports at competitive prices.

Besides, foreign direct investment (FDI) has been liberalised subject to certain conditions and foreign institutional investors have been permitted to invest in equity and debt securities in the Indian stock market. All these measures of deregulation and liberalisation of foreign trade and investment have produced beneficial effects on India's balance of payments and accumulation of foreign exchange reserves.

Balance of Payments on Current Account

Balance of payments on the other hand is more comprehensive in scope than balance of trade. It includes not only imports and exports of goods which are visible items but also such invisible items as shipping, banking, insurance, tourism, interest on investments, gifts, etc.

A country, say India, has to make payments to the other countries not only for its imports of merchandise but also for banking, insurance and shipping services rendered by other countries; it has to pay further the royalties for foreign firms, expenditure of Indians in foreign countries, interest on foreign investments in India, or on loans obtained by India from other countries and such international organizations as the I.M.F., I.B.R.D., etc. These are debit items for India, since these transactions involve payments abroad. In the same way, foreign countries import goods from India, make use of Indian films and so on, for all of which they make payments to India. These are the credit items for India as the latter receives payments. Balance of payments thus gives a comprehensive picture of all such transactions including imports and exports of goods and services.

The Table 29.1 (given below) we give the position of India's balance of payments on current account for the years 2005-06 to 2012-13. In this table of balance of payments are given the visible as well as invisible items of trade. The *visible items* are export-import trade and the *invisible items of balance of payments on current account are travel, transportation and insurance, interest on loans given and other investment income and private transfers such as remittances from Indians living abroad.* Both visible and invisible items together make up the *current account*. Invisible items such as interest on loans, tourist expenditure, banking and insurance charges, etc., are similar to visible trade since receipts from selling such services to the foreigners are very similar in their effects on receipts from sales of goods; they provide income to the people who produce the goods or services.

Table 29.1. India's Balance of Payments on Current Account ***(in Billion US $)***

S.No. Items	2005-06	2006-07	2007-08	2008-09	2009-10	2010-11	11-12	12-13
1. Exports	105.1	128.9	166.2	189.0	182.2	256.2	309.8	305.6
2. Imports	157.1	190.7	257.6	307.6	300.6	383.5	499.5	502-2
3. **Trade Balance**	–52.0	–61.8	–91.5	–118.6	–118.4	–127.3	–189.9	–195.7
	(–6.2)	(–6.5)	(–7.4)	(–9.8)	(–8.6)	(–7.8)	(–10.1)	(–10.6)
4. **Invisibles (Net)**	42.0	52.2	75.7	89.9	79.9	79.3	111.6	–
(*i*). Non-factor Services	23.2	29.5	38.9	49.6	35.7	44.1	64.1	–
(*ii*). Investment Income	–5.9	–7.2	–5.1	–4.0	–8.0	–17.9	–16.0	–
(*iii*). Private Transfers	24.5	29.8	41.7	44.6	52.3	53.1	63.5	–
5. **Goods and Services Balance**	–28.7	–32.3	–52.6	–69.0	–83.0	–83.2	–125.7	–130.7
6. **Current Account Balance (Net)**	**–10.0**	**– 9.6**	**–15.7**	**–28.7**	**–38.4**	**–48.1**	**–78.2**	**–87.8**
	(–1.2)	**(–1.0)**	**(–1.3)**	**(–2.4)**	**(–2.8)**	**(–2.7)**	**(–4.2)**	**(–4.8)**

Source : RBI

Note : *Figures in brackets show per cent of GDP at market prices.*

It will be noted from Table 29.1 above that the most important item in the balance of payments on current account is balance of trade which refers to imports and exports of goods. In the Table 29.1 balance of trade does not balance and shows a deficit in all the seven years. In the years 2011-12 and 2012-13 trade deficit has substantially increased. Trade deficit was over 10 per cent of GDP in both these years. In fact, it is huge trade deficit in these two years that has caused huge current account deficit of over 4% of GDP in these two years Economic slowdown in advanced countries and its spill over effects on Emerging Market Economies coupled with high crude oil and gold prices were responsible for sharp increase in trade deficit. Due to *surplus in invisibles account*, there was a surplus on current account for three years, 2001-2002, 2002-03 and 2003-04. In India's balance of payments on current account for three years, 2004-05 onwards there has been a deficit. Contrary to popular perception, deficit on current account is not always bad provided it is within reasonable limits (which in case of India is estimated to be 2.5% of GDP) and can be easily met by non-debt capital receipts. In fact, *deficit on current account represents the extent of absorption of capital inflows in India during a year*.

It may be noted that when there is deficit on the current account, it is financed either by using *foreign exchange reserves* held by Reserve Bank of India or by *capital flows* that come into the country in the form of foreign direct investment (FDI) and portfolio investment by FIIs, external commercial borrowing (ECB) from abraod and by NRI deposits in foreign exchange account in our banks. However, due to global financial crisis in 2008-09, there was first slowdown and then decrease in exports. As a result, there was a large deficit of 2.4 of per cent of GDP on current account which could not be met by capital inflows as they were quite meagre ($ 8.6 billion) as a result of global financial crisis. Therefore, to finance the deficit on current account in 2008-09 we had to withdraw US $ 20 billion from our foreign exchange reserves. Again in the last two years 2011-12 and 2012-13 the current account deficit (CAD) has been quite high.

It may be noted that high current deficit tends to weaken the rupee by raising the demand for US dollars. In 2011-12, current account deficit tended to weaken the rupee by raising the demand for US dollars. In 2011-12, the current account deficit was 4.2 per cent of GDP. Since capital inflows in this year were not adequate to finance the current account deficit, RBI had to withdraw 12.8 billion US dollars from its foreign exchange reserves to meet the demand for US dollars (see Table 34.2) . In the year 2012-13 the current account deficit was estimated to be even higher at 4.8 per cent of GDP, capital inflows through portfolio investment by FIIs picked up in the latter half of 2012-13 but capital inflows through FDI had fallen. However, in 2012-13 we were able to finance the current account deficit with capital inflows without withdrawing from our foreign exchange reserves.

In 2013-14 current account deficit situation has worsened as FIIs have pulled out both from debt and equity markets since June 2013. This has led to the sharp depreciation of rupee by increasing demand for dollars. Thus current account deficit poses a serious challenge to macroeconomic management of the economy. The dependence on volatile capital inflows through FIIs to meet the current account deficit is unsustainable as these capital flows go back when economic situation in their home countries improve and thereby causes sharp depreciation in exchange rate of rupee and crash in stock market prices.

Since in the recent years, 2011-12, 2012-13 and 2013-14 current account deficit has widened, which has increased the balance of payments vulnerability to sudden reversal of capital flows, especially when sizable flows are comprised of debt and volatile portfolio investment by FIIs. The priority has therefore been to reduce current account deficit (CAD) through improving trade balance. Efforts have been made to promote exports by diversifying the export commodity basket and export destinations. One way to limit imports is to bring prices up to the international level so that users bear the full cost. Accordingly, petrol has been decontrolled and diesel prices have been revised upward in Jan. 2013 to curtail subsidy on it. To discourage the imports of gold which has played a significant role in causing trade deficit, customs duty on its import was first raised from 6% to 8% and then to 10 per cent.

Further, to improve the current account deficit emphasis has been on facilitating remittances and encouraging software exports that have been responsible for surplus on the invisible account. In recent years this surplus has lowered the impact of widening trade deficit on current account deficit (CAD) significantly. The two components together constituted nearly two thirds of the trade deficit that was more than 10 per cent of GDP in 2011-12 and 2012-13. Remittances particularly are known to exhibit resistance when the country is hit by external shock as was evident during the global crisis of 2008. Besides, several incentives have been given to NRIs to deposit their foreign exchange savings in Indian banks.

Balance of Payments on Capital Account

In the balance of payments on capital account given in Table 29.2 important items are borrowings from foreign countries and lending funds to other countries. This takes two forms: (*i*) *External assistance* which means borrowing from foreign countries under concessional rate of interest; (*ii*) *Commercial borrowing* under which the Indian Government and the Private sector borrow funds from world money market at higher market rate of interest. Besides *non-resident deposits* are another important item in capital account. These are the deposits made by non-resident Indians (NRI) who keep their surplus funds with Indian Banks. Another important item in balance of payments on capital account is *foreign investment* by foreign companies in India. There are two

Table 292. India's Balance of Payments on Capital Account ***(in Billion US $)***

	2005-06	2006-07	2007-08	2008-09	2009-10	2010-11	2011-12
External Assistance (Net)	1.7	1.8	2.1	2.6	2.9	4.94	2.3
Commercial Borrowing (Net)	2.5	16.1	22.6	7.0	2.8	12.16	10.3
Non-Resident Deposits (Net)	2.8	4.3	0.2	– 4.3	2.9	3.14	11.9
Foreign Investment (Net)	15.5	14.8	43.3	3.5	50.4	42.13	39.2
of which							
(*i*) FDI net	3.0	7.7	15.9	17.5	18.0	11.83	22.1
(*ii*) Portfolio Investment (Net)	12.5	7.1	27.4	–15.0	32.4	30.3	17.2
(*iii*) Other capital flows (Net)	2.4	9.2	39.7	–9.7	–13.1	–10.48	–7.0
Capital Account Balance (Net)	**24.9**	**46.1**	**107.9**	**8.6**	**51.6**	**63.74**	**67.8**
Use of Exchange Reserves*	–15.0	–36.6	–92.2	+20.1*	–13.4*	(–13.1)*	(+12.8)*

*** Also includes errors and omissions***

Source: RBI Annual Report 2012-13. Use of foreign exchange reserves (–indicates increase of reserves, and + indicates decrease of reserves on BOP basis.

types of foreign investment. First is *portfolio investment* under which foreign institutional investors (FII) *purchase shares (equity) and bonds* of Indian companies and Government. The second is *foreign direct investment* (FDI) under which foreign companies set up plants and factories on their own or in collaboration with the Indian companies. Still another item in capital account is other capital flows in which the important source of funds is remittances from abroad sent by the Indian citizens working in foreign countries. The Table 29.2 gives the position of India's capital account for the years 2004 -05 to 2011-12.

Capital inflows in the capital account can be classified into ***debt creating*** and ***non-debt creating.*** Foreign investment (both direct and portfolio) represents non-debt creating capital inflows, whereas external assistance (i.e. concessional loans taken from abroad), external commercial borrowing (ECB) and non-resident deposits are debt-creating capital inflows.

It will be seen from Table 29.2, during 2007-08, there was net capital inflow of 43.3 billion US dollars on account of *foreign investment (both direct and portfolio)*. The Table 29.2 gives the position of India's balance of payments on capital account for seven years, 2005-06, 2006-07, 2007-08, 2008-09 and 2009-10, 2010-11 and 2011-12. When all items of balance of payments on capital account are taken into account we had *a surplus* of 107.9 billion US dollars in 2007-08. Taking into current account deficit of $ 15.7 billion on current account in year 2007-08 there was accretion to our foreign exchange reserves by $ 92.2 billion in 2007-08. Global financial crisis affected our capital account balance as there was ***reversal of capital flows after Sept. 2008*** with the result that ***we used*** $ 20.1 billion of our foreign exchange reserves in 2008-09 resulting in *decrease* of our foreign exchange reserves. That is, because we used our foreign exchange reserves equal to $ 20.1 billion, there was decline in our foreign exchange reserves by $ 20 billion in 2008-09. The situation improved in 2009-10 as foreign direct investment (FDI) and portfolio investment by FIIs picked up. As a result there was net capital account surplus of $ 51.6 billion in 2009-10 and after meeting the current account deficit of $ 38 billion there was addition to our foreign exchange reserves by $ 13.4 billion in 2009-10. In 2010-11 also there was surplus on capital account of $ 63.74 billion and after meeting current deficit we added $ 13.1 billion in our foreign exchange reserves in 2010.11.

However, in 2011-2012 and 2012-13 the situation regarding capital flows changed significantly and capital flows were not sufficient to meet the large current account deficit (CAD). Consequently, in 2011-12 withdrawal from foreign exchange reserves of 12.8 billion US dollars was made. However, in 2012-13 we were able to finance large deficit on current account by capital inflows and therefore without withdrawal from our foreign exchange reserves.

Capital flows are driven by pull factors such as economic fundamentals of recipient countries and push factors such as policy stance of source countries. The capital flows have implications for exchange rate management, overall macroeconomic and financial stability including liquidity conditions. Capital account management therefore needs to emphasize promoting foreign direct investment (FDI) and reducing dependance on volatile portfolio capital. This would ensure that to the extent current account defect is bridged through capital surplus it would be better if it is done through stable and growth enhancing foreign direct investment flows. In the present international financial situation, reserves are the first line of defence against the volatile capital flows. However, the decline in reserves as a percentage of GDP is a source of concern.

THE PROBLEM OF WIDENING CURRENT ACCOUNT DEFICIT OF INDIA

In the last three years India is faced with a serious problem of current account deficit. The deficit in current account has been mainly due to the large merchandise trade deficit. Our imports of goods rose in relation to our exports due to lagging competitiveness of our exports and failure of our government to diversify market for exports. Crude oil and gold in recent years constitute almost half of our imports. Demand for gold in India is quite large as it is demanded both for making jewellery and as hedge against inflation.

India's current account deficit plumbed new depths as gold and oil imports soared, putting pressure on the government to come up with new measures to attract foreign investments and increase exports to cut the deficit. Current account deficit, or CAD, the excess of spending overseas than earning, rose to 6.7% of the GDP in the third quarter of the year 2012-13 (from Oct. to Dec. 2013) from 5.4% in the previous quarter, smashing optimistic estimates. This is more than double of what was prevalent during the 1991 currency crisis. The country got a relief when at the and of June 2013, the RBI said that for the whole year 2012013 current account deficit was 4.8 per cent of GDP.

Due to pick up of exports in the 4th quarter of 2012-13 though in this quarter CAD was quite high (3.6% of GDP) it was lower than 6.7% of the third quarter of 2012-13 and 5.4 per cent of its second quarter. The deterioration was all-round, with software exports – India's mainstay when it comes to US dollar earnings – remaining flat at $18.9 billion in the quarter from a year ago. Remittances from workers and Indians overseas fell as a weakening currency and lower interest rates deterred fresh inflows.

Table: 29.3. Trade Deficit, Net Invisibles, Current Account Deficit and Net Capital Inflows during 2007-08 to 2011-12 (per cent of GDP)

Year	*Trade Deficit*	*Net Invisibles*	*Current Account Deficit (CAD)*	*Net Capital Inflows*
2007-08	–7.4	6.1	–1.3	5.6
2008-09	–9.8	7.5	–2.3	0.6
2009-10	–8.7	5.9	–2.8	3.7
2010-11	–7.4	4.6	–2.8	3.7
2011-12	–10.2	6.0	–4.2	3.6
2012-13	–10.6	–	–4.8	–

Source, *Economic Survey,* 2012-13

Current account deficit for the financial year (2012-13) still works out to be record of high 4.8 per cent of GDP indicating that the economy is still not out of the woods on the external front. The high CAD essentially reflects the fact that export earnings fall short of the huge import bill. It will be observed from the Table 29.1 that net invisible (which represent net exports of services is *positive* throughout). It is therefore on account of trading in goods that shows a large deficit and is responsible for overall current account deficit.

It is worth mentioning that ***huge dependence on imports of certain items such as oil, coal and gold is the major reason for the large current account deficit.*** As a result of huge current account deficit, rupee came under pressure since a large current account deficit implies more demand for US dollars for excess of imports over exports. This resulted in sharp depreciation of rupee from June 2013 when value of the Indian rupee to a US dollar fell from about ₹ 56 to a dollar in the first week of June to over ₹ 60.73 to a dollar on June 26, 2013, further to ₹ 61.21 to a US dollar on July 8, 2013, a 10 per cent decline in the value – rupee is a single month. As a result of capital outflows and uncertainity in Government policy, depreciation of rupee continued and it fell to ₹ 66 to a dollar on Aug. 16, 2013 and hit the rocord level of ₹ 68.8 on August 28, 2013.

The outflow of capital is taking place partly because of large current account deficit hurting the foreign investor confidence for investment in the Indian economy and also the announcement of the governor of the US Federal Reserve about reducing the **'quantitative easing'** (*QE*) following the signs of the recovery of the American economy prompted the foreign portfolio investors to withdraw from the debt and equity markets in the month of May and June 2013 of India for safe investment in the US. Around $7 billion were pulled out from the Indian debt and equity markets in the months of May end June 2013 and this not only resulted in crash in India's stock market but also further raised the demand for dollars. As a result, the rupee fell below ₹ 68 to a US dollar on Aug. 28, 2013 despite the intervention by the RBI to stall the process of more depreciation by selling US dollars from its reserves. However, with the postponement of unwinding of quantitative easing by the US Federal Reserve, rupee rose to around ₹ 62 to a US dollar at end September 2013.

The Indian government also tried to reduce current account deficit by ***raising import duty on gold*** from first 6 per cent to 8 per cent and then to 10 per cent. Further, the government is also wooing foreign investment by raising the caps (*i.e.*, upper limits) on *foreign direct investment* (FDI) in various sectors of the economy such as telecom, oil refineries, defense production, insurance. Recall that FDI is a stable source of foreign capital that can help to finance the current account deficit. Further, the government is hoping that since rate of return in India is higher than that in the US and European countries, even portfolio capital by FII which is now flowing out will ultimately return to India.

The basic solution to our widening current account deficit is to frame economic policies that improve productivity of our manufacturing sector substantially so that their exports may be increased. Over the years manufacturing exports have struggled while service exports have surged. To boost manufacturing exports we need better infrastructure such as adequate availability of power, good ports, good highways, relaxation of rigid labour laws, lower transaction costs in terms of lesser paper works, quick environment clearances of projects so that projects are not stalled for a long period. The government should also guide exporters to diversify into new markets, for example, in African nations where growth is strong.

The large current account deficit poses a great challenge for the Indian economy to tackle it. If foreign investment, direct and portfolio, is not coming in adequate quantity we will use our own foreign exchange reserves to finance CAD. However, these foreign exchange reserves are available only in a limited quantity. In August 2013, foreign exchange reserves of only $285 billion were available which was sufficient to cover only 7 months of imports. Thus, to solve the problem of CAD, either we have to attract sufficient foreign capital inflows or we have to cut our imports if we fail to expand our exports.

Two types of measures to solve the problem of current account deficit must be distinguished. First type of measures is to find ways of ***financing current account deficit*** which in recent years has become much larger than the comfort level of 2.5% of GDP. **The second type of measures is to reduce this current account deficit (CAD) by increasing exports and curtailing imports**. We first discuss the second type of measures. In recent years the imports of gold have largely risen adding to the current account deficit. The imports of gold have to be reduced. In 2009-10 we imported about $30 billion of gold and silver. Before that it was $22 – $24 billion of which about $7 billion was re-exported as jewellery. Financing that was not a problem but when imports of gold went up to $62 billion in 2011-12 it became a problem. In 2011-12 and 2012-13, a large part of imports of gold had gone into gold coins and biscuits. Even banks were selling gold coins to the public. The many households buy these coins and biscuits as hedge against inflation. Therefore, it was necessary to reduce the imports of gold. Finance Minister raised the import duty on gold first from 6% to 8% and then 8% to 10% to discourage the imports of gold. The RBI also made the imports of gold tougher. The RBI announced that 20% of imports of gold by businessmen *must be exported* in the form of jewellery. If any importer of gold fails to export 20% of its imports of gold, he would he debarred from importing any more gold. This would have a dual effect. On the one hand, 20% export condition will lower imports of gold, on the other hand it would encourage exports of gold jewellery. This will help in reducing current account deficit.

Further, **our exports of iron has been drastically reduced** because of restrictions on mining of iron as there was a lot of corruption and violation of law regarding mining. To reduce current account deficit these mining restrictions on iron have to be relaxed so that their exports are increased. Similarly, our ***imports of coal*** have significantly increased that have led to the widening of current account deficit. The government alloted quotas of coal mining to those who had no experience of mining coal and there has been *coal scam* involving thousands of crores which has worsened domestic coal-supply scenario. We must improve our policy on coal mining so that larger requirements of coal should be met by domestic production. Our Finance Minister rightly says that "*the only way to contain CAD is to increase the domestic production of oil and coal and restrain the consumption of gold*". Further, a lot of foreign exchange is used for importing ***electronic goods*** such as laptops, desktops, smart phones, mobiles, their imports must be curbed by imposing heavy import duties and also through some suitable way of quantitative restrictions such as adopted in case of gold (Note that ***outright quantitative restrictions on imports of goods*** are not permitted under WTO rules. To promote overall exports, 3% subsidy on interest has been announced on exports. This is a step in right direction.

Now we turn to explain the ***ways of financing current account deficit (CAD)***. Our present stock of foreign exchange reserves ($ 281 billion) are insufficient to meet the current account deficit as they only cover 7 months of imports. Besides, we have to use them to payback our short-term loans taken from abroad which mature in a year. It is therefore important to ***finance*** CAD than to draw upon foreign exchange reserves. We have been relying on capital inflows by FIIs, which are quite volatile and unstable. Therefore, to attract foreign direct investment (FDI), government has recently raised the caps (*i.e.,* limits) on FDI in various industries such as telecom, oil refineries, defence production, insurance and make its entry easier by permitting a large percentage of FDI through ***automatic route,*** that is,. without the approval of Foreign Investment Promotion Board (FIPB).

The economic growth dipped to a decade low of 5% in 2012-13 and FDI inflows during 2012-13 declined by 38% to $22.42 billion. Despite all odds the government was able to finance CAD and also added $3 billion in 2012-13 to foreign exchange reserves. What is required in 2013-14 for which CAD is estimated to be 4.3% of GDP is to attract foreign direct investment (FDI) which is quite stable source of funding CAD by raising its limits in various industries and make its entry into the country easier as has been now done by the government. All European countries at present are in recession and so is the case with Japan, and other developed countries. Only tho US economy is showing some signs of revival. India still continues to remain a desired destination for foreign direct and institutional investment. To attract them therefore we need to adopt proper policy and restore confidence among foreign investors.

Finally, policy makers in India have been considering the idea of *issuing sovereign bonds* to overseas investors to attract dollar inflows to meet the current account deficit (CAD). However, according to former RBI governor D. Subbarao, issuing of sovereign bonds to overseas investors may not be good for the long-term financial stability of the economy as it would further increase external indebtedness of the economy making it more vulnerable to external shocks.

In our view if by ***raising interest rate on non-India resident Indian* deposits** (*i.e.,* NRI deposits) in Indian banks as RBI has now permitted good amount of dollars can be attracted which can be used to finance current account deficit.

EXTERNAL SECTOR REFORMS IN INDIA SINCE 1991

To overcome balance of payments crisis 1991, and restore economic health to the external sector, various measures of stabilisation and structural reforms were undertaken by the new Congress Government with Dr. Manmohan Singh as the Finance Minister. They are breifly explained below.

1. Devaluation of Rupee in 1991. Before 1991, the Indian rupee was overvalued in terms of US $ and other important currencies. This overvaluation of the Indian rupee discouraged our exports and encouraged imports. This foreign exchagne policy had therefore *anti-export* bias. To discourage imports and encourge exports rupee was devalued on July 1, 1991 and again on July 3,

1991. In the two doses of devaluation, the rupee value in terms of trade-weighted basket of foreign currencies declined on an average by 22.8 per cent. The devaluation of the rupee in July 1991 was followed by the *withdrawal of cash compensatory subsidy to exporters* which prevailed before. Thus, devalaution was expected to act as a substitute of export subsidy as the exporters would get more rupees in exchange of foreign currencies. The devalaution was also expected to promote the flow of funds from Non-Resident Indians (NRIs) to India. Besides, exports were expected to go up as the competitiveness of exportables improved. However, devaluation made the imports costlier. As a result, it would have an adverse impact on import-sensitive export industries and would have given a fillip to cost-push inflation. However, suitable monetary and fiscal policies aimed at stabilisation of price level measures were adopted to check cost-push inflation.

2. Trade Liberalisation and Reduction in Customs Duties. An important policy in external sector has been to open up the Indian economy to foreign trade. In place of import-substitution, export-led growth strategy has been adopted. Towards that end customs duties on non-agricultural imports have been reduced so that doemstic industries should get cheaper imported raw materials and capital goods, to produce goods for exports at lower prices. Accordingly, the peak customs tariff rate which was over 300 per cent in 1990 was reduced in a phased manner to 35 per cent in 2002-03 budget and further to 15 per cent in 2005-06 and to 12.5 per cent in 2006-07 budget. Customs duties on imports were lowered not only to increase the competitiveness of Indian exports but to serve other purposes. First, it checked cost-push inflation which arose due to devaluation of India rupee. Second, it reduced the prices of exportable goods which used a large quantity of imported raw materials and capital goods. This further increased the competitiveness of Indian exportables. Thirdly, lowering of custom duties exposed Indian industries to foreign competition. It was expected that this increased competition would lead to higher productivity in Indian industries.

3. Assistance from IMF and World Bank. To overcome balance of payments problem, an emergency measure taken was to obtain financial aid from IMF and World Bank. IMF agreed to provide aid only if India fulfilled its preconditions. Its preconditions were that we should devalue our rupee, liberalise imports by lowering customs duties and introduce structural reforms by undertaking various measures of domestic liberalisation and opening up the Indian economy to foreign trade and investment. India accepted these conditions and got assistance from IMF. Dr. Manmohan Singh argued that these structural reforms were in fact needed by the economy not only to restore confidence of the foreign and domestic investors and thereby to solve balance of payments problem but also to accelerate economic growth. Later events proved him right.

4. Cut in Fiscal Deficit for Macroeconomic Stabilisation. As explained above, rising fiscal deficit in the eighties was an important cause of worsening of the balance of payments. Therefore, an important measure taken to tackle the problem of balance of payments was to reduce fiscal deficit. The fiscal deficit of the Central Government which was 8.5 per cent of GDP in 1987-88 and 7.3 per cent of GDP both in 1988-89 and 1989-90 was reduced to 4.7 per cent in 1991-92 by reducing Government expenditure and introducing tax reforms[9]. Fiscal deficit of Central Government however deteriorated to 6.4 per cent of GDP in 1993-94 but was again brought down to 4.0 per cent in 1995-96 and further to 2.5 per cent in 2007-08. Reduction in fiscal deficit caused growth in aggregate demand to decline which helped in lowering the rate of inflation. Lower inflation rate in the Indian economy increased exports and discouraged imports of goods. Besides, reduction in fiscal deficit ensured smaller government borrowing from abroad. This worked to lower the interest burden and debt-service charges over a span of time. However, it may be noted that due to fiscal stimulus programme adopted in 2009 and 2010 to prevent economic slowdown fiscal deficit of the Central Government as per cent of GDP rose to 6 per cent in 2008-09 and 6.3% in 2009-10.

5. Switch-over to Market-determined Exchange Rate. An important measure adopted to tackle the balance of payments problem was that after a two year transition exchange rate was made market determined with effect from 1993. With this exchange rate began to be determined by demand for and supply of foreign currencies and Indian rupee. The Indian rupee was made *convertible on current account transactions*. This facilitated the foreign exchange transactions at the exchange rate determined by market forces. This meant that correction in balance of payments which influences demand for and supply of foreign exchange, say US $, could be made to some exent by changes in foreign exchange rate. As a matter of fact, since 1993 there has been substantial depreciation of Indian rupee. The exchange rate of rupee which was 24.47 rupees per US $ fell to 31.94 in 1994-95 and further to ₹ 35.50 per US $ in 1996-97, to ₹ 47.69 in 2001-02 and further to 48.40 in 2002-03. This improved greatly the incentives to exporters and to NRI remitting funds to India. Imports became more expensive which restrained their growth. However, from 2002-03 to 2008-09 there was appreciation of Indian rupee. The *average value* of rupee in terms of number of rupees for a US dollar changed from ₹ 45.95 in 2003-04, to ₹ 44.93 in 2003-04, ₹ 45.28 in 2005-06 and further to ₹ 45.99 in 2008-09 to ₹ 47.42 in 2009-10. During 2010-11 it appreciated to ₹ 45.68. However, from Sept. 2011, due to large capital outflows from India, it started depreciating sharply and was hovering around ₹ 53 to a US dollar in Dec. 2011. Though exchange rate is allowed to be determined by the market forces of demand and supply, Reserve Bank of India intervenes in the foreign exchange market by selling or purchasing dollars to prevent large volatility in the exchange rate. However, RBI has no fixed exchange rate target to achieve.

6. Elimination of Anti-Export Bias. An important reform in the external sector was change in India's trade policy which had anti-export bias and pro-import-substitution bias. The new trade policy was to lower customs duties so as to reduce protection to large-scale industries. Protection reduces productivity and efficiency through eliminating foreign competition. To remove the pro-import-substitution bias and liberalise imports, in 1992-93 the peak custom duty on imports was reduced from 150 per cent to 110 per cent. The maximum import duty was further reduced to 85 per cent in 1993-94, to 65 per cent in 1994-95 and to 50 per cent in 1995-96 and to 45 per cent in 1997. The peak customs duty was further reduced to 35 per cent in 2002-03 and to 15 per cent in 2005-06 budget, to 12.5 per cent in 2006-07 budget and to 10 per cent in 2008-09. The lowering of customs duties on imports also removes anti-export bias. The lower custom duties enable the domestic industries to get cheaper imported raw materials and capital goods to produce goods for exports at competitive prices.

Another important reform in the external sector relates to the reforms in foreign investment policy. For Reforms in India's Foreign Investment Policy see next Chapter 30.

7. FEMA Replaces FERA

Another important reform in the external sector was Foreign Exchange Regulation Act (FERA) was replaced by Foreign Exchange Management Act (FEMA). The stringent provisions of FERA had become obsolete in the context of liberalisation of foreign trade, foreign investment and foreign exchange market in the early nineties. Stringent provisions of FERA was thought to be impeding the speedy globilisation of the Indian economy. The aim of FEMA is to achieve the following objectives.

1. In seeks to a facilitate foreign trade and payments involving foreign exchange.
2. It seeks to promote orderly maintenance of the foreign exchange market.

The following are the main provisions of FEMA.

1. Under the provisions of this act a person resident in India is permitted to hold, own, transfer or invest in foreign currency, foreign security or any immovable property situated outside India provided such currency, security or property was acquired, held or owned by him when he was resident outside India

2. Similarly, the act provides that a person resident outside India has been permitted to hold shares, securities and properties acquired by him or her while he or she was resident in India. It also permits a non-resident Indian to hold such properties which have been inherited by him or her from a person resident in India.

Table 29.4. Performance of India's External Sector

	1990-91	1995-96	2000-01	2001-02	2002-03	2003-04	2004-05	2005-06	2006-07	2007-08	2008-09	2009-10*
As % change over the previous year												
1. Growth of Exports – BOP (%)	5.8	20.8	21.1	– 1.6	20.3	23.3	28.5	23.4	22.6	28.9	13.7	–3.6
2. Growth of Imports – BOP (%)	8.8	28.0	4.6	1.7	14.5	24.1	48.6	32.1	23.4	35.2	19.8	–2.6
3. Exports/Imports (BOP %)	66.2	74.0	78.5	79.4	83.4	82.9	71.7	67.0	67.6	64.5	61.4	60.6
4. Import Cover of FER (No. of months)	2.5	6.0	8.8	11.5	14.2	16.9	14.3	11.6	12.5	14.4	9.8	11.2
5. External assistance (Net)/TC(%)	26.2	–	4.8	13.4	– 29.4	– 16.5	6.9	6.7	3.9	2.0	36.1	5.4
6. ECB (net) /TC (%)	26.8	–	50.6	–19.0	–15.9	– 17.5	18.5	9.8	35.6	21.0	116.2	5.3
7. NR-Deposits /TC (%)	18.3	–	27.2	33.0	28.8	21.8	– 3.4	11.0	9.6	0.2	63.4	5.5
As % of GDP at current mrket prices												
8. Exports	5.8	9.2	9.9	9.4	10.6	11.1	11.8	12.6	13.6	13.5	15.4	13.2
9. Imports	8.8	12.3	12.6	11.8	12.7	13.3	16.5	18.8	20.1	21.0	25.1	21.7
10. Trade Balance	– 3.0	– 3.1	– 2.7	– 2.4	– 2.1	– 2.3	– 4.8	– 6.4	– 6.8	– 7.4	–9.8	– 8.6
11. Invisible (Net) Balance	– 0.1	1.6	2.1	3.1	3.4	4.6	4.5	5.2	5.7	6.2	7.4	5.8
12. Current account balance	– 3.1	– 1.7	– 0.6	0.7	1.2	2.3	– 0.4	1.2	1.1	–1.3	–2.4	– 2.8
13. External Debt	28.7	27.0	22.5	21.1	20.3	17.8	18.5	17.2	17.9	18.1	20.5	18.0

* Revised data

Notes . (1) TC stands for Total Capital Flows (Net), (2) ECB for External Commercial Borrowing and (3) FER for Foreign Exchange Reserves

Source : GOI, Various Issues of *Annual Economic Surveys.*

3. FEMA provides that any person may sell foreign exchange to any authorised person or dealer or draw foreign exchange from such authorised person if such sale or drawal is a current account transaction (that is, exports and imports of goods and services). However, the government with consultation with RBI can impose reasonable restrictions on such transactions.

4. Further, the FEMA provides that subject to the class of capital account transactions, a person can sell or draw foreign exchange to or from an authorised person. These is limit up to which such capital account transactions are permitted. Besides, RBI has been authorised to regulate the foreign exchange transactions on capital account.

5. Under the provisions of FEMA, every exporter of goods and services will furnish to RBI full particulars including the export-value of goods and services exported and ensure the realisation and repatriation of export proceeds within a period of time and manner prescribed by RBI.

6. Another important liberalisation measure of the use of foreign exchange is that Indian residents going abroad for business purposes or for participating in conferences and seminars need not seek RBI's permission to avail themselves of foreign exchange upto $ 25000 per trip irrespective of the period of stay.

7. **Gifts and Donations.** FEMA has substantially increased the prescribed limits in respect of certain payments abroad. In respect of gifts payments limit in foreign exchange has been raised from $ 1000 to $ 5000 and in respect of donations from $ 3000 to $ 5000.

8. **EEFC and RFC Account Holders.** The Exchange Earners' Foreign currency (EEFC) account holders have been permitted to freely use the funds held in EEFC for payment of all permissible current account transactions. Similarly, the Residents' Foreign Currency (RFC) account holders have also been permitted to freely use the funds held in RFC for payment of all permissible current account transactions.

9. **GDR and ADR Permissions**. Under FEMA, the Indian firms of good standing have been permitted, with government approval to issue equity and convertible bonds through Global Depository Receipts (GDR) and American Depository Receipts (ADR) in European and US capital markets respectively up to certain specified limits.

10. **Violations and Penalities under FEMA**. FEMA differs from the earlier exchange regulation Act FERA with regard to penalities and punishment in case of violation of the act. Under FEMA, the *receiver* of laundered money is to be made culpable, instead of sender/distributor. Thus, only the recipient of hawala money is culpable. Further, the violators of FEMA would no longer be treated as criminals as was the case under FERA but as civil offenders. The contravention of FEMA provisions would invite a monetary penalty amounting to a maximum of three times of the sum involved in contrast to five times prescribed in the repealed FERA. Besides, under FEMA, although there would be no prosecution in the foreign exchange violation cases, yet in case an offender fails to pay the penalty, the Enforcement Directorate could move court, which could sent him to jail. In jail also the offender would be treated like a civil prisoner, who has to pay for his stay behind bars. Moreover, under FEMA, search and seizures can be carried out only if Enforcement Directorate has reasons to believe that the surpect will not show up when summoned.

Evaluation. It is evident from the provisions of FEMA that it has greatly relaxed the conditions for dealings in foreign exchange. This is what was required in the economic environment when the Indian economy has been opened up to expand foreign trade and investment. This act has facilitated the growth of India's exports and made the procurement of imported raw materials and capital goods required for rapid industrial growth. None that when the private sector is playing an important role in promoting economic growth, it is quite appropriate that foreign exchange regulation should be relaxed so that private sector can get the foreign exchange needed for giving a big push to the industrial growth. Moreover, in India foreign exchange reserves are currently quite large and there is need for its use for productive purposes. It is because of FEMA that foreign institutional investors have brought in capital inflows to invest in equity and debt securities in the Indian capital market. This has resulted in a boom in the Indian capital market.

SUCCESS OF EXTERNAL SECTOR REFORMS

The balance of payments crisis of 1991 resulting in the depletion of foreign exchange services provided an opportunity to the government to undertake reforms in the external sector. In Table 29.4 we present the key indicators of the external sector. It will be seen from table 29.4 that the reform measures improved the performance of India's external sector and brought good dividends. Export growth zoomed to 20.8 per cent in 1995-96. After registering slow growth in the next four years due to global slowdown, growth rate of 21 per cent and 20.3 per cent in 2000-01 and 2002-03 respectively was attained. In the next three years (2003-06) this high growth rate in exports had been maintained. *Fears that imports will rapidly increase due to import liberalisation, would swallow domestic industries and result in large increase in deficit in current account balance have not come true.* This is due to more efficient management of changes in foreign exchange rate as an essential part of economic reforms. Further, as a result of liberalisation of capital flows, NRI deposits increased two times from 1.5 billion US dollars in 1990-91 to 2.8 billion US dollars in 2001-02 and to 3.6 US billion dollars in 2003-04 and rose further to 4.3 US dollars in 2006-07 (see Table 29.4). However, in 2007-08 increase in NRI deposits was quite small but they again rose to 4.3 billion dollars in 2008-09. In 2009-10 and 2010-11 NR deposits were $ 2.9 billion and $ 3.18 billion respectively.

An important benefit of external sector reforms has been improvement in current account balance of payments. The deficit in current account balance which was 3.1 per cent of GDP_{mp} in 1990-91, fell to 1.7 per cent in 1995-96, 1 to 1.4 per cent in 1997-98 and further fell to 0.6 per cent in 2000-01. The significant point to note is that throughout the nineties after 1991, current account deficit in balance of payments never exceeded two per cent of GDP_{mp}. This is no means achievement of economic reforms in the external sector. It is important to note that in the three years (2001-02, 2002-03 and 2003-04), *the surplus in current account* was achieved (see Table 29.4 above). After 2003-04 there was current account deficit but it remained at low level except in 2008-09 and 2009-10 when current deficit went up to 2.4 and 2.8 per cent of GDP due to global economic slowdown following the global financial crisis. In 2010-11, the current account deficit was 2.6 per cent of GDP. It may however be noted that deficit in current account balance is not bad provided it is within reasonable limits and there are either enough foreign exchange reserves in the country or enough net current capital inflows into India. In fact, as mentioned above, current account deficit represents absorption of foreign capital by the Indian economy.

Another big achievement of the external sector reforms is the flows of foreign investment in India which has contributed a good deal to the growth of industrial production and as result Indian exports rose sharply. Foreign investment (net) increased from only 103 million US $ in 1990-91 to around 5.35 billion US $ in 1997-1998 and further increased to around 15.5 billion US $ in 2005-06 and to 43.4 billion US $ in 2007-08 (see Table 29.4). Of course, foreign capital flows into India are lower than those into China. However, due to economic slowdown, foreign investment declined to 3.5 billion US$ in 2008-09 because of *net outflows* of portfolio capital. But again went up to 51.2 billion. In 2010-11 net foreign investment in India was $ 44.3 billion.

Of greater significance is the inflows of foreign exchange. Foreign exchange reserves in India which were a meagre amount of 5.8 billion US $ in 1990-91 climbed to 26 billion US $ in 1997-98, 5 times increase in seven years. There has been greater inflows of foreign exchange in the last few years with the result that foreign exchange reserves in India reached a level of 150 billion US dollars in March 2006 and further to US $ 309 billion at end-March 2008. But as a result of capital outflows in 2008-09 due to global financial crisis foreign exchange reserves fell to $252 billion at end-March 2009 but again picked up and stood at $ 304 billion at end-March 2011. As a matter of fact, such a large stock of foreign exchange reserves has created problem for us as this has economy. However, they served as cushion in case of capital outflows from India as it is happening in the later half of 2011-12.

It will be seen from Table 29.4 (Row 4) that foreign exchange reserves which in 1990-91 covered imports required for only 2.5 months rose to such an extent that the foreign exchange reserves covered Indian imports for 8.2 months in 1992-2000 and for as high as 16.9 months in 2003-04 and 14.4 months in 2007-08. At present (2013-14) foreign exchange reserves are US $ 275 billion (Sep. 2013) and cover about 70 months of imports.

External Debt Situation

It will be observed from Table 29.5 that external debt which as per cent of India's GDP was 28.7 per cent in 1990-91 fell to 22.1 per cent in 1999-2000 and further to 18.0 per cent at end March 2008 and was also at 18% at end-March 2010 but again rose to 19.7 per cent at end-March 2012. High external debt service ratio (that is, ratio of external debt service to current receipts) of 35 per cent in 1990-91 which contributed to our balance of payments crisis in 1991, was brought down to about half of that (*i.e.* 17 per cent) in 1999-2000 (See Table 29.5) and further to 4.3 at end-March 2009 and stood at 4.3% at end-March 2011 but rose to 6% at end-March 2012. This significantly reduced our burden of external debt relative to our GDP.

Table 29.5. Parameters of India's External Debt

End March of the year	*External Debt-GDP Ratio*	*External Debt-Service ratio*	*Raio of foreign exchange reserves to total External Debt*	*Ratio of Short-Term Debt to Total External Debt*	*Percentage of Short Term Debt to Foreign Exchange reserves*
1990-91	28.7	35.3	7.0	10.2	146.5
1991-92	38.7	30.2	–	8.2	141.6
1992-93	37.6	27.5	–	7.1	98.3
1993-94	33.8	25.0	–	3.9	24.4
1994-95	30.9	26.2	–	4.5	20.4
1995-96	27.1	24.3	23.1	5.4	23.2
1996-97	24.7	21.2	–	7.2	25.5
1997-98	24.4	19.0	–	5.4	17.2
1998-99	23.6	18.8	–	4.4	13.2
1999-2000	22.1	17.1	–	4.0	10.3
2000-01	22.6	16.2	–	3.6	6.6
2001-02	21.1	16.1	–	2.8	–5.1
2002-03	20.4	16.0	54.7	4.5	6.5
2003-04	17.8	15.9	100.3	3.9	3.9
2004-05	18.5	5.9	105.0	13.2	12.5
2005-06	17.2	10.1	109.0	14.1	12.9
2006-07	18.1	4.7	115.6	16.3	14.1
2007-08	18.1	4.8	138.0	20.4	14.8
2008-09	20.5	4.4	112.1	19.3	17.2
2009-10	18.0	5.8	106.8	20.1	18.8
2010-11	17.5	4.3	99.6	21.2	21.3
2011-12	19.7	6.0	85.2	22.6	26.6

Note : 1. Flows refer to fiscal year indicated while stocks relato to the end March of the year indicated

2. Debt-service ratio is the proportion of gross debt service payments to external current receipts (net of official transfers)

Source : Shankar Acharya, Macroeconomic Management in the Nineties, *EPW*, Apirl 20, 2002 and *Economic Survey* 2004-05, 2007-08, 2009-10, 2010-11 and 2012-13.

The ratio of short-term foreign debt to foreign exchange reserves is very critical from the viewpoint of foreign exchange management when there is flight of capital from a country. If it is very high as was the case in East Asian crisis of 1997-98, it can land a country into a great trouble. It goes to the credit of India's external sector reforms that ratio of short-term debt to foreign exchange reserves was brought down from an extremely high level 146.5 per cent in 1990-91 to just 10.3 per cent in 1999-2000. With greater inflows of foreign exchange reserves during three years (2000-2003) and payback of a part of short-term debt, the ratio of short-term debt to foreign exchange reserves fell to just 3.9 per cent at the end of March 2004 but rose again to 14.8 per cent at the end of March 2008 (Table 29.5). It is now widely recognised that while East Asian countries experienced a severe crisis in 1997-98, India successfully weathered the storm. Thus a prudent external debt policy has placed India's external debt in a comfortable position. Recently, policy focus has been on concessional and relatively less expensive source of external funds. In this policy focus preference for long maturity loans, monitoring of short-term debts and emphasis on non-debt creating capital flows is being given. Recent initiatives towards reducing burden of external debt include prepayment of costly Government and non-Government external loans, rationalising interest rates and structure of NRI deposits, and making end -use specifications for external commercial borrowing (ECB).

QUESTIONS FOR REVIEW

1. Distinguish between balance of trade and balance of payments.
2. What is meant by balance of payments on current account? Explain the visible and invisible items on the current account.
3. Distinguish between current account and capital account of the balance of payments. Mention the various items on both these accounts of the balance of payments.
4. When is country's balance of payments said to be in equilibrium ? Explain the factors that cause disequilibrium in the balance of payments.
5. Balance of payments must always balance. Is it true? Explain.
6. What is devaluation ? Is it an effective way of correcting disequilibrium in the balance of payments.
7. Explain the various measures that can be adopted to correct disequilibrium.
8. What is expenditure reducing fiscal policy ? How does it help to maintain the current account of the balance of payments in equilibrium?
9. What is meant by devaluation ? Under what conditions is it expected to improve the balance of payments position of an economy ?
10. Discuss the absorption approach to devaluation as a measure of correcting balance of payments deficit.
11. Distinguish between Expenditure Reducing and Expenditure Switching policies to correct the balance of payments disequilibrium.
12. Explain India's external debt situation. Explain how when in 1997-98 East Asian countries experienced a serious crisis with regard to foreign debt problem,,India successfully escaped from this crisis situation.

CHAPTER 30

Foreign Capital and Multinational Corporations

Introduction

After the Second World War, the developing countries are making concerted efforts to achieve rapid economic growth so as to alleviate problems of poverty and unemployment. Besides, there has been rapid growth of international trade. The developing countries like India have been facing the problem of shortage of capital. To meet this shortage, capital flows from the developed countries to the developing countries in the last two decades have substantially increased.

Immediately after the Second World War, capital flows were largely in the form of *foreign aid* from the Governments of the developed countries and international institutions such as IMF and World Bank to the Governments of the developing countries. In the last two decades the capital flows in the form of foreign aid on Government to Government basis have dried up, whereas aid from IMF and World Bank is based on certain conditionalities of undertaking some structural economic reforms which the developing countries often find them difficult to implement to the entire satisfaction of these institutions. Besides, the capital needs of the developing countries are so large that IMF and World Bank alone cannot meet them. Therefore, there is great need for *capital flows on private account* on a large scale. Fortunately, capital flows on private account have substantially increased in the last two decades. These capital flows on private account are of the following two types :

1. Foreign Portfolio Investment
2. Foreign Direct Investment (FDI)

We discuss below the roles of the above two types of capital flows briefly.

ROLE OF FOREIGN CAPITAL

Foreign Portfolio Investment

This is important type of capital flow under which foreign institutions such as banks, insurance companies, companies managing mutual funds and pension funds purchase stocks and bonds of companies of other countries in the secondary markets (*i.e.*, stock markets). They get returns in the form of capital gains and yearly payable dividends but do not exercise any direct control in running these companies. Pension funds, mutual funds and insurance companies have been very active in moving portfolio capital in the last two decades because restrictions on foreign equity investment by various countries have been reduced or removed in recent years allowing pension and mutual funds and insurance companies to diversify their portfolio in order to reduce risk. Besides, the growth of portfolio foreign capital in the last two decades has also been due to the policies of liberalisation followed by the developing countries. In India following the adoption of policy of liberalisation the flow of portfolio capital was permitted in 1991. Consequently, foreign portfolio capital flows have come to India in large amounts in the last ten years (1991-2001). However, Mexico has been the chief beneficiary of portfolio capital flows. Portfolio capital flows now account for one third of net capital flows to the developing countries.

Benefits of Portfolio Capital Flows

Benefits and costs of portfolio capital flows have been a subject of severe controversy. Private foreign portfolio investment in stocks, equities and bonds has been made by foreign investors in order to get higher return or higher interest on their investment and also to diversify their portfolio in order to reduce risk. Thus, Prof. Todaro rightly writes, "From the investor's point of view, investing in the stock markets of emerging countries permits them to increase their returns while diversifying their risks.[1]"

In the early 1990s the return on the portfolio investment in the so called 'emerging' developing countries was quite high, for instance it was 39 percent during 1988-93 in Latin America which is main recipient of portfolio capital flows. But the high returns were marred by *high volatility* of stock markets of these countries. Many mutual-funds based US companies which were lured by high returns had to suffer heavy losses when there was collapse of Mexican stock market following 35% devaluation of Mexican currency in Dec. 1994. The experience of these heavy losses resulted in drastic fall in portfolio capital flows in 1995 not only in Mexico but also in other developing countries. In fact, there was net capital outflows from the developing countries for some months.

From the perspective of developing countries private portfolio capital flows are generally considered as a welcome means for raising capital for private domestic companies. However, it has been argued whether it is prudent to rely on large and volatile private capital flows as they have a destabilising influence in both the financial markets and in the overall economy. It has been pointed out that when the developing countries run into trouble, the portfolio capital flows disappear in few days as happened in case of Mexico in 1995 and recently in South East Asian countries in 1997-98. However, it may be noted that a developing country should not cover up its structural weakness by obtaining private capital flows. If they want to ensure that there private portfolio capital flows continue occurring year after year on a sustained basis, they should manage the foreign exchange rates efficiently by controlling deficits on current account and also keeping adequate reserves of foreign exchange so that their currencies should not remain overvalued which might lead to severe long-term consequences.

From above it follows that private portfolio capital flows are welcome as they provide needed finance for developing countries and also bring in required foreign exchange. However, one should not consider them as substitutes for making structural changes in these economies such as maintaining exchange rate at the right level, controlling deficits in balance of payments, checking rate of inflation and adoption of proper monetary policy which should ensure relatively higher interest rates. We agree with Prof. Todaro who while commenting on portfolio capital flows write, "Like multinational corporations, portfolio investors are not in the development business. If developed country interest rates rise or expected Third World profit rates decline, foreign speculator will withdraw their 'investments' as quickly as they brought them in. What LDCs need is true long-run economic investment (plants, equipment, physical and social infrastructure etc.) and not speculative equity capital."[2]

FOREIGN DIRECT INVESTMENT (FDI)

The foreign direct investment (FDI) is the investment in the construction of physical capital such as building factories and infrastructure (*i.e.*, power, telecom, ports etc.) in the capital-importing country. It may be done in several ways. Companies or corporations may be specially set up for the purpose in the capital-exporting country to carry out trade and industry in an under--developed country. This is how the East Company operated in India or railways were constructed in India. The head office is in the investing country and the operations are in the developing

1. Michael P. Todaro, *Economic Development*, 6th edition, P. 544.
2. *Op. cit.*, p. 545.

country. Another method is that an already existing corporation spreads out its business in another country by establishing branches. Thus, many foreign companies producing cars, colour TVs have set up branches in India and are producing these items in India. There is another way open to the foreign entrepreneur, that is, to form companies and register them in the borrowing country without having any connection in the lending country. When India adopted protection, it became profitable, and quite fashionable too, for the foreign entrepreneurs to set up so called "India limited," to jump over the tariff wall and to avail themselves of the various concessions which the government extended to national concerns. These were in fact disguised branches of the foreign firms. The Indian match industry, for instance, is dominated by Swedish concerns. There is still another possibility which is now becoming common in India, *viz.*, of joint ventures or joint participation. The foreign firms start industrial concerns in collaboration with Indian firms. This form of foreign investment has some special advantages. The standing and reputation of foreign firms inspire confidence in the domestic and foreign capital. The long experience and efficient techniques are placed at the disposal of the domestic companies. It avoids evils of absentee ownership; it provides full opportunities for developing local skills, and also a large proportion of profits is retained in the country. It is also advantageous to the foreign investor. He is able to ward off in this manner any danger of discriminatory treatment by the government. A developing country lacks capital for development and it will have to depend on foreign capital.

Merits of Foreign Direct Investment (FDI)

Several advantages can be claimed for foreign direct investment (FDI).

(1) Such investment does not burden the tax payer since no interest at fixed rate is to be paid as in the case of foreign borrowing. The foreign investor is compensated by the profit he gets.

(2) In private investment, the investor is actuated by the profit motive; hence the business operations are subjected to careful calculations. This is a guarantee that the capital resources are most efficiently employed and are not frittered away in some reckless investment as may happen in the case of borrowing.

(3) Direct investment by foreign companies introduces, in the developing country, new technology, modern skills, innovations and new ideas. This is a great gain because the developing country is backward in technology and skills. The local entrepreneurs take a clue and start similar concerns. The Indian cotton textile industry was inspired by the Indian jute industry established by British entrepreneurs. Thus, direct foreign investment serves as an instrument for transferring modern technology to the developing countries.

(4) Another advantage is that a part of the profit is ploughed back into business and is not drained off from the country as it happens in the case of portfolio investment. The profits are invested either in modernisation and expansion of existing concerns or for establishing ancillary or subsidiary concerns in related fields. There is thus a continuing advantage for the developing country.

(5) Foreign direct investments are most likely to flow into export industries. By increasing exports and reducing imports, it will improve balance of payments of the developing country. It has a specially favourable effect on balance of payments position during recession because direct investment is serviced by dividends which are related to profits and not by fixed interest charges as in the case of loans. This flexibility of pressure on the balance of payments is of great advantage.

(6) Even otherwise flexible return on direct investment is a great advantage as compared with rigid interest and amortization requirements associated with public foreign loans.

(7) Direct foreign investment induces domestic investment also either in the form of joint participation or in local ancillary industries. Thus, foreign capital activates otherwise inert

domestic capital. The domestic capital sheds off its shyness and enters into fields opened by direct foreign investment.

(8) The direct foreign investment makes a real addition to the productive capacity of the capital importing country. There is no question of foreign capital coming in this form being used for unproductive purposes. In the case of other types of foreign borrowings, there is nothing to prevent them from being utilised unproductively.

(9) Another important advantage of direct foreign capital is that it can be induced to be invested in infrastructure such as power, telecom, development of ports which is an obstacle to accelerating economic growth in the developing countries. Such direct foreign investment enables the developing countries to overcome supply-side bottlenecks which will spur domestic investment. It should be mentioned that in recent times the Indian Government has been wooing foreign investors to invest in the infrastructure sector. The foreign companies have the resources, technology and technical knowhow to start productive ventures in the infrastructure.

(10) The capital that comes through foreign direct investment has a distinct advantage over portfolio investment. While foreign institutional investors can sell their shares and take capital out of the developing countries in a very short time and thus destabilise these economies as recently happened during East Asia Crisis, it is not easy to close down foreign concerns established through direct investments. Foreign Direct Investment (FDI) enters the developing economics to build factories and these factories (*i.e.*, physical capital) stay even if the investors decide to sell out later to domestic buyers.

The direct foreign investment (DFI) is opposed on the ground that it seeks to establish *'financial imperialism'*. It leads to political domination and economic exploitation. That is why foreign capital was so unpopular in India. The strength of this objection really rests on the nature of political set up. A free democratic country of the continental size such as India need not entertain such fears.

In order to promote private foreign direct investment, it is necessary both for the lending and borrowing countries to remove the impediments to free flow of capital and to grant the necessary facilities. The borrowing country should guarantee immunity from nationalisation and repatriation of profits. The crux of the problem is to assure higher returns and minimum risk. At present investment is deterred by political and social instability, uncertainty about the jurisdiction of courts, exchange controls and currency inconvertibility, controls on capital issues, fear of discriminatory legislation and fear of nationalisation, the practice of shutting out some industrial fields for foreign investors, employment of nationals in superior posts etc. Among the measures to minimise risks and allay fears may be mentioned investment treaties, government guarantees, tax incentives, joint ventures, relaxation of restrictions and granting of concessions. In short, the investment climate must be made most favourable by ensuring the following :

(*i*) Political stability and freedom from external aggression.

(*ii*) Security of life and property.

(*iii*) Availability of opportunities for earning profits.

(*iv*) Prompt payment for fair compensation and its remittance to the country of origin in the event of compulsory acquisition of a foreign enterprise.

(*v*) Facilities for the remittance of profits, dividends, interest, etc.

(*vi*) Facilities for the immigration and employment of foreign technical and administrative personnel.

(*vii*) A system of taxation that does not impose an excess burden on private foreign enterprise.

(*viii*) Freedom from double taxation.

(*ix*) A general spirit of friendliness for foreign investors.

The department of commerce of the United States mentions certain factors which stand in the way of private investment of American capital are uncertainty created by the present political situation, the policies and practices with respect to foreign investment, the relatively low level of economic infrastructure and the lack of trained labour, and the limited knowledge of the developing countries on the part of American businessmen. The particular impediments mentioned in the case of India are the nature of India's screening policy shutting out foreign investment in certain spheres and controls on imports, exports and foreign exchange and the absence of a double taxation agreement, obligation to employ and train Indian labour. India also offers some special inducements, *e.g.*, special tax exemptions, increased depreciation allowance and other benefits available to domestic industry, guarantee of exchange facilities for profit remittances, capital repatriation and import of essential requirements, government assistance in the acquisition of land, transport facilities, etc., the right to hold controlling interest. This compares quite favourably with many other countries. But there are still some countries with more attraction in the form of higher returns and better guarantees and they can absorb a substantial supply of foreign U.S. capital.

However, in the opinion of the present author direct foreign investment in the field of infrastructure in India may not be as much as expected because infrastructure projects relating to power, telecom, ports are of the nature of public utilities and therefore, the price of their end-product (for example, electricity charges) have to be controlled which may not yield sufficient profits to attract foreign investment.

Reforms in Foreign Investment Policy

Policy of economic liberalisation pursued since 1991 also involved changes in foreign investment policy. Until 1991 foreign investment played a minimal role in India's growth process. The current account deficit during 1980s was met largely by external commercial borrowing, external assistance and inflows under non-resident bank deposits. All these three types of capital inflows were of debt-creating nature which created problem in paying them back. However, since the initiation of economic reforms foreign investment, both foreign direct investment and portfolio investment through investment by FII in the Indian equity and debt securities, has also played an important role. Foreign investment has been sought by India for three reasons. First, foreign investment increases the total investible resources for accelerating capital formation. Second, foreign investment can be utilised for developing physical infrastructure which is badly needed for achieving a higher rate of economic growth. Third, foreign investment is expected to bring advanced technology and modern managerial skills which are required for technological ungradation of the Indian economy. To attract foreign investment various reforms were made in India's foreign investment policy.

Prior to 1991 foreign investment was restricted to certain priority sectors and foreign investment was permitted up to only 40 per cent of equity capital of a business enterprise. This was relaxed under liberalised foreign investment policy. Under this, foreign direct investment (FDI) upto 51 per cent of equity capital of a company was allowed in 34 high priority industries under automatic approval route. Besides, foreign equity participation up to 100 per cent equity capital of a production unit was allowed in 100 per cent export-oriented units (EOUs)

Another important foreign investment policy reform is that for infrastructure projects such as building of roads, highways, ports and harbours and vehicular tunnels and bridges, foreign equity participation upto 100 per cent subject to the maximum of Rs. 1500 crores has been allowed under automatic approval route. In case of 100 *per cent foreign equity participation in projects involving electricity generation, transmission and distribution*, the upper limit of Rs. 1500 crores has been withdrawn.

Furthermore, foreign investment in equity capital upto 100 per cent in e-commerce, oil refining, and drugs and pharmaceuticals, 49 per cent in telecommunication, 50 per cent in mining,

50 per cent in hotels and tourism has been allowed. The foreign direct investment under automatic approval route has been permitted up to 100 per cent for all manufacturing activities in Special Economic Zones (SEZs) except certain specified activities.

Even insurance and banking have been opened up to foreign investment and many foreign banks and insurance companies have opened their own branches and also invested in other private banks. Another important foreign investment reform has been that the registered foreign institutional investors have been permitted to buy equity and debt securities directly in the Indian capital market. Last but not the least important reform has been that Indian firms of good standing have been permitted, with government approval, *to issue equity and convertible bonds* through Global Depository Receipts (GDRs) and American Depository Receipts (ADRs) respectively in European and American markets. Recently in 2006, retail foreign investment in single foreign brands has been permitted.

It is evident from above that foreign private investment has been liberalised to the same extent.

FOREIGN DIRECT INVESTMENT FLOWS IN INDIA, 2003-2011

Domestic savings in India have not been large enough to wholy meet investment requirements. Therefore, capital inflows from other countries have become important. The ratio of domestic savings to GDP ratio has been generally lower than that of gross capital formation (GCF) to GDP. During 2004-05 this gap between domestic saving and gross capital formation (GCF) was 1.3 per cent of GDP which was filled up by foreign direct investment. FDI Equity inflows are more stable and bring in managerial skills and technological know-how together with investment.

Table 30.1: Growth in FDI inflows

(US$ billion)

Financial Year	FDI Inflows As per International practices	Percentage Growth	FDI Equity Inflow	Percentage Growth
2003-04	4.32	(–) 14 %	2.19	(–) 19
2004-05	6.05	(+) 40 %	3.22	(+) 47
2005-06	8.96	(+) 48 %	5.54	(+) 72
2006-07	22.83	(+) 146 %	12.49	(+) 125
2007-08	34.84	(+) 53 %	24.58	(+) 97
2008-09	41.87	(+) 20 %	31.40	(+) 28
2009-10 (P)	37.75	(–) 10	25.83	(–) 18
2010-11 (P)	34.85	(–) 08	21.38	(–) 17
2011-12 (P)	46.55	(+) 34	35.12	(+) 64
2012-13 (P) (Apr-Nov.)	24.65		15.85	

Source : Office of the Economic Adviser, DIPP.

Note : * As per Reserve Bank of India (RBI) estimates. Note that *International practices of measuring FDI includes not only equity investment but also reinvested earnings and intra company loans.*

As per DIPP estimates.

Since the liberalisation of the Indian economy inflows of foreign direct investment has greatly increased. The total foreign direct investment inflow (net) was mere 0.13 billion US dollars in 1991-92, rose to 2.15 billion US dollars in 1999-2000 during April-November 2012-13, FDI inflow (including equity inflows, reinvested earnings and other capital) was US $24.65 billion (Table 30.1). FDI equity inflows during April-Nov. 2012-13, were US$ 15.85 billion showing a decline of 43 percent as compared to the corresponding period of the previous year. Commulative FDI inflow from April 2000 to November 2012 stood at US $277.86 billion. Note that foreign direct investment (FDI) is made both by foreigners and NRI. In Table 30.1 break-up of foreign direct investment by foreigners and NRI together has not been given.

To encourage FDI inflows, FDI policy has continued to be fine-tuned and progressively liberalized, allowing FDI in more and more industries under the automatic route. In the year 2000, Government allowed FDI up to 100 per cent on the automatic route for most activities; a small negative list was notified where either the *automatic route* was not available or there were limits on FDI. Since then, the policy has been gradually simplified and rationalized and more sectors have been opened up for foreign investment. In July 2013 as will be dicussed lataer in thus chapter there has been further liberalisation of FDI and caps of FDI in various sectors and industries have raised and further muuch of FDI has been permitted through *automatic route* which will make entry of FDI easier. Growth in FDI inflows is given in Table 30.1. There has been tremendous growth in FDI inflows to India since 2003-04. Equity inflows have risen nearly thirteen-fold, from US$ 2.19 billion in 2003-04 to US$ 31.40 in 2008-09,US$ 25.83 billion in 2009-10 and further rose to US $32.12 billion in 2011-12. *This represents only the equity capital component.* Under international practices of reporting, which includes equity capital, reinvested earnings, and intra company loans, the total FDI inflows as against US$ 4.32 billion in 2003-04, rose to US $ 41.87 billion in 2008-09, and rose US $ 37.75 billion in 2009-10 and rose to US $ 46.55 billion in 2011-12. (see Table 30.1).

In FDI equity investments, Maurtius tops the list of first ten investing countries, followed by Singapore, the UK, Japan, the US, the Netherlands, Cyprus, Germany, France, and the UAE. The United Nations Conference on Trade and Development (UNCTAD) World Investment Report, 2012 in its analysis of the global trends and sustained growth of FDI inflows continues to report India as the third most attractive location for 2012-14. Among the sectors attracting highest FDI are services, telecommunications, computer software and hardware, housing and real estate, and construction. Sectors like agricultural services, sea transport, and electrical equipment had shown a quantum jump in FDI inflows during 2009-10. Sector-wise FDI inflows into some of the key industrial and infrastructure sectors are given in Table 30.2.

During 2012-13, services, hotels and tourism, metallurgical industries, automobile industry, construction, drugs and pharmaceuticals, industrial machinery were the sectors that attracted maximum FDI inflows. Sector-wise FDI inflows into industry and infrastructure are given in Table 30.2.

Note that foreign investment has two components : **foreign direct investment (FDI) and portfolio investment**. The latter have two sub-components – FII and Euro equities and others. It will be seen from Tables 30.1 and 30.3 that there have been large increase in foreign investment flows. *Since outflows of foreign direct investment from India have also greatly increased, net direct foreign investment will be less*. In fact due to sustained economic growth in income (except for the years 2011-12 and 2012-13), India offers a very high return on investment and has therefore become one of the world's largest market for manufactured goods and services.

In Table 30.3 we have given the net capital flows into the Indian economy for the years 2011-12 and 2012-13. It may be noted that capital flows comprise (1) foreign direct investment (FDI) (2) portfolio investment by foreign institutional investors (FIIs), (3) external assistance (4) external commercial borrowing (ECB) (5) NRI deposits and (6) short-term trade credit. It will be seen from **Table 30.3** that *net* capital flows to India were US$ 80.7 billion in 2010-11 and $85.4 billion in 2011-12. The major portion of these net capital inflows (*i.e.* after allowing for outward capital flows by Indians) was on account of foreign direct investment and portfolio investment by FIIs.

Table 30.2 : Sector-wise FDI inflows into industry and infrastructure

(US $ million)

	1991-2000	2000-10	2010-11	2011-12	April-Oct 2011-12	April-Oct 2012-13
Food Products	704.4	1237.3	246.9	239.7	122.3	368.4
Fermentation Industries	24	770.1	57.7	69.7	53.1	43.7
Textiles	241.8	828.6	129.8	164.7	74.3	91.3
Wood Products	0.0	18.8	1.6	29.6	8.1	28.7
Paper	250.5	716.9	44.0	454.7	29.6	3.1
Leather	33.5	42.6	9.3	8.3	5.6	34.7
Chemicals	1480.9	4461.1	2690.2	7534.1	7007.6	789.4
Rubber, Plastic, & Petroleium Products (including oil exploration)	90.3	2953.6	573.6	2217.4	2097.8	476.3
Non-metallic Minerals	261.1	2263.6	657.3	310.0	203.4	189.7
Metals and Metal products	186.2	3143.2	1098.1	1786.1	1436.9	1215.1
Machinery and Equipments	2043.1	15670.4	1836.3	4147.5	2894.2	1171.2
Transport Equipments	0	4603.2	1299.4	923.0	563.7	743.2
Other Manufacturing	1761.0	5705.6	1495.6	850.5	625.7	206.3
Mining (inclding mining services)	0	730.9	79.5	142.7	135.0	15.9
Power*	1038.9	5220.9	1486.2	2104.6	1440.8	771.0
Telecommunications	1089.4	8915.9	1664.5	1997.2	1964.1	48.4
Total	**9208.7**	**57267.7**	**13369.9**	**22979.7**	**18662.0**	**6196.4**

Source: GOI, *Economic Survey*, 2012-13.

Note : Total excludes inflows to services sector and other schemes;

* Includes non-conventional energy sector.

While the procedures for sanctioning foreign direct investment have been greatly simplified and more sectors such as single brand retail foreign investment, foreign investment up to 49 per cent in airports, further opening up of telecom sector, has been permitted, there is a need for a holistic approach to attract more foreign investment. There is also a need to address regional disparities in attracting foreign investments. It is understood that the Centre may work with state governments to evolve a concerted strategy to ensure more equitable distribution of such inflows. Maharashtra topped the list of FDI recipient states in India, followed by Delhi, Tamil Nadu, Karnataka and Gujarat.

Table 30.3: Desaggregated Items of Financial Account (Capital Inflows)

(US $ billion)

	2010-11 (P)	2012-13 (P)	2012-13			
			Q1 (PR)	Q2 (PR)	Q3 (PR)	Q4 (P)
1	2	3	4	5	6	7
1. Direct Investment (net)	**22.1**	**19.8**	**3.8**	**8.2**	**2.1**	**5.7**
1.(a) Direct Investment to India	33.0	26.9	5.9	9.5	4.3	7.2
2.(b) Direct Investment by India	–10.9	–7.1	–2.1	–1.4	–2.2	–1.4
2. Portfolio Investment (net)	**16.6**	**26.7**	**–2.0**	**7.6**	**9.7**	**11.3**
2(a) Portfolio Investment in India	16.8	27.6	–1.7	7.9	9.8	11.5
2(b) Portfolio Investment by India	–0.2	–0.9	3.5	3.3	5.9	–1.6
3. Financial Derivatives & Employees Stock Options	**–**	**–2.3**	**–0.6**	**–0.5**	**–0.4**	**–0.9**
4. Other Investment	**29.2**	**45.2**	**15.4**	**5.6**	**20.0**	**4.2**
4(a) Other equity (ADRs/GDRs)	0.6	0.2	0.1	0.1	0.0	0.0
4(b) Currency and deposits	12.1	15.3	6.4	3.5	2.0	2.8
Deposit-taking corporations except the central bank (NRI Deposits)	11.9	14.8	6.6	2.8	2.7	2.8
4(c) Loan	16.8	10.7	3.5	3.0	5.7	4.6
4(c)i Loans of India	15.7	11.1	3.5	3.3	5.9	–1.6
Deposit-taking corporation, except the central bank	4.1	1.3	3.0	2.0	2.7	2.8
General government (External Assistance)	2.5	1.3	–0.1	–0.3	–0.2	0.0
Other sectors (ECRs)	0.1	8.6	0.1	–0.1	–0.1	–0.1
4(c)ii Loans by India	1.0	–0.4	0.1	–0.3	–0.2	0.0
General government (External Assit.)	–0.2	–0.3	–0.1	–0.1	–0.1	–01
Other sectors (ECRs)	1.2	–0.1	0.1	–0.1	0.3	0.1
4.(d) Trade credit and advances	6.7	21.7	5.4	4.1	7.7	4.5
4.(c) Other accounts receivable/payable	–6.8	–2.7	–0.1	–5.1	4.0	–1.5
5. Reserve assets	**12.8**	**–3.8**	**–0.5**	**–0.2**	**–0.8**	**–2.7**
Financial Account (1+ 2+3+4)	**80.7**	**85.4**	**16.1**	**21.0**	**30.8**	**17.6**

Source : RBI, *Macroeconomic and Monetary Developments: First Quarter Review 2013-14*, Total of sub-components may not tally with aggregate due to rounding off.

P. Preliminary PR. Partially Revised

Significant Increase in FDI Since 2004

Gross FDI inflows increased from $8.96 billion in 2005-06 to $22.8 billion in 2006-07 and as will be seen from Table 30.3 FDI inflows (inward) to India further rose to $33.1 billion in 2009-10 and 2011-12 but declined to $ 26.9 billion in 2012-13. It may be noted that gross FDI reported consists of *FDI inflows and FDI outflows* from the country.

India has now emerged as the favourite destination for foreign direct investment. Booming stock market, robust growth of the Indian economy, expectations of Indian corporates doing well are the reasons for pouring of private equity investment into India in recent years. *Information*

Technology and IT-Enabled Services (IT & ITES) industry has been a favourite among PE investors in 2007 led by HDFC, banking, financial services and insurance sectors emerged as the second most popular sectors among PE investors in 2007.

Several international observers have opined that a developing country like India should try to attract much larger *foreign direct investments* (FDI) rather than encourage *portfolio investment.* Sir William Ryrie, former chairman of the International Finance Corporation, who has for decades closely watched developments in several developing countries, including India, says that portfolio investments do not result directly in "real" investment in the economy, though they do help "free" resources which can be used for real investment. Portfolio capital inflows can be volatile and cause problems when confidence weakens and funds are withdrawn. The recent Mexico and South East-Asian countries experience has shown how a country can be driven to a crisis when foreigners resort to a massive withdrawal of funds.

India has the basic ingredients to attract much larger foreign direct investments. Its vast domestic market, a low cost production base along with the availability of skilled labour, adequate repatriation facilities and a good legal system have placed the country ahead of several others for foreign investors. If these favourable features are reinforced by a stable economic environment, the country should be able to attract larger direct inflows of funds. China attracted over $ 60 billion of direct foreign investment in 2004 which constitutes 9.3 per cent of global foreign investment as compared to $ 5.34 billion of India in the year 2004.

According to recent UNCTAD report India is the second most preferred destination for foreign direct investment, ahead of US, UK and Germany but below China. During 2009-10 on *a gross basis* FDI inflows into India reached 33.1 billion US $. UNCTAD in its recent report '*World Investment Report 2010' ranked India as the 9th most attractive destination for foreign direct investment* (FDI) in 2009 up from the 13th rank in 2008. According to its estimates, in 2009, India received FDI inflows to the tune of $35 billion as against $24.6 billion in 2008. FDI inflows in 2009 in 10 countries (including India are shown in Fig. 30.4) below. It will be seen from this figure that the largest receipent of foreign direct investment (FDI) is the US followed by China and and France.

World Investment Report 2010 paints a brighter picture of trends in global FDI flows and estimates that global FDI inflows would reach the pre-crisis level of $1.6, trillion. Key features of trends in global FDI inflows are (1) the increase in the relative share of developing countries in these global inflows, and (2) flows to the services sectors gaining over manufacturing.

It may be noted that the large increase in FDI inflows into India in recent years till 2011-12 is due to robust economic growth, improved investment environment and further opening of telecommunication, retail and other sectors. In the beginning of the year 2008-09 the government had announced major changes in FDI policy raising foreign investment limits in several key secotrs including real estate, petroleum refenery, commodity exchanges, mining and civil aviation. However, the recent global financial crisis (2007-09) has created liquidity crunch in the US and European Countries. This affected the foreign direct investment flows into the Indian economy. Despite the global financial termoil during 2008-09, the total equity inflows (*i.e.*, FDI inflows) into India stood at US $ 27.3 billion signifying a growth of 11 per cent in terms of US dollar over the previous year. On the other hand, India has clearly emerged as a better market for foreign portfolio investment. Most fund managers rate India above China, the Philippines, South Korea and Indonesia among Asian markets. India is also rated higher than some of the Latin American markets like Colombia and Peru and European markets like Greece and Hungary.

FDI Inflows to Infrastrucutre

Lack of infrastructure facilities has been an important bottleneck for accelerating economic growth. In India a good amount of foreign direct investment has been made in the infrastructure which has therefore contributed to economic growth of the country. In 2007-08 foreign direct investment of $ 5168 million was made in the infrastructures which rose to $ 5659 million in 2009-10. It will be seen from Table 30.4 that in telecommunication, petroleum and natural gas, and power foreign direct investment has been quite significant. The total FDI inflows during Financial Year 2010-11 (April-November 2010) have been comparatively lower as compared to the inflows during the same period in the previous year 2009-10. However, FDI inflows into the petroleum and natural gas and air transport have been comparatively higher during the Financial year 2010-11. FDI inflows into power, telecommunication and information and broadcasting sectors have been comparatively lower during 2010-11 (see table 30.4).

Table 30.4: FDI flows to infrastructure (US$ million)

Sector	2007-08	2008-09	2009-10	Apri-Nov. 2009	April-Nov. 2010
Power	968	984.8	1,437.3	1237.8	984.0
Non-conventional Energy	43.2	85.3	497.9	67.0	44.1
Petroleum & Natural gas	1426.8	412.3	272.1	218.7	529.4
Telecommunications	1261.5	2558.4	2554.0	2223.3	1092.8
Information & Broadcasting*	299.1	748.7	491.2	419.9	272.4
Air Transport**	99.1	35.2	22.6	15.7	115.6
Sea Transport	128.4	50.2	284.9	279.8	288.6
Ports	918.2	493.2	65.5	65.4	10.9
Railway-related Components	12.4	18	34.2	25.1	0.4
Total (of above)	**5168.8**	**5386.1**	**5659.6**	**4552.7**	**3338.2**

Source : Department of Industrial Policy & Promotion.

Notes: * Information & broadcasting including print media;

** Air transport including air freight. Variation in data is due to reclassification of some sectors.

Volatile Nature of Capital Flows

The events of 2007-08 and the outflows and inflows of FII equity have brought home with renewed force the volatile nature of certain capital flows. Global capital flows to emerging and developing economies tripled from US$ 202.8 billion in 2006 to US$ 617.5 billion in 2007 and then collapsed to US$ 109.3 billion in 2008. India shared in the global boom in private *capital flows to emerging economies* with gross private capital inflows more than doubling from about US$ 36.7 billion in 2006 to about US$ 88.8 billion in 2007, then falling back to US$ 31.2 billion in 2008. Total net *capital inflows* into India consequently increased from 4.4 per cent of GDP in 2006 to 9.1 per cent of GDP in 2007 and back to about 3.3 per cent of GDP in 2008. Though *the private flows provide critical risk capital with long-term benefits to the economy, the volatile nature of these flows creates a negative externality for the real sectors in the short term.* We shall discuss in detail the volatile nature of capital flows in Appendix to this chapter.

FOREIGN DIRECT INVESTMENT (FDI) POLICY IN INDIA

Foreign direct investment (FDI) is at present very necessary for India not only for accelerating economic growth but also for meeting current account deficit which in recent years has significantly increased and is posing a serious challenge for India's economy. In Oct. 2012, the Parliament approved 51% FDI in multi-brand retail business. But due to stringent conditions imposed not a single company has come forward to open a multi-brand retail store. Besides, in other fields or sectors where FDI has been permitted long ago, the caps or limits imposed are not large enough to bring FDI in adequate quantity. Therefore, in 2013 government decided to raise these caps so as to attract more foreign direct investment. There is a need for building consensus on the role of foreign direct investment in India. In China's success growth story, foreign direct investment has played a significant role as China has not imposed much conditions on the entry of MNCs. Rate of return on investment in both India and China are much larger compared to the home countries of MNCs and, therefore, the right policy towards FDI will go a long way in attracting FDI to finance the projects needed for economic growth and to fill the gap in our current account deficit. To woo foreign direct investment we must give it a fair deal and ensure the security of their investment. Our treatment of FDI has not been good in the past. In the 1970s India chucked out IBM and Coca-Cola in a fit of nationalist spirit. In the late 1990s we sent back a power producing company 'Enron' which lost billions of dollars in setting up a power plant in Maharashtra due the differences in pricing of power generated. Recently, Sweden's IKEA faced problems in selling Nordic Comfort food and furniture. Recent acquisitions by a multinational firm Vodafone, British mobile telecoms firm, and Dai- chi Sankyo a Japanese drug firm have recently been facing problems.

Despite the problems faced by MNCs in India, as per data furnished by the Reserve Bank of India the stock of FDI in India is now quite large equal to about \$ 220 billion or 12% of our GDP. This includes all things from research centers in Bangalore to cement plants. The balance of payment data reveals that overall return on equity capital for foreign investors is probably below 10 percent and slumped in the year 2011-12. However, balance of payments data does not fully show the rate of return earned by foreign investors. A recent survey by the RBI estimated the return on equity capital by 745 firms with a significant foreign shareholders. According to it, the overall return on equity of these 745 firms with significant foreign shareholders was 13% in the year 2010-11.

Technology firms, car makers and chemical makers did well, transport and telecoms firms less so. *Unlike FDI in China, which has been directed at building factories for export, foreign direct investment into India is aimed at the domestic market—only 12% of the firms's sales were foreign.*

Successful Foreign Firms in India. It is worth mentioning that a number of foreign firms has been highly successful and they have invested a large amount of capital and have earned a lot. These high profile firms are listed in Indian stock market while being controlled by foreign firms such as Suzuki, Nestle, Unilever and Siemens (see chart). These are well established businesses with deep roots in India and high profitability.

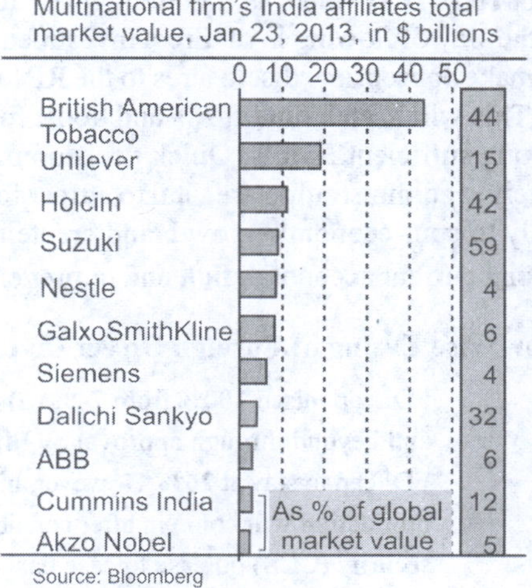

Figure 1: Multinational firms' India affiliates total market value, Jan 23, 2013, in \$bn

Foreign-controlled firms among the top 100 companies listed in India made a 24% return on equity in the year 2010-11 better than domestic firms' returns. Their market value doubled over the five preceding years. Although the foreigners will never admit it, some of these operations have gone from backwaters within multinationals to vital sources of growth.

That in turn has presented a different set of problems. Some foreign firms had the foresight to convert minority stakes in good Indian firms in to controlling ones. Suzuki took control of Maruti, India's biggest car manufacturer by volume, in 2002. Others have failed. After a botched effort to take control almost decades ago, British American Tabacco still owns only 31% of ITC, that has grown so fast it is now a global player in its own right. Faced with no prospect of control, some foreigners have pulled out. Honda sold its stake in Hero, an Indian motorbike-maker, in 2010 and is now competing directly against it. Those firms that have control of fast-growing subsidiaries have been keen to boost their stakes still further. Siemens raised its stake in its unit from 55% to 75 % in 2011. But often the valuations of Indian subsidiaries are quite high. Nestle India is valued at 50 times its profits—more than double the ratio of its Swiss parent.

Faced with lower stakes than they would like, foreigners have found another, shabby way, to extract more value from their Indian subsidiaries: charging them "royalty fees". They argue that these reflect the brand and technology benefits of being part of a global group. On 22nd January Hindustan Unilever became the latest firm to do so—announcing that the fee paid to its foreign parent would rise from 1.4% to 3.15% of sales. The minority investors in those companies complain that they are not being given fair deal. Still, for India the trend towards higher royalty payments is a backhanded compliment, It shows that some foreign-run firms in India make heavy profits. That is why their parent companies want to grab more of them. As a signal about outsiders' appetite for exposure to India, that may be rather important.

Latest Liberalisation of Foreign Direct Investment (FDI)

Faced with a harsh economic environment of sluggish economic growth and widening current deficit (CAD) and rapidly depreciating Indian rupee, government in its significant latest reform opened the doors to greater foreign direct investment by *raising 'caps'* on foreign direct investment in about a dozen sectors including telecom and highly sensitive sector of defence production (for state of the art technology') Not only have the '*caps*' (that is, upper limits) have been raised in several sectors but the norms of their entry into India has been eased by allowing much foreign directs investment to come through **automatic route,** that is, without the approval of **Foreign investment promotion Board (FIPs)** which is a nodel agency to vet FDI applications in India. Often FIPB put hurdles in the way of flowing in of direct investment. Under automatic route foreign investors will only need to make appropriate disclosures to the RBI instead of routing the investment application through FIPB. This will hasten fund flows and boost foreign investment, provided they see the possibilities of making sufficient Profits. Quick decision making, speedier implementation of decisions and non- interfering administration are vital to attract foreign direct investment which is badly needed today not only to spur economic growth and create more employment opportunities but also to meet the increasing current account deficit and to prevent the fast depreciation of rupee.

Sector-Wise Easing of Foreign Direct Investment Norms

1. ***Telecom***	FDI cap raised 100% from 74% (*a*) up to 49% through automatic route and beyond through approval by FIPB
2. ***Defence Production***	FDI cap to stay at 26%. However, higher foreign investment in defence production will come in after consideration by cabinet committee on security (CCS) on case to case basis
3. ***Single brand Retail***	The existing limit as 100 per cent but norms have been changed; 49% of FDI in single brand retail through automatic route and between 49 to100% through FIPB.

4. ***Insurance***	FDI limit raised from 26% to 49% subject to Parliament Approval.
5. ***Basic Cellular Services***	Up to 49 automatic and 49% to 100% through FIPB
6. ***Courier Service***	Cap at 100%, fully automatic.
7. ***Asset Reconstruction Companies***	FDI limit raised to 100 percent from the existing 74%—49% through automatic route and the rest with approval of FIPB
8. ***Credit Information Bureaus***	FDI limit raised to 74% from the existing 49% through automatic route
9. ***Petroleum and Natural Gas Refineries***	FDI limit retained at 49% but will be allowed through automatic route
10. ***Commodity Exchanges.***	FDI limit retained at 49% but allowed through automatic route
11. ***Stock Exchanges***	49% through automatic route
12. ***Power Exchanges***	49% through automatic route

FDI cap on civil aviation has been fixed at 46%. Besides civil aviation, decision was taken on relaxing FDI caps in airports, medicine Brownfield pharma and multibrand retail. While most of these caps can be fixed through executive orders, raising the multibrand FDI limit in insurance requires Parliament approval.

It is evident from above that intended objective of liberalisation of foreign direct investment policy is to send right signals to the existing and potential foreign investors to revive Indian economic growth which until recently was an engine for global growth. Besides spurring economic growth, the new FDI policy has been guided to meet the current account deficit and to stem the slide of the Indian rupee. Though new FDI policy of raising FDI caps in a number of industries is a step in the right direction but more need to be done to improve India's image as a global investment decision through speeder implementation of projects and non-interfering administration. Flowing in of much foreign investment is vital to spur economic growth and create new employment opportunities. We need foreign investment in insurance sector to build enough capital base of the insurance companies, offer a wide range of products and protect customers' interests against insolvency. The Indian economy battling to get out of slowdown in economic growth which is now (2012–13) down to 5 per cent is in need of resources to fund its infrastructure projects, to build highways, ports, airports and railways. Foreign funds flow will also release government resources to be spent on the infrastructure projects.

The government's attempt to open up to more foreign direct investment (FDI) might not bring in a flood of dollars immediately but is an important policy reform. Just setting FDI limits higher is not enough to get capital flows coming in, we need better and cleaner governance at all levels. That requires political resolve at the highest level because corruption in India is systemic to how political parties are funded.

ROLE OF MULTINATIONAL CORPORATIONS (MNCs)

Multinational corporations are those large firms which are incorporated in one country but which own, control or manage production and distribution facilities in several countries. Therefore, these multinational corporations are also known as *transnational corporations.* They transact business in a large number of countries and often operate in diversified business activities. The movements of private foreign capital take place through the medium of these multinational corporations. Thus multinational corporations are important source of foreign direct investment (FDI). Besides, it is through multinational corporations that modern high technology is transferred to the developing countries.

The important question about multinational corporations is why they exist. The multinational corporations exist because they are highly efficient. Their efficiencies in production and distribution of goods and services arise from *internalising* certain activities rather than contracting them out to other firms[1]. Managing a firm involves which production and distribution activities it will

1. See Ronald Coase, "The Nature of the Firm, *Economica*, Nov. 1937, pp.368-405.

perform itself and which activities it will contract out to *other firms and individuals*. In addition to this basic issue, a big firm may decide to set up and operate business units in other countries to benefit from *advantages of location.* For examples, it has been found that giant American and European firms set up production units to explore and refine oil in Middle East Countries because oil is found there. Similarly, to take advantages of lower labour costs, and not strict environmental standards, multinational corporate firms set up production units in developing countries

Alternative Methods of Foreign Investment by Multinational Companies

In order to increase their profitability many giant firms find it necessary to go in for horizontal and vertical integration. For this purpose they find it profitable to set up their production or distribution units outside their home country. The firms that sell abroad the products produced in the home country or the products produced abroad to sell in the home country must decide how to manage and control their assets in other countries. In this regard, there are three methods of foreign investment by multinational firms among which they have to choose which mode of control over their assets they adopt. There are three main modes of foreign investment.

1. Agreement with Local Firms for Sale of MNCs Products. A multinational firm can enter into an agreement with local firms for exporting the product produced by it in the home country to them for sale in their countries. In this case, a multinational firm allows the foreign firms to sell its product in the foreign markets and control all aspects of sale operations.

2. Setting up of Subsidiaries. The second mode for investment abroad by a multinational firm is to set up a *wholly owned subsidiary* to operate in the foreign country. In this case a multinational firm has complete control over its business operations ranging from the production of its product or service to its sale to the ultimate use or consumers. A subsidiary of a multinational corporation in a particular country is set up under the company act of that country. Such subsidiary firm benefits from the managerial skills, financial resources, and international reputation of their parent company. However, it enjoys some independence from the parent company.

3. Branches of Multinational Corporation. Instead of establishing its subsidiaries, multinational corporation can set up their branches in other countries. Being branches they are not legally independent business unit but are linked with their parent company.

4. Foreign Collaboration or Joint Ventures. Thirdly, the multinational corporations set up joint ventures with foreign firms to either produce its product jointly with local companies of foreign countries for sale of the product in the foreign markets. A multinational firm may set up its business operation in collaboration with foreign local firms *to obtain raw materials* not available in the home country. More often, to reduce its overall production costs multinational companies set up joint ventures with local foreign firms to manufacture inputs or sub-components in foreign markets to produce the final product in the home country.

Role of Multinational Corporations in the Indian Economy

Prior to 1991 Multinational companies did not play much role in the Indian economy. In the pre-reform period the Indian economy was dominated by public enterprises. To prevent concentration of economic power industrial policy 1956 did not allow the private firms to grow in size beyond a point. By definition multinational companies were quite big and operate in several countries. While multinational companies played a significant role in the promotion of growth and trade in South-East Asian countries they did not play much role in the Indian economy where import-substitution development strategy was followed. Since 1991with the adoption of industrial policy of liberalisation and privatisation rote of private foreign capital has been recognised as important for rapid growth of the Indian economy. Since source of bulk of foreign capital and investment are multinational corporation, they have been allowed to operate in the Indian economy subject to some regulations. The following are the important reasons for this change in policy towards multinational companies in the post-reform period.

Some of world's largest multinational corporations are given below.

World's Some Important Non-Financial Multinational Corporations

S.No.	*International Corporation*	*Parent Country*	*Industry of operation*
1.	General Electric	United States	Electronics
2.	Exxon Mobil Corporation	United States	Petroleum (exploring, refining and distributing)
3.	Royal Duch Shell Group	Netherland/UK	-do-
4.	General Motors	United States	Motor Vehicles
5.	Ford Motor Co.	United States	Motor Vehicles
6.	Toyata Motor Co.	Japan	Motor Vehicles
7.	IBM	United States	Computers
8.	BP	United Kingdom	Petroleum (Exp/Ref./Distt.)
9.	Nesle SA	Switzerland	Food/Beverages
10.	Nippon Oil Co.	Japan	Petroleum/Expl., Ref./Distt.
11.	Sieman AG	Germany	Electronics
12.	BMW AG	Germany	Motors Vehicles
13.	ABB	Switzerland	Electrical equipment
14.	Sony Corporation	Japan	Electronics
15.	Seagram	Canada	Food/Beverages
16.	Aventis	France	Pharmaceuticals/Chemicals
17.	Roche Group	Switzerland	Pharmaceuticals
18.	Honda Motor Co.	Japan	Motor Vehicles
19.	Phillips Electronics	Netherland	Electronics
20.	Hewlett-Packard	United States	Electronics/Computers

1. Promotion Foreign Investment. In the recent years, external assistance to developing exintries has been declining. This is because the donor developed countries have not been willing to part with a larger proportion of their GDP as assistance to developing countries. MNCs can bridge the gap between the requirements of foreign capital for increasing foreign investment in India. The liberalised foreign investment pursued since 1991, allows MNCs to make investment in India subject to different ceilings fixed for different industries or projects. However, in some industries 100 per cent export-oriented units (EOUs) can be set up. It may be noted, like domestic investment, foreign investment has also a multiplier effect on income and employment in a country. For example, the effect of Suzuki firm's investment in Maruti Udyog manufacturing cars is not confined to income and employment for the workers and employees of Maruti Udyog but goes beyond that. Many workers are employed in dealer firms who sell Maruti cars. Moreover, many intermediate goods are supplied by Indian suppliers to Maruti Udyog and for this many workers are employed by them to manufacture various parts and components used in Maruti cars. Thus their incomes also go up by investment by a Japanese multinational in Maruti Udyog Limited in India.

2. Non-Debt Creating Capital inflows. In pre-reform period in India when foreign direct investment by MNCs was discouraged, we relied heavily on *external commercial borrowing* (ECB) which was of debt-creating capital inflows. This raised the burden of external debt and debt service payments reached the alarming figure of 35 per cent of our current account receipts. This created doubts about our ability to fulfil our debt obligations and there was a flight of capital from

India and this resulted in balance of payments crisis in 1991. As direct foreign investment by multinational corporations represents non-debt creating capital inflows we can avoid the liability of debt-servicing payments. Moreover, the advantage of investment by MNCs lies in the fact that servicing of non-debt capital begins only when the MNC firm reaches the stage of making profits to repatriate Thus, MNCs can play an important role in reducing stress strains and on India's balance of payments (BOP).

3. Technology Transfer. Another important role of multinational corporations is that they transfer high sophisticated technology to developing countries which are essential for raising productivity of working class and enable us to start new productive ventures requiring high technology. Whenever, multinational firms set up their subsidiary production units or joint-venture units, they not only import new equipment and machinery embodying new technology but also skills and technical know-how to use the new equipment and machinery. As a result, the Indian workers and engineers come to know of new superior technology and the way to use it. In India, the corporate sector spends only few resources on Research and Development (R&D). It is the giant multinational corporate firms (MNCs) which spend a lot on the development of new technologies can greatly benefit the developing countries by transferring the new technology developed by them. Therefore, MNCs can play an important role in the technological upgradation of the Indian economy.

4. Promotion of Exports. With extensive links all over the world and producing products efficiently and therefore with lower costs multinationals can play a significant role in promoting exports of a country in which they invest. For example, the rapid expansion in China's exports in recent years is due to the large investment made by multinationals in various fields of Chinese industry. Historically in India, multinationals made large investment in planlations whose products they exported. In recent years, Japanese automobile company Suzuki made a large investment in Maruti Udyog with a joint collaboration with Government of India. Maruti cars are not only being sold in the Indian domestic market but are exported in a large number to the foreign countries.

As a matter of fact until recently, when giving permission to a multinational firm for investment in India, Government granted the permission subject to the condition that the concerned multinational company would export the product so as to earn foreign exchange for India. However, in case of Pepsi, a famous cold -drink multinational company, while for getting a product license in 1961 to produce Pepsi Cola in India it agreed to export a certain proportion of its product, but later it expressed its inability to do so. Instead, it ultimately agreed to export things other than what it produced such as tea.

5. Investment in Infrastructure. With a large command over financial resources and their superior ability to raise resources both globally and inside India it is said that multinational corporations could invest in infrastructure such as power projects, modernisation of airports and posts, telecommunication. The investment in infrastructure w1ll give a boost to industrial growth and help in creating income and employment in the India economy. The external economies generated by investment in infrastructure by MNCs will therefore *crowd* in investment by the indigenous private sector and will therefore stimulate economic growth.

In view of above, even Common Minimum Programme of the present UPA government provides that foreign direct investment (FDI) will be encouraged and actively sought, especially in areas of (*a*) infrastructure, (*b*) high technology and (*c*) exports, and (*d*) where domestic assets and employment are created on a significant scale.

A Critique of Multinational Corporations

In recent years foreign direct investment through multinational corporations has vastly increased in India and other developing countries. This vast increase in investment by multinational corporations in recent years is prompted by factors (1) the liberalisation of industrial policy giving greater role to the private sector, (2) opening up of the economy and liberalisation of foreign trade and capital inflows. In this economic environment multinational corporations which are in search for global profits are induced to make investment in developing countries. As explained above, foreign direct investment by multinational firms bring many benefits to the recipient countries but there are many potential dangers and disadvantages from the viewpoint of economic growth and employment generation. Therefore, role of multinational corporations in India and other developing countries have been criticised on several grounds. We discuss below some of the criticisms levelled against multinational corporations.

Capturing Markets

1. First, it is alleged that multinational corporations invest their capital and locate their manufacturing units on their own or in collaboration with local firms in order *to sell their products and capture the domestic markets of the countries where they invest and operate.* With their vast resources and competitive strength, they can weed out their competitive firms. For example, in India if corporate multinational firms are allowed to sell or produce the products presently produced by small and medium enterprises, the latter would not be able to compete and therefore would be thrown out of business. This will lead to reduction in employment opportunities in the country.

2. **Use of Capital-intensive Techniques**. It has been seen that increasing capital intensity in modern manufacturing sector is responsible for slow growth of employment opportunities in India's industrial sector. These capital-intensive techniques may be imported by large domestic firms but presently they are being increasingly used by multinational corporations which bring their technology when they invest in India. Emphasising this factor, Thirwall rightly writes, "*In this case the technology may be inappropriate not because there is not a spectrum of technology or inappropriate selection is made but because the technology available is circumscribed by the global profit maximising motives of multinational companies investing in the less-developed country concerned* "[3]

3. **Encouragement to Inessential Consumption.** The investment by multinational companies leads to overall increase in investment in India but it is alleged that they encourage conspicuous consumption in the economy. These companies cater to the wants of the already well-to-do people. For example, in India very expensive cars (such as City Honda, Hyundai's Accent, Mercedes, Opal Astra, etc.) the air conditioners, costly laptops, washing machines, expensive fridges, 29" and Plasma TVs are being produced/sold by multinational companies. Such goods are quite inappropriate for a poor country like India. Besides, their consumption has a demonstration effect on the consumption of others. This tends to raise the propensity to consume and adversely affects the increase in savings of the country.

4. **Import of Obsolete Technology.** Another criticism of MNCs is based on the ground that they import obsolete machines and technology. As mentioned above, some of the imported technologies are inappropriate to the conditions of Indian economy. It is alleged that India has been made a dumping ground for obsolete technology. Moreover, the multinational corporations do not undertake Research and Development (R&D) in India to promote local technologies suited to the Indian factor-endowment conditions. Instead, they concentrate R & D activity at their head quarters.

5. **Setting up Environment-Polluting Industries.** It has been found that investment by multinational corporations in developing countries such as India is usually made for capturing domestic markets rather than for export promotion. Moreover, in order to evade strict environment control measures in their home countries they set up polluting industrial units in India. A classic example of this is a highly polluting chemical plant set up in Bhopal resulting in gas tragedy when

3. A.P. Thirwal *Growth and Development,* Pelgrave, Macmillan, seventh edition, 2003. p. 435.

thousands of people were either killed or made handicapped due to severe ailments. "With the tighening of environmental measures in the such countries, there is a tendency among the MNCs to locate the polluting industries in the poor countries, where environmental legislation is non-existent or is not properly implemented, as exemplified in the Bhopal gas tragedy".[4]

6. Volatility in Exchange Rate. Another major consequence of liberalised foreign investment by multinational corporations is its impact on the foreign exchange rate of the host country. Foreign capital inflows affect the foreign exchange rate of the Indian rupee. A large capital inflows through foreign investment brings about increase in the supply of foreign exchange say of US dollars. With demand for foreign exchange being given, increase in supply of foreign exchange will lead to the appreciation of exchange rate of rupee. This appreciation of the Indian rupee will discourage exports and encourage imports causing deficit in balance of trade. For example, in India in the fiscal years 2004-05 and 2005-06, there was large capital inflows by FII (giant financial multinationals) in the Indian economy to take advantage of higher interest rates here and also booming of the Indian capital market.

On the other hand, when interest rates rise in the parent countries of these multinationals or rates of return from capital markets go up or when there is loss of confidence in the host country about its capacity to make payments of its debt as happened in case of South-East Asia in the late nineties there is large outflow of capital by multinational companies resulting in the crisis and huge depreciation of their exchange rate. Thus, capital inflows and outflows by multinationals have been responsible for large volatility of exchange rate.

Then there is the question of *repatriation of profits* by the multinationals. Though a part of profit is reinvested by the multinational companies in the host country, a large amount of profits are remitted to their own parent countries. This has a potential disadvantage for the developing countries, especially when they are facing foreign exchange problem. Commenting on this Thirwall writes "FDI has the potential disadvantage even when compared with loan finance, that there may be outflow of profits that lasts much longer.[5]

Transfer Pricing and Evasion of Local Taxes. Multinational corporations are usually vertically integrated. The production of a commodity by multinational firm comprises various phases in its production the components used in the production of a final commodity may be produced in its parent country or in its affiliates in other countries. *Transfer pricing refers to the prices a vertically integrated multinational firm charges for its components or parts used for the production of the final commodity, say in India.* These prices of components or parts are not real prices as determined by demand for and supply of them. They are arbitrarely fixed by the companies so that they have to pay less taxes in India. They artificially inflate the transfer prices for intermediate products (i.e., components) produced in their parent country or their overseas affiliates so as to show lower profits earned in India. As a result, they succeed in evading corporate income tax

Conclusion. We have seen above foreign investment by multinational companies have both advantages and disadvantages. Therefore, they need regulation and should be permitted in selected sectors and also subject to a cap on their investment in particular fields. If objective of economic growth with stability and social justice is to be achieved, there should not be complete open door policy for them.

It is true that multinational corporations take risk in making investment in India, they bring capital and foreign exchange which are non-debt creating, they generally promote technology and can help in raising exports. But they must be regulated so that they serve these goals. They should

---

4. Bipalab Dasgupta, *Globalisation : India's Adjustment Experience,* Sage Publications, New Delhi, 2005, P. 81.

5. A.P. Thirwall, of. cit.

be allowed to invest in infrastructure, high-technology areas, and in industries whose products they can export and if they help in generating net employment opportunities. We agree with Colman and Nixon who write :

"Transnational corporations cannot be directly blamed for lack of development (or the direction development is taking) within less developed countries. Their prime objective is global profit maximisation and their actions are aimed at achieving that objective, not developing the host less developed country. If the technology and products that they introduce are inappropriate, if their actions exacerbate regional and social inequalities, if they weaken the balance of payments position, in the last resort it is up to the government of less developed country to pursue policies which will eliminate the causes of these problems".[6]

---

6. D. Colman, D and F Nixon, *Economics of Change in Less Developed Countries,* Oxford University Press, 1978.

APPENDIX TO CHAPTER 30

Foreign Direct Investment (FDI) in Multi-brand Retail Sector

Introduction

In a significant, decision on Nov. 24, 2011, the Central Government gave approval to the proposal to allow 51 per cent foreign direct investment FDI in multibrand retail as well as 100 per cent FDI in single brand retail. The decision was hailed as a big reform measure adopted by the Government which will benefit both consumers and farmers. It was pointed out that this would lead to the creation of supply chains, logistic support, storage facilities, and cut middlemen to ensure better prices for farmers' products and cheaper goods for the consumers and generate for employment for 10 million persons in three years. It will bring not only foreign capital so badly needed for the growth of the Indian economy but also superior technology and better managerial techniques.

At present 100 per cent FDI is permitted under the automatic route for *wholesale trade* subject to certain end-sale limitations and restrictions while in single brand retail it is permitted up to 51 per cent with government approval. But due to stiff opposition by the opposition parties FDI is multi-brand retail was not permitted for it is feared that it would hit small shopkeepers and neighbour stores. In March 2010, the Central Government came out with a blue print for discussion describing the merits of throwing open the multi-brand retail trading to foreign direct investment (FDI). The policy of allowing FDI in multi-brand retail trade will permit global giants such as Wall-Mart, Tesco and Correfour to set up huge market stores in India with back-end infrastructure. It is contended that FDI in multi-brand retail trading will help both farmers and consumers. Government proposal provides for safety clauses and appointment of a regulator to protect various interests.

The government decision regarding entry of FDI in retail comes with certain conditions to address the fears of small traders that the global giants setting up big stores selling multi-brand products would drive them out of business and render them unemployed. These conditions are stated below :

1. Minimum investment by the big global retailers setting up stores in India should be $ 100 million.

2. 50 per cent of the investment by multibrand retail giants must be in *back-end infrastructure* such as cold chains, storage facilities (i.e. ware housing), logistic support and transportation.

3. At least 30 per cent of goods purchased for sale in these multi-brand stores must be sourced from small-scale and medium enterprises (SME).

4. These giant multi-brand retail stores can only be opened in cities with at least 10 lakh population. India has about 43 such cities. The Government will have the first right of procurement of agricultural produce.

5. Since retail trade is a state subject, the different states are free to allow or not for the opening up retail shops by these international retail giants.

Against the opening up of multi-brand to foreign investment (FDI) it is pointed out that it would adversely affect the large unorganised sector which will not stand up to the competition of FDI in this sector.

The government proposal contains enacting a law called *Multi-Regulation Act* to protect small retailers and setting up a centrally administered agency to monitor compliance with the rules. It is mentioned that despite without any restrictions at present only 5 per cent of the nearly $ 500 billion or about ₹ Rs. 23 lakh crore of retail trade is in the organised sector.

Case for FDI in Multi-brand Retail

The inter-mnisteral committee headed by chief economic advisor favoured the opening up of multi-brand retail trade on the ground that *it will help to fight inflation, especially food inflation.* Today it is estimated that about 40% of all farm products get rotten by the time they reach the final point of sale. Apart from the enormous waste that this generates, it creates upward pressure on food prices, hitting consumers hard with no benefit to the farmers. The lack of organised storage and transport chains is the main culprit behind these losses. To quote the DIPP paper "*there is the need to address issues relating to the farmers through removal of structural inefficiencies, as also to improve post-harvest management that requires investment in backend logistics and storage infrastructure. A week supply chain result in large-scale wastage and more often than not, the ultimate consumer pays a lot more than what reaches the farmer*. It is important to provide for steadier incomes to farmers either through direct marketing or contract farming programmes. Further, allowing FDI on this multi-brand retail sector will not only bring financial capital into the Indian economy, *it will also bring in new technologies for storage and transport*".

The DIPP paper further mentioned that to ensure the advantages of opening up of the multi-brand retail trade to FDI, the government could make 50 per cent total FDI for multi-brand retail mandatory to be invested in creation of back-end infrastructure and reserve half of all in the retail sector for rural youth. Besides, this will help in boosting investment in warehouses and cold chains to cut wastes of agricultural products. *Foreign investment in multi-brand retail will eliminate high margins of middlemen that will not only benefit farmers but ensure lower prices to the consumers.* Thus from the perspective of consumers there is urgent need to check food inflation and control the demand -supply inmalances.

The retail sector needs large-scale investments. A substantial portion of these investments are expected from private enterprises, hence, it is imperative to make it financially worthwhile for them. It has long been argued that the *entry of foreign retailers through joint ventures would help develop backward linkages to sources of supply and thus develop a domestic supply chain of international standards*. Eventually, this would improve productivity benefiting the farmer, and the competition may eventually help bring down prices for consumers. The government believes that permitting FDI in the sector will also help bring in technical and management knowhow which is in India's long-term interest.

Addressing people's concern about opening up the multibrand retail sector to foreign direct investment the department of *Industrial Policy and promotion* or DIPP moved its amended proposals for approval by the cabinet in this regard. In its 24 November 2011 decision the cabinet approved these proposals. According to these proposals 51 per cent of foreign direct investment (FDI) in multi-brand retail shall be permitted subject to a minimum investment of $100 million. It is also proposed that state governments will have the final say in whether they have front-end retail stores in their states. Further, the Government claims that draft framework for FDI in multi-brand retail has been prepared keeping adequate safeguards to protect small shopkeepers and to ensure that FDI in multi-brand retail actually helps in development of back-end infrastructure. According to the Government framework, at least 50 per cent of FDI in multi-brand retail projects should be in infrastructure. Multinational retailers will have to file a statement of account with the RBI and Foreign Investment Promotion Board showing the investment in back-end functions.

The government is very clear that *FDI in multi-brand retail should create large scale employment and bring quality investment into the country* leading to development of back-end infrastructure. According to industry estimates, lack of cold chains leads to a loss of about 40% of the country's farm produce or Rs. 50,000 crore, every year. Because of this, Dr. Kaushik Basu, Economic Adviser,

Ministry of Finance asserts that *FDI in multi-brand retail will serve as an important measure to fight food inflation* which arises due to supply-side bottlenecks, one of them being lack of back-end infrastructure such as cold chain and warehouses to store food grains.

For easier monitoring, the government will also allow back-end infrastructure to be executed through a dedicated entity. Multi-brand retail stores would be required to source at least 30% of their products, including food items, from small and medium enterprises, according to the draft framework. These stores will be allowed only in cities with a population of more than 1 million.

At least 30% of the turnover of these ventures will have to come from small traders through wholesale cash-and-carry stores set up for the purpose. In order to address concerns of some States that multi-brand FDI will drive out local shops, the draft framework proposes powers to State governments to impose additional conditions on MNC retailers, such as measures to integrate 'kirana' or local retailers into the value chain.

Case Against FDI in Multi-brand Retail

But the Government's decision to allow global retail giants to open their shops in India has met with a stiff opposition. The reasons for which the decision ha been opposed are stated below :

1. First, the crucial disadvantage of opening up to multi-brand retail sector to foreign direct investment (FDI) by global retail giants is that it will badly hurt small traders and shopkeepers who would be competed out by these giant retailers. It is because of the economies of scale and procuring goods from cheaper sources, even from abroad, they will be able to sell goods at cheaper prices. It is pointed out that retail sector in India employs over 40 million people, next only to agriculture. Being unable to compete with the giant retailers, they would be forced out of business and thus deprived of their livelihood. As a result there will massive loss of jobs. This has been the experience of most countries which have permitted the entry of FDI in retail.

Besides, not only will the small traders and shopkeepers who are engaged in self employment in retail business will lose their jobs but also other workers who are employed in these relatively small shops and retail outlets will be rendered unemployed as due to deficient in skills, the majority of them are unlikely to be absorbed in the global giant retail stores. As a result, *unemployment in the country will increase.*

The government and the supporters of its decision to allow entry of global giants in retail business point out that 10 million jobs will be created by them in three years. This is quite a tall claim without any evidence. Of course, they will employ people in retail shops, in cold chain, warehousing etc. but they will displace more than they employ. It may be noted that many workers who do not find employment in agriculture find jobs in the unorganised service sector (i.e. retail business) to make meagre earnings as they fail to get employment in the organised sector at higher wages. A majority of them are unskilled and are therefore unlikely to get jobs in the supermarket shops set up by the global giants. The entry of big giants in the organised retail sector will add to their miseries and send them below the poverty line. Prime Minister Manmohan Singh is of the view that there is no reason why the small traders will not be able to compete with retail giants. This is only a wishful thinking without any facts and evidence.

Another outcome of the entry of FDI multiband retail giants is that the supermarket stores set up by them will *source most of their manufactured goods from abroad* to sell in their stores in India. Already crazy of foreign goods, a major chunk of middle class in India will bring foreign goods which are supposed to be of better quality. This will lead to more imports of manufactured goods which will hurt the Indian manufacturing industries, especially small-scale and medium enterprises. The Government has stipulated that for their big retail stores, foreign global giants must source 30 per cent of the goods from local small and medium enterprises. However, this will be difficult to enforce.

Thus, with FDI retail giants setting up shops in India will not only displace small traders they will also cause loss of jobs in their manufacturing sector as these supermarkets opened with FDI by global giants will source their goods internationally and not from domestic sources. This will hurt small Indian investors and producers who cannot compete will these global giants. This will lead to greater loss of jobs. This has been the actual experience of most countries which have allowed the entry of FDI in retail.

In our view comparison between China and India is quite misplaced. China is major manufacturing country and the largest supplier of manufactured goods to Wall-Mart and other international retail giants. It obviously cannot say no to these international chains opening stores in China when it is global supplier to them. India, in contrast, will lose both retail services and manufacturing jobs.

The claim that opening up of multi-brand retail trade spur competition and improve farm productivity has been contested. The obstacle to growth of agricultural productivity are tiny farm holdings and that too are fragmented. Agricultural productivity per hectare in India is one of the lowest in the world, Besides small and fragmented land holdings, there is a lack of irrigation facilities. Even after sixty years of planning and rural development only 40 per cent of arable land is irrigated, the remaining 60 per cent of the arable land is still rained. Increasing fluctuations in rainfall, depleting ground water level and lower and improper fertilizer usage are also issues of great concern. So, who is going to benefit from *efficient back-end operations and improved infrastructure of business* ? Certainly not the common Indian farmers !

There would be further land consolidation in favour of the already rich and resourceful farmers, creating conditions for further widening of the gap between the well-to-do and poor farmers.

Rural infrastructure is another area of worry. One cannot drive high speed, air-conditioned trucks carrying fresh perishable fruits or milk products on roads unsuitable even for bullock-carts. During the monsoon, when a considerable amount of agriculture inputs is expected to be moved to villages, more than 30 per cent of the villages in flood prone states become unapproachable by road. How FDI in multi-brand retail trade will help in building rural infrastructure is open to question ?

Lastly "farming is the riskiest profession" observes Dr. M.S. Swaminathan, eminent agriculture scientist. In spite of being an agricultural country, our farmers are not insulated from risk. The existing insurance system is either beyond their reach or too complicated to be relied upon. The arrival of retail in a big way will certainly make farming riskier. Meeting customers' (mostly urban) demands and quality specifications require more resource-intensive farming. We need to learn lessons from the innumerable incidents of farmers' suicides being reported across the country. Only time will tell how much risk these big retail players will be willing to shoulder.

Finally the argument advanced by the Government in favour of its decision permitting FDI in retail giants that it will create the supply chain, back-end infrastructure such as storage facilities, refrigeration, transportation for farm's produce is quite misleading. Foreign multinational giants cannot be expected to make large investment in rural infrastructure including power generation and transportation. Why plan after plan in the 60 years of planning (1951-2011) which has been allocating quite a good chunk of plan resources to them has failed to accomplish this task. Further, why to rely on foreign multinationals for building up cold chain infrastrucutre and warehousing. Cannot the Government itself or India's big businessmen can do this job ?

To conclude, the Government argument that FDI in retail will solve all problems like back-end infrstructure, generate employment on a large scale and check inflation, especially food inflation is making a tall claim. In fact, FDI in retail is no solution for these fundamental problems of supply-side bottlenecks and of rising inflation and unemployment. They have to be solved through prudent resource allocation in development planning for India.

In view of above we are of the view that opening up multi-brand retail trade to FDI is not a panacea for the problems of Indian agriculture. It will create more distress not only for our retail shopkeepers and create large-scale unemployment but will also not benefit farmers.

EASING OF RULES FOR FDI IN MULTI-BRAND RETAIL BUSINESS

It is now over a year that government got sectioned from the parliament allowing FDI in multi-brand retail business. The limit of 51 per cent of FDI in this multi-brand retail business was fixed. Besides, it was stipulated that the retail giants would purchase or source goods from small and medium enterprises to be sold by them. Further, each multi-brand retial giant had to deposit ₹ 100 crore with the government. They were also required to make 50% investment in building back-end infrastructure. They were also to set up their supermarket shops in cities with 10 lakh population or more. But in the last twelve months, no global FDI retail giant has come forward to set up their supermarket in India. Therefore, to woo them the government has eased of rules for them. It has now rolled back the policy concerning investment in back-end infrastructure. It has also diluted the condition of sourcing goods to be sold by them from small and medium enterprises. These were the two key conditions of the policy of FDI in multi brand retail business. Thus the commerce and industry minister Mr. Anand Sharma says, "*No policy can be divorced from the socio-economic conditions of the nation. These conditionalities are a reflection of the realities. The purpose of the policy is creation of infrastructure, jobs and reduction of post harvest losses. Sourcing has to be given priority and reflected.* However, be added, **"the government will look at providing flexibilities wherever possible".**

It has been clarified by the government that relaxation would involve that instead of confining the purchase of goods from SMEs, the multi-brand retail FDI companies could include procurement from cooperatives such as Amul or Nafed to comply with the 30 per cent sourcing requirement. In the meeting of the Minister with domestic and international big retailers a special mention of this was made. Besides, the commerce and industry was also considering to allow foreign retailers to set up shop in tier-2 and tier 3 cities.

Foreign retailers want agro sourcing to be a part of the minimum 30% sourcing from MSMEs. The DIPP, however, says the policy only allows processed products' sourcing from MSMEs. The department's clarifications also said that all front-end stores will be company-owned and operated, which means, these chains cannot operate through the franchise route. "We will have to do some handholding for them, like in single-brand, in the form of a fast-track approval mechanism. If there is need for greater clarity, we shall do so (issue more clarifications)".

The other major area of concern for global retailers was investment in infrastructure, where existing rules mandate that at least 50% of the initial $100 million is ploughed into creating the back-end architecture, which includes warehouses and cold chains.

Easing of Retail Giants' Entry

The government in July 2013 relaxed investment rules in multi-brand retail, significantly easing the condition that global giants will have to procure 30% of the goods they sell in India from local small firms and artisans, a condition that the industry had argued was restrictive. *It also allowed global chains to open stores in smaller cities by removing the restriction that only the 53 urban centres with a minimum population of one million can house such supermarkets.* The rules were eased to woo MNCs like Walmart, Carrefour and Pesco which had sought several clarifications, which the government has sought to address. Goods bought from companies that have invested at least $2 million in plant and machinery will now quality as part of the "mandatory 30% sourching requirement" for big retailers has been decided by the cabinet. This is double the earlier investment threshold of $1 million. Besides, such suppliers will continue to make the grade as small enterprises even if investments made subsequent to their first association with retail giants take the value of their plant and machinery beyond $ 2 million.

In addition, farmers' and agricultural cooperatives will be counted as small firms for meeting the mandatory sourcing condition, implying that the processing fruits and vegetables procured from Indian farmers will form part of the 30% local sourcing obligation.

Retailers will have to source an average of 30% from Indian suppliers over a period of the first five years. This means they can import less in the initial years and raise the level in subsequent years. Earlier, retailers had been asked to invest half their at least $ 100 million (about ₹ 600 crore) in back-end infrastructure. Under the new rules, retailers will have to meet this condition within three years only with their first tranche of investment, allowing them the freedom to deploy capital subsequently according to "need based" necessity.

With the above relaxation of rules, it was expected FDI inflows by retail giants would occur in adequate quantity and provide stimus to the growth of the Indian economy. However, even with the above relaxation of rules for giant retailers no one so far (Nov. 2013) has shown willingness to set up these super-market shops. Some giant retailers have indicated they are waiting for the outcome of 2014 parliamentary elections. They are afraid that the new government may ban the entry into India of multi-brand FDI retail giants.

CHAPTER 31
Globalisation and Its Impact on Indian Economy

Introduction : Meaning of Globalisation

In this chapter we will discuss the integration of the Indian economy with global economy. Globalisation is one of the most frequently used word which means different things to different people. In true economic meaning, globalisation refers to the increased openness of an economy to the international trade, capital flows (both portfolio and foreign direct investment, FDI), transfer of technology and free movement of labor or people. Thus **globalisation means the integration of economies of the world resulting from free flows of trade, capital, labor (or people) and technology.** The term globalisation signifies new international economic order which envisages the following:

(*a*) free flow of trade of goods and services between different countries of the world.

(*b*) free flow of capital among countries.

(*c*) free flow of technology among different countries of the world.

(*d*) free movement of labor or people internationally.

The growing interaction between different countries of the world has made the idea of globalisation increasingly popular in recent years. In the past there has been a movement to form regional groupings such as European Union (EU) formed by European countries and NAFTA (North American Free Trade Association) set up by North American countries to promote their regional interests by removing trade barriers among them. However, these regional groupings (also called *custom unions*) were found to be inadequate as they did not enable the countries forming these unions to produce on a global scale and enjoy all economies of scale and take full advantages from the modern technologies. Therefore, the developed countries pleaded for globalization to get benefits from widening of the size of the market for their products, locating and spreading optimally capital investment across different countries.

For developing countries like India globalisation carries benefits and opportunities as well as costs and risks. Both India and China have been recently using globalisation as an opportunity to accelerate rate of economic growth so as to catch up with the developed countries.

CASE FOR GLOBALISATION OF INDIAN ECONOMY

Several arguments have been given for integrating Indian economy with the global economy since 1991 when structural reforms were initiated in India. Tariffs and non-tariff barriers have been removed to promote free trade, the Indian economy has been opened up to foreign investment and import of technology from the developed countries. The following benefits of liberalisation and globalisation of Indian economy have been emphasised.

1. Shift from Import-Substitution to Export-Led Growth Strategy. The failure of import substitution strategy of industrial growth to achieve sustained growth forced India and other developing countries to pursue export-led growth strategy (which is also called outward looking strategy of development). It has been argued that by expanding exports to the other countries and getting required imports from them based on their respective *comparative costs*, developing countries will be able to achieve faster rate of economic growth. An important argument for trade liberalisation from the viewpoint of the developing countries is that they will gain from it as they have a comparative advantage in abundant, low-cost unskilled labor. If they specialise in the production of those goods which are labor-intensive, greater integration into global markets would increase their exports and production. This will help in generating more employment opportunities for the poor.

The strategy of development focussed on export promotion requires that other countries, especially developed countries should not prevent the imports to their countries through imposition of tariffs and non-tariff barriers. This is possible in the framework of a global economy with free movements of trade, capital and technology among countries. The setting up of WTO on Jan 1, 1995 was a step towards that direction. Accordingly, the entry of India in WTO in 1995 was a step to further globalise its economy.

2. Foreign Capital Inflows. The globalisation or integration of the Indian economy with the world economy is also beneficial because it would give a boost to foreign capital inflows in the form of portfolio investment and foreign direct investment (FDI). Portfolio investment will bring valuable foreign exchange currencies in India and free us of balance of payments difficulties. With sufficient foreign exchange reserves, balance of payments constraint on accelerating the growth process will be removed.

In the eighties due to shrinkage of foreign assistance, India had to resort to external commercial borrowings (ECB) which carried relatively higher rates of interest and increased the burden of external public debt. It may be noted that small foreign exchange reserves led to the economic crisis of 1991. As shall be explained later, the role of foreign direct investment is more important than portfolio foreign investmenet as it raises the rate of real investment in the economy and helps us to achieve a faster rate of economic growth. Foreign direct investment (FDI), like domestic investmenet, has a multiplier effect on output and employment.

3. Globalisation and Transfer of Technology. Another benefit flowing from globalisation of the Indian economy is that it acts as a mechanism for the transfer of technology from the developed countries. Due to financial constraints, Indian companies are in a position to invest only a small amount of funds on R & D. Therefore, it is through globalisation of its economy that we will be able to get advanced technology from the developed countries. The technological upgradation of the Indian industries will lead to higher productivity and help us to achieve a higher rate of industrial growth. It is worth noting that it is the multinational corporations (MNCs) that are carriers of technolgy to the developing countries through technological and financial collaboration with doemstic enterprises.

Globalisation makes faster diffusion of new ideas and advanced technologies in the world. This will make possible for the developing countries like India to catch up the developed countries more quickly.

4. Increased Market Access. An important benefit of globalisation is increased market access. Long ago Adam Smith wrote in 1776 that division of labor is limited by the size of market. Free trade accompanying globalisation widens the markets for products of industries. The larger the market in which products can be sold, the greater the benefit that will accrue as a result of economies of scale and specialisation. This will lower unit cost of production and increase the competitiveness of manufactured products. Thus globalisation will ensure greater gain from trade. In addition, the wider market increases the incentives for investing in new innovations as the potential return on investment in them will increase.

5. Faster Economic Growth and Poverty Reduction. Above all, it has been argued by some prominent economists such as Jagdish Bhagwati, T.N. Srinivasan, Arvind Panagariya, that globalisation will help in faster rate of reduction in poverty through acceleration of economic growth. To quote professor Arvind Panagariya, "Countries that have achieved significant poverty reduction are generally those that have grown rapidly and have, in turn, been open to trade. The most obvious example are the Newly Industrialized Economies (NIEs) including Hong Kong, Singapore, Republic of Korea and Taiwan that have entirely eliminated poverty according to the *dollar-a-day poverty line*. On the other hand, countries such as India that remained autarkic[1] and grew at less than 1.5% in per capita terms until late seventies experienced little reduction in the trend poverty ratio. Both India and China achieved poverty reduction after they began to dismantle *autarkic policies* and began to grow rapidly".[2]

6. Employment Arguement. An important arguement for libaration of trade and capital flows is that it will generate more employment oportunities. Employment increases on two counts. First, the growth in exports based on comparative cost advantage will lead to the creation of more employment opportunities. Secondly, employement opportunities also increase following the removal of restrictions on capital flows. The greater capital inflows, especially in the form of foreign direct investment (FDI), create not only more direct employment for labour but they have also a multiplier effect on the growth of employment and output.

DANGERS AND RISKS OF GLOBALISATION

Globalisation is not without dangers and risks. Stakes of poor countries like India are much higher for pursuing pro-globalisation policies. The historical experience of the colonial period shows that free trade and capital inflows helped imperialist countries more than the poor under-developed countries. With help of free trade and capital investment in some particular spheres, the developed countries exploited the poor countries which happened to be their colonies and drew away resources from them. With achievement of independence by the developing countries, though the situation today is vastly different but the developed countries has not shed their behaviour of promoting their own interests at the cost of developing countries. In fact, as has been stressed by Joseph Stiglitz, a Nobel Laurate in economics, *that while US and European countries preach free trade and globalisation, they actually practice protectionist polices to safeguard their domestic industries. Imposition of tariffs on imports of steel and grant of subsidies on farm products and cotton textiles by the developed countries such as the USA to protect their domestic industries which caused widespread protests around the world is a shining example of such double standards.*[3] To quote Stiglitz, "*I have always been struck by the divergence between the policies that America pushes on developing countries and those practiced in the US itself*".[4] Therefore, he advises that the developing countries should look carefully not what America says but at what it did in the years when America emerged as the industrial power, and what it does today.

Even Dr. Manmohan singh who has been the votary of free trade and free capital flows between countries in his address to the United Nations General Assembly in September 2011 said that recent events had called into question that globalisation would always do social good. He lamented the tendency on the part of developed countries to adopt protectionist policies to protect their own interest at the cost of the developing countries. To quite him, "*Till a few years ago, the world had taken for granted the benefits of globalization and global interdependence. Today we are being called upon to cope with the negative dimensions of those very phenomena.*"

An important disadvantage of globalisation is the danger posed by free flows of capital, especially portfolio capital, which are highly volatile and are a source of great macroeconomic instability. When there are large capital inflows into a country, the currency of a currency appreciates which makes its exports costlier and therefore cause reduction in them which not only adversely affects its

1. Autarkic means the closed nature of the economy having not much trade transactions with other country and which aims at achieving self-sufficiency.
2 Arvind Panagariya, Open up trade, get rich, *The Economic Times*, April 25, 2003.
3. Joseph Stiglitz, Protectionism : US Style, *Economic Times*, May 8, 2002.
4. Joseph Stiglitz, "Do what we did, not what we say" *The Economic Times*, Nov. 3, 2003.

current account balance of payments but also adversely affects its levels of GPP and employment. Besides, excess capital inflows in an economy lead to the expansion on money supply and if not sterlised by the RBI will add to the inflationary pressures in the economy.

On the other hand, when there are large capital outflows from an economy they cause depreciation of the national currency which though tend to increase its exports but carry some risks. First, depreciation makes the imports more expensive and therefore leads to the rise in prices of commodities and raw materials imported from abroad and causes cost-push inflation in the economy. Further, depreciation of a national currency, say the Indian rupee, will raise the burden of external debt as more rupees are required to pay for a US dollar. Further, countries like India badly need foreign capital flows to finance its current deficit. In the absence of adequate capital flows, some US dollars will have to withdrawn from foreign exchange reserves resulting in the decline in our foreign exchange reserves. As foreign exchange reserves are available in limited quantity in the absence of adequate capital flows to India year after year deficit in current account cannot be easily financed.

Therefore, in view of the present author, case for globalisation, is theoretically quite sound. If promoted in its true spirit by all countries, it would lead to rapid economic growth in both the developed and developing countries. But, the developed countries are interested in promoting their own interests even at the cost of the poor developing countries on whom they impose policies of liberalisation and globalisation through their greater say in World Bank and IMF. Therefore, globalisation and reduction of tariffs and removal of quantitative restrictions on imports from US, Japan and European countries, carry a good deal of risk for them. This is quite evident from the recent failure of talks held under the auspices of WTO at Doha, Seatle and Cancun. These talks to liberalise trade between the developed and developed countries failed because US and EU (European Union) were not willing to reduce huge subsidies they are providing to their farmers on agricultural products and also subsidies on exports of these products. This support by the developed countries to their farmers prevent agricultural exports from the developing countries. In this way exports from developing countries are prevented even when they enjoy comparative advantage in their production. That is why the people of the developing countries of Asia, Africa and Latin America are protesting against them during the multilateral talks being held under the auspices of WTO.

US's Tariffs on Imports of Steel and Subsidies on Cotton Textiles. Besides, another example of protectionist's policy of US is its imposition of the higher tariffs on imports of steel and subsidies on cotton testiles which prevent exports of these commodities from the developing countries, especially African countries and India. USA tried to use some provisions of WTO agreements regarding use of "safeguards for protecting employment" to defend these import tariffs and subsidies on cottons textiles. Recently, in Nov. 2003, WTO dispute settlement body has given its verdict against the imposition of higher tariffs on steel by the USA and has asked it to scrap them. The reluctance of USA to remove tariffs on imports of steel and subsidies on cotton textiles is against the spirit of globalisation.

Efforts in USA to ban BPO. Through business process outsourcing (BPO), American firms and businesses are getting various types of services such medical transcription, insurance connected work, various types of office jobs done through telecommunication and computer internet in call-centres from India.

This BPO has created good deal of employment opportunities for Indian educated youth. But recently there is anti-BPO campaign in the USA and UK. Some US states are even trying to enact laws to prvent BPO and thereby use of foreign (Indian) cheap skilled labour. This is against the spirit of free trade as India has a comparative advantage in these business processing services because of its educated skilled labor is available at comparatively much lower wages. Some Americans have argued "our resources should not be used to create jobs overseas when we have skilled workers and unemployment at home". But business processing services for American business firms are like exports from India based on comparative costs advantage and therefore to prevent them to protect employment of American labor is an argument in favour of protection.

MEASURES ADOPTED IN INDIA TO PROMOTE GLOBALISATION

The first Iraq war in 1991 involving gulf countries resulted in sharp rise in oil prices which landed India in acute balance of payments. To overcome this crisis and restore economic health of Indian economy many far-reaching changes in economic policy were made to promote globalisation of the Indian economy. The following measures are worth mentioning in this regard.

1. **Import Liberalization**. For liberalising foreign trade, *import controls through licesing was* abolished. With this almost all items of capital goods, raw materials, intermediate goods can be freely imported subject only to payment of customs duties. For some time quantitative quantitative restrictions on consumer goods remained but with effect from 1995 all quantitative restrctions, even on imports of consumer goods, have been lifted.

To liberalise imports peak customs duties which in some cases were as high as over 300 per cent were lowered in stages to 150 per cent in July 1991, to 85 per cent in Feb. 1993, 50 per cent in 2002. The average import duty was further reduced to 31 per cent in 2003 and to 20 percent in Jan. 2004, to 15 per cent in 2005 and further to 12.5% in 2006. Import duties on capital goods have been reduced even below 20 per cent for certain categories. This phased reduction in exceptionally high custms duties and a phased removal of quantitative restrictions on imports has substantially reduced anti-export bias in the earlier trade and balance of payment policies.

2. **Imports of Gold and Silver** have been considerably liberalised. This reduced the incentive for smuggling. In Jan. 2004 imports of gold were made free from any commission charged for it.

3. **Market-Determined Exchange Rate**. An important measure in external sector was to devalue the rupee in July 1991 and after about 2 years in 1993 exchange rate was changed from basket based pegged exchange rate system to *market-determined exchange rate*. With this the exchange rate of the rupee today is determined by demand and supply conditions in the foreign exchange markets.

4. **Convertibility of Rupee**. Another important reform for globalising the Indian economy was the convertibility of rupee on balance of payments on current account. This implies the importers can get their required quantity of foreign exchange by converting their rupee resources into dollars from the foreign exchange market. The exporters do not have to surrender their foreign exchange (US dollar or EU Euro) earned abroad to RBI but can now sell them in the foreign exhcnage markets.

5. **Liberalisation of Foreign Investmenet**. The new economic policy adopted since 1991 considerably liberalised the scope of foreign investment, both direct and portfolio. Earlier investmenet by foreign companies required prior approval of the government and was restricted to 40 per cent equity participation and was also subjected to the conditions of technology transfer to India. Besides, foreign investmenet was permitted in priority areas only. Foreign portfolio investmenet was allowed mainly into a limited number of public sectors bond issues. The new economic policy of 1991 plrovided for automatic approval of foreign direct investment, that is, no prior permission from the government is required upto 51 per cent of the total equity capital of the firms in 34 priority industries. In 1996, the government raised this ceiling limit for auotmatic approval from 51 per cent to 74 per cent for foreign equity participation.

Criteria for approval of foreign investment greater than 51 per cent equity participation prior to 1996 (and greater than 74 per cent after 1996) in priority industries and foreign equity participation in non priority industries which was approved on case to case basis was quite liberalised to attract more foreign investmenet. Besides, it is worth mentioning that elimination of industrial licensing restrictions, openning up to the private sector of a number of industries previously reserved for the public sector which increased the growht of domestic corporate sector also served to promote foreign private investment.

Portfolio Foreign Investment. An important feature of new economic policy adopted since 1991 is that it has laid stress on *non-debt creating capital inflows*, such as direct foreign investment and foreign portfolio investment for reducing reliance on *debt flows* as the chief source of external resources. Accordingly, in addition to foreign direct investment, foreign portfolio investment has also been liberalised. Portfolio foreign investment refers to the foreign firms, foreign institutional investors and NRI who invest in the equity bonds and securities of Indian firms. In case of foreign portfolio investment foreign investors get returns in the form of yearly payable dividents/interest and capital gains accrued but do not excercise any direct control in running these companies. Foreign private portfolio capital inflows are welcome as they provide needed finance to the Indian firms and also bring the much needed foreign exchange. But it is important to mention that they are prone to greater volatility. The currency crisis of East Asian countries in 1997-78 was mainly precipitated by the sudden flight of portfolio foreign capital. Therefore, sufficient foreign exchange reserves must be maintained to save the domestic currency from such sudden capital flight. In the new economic policy of 1991, foreign portfolio investment was also liberalised. In Feb. 1992 the Indian firms of good standing were allowed to raise funds through equity and convertible bond issues in Euromarkets and in September 1992 registered Foreign Institutional Investors (FII) were allowed to purchase both equity and debt securities directly in the Indian markets.

The Foreign Exchange Regulation Act (FERA) has been replaced by Foreign Exchange Managment Act (FEMA) to remove a number of constraints earlier applicable to firms with foreign equity operating in India. Besides, FEMA makes it easier for Indian companies to operate abroad. Further, procedure for Indian companies to invest abroad and also raise funds abroad through ECB (*External Commercial Borrowing*), that is, through ADR (American Depository Receipts) and GDR (General Depository Receipts have been simplified.

Foreign institutional investors (FII) found Indian stocks particularly attractive for the purpose of risk diversification. Both 'pull' factors and 'push' factors worked to attract foreign portfolio investment into India. The pull factors include the improvement in Indian macroeconomic environment following the abolition of licensing system and banking and financial sector reforms. On the other hand, 'push' factors included the fall in interest rates and yields and slowdown in economic growth in USA and other developed countries. These prompted foreign investors to invest in India and other developing countries, especially China, to get higher yields on their investment.

IMPACT OF GLOBALISATION ON INDIA

We have explained above the case for and against globalisation. In what follows we explain what has been the impact of globalisation and liberalisation on the Indian economy.

1. **Effect on Economic Growth**. The chief argument for globalisation and liberalisation was that they would lead to higher economic growth. As a result of balance of payments crisis in 1991, growth in GDP which collapsed to 1.3 per cent in 1991-92 gained momentum thereafter in the next 5 years period (1992-2001), the annual average growth rate in GDP achieved was 6.1 per cent. However, in the 10th plan period as a whole (2002-07), average annual growth achieved had been 7.8 per cent. Besides, in the last three years of the 10th plan (2005-06 , 2006-07 and 2007-08) growth rate in GDP rose to 9.5 and 9.6 and 9.3 per cent respectively.Thus, it was claimed that policy of liberalisation and globalisation has accelerated economic growth.

Howevr, under the impact of crisis of 2008-09 GDP growth rate fell to 6.7 per cent in 2008-09. It was because of fiscal stimlus provided by the government and expansionary monetary policy of RBI that economic growth could be revived to 8.6 per cent in 2009-10 and 9.3 per cent in 2010-11. However, due to adverse global factors such as slowdown in US economic gorwth and recession in

European countries and Eurozone crisis affected our export growth in several months. As a result our economic growth was badly affected. Growth rate in 2011-12 fell to 6.2 per cent and in 2012-13 to 5 per cent – lowest in a decade. Volatility of capital flows added to uncertainty. In 2013-14, growth rate is also expected to be around 5 per cent. It is thus evident that *globalisation could not ensure sustained rate of higher economic* growth. In 2013-14 Indian economy is said to be in crisis due to operation of mainly global factors.

Table 31.1: GDP, Industry and Services Growth Rates (Per cent per annum)

Indicator	1981-82 to 1990-91	1992-93 to 2000-01	2002-03 to 2006-07	2007-08	2008-09	2009-10	2010-11	2011 – 2012
GDP	5.6	6.1	7.8	9.3	6.7	8.6	9.3	6.2
Agriculture	3.6	3.2	2.5	5.5	0.4	1.5	7.5	1.9
Industry	7.1	6.4	8.9	10.3	4.7	9.5	9.5	1.2
Services	6.7	7.8	9.3	10.2	10.0	10.0	9.4	6.8

Source : World Bank, *India: Sustaining Reform, Reducing Poverty*, Oxford Univesity Press, 2003 and GOI, *Economic Survey*, 2011-12 and 2012-13.

* Estimates for 2007-08, 2008-09, 2009-10 and 2010-11, 2011-12 and 2012-13 are at 2004-05 prices.

Impact on Foreign Trade and Balance of Payments

The effect of trade liberalisation and globalisation on foreign trade and balance of payments has been favourable. Export growth zoomed to 20 per cent in 1993-94, 18.4 per cent in 1994-95, and to 20.8 per cent in 1995-96. Growth of exports in recent years has also been quite impressive. Growth in exports in 2003-04, 2004-05 and 2005-06 was 23.3% 28.5% and 23.4% respectively (See Table 31.2). In 2006-07 and 2007-08, the growth in exports 22.6 and 28.9 per cent respectively. Though imports also grew but due to roxbust growth in invisibles, current account deficit

Table 31.2. Globalisation and External Sector

	1995-96	99-2000	03-04	04-05	05-06	06-07	07-08	08-09	09-10	10-11	11-12
Growth of Exports (BOP (%) dollar terms)	20.8	17.8	23.3	28.5	23.4	22.6	28.9	13.9	–3.6	29.5	21.8
Growth of imports (BOP (%) dollar terms)	28.0	17.2	24.1	48.8	32.1	21.4	35.1	19.8	–2.6	19.0	32.3
Trade balance (% of GDP_{mp})	–3.1	–4.0	–2.3	–4.8	–6.4	–6.5	–7.4	–9.8	–8.6	N.A	–
Net Invisibles (% of GDP_{mp})	1.6	3.0	4.6	4.5	5.0	5.5	6.1	7.5	5.8	N.A	–
Current Account Balance (%) GDP)	–1.7	–1.1	2.3	–0.4	–1.2	–1.0	–1.3	–2.3	–2.8	–2.6	–4.2

Source : *Economic Survey,* 2007-08, 2010-11, p1

remained below 2 per cent of GDP upto the year 2007-08 as compared to 1990-91 when this deficit was over 3.1 per cent of GDP. In three years period (2001 to 2004) current account balance turned into surplus. Along with surpluses on capital account this resulted in large increase in foreign exchange reserves.

As will be seen from Table 31.2 from 2005-06, 2006-07 and 2007-08 due to good growth in exports in these three years, current account deficit was less than 2 per cent of GDP which was easily financed by capital flows into the Indian economy. Thus the fears that liberalisation of imports by reducing tariffs and removing quantitative restrictions would open the flood- gates for massive imports which would not only worsen India's balance of payments but would also kill domestic industries and slow down industrial growth have not come true. In fact globalisation, according to this view, not only helped in the acceleration of industrial growth but also in improvement of balance of payments position. Liberalisation of trade and removing restrictions on foreign investment have led to increase in investment inflows from abroad which have helped the growth process. However, globalisation has not been without disadvantages and risks. Foreign capital flows by FIIs are highly volatile. When they come they lead to appreciation of rupee which discourages exports by making them costlier and encourages imports by making them cheaper. However, when capital outflows by FIIs occur as has been the case since the last week of May, 2013 to end of August, 2013 due to the announcement by the governor of US federal Reserve that it would soon start *unwinding quantitative easing (QE) policy* because of the signs of revival of the US economy. The capital-outflows by FIIs in months (June, July and Aug. 2013) led to the sharp depreciation of rupee and crash in India's stock market. These capital outflows also make it difficult to finance current account deficit (CAD) which have adversely affected the sentiments of foreign investors.

Impact on Poverty

Advocates of globalisation and trade liberalisation claimed that it would ensure greater reduction in poverty and unemplyoment in developing countries through acceleration of economic growth. The issue of reduction in poverty has been a highly controversial issue. Due to changes in methodology for measuring poverty in various rounds of NSS, it could not be said to *what extent poverty declined in the post-reform period on account of the policies of liberalisation, privatisation and globalisation.* However, NSS Survey 2004-05 made corrections in the data so as to be comparable with the 1993-94 survey data of poverty ratio. On the basis of *uniform recall period* (URP) the percentage of population in all India below the poverty line fell from 36 per cent in 1993-94 to 27.8 per cent in 2004-05 which amounts to 0.74 per cent annual reduction in poverty ratio in this post-reform period. This is much less than rate of reduction in poverty rate in the pre-reform period when percentage of population below the poverty line declined from 51.3 per cent in 1977-78 to 38.9 per cent in 1987-88 which works out to be 1.2 per cent annual fall in poverty ratio.

However, an expert committee headed by Late Prof. Suresh Tendulkar suggested moving away from taking the calorie intake as defining parameter for poverty line to make a more comprehensive method of using per capita expenditure data on basic needs such as food, clothing, housing and services such as health and education. Using this criteria for measuring poverty even from the data collected by *NSSO for the year 2004-05, it was estimated that for all India 37.2 per cent of population lived below the poverty line.* Further, on the basis of special NSSO survey conducted in 2011-12 and *using Tendulkar Committee methodology, it has been estimated by the Planning Commission* that *in 2011-12, 21.9 per cent of India's population lived below the poverty line, that is, a decline by 15.3 per cent points in poverty in seven years between 2004-05 and 2011-12.* In absolute numbers, the number of poor people declined from 407 million in 2004-05 to 269 million in 2011-12, that is, 138 million persons were lifted out of poverty line. This was attributed to higher average rate of economic growth over 8 per cent per annum achieved during this period which was claimed by the government was due to the policy of liberalisation and globalisation pursued. This proved to be a highly controversial issue as critics pointed out that the estimates of poverty for the year 2011-12 was very low because of a low poor line, *a daily expenditure of ₹27.2 per capita for rural areas and ₹33.3 per capita for urban area.* It was said one could not survive on such a low expenditure. Some critics went to the extent of saying that such lower expenditure as a norm for poverty was a cruel job on the poor. In 2009-10, even Supreme Court of India rejected these poverty norms as too low for the people to survive. Therefore, under the pressure the government decided to appoint a new Committee headed by Dr. C. Rangarajan to suggest an alternative methodology for measuring poverty in India.

Further, in our view, reduction in poverty is not necessarily due to higher rate of economic growth which has been achieved by the use of highly capital-intensive technology generating little employment opportunities in the organised sector as will be seen later. Of course, under the export-oriented trade policy under economic reforms with globalisation as its important feature a good number of employment opportunities has been generated in the export sector. However, liberalisation of imports under the policy of globalisation has tended to displace labour in many industries. However, whether, there has been a *net increase* in employment under the policy of liberalisation and globalisation is difficult to say.

Impact on Employment

It is generally alleged that liberalisation and globalisation had adverse effect on growth of employment. All the three unemployment rates, namely, unusual status, weekly status and daily status, based on National Sample Survey, increased during the period 1993-94 to 2004-05 whereas they had declined earlier. As will be seen from Table 31.3 that on the basis of *current daily status* (CDS) (*i.e.* unemployment on an average in the reference week) the rate of unemployment which was 6.1 per cent in 1993-94, rose to 7.3 per cent in 1999-2000 and further to 8.3 per cent in 2004-05. With this the number of unemployed which was 20 million in 1993-94 went up to 26.7 million in 1999-2000 and further to 34.7 million in 2004-05.

Table 31.3. Unemployment (on CDS Basis)

	1993-94	1999-2000	2004-05	2009-10	2011-12
Unemployment rate	6.1	7.3	8.3	6.6	5.6
No. of Unemployed (in millions)	20.3	26.7	34.7	N.A	N.A

Source : Various Rounds of NSSO Survey

It may be noted that the growth of employment, according to National Sample Surveys, in the post-reform period from 1999-2000 to 2004-05 increased by 2.62 per cent annum as against 1.25 per cent in 1993-94 to 1999-2000. But all this growth of employment was *in the unorganised and informal sector*. In fact, as can seen from Table 31.4, the *rate of growth of employment in the organised sector* in the post-reform period 1994-2008 has been found to be only 0.05 per cent per annum whereas during the pre-reform period (1983-94) employment grew at 1.2 per cent per annum. It will be noticed from Table 31.4 that in this post-reform period (1994-2008) there has been *negative employment growth* in the public sector, employment in the organised private sector showed some acceleration in employment growth from 0.44 per cent per annum during 1983-94 to 1.75 per cent per annum during 1994-2008. However, since the labour force grew at a higher rate of 2.84 per cent per annum than the growth in employment during this period the unemployment rate on current daily status (CDS) basis increased from 7.3 per cent in 1999-2000 to 8.3 per cent in 2004-05. However, in NSS surveys for the years 2009-10 and 2011-12 unemployment on current daily status (CDS) basis fell to 6.6 per cent and 5.6 per cent of labour force respectively. But, according to our view this is due to the starting of Mahatma Gandhi National Rural Employment Gurantee Scheme (MGNREGA) rather than the result of growth in the organised sector. However, employment created under MGNREGS is quite unproductive. Though wages are paid to the workers for the number of days employed but no durable assets are built by them. Therefore, employment generated under the scheme is not sustainable. Further, it may be noted that though man-days of emplooyment generated under the scheme have resulted in the declined in daily status unemployment in 2009-10 and 2011-12, there is no any increase in productive employment.

Table 31.4. Rate of Growth of Employment in the Organised Sector

% per annum

	1983-94	1994-2008	2010/2009	2011/2010
Public sector	1.53	– 0.65	0.4	–1.8
Private Sector	0.44	1.75	4.5	5.6
Total Organised Sector	1.20	0.05	1.9	1.0

Source : Planning Commission, *Eleventh Plan Document*, 2010-11and *Economic Survey* 2011-12 p.275

For the increase in unemployment in the formal sector since 1993-94, the policies of liberalisation and globalisation adopted since 1991 are often blamed. First, under this policy the import tariffs have been substantially reduced making imports cheaper. Deprived of protection many Indian small-scale industries could not compete with the imported products. As a result, many small scale industries closed down rendering many workers unemployed. Many large-scale industries undertook modernisation of their plants using updated capital-intensive technology in order to compete with the cheap imported products and also to export more in foreign competitive markets. This did not help in the generation of a large number of new employment opportunities. In fact, even some large-scale corporate firms cut down jobs. That there has been jobless growth is revealed by 68th round of special employment and unemployment survey, 2011-12. This latest 68th NSSO survey reveals that the percentage of employed persons to the total population declined in 2011-12. According to this, on the basis of usual principal and subsidiary status approach the proportion of population gainfully employed for better part of the year fell from 36.5 per cent of population in 2009-10 to 35.4 per cent in 2011-12 despite GDP growth of 8.6% in 2009-10, 9.3% in 2010-11 and 6.2 per cent in 2011-12. Though in percentage terms fall in employment appears to be small, in absolute numbers it will amout to several lakhs. As a result, usual principal and subsidiary status unemployment rose from 2.5 per cent in 2009-10 to 2.7% in 2011-12.

Strangely enough, some prominent economists are arguing for labour reforms under which the large firms are permitted to hire and fire workers feeely. They argue that the firms are reluctant to hire and employ more labour because under the present labour laws, it is difficult for them to retrench them. Likewise, they argue that foreign direct investment is not coming to India in sufficient amount because of inflexible labour legislation. They point out once labour reforms are undertaken, adequate employment opportunities will be created. However, in our view, this is a very simplistic view because growth of employment primarily depends on the rate of investment and the nature of technology used in the manufacturing industries and other sectors of the economy. If preference for use of capital-intensive technology to achieve higher productivity of labour, as has been the case so far, remains unchanged, adequate growth in employment will not take place. This will lead to the increase in unemployment. Therefore, we cannot rely on market forces to generate enough employment opportunities. Conscious efforts have therefore to be made to promote labour-intensive techniques to take care of the presently about 37 million unemployed workers on current daily status basis found in 2007-08.

Similarly, increase in unemployment is due to the increase in capital intensity in production in agriculture, lack of investment in agriculture, non-implementation of land reforms, rapid growth in labour force. Plan after plan has been paying lip service to increasing labour-intensity of production to promote employment growth but policies to ensure this have not been implemented.

Exports, Imports and Employment. In fact the expansion in exports following globalisation of the Indian economy has led to a large expansion in employment in the export sector. One of the objectives of foreign trade policy has been to make it an instrument of employment generation. In 2004-05 against exports of US $ 80 billion total employment growth in the export sector was 16 million (9 million direct and 7 million indirect)[1]. In 2004-05, in the export sector the maximum employment created was in agricultural products (6.2 million) followed by mineral products (1.7 million), textiles and textile articles (1.7 million) and prepared foodstuffs and beverages etc (1.6 million).[2] However, while exports has recorded robust growth in recent years, the corresponding growth of labour-intensive goods has slowed down[3]. We thus see that export promotion under globalisation has promoted employment growth rather than reducing it.

1. GOI, *Economic Survey*, 2006-07, p. 122
2. *Ibid.*
3. *Ibid.*

However, it is claimed by many that liberalisation of imports as a result of globalisation of the indian economy has adversely affected employment situation in the Indian economy. This is because small and medium enterprises which have large employment potential could not compete with the cheap imports from the developed countries and China. This led to closure of several small and medium enterprises resulting in loss of employment opportunities. Thus whereas growth of exports has tended to increase employment opportunities, cheap imports from abroad have tended to reduce them. Which effect on employment has been stronger is anybody's guess. However, as seen from Table 31.4, in the organised sector there has been net 0.05 per cent growth in employment per annum in the organised sector (in the public and private sectors taken together) during 1994-2008.

Foreign Capital Inflows : FDI and Portfolio Investment

Policies of liberalisation of private capital inflows have led to the increase in foreign investment flows in the country both in terms of direct investment (FDI) and portfolio investment. Profile of foreign investment flows is given in Table 31.5. It will be seen from this table that annual total investment inflows which were about US $ 4.15 billion in 1993-94 rose to about 6.1 billion US dollars in 1996-97 and varied a lot after that but reached US $ 15.7 billion in 2003-04 and a record figure of US $ 29 billion in 2006-07. In the year 1998-99, there was *negative* portfolio investment inflows following the East Asian currency crisis in 1997-98.

In the year 2006-07 and 2007-08 foreign investment inflows in India had been quite substantial indicating the rising confidence of international investors in the Indian economy. In the year 2006-07, foreign direct investment (FDI) 22.8 billion US $ and portfolio investment of 7 billion US

Table 31.5. Foreign Investment Inflows in India

(in US $ millions)

Year	Foreign Direct Investment (*Receipts*)	Portfolio Investment (net)	Total Foreign Investment
1991-92	129	4	133
1992-93	315	244	559
1993-94	586	3567	4153
1994-95	1314	3824	5138
1995-96	2144	2748	4892
1996-97	2821	3312	6133
1997-98	3557	1828	5385
1998-99	2462	(-)61	2401
1999-2000	2155	3026	5181
2000-01	4031	2760	6791
2001-02	6130	2021	8151
2002-03	5035	979	6014
2003-04	4322	11377	15699
2004-05	6051	9315	15366
2005-06	8962	12492	21454
2006-07	22826	7004	29830
200708	34844	27230	62114
2008-09	37837	–13854	23983
2009-10	37762	32396	70158
2010-11	34850	–	–
2011-12(P)	33000	16600	49600
2012-13(P)	19800	26700	46500

(*ii*) Foreign portfolio investment includes capital inflows by FII, Funds raised by Indian companies through GDR/ADR, Eruo equites and others. PR : Provisionally revised.

Source : GOI, *Economic Survey*, 2007-08, 2009-10 and 2012-13.

dollars came into India. In 2007-08 foreign direct investment (FDI) of 34.8 billion US $ was made in India. In fact India became a favourite destination for foreign direct investment. Besides, in the year 2007-08, about 27.2 billion US dollars were brought into India by FIIs for purchase of equity shares (i.e. portfolio investment). However, in 2008-09 following the sub-prime housing loans provided by American banks, financial crisis occurred in American and Western Europe which created liquidity crunch in their economies and redemption pressure on securities held by FIIs increased very much. To fulfill the liquidity needs of their parent countries FIIs sold shares in the Indian stock market on a large scale and repatriated dollars. The large-scale sale of shares by FIIs and capital outflows not only caused crash in Indian stock market but also resulted in large depreciation of Indian rupee. Besides, the world financial crisis caused global meltdown which affected capital inflows into India through FDI. However, there was reversal of portfolio capital flows in 2009-10. In 2009-10, India attracted foreign direct investment (FDI) of $ 37.7 billion and portfolio investment of $32.3 billion in 2009-10 and therefore total foreign investment of S 70.1 billion in 2009-10. Foreign investment in inflows further declined in 2011-12 and 2012-13.

Effect on Foreign Exchange Reserves

An important beneficial effect of the globalisation of the Indian economy has been that its foreign exchange reserves have been substantially increased. In Dec. 2003, our foreign exchange reserves crossed 100 billion US dollars and increaed to 309.7 billion US dollars on February 2008. In 1991 we faced an acute foreign exchange crisis arising from continued deficits in balance of payments for several years. It is this crisis that compelled us to shift to the policy of liberalisation and globalisation. At the end of March 1991 we had forex reserves of only about 6 billion US dollars which were sufficient to cover only 2.5 months of imports. At the end-March 2007-8 foreign exchange reserves of nearly 310 billion US dollars were adequate enough to cover imports of 16 months.

However, during 2008-09 there was decline in foreign exchange reserves due to net capital outflows. At end-March 2009 foreign exchange reserves declined to 252 billion US dollars, but there was reversal of capital flows in 2009-10. As a result due to large capital inlfows into the Indian economy the foreign exchange reserves rose to $279 billion in end-March 2010 and stood at around $306 billion at end-March 2011.

Table 31.6. Foreign Exchange Reserves (Billion US Dollars)

Year end	1900-91	2000-01	03-04	05-06	06-07	07-08	08-09	09-10	10-11	11-12	12-13
Forex reserves	5.83	39.6	113	152	199	310	252	279	306	294.4	295
Forex reserves as months of import cover	2.5	8.6	16.9	11.6	12.5	16	14	11	10	8	8

Source : RBI Annual Reports

This huge accumulation of foreign exchange reserves has been possible because of the policy of liberalisation of foreign investment. The major contributor to dollar inflows in the Indian economy was Foreign Institutional Investors (FII) who invested in the Indian equity and debt markets. In the year 2003-04 alone capital inflows of 11.4 billion US dollars were brought by FIIs alone who invested in the Indian equity and debt markets. In the year 2007-08 appreciation of rupee caused large inflow of portfolio capital by FIIs resulting in increase in foreign exchange reserves to $310 billion in end-March 2008.

Quite a good part of foreign exchange inflows has also been due to NRI deposits. NRI brought their money to India in order to take advantage of the interest rate differentials between India and the US. A big chunk of these reserves was also due to external commercial borrowings (ECB) by Indian corporate firms. Capital inflows through foreign direct investment (FDI) also gained momentum in

2006-07, 2007-08 and 2008-09. What are the reasons for a flood of inflows of foreign exchange in these years ? Booming stock market of India, a robust growth of the order of over 9 per cent in the the three years 2005-06, 2006-07 and 2007-08 and expectations of Indian corporates doing well and a high rate of return on investment in India were the important reasons for large inflows of foreign exchange reserves in these years.

An important thing to note about the accumulation of foreign exchange reserves has been that much of them *had not occurred* on account of foreign trade, that is, exports and imports of goods and services. With the exception of three years (2001-02, 2002-03 and 2003-04) there has been continued deficits in balance of payments on current account. However, a good thing about these reserves is that ***most of the increase in foreign exchange reserves were of non-debt variety and had not added to our external debt. In fact, we pre-paid a part of costly external debt by using some foreign exchange reserves.*** The large foreign exchange reserves provided India a sense of security against any contingencies in future and permit us to take economic policy decisions independently without any preconditions by IMF and World Bank. In fact during 2008-09 when due to global financial crisis there were capital outflows on a large scale from India $20 billion of foreign exchange were withdrawn from our foreign exchange reserves to finance current account deficit.

This global financial crisis also caused a drastic depreciation of the Indian rupee. The rupee which had appreciated to ₹ 39.4 to a dollar in Oct. 2008 fell to ₹ 45 in July 2008 and to ₹ 49.30 to a dollar on in Oct, 2008 and further to around ₹ 50 in Nov. 2008. This depreciation in value of rupee made our imports including crude oil costlier which adversely affected our balance of payments in 2008-09. Therefore, to finance current account deficit we had to draw upon our foreign exchange reserves equal to $ 57.7 billion in 2008-09. Therefore, our foreign exchange reserves fell from $ 310 billion in 2007-08 to $ 252 billion in 2008-09 (end-March). During 2009-10 and 2010-11 there was net capital inflows and as a result our foreign exchange reserves increased to $ 279 billion in 2009-10 and to $ 304.8 billion in 2010-11. Again in 2011-12, our current account deficit (CAD) was very large and capital inflows were insufficient to finance it fully. Therefore we had to withdraw $ 10.4 billion from our foreign exchange reserves.

GLOBAL FINANCIAL CRISIS AND ITS IMPACT ON INDIA'S GROWTH

The global financial crisis surfaced around August 2007. Its origin lay in structured investment instruments (Collateralized Debt Obligations, synthetic CDOs) created out of sub-prime mortgage lending in the United States. The securitization process however was not backed by due diligence and led to large-scale default. The complexity of the instruments and the role of credit rating agencies played a contributory role. The high ratings assigned to certain CDO trenches, which were then quickly reversed with the onset of the crisis, created a panic situation among investors and precipitated the crisis.

While the initial effect of the crisis was profound on the US financial institutions and to a lesser extent on European institutions, the effect on emerging economies was less serious. In the initial stages, the capital flows to the emerging economies actually increased, giving rise to what is termed as "*positive shock*" and the "*decoupling*" debate. In the case of India, for example, the net FII inflows during the five-month period from September 2007 to January 2008 was US$ 22.5 billion as against an inflow of US$ 11.8 billion during April-July 2007, which were the four months immediately preceding the onset of crisis.

The effect of the global financial crisis on emerging economies (including India) thereafter was mainly through *reversal of portfolio capital flows* due to unwinding of stock positions by FIIs to replenish cash balances abroad. Withdrawal of FII investment led to stock market crash in many emerging economies and depreciation or decline in the value of local currencies vis-a-vis US dollar as a result of supply-demand imbalances in domestic markets. In the case of India, the extent of reversal of capital flows was US$ 15.8 billion during five months (February-June, 2008) following the end of "positive shock" period in January 2008.

Following the collapse of Lehman Brothers in mid-September 2008, there was a full-blown meltdown of the global financial markets. It created a crisis of confidence that led to the seizure of inter-bank market and had trickle-down effect on *trade financing* in the emerging economies. Together with slackening global demand and declining commodity prices, it led to fall in exports, thereby transmitting financial sector crisis to the real economy. Countries with export-led model of growth, as in many South-East Asian countries, and that depended upon commodity exports, were more severely affected. The impact on Indian economy was less severe because of lower dependence of the economy on export markets and the fact that a sizeable contribution to GDP is from domestic sources. India's trade reforms since 1991 have moved progressively towards neutral regime for exports and imports, eschewing tax and other incentives for exports.

The direct impact of the crisis on financial sector was primarily through exposure to the toxic financial assets and the linkages with the money and foreign exchange markets. Indian banks however had very limited exposure to the US mortgage market, directly or through derivatives, and to the failed and stressed international financial institutions. The depending of the global crisis and subsequent deleveraging and risk aversion however affected the Indian economy leading to slowing of growth momentum.

The overall balance of payment situation however remained resilient despite signs of strain in the capital account that manifested in the net reversal of FII flows of US$ 15.0 billion during fiscal year 2008-09 and on current account through decline in exports. In 2008-09, *the merchandise exports* recorded a growth of 13.6 per cent reaching US$ 189 billion. While export growth was robust till August 2008, it became low in September and became negative from October 2008 to July 2009. The rupee depreciated by 21.2 per cent against the US dollar during the fiscal year 2008-09. The US dollar however appreciated by 17 per cent against the broad index (FRB, New York) between March 2008 and March 2009, suggesting that only 5 percentage points of the rupee *depreciation was due to India-specific factors*.

Money and credit markets had been affected indirectly through the dynamic linkages. The drying up of liquidity, a fallout of repatriation of portfolio investments by FIIs, affected credit markets in second half of 2008-09. This was compounded by the "risk aversion" of banks to extend credit in the face of general downturn. The extent of the external financial and monetary shock on the Indian monetary financial system is best captured by the precipitous contraction in reserve money by more than 15 per cent between August 2008 and November 2008 (compared to 0.5 percent increase in the corresponding period of the previous year). Reserve money growth (y-o-y) collapsed from 26.9 per cent in August 2008 to 10.3 per cent in November 2008 and further to 6.4 per cent in March 2009. The various monetary policy measures taken by RBI kept narrow money M1 and broad money M3 from falling as precipitously. Despite these, however, M1 growth declerated from 19.4 per cent in August 2008 to 10.3 per cent in November 2008 and further to 8.2 per cent in March 2009, while M3 growth decelerated from 21 per cent in August 2008 to 18.7 per cent in March 2009. A series of unconventional measures actually helped to push up the rate of growth of bank credit from 25.4 per cent in August 2008 to 26.9 per cent in November 2008. However, this only partly offset the effects on short-and long-term credit to Indian companies in the United States and EU markets, because of the freezing of financial markets. Subsequently, credit growth decelerated sharply to 17.1 per cent in March 2009, partly because of transmission of OECD recession effects to Indian exporters and organized manufacturing.

Despite these developments, the macroeconomic impact of the global financial turmoil, particularly on the GDP growth, has been relatively muted due to the overall strength of domestic demand in India and the predominantly domestic nature of investment financing.

Impact of Global Financial Crisis on India's Growth

In the last two decades (1990-2009) fluctuations in India's economic growth were not closely linked to the cycles in developed countries or high-income OECD countries. The upward jump in Indian growth between 2003-04 and 2008-09 however seems to coincide with a similar jump in global and OECD growth. The sharp decline in growth to 5.8 per cent in the second half of 2008-09 from 7.8 per cent in the first half of 2008-09, following the US and global financial meltdown in August 2008, seemed to support this perspective. Following the global recession, there was a view among global market analysts, that growth in emerging markets and developing countries was driven by the global excess liquidity/monetization, the associated capital flows from developed countries and the demand for commodities. Consequently, with the bursting of the bubble the initial impact would be a growth collapse, followed by a return in the medium term to growth rates that prevailed before 2004-05, because of the painful process of de-leveraging and collapse of capital flows. It was therefore concluded by some of these analysts belonging to World Bank and IMF that India's growth would collapse to around 4 per cent during the subsequent four to six quarters and thereafter it may revert to around 5 to 5.5 per cent over the medium term. An analysis of the growth history of India during 2008-09 suggests that this superficial generalization of a plausible global analysis to India was erroneous.

The first half (H1) of 2008-09 saw the Indian economy recording a growth of 7.8 per cent in GDP, despite the build-up of uncertainty in the international commodity and financial markets. Among the domestic growth drivers, gross fixed capital formation (GFCF) retained some of its momentum from the preceding years with a growth of nearly 11 per cent. Consumption - both private and government however declined significantly. The growth in private final consumption expenditure (PFCE) in of the first half 2008-09 was 3.3 per cent, which was less than half of the corresponding period in 2007-08. Similarly, government final consumption expenditure (GFCE) in the first half of 2008-09 grew at less than 1 per cent, or just one-third of the growth in first half of 2007-08.

In the second half (H2) of 2008-09, GDP growth declined to 5.8 per cent, with a further decline in private consumption growth to 2.5 per cent and a significant moderation in growth rate of GFCF to about 6 per cent over the corresponding period of 2007-08. However, with the roll-out of the fiscal stimulus, primarily in the shape of implementation of the Sixth Pay Commission recommendations in Q3, as well as the second round of fiscal expansion announced in Q4, the growth in government final consumption expenditure shot up by nearly 36 per cent, partly making up for the shortfall in other components of the domestic aggregate demand. The overall GDP growth for the fiscal 2008-09 at 6.7 per cent surpassed all estimates and forecasts, mostly ranging from 5.5 per cent to 6.5 per cent, made by international agencies and analysts.

As expected, outcome of the recession in countries to which India exports its goods has been the sharp fall in growth of Indian organised manufacturing. The trend in India's manufacturing sector started in the second quarter of calender year 2007 with the slowing of the US economy and its imports of several products from India. The trend was merely accelerated after the US meltdown and the onset of the global recession. Services sector growth of India was not expected to slow sharply because of its well-known insensitivity to demand cycles and relatively small contribution of service *exports* to GDP. *In fact, there was a sharp increase* in the growth of community, social and personal services which includes GDP from government administration. It is also important to note that in 2009-10 the Indian economy recovered faster and GDP growth rate in 2009-10 was 8.6 per cent and in 2010-11 it was 9.3 per cent. This shows the resilience of the Indian economy against external shocks.

APPENDIX TO CHAPTER 31

FOREIGN CAPITAL FLOWS AND THEIR IMPACT ON MACROECONOMIC STABILITY

VOLATILITY OF CAPITAL FLOWS INTO INDIA

As explained in the previous chapter capital flows in the form of foreign direct investment (FDI) and portfolio investment by FII play not only an important role in economic growth of the country but also are badly needed to finance the deficit in current account of our balance of payments. However, volatility of capital flows creates a lot of macroeconomic instability in the Indian economy. This volatility creates sometimes boom in stock market and some times crash in it. Capital inflows cause appreciation of exchange rate of rupee and thereby adversely affect our exports and through creating excess liquidity they add to inflationary pressures in the economy. On the other hand, capital outflows cause depreciation of rupee and thereby encourage exports but make our imports costlier.

Volatile capital movements have influenced the domestic stock price movements, exchange rate and domestic liquidity conditions significantly in the past. In 2009-10, the and current account deficit widened to 2.8 per cent of GDP in 2010-11 and it is estimated at 3.6 percent of GDP in 2011-12. Volatile capital flows have been a potential source of instability for emerging market economies (EMEs). Costs of volatility of the capital flows could magnify for an economy during periods of both too little and too much of capital flows, unless they are managed judiciously. India, in recent years, had to manage phases of capital flows characterised by large net inflows as well as sudden outflows in the midst of a global crisis. *A judicious mix of flexible exchange rate, sterilisation of the impact of inflows on domestic liquidity, cautious approach to liberalisation of the capital account and the cushion of foreign exchange reserves has been used to deal with the adverse ramifications of capital flows.*

Volatility of capital flows is caused mainly by investment by FIIs. In India it is the inflows and outflows of portfolio capital by FIIs that have caused a lot of macroeconomic instability in the Indian economy. The total *net* FII flows to India in 2009 stood at US $ 18.51 billion. These flows grew remarkably in 2010 and India received FII investment worth US $ 39.71 billion in 2010 which was the highest in the last decade. These inflows were largely driven by equity inflows which remained buoyant on the back of strong domestic macroeconomic fundamentals and high GDP growth. FIIs had been quite active in the debt segment as well in 2010. However, against the high net FII inflows of the year 2010, the flows during the year 2011 were quite low. During the first ten months (Jan.-Oct.) of the calender year 2011 India received only $ 4.66 billion against US $ 39.47 billion during 2010. FII investment in India during 2007-11 is given below in Table 31A.1.

Table 31A.1 FII Investment in India

Segment	2007	2008	2009	2010	2011*
Equity	17.65	–11.97	16.87	29.36	0.39
Debt	2.34	2.63	1.64	10.11	4.27
Total	19.99	–9.34	18.51	39.47	4.66

Source: MOF *Mid-year Review* 2011-12. * Investment upto Oct. 31, 2011

Capital Inflows and Economic Instability

While capital inflows during 2009 remained moderate, in 2010 there was a return of another phase of surge in capital flows to India in response to global search for higher yields in an environment of easy liquidity conditions in advanced economies and the prospect of relatively higher return on investment in India in view of its superior growth outlook. The Indian economy grew at 8.4 per cent during 2010-11 which is the second highest growth rate in the world, next only to China. While stronger growth could help in absorbing higher magnitude of foreign capital within the limits of sustainable current account deficit, excess capital inflows would entail the risk of exerting *appreciation pressure on the exchange rate of the rupee*, which in turn could weaken the competitive advantage of Indian exports. Sterilised intervention by RBI could limit the pressure on appreciation of the rupee on account of capital inflows, but may lead to a higher interest rate environment. *Unsterilised intervention* by the RBI that could relieve the pressure on both exchange rate and interest rate, however would involve excess liquidity creation in the economy. In an environment of high inflation, this could only increase the inflationary situation further.

High inflation would also adversely impact export competitiveness through appreciation of the real effective exchange rate (REER), which would further widen the current account deficit. Excess capital inflows, thus, would continue to pose challenges for the country's exchange rate, interest rate and inflation environment and through these channels, may at times also weaken the beneficial impact of capital flows on economic growth. Unlike the pre-global crisis period, international perception now seems to have changed significantly *in terms of support for use of soft capital controls to deal with excessive capital flows*. In the case of emerging market economies (EMEs), surges in capital flows into them have contributed to asset price build up, along with exchange rate appreciation. Given the complications, asset price build-up could pose problem for monetary policy and potential risks to financial stability. Therefore, management of capital flows into India would need to strike a balance between the objectives of growth and financial stability.

Stronger recovery in India in 2009-10 and 2010-11, ahead of the global recovery along with positive sentiments of global investors about India's growth prospects, encouraged a revival in capital flows into India during 2009-10. The turnaround was mainly driven by large capital inflows under profitfolio investment by FIIs and short-term trade credits. As a result *net* capital flows into India at US $53.4 billion (3.8% of GDP were much higher during 2009-10 as compared to US $6.8 billion (0.5 per cent of GDP) in 2008-09. The strong domestic demand for goods in India, unlike many other emerging markets which depend on exports to the West where consumer confidence is waning, was an added attraction. Net equity inflows hit $ 23-25 billion in 2010-11, while net debt flows will also be significantly higher. Globally, with debt investment yields so low, money continues to be allocated to equities and gold. And within the equity universe, emerging markets, especially India, witnessed increased capital inflows and many new investors in 2009-10 and 2010-11.

The fact that when a country witnesses a volatile capital inflows comprising short-term capital flows while stable capital flows represented by FDI slows down, country faces an acute problem of economic instability. This forced Brazil with an emerging economy to go in for capital controls in April 2011 to ensure economic stability. The too much inflows of volatile capital in Brazil threatened to fuel an *asset bubble*. Surprisingly enough, the champion of free flow of capital, International Monetary Fund conceded in April 2011 that governments can resort to capital controls when they have to prevent economic destabilisation.

Now, the pertinent question where does India, a prominent emerging market economy, stand ? It is a very different situation. The emerging economies of Brazil, Russia, India and China – normally known as BRICs for their uniform opportunities in the past – are beginning to diverge. Inflation is a common theme running across these countries. So are slowing domestic growth and investment opportunities, but not the current account deficit. That throws up a peculiar problem for Indian policy makers who need the foreign capital flows to keep the economy growing by financing its current account deficit. But we also need to prevent rise in inflation due to large capital inflows. This requires fine-tuning *capital flows management*. We cannot resort to controlling capital inflows whether through FDI or FII for we need them to finance our current account deficit which is now of a significant size. For India it is a big problem to rely on volatile capital inflows by FIIs for financing our current account deficit. What we need are *stable and long term* capital flows of foreign direct investment.

Capital Outflows and Economic Instability

There was capital flight from the Indian markets in Feb, 2011 but it returned to India in April and there was *net inflow of capital* of US $3.1 billion by FIIs in April-July 15, 2011 bringing boom in the Indian stock and bond market and also led to appreciation of rupee to some extent. However, from Aug. 2011 there had again been outlow of capital due to worsening of sovereign debt crisis of European countries and slowdown of the US economy. This caused Bombay Stock Exchange Index (SENSEX) to fall heavily from over 18000 to 16200 on September 24, 2011 and further to 15500 in Mid-December 2011, Besides, this capital outflow led to a large depreciation of rupee from September 2011. The Indian Rupee which was around ` 44 to a US dollar in July 2011 fell to nearly ` 52 to a US dollar on Nov. 22, 2011 and further to ` 53.7 to a US dollar in mid-December 2011. The sharp-depreciation of the Indian rupee caused by capital outflows from Sept. 2011 proved to be highly harmful for the Indian economy. To prevent excessive depreciation of the Indian rupee the RBI used its foreign exchange reserves to sell US dollars in foreign exchange market. This caused decline in foreign exchange reserves which are needed to cover imports of goods and services needed for industrial growth. Further, lack of adequate foreign exchange reserves with the RBI will lead to the loss of confidence among foreign investors about the ability of the country to pay back the loans from foreign financial institutions. Besides, weakening of the rupee is likely to cause losses to the foreign investors who repatriate their profits to their home countries. This will discourage inflows of foreign direct investment needed for economic growth of the country. To attract capital inflows Reserve Bank of India also relaxed norms for external commercial borrowing and removed the cap on NRI deposits in Indian banks. It is evident from above the that capital outflows create a lot of macroeconomic instability and therefore they need to be prudently managed. As mentioned above, India faces a different problem from other emerging economies as it has to contend with a large deficit on current account balance which during the year 2011-12 may go up to 3.6 % of GDP or more for which we need foreign exchange. In this context it is not advisable for India to impose any control on foreign capital inflows. Our foreign exchange reserves stood at around US $272 billion at end-January 2012 and if monthly deficit on current account goes on occurring at the present rate, due to small capital outflows we may find it difficult to meet our current account deficit and as a result we will have to use some of our foreign exchange reserves for this purpose.

Further, of late there is another adverse situation that is developing is the falling cover of our exchange reserves for our imports which means the number of months of imports that our foreign exchange reserves can finance. After touching a peak of being able to Finance 16.5 months imports in February 2010, it fell to 8 months in Feb. 2012.

However, things go on changing dramatically depending on the global economic and financial situation. When there are large capital outflows causing depreciation of rupee as it occured in Sept.-Dec. 2011, there is need for intervention by RBI to sell US dollars from its foreign exchange resourves to check excess depreciation of rupee. On the other hand, when there is excess capital inflows causing appreciation of exchange rate of rupee, the RBI can intervene and buy or absorb some foreign exchange (*i.e.* dollars) coming into the country.

Composition of Capital Flows : A Problem

But the problem for India is more of the adverse nature of the composition of capital flows. In the recent past *capital flows are more of portfolio route by FIIs* which was the largest component of total capital flow in FY 2010-11. The difficult problem posed by these volatile capital flows, as mentioned above, is that they are being used to finance widening deficit in current account balance of payments. Foreign direct investment (FDI) which prior to 2010 was the largest component of capital inflows declined in 2010-11 The NRI deposits also slowed down in 2010-11. Even the external commercial borrowing (ECB) had also not risen much in 2010-11 as compared to 2009-10. Because of these the Reserve Bank had to use its policy regarding management of capital flows and foreign exchange rate more proactively than adopt a mere reactive policy in this regard. Even though with the use of proper foreign exchange rate policy the RBI can encourage imports to fight inflation, but it has refrained from doing so. The extent of the RBI intervention in the foreign exchange market had been much less in the years 2009-10 and 2010-11. Exchange rate policy had not been used to promote exports or to encourage imports to fight inflation. The latest situation regarding composition of capital flows is given in Table 31A.2.

It is due to the lack proactive policy of management of capital flows and foreign exchange rate that there is a lot of macroeconomic instability in the Indian economy. When capital outflows by FIIs occur we face a problem of crash in Indian stock market and depreciation of exchange rate of rupee as it occurred during Sept.-Dec. 2011 and again in June-August 2013. By increasing the costs of imports (including crude oil) this results in rise in inflation which adds to the problem of ongoing inflation unless they are offset by fall in international commodity prices.

On the other hand, when there is excess capital inflows beyond our absorptive capacity as occurred during April-July 2011 this leads to the appreciation of rupee which makes our exports less competitive and increases excess liquidity in the economy. Intervention by the RBI in such a situation is called for but it has been hesitant to intervene. Explaining this non-intervention Dr. D. Subba Rao, the former Governor of the RBI, states, "*If this resultant liquidity is left unsterilised, it fuels inflationary pressures. If the resultant liquidity is sterilized, it puts upward pressure on interest rates which, apart from hurting competitiveness, also encourages further flows*". This is arguing for unfettered free market in foreign exchange and no regulation of the capital flows.

In our view the RBI should be more watchfal of the movement of capital flows and foreign exchange rate of rupee and should actively intervene in forex market to ensure exchange rate stability and to encourage stable long-run capital flows into the Indian economy.

Macroeconomic Instability. It follows from above that the capital flows, if not regulated properly, can lead to macroeconomic instability. They cause changes in foreign exchange rate which affect exports and imports and therefore the balance of payments of a country. They also lead to the changes in foreign currency assets of Reserve Bank of India bringing about changes in money supply and thus causing price instability. Thus large capital inflows, if not regulated properly, cause inflation in the economy by bringing about expansion in money supply. Besides, as seen above, the large capital inflows of portfolio type affect stock market prices; when they come into the country, they generate boom in the stock market but when there is reversal of these flows, they cause crash in the stock market.

Controlling Capital Inflows

It may be noted that the central banks of the US and Japan have reduced their interest rate to almost zero and bought government securities from the market to pump more money into the market. From Nov. 2010 to June 2011 the US Federal Reserve pumped in $ 600 billion in the US economy which led to capital outflow from the US economy to the emerging economies and caused depreciation of US dollar. Besides, their Central Banks have given loans to their FIIs which are investing in India, and other emerging economies. This has created surplus liquidity in the financial system of some emerging economecs such as Brazil. Besides, the depreciation of the US dollar will make its products cheaper which will boost its earnings from exports. These funds are being brought by FIIs into the emerging economies like Brazil, China and India where growth prospects are very bright and rates of return on capital are quite high. Besides, capital inflows will cause appreciation of rupee which will affect our GDP growth. This is because exports at present are not a negligible part of our GDP. Goods and services put together (that is, both merchandise and invisible exports) add up to about 22 per cent of our GDP. This implies that we cannot afford to let our exports decline on account of appreciation of our rupee. Therefore, when there are large capital inflows in the foreign exchange market is absolutely necessary that the RBI intervenes to check the appreciation of rupee rather than go on waiting and watching. There are two main ways of capital control. First, the RBI intervenes in the foreign exchange market in a big way and buy US dollars. This leads to the expansion in money supply that will further accelerate the inflation rate which was at the uncomfortable level of 8.53 per cent in December 2010 (year-on-year basis) with 2004-05 as the base. But this inflation can be checked by ***sterilization measure*** adopted by the RBI.

Second, excessive capital inflows can be reduced by imposing tax on purchase of bonds or shares by FIIs. To control capital inflows and protect their currency from appreciation, Brazil imposed a tax on foreign investment in bonds and recently doubled its tax rate. Similarly, to protect their exports, Thailand has also introduced a similar tax on foreign investment in bonds and shares. South Korea is also said to be thinking on the same lines to control capital inflows. Even China has been resisting efforts by the US and Europe to let its currency, Yuan, appreciate. In fact in the world today ***currency war*** is going on and each country is trying to protect exports by taking steps to prevent appreciation of their national currency to boost their exports. But the problem with imposition of capital controls by India is that these may adversely affect the long-term capital flows into India and other developing countries for investment in productive projects which are crucial for long-term growth of these economies.

We are therefore of the view that in the end no country will gain from following this "***beggar thy neighbour policy***". It is necessary that the leaders of both developed and developing countries evolve a consensus about adoption of appropriate policy measures to protect the interests of all countries and save the world from another global crisis.

Need for Capital Flows in Case of India. However, it may be noted that **problem facing India is quite different**. At present (October 2013) adequate capital flows into India are useful for meeting its current account deficit which is estimated at 4.2% per cent of GDP in 2011-12 and 4.8% of GDP in 2012-13. The matter of concern for us is that in view of decline in capital inflows through foreign direct investment (FDI) we are meeting our large current deficit with portfolio capital inflows by FIIs which are quite volatile and when there is reversal of these flows it creates problems for the Indian economy. For instance, after a surge of these portfolio capital inflows prior to August 2011, there was reversal of these flows from September 2011 onwards which put pressure on stock market prices and exchange rate of rupee. Therefore, what is needed for India is to encourage capital inflows through foreign direct investment to build infrastructure facilities and to meet to a large extent the country's current account deficit through these stable FDI inflows. However, at present in view of large current account deficit *there is no need for India for imposing any control on inflows of portfolio capital*. In fact Reserve Bank of India and the Indian Government are taking steps to encourage these capital inflows to finance our large current account deficit.

At present, if adequate capital flows into India do not occur, it will be difficult to finance our increasing current account deficit. In these circumstances we will have to draw upon our mearge foreign exchange reserves ($ 275 billion in September 2013) to finance our current account deficit. Our present foreign exchange reserves are sufficient to finance only 7 months of our imports.

LATEST SITUATION REGARDING CAPITAL FLOWS IN INDIA

Capital flows became volatile in India in 2013

Although net capital flows moderated in Q4 of 2012-13, they were adequate to finance the CAD, and indeed there was net aqccretion of USS 2.7 billion in india's foreign exchange reserves during 2012-13. The lower net capital inflows in Q4 of 2012-13 were mianly due to higher repayments of short-term trade credit and overseas borrowings by banks compared with Q3. Net FDI flows were, however, significantly higher in Q4 of 2012-13 than in the preceding quarter (Table 31A.2). Trends till July 18, 2013 in 2013-14 suggest an uptrend in capital flows in the form of FDI and NRI deposits, while ECBs (External Commercial Borrowing) showed a decline as compared with previous quarter (Table 31A.2), net FII flows were substantial until the third week of May, 2013, followed by a significant outflow in the subsequent period. Since the last week of May 2013, there was a net outflow of USS 12.1 billion on account of FIIs (till July 18). The reversal of FII flows from the domestic market was mainly evident in the debt segment. The outflows of FIIs from the domestic debt market was led by the global bond sell-offs on US Federal Reserve signals about tapering of quantitative easing (QE) that raised the prospects of global interest rates hardening, shifts in yeild spreads and the elevated cost of hedging a volatile rupee. Fig. 31A.2.

Table 31A.2. Trend in Capital Flows

(USS billion)

	2012-13 (Monthly Average)				2013-14
	Q1	Q2	Q3	Q4	April-May
FDI *in* India	2.0	3.2	1.4	2.4	2.7
FDI *by* India	0.7	0.5	0.7	0.5	0.3
FIIs	–0.6	2.6	3.3	3.8	–0.2#
ADRs/GDRs	0.03	0.03	0.0	0.0	0.0
ECBs	0.1	0.4	1.0	1.4	0.8
NRI Deposits	2.2	0.9	0.9	0.9	1.5

#: Apr-Jun 2013, Source : RBI

Rupee depreciated significantly in Q1 of 2013-14

In line with most Emerging Economies, as a result of capital outflows, the indian rupee depreciated by around 9 per cent during Q1 of 2013-14. The Rupee appreciated in April 2013, but the trend reversed from the start of May, with dollar gaining strength on better growth prospects. *Wider trade deficit and rising gold imports also put pressure on the rupee.* Since the Federal Reserve Chairman's May 22, 2013, testimony before the US Congress that it would soon start unwinding of quantitative easing (QE) under which it was purchasing bonds to stimulate the US economy the rupee deprreciated significantly (by 7.5 per cent till July 15 as global investors began unwinding their risky positions in emerging markets, anticipating that the US Fed could begin tapering its bond purchase. The dollar strengthening against major currencies, coupled with widening trade deficit drove the rupee to a new low of 61.05 against the dollar on July 8, 2013. The depreciation of rupee further gained momentum in Aug. 2013 and the value of rupee fell to a record low level of ₹ 68.83 to a US dollar on Aug 28, 2013.

The Reserve Bank's measures on July 15, 2013 to address exchange rate volatility helped stabilise the rupee subsequently. The government's announcement on july 16, 2013 proposing to liberalise FDI in single-brand retail, pertroleum and natural gas, pension and insurance sectors defence production and some other sectors also improved sentiments and worked towards bringing some stability to the rupee.

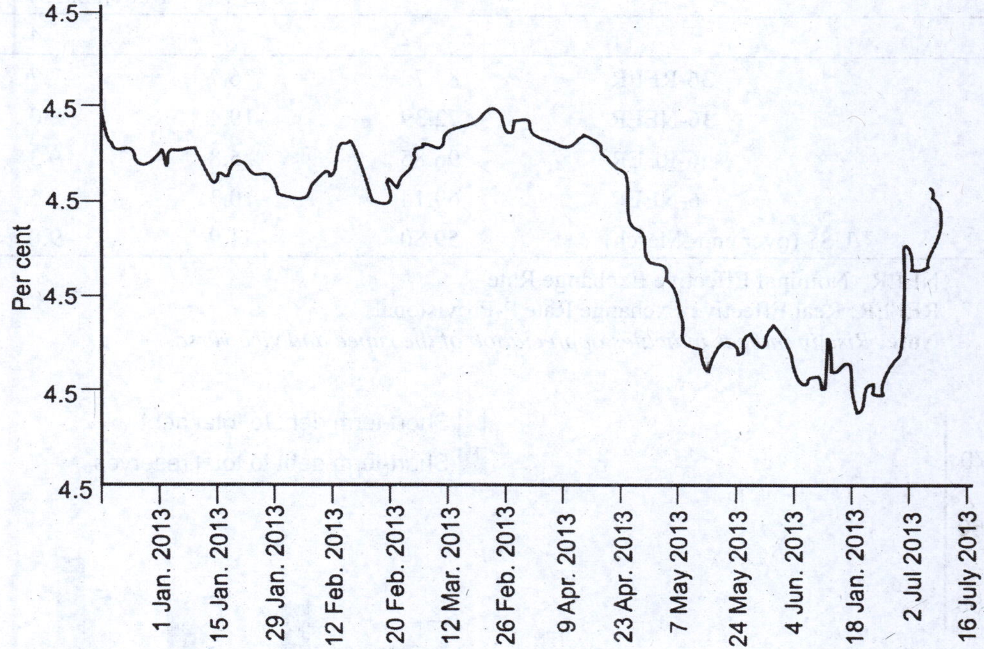

Fig. 31A.1. *Spread between 10 year sovereign yield of India and USA*

In terms of the real exchange rate, as at the end of Q1 of 2013-14, the 6-currency and 36-currency REER showed depreciation of 9.3 per cent and 7.7 per cent respectively over march 2013, reflecting weakening of the rupee in nominal terms (Table 31A.3).

External Debt Rose Further in Q4 of 2012 -13

The widening CAD, financed through higher debt flows resulted in significant rise in India's external debt which stood at US$ 390 billion at end-March 2013. There has been a sizeable rise in external commercial borrowings (ECBs) and rupee-denominated non-resident Indian deposits. Short-term debts on residual maturity basis at end-March 2013 surged by about US$ 25 billion over end-March 2012.

Table 31A.3 : Nominal and Real Effective Exchange Rates : Trade-Based

(Base: 2004-05 = 100)

	Index July19 2013 (P)	y-o-y Variation (Average) 2012-13	FY Variation (July19,2013 over March 2013)
1	2	3	4
36-REER	87.72	–6.7	–7.7
36-NEER	72.39	–10.4	–8.0
6-REER	96.85	–5.8	–9.3
6-NEER	69.14	–10.3	–9.5
₹/US$ (over end- March)	59.80	–11.9	–9.0

NEER : Nominal Effective Exchange Rate
REFER: Real Effective Exchange Rate P-Provisional
Note: *Rise in indices indicates appreciation of the rupee and vice versa.*

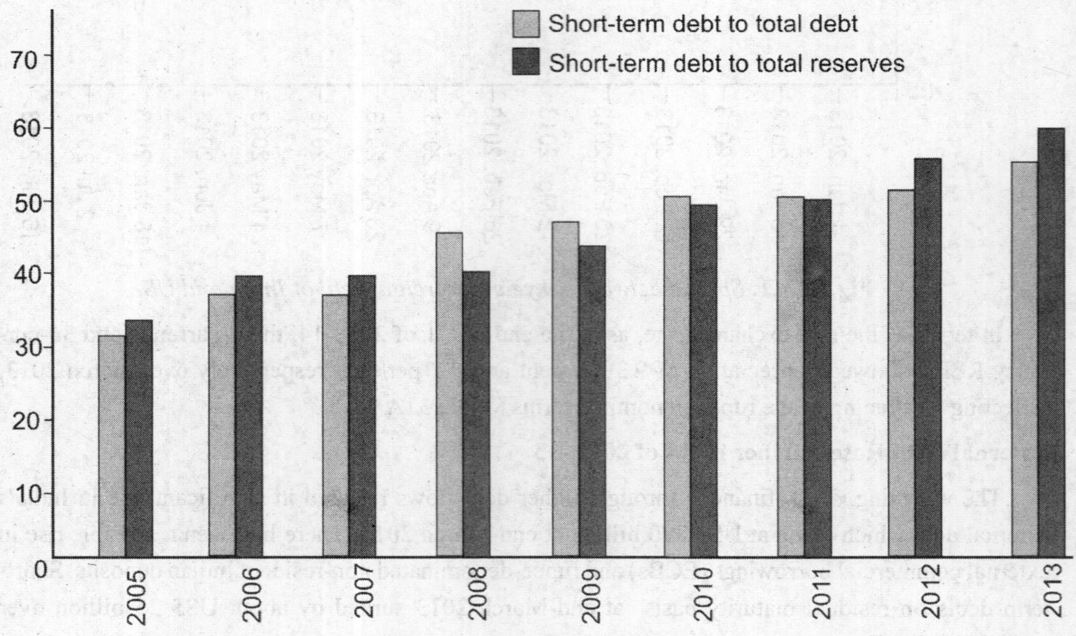

Fig. 31A.1. *Short-Term Debt Indicators (based on residual maturity)*

billion in 2012-13 9 Table 31A.4). In view of the rise in external debt and shortening maturities, there is a need to keep a close vigil on external debt levels and its components, especially private corporate debt. In this milieu, the Reserve Bank has proposed to levy capital and provisioning requirements for corporate that have unhedged foreign currency exposure and issued draft guidelines for the same.

Table 31A.4. India's External Debt (in US $ billion)

Item	End-March 2011 (PR)	End-March 2012 (PR)	End-December 2012 (PR)	End-March 2013 (P)	Vriation (end-March 2013 over end-December 2012 Per cent
1	2	3	4	5	6
1. Multilateral	48.5	50.5	51.6	51.6	0.0
2. Bilateral	25.7	26.9	26.4	25.1	–4.8
3. IMF	6.3	6.2	6.1	5.96	–2.5
4. Trade Credit (above 1 year)	18.6	19.1	18.6	17.7	–4.7
5. ECBS	88.5	104.8	112.7	120.9	7.2
6. NRI Deposits	51.7	58.6	67.6	70.8	4.8
7. Rupee Debt	1.6	1.4	1.3	1.3	0.3
8. Long term	240.9	267.3	284.3	293.3	3.2
9. Short-term (Original Maturity)	65.0	78.2	93.3	96.7	3.6
10. Short-term (Residual Maturity)#	129.1	147.4	166.1	172.3	3.7
Total (8 + 9)	**305.9**	**345.5**	**377.6**	**390.0**	**3.3**

PR : Partially Revised, P: Provisional, # : RBI Estimate
Note: Growth rates are based on data up to 3 decimal points.

Vulnerability Indicators Show Further Worsening.

With rising debt and deceleration in GDP growth, external sector vulnerability increased in 2012-13 compared with the previous year. India's external debt to GDP ratio increased to 21.2 per cent at end-March 2013 from 19.7 per cent at end-March 2012. Moreover, the ratio of short-term debt (both original and residual maturity) to total external debt increased further at end-March 2013. The ratio of reserves to total debt deteriorated through 2012-13 and stood at 74.9 per cent by the end of March 2013. Reflecting widening CAD, the net international investment position (IIP) as a ratio to GDP worsened from (–) 14 per cent at end-March 2012 to (–) 16.7 per cent at end-March 2013 (See table 31A.5).

CAD may moderate in 2013-14. but risks to its financing remain.

The CAD narrowed somewhat in Q4, but it remained above the sustainable level. It is likely that the widening trade deficit in Q1 of 2013-14 compared with the corresponding period of the previous year may manifest in a wider CAD in the quarter. However, the CAD could moderate over subsequent quarters if gold imports shows significant contraction, global crude oil prices stay low and exports will get some support from global recovery. Nevertheless, the CAD is likely to stay significantly higher than the substantiable level of 2.5 per cent. As such, a strategy aiming at its reduction and at the same time ensuring its financing with stable and non-debt resources such as FDI will be necessary. It is also important to remove structural impediments constraining India's export competitiveness and to sustain non-debt-creating flows over the medium term.

Table 31A.5. External Sector Vulerability Indicators

Indicator	*End Mar 2011*	*End Mar 2012*	*End Mar 2013*
1	**2**	**3**	**4**
1. Ratio of Total Debt to GDP	17.5	19.7	21.2
2. Ratio of Short-term to Total (Original Maturity)	21.2	22.6	24.8
3. Ratio of Short-term to Total Debt (Residual Maturity)#	42.2	42.6	44.2
4. Ratio of Concessional Debt to Total Debt	15.5	13.9	11.7
5. Ratio of Reserve to Total Debt	99.7	83.2	74.9
6. Ratio of Short-term Debt to Reserves	21.3	26.6	33.1
7. Ratio of Short-term Debt (Residual Maturity) to Reserves#	42.3	50.1	59.9
8. Reserves Cover of Imports (in months)	9.6	7.1	7.0
9. Debt-Service Ratio (Debt Service Payments to Current Receipts)	4.4	6.0	5.9
10. External Debt (US$ billion)	305.9	345.5	390.0
11. International Investment Position (IIP) (US$ billion)	–207.0	–249.5	–307.3
12. IIP/GDP ratio	–11.9	–14.0	–16.7

RBI Estimates

Global Risks. There are certain global risks that call for appropriate policy attention. International crude oil prices, though showing a downtred since February 2013, would largely be impacted by the outlook on global growth, geopolitical uncertainities and supply-side factors. High remittances underpinned by significant depreciation of the rupee in recent months and anticipated recovery in source countries may attenuate concerns relating to financing the CAD. However, the most important risk is that at some stage, exit from accommodative monetary policy in the US may tighten global liquidity, with implications for capital flows to EMDFs, including India. The resulting volatile capital flows could impede smooth financing the CAD in 2013-14. In this context, continued policy reforms assume utmost importance to ensure a conducive economic and business environment to attract more stable capital flows to the Indian economy.

Capital Inflows through FDI and NRI Deposits Increase from July 2013

As a result of measure taken by RBI and government, capital inflows through FDI and NRI deposits have started increasing as will be seen from Table 31A.6. FDI rose 58% on a net basis to $8.7 billion during April-July 2013, despite a moderation in the pace of inflows from abroad.

On a gross basis, inflows rose 9.2% to $10.7 billion as companies pumped in over $7.3 billion as equity capital while $2.2 billion was reinvested earnings. Of this around $2.2 billion was repatriated or disinvested in India by foreign companies. As a result, *inflows were up a little over 6% at $8.5 billion during the first four months of the financial year 2013-14*, latest data released by RBI in the monthly bulletin (August 2013) showed.

What boosted the net flows was the fact that repatriation and disinvestment by Indian companies overseas rose to $3.1 billion during April-July 2013, compared to $1.3 billion in the corresponding period last year. Add to that a moderation in investment abroad, FDI outflows of $2.5 billion also turned into inflows. What contributed to the sharp reversal is unclear but analysts believe that Indian companies have become more cautions in recent months as several of them are saddled with high debt burden and are looking to sell some of their assets abroad.

Table 31A.6. FDI Flows and NRI Deposits

FDI	2012	2013	%
	April-July		change
Inflows	8.0	8.5	6.3
Outflows	2.5	–0.2	NA
Net FDI	5.5	9.7	58.2

Outstanding NRI Deposits*	US $ billion
March '13	70.8
Apr '13	72.7
May '13	71.7
June '13	71.1
July '13	73.0

Sources: RBI

Apart from FDI, the other good news for the government with a *reversal in the flow of non-residents deposits*, which witnessed the first accretion to the stock during the current financial year 2013-14. The stock of deposits by expatriates had been falling every month since March 2013. While bankers believed that several NRIs were pulling money from India to avoid an erosion of their base on account of the rupee depreciation, the trend seems to have been turned after a series of steps announced by the government and RBI. In fact, more steps had come in April and bankers are expecting a sharper turnaround, if the rupee retains its recent momentum.

Chapter 32

India and World Trade Organisation (WTO) and Bilateral and Regional Trade Cooperation

Introduction

World Trade Organisation (WTO) is the most important trade organisation set up on January 1, 1995 to promote free trade among different countries. Protection has harmful affects on economic growth and consumer welfare. Bretton Woods Conference held in 1944 which recommended the setting up of International Monetary Fund (IMF) and World Bank (WB) also recommended the establishment of an International trade organisation to promote free trade among nations. However, while IMF and World Bank were established in 1946, agreement to set up International Trade Organisation could not be finally reached. Instead, a less formal organisation called GATT (General Agreement on Trade and Tariff) were set up to guide the international trading system based on rules and principles agreed between the member countries. However, it was found to be weak and ineffective although it succeeded in achieving its objective of promoting world trade to some extent by bringing down the level of tariffs on manufactured products in the developed countries. The process of liberalisation of trade, however, suffered a set back since 1974. Although the process of reducing tariff barriers continued, Non-Tariff Barriers (NTB's) were substantially increased by various countries including the developed countries. Strangly enough, it was found that while the developed countries were adopting Non-Tariff Barriers such as quantitative restrictions to protect their industries, the developing countries were liberalising their trade by reducing tariff on the imports from the developed countries.

The Uruguay Round. From 1986 onward several rounds of talks were held under the auspices of GATT to promote free and fair trade among the nations so that world resources be optimally utilised and well-being of the people be increased. After several years of talks agreement was reached on a set of proposals, which is popularly known as *Dunkel Draft* as it, was prepared by Arther Dunkel who was then the Director General of GATT.

Thus, WTO was created at the end of the 1986-93 Uruguay Round of international trade negotiations when agreement was finally formalised. Started on January 1, 1995, WTO replaced General Agreement on Tariff and Trade (GATT) which had acted as an interim World Trade Organisation as a watch dog since 1948.

WTO : STATUS, ADMINISTRATION AND FUNCTIONS

WTO is officially defined as the legal and institutional foundation of the *multilateral trade system*. Unlike GATT, the WTO is a permanent organisation created by international treaty ratified by the governments and legislatures of member states. As the principal international body concerned with solving trade problems between countries and providing a forum for multilateral trade negotiations, it has global status similar to that of the International Monetary Fund and the World Bank.

Administrative Structure of WTO. WTO is headed by a director-general (currently Mr. Renato Ruggiero, former Italian trade minister) who has four deputies from different member states. The WTO's ruling body is the General Council, comprising each member country's permanent envoys. It sits in Geneva on an average once a month. Its supreme authority is the *ministerial conference,* to be held every two years. The General Council appoints the director-general to a four-year term after consultations among member countries.

WTO started with 125 countries. But seven more states including China, Russia were admitted later on as members. Members range from the top four world trade powers—the United States, the European Union, Japan and Canada—to the increasingly influential emerging developing economies of Asia to some of the world's poorest countries, like Bangladesh, Guinea.

WTO Bodies for Administration

The two important bodies in WTO have been set up to perform its various functions.

1. Dispute Settlement Body (DSB). The DSB, on which all member countries can sit, usually meets twice a month to hear complaints of violations of WTO rules and agreements. It sets up expert panels to study disputes and decide if the rules are being broken. The DSB's final decisions, unlike those of a similar but less powerful body in the old GATT, cannot be challenged.

2. Trade Policy Review Body (TPRB). The TPRB is a forum for the entire membership to review the trade policies of all WTO member countries. Major trading policies are reviewed every two years, others every four years.

Other major bodies are the Council for Trade in Goods, the Council for Trade in Services and the Council for *Trade-Related Aspects of Intellectual Property Rights* (TRIPS).

Functions of WTO

WTO has the following five functions to perform :

(1) The WTO provides the framework for implementation, administration and operation of multilateral trade agreements reached at Uruguay Round.

(2) The WTO provides the forum for further negotiations among its member states concerning their multilateral trade relations with regard to the matters included in the agreements reached at Uruguay Round.

(3) The WTO undertakes the task of *settlement of disputes* among the member states, which arise from their different understandings of the rules and procedure agreed upon.

(4) The WTO administers the '*Trade Review Mechanism.*'

(5) In order to evolve a coherrent global economic policy to promote free and fair trade among the different countries, WTO cooperates in an appropriate manner with the IMF; World Bank and its affiliated agencies.

THE GUIDING FUNDAMENTAL PRINCIPLES AND FEATURES OF WTO

The following fundamental principles have been provided for the functioning of WTO as a multiple trading system. These principles represent the salient features of WTO.

(*a*) **Non-Discrimination.** This is the most important principle on which WTO has been founded. The principle of non-discrimination means two things. (1) All trading partners will be granted the *most favoured nation (MFN) status*, that is, each member state of WTO will treat every other member state equally as the most favoured nation doing trade. No discrimination will be done by a member of state between different trading states who are also members of WTO. However, some exceptions have been provided in this regard, for example, in case regional trade agreements exist. (1) Foreign goods, services, trade marks, patents and copyrights shall be given the same treatment as is given to nationals of a country.

(b) **Free Trade.** The objective of WTO, as in case of GATT, is to promote free trade among nations through negotiations. For this purpose WTO has to work for progressive liberalisation of trade through reduction in tariffs and removal of quantitative restrictions on imports by member countries.

(*c*) **Stability in the Trading System.** Under WTO agreements member states are committed not to raise tariff and non-tariff trade barriers arbitrarily. This provides stability and predictability to the trading system.

(*d*) **Promotion of Fair Competition.** WTO system of multilateral trading system provides for transparent, fair and undistorted competition among the various countries. Rules such as Most Favoured Nation (MFN) treatment to all trading parties, equal treatment to foreign goods, patents and copyrights as with nationals ensure fair competition among trading countries. Besides, WTO agreement provides for discouraging unfair competitive practices such as export subsidies and dumping (that is, selling products abroad below domestic prices to gain market access).

(*e*) **Special Concern for Developing Countries.** WTO has shown special concern for the developing countries as it has given them more time to adjust to agreements under it and also some special privileges. An important feature of WTO is that it would deal with not only the disputes in the area of trade in goods but a whole range of issues such services and intellectual property rights.

(*f*) **Market Access Commitment.** WTO agreements which seek to establish multilateral trading system require the member countries to undertake market access commitment on reciprocity basis. In fact, market access is ensured by abolsihing non-tariff barriers as well as by reducing tariffs. The understanding on market access requires that member countries will cut tariffs on industrial goods and agricultural products by about 37 per cent. In order to provide market access for the products of developing countries to the USA, USA agreed to cut down farm subsidies. The developing countries are also required to reduce agricultural subsidies to the level of 10 per cent of the value of agricultural produce.

In the area of trade in services, market access has been ensured by giving foreign service suppliers the same treatment as demestic service suppliers.

(*g*) **Decision at the Ministerial Level Meeting**. Another feature of WTO agreement is that it has upgraded decision-making at the ministeral level. Important decisions regarding trade related matters are to be taken at the Ministerial level meetings. Ministerial level meetings have now been incorporated in the legal structure of WTO.

(*h*) **Wider Range of Issues.** Another important feature of WTO is that it wil deal with not only issues and disputes relating to trade in goods but also the whole range of issues concerning *trade in services and intellectual property rights*.

(*i*) **Multlateral Trading System.** The most important features of WTO is that it seeks to establish just and fair multilateral system of international trade wherein the developed countries, the developing countries, and the least developing countries all have equal opportunities for market access for their products in foreign countries and wherin discriminatory trade barriers and unjust Government support to exports by different countries have been eliminated.

Object of WTO

The objective of WTO agreements is *to establish a multilateral trading system* in order to promote free and fair trade among nations. Thus, Dunkel Act on which WTO has been founded is wedded to liberalisation of trade based on comparative costs. For the purpose of trade liberalisation, it provides for a *multilateral trading system*. Accordingly, this provides for a multilateral framework for trade not only in industrial and agricultural goods but also in services and and also to protect trade related intellectual property rights (TRIPS. By committing the member countries to give Most Favoured Nation (MFN) treatment to all trading partners, it has sought to discourage bilateral trading so as to encourage multilateral trading system.

WTO AGREEMENTS AND LIBERALISATION

We discuss below various WTO agreements which seek to promote liberalisation of trade.

(1) Liberalisation of trade in manufactures
(2) Liberalisation of agricultural trade
(3) Liberalisation of trade in services (GATS)
(4) Trade Related Intellectual Property Rights (TRIPS)
(5) Trade Related Investment Measures (TRIMS).

Liberalisation of Trade in Manufactures : Agreement on Tariff Bindings and Tariff Reducton

The main agreements with regard to trade liberalisation in manufactures are:

1. Firstly, the provision for *expansion of tariff bindings* which prevent the developed countries from increasing tariff rates in future beyond a particular level. Tariff bindings cover 99 per cent of imports. Secondly, the agreement provides for *reduction in tariff rates* by the developed countries by 40 per cent from 6.2 to 3.7 per cent. Thirdly, the agreement provides for *expansion of duty free access* from 20 to 43 per cent of their imports by the developed countries.

It is however important to note that gain to the developing countries from tariff reduction by the developed countries is not very significant. The average reduction of tariffs on their imports to the developed countries is estimated at 30 per cent and in case of labour-intensive industrial products such as textiles, clothing, leather goods and certain processed primary products such as fish products which are regarded as sensitive, the reduction in tariffs is less than even the average reduction of 30 per cent.

On the other hand, the offers of tariff cuts on imports of manufactures by the developing countries are estimated at about one-third of the average tariff reduction by the whole world. The expansion of tariff bindings which prevent the developing countries from increasing tariffs in future represent significant gains for the developed countries.

Agreement on Agriculture

To achieve liberalisation of agricultural trade, agreement on agriculture was also reached during multinational trade negotiations resulting in the establishment of WTO in 1995. Agreement on agriculture was highly significant as agriculture was a highly protected sectors in the developed countries. This distorted world prices of agricultural products prevented the developing countries to realise the benefits of their comparative advantage. As a result, exports of developing countries could not increase significantly. Agreement on agriculture includes the following conditions :

(*a*) **Tariffication.** It was agreed that existing non-tariff barriers imposed by the member countries would by replaced by suitable tariffs which would provide almost the same level of protection. This is called tariffication.

(*b*) **Tariff Bindings.** The agreement on agriculture also required that developed countries would reduce their tariff bindings by an average of 36 per cent within six years from 1995. The developing countries were required to reduce tariffs by an average 24 percent over a period of 10 years, while the least developed countries are not required to make any commitment regarding reduction of tariffs on their farm products.

The developing countries were permitted to indicate only their maximum bindings. For example, India declared maximum bindings of 100 per cent on farm products and 300 per cent on edible oils.

(*c*) **Subsidies and Domestic Support Policies.** Reduction in Agricultural subsidies and domestic support prices is another important aspect of agreement on agriculture. The developed countires such as USA and the countries of East European Union (EU) maintain high level of agricultural subsidies and other domestic support programmes to protect their farmers and prevent the imports from the developing countries. As a result, exports of farm products of the developing countries suffer a lot. WTO agreement on agriculture requires that subsidies on farm products should not exceed 10 per cent of the value of agricultural production.

Besides, it was agreed that product specific subsidies, non-product specific subsidies on fertilizers, irrigation, power and seeds etc were also not to exceed 10 per cent of the value of agricultural output. Agreement on agriculture also provided that countries with closed agricultural markets will have to import agricultural commodities to the extent of 3 per cent of their domestic consumption, going up to 5 per cent over six years. However, developing countries which were facing balance of payments problems were exempted from this rule of compulsory imports.

Agrement on agriculture also provides that countries are free either to give patents on agricultural products or to evolve an effective *sui genris* (*i.e.* special) system of protection for plant breeder rights. It implies freedom of multiplication and exchange of indigeneously produced seeds or plants in the country. In other words, the farmers are free to retain seeds from their own harvests for their uses and exchange with each other. The only exception is seeds evolved genetically through the tools of high-tech biotechnology. The patent fee would be payble if the seed or plant varieties bought are genetically superior to and more productive than the local varieties. Thus, the farmers will have to pay a patent fee on branded seeds or plant varieties imported from developed countries. The commerrcial sale of such seeds would be affected by patents.

GATS (General Agreement on Trade in Services)

The General Agreement on Trade in Services (GATS) has been one of the major achievements of Uruguay Round of negotiations which now forms part of WTO legal framework GATS covers all service sectors including financial services, telecommunications, transport, tourism, audio visual and professional services. GATS requires some basic obligations to be fulfilled by all member countries of WTO with regard to international trade in services. GATS applies to services provided by service suppliers of one country and sold to consumers of another country (for example tourism). It also applies to services provided by the commercial presence of a supplier of one country in the territory of another (for example bank of a country providing banking service in another country). It is equally applicable to services supplied by companies of one country in the territory of another. However, GATS shall not cover services provided by the government which are not supplied on a commercial basis.

GATS requires countries to provide most-favoured nation treatment (MFN) to all member countries. It implies that equally favourable treatment is to be accorded to service suppliers of all member foreign countries. GATS also requires that member countries should have transparency in their trade in services. This implies that each country to promptly publish all its relevant law and regulations pertaining to services including international agreements pertaining to trade in services to which the country is a signatory. Besides, each member country shall provide all information sought by any other member country relating to any service covered by GATS. Further, the countries are required to accord foreign service suppliers the same treatment as domestic service suppliers.

The countries may be exempted from GATS if they face balance of payments difficulties. They may also be exempted from GATS for national security reason as well as for purposes of protecting public order. The GATS requires that the countries would provide market access to foreign service suppliers. Hence, they would not impose restrictions on the number of service suppliers, total value of service transactions, the total number of service operations, joint ventures through which service may be supplied and the participation of foreign capital. The GATS has excluded labour movement from its purview. It allows countries to apply immigration laws to regulate the entry of persons into their territories. Countries are specifically allowed to apply *visa* requirements selectively to some countries and not to others.

TRIPS (Trade Related Intellectual Property Rights) Agreement

One of the most controversial agreement of Urugay Round of negotiations relates to Trade Related Intellectual Property Rights or briefly known as TRIPS. The agreement regarding TRIPS requires member countries to provide patent protection to all products or processes in all fields of technology. This protection is granted subject to the following three conditions :

(1) The product or the process is a new one
(2) It contains an inventive step
(3) It is capable of industrial application for 20 years from the grant of the patent.

TRIPS agreement corers the following seven intellectual properties.

(*i*) Patents
(*ii*) Copyrights and other related rights
(*iii*) Geographical indications
(*iv*) Industrial designs
(*v*) Trade marks
(*vi*) Layout designs of integrated circuits
(*vii*) Undisclosed information including trade secrets.

Patents shall be available without discrimination as to the place of invention, the field of technology and whether products are imported or locally produced. The patent-holder would enjoy exclusive marketing rights for a particular period. Any body else seeking to manufacture and sell the product would have to establish that there has been no violation of the patent-holder's rights. The term of patent under the new regime would be 20 years from the date of the filling of the application.

Since the patent would be available for products or processes, it would be possible in chemical-base products like drugs and pharmaceuticals, agro-chemicals, alloys and food products to take patents for new products for 20 years and process patents thereafter for another 20 years. The countries which do not have product patent in certain areas (in India, agriculture and horticulutre, technologies relating to atomic energy and chemical based products like chemicals, alloys, drugs and pharmaceuticals, agro-chemicals, food products and so on are exempt from product patents) are given 10 years transition period for the introduction of product patents.

The countries are free to give patents or adopt an *effective sui genris* system of protection for plant breeder rights enshrined in the International Union for Protection of new Plant Varieties UPOV) convention.

A period of five years was given to implement the provisions of the TRIPS agreement. In respect of Copyrights and related rights India is a signatory to the Berne convention. Likewise, in respect layout designs and integrated circuits India is signatory to Washington Treaty whose main obligations have also been incorporated in the TRIPS.

TRIMS (Trade Related Investment Measures) Agreement.

TRIMS agreement refers to conditions or restrictions imposed on *foreign investors*. This agreement requires that investment regulations by member countries have to give same treatment to domestic products and imports. The TRIMS agreement specifically forbids imposing restrictions on operations of an enterprise which result in protecting domestic products and making imports disadvantageous. The foreign trade related restrictions on investment by foreign enterprises were generally imposed by developing countries including India. The following conditions which favour domestic production were prohibited under TRIMS agreement.

1. **Local content requirement.** That is, foreign enterprises must use a certain amount of locally produced inputs in production of products.

2. **Trade balancing requirement.** That is, imports by a foreign enterprise shall not exceed a certain proportion of exports by it.

3. Trade and foreign exchange balancing requirements.

4. **Domestic sales requirement.** This requires an enterprise to sell a certain proportion of its output locally.

However, it was agreed that subsidies applicable solely to domestic enterprises and government procurement policy in favour of domestic producers will not violate the TRIMS agreement. Thus, under TRIMS Agreement, investment regulations have to accord same treatment to domestic products and imports. *The TRIMS agreement requires removal of quantitative restrictions on imports and exports*. However, exemptions are allowed if a country is suffering from balance of payments problems.

The industrialised countries were required to eliminate conditins covered under TRIMS by July 1, 1997. Developing countries were required to do so by 2000 and least developed countries were required to eliminate them by 2002.

India notified the TRIMS required by it before 2000. It notified two TRIMS conditions (1) relating to local content requirements in the production of certain pharmaceutical products and (2) dividend balancing requirements in the case of investment in 22 categories of consumer items. These were to be eliminated by 1-1-2000. The developing countries, including India, requested for extension of transition period for the elimination of the notified TRIMS. In view of the failures of the Seatle Ministerial Conference and Cancun conference no final decision was taken on this request of the developing counties.

INDIA'S ROLE IN WTO TALKS

India has consistently taken the stand that the launch of any new round of talks depends on a full convergence of views amongst the entire WTO membership on the scope and framework for such negotiations. Our more urgent task is to resolve the concerns of developing countries on implementation of the Uruguay Round agreements. We are against calls for new commitments from the developing world for achieving symmetry and equity in the existing agreements. It is in favour of '*non-trade' issues* be permanently kept off the negotiating table.

Incorporating Livelihood Clause. Ensuring food and livelihood security is critical, particularly for a large agrarian economy like India. India's proposal in ongoing negotiations includes suggestions like allowing developing countries to maintain appropriate level of tariff bindings, commensurate with their developmental needs and the prevailing distortions in international markets. We are also seeking a separate safeguard mechanism including provision for imposition of quantitative restrictions under specified circumstances, particularly in case of a surge in imports or decline in prices; exemptions for developing countries from obligations to provide minimum market access; exemptions of all measures taken by developing countries for poverty alleviation, rural development and rural employment.

Our immediate priority is that the agreements reached earlier with the developing countries should be implemented so as to correct inherent imbalances in some of the Uruguay Round agreements. Sincere and meaningful implementation of commitments undertaken by developed countries and operationalisation of all special and differential treatment clauses for developing countries in the various agreements be made.

We also strongly favour extension of higher levels of protection to the geographical indications for products like Basmati rice, Darjeeling tea, and Alphonso mangoes at par with that provided to wines and spirits under the Trade-related Aspects of Intellectual Property Rights (TRIPS) agreement. In the TRIMS (Agreement on Trade-Related Investment Measures) review we want flexibility for developing countries in adopting appreopriate domestic policy while permitting foreign investment.

Developed Countries Demand and Singapore Issues. Developed countries are pushing for a comprehensive agenda like *rules on investment, environment, competition policy, trade facilitation, transparency in government procurement*, labour standards etc. They are pressing for incorporating non-trade issues of environment and labour standards. Using as an excuse that production of products in developing countries are not being done under proper environment and labour standards they can ban the imports of their products or impose other non-tariff restrictions. The developing countries are opposed to these non-trade issues

WTO and Indian Agriculture and Farmers

Some critics of WTO have expressed the fears that Indian farmers are threatened by the WTO. There is however no adverse impact. India has bound its tariff to the extent of 100 per cent for primary agricultural products, 150 per cent for processed agricultural products and 300 per cent for edible oils. A few agricultural products had been bound historically at low levels but these bindings have been raised following the Article XXVIII negotiations held in this regard.

It has also been possible to maintain without hindrance the domestic policy instruments for promotion of agriculture or for targeted supply of food grains. Domestic policy measures like the operation of minimum support price, public distribution system as well as provision of input subsidies to agriculture have not in any way been constrained by the WTO agreement. Certain provisions in the Agreement on Agriculture (AoA) also give us flexibility to provide support for research, pest and disease control, marketing and promotion services, infrastructure development, payments for relief from natural disasters, payments under the regional assistance programmes for disadvantaged regions and payments under environmental programmes. Indian farmers now need to take advantage of the opportunity provided by the AoA, by addressing productivity issues and making their products more competitive globally.

WTO and Indian Industries

Indian industry has had to face greater competition in the wake of globalisation. But it has successfully competed, as can be inferred from the fact that there has been no particular surge in imports. In fact, as per the provisional data for 2000-01 our non-oil imports declined by 14 per cent while our exports rose by over 20 per cent in the same period. A close watch is also being kept to ensure that Indian industry does not have to face unfair competition from dumped or subsidised imports of other countries.

As for drug prices, safeguards are provided like compulsory licensing, price controls, and parallel imports which should help address this concern. It must also be recognised that the prices of medicines are influenced by several factors including the level of competition, size of market, purchasing capacity etc. The issue of affordable access to treatment for AIDS, which has gathered international attention in recent months, is hopefully a pointer in the right direction. The TRIPS agreement should not be allowed to hinder the efforts of developing countries to provide affordable access to medicines.

The apex Indian organisations representing various industries are sincerely working towards ensuring a gainful transition with least disadvantage into the global economy. The government also has to strive to improve infrastructure and provide a facilitating environment for inducing acceleration in trade. Developed countries have been putting pressures on inclusion of non-trade issues such as labour standards, environment protection, human rights, rules on investment, competition policy in the WTO agreements. This is because by asserting that particular developing countries are not observing and implementing the rules in regard to the non-trade issues so that the developed countries can ban the imports of some goods in their countries, as the USA has been trying to do so from time to time. We are against any inclusion of non-trade issues that are directed in the long run at enforcing protectionist measures, particularly against developing countries.

INDIA'S GAIN FROM WTO

Now almost a decade has passed when India joined WTO from the very beginning in Jan. 1,1995. India has benefitted from joining WTO, despite the failures of two ministerial level conferences at Seatle and Cancun. We explain below the gains India has achieved by joining WTO.

Exports and Imports. According to the recent estimates. India's exports have almost doubled in less than a decade. With exports going up from $26.33 billion in 1994-1995 when India joined WTO to $51.7 billion in 2002-03. Besides, India's share in total world exports of goods and commercial services increased from 0.6 in 1995 to 0.86 in 2001 whereas its total world imports of goods and commercial services increased from 0.78 in 1995 to 0.99 per cent during the same period.

Exports of Textiles and Clothing. According to a WTO agreement known as Multi-Fibre Agreement (MFA) entire quotas in textile and clothing trade will come to end from January 1, 2005. Till now WTO agreement has required the member countries to phase out their existing quotas by the Dec. 31, 2004. It has further restrained them from expanding the size of quotas annually. These measures have helped India to increase its market access for its textile and clothing products. With effect from January 1, 2005, the entire textiles and clothing trade would get integrated into the multilateral trade framework of WTO. According to recent report (Feb. 2004), after China, India is largest gainer from the end of quotas and the consequent free trade in textiles and clothing. It is estimated that export market of $500 billion in garments alone with employment potential of 30 million jobs will be up for grabs from which India can get a good share.

Five years ago, Indian economists feared the country's fabrics sector would be steam-rollered by China. But recent reforms in the industry have given hope. India could see apparel exports rise between 40-100 per cent ($6.7 billion in 2001). A target of $50 billion in textile and clothing exports by 2010 is no longer a pipe dream.

Gain in Exports of Software Services. Further, thanks to WTO agreement on free trade in services India has become a world leader in software services which are contributing a lot to foreign exchange earnings and employment generation for Indians.

A Good Deal of Earnings from BPO. BPO (Business Processing Outsourcing Services) from USA and UK are coming to India which have enabled us to earn not only foreign exchange but also to generate a large number of employment opportunities for educated Indian youth. Recently, there is resentment in the USA against BPO to India and other countries because it is causing loss of jobs in the USA and UK. But BPO to India and other developing countries are in accordance with the comparative advantage principle and raises profits of American companies which on being used for further investment will generate more employment opportunities in the USA

India's Demand from the Industrialised Countries about Agricultural Subsidies and Movement of Labour. In its negotiating proposal, India has demanded substantial reduction in tariffs, elimination of trade-distorting domestic support and export subsidies in developed countries. The movement of professionals (*i.e.*, labour) from developing countries is constrained by a number of factors such as lack of specific sectorial commitments, lack of mutual recognition of qualifications, lack of transparency in administration of *visa* regimes, discriminatory practices in use of Economic Needs Test and social security contributions. India has, therefore, sought liberalisation of movement of professionals through removal of these constraints and submitted a paper for discussion at the ongoing negotiations.

Failure of WTO Talks at Cancun

From Sept. 10 to 14,2003 trade ministers of developed and developing countries met for the next stage of talks on multilateral trading system. In an earlier meeting at Doha is Nov. 2001 ministers recognised the inequities of Uruguay Round of negotiations. It was expected that the developing countries would get a just and fair global trading system at the conclusion of Cancun meeting. But these hopes were not fulfilled and Cancun meeting ended in a failure. At Cancun, a group of 21 developing countries led by India, Brazil and China frustrated the attempts of US-European Union Cambine to pressurise the developing countries to accept the agenda that suited them most and was against the interests of the developing countries. Draft declaration prepared by WTO allowed the developed countries to maintain or keep domestic subsidies and support for their agriculture and farmers and avoided eliminating export subsidies and credit concessions on their exports, especially on farm products and textiles. On the other hand, draft declaration sought even stiffer tariff cuts by developing countries. In this way, developing countries were badly treated with regard to market access of their products to the developed countries. All these were not acceptable to the developing countries including India. African countries who are badly hit by the subsidies and domestic support on the farm products by the developed countries walked out of the meeting. As a result, Cancun meeting ended without adopting any declaration. The lesson from the failure of Cancun meeting is that unless the developed countries look beyond their own interests and try to evolve multilateral trading system which is just and fair to the developing countries talks cannot succeed.

WTO'S HONG KONG DECLARATION

After failures at Seatle and Cancun, the ministerial meeting in Hong Kong in December 2005 negotiated trade liberalisation to conclude Doha Round on Development. In Nov. 2001 in the Ministerial meeting at Doha the developed countries (the US and EU) and developing countries, it was agreed to start new round of talks to *promote development through trade liberalisation*. Hence the name '*Doha Round on Development*'. The two successive ministerial meetings at Seatle and Cancun failed to arrive at an agreement acceptable to the LDCs and developing countries. It may be noted that Uruguay Round of 1994 resulted in setting up of WTO in Jan. 1995. It may be further noted that the agenda of Uruguay Round as well as its outcome discriminated against developing countries. The trade negotiations of Doha Round are meant to remove this discrimination against the developing countries[1]. During the negotiations developed countries have been raising irrelevant issues so as to protect their agriculture and textiles industry through tariffs and non-tariff barriers (NTB) so as to prevent free and fair trade from the viewpoint of developing countries. On the other hand, at the conclusion of Uruguay Round, the developed countries succeeded in extracting an agreement regarding the *inclusion of services and intellectual property rights* – the two issues which concern them most. In return for this agreement on services and intellectual property rights – they agreed to *eliminate* over a period of 10 years high tariff and non-tariff barriers on textiles, agricultural products, sugar – the products which are of special interest for developing countries However, the developed countries did not fulfil promise on one protext or the other. Commenting on this duplicity on the part of developed countries Stiglitz writes, "When the Uruguay Round began there was a grand bargain to expand the trade agenda to include services and intellectual property rights—the two

1. See Joseph E Stiglitz, *Fair Trade for All : How Trade Can Promote Development,* Oxford University Press, 2006.

issues which are of particular concern to developed countries. In return *developed countries were to make major concessions on agriculture*—the livelihood of the vast majority of people in developing countries — and textile quota the only trade area (besides sugur) in which quantitative restrictions persist. In the end developed countries got what they wanted, and developing countries were told to be patient : eventually the developed countries would fulfil their part of the deal. Even as the rich countries urged *developing countries to make quick adjustments*, they claimed that *they needed a decade to make the transition to a quota-free-textile regime.* In truth they were buying time; *they did nothing for a decade* and when the quota finally ended last January (i.e., Jan. 2005) they pleaded they were still not prepared and thus concluded a three year extension with China.[2]

Singapur Conference was meant to negotiate trade issues relating to agriculture, non-agriculture services and intellectual property rights so as achieve trade liberalisation for promoting economic development. The problem with regard to agriculture is that the developed countries, the US and EU provide export subsidies and also give financial support on a large scale to their agriculture resulting in cheapening of their agricultural products. This distorts trade between the countries as it prevents market access in developed countries for products of developing countries which have comparative advantage in their production. Developing countries discovered that their gain from trade with developed countries were far less than they were made out to be and LDCs (Least Developed Countries) felt than they were actually worse off by agreeing in Uruguay Round of talks resulting in establishment WTO. Thus developed countries lost their credibility.

With the above in background the Ministerial Conference at Hong Kong adopted a declaration which called for conclusion in 2006 of trade negotiations launched at Doha in Nov. 2001. This Hong Kong declaration established timeframe and targets in specific areas of trade liberalisation. The following agreement which addresses some of the concerns of developing countries related to agriculture was reached.

1. First it was resolved to complete Doha Round on Development in 2006 and conclude negotiations for liberalisation of trade between members of WTO.

2. **Elimination of Agricultural Export Subsidies.** The agreement was reached in Hong Kong that export subsidies given by the developed countries will be eliminated by the year 2013 in a phased manner. While the earlier proposal was to phase these export subsidies by 2010, the EU the largest provider of export subsidies sought a longer phase-out period. Thus, the agreed end-date of 2013 gives the EU a level of comfort of phasing out its export subsidies as a part of its next phase of reforms of the common agricultural policy (CAP). This is an achievement of the developing countries as it was contended earlier by its the earlier Trade Commissioner of WTO Pascal Lamy that Doha declaration had not mandated elimination of export subsidies in the developed countries. It may be noted further that under the agreement developing countries like India will continue to have the right to provide marketing and transport subsidies on agricultural exports for 5 years beyond the date for elimination of all forms of subsidies.

Agricultural Tariffs. To increase market access in the developed countries for the agricultural products of developing countries, the Hong Kong declaration has agreed to banding approach suggested by the group G-20 of developing Countries, According to this approach, agricultural tariffs have been put in *four bands* ranging from the lower to the high level, with the provision that tariff in the higher band will be subject to deeper cuts. The extent of cut in agricultural tariffs in each band is yet to be agreed upon in future negotiations. The higher cuts

2. Joseph Stiglitz, The Development Round that wasn't, *The Economic Times,* December 15, 2005.

in tariffs in the higher bands will greatly bring down the agricultural tariffs of the developed countries and will therefore improve market access for agricultural exports of the developing countries in the developed industrialised economies. However, it will also mean substantial reduction in agricultural tariffs of developing countries such as India who have higher tariff bindings. Indias tariff bindings for agricultural products are in the range 100 to 150 per cent and will therefore require to reduction about 35 per cent which is quite large.

However, in the Hong Kong declaration, the developing countries have been provided some special safeguards in connection with the cuts in agricultural tariffs. Firstly, the developing countries have been given the flexibility to self-designate an appropriate number of tariff lines as *special products* (SPs). However, the self-designation of a number of tariff lines as special products will require the satisfaction of some criteria such as needs of food security, livelihood security and rural development.

Secondly, under Hong Kong agreement on agriculture (AoA) the developing countries are also entitled to adopt *Special Safeguard Mechanism* (SSM) based on import quantities and price triggers. This means under special safeguard mechanism, developing countries can raise their tariff on imports of agricultural products in the event of a sudden increase in imports or fall in prices of imports. However, they are not allowed to reintroduce quantitative restrictions (QRs) which both the developed and developing countries have already eliminated

Domestic Support for Agriculture. In Hong Kong developed countries agreed to the proposal of G-20 (i.e., the group of developing countries including India and Brazil) for reduction of trade-distorting agricultural subsides with higher linear cuts in higher bands. However, the extent of reduction in these subsidies were left for future negotiations. It may be noted that Blue Box and Green Box agricultural subsidies have been excluded from the scope of reduction. But there is a provision for review of the criteria of the Green Box subsidies in which most of the EU domestic subsidies are included.

In Doha Round on development it was agreed to reduce the minimum level of support (de minimis) allowed to be exempted from reduction for both developed and developing countries. Developing countries are entitled to a de minimis of 10 per cent of the value of total production. In Hong Kong it was agreed that those developing countries whose domestic support to agriculture was below 10 per cent of the value of production and therefore no commitment to reduce them will be exempt from reductions in de minimis as well as overall trade-distorting agricultural subsidies.

Under the Hong Kong agreement export subsidies on cotton will be eliminated by developed countries in 2006 and trade distorting domestic subsidies on agricultural products will be reduced drastically over a storter period of time.

Non Agricultural Market Access (NAMA). The Hong Kong declaration provides for the reduction or elimination of tariffs including peak levels of tariffs, high levels of tarifs and tariff escalation on non-agricultural goods, particularly on the products of exports which are of great interest for the developing countries. In this context of market access for non-agricultural products it has been agreed to apply *Swis formula.* According to this formula, deeper cuts in tariff rates on a line-by-line basis have to be made by countries levying higher tariffs. How larger will be the cut in tariff levels will depend on the coefficients to be agreed.

However, in Hong Kong declaration the provision for *special and differential treatment* (S&DT) and *less than full reciprocity* for developing countries have been included. According to this provision, a certain proportion of tariff lines of the developing countries may be subjected to tariff cuts lower than that permitted by applying Swis formula and a certain percentage of the tariff lines of these countries may be kept unbound (that is, without any binding for tariff reduction). Thus flexibilities granted under S&DT include the longer implementation period as well as applying less than Swis formula cuts or no cuts for a specified list of tariff lines as unbound. These have been declared as an integral part of the modalities for negotiations under NAMA. On the sectoral initiatives, India and most of the developing countries has emphasized that formula approach should be the main modality for negotiations and sectoral initiative can only be a voluntary exercise.

Services. In the Hong Kong declaration it has been decided to achieve a higher level of liberalisation of trade in services and towards that negotiations will be intensified. New date lines have been fixed for submission of revised offer and draft schedules of commitments by the member countries. These negotiations on trade in services will be conducted in accordance with principle of GATS and the Guidelines and Procedures for the Negotiations on Trade in Services. According to GATS and these guidelines, the developing countries are required to liberalise the service sectors and modes of supply of their own choice and determine the extent of liberalisation.

India is particularly concerned with liberalisation of trade in services as it wants to increase its access to the markets of developed countries for the services such as ITES in which it has a comparative advantage. In services, India submitted its Revised offer in August 2005. Eleven service sectors and 94 sub-sectors are covered in the Revised offer.

It is thus clear that with regard the services much depends on revised services offer by the member countries and the future negotiations.

Market Access for LDCs. An important feature of Hong Kong Declaration is that it was decided to provide *duty-free* and *quota free* market access for all LDCs (Least Developed Countries) products to *all developed countries.* The developing countries which are in a position to provide such access to LDCs are expected to do so.

Agreement on TRIPS. On December 6, 2005, the General Council of WTO adopted the amendment to the TRIPS to address public health concerns of developing countries which was reaffirmed by Hong Kong Declaration. This amendment enables manufacturing and export of pharmaceutical products under compulsory license to countries with limited or no manufacturing capacities in the pharmaceutical sectors. On Trips, CBD (Convention of Bio-Diversity) on relationship and protection of traditional knowledge, India along with a number of other developing countries which are rich in bio-diversity proposed that the Trips Agreement of WTO should be amended to provide for : (*i*) disclosure of source of the traditional knowledge used in the invention; (*ii*) disclosure of evidence of prior informed consent under the relevant national regime; and (*iii*) disclosure of evidence of benefit sharing under the relevant national regime. With this amendment the use of India's natural herbs such as Neem, Arjuna, Ashavgandha and others for preparing medicines and also certain plant varieties such as Basmati rice will get protection from the use by multinational companies.

DOHA ROUND NEGOTIATION UNDER WTO

In Hong Kong India made some modest gains in the field of agriculture, industrial products and TRIPS. A good number of issues concerning liberalisation of global trade are yet to be resolved. However, much depends on future negotiations during which several issues particularly regarding market access for manufactured goods (NAMA) and services are to be resolved. Whether in these future negotiations, developed countries will adopt an attitude which ensure fair and free trade from the viewpoint of LDCs and developing countries. The developed countries proposed to link lower farm subsidies by them to gain greater market access for non-agricultural goods in the developing countries. This is against the letter and spirit of Hong Kong Declaration. And it is these kinds of tactics of the developed countries that Juseph Stiglitz predicted and thought that due to this Doha Round Negotiations for Development will collapse.

In our view it must be made clear to the developed countries that the artificiality of prices arising out of the substantial domestic agricultural subsidies provided by them must be dealt with firmly if we are to make any headway towards fair trade in agriculture. Developing countries have a right to use the flexiblities provided in Hong Kong declaration to protect their small and medium enterprises and their infant industries like automobiles. Therefore, in future trade negotiations no compromise be made on flexibilities in conection with agriculture and industrial products granted to the developing countries in Hong Kong declaration. We agree with Muchkund Dubey who have been associated with earlier Uruguay Round negotiations when he writes "The initiatives of India, Brazil and other major developing countries have indeed brightened up the prospects of concluding the Doha Round by the end of 2006 or thereafter. However, the magnitude of the problems still remaining unresolved should not be underestimated. There are still seemingly irreconcilable differences on some of major elements of modalities. The time available is too short. Therefore, one cannot rule out the possibility of the agreement reached in Hong Kong falling apart and the Doha Round being delayed indefinitely posing new threats to the multilateral trading system.[3]

The Doha Round of trade negotiations are under way for the last ten years (since 2001). Negotiations pasued in December 2008 but again resumed but so far talks have not been concluded and also there has not been much progress in this regard too. It may recalled that main purpose of setting up WTO was to usher in era of trade liberalisation. Thus, if Doha Round which focuses on the *developmental dimension* fails, it would affect free trade and the countries would enter into bilateral trade agreements providing for trade preference to the parties to the agreements. To promote multilateral trade mechanism India is working with coalition groups in the WTO towards an early conclusion of the Doha Round. *Its stands has been made quite clear that it favours the protection of poor, substance farmers of developing countries and gives priority to vulnerable industries of the developing countries.*

Doha Round Talks in the Area of Agriculture. In the area of agriculture discussions are still taking place on the basis of revised Draft of *agriculture modalities* of December 2008. According to this draft, developed countries would have to reduce their bound tariffs in equal annual instalments over 5 years with an overall minimum average cut of 54 per cent. And developing countries have to reduce their bound tariff with a maximum overall average cut of 36% per cent over a larger implementation period of 10 years. Developing countries would have a special products (SP) entitlement of 12 per cent of agricultural tariff lines. An average tariff cut of 11 per cent is proposed on SPs including 5 per cent of total tariff lines at zero cuts. There are also reductions proposed for various categories of domestic and export subsidies.

Non-Agricultural Market Access (NAHA) Negotiations.

In the case of Non-Agricultural Market Access (NAMA) negotiations, the tariff reductions are proposed through a non-linear swift formula with three coefficients of 20, 22 and 25 for formula reductions linked to specific flexibilities for protecting sensitive NAMA tariff lines of developing countries.

India has said any attempt to dilute the development agenda of the Doha round of the WTO talks will not be acceptable and demands for more market access from developing countries by developed countries cannot be entertained. The US has asked large developing countries including India, Brazil and China to remove duties on some industrial goods but has been refused as these countries claim that it goes beyond the commitments that they have to undertake in the on-going round. This is now the primary issue holding up the Doha negotiations which is into its tenth year. According to WTO Director General Pascal Lamy, while the Doha round is stuck in a deadlock, the relevance of the multilateral institute has not yet waned. WTO is a member driven organization and its negotiations are a collective enterprise, India is a good example of how trade can be leveraged

3. Muchkund Dubey, WTO Hong Kong Declaration : An Appraisal, *EPW*, Jan. 7, 2006.

to achieve growth and reduce poverty," he added. As per WTO estimates, the Doha round that seeks to open up trade further in goods and services, is expected to result in gains worth $282 billion.

Another important aspect of NAMA negotiations pertain to *Non-Tariff Barriers* (NTBs). With regard to this, India is one of the initial proponents of the Horizontal Mechanism (HM) proposal. It aims to bring in a ministerial decision on "Procedures for the facilitation of NTBs.. This proposal has received the support of more than 100 WTO Member countries. Though the Doha mandate refers to NTBs in the context of 'products of export interest to developing countries', there have been some moves to utilise this increasing market access of remanufactured goods by some countries, led by United States of America.

The Services Negotiations at the WTO

In services India has been a demandeur. It has also offered substantial sectoral and modal coverage in its initial and revised offers which are subject to the conditions of receiving satisfaction in respect of its Mode 1 and Mode 4 requests. India is the coordinator of the plurilateral requests in Model (cross-border supply) and Mode 4 (Movement of Natural Persons) - the crore areas of its interest in the services negotiations. India is also co-sponsor of plurilateral requests in computer and related services (CRS) and architectural, engineering and integrated engineering services.

India has shown considerable movement from Uruguay Round commitments to revised offers; however its primary requests in Modes 1 and 4 have not been addressed by key developed countries. Some of the major developed country members have shown little or no movement in their Mode 4 offers which is a major cause of concern to India. The US and other developed countries such as Australia are trying to introduce a new approach to services negotiations by way of the clustering initiative. India has opposed this cluster approach on procedural as well as substantive grounds. The lack of progress in services under the Doha Round is not due to problems with the approach of negotiations but because of lack of political will, inadequate response from developed countries in sectors and areas of export interest to developing countries, and little movement in agriculture and NAMA.

Rules Negotiations at Doha Round Talks

Negotiations are taking place in the Negotiating Group of Rules (NGR) aimed at clarifying and improving disciplines under the Anti-Dumping Agreement and the Agreement on Subsidies and Countervailing Measures (ASCM), while preserving the basic concepts, principles, and effectiveness of these agreements and their instruments and objectives. Members are also discussing new disciplines for fisheries subsidies.

Consensus eludes on the bigger issues in anti-dumping such as zeroing, sunset reviews, lesser duty rule, public interest, causation, and anti-circumvention. In Subsidies Agreement, considerable divergence remains in the proposals on specific subsidies in the case of inputs provided at regulated prices, and benchmarks for export finance. India has been seeking strengthened anti-dumping rules so as to prohibit the use of zeroing in dumping margin calculation, strengthening of the rules for conduct of sunset reviews, and mandatory application of lesser duty. In the Subsidies Agreement, India is opposed to the enlargement of the scope of prohibited subsidies in the ASCM and /or limiting of the existing flexibilities for the developing countries. In the negotiations on the new disciplines on fisheries subsidies, India is seeking effective special and differential (S&D) treatment for the developoing countries, particularly in the light of employment and livelihood concerns for small, artisanal fishing communities and for retaining sufficient 'policy space' so as to enable it to develop its infrastructure.

Trade Facilitation at Doha Round Negotiations

Another important area of the Doha round is the negotiations on trade facilitation. Simplification of trade procedures by reducing trading costs is in the interest of all WTO members. A Draft Consolidated Negotiation Text on Trade Facilitation was worked out by the WTO members on 14 December 2009. The draft text has since been revised six times in 2010 through discussions in the meetings of the Negotiating Group on Trade Facilitation. India has been actively participating in these meetings and has also tabled a few proposals on 'Customs Cooperation', Rapid Alerts System of Customs Union', and 'Appeal Mechanism', Developed countries do not want to change their trade procedures but expect others to do so. Developing countries have, by and large, adopted an extra defensive approach to negotiations. Least developed countries, in general, do not want to undertake any binding commitment. Capacity constraints and lack of resources are two major factors that prevent developing countries (and least developed countries) from taking on binding commitments in trade facilitation. The current scenario indicates that developed countries and other donors may not invest in building physical infrastructure in these countries, although the July 2004 Framework Agreement clearly links commitments to support and assistance for infrastructure development. It is important that this linkage is respected by the entire WTO membership particularly the developed countries and that of adequate assistance is provided for implementation of commitments so that a high standard agreement on trade facilitation can be reached.

The Doha Round of trade negotiations in the WTO which began in 2001 remains unfinished due to differences among members on various issues. The Eighth Ministerial Meeting of the WTO which was held in December 2011 in Geneva provided political guidance to the members to resolve the issues involved. However, there was no significant progress in 2012. Efforts are being made for an early progress on some issues in time for the Ninth Ministerial Conference of the WTO (MC9) to be held in December 2013. India is of the view that any yearly outcome of the negotiations should in invariably address issues of interest to the developing countries, especially the least developed countries (LDCs) and the small vulnerable economies.

A Draft Consolidated Negotiating Text on Trade Facilitation was worked out by the WTO members on 14 December 2009. The Draft Text has since been revised fourteen times (till December 2012) through discussions in the meetings of the **Negotiating Group on Trade Facilitation** (NGTF). India is actively engaged in these negotiations and has also tabled a few proposals on 'Customs Cooperation', 'Rapid Alerts System of Customs Union', and 'Appeal Mechanism'. The Draft Text, however, lacks internal balance. The developed countries are holding up the laws and procedures of their own countries as benchmarks and want the developing countries to replicate them. Developing countries have by and large adopted a defensive approach in the negotiations. The developed countries and a few developing countries are making efforts to achieve '*Trade facilitation*' for an early outcome, in time for the Nineteenth Ministerial Conference. *India along with most of the developing countries wants issues of market access and trade facilitation to be balanced with developmental issues such as duty free quota, free market access for LDCs, and acceptance of the modalities for reducing cotton subsidies.* The G33 group of countries, which is a coalition of 46 developing countries, including India, has tabled a proposal on food security in the WTO on 16 November 2012. The proposal is for an amendment to certain provisions of the WTO Agreement on Agriculture to allow developing countries great flexibility in their public stockholding operations for food security purposes. The issue of food security is very important for India and any concession on the trade facilitation front needs to be balanced by acceptance of the G33 proposal in any package deal for the Nineteenth Ministerial Conference.

During the 2012-13 some of the developed countries members of the **Information Technology Agreement** (ITA) of WTO viz, the USA, European Union, and Japan, have proposed expansion of the agreement (called ITA-2) to increase the coverage of IT products on which customs duty would be bound at zero, addressing non-tariff measures, and expanding the number of signatory countries to include new signatories such as Argentina, Brazil and South Africa. The proponents of ITA expansion have prepared a consolidated list containing around 350 IT products (combining products of interest to all proponents of ITA-2) on which tariff reductions are being sought. This is under active discussion in the WTO and India is carefully examining the proposal.

Negotiations in services have continued primarily in the plurilateral format. Intensive negotiations were held in 2009, 2010, and also till the first half of 2011. These efforts culminated in a report by the **Chair of the Committee on Trade in Services (CTS)** and all subsidiary bodies under the CTS in April 2011. The Chair's report puts forth two views. The developed countries' view is that further progress on market access could include the binding of autonomous liberalization where possible, improved levels of access under commercial presence mode, that is, Mode 3 (including restrictions on foreign equity participation and forms of commercial presence). The developing countries view is that there is imbalance in market access negotiations as sectors of export interest to them are not being fully reflected in developed countries' offer.

BTIATERAL AND REGIONAL COOPERATION

While India has always stood for an open, equitable, predictable, non-discriminatory, and rule based multilateral trading system(MTS), it has also been active in recent years with regional trading arrangements (RTAs), to serve as 'building blocks' for achieving trade liberalization and complementing the MTS. So far, India has signed 10 free trade agreements (FTAs) and 5 preferential trade agreements (PTAs) and these FTAs/PTAs are already in force. Further, India is currently negotiating 17 FTAs, including review/expansion of som existing ones. Some of India's recent trade arrangements/aggreements are briefly explained below :

1. **Agreement on South Asia Free Trade Area (SAFTA):** The SAFTA Agreement was signed on 1 January 2004 and came into force on 1 January 2006. Under SAFTA, India has granted zero basic custom duty to all LDCs, viz. Afghanistan, Bangladesh, Bhutan, and Maldives, on all items except 25 items relating to alcohol and tobacco. Under the SAFTA Agreement, India has reduced the SAFTA Sensitive List for non-LDCs from 878 to 614 by reduction of 264 tariff lines w.e.f. 6 September 2012. As per the schedule of Tariff Liberalisation Programme (TLP) under SAFTA, India has brought down its peak tariff rates to 5 per cent w.e.f. 1.1.2013

2. **India-Thailand FTA, Early Harvest Scheme (EHS) under the Framework Agreement for establishing India- Thailand FTA:** On 9th October 2003, India and Thailand signed a Framework Agreement for establishing an India-Thailand FT A, which includes trade in goods, trade in services, investment, and other areas of economic cooperation, to be concluded as a single undertaking. Under the Early Harvest Scheme (EHS), tariff has gradually been eliminated on a list of 82 common items simultaneously by both sides between 1 September 2004 and 31 August 2006. Under the India-Thailand FTA, it is proposed to provide ASEA plus tariff concessions. So far 26 rounds of the India-Thailand Trade Liberalisation Committee (IIT C) meetings have been held. The last round was held on 26-27 November 2012 in New Delhi.

3. **India-ASEA Comprehensive Economic Cooperation Agreement (CECA):** *Services and Investment Agreements.* The Trade in Goods Agreement, which was signed on 13 August 2009 under the broader framework of the CECA between India and ASEAN has already come into force. Conclusions of negotiations for trade in Services Agreement and Investment Agreement have been announced during the ASEAN-India Commemorative Summit held on 20 December 2012 in New Delhi. Legal framework for these Agreements was to be finalized by February, 2013. The Agreement was signed during ASEAN Economic Ministers (AEM) India Consultations in August 2013.

4. **Regional Comprehensive Economic Partnership (RCEP) Agreement among ASEAN + 6 (Australia, China, India, Japan, Korea, and New Zealand):** During the 20th ASEAN Summit held in Cambodia in April 2012, ASEAN States agreed to move towards establishing an RCEP involving ASEAN and its FTA partners. The objective of launching RCEP negotiations is to achieve a modem, comprehensive, high-quality, and mutually beneficial economic partnership agreement among the ASEA member States and ASEAN's FT A partners. The RCEP will cover trade in goods, trade in services, investment, economic and technical cooperation, intellectual property, competition, dispute settlement, and other issues.

5. **India - EU Broad Based Trade and Investment Agreement (BTIA):** Fifteen rounds of negotiations and a number of international and Chief Negotiator level meetings have been held till date. The 15th round was held during 4-7 December, 2012 in New Delhi. Chief negotiator level meeting was held on 29-30 January, 2013 in New Delhi.

6. **Global System of Trade Preferences (GSTP):** The Agreement establishing the GSTP among developing countries was signed on 13 April 1988 at Belgrade following the conclusion of the First Round of Negotiations. Forty-three countries have ratified the Agreement and become participant. India has offered tariff concessions on 70.08 per cent of dutiable tariff lines with an across-the-board *margin of preference* (MoP) of 20 per cent on the applied tariffs prevailing on the date of import. India has also unilaterally offered special concessions to LDC participants by granting an MoP of 25 per cent on 77 per cent of all its dutiable tariff lines. The Cabinet Committee on Economic Affairs (CCEA), in its meeting on 23 August 2012, has granted approval for implementing India's schedule of concessions. The tariff concessions are to be implemented thirty days after a minimum of four participants ratify their schedules of concessions . So far India and Malaysia have ratified their schedules.

Diversifying Technology-Intensive Export Products through the Regional Agreement[1]

In the current situation when WTO negotiations are stalled world trade has slowed down and the shadow of protectionist measures loom large, a strategy of diversifying technology-intensive exports through the regional process could lead to further trade promotion with trade liberalisation.

Two trends in international trade are of great importance in the current global economic environment. One, the growing importance of technology-intensive exports and two, the increasing role of regional trade. Tradable products can be classified into five different groups based on the technology intensity. (1) Primary products have very little technology basis for retaining comparative advantage, (2) resource-based products having competitive advantages, generally arising from local availability of natural resources and using simple and labour-intensive technology, (3) low technology products having simple technologies mainly embodied in capital equipment. With labour constituting a major clement of cost in competitiveness and operating under low-scale economies with low entry barriers, (4) medium technology products comprising skill- and scale-intensive technologies in capital and intermediate products where product development takes place with complex technologies, involving high level of research and development (R&D) expenditure and which require lengthy learning periods and are subject to high entry barriers, and (5) high technology products having advanced and fast changing technologies with emphasis on product design requiring high R&D investment, sophisticated infrastructures, high levels of specialized technical skills, and close interactions between firms and universities' research institutions.

Trends in global trade indicate that there has been a proliferation of trade in technology-intensive manufacturing products. Among the globally dynamic products of trade, a significant proportion of items are high and medium technology-intensive items. India has been diversifying into technology

1. This analysis is based on study by S.K. Mohanty, (2013), '*Examining Diversification of India's Exports to Developing Countries in a Situation of Partially Affected Global Economy by Recession*'.

intensive products with a fair amount of success with exports of high technology and medium technology products growing faster than the total exports of India during 2004-2011 (Table 32.1). Further, diversifying India's exports to include more technology-intensive product groups is of vital importance.

Table 32.1. India's Trade with technology Intensive products

	CAGR		
	2004 to 2007	2007 to 2011	2004 to 2011
1.Primary products	25.3	17.6	20.8
2.Resources based products	32.4	20.0	25.2
3.Low technology products	13.3	14.5	14.0
4.Medium technology products	27.0	20.0	23.0
5.High technolgoy products	26.6	26.9	26.8
Total exports	24.3	18.8	21.2

In the present global trading environment, export promotion is more strategically pursued through the regional approach., India's export compound annual growth rate (CAGR) is faster with most of the 21 RT As (covering more than 100 countries) considered here (based on India's level of exports with them, India's membership in some of them, and India's engagement with other continents including Africa), than its overall export CAGR of 19.1 per cent during 1999-2000 to 2010-11. Asia is emerging as the most important destination for India's exports through the regional process.

Export potential in medium and high technology-intensive products varies across different RTAs. Decomposition of export potential products into their technology intensities in different regional blocs shows possibility of trade diversification for India in hi-tech product segments. Empirical evidence suggests that India can diversify its exports of technology-intensive products to RTAs. The EU, NAFTA, RCEP, APTA, ASEAN, IOR-RAC, etc. could be some important export destinations with sizeable trade opportunities for technology-intensive exports, though some of these regional arrangements overlap.

Focused product-market diversification trade and marketing strategies should necessarily entail diversifying India's trade basket, particularly in favour of high and medium technology-intensive products in the targeted RTAs, While this type focus could also help in avoiding the adverse effects of some RTAs concentrating on primary products involving livelihood concerns of a significant portion of our agricultural and rural communities, care should be taken to *avoid* inverted duty structures in the 'quid-pro-quo' during RT A negotiations.

The challenges for India on the trade front are many. While India has successfully diversified its export basket, more needs to be done on the market diversification front. It also has to reposition itself in its traditional areas of strength like textiles and leather & leather manufactures where it has lost considerable ground, while at the same time making forays into new areas, With multilateral trade negotiations stalled, and RTAs on the rise, India also has to follow a strategic regional trading policy focusing on the potential technology-intensive items in the more important RTAs, Though geopolitical considerations are important, India may have to bargain more in its regional trade negotiations, particularly in cases where livelihood concerns of large pockets of the population are involved, There is also need to address the inverted duty structure in sectors like electronics, textiles, and chemicals and the artificial inverted duty structure caused by some FTAs/RTAs, In the case of services trade, a gold mine of opportunity in sectors like tourism including health tourism is waiting to be tapped.

QUESTIONS FOR REVIEW

1. Why has WTO been established? Explain its role in promoting world trade.
2. Explain how India has gained from becoming a member of WTO.
3. How agreements reached at WTO will affect (a) Indian agriculture and farmers (b) Indian industry.
4. Discuss the objects and functions of WTO (World Trade Organisation)
5. What are the main features of WTO ? What are its functions ?
6. What is meant by globalisation? How does WTO promote globalisation?
7. What is liberalisation of trade? What steps have been taken by WTO to promote trade liberalisation?
8. What is multilateral trading system ? How is it better than bilateral trade agreement ?
9. Explain briefly why ministerial level talks udner the aegis of WTO at Cancun failed.
10. What is 'Doha Round of Development'? What progress has been made in this regard ?
11. Explain the main features of WTO's Hong Kong Declaration. Critically exame how India and other developing countries will gain from it ?
12. Explain the TRIPS agreement. What progress has been made in implementing this agreement ?
13. Describe Doha Round negotiations with regard to trade in (1) agriculture,. (2) manufactured products (3) services. What are the hindrances to the conclusion of these negotiations.
14. Explain briefly various bilateral and regional trade agreements signed by India. How will they benefit India ?
15. Explain how through regional agreements India has attempted to diversity *technology-intensive* export products.

PART — VII

SOME ASPECTS OF INDIA'S BUSINESS ENVIRONMENT

- Role of Fiscal Policy and Taxation in Economic Development
- Fiscal Policy: Government Borrowing for Financing of Budget Deficit
- Resource Mobilisation through Money Financing of Fiscal Deficit
- Fiscal Deficit and Economic Growth
- India's Financial Sector Reforms
- Industrial Policy in India
- Public Sector and Privatisation in India
- Industrial Sickness in India
- Consumer Rights and Consumer Protection
- Planning in India
- Global Financial Crisis and its Impact on the Indian Economy
- Environment, Climate Change and Sustainable Development

Chapter 33

Role of Fiscal Policy and Taxation in Economic Development

Introduction

In this chapter we shall explain the role of fiscal policy for mobilising resources for economic growth and for achieving the objectives of equity and stability. We will first explain the various sources of public revenue and pattern of government expenditure. We shall examine the implications of fiscal deficit in the next chapter. Today, since Government plays a crucial role in the working of an economy, understanding of its budget is of great importance. *Budget is a statement of the estimates of revenue and expenditure of the government for a year.* The year for which the government presents its annual budget is called the *fiscal year.* In India, both for the central and state governments the fiscal year starts from April 1 of a year and ends on March 31, next year.

The Government announces its fiscal policy in its annual budget. Fiscal policy relates to how the government raises its revenue and how it spends it. What new taxes are levied, what changes in the existing tax rates are made, how much expenditure government wants to spend on defence, education, health, capital formation, economic infrastructure are all proposed in the budget. Since budget affects the economic life of the people, especially the business class, presentation of annual budget by the Finance Minister is eagerly awaited by every body.

Classical economists were of the view that sound budget should always be balanced, that is, government expenditure should equal Government revenue. They thought that deficit budget meant more borrowing by the government to meet the increased expenditure. According to them, this increases public debt which raises the burden on future generations. However, after Keynesian revolution role of budget has underwent a basic change. Today budget is not regarded as a mere *instrument for raising revenue for the government. Instead, budget is an important tool of economic policy to achieve certain objectives.* At times of recession, there is a need to increase aggregate demand. To overcome recession, the government should increase its expenditure and lower taxes and make a deficit budget. This will help to raise aggregate demand and achieve equilibrium at full-employment. On the contrary, at times of severe inflation government has to reduce its expenditure and increase direct taxes so as to eliminate excess demand. Thus, balanced budgets are no longer considered as sacred. Whether government budget should be balanced, deficit or surplus depends on the prevailing economic situation and the objectives of economic policy. Thus, after Keynesian revolution budget making has acquired a functional role of maintaining economic stability at full-employment level. Later, promoting steady growth in the long run also became the objective of fiscal policy both in the developed and developing countries. Therefore, *the present view of budget making is not one of mere resource raising for the government but one of serving as an instrument for promoting full employment, price stability and steady economic growth.* This view of budget making as a tool for performing some economic functions or achieving certain economic policy objectives has been called as *Function Finance.*

Government Budgeting in India

As mentioned above, the *Government budget is annual financial statement giving the estimates of revenue and expenditure of the government for a year.* Budget of the government has two parts:

1. Revenue Account
2. Capital Account

Revenue Account. In the revenue account, on the receipts side, revenue raised through taxes, both direct and indirect, fees, dividends and profits of public undertakings are given. It is important to note that the *revenue receipts are those that neither create a liability for repayment, nor cause any reduction in assets of the government*. On the expenditure side of the revenue account, *recurrent or consumption expenditure of the Government* on purchases of goods, on health and education and on services required to meet the needs of defence, public administration, and expenditure on subsidies on food, fertilisers and exports, and interest payments on the public debt are given for a fiscal year.

Capital Account. In the capital account the main items of receipts are (*a*) recoveries of loans which the government has given to the State and local governments (*b*) market borrowing by the government from the public, banks and other financial institutions (*c*) small-savings (*i.e.*, Provident Fund, National Savings Scheme etc.) (*d*) proceeds from disinvestment of public sector enterprises (*e*) foreign assistance from other countries. *The distinguishing feature of capital receipts is that they either create a liability for the government or cause disinvestment of government assets.*

The important items of the expenditure in the capital account are defence expenditure, loans to public enterprises for development purposes, loans to governments of States and Union Territories. *The distinguishing feature of capital expenditure is that it is incurred on building durable assets* such as machinery and equipments, buildings, roads and highways, dams, irrigation facilities, steel plants etc. It is in fact investment expenditure. Capital expenditure is therefore highly important because it promotes growth and development.

Direct and Indirect Taxes

The taxes have been classified into two types: direct and indirect taxes. They can be progressive, proportional or regressive. Further, indirect taxes can be *specific or ad valorem*. The distinction between direct and indirect taxes is based on whether or not the burden of a tax can be shifted wholly or partly to others. If a tax is such that its burden cannot be shifted to others and the person who pays it to government has also to bear its burden, it is called a direct tax. Income tax, corporation tax, gift tax annual wealth tax, expenditure tax, capital gains tax are examples of direct taxes. In case of a direct tax there is a direct contact between the tax payer and tax-levying public authority.

On the other hand, indirect taxes are those whose burden can be shifted to others so that those who pay these taxes to the government do not bear the whole burden but pass it on wholly or partly to others. Excise duties, customs duties and service tax are important examples of indirect taxes levied by the central government in India. For instance, excise duty on the production of sugar is an indirect tax because the manufactures of sugar include the excise duty in the price of the product and pass it on to the buyers. Ultimately, it is the consumers on whom the incidence of excise duty on sugar falls as they will pay higher price for sugar than before the imposition of the tax. Thus, though excise duties are taxes on the production of commodities but they can be shifted to the consumers. Similarly, the *service tax* is a recent indirect tax levied by the central government in India. It is imposed on such services as telephone, insurance, transport etc. The burden of service tax is also passed on to the users of the services. Likewise, sales tax on commodities can also be passed on to the buyers or consumers in the form of higher prices charged for the commodities. Therefore, excise duties and sales taxes on commodities are examples of the indirect taxes. They are also known as *commodity taxes*. In the case of indirect taxes, there is an indirect relation between the government and those who ultimately bear the burden of the taxes.

Objectives of Fiscal Policy in India

In a developing country such as India taxation, Government expenditure and borrowing have to play a very important role in accelerating economic development. In fact, fiscal policy is a powerful instrument in the hands of the Government by means of which it can achieve the objectives of economic growth. Rapid economic growth is needed to solve the problem of poverty and unemployment. There are several peculiar characteristics of a developing country which necessitate the adoption of a special fiscal policy which ensures a rapid economic growth. There are vast and diverse resources, human and material, which are lying underutilised in a developing country. Such countries have weak infrastructure, *i.e*, they lack adequate means of transport and communications, roads, ports, highways, irrigation and power. They also lack technical know-how. Indian population is increasing at a rapid rate which necessitates rapid economic growth to meet the requirements of the rapidly-growing population. Above all, there are acute problems of mass poverty and unemployment which for their solution require proper economic policies. In order to tackle these problems, a suitable fiscal and taxation policy is called for.

The principal objectives of fiscal policy in a developing economy are:

1. to mobilise resources for economic growth, especially for the public sector;
2. to promote economic growth in the private sector by providing incentives to save and invest;
3. to restrain inflationary forces in the economy in order to ensure price stability; and
4. to ensure equitable distribution of income and wealth so that fruits of economic growth are fairly distributed, that is, to achieve **inclusive growth**.

In developing countries like India, budget has to play a more important role.The developing countries face a more difficult problem of how to generate a higher economic growth so as to tackle the problems of poverty and unemployment. Therefore, fiscal policy has to play a special role of promoting economic growth in the developing countries like India so as to tackle the twin problems of poverty and unemployment. Besides, like the industrialised developed countries, India has been facing the problem of *inflation* from time to time. Inflation adversely affects economic growth and hurts the poor most. Therefore, besides accelerating economic growth, fiscal policy has to control inflation and thus to ensure price stability. Besides, fiscal policy has to reduce large inequalities of income distribution and to ensure just distribution of fruits of economic growth. In the words of our Finance Minister P. Chidambaram budget has to "*strike a fine balance among three mutually reinforcing objectives of growth, stability and equity.*"[1] Further, for developing countries mere economic growth is not enough; the budgetary policies should be so designed so as to ensure removal of poverty and unemployment. Therefore, the function of the government budget has not only to raise resources for development and to achieve optimum allocation of resources, but also has to promote fair distribution of income and expansion in employment opportunities. This is the functional view of public finance in the context of the developing countries.

ROLE OF FISCAL POLICY FOR MOBILISATION OF RESOURCES FOR ECONOMIC GROWTH

In the Indian economy, the Government has to play a very active role in promoting economic growth and fiscal policy is an important instrument that the state must use. In a democratic society, there is an inherent dislike for direct (physical) controls and regulation by the state. The entrepreneurs would not like to be ordered about to produce this or that, how much to produce or where to produce. Fiscal incentives in the form of tax concessions, rebates or subsidies are, therefore, preferable. Similarly, the consumers would not like to be told directly to curtail their consumption or to consume this and not to consume that. Taxation of commodities and services whose consumption is to be discouraged is therefore preferable. Hence, a democratic state must rely on indirect methods of control and regulation and this is done through fiscal and monetary policies. Thus, in democratic countries, fiscal policy is a powerful and least undesirable weapon on which government can rely for promoting economic growth.

Capital formation is of strategic importance for bringing about rapid economic growth. It is, therefore, necessary to achieve a higher ratio of savings to national income. In early days of capital-

1. Budget Speach while presenting Budget for 2004-05, July 8, 2004.

ism, payment of low wages and the existence of inequalities of income helped capital formation is the present-day developed countries. But no democratic country can adopt this method in modern times; the effort rather is to raise wages and reduce inequalities of income and wealth. Under a regime of socialist dictatorship such as that prevailed in erstwhile Soviet Russia capital formation was brought about by ruthlessly curtailing consumption and keeping down the standards of living. But in modern democracies with every adult person having a right to cast vote very low levels of living for a long time is not feasible. *Hence the state must rely on instruments of fical policy to mobilise resources for economic development.* Taxation can be used to to raise collective savings for public investment and also at the same time to promote private investment. A well-conceived scheme of taxation is an important way of raising ratio of savings to national income which is one of the crucial determinants of the rate of economic growth. However, is a liberal mixed economy such as ours the task of fiscal policy is not only to raise saving ratio for acceleration of growth but also to improve investment elimate for private sector so that higher rate of investment be achieved. As Nurkse says, "*public finance assumes a new significance in the face of the problem of capital formation in underdeveloped countries.*"[2]

On the expenditure side, there is positive need for public investment, especially in those spheres of economic activity where the private investments are not easily attracted, for example, the development of power resources, roads and highway, ports and airports, means of transport and communications, basic heavy industries, social infrastructure such as education and research, public health etc. Such investments are very often the very foundations of rapid economic advance. Thus, fiscal policy is of crucial importance in accelerating the pace of economic growth in developing countries.

As mentioned above, capital formation is an important determinant of economic growth. For accelerating the rate of capital formation, savings and investment rate in the economy has to be stepped up. For this purpose savings have to be mobilised and channelled into productive investment. The alternative means other than fiscal policy available to promote savings and investment in the developing countries are not very effective in mobilising enough resources for investment and capital formation.

Fiscal policy has also to promote *voluntary savings*. There exist large inequalities of income in these countries and this should ensure a large voluntary savings by the richer sections of the society. But the richer sections in them indulge in conspicious consumption such as building of luxury houses, indulging in five star culture, buying air-conditioners and such other things and, therefore, the volume of their voluntary savings is inadequate. This propensity to indulge in conspicuous consumption is reinforced by demonstration effect which is operating strongly these days due to the development of better communication system and superior means of advertisement. Further, rich people tend to invest their rising incomes on unproductive investment such as gold and jewellery, real estate etc., which yield high profits due to their appreciation. In view of these, without proper fiscal policy savings cannot be made available for raising significantly the rate of capital formation.

Fiscal policy, if properly designed, is an efficient and equitable way of mobilising resources for augmenting public investment. Through it not only collective public savings can be raised for financing public investment but also at the same time private savings and investment can be encouraged. In fact *taxation may be the most effective means of increasing the total volume of savings and investments in an economy where the propensity to consume is normally high*. Further, the fiscal policy can be so devised that not only the objective of rapid capital accumulation or growth, but also other objectives of economic policy such as equitable distribution of income and wealth, price stability and promotion of employment opportunities can be achieved.

In what follows we shall explain how the various instruments of fiscal policy such as taxation and Government borrowing can be used to mobilise resources for economic development.

2. Ragnar Nurkse, *Problems of Capital Formation in Underdeveloped Countries.*

Government Budget Constraint : Role of Taxation in Financing Economic Development

Government Budget Constraint. The government normally finances its expenditure through receipts from taxes, both direct and indirect. When government expenditure increases and it finds it difficult to raise more resources from taxation, it resorts to borrowing from the public or printing money to finance its budget deficit. Increase in rates of income and other taxes not only adversely affects incentives to work more, save and invest more but also promotes tax evasion. Further, as Laffer curve concept shows increase in rate of a tax beyond a point causes revenue from taxes to decline. Thus there are limits to increasing revenue from taxes to finance the increased expenditure of the government. As result, when government finds it difficult to raise adequate resources to finance its increased expenditure fully through normal taxes, it faces a resource constraint resulting in *budget deficit* which in recent years is also called *fiscal deficit*. Thus government budget constraint *refers to the limit to which the Government can finance its budget deficit by taxation, borrowing from the market (i.e., through sale of its bonds) or using printed money*. The Government has to make a choice between the magnitude of borrowing from the market and the magnitude of using printed money to finance its budget deficit written as :

The general from of government budget equation is :

$$G = T + \Delta B + \Delta M \qquad ...(1)$$

Where G stands for government expenditure (including subsidies and interest payments on past debt), T is tax revenue, ΔB is the new borrowing from the market (through sale of bonds or securities) and ΔM is the new printed money issued to finance Government expenditure. According to the budget constraint equation (1), government expenditure in a year can be financed by tax revenue (T), new borrowing (ΔB) by the government from the market (both within and outside the country) through sale of its bonds, and by creating new high powered money (ΔM) which is also called *money financing*. The Government budget constraint can be rewritten as :

$$G - T = \Delta B + \Delta M \qquad ...(2)$$

$G - T$ represents budget deficit (also called fiscal deficit) that must be financed by new borrowing (ΔB) by the government through sale of bonds and by creation of new high powered money (ΔM) which is called *money financing*. Thus

Budget Deficit = New Borrowing (*i. e.,* Sale of Bonds by the Government) + Printed Money

The budget deficit (fiscal deficit) can be financed either by *printing money* (also called *seiniorage*) by the government or by *selling bonds* to the public (which includes banks, insurance companies, mutual funds and other financial institutions). It is through sale of bonds that the government borrows from the market which adds to the government debt. The government has to pay interest annually on its debt and have also to pay back the principal sum borrowed at the maturity of bonds or securities. Besides, borrowing by the Government leads to the rise in interest rate which crowds out private investment. On the other hand it Government finances its budget deficit by using printed money, it can lead to inflation. Thus due to budget constraint, the Government has to make a difficult choice between borrowing from the market and using printed money to finance its budget deficit. Financing through the use of printed money is also called *money financing*.

In times of recessionary conditions which arise due to the deficiency of aggregate demand J.M. Keynes argued for the adoption of deliberate policy of framing a budget deficit to get rid of recession and restore full-employment equilibrium. In recent years there has been a considerable debate among economists about the appropriate methods of financing the budget deficits and their consequences. It is important to discuss the consequencies of budget deficit and the mode of its financing as there has been persistent large budget deficits year after year not only in developed countries such as the United States but also in the developing countries such as India resulting in mounting burden of public debt on the one hand and inflation on the other.

Direct Taxes and Mobilisation of Resources

Now the question arises what should be the taxation structure of a developing economy which will mobilise the potential economic surplus to the maximum, that is, what kinds of taxes be levied, how much progressive should be their rates and what should be the exemptions and concessions in various taxes. This is, however, a highly controversial issue. It has been suggested that an appropriate tax which would mobilise resources or mop up economic surplus is the progressive income tax. Income tax is imposed not only on the incomes of individuals but also on the profits of the corporate companies. Thus there is *personal income tax* and *corporate income tax* (that is, tax on net profits earned by corporate companies). In India and the other developing countries income has been regarded as a good base for direct taxation. And the imposition of highly progressive income tax not only mops up relatively greater amount of resources but also tend to reduce inequalities of income. However, a progressive income tax with a high marginal rates of taxes adversely affects private saving and investment and also raises the propensity to evade the tax. In view of this, two proposals have been put forward to make the income tax both as an effective instrument of resource mobilisation for the public sector and of providing incentives to save and invest. First, Prof. Kaldor of Cambridge University, who in 1956 was invited by Government of India to suggest reforms in the Indian tax system for mobilising resources for development, suggested that whereas the marginal rate of income tax be reduced to, say, 45 to 50 per cent, expenditure tax be levied to discourage the people belonging to upper income brackets from dissipating their income in conspicuous consumption. According to him, this will also reduce the tendency to evade income tax on the one hand and promote private savings on the other. The second proposal to reform the income tax put forward by others is that whereas marginal rates of income tax be kept high but some exemptions for approved forms of saving and investment be allowed to the individuals. This will channel individual savings along desired lines and at the same time mobilise resources for development.

Apart from the income tax on individuals and companies, the imposition of other direct taxes such as capital gains tax, wealth tax, gift tax, and estate duty are also needed to mobilise sufficient resources for capital formation. Unlike income tax, these capital taxes do not have any adverse effects on incentives to save and invest.[3] They are also important instruments of reducing inequalities of income and wealth. Because of these advantages, Professor Kaldor in his report of taxation reforms in India recommended the imposition of these capital taxes and this recommendation was accepted and the annual wealth tax and gift tax were levied in 1957 with estate duty having been already introduced in 1954.

Agricultural Taxation and Resource Mobilisation. A major part of national income in India and other developing countries originates in the agricultural sector which has substantial economic surplus which can be tapped for capital formation. This economic surplus mainly goes to rich farmers, landlords, merchants and other intermediaries and, in the absence of suitable taxation on agriculture, this is used for conspicuous consumption and for investing in unproductive activities such as buying gold, jewellery, real estate. Thus, according to Professor Kaldor, "*the taxation of agriculture by one means or another has a critical role to play in the acceleration of economic development*."[4] Further, owing to economic growth in general and agricultural development in par-ticular income of the agricultural class and therefore economic surplus enormously increases and therefore need to be mopped up for further development. Besides, the agricultural sector has to be taxed not only because it has a potential surplus but also to achieve maximium utilisation of land through devising a system of land taxation which would penalise poor use of good land. In this regard, a progressive land tax "the effective rates of taxation of which vary with the total value of landholdings of the family unit" may be suitable one. Besides this, progressive agricultural income

3. See, S. Gulati, *Capital Taxation in India*, Orient Longman, 1957.
4. N. Kaldor, The Role of Taxation in Economic Development, in E.A.G. Robinson (ed.), *Problems in Economic Development*, 1965, p. 177.

tax with appropriate exemption may be levied to tap resources from affluent sections of the agricultural sector.

It may be noted that as compared to the non-agricultural sector, agricultural sector in India and other developing countries is quite under-taxed. Land revenue which was at one time the greatest source of revenue for government has now become an insignificant yielder of revenue. In the context of India, Agricultural Taxation Committee under the Chairmanship of Dr. K.N. Raj recommended Agricultural Holdings Tax (AHT) which was to be imposed at a progressive rate on the rateable value of an agricultural holdings of ₹ 5000 and above. It was expected to yield annually ₹ 200 crores. However, Agricultural Holdings Tax was found to be difficult to assess and administer. In our view, a *graded surcharge on the existing land revenue* will be far easier to assess and administer and make land revenue a more elastic source of revenue. In 2002, Kelkar Committe on tax reforms also recommended imposition of tax on agricultural income, proceeds from which were to be distributed among the states. But this was vehemently opposed by the members of the ruling party. However, it may be noted that in India agricultural taxation is a state subject and there is lack of political will on the part of the State Governments to raise the level of land taxation in a country. But if sufficient resources are to be mobilised for development, the level of agricultural taxation has to be raised.

Merits of Direct Taxes for Resource Mobilisation

As seen above, as an instrument of resource mobilisation for development direct taxes enjoy several advantages. (1) They raise resources in a non-inflationary way. Indeed, by reducing disposable incomes of the people direct taxes tend to check inflation by curtailing consumption demand. (2) If they are made progreessive, they help to reduce inequalities of income and wealth, and thus help in achieving the equity objective, and (3) Progressive direct taxes discourage conspicuous and non-necessary consumption and thereby enlarge economic surplus. But the direct taxation of income and wealth has its own limits. The coverage of direct taxes is quite narrow and difficult to expand. For instance, in India out of 125 crore of population only about 3 crore individuals of the population come within the purview of income tax as incomes of the majority of the people fall below the exemption limit which in 2012-13 budget was raised to the annual income of ₹ 200,000. Moreover, there is a considerable evasion of income tax. Yield from other direct taxes such as wealth tax, gift tax is quite meagre due to very small coverage, low rates and considerable evasion of them. However, in India due to buyoncy of personal income tax and corporate tax percentage share of direct taxes in gross tax revenue of the central Government greatly went up to 58.9 per cent in 2009-10 from 41 per cent in 2003-04. This reflects sharp improvement in equity of our tax system. In 2011-12, the share of direct taxes (personal income tax and corporation tax) was 54.9 per cent.

Role of Indirect Taxes in Resource Mobilisation

As a result of limitations of direct taxes, developing countries have resorted to extensive use of indirect taxes. *In India, almost all commodities have been brought within the net of indirect taxes such as excise duties and sales tax. Besides, there are custom duties* (*i.e., taxes on imports and exports*). Indirect taxation is an important source of development funds in a developing country such as India. In the last five decades of planned development, revenue from several indirect taxes has been rising . It has been pointed out by some economists that indirect taxes are better suited to the conditions obtaining in developing countries for reducing current consumption and mobilising resources for development. This is because in such countries quite a large proportion of national income tends to be diverted to current consumption instead of being productively invested. The average propensity to consume in such countries is much higher than is the case in advanced countries. Indirect taxes which reduce consumption must thus play a more important part. They will raise the rate of savings which are so essential for economic growth. It may be noted that indirect tax system can also be made progressive by levying higher indirect taxes on income-elastic *luxuries* such as cars, air conditioners, air travel. This will serve the equity objective, apart from making larger contribution to resource mobilisation for economic growth. Similarly, imposing higher indirect tax on harmful commodities such as cigaretless and alcohol will serve a useful social purpose of discouraging their consumption. *"High rates of taxes on commodities with a high income elasticity of demand are quite effective in siphoning a substantial proportion of increase in output into the resources of the public sector needed for development financing and a higher rate of commodity taxes on luxury articles tends to introduce an element of progressiveness in an otherwise predominantly regressive tax structure in developing countries."*[5]

But in order to make sure that the resources raised through commodity taxes are adequate, it will be necessary to extend their coverage to include some goods of mass consumption. In the poor countries, it is not possible to exempt entirely goods of general and necessary consumption, because they are the only goods that provide a base broad enough to assure an adequate amount of resources. It may be noted that revenue from indirect taxes has substantially increased during the six decades of development (1951-2010). From a small sum of ₹ 227 crore in 1950-51, the revenue raised from indirect taxes rose to about ₹ 5,04,423 crore in 2012-13 (BE). Moreover, the share of indirect takes to gross tax revenue (direct plus indirect taxes) was about 44 per cent in 2012-13.

It is thus clear that for mobilisation of resources for growth and capital formation indirect taxes have made an important contribution. But due to reduction in customs duties and union excise duty on the one hand and a large increase in revenue from direct taxes such as personal income tax and corporation tax on the other, share of indirect taxes in gross tax revenue of Central Government has declined from 78.4 per cent in 1990-91 to 44 per cent in 2011-12. Now, about 55 per cent of GDP in India comes through 'services'. Therefore, to increase the tax base for indirect taxation, more than 120 services have been brought in the net of the service tax. In 2011-12, revenue from service tax was estimated at ₹ 97,579 crores and for 2013-14 service tax is estimated to yield 1.80 lakh crore. It is expected that in future service tax will make a substantial conribution to the mobilisation of resources for economic growth. To improve the indirect tax structure, broaden its base and rationalise the rates a single indirect tax called **'Goods and Services Tax (GST)'** is proposed to be introduced in near future. This new indirect tax GST will replace CENVAT (which is a central excise duty levied by the central government on the basis of value added) and service tax levied by the Centre and VAT levied by the States. We will explain GST in detail later in this chapter.

Limitations. But there are some limitations of raising resources through indirect taxes. First, they lead to *cost-push inflation*. The burden of indirect taxes are passed on to the consumers in the form of higher prices charged from them. In India excise duties on sugar, cloth, kerosene oil, petrol etc., has raised the prices and have contributed a good deal to cost-push inflation witnessed in past some years. Secondly, levying of custom duties on imports of capital goods, raw materials used for industrial production have accelerated cost-push inflation in the Indian economy. Thirdly, imposition of custom duties on imports of goods also protect inefficiency in domestic industries. This also contributes to high-cost production and promotes inefficiency. Fourthly, indirect taxes are *regressive* in nature; both the rich and poor have to pay the same rate on the taxed commodities. The regressive character of indirect taxes have been attempted to be reduced by imposing higher rates of excise and custom duties on luxury items and smaller rates of duties on goods of mass consumption. However, the need for mobilising greater resources have forced the finance ministers to levy higher indirect taxes even on articles of mass consumption. Lastly, the higher excise duties, customs duties and service tax lead to higher prices of Indian goods and thus adversely affect competitiveness of Indian goods in the foreign markets. Due to these shortcomings of indirect tax the reforms undertaken in India since 1991 seek to bring about a compositional shift from excessive

5. R.N. Tripathy, *Public Finance in Developing Countries*, 1966, p. 200.

dependence on indirect taxes to direct taxes and provide for increased competitiveness of the Indian Industry.

Role of Taxation in Promoting Private Saving and Investment

It is worth mentioning that in a mixed economy such as ours, there is need to raise not only the public savings and investment but also to promote private saving and investment so that the overall rate of saving and investment in the economy is stepped up. This implies that taxation measures should not impair incentives to save and invest of the people. Therefore, a developing economy encounters a crucial dilemma in augmenting larger resources for public investment on the one hand and to promote private savings and investment on the other. Thus, according to Prof. Heller, "Tax Policy faces a basic dilemma in its role as a an instrument of capital formation for economic development. On the one hand, high levels of taxes are necessary to finance that part of the development which falls in the government share and to mobilise for investment the private resources that might otherwise be dissipated. On the other hand, the lower the taxes the greater will be the inducement to private investment. The dilemma is worsened by the fact that those taxes which are most effective in capturing a large share of the gains from economic development for further capital formation are the ones most likely to affect the returns from private investment. *Only way of the dilemma may be to combine high rates of taxation in general, with preferential treatment for categories of desired development activity*."

However, the empirical evidence of the last 20 years of tax reforms in India confirms the *Laffer Curve* concept that increase in tax rate beyond a point causes Government revenue to fall. Therefore in our view, moderate rates of tax on income with preferential treatment of some desired development activities such as building of infrastructure can ensure higher private saving and investment. Private savings can be promoted in several other ways. First, interest on several types of private savings such as bank deposits, investment in units of Unit Trust of India and National Savings Certificates, and other approved forms of saving be exempted from taxation to a reasonable extent. This will encourage private savings through raising the rate of return on savings as the savers would earn some interest income free of income tax. Secondly, voluntary savings in certain selective lines such as voluntary contributions to provident fund, life insurance premium, certain specific units (of UTI) and National Savings Certificates be substantially exempted from income tax. This will also stimulate private savings by raising the rate of return on these savings. For, people will not only earn rate of interest or dividend but will save a good amount of income tax on these approved forms of savings.

Thirdly, as noted above, if very high progressivity in tax rates is avoided (that is, if rates of income taxes do not increase much with the increase in income) private saving and investment will be boosted up. The *Laffer curve concept* shows that the policy of moderate progressivity in tax rates will not only help to maintain incentives to save and investment but will also yield more revenue to the Government. In view of the present author, the lower marginal rates of taxes will place more disposable income in the hands of higher income brackets which will tend to raise their conspicuous consumption, especially when goods catering to their frivolous wants are available in abundance these days through both domestic production and imports. As mentioned above, this is reinforced by the international demonstration effect which exercises a strong influence on the consumption behaviour of the richer sections of the Indian society. The increase in consumption can be discouraged by leving expenditure tax as proposed by Nicholas Kaldor.

Besides private savings, private investment can be directly encouraged through taxation. Firstly, in order to stimulate private investment, the *retained profits* which are reinvested by the business firms instead of distributing them among the shareholders can be exempted from taxation or taxed at preferential rates. Secondly, to boost private investment *liberal depreciation and investment allowances* can also to be allowed to the business firms which will be used for purposes of investment in new plant, equipment and machinery. Further, **subsidies on investment**, that is, tax break or tax rebate can also be provided by the Government which generally prove to be a very effective way of promoting private investment.

Another important fiscal method of stimulating private investment in developing countries is *granting of tax holidays or relief from tax on the profits of new enterprises* for some specified period of time. Further, indirect taxes can also be manipulated in a variety of ways to promote private investment in certain selected fields of industrial activity. Thus exemption or lowering of sales tax or excise duties on some domestically produced important raw materials or lowering of import duties on raw materials and capital goods from abroad can provide a boost to private investment. Likewise, reduction of export duties may also bring about a healthy effect on investment outlook.

It needs to be stressed that various incentives to promote private savings and investment will prove effectively only if they are kept as simple, transparent, certain and stable as far as possible. A complicated schemes of incentives with frequent and arbitrary changes are likely to defeat the very purpose of these incentive schemes. Prof. Prest rightly points out, "*If the main purpose of investment incentives is to raise the long-term level of investment rather than offset cyclical downturns and this clearly is the case in underdeveloped countries ... the emphasis should be on the stability of these tax arrangements rather than their variability.*"[6]

It is important to note that private investment depends upon several factors such as size of the market (i.e., aggregate demand), cost of inputs, availability of infrastructure facilities such as power, coal, oil, transport, availability of technical know-how. Tax incentives will prove effective only if conditions regarding these other factors are not unfavourable. Further, unless there is an efficient and competent system of tax administration it is very likely that incentives become tax loopholes. The businessmen in the developing countries tend to take advantages of these tax exemptions on bogus basis without fulfilling and carrying out the underlying intent of such concessions. An honest and efficient administrative machinery, therefore, remains the basic precondition for the purposeful use of incentives.[7]

It will be seen from Table 33.1 that there has been revenue deficit throughout since 1980-81 which as per cent of GDP increased from 3.4 % of GDP in 1990-91 to 4.4% in 2001-02 and to 5.2 per cent in 2009-10 but declined to 3.2 per cent in 2010-11 but again rose to 4.3% of GDP in 2011-12. It is important to note that *revenue deficit of the government indicates public disavings*. This shows that far from contributing to resources for investment and capital formation receipts from tax and non-tax revenue have not been sufficient to meet Central government current (*i.e.* consumption) expenditure. As a result, borrowed funds (*i.e.* capital receipts) have been used to finance the current government expenditure. Thus *revenue deficit has been a great impediment to economic growth*. This is because resources which could have been used to step up investment expenditure have been used to meet revenue expenditure. Recognising this lacuna in India's fiscal system, 'Fiscal responsibility Budget Management Act (FRBMA)' was passed in 2003 which prescribed reduction of revenue deficit to zero by 2008-09. Accordingly, effort was made to raise more resources through taxation so as to achieve the target of zero revenue deficit by 2008-09. As percentage of GDP revenue deficit declined to 2.5% in 2005-06, to 1.9 per cent in 2006-07 and to 1.1 per cent in 2007-08. But afrter 2007-08, revenue deficit as per cent of GDP again went up (see Table 33.1). During 2008-09 to prevent the slowdown in the Indian economy and keep the growth momentum following global financial crisis, the government had to raise its expenditure and cut customs duties and excise duties to give *fiscal stimulus*. Consequently, revenue deficit rose to 4.5 per cent of GDP in 2008-09. 5.2 per cent of GDP in 2009-10 but fell to 3.2 per cent in 2010-11 again rose and to

6. See A.R. Prest, Fiscal Measures and Capital Accumulation in Agarwala and Singh (ed.), *Accelerating Investment in Developing Countries*, Oxford University Press.
7. A.R. Prest. *op. cit., p.* 445.

4.3% in 2011-12. Accordingly, due to increase in Government expenditure and cut in taxes to fight global meltdown following global financial crisis, gross fiscal deficit which had been reduced to 2.5 per cent of GDP in 2007-08 rose to 6.0 per cent in 2008-09 and 6.5 per cent of GDP in 2009-10 and was estimated at 5.7% in 2011-12 and 5.1% in 2012-13.

TAXATION IN INDIA

In what follows we explain the major direct and indirect taxes in India and the revenue collected from them.

Income Tax. Income tax is an important direct tax levied by the central government but the proceeds obtained from it are shared between the centre and states according to the recommendations of the Finance Commission which decides about the sharing after every five-year period. Income tax is levied on the personal incomes of the individuals and Hindu undivided families. In order to ensure equitable distribution of the tax burden, income tax levied in India is a progressive tax, that is, individuals with higher income brackets have to pay a higher rate. According to the latest provisions, taxable income up to ₹ 200,000 is exempted from income tax[8]. In 1950s, rates of income tax were quite high (marginal income rates was even higher than 70 per cent) which served as a disincentive to work, save and invest more. In the new economic policy adopted since 1991 the rates of income tax have been greatly reduced. The maximum income tax rate is now 30 per cent on incomes above ₹ 10,00,000. At present (financial year2013-14) the tax rate on different income brackets are:

Upto ₹ 2,00,000	=	NIL
₹ 2,00,000 to ₹ 500,000	=	10%
₹ 500,001 to ₹ 10,00,000	=	20%
Above ₹ 10,00,000	=	30%

Super-rich to pay surcharge. To augment revenues, a surcharge of 10 per cent has been levied on persons (other than companies) whose annual taxable income exceeds ₹ 1 crore, with effect from 2013-14.

It is important to note that lower income tax rates have resulted in greater tax revenue because incentive to evade tax has become less and, therefore, there has been a greater tax compliance. Surcharges on income tax are also sometimes levied to meet certain contingencies. These surcharges are only temporary and are withdrawn after some time. Now, a 2 per cent *education cess* on income tax was imposed with effect from the financial year 2004-05 which in the budget for 2007-08 was raised to 3 per cent. In order to give incentives to the individuals to save more, contribution to PPF, premium on life insurance, *equity linked saving schemes* (ELSS) of Mutual Funds, contribution by an employee to pension funds, and investment in fixed deposits in scheduled commercial banks (for a term of 5 years) are exempted from income tax subject to overall ceiling of ₹ 100,000. In the budget for 2004-05 a major relief was provided in the form of *abolition of income tax on long-term capital gains* and reduction in tax on short-term capital gains from 30 per cent to a flat rate of 10 per cent on *shares and securities transactions*. In 2012-13, income tax other than corporation tax was estimated to yield ₹ 1,90,000 crore (BE).

Corporation Tax. The corporation tax is the tax on the income (*i.e.* profits) of public limited companies. Initially, corporation tax rate was high which discouraged investment by the companies. Since the adoption of new economic policy in 1991, the corporation tax rate has been reduced in a phased manner to 30 per cent of the net profits of the companies. Thus, there is a single rate of corporation tax. However, like that on personal income tax, surcharge is imposed on the corporation tax from time to time to meet some contingencies. With effect from 2007-08, a 3 per cent education cess on corporation tax has been levied to meet the expenses on promotion of education. In calculaton

---

8. According to the latest budget for the financial year 2013-14, exemption limit for senior citizens is ₹ 2,50,000.

of profits, rate of depreciation on plant and machinery permitted has been reduced from 25% to 15 per cent with effect from the financial year 2006-07. Further, due to several exemptions about 40% of companies pay effective corporation tax of only 19% or even less though they make large profits. For them there is *Minimum Alternative Tax* (MAT) based on their *book profits*. In 2010-11 budget, rate of Minimum Alternate Tax was raised to 18.5 per cent of book profits of the companies. Further, long-term capital gains arising out of shares/securities have been included in calculating book profits. The surcharge on domestic companies with taxable income exceeding ₹ 10 crore has been increased from five per cent to 10 per cent with effect from 2013-14. For foreign companies, which pay a higher corporate tax, the surcharge will increase from two per cent to five per cent, with effect from 2013-14 if the taxable income exceeds ₹ 10 crore. Manufacturing companies that invest more than ₹ 100 crore in plant and machinery during the period April 1, 2-013 to March 31, 2015, have been permited investment allowance at the rate of 15 per cent.

Corporation tax was estimated to yield revenue of ₹ 3,73,000 crore in 2012-13 (BE) which was about 40 per cent of gross tax revenue of central government.

Expenditure Tax. In India, an expenditure tax was levied on the recommendations of a British economist, Prof. Kaldor in 1957, but because of small revenue receipts from it, it was withdrawn. Now, a new expenditure tax has been levied on expenditure incurred by the people on expenses in luxury hotels with residential accommodation of ₹ 400 or more per day for an individual and on bills of restaurants providing superior facilities of air conditioning.

Wealth Tax. Wealth tax is another direct tax imposed in India but revenue from it is very small. Wealth below ₹ 2.5 lakh is exempted from wealth tax since 1992-93. At one time rate of wealth tax was very high, namely 15 per cent of taxable wealth. In 1992-93 when Manmohan Singh was the Finance Minister, rates of wealth tax were reduced on the recommendation of Raja Chelliah Committee on tax reforms. Now, the rate of tax ranges from 0.5 per cent to 2 per cent of taxable wealth levied on the basis of slab system. Assets such as shares, bank deposits and one residential house are exempted from wealth tax. Wealth tax yields only very small revenue for the Central government. But it is an important tax to achieve the objective of equity or social justice. In 2011-12, wealth tax was estimated to yield Rs. 635 crores. To increase the revenue in the budget for 2013-14, tax deducted at source (TDS) has been levied at the rate of one per cent on the *value of transfer of immovable properties* where consideration exceeds ₹ 50lakh. Agricultural land has been exempted.

Securities Transactions Tax (STT) with effect from 2004-05, securities transaction tax (STT) has been levied, The STT is administratively simple and easy to enforce. For those presently paying capital gains tax, the rate of STT is 15 per cent of the value of transactions of *equities delivered.* In this case the tax has to be split up equally between buyer and seller. For unit holders holding units in equity-oriented mutual funds, rate of STT is 0.15 per cent of the value of transactions. However, for (*a*) *day traders and arbitragers* of the equities/securities, and (*b*) *traders of derivatives* (futures and options) rate of STT is 0.017 per cent and 0.01 per cent respectively of the value of transactions made. In the budget for 2013-14 Securities Transaction Tax on *equity futures* has been cut from 0.017 per cent to 0.01 per cent.In 2013-14 security transction tax (STT) was expected to yield ₹ 6,720 crore.

Indirect Taxes in India

Receipts from indirect taxes are a very important source of tax revenue for the Central Government in India. Three important indirect taxes levied by the central government in India are:

1. **Union Excise Duties** 2. **Customs Duties** 3. **Service Tax**

As economic growth takes place and production of commodities and services increases, revenue from indirect taxes will increase. Therefore, imposition of indirect taxes gives great buoyancy to tax system in India. We discuss below these indirect taxes in some detail.

Union Excise Duties. Union excise duties are levied by the central government on the production of the commodities and they are the most important source of government revenue. Initially, excise duties on the production of few commodities, such as, sugar, matches, cigarettes, tobacco, cement were levied by the centre, but in recent years a very large number of commodities have been brought within the net of indirect taxes. Moreover, initially, the rates of excise duties were high but under the economic reforms since 1991 the rates of excise duties have been lowered to promote industrial growth by increasing their competitiveness. On a number of commodities, at present Central Exercise Duty at the rate of 12% is levied on the basis of *value added* by a firm in the production of a commodity. Therefore, it is called CENVAT. Every year more commodities are brought under CENVAT. The revenue from Union excise duties are estimated at around ₹ 1,94,000 crore in 2012-13 (BE) which amount to 15 per cent of total central revenue.

Customs Duties. Customs duties are another important indirect tax which yields a good amount of revenue for the central government. Customs duties refer to the duties imposed on the commodities imported in India. These import duties on the import of foreign goods raise their prices and therefore, they provide protection to the domestic industries. Initially, the customs duties were very high and, in some cases, they were fixed at over 300 per cent of the value of imported goods. Under new economic reforms undertaken since 1991 wherein import liberalisation is an important measure of reform, customs duties have been substantially reduced. In the budget for 2007-2008, the peak rate of customs duties for non-agricultural products was reduced from 12.5% to 10 per cent. Even in the budget for 2012-13, the peak rate of customs duty was retained at 10 per cent. Despite reduction in customs duties a higher revenue of ₹ 12,400 crores was estimated for 2012-13 (BE) due to the estimated increase in imports.

Service Tax. Service tax is an indirect tax levied on services provided to the people, Services contribute about 51 per cent to Gross Dometic Product (GDP) but its contribution to the revenue of the government is much less. Initially, service tax was levied in 1994-95 on services provided by hotels, restaurants, telephone services etc. but in the budgets for the year 2001-2002 to 2010-11 service tax 2011-11 has been broadened by bringing more services within the net of service tax. Important new services on which service tax has been imposed are specialised banking and financial services, port services, telex services, video tape productive services, broadcasting services, services of authorised stations for servicing vehicles etc. Thus, at present on more than 100 services, service tax is payable. In budget for 2012-13 rate of service tax has been raised to 12 per cent per cent and further education cess of 3 per cent has been imposed on it. Note that excise duty is levied on goods while service tax is levied on services. It is proposed that in the medium term a unifrom **integrated Goods and Service Tax** (GST) will be levied on both goods and services. Service tax has become a good source of revenue for the government. In 2013-14 it was expected to yield ₹ 1.80 lakh crore (BE).

REFORMS IN INDIA'S FISCAL POLICY AND THEIR PERFORMANCE

Fiscal policy is a critical component of the policy framework pursued since the initiation of economic reforms in India in 1991 to achieve the objectives of economic growth, price stability and equity. To achieve these objectives, it was necessary to raise more resources through taxation and restrain the growth of unproductive and non-plan expenditure. During the mid-nineties there was set back in this policy when Fifth Pay Commission's recommendations of sharp hike is wages and salaries were accepted resulting in large increase in non-plan government expenditure and consequently rise is fiscal deficit. But since 2001-02, the Central Government has continued to follow prudent fiscal policy comprising (*i*) balanced tax structure of direct and indirect taxation based on ***moderate tax rates with*** minimum exemptions covering a wider class of tax payers and (*ii*) an expenditure policy that aims to restrain the growth in non-developmental expenditure and adequately provide for pressing social and infrastructure needs of a developing economy. In the last some budgets, especially the budgets for the years 2005-06, 2006-07, 2007-08, 2010-11, 2011-12 and 2012-13 the fiscal strategy for achieving the above stated objectives has been primarily ***revenue led*** without expenditure compression. However, within the limits of fiscal deficit set under Fiscal Responsibility and Budget Management

(FRBM) Act passed in 2003-04, there *has been* ***re-prioritisation of public expenditure*** along with ***revenue-led strategy*** of fiscal consolidation.

To raise more revenue for achieving growth with macroeconomic stability, *tax-GDP ratio has been sought to be raised*. As a result of tax effort made for mobilisation of tax-GDP ratio rose to 12.6 per cent (for both the centre and states combined) in 2007-08. For this purpose various tax reforms both in the spheres of direct and indirect taxes have been carried out. It is felt that while the policy of moderate tax rates have to be followed, the base of taxation has to be broadened. With this end in view the tax reforms undertaken since the beginning of nineties have sought to bring about a ***compositional shift*** in the structure of the tax system away from the excessive dependence on regressive indirect taxes to progressive direct taxes for raising resources for accelerating economic growth with stability. Besides, to ensure competitiveness of the products of Indian industry excise duties and custom duties have been reduced so that rapid growth of Indian exports is possible. Moreover customs duties were reduced to open up the Indian economy and to obtain gain from free trade. To compensate for this and realising that more than per cent of India's GDP came from *services*, service tax was levied which has now become an important source of Government revenue. In 2013-14 service tax was expected to yield ₹ 1.80 lakh crore (BE).

Table 33.1. Centre's Fiscal Position
(As per cent of GDP at current market prices)

	2001-02	2004-05	2005-06	2006-07	2007-08	08-09	09-10	10-11	11-12	12-13 (BE)
1. Revenue receipts (a + b)	8.8	9.6	9.4	10.1	11.0	9.7	8.8	10.1	8.4	9.3
(*a*) Tax revenue (net of States' share)	5.9	6.9	7.3	8.2	8.8	7.9	7.0	7.3	7.0	7.7
(*b*) Non-tax revenue	3.0	2.5	2.1	1.9	2.1	1.7	1.8	2.8	1.4	1.6
2. Revenue expenditure	13.2	11.9	11.9	12.0	11.9	14.2	14.1	13.4	12.7	12.8
of which										
(*a*) Interest payments	4.7	3.9	3.6	3.5	3.5	3.4	3.3	3.0	3.0	3.2
(*b*) Major subsidies	1.3	1.4	1.2	1.2	1.4	2.2	2.1	2.1	1.6	1.8
(*c*) Defence expenditure	1.7	1.4	1.3	1.2	1.1	1.3	1.4	1.2	1.1	1.1
3. Revenue deficit (2-1)	**4.4**	**2.4**	**2.5**	**1.9**	**1.1**	**4.5**	**5.1**	**3.2**	**4.3**	**3.5**
4. Capital receipts (a + b + c)	7.1	5.9	4.3	3.5	3.4	6.2	7.0	5.2	6.0	5.5
(*a*) Recovery of loans*	0.7	1.1	0.3	0.1	0.1	0.1	0.1	0.2	0.2	0.1
(*b*) Other receipt (mainly PSU disinvestment)	0.2	0.1	0.0	0.0	0.8	0.0	0.4	0.3	0.2	0.3
(*c*) Borrowings and other liabilities	6.2	3.9	4.0	3.3	2.5	6.0	6.5	4.8	5.7	5.1
5. Capital expenditure	2.7	3.5	1.8	1.6	2.4	1.6	1.7	2.0	1.8	2.0
6. Total expenditure (2+5=6(a)+6(b)]	15.9	15.4	13.7	13.7	14.3	15.8	15.8	15.4	14.5	14.9
of which										
(*a*) Plan expenditure	4.4	4.1	3.8	4.0	4.1	4.9	4.7	4.9	4.6	5.2
(*b*) Non-plan expenditure	11.4	11.3	9.9	9.6	10.2	10.9	11.1	10.5	9.9	9.7
7. Fiscal deficit [6-1-4 (a)=8(a)+8(b)]	**6.2**	**3.9**	**4.0**	**3.3**	**2.5**	**6.0**	**6.5**	**4.8**	**5.7**	**5.1**
8. Primary deficit [7-2 (a)=8(a)+8(b)]	**1.1**	**0.0**	**0.4**	**– 0.2**	**– 0.9**	**2.6**	3.2	1.8	2.6	1.9
(*a*) Primary deficit consumption	1.6	0.0	0.0	–0.7	–1.6	1.7	–	–	–	–
(*b*)Primary deficit investment	-0.1	0.0	0.4	0.5	0.7	0.8	–	–	–	–

Source: GOI, *Economic Survey* (various issues), and Budget for 2010-11.

However, as stated above, to achieve fiscal consolidation (i.e., reduction of fiscal deficit) for controlling inflation and ensuring release of resources for economic growth and employment generation, raising revenue from taxation has been given priority along with improving the quality of public expenditure (that is, restraining the growth of non-developmental expenditure and raising plan expenditure). Since, much of public expenditure is of committed nature such as interest payments for servicing past public debt, expenditure on defence, pensions and wages and salaries of government employees, there is very little room for compression of expenditure in the short run, the objective of accelerating growth and employment generation have to be achieved by raising revenue and improving the quality of expenditure. However, *in the financial year 2012-13 in order to contain fiscal deficit, Finance Minister, Mr. Chitambram reduced planned expenditure by ₹90,000 crore which worked to reduce rate of ecomomic growth.* In what follows we first explain the reforms in both direct and indirect tax systems that have been undertaken in the last two decades.

Reforms in Direct Taxation

It is important to note that over the last two decades, there has been significant reforms in the tax system so that it can make larger contribution to resource mobilisation for economic growth and at the same time serves the objective of achieving equity as well. First, in the sphere of direct taxation *rate of income and corporation taxes have been lowered to moderate levels.* With lower tax rates revenue buoyancy from these taxes can be achieved through better compliance and minimal exemptions. Until the early eighties, direct tax rates were exorbitant, evasion of these taxes was rampant which gave birth to the enormous black money in the Indian economy. It was realised that moderate rates of these taxes would yield more revenue by increasing tax compliance. Lower rates of *direct texes also provide incentives to work more, save more and invest more* as lower rates increases after-tax returns on work, saving and investment. Long-term fiscal policy announced in 1985 rightly emphasised that "*a broader base of taxation combined with moderate rates of taxes and strict enforcement, can yield better revenue results*".[9]

Acting on the long-term fiscal policy V.P. Singh in his 1985-86 budget cut the maximum marginal rate of income tax to 50 per cent and reduced personal income tax slabs from eight to four. Seven years later Dr. Manmohan Singh reduced the maximum marginal income tax rate to 40 per cent in his budget for 1992-93 and reduced the personal income tax slabs to only three. Mr. Chidambaram in his dream budget 1997-98 further reduced top marginal rate of income tax to 30 per cent. Moreover, education cess of 3 per cent has been levied on both income tax and corporation tax.

As regards corporation tax, acting on the Chilliah Committee recommendations Dr. Manmohan Singh attempted rationalisation of corporate taxation and cut the corporation tax rate to 40 per cent and reduced exemptions in 1994-95 budget to broaden the base of the tax. Three years later Mr. Chidambaram further reduced corporation tax to 35 percent in his budget for 1997-98 and again as Finance Minister in UPA Government he further reduced the corporation tax rate to 33 per cent in 2004-05 budget. However, to broaden the base of corporation tax so as to increase tax revenue he lowered the depreciation allowance from 25 per cent to 15 per cent in 2007-08. Besides, to raise revenue from corporate taxation, **fringe benefit tax** (FBT) was levied payable by corporate employee. Besides, **Minimum Alternate tax** (MAT) which was fixed at 7.5 per cent to 10 of book profits of the corporate companies has now been raised to 18.5 per cent in 2011-12 budget and long-term capital gains have been included in the book-profits. Further, **securities transaction tax** (STT) has been levied on the sale and purchase of shares/securities.

9. Finance Minister, Mr. Chidambaram in his Budget Speech, July 8, 2004

It is thus evident from above that in the last over two decades, efforts have been made to move to moderate direct tax rates and broaden the base of direct taxation by withdrawing certain exemptions. This has improved the compliance to pay taxes and resulted in increase in revenue from direct taxes. However, there is still a vast potential for revenue buoygency of direct taxes since there are still a large number of exemptions, for example, in case of various types of financial savings and exports. As recommended by the Task Force headed by R. Vijay Kelkar, *more resources can be mobilised from direct taxes if a large number of existing exemptions which have outlived their utility* are withdrawn and direct tax system is simplified and made transparent. It is now proposed to implement *direct tax code* without much exemptions which is now awaiting the approval of parliament.

An important outcome of fiscal policy pursued after 2002-03 was decline in fiscal deficit till 2007-08 which helped to keep inflation rate at around 5 per cent per annum as measured by WPI of all commodities. It will be seen from Table 33.1 that fiscal deficit which was 6.2 per cent of GDP in 2001-02 fell to 2.5 per cent in 2007-08, but again rose to 6.5 percent in 2009-10 due to fiscal stimulus package adopted to prevent slowdown of the Indian economy due to global financial crisis. High fiscal deficit of the order of 6 per cent and more is bad and against fiscal prudence. Fiscal deficit can be either financed by the Government *monetisation*, that is, printing of new money by RBI or by *borrowing from the market*. Monetisation of fiscal deficit is avoided as it leads to inflation in the economy. The excessive Government borrowing is also had because it causes increase in public debit which raises the burden on future generations. Besides, excessive Government borrowing from the banks dries up banking resources for the private sector, that is, reduces the *availability of credit* for the private sector. Further, Government borrowing from the market tends to raise interest rate. Higher interest rate causes increase in cost of credit for the private sector which impinges on their profit margins. Therefore, on the recommendation of IMF, Fiscal Responsibility and Budget Management (FRBM) Act was passed in 2003-04. After this, fiscal deficit consistently declined to 4.0 per cent of GDP in 2005-06 and to 2.6 per cent in the year 2007-08. This decline in fiscal deficit in these years was achieved by reducing revenue deficit from 4.4 per cent of GDP in 2001-02 to 2.5 per cent in 2005-06 and further to 1.1 per cent in 2007-08 on the one hand and restraining the growth of expenditure (See Row 6 of Table 33.1), especially non-plan expenditure. Under Fiscal Responsibility and Budget Management Act (FRBMA) it was planned to eliminate revenue deficit completely by 2008-09 and fiscal deficit to be reduced to 3 per cent of GDP in 2008-09. This was expected to release more resources for economic growth and social sector development. However, fiscal deficit rose to 6.0 per cent of GDP in 2008-09 and to 6.5 per cent of GDP in 2009-10. This is because to fight economic slowdown following the intensification of global financial crisis in 2008, the Central Government came out with fiscal stimulus programmes wherein Government expenditure had to be increased and indirect taxes reduced to keep the momentum of economic growth. However, it was reduced by the 4.8 per cent in 2010-11 and to 4.6 per cent of GDP in 2011-12, but it again rose to 5.7% of GDP in 2011-12 and 5.1% in 2012-13. In his budget for 2013-14, the Finance Minister has set the target of fiscal deficit for 2013-14 at 4.8% of GDP.

Changes in Taxation Structure : Increase in Share of Direct Taxes

It is interesting to note that tax-GDP ratio which rose to 11.9 per cent in 2007-08 declined to 10.8% and 9.6 per of GDP in 2008-09 and 2009-10 respectively due to lowering of indierect taxes in 2008-09 and 2009-10 to prevent large economic slowdown. Besides, there has been also improvement in the taxation structure (See Table 33.2). While there has been decline in the share of regressive and resource-distorting indirect taxes in the revenue of the Central Government, there is rise in the share of direct taxes. Thus, as will be seen from Table 33.2, whereas the share of direct taxes as per cent of GDP rose from 2.8% in 1995-96 to 5.9 percent in 2007-08, the share of indirect taxes (customs duties, excise duties and service tax) as per cent of GDP fell from 6.4 per cent in 1995-96 to 5.6 per cent in 2007-08 and further to 3.8% in 2009-10 but for 2012-13 it was budgeted to rise to 5% of GDP. On the other hand, the share of direct tax as percentage of GDP which was 3% of GDP rose to 5.6 per cent of GDP in 2012-13. This increase in share of direct taxes and fall in indirect tax in total tax revenue of Central Government has made the Indin tax system more equitable.

Table 33.2. Share of Direct and Indirect Taxes in Central Government's Revenue : Tax Revenue as per cent of GDP

	1995-96	2001-02	04-05	05-06	06-07	07-08	08-09	09-10	10-11	11-12	2-13(BE)
Direct (a)	**2.8**	**3.0**	**4.1**	**4.3**	**5.1**	**5.9**	**5.7**	**5.7**	**5.6**	**5.5.**	**5.6**
Personal income tax	1.3	1.4	1.5	1.5	1.8	2.1	1.9	1.9	1.8	1.9	1.9
Corporation tax	1.4	1.6	2.6	2.7	3.4	3.9	3.8	3.8	3.8	3.6	3.7
Indirect (b)	**6.4**	**5.1**	**5.3**	**5.4**	**5.6**	**5.6**	**4.8**	**3.8**	**4.4**	**4.4**	**5.0**
Customs	3.0	1.8	1.8	1.8	2.0	2.1	1.8	1.3	1.7	1.7	1.9
Excise	3.4	3.2	3.1	3.0	2.7	2.5	1.9	1.6	1.8	1.6	1.9
Service tax	0.1	0.1	0.4	0.6	0.9	1.0	1.1	0.9	0.9	1.1	1.2
Gross Tax Revenue	**9.4**	**8.2**	**9.4**	**9.9**	**11.1**	**11.9**	**10.8**	**9.6**	**10.2**	**9.9**	**10.7**

Source : GOI, *Economic, Survey* 2009-2010, p.42

1. Direct taxes also include taxes pertaining to expenditure, interest, wealth, gift and estate duty.
2. The ratios to GDP at current market price sare based on the CSO's National Accounts 2004-05 series.

This change in tax structure a creditable achievement of mobilising resources from direct taxes, as this has been done despite the fact that rates of both personal income tax and corporation tax have been substantially reduced. This will also ensure equitable distribution of burden of overall tax among the people.

Reforms in the Indian Indirect Tax System

The Indian indirect tax system as it existed in the early nineties had several drawbacks. First, the excise duties and sales tax were levied on inputs which had a *cascading effect* on raising prices of final products. In a way, there is 'a tax on tax'. As regards sales tax which is levied by State governments, a uniform value added tax (VAT) is proposed to be levied. VAT tax will replace different rates of sales tax levied by the state governments. Legislation has already been enacted but its implementation was deferred due to protest by traders and due to general elections in April 2004. Now, as per decision of UPA government VAT has come into effect from April 1, 2005. Implementation of VAT will eliminate the **cascading effect** of sales tax and also help in achieving price stability. The experience of Haryana and Delhi which have implemented VAT shows that government revenue increased when VAT was introduced.

Reforms in Excise Duty. To rationalise the indirect tax system at the centreby removing distortion in the structure there is a need to remove multiplicity of tax rates of central excise duties on various goods and services. With tax reform initiated since 1991, this has been now achieved with few exceptions. Now, there is a single excise duty called CENVAT (which is in the form of value added tax) at the rate of 16 per cent on all products which enter a production chain. The argument for a single 16 per cent CENVAT is that it will remove the distortions in the tax system as a result of multiplicity of rates of excise duties. This is of course a correct approach in general but in the view of the present author *the final consumption goods of the nature of income-elastic luxuries* such as cars and air conditioners should be taxed at a much higher rate than CENVAT. This will enable the government to raise more revenue without harming production incentives and will thus serve well the equity objective. To simplify the indirect tax system, it is now planned to introduce *Goods and Services Tax* (GST) in near future. This GST will replace the service tax Central CENVAT and states VAT and a uniform rate of GST by all states will be fixed.

Revenue Mobilisation through Service Tax. While the revenue from existing three sources, namely, direct, excise and customs taxes, is expected to increase by ensuring greater tax complaince and withdrawal of exemptions, the government seeks to collect more revenue from service tax by bringing more services under its net. Over the last four decades there has been a structural change in the Indian economy with relative contribution of agricultrue to GDP significantly decreasing and of services sector sharply increasing to 54 per cent of GDP. With more services which have been brought within the service tax net in the last four budgets for the years, 2004-05, 2005-06, 2006-07, 2007-08 the total number of services on which service tax is levied has risen to more than 100. In the year 2013-14 service tax was expected to bring in about ₹ 1.80 lakh crore (BE). It is now well recognised that for more revenue mobilisation as well as for achieving equity and price stability there is a need to look at the whole *value addition chain covering both goods and services* from the viewpoint of taxation. Government intends to expand the scope of taxation of services by not only bringing additional services within the tax net, but also covering a larger number of assessees under the service tax.

Reforms in Customs Duties. Since the early ninties revenue from customs duties as a percentage of GDP has been falling due to the reduction in customs duty rates following the policy of trade liberalisation. Dr. Manmohan Singh, the Finance Minister in his five budgets between 1991 and 1996 reduced India's absurdly high customs duties. He reduced peak tariff rates from over 200 per cent to 50 per cent and the import weighted average tariff rate from over 80 per cent to below 30 per cent. Since 1996, successive finance ministers further reduced the *peak tarif rate (i.e. customs duty) first* to 35 per, and then to 20 per cent in Jan. 2004. The peak rate of customs duty has been further reduced to 15 per in 2005-06 and to 12.5 per cent in 2006-07 and to 10 per cent in 2007-08. But there are several exceptions to this peak rate. It is now planned to reduce the peak customs duties to the ASEAN level. Though India is committed to reduce tariff duties under trade liberalisation agreement of WTO, we should try to provide effective protection to some of our crucial industries such as textiles and agriculture by fixing higher customs rates than peak customs duty making a cause for their exceptional treatment. It is quite surprising to note that Kelkar Task Force on implementation of Fiscal Responsibility and Budgetary Management Act (FRBMA) proposed a shift to a three rate structure on customs duties consisting of 5 per cent, 8 per cent and 10 per cent. In our view this is going too far in trade liberalisation. This will involve not only a loss of tax revenues but will also reduce effective protection to Indian industries.

Changes in Quality of Expenditure

Changes in pattern of expenditure is also worth mentioning. It will be seen from Table 33.4 that prior to 2007-08 through the adoption of prudent fiscal policy the Government had been able to reduce *total expenditure* both revenue and capital, which as percentage of GDP fell from 17.3 per cent in 2001-02 to 15.4 per cent in 2004-05 and further fell to 13.6 per cent in 2006-07, and rose marginally to 14.1% in 2007-08. As compared to plan-expenditure which as a percent of GDP rose from 3.8 per cent in 2005-06 to 4.9% in 2008-09 and 5.3% in 2009-10 non-plan expenditure *fell sharply* from 12.3 per cent of GDP in 2002-03 to 9.7% in 2006-07 and to 10.3 per cent in 2007-08. It is only in 2008-09 and 2009-10 that due to need of increasing public expenditure to overcome recession or slowdown of the Indian economy and to keep the growth momentum that non-plan expenditure slightly increased to 10.9% and 11.3% in 2008-09 and 2009-10 respectively (See Row 6 (a) and 6 (b) of Table 33.1. Further, as seen from Table 33.4 that Government has succeeded in restraining the growth of non-devlopment expenditure incurred on interest payments, major subsidies and defence till 2007-08. It is only in 2008-09 and 2009-10 under well-designed contra-cyclical policy that Government increased its expenditure and borrowed heavily for this purpose to fight slowdown of the Indian economy and to keep the growth momentum. This resulted in increase in expenditure on interest and subsidies. As plan expenditure represents development expenditure and non-plan expenditure represents non-development expenditure, the changes witnessed in the pattern of expenditure therefore show improvement in the quality of expenditure.

Table 33.4. Public Expenditure on Some Important Items

As per cent of GDP

	1990-91	01-02	02-03	03-04	04-05	05-06	06-07	07-08	08-09	09-10	10-11	11-12
Total Public Expenditure	17.3	15.9	16.3	15.5	15.4	13.6	13.6	14.4	15.7	15.8	15.4	14.5
(*i*) Interest payments	3.8	4.7	4.8	4.5	3.9	3.6	3.5	3.5	3.4	3.3	3.0	3.0
(*ii*) Major subsidies	1.7	1.3	1.7	1.6	1.4	1.2	1.2	1.4	2.2	2.1	2.1	1.6
(*iii*) Defence revenue expen.	1.9	1.7	1.7	1.6	1.4	1.3	1.2	1.1	1.3	1.4	1.2	1.1

Source : Economic Survey, 2006-07. p.21, 2007-08, p.33., 2010-11, p.45, 2012-13, p.59

For achieving 8 per cent rate of growth in GDP on a sustained basis, it is necessary to step-up public investment expenditure on agriculture and infrastructure. This *requires to effect a shift in the composition* of total expenditure in favour of capital expenditure. This can be done only if revenue deficit is bridged by raising more resources through taxation on the one hand and cutting non-plan expenditure on the other. One of the major objectives of Fiscal Responsibility and Budget Management (FRBM) Act, 2003 was to eliminate revenue deficit by the year 2008-09. With revenue deficit reduced to zero, But in 2008-09 partly due to fiscal stimulus in which tax cuts were made and government expenditure increased to maintain the growth momentum and partly due to the populist programme such as waiving loans of farmers to the time of ₹ 70,000 crore the target of zero revenue deifict was not achieved. As a result revenue deficit which was lowered to 1.1 per cent of GDP in 2007-08 went up to 4.6 per cent in 2008-09. Therefore, the expectation that with zero revenue deifict, the government would be able to increase capital expenditure for investment in agriculture, industry and infrastructure was not realised. Large revenue deficit is quite bad because large expenditure incurred on revenue account does not lead to creation of durable assets which are essential to sustain growth.

Thus, what is a matter of concern is the **decline in capital expenditure** which mostly represents investment expenditure in physical assets. As a proportion of of GDP, fall in total government expenditure from a level of 17.1 per cent in 2003-04 to 14.4 per cent in 2007-08 was largely driven by the steep fall in capital expenditure with revenue expenditure remaining almost steady between 2004-05 and 2007-08 (see rows 5 and 6 in Table 33.1).

It may be however noted that *revenue expenditure* includes some expenditure on social sector (mainly *elementary education and literacy*) under Sarv Shiksha Abhiyan and Mid-day Meals; health and family welfare (National Rural Health Mission), rural employment, and physical infrastructure including rural roads which are also of developmental nature. Even accounting for these the fact remains that fall in capital expenditure is disturbing and must be reversed.

As regards expenditure on subsidies, the government's recent policy is to make them targeted to the poor and weaker sections of the society. To ensure that benefits of expenditure on subsidies are not usurped by those not intended be the beneficiaries of these subsidies. Delivery mechanism for providing these subsidies should be improved and made more efficient. Under NCMP, Government is committed to control inefficiencies that increase the food subsidy burden and to target all subsidies sharply at the poor and the truly needy like small and marginal farmers, farm labour and the urban poor. To reduce expenditure on subsidies government has raised the price of cooking gas and restricted its use by a family to 9 cylenders per year. Besides, it has decontrolled petrol and raising price of diesel by 50 paise every month. However, due to enactment of *Food Security Bill*, its expenditure on food subsidy will rise.

Reduction in Fiscal Deficit

A large fiscal deficit has been a major macro-economic problem. It is persistent large fiscal deficits in the nineteen eighties that landed the Indian economy in a state of severe economic crisis reflected in the acute balance of payments problem. This acute economic crisis compelled us to approach IMF for help to tide over the crisis. Fiscal deficit is the difference between the total government expenditure on revenue and capital accounts and the total sum of revenue receipts and non-debt capital receipts. Thus fiscal deficit measures the total borrowing from the market, net borrowing from the Reserve Bank of India (i.e. monetisation of deficit), small savings and external assistance (i.e. borrowing from abroad at concessional rate of interest). For the achievement of macroeconomic stability, fiscal deficit should not exceed 3 per cent of GDP. Fiscal Responsibility and Business Management (FRMB) Act 2003 has prescribed to achieve the target of fiscal deficit to 3 per cent of GDP by the year 2008–09. This is generally called fiscal consolidation. But how this fiscal consolidaton, that is, reduction in fiscal deficit is to be achieved so as to achieve economic growth with stability and equity. As explained above, this can be done by raising tax-GDP ratio on the one hand and reducing non-plan expenditure on the other.

Tax-GDP ratio can be raised by widening the base of direct taxes, especially personal income tax and corporation tax. One important way of broadening the base of the direct taxes is to withdraw many of such exemptions which have outlived their utility and are merely used to evade these taxes. As result of these exemptions, the effective rate of corporation tax is much smaller. *Economic Survey* 2005-06 found that 40 per cent of corporate companies pay only 10 per cent or less corporation tax as against 30 per cent levied on them. This has also been found by Task Force headed by Vijay Kelkar. It is interesting to note that because of these exemptions *Reliance Industries* which made huge profits throughout its career did not pay any corporation tax for several years. Similarly, many other profitable companies also took advantage of these exemptions and did not pay any tax for several years. Therefore, the Central government enacted '*Minimum Alternative Tax (MAT)* according to which these profitable companies which did not pay corporation tax would have to pay this minimum alternative tax.

The efforts have been to raise more resources through leveying new taxes in order to reduce fiscal deficit. The introduction of service tax in 1994-95 ushered in a major change in indirect taxes in the (BE) form of wider base and facilitated the process of rationalisation of excise duties resulting in lower tax burden on productive sectors. Over the years, the number of services subject to service tax has increased and now stands at around 114. However, a further reform in the indirect tax system in the form of Goods and service tax (GST) is to be introduced from April 2012.

It is also worth noting that long-term capital gains from shares has been exempted in the budget w.e.f. 2004-05 and has been replaced by Securities Transaction Tax. Along with it, short-term capital gains tax was reduced from 20% to 10%. This is quite contrary to broadening the tax base. Indeed, there is good economic case for imposing a tax on long-term capital gains on shares, its rate may be kept lower than the general income tax rate because of the risk involved in investing funds in equity capital. The total abolition of capital gains tax on equity capital will introduce large distortions (relative to capital gains from other assets) and also results in loss of revenue for the government. This loss is unlikely to be made up by levying a small securities transaction tax.

FISCAL POLICY, INCLUSIVE GROWTH, EQUITY AND PRICE STABILITY

Fiscal Policy Inclusive Growth and Equity

Let us now explain how fiscal policy can be used to achieve equitable distribution of income. Attainment of a wider measure of equality in incomes, wealth and opportunities must form an integral part of economic development and social advance. Existence of gross inequalities is a social evil and no measure of economic growth will increase economic welfare unless an equitable distribution of the rising national product is assured. Instrument of taxation and certain types of government expenditure are used as a means of bringing about a redistribution of income in favour of the poorer sections of the society. It is worth noting that in a poor underdeveloped country the objective of equity can be achieved if *fiscal policy seeks to reduce mass poverty and unemployment that prevails in it.* A caution is, however, necessary. It is essential to strike a balance between the two objectives of lessening economic inequalities and that of sustaining and strengthening incentives to invest and accelerating economic growth. Fiscal policy must maintain unimpaired the flow of savings and investment which makes for continued progress of productive enterprises. Higher economic growth and greater equality are both objectives of high importance. Higher incomes can be taxed without adverse repercussions on private productive effort and enterprise. To achieve equity, income tax in India has been made progressive. Rate of income tax at present is 10 per cent in the tax slab of ₹ 2,00,000 to 5,00,000, 20 per cent in the slab of ₹ 5,00,000 to 10,00,000 and 30 per cent in the income above ₹ 10,00,000. Besides, there was surcharge of 10 per cent on income above ₹ 10 lakhs, which was withdrawn in 2009-10 budget. Besides, there are wealth tax and expenditure tax on the rich persons. In 2013-14 to achieve equity 10 per cent surcharge on personal income of over ₹ one crore has been levied. This is only token super rich tax which needs to be raised if the objective of equity is to be realised. Optimum rate of growth and maximum social welfare are not irreconcilable. It will be possible to reconcile these two objectives by the formulation of a well-balanced fiscal programme.

But lessening inequalities through taxing higher incomes is only one form of fiscal operations. A better and complementary fiscal policy consists of *increasing public expenditure for promoting welfare of the poor and less privileged classes.* Increasing public expenditure on anti-poverty programmes such as National Rural Employment Guarantee (NREG) Scheme and Antyodaya Anna Yojana, Bharat Nirman Yojna will ensure equity in income distribution. Stepping up of public expenditure on primary education and public health will greatly improve the economic conditions of the poor people. In fact, international experience shows that active public expenditure policies aimed at raising the consumption of the poor are far more effective in promoting equity as compared to tax policies aimed at containing the incomes of the rich. It is in this context that economic policy of new UPA government lays emphasis on achieving through fiscal policy generation of employment opportunities in agriculture, manufacturing and services by promoting investment, providing 100 days employment to the bread earner in each family at minimum wages, food for work programme in 150 districts of the country, ensuring universal access to quality basic education and health. For this purpose adequate funds are being provided for Sarv Shiksha Abhiyan, Midday Cooked Meal scheme, basic health care, drinking water facilities in villages. In this connection P. Chidambaram, our former Finance Minister says, "*The poor want education for their children: we shall provide it . . . . we shall also make sure that the child is not hungry while he or she is at school. The poor want drinking water : we shall ensure that every habitation has an assured source of drinking water. The poor want basic health care, medicines at fair prices and doctor within a reasonable distance : we shall ensure that the public health system has adequate human and financial resources to provide basic medical care. The poor want jobs for their children we shall ensure through higher investment, and through targeted intervention, jobs are available to them*[10]. 3 per cent education cess on all central taxes such as income tax, corporation tax, excise duties has been imposed to collect funds necessary for achieving objective of universal elementary education. However, the above promises by the Finance Minister are tall claims. Up till 2014 we are far away from the achievement of these goods.

Fiscal Policy and Price Stability

India as well as other developing countries have been experiencing the problem of rising prices or inflation. Inflation in them has been of both demand-pull and cost-push types. The main cause of demand-pull inflation has been the *fiscal deficit* in Government's budgets which has arisen because Government has not been able to finance the mounting public expenditure through revenue from taxes and public sector surpluses. In India in the year 1986-87, fiscal deficit of the Central government rose to 8.5 per cent of GDP (Gross Domestic Product) and even after 5 years of efforts, the

Indian Government had not been able to achieve a significant reduction in fiscal deficit. In 1990-91, fiscal deficit was estimated to be of the order of 6.6 per cent of GDP, whereas to achieve price stabilisation IMF recommended its reduction to 3 per cent of GDP.

Therefore, under the New Economic Policy adopted since 1991, efforts were made to reduce fiscal deficit by reducing Government expenditure and raising more resources through taxes. As a result, fiscal deficit the Central Government was reduced to 5.4 per cent in 1999-2000 and this helped in bringing inflation under control. However, to fight recessionary conditions in Indian industrial sector during three years period (2000 - 2003), the Government had to raise its expenditure resulting in higher deficit of 5.7 % of GDP in 2000-01, 6.2% in 2001-02 and 5.9 per cent in 2002-03.

To follow fiscal prudence in fiscal policy, Fiscal Responsibility Budget Management Act FRBMA was enacted in 2003 to reduce fiscal deficit to 3 per cent by 2008-09, As a result of fiscal efforts fiscal deficit was brought down to 2.7 per cent of GDP in 2007-08. However, again in 2008 there was slowdown in the Indian economy as a result of global financial crisis. To keep the growth momentum the Government had to increase its expenditure and cut certain taxes to provide fiscal stimulus to the economy. Consequently fiscal deficit rose to 6.0 per cent in 2008-09 and 6.4 per cent in 2009-10 . This had inflationary potential. Food inflation rose to over 18 per cent in Jan. 2010. Though inflation measured by CPI had risen to 11.5 per cent in Jan. 2010, inflation rate as measured by WPI rose to 10.56 per cent in June 2010. Initially it was believed that WPI inflation was driven by supply-side factors, but later it was realised that demand pressures contributed a good deal to this double-digit WPI inflation. Apart from planned reduction in fiscal deficit to 5.1 per cent 2010-11 and to 4.6 per cent in 2012-13 no concrete fiscal policy measures were announced to fight this higher inflation rate. The consumer price Index (CPI) for Industrial workers rose to 9.85 per cent (YOY) in September 2013 and food inflation increased has risen above 18 per cent in September 2013. Despute some measures taken by the Government and the RBI rates of retail inflation and food inflation have remained high in 2012-13 and 2013-14.

A huge fiscal deficit of Central Government is financed in two ways: (1) by Government borrowing from the market, (2) by monetising the deficit which is commonly called deficit financing in India. A high degree of fiscal deficit leads to excess market borrowing by the Government which causes expansion in bank credit to the Government and therefore leads to increase in money supply in the economy causing prices to rise. Besides, excessive Government borrowing from the market leads to the rise in interest rate which discourages private investment. Further, a part of fiscal deficit is financed through borrowing from Reserve Bank of India which issues new currency (which is called reserve or high powered money) for the Government. This causes greater expansion in money supply through the process of money multiplier and generates inflationary pressures in the economy. Thus, to check the rate of inflation, fiscal deficit has to be reduced through both raising revenue of the Government and reducing non-plan Government expenditure.

Goods and Service Tax (GST)

An important fiscal reform recommended by Kelkar committee was the introduction of a "Goods and Services Tax (GST)" which will replace all multistage value added taxes such as CENVAT and service tax levied by the Centre sales tax, entertainment tax, luxury tax and VAT levied by the States. This comprehensive tax on goods and services will not only simplify the indirect tax structure in the country but will also yield more revenue for the Government. The significant cause of complexity of the present indirect tax system is related to the existence of various exemptions and multiple rates of CENVAT on various commodities and different rates of VAT levied by the States. The starting base for central excise duty or CENVAT is narrow and is further eroded by a variety of area-specific and conditional and unconditional exemptions. Therefore, the introduction of Goods and Services Tax (GST would thus be appropriate for deepening tax reforms.

Thus, the Goods and Service Tax (GST) is a final tax on buying goods and services as taxes paid on inputs that go into the production of a particular good or service have been excluded so that there is no ***cascading effect*** of taxes. To put it simply, GST is levied only on the value added at every stage of production. Thus goods and service tax system ensures that when the final tax is calculated, tax paid on inpuls is taken out and the tax is paid on the cost of the final good produced.

GST rate. There is no decision yet on the rate structure of GST. A task force set up by the Thirteenth Finance Commission in its report recommended a rate of 12%. States, however, have said they will not settle for a rate less than 15%. Internal studies carried out by the Centre and various states point to rate of 14-16%. At present, the talks have veered round to the view that there should be two slabs – one lower or floor rate for essential items and another higher or effective rate for most items. There will also be an exempted list of items and a lower rate of 1% for precious metals such as gold, platinum, silver.

Impact of GST on Prices ? If the GST rate is pegged at 16%, it will lower the price of goods but push up the cost of services. For example, a good attracting 8% excise duty and 12% VAT faces a total tax of 20%. That will fall to 16%. However, cost of consuming services will go up, as service tax rate is currently 10%.

GST is a broad-based consumption tax which is expected to yield more revenue both for the States and Centre. The Empowered Committee of State Finance Ministers in November 2007 had recommended a "dual" GST levied concurrently by both levels of government (*i.e.* Centre and States). The dual GST tax strikes a good balance between fiscal autonomy of the Centre and States and the need of harmonisation of tax structure. The empowered committee recommended that both levels of government (i.e. Centre and States) should apply this GST tax to a comprehensive base of goods and services at all points in the supply chain. It will also eliminate the tax cascading, which occurs because of truncated or partial application of the Centre and State taxes.

GST will benefit both industry and government. GST will eliminate the cascading effects of multiple layers of taxation all over the country. It will also help create a seamless national market, as the plethora of taxes and checks that movement of goods faces will go. For both the centre and state governments, integration of goods and services taxation across the country will create a world-class tax system and improve tax collections as it will end the long standing distortions of differential treatments of manufacturing and service sector and end exemptions. Moreover, GST is a tax on consumption and will reduce the incidence of evasion.

APPENDIX TO CHAPTER 33

DIRECT TAX CODE (DTC) : REFORMS IN THE INDIAN DIRECT TAX SYSTEM

Introduction

In August 2009, the Finance Minister proposed to do away decades old complex direct tax regime which was riddled with a large number of the unnecessary exemptions. These exemptions caused not only a huge loss of revenue to the government but also violated the cannon of horizontal equity. The Direct Tax Code (DTC) was proposed to do away these exemptions in the direct tax system so as to simplify it and make it *rule-based system* so that it becomes more transparent by removing the plethora of exemptions. It was thought that this simplified and transparent tax regime without much exemptions would enable the government to lower tax rates and widen the tax net to make it more equitable and at the same time yield more revenue for the government. The original Direct Tax Code (DTC) was released for public discussion in Aug. 2009 and after receiving suggestions the modified draft was again brought out for discission in June 2010. Then with revisions in the light of suggestions received, the final version of DTC was introduced as a bill in Lok Sabha on Aug. 30, 2010.

The Direct Tax Code Bill when passed by the parliament will replace Income Tax Act 1961 and is now proposed to come into effect from April 1, 2012. This Direct Tax Code Bill is quite comprehensive and covers personal income tax, corporate tax, wealth tax. It is worth noting that the Direct Code Bill as introduced in the Parliament has undergone a number of changes aimed at diluting the originally proposed rule-based direct tax system and lower tax regime. Thus modified direct tax code incorporated in the bill presented in the parliament is a greatly watered-down version of the original direct tax code. Even then it makes the direct tax system more equitable and less discretionary than the existing one. We explain below in detail the various provisions of the modified Direct Tax Code regarding personal income tax, corporate tax and wealth tax.

PERSONAL INCOME TAX

The Direct Tax Code promises radical overhaul of the income tax slabs and rates to reduce the overall tax burden on individual income tax payees. We explain below the proposals regarding personal income tax:

Exemption Limit. The DTC bill seeks to increase exemption limit of individual income tax payers from 1.6* lakh to ₹ 2 lakhs. Higher exemption limit for working women have been withdrawn and they have been clubbed with other non-senior citizens by fixing their exemption limit also at ₹ 2 lakh. For senior citizens (i.e. those with more than 65 years) exemption limit has been marginally raised from ₹ 2.40 lakh to 2.50 lakh per annum.

Income Tax Slabs. For individuals the following tax slabs have been proposed. Along with these on the right hand side we have given existing tax slabs to show how the individuals with various income brackets will benefit from the tax provisions of the new DTC Bill, 2010.

---

*Note that on 2011-12 budget exemption limit for individual tax payers has already been raised to 1.80 lakh

Increase in basic exemption limit will benefit the individual tax payers as they will result in tax saving for all to the varying degree depending upon the income bracket in which they fall. Besides, education cess and surcharge on income tax has been removed which benefit all income tax payers.

Table 33A.1. Personal Income Tax Slabs

Tax Slabs in the New DTC Bill	*Slabs Existing Income Tax*
upto 2 lakh . . . . Nil	upto 1.6 lakh .... Nil
2 lakhs to <5 lakhs 10%	1.6 lakh to 5 lakh 10%
5 lakhs to < 10 lakhs 20%	5 lakh to 8 lakh 20%
over 10 lakh 30%	above 8 lakhs 30%

Income Tax Slabs for Senior Citizen

Slabs in DTC	*Existing Slabs*
Upto 2.50 lakh .... Nil	Upto 2.40 lakh* .... Nil
2.50 lakhs to < 5 lakh 10%	2.40 lakh < 5 lakh 10%
5 lakh to < 10 lakh 20%	5 lakh < 8 lakh 20%
above 10 lakh 30%	above 8 lakh 30%

It may be noted that income tax slabs that the DTC bill has been greatly diluted as compared to those originally proposed in Aug. 2009 version. In the original DTC the first slab went up to ₹ 10 lakh and carried 10% tax rate; the second slab was of ₹ 10 lakh to ₹ 25 lakh carrying 20% tax rate and the third slab was of income above ₹ 25 lakh with tax rate of 30%. Thus the promise that direct tax code would drastically cut income tax rate after withdrawing most of the exemptions to make rule-based and less directionary stands belied. It appears that government had a second thought over the issue and since it could not withdraw several exemptions to provide not only incentives for saving but also for investing in shares of corporate companies. We spell out later the exemptions provided in the new Direct Tax Code Bill.

In a significant departure from its original plan of doing away with various exemptions DTC retained the existing ₹ 100,000 overall exemptions for providing incentives for savings. Apart from contribution to Employees provident Fund (EPP), Public Provident Fund PPF), superannuation fund (including New Pension scheme), gratuity fund and the other approved securities constituted the various components of this list of exemptions within the overall limit of ₹ 100,000. Besides, the Direct Tax Code (DTC) Bill has proposed to introduce a new investment scheme to avail tax exemptions. In this scheme investment upto ₹ 50,000 in Life Insurance Policies, health insurance (i.e. mediclaim) and children's education fees are exempted from income tax. This is expected to give boost to life and health insurance and to promotion of children's education.

Thus the exemption limit under this head has been marginally increased from 1 lakh to 1.5 lakh but it has been split into two parts. So the freedom to invest most of the income in any one particular scheme has been curtailed.

ELSS, ULIPS, Bank Fixed Deposits Withdrawn from Exemption List

It is important to note that deposits/investment in some important instruments such as equity linked saving schemes (ELSS), Unit linked insurance Plans (ULIPS) and Bank's Fixed Deposits (for fixed five years period) have been removed from the qualifying list of tax exemption under this list. As a result, investment in ELSS and ULIPS will lose much of sheen.

*Note that in the budget for 2011-12 exemption limit for senior citizens has already been raised to 2.50 lakhs.

Other Exemptions from Salary Income. Apart from the general exemptions from taxation mentioned above, there are certain other exemptions from income tax that are allowed from salary income.

First, as at present, *house rent allowance* (*HRA*) obtained by salary earners is exempted from income tax even under the new DTC bill. This will ensure parity between employees staying in own houses and those staying in rental houses. Secondly, as at present, employees will continue to avail of *exemption for leave encashment on retirement* upto, a certain limit that are yet to be specified. In the present tax regime leave encashments on retirement by government employees is fully exempted from income tax. However, in some specified cases exemption from income tax is available up to ₹ 3 lakh.

Thirdly, as at present, in the new direct tax code also *medical treatment facilities* in some specified hospitals will not be taxable. Besides, *reimbursement of medical expenses upto ₹ 50,000* has been exempted from income tax as against ₹ 15000 at present. Fourthly, exemption for *leave travel concession* (*LTC*) in respect of travel expenses for self/family from income tax (subject to certain conditions) that is available at present has been removed in the new direct tax code.

Retirement Benefits. As at present, DTC exempts from income tax terminal benefits as such as gratuity, VRS, commuted pension (subject to some conditions). This mitigates the financial hardship of salary earners after retirement.

It is evident from above that except in case of LTC concession all other exemptions from income tax in case of salaried class will continue even in the new direct tax code.

Life Insurance Policies and Taxation

It will be useful to examine Direct Tax Code (DTC) bill with regard to the benefits or other wise of life insurance policies. First, as mentioned above, *life insurance premium* eligible for deduction from income has been limited to ₹ 50,000 only along with mediclaim premia and children's tuition fees. Second, *premium paid on life insurance policy which exceeds* 5% of the capital sum insured *are not eligible* for deduction for calculating taxable income. Third, *maturity proceeds* of a life insurance policy received on the original insurance period will be exempted from income tax only if the premium paid on it in any year is less than 5 per cent of the sum insured. However, the proceeds received on the death of the insured will be exempted irrespective of the amount of annual premia paid. Since threshold of the annual premium of 5% of the sum assured seems to be low it will adversely affect the issue of even genuine insurance policies.

Lastly, *5% tax on distribution of income of equity linked insurance policies* has been levied in the hands of individuals. This would lower the effective yield of such instruments and as a result they will lose much of the sheen they have at present.

Capital Gains Taxation

With the introduction of modified New Direct Tax Code bill in Parliament on Aug. 31, 2010 there has been a big relief to the investors in the capital market. The original draft on Direct Tax Code (DTC) had proposed to adopt graded tax system for long-term capital gains on the basis of period of investment while doing away with zero tax system for long-term capital gains. In the graded tax system, if one remains invested for a longer period in listed securities, the effective tax rate would be lower and vice-versa. Stock-market investors criticized this proposal as it would have adversely affected the net return from investment in equities. The DTC bill introduced in Parliament decided to continue with the existing system of zero tax on the long term capital gains from sale of shares and equity linked other schemes. In the new modified DTC bill though no specific distinction has been made in the long-term and short-term capital gains, they have been treated more favourably as compared with the existing system of taxing them. For the short-term small investors, the DTC bill has reduced the tax burden substantially. Besides, the DTC bill is positive for the stock market. We explain below the treatment of capital gains in the new modified Direct Tax Code.

Securities Transaction Tax (STT). The securities transaction tax (STT) is leviable on sale/ purchase transaction of securities (equity shares, equity linked mutual funds, debentures) made in the recognised stock exchange at the rate of 0.25 per cent. The modified DTC Bill has proposed to continue levying securities transaction tax (STT) in the same way as at present.

Capital Gains. As regards capital gains the modified DTC draws the distinction between the transaction of shares/securities held by a person for more than 12 months and those held for less than 12 months. If securities (shares, equity linked mutual funds, debentures etc) are held by person or a company for more than 12 months, 100 per cent capital gains would be allowed as deduction from income if securities transaction tax (STT) has been paid. In other words, entire capital gains from sale of securities held by persons for more than a year are not taxable if securities transaction tax (STT) has been paid. On the other hand, transaction of securities (shares, debentures, equity linked mutual funds) held for less than 12 months by a person, 50 per cent of capital gains from their sales will be allowed deduction for calculating taxable income (if STT has been paid for them) and the remaining capital gains will be clubbed with other regular income of individuals and taxed according to the tax slab applicable to them. In other words, this means investors have to pay half of the tax rate applicable to their income tax slab.

At present, tax on short-term capital gains (i.e. for investment less than one year) is 15 per cent. Along with surcharge and education cess, the tax amount becomes 17%. This rate *is presently applicable to everybody irrespective of the investor's income level in the different tax slabs of 10%* or 20% or 30%. So in the existing tax regime big investor who fall in 20% or 30% tax slab pay 17% tax on short-term capital gains, instead of 20% or 30% in which tax slab his income level falls. But in the new modified DTC small investor having income between ₹ 2 lakh and 5 lakh will pay only 5% short-term capita gains tax, that is, half of 10% tax they will have to pay in this income slab. This is less than one-third of the existing short-term capital gains, tax of 17%. Investors having income between ₹ 5 lakh and 10 lakh will pay the short-term capital gains at the rate of 10% as the modified Direct Tax Code proposes 20% tax on income slab of 5 lakh to 10 lakh. However, even big investors having income over ₹ 10 lakh will pay the short-term capital gains tax at 15% compared to their income tax of 30%. Thus even big investors gain as in the present system they also have to pay 17% tax rate. But, as explained above, small investors gain more.

Capital Losses. However, investors suffering losses on their equity transactions will not be better off than the present regime. There would be no relief on long-term capital losses, as the same has to be set-off only against long-term capital gain; the latter being nil.

In the case of *short-term capital losses*, only 50 per cent such losses can be set off against the total *short-term capital gains*. In other words, if an investor had, say a ₹ 50 short-term capital loss, only ₹ 25 would be allowed to be set off against the short-term capital gains. In the present tax regime, the entire losses are be allowed as set-off against short-term capital gains.

EEE is Restored in the Modified Direct Tax Code

EEE or Exempt, Exempt and Exempt of an investment scheme implies all three stages, namely, (i) deposit or investment in a scheme, annual income from it and withdrawal of the sum on maturity are exempted from income tax. When the first draft of Direct Tax Code (DTC) was released and fears were expressed that *withdrawal of money* from provident fund account and other such schemes would be taxed though deposit (i.e. investment) in them in the first instance and yearly income from them were exempted from income tax. That is Exempt, Exempt and Exempt (EEE), would no longer apply. However, the modified version of DTC as presented in the bill introduced in the Parliament EEE method of treatment of most of tax-saving schemes such as provident fund account superannuation fund has been restored. Thus, in their case deposit (or investment) in them (upto a certain limit), annual income from them and final withdrawal from them on maturity would be exempted from tax as is displayed in the Table 33A.2.

Table 33A. 2. Small Savings Instruments – Taxability in the Hands of the Investor

Instrument	Stage	Existing	Proposed in DTC
Provident fund	Investment	Exempt	Exempt
	Income	Exempt	Exempt
	Withdrawal	Exempt	Exempt
Superannuation fund	Investment	Exempt	Exempt
	Income	Exempt	Exempt
	Withdrawal	Exempt	Exempt
Mutual funds – Equity linked Schemes	Investment	Exempt	–
	Income	Exempt	Exempt
	Withdrawal	Long term Capital gains Exempt	Short-term Capital gains Taxable
Mutual funds Debt	Investment	Exempt	Exempt
	Income	Taxable	Taxable
	Withdrawal	Exempt	Exempt

However *in case of equity-linked mutual funds* short-term capital gains are taxable on withdrawal when they mature and on case of debt linked mutual funds annual income from them is taxable though final withdrawal at the time of maturity is exempted from tax (see Table – 33A.2) Besides, according to final DTC tax exemption on interest paid on housing loan will continue subject to a ceiling of ₹ 1.5 lakh.

Tax on Property Income

DTC bill proposes to levy tax on income (rent) on housing property only *when rent is actually received or receivable*. That is, DTC bill has removed the tax on **notional rental income** from the house property. This removes the anomaly in the present taxation system which levies income tax on house property (other than self-occupied one) even if it is not actually let out. The present system levied tax on house property which is not let out on deemed rent basis. This was quite unjust and unfair.

New modified DTC allows 20% on gross rent towards repairs etc and therefore not taxable as against deduction of 30% on gross rent on account of repairs in the present tax regime.

In addition to the above modified deduction upto ₹ 1.5 lakh on interest instalment on loan for self-occupied house has been allowed in the new modified DTC. This will boost investment in the construction of houses. However, *tax benefit on repayment of the principal of home loan* has been withdrawn in the new DTC.

CORPORATE INCOME TAX

Corporate income tax yields a good amount of revenue for the government. In the DTC bill rate of corporate tax has been reduced to 30% with no extra surcharge and cess as against the current rate of 33.22 per cent (inclusive of surcharge and cess). Though the original DTC draft released in Aug. 2009 had proposed 25% rate of corporate tax along with *2% asset-based MAT* which was called Gross Asset Tax (GAT). Since asset-based MAT was strongly opposed on the ground that even loss-making companies will have to pay such a tax, less revenue-yielding MAT on profit basis has therefore been proposed in the DTC bill, while corporate tax rate has been fixed at a higher level of 30 per cent with no extra surcharge and cess as compared to 33.22% tax (inclusive of surcharge and cess). Thus, the reduction in corporate tax by 3.22 per cent in our view is quite a significant relief for the companies which will result in lot of tax saving by them. Further, New DTC bill also allows the companies to offset losses made on infrastructure projects against corporate income. This is a also beneficial for the companies especially those engaged in power, road, oil and gas companies.

Further, in addition to corporate income tax in DTC bill also there is *dividend distribution tax* on corporate companies at the rate of 15% as against 16.6% at present. This also gives relief to the companies.

Minimum Alternative Tax (MAT)

It is proposed to raise minimum alternate tax (MAT) to 20 per cent on book profits but diluted the earlier proposal to impose it on gross assets that had drawn protests from firms. MAT was introduced in fiscal 1998 to address the inequity. Many companies, despite marking book profits as per their profit and loss account, were hardly paying any tax because income computed as per provisions of the Income-Tax Act, was either nil, or insignificant.

Besides exemptions, there were several deductions permitted from gross total income. The result of such exemptions, deductions, and other incentives under the Act in the form of liberal rates of depreciation was the emergence of Zero tax companies which in spite of having high book profits were able to reduce their taxable income to nil.

Special economic zone (SEZ) developers and units operating there are also included under the MAT regime. Under DTC, all the corporate taxpayers will now be liable to MAT including those availing the investment-linked incentives and profit-linked incentives.

Besides, in new modified DTC companies will be allowed to carry forward credit for taxes paid at MAT for 15 years (as against 10 years at present) when it begins to pay the regular corporate tax rate. Like other corporate companies the companies paying MAT to the government are also liable to pay dividend distribution tax at the rate of 15% as against 16.6% at present.

Special Economic Zone (SEZ) and MAT. Special economic zones (SEZ) developers and the units operating there have also been brought under the MAT regime and therefore they will also pay 20% tax on their book profit. However, the Direct Taxes Code (DTC). Bill has offered a reprieve to Special Economic Zones (SEZ) from payment of MAT till 2014.

At present, SEZs enjoy income tax holidays on the principle that *location-based exemptions promote regional development*. Under the present regime, SEZ units get 100 per cent tax exemption on profits earned for the first five years, 50 per cent for the next five years and another 50 per cent on reinvested profits in the following five years.

SEZ *developers*, on the other hand, get 100 per cent tax exemption on profits for ten years, which they can choose in the block of the first fifteen years. In the Bill, the government has proposed that deduction under section 10AA of the repealed Income-tax Act shall continue to be allowed under DTC. However, this is conditional upon the fact that SEZ units should begin to manufacture or produce articles in zone on or before March 31, 2014. For existing units set up under the repealed Income-tax Act, deduction would be allowed only for the un-expired period.

Charitable and Not-For-Profit Organisation

The government has proposed to exempt income of charitable and not-for-profit organisations up to ₹1 lakh from tax and levy a tax of 15 per cent on all income above that ceiling. However, according to the Direct Taxes Code (DTC) Bill, these provisions would not apply to specified organisations. According to DTC Bill, charitable activity does not include the carrying on of any activity in the nature of trade, commerce or business or any activity of rendering any service for a fee except where the gross receipts during the financial year from such activity exceed ₹ 10 lakhs.

It has also dropped the earlier controversial proposal to enforce a compulsory registration of such institutions with the income tax department. The Bill specifies that fresh registration would not be required for such organisations having existing income tax registration. At present trusts and institutions established for charitable purposes do not pay income tax on donations received by them. The DTC Bill proposes to tax anonymous donations at the rate of 30% as against 15% applicable to other donations.

Taxation of Foreign Companies

A significant feature of DTC bill is that tax rate for foreign corporate companies has also been fixed at 30% (that is, at par with the domestic companies) as against 42.23% in the current tax regime in case income exceeds ₹ one core. This represents a great relief for the foreign companies of about 12 per cent on the tax rate. This seeks to ensure level playing field for the foreign companies. However, profits of Indian branches of foreign companies will be subject to additional **'Branch Profit Tax (BPT)'** leviable at the rate of 15% on total income. It may however be noted this 'branch profit tax BPT' on total income of Indian branches of foreign companies is comparable to 15% tax on the amount of dividends distribution by the Indian domestic companies. However, while dividend distribution tax is payable at the time of distribution of dividends to the shareholders, BPT is however not linked to remittance of profits to their head office abroad.

Further, the proposed Direct Tax Code (DTC) has introduced the concept of *Controlled Foreign Companies* (CFC) which, among other things, provides for taxing income earned by *a foreign company controlled directly or indirectly* by a resident in India. The purpose of this provision in DTC is to capture the income earned by CFC during a fiscal year opportioned to the Indian shareholder to the extent of its share in the profits of CFC less any amount received during the fiscal year as a dividend from such a company. Under CFC rules even income of such foreign company not distributed to shareholders would be deemed to be distributed and consequently taxable in India in the hands of resident shareholders as dividend received from the foreign company.

However, in our view, since in the rules prescribed in this connection no credit for taxes paid abroad by foreign subsidiary has been provided, this will lead to effective double taxation which is quite unjust.

Critical Evaluation

The idea of the direct tax code (DTC) was to restructure the Indian direct tax system so as to make economically efficient, effective and equitable by removing the unnecessary exemptions. It was estimated that because of these exemptions, there was a loss of government revenue to the tune of 6.5 per cent GDP. It was thought that if we could plug this loophole from the Indian tax system, tax GDP ratio could rise significantly. The higher tax GDP ratio would not only help to eliminate revenue deficit but also make sufficient resources available to take third of its people out of poverty and provide rudimentary health care and equip them with basic skills needed to be engaged in productive employment.

It was thought that with the plethora of unnecessary exemptions removed it would be possible to drastically lower tax rates and broaden the tax net for raising government revenue through greater tax compliance. But the originally proposed Direct Tax Code (DTC) has been so much diluted and watered down that earlier expectations of raising enough revenue by making the tax system economically efficient and effective stand belied. The revised direct Tax Code bill as introduced in Parliament is just old wine in old bottle as it has finally tampered only with tax slabs, rather than making sweeping changes in the direct tax system. The existing talk slab of 1.6 lakh to 3 lakh has been substituted by the slab of 2 lakh to 5 lakh; the slab of ₹ 3 lakh to ₹ 10 lakh has been substituted by that of ₹ 5 lakh to ₹ 10 lakh; and slab of over ₹ 8 lakh has been replaced by that of over ₹ 10 lakh. Even without any bill such adjustments in tax slabs would have made keeping in view higher inflation rate in the last two years. Taxing income above ₹ 25 lakh at 30% as proposed in the original draft DTC does not remotely resemble the plan to apply the same rate at above a mere ₹ 10 lakh.

Exemption limit for senior citizens has been only marginally increased from ₹ 2.40 lakh to ₹ 2.50 lakh which is only a meagre increase in view of double digit inflation as measured by CPI in the last two years. (Note that exemption limit for senior citizens has already been raised to ₹ 2.50 lakh in the budget, 2011-12). Further, bringing women tax payers at par with men is a retrograde step for only 0.27 per cent of working age women are estimated to pay income tax. So the aim should have been to incentivise more women to join the work force by their preferential treatment in the tax system. Regarding personal income tax, taxpayers falling in income bracket of up to ₹ 5 lakh will benefit the most. It is now well known that location-based tax employees for various corporate companies have failed to provide regional development. Several other exemptions such as liberal depreciation allowance, liberal permission of huge expenditure on advertising in print and electronic media as cost expenditure allowed as deduction to calculate taxable income are not justified. The retention of several exemptions in the direct tax system that make it rule-based rather than discretionary as a result of lobbying by the rich industrialists and their organisations prevents the government to lower taxes and broaden the tax net and also make it effective and equitable. Several of these exemptions have not served the intended purpose of promoting research and development (R&D) and to encourage discover new innovations.

Besides, if employment objective has to be pursued vigorously then not only labour-intensive small-scale industries deserve preferential treatment in taxation but also income tax breaks should be available on the basis of employment generated by an a corporate enterprise rather than liberal depreciation on the basis of in capital assets. Besides, capital gains has been treated more favourably in the direct tax code bill. There is no valid reason for exempting from income tax long-term capital gains entirely. Imposition of short-run capital gains at half of the tax slab rates, namely, at 5% 10% and 15% is preferential treatment for speculative investment rather than promoting genuine productive investment. It is ironical that while government is borrowing heavily to fund its welfare programmes and poverty reduction, it exempts long-term capital gains from income tax and levies only at half the tax rate on the short-term capital gains than that of regular income of the relevant slab.

Preferential tax treatment in India's emerging economy is required only for saving which needs to be promoted for accelerating investment. Tax rationalisation requires removing unnecessary exemptions wherever possible. Thus, the DTC which is more or less the same as the existing tax regime. By merely timbering at the margins, it misses the chance to be an effective instrument to move the Indian economy onto a higher growth trajectory.

CHAPTER 34

Fiscal Policy : Role of Government Borrowing for Financing of Fiscal Deficit

Government borrowing is another fiscal method by which savings of the community may be mobilised for economic development. In developing economies, the Governments resort to borrowing in order to finance schemes of economic development. Government or what is also called public borrowing becomes necessary because taxation alone cannot provide sufficient funds for economic development. Besides, too heavy taxation has an adverse effect on private saving and investment. It may noted that when there is fiscal deficit (i.e. budget deficit). It can be financed in two ways. First, by borrowing by the Government from the market and this borrowing leads to the increase in public debt. Borrowing as a means to finance the fiscal deficit is therefore also called **debt-financing of budget deficit.** Second, budget or fiscal deficit can be financed by *printing new money* and therefore it is called *money financing* of fiscal deficit. The debt-financing of budget deficit will be discussed in the present chapter and money financing of fiscal or budget deficit will be discussed in the next chapter.

BORROWING OR DEBT-FINANCING OF FISCAL DEFICIT

Under debt-financing of fiscal deficit or borrowing the government issues bonds and sells it in the market. Generally, sale of interest-bearing bonds to the public is indirect through financial intermediarises such as banks. Banks buy the bonds floated by the government with the currency deposits of the public. Therefore, debt-financing of budget deficit is also known as *bond-financy of budget deficit*. With the borrowed money in this way the government is able to expand its expenditure but at the same time it adds to public debt which has both short-run and long run consequences. It may also be noted that budget deficit also comes about when taxes are reduced, keeping government expenditure constant. This type of budget deficit can also be financed through incurring debt by selling bonds to the banks or public. The government has not only to pay annually interest on borrowed funds but has to pay back also the principal sum borrowed for which it may levy higher taxes in future.

The Keynesians have emphasised the expansionary effect of debt financing of government expenditure or budget deficit. In the Keynesian model with a fixed price level, the increase in government expenditure through use of borrowed money causes an upward shift in aggregate expenditure ($C + I + G$) curve. If the economy is working at less than full-employment level of national income so that output gap exists in the economy, the increase in debt-financed government expenditure will bring about expansion in output or income. With the increase in income at the given tax rate, tax revenue collected will rise which will over time reduce the budget deficit or even ultimately eliminate it so that budget becomes balanced. This can also be illustrated through *IS-LM* model in Figure 34.1 where *IS* and *LM* curves are drawn, given the money supply in the economy. Y^* is the full-employment level of output. Initially, the equilibrium is at income level Y_0. Now, with debt-financed increase in government expenditure *IS* curve shift to the right from IS_0 to IS_1 with *LM* curve remaining the same. As a result, as will be seen from Fig. 34.1, national income increases to Y_1. This will bring about increase in tax revenue collected by the government and over time budget deficit will be

However critics have pointed out that debt-financed government expenditure is largely offset by the *crowding-out effect* of debt financing on private investment. The crowding-out effect on private investment takes place in a variety of ways. First, it has been pointed out that government's borrowing funds to finance budget deficit will lead to the increase in demand for lendable funds which will cause the rate of interest to rise. The rise in interest rate will cause private investment to decline. Thus, debt-financed increase in government expenditure crowds out private investment. According to this

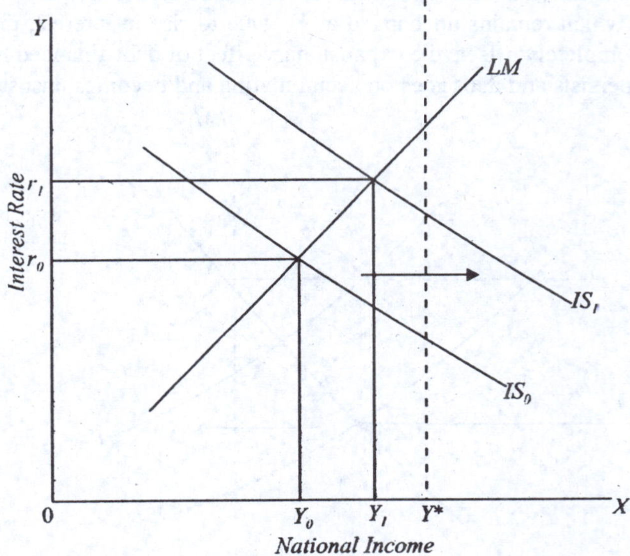

Fig. 34.1. *Expansionary Effect of Debt-financed Increase in Government Expenditure*

view, due to crowding-out effect on private investment net expansionary effect of increase in government expenditure is negligible. On the other hand, the society will have to bear the burden of increase in public debt as a result of debt-financed expansion in government expenditure. If budget deficit arises due to reduction in taxes, keeping government expenditure constant, this will also lead to rise in interest rate and will therefore cause crowding-out effect on private investment. This happens because reduction in taxes stimulates consumption expenditure of the people which reduces savings. The decline in savings causes interest rate to rise resulting in fall in private investment.

Wealth Effect of Debt-Financing (i.e., Government Borrowing)

In our above analysis we have not taken into account the *wealth effect* of debt financing. When the government issues bonds to finance its budget deficit, it creates private wealth. This is because bonds are considered as wealth by the people. Patinkin and Friedman in their models include wealth in their money demand function. That is, according to them, demand from money depends on the real value of wealth, apart from other factors. If this wealth effect of bond-financing of budget deficit is recognised, then it exercises an important influence on the dynamic behaviour of the economy. When through debt-financing of budget deficit, more bonds are issued and sold by the government, the wealth of the people increases which will raise the demand for money.[1] The increase in demand for money, money supply remaining the same, causes a leftward shift in the *LM* curve, for instance, from LM_0 to LM_1 in Figure 34.2. This is because borrowing which raises demand for money, given the supply, causes interest rate to rise. (Note that financing of Government expenditure through creation of printed money, causes *LM* curve to the right). Thus, while with the increase in government

1. See R. Dornbusch, S. Fischer, & R. Startz, *Macroeconomics*, Tata McGraw Hill, 8th edition, P.476.

expenditure *IS* curve shifts to the right to the new position IS_1 which tends to raise aggregate income, the wealth effect of bonds issued to finance the deficit causes leftward shift in the *LM* curve which tends to raise rate of interest and thereby crowds out private investment. According to Friedman, the wealth effect is quite substantial so that it completely offsets the expansionary effect of increase in government expenditure. In Figure 34.2, initially the equilibrium is at Y_0 level of income. With bond-financed increase in government expenditure *IS* curve shifts from IS_0 to IS_1 and due to wealth effect *LM* curve shifts leftward to LM_1. It will be seen that interest rate rises from r_0 to r_1 with no net effect on the level of income which remains unchanged at Y_0. Due to rise in interest, private investment declines so much that completely offsets the expansionary effect of debt-financed budget deficit. As a result, budget deficit persists and debt goes on accumulating and becomes unsustainable.

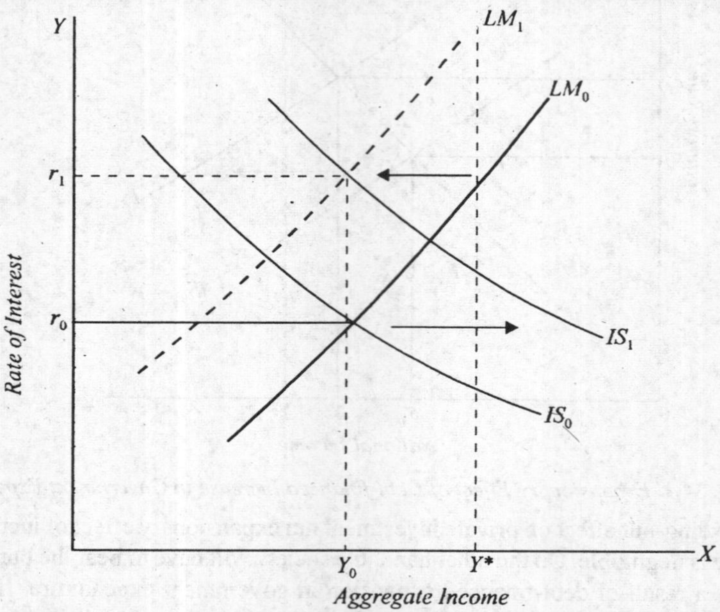

Fig. 34.2. *Debt-financing of Budget Deficit with Wealth effect of Bonds Sold by the Government*

In the above analysis of crowding-out effect of debt-financing it is assumed that price level remains fixed. However, when the aggregate supply function is vertical as is the case when the economy is working at full capacity output (i.e., full-employment level), increase in aggregate demand (*AD*) brought about by debt-financed increase in government expenditure will result in rise in price level, equilibrium income remains unchanged as shown through *AS-AD* model in Figure 34.3. Since income remains unchanged, tax-revenue, will not increase and therefore budget deficit persists and debt will go on accumulating and over time become unsustainable.

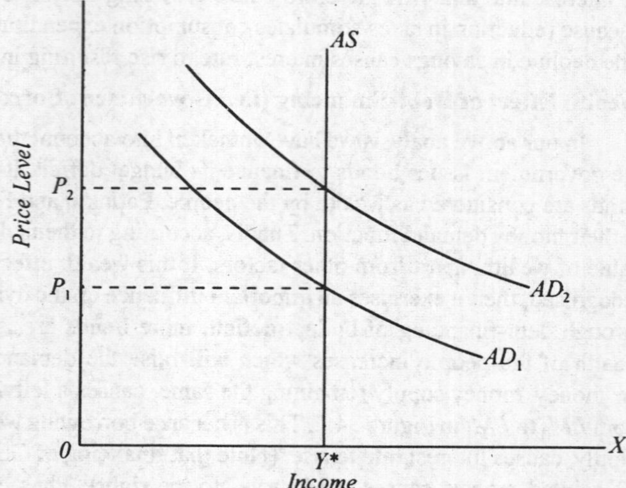

Fig. 34.3. *Rise in price level offsets the expansionary effect of debt financing of budget deficit.*

Conclusion: We have seen above that expansionary effect of debt-financed budget deficit has been challenged on the ground of its crowding-out effect. However, in our view, the crowding-out effect of debt-financing has been belown out of all proportions. As a matter of fact, crowding-out effect of debt financing of budget deficit is negligible, especially when the economy is working at less than full-employment level of income. Generally, budget deficit and its financing through floating of bonds is recommend to overcome depression when there is under-employment equilibrium and therefore output gap exists. For planned development in developing countries where there *exists potential for growth*, debt-financing or borrowing by the Government can be used for mobilising resources for projects of economic growth, expecially infrastructure. *Empirical evidence also shows that wealth effect of sale of bonds is not significant.* As shall be discussed below in detail, even in developing countries where there is gross under-utilisation of resources or when they work at less than their full-production capacity, policy of budget deficits and financing it through debt to a reasonable degree is a useful instrument for stimulating economic growth and raise income.

GOVERNMENT BORROWING OR DEBT-FINANCING OF FISCAL DEFICIT : THE CASE OF INDIA

In India there has been a problem of persistent budget deficits which has been largely financed by borrowing from the banks and public and thus adding to the public debt. In 1991 as a measure of economic reforms IMF directed that fiscal deficit of the central government should be reduced to achieve economic stability. The economists associated with IMF and World Bank hold the view that large fiscal deficit raises inflation rate of the economy on the one hand and since it is financed largely by borrowing from the market, this raises rate of interest and therefore crowds out private investment and adversely affects economic growth. Besides, it has been pointed out that the persistent budget deficit year after year adds to public debt and as a result ratio of public debt to national income (Debt/ GDP ratio) will greatly increase which will land the country in debt trap[2].

In view of the above it is appropriate to discuss the above issues relating to debt-financing of budget deficit in the light of the recent Indian experience. It is worth mentioning that from the years 1997 to 2002-03 and again in 2008 and 2009 the Indian economy experienced slowdown in economic growth due to lack of aggregate demand resulting mainly from the fall in public investment and poor performance in agriculture. In this situation *output gap* in the Indian economy emerged as the existing production capacity was not fully utilised. Besides, there has been lack of infrastructure facilities which stands in the way of raising private investment.

With their focus on reducing fiscal deficit the government reduced its capital expenditure (i.e. investment expenditure) because it failed to curb its consumption expenditure and subsidies. Thus, Mihir Rakshit, a leading Indian macroeconomist, rightly states. "With their focus on fiscal deficit, policy makers seem to think that what matters primarily is curbing government expenditure .... irrespective of changes in their composition. The period 1995-2000 was marked by 9.6 per cent and 12.6 per cent growth in government consumption and subsidies respectively, but public sector capital accumulation grew at snail's pace of 1.9 per cent and its two crucial constituents, namely, investment in agriculture and infrastructure actually declined by 5.6 per cent and 0.2 per cent respectively"[3]

The consequences of debt-financed budget deficit in the case of India depends on whether or not output gap exists due to lack of demand and infrastructural facilities. If the output gap exists, then increase in government expenditure on consumption and subsidies will raise aggregate demand

2. For this view, see Shankar Acharya, former Chief Economic Advisor who puts forward this view in a forcefull manner in 'How Fiscal Deficit Hurts Economic Growth. We have explained in detail this mainstream view in the next chapter.
3. Mihir Rakshit, "Some Macroeconomics of India's Reforms Experience" in *India's Emerging Economy* (e.d.) Kaushik Basu, Oxford University Press, 2004, p,104.

and help in utilising more fully the existing production capacity and over time will cause private investment to rise. But this will not raise public saving and public investment and therefore will not result in much higher growth of the economy. This may also raise ratio of public debt to GDP since due to slow growth in GDP, tax collection will not appreciably rise. Mihir Rakshit aptly points out that, "The Indian economy since 1997[3] has also been characterised by output gap, high fiscal deficit and growing debt/GDP ratio. The mainstream view in India is that despite the output gap fiscal deficits crowd out private investment and are unsustainable"[4].

The mainstream view of debt-financed fiscal deficit is not correct and has been rightly challenged by some prominent India economists such as Mihir Rakshit, V.N. Pandit and Prabhat Patnaik, among others. Under the circumstances when there exists output-gap and under-utilisation of production capacity, the increase in government expenditure, especially of investment nature will *crowd in* private investment and speed up rate of economic growth. To quote Mihir Rakshit, "contrary to wide-spread perception among commentators *budget deficits associated with closing the output gap in fact crowds in private investment*.......... crowding in will be much more pronounced in countries like India where government's infrastructural investment favourably affects private investment even while projects are being executed : the fact that highways are being built in some area or that it will soon have abundant supply of power, communication facilities is likely to induce private investors to start setting up new units and expending existing ones even in the shrot run"[5].

When there is output-gap in a developing economy such as India, even increase in Government's consumption expenditure will crowd in private investment through the former's demand effect. But, as has been pointed out by Dr. Mihir Rakshit, crowding-in effect of government's investment expenditure will be greater because it expands the infrastructural facilities (i.e. supply-side factors) badly needed for increase in private investment.

In our view, the expansionary effect of government's investment expenditure and also its crowding-in effect on private investment in a developing country like India is not confined to the situation when output gap and under-utilisation of capital stock exists due to demand deficiency but also when such an economy functions at its normal capacity. Besides, even in normal times, debt-financed government investment expenditure which brings about rapid economic growth, budget deficits and debt/GDP ratio over time can be reduced. An *important rule of public finance, which is sometimes* described as a *golden rule* is that if borrowed money by the government is used for investment or developmental purposes, it leads to growth in GDP or national income. Given the tax rate, this increase in income will ensure collection of more tax revenue possible. As a result, budget deficit or what is also called fiscal deficit will be reduced and debt/GDP ratio will decline. This has actually happened in India.

As a matter of fact long ago (in 1994) E.D. Domar had stated the condition for sustainability of persistent budget deficits and consequently of mounting public debit. According to Domar, *debt-financed deficits are sustainable if growth rate exceeds the rate of interest*. This is because economic growth means increase in income or GDP from which annual interest payments can be made and if growth in income exceeds the rate of interest, the part of increase in income may be used for retiring public debt. In this way with the growth of the economy budget deficit and debt/GDP ratio can be reduced Elaborating Domar's condition. Mihir Rakshit writes, "According to Domar, if the government finances part of its expenditure (amounting to a given fraction of full-employment output) through borrowing, in a growing economy public debt and the government interest outgo as proportion of GDP will be stable in the long run provided the growth rate exceeds the interest rate.

---

4. Budget Deficit: Sustainability, Solvancy and Optimality, printed in Amaresh Bagchi, "*Readings in Public Finance*" Oxford University Press, 2005, pp. 342-343.
5. Mihir Rabshit, op. cit. p.345
6. Mihir Rakshit, op. cit. (2005), p. 340.

The implication is that when this condition is satisfied, maintenance of full employment through debt financing of budget deficit does not erode fiscal viability or produce a debt trap"[6]

The viability and sustainability of debt-financed budget deficits in a growing economy must be based on the magnitude of Government investment expenditure (I_g) in the total expenditure ($I_g + G$). Suppose the economy is working at the full capacity output, and government increases its investment expenditure, say, in infrastructure and finances the budget deficit through incurring debt. This increase in government investment expenditure will raise income through both demand effect and capacity effect and will therefore stimulate private investment which depends on change in income (i.e. $Y_1 - Y_{t-1}$). This increase in both government and private investment will over time cause rapid growth in income which in turn will result in more tax revenue. Thus, in this way budget deficit will be reduced with favourable effect on public debt/GDP ratio, if rate of growth in income (GDP) exceeds rate of interest.

It is thus clear that sustainability of budget deficit and public debt (*i.e.* government borrowing) depends on *shifting the composition of government expenditure towards investment.* To quote Mihir Rakshit, "Budgetary viability requires an improvement in revenue balances in the medium term and the long run....... public investment in agriculture aided by crowding-in effect, raises agricultural productivity and acts as a stimulant to a rural economy, brings down poverty and *enables the government to reduce over time expenditure on food or fertilizer subsidies and poverty alleviation measures.* An increase in government investment in rural and urban infrastructural facilities will through increased revenue receipts and decreased subsidies will strengthen budgetary position not only in the medium term and the long run but in the short run as well"[7]. It is interesting to note that when with effect from year 2003 the Government investment expenditure in India had been raised, tax revenue collection significantly increased and also fiscal deficit, revenue deficit and debt/GDP ratio declined. Besides, private investment had also gone up (*i.e.* crowed in) rather than crowding out by increase in debt-financed increase in government expenditure.

Thus, in the nineties when the focus in our strategy was to reduce fiscal deficit, no matter reducing capital expenditure of the government for this purpose, the Indian economy experienced slowdown in growth and our fiscal situation worsened. On the other hand, when from March 2003 we shifted the focus toward increase in government investment expenditure on power, ports, highways, rural roads in a big way, private investment also croweded in, generated higher economic growth which resulted in lower fiscal deficits and lower debt/GDP ratio.

Now-a-days, the Central Government borrows mostly from the market through sale of its bonds of different maturities carrying different rates of interest by RBI.

Borrowing is the quickest mode of raising funds. Financing through taxation is not so expeditious because passing of tax laws, assessment of taxes based on those laws and their collection involves considerable delay. On the other hand, bonds can be issued any time during a year. It is bankes, insurance companies, mutual funds that usually invest their funds in government bonds. **Public borrowing generates additional productive capacity.** The funds raised by public borrowing can be utilised for building up economic infrastructure for the economy through schemes for the development of irrigation, transport, power and communication. They can help also in building up of the agricultural and industrial base of the economy. All such investments facilitate further economic growth. There is no doubt, therefore, that the public borrowing plays a very useful and important role in accelerating economic development of underdeveloped economies. Public debt promotes saving and investment, the two most crucial determinants of economic growth.

But there are three problems concerning government borrowing. First, government borrowing leads to increase is public debt whose burden falls on future generations who have to pay higher

7. Mihir Rakshit, op. cit. 2005 p.105

taxes to the government for paying back the borrowed funds. Besides, every year the Government has to pay interest on the borrowed funds and these annual interest payments which are very large due to accumulated large public debt generally cause large deficit in revenue account of the Government budget. As a result, a large chunck of new borrowings every year are used to make interest payments. Thirdly, borrowing by the government from the market leads to increase in demand for loanable funds and *causes rise in interet* rate. At a higher interest rate private investment falls. Thus it is often asserted that *Government borrowing crowds out private investment*. However, when there is ample liquidity in the banking system, the banks can make adequate funds available for meeting the demand for funds for the corporate sector.

However, Government borrowing has often been used to finance Governments's current or consumption expenditure as there has been *large revenue deficit* year after year and Government borrowing has been used to meet this revenue deficit with the result that financing of capital expenditure through Government borrowing has been very small. *Golden rule of Government borrowing* is that it should be used for financing investment or productive projects so that it yields returns which can be used to pay interest on the borrowed funds as well as pay back the principal amount. In this way Government borrowing would not involve any burden on future generations and instead higher economic growth will occur which will benefit the future generations.

Another problem of Government borrowing to finance large fiscal deficit is that it causes large increase in government expenditure which leads to *excess demand conditions* in the immediate future which cause inflation in the economy. Therefore, financial prudence requires that fiscal deficit should be of reasonable degree and the funds borrowed by the Government should be used for investment and productive purposes so that inflationary pressures can be contained.

Obstacles. But there exist a number of obstacles which hinder the success of borrowing policy in developing countries. The resources of the organised financial market may be too inadequate to fulfil the needs both of the private and public sectors. Further, in the financial market the competition for funds between the government and the private sector will raise rate of interest and this will have a highly disincentive effect on the expansion of investment in the private sector. More borrowing by the Government leads to the rise in market rates of interest. The higher interest rates tends to reduce private investment. Therefore, it is often asserted that the *higher borrowing target by the Government `crowds out' private investment*. In India the rates of interest on loans (on bonds or securities) of Government have been raised quite substantially. Since banks and others prefer to invest in Government securities because they are safe (*i.e.*, riskless). This has reduced funds for private investment. However, in our view, this can be avoided if RBI through its monetary measures ensure adequate availability of funds available with the banks so that rate of interest does not rise when Government borrows from the market.

For the success of government's borrowing policy, it is necessary that financial institutions be developed and extended into the rural areas of the economy in order to inculcate the habit of thrift in the population and to mobilise for productive purposes the amount of savings originating in this sector. Besides, for the mobilisation of savings it will be necessary to check and regulate the diversion of savings into unproductive investment such as real estate, gold and jewellery and inventory accumulation.

Suitable techniques of borrowing must also be devised. For example, bonds issued by the Government should be adjusted to the preferences of the general public; bonds of large denomination and long maturity may be offered to the institutional investors, whereas those of small denomination and short maturity may be reserved for the non-institutional public. If properly devised and conducted small savings campaign can mobilise a sizable amount of resources. Further, the mobilisation of the hoardings of gold and jewellery through government programmes constitutes a highly desirable source of resource mobilisation. Of course, suitable techniques of public borrowing for the mobilisation of these resources have to be evolved.

CHAPTER 34A

Fiscal Policy : Resource Mobilisation Through Money Financing of Budget Deficit

Resource Mobilisation through Money Financing of Budget Deficit

The government can mobilise resources for economic growth by financing its budget deficit through printing high powered money. This is therefore called *money financing of budget deficit*. It is important to note that in the old or earlier terminology printing of new money to finance the budget deficit was called **deficit financing**. It is now called **money financing** of budget deficit for mobilising resources by the government. The printing of money to raise revenue by the government is also called **seigniorage**.

When government finances its budget deficit through printing money, money supply in the economy increases. There are two views regarding the effect of increase in money supply on inflation. According to the Keynesean view, when money supply is increased in times of depression when both productive capacity and labour are lying idle due to deficiency of aggregate demand, price level is not likely to rise much and the effect of increase in money supply is to raise output or income. The increase in real income, given the rate of taxation will bring about increase in revenue from taxation, which will *tend to reduce budget deficit in the short run*. However, if the economy is operating at or near full employment, printing money to finance the deficit will cause inflation. Printing money to raise revenue for financing the budget deficit which causes inflation is like an *inflation tax*. This is because the government is able to get resources through printed money which causes inflation and reduces the real value of the holdings of money by the public.

Let us first explain the Keynesian model with a fixed price level when the economy is in recession due to demand deficiency and a lot of unemployment of resources prevails. The tax function can be written as

$$T = t(Y)$$

where t is the rate of tax and Y is real income and T is the total tax revenue. If G is government expenditure, then budget deficit (BD) is given by

$$BD = G - t(Y) \qquad \ldots (i)$$

If $G - t(Y) = 0$, budget deficit will be zero and therefore the budget will be balanced one. If $G - t(Y) > 0$ there will be budget deficit.

If the Government finances its deficit through money creation, then the short-run macro equilibrium can be written as

$$Y = Y(G, M) \qquad \ldots (ii)$$

The short run equilibrium in simple $IS - LM$ model is shown rated in Fig. 34A.1 where IS and LM curves intersect at point E and determine equilibrium income Y_0 and equilibrium interest rate r_0. Suppose in this equilibrium the government has a budget deficit so that $G - t(Y) > 0$. Further, government finances this budget deficit through creating high powered money. As a result, money supply in the economy increases and LM curve shifts to the right to the new position LM_1. With this, as will be seen from the figure, level of equilibrium income increases to Y_1 and rate of interest falls to r_1. Since we are assuming an economy with a depression, increase in demand brought about by expansion in money supply will not cause any rise in price level.In the above model of an economy representing

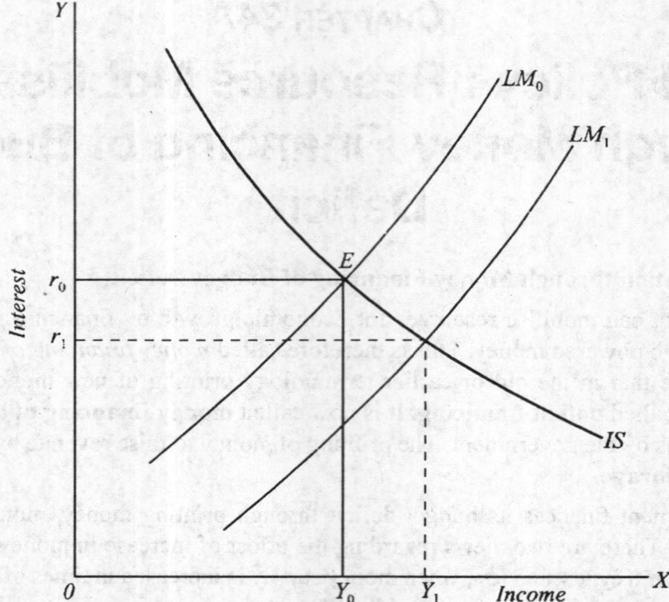

Fig. 34A.1. *IS-LM Model ; The Effect of Budget Deficit Financed by Printing Money*

the period of recession price level remains unchanged as more money is created to finance budget deficit. In an important contribution. *Fischer and Easterly explain the condition for non-inflationary printing of money.* They write, "the amount of revenue that the government can expect to obtain from the printing of money is determined by the demand for *base or high-powered money* in the economy, the real rate of growth of the economy and the elasticity of demand for real balances with respect to inflation and income"[1]. Further, assuming income elasticity of demand equal to unity and currency to GNP ratio equal to 13, they conclude that "for every one percentage point that GNP increases, the government can obtain 0.13 percentage points of GNP in revenue through the printing of money that just meets the increased demand for real balances. With an annual economic growth rate of 6.5 per cent of GNP the government should be able to obtain nearly 0.9 per cent of GNP for financing the budget deficit through the non-inflationary printing of money, increasing the high powered money stock at an annual rate of 6.5 per cent".[2] If rate of growth of money exceeds this and, given a stable demand function for currency, inflation will result.

Printed Money and the Inflation Tax

It follows from above that if the economy is operating at full-employment level of GNP or growth rate of money due to persistent budget deficits over time is in excess of rate of growth of GNP, inflation will come about. It has been pointed out by some economists that inflationary financing through the creation of high powered money is an alternative to explicit taxation. Though in most of the industrialised economies (including the United States) the creation of high-powered money or inflationary financing of budget deficits is only a minor source of revenue, in other countries (including India), the creation of high-powered money has been a significant source of raising revenue to finance government expenditure. Before March 1997, in India the creation of money to finance the budget deficit was called '*deficit financing*' which has been a significant source of revenue for the Central Government in the sixties, seventies and eighties of the last century. Though, as explained

1. Stanley Fischer and William Easterly, Economics of the Government Budget Constraint, *World Bank Research Observer*, Vol. 5 No. 2, July 1990, pp 127-42.
2. Fischer and Easterly, op. cit.

above, it is not entirely correct that financing government expenditure through creation of high-powered money necessarily leads to inflation, though traditionally every creation of high-powered money or deficit financing has been called inflationary.

Why is the creation of high powered money that causes inflation is called *inflation tax* and is an alternative to explicit taxation as a source of financing government expenditure. When government uses printed money to finance its deficit year after year, it uses it to pay for the goods and services it buys. Thus in this process the government get the resources to buy goods and services and as a result, money balances with the people increase a part of which they will save and the rest they will also spend on goods and services.

However, due to inflation *real value of money balances* held by the people decreases. That is, with their given money balances, people can buy fewer goods and services due to inflation. Thus when the government finances its budget deficit through creation of new high powered money and in the process causes inflation, the purchasing power of old money balances held by the public falls. Hence *inflation caused by creation of new money is like a tax on holding money. Though, apparently people do not pay inflation tax, but since their old money balances can buy fewer goods and services due to inflation they in fact bear the burden of inflation in terms of decline in their purchasing power.* To conclude in the words of Dornbusch and Fischer, *"Inflation acts just like a tax because people are forced to spend less than their income and pay the diference to the government in exchange for extra money*. The government thus can spend more resources, and the public less just as if the government had raised taxes to finance extra spending. When the government finances its deficit by issuing new printed money which the public adds to its holdings of nominal balances to maintain the real value of money balances constant we say the government is financing itself through the *inflation tax*.[3]

We can even estimate the revenue raised through inflation tax as under :

Inflation tax revenue = Inflation tax × real monetary base

Note that monetary base is the amount of the high powered money. It may be mentioned that in the eighties of the last century the inflation rate due to excess creation of high powered money in the Latin American Countries was very high and therefore the revenue raised through inflation tax was very high[4]. In fact some Latin American countries experienced *hyper inflation*. Thus, during 1983-1988 average annual inflation rate in Argentina was 359 per cent, in Boliva 1,797 per cent, Brazil 341 per cent, Mexico 87 percent and Peru 382 per cent.

Inflation Tax Revenue. In the Latin American countries, the governments raised large revenues due to high inflation rates caused by creation of large amount of printed money due to budget deficits year after year. From the above equation it is evident that inflation tax revenue of the government depends on the inflation rate and real money base. When the inflation rate is zero, inflation tax revenue obtained by the government will also be zero. As the *inflation rate rises, the revenue obtained by the government through inflation tax increases*. But as the inflation rate rises, the people tend to reduce their holdings of the real money balances as the purchasing power of money holdings declines. As a result, as the inflation rate rises the public holds less currency and banks hold less excess reserves with them. With this the real money balances with the public and banks decline so much that inflation tax revenue collected by the government declines after a point.

3. Rudiger Dornbusch, Stanley Fischer and Richard Startz, *Macroeconomics*, TATA McGRAW HILL, 8th edition, p. 436.
4. Ibid, p. 437.

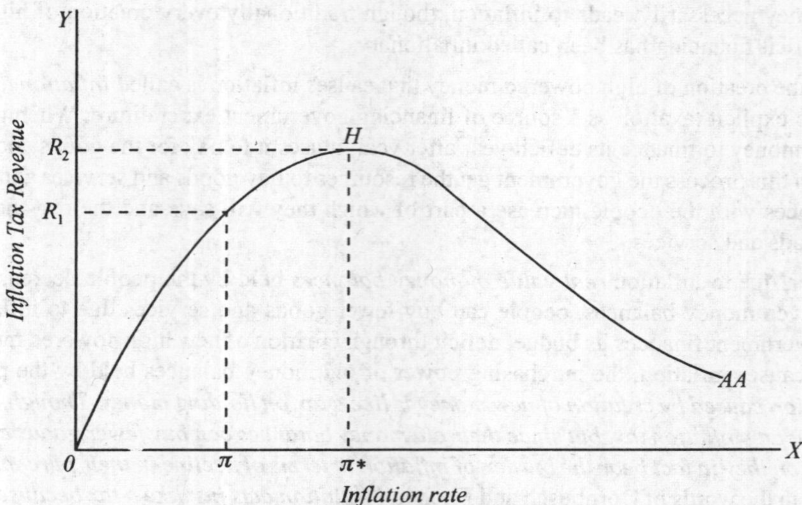

Fig. 34A.2. *Inflation Tax Revenue*

The change in the tax revenue received by the government as the inflation rate rises is shown by *AA* curve in Figure 34A.2. Initially, in the economy there is no budget deficit and therefore no printing of money, inflation rate is zero, inflation tax revenue received by the government is also zero and the economy's situation lies at the point of origin. Now suppose the government reduces taxes, keeping its expenditure constant, budget deficit emerges which is financed by printing high powered money and suppose the resulting inflation rate is π at which the government collects tax revenue equal to OR_1. But as the inflation rate further rises as a result of increase in printed money, the tax revenue collected increases until inflation rate π* is reached. At inflation rate π* brought about by a certain amount of increase in printed money, the tax revenue collected by the government is OR_2. Beyond this growth in printed money and rise in inflation rate greater than π*, tax revenue collected declines because real money balances with the public and banks decline, as explained above. Thus OR_2 is the maximum of tax revenue raised by the government through inflation tax and the corresponding inflation rate is π*.

In the developed industralised countries where the real money base is relatively small, the government collects a small amount of inflation tax revenue. For example, in the United States where money base is only about 6 per cent of GDP the government raises revenue through inflation tax equal to only 0.3 per cent of GDP. corresponding to 5 per cent rate of inflation[5]. However, some developing countries such as Argentina, Brazil, Mexico, Peru have collected 3.5 per cent to 5.2 per cent of their GDP as inflation tax revenue[6]. But for this they had to pay a heavy price in terms of a very high rate of inflation. Dornbusch, Fischer and Startz righly comments, "In countries in which the banking system is less developed and in which people hold large amounts of currency, the government obtains more revenue from inflation and is more likely to give much weight to the revenue aspects of inflation in setting policy. Under conditions of high inflation in which the conventional tax system breaks down, the inflation tax revenue may be the government's last resort to keep paying its bills. But whenever the inflation tax is used on a large scale, inflation invariably becomes extreme".[7]

5. Dornbusch, Fischer, and Startz, op. cit. p. 438
6. Ibid, p. 438
7. *op. cit.* p. 439

Evaluation of Inflation Tax Revenue

The above view of inflation tax revenue is based on the assumption that every increase in printed money causes inflation. In our view this is not correct. When the economy is working much below its full production capacity due to deficiency of aggregate demand as it happens at times of recession or depression, then more printed money can be created by the government to finance its projects. The increase in demand resulting from this will help in fuller utilisation of idle production capacity and will also generate employment for unemployed labour. This will not lead to inflation as output of goods and services will increase in this case to meet the increased demand. This case was analysed by J.M. Keynes who advocated for the adoption of budget deficit to overcome depression and financing it through printed money without causing inflation . It is only when there exists full employment in the economy that financing government expenditure through printed money causes inflation.

Similarly, in developing countries like India where growth in GDP is taking place annually and also the economy is getting more monetised, the demand for money is increasing. Besides, a lot of resources are unutilised or underutilised in the Indian economy. Therefore, a reasonable amount of printed money can be created, which before 1997 was called deficit financing, to finance the investment expenditure of the government without causing inflation. Therefore, it is not true that the use of printed money for financing government expenditure necessarily leads to inflation. It all depends on whether or not newly printed money is used for productive purposes which generates higher growth in GDP.

In our view in a developing economy such as ours, a fine balance needs to be striked between how much resources have to be raised through taxation, borrowing (i.e. debt financing) and newly created money (i.e. money financing).

CHAPTER 34B
Fiscal Deficit, Inflation and Economic Growth

Introduction

Government expenditure on goods and services and resources mobilised by it through taxes, etc., are important factors that determine aggregate demand in the economy. When there is a deficit in the budget of the government, it spends more than it collects resources through taxes and non-tax revenue. In recent years there have been huge fiscal deficits in India which have created large excess demand in the economy. This has resulted in inflation or sharp rise in the general level in prices. The deficit may occur either in the revenue budget or capital budget or in both taken together. When there is an overall budget deficit of the Government, it has to be financed by either borrowing from the market or from the Reserve Bank of India which is the nationalised central bank of the country. RBI has the power to create new money, that is, to issue new notes. Thus, to finance its fiscal deficit, the government may borrow from Reserve Bank of India against its own securities. This is only a technical way of creating new money because the government has to pay neither the rate of interest nor the original amount when it borrows from the Reserve Bank of India against its own securities. It is thus clear that fiscal deficit implies that government incurs more expenditure on goods and services than its normal receipts from taxes and non-tax revenue. This excess expenditure by the government is financed by either borrowing from the market or by newly created money which leads to the rise in incomes of the people. This causes the aggregate demand of the community to rise to a greater extent than the actual amount of deficit financing undertaken through the operation of what Keynes called *income multiplier.*

In the opinion of many economists, the expansion in money supply caused by monetisation of fiscal deficit leads to the excess aggregate demand in the economy, especially when aggregate supply of output is inelastic. The excess aggregate demand causes rise in the price level or brings about inflation in the economy.

Revenue Deficit

As mentioned above, the budget has two parts : *Revenue Budget* and *Capital Budget.* Receipts in the revenue account come from such sources as various types of direct and indirect taxes and also from non-tax sources such as interest received on loans given, dividend and profits of public enterprises. The items of expenditure in the revenue account are of the type that represents *collective consumption* of the society and therefore, creates no earning assets. The various types of expenditure on the revenue account are incurred on : (1) Interest payments on public debit, (2) Civil administration, (3) Defence, (4) Subsidies on food, fertilisers, exports and (5) Social services such as education, health, etc.

Revenue deficit refers to the excess of revenue expenditure over revenue receipts. Prudent management of public finance requires that receipts on revenue account should not exceed expenditure on revenue account. In other words, there should be surplus on revenue account so that this surplus should be used for investment in development projects or building assets which yield returns. In fact, surplus on revenue account of the budget represents *public or government savings* which can be used for financing developmental activities. However, in India, for the past several years, there has been deficit on the revenue account. That is, there has been *government dissaving* for the last some years in

India. Therefore, borrowed funds from the capital account have been used to meet a part of consumption expenditure of the government. This has bad consequences for the economy. Revenue deficit as percentage of gross domestic product (GDP) has been quite high in recent years. Revenue deficit of the central government of India for the last some years is given in Table 34B.1.

Table 34B.1: Trends in Budget Deficit of Central Government as % of GDP

	Fiscal deficit	*Revenue deficit*	*Primary deficit*	*Revenue deficit as % of fiscal deficit*
1996-97	4.1	2.4	–0.2	58.2
1997-98	4.8	3.0	0.5	63.5
1998-99	5.1	3.8	0.7	74.8
1999-2000	5.4	3.5	0.7	64.6
2000-01	5.7	4.1	0.9	71.7
2001-02	6.2	4.4	1.5	71.1
2002-03	5.9	4.4	1.1	74.4
Enactment of FRBMA				
2003-04	4.5	3.6	0.0	79.7
2004-05	4.0	2.5	–0.1	62.6
2005-06	4.0	2.5	0.4	63.0
2006-07	3.3	1.9	–0.2	56.3
2007-08	2.5	1.1	–0.9	47.4
2008-09	6.0	4.5	2.6	75.3
2009-10	6.5	5.1	3.1	81.0
2010-11	4.8	3.5	1.7	67.5
2011-12	5.7	4.3	–	75.5
2012-13	5.1	3.9	–	68.2

As per cent of GDP, revenue deficit rose from 2.4 per cent in 1996-97 to 4.4 per cent in 2002-03 but fell to 1.1 per cent in 2007-08 . Fiscal Responsibility Budget Management (FRBM) Act passed in 2003 required to eliminate it by 2008-09. However, due to global financial crisis in 2008, it could not be achieved. As a part of fiscal stimulus package the government increased its expenditure and cut customs and excise duties in 2008 and 2009 to prevent large slowdown of economic growth following the global financial crisis. As a result, revenue deficit rose to 4.5 per cent of GDP in 2008-09 and 5.2% of GDP in 2009-10. Waving of loans of farmers in 2008-09 and rise in salaries of central government employees following the implementation of Sixth Central Payment Commission in 2008 and 2009 also caused the revenue deficit, to go up in 2008-09 and 2009-10. Since revenue deficit

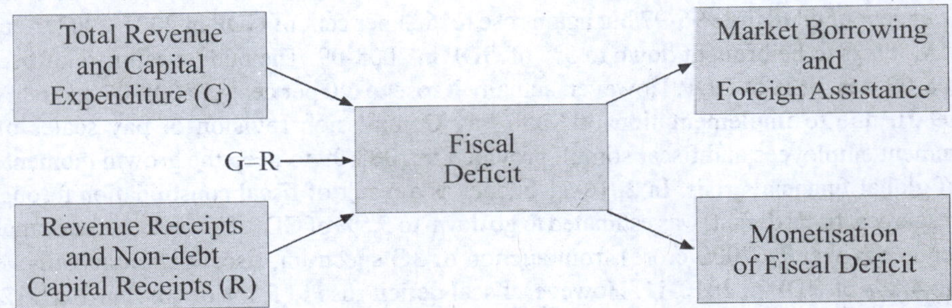

Fig. 34B.1. *Financing of Fiscal Deficit*

represents *negative savings* of the government it leads to lower investment by the government and slows down economic growth of the country in the long run. Central government has been trying to achieve fiscal consolidation by raising more tax revenue by roll-back of tax concession withdrawing tax exemptions. As a result, the Central Government revenue deficit in 2010-11 fell to 3.5% of GDP, revenue deficit again rose to 3.9% of GDP. The Finance Minister plans to reduce it to 3.4% GDP in 2013-14, to 2.7% 2014-15 and further to 2% of GDP in 2014-15 (see Fig. 34B.2). Government expenditure to meet revenue deficit does not lead to increase in durable assets and therefore does not cause expansion in productive capacity to ensure sustained economic growth in future.

Fiscal Deficit

Fiscal deficit in the budget is an important measure of deficit. IMF and the World Bank generally prescribe targets for budget deficit in terms of fiscal deficit. *Fiscal deficit is the excess of total expenditure (both on revenue and capital accounts) over revenue receipts and non-debt type of capital receipts such as recoveries of loans.*

Thus,

Fiscal Deficit = *(Total Expenditure both on Revenue Account and Capital Account)* – *(Revenue Receipts + Non-debt Capital Receipts)*

Fiscal deficit is a more comprehensive measure of budgetary imbalances. Thus, we see that when the government's total expenditure, both revenue and capital expenditure, exceeds its receipts from taxes and other normal non-revenue and non-debt capital resources, *a fiscal deficit* is created. Now, this fiscal deficit can be financed in two ways. First, through borrowing by the government from the market, both inside and outside the country. On this borrowing, the government has to pay rate of interest annually. Apart from that it has to pay back the internal and external debt taken. Secondly, the government can finance the fiscal deficit by borrowing from the Reserve Bank of India which issues new notes against government securities. Thus, borrowing from the Reserve Bank results in expansion of high powered money in the economy and is popularly called deficit financing. It is in fact *monetisation* of fiscal deficit which, if undertaken to an excessive extent, leads to inflation in the economy. On the other hand, Government borrowing from the market to finance fiscal deficit adds to the public debt and increases burden on future generations on whom heavy taxes have to be imposed for repaying the loans.

In the Table 34B.1, fiscal deficit of the Central Government of India has been calculated for the last fifteen years. Fiscal deficit had been quite large prior to 2003-04 which led to inflation or rise in prices in the economy on the one hand and increase in public debt on the other. Therefore, to ensure economic growth with stability in 2003 it was decided to follow a *prudent fiscal policy* and accordingly to reduce fiscal deficit to 3 per cent of GDP by the fiscal 2008-09. In the budget for 2007-08, the Finance Minister planned to reduce it to 3.1 per cent and actually succeeded to reduce it to 2.5% of GDP. In 1990-91, fiscal deficit of the Central Government which was around 8% of GDP came down to 4.1 per cent of GDP in 1996-97 but again rose to 6.2 per cent of GDP in 2001-2002. According to FRBMA, it was to be brought down to 3% of GDP in 2008-09. The budget estimate of fiscal deficit for 2008-09 was 4.5% of GDP. However, actually it rose to 6.0 per cent in 2008-09 and 6.5% of GDP in 2009-10 due to implementation of Sixth Pay Commission revision of pay scales of Central Government employees and fiscal stimuli provided in 2008-09 to keep the growth momentum in the light of global financial crisis. In 2010-11 budget as a result of fiscal consolidation through raising more resources, fiscal deficit, was estimated to go down to 5.5% of GDP. However, revenue mobilisation of revenue of (over ₹ 67000 crore) from auction of 3G spectrum, fiscal deficit actuallywent down down to 4.8% of GDP in 2010-11. However, fiscal deficit rose to 5.7% of GDP in 2011-12 and was 5.1 per cent of GDP for 2012-13 (RE). In the budget for 2013-14 the Finance Minister provides for fiscal deficit of 4.8% and has promised to stick to it. Further, in his budget speech for 2013-14, he has

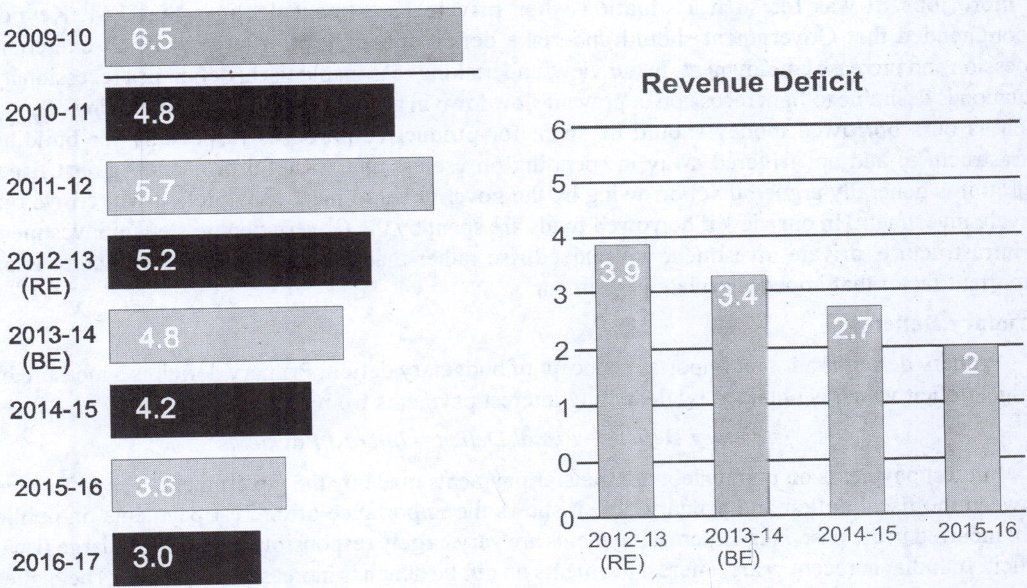

Fig. 34B.2. *Roadmap of Reduction in Central Government's Fiscal and Revenue Deficits As Per Cent of GDP*

presented the the whole roadmap of reducing fiscal deficit to 4.2 per cent in 2014-15, to 3.6% in 2015-16 and 3.0 per cent of GDP in 2016-17 (see Fig. 34B.2).

Implications of Large Fiscal Deficit. There are four implications of fiscal deficit. First, a good part of it is financed through borrowing from within and outside the country. This *leads to the increase in public debt and its burden*. Secondly, if a part of fiscal deficit is financed through monetisation of fiscal deficits, it leads to the creation of new money and *rise in prices or inflation*. To check inflation and achieve price stability, IMF and World Bank had recommended that fiscal deficit in India should be reduced to 3 per cent of GDP in a phased manner. Thirdly, a large fiscal deficit *adversely affects economic growth*. Due to large revenue deficit, a very large part of borrowed funds by the Government is used to finance current consumption expenditure of the Government. As a result, a smaller amount of resources are left for productive investment in infrastructure and social capital (*i.e.* education and health) by the Government. This lowers the rate of economic growth. Lastly, more borrowing by the Government leaves less resources for private sector investment.

To reduce fiscal deficit to 3 per cent requires a drastic cut in non-productive revenue expenditure which is a difficult task. *In India, in the past attempts have been made to reduce fiscal deficit by curtailing capital expenditure which is incurred on projects of capital formation and other developmental activities*. This is not a desirable way of reducing fiscal deficit because this adversely affects economic growth. For sound management of Government finances there is need to cut revenue expenditure and raise revenue receipts by mobilising resources through taxation. Attempts to reduce fiscal deficit by curtailing capital expenditure, as has been the practice in India so far, adversely affects economic growth and should therefore be avoided.

However, as shall be discussed below in detail fiscal deficit, even a large one, is not *always* bad. In times of recessionary situation or slowdown in economic growth such as the one that prevailed in 2008-09 large fiscal deficit is needed to fight recession and prevent slowdown of economic growth. All over the world (including the US and European countries), the governments resorted to a large dozes of fiscal deficit to stimulate the economy and prevent further deepening of recession and losses of more jobs. It was for such a situation when private investment declines that J.M. Keynes recommended that Government should undertake deficit spending on a large scale to overcome recession and increase employment. In our view, undertaking reasonable fiscal deficit in a recessionary situation is desirable to fight recession or prevent slowdown in growth. However, in developing country such as ours borrowed money should be spent for productive purposes (especially for building infrastructure) and not frittered away in spending on useless and wasteful projects. Against fiscal deficit it is generally argued that borrowing by the government to meet fiscal deficit will crowd out private investment. In our view if borrowed funds are spent by the Government to step up investment in infrastructure, private investment will indeed rise rather than fall as lack of infrastructure is an important factor that impedes private investment.

Primary Deficit

Primary deficit is another important concept of budgetary deficit. Primary deficit is a measure of budget deficit which is obtained by deducting interest payments from fiscal deficit. Thus,

Primary Deficit = Fiscal Deficit – Interest Payments

Interest payments on public debt are transfer payments made by the government. The difference between the fiscal deficit and primary deficit shows the importance of interest payments on public debt incurred in the past. Huge interest payments are very largely responsible for causing a large fiscal deficit. In India, in recent years, interest payments on public debt has increased very much. The higher interest payments on the past borrowings by the Government has greatly increased the fiscal deficit. Therefore, primary deficit is much lower than the fiscal deficit. In India, in the year 1990-91 primary deficit was 2.8 per cent of GDP, whereas fiscal deficit was 6.3 per cent of GDP. The primary deficit came down to 0.4 per cent of GDP in 1995-96 and negative (–0.2) in 1996-97, went up to 0.7 per cent of GDP in 1999-2000 and to 1.5 per cent in 2001-2002. Primary deficit as per cent of GDP again fell to around zero per cent of GDP in 2003-04, 2004-05, 2005-06. It was negative in 2006-07 and 2007-08. It may be noted that only when primary deficit is positive, a part of it can be used to meet consumption expenditure and a part to use for investment purpose. If primary deficit is negative, then borrowing by the Government is not even sufficient to make the entire interest payments on the past debt. As mentioned above, interest payments is an item of liabilities on the revenue account of the budget. Therefore, if fiscal deficit has to be reduced, interest payments on the revenue account should be reduced which can be done if past public debt is quickly retired by mobilising more resources and by curtailing non-developmental public expenditure.

Monetisation of Fiscal Deficit

It may be noted that fiscal deficit can be financed by borrowing from the Reserve Bank of India by the central government against its own securities or treasury bills. The fiscal deficit is financed by borrowing from the Reserve Bank which issues new money or currency against government securities, which leads to the expansion in money supply. In the old terminology, it was known as *deficit financing in India.* Financing the fiscal deficit by issuing new money through borrowing from the Reserve Bank against securities in the new terminology is called *monetisation of fiscal deficit.* It may be noted that in the earlier years separate data regarding the budgetary deficit and therefore, the magnitude of deficit financing undertaken in a year were provided by the government. However, in recent years the data regarding budgetary deficit is not separately provided by the government and it has become a part of fiscal deficit which is shown to be financed by *government borrowing and other new liabilities.* Now the data regarding these deficits, namely, (1) revenue deficit, (2) fiscal deficit and (3) primary deficit are provided in the budget documents.

MEASURES FOR FISCAL CONSOLIDATION

By fiscal consolidation we mean raising more resource and reducing non-essential expenditure by the government so as to reduce fiscal deficit to a reasonable level. Reducing fiscal deficit is a formiddle challenge for control of inflation and achieving 8% growth in the 12the plan period (2012-17) large fiscal deficit has two bad consequences. First, it leads to excessive Government borrowing from the market which causes rise in market interest rate. Higher market interest rate tends to reduce private investment. Further, it reduces the resources available for private sector investment. Second, the extent to which a large fiscal deficit is financed by borrowing from the Reserve Bank of India which issues new currency (which is called reserve money or high-powered money) for the government. This causes greater expansion in money supply through the process of money multiplier and generates inflationary situation in the economy. Thus, to check the rate of inflation, fiscal deficit has to be reduced through both raising revenue of the government and reducing government expenditure. In the Indian context, the following measures can be adopted to reduce fiscal deficit and thereby to reduce inflationary pressures in the economy. We first spell out the measures which may be adopted to reduce government expenditure and then describe measures for raising Government revenue.

Measures to Reduce Public Expenditure. In the context of the Indian economy, the following measures can be adopted to reduce public expenditure for reducing fiscal deficit and thereby check inflation.

1. A drastic reduction in expenditure on major subsidies such as food, fertilisers, and petroleum products is required to curtail public expenditure. A huge sum of money is spent on major subsidies on food, fertilisers, petroleum products by the central government. Without a drastic cut in subsidies over time it is difficult to reduce public expenditure to an appreciable degree. In June 2012, the government rightly decontrolled petrol so that its price is aligned with global price level. Besides, to reduce its expenditure on subsidies diesel prices were increased in September 2012 by ₹ 5 per litre and now it has been decided to increase diesel price by around 50 paise every month. As regards checking leakages the policy of direct cash transfers to the beneficiaries has been adopted. To reduce subsidy on LPG, the supply of subsidised LPG cylinder to each consumer was capped at 6 per annum which together with hike in diesel prices was expected to lower government expenditure by ₹ 2300 crore. However, in the budget for 2013-14 expenditure on subsidies as per cent GDP is planned to be reduced marginally to 2 per cent of GDP compared to 2.2% of GDP for the years 2009-10 and 2010-11.

2. The huge sum of money is spent by the government on LTC (Leave Travelling Concessions), bonus, leave encashment etc. A reduction in expenditure on these is necessary if the government is determined to cut public expenditure.

3. Another useful measure to cut public expenditure is to reduce interest payments on past debt. In India, interest payments account for about 40 per cent of expenditure on revenue account of the central government. In our view, *funds raised through disinvestment in the public sector should be used to retire a part of old public debt rather than financing current expenditure*. Retirement of public debt quickly will reduce burden of interest payments in future.

4. Budgetary support to public sector enterprises other than infrastructure projects should be substantially reduced. Further, public sector enterprises should be asked to raise funds from the market and banks.

5. *Austerity measures* should be adopted to curtail non-plan expenditure in all government departments.

Increasing Revenue from Taxation

To reduce fiscal deficit and thereby check rise in inflation rate, apart from reducing government expenditure, government revenue has to be raised. However, in recent years tax-GDP ration has declined. In 2007-08, tax GDP ratio was 12 per cent which came down to 10.4 per cent for the year 2012-13. Continuing on the path of fiscal consolidation with a view to narrowing the gap in Government spending and resources, the tax-GDP ratio has been targeted at 10.9 per cent in the 2013-14 (BE) with a nominal growth rate of 19.1 per cent. However, this is not enough for fiscal consolidation to reduce fiscal deficit to 3% of GDP. The Finance Minister has not made genuine efforts to raise more resources through taxation. He has in his budget for 2013-14, has only levied a surcharge of 10% on income of those earning ₹ 1 crore or more. This is too low to yield enough tax revenue. With current income tax rate of 30% in this income bracket, it will means a super rich person will pay only ₹ 3 lakh more tax on his or her income of ₹ one crore per annum which is too small.

1. As regards mobilising resources to increase public revenue, it may be noted that the policy of moderate taxes with simplified taxation structure should be followed. This will help to increase public revenue rather than reduce it. High marginal rates of taxes should be avoided as they serve as disincentives to work more, save more and invest more. Further, high marginal rates of direct taxes cause evasion of taxes. However, *in our view, the present marginal rate of tax in India is 30 per cent for above 10 lakh income per annum*. This is too small. Besides, due to various exemptions effective rate has been estimated to be around 20 per cent. Therefore, there is need for introducing a higher income tax slab with 35% rate of income tax.

2. In India, the *tax base is narrow for both direct and indirect taxes*; only about 2.7 per cent of population pays income tax. To increase revenue from taxation, tax base should be broadened by taxing agricultural incomes and incomes derived from unorganised industrial and services sectors. *The various exemptions and deductions provided in the income and wealth taxes should be withdrawn to broaden the tax base and collect more revenue.* It may be noted that the Indian experience of the last 50 years reveals that these exemptions and deductions do not promote the intended objectives.

3. As is well known, there is a huge amount of black money in the Indian economy which has come into existence as a result of tax evasion. A good part of black money is parked in Swiss banks. In the last VDIS (Voluntary Disclosure Income Scheme) in 1997-98, more than, 10,000 crores of rupees were collected. However, there has been huge increase in the amount of black money since then. Not only the current black money has to be mopped up but also tax evasion that occurs every year has to be prevented by strict enforcement of the tax laws.

4. The past experience has shown that various tax concessions which have been given in income taxes and indirect taxes for promoting employment, industrial development of backward regions and for other such social objectives do not actually serve the intended purposes and are largely used for evading taxes. These *concessions should therefore be withdrawn to collect more revenue from taxes and the social objectives should be served by adopting more effective policy instruments.* Long-term capital gains on equity shares are exempted from income tax. In the context of boom conditions in the stock market, their exemption should be withdrawn to increase public revenue. They represent *unearned incomes* and canon of equity in taxation demands that this exemption should be withdrawn

To sum up, with the adoption of above measures of reducing public expenditure and enhancing public revenue, it will be possible to reduce fiscal deficit to a safe limit. The reduction in fiscal deficit will prevent the emergence of excess demand in the economy and thereby help in controlling inflation and achieving price stability.

FISCAL DEFICIT AND ECONOMIC GROWTH

How does fiscal deficit affect economic growth is a hotly debated issue. A number of Keynesian economists argue that fiscal deficit promotes growth. In India where in the last some years since 1996, a good deal of industrial capacity has been lying idle due to lack of aggregate demand, and there has been enough stocks of foodgrains, it was asserted that fiscal deficit would stimulate demand and thereby ensure rapid economic growth. In the prevailing economic situation especially from 1996 to 2004 the Indian economy was a *demand-constrained economy* and therefore the increase in aggregate demand through larger fiscal deficit did not generate inflationary pressures in the economy. If the increase in public expenditure made possible by large fiscal deficit is used for productive investment, especially for investment in infrastructure and rural development, it will boost production and help increase employment opportunities in the economy. In fact, increase in public investment in infrastructure such as irrigation, roads, highways, is doubly beneficial from the viewpoint of accelerating economic growth. It helps in increasing aggregate demand on the one hand and helps to reduce supply constraints on economic growth on the other. So the focus should not be so much on reducing fiscal deficit but on reducing revenue deficit. Recall that revenue deficit is the excess of government revenue expenditure (*i.e.* current consumption expenditure) over revenue receipts. From the beginning of the nineties since economic reforms have been initiated, there has been large revenue deficits so that a large part of borrowings by the government has been used to bridge the revenue deficit. As a result, capital expenditure on investment in infrastructure and rural development as a percent of GDP declined which has adversely affected economic growth.

Alternative View

However, from the above it should not be understood that any amount of fiscal deficit or government borrowing is good for economic growth and employment generation. Higher fiscal deficit, that is, borrowing by the government involves payment of interest and raises the burden of public debt. The large increase in public debt involving large interest payments year after year will not only make the process unsustainable but adversely affect economic growth through reducing investible resources for spending on infrastructure and social sectors. Reviewing the Indian growth scenario World bank Study made in 2004[1] concludes "Interest payments consumed less than 20% of total revenues in the pre-crisis period, compared with over 30% during the Ninth Plan period (1997-2002). Revenue deficits doubled from less than 3% in the second half of the 1980s to 6% during the Ninth Plan period and beyond *representing a deterioration in the fiscal stance with spending on social and physical infrastructure crowded out by rising interest and other current payments*". It will be seen

Table 34B.2 : General Government Fiscal Trends, 1985-86 to 2002-03 (Centre and States Combined) (% of GDP)

	1985-86 to 1989-90	*1992-93 to 1996-97 (Eighth plan)*	*1997-98 to 2001-02 (Ninth plan)*	*2002-03*
Revenue deficit	2.6	3.6	6.1	6.9
Gross fiscal deficit	9.0	7.2	9.3	10.4
Interest payments	3.8	5.1	5.8	6.5
Capital expenditure	6.4	3.6	3.2	3.5
Current expenditure on social services (education, health, housing anti-poverty	5.4	5.0	5.6	5.7
(Irrigation + power + transport)/GDP	4.7	3.5	3.5	3.8

Source : World Bank Study, *India: Sustaining Reforms, Reducing Poverty*, OUP, 2004 p.14

from Table 34B.2 that as compared to the later half of the Eighties, (1985-86 to 1989-90), revenue and gross fiscal deficits (of the Centre and States combined) went up in the 9th plan period (1997-98 to 2002), especially revenue deficit. As a result, interest payments as per cent of GDP greatly increased. The higher revenue deficits and large interest payments during the nineties caused a drastic decline in capital expenditure and public investment in physical infrastructure (irrigation + power + transport) as compared to the later half of the eighties (1985-86 to 1989-90). It will be seen from Table 34B.2 that current expenditure on social services (such as education, health, housing, anti-poverty schemes) remained almost stagnant. This shows, according to this view, fiscal and revenue deficits (especially revenue deficit) have worked to lower economic growth.

1. The World Bank, *India : Sustaining Reforms, Reducing Poverty*, Oxford University Press, 2003, 17-18.

Table 34B.3: Fiscal Deficit, Savings, Investment and Economic Growth

	1990-91	1995-96	1999-2000	2000-01	2001-02	2002-03	10th Plan (Annual Average)
Fiscal Deficit (Centre & States)	9.4	6.5	9.4	9.6	9.9	10.1	8.4
Revenue Deficit (Centre & States)	4.2	3.2	6.2	6.6	7.0	6.7	4.26
Gross Domestic Savings	23.1	25.1	24.2	23.7	23.5	26.4	31.4
(a) Public Savings	1.1	2.0	-1.0	-2.3	-2.7	–0.6	1.7
(b) Private Savings	22.0	23.0	25.2	26.1	25.5	27.0	29.7
Gross domestic investment	26.3	26.8	25.3	24.4	22.8	25.2	31.4
Rate of economic growth (Annual % change in GDP_{FC})	5.6	7.3	6.1	4.4	5.8	4.4	7.8

Note : Data of fiscal deficit, revenue deficit, saving and investment are per cent of GDP

Source : GOI, *Economic Survey*, 1995-96, 2003-04, 2006-07, 2007-08.

Adverse impact of fiscal deficit on economic growth has also been shown through its effect on saving and investment in the Indian economy. For example, Shankar Acharya, a former chief economic adviser to the Government of India, has contended that a *large* fiscal and revenue deficits during 1996-2003 as compared to 1995-96 slowed down economic growth in the second half of nineties and from 2000 to 2003 in India[2]. He argued that as a result of fiscal consolidation achieved between 1990-91 and 1995-96, combined fiscal deficit of Centre and States as percentage of GDP declined from 9.4 percent in 1990-91 to 6.5 percent in 1995-96 and revenue deficit fell from 4.2 percent in 1990-91 to 3.2 per cent in 1995-96 (See Table 34B.3). This freed resources for private investment and in fact brought about investment boom of 1993-96. Gross domestic investment rose from 22.5 percent of GDP in 1991-92 (to which it had fallen during the crisis) to a peak of 26.8 percent GDP in 1995-96 (See Table 34B.3). Gross domestic saving also rose to a record level of 25.1 per cent of GDP in 1995-56. This increase in gross domestic saving and investment, according to Dr. Shankar Acharya, "helped propelled Inida's growth to 7 per cent plus for three successive years in the mid-nineties" (1995-96, 1996-97 and 1997-98).

As will be seen from Table 34B.3 after the mid nineties, fiscal deficit and revenue deficit increased which caused the decline in gross domestic saving and investment and thereby contributed to slowdown in economic growth. To quote Dr. Shankar Acharya, "*It would be hard to find more telling evidence of the adverse impact of deficits on savings and investment*"[3]. Of course, other factors were also dampening investment, including the slowdown in reforms, the higher uncertainties associated with coalition government and a worsening international economic environment. But increased borrowing by government (rising fiscal deficits) and the associated high real interest rates clearly played a role in slowing private investment. The drop in aggregate savings and investment took its toll of economic growth, which slowed from 7 percent plus of the mid nineties to around 5 percent in recent years"[4].

According to him, high fiscal deficits during the eighties created balance of payments deficits as it was mainly financed by external commercial borrowing and therefore did not adversely affect economic growth. But in the later half of nineties rising fiscal deficits were financed by domestic borrowings which were largely used to meet current consumption expenditure and resulted in *public dissavings* (see Table 34B.3). It may be noted that the implementation during (1997-2000) of Eighth Pay Commission report enhancing the salaries of Government staff both at the Centre and States

2. See his article 'Fiscal Deficits Hurt Economic Growth, *The Economic Times*, Nov. 1, 2001 and 'Why Large Fiscal Deficits are bad for us ? *CNBC*, January 2003.
3. *Op. cit.*
4. Shankar Acharya, 'High Fiscal Deficit Hurts Growth, *The Economic Times*, Nov. 1, 2003.

sharply increased the revenue expenditure of the governments and increased public dissavings. This adversely affected domestic rate of saving and investment and lowered rate of economic growth.

The high and rising fiscal deficits during the period from 1997 to 2003 which resulted in larger government borrowings from the market preempted the needed resources for investment by the private sector. This had an adverse effect on private investment and was mainly responsible for slowdown in economic growth.

Dr. Shankar Acharya's argument also applies to the growth experience in the 10th plan period (2002-07). As will be seen from Table 34B.3, in the five years of 10th plan on an average annual combined fiscal deficit of Centre and States was reduced to 8.4 per cent as compared to 9.4 to 9.9 per cent in the previous three years which resulted in higher domestic saving (28.2%) and higher domestic investment (27.2%) of GDP. As a consequence public saving turned positive (1% of GDP) and rate of economic growth rose to 7.8 per cent per annum during this period.

Thus in our view both supply-side and demand-side factors play a role in determining economic growth. The growth experience of a country cannot be explained by one type of factors alone.

Role of Fiscal Deficit and Economic Growth : Our View

However, we do not fully agree with Dr. Shankar Acharya's view which is similar to that of World Bank. They consider only supply-side factors determining economic growth.The fall in growth rate during the period from 1997 to 2002 was largely due to demand recession in the economy caused by (1) reduction in the capital expenditure by Government as a matter of new economic policy initiated since 1991, (2) sluggish performance in agriculture during the period, and (3) world-wide recession during the period. Thus demand recession caused a slowdown in the Ninth Plan period (1999-2002) As a result, gross saving and investment rate and GDP growth slowed down. As will be seen from Table 33.5 of the previous chapter, capital expenditure of government increased substantially in 2003-04 and 2005-06 and with multiplier effects led to the increase in aggeregate demand. This increase in demand also caused increase in private investment and the two together ensured a higher rate of economic growth. In the two years (2005-07) even when Government's capital expenditure as per cent of GDP fell, under pressure of rise in aggregate demand it was made up by increase in private investment in the two years 2005-06 and 2006-07 which kept the momentum of higher economic growth.

Thus in our view both supply-side and demand-side factors play a role in determining economic growth. The growth experience of a country cannot be explained by supply-side factors alone. In fact, in 2008 and 2009 as a result of global financial crisis there was economic slowdown in India which caused huge job losses. To prevent the situation from worsening further the Government came out with three fiscal stimulus packages to keep the growth momentum. In these stimulus packages Government raised its expenditure, especially on infrastructure on the one hand and cut taxes on the other to stimulate aggregate demand. To increase its expenditure Government borrowed from the market about ₹ 300,000 crore in 2008-09 ₹ 400,000 crore in 2009-10. As a result, its fiscal deficit went up from 2.7 per cent of GDP in 2007-08 to 6.0 per cent in 2008-09 and 6.4% of GDP in 2009-10. *But this did not produce bad results for the private sector investment, nor did it result in higher rate of interest.* Of course RBI reduced cash reserve ratio to increase liquidity in the banking system and lowered its repo rate to enable banks to lower the lending rates of interest. As a matter of fact, increased borrowing and expenditure by the Government in 2008-09 and 2009-10 led to the increase in demand for the products of private sector. Therefore, from May 2009 onward there were signs of revival of the Indian manufacturing sector. Manufacturing sector output grew at 9.6% in Sept. 2009 year-on-year basis and this growth further picked up to 17.6% year-on-year basis in Dec. 2009

Manufacturing sector registered growth of 13.5 per cent in March 2010, 16.5% in April, 2010 and 11.1% in May 2010 year-on-year basis. This shows despite 6.0 per cent fiscal deficit in 2008-09 and 6.4 % in 2009-10 and consequently heavy borrowing by the government in these two years manufacturing output recorded high growth.

Besides, it is because of the fiscal stimulus packages and increase in government expenditure made possible by heavy borrowing and fiscal deficit that India could achieve 6.8 per cent rate of economic growth in 2008-09 and 8.6% in 2009-10, 9.3 % in 2010-11 which is quite high, especially when there were recessionary conditions in the US and Europe. So in our view fiscal deficit of more than 3% in a year is not always bad. All depends on the economic situation in the country and the purposes for which borrowed funds are spent. If there is recession or slowdown in the economy, the fiscal deficit of 6 to 7 per cent of GDP is necessary to lift the economy out of recession or to prevent sharp slowdown in the growth of the economy. If borrowed funds are spent by the Government for investment or building durable assets, it will lead to the expansion in productive capacity and therefore ensure sustained economic growth.

It is evident from above that larger fiscal deficit at the time of recession or economic slowdown far from reducing private saving and investment is helpful for fighting recession or keeping growth momentum of the economy. In fact, the present economic thinking is that even 3 per cent of fiscal deficit should be treated as *cyclically adjusted number*; that is, the fiscal deficit should go up at times of recession or economic slowdown and should come down in normal or boom period.

We have explained above the two alternative views regarding the impact of fiscal deficit on our economic growth. One view is of the Keynesian economists who think that in developing economies such as India when they suffer from demand constraint, fiscal deficit provides stimulus to economic growth by bringing about increase in aggregate demand. In the situation prevailing in India from 1997 to 2002, and then in 2008-2009 the Indian economy in fact suffered from lack of aggregate demand for manufactured products. This demand deficiency problem arose due to *bad agricultural performance in some years* (there was a negative agricultural growth in 1995-96, 1997-98 1999-2000 and 2000-01 and 2002-03 and also due to sharp *decline in public sector investment* which started in early nineties following the initiation of economic reforms since 1991.

Thus, during 1997-2002 there was a decline in public investment not only because a good deal of borrowing by the government was used to meet revenue deficit but also because of change in economic policy which aimed at reducing the role of public sector. Besides, public sector investment could not be raised also because of the fiscal policy stance of reducing fiscal deficit as recommended by IMF, World Bank and economists associated with these institutions. *In fact the focus of fiscal consolidation was reducing fiscal deficit rather than revenue deficit*. In fact, rates of income tax, corporation tax, excise and customs duties were reduced which resulted in fall in tax-GDP ratio till 2001-02 and caused revenue deficit to rise and therefore much of the borrowing by the government was used to bridge the revenue deficit. Thus, the fall in public investment was embedded in the new economic policy of reforms. *Fall in public sector investment resulted in decrease in aggregate demand on the one hand and shortage of infrastructure on the other which caused slowdown in economic growth during the period 1997-2002*. Again in 2008-09 and 2009-10 it was increase in Government expenditure made possible by heavy borrowing and large fiscal deficit that helped India to achieve GDP growth of 6.7% in 2008-09 and 8.6% in 2009-10.

After, 2003-04, the focus of the fiscal strategy of the Government has been to reduce fiscal deficit and revenue deficit by raising more resources through taxes. As a result, the Government succeeded in increasing tax-GDP ratio from 8.1 per cent in 2001-02 to 12.5 per cent in 2007-08, reducing revenue deficit to 1.1% of GDP and fiscal deficit to 2.5 percent in 2007-08. This enabled the

Government to raise public sector investment and also private sector investment with the result that investment rate went up to 38 per cent of GDP in 2007-08. This caused on an average economic growth rate of over 9 per cent in three successive years, 2005-06, 2006-07 and 2007-08. Thus, *in order to ensure economic growth of 9 percent per annum on a sustained basis, focus should be shifted to reducing revenue deficit.* To reduce revenue deficit, steps should be taken to raise tax-GDP ratio and curtail unproductive consumption expenditure of the government so as to eliminate revenue deficit. The borrowings in the capital account should be used for financing public investment in physical infrastructure and social sectors. This will ensure sustained economic growth at the rate of 8 per cent per annum - the objective fixed under the Twelfth Year Plan (2012-17).

Here it may be recalled the **Golden Rule of Public Finance**, namely. *borrowing by the government should be used only for investment purposes and not to meet excess current consumption expenditure except during times of recession.* In times of recession even government consumption expenditure will promote GDP growth. Thus, the focus on merely reducing fiscal deficit at all times and treat it as fetish is not right. In fact, in a demand-constrained economy, a moderate doze of fiscal stimulus is needed. Fiscal responsibility should not be conceived in ritualistic terms of reducing fiscal deficit alone regardless of its effect on the public investment and the economy. In fact, the increase in public investment in infrastructure will also stimulate private investment. The question of containing Government consumption expenditure, except during periods of recession or economic slowdown, is important but reduction in fiscal deficit should not be elevated to a dogma. A moderate amount of fiscal deficit and associated borrowing is good as long as it is used for increasing public investment in physical infrastructure, education and health of the people. Even foreign investment depends on our success in improving infrastructure.

5 Sudipto Mundle, "Finessing the Deficit" in the *Times of India*, Aug. 26, 2010.

6. *Ibid.*

7. Sudipto Mundle, op. cit.

CHAPTER 35

Financial Sector Reforms and Banking in India

Importance

Financial sector reforms refer to the reforms in the banking system and capital market. An efficient banking system and a well-functioning capital market are essential to mobilise savings of the households and channel them to productive uses. The high rate of saving and productive investment are essential for economic growth. Prior to 1991 while the banking system and the capital market had shown impressive growth in the volume of operations, they suffered from many deficiencies with regard to their efficiency and the quality of their operations. The weaknesses of the banking system was extensively analysed by the committee (1991) on financial sector reforms, headed by Narasimham. The committee found that banking system was both over-regulated and under-regulated. Prior to 1991 system of *multiple regulated interest rates* prevailed. Besides, a large proportion of bank funds was preempted by Government through high Statutory Liquidity Ratio (SLR) and a high Cash Reserve Ratio (CRR). As a result, there was a decrease in resources of the banks to provide loans to the private sector for investment.

This preemption of bank funds by Government weakened the financial health of the banking system and forced banks to charge high interest rates on their advances to the private sector to meet their needs of credit for investment purposes. Further, the lack of transparency in the accounting practice of the banks and non-application of international norms by the banks meant that their balance sheets did not reflect their underlying financial position. This was prominently revealed by 1992 scarcity scam triggered by Harshad Mehta. In this situation the quality of investment portfolio of the banks deteriorated and culture of 'non-recovery' developed in the public sector banks which led to a severe problem of *non-performing assets* (NPA) and low profitability of banks. Financial sector reforms aim at removing all these weaknesses of the financial system. Under these reforms, attempts have been made to make the Indian financial system more viable, operationally efficient, more responsive and improve their allocative efficiency. Financial reforms have been undertaken in all the three segments of the financial system, namely banking, capital market and Government securities market. We explain below various reforms in these three segments in financial sector initiated since 1991.

1. Reduction in Statutory Liquidity Ratio (SLR) and Cash Reserve Ratio (CRR)

An important financial reform has been the reduction in Statutory Liquidity Ratio (SLR) and Cash Reserve Ratio (CRR) so that more bank credit is made available to the industry, trade and agriculture. The statutory liquidity ratio (SLR) which was as high as 39 per cent of deposits with the banks has been reduced in a phased manner to 25 per cent. It may be noted that under statutory liquidity ratio banks are required to maintain a minimum amount of liquid assets such as government securities and gold reserves of not less than 25 per cent of their total liabilities. In 2008, statutory liquidity ratio was reduced to 24 per cent by RBI.

Similarly, cash reserve ratio (CRR) which was 15 per cent was reduced over phases to 4.5 per cent in June 2003. It may be noted that reduction in CRR has been possible with reduction of monetised budget deficit of the government and doing away with the *automatic system* of financing government's budget deficit through the practice of issuing *ad hoc* treasury bills to the Central Government.

On the other hand, reduction in Statutory Liquidity Ratio (SLR) has been possible because efforts have been made by government to reduce fiscal deficit and therefore its borrowing requirements. Besides, reduction in SLR has become possible because of a shift to payment of market-related rates of interest on government securities. Since the government securities are free from any risk and now bear market-related interest rates, the banks may themselves feel inclined to invest their surplus funds in these securities, especially when demand for credit by the industry and trade is not adequate.

The reduction in CRR and SLR has made available more lendable resources for industry, trade and agriculture. Reductions in CRR and SLR also made possible for Reserve Bank of India to use open market operations and changes in bank rate as tools of monetary policy to achieve the objectives of economic growth, price stability and exchange rate stability. Thus, Dr. C. Rangarajan, the former Governor of Reserve Bank of India, says, "*As we move away from automatic monetisation of deficits, monetary policy will come into own. The regulation of money and credit will be determined by the overall perception of the Central monetary authority on what appropriate level of expansion of money and credit should be depending on how the real factors in the economy are evolving*"[1].

2. End of Administered Interest Rate Regime

A basic weakness of the Indian financial system was that interest rates were administered by the Reserve Bank/Government. In the case of commercial banks, both deposit rates and lending rates were regulated by Reserve Bank of India. As stated above, before 1993, rate of interest on Government Securities could be maintained at low levels through the means of high Statutory Liquidity Ratio (SLR). Under SLR regulation commercial banks and certain other financial institutions were required by law to invest a large proportion of their liabilities in Government securities. The purpose behind the administered interest-rate structure was to enable certain priority sectors to get funds at concessional rates of interest. Thus the system of administered interest rates involved cross subsidisation; concessional rates charged from primary sectors were compensated by higher rates charged from other non-concessional borrowers.

The structure of administered rates has been almost totally done away with in a phased manner. RBI no longer prescribes interest rates on fixed or time deposits paid by their banks to their depositors. Banks have also been freed from any prescribed conditions of premature withdrawal by depositors. Individual banks are free to determine their conditions for premature withdrawal. Currently, there is prescribed rate of 3.5 per cent for Savings Bank Accounts. Note that Savings Bank Account are actually used by the individuals as current account even with cheque-book facility. Since the banks' cost of servicing these accounts is high, rate of interest on them is bound to be low. Besides, there is lower interest rate ceilings prescribed for foreign currency denominated deposits from non-resident Indians (NRI). Such a lower prescribed ceiling is required for managing external capital flows, especially short-term capital flows, till we switch over to liberalisation of capital account.

Lending rates of interest for different categories which were earlier regulated have been gradually deregulated. However, RBI insists upon transparency in this regard. Each bank is required to announce prime lending rates (PLRs) and the maximum spread it charges. Maximum spread refers to the difference between the lending rate and bank's cost of funds. Interest on smaller loans up to ₹ 2,00,000 are regulated at concessional rates of interest. At present, the interest rate on these smaller loans should not exceed the prime lending rates. Besides, lending interest rates for exports are also prescribed and are linked to the period of availment. Changes in prescribed interest rates for exports have been often used as an instrument to influence repatriation of export proceeds.

Thus, except prescribed lending rates for exports and small loans up to ₹ 2,00,000, the lending rates have been freed from control. Banks can now fix their lending rates as per their risk reward perception of borrowers and purposes for which bank loans are sought.

1. C. Rangarajan, '*Structural Reforms in the Financial Sector*', Inaugural Address at the FICCI Conference on Banking and Finance, Bombay, May 21, 1993.

3. Prudential Norms : High Capital Adequacy Ratio

In order to ensure that financial system operates on sound and competitive basis, prudential norms, especially with regard to capital-adequacy ratio, have been gradually introduced to meet the international standards. *Capital adequacy norm refers to the ratio of paid-up capital and reserves to deposits of banks*. The capital base of Indian banks has been very much lower by international standards and in fact declined over time.

As a part of financial sector reforms, capital adequacy norm of 8 per cent based on risk-weighted asset ratio system has been introduced in India. Indian banks which have branches abroad were required to achieve this capital-adequacy norm by March 31, 1994. Foreign banks operating in India had to achieve this norm by March 31, 1993. Other Indian banks had to achieve this capital adequacy norm of 8 per cent latest by March 31, 1996. Banks were advised by RBI to review their existing level of capital funds as compared to the prescribed capital adequacy norm and take steps to increase their capital base in a phased manner to achieve the prescribed norm by the stipulated date.

It may be noted that Global Trust Bank (GTB), a private sector bank, whose operations had to be stopped by RBI on July 24, 2004 had a capital adequacy ratio much below the prescribed prudent capital adequacy ratio norm. In this regard, link between capital adequacy and provisioning is worth noting. Capital adequacy norm can be met by the banks after ensuring that adequate capital provisions have been made. To achieve this capital adequacy norm, Government had come in to provide capital funds to some nationalised banks. Some stronger public sector banks raised funds from the capital market by selling their equity. Law was passed to enable the public sector banks to go to the capital markets for raising funds to enhance their capital base. Banks can also use a part of their annual profits to enhance their capital base (that is, ploughing back of retained earnings into investment).

4. Competitive Financial System

After nationalisation of 14 large banks in 1969, no bank had been allowed to be set up in the private sector. While the importance and role of public sector banks in Indian financial system continued to be emphasised, it was however recognised that there was urgent need for introducing greater competition in the Indian money market which could lead to higher efficiency of the financial system. Accordingly, private sector banks such as HDFC, Corporation Bank, ICICI Bank, UTI Bank, IDBI Bank and some others have been set up. Establishment of these banks has made substantial contribution to housing finance, car loans and retail credit through credit card system. They have made possible the wider use of what is often called *plastic money*, namely; ITM cards, Debit Cards, and Credit Cards.

In addition to the setting up of private sector Indian banks, competition has also sought to be promoted by permitting liberal entry of branches of foreign banks, therefore, CITI Bank, Standard Chartered Bank, Bank of America, American Express, HSBC Bank have opened more branches in India, especially in the metropolitan cities

An important recent step is the liberalisation of foreign direct investment in banks. In the budget for 2003-04, the limit of foreign direct investment in banking companies was raised from 49 per cent to the maximum 74 per cent of the paid up capital of the banks. However, this did not apply to the wholly owned subsidiaries of foreign banks. A foreign bank may operate in India through any one of three channels, namely (1) as branches of foreign banks, (2) a wholly owned subsidiary of a foreign bank, (3) a subsidiary with aggregate foreign investment up to the maximum of 74 per cent of the paid-up capital.

The above measures are expected to facilitate setting up of subsidiaries by foreign banks. Besides fostering competition among banks they have also increased transparency and disclosure standards to reach the international standards. Banks have to submit to RBI and SEBI, the maturity pattern of their assets and liabilities, movements in the provision account and about non-performing assets (NPA).

RBI's annual publication '*Trends and Progress of Banking in India*' provides detailed information on individual bank's financial position, that is, their losses, assets, liabilities, NPA etc which enable public assessment of the working of the banks.

5. Non-Performing Assets (NPA) and Income Recognition Norm

Non-performing assets of banks have been a big problem of commercial banks. Non-performing assets mean *bad loans*, that is, loans which are difficult to recover. A large quantity of non-performing assets also lowers the profitability of bank. In this regard, a norm of *income recognition* introduced by RBI is worth mentioning. According to this, income on assets of a bank is not recognised if it is not received within two quarters after the last date.

In order to improve the performance of commercial banks recovery management has been greatly strengthened in recent years. Measures taken to reduce non-performing assets include restructuring at the bank level, recovery of bad debt through Lok Adalats, Civil Courts, setting up of Recovery Tribunals and compromise settlements. The recovery of bad debt got a great boost with the enactment of '*Securitisation and Reconstruction of Financial Assets and Enforcement of Security Interest*' (SARFAESI). Under this Act, Debt Recovery Tribunals have been set up which will facilitate the recovery of bad debts by the banks.

As a result of the above measures gross NPA declined from ₹ 70,861 crores in 2001-02 to ₹ 68,715 crores in 2002-03. But there are substantial amounts of non-performing assets whose recovery is still to be made. Besides, as a result of introduction of risk-based supervision by RBI, the ratio of gross NPA to gross advances of scheduled commercial banks declined from 12.7 per cent in 1999-2000 to 8.8 per cent in 2002-03.

6. Elimination of Direct Credit Controls

Another significant financial sector reform is the elimination of direct or selective credit controls. Selective credit controls have been done way with. Under selective credit controls RBI used to control through the system of changes in margin for provision of bank credit to traders against stocks of sensitive commodities and to stock brokers against shares. As a result, there is now greater freedom to both the banks and borrowers in respect of credit.

But it is worth mentioning that banks are required to observe the guidelines issued by RBI regarding lending to priority sectors such as small scale industries and agriculture. The advances eligible for priority sectors lending have been increased at *deregulated* interest rates. This is in accordance with the recognition that the main problem is more of availability of credit than the cost of credit. In June 2004 UPA Government announced that credit to farmers for agriculture will be available at 2 per cent below PLR of banks. Further, credit for agriculture will be doubled in three years time.

7. Promoting Micro-Finance to Increase Financial Inclusion

To promote financial inclusion the government has started the scheme of micro finance. RBI provides guidelines to banks for mainstreaming micro-credit providers and enhancing the outreach of micro-credit providers *inter alia* stipulated that micro-credit extended by banks to individual borrowers directly or through any intermediary would henceforth be reckoned as part of their priority-sector lending. However, no particular model was prescribed for micro-finance and banks have been extended freedom to formulate their own model(s) or choose any conduit/intermediary for extending micro-credit.

Though there are different models for pursuing micro-finance, the Self-Help Group (SHG)-Bank Linkage Programme has emerged as the major micro-finance programme in the country. It is being implemented by commercial banks, regional rural banks (RRBs), and cooperative banks. Under the SHG-Bank Linkage Programme, as on 31 March 2012, 79.60 lakh SHG-held savings bank accounts with total savings of ₹ 6,551 crore were in operation. By November 2012 another 2.14 lakh SHGs had come under the ambit of the programme, taking the cumulative number of savings-linked groups to 81.74. As on 31 March 2012, 43.54 lakh SGHs had outstanding bank loans of ₹ 36,340 crore (Table 35.1). During 2012-13 (up to November 2012), 3.67 lakh SHGs were financed with an amount ₹ 6,664.15 crore.

Table 35.1 : Progress of Micro-finance Programme

Year	*SHGs Financed by Banks during the year**			*Bank Loan Outstanding*		
	No. (lakh)	*Amount (₹ crore)*	*Growth (%)*	*No. (lakh)*	*Amount (₹ crore)*	*Growth (%)*
2007-08	12.28	8849.26	-	36.26	16999.90	-
2008-09	16.09	12256.51	38.50	42.24	22679.85	33.41
2009-10	15.87	14453.30	17.90	48.52	28038.28	23.62
2010-11	11.96	14547.73	0.65	47.87	31221.17	11.35
2011-12	11.48	16534.77	13.66	43.54	36340.00	16.40

Source: NABARD.
*Note: *Includes new as well as repeat loans to SHGs.*

Extension of Swabhimaan Scheme

Under the Swabhimaan financial inclusion campaign, over 74,000 habitations with population in excess of 2,000 had been provided banking facilities by March 2012, using various models and technologies including branchless banking through business correspondents (BCs). The Finance Minister in his Budget Speech of 2012-13 had announced that Swabhimaan would be extended to habitations with population more than 1,000 in the north-eastern and hilly states and population more than 1,600 in the plains areas as per Census 2001. Accordingly, about 45,000 such habitations had been identified for coverage under the extended Swabhimaan campaign. As per the progress received through the conveners of State Level Bankers' Committee (SLBC), out of the identified habitations, 10,450 have been provided banking facilities by end of December, 2012. This will extend the reach of banks to all habitations above a threshold population.

8. Setting up of Rural Infrastructure Development Fund (RIDF)

The Government of India set up the RIDF in 1995 through contribution from commercial banks to the extent of their shortfall in priority sector lending by banks with the objective of giving low cost fund support to states and state-owned corporations for quick completion of ongoing projects relating to medium and minor irrigation, soil conservation, watershed management, and other forms of rural infrastructure.

The Fund has continued, with its corpus being announced every year in the Budget. Over the years, coverage under the RIDF has been made more broadbased in each tranche and, at present, a wide range of 31 activities under various sectors is being financed. The annual allocation of funds for the RIDF announced in the Union Budget has gradually increased from ₹ 2000 crore in 1995-96 (RIDF 1) to ₹ 20,000 crore in 2012-13. Further, a separate window was introduced in 2006-07 for funding the rural roads component of the Bharat Nirman Programme with a cumulative allocation of ₹ 18,500 crore till 2009-10.

From inception of the RIDF in 1995-6 to March 2012, 462,229 projects have been sanctioned with a sanctioned amount of ₹ 1,43,230 crore. Of the cumulative RIDF loans sanctioned to state governments, 42 per cent have gone to the agriculture and allied sector, including irrigation and power; 15 per cent to health, education, and rural drinking water supply; while the share of rural roads and bridges has been 31 per cent and 12 per cent, respectively. The annual allocation of funds under the RIDF has gradually increased from ₹ 2,000 crore in 1995-6 (RIDF I) to ₹ 20,000 crore in 2012-13 (RIDF XVIII).

As against the total allocation of ₹ 1,72,500 crore, encompassing RIDF I to XVIII, sanctions aggregating ₹ 1,51,154 crore have been accorded to various state governments and an amount of ₹ 1,00,051 crore disbursed up to the end of November 2012. Nearly 55 per cent of allocation has been made to southern and northern regions. The National Rural Roads Development Agency (NRRDA) has disbursed the entire amount of ₹ 18,500 crore sanctioned for it (under RIDF XII-XV) by March 2010. During 2012-13 (up to end November 2012), ₹ 5,829 crore was disbursed to the states under the RIDF (Table 35.2)

Table 35.2 : Sanctions and disbursements under the RIDF and Bharat Nirman (Rural Roads Components)

(₹ *crore*)

Region	*2012-13 (up to November 2012)*			*Bank Loan Outstanding*		
	Target	*Achievement*	*Achievement (%)*	*Sanction*	*Disbursement**	*Disbursement as % of Sanction*
South	3775	1420	37.6	37899	26529	70.0
West	2170	1134	52.3	22149	15693	70.9
North	4850	1810	37.3	44668	30092	67.4
Central	1480	356	24.1	13080	8078	61.8
East	3800	863	22.7	26600	15625	58.7
NER & Sikkim	725	145	20.0	6758	4034	59.7
Sub total	**16800**	**5728**	**34.1**	**151154**	**100051**	**66.2**
Warehousing	-	101	-	2512	1208	48.1
Bharat Nirman	-	-	-	18500	18500	100.0
Grand total	**16800**	**5829**	**34.7**	**172166**	**119759**	**70.0**

Source: NABARD.
Note : NER is north-eastern region.

Roll Out of Direct Benefit Transfer Scheme

The Government of India has decided to introduce a Direct Benefit Transfer (DBT) scheme with effect from 1 January 2013. To begin with, benefits under 26 schemes will directly be transferred into the bank accounts of beneficiaries in 43 identified districts across respective states and union territories (UT). Banks will ensure that all beneficiaries in these districts have a bank account. All PSBs and RRBs have made provision so that the data collected by the Departments/Ministries/ Implementing agency concerned can be used for seeding the bank account details in the core banking system (CBS) of banks with Aadhaar. All PSBs have also joined the Adhaar Payment Bridge of the National Payment Corporation of India for smooth transfer of benefits.

Termination of Automatic Monetisation of Budget Deficits

This is significant reforms measure to put a check on the growing fiscal deficit of the Central Government. Before 1997 whenever there was a deficit in Central Government budget this was financed by borrowing from RBI through issuing of *ad hoc* treasury bills. RBI issued new notes against these treasury bills and delivered them to the Central Government. Since Government incurred deficits year after year, the question of retiring these *ad hoc* treasury bills did not arise. In this way there was automatic monetisation of Central Government's budget deficit resulting in the increase in reserve money in the economy. With the operation of money multiplier, the increase in reserve money led to a manifold increase in money supply in the economy which contributed to inflationary tendencies in the Indian economy. Dr. C. Rangarajan in an important contribution to financial management highlighted the adverse effects of automatic monetisation of Government's budget deficits through *ad hoc* treasury bills.[2]

Since in the eighties and nineties Government borrowed heavily due to large fiscal deficits, expansionary impact of these deficits had to be countered by RBI by raising CRR and SLR from time to time. Besides, in the context of heavy borrowing by the Central Government the need to counter the impact on the money supply by raising CRR to mop up excess liquidity increased so as to control inflation. In this environment RBI could not use the instrument of open market operations to regulate the money supply and rate of interest. At a time when Government borrowed heavily in the market to meet its large deficit, the use of open market operations (*i.e.* selling Government securities in the open market from its own reserves by RBI) would have resulted in sharp rise in interest rate.

Dr. Rangarajan succeeded in getting abolished the system of automatic monetisation of ever-rising budget deficits through the issue of *ad hoc* treasury bills by the Government. In its place the system of *Ways and Means Advances (*WMA) were introduced from April 1, 1997. Under this new system of Ways and Means Advance (WMA) financial limits are fixed to accommodate *temporary mismatches* in Government receipts and payments and further that market related interest rate is charged on these advances. The limit for WMA and rate of interest charged on them are mutually agreed between RBI and Government from time to time. Further, after 1999 no overdrafts by the Government are permitted for a period beyond 10 consecutive days. Thus, ways and means advances are in fact loans to the Government given by RBI for a short period of time.

It is important to note that with the abolition of *ad hoc* treasury bills, the system of 91 days tap treasury Bills has also been discontinued with effect from April 1, 1997. Accordingly, with the introduction of the system of Ways and Means Advances (WMA), the conventional concept of budget deficit and deficit financing have also lost their relevance. Therefore, the earlier practice of showing budgetary deficit in Government's budget and the extent of deficit financing has been abandened. Instead, at present the magnitudes of fiscal deficit, revenue deficit and primary deficits are provided in the budget and become key indicators of Government's fiscal position.

It is clear from above that the new system of Ways and Means Advances (WMA) has given more autonomy to RBI for conducting its monetary policy. Another related important financial reform is the enactment of '*Fiscal Responsibility and Budget Management (FRBM)*' Act, which provides a relationship between Government's fiscal stance and RBI's monetary management. According to FRBM, Central Government will take appropriate measures to reduce fiscal deficit to 2 per cent and to eliminate entirely revenue deficit in a time-bound manner by March 31, 2008.[3] It has been provided in the law that revenue deficit and fiscal deficit may exceed targets specified in the rules only on grounds of national security or natural calamity or such other exceptional circumstances as specified by Central Government. An important provision of the Act is that the Central Government shall not borrow from RBI except by Ways and Means Advances. Further, an important feature of FRBM Act is that RBI will not subscribe to the *primary issues* of Central Government securities from the year 2006-07.

Pension Reforms

Since October 2003, a New Pension Scheme (NPS) was introduced by the Central Government for its employees. Later many States have also joined the scheme for their employees. The **New Pension Scheme is a contributory** retirement scheme.

---

2. See C. Rangarajan, '*Issues in Monetary Management*', Presidential Address at the 71st Annual Conference of the Indian Economic Association at Jadavpur University, Calcutta, Dec. 29,1988
3. Finance Minister P. Chidambaram extended this date of eliminating revenue deficit by one year. He proposed to reduce revenue deficit to zero by March 31, 2009.

All employees joining Central Government after January 1, 2004 have to join the scheme and contribute to it to obtain pension after their retirement. Later many states have also joined the scheme for their employees. It is now also open to private individuals and eight fund managers manage the scheme. The pension authority was named as Pension Fund Regulatory and Development (PFRDA). Till September 2013, this pension authority has been functioning under executive authority since October 2003. Now in September 2013, the Indian Parliament passed the Pension Fund Regulatory Development Authority Bill, eight years after it was introduced in March 2005. This bill seeks to empower PFRDA to regulate the pension scheme (NPS). The corpus of PFRDA has ₹ 34,965 crore. NPS has been there with us for nine years and to manage such a large amount of ₹ 35,000 crore was not good to be managed by a non-statutory authority. It should be managed by a statutory authority. All that this new legislation does is to make the non-statutory authority a statutory authority.

The legislation regarding Pension Fund Regulatory and Development Authority passed by the Parliament *is an important financial reform that will pave the way for foreign investment* in the sector. At present the new pension scheme has about 5.3 million subscribers and as mentioned above the scheme has a corpus of around ₹ 35,000 crore.

The Finance Minister has clarified that foreign investment in the pension sector will be 26% and linked to that in the insurance sector. The government has already approved 49% foreign investment in the insurance sector.

"I am confident that the Pension Bill will be passed in Rajya Sabha," Chidambaram said adding that the government had accepted all but one suggestion of the Standing Committee on Finance that gave its recommendations on the Bill in August 2011. The PFRDA will notify New Pension System schemes that provide minimum assured returns, incorporated after the standing committee suggested some sort of guaranteed returns.

The NPS will also provide for withdrawal for some limited purposes, which was not the case earlier. The reform will go a long way in increasing the coverage of formal pension and social security plans in India, where only about 12% of the active workforce has any formal pension or social security plan. The opening of the pension sector, even at 26%, will encourage foreign investors to put their money, as India has a huge population that needs social security cover. We do not have much pension products now but once there are more players, there will be more products which will help to channelise this pension money into the economy.

The Bill will further empower the PFRDA to regulate the NPS and other pension schemes that are not covered under any Act.

MARKET STABILISATION SCHEME (MSS)

A significant reform has been the introduction of Market Stabilisation Scheme to sterilise the inflationary impact of huge foreign exchange inflows into the Indian economy in recent years. During 2002-03 and 2003-04 foreign exchange reserves with RBI soared so much that they crossed US $ 107 billion at the end of March 2004. To prevent the undue appreciation of Indian rupee as a result of this huge inflow of foreign exchange, RBI intervened to buy US dollars and paid for it newly issued rupee currency. As a result, liquidity in the banking system increased. But this higher liquidity in the banking system posed a threat to the price stability. Rate of inflation which remained low in the last six years tended to rise . To prevent the inflationary pressures in the Indian economy Reserve Bank of India *sterilised* much of the liquidity in the banking system by selling Government securities held by it to the banks. In this way the *excess rupee currency reserves* swelled with RBI.

But the exchange inflows continued unabated and the sale of Government securities by RBI to banks and other financial institutions could not be made because the stock of Government securities with RBI was exhausted.

To deal with this strange situation, RBI entered into an agreement with Central Government in April 2004 which resulted in a novel scheme called as *Market Stabilisation Scheme* (MSS). Under this scheme, Government of India issued special *treasury* bills or dated securities in addition to normal requirements. The purpose of this Market Stabilisation Scheme (MSS) is to enable RBI to absorb excess liquidity in the banking system. The ceiling limit for the issue of additional securities for the stabilisation purpose was fixed at ₹ 60,000 crores for the year 2004-05, These special securities are sold by RBI to banks and other financial institutions. The funds raised under this MSS scheme (₹ 60,000 crores for 2004-05) are held in specific cash account maintained and operated by RBI. But under the agreement the Central Government cannot use these funds.

Capital Market Reforms

An important type of financial reforms relates to reforms undertaken to improve market efficiency, increase transparency and prevent unfair practices regarding trading in the capital market. A set of reforms comprising measures to liberalise, regulate and develop capital markets has been introduced since 1991.

1. Establishment of SEBI. An important measure regarding capital market reforms is the setting up of Securities and Exchange Board of India (SEBI) as the regulator of equity market in India. Regulation of stock markets is important to ensure (*a*) that the equity markets operate in a fair and orderly manner, (*b*) that the brokers and other professionals of the stock markets deal justly with their customers, (*c*) that the corporate firms who raise funds through the market provide all information about themselves which the investors need to make intelligent investment decisions. Since its inception SEBI has been addressing itself to these tasks.

SEBI has introduced various guidelines and regulations for the functioning of capital markets and assuming and selling of shares in the primary market. The following important regulatory measures have been introduced by SEBI.

(*a*) SEBI has introduced a code of advertisement for public issues by companies for making fair and truthful disclosures. The companies are now required to disclose all material facts and specific risk factors associated with their projects while making public issues.

(*b*) It has required the stock exchanges to amend their listing agreements to ensure that a listed company furnishes annual statements to them showing variations between financial projections and project utilisation of funds made in the offer documents and actuals. This will enable shareholders to make comparisons between performance and promises made by of company.

(*c*) An important reform SEBI has introduced is that it has brought *merchant banking* also under its regulatory framework. The merchant bankers are required to follow the code of conduct issued by SEBI in respect of *pricing and premium fixation of issues* of shares a companies.

(*d*) The practice of making preferential allotment of shares *at prices* unrelated to the prevailing price has been stopped by SEBI. Besides, to ensure transparency insider trading has also been banned.

(*e*) As a part of the process of establishing transparent rules for trading in stock exchanges, a notorious *BADLA* system has been banned and in its place Rolling Settlement System has been introduced.

2. Setting up of Private Mutual Funds. Another important reform is the permission granted to the private sector firms to start Mutual Funds. Many private sector companies such as Tata, Reliance, Birla have set up their mutual funds through which they raise money from the public. In this way monopoly position of UTI in Mutual Fund business has come to end. Mutual Funds raise money by selling units to the public and the funds so raised are invested in a number of equities and debentures of companies. A mutual fund may be entirely equity-based or debt-based or a balanced one having a particular combination of investment in equities and debentures of a number of companies. Investment in mutual funds enables the investors to reduce risk. Mutual funds have also been allowed to open offshore funds to invest in equities abroad. UTI has also been brought within the regulatory framework of SEBI.

3. Opening up to Foreign Capital. A significant reform has been that Indian capital market has been opened up for *foreign institutional institutions* (FII). That is, FII can now buy shares and debentures of private Indian companies in the Indian stock market and can also invest in government securities. This has been done to attract foreign capital. Foreign Institutional Investors (FII) *have been permitted full capital convertibility*

4. Access to International Capital Markets. The Indian corporate sector has been allowed to raise funds in the international capital markets through American Depository Receipts (ADRs), Global Depository Receipts (GDR), Foreign Currency Convertible Bonds (FCCBs) and External Commercial Borrowings (ECBs). Similarly, Overseas Corporate Bodies (OCBs) and Non-resident Indians have been allowed to invest in the equity capital of the Indian companies. As mentioned above, FIIs have been allowed to invest in equities of private corporate Indian companies as well as in Government securities.

5. Banks and Capital Markets. Another important step to strengthen the Indian capital market is that banks have been allowed to lend against various capital market instruments such as corporate shares and debentures to individuals, investment companies, trusts and endowment share and stock brokers, industrial and corporate buyers and SEBI-approved market makers.[4] Lending by banks against various capital market instruments to individuals, share and stock brokers, market makers is made in accordance with certain norms regarding purpose, capital adequacy, transparent transactions, maximum possible amount or ceiling, or duration of the loan. Bank lending against shares and debentures, according to C. Rangarajan, will "*enable partial liquidity to scrips, to help reduce volatility in price movement, encourage the presence of market makers so as to reduce market concentration and help in widening and deepening of trading in the secondary market.*"[5]

Reforms in Government's Securities Market

The Government securities market will gradually emerge as a vibrant segment of the Indian capital market. Therefore, major reforms have been carried out in Government securities market since 1991 in tune with general policy of liberalisation, privatisation and globalisation. In the pre-reform period, through the medium of increase in statutory liquidity ratio (SLR), the banks were forced to invest in government securities at administered interest rate. In this way a large amount of bank resources were pre-empted by government through the medium of SLR. Thus, Rakesh Mohan, the Deputy Governor of Reserve Bank of India, writes, "Prescription of a statutory liquidity ratio (SLR), though originally devised as a prudential measure, was used as the main *instrument of pre-emption of bank resources in the pre-reform period.* The high SLR requirement created a captive

4. See C. Rangarajan, "The Indian Financial System : The Emerging Horizon," printed in his *Indian Economy : Essays on Money and Finance*, UBS Publishers, 1998.
5. C. Rangarajan, *op. cit.*

market for government securities, which were issued at low administered interest rates."[6] Since 1991, a number of reforms have been undertaken to widen and deepen government securities market and to increase transparency in sale of these securities.

(1) First, the statutory liquidity ratio has been reduced over stages from 45 per cent to 25 per cent which is the statutory minimum liquidity ratio. With this a lot of bank resources have become available for lending to private sector. Of course, the banks, if they think profitable, can invest more than 25 per cent in government securities.

(2) In place of the system of administered rates on government securities, these securities are sold through an auction system. As a result, interest rates on government securities are determined at levels which are close to market rates of interest.

(*c*) To widen the market for government securities foreign institutional investors (FII) have been allowed to invest in government securities.

(*d*) Primary dealers (PD) were introduced as market makers in government securities markets. Besides, to ensure transparency in sale and purchase of government securities Delivery versus Payment (DvP) settlement system has been introduced.

(*e*) An important reform concerning trading in government securities is the Repurchase agreement (Repo) which is currently operated under the Liquidity Adjustment Facility (LAF) scheme. LAF scheme operates through repo and reverse repo auctions by RBI. The sale and purchase of government securities through repo and reverse repo operations are for only a short period, a day or few days. When there is shortage of liquidity funds with banks Reserve Bank of India lends funds to them at a fixed *repro interest rate* through purchasing of securities from them for a very short period. On the other hand, when there are surplus liquid funds with the banks, they park these funds with RBI at a fixed *reverse repo rate* and in return get the government securities. Thus, in this way RBI is able to adjust and regulate the liquidity position of the banks.

The other reforms related to government securities are the (*i*) termination of automatic monetisation of budget deficits and (*ii*) the introduction of Market Stabilisation Scheme, which have been discussed above.

PERFORMANCE OF THE FINANCIAL SECTOR UNDER THE REFORM PROCESS

We will now discuss how the various segments of the financial system, namely, banking, capital market and government securities market have performed. The banking sector reforms have sought to increase efficiency and productivity of the banking system through enhanced competition. At the same time these banking reforms have aimed at achieving social obligations such as increase in lending to the priority sectors such as small-scale industries and agriculture. A major achievement of banking sector reforms has been marked improvement in the financial health of banks as reflected in capital adequacy norms and improved asset quality[7]. We give in Table 35.4 the distribution of commercial banks according to risk-weighted capital adequacy. Note that capital adequacy of a bank below 10 per cent reveals the risk of default by it and is therefore considered as financially unhealthy. As many as 50 commercial banks had risk-adjusted adequacy ratio below 10 per cent norm in 1995-1996, the number of such banks below 10 per cent capital adequacy norm came down to mere 6 in 2002-03. This is appreciable achievement.

---

6. C. Rangarajan, *op.cit,* and Rakesh Mohan, *op.cit.*
7. Rakesh Mohan, "Financial Sector Reforms in India; Policy and Performance Analysis", *Economic and Political Weekly,* March 2005, p.1108.

Table 35.4. Distribution of Commercial Banks according to Risk-Weighted Capital Adequacy

(No. of Banks)

Year	*Below 4 per cent*	*Between 4-9 per cent*	*Between 9-10 per cent*	*Above 10 per cent*	*Total No. of Banks*
1995-96	8	9	33	42	92
1999-00	3	2	12	84	101
2000-01	3	2	11	84	100
2001-02	1	2	7	81	91
2002-03	2	0	4	87	93

1. Note that number of banks has also declined due to merger of some banks.

Source : (1) Rakesh Mohan, "Financial Sector Reforms in India : Policies and Performance" *EPW,* March 2005, and (2) Reserve Bank of India.

Progress of Commercial Banking in India : 1969 to 2003: After the nationalisation of big banks in 1969 there has been rapid progress of commercial banking in India in terms of expansion of branches (especially in the rural and semi-urban areas), and growth of credit, especially for the priority sectors such as small scale industries and agriculture during the seventies and eighties. Under the financial reforms since 1991, as will be seen from Table 35.5, there has not been much progress in the expansion in number of bank branches (offices) and the number of population served by a bank branch which has remained at around 15,000. But, as rightly pointed by Rakesh Mohan, "the reform *maintained the gains* in terms of the outreach of bank branches achieved in the priority sector advances by banks"[8] after nationalisation in 1969. Besides, banking reforms have led to the *gains in terms of deposits per capita of population and credit issue per capita* by banks. Whereas deposits per capita rose from ₹ 2,368 at end-March 1991 to ₹ 12,253 at end-March 2000 – about 6 times increase, per capita credit rose from ₹ 1,434 at end-March 1991 to ₹ 7,275 at end-March 2003. Besides, deposits in commercial banks as per cent of national income increased from 48.1 at end-March 1991 to about 52 at end-March 2003.

Table 35.5. Progress of Commercial Banking in India : From 1969 – 2000

	Indicators	*June* 1969	*June* 1980	*March* 1991	*March* 1995	*March* 2000	*March* 2003
1	No of commercial banks	73	154	272	284	298	292
2	No of bank offices	8,262	34,594	60,570	64,234	67,868	68561
	Of which						
	Rural and semi-urban bank offices	5,172	23,227	46,550	46,602	47,693	47496
3	Population per office ('000s)	64	16	14	15	15	16
4	Per capita deposit (₹)	88	738	2,368	4,242	8,5423	12253
5	Per capita credit (₹)	68	457	1,434	2,320	4,555	7,275
6	Priority sector advances @ (per cent)	15.0	37.0	39.2	33.7	35.4	33.7
7	Deposits (per cent of national income)	15.5	36.0	48.1	48.0	53.5	51.8

@ : Share of priority sector advances in total non-food credit of scheduled commercial bank.

* : As at end-March 2002.

Source : Reserve Bank of India

8. *op. cit.* p.1110 (italics added)

An aspect of banking in respect of which there has been deterioration rather than progress relates to the lending to the priority sectors. It will be seen from Table 35.2 that there has been decline in priority sector advances which as per cent of total non-food credit of scheduled commercial banks fell from 39.2 per cent at end-March 1991 33.7 per cent at end March 2003. However, in the credit policy statement 2005-06 RBI has provided some incentives to the banks for providing more credit to the priority sectors such as agriculture and small and medium enterprises.

Despite the reduction of SLR requirements to invest in government and other approved securities banks voluntarity made large investment in these securities since the mid-1990s. This was due to slowdown in industrial growth from 1997 to 2002 which accounted for lower credit demand by the industrial sector resulting in larger investment by the banks in risk-free government securities. During the last three years (2003-06) due to revival and acceleration in industrial growth demand for bank credit by the commercial sector has increased and as a result the commercial banks are undertaking their core functions of providing loans and advances to the commercial sector to a greater extent. In fact, liberalisation of banking system and reduction in SLR banks seem to have struck a proper balance between investment and providing loans and advances as per their rational profit-maximising strategy.

Further Aspects of Progress of Commercial Banking in India, 2000 to 2009. The commercial banking as measured by the amount of deposits in them and advances by them increased significantly between 2000 and 2009. As will be seen from Table 35.6. The total deposits in scheduled commercial banks (SCB) increased from 852 thousand crore in 2000 to 4063 thousand crore in 2009, that is, five times during these nine years, while advances by them grew from 454 thousand crore to 3000 thousand crore (see Table 35.6). During these nine years interest income by SCBs increased by 9.5 times from 40.8 thousand crore to 38.8 thousand crore. However, number of employees in the banks increased very slowly from 840 thousand crore in 2000 to 885 thousand in 2009, that is, only by 5 per cent.

Table 35.6. Further Aspects of Progress of Commercial Banking (Schedule Commercial Banks)

(in ₹ crore)

	2000	2009
GDP (in crore)	19,25,017	54,75,833
Capital & reserves and surplus	–81,000	3,68,255
Deposits	8,51,593	40,63,203
Advances	4,54,069	30,00,906
Interest income	40,866	3,88,816
Interest expenses	52,628	2,63,219
Operating expenses	–31,000	89,268
Total employees (*in numbers*)	8,40,000	8,85,414
Return on assets (in %)	0.87	1.0
Net NPA ratio (in %)	6	1.4
Deposit-to-GDP ratio (in %)	44	74
Credit-to-GDP ratio (in %)	24	55

During 2000-09 our gross domestic product (GDP) nearly trebled from ₹ 19,25,000 crore to ₹ 54,75,000 crore, *return on assets* (RoA), which varies between 0.25% and 1.5% worldwide, rose from 0.87% in 2000 to 1.0 per cent in 2009 in India. At 1.4% in 2009 the net non-performing assets (NPA) ratio is a far cry from 6% level 10 years ago.

In contrast to most countries, in India, retail deposits form a sizeable chunk of gross domestic savings, creating a large potential for investment. The ratio of total deposits-to-GDP, which stood at

44% in 2000 climbed to 74% in 2009. However, the credit-to-GDP ratio presents an opposite picture, and India with a credit-to-GDP ratio 55%, lags behind many countries whose banks lend more than the size of their economies. We also have to catch up with the world's best-run banks in the area of cost management – at anywhere between 37% and 66% our cost-income ratio is no match for international bench marks of 30-35%.

The better performance of the banking system till 2009 as a result of financial reforms is reflected in greater efficiency and productivety through enhanced competition. This has resulted in greater profitability of banks in the 1990s. The profitability of not only private sector banks but also of the public sector banks has greatly improved. Thus, according to Rakesh Mohan, "*public sector banks have responded to the new challenges of competition which is reflected in the increase in share of these banks in the overall profits of the banking sector. From the position of net loss in the mid-1990s, in recent years the share of public sector banks in the profits of the commercial banking system has become broadly commensurate with their share of assets, indicating a broad convergence of profitability across various bank groups*."[9]

Increase in Non-Performing Assets (Bad Loans)

Because of the slowdown and high levels of leverage, banks are experiencing a rise in NPAs. Overall NPAs of the banking sector increased from 2.36 per cent of total credit advanced in March 2011 to 3.57 per cent of total credit advanced in September 2012 (Figure 35.1). While there has been an across-the-board increase in NPAs, the increase has been particularly sharp for the industry and infrastructure sectors, with NPAs as a percentage of credit advanced increasing from 1.91 per cent in March 2011 to 3.44 per cent as in September 2012. Sectors particularly under stress include textiles, chemicals, iron and steel, food processing, construction, and telecommunications.

As per RBI data, gross NPAs (GNPA) of PSBs have shown a rising trend during the last three years from ₹ 59,972 crore (March, 2010) to ₹ 71,080 crore (March, 2011), ₹ 1,12,489 crore (March, 2012), and ₹ 1,44,437 crore (September, 2012). **As a percentage of credit advanced, NPAs were at a level of 4.01 per cent in September 2012** compared to 2.09 per cent in 2008-09. Although GNPAs have increased at system level, the GNPA ratios of PSBs are still at manageable levels. However, given their rapid growth, albeit partly for technical reasons, they need to be closely monitored.

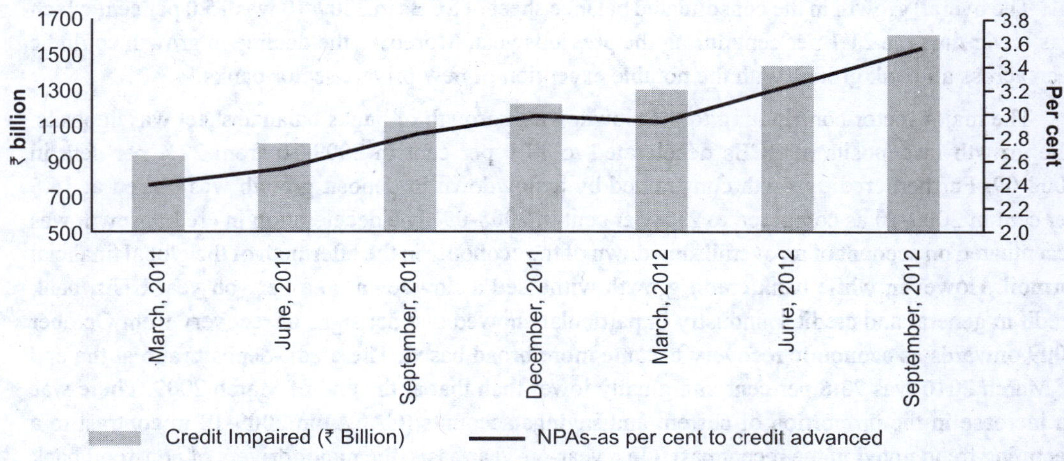

Fig. 35.1 : Non-Performing Assets of the Banking Sector

9. Rakesh Mohan, *op. cit.*, p. 111.

The main reasons for increase in NPAs of banks are (*a*) switchover to system-based identification of NPAs by PSBs; (*b*) current macroeconomic situation in the country; (*c*) increased interest rates in the recent past; (*d*) lower economic growth; and (*e*) aggressive lending by banks in the past, especially during good times.

Some recent initiatives taken by the government to address the rising NPAs include (*a*) appointment of nodal officers in banks for recovery at their head offices/zonal offices/ for each Debts Recovery Tribunal (DRT); (*b*) thrust on recovery of loss assets by banks; (*c*) close watch on NPAs by picking up early warning signals and ensuring timely corrective steps by banks; (*d*) directing the state-level Bankers' Committee to be proactive in resolving issues with the state governments; and (*e*) designating asset reconstruction companies (ARCs) resolution agents of banks. Pursuant to the second review of the Monetary Policy, the RBI has also announced the following remedial measures:

1. The provision for restructured standard accounts is to be raised from the existing 2 per cent to 2.75 per cent;
2. The sanction of fresh loans/*ad hoc* loans from 1st Jan 2013 will be made on the basis of sharing of information among banks;
3. Banks will conduct sector-/activity-wise analysis of NPAs; banks will put in place a robust mechanism for early detection of sign of distress, amendments in recovery laws, and strengthening of credit appraisal and post-credit monitoring.

Steps taken by the government and the RBI have resulted in improvement in recovery of NPAs by the PSBs which has increased from ₹ 9,726 crore as in March 2010 to ₹ 13,940 crore as in March 2011 and ₹ 17,043 crore as in March 2012.

Financial Performance of Banks, 2008-09 and 2009-10

The consolidated balance sheet of the SCBs in India during 2009-10 showed relatively sluggish growth performance, marked mainly by slow deposit growth. The growth in profits of SCBs too was lower in 2009-10 than in the previous year. Further, there was a rise in the NPA ratio of SCBs in 2009-10. Though asset quality emerged as a concern for the banking sector, its capital adequacy remained fairly robust during the year, providing cushion for any future losses.

The overall growth in the consolidated balance sheet of SCBs in 2009-10 was 15.0 per cent which was lower than the 21.1 per cent during the previous year. Moreover the decline in growth could be seen across all bank groups with the notable exception of new private sector banks.

The major factor contributing to the slowdown in growth of banks balance sheet was deposits. The growth in deposits of SCBs decelerated to 17.0 per cent in 2009-10 from 22.4 per cent in 2008-09. Further, credit growth constrained by a slowdown in deposit growth was placed at 16.6 per cent in 2009-10 as compared to 21.1 per cent in 2008-09. The deceleration in credit growth was accentuated on account of an overall slowdown of the economy in the aftermath of the global financial turmoil. However, while bank credit growth witnessed a slowdown on a year-on-year basis, bank credit in general and credit to industry in particular showed distinct signs of recovery from October 2009 onwards as economic recovery became more broad based. The credit-deposit ratio at the end of March 2010 was 73.6 per cent, marginally lower than that at the end of March 2009. There was an increase in the proportion of current and savings accounts (CASA) in 2009-10 in contrast to a declining trend noted in the recent past. On a year-on-year basis, the major drivers of non-food bank credit in 2009-10 were industry and agriculture. There was considerable slowdown in the growth in personal loans and also credit to the services sector during the year.

The growth in investments of banks decelerated to 18.6 per cent in 2009-10 from 23.1 per cent in 2008-09. Also, there were notable changes in the investment portfolio of banks. The percentage contribution of investments in approved securities declined in 2009-10 in contrast to an increase in 2008-09, which was mainly due to banks' preference to park their funds in low-risk instruments against the backdrop of prevailing global uncertainties. Consequently, the percentage contribution of investments in non-SLR (statutory liquidity ratio) securities by banks showed an increase in 2009-10 driven mainly by an increase in investments in mutual funds.

Similar to the slowdown in growth in balance sheets, there was a moderation in the financial performance of SCBs in 2009-10. The growth in both income and expenditure of the SCBs slowed down leading to a deceleration in the growth of operating and net profits of SCBs. Every indicator of profitability also showed a decline in 2009-10. The most salient indicator of profitability, return on assets (RoA), declined to 1.05 per cent in 2009-10 from 1.13 per cent in 2008-09. Further, return on equity (RoE) too declined to 14.3 per cent in 2009-10 from 15.4 per cent in 2008-09.

After abstaining during 2008-09, banks started resorting to the capital market for raising resources in 2009-10. The resources raised from the capital market by banks were in the form of both public issues and private placement in 2009-10.

Financial Performance of Banks, 2010-11 and 2011-12

Performance of Indian banks during the year 2011-12 was conditioned to a large extent by fragile recovery of the global financial markets as well as a challenging operational environment on the domestic front, with persistent high inflation and muted growth performance. In addition, stressed financial conditions of some State Electricity Boards and airline companies added to the deterioration in asset quality of banks. The consolidated balance sheet of SCBs grew at a slower pace during 2011-12 as compared to the previous year due to slower growth of credit as well as deposits. In addition, net profit of banks slowed down. Though Indian banks remained well-capitalized, concerns regarding growing non-performing assets (NPAs) persisted.

The operating performance of the SCBs as shown in Table 35.7 can be summed up as follows:

1. PSBs had a dominant share and accounted for 72 per cent of the total income of the SCBs and 72.8 per cent of aggregate assets.
2. In 2011-12, there was a sharp increase in the expenditure on provisioning and contingencies; the rate of growth, however, varied across the bank categories. While contingency and provisioning expenses recorded a growth of 16.1 per cent for all commercial banks, the rate of growth was 21.3 per cent for PSBs and only 3 per cent for the new private sector banks. As percentage of PSB assets, the provisioning expenditure increased from 1.04 per cent in 2010-11 to 1.11 per cent in 2011-12.
3. PSBs were able to increase their interest spread from 2.55 per cent in 2010-11 to 2.59 per cent in 2011-12. The interest spread declined for old private sector banks and foreign banks. An increase in interest spread for all SCBs during 2011-12 with a relatively moderate growth in credit disbursement is significant.
4. Net profit as percentage of assets remained sticky at 0.98 per cent in 2010 and 2011-12. However, in case of the PSBs, this declined from 0.85 per cent in 2010-11 to 0.82 per cent in 2011-12. Foreign banks and old and new private sector banks, however, were able to increase the ratio of net profit to assets.

Table 35.7 : Operating Parameters of Commercial Banks

Items	*Income*	*Interest Income*	*Expenditure*	*Interest Expended*	*Provisions and contingencies*	*Net Profit*	*Total Assets*
				2010-11			
PSBs	414099	366135	369199	231153	55080	44901	5294006
Foreign banks	39505	28493	31786	10623	8595	7719	491175
Old private sector banks	26328	23299	23226	14768	2858	3101	309011
New private sector banks	91259	73414	76649	42381	12261	14610	1089206
All SCBs	571191	491341	500860	298925	78795	70331	7183398
				2011-12			
PSBs	535098	484740	485584	328539	66831	49514	6037982
Foreign banks	47223	36340	37797	15195	9056	9426	583600
Old private sector banks	35975	32592	32051	22506	3005	3924	375015
New private sector banks	122503	101387	103709	64279	12626	18794	1302786
All SCBs	740799	655059	659141	430519	91517	81658	8299383
				As percentage to Assets			
				2010-11			
PSBs	7.82	6.92	6.97	4.37	1.04	0.85	2.55
Foreign banks	8.04	5.80	6.47	2.16	1.75	1.57	3.64
Old private sector banks	8.52	7.54	7.52	4.78	0.92	1.00	2.76
New private sector banks	8.38	6.74	7.04	3.89	1.13	1.34	2.85
All SCBs	7.95	6.84	6.97	4.16	1.10	0.98	2.68
				2011-12			
PSBs	8.86	8.03	8.04	5.44	1.11	0.82	2.59
Foreign banks	8.09	6.23	6.48	2.60	1.55	1.62	3.62
Old private sector banks	9.59	8.69	8.55	6.00	0.80	1.05	2.69
New private sector banks	9.40	7.78	7.96	4.93	0.97	1.44	2.85
All SCBs	**8.93**	**7.89**	**7.94**	**5.19**	**1.10**	**0.98**	**2.71**

Capital Adequacy Ratio (CAR)

One of the major indicators of growing financial soundness of the Indian banking system was the improvement in the *capital to risk-weighted assets ratio* (CRAR). The CRAR of all SCBs (Scheduled Commercial Banks) under Basel 1 framework improved to 13.6 per cent by end-March 2010 from 13.2 per cent a year earlier, thus remaining significantly above the stipulated minimum of 9.0 per cent. As all commercial banks in India excluding RRBs (regional rural banks) and local area banks became Base I compliant as on 31 March 2009, it is also essential to look at the capital adequacy position under this framework. Under the Base II framework too, the CRAR of SCBs showed an increase in 2009-10; the CRAR improved to 14.5 per cent at the end of March 2010 from 14.0 per cent at the end of March 2009. At the bank group level, every bank group reported CRAR, on an average, of over 13 per cent under the Basel II framework.

Following the uncertainties prevailing in the domestic market and relatively subdued performance of the equity market during the first half of 2011-12, *banks abstained from raising resources through public issues during 2011-12.* During 2011-12, banks' resource mobilization through private placements also slowed down as compared to the previous year. However, this reduction was seen in the case of PSBs, while private sector banks continued to raise resources through private placements.

The capital to risk-weighted assets ratio (CRAR) remained well above the RBI's stipulated 9 per cent for the system as a whole as well as for all bank groups during 2011-12, indicating that Indian banks remained *well-capitalized.* Also, the CRAR at system level improved marginally compared to the previous year. *The CRAR (under Basel II) at system-wide level stood at 14.24 per cent as at end-March 2012, as compared to 14.19 per cent as at end-March 2011.*

As capital is a key measure of banks' capacity for generating loan assets and is essential for balance sheet expansion, the Government of India has regularly invested additional capital in the PSBs to support their growth and keep them financially sound so as to ensure that the growing credit needs of the economy are adequately met. A sum of ₹ 12,000 crore was infused in seven PSBs during 2011-12 to enable them to maintain a minimum Tier-I CRAR of 8 per cent and also to increase shareholding of the Government of India in these PSBs. In 2012-13 also, the Government infused capital in PSBs to augment their Tier-I capital so that they maintain their Tier-I CRAR at a comfortable level and remain compliant with the stricter capital adequacy norms under BASEL-III. This will also support internationally active PSBs in their national and international banking operations undertaken through their subsidiaries and associates. For this purpose an amount of ₹ 12,517 crore was allocated in the Revised Estimates (RE) 2012-13 under Plan.

In 2013-14, the Finance Ministry planned to infuse ₹ 14,000 crore in the public sector banks (PSBs) in the first quarter of 2013-14 but deferred its infusion plan till the next quarter as it wanted to assess their needs after the second quarter results before pumping cash to shore up their capital adequacy ratio (CAR). The Finance Ministry wants to assess the capital requirements of banks such as credit growth, non-performing assets, their recoveries, and profitability. The Finance Ministry feels there's no urgent need of capital infusion in banks and the government can take a call after the half-yearly results. *Barring four, all other public sector banks are quite comfortably placed at 8% CAR, which is much above the required 6%,* as prescribed by the Reserve Bank under the Basel III norms. The CAR requirement will increase by 50 basis points to 6.50% from March 2014.

The Finance Minister in his budget speech for 2013-14 has said that all banks with capital adequacy ratio of less than 8% will be given preference for capitalisation. Dena Bank has the lowest CAR at 7.26% followed by Bank of Maharashtra (7.57%), IDBI (7.68%) and Indian Overseas Bank (7.80%).

He had also said that banks will plough back retail earnings and also find other ways to raise capital. "We have asked banks to explore other options. In cases where government holding is more than 75%, both banks and the government will evaluate if options other than direct cash infusion can be explored."

Sectoral Deployment of Bank Credit

Details of sectoral deployment of credit are maintained by the RBI on a regular basis for 47 scheduled banks accounting for nearly 95 per cent of total credit flow. Industry has remained the dominant sector accounting for around 45 per cent of total credit disbursed by the banks. While food credit, primarily advanced for food procurement, has fluctuated, *credit to the agriculture* and allied sector has grown in percentage terms after Q3 of 2011-12. While the percentage growth of credit for the industry and services sectors has declined in 2012-13 growth in personal loans appears to have bottomed out and some recovery was visible in Q3 of 2012-13 (Table 35.8). Inflation affected the consumption of non-food items. *Sectoral shares in the credit flow have generally remained stable.*

Table 35.8. Sectoral Deployment of Credit

	2010-11	2011-12	2012-13 Q1	Q2	Q3
Credit disbursed (₹ billion)					
Total credit	**33359**	**39506**	**44190**	**44610**	**46386**
Food credit	546	726	949	950	1018
Agriculture & allied activities	4159	4561	5217	5266	5479
Industry	14461	17656	19772	19890	20752
Services	7859	9298	10405	10383	10617
Personal loans	6333	7255	7847	8121	8520
Shares of the broad sectors in credit disbursed (per cent)					
Total credit	1.64	1.84	2.15	2.13	2.20
Food credit	12.47	11.55	11.81	11.80	11.81
Agriculture & allied activities	43.35	44.69	44.74	44.59	44.74
Industry	23.56	23.53	23.55	23.28	22.89
Services	18.99	18.36	17.76	18.20	18.37
Personal loans					
Average annual rate of growth (per cent)					
Total credit	**20.84**	**18.43**	**17.76**	**16.48**	**16.09**
Food credit	16.03	32.91	51.95	40.01	32.38
Agriculture & allied activities	19.82	9.67	15.32	20.02	22.86
Industry	26.48	22.10	19.54	16.17	15.52
Services	19.55	18.30	16.87	16.10	13.01
Personal loans	11.96	14.54	13.19	13.92	15.61

Source : Economic Survey, 2012-13

Sectoral deployment of credit indicates deceleration across most sectors in 2013-14*

An analysis of the sectoral deployment of credit based on data from select banks (which cover 95 per cent of total non-food credit extended by all SCBs) for June 2013 reveals that deceleration in credit growth was observed in all major sectors (*viz*., agriculture, industry and services), except for personal loans. The y-o-y bank credit growth to industry moderated to 14.1 per cent in June 2013 from 20.7 per cent in June 2012. Deceleration in credit growth to industry was observed in all the major sub-sectors, barring food processing, textiles, leather & leather products, cement & cement products and infrastructure. Credit growth to industry *excluding infrastructure* was much lower, at 11.7 per cent in June 2013 compared with 22.4 per cent a year ago.

Despite a comfortable liquidity situation and a marginal decline in WALR during Q1 of 2013-14, SCBs non-food credit growth remained below the Reserve Bank's indicative trajectory. On the demand side, the deceleration in domestic growth adversely affected the demand for credit in India. The deterioration in credit quality, on the other hand, impeded the supply of domestic credit. The deceleration was observed across all bank groups, being high for PSBs and private sector banks, which jointly account for above 90 per cent of the SCB credit.

* RBI, Macroeconomic and Monetary Developments, *'First Quarterly* Review' July 29, 2013

Risk aversion impacting credit, as asset quality concerns persist

Besides sluggish demand, a major factor that could have led to the low credit growth of public sector banks (PSBs) over the past quarters relates to deterioration in their asset quality. Asset quality indicators of the banking sector, which had suffered significantly during 2011-12, worsened in 2012-13. Although data indicate worsening asset quality across bank groups during 2012-13, it continued to be led by public sector banks (PSBs), which account for the major portion of bank advances. Deterioration in both asset quality and in macroeconomic conditions resulted in risk aversion in the banking sector.

Priority Sector Lending

In view of the need to ensure adequate institutional credit flow to the vulnerable sectors, the RBI has mandated that banks should lend a minimum of 40 per cent of their advances to the priority sectors. Priority sector broadly includes advances to agriculture, small scale industries, weaker section, exports, education, SHGs, etc. Revised guidelines issued by the RBI on priority sector lending (PSL) on 20 July 2012 mandates commercial banks and foreign banks with 20 or more branches to allocate 40 per cent of their adjusted net bank credit (ANBC) or credit equivalent amount of off-balance sheet exposures (OBE), whichever is higher, to the priority sector. Within this, sub-targets of 18 per cent and 10 per cent of ANBC or credit equivalent amount of OBE have been mandated for lending to agriculture and the weaker sections respectively. For foreign banks with less than 20 branches, the target PSL is 32 per cent of ANBC or credit equivalent amount of OBE, whichever is higher. Foreign banks have been given a period of 5 years beginning April 2013 to achieve their PSL target. Their action plan, however, is required to be approved by the RBI.

Table 35.8. Particulars of Priority Sector Advances (₹ *crore*)

	Public Sector Banks			Private Sector Banks			Foreign Banks		
	Mar-10	Mar-11	Mar-12	Mar-10	Mar-11	Mar-12	Mar-10	Mar-11	Mar-12
Total Priority Sector Advances	863777	1021496	1129993	214669	249099	286420	59959	66737	80559
Advances to Agriculture#	372463	414973	475148	90737	92146	100900	121	56	111
Advances to Micro and small enterprises	276318	369930	396343	64824	88115	110513	21147	20981	21760
Advances to weaker sections	211376	240321	293960	25532	28575	38929	0.00	0.00	0.00
Advances to Exports	NA	NA	NA	NA	NA	NA	35167	43322	51742
Priority Sector Advances as percentage of total advances									
Total Priority Sector Advances	41.50	40.90	37.40	45.80	46.60	39.40	36.00	39.70	40.90
Advances to Agriculture#	17.90	16.60	15.70	19.30	17.20	13.80	0.00	0.00	0.00
Advances to Micro and small enterprises	13.20	14.80	13.10	13.80	16.50	15.20	12.70	12.40	11.00
Advances to weaker sections	10.10	9.60	9.70	5.40	5.30	5.30	0.00	0.00	0.00
Advances to Exports							21.10	25.70	26.20

Source: RBI.

Note : Indirect agriculture is reckoned only up to 4.5 per cent of the ANBC (Adjusted net bank credit) or credit equivalent of off-balance sheet exposures, whichever is higher; NA = Not Applicable

The total outstanding priority sector advances of public sector banks (PSB) increased from ₹ 10,21,496 crore as on the last reporting Friday of March 2011 to ₹ 11,29,993 crore as on the last reporting Friday of March 2012, showing a growth of 10.6 per cent. The achievement of PSBs as a group was 37.4 per cent as on the last reporting Friday of March 2012. The outstanding priority sector advances of private sector banks grew by 14.9 per cent in 2011-12 and these were 39.4 per cent of their total advances as on the last reporting Friday of March 2012. The outstanding priority sector advances of foreign banks had reached the targeted level of 40 per cent as on March 2012, though these advances have largely been in export sector (See Table 35.8).

Technological Developments in Banks

Banks in India are using information technology (IT) not only to improve their own internal processes but also to increase facilities and services to their customers. Efficient use of technology has facilitated accurate and timely management of the increased volumes of transactions of banks, consistent with a larger customer base. Of the total number of PSB branches, 97.8 per cent were fully computerized at the end of March 2010. ATMs, particularly off-site ATMs, act as substitutes for bank branches in offering a means of anytime cash withdrawal to customers. Growth of ATMs, which had generally been steadily rising in recent years, was observed to be 37.8 per cent in 2009-10. More importantly, the growth in off-site ATMs too was comparably high at 44.6 per cent during the year. At the end of March 2010, the percentage of off-site ATMs to total ATMs stood at 45.7 per cent for all SCBs.

Another important technological development in 2009-10 was a significant increase in the percentage of PSB branches implementing CBS from 79.4 per cent at the end of March 2009 to 90 per cent at the end of March 2010. The percentage of branches under CBS (Computer Based System) was much larger for the SBI group as compared to nationalized banks.

With computerization in general, and CBS (Computer based system) in particular, having reached near completion, it is important to leverage this technological advancement to look at areas beyond CBS that can help in not just delivering quality and efficient services to customers but also generating and managing information effectively. With regard to the second aspect of information management, a system of receiving data from banks by the RBI in an automated manner without any manual intervention is under examination.

Going forward, there are a number of issues with regard to development of banking technology that need to be addressed. These relate to further improvement in back office management in the form of streamlining the management information system (MIS), strengthening centralized processing, customer relationship management (CRM), and IT Governance. Back office technological advancement would help divert banks' resources more towards front office management, thereby increasing the customer focus of their services and supporting greater financial penetration and inclusion.

PERFORMANCE OF CAPITAL MARKET

The reforms undertaken in the capital market since 1991 have brought about a healthy growth in the capital market, except for a few stock market scams engineered by Harshad Mehata in 1992 and Ketan Parikh in the late nineties. The equity market has registered substantial growth in terms of resource mobilisation, the number of stock exchanges, the number of listed companies, trading volume in the stock exchanges (see Table 35.9). The significant improvement in efficiency resulting in reduction in transaction costs, the improvement in transparency and safety in transactions in stock exchanges have taken place, thanks to regulation by SEBI. The introduction of rolling settlement system, abolition of Badla system, sophisticated risk management system and trading in derivatives have greatly improved the efficiency of the stock markets.

Table 35.9 : Some Stock Market Indicators in India

Year (end-March)	1961	1971	1980	1991	2000	2002	2003
1. Number of Stock Exchanges	7	8	9	22	23	23	23
2. Number of listed companies	1,203	1,599	2,265	6,229	9,871	9,644	9,413
3. Market Capitalisation (₹ billion)	12	27	68	1103	11,926	7,493	6,318

The reforms in the capital market have induced the foreign institutional investors to make investment in both equity and debt instruments of the Indian corporate companies. As a result, *portfolio investment in India has substantially increased, especially in recent years. "India has emerged as a major recipient of portfolio investment among the emerging market economies. ...The stability of portfolio investment towards India is in contrast with large volatility of portfolio flows in most emerging markets."*[10] However these remarks of Rakesh Mohan are not valid in the context of post-crisis period. From Feb. 2008, there were large outflows of capital from India causing stock market crash and depreciation of rupee. Again from Sept. 2011 there had been large-scale capital flight by FIIs from India causing crash in Indian stock market and a sharp depreciation of rupee. Further, in May-August 2013, there was large-scale capital outflows causing a sharp depreciation of rupee. The depreciation of rupee has raised the costs of imports, especially of crude oils and other international commodity prices which have added to the inflationary pressures in the Indian economy.

As a result of the improvement in efficiency and transparency in trading in the Indian stock exchanges the BSE sensex crossed 12,000 mark in March 2006 and 2000 in January 2008. A large-scale portfolio investment by FII had brought large dollar inflows in India, apart from increasing the capitalisation of the Indian companies. At present (October 2013) BSE sensex has risen above 20500 mark.

Performance of Government Securities Market.

The reform measures undertaken in respect of government securities market have also yielded good results. As mentioned above, government *finances its fiscal deficit* mostly by borrowing from the market through sale of its securities. Banks and insurance companies buy these government securities and therefore act as financial intermediaries between the public and government. The fiscal deficit of the central government has varied in the range of 6 to 4.6 per cent since 1992. As a result, as will be seen from Table 35.10, the outstanding debt, *i.e.*, stock of central and state government securities has increased by about 10 times in respect of both the Centre and States.

Table 35.10 : Outstanding Stock of Government Securities

	1992	1995	2000	2003	2004
Centre	769	1,375	3,819	6,739	8,243
	(10.3)	(11.6)	(18.1)	(27.3)	(29.7)
States	190	312	739	1,331	1,795
	(2.5)	(2.6)	(3.5)	5.4	6.5

Note : Figures in brackets show outstanding debt as per cent of GDP at current market prices.
Source : RBI

It will also be seen from Table 35.10 that outstanding government debt as a per cent of GDP at current market prices rose from 12.8 per cent in 1992 to 36.2 per cent in 2004. Despite such a large increase in government borrowing to finance its fiscal deficit, the yield and interest rate (*i.e.*, cost of borrowing) has sharply declined. This is due to high liquidity position of banks and also deliberate policy of lower administered interest rates pursued during the major part of the period. The yield on primary issues of government securities of the maturity period of 5 to 10 years which ranged between 13.25 and 14.0 per cent during 1995-96 fell to 4.62 to 5.73 per cent in 2003-04. Despite the reduction in yield and interest rate on government securities the turnover (*i.e.*, sale and purchase) of government securities in the market has increased over ten times between 1998-99 and 2003-04.[11] This shows the buoyancy of risk-free and fixed income government securities.

10. Rakesh Mohan, *op. cit.*
11. See Rakesh Mohan, *op. cit.*, p. 1116.

Chapter 36

New Industrial Policy of 1991 in India

Introduction

In India as early as the First Five Year Plan the economic policy adopted was that the State must not only assume the responsibility for providing the infrastructure facilities, but also undertake direct production work. The need for the intervention of the state in the industrial field was recognised and the development of basic and strategic industries was earmarked for the public sector. At the same time, policy of nationalisation of the private sector was given up; as it was clear that the task before the country was so large that the initiative of both public and private sectors was necessary to secure maximum growth. A complementary role was assigned to the private sector and a large field of operation was left open for private sector activities. The concept of mixed economy was evolved, envisaging the operation of both public and private sectors with an expanding role to the former. Over a greater part of the activities including not only the organised industries but also agriculture, small-scale industries, trade and construction, individual effort and private initiative were regarded as necessary and desirable.

Industrial Policy Resolution 1956

The concept of mixed economy was given a concrete shape and policy direction at the commencement of the Second Five Year Plan by the announcement of the Industrial Policy Resolution of April 1956. This Policy Resolution with some amendments made from time to time continued till 1991 when the policy of liberalisation was adopted.

The basic consideration underlying Industrial Policy Resolution of 1956 was that public sector should venture into new field and to provide the country with the foundations of economic development by strengthening the basic industrial structure of the country. This implied long-term programme and substantial investment by the State not only for the development of basic and heavy industries such as iron and steel, machine building, fertilizers and chemicals, but also providing essential infrastructure such as irrigation, power, transport and communications. The Government was also to undertake direct promotional work of providing finance, marketing facilities, technical advice and other assistance to promote industrial development in the private sector.

The Industrial Policy Resolution, 1956 spelt out the role expected to be played by the private and public sectors. As the Resolution puts it, 'the need for planned and rapid development requires that all industries of basic and strategic importance or in the nature of public utility services should be in the public sector. Other industries which are essential and require investment on a scale which only the State, in the present circumstances, could provide, have also to be in the public sector. The *State has, therefore, to assume direct responsibility for the future development of the industries over a wide area.*"

Two schedules were drawn up: Schedule 'A' consisting of 17 industries, the future development of which was the *exclusive responsibility of the State,* and Schedule 'B' containing a list of 12 industries which were *to be progressively State-owned* in which the State would, therefore, generally take the initiative in establishing new industries. But in this Schedule 'B' private enterprise was also expected to supplement the efforts of the State. All the remaining industries were in general left to the initiative and enterprise of the private sector. This classification was, however, not rigid. The Resolution had left open considerable flexibility so as to permit the entry of the private sector wherever necessary in the fields which were generally allotted to public sector, and *vice versa.*

Within the broad framework of the Industrial Policy Resolution of 1956, the *Industries (Development and Regulation) Act, 1951* provided the main instruments through which the development of the industries in the Private Sector was regulated. The industrial licensing system was designed to canalise investment in the desired directions in accordance with Plan priorities and targets, so as to prevent concentration of economic power and to bring about progressively economic and technological improvements in the industries in the Private Sector.

The roles of public sectors as described in the Industrial Policy Resolution of 1956 continued for 35 years though some modifications and amendments, especially in the licensing policy, were made from time to time. In the industrial policy statements of 1980 and 1985 licensing system was liberalised so that it should not work as an obstacle to the industrial production in the private sector. But in 1991 when Congress Party came into power again under the leadership of Narasimha Rao with Prof. Manmohan Singh as Finance Minister, industrial policy was drastically revised. As shall be discussed below, in the Industrial Policy 1991, the role of public sector has been greatly reduced and policy of liberalisation has been adopted. Under the policy of liberalisation, private sector has been given greater role in the industrial development of the Indian economy.

Need for Revision of Industrial Policy in 1991

It is important to know why industrial policy had to be revised drastically in 1991. In the late eighties it was felt that importance given to the public sector in the strategy of industrial development and stiff controls over the working and expansion of the private sector were obstructing economic growth and *promoting inefficiency.* Further, India experienced serious problems of a *high rate of inflation* on the one hand and *huge deficit in the balance of payments* on the other. To overcome these problems some economists such as I.M.D. Little, Jagdish Bhagwati, Bela Balassa who had been advisors of World Bank and IMF argued for the adoption of the policy of economic liberalisation by India and other developing countries to promote growth, check inflation and solve the problem of balance of payments. They advocated that *free markets and greater role of private sector (including foreign investors) would ensure efficiency by encouraging competition.*

The experiment of a mixed economy as described in the Industrial Policy Resolution of 1956 and later amendments made in it wherein public sector was given a prominent role in industrial development of the Indian economy seemed to be a success in the beginning. It was through public sector investment that a lot of infrastructure such as irrigation, transport, power was developed. Many basic and basic heavy industries such as steel, fertilizers, machine-making industries were built by the public sector. But during the eighties several shortcomings of the working of public sector were observed. First, the *public sector which was expected to generate adequate resources* for the growth of the economy not only failed to do so but *in fact was incurring huge losses* which raised the expenditure of the Government. The losses of the public sector were said to be due to the inefficiency of the public sector enterprises. Secondly, the *problem of macroeconomic imbalances,* both in the internal and external sectors, emerged and assumed serious proportions in 1990-91. The huge budget deficits of the Government and expansion in money supply led to the serious problem of inflation. On the external front, higher commercial borrowing from abroad at higher rates of interest resulted in the serious problem of persistent deficit in the balance of payments. This caused a *sharp decline in the foreign exchange reserves*. The foreign exchange reserves fell to such a meagre amount that it could meet the payments for imports only for 15 days. This compelled the Government to approach IMF and World Bank for necessary help to tide over the foreign exchange crisis. IMF and World

Bank agreed to help only if policy of economic liberalisation is adopted and accordingly greater role be assigned to the private sector in boosting industrial investment and production in a competitive environment. *It was believed that competition in the industrial sector would ensure efficiency and stimulate economic growth.*

Thus the year 1991 is a landmark in the economic history of India. The country faced a severe economic crisis triggered in part by a serious economic situation. Through fundamental changes in economic policy, this crisis was converted into an opportunity. The objective of new industrial policy was to improve the efficiency of the economic system by eliminating the regulatary mechanism that involved various licences and permits which reduced competition even in private sector. To quote Dr. C. Rangarajan, "The thrust of the new economic policy was towards creating a more competitive environment in the economy as a means to improving the productivity and efficiency of the system. This is to be achieved by removing the barriers to entry and restrictions on growth of the firm. While the industrial policy seeks to bring about a greater competitive environment domestically, the trade policy seeks to improve international competitiveness subject to the protection offered by tariffs which are coming down.[1]"

NEW INDUSTRIAL POLICY OF 1991

We discuss below the new industrial policy decisions regarding industry announced in 1991 under the following heads:

1. Abolition of Licensing and Role of Private Sector
2. Public Sector and Privatisation
3. MRTP Policy and Role of Large Business Houses
4. Foreign Investment and Foreign Technology

1. Abolition of Industrial Licensing

Until the early 1980s, the Indian industrial sector had functioned under a system of tight controls and regulations, represented by industrial licensing which was meant to allocate the scarce resources towards building the industrial base of the economy. Now that the Indian industrial economy had acquired quite a wide and diversified base, the new industrial policy of 1991 abolished all industrial licensing irrespective of the level of investment except for 18 industries for which licence was still required. Later, in April 1993 more industries were dereserved and thrown open to the private sector. These three industries dereserved later were (1) motor cars, (2) white goods (such as domestic referigerators, washing machines, microwave ovens, airconditioners) and (3) raw hides, skins and leather. *The remaining fifteen industries which remain reserved for the public sector are those which are essential for security and strategic reasons, safety purposes and for protection of environment.* For granting of licences for even these 15 industries procedure has been greatly simplified. For getting licences only certain vocational guidelines are to be fulfilled so that polluting industries should not cluster around the major urban centres.

The 15 specified industries which continue to be subject to compulsory licensing are:

(1) Coal and Lignite

(2) Petroleum (other than crude) and its distillation products

(3) Distillation and Brewing of Alcoholic drinks

(4) Sugar

(5) Animal Fats and Oils

1. C. Rangarajan, "Growth and Challenges Ahead," *Survey of Indian Industry* 2011, *The Hindu.* pp. 9–10.

(6) Cigars and Cigarettes of Tobacco and Manufactured Tobacco Substitutes

(7) Asbestos and Asbestos based Products

(8) Raw hides and skins, leather

(9) Tanned or dressed furskins

(10) Paper and Newsprint except bagasse based units

(11) Electronic aerospace and defence equipment (all types)

(12) Industrial explosives, safety fuse, gun powder and matches

(13) Drugs and Pharmaceuticals

(14) Plywood and other wood-based products

(15) Hazardous chemicals.

The Industrial Policy, 1991 hoped that with the removal of licensing control for most of the industries, the Indian industries would benefit by becoming more competitive, more efficient and modern which would ensure its rightful place in the world of industrial progress.

2. Freedom to Create New Capacity and Manufacture Any Product. It is worth noting that with the abolition of licensing control, existing private industrial enterprises have been allowed to expand and create new capacity according to the demand in the market without obtaining prior permission or capacity clearance from the Government. Further, in the earlier licensing system existing private enterprises were required to produce *specific* products. With the abolition of industrial licensing, firms will now be free to manufacture any article in response to market demand (except for those subject to compulsory licensing). Big industrial houses have been allowed to expand, diversify, merge and take over.

3. Role of Public Sector and Privatisation

In the earlier industrial policy public sector investment was a crucial element in the strategy of industrial development. It was planned that public sector would occupy the commanding heights of the Indian economy. Public sector was originally given importance because it was required to make adequate investment in infrastructure (power, irrigation, transport and communication) and basic heavy industries so as to lay the basis for future industrial growth. Besides, role of public sector was considered essential to prevent the concentration of economic power in a few private hands, and to promote balanced regional development.

But after the initial success in its original role some problems emerged in the working of public enterprises. Low productivity and inefficiency, poor project management, over-staffing, lack of continuous upgradation, lack of concern for R&D are some of the problems faced by public sector enterprises. But the most important problem was that public sector enterprises suffered heavy losses and were yielding a very low rate of return. As a result, instead of being a source of investible surplus for industrial development, public sector enterprises became a burden on the Government rather than being an asset.

It may also be noted *over a period of time public sector made a departure from its original role.* First, for protecting the interests of workers, the Government had to take over the sick industrial units from the private sector. This category of public sector enterprises accounts for about one-third of the losses of the central public sector enterprises. Second, the public sector had also entered into the production of consumer goods and service sectors such as cars, hotels etc.

In view of the above, Industrial Policy of 1991 adopted a new approach to the public sector. According to this new approach, *the priority areas for future growth of public enterprises are*:

1. Production of essential *infrastructure goods and services*.
2. Exploration and exploitation of oil and mineral resources.
3. *Technological development* and investment in manufacturing capabilities in areas *which are essential for long-term development* of the economy and where private sector will not make adequate investment.
4. Manufacturing products which are of paramount importance on account of *strategic considerations*.

De-Reservation of Industries of the Public Sector. In the new industrial policy 1991 far-reaching structural reforms had been initiated to lead industries away from excess direct controls and regulations to a free, market-oriented economic system. The list of industries reserved for the public sector has been pruned. In the Industrial Policy of 1956, 17 industries were reserved for investment by the public sector. Now, only 8 industries remain reserved for the public sector. Among the industries reserved earlier included many core industries like iron and steel, electricity, air transport, ship building, heavy machinery industries such as heavy chemical plants and telecommunication cables and instruments. The new industrial policy of 1991 threw open all these industries for the private sector for investment and growth. Thus the *new policy of 1991 indicates the Government's intentions to invite a greater degree of participation by the private sector* in important areas of the economy. From March 1993, two more industries, namely, (1) mining of iron are, manganese ore, sulphur, gold and diamond and (2) mining of copper, lead, zinc, tin etc. were dereserved. The six remaining industries reserved for the public sector are (1) Arms and ammunition, other defence equipment, warships, aircraft, (2) Atomic Energy, (3) Coal and Lignite (4) Mineral Oils, (5) Minerals used for producing atomic energy and (6) Railway transport. Thus, six industries which continue to be reserved for the public sector are *in areas where security and strategic considerations predominate.* According to the new policy, as stated above, *the resources in the public sector are now to be used for strategic, high technology and essential infrastructure areas.*

The New Industrial Policy 1991 stipulated that the Government would strengthen those public enterprises which fall in the reserved areas for public sector operation or belong to high priority areas or are yielding reasonable profits. To strengthen them, such public enterprises will be given a *much greater degree of management autonomy* through the system of memoranda of understanding (MOU). *Competition will also be induced* in these areas by inviting private sector participation.

Public Sector Disinvestment. Another important decision of Industrial Policy of 1991 was that in case of *selected public sector companies,* a part of the Government holdings in the equity share capital of these will be disinvested. Apparently this disinvestment was to subject them to market discipline so that they can increase their efficiency. These selected enterprises would be those which are non-essential and commercial in nature. In accordance with this year, beginning from 1991 a target of realising an amount through public disinvestment is set. Revenue so raised is used to reduce budget deficit. So far disinvestment in BALCO, Modern Bread, Indian Tourism Development Corporation, Asoka Hotel, Hotel Corporation of India, Maruti Udyog Limited, IPCL etc. has been carried out and more are in queue for this purpose.

4. MRTP Policy and Large Business Houses

Removal of Investment Controls on Large Business Houses. Under the Restrictive Trade Practices Act (MRTP Act), all firms with assets above a certain size (₹ 100 crores since 1965) were classified as MRTP firms. Such firms were permitted to enter selected industries only and this also on a case-by-case approval basis. In addition to control through industrial licensing separate approval from MRTP Commission was required by such large firms for any investment proposals. This produced a significant adverse effect on the freedom of many of the large private firms in their planning for growth and diversification. In the Industrial Policy 1991, the threshold limits of assets in respect of MRTP and dominant undertakings were removed. These firms will now be at par with others and no prior approval from the Government for investment in the delicensed industries was required.

This is a significant change in the policy regarding the Government control on growth of big business and private monopolies through MRTP Act 1991. According to this policy, to achieve economies of scale by the firms and thereby to ensure higher productivity and competitive advantage, the check by the Government through *Monopoly and Restrictive Trade Practices Act* (MRTP) was not needed. Therefore, industrial policy 1991 limited and restricted the role of MRTP Act. The following decisions were taken in this regard:

(1) Prior Government approval of investment proposals regarding expansion of present undertaking and establishment of new undertaking by big industrial companies which came within the purview of *MRTP Act was not required.*

(2) It was decided to repeal the provisions which prohibited the companies for merger, amalgamation and takeover of other firms by a firm.

(3) It was decided that emphasis would now be on controlling monopolistic, restrictive and unfair trade practices. In accordance with this, provisions of MRTP Act were strengthened in order to enable MRTP Commission to take appropriate action in respect of monopolistic, restrictive and unfair trade practices.

Accordingly, the newly appointed monopoly commission would be asked to investigate the complaints received from industrial consumers or various other specific classes of consumers.

5. Foreign Trade Liberalisation

Prior to 1991 India followed the policy of *import substitution* under which goods were produced within the country instead of importing them. A significant policy reform was to free trade, that is, to reduce tariffs on imports and remove tight *quantitative restrictions on imports*. Besides, *export-oriented* industrial policy was adopted so as to boost exports of India to raise growth of both output and employment. Prior to 1991 imports of consumer goods were banned. Capital goods, raw materials and intermediates were freely importable, subject to indigenous unavailability. The criteria for issuing of licences were non-transparent; delays were order of the day and corruption unavoidable. The first series of economic reforms sought to phase out import licensing and also to reduce import duties.

Import licensing was abolished relatively early for capital goods and intermediates in 1992 simultaneously with the switch to a flexible exchange rate regime. "Import licensing had been traditionally defended on the grounds that it was necessary to manage the balance of payments, but the shift to a flexible exchange rate enabled the government to argue that any balance of payments impact would be dealt with through exchange rate flexibility"[2]. Removing quantitative restrictions thrust on finished goods was much more difficult because the number of domestic producers was very large. Quantitative restrictions on imports of consumer goods and agricultural produce were finally removed on April 1, 2001 in phases primarily because of a ruling by WTO Dispute Panel on a complaint brought by the US.

6. Foreign Capital and Foreign Technology

The new Industrial Policy 1991 also made a significant change towards the approach to foreign capital and technology. Till 1991 the import of foreign technology was strictly regulated. In case of foreign technology transfer agreements sought by the Indian firms, it was necessary to obtain specific prior approval from the Government for each project. This involved delays and hampered business

---

2. Ramu S. Deora, "On Course to Regain Past Glory" in Hindu, *Survey of Indian Industry.* 2011, p.14

decision-making for the import of technology by Indian firms. With a view to promoting technological advancement of the Indian industry, Industrial Policy 1991 announced that *now the Government would provide automatic approval to technological agreements relating to high-priority industries within specified guidelines.* Similar facilities will also be available for other industries as well if technology agreements do not require expenditure of *free* foreign exchange. Indian companies were given freedom to negotiate the terms of technology transfer with the foreign companies according to their own commercial judgement.

The new Industrial Policy 1991 emphasised that opportunities for foreign investment in India should also be utilised to ensure rapid industrial growth. It welcomed foreign capital to supplement domestic efforts for mobilisation of resources. In keeping with this approach Government liberalised its policy regarding foreign investment. To attract foreign direct investment (FDI), it decided to grant automatic approval to private foreign investors to hold equity in Indian companies up to 51 per cent of the total equity shares of a company in 34 high priority industries. This facility would be available to those firms which are able to finance their capital equipment imports through their foreign equity. This is a major departure from the previous policies which required a case-by-case approval of foreign investment normally limited to 40 per cent equity participation. The priority sector industries include power generation and petroleum refining. Further, the Government has given a guaranted 16 per cent return on foreign investment in priority sectors.

Foreign capital flows are not only of the type of foreign direct investment (FDI) but also of *portfolio capital* type. Under portfolio capital foreign institutional investors (FIIs) invest in our equity (*i.e.*, shares) of the Indian companies and also in bonds or securities of government and corporate sector. Portfolio capital flows are generally *volatile*, they come in when market conditions in a country are favourable and go out when uncertainty prevails in the domestic economy or in the international business environment.

7. Further Liberalisation of Industrial Policy

In pursuance of liberalisation policy initiated in 1991, Government has taken more measures to remove restrictions on industrial enterprises, both domestic and foreign. Some important measures are :

(i) Promoting Competition. To prevent monopolistic practices and to promote competition Competition Act 2002 was enacted. The main objectives of this Competition Act are to provide for the establishment of a commission to prevent practices which adversely affect competition and also to sustain competition in markets in India. The competition commission is expected to protect the interests of consumers and to ensure freedom of trade carried on by the participants in market in India. *Competition Commission of India* was established on October 14, 2003.

In his budget for 2004-05 the new Finance Minister has announced to set up a *National Manufacturing Competitiveness Council*. This council will be a continuing forum to advise the government for energising and sustaining the growth of manufacturing industries. The council will also be asked to suggest measures to increase competitiveness in manufacturing sector. The council may also recommend industry-specific policies to enhance competitiveness.

(ii) Dereservation of Items for Small Scale Industries (SSI). Another important measure of economic reforms initiated in 1991 is that several items reserved for exclusive production in the small-scale sector should be de-reserved so that large firms can also produce these items. The policy of reservation of items for manufacturing in small-scale industries (SSI) was introduced in 1967. With 47 items reserved initially in 1967 for small-scale industries, the number of items reserved for SSI went up to 887 in 1984. It has been argued that dereservation of items reserved for small-scale industries will enable the large firms to enter in these fields and produce the products on a large scale and enjoy economies of scale. Besides, the large firms producing on a larger scale and having higher productivity can compete successfully in international markets. Thus, dereservation of items for exclusive manufacturing by SSI will boost both industrial production and growth of exports. Under the new economic policy of liberalisation as many as 75 items consisting of chemicals and their products, leather and leather products, paper products, laboratory reagents etc were dereserved in June 2003. Besides, investment limit (in plant and machinery) for small-scale industries (SSI) was increased from ₹ 1 crore to ₹ 5 crore to enable SSI for making technological upgradation and modernisation so as to enhance productivity and to compete successfully in global markets.

Even though the new UPA government regards small-scale industry as an engine of growth, Finance Minister Chidambaram has carried the dereservation policy further. In budget for 2004-05, 85 more items reserved for exclusive manufacturing in SSI have been dereserved. But to promote technological upgradation of SSI units so that they can grow in competitive environment, capital subsidy scheme for them has been liberalised.

Liberalisation of Foreign Direct Investment

In pursuance of industrial policy of 1991, the government has been trying to woo foreign investors to make direct investment. Foreign direct investment gives opportunity to Indian industry for technologyical upgradation, gaining access to global managerial skills, helping in optimal utilisation of natural and human resources. More importantly, FDI is central for India's integration into global production chain which involves production by multinational corporations working all over the world. Foreign Investment Promotion Board (FIPB) was set up to facilitate foreign direct investment in India has also one of the most liberal policy framework for FDI and foreign technological transfer. In most of the sectors foreign direct investment (FDI) up to 100 per cent is permitted under *automatic approval route*. Note that under automatic approval route, no prior permission is required for foreign direct investment; only post-entry notification is needed.

The consolidated press note released in June 2008 by the Department of Industrial Policy and Promotion (DIPP) specified the sectors in which FDI is prohibited as: retail trading (except single brand product retailing), atomic energy, lottery business, gambling and betting, business of chit fund, Nidhi companies, trading in transferable development rights (TDRs) and activities/sectors not opened to private sector investment. Except these sectors, FDI is allowed in all the other sectors of the economy, at varying specified degrees, either through the Government approval route or the automatic route of the Reserve Bank of India.

In recent years following policy measures have been announced to further liberalise foreign investment:

1. 49 per cent FDI in credit information companies has been allowed.
2. FDI up to 26 per cent and FII up to 23 per cent in commodity exchanges, subject to no single investor holding more than 5 per cent, has been allowed.
3. FDI up to 100 per cent under the automatic route has been allowed both in setting up and in established industrial parks.
4. FDI cap in the civil aviation sector, which includes 74 per cent FDI in non-scheduled airlines, chartered airlines and cargo airlines has, been relaxed. 100 per cent FDI in maintenance and repair organizations, flying training institutes, technical training institutions, and helicopter services/seaplane services has been allowed.
5. FDI policy in the petroleum and natural gas sector has been rationalized.
6. FDI up to 100 per cent (with prior government approval) in mining and mineral separation of titanium-bearing minerals and ores, its value addition, and integrated activities has been allowed.

The *National Common Minimum Programme (NCMP) of UPA-1* government also declared that FDI would continue to be encouraged and actively sought, particularly in areas of infrastructure, high technology. *In accordance with this policy, Finance Minister in his budget for 2004-05 had proposed to raise the sector cap. (i.e. maximum limit) for FDI in telecommunication from present 49 per cent to 74 per cent; in civil aviation from present 40 per cent to 49 per cent and in insurance from 26 per cent to 49 per cent*. There is urgent need for infusing huge amounts of capital in these three sectors, telecommunication, civil aviation, and insurance. However, the left parties which were supporting UPA -1 government were opposed to increasing the limits for FDI.

(iv) Establishment of Investment Commission. The policy of the new UPA government is to make the environment in India attractive for investors. In order to achieve that goal, Finance Minister in his budget for 2004-05 has announced the setting up of *Investment Commission*. This investment commission will have the authority to discuss with and invite domestic and foreign business men to invest in India. Efforts will be made by it to woo domestic and foreign investors to make adequate investment so as to promote growth and employment in India.

A CRITICAL EVALUATION OF NEW INDUSTRIAL POLICY, 1991

It is evident from the changes made in industrial policy that from a planned economy we have moved towards a free-market economy. Though we still have a mixed economy with the both public and private sectors coexisting but the role of private sector, which is governed by market forces, has been greatly increased and that of the public sector greatly diluted. So now, we have mixed economy with greater orientation towards a free market and private sector.

Now, 20 years have passed by when we initiated industrial policy reforms in 1991 laying greater emphasis on liberalisation and privatisation. Now, the pertinent question is whether these industrial reforms have ensured higher and sustained industrial growth which the supporters of these reforms argued they would, whether these reforms have led to a higher growth rate and to the reduction of unemployment which was expected of them. It may be said in favour of industrial policy reforms that today we face no longer any foreign exchange crisis which prompted the initiation of these reforms. Foreign exchange resources which had gone too low in 1991 substantially increased in the post-reforms period. Foreign exchange reserves crossed 100 billion US dollars in December 2003 and reached 152 billion US dollars in March 2006 and further to 309 billion US dollars at end-March 2008. This made foreign exchange reserves situation quite comfortable to deal with any future contingency. However, this huge amount of foreign exchange reserves also created problems as it led to the rapid increase in money supply causing inflationary pressures in the Indian economy. Besides, it also created the problem of how to use the vast amount of foreign exchange reserves for developmental purposes.

The annual rate of inflation as measured by the change in wholesale price index (WPI) which had been brought down from about 14 per cent in 1991-92 to 4.5 per cent in 1997-98, again went up to 8.2 per cent in January 2001. But, it was again brought down to 5.2 per cent in July 2001 and to around 2.6 per cent in July 2002. Annual average rate of inflation based on WPI of all commodities was 3.4 per cent in 2002-03 but it again went up to 4.3 per cent in 2005-06. In the year 2006-07 annual inflation rate as measured by WPI rose to 6.8 per cent. In 2007-08 it fell to 4.8 per cent but rose sharply to 8.0 per cent in 2008-09 and fell to 8.3 per cent in 2009-10. However, inflation has been a matter of serious concern from March 2010 and in 2010-11 the average WPI inflation rate went up to 9.4 per cent and during 2011 it continued to be at an elevated level. In September 2011, WPI inflation was at 10 per cent level compared to the corresponding period of the previous year. The average rate of inflation as measured by CPI (workers) has been more than two digit levels; it was measured at 12.4 per cent in 2009-10 and 11.0 per cent in 2010-11. This has raised the cost of living of the people and eroded their income and there are loud protests against this.

However, it is worth noting that the recent inflation has nothing to do with the economic reforms undertaken since 1991. Various supply-side and demand-side pressures originating both from external sources and domestic developments are responsible for the high inflation rate during 2010-2011 and 2011-2012.

Growth of Indian Economy

As regards growth of the Indian economy in the post-industrial reform period, a significant increase in growth rate of Gross Domestic Product (GDP) has been achieved. As will be seen from

Table 36.1, average annual growth rate of GDP at factor cost which was 5.6 per cent during the eighties (1981-82 to 1990-91), rose to 6.1 per cent during 1992-93 to 2000-01 (that is, omitting the year of crisis, 1991-92). However, the performance of industrial growth rate achieved is a mixed one. The average annual industrial growth in the nineties (1992-93 to 2000-01) fell to 6.4 per cent as compared to 6.6 per cent achieved during 1980-81 to 1990-91 (See Table 36.1).

However, the proper evaluation of industrial growth during the nineties can be made if we break up the decade of nineties into two periods, 1992-93 to 1996-97 and 1997-98 to 2001-2002. Whereas average annual industrial growth in the period 1992-93 to 1996-97 was quite high, namely, 7.6 per cent, in the later period (1997-98 to 2001-02) average industrial growth fell to 4.6 per cent per annum. This slowdown in industrial growth rate in the later half of nineties is due to fall in public sector investment on the one hand and lower rate of growth of exports due to global slowdown during this period on the other. Fall in public sector investment not only created infrastructure bottlenecks but also adversely affected aggregate demand for industrial goods. These factors also adversely affected overall growth of Gross Domestic Product which increased at the rate of 5.5 per cent per annum during the period 1997-98 to 2001-02. (See Table 36.1).

But starting from the year 2002-03 there had been revival of industrial growth. The rate of industrial growth rose to 7.1 per cent in 2002-03 to 7.0 per cent in 2003-04, to 8.4 per cent in 2004-05, to 8.2 per cent in 2005-06. In the entire 10th Plan period the higher industrial growth rate of 8.7 per cent per annum was achieved (see Table 36.1). In the entire 10th Plan period (2002-07) average annual industrial growth was estimated at 8.74 per cent (RE). Thus there has been significantly higher industrial growth in the 10th Plan period (2002-07) and this can be validly attributed to the industrial policy of liberalisaton adopted since 1991. However, it may be noted that apart from industrial policy reforms, a large increase in public sector investment in infrastructure and easy monetary policy of lower interest rates from 1997 to 2005 and greater availability of credit for private sector since 1997 are also the important driving forces of recent spurt in industrial growth. Lower lending interest rates particularly accelerated the growth rate in automobile and consumer durable goods industries during the recent years. Besides, the sustained annual growth of exports at the rate of 20 per cent and more has also contributed to higher industrial growth rate achieved in the last five years (2002-07). The industrial growth will further brighten if constraints like infrastructural bottlenecks are removed.

Table 36.1: Average Annual Growth Rate

Sector	1980-81 to 1990-91	1992-93 to 2000-01	1992-93 to 1996-97	Ninth Plan 1997-1998 2001-02 (Annual average)	10th Plan 2002-07 (Annual average)
Agriculture	3.4	3.2	4.7	2.0	2.5
Industry	**6.6**	**6.4**	**7.6**	**4.6**	**8.74**
Services	6.7	7.8	7.6	8.1	9.28
GDP (factor cost)	5.6	6.1	6.7	5.5	7.8

Source : Dr. Shankar Acharya, "Growth has slowed," *Economic Times,* 22 May, 2001 and *Economic Survey,* 2006-07, 2007-08, 2008-09 and 2009-10.

It may be noted that overall growth rate achieved in the post-reforms period during 1992-93 to 2000-01 was higher, though during the 9th Plan period (1997-98 to 2001-02) it slowed down. However, *it is important to note that 5.5 per cent annual growth in overall GDP during the period had also been achieved due to higher growth rate achieved in services during the 9th Plan period.*

Services such as transportation, communication, travel and tourism have strong linkages with industrial growth. However, in the 10th Plan period, a higher annual growth in GDP of 7.8 per cent was achieved due to higher growth both in industry (8.74%) and services (9.28%).

In Table 36.2 we give growth rate of GDP at factor cost since 2005-06 at 2004-05 prices and will be seen for three successive years (2005-08) in a row, the economy grew at the rate more than 9 per cent growth rate. Even when the developed countries such as US, UK, Germany, France were reeling under severe recession in 2008-09 there was 6.8 per cent growth in India's GDP and after that the Indian economy grew at the rate of 8 per cent in 2009-10 and 8.6 per cent in 2010-11. This is a significant improvement over the pre-reform period. As will be seen from Table 36.2, manufacturing industries growth was over 10 per cent per annum in three successive years, 2005-06 to 2007-08 and after falling to 4.2 per cent in 2008-09, the year of global financial crisis, recovered to 8.8 per cent in 2009-10 and 2010-2011.

Table 36.2: Growth rate of GDP since 2005-2006.

	2005-06	2006-07	2007-08	2008-09	2009-10	2010-11
GDP growth rate	9.5	9.6	9.3	6.8	8.0	8.6
Manufacturing Industries	10.1	14.3	10.3	4.2	8.8	8.8

Source : GOI *Economic survey, 2010-2011.*

However, as will be seen from Table 36.1, from the mid-nineties agricultural growth has slowed down which is a matter of serious concern. In the Ninth Plan period (1997-98 to 2001-02) and the Tenth Plan period (2002-07), annual agricultural growth had been 2 per cent and 2.5 per cent respectively. Economic reforms initiated in 1991 have not paid any attention to accelerating agricultural growth.

Impact on Employment. The new industrial policy has not affected favourably employment generation in the industrial sector. There was only little change in employment opportunities in the industries. In the recent years there has been **continuous decrease** in the eight key sectors over the years as is seen from Table 36.3.

As per the Labour Bureau Survey, there was overall significant decline in employment growth in 2012-13. Whereas in 2009-10, there was 1.07 million growth in employment in the eight key sectors, the overall employment growth in them during 2012-13 fell to 0.35 million in 2012-13. The IT/BPO sector, which has been taking the lead in employment generation, performed badly during 2012-13 due to non-favourable situation across the globe.

Table 36.3. Changes in Employment

(million)

Industry/Group 1	2009-10 2	2010-11 3	2011-12 4	2012-13 5
Textiles, including Apparel	0.06	0.1	0.09	0.14
Leather	0.01	0.03	–0.02	0.01
Metals	0.09	0.09	0.08	0.04
Automobiles	0.08	0.11	0.03	0.02
Gems and Jewellery	0.07	0.00	0.03	0.02
Transport	–0.01	0.00	0.04	0.02
IT/BPO	0.69	0.67	0.58	0.12
Handloom/Powerloom	0.07	–0.01	0.00	0.00
Overall	**1.07**	**0.98**	**0.83**	**0.35**

Source: Employment Surveys, Labour Bureau.

It may be further noted that it is claimed by the Planning Commission that the employment opportunities during the 10th Plan period were created for 47 million persons as against the target of 50 million. However, all new employment opportunities that are claimed to have been created during 1994-2005 are in the *unorganised sector.* There has been in fact net negligible *growth of employment opportunities in* the organised sector as shown in Table 36.4.

Table 36.4. Rate of Growth of Employment in the Organised Sector

(% per annum)

	1983-94	1994-2008
Public Sector	1.53	– 0.65
Private Sector	0.44	1.75
Total Organised	1.20	0.05

Source : GOI, *Economic Survey 2010-11.*

It will be seen from Table 36.4 that while in the pre-reform period (1983-94) employment growth in the total organised sector was 1.20 per cent per annum, in the post-reform period (1994-2008) in the organised sector there was employment growth of only 0.05% per annum. In the post-reform period (1994-2008) while there was negative growth rate (– 0.65%) in the public sector, the employment in the private organised sector increased at the rate of mere 1.75 per cent per annum. Thus there has been neglible growth of employment in the organised sector (both public and private sectors taken together) in the post-reform period despite a high rate of economic growth achieved. This shows a significant failure of economic growth.

This was only to be expected. The chief drawback of New Industrial Policy is that it involves the use of labour-saving modern technology, the competition from the imported products to be faced by the domestic industries and public sector disinvestment on a large scale. The use of capital-intensive technology not only displaces labour already employed but also lowers the growth of employment from the new investment and capital accumulation. Besides, due to the greater role assigned to the private sector, big business houses, foreign capital (MNCs) without ensuring sufficient employment generation by them the already existing inequalities will further increase. This is against the objective of social justice which has been the cherished goal of the Indian planning.

Slower Reduction in Poverty

While higher rate of growth of GDP is important, but it is only one aspect of measuring performance and achievement of an economy. It is equally important who benefits from growth. In fact, higher economic growth was expected to generate adequate employment opportunities and to reduce poverty at a greater rate. There is a good deal of dispute in India about estimating the number of people below the poverty line. There is yet no consensus what is the appropriate poverty line. According to *uniform recall period (URP) methodology* used by the Planning Commission until recently, the number of people below the poverty line in India was 36 per cent in 1993-94 which came down to 27.8 per cent in 2004-05, that is, 8.2 per cent fall in 11 years. Under the same methodology the percentage of people below the poverty line was 44.5 in 1983 which came down to 36 in 1993-94, that is, 8.5 per cent decline in poverty ratio in these 10 years.

Recently, a committee headed by Late Prof. Suresh Tendulkar by adopting a slightly different methodology came to the conclusion that overall poverty ratio in India was 45.3 per cent in 1993-94 and 37.2 per cent in 2004-05, again 8.1 percentage point in 11 years. This clearly shows that despite higher economic growth in the post-reform period, poverty ratio has not been reduced at a higher rate that was expected. The objective of inclusive growth has not been achieved. In our view unless drastic changes in development strategy with greater emphasis on generation of gainful employment opportunities, poverty will not decline much. For elimination of poverty, mere keeping momentum of higher growth is not enough.

What has caused this slow reduction of poverty ratio in the post-reform period ? First, increase in unemployment rate as adequate number of employment opportunities were not created due to use of capital intensive nature of technologies used in the growth process in the post-reform period. Secondly, due to liberalisation of cheap imports of goods from abroad, the small and medium enterprises (SME) could not compete with them resulting in fall in employment. Thirdly, in the growth strategy pursued in the post-reform period, the rate of investment in agriculture has not been increased. As a result, there has been low growth in agriculture in the post-reform period. This reduced relative supply of wage goods, especially foodgrains which led to the problems of hunger and malnutrition in various vulnerable sections of population in various parts of the country.

However, in a recent special NSS Survey conducted in 2011-12, the Planning Commission has estimated on the basis of Tendulkar Committee methodology that the percentage of population living below poverty line declined from 37.2 per cent in 2004-05 to 21.9 per cent in 2011-12, that is, at the rate of 2.2 per cent per annum and this higher rate of decline in poverty has been attributed to higher rate of economic growth (of over 8 per cent per annum on an average). However, this has been challenged on the ground that poverty line has been fixed at a very low level ₹ 27.2 per person per day expenditure in the rural areas and ₹ 33.3 per person per day expenditure in the urban areas. The critics have pointed out that in view of higher rate of inflation based on CPI, it is not possible to live on such low expenditure.

Market Failures and Role of Government

The supporters of economic reforms who argued for diluting the role of public sector as it does not ensure efficiency in production laid great stress on '*government failures*' in promoting economic growth. They however turned a blind eye to the *market failures*. To quote an eminent American economist, Dr. Joseph Stiglitz, "*Market failures are a fact of life, as are government failures. Neoliberal ideologies assume perfect markets, perfect information, and a host of other things which even the best performing market economies cannot satisfy*"[3]. He therefore forcefully argues for a balanced approach to government and markets recognising that both are important and complementary. What is required is that markets need to be regulated effectively by the Government if the objective of growth with equity is to be realised.

3. Shankar Acharya, "Macroeconomic Management in the Nineties," *EPW*, 2002.

Chapter 37

Public Sector and Privatisation

Introduction

Industrial policy resolutions of 1948 and 1956 gave an important role to the public sector in the industrial development of the country. At the time of independence, Indian economy was industrially underdeveloped. In fact, it was predominantly an agrarian economy with a weak industrial base and lack of infrastructural facilities. Therefore, Indian economy needed a big push and it was visualised that public sector would provide this big push. It was thought that private sector had neither adequate resources, nor the right mindset to invest and develop the basic heavy industries. The First Five Year Plan allocated relatively more resources to agriculture and infrastructure development. From the Second Plan onwards and till the mid-seventies public sector was assigned the role of developing basic heavy industries and plan resources were allocated accordingly.

Further, the Mahalanobis strategy of development which was adopted from the Second Plan onwards, import-substitution type of industrial development was considered so that public sector would mainly invest in those industries which would substitute imports. With import-substitution, it was thought, Indian economy would become self-reliant.

In this chapter, we discuss the role of public sector in India's economic development and will see how this role has been greatly diluted in the New Industrial Policy of 1991. We also examine the growth and performance of public sector in India. At the end we will explain the new policy of privatisation or disinvestment of the public sector enterprises.

ROLE OF PUBLIC SECTOR IN INDIA'S MIXED ECONOMY

It is noteworthy that in India's mixed economy public sector was accorded a vital role not only in initiating and accelerating economic growth but also for ensuring just distribution of the fruits of economic growth. Besides, the expansion of public sector was considered as an essential instrument of socialising means of production, economic planning was adopted as important method of promoting economic growth with social justice. It needs to be stressed that the attainment of socialism in an economically backward country like India does not involve merely redistributing existing incomes and wealth because that would mean distributing poverty. If the objective of socialism is to be realised in a developing country like India, economic growth has to be accelerated along with the promotion of social justice.

The functions and importance of public sector and economic planning for promotion of economic growth and socialist transformation of the Indian economy are explained below:

Accelerating Economic Growth. First, public sector and planning are required to initiate and speed up the process of economic growth. As is quite well known, developing countries are caught up in vicious circle of poverty. Only through economic planning and expansion of public sector it would be possible to break the vicious circle of poverty and accelerate the rate of economic growth. The free private enterprise working in an unplanned manner would fail to bring about rapid economic development. Prof. Galbraith rightly points out that, "What is not in doubt is the need for planning by the less developed country ..... there is much that the market can usefully encourage and accomplish.

But the market cannot reach forward to take great strides when these are called for. As it cannot put a man into space so it cannot bring quickly into existence a steel industry where there was little or no steel making capacity before. Nor can it quickly create an integrated industrial plant. *Above all no one can be certain that it will do so in countries where development has lagged and where there is not only a need for development but an urgent demand that it should occur promptly.* To trust the market is to take an unacceptable risk that nothing or too little will happen"[1]. This clearly shows that economic planning and expansion of public sector alone can guarantee quick economic growth in less developed countries like India.

Building up of Economic Infrastructure. Second, building up of what is often called *economic infrastructure,* such as power, fuel, transport and telecommunication in the Indian economy. Without the expansion of the basic infrastructure process of economic development cannot be speeded up and optimum utilisation of a country's resources cannot be made . However, it is noteworthy that investment in the economic infrastructure is not profitable from the viewpoint of private enterprise since most of the gains from them accrue in the form of external economies for the growth of other enterprises and industries rather than money profits for the investors themselves. Moreover, profits from these infrastructure take a long time to accrue. Private enterprise is generally interested in quick returns and therefore does not feel interested in making investment in them. Therefore, it is the task of public sector to make adequate investment in them so as to remove bottlenecks to economic development.

Investment in Basic Heavy Industries. Third, the public sector in the Indian economy has to expand the *basic heavy industries* such as steel, fertilizers and other chemical industries, engineering industries (*i.e.* industries which make machines). The investment in these industries, as has been brought out by Prof P.C. Mahalanobis in his well-known growth model, would ensure rapid capital formation which crucially determines rate of economic growth and employment generation in the economy and help achieve self-reliance. But, as in case of infrastructure, private entrepreneurs hesitate to make sufficient investment in them, for they do not yield quick and high rate of profits. Besides, investment in them requires a huge amount of resources which private enterprise may not be able to mobilise.

Occupying Commanding Heights of the Economy. Fourth, in the industrial policy resolution, 1956 public sector in India was expected to occupy the *commanding heights of the economy* such as banks, other financial institutions, Life and General Insurance so as to regulate the functioning of the private enterprise in the public interest and in accordance with the priorities of planning. It is on the basis of these considerations that Industrial Policy Resolution of 1956 visualised that efforts would be made to expand the public sector so that it occupies the commanding heights in the Indian economy.

Preventing Concentration of Economic Power. Fifth, the public sector has to be expanded so that it not only provides countervailing power to the big business houses but also to check the concentration of economic power in a few private hands. This implies that sphere of public sector should not remain merely confined to the infrastructure and basic heavy industries but if it is to check the emergence of monopolistic conditions it should include investment in and production of those consumer goods industries which due to technological considerations require large-scale production.

Balanced Regional Development. Sixth, the public sector has an important role to set up industries in the economically backward regions of the country which in spite of having natural resources have remained poor. This would help in ensuring balanced regional development and generate income and employment opportunities for poor people all over the country.

1. J.K. Galbraith, *Economic Development in Perspective*, p. 29.

Investment in Social Sectors. Finally, the public sector has a significant role to play in promoting social sectors such as education, healthcare, poverty alleviation and to ensure drinking water supply in all parts of the country. Development economists such as Amartya Sen call for more public action with regard to factors such as education, healthcare, nutrition, drinking water supply to promote economic growth and improve the quality of life. Therefore, government and public sector have to play more active role in these areas of social development.

It is worthwhile to mention that it was expected of the public sector that it would work with efficiency so as to minimise cost of production and also to generate surpluses or savings which when ploughed back into investment would help accelerate overall rate of investment and capital formation in the economy.

Dilution of the Role of Public Sector in the New Economic Policy

It is worth mentioning that under the ongoing economic reforms being implemented since July 1991 under the *New Economic Policy of Structural Adjustment* the role of public sector has been greatly reduced. In the New Economic Policy, private sector and foreign investment have been given more important role to promote economic growth in India.

GROWTH OF PUBLIC SECTOR IN INDIA

Since 1956, there has been an impressive growth of the public sector enterprises. Both the Central and State Governments have set up industrial enterprises for production of *both goods and services.* The amount of investment in public sector enterprises has been rapidly increasing. The growth of public enterprises started by the Central Government can be observed from Table 37.1. It will be seen from this table that whereas there were 5 industrial public sector units of Central Government with a capital investment of ₹ 29 crore in 1951, the number went up to 244 in 1990 with investment of ₹ 99,330 crore. At the end of March 2008, the number of Central Government Public Enterprises stood at 242 with a total cumulative investment of ₹ 4,55,409 crore. At the end of March 2010, the total number of public sector units fell to 217 but cumulative investment in them rose to ₹ 5,79,920 crore.

Table 37.1. Growth of Central Public Sector Enterprises

As at End of March	*No. of Total Units*	*Cumulative Investment (₹ Crore)*
1951	5	29
1961	47	950
1980	179	18,150
1990	244*	99,330
2000	240*	252,745
2001	242*	274,114
2005	237	357,849
2007	244	421,089
2008	242	4,55,409
2010	217	5,79,920
2012	200**	—

[*Note: Some of them have been privatised and therefore do not strictly fall in the category of public enterprises].

** Out of 260 CPSEs in 2012-225 were in operation and 35 under construction.

Pattern of Public Sector Investment. It would be of great interest to describe the pattern of investment by the Central Government. It will be seen from Table 37.2 that in keeping with role assigned to the public sector by India's plans in the fields of development of economic infrastructure (power, transport, telecommunications) and basic heavy industries (power, steel, petroleum, coal, fertilizers. etc.), of the total (both equity capital + long-term loans) investment of ₹ 3,57,849 crore, in 2004-05, ₹ 75,300 crore (21%) were invested in the power production, followed by ₹ 34,860 crore (9.7 per cent) in petroleum, ₹ 22,932 crore (6.4 per cent) in coal and lignite, ₹ 13,710 crore (3.8%) in fetrilizers, ₹ 18,062 crore (5.0%) in steel, ₹ 21,608 crore (6.0 per cent) in telecommunication services.

Table 37.2

Pattern of Investment in Central Government Public Enterprises, 2004-05

	2004-05		
Name of the Industry	*Investment*	*Per cent of total*	*2007-08 per cent*
1. Enterprises under Construction	6,618	1.8	
2. Enterprises Producing/Selling Goods	**2,11,058**	**59.0**	**27.8**
(*i*) Power	75,300	21.0	
(*ii*) Steel	18,062	5.0	
(*iii*) Coal and Lignite	22,932	6.4	
(*iv*) Petroleum	34,860	9.7	
(*v*) Fertilizers	13,710	3.8	
(*vi*) Chemicals & Pharmaceuticals	2,598	0.7	
(*vii*) Minerals and Metals	3,801	1.1	
(*viii*) Engineering	12,712	3.6	
(*ix*) Textiles	19,663	5.5	
(*x*) Consumer Goods	4,129	1.2	
(*xi*) Transportation equipment	3,221	0.9	
(*xii*) Agro-based industries	71	0.0	
3. Enterprises Producing Services	**1,40,173**	**39.2**	**44.4**
(*i*) Financial Services	80,100	22.4	
(*ii*) Industrial Development and Technical Consultancy Services	16,720	4.7	
(*iii*) Transportation Services	4,678	1.3	
(*iv*) Telecommunication Services	21,608	6.8	
(*v*) Other Services	17,067	4.8	
Total	3,57,849	100	

Source: Public Enterprises Survey, 2004-05.

At the end of 2007-08, the total cumulative investment in all the CPSEs stood at ₹ 4,55,409 crore. The largest share in this total investment belonged to the services sector (44.4%) followed by power (i.e., electricity 27.95%), mining sector (8.83%) and agriculture (0.04%). The remaining investment (10.55%) of CPSEs was under construction. Thus, a major part of public investment by Central Government has been made in infrastructure such as power, coal, petroleum and basic heavy industries such as steel, fertilizers, engineering. Public investment in financial services (which include commercial banks, nationalised insurance companies) ₹ 80,100 (22.4 per cent of total public sector investment) was made till the year 2004-05. It may however be noted that a great deal of investment in CPSEs is being made through internal resources rather than through investment from outside.

On the other hand, it will be noticed that a relatively low per cent of capital investment by Central Government has been made in textiles and consumer goods. However, it is important to note that a good number of sick industrial units belonging to textiles and consumer goods was taken over by the Central Government from the private sector. In 2004-05, ₹ 19,663 crores (5.5%) remained invested in textiles. This was done for the purpose of protecting the interests of workers who would have become unemployed if these sick private sector enterprises would have closed down.

PERFORMANCE OF PUBLIC ENTERPRISES

The performance of public enterprises like the private sector enterprises are generally judged on the profitability criterion. Public enterprises are generally criticised on the ground that their performance has been very poor in terms of *rate of return or profit made on capital investment*. In Table 37.3 we have provided the data showing various measures of profitability of Central Public Sector Undertakings. It will be seen from this table that in the year 1991-92 when the process of privatisation or disinvestment was started, profitability of Central Public Enterprises was relatively low. Profitability measured in terms of per cent of gross profits to capital employed was 11.6 in 1991-92 and 11.4 in 1992-93. Profitability measured in terms of net profit after tax to capital employed was 2.3 per cent in both 1991-92 and 1992-93.

However, an important point worth noting from Table 37.3 is that beginning from 1994-95, profitability of Central Public Undertakings has greatly improved. Thus, ratio of gross profit to capital employed, which was 11.6 per cent in 1991-92, rose to around 14 per cent in 1994-95 and to 16 per cent in 1995-96. In more recent years, rate of gross profits to capital employed rose to 16.2 per cent in 2001-02, 17.7 per cent in 2002-03, 21 per cent in 2003-04 and 21.5 per cent in 2004-05. Corresponding ratio of net profit after tax to capital employed rose to 6.7%, 7.8%, 11.7% and 13.0% in 2001-02, 2002-03, 2003-04 and 2004-05 respectively. However, *a very significant fact about the profits of public enterprises is that a major part of them is contributed by the petroleum sector enterprises*. For example, in 2004-05 the net profit after tax of all central public sector enterprises amounted to ₹ 65,429 crores of which about 41 per cent was contributed by petroleum sector enterprises alone. It will be seen from Table 37.3 that rate of gross profit to capital employed was 21.1% in 2007-08, 18% in 2008-09 and 17.6% in 2009-10.

It may be further noted that in order to improve the efficiency and profitability of public undertakings, they have been given autonomy by the Government in their working and decision-making through signing of Memoranda of Understanding (MOUs). In 2000-2001, 107 PSUs signed Memoranda of Understandings. It is expected that with the autonomous functioning the efficiency and profitability of these enterprises will further improve.

Other Efficiency Criteria of Evaluating Public Sector Enterprises

Public sector enterprises should not be judged on the basis of profitability alone. There are other criteria by which they can be judged. They are[2] (1) *technical efficiency*, (2) *allocative efficiency*, and (3) *dynamic efficiency*. Technical efficiency implies ratio of output produced by an enterprise to inputs

2. See C. Rangarajan, "Disinvestment Strategy and Issues", printed in *Indian Economy: Essays on Money and Finance*, UBS Publishers, 1998.

Table 37.3. Financial Performance of Centre's Public Enterprises

(Running Enterprises excluding insurance companies)

₹ *Crores*

	No. of Operating Enterprises	Capital Employed	Gross Profit before Interest & Tax	Net Profit before Tax	Net Profit after Tax	Rate of return: Gross Profit to Capital Employed (%) $6=\frac{3}{2}\times 100$	Rate of return: Net Profit After Tax to Capital Employed (%) $7=\frac{5}{2}\times 100$
	1	2	3	4	5	6	7
SIXTH PLAN							
1980-81	168	18.207	1,418	19	–203	7.8	–1.1
1981-82	188	21,935	2,654	1,025	446	12.1	+2.0
1982-83	193	26.590	3,469	1,547	618	13.1	+2.3
1983-84	201	29,856	3,564	1,480	240	11.9	+0.8
1984-85	207	36,382	4,628	2,099	909	12.7	+2.5
SEVENTH PLAN							
1985-86	211	42,965	5,287	2,173	1,172	12.3	+2.8
1986-87	214	51,835	6,521	3,101	1,771	12.6	+3.4
1987-88	220	55,617	6,940	3,353	2,030	12.5	+3.6
1988-89	226	67,629	8,572	4,404	2,993	12.7	+4.4
1989-90	233	84,760	10,622	5,293	3,789	12.5	+4.5
1990-91	236	1,01,702	11,359	3,820	2,368	11.2	+2.3
1991-92	237	1,17,991	13,675	4,003	2,355	11.6	+2.0
EIGHTH PLAN							
1992-93	239	1,40,110	15,957	5,076	3,271	11.4	+2.3
1993-94	240	1.59,836	18,555	6,654	4,544	11.6	+2.8
1994-95	241	1,62,451	22,630	9,768	7,187	13.9	+4.4
1995-96	239	1,73,948	27,587	13,621	9,574	15.9	+5.5
1996-97	236	2,31,178	30,915	15,378	10,188	13.4	+.44
NINTH PLAN							
1997-98	236	2,49,855	37,206	19,216	13,582	14.9	5.4
1998-99	235	2,65,093	39,727	19,702	13,203	15.0	5.0
1999-00	232	3,02,947	42,270	22,037	14,331	13.9	4.7
2000-01	234	3,31,372	48,767	24,967	15,653	14.7	4.7
2001-02	231	3,89,934	63,190	38,233	25,978	16.2	6.7
TENTH PLAN							
2002-03	226	4,17,160	72,539	48,616	31,119	17.4	7.5
2003-04	230	4,52,336	95,039	71,144	49,010	21.0	10.8
2004-05	227	5,04,407	1,08,420	85,550	63,889	21.5	12.7
2005-06	226	5,85,484	1,14,422	90,714	66,344	19.5	11.3
2006-07	217	6,61,338	1,39,008	1,11,527	77,175	21.0	11.7
2007-08	214	7,24,009	1,52,579	1,20,453	79,704	21.1	11.0
2008-09	213	7,92,232	1,42,395	1,03,095	69,267	18.0	8.7
2009-10	217	9,08,842	1,59,846	1,24,126	84,119	17.6	8.7

[Note: Gross Profits before Tax = (Net Profits + Interest + corporate tax paid)

Total Capital Employed = (Fixed Assets – Depreciation + Working Capital)

Source : Public Enterprises Survey (2009–2010), Vol. 1.

used, which is also called *total factor productivity*. Allocative efficiency refers to the correction of market failures by the production of certain essential products by public enterprises which private enterprises will not produce on the basis of free working of price mechanism. In this case production by public enterprises leads to better allocation of resources. Dynamic efficiency relates to introduction of innovations and upgradation of technology. On these criteria, public enterprises do not fare badly as compared to private enterprises. In addition to these, public enterprises have made significant contribution to increase in investment or gross domestic capital formation (GDCF) and for achieving broad-based industrial growth. When there was a decline in public investment from mid-sixties to mid-seventies and during the late nineties, there was a slowdown in industrial growth.

The major highlights of the performance of CPSEs during 2009-10 are given in Table 37.3. It will be seen from this table that net profit after tax of central public sector enterprises stood at ₹ 84,119 crore as compared to ₹ 69,267 crore in 2008-09. Besides, the gross profit (before interest and tax) to capital employed of these enterprises in 2009-10 was 17.6 per cent as compared to 18 per cent in 2008-09. The year 2009-10 also witnessed severe financial *under-recoveries* by public sector oil marketing companies as they had to keep the prices low in the domestic market on sales of petroleum products.

Table 37.4. Indicators of Financial Performance of Central Public Sector Enterprises

Sl.No.	Particulars	2009-10	2008-09	% Change over previous year
		(in ₹ crore)		
1.	Investment (long-term loan + equity)	579,920	513,532	12.93
2.	Capital employed (net fixed assets + working capital)	910,120	793,240	14.73
3.	Total turnover	1,235,060	1,271,529	–2.87
4.	Profit of Profit Making CPSEs	108,435	98,488	10.10
5.	Loss of Loss Making CPSEs	15,842	14,621	8.35
6.	Net worth	660,245	665,686	–0.82
7.	Dividend declared	33,223	25,501	30.28
8.	Corporate tax	119,529	131,583	–9.16
9.	Interest paid	35,720	39,300	–9.11
10.	Contribution to Central Exchequer	139,828	151,529	–7.72
11.	Foreign Exchange Earnings	77,745	74,206	4.77
12.	Foreign Exchange Outgo	420,415	433,332	–2.98

Source: Department of Public Enterprises.

It will be seen from Table 37.4 that cumulative investment (paid-up capital plus long term loans) in all the CPSEs stood at ₹ 5,79,920 crore as on 31 March 2010, an increase of 12.93 per cent over 2008-09. The capital employed in all the CPSEs went up by 14.73 per cent during the same period. A great deal of investment in CPSEs is accounted for by internal resources rather than through investment from outside.

The net profit of the profit-making CPSEs (158) stood at ₹ 1,08,434.68 crore in 2009-10. The net loss of the loss-making enterprises (59), on the other hand, stood at ₹ 15,842 crore during the same period. The year also witnessed severe financial under-recoveries by public sector oil marketing companies (OMCs) as they had to keep prices on sale of petroleum products low in the domestic market. The foreign exchange earnings of the CPSEs amounted to ₹ 77,745 crore during 2009-10 and were clearly overtaken by the foreign exchange outgo of ₹ 4,20,415 crore (Table 37.4).

It will also be seen from Table 37.4 that net worth of Central Public Sector Enterprises (CPSEs) decreased by 0.82 per cent in 2009-10 over 2008-09, dividend declared increased by 30.28 per cent, corporation tax paid declined by 9.16 per cent and contribution to central exchequer decreased by 7.7 per cent. Besides, CBSEs earned foreign exchange amounting to ₹ 77,745 crore during 2009-10. Thus, the overall performance of Central Public Sector enterprises is not bad keeping into account that many public sector enterprises lay greater emphasis on achieving non-financial social objectives.

The Recent Performance of CPSEs in Terms of Turnover and Net Profit

The latest complete results are available for the year 2011-12. CPSEs in the mining sector registered the highest increase in net profit (29.5 per cent) in 2011-12. CPSEs in manufacturing sector recorded a decline of 22.7 per cent in net profit in 2011-12 despite 27.7 per cent increase in their turnover. The electricity sector recorded growth of 16 per cent in turnover and 13.4 per cent in profit (Table 37.5).

Table 37.5. Performance of Industrial CPSEs, 2010-11 to 2011-12

(₹ crore)

Sl.No.	*Sector*	*2010-11*	*2011-12*	*Per cent change*
I.	Manufacturing (28.31 per cent) @			
	1.1) Turnover	947,411.7	1,210,087.6	27.7
	1.2) Net Profit	30,668.2	23,720.5	(22.7)
II.	Mining (23.53 per cent) @			
	2.1) Turnover	15,968.3	188,011.1	17.7
	2.2) Net Profit	47,594.8	61,610.6	29.5
III.	Electricity (25.62 per cent) @			
	2.1) Turnover	84,032.4	97,623.0	16.2
	2.2) Net Profit	18,727.5	21,239.9	13.4

Source : Department of Public Enterprises.

Note : @ shows the percentage share, in total investment in terms of gross block;

Causes of Poor Performance or Low Profitability of Public Enterprises

We have explained above that whatever important contribution to industrial development the public enterprises have made, their commercial profitability has been found to be low. In fact many public enterprises have been incurring losses. We discuss below the reasons for their poor performance in terms of rate of profit on capital investment made in them.

1. Lack of Importance to Profit Motive. In the working of public enterprises profitability criteria was not given proper place. Some of the persons and economists associated with our Planning Commission who formulated policies on public sector enterprises as well as those who were entrusted with setting them up and running them played down the idea of profit making by public enterprises and unduly emphasised the social obligations of public enterprises. It is only recently that profit aspect of public enterprises has been given due recognition.

2. Inappropriate Location. An important reason for the low profitability of public enterprises is their uneconomic location. Usually, public enterprises are set up on the basis of political considerations rather than economic criteria. There is clamour for locating these enterprises in certain regions on the part of the ruling party bosses, influential ministers and public leaders even at the threat of fasts.

3. Underutilisation of Installed Capacity. Low utilisation of capacity has been a very important reason for the low profitability of the public undertakings. Enormous installed capacities have been created with the help of foreign credits and know-how on easy terms, but fuller use of them has not been made. The phenomenon of underutilisation of capacities has arisen on account of overestimating demand, administrative deficiencies, lack of proper working techniques, labour troubles or failure to install balancing equipment or making technical improvement essential for fuller utilisation of capacity.

4. Not Making Proper Technical Feasibility Studies. The technical factors determine the scale of operations of production enterprises. Technical considerations require that there should be a thorough investigation into the processes to be used and the availability of the essential factors of production like raw materials, fuel, power, water supply, skilled and unskilled labour, credit facilities, transport, proximity of the markets, etc. In several cases, there is no evidence that a proper study of these aspects was made before the project was launched. The scale was determined more by a bias for launching a big project rather than on the basis of economic calculation of production potential and likely demand.

The Committee on Public Undertakings pointed out that tenders were invited without any project reports in the case of Trombay Fertilizer Project, Hindustan Insecticides and Indian Telephone Industries.

5. Delay in Project Completion. Also, very little consideration is given to the time-schedule in the construction of the public sector projects. The inevitable result is that the projects are commissioned much later than scheduled. It unnecessarily raises the cost of construction. Trombay Fertilizer Project, for instance, took 6-7 years to complete against time schedule of 3 years and this heavily raised the cost of the project.

6. Absence of Professional Management. The composition of the Boards of Directors indicates the absence of professional managers. These boards are dominated invariably by IAS officers from the civil service, a number of whom owe their position to political patronage rather than their professional managerial abilities.

The Committee on Public Undertakings remarked that the civil servants are costly on account of the burden of deputation pay and leave-salary and pension contribution. The use of civil servants such as IAS officers is not conducive to efficiency as by their attitude and training, they are used to a different way of working, which hardly fits into a business organisation.

7. Overstaffing, Defective Recruitment and Promotion Policy. With regard to staffing, recruitment and promotion policy a deplorable situation exists in our public sector. Recruitment is haphazard; there is overstaffing, drift of personnel and a lack of regular schemes of 'executive development'. The Committee on Public Undertakings pointed out the bureaucratic approach to the administration of these undertakings and warned against the regular practice of dumping retired and superannuated Government officials into their service.

8. Lack of Rational Pricing Policy. The public enterprises in India have failed to evolve an appropriate pricing policy for their products. Should public enterprises follow marginal cost pricing or average cost pricing or the mark-up pricing policy? In the absence of an appropriate pricing policy, optimal utilisation of resources and profitability cannot be achieved. Most of the public enterprises are regulated by the Government and do not aim at maximising profits. It is worth noting that most of the products produced by the public enterprises such as steel, fertilizers, oil etc. are essential inputs for other industries or sectors of the economy. It will be anti-growth and socially improper if the public enterprises follow profit-maximising pricing principle and fix high prices of the essential products produced by them. The appropriate pricing policy for public enterprises is to follow mark-up pricing principle with reasonable profit margin.

9. Political Interference. The political interference has been forcing the management of public enterprises to give up sound commercial principles in arriving at vital decisions pertaining to investment, location, production and pricing policies of public enterprises.

Most often political considerations guide the decision making of the public enterprises. Ministers and Members of Parliament put pressure on the government about the location of the public sector projects in their constituencies regardless of any economic criteria and feasibility studies made. This leads to considerable wastage of capital resources.

Conclusion

The relatively low surpluses created by the public enterprises are attributed to their long gestation period, the lack, in the initial period, of expert and trained personnel, defective planning, wrong selling policies and monopolistic nature of various public enterprises which produced lethargy among the managerial staff. It is true that there may be losses in the initial stages but the losses should not have become a permanent phenomenon. *The public enterprises suffer from inefficiency and low productivity due to lack of an effective system of accountability.* It is the system of accountability in the private sector which leads to an efficient utilisation of resources which ensures profitability.

DISINVESTMENT AND PRIVATISATION OF PUBLIC SECTOR ENTERPRISES

An important aspect of present industrial policy of the Government is that it should not operate commercial enterprises. With that end in view the Government has decided to disinvest the public enterprises. The Government can sell its enterprises completely to the private sector or disinvest a part of its equity capital held by it to the private sector companies or in the open market. Distinction may be drawn between *disinvestment and privatisation.* Strictly speaking, disinvestment means the dilution of stake of the Government in a public enterprise. This can be done in two ways. When the Government sells a part of its equity of a public enterprise less than 50 per cent of its total stock, it is called merely disinvestment and in this case control and management of the business enterprise remains in the hands of Government. On the other hand, when disinvestment or sale of its equity capital by the Government exceeds 50 per cent so that the majority ownership and therefore control and management of the enterprise is transferred to private enterprise, it results in privatisation.[3] Therefore, in many disinvestment programmes government retains 51 per cent or more of the total equity capital of the public enterprises so that control and management remains in its hands. Through disinvestment or privatisation, the Government can mop up a good amount of resources which can be used for various purposes. The released resources can be used to restructure and strengthen the public sector enterprises which are potentially viable. These resources can also be used to pay back a part of public debt. These resources can also be used to finance budget deficits.

Case for Public Sector Disinvestment

What are the reasons for the policy of public sector disinvestment or privatisation ? First, resources available with the Government are scarce. The Government needs resources to reduce its budget deficit. Second, the Government urgently requires resources to make investment in infrastructure, social sectors such as education, public health and for poverty alleviation programmes. Resources released through disinvestment can be used for investment in these crucial sectors. Thirdly, a good number of existing public enterprises are working inefficiently and incurring huge losses. Disinvestment can lead to the improvement of efficiency of these enterprises. When government divests a good part of its stake to a private enterprise or public at large, it increaes accountability of management of an enterprise which have a beneficial effect on the efficient working of the enterprise. "The shareholders would require to be compensated and this will, in turn, compell the enterprise to run more efficiently and earn more profits". Thus, Dr. C. Rangarajan is of the view that, "There is a compelling need to expand the activities of the state in areas such as education, health and medicine. It is therefore legitinate that a part of the additional resources needed for supporting these activities come out of the sale of shares of public enterprises built up earlier by the Government out of its resources."[4]

---

3. See C. Rangarajan, "Disinvestment : Strategy and Issues," printed in *Indian Economy* : *Essays on Money and Finance*, UBS Publishers, 1998
4. C. Rangarajan, *op.cit.*

Another important use of disinvestment of public enterprises is the resources raised from them can be used to pay off past debts of the Government and thereby reducing the interest burden of the Government. The proposal of the use of proceeds from disinvestment for retiring a part public debt has been put forward by several economists. However, in our opinion, it does not make much difference if the resources raised from disinvestment of public enterprises are used as receipts to be spent on education, health and employment generation schemes or used for retiring a part of the past public debt. In the former case of disinvestment receipts being used for making worthwhile expenditure will result in a lower borrowing by the Government, that is, less increment in public debt.

Disinvestment, especially privatisation of public sector enterprises, will ensure that the working of these enterprises will be governed by professional managers guided by market mechanism instead of being administered by bureaucrats. Functioning of these enterprises in the competitive environment of free markets will lead to higher efficiency and productivity. Privatisation will also lead to the closing down of *unviable and sick public sector enterprises.* A private company which buys such sick public sector units will benefit only from the real estate and assets of the sick public sector units.

Privatisation of public enterprises through public sector disinvestment is also beneficial because this will enable these enterprises to attract private foreign investment in setting up joint ventures. It may be noted that capital inflow through private direct foreign investment is better than that procured through foreign aid or commercial borrowing from abroad.

In support of privatisation of public enterprises it is also argued that it will end state monopolies in certain industries. State monopoly is said to be as bad and undesirable as private monopolies. The privatisation of some monopolistic public enterprises would infuse competition which will lead to increase in efficiency and productivity. As a result of privatisation underutilised capacity will be fully utilised.

Arguments Against Disinvestment and Privatisation

Privatisation has also been opposed by some who say that dismantling of public sector which has been built at a very heavy cost to the society would do no good. The following arguments are given against privatisation, that is, disinvestment of public sector enterprises.

1. Disinvestment of public enterprises is criticised by left-oriented economists on the ground that *it amounts to selling 'family silver'*. This in our view is not a valid criticism. This is because original investment on these public enterprises was made by the Government out of its revenue and capital receipts in the past. If some part of these public enterprises are sold and the resources so released are spent on certain beneficial schemes of promotions of education and health or reduction of poverty and unemployment, it cannot be called an undesirable act.
2. Second, it is pointed out that privatisation of some public enterprises would, in the absence of anti-trust law, lead to the emergence of private monopolies under which resources are misallocated. As a result, consumer welfare will be reduced. Besides, adoption of monopolistic practices will lead to higher prices and lower levels of output and employment.
3. It is argued that mere change of ownership, from public to private, does not ensure higher efficiency and productivity of industrial enterprises. In the modern corporate form of business organisation, management has been separated from ownership. In case of both public and private enterprises professional managers can be employed to manage the industrial enterprises to ensure efficiency in working. Thus, it is argued that for professionalisation of management, privatisation of public enterprises is not needed.
4. The disinvestment of public enterprises is also opposed on the ground that it will lead to the concentration of economic power in a few private hands. This economic power can be used to exploit the consumers on the one hand and workers on the other. Further, greater

concentration of economic power in private hands will also lead to increase in inequalities of income and wealth. Thus, disinvestment and privatisation is a negation of the objective of promoting equality.

5. An important argument against privatisation is that it will lead to retrenchment of workers who will be deprived of the means of their livelihood. Further, private sector, governed as they are by profit motive, has a tendency to use capital-intensive techniques in production. This will not lead to generation of many employment opportunities. As a result, unemployment problem in India will worsen.
6. Disinvestment is also opposed on the ground that it is no solution for loss-making sick public sector undertakings. In fact, it is pointed out that about 50 per cent of loss-making public enterprises, especially in the field of textiles, are those sick units which were taken over by the Government from the private sector to protect the jobs and interests of the workers.
7. Last but not the least, it is argued that public enterprises should not be privatised because, though they may not be yielding enough profits, *they are socially profitable* and have made important contribution to build up a strong base for industrial development of the country. But for the growth of public enterprises in the industries such as machine making, heavy chemicals, fertilizers, steel and power, and communication, these industries would not have been developed as has been actually the case. In the absence of this strong base, rapid industrial development would not have been possible. If they are privatised, the private sector would encash the benefits from the basic heavy industries for whose development heavy social costs have been incurred. Further, many public enterprises come under *public utilities* which must be run in public interest and not on the basis of maximising private profits.

Conclusion

Now, whatever the reasons for and against privatisation of public enterprises, the need for resources by the Government are very large and therefore it has been decided by the Government to go in for disinvestment of the public sector enterprises. The Government claims that Monopolistic and Restrictive Trade Practices Commission (MRTPC) will check the monopolistic practices, if any, adopted by private enterprises. Further, the Government claims that while making strategic sale to a buyer, interests of the workers will be protected. If a private enterprise after buying the equity capital controls and manages the enterprise, it will be permitted to reduce manpower employed only if VRS (Voluntary Retirement Scheme) is introduced and golden hand-shake is provided to the workers whose services are not required.

Disinvestment Process and Valuation

Disinvestment of public enterprises can be made in a number of ways.

1. The entire public enterprise can be sold to a private sector firm which is the highest bidder or otherwise. In this case both the ownership and control or management is transferred to the private firm. This happened when 'Modern Food', a public company, was sold to Hindustan Lever and Centaur Hotel in Bombay was sold to a private company.
2. The second way in which disinvestment in a public enterprise can be made is selling a part of the Government stake to a *strategic private company.* A strategic company is one which has a strategic interest in the public enterprise and has a capability to run it efficiently. The strategic buyer can be chosen by inviting tenders from the private companies.
3. Thirdly, the Government can *offer for sale its shares of a public enterprise to the general public* through the stock-market intermediaries.
4. Finally, sale of a certain number of Government shares in a public enterprise can be made *through auction of shares* among a selected number of private firms. The reserve price of shares of a company for auction can be determined with the help of merchant bankers.

Table 37.5. Disinvestment of Public Sector Undertakings

Year	*Target* (₹ *Crore*)	*Proceeds* (₹ *Crore*)
1991-92	2,500	3,038
1992-93	2,500	1,913
1993-94	3,500	
1994-95	4,000	4,843
1995-96	7,000	168
1996-97	5,000	380
1997-98	4,800	910
1998-99	5,000	5,371
1999-2000	10,000	1,860
2000-01	10,000	1,871
2001-02	12,000	5,632
2002-03	12,000	3,348
2003-04	14,500	15,547
2004-05	4,000	2,765
2005-06	No Target	1,568
2006-07	"	Nil
2007-08	"	38,795
2008-09	"	546
2009-10	"	1,120
2010-11	"	24,557
2011-12	40,000	13,854

Accordingly, as a part of the economic reforms policy, the Government has started reforms in public sector enterprises. The main elements of Government policy towards Public Sector Enterprises (PSU) are:

1. Disinvestment of Government equity in all non-strategic Public Sector Undertakings (PSU) to 26 per cent or lower if necessary.
2. Those public sector enterprises which are potentially viable have to be restructured and revived.
3. Those Public Sector Undertakings (PSU) which cannot be revived would be closed down.

There is a need for evolving a fair, transparent and equitable procedure for disinvestment in selected public sector enterprises. The achievement made with regard to disinvestment of Public Sector Undertakings which started in 1991-92, are given in Table 37.5. For the year 2001-2002, the Government set the target of ₹ 12,000 crore regarding public sector disinvestment, but equity worth ₹ 5,632 crores was sold to the private sector. 100 per cent equity of Modern Food (a non-strategic public sector undertaking) has been sold to Hindustan Lever. 51 per cent of Government equity holding of BALCO (Bharat Aluminium Company Ltd.) has been sold to private sector firm Sterlite Industries at 826.5 crore rupees. 51 per cent of Government equity holdings in CMC has been sold to TATA. 25 per cent of Government equity in VSNL has been sold to TATA at 3689 crore rupees, 25 per cent of Government equity in IPCL has been sold to Reliance Industries at 1490 crore rupees. The per cent of Government equity sold and the money received from its sale of different Public Sector Undertakings are given in Table 37.6. This table also gives which private company has purchased the equity of Government and at what price. The pace of public sector disinvestment greatly quickened in the year 2003-2004. In 2003-04 government equity worth ₹ 15,547 crores was sold as compared to ₹ 3348 crores in 2002-03.

Table 37.6. Public Sector Disinvestment through Strategic Sales

PSUs	*Equity sold (in %)*	*Accruals (in ₹ cr)*	*Buyer*
Modern Food	74	149	Hindustan Lever
Balco	51	826.5	Sterilite Industries
CMC	51	152	Tatas
HTL	74	55	Himachal Futuristic
LJMC	74	2.53	
ITDC (13 Hotels)	—	264.66*	Bharat Hotels, Tulip among buyers
HCl	—	242.51	—
IBP	33.58	1153.68	Indian Oil Corp.
VSNL	25	3689	Tatas
PPL	74	151.70	Zuari-Maroc
Jessop	72	18.18#	Ruia Cotex
HZL	26	445	Sterlite
Maruti	—	2424	Suzuki
IPCL	25	1490.84	Reliance Ind
	Total:	11064.60	

to be approved by BIFR. *Includes outright sales plus lease payments. Includes dividend and dividend tax.

Strategic Sale Approach to Public Sector Disinvestment

Another approach adopted for public sector disinvestment is called '*strategic sale*'. Simply put, it means that the Government, instead of offloading a minority percentage of its equity in market either at home or abroad, chooses to sell blocks of shares, usually more than 26 per cent of its stake, *to an investor ideally having a strategic interest in the company.* This is accompanied by the transfer of management control.

This has worked wonders. Not only have a wide range of companies been disinvested, but they have reaped handsome dividends for the Government as well (see Table 37.5). Importantly, a mere 14 companies were involved in these sell-offs. Compare this with ₹ 18,368 crore obtained through the public offer route between 1992 and 1999, in the recent strategic sales of 45 PSUs, some important companies like Concor, VSNL and Gail (Gas Authority of India, Ltd.) were involved. The P/E (price-to-equity) ratios of shares of the companies sold in strategic sales have been phenomenal. IBP shares were sold at P/E ratios of 63 and IPCL at 58. Compare them to the P/E ratios of 4 to 6 obtained, when the Government sold minority shares in VSNL, HPCL and BPCL in the early 90s.

The New Approach to PSU Disinvestment : Public Sale of Shares

The strategic sales approach to public sector disinvestment during 2001-2002, and 2002-03 was quite successful. But Supreme Court in its judgement in September, 2003 restrained the Central Government from proceeding with disinvestment in Hindustan Petroleum Corporation Ltd

(HPCL) and Bharat Petroleum Corporation Ltd (BPCL) through strategic sales without amending the law by the parliament. Therefore, the Central Government decided that the various public sector companies such as HPCL, BPCL which were making profits will make *initial public offers* (IPO) of selling their shares to the public in the primary market. In this way they hoped to mop up huge funds. The Government believed that with the public issue of profitable public sector companies, the capital markets which were in depressed mode at that time would also revive. It was argued that by offloading Government stake in profitable Public Sector Undertakings (PSUs) in the market, it will not only revive the capital market but also strengthen the financial position and liquidity of the public sector companies. Various public sector comapnies made public offer for sale of a part of government equity. As a reuslt of this ₹ 15,547 crores were realised during 2003-04. The names of various public sector companies which made disinvestment through public sale and the proceeds realised by them are given in Table 37.7.

Table 37.7. Public Sector Disinvestment through Public Sales Offer (IPO) during 2003-04

Name of the company	*Type of the Sale*	*Percentage of equity disinvested*	*Proceeds Realised (₹ crores)*
Maruti Udyog Ltd	Public offer for sale	27.5	933.3
Jessop & Co. Ltd	Strategic sale	72.0	18.2
HZL*	Call option	18.9	323.9
ICIL	Limtied Auction	9.2	77.1
IBP	Public offer for sale	26.0	350.7
IPCL	Public offer for sale	28.9	1202.9
CMC	Public offer for sale	26.3	190.4
DCIL	Public offer for sale	20.0	221.2
GAIL	Public offer for sale	10.0	1627.4
ONGC	Public offer for sale	9.9	10542.4
Total			**15,547.4**

* Exercise of call option by the strategic partner

Source : GOI, *Economic Survey*, 2003-04, p.148

In 2011-12, public sector disinvestment through offer for sale in Oil and Natural Gas Commission (ONCC) amounted to ₹ 1274.9 crore. Disinvestment through the public offer route has been attempted in other countries, such as Britain where the aim was to widely disperse shares. Companies like British Airports Authority were 100 per cent privatised through this route. They were then run by professional managements. Thus in India the Government can continue with a high stake in the PSUs and make a very large public offer to ensure a widely dispersed holding of equity capital of these companies. However, if the objective is that the management should change, then a strategic sale is a more viable option in Indian conditions. However, some analysts are skeptical of this strategy of public offer route to disinvestment. According to them, true disinvestment and privatisation would not take place if Government control and management of the public sector companies continue after public offer to retail investors. True disinvestment and privatisation occur when the companies are controlled and managed by the private professional managers. However, in our view, professional managers can be appointed even in public enterprises controlled by government. In fact, through public sale of equity, profitable public sector companies can raise resources through the capital market.

UPA Government Approach to Public Sector Disinvestment

An important issue before UPA government was to clarify its policy towards public sector disinvestment. As a part of Common Minimum Programme (CMP), it was decided that public sector companies which were making profits would not be privatised though they could raise resources from the capital market.

In 2009 with no need for support of left parties, the Government announced public sector disinvestment through sale of a part of its equity in some public sector enterprises though the Government would retain their public character and control management by not allowing its equity to drop below 51%. Though Finance Minister Pranab Mukherjee was silent in his budget for 2009-10, he made the statement to this effect in the Parliament on July 14, 2009. The PSUs such as NHPC, OIL, Tyre Corporation of India (TCA) and Central Inland Water Transport Corporation (CIWTC) have been identified for disinvestment. Further, these PSUs have been permitted to float IPOs simultaneously to raise the required funds to meet their needs. In defence of such disinvestment through a part sale of government equity and issue of IPO by PSUs would enable the people to have a partial ownership of state-run units.

Navaratna PSUs

UPA government pledged to devolve full managerial and commercial autonomy to successful, profit-making public sector companies operating in a competitive environment. All privatisation will be considered on a transparent and case by case selective basis. The existing public sector "*navaratnas*" will remain in the public sector but they can raise resources from the capital market.

The Government has delegated enhanced financial and operational powers to the **Navaratnas** and **Miniratnas** and other profit-making central public sector enterprises (CPSE). In addition to professionalising the Board of Directors of CPSE, it has also issued the guidelines to them on corporate governance While every effort will be made to modernise and restructure sick public sector companies and to revive sick industries, chronically loss-making firms will either be sold off or closed after all workers have got their legitimate dues and compensation. The government will induct private industry to turn around companies that have potential for revival.

The *Board for Reconstruction of Public Sector Enterprises (BRPSE)* has been established to advise Government on revival of sick and loss-making enterprises. The BRPSE has made recommendations in 47 cases including two for closure till Oct. 31, 2007 . The proposals for revival of 26 Central Public Sector enterprises and closure of two have been approved by the Government. The total assistance approved by the Government up to Dec. 2007 in this regard is ₹ 8, 285 crores including ₹ 1,955 crore cash assistance and ₹ 6,330 crore non-cash assistance.

In 1997 when Mr. Chidambaram was finance minister he announced that nine profit-making public sector companies *had the capacity and resources to become* '*global giants*'. He called them ***navaratnas***. These navaratanas are : IOC, ONGC, HPCL, IPCL, VSNL, BHEL, SAIL, and NTPC. Due to stiff opposition from the left, the UPA government put the disinvestment process in profit-making enterprises on hold. However, Maruti Udyog Ltd was permitted to raise resources from the market through sale of some government shares in the market in Feb. 2006. Maruti Udyog succeeded in raising ₹ 1600 crores from the open sale of Government shares in Feb. 2006. In 2006-07, the Government created *national investment fund* (*NIF*) to park funds raised through proceeds of disinvestment of the Centre's stake in public sector enterprises. It was stipulated that while 75 per cent of NIFs funds would have been invested in social sector projects on education, healthcare and employment, the rest would be ploughed in capital investment in select profitable and revivable PSUs. Since disinvestment process was put on hold because of stiff opposition by the left adequate funds from disinvestment could not be raised. This affected not only the revival of PSUs but also the expenditure on education, healthcare and employment.

CHAPTER 38

Industrial Sickness in India

The Meaning of Industrial Sickness

The strength of the industrial sector, by and large, determines the soundness of the economy. A developing economy like India cannot afford the growing sickness in industries as it results in a colossal wastage of physical, financial and human resources. In the presence of the resource crunch, the industrial sickness becomes all the more an alarming problem. Industrial sickness usually refers to a situation when an industrial firm performs poorly, incurs losses for several years and often defaults in its debt repayment obligations. The Reserve Bank of India has defined a sick unit as one "*which has incurred a cash loss for one year and is likely to continue incurring losses for the current year as well as in the following year and the unit has an imbalance in its financial structure, such as, current ratio is less than 1 : 1 and there is worsening trend in debt-equity ratio*." The State Bank of India has defined a sick unit as one "which fails to generate an internal surplus on a continuous basis and depends for its survival upon frequent infusion of funds." However, prior to the enactment of Sick Industrial Companies Act (SICA) in 1985, there was no agreement on the criteria to be used to describe an industrial unit as sick. According to SICA, as amended in 1992, *an industrial company can be declared as sick which has at the end of any financial year accumulated losses equal to or exceeding its entire net worth*. It may be noted that Sick Industrial Companies Act (SICA) applies to registered companies which have been in existence for at least 5 years. In case of small scale industrial unit (SSI), it is regarded as a sick unit if it has (i) incurred a cash loss in the previous accounting year and was likely to continue with losses in the current accounting year and further its cumulative cash losses are equal to 50 per cent or more of its peak net worth during the last five years and (ii) it has defaulted in meeting four consecutive instalments of interest.

According to the Development Commissioner, a small scale industrial unit (SSI) becomes sick if its :

(*a*) capacity utilisation is less than 50 per cent of the highest achieved during the preceding five years (*incipient sickness*);

(*b*) net worth has been eroded by more than 50 per cent; and

(*c*) the unit has remained closed for a period more than six months.

On the basis of the above definitions of a sick industrial unit, it emerges that the symptoms of the sickness of an industrial unit manifest themselves in the form of imbalanced financial structure, erosion of more than 50 per cent of its net worth, absence of the generation of internal surplus, under-utilisation of capacity and survival of the unit upon frequent infusion of funds.

Incidence of Industrial Sickness

A very disquieting feature of the industrial scenario is the mounting incidence of industrial sickness. It is a matter of deep concern not only for shareholders and creditors of the sick concerns but also to the society at large. There is sickness of industries both in the large-scale sector (*i.e.*, Non-SSI sector) and in the small-scale industries (SSI). Growing incidence of sickness has been one of the pressing problems faced by the industrial sector in India. Substantial amounts of banking funds are locked up in these sick industrial units. There was a problem of increasing industrial sickness even before the new policy of liberalisation and globalisation adopted in 1991. Thus the number of SSI sick units increased from 58,551 in 1982, rose to 2.21 lakhs in March 1991 and to 2.52 lakhs in end-March 2001. Table 38.1 gives the number of sick industrial units both in the small scale industrial (SSI) sector and non-small scale industrial (non-SSI) and the outstanding bank credit locked in them. It will be seen from Table 38.1 that though the number of large and medium sick industrial enterprises (*i.e.,* non-SSI sick units) is much smaller than SSI sick units, the outstanding bank credit locked in them is much greater than that in SSI sick units.

It may be noted that in the sick industrial companies, a lot of resources of banks are locked up. The data reveal that as on March 31, 2001, 3,317 non-SSI sick industrial units accounted for an outstanding bank credit of ₹ 21,270 crores. *Industry-wise data show that five industries, namely, textiles, engineering, electrical, chemicals and iron and steel accounted for about 56 per cent of total outstanding bank credit.*

There has been a phenomenal rise of industrial sickness over the last few years. It is significant to note that sickness has been growing faster in the small-scale sector than in large and medium-scale sectors. At the end of March 2001, there were 252,947 sick units. Out of these, 249,630 were small-scale sick units against whom outstanding bank credit was ₹ 4,506 crores. (See Table 38.1)

Table 38 .1 : Industrial Sickenss – End-March, 2001

Category	No. of Units	Outstanding Bank Credit (₹ *Crores*)
1. SSI Sick Units	249,630	4,506
2. Non-SSI Sick Units	3,317	21,270
Total	252,947	25,776

Source : Tata Services Ltd., *Statistical Outline of India,* 2002-03.

NATURE AND CAUSES OF INDUSTRIAL SICKNESS

Competition breeds efficiency but adversely affects weak industrial units and makes them sick. The clear directional changes since 1982-83 towards liberalisation of industrial licensing policies, foreign collaboration approvals, the concept of minimum-size plants are welcome from consumers' point of view. But the weaker units have to pay the price. The inevitable cost of achieving competitive efficiency is that the weak must be allowed to fade. But the country cannot allow this to happen. The Sick Industrial Companies (Special Provisions) Act, 1985, was enacted to help and revive the sick units. The substantive portions of the Act came into force from May 15, 1987. The Act provided for setting up of a quasi-judicial body designated as the **Board for Industrial and Financial Reconstruction (BIFR)** to deal effectively with the problem of sick industrial companies. The Reserve Bank of India has issued guidelines to banks to strengthen the monitoring system and to arrest industrial sickness at the incipient stage. These remedial measures to deal with the problem of industrial sickness by BIFR and Reserve Bank of India will be discussed later in this chapter.

Nature of Sickness

Sickness in industry can be classified into :

(a) Genuine sickness which is beyond the control of the promoters of the concern despite the sincere efforts by them, (b) Incipient sickness due to basic non-viability of the project, and (c) Induced sickness which is due to the managerial incompetence and wrong policies pursued deliberately for want of genuine stake. This is a man-made sickness in which some unscrupulous promoters adopt fraudulent practices to start a concern and to get away with the money obtained by fraud and deceit.

The FICCI study entitled '*Industrial Sickness — Dimensions and Perspectives*' says that the causes of sickness are both internal and external, often operating in combination. External factors are government policies on pricing, duties, taxes, high interest rates, taxes on profit, slackness in demand, sluggishness in export markets, high labour cost, inadequate availability of inputs, lack of infrastructure and the like.

The internal factors which contribute to sickness are wrong planning in relation to location, technology, capital cost, technological obsolescence, management deficiencies and industrial unrest. We explain below these external and internal factors in some detail.

External Factors

The following are some of the external factors causing industrial sickenss in India :

(*i*) *General Recessionary Trend.* Sometimes a general depression hits industrial units. This is reflected in lack of demand for industrial products in general. An overall slowdown in economic activities affects the performance of individual projects. Improper demand estimation for the products to project lands the industrial units in difficulties.

(*ii*) *High Prices of Inputs.* When the costs of manufacture are high and sales realisation low, the industrial unit cannot stand in the market. This happens when the prices of inputs such as price of fuel such as petroleum during energy crisis goes up whereas the competitive forces keep down the prices of the products.

(*iii*) *Non-Availability of Raw Materials.* When the supplies of raw materials are not available regularly or in good quality, the industrial units are bound to be in trouble. This often occurs in case of supply of imported raw materials.

(*iv*) *Changes in Government Policies.* The industrial sickness is also caused by certain changes in policy designs of the government. These frequent changes affect the long-term production, financial and marketing planning of an industrial unit. Changes in Government policies regarding imports, industrial licensing, taxation can make viable units sick. For example, liberal import policy since 1991 has rendered many small-scale industrial units sick.

(*v*) *Infrastructure Bottlenecks.* Often the infrastructure difficulty is responsible for industrial sickness. No industrial unit can survive prolonged transport and power bottlenecks.

Internal Factors

The following are the important internal factors which are often responsible for industrial sickness :

(*i*) *Project Appraisal Deficiencies* : The industrial unit becomes sick when the unit has been launched without a comprehensive appraisal of economic, financial and technical viabilities of the project.

(*ii*) *Industrial Unrest and Lack of Employee Motivation.* When there is labour discontent, no industrial unit can function smoothly and efficiently. When labour lacks motivation no good results can be expected and this results in sickness and non-viability of several industrial units.

(*iii*) *Wrong Choice of Technology.* If the promoters use wrong technology, results are bound to be unsatisfactory. Many industrial units, especially in the small-scale sector, do not seek professional guidance in installing the correct machinery and plant. If the machinery and plant installed turn out to be defective and unsuitable, they are bound to suffer losses and become sick and non-viable.

(*iv*) *Marketing Problems.* The industrial unit becomes sick due to product obsolescence and market saturation. The industrial unit becomes sick when its product-mix is not attuned to the consumers' demand.

(v) *Wrong Location.* If the location of an industrial unit happens to be defective either from the point of the market or the supply of inputs, it is bound to experience insurmountable difficulties.

(vi) *Lack of Finance.* Inadequate financial arrangements or in the absence of timely financial aid an industrial unit is bound to come to grief. It will not be able to withstand operational losses.

(vii) *Improper Capital Structure.* If capital structure proves to be unsound or unsuitable especially on account of delayed construction or operation, it will result in cost overruns or unduly large borrowing and create financial trouble for the unit concerned.

(viii) *Management Deficiencies.* The biggest cause of industrial sickness is the managerial inefficiency. Lack of professional management or experienced management and the existence of hereditary management is an important cause of industrial sickness. Inefficient management results in inability to preceive things in proper perspective devoid of routine considerations. Inefficient management is also unable to build up good team and inspire confidence for an organised collective effort and takes autocratic and high-handed decisions.

(xiv) *Voluntary Sickness.* There is some sickness which is voluntarily invited by the entrepreneurs for various motives like getting government concession or aid from financial institutions.

Thus industrial sickness cannot be attributed to any single, or simple cause but may be the result of a combination of number of allied causes.

An analysis of 637 large-scale units identified that *deficiency in management* was responsible for 52 per cent cases of sickness. While labour troubles caused sickness only in 2 per cent of the industries, *market recession and environmental* factors came second with 23 per cent. The other causes were *technical factors and faulty initial planning* (14 per cent) and *infrastructural factors* such as power cuts and shortage of critical inputs (9 per cent). Of the 637 large units, 350 could be put back on the track. Of these, 221 units, with the outstanding credit of ₹ 1,125.06 crores were put under the nursing programme.

Suggestions for Rehabilitation of Sick Units

The rehabilitation of sick units or restoring them to normal health is a matter of great urgency in view of the serious social, economic and political consequences of industrial illness. The following measures may be suggested :

(i) *Cooperation between Term-Lending Institutions and Commercial Banks.* Since commercial banks provide working capital, they are in a position to know about the working of industrial concern. But assistance from term-lending institutions is also essential for rescue operations.

(ii) *Coordination between Various Government Agencies.* All government agencies, both regulatory and promotional, must join hands to restore sick units to health.

(iii) *Full cooperation* from various suppliers, unsecured creditors and other stakeholders, particularly from the employees, is also essential to take the concern out of the difficulties in which it is involved.

(iv) *Willing Cooperation and Clear Understanding with the Project Promoters.* Generally there is a lack of trust and confidence among the various interests concerned. It is found that government agencies and dealing institutions are more worried about their money and are anxious to recover them instead of curing of the health of the sick units.

(v) *Checking Over-Valuation of Inventories.* The banks should verify on a regular basis the valuation of inventories both in terms of quantity and price. This would prevent over-borrowing on the hypothecation of inventories.

(*vi*) *Marketing*. There should be well organised and scientific marketing by the project promoters otherwise launching of a project will be a leap in the dark. Good marketing arrangements will prevent industrial sickness.

(*vii*) *Recovery of Outstandings*. Every effort should be made to realise outstanding advances so that the concern is able to gather funds to avoid sickness.

(*viii*) *Modernisation of Machinery*. If the sick unit is to be restored to health, old and obsolete machinery and outdated technology should be discarded at the earliest.

(*ix*) *Improving Labour Relations*. Restrictive labour and unreasonable trade unions are great obstacles. Improving labour relations will go a long way in curing industrial sickenss.

(*x*) *Efficient Management*. If necessary inefficient management should be replaced. The key to industrial health lies in alert and efficient management. The management should show a calm approach, patience and perseverance, courage and ability to steer in bad weather.

(*xi*) *Performance Incentives*. It is necessary to offer performance incentives to the executives and the workers to induce them to put in their best efforts. This will be quite helpful in curing industrial sickness.

(*xii*) *Sympathetic Government Attitude*. During periods of industrial illness the government agencies should adopt a sympathetic and understanding attitude so that the problem is not aggravated but moves towards a solution instead.

(*xiii*) *Austerity and Economy*. Austerity and disciplines should be enforced at all levels. Every effort should be made in raising funds internally through the sale of excess assets, surplus machinery, etc. Uncalled for tours, lavish entertainments, unnecessary personal expenses should be ruthlessly cut down.

Conclusion

In view of the large-scale industrial sickness it would be necessary to organise a task force consisting of competent and experienced executives in various branches of business to go into the case and monitor recovery. Rehabilitation of sick units is not an easy and simple affair. An all-round effort is necessary to root out the disease, first necessary step is the *identification of sick units* which can be made viable through renovation, expansion, and diversification. Units beyond recovery should be wound up. The second step is the *reconstitution of management*. Where the management is unwilling or unable to play its proper role, the financial institutions and the government agencies should intervene to fulfil their large social responsibility of ensuring efficient use of national resources. Since industrial sickness is due both to external causes, e.g., general recession, and internal causes like dishonest and inefficient management, the remedy must also lie in both directions.

With a view to meeting the situation, the early warning system is strengthened. Viability studies should be undertaken to identify the sick units including creeping sickness which could be eventually restored to health with additional financial aid on liberal and easy terms. To an extent increase in industrial sickenss is inevitable result of the very process of modernisation or technological development industry. It is natural that the units which cannot keep pace with the ongoing technological change will become sick, they should be allowed to wind up.

GOVERNMENT'S REMEDIAL POLICY MEASURES

The Government has initiated a number of measures for the revival of the sick industrial units as well as to prevent the incidence of industrial sickness. The policy measures are as follows :

1. In October 1981, the Government announced guidelines to its Ministries, State Governments and financial institutions, regarding the sick industrial undertakings. Accordingly, responsibility was assigned to the concerned ministries for the prevention of such sickness as also for coordinated

remedial action. Banks and other financial institutions providing credit facilities to the sick units were requested to ensure that such credits are utilised properly. The aided sick units are required to submit periodical returns to financial institutions. Besides, banks are required to refer the cases of all sick units to the Industrial Reconstruction Corporation of India (IRCI) where term-lending institutions are not involved. (The IRCI has since been converted into Industrial Reconstruction Bank of India or IRBI).

2. The Government also announced a 'margin money' scheme (effective from January 1, 1982) for reviving viable sick small-scale units. Under the scheme, a sick small-scale unit was sanctioned a minimum loan of ₹1,000 and a maximum of ₹ 20,000. These minimum and maximum amounts have now been raised.

3. In April 1983, the RBI advised financing banks that they should evolve methods to diagnose sickness in industrial units at the incipient stage itself and bring it to the notice of the concerned Ministries and Finance Ministry.

4. In August 1984, through a Parliamentary Act, the Industrial Reconstruction Corporation of India (IRCI) was converted into a statutory body called the **Industrial Reconstruction Bank of India** (IRBI). This new bank has been established with a capital base of ₹ 50 crores which could go up to ₹ 200 crores, for the purpose of rehabilitating and reconstructing ailing industrial concerns. With its head office in Kolkata, the IRBI is wholly owned by the Central Government. Apart from its role as the principal credit and reconstruction agency for industrial revival, the IRBI has been given powers to take over the management, lease out or sell the undertaking as a running concern or prepare schemes of merger or amalgamation and submit them for Central Government's approval.

5. In 1985, the Sick Industrial Companies (Special Provisions) Act (SICA) was passed. According to it the Government has removed sick industrial companies from the purview of the Monopolies and Restrictive Trade Practices Act, 1969, for purposes of modernisation, expansion, amalgamation or merger. Besides, for the early detection of industrial sickness, instructions have been given to the banks to monitor the progress of sick industrial units. In cases, where the net worth has been substantially eroded, financial institutions have been directed to stop assistance to the concerned units.The Act also provides for the setting up of a board of experts for industrial and financial reconstruction.

The Reserve Bank's Guidelines for Checking Industrial Sickness

The Reserve Bank of India has suggested to all scheduled commercial banks parameters within which they are considered viable. The Reserve Bank of India has issued guidelines to the banks for restrengthening the monitoring systems and for arresting industrial sickness at the incipient stage so that corrective measures could be taken in time. It has also asked banks to formulate rehabilitation packages for the revival of potentially viable units.

Some of the fresh guidelines issued by the RBI to scheduled commercial banks regarding the revival of sick units are as under :

(*a*) Banks participating under consortium arrangement of financing a healthy unit should provide for a clause to the effect that in case the unit turns sick, they would participate in the rehabilitation package in accordance with the instructions issued by the RBI.

(*b*) In the case of sick units where workers are interested in taking over the management by forming workers' cooperatives, banks have been advised to actively support the rehabilitation packages.

(*c*) Banks are given the option of selling their debts in respect of a sick unit to other willing banks at a discount as per the guidelines issued by the RBI.

The Reserve Bank of India has evolved a coordinated approach between banks and term-lending institutions in assessing the viability of a unit once it is identified sick. The earlier *ad hoc* approach of nursing sick units has given place to a pragmatic package approach to tackle problem of sickness. The new approach puts emphasis on prevention of sickness rather than resorting to remedial measures after the unit becomes sick.

In October 1989, the Government introduced the scheme for the grant of excise loan to sick/ weak industrial units. Under the scheme, the sick units are eligible for excise loan not exceeding 50% of the excise duty actually paid for 5 years from the date of approval of the rehabilitation package subject to the ceiling of 33% of the total cost of the rehabilitation.

BOARD FOR INDUSTRIAL AND FINANCIAL RECONSTRUCTION

The Government of India set up a Board for Industrial and Financial Reconstruction (BIER) under the Sick Industrial Companies (Special Provisions) Act (SICA) 1985. The board became operational from May 15, 1987. The amendment in the Sick Industrial Companies Act (SICA) in December 1991 brought public sector enterprises also within the purview of BIFR. The industrial companies (other than those specifically exempted under the Act) whose net worth has been eroded completely or by 50 per cent or more are required to make a reference to the BIFR under sections 15 and 23 of the Act, respectively. The present BIFR norms lay down that a unit must be in existence for a minimum period of five years for it to qualify for classification under the BIFR Act in case of sickness. The powers of BIFR are wide ranging and extend to the framing of the scheme of amalgamation, merger and financial reconstruction. The scheme relating to revival of any sick industrial company offered by BIFR could provide for financial assistance by way of loans, advances, guarantees, reliefs etc. from official financial institutions. The scheme offered by BIFR for the revival of a sick industrial company may provide for any one or more of the following measures :

1. The financial reconstruction of the sick unit so as to make it viable.
2. Change in the management of the sick company or to arrange for its takeover by a non-sick efficient company.
3. Merger of the sick industrial unit with any other company.
4. The sale or lease a part or whole of the sick industrial undertaking.

BIFR follows a clear-cut policy of holding the large groups responsible for their sick units. Large houses will have also to make the maximum sacrifice in the revival process. The bulk of financial pakage will have to be borne by the healthy units in the group. If it is found that large corporate houses are dithering in their help to sick units, the RBI's group concept will be applied.

Where the BIFR finds that it is not possible to revive the sick unit through financial reconstruction, change in management or takeover by others and that its net worth cannot be increased to exceed its accumulated losses within reasonable time, it then recommends that the sick company should be wound up. It can then approach the High Court of a State for winding up of the company. It is worth mentioning that the decision of BIFR is binding on all concerned.

References to BIFR for Revival of Sick Industrial Companies

As mentioned above, those industrial companies whose net worth has been eroded completely or by 50 per cent or more are required to make reference to BIFR for taking appropriate measures for their revival. As will be seen from Table 38.2, since its inception in May 1987 till the end of September 2006, the Board of Industrial and Financial Reconstruction (BIFR) received 6,991 references under the Sick Industrial Companies (Special Provisions) Act (SICA), 1985. These references included 296 references from Central Public Sector Undertakings (CPSUs) and State Public Sector Undertakings.

Table 38.2: References to BIFR as on September 30, 2006

Sl.No.	Status	Private	Central PSUs	State PSUs	Total PSUs	Total
1.	References received	6,695	108	188	296	6,991
2.	Registration declined	1,484	17	66	83	1,567
3.	Under Scrutiny	12	0	0	0	12
A	References registered (= 1-2-3)	5,199	91	122	213	5,412
	DISPOSALS OF CASES					
5.	Dismissed					
	(i) as non-maintainable	1,660	11	36	47	1,707
	(ii) as multiple registered	218	0	0	0	218
6.	Rehabilitation schemes approved/sanctioned					
	(i) by BIFR	695	27	26	53	748
	(ii) by AAIFR/SC	11	1	0	1	12
7.	Declared no longer sick out of Sl. No. 6	462	9	14	23	485
8.	Winding up recommended to the concerned high courts	1,234	29	40	69	1,303
9.	Dropped now	119	5	3	8	127
B	Total (5 + 6 + 8 + 9)	3,937	73	105	178	4,115
C	PENDING					
10.	Draft schemes circulated	42	2	0	2	44
11.	Winding up notice issued	85	1	4	5	90
12.	Pending for sickness determination	357	2	1	3	360
13.	Declared sick	678	11	10	21	699
14.	Schemes failed and reopened	8	1	0	1	9
15.	Pending cases remanded by AAIFR	43	1	2	3	46
16.	Stay ordered by courts	46	0	3	3	49
	Total (C = A–B)	1,262	18	17	35	1297

Source : BIFR, Department of Economic Affairs, Ministry of Finance

With 6,991 references received, 1,707 were dismissed as non-maintainable under the Act. 760 rehabilitation schemes (including 12 by Appellate Authority of Industrial and Financial Reconstruction (AAIFR) (Supreme Court), were sanctioned and 1,303 companies were recommended to be wound up. 485 companies have been declared 'no longer sick' and were discharged from the purview of SICA as their net worth turned positive after the implementation of the schemes.

Among the 296 references for Public Sector Undertakings (PSUs) registered up to Sept. 30, 2006, Rehabilitation Schemes were sanctioned for 28 CPSUs and 26 SPSUs. It was recommended that 29 CPSUs and 40 SPSUs be wound up. Besides 9 CPSUs and 14 SPSUs were declared no longer sick. As on Sept. 30, 2006, the gross disposal of cases by BIFR stood at 4,115.

RECOMMENDATIONS OF THE COMMITTEE ON INDUSTRIAL SICKNESS AND CORPORATE RESTRUCTURING

Government of India appointed a Committee on Industrial Sickness and Corporate Restructuring in May 1993. The committee submitted its report in July 1993. The major recommendations of the Committee are as follows :

1. The industrial unit should be treated as a sick unit if it makes :

(a) Default of 180 days or more on repayment to term lending institutions; and

(*b*) Irregularities in cash credits or working capital for 180 days or more.

2. A sick company's own reference to BIFR should be voluntary, not mandatory.

3. The BIFR should act as a fast track facilitator and occasionally an arbitrator.

4. There should be five fast track winding up Tribunals to reduce the problem of delays in winding up.

5. The Industrial Disputes Act (IDA) should be amended so that there is no need for seeking prior approval of the Government for lay-off and retrenchment of workers and for a permanent closure. Further, for the operation of the provisions relating to lay-off, retrenchment and closure, the number of workers in an undertaking should be raised from 100 to 300. The compensation for retrenchment and closure may be increased from 15 days' wages to one month's wage per year of the completed service.

Conclusion

A viable policy for dealing with the sick units must provide for orderly closure of the units which have no chance of survival. In the past, the Government was compelled to take over sick units because of the socio-economic reasons for maintaining employment and to avoid sudden and undue hardship to the workers' families. But this is not a rational way of bailing out uneconomic industrial units.The previous management must be held accountable for the lapses which impaired the economic viability of the units concerned. The inept and fraudulent managements must receive adequate punishment. Needless to say that sick units with no prospect of becoming viable should not be kept alive artificially at heavy cost. Special institutional arrangements are needed to deal with this complex problem of industrial sickness.

As the mismanagement by the private businessmen has been the main factor the policy of takeover of these private sick units by the Government has been widely criticised. Dr Prem Shankar Jha rightly writes, "In fact as the takeover of sick engineering units and textile mills has shown in every case what the Government has inherited is a load of worn-out machinery, a mountain of debts and a distrust of work-force. Nationalization in such circumstances has become a means of indemnifying the entrepreneur against the consequences of his misdeeds instead of punishing him — first he milks an enterprise dry, then hands it over to the Government for salvage".[1] Further in our view the approach towards the rehabilitation of sick industrial units has to be very selective and systematic. There is no point in throwing away further resources in support of units which are irretrievably sick. Only such units as are found to be potentially viable need to be taken up for the formulation of rehabilitation packages to restore them to health.

1. Prem Shankar Jha, 'To Nationalise or Not to Nationalise', *The Illustrated Weekly of India*, Feb.18, 1979, p.8.

CHAPTER 39

Consumer Protection : Consumer Rights and Redressal Mechanism

Introduction

Consumer awareness about their legitimate rights has been constantly growing in recent years. Consumer protection movement is a part of global recognition and concern that consumers are a weak party in buying goods and services as compared to the manufacturers and traders producing and selling them. Ideally, a market economy where firms compete to sell goods and services to the consumers should serve the interests of consumers better but more often than not the consumers are exploited by the adoption of unfair and restrictive trade practices. Far from being a sovereign the consumer is a child who is too weak to resist or challenge the suppliers of goods and services. Therefore, even in a free market economy he needs protection of his rights by a legal authority. Consumer protection is necessary even in a controlled economy where public enterprises play a dominant role since consumers are likely to be denied their rights in their case too.

Most consumers buy goods and services after being lured by advertisements exaggerating the contents and quality of their products or services. Legal support to them is required if they are to be protected from the exploitation and deception by the suppliers so that erring vendors are brought to book. It is this increasing realisation of the helplessness of the consumers and to ensure their legitimate rights that led to the resolution of the United Nations General Assembly in 1985 recommending to the member states for adopting preventive, protective and curative measures for the benefit of consumers. Thus this resolution required the member states to create agencies for adjudication of consumer claims and to create conducive environment for protection of consumers. In the UN General Assembly resolution Consumer Councils were recommended to be set up for redressal of the complaints and claims of consumers. In what follows we first spell out the consumers' rights and then explain the need for consumer protection. We will then proceed to explain the important methods for consumer protection and Consumer Protection Act 1986 and later amendments made in it in 2002 for protection of consumer rights and redressal of consumer disputes.

Consumer Rights

Consumers in the developed countries such as the USA and UK are much more conscious of their rights. But in countries such as India consumers are quite a vulnerable lot due to their poverty, illiteracy and lack of awareness of legal rights. As a result, manufacturers and suppliers of goods and services generally exploit the consumers by adopting unfair and restrictive trade practices. However, consumer awareness is constantly increasing in India too and the consumers who have been deceived or exploited are increasingly approaching the consumer forums or councils set up by the government for redressal of their complaints and settlement of their claims or damages.

The following are the important consumer rights :

1. **The Right to be heard.** The consumer has the right to be heard if he has any complaint or grievance regarding the good or service received. This implies that consumers' complaints and grievances must receive due attention and consideration at an appropriate forum.

2. The Right to safety. The consumers are entitled to protection of their health and safety from the goods and services they buy. They should not be supplied goods or services which are hazardous to their health and safety.

3. The Right against exploitation. This covers right to protection from unfair trade practices and unscrupulous exploitation of consumers by charging excessive prices by suppliers of goods or services.

4. The Right to be informed. This implies that consumers should be given correct and full information about the quality of goods that they buy. They should be provided information about the ingredients of the product, freshness of the product, any side effects that may occur as a result of consumption of a commodity. This right applies especially to the drug manufacturers and suppliers.

5. The Right to choose. This implies that consumers should be provided a variety of products from which they can make a choice of their liking. The opportunity to choose from limited options restricts their right to choose.

6. The Right to get redress. This implies that consumers' complaints and grievances about the products and services supplied to them must be redressed. That is, they should not only be heard but their complaints must be redressed and compensated adequately.

In India, the Consumer Protection Act 1986 was passed which was later amended in 2002, wherein most of the consumer rights have been provided and mechanism for redressal of their complaints have been put in place. We shall explain the Consumer Protection Act 1986 and amendment in it later in 2002.

THE NEED FOR CONSUMER PROTECTION

As mentioned above, consumers are largely denied their due rights, especially in developing countries such as India. The consumers are spread widely all over a country and are poor, illiterate and are generally not aware of their rights, though their awareness has recently increased.

The manufacturers and suppliers of goods or services often exploit consumers by adopting a number of unfair and restrictive trade practices. They often merge and also form tacit cartels to raise prices for maximising their profits at the expense of consumers. For instance, in case of drugs manufacturers generally charge high prices which are much above their cost of production. Some pharmaceutical companies misuse their patent rights to exploit consumers. They therefore need protection from unfair and restrictive trade practices of producers and suppliers of goods or services.

Misleading advertising is another means by which the producers deceive the consumers. Advertisement is of two types. One is *informative advertisement* which informs the consumers about the availability of certain products at certain prices. This is not objectionable as it provides information to the consumers. However, more often the purpose of advertisement by the manufacturers and suppliers is to mislead the ill-informed consumers about the quality and contents of their products and services. They indulge in what is called *persuasive advertisement* to compete away customers from their rivals. Such persuasive advertisements serve no useful social purpose and lead to deception of consumers. The cost of advertisement is added to the cost of production and this leads to very high prices being charged from the consumers. The Indian readers will be knowing well that crores of rupees are spent on film actors and cricket players as brand ambassadors and on advertisements on print and electronic media to promote the sale of their products. From whom such heavy costs incurred on advertising are recovered ? Such heavy advertising expenditures just enable the manufacturers at the most to maintain their market shares of the product without adding much to its total output. The consumers need protection from such deception of persuasive advertisements. The government should not allow such heavy advertising cost to be incurred as valid cost for calculation of taxable profits of the firms.

The other and highly injurious practice by the suppliers, especially in India, is *widespread practice of adulteration of commodities*. The adulteration by private sector can take place right from the manufacturing point to the ultimate supplier of the products to the consumers. It has been found that small pebbles and dust are mixed with wheat, maize, jawar and bajra to increase weight, sand is mixed with cement, leaves and barks of some trees are mixed with tea leaves. Again Vanaspati is often mixed with *Desi ghee* and butter, etc. All these practices of adulteration are hazardous to health and life of the consumers and they need protection from them. But the most injurious is the widespread practice in India by manufacturers and dealers of *spurious drugs* which do immense harm to the health and life of the people.

It is due to the above practices of the manufacturers and suppliers which have resulted in consumer protection movement and have forced the governments to enact legislation to protect the consumers.

Consumerism. *Social movement to protect the consumers from unfair and unhealthy restrictive trade practices by the manufacturers and suppliers is also called consumerism.* An eminent management expert states, "*Consumerism is a social movement seeking to augment the rights and powers of consumers*".[1] Similarly, Boyd and Allen state, "Consumerism may be defined as the dedication of those activities of both public and private organisations which are designed to protect individuals from practices that impinge upon their rights as consumers"[2].

IMPORTANT METHODS OF CONSUMER PROTECTION

How to ensure consumer protection from unfair, restrictive, deceptive and exploitative practices of manufacturers and suppliers ? The important ways for consumer protection are :

1. Imposition of self-regulation and discipline by the manufacturers and suppliers of goods and services for working in the interests of consumers.

2. The role of government which can enact laws for the protection of consumers and make arrangements for their enforcement.

3. Voluntary organisation of consumers to form groups such as NGO, cooperative societies to safeguard the interests of consumers.

We explain below in detail the above three ways of protection of consumers.

Imposition of Self-Regulation and Discipline by Manufacturers and Dealers

The important way for consumer protection is the voluntary imposition of self-regulation and discipline by the manufacturers and others engaged in supplying and distributing goods and services. If they are self enlightened, they would pay due attention to the consumer rights. Of course, producers' main aim is to maximise their profits but this should be achieved by raising their efficiency in production and quality of their products rather than deceiving and exploiting consumers. The socially responsible producers and distributors must not form cartels and adopt monopolistic practices to fleece consumers by charging high prices. Prime Minister Dr. Manmohan Singh in the annual session of Confederation of Indian Industry (CII) in May 2007 rightly urged the captains of Indian industries to exercise self-restraint in charging and raising prices by using their monopolistic power. To quote him, "The operation of cartels by groups of companies to keep prices high must end. It is unacceptable to obstruct the forces of competition from having free play. It is even more distressing in a country where the poor are severely affected by rising commodity prices. Cartels are a crime and go against the grain of an open economy". He further adds. "*Maximisation of profits*

1. Philip Kotler, 'What Consumerism Means for Marketers', *Harvard Business Review*, May-June 1972, p.49.
2. Harper, W. Boyd Jr. and David B. Allen Jr., "Caveat Emptor, Caveat Venditor, Caveat Omnis" in Neelegham S, (ed.). *Market Management and the Indian Economy*, Vikas Publishing House Pvt. Ltd, 1982, p.310.

should be within the bounds of decency and greed". Similarly, long ago, Mr. T. Thomas, a former chairman of *Hindustan Lever Limited* in his speech at the 44th Annual General Body Meeting in 1977 stated, "Restraint is best exercised voluntarily than through legislation which will otherwise become inevitable. Advertising agencies and marketing management have a very important role to play in this respect. By over-playing the claims they will be cutting the very branch on which they are pearched".

However, in our opinion it is idle to expect that private business executives will impose self-discipline on them and exercise restraint on deceiving and exploiting the consumers for maximising their profits. The fact is they regard making large profits as a symbol of their success in business and it has therefore become a mission of their life.

However, a novel way to ensure compliance of business for paying due regard to the consumer rights and the promotion of social welfare is to 'publicise' certain important information about proper code of conduct and require businesses to report their degree of compliance to this information. For example, in the USA, the government provides and widely publicises information about industrial pollutants and require the manufacturers to report about the extent of pollution generation by them. The submission of reports about their emission of pollutants and Government's publicity about them induces some compliance by them in maintaining standards of safety. A noted example is the **'US Toxic Release Inventory'**. According to this, manufacturers are required to submit reports about the toxic materials they release in the environment. This induces them to reduce pollution to maintain their reputation.[3]

Voluntary Organisation of Consumers to Protect their Rights

In some countries the consumers have organised themselves on a voluntary basis to form consumer groups or councils. They are non-government organisations (NGOs) to protect consumer rights. These voluntary consumer groups or councils protect consumer rights in the following ways:

1. They issue leaflets providing information so as to educate consumers on matters affecting them.

2. They have been pressing for proper labelling of the products with maximum price to be charged, the contents of the product, especially drugs, side effects if any, of the product etc.

3. Organising movements against the malpractices of manufacturers and traders of the products.

In Delhi, Mumbai and other important cities voluntary consumer organisations came into existence in sixties and seventies when prices of goods rose very high to resist the hike in prices by traders arbitrarily. The idea of Super Bazar on cooperative principles emerged from this price resistance movements of consumers. Besides, an organisation named **'Common Cause'** established by late. Mr. H.D. Shourie and based in Delhi did a very useful work in protecting the rights of consumers.

Consumer cooperative movement also started to protect the consumers against the malpractices and traders of goods. A consumer cooperative is a voluntary association of consumers formed to promote their interests. The consumers enhance their bargaining power as against traders and manufacturers.

The consumer cooperatives protect the consumers in the following ways :

1. Since these cooperatives purchase commodities in bulk and generally directly from the manufacturers they are able to provide goods to the consumers at reasonable prices.

2. Secondly, the consumers themselves control the cooperatives. They are therefore assured of standard quality and unadulterated goods.

3. Correct weights and measures are used by the cooperative societies and therefore consumers are saved from any deception in this regard.

---

3. See UNDP, *Human Development Report*, 1998, p.11

4. In India consumer cooperatives are especially engaged in distributing essential commodities at controlled prices.

Despite the efforts of voluntary organisations to protect consumers and safeguard their legitimate rights, these voluntary organisations have not succeeded much in protecting consumers. Their growth has been limited mainly to house building societies. Other voluntary cooperative societies work at the level of distributing goods and are able to eliminate malpractices of middlemen. But, the real problem is to save the consumers from monopolistic, unfair and restrictive trade practices of manufacturers of goods and services and misleading advertisements by them to exploit the consumers.

Government Role in Consumer Protection

The government can play an important role for protection of consumers. It can enact various legislations for protection of consumers. According to the *UN Guidelines for Consumer Protection*[4], "the government role in consumer protection is vital and finds expression through policy making legisiations and establishment of institutional authority for its enforcement. To provide a legal basis for its enforcing basic consumer rights every country needs to have irreducible minimum of consumer protection legislation covering physical safety, promotion and protection of consumers' economic interests, standards for the safety and quality of goods and services, distribution facilities, redress, education and information programmes. Governments also require the necessary machinery to enforce such legislation." In both the developed and developing countries the governments have taken several measures to protect consumers. Laws relating to cooperative societies have been enforced in India for quite some time now.

Besides, consumers have been sought to be protected by enactment of several laws by government. The important laws have been passed by the government to protect consumers and uphold their rights. These laws include (1) Prevention of Food Adulteration Act, 1954, (2) the Essential Commodities Act, 1985, (3) Agricultural Produce (Grading and Marketing) Act, (4) Drugs Control Act, (5) Drugs and Cosmetics Act, (6) Standards of Weights and Measures Act, (7) Drugs and Magic Remedies (Objectional Advertisement) Act, (8) Water (Prevention and Control of Pollution) Act, (9) Prevention of Black Marketing and Maintenance of Essential Commodities Act, and (10) Air (Prevention and Control of Pollution) Act.

Besides, Monopolistic and Restrictive Trade Practices (MRTP) Act was passed in 1969 to check monopolistic and restrictive trade practices. This Act was based on the economic theory that control of monopolies and prevention of mergers will lead to competition among the manufacturers and suppliers of goods and therefore cause expansion in their output and will therefore also provide benefits to the consumers. Under Section 12B of the MRTP Act, MRTP Commission has been given the necessary powers to award compensation in the matter of unfair trade practices.

Above all, in 1986, the Indian government passed *Consumer Protection Act*. Under it the consumers have the right to approach appropriate consumer forum or commission set up under the Act to get their complaints redressed. In what follows we will explain the provisions of Consumer Protection Act 1986.

THE CONSUMER PROTECTION ACT 1986

The Consumer Protection Act 1986 was passed by the Indian Parliament to protect consumer rights and to redress consumer complaints and resolve consumer disputes. Every individual is a consumer of goods and services and expects a fair deal against unfair exploitation. This Consumer Protection Act applies to the whole of India except the State of Jammu and Kashmir and covers all goods and services purchased by the consumers and to all sectors — private, public and cooperative. The objective of the Act is "to provide for better protection of the interests of consumers and for that

4. These guidelines were adopted by the UN General Assembly in April 1985.

purpose to make provisions for the establishment of *Consumer Councils* and other authorities for the settlement of consumer disputes and for matters connected therewith". It protects the consumers from unfair trading or unfair trade practices.

It is important to note that the Indian Consumer Protection Act is *a social welfare legislation and has been designed to avoid technicalities, procedural delays, procedural requirement, court fees and costs*.

The Consumer Protection Act, 1986 provides for the following rights to the consumers :

(*a*) Right to be heard and to be assured that consumers' interests will receive due consideration at appropriate forum;

(*b*) Right to seek redressal against unfair trade practices or unscrupulous exploitation of consumers; and

(*c*) Right to consumer education.

The Consumer Protection (Amendment) Act 1993 adds the following consumer rights :

(*d*) The right to be assured wherever possible, access to a variety of goods and services at competitive prices;

(*e*) The right to be informed about the quality, potency, purity, standard and price of goods (or services as the case may be) so as to protect the consumers against unfair trade practices; and

(*f*) The right to be protected against the marketing of goods (and services) which are hazardous to life and property.

Redressal Agencies

We explain below the various authorities set up under the Consumer Protection Act 1986.

Consumer Protection Councils. The Act provides for setting up a Central Consumer Protection Council by the Central Government and State Consumer Councils by each state of India. The Central Consumer Protection Council shall consist of (1) the Minister in Charge of Consumer Affairs in the Central Government who shall be its chairman and such number of other official or non-official members representing such interests as prescribed. It is required by the Act that Central Consumer Protection Council will meet as and when necessary. However, at least one meeting of the Central Council must be held every year. The objects of the council are to protect the rights of consumers and promote their interest as listed above from (*a*) to (*f*).

The State Consumer Councils to protect consumer rights as per amendment in the Act in 1993 will consist of (1) the Minister in Charge of Consumer Affairs in the State Government concerned and members of other officials and non-officials representing such interests as may be prescribed by the State Governments. As in the case of the Central Council, the objects of State Councils will be to protect the rights of consumers as listed above from (a) to (f) within the State.

CONSUMER DISPUTES REDRESSAL SYSTEM

Under the Consumer Protection Act 1986 three-tier consumer disputes redressal system at the District, State and National levels has been set up. Thus the Act provides for establishing the following consumer redressal agencies :

1. *District Consumer Forum* in each district of a state set up by the State Government.
2. *State Consumer Commission* in each state set up by each State.
3. *National Consumer Commission* set up by the Central Government.

Composition of Consumer Redressal Agencies

According to Consumer Protection Act 1986 each District Consumer Forum set up in each district of a State shall consist of a person who is or has been or is qualified to be a district judge. This person will work as president of the district consumer forum.

Two eminent members who have adequate knowledge and experience and have the ability in dealing with problems concerning law, commerce, economics, accountancy, industry, public affairs or administration and one of whom shall be a lady member, especially who is a social worker.

A **District Forum** has the jurisdiction to deal with the complaints where the value of good or service and the compensation claimed, if any, does not exceed Rs. 20 lakh (as per amendment in the Act in 2002). A complaint by consumers will be filed in a District Forum in case when the opposite party or each of the opposite party if there are more than one resides or carries on business within the district concerned at the time of filing the complaint or *any one of the party* (if there are more than one) residing or carrying on business in the district at the time of the filing of the complaint if the district forum grants permission for this.

The **State Consumer Commission** shall consist of (1) a person who is or has been a judge of a high court appointed by the State Government, (2) two other members of high standing and eminence who have adequate knowledge or experience concerning the problems relating to law, commerce, economics, industry, public administration etc one of whom shall be a woman.

The State Consumer Commission as per the amendment of the Act in 2002 shall have the jurisdiction to entertain complaints where the value of goods or services and compensation claimed if any exceeds ₹ 20 lakh but is not more than ₹ 1 crore.

The State Consumer Commission will also entertain appeals against the orders of District Forums within the State. Besides, the State Consumer Commissions have been authorised to call for the records and give appropriate orders in case of any consumer dispute pending before the District Forum within the State or has been decided by it if the State Commission finds that a District Forum has exercised a power not vested in it by the Act or has failed to exercise a power or jurisdiction vested in it or acted illegally in exercise of its powers.

The **National Consumer Commission** will consist of (a) a person who is or has been a judge of the Supreme Court and is appointed by the Central Government in consultation with Chief Justice of India. He will also work as president of the national commission, (b) four other members of eminence having good knowledge or experience and ability to deal with the problems relating to commerce, economics, law, industry, public affairs or administration and one of whom shall be a woman.

National Consumer Commission has the jurisdiction : (1) to entertain complaints where the value of goods or services and compensation claimed if any is, according to Amendment Act 2002, one crore or more; (2) National Commission is authorised to hear appeals against the order of any State Consumer Commission; (3) The Central Commission has the right to call for the records from the State Commissions.

It is important to note that *all forums, commissions appointed under the Consumer Protection Act are in substantial matters not different from the ordinary civil courts. They are quasi-judicial tribunals created to render speady justice.*[5]

Remedial Action

It may be noted that a complaint to a redressal agency may be filed by (a) an individual, consumer; (b) recognised consumer association, (c) more than one consumers who have the same

5. G.L. Sanghi, Consumer Protection Law in India, a paper presented at 5th LAWASIA Business Law Conference, New Delhi, Jan.2003.

interest; and (d) the State or Central Government. The complaint to a redressal agency must be in relation to goods sold or delivered or service provided to the complainant.

If the redressal agency is convinced that any of the allegations in the complaint filed before it is true, it shall issue an appropriate order to the opposite party. This order may be any of the following types :

1. to remove the defect if found to be true by the appropriate laboratory from the good in question;
2. to replace the defective goods with the new goods of the same type free from the defects;
3. to return to the complainant price of the defective good or charges paid by him;
4. to pay the compensation to the complainant as may be decided by the redressal agency for the loss suffered by him;
5. to remove the defects or deficiencies in the service rendered to the individuals;
6. to stop the unfair or restrictive trade practice or give undertaking not to repeat in future;
7. not to supply hazardous goods;
8. to withdraw the hazardous goods being offered for sale; and
9. to give adequate costs to the parties in question.

Penalties

The Consumer Commissions are authorised to impose penalties on trader or person against whom complaint is made if he fails to comply with the order of the redressal agency. The penalty or punishment may involve imprisonment for a period not more than 3 years or a fine of not more than 10 thousand rupees or both.

The Consumer Protection Amendment Act 2002

The Consumer Protection Act 1986 held great hopes for the helpless consumers who have been denied fair deal by the unscrupulous producers or traders. In the implementation of Consumer Protection Act 1986 some deficiencies in the Act were noticed. Therefore, some important amendments were made in the Act by Consumer Amendment Act 2002. With this amendment all the redressal agencies (District Forums, State Consumer Commissions and Central Consumer Commission) have been given the powers of a judicial magistrate of a first class for trial of offences within their jurisdiction, subject of course to the right of appeal from a lower redressal agency to a higher one.

The important changes made by the Consumer Protection Amendment Act 2002 are the following :

1. Both MRTP Act and Consumer Protection Act deal with unfair and restrictive trade practices. Amendment made in Consumer Protection Act in 2002 has clarified that the expression '*restrictive trade practices*' will also include delay in supply of goods or services and rise in prices in the mean time.

2. Provisions regarding unfair trade practices have been made more stringent. It is now provided that if the representations contained in an advertisement for the sale or supply of a good or service are misleading, the advertiser can be held responsible for taking corrective steps at his own cost apart from other obligations.

3. The District Forums would be able to deal with cases involving the payment of compensation of ₹ 20 lakhs against the pre-existing ₹ 5 lakhs. Similarly, the State Consumer Commissions can now deal with cases involving compensation up to ₹ 1 crore while National Consumer Commission can deal with cases involving compensation of Rs. 1 crore or more instead of pre-existing ₹ 25 lakhs.

4. In the event of the death of the complainant, amendment in the Act in 2002 now provides for substitution of his legal representatives. Surviving legal representatives can file a complaint or get substitution in place of the existing one.

5. In regard to goods hazardous to life or safety of the public, traders supplying goods will be liable if it can be proved that the supplier could have known with due care that the goods or services supplied were hazardous to the public. Besides, liability of suppliers of spurious products and services is made clear in the Amendment Act 2002.

6. An important amendment relates to the meaning of expression 'manufacturing'. Manufacturing has now been defined to include merely *assembling parts of goods made by others* or *putting one's own mark on any good manufactured by others*.

7. Amendment Act 2002 makes the restrictive trade practices more stringent by including under it trade practice which tends to the manipulation of price or the conditions of delivery of goods or affect the flow of supplies of goods in the market in a manner that imposes undue costs or restrictions on the consumers. Restrictive trade practice also includes delay in the delivery of goods beyond the period agreed to by the traders or delay in providing services when such delay is likely to lead to rise in their prices.

8. According to an important provision in the 2002 Amendment Act, in trading or commerce of goods or services misleading or deceptive conduct of traders or suppliers would be treated as unfair trade practice. Those who make misleading or false representation luring consumers to buy goods or services would fall within unfair trade practice and would be held liable. Under the Consumer Protection Amendment Act 2002 the consumers who are lured to enter into such a contract would be entitled to get the damages.

Similarly, Amendment Act 2002 also covers the unfair treatment to the consumers who have suffered by being lured in the schemes offering gifts, concessional prices or some items free of charge depending on the official results of a particular scheme. This amendment provides remedy to the consumers who might be unfairly treated in such schemes by requiring the promotor to disclose proper information regarding the results of a scheme by appropriate timely publication of results in newspapers, etc.

Proposed Amendments in Consumer Act, 2010

The Cabinet has given clearance to the proposed amendments to the Consumer Protection Act which is likely to be passed by the parliament in winter session of 2010. These amendments seek to make the *consumer protection law more responsive to consumer complaints* through quicker disposal of cases. The proposed amendments have widened the scope of the law, specified time limit for quicker disposal of cases and rationalised qualifications for appointment of members of consumer forums at the state and national level.

Evaluation of Consumer Protection Act

Consumer Protection Act with amendments made in it in 2002 is a quite comprehensive piece of legislation that seeks to protect the consumers against unfair and exploitative practices of manufacturers. Consumer awareness in India is now fast growing. As a result, the number of complaints by the end of 2002 before District Forums had been about 14 lakhs, that before State Commissions 2 lakhs and that before National Commission about 21,000 all of which amount to the total of about 162,100[6].

6. G.L. Sanghi, Consumer Protection Law in India, a Paper presented at 5th LAWASIA Business Law Conference, New Delhi, Jan 2003.

It is important to note that Consumer Protection Act is additional law protecting consumers but not a derogation of any other laws which protect consumers. Services or goods provided by those dealing in information technology, electronic commerce (E-Commerce) are also liable under the Consumer Protection Act apart from the Act governing Telecommunication Regulatory Authority of India (TRAI) which regulates not only transactions between competing providers of telecommunication services but also regulate them to protect consumer interests.[7]

Similarly, the Consumer Protection Act is in addition to MRTP Act which also tries to protect the interests of consumers by controlling monopolistic and restrictive trade practices. According to G.L. Sanghi, "The tribunals created under the Consumer Protection Act are in substantial matters not different from the ordinary civil courts. They are quasi-judicial tribunals created to render inexpensive and speedy justice. They provide additional remedies through the newly created forums".[8]

A Comprehensive Act. The Consumer Protection Act is quite a comprehensive legislation. Under the Consumer Protection Act not only manufacturers and suppliers of goods but also of such services as insurance providers, medical treatment, lending and recovery of bank loans also come within the purview of the Act. A few such important cases are worth explaining.

Consumer Protection Act and Medical Practitioners

The applicability of Consumer Protection Act to medical practitioners is a highly complicated issue and the case relating to it went even up to the Supreme Court of India. In defence of medical practitioners it was argued that their services are excluded category being services under "Control of Personal Services". Supreme Court rejected these arguments and brought medical practitioners, hospitals and nursing homes where services are rendered for valuable consideration under the purview of Consumer Protection Act. Doctors and hospitals committing medical negligence have therefore become liable and damages for medical negligence can be claimed from them. Though this has created fear and concern among medical practitioners and private hospitals but this will help in preventing medical negligence on the part of doctors and hospitals. It has been widely reported in the media about medical negligence, for example, of operating a wrong eye, removing a kidney of a person without his consent, leaving screw, scissors and a towel in the abdomen of a patient, giving a wrong injection leading to the death of a patient. For all these acts of negligence compensation can be claimed from doctors and hospitals and also penalties can be imposed on them. In an important case Supreme Court held that *a medical practitioner may be liable if there was a negligence in respect of diagnosis and/or treatment given to a patient provided it can be demonstrated that the negligent act was not based on reasonable and responsible information as to the kind and quality of treatment.*"[9]

Insurance Companies and Consumer Protection Act

One of the important categories where Consumer Protection Act has been usefully applied is the claims against insurance companies. Many insurance companies (including public sector insurance companies) often deny mediclaims to the insurers on one pretext or the other. Generally insurance companies deny claims or damages to the insurers that they did not disclose the pre-existing disease they were suffering from at the time of getting insured. In many cases consumer commissions have rejected the arguments of insurance companies and have awarded damages to the insurers and require insurance companies to fulfil their contractual obligations.

In a recent case of accident claim the United India Insurance Company denied to pay the damages on a car which met with an accident on the ground that it was being plied without the 'fitness certificate' as required under the Motor Vehicles Act. In this case in Nov. 2007, National Consumer

---

7. *Ibid.*
8. G.L. Sanghi, *op. cit.*
9. Referred to in G.L. Sanghi *op. cit.*

Commission held that the insurance companies, if the terms of the policy were not breached, cannot refuse to entertain claims on the pretext that the *insured violated some other laws or conditions* "as the insurance is a matter of contract between the two parties."[10]

Recovery of Bank Loans and Consumer Protection Act

The wide applicability of Consumer Protection Act can be understood from the recent judgement of the State Consumer Commission of Delhi which slapped a fine of Rs. 55 lakhs on ICICI Bank for trying to recover a vehicle loan by hiring musclemen. The goons of recovery agent of the bank forcibly dragged out a youth from the car, beat him up with iron rods and left him bleeding and drove away with the vehicle. Justice J.D. Kapoor, president of the commission, said, "We hold ICICI Bank guilty of the grossest kind of deficiency in service and unfair trade practice for breach of terms of contract of hire-purchase/loan agreement by seizing the vehicle illegally."[11]

Conclusion. In view of the above usefulness and wide applicability of Consumer Protection Act, Mr. G.L. Sanghi is right in concluding, "In each and every area involving sale of goods and services for valuable consideration a consumer stands protected. The polarity of this law is unlimited. Its machinery is effective and awesome to the delinquent trader with solace to the consumer. As experience grows further improvements will undoubtetedly make this remedy more and more useful".[12]

10. Reported in the *Economic Times*, November 5, 2007
11. Reported in *Times of India*, Nov. 3, 2007
12. G.L. Sanghi, *op. cit.*, p.45

Chapter 40

Capital Market in India

Financial Infrastructure and Economic Growth

The financial infrastructure has a strong bearing on the process of economic growth. In fact, it is as imperative for economic growth as a runway for an aeroplane to take off. It implies that the growth of financial infrastructure is a precondition for launching the process of economic growth and also for its acceleration. The term financial infrastructure signifies *financial assets* (primary securities as well as secondary securities), *financial markets* (money market and capital market) and *financial intermediaries* (banks and non-bank financial institutions). Thus the financial assets, financial markets and financial intermediaries are the three ingredients of the financial system of a country.

Though finance is not a substitute for real resources, it has a crucial role in the process of economic growth. It is for this reason that economic growth and growth of financial infrastructure go hand in hand. Schumpeter regarded *the banking financial intermediaries* as one of the two key agents (the other being entrepreneurship) in the whole process of economic growth. He held the view that credit-creation by the commercial banking system is a monetary complement of the innovation process in the course of economic growth. Gurlay and Shaw, on the other hand, have considered *non-bank financial intermediaries* as highly essential to the growth process, because economic growth is accompanied by a process of financial innovation, in which primary securities become differentiated. It implies that the non-banking financial intermediaries, on the one hand, mobilise funds from *surplus-spending units* (households) by issuing them their own securities, called *secondary securities* and, on the other hand, they put funds at the disposal of the *deficit-spending units* (corporate firms) by acquiring their securities, called *primary securities.*

The growth of financial infrastructure in an economy embraces within its purview :

(*a*) the expansion in size and number of specialised financial intermediaries;

(*b*) the diversification and increase in financial instruments and financial assets; and

(*c*) the growth of an organised network of supporting financial markets.

Financial Markets

It needs to be emphasised that financial markets provide mechanism to trade in financial assets, through financial intermediaries. Thus, the financial markets by acting as a link between savers (households) and investors (firms) provide institutional arrangements to facilitate transfer of resources between them. Functionally, financial markets are broadly sub-divided under two heads : money market and capital market. Money market deals with short term funds, borrowed and lent for working capital to finance current assets. In fact, money market *is a short-term credit market.* **The capital market, on the other hand, deals with long-term funds, demanded and supplied to finance the creation or requisition of fixed assets.** The points of distinctions between money market and capital market can be summed up as follows :

(*a*)**Money Market** is a mechanism of the transfer of funds for a short period from surplus-spending units to deficit-spending units, whereas the **Capital Market** channelises long-term funds.

(*b*)In money market, the important financial instruments used are Bills of Exchange, Certificates of Deposits (CDs), Commercial Papers (CP), Inter-Bank Participations (IBPs) and Treasury Bills, whereas in capital market, the important financial instruments in use are shares, bonds, Government Securities and UTI's units.

(*c*)In money market, the important sub-markets are Inter-Bank call money market, Treasury bills market, Commercial bills market and Discount and Finance House of India (DFHI), whereas in capital market, the business is transacted through Industrial Securities Market (New Issue Market and Stock Exchange) and Government Securities Market (Gilt-edged Market).

(*d*)In money market, the main participants are commercial banks, whereas in capital market, the non-bank financial intermediaries are the main transactors.

(*e*)The money market is regulated by the Reserve Bank of India, whereas the capital market is regulated by the Securities Exchange Board of India (SEBI).

(*f*)The money market signals trends in liquidity and interest rates, thereby furnishing information for monetary policy formulation and management. In case of *Capital Market,* the role of monetary policy is *indirect* through bridge loans that banks provide to the corporate sector and *direct* through RBI's open market operations in the gild-edged market.

To sum up, money market and capital market, despite being operative in different spheres, constitute the *funds transfer mechanism* of the financial infrastructure of a country. Since *transfer mechanism* is crucial to the process of capital formation and economic development, the growth of financial infrastructure is a necessary condition for economic development. In view of this, since 1951, the RB1 and the Government of India have been pursuing policies to build up a strong financial infrastructure. It may be noted here that the recent measures, on the lines of the recommendations of the Narasimham Committee, to liberalise the financial sector would lead to speedy growth of India's financial infrastructure.

EQUITY MARKET IN INDIA

The capital market of a country represents a series of channels through which the savings of the community are made available for industrial and commercial enterprises and for public authorities. One of the channels of the transfer of community's savings to the investors is the mechanism of the purchase and sale of securities. The term *securities* refers to financial claims held by investors against the corporate entity at whose disposal the funds are placed. The three types of securities through which the joint stock companies raise funds are (*a*) *Equity Shares or Ordinary Shares or Common Stock,* (*b*) *Preference Shares*, and (*c*) *Bonds or Debentures*. These are often called *industrial securities*. The securities through which the Government of India, State Government and Local authorities raise funds are called the *Gilt-edged securities*.

The *securities market* refers to the buyers and sellers of securities and also the structure comprising all these agencies and institutions which help in the sale and resale of securities. The structure of securities market in India is depicted in Table 40.1. The scope and structure of the securities market can be analysed on the basis of this Table 40.1.

Table 40.1. The Structure of Securities Market

Securities Market

- Industrial Securities Market
  - New Issue Market
  - Secondary Market
    - Organised Stock Exchange
    - Over-the-Counter Market
      - Bonds
      - Equities
      - Preference Shares
- Government Securities Market
  - Over-the-Counter Market
    - New Issue Market
    - Secondary Market

1. Industrial Capital Market

The Industrial capital market refers to the market for shares and bonds of the existing companies, as well as those of new companies. This market is further divided into New Issue Market (NIM) and Old Issue Market. The New Issue Market is also called *Primary Market.* Likewise, the Old Issue Market is also called *Secondary Market* or Stock Exchange. However, it is important to emphasise that the New Issue Market and Stock Exchange are inter-linked and work in conjunction with each other. Although they differ from each other in the sense that the New Issue Market deals with 'new securities' issued for the first time to the public and Stock Exchange deals with those securities which have already been issued once to the public.

(*a*) **Primary Market:** The primary market is concerned with the floatation of new issues of shares or bonds. The firms floating new issues to raise funds may be new companies or existing companies planning expansions. The Merchant Banking Division of a commercial bank is asked by the company to advise on the viability of floatation of an issue before an issue is actually floated in the market. The stock issuing company also approaches the institutional underwriters like LIC, UTI, ICICI and IDBI, to ensure the marketability of an issue. The underwriters like LIC and UTI purchase securities from the New Issue Market to hold these in their own asset portfolio.

In Indian capital market, there are two main *ways of floating* new issues: (*a*) Public issues, and (*b*) Rights issues.

(*a*) **Public Issues** — The most popular method for floating securities in the New Issue Market is through a legal document called the " Prospectus". It is an open invitation to the public to subscribe to the issue at par or at premium.

(*b*) **Right Issues** — This method of the sale of stock is normally used by existing companies whose shares are already listed in the Stock Exchange. Right issue represents an invitation to the existing shareholders to subscribe to a part or the whole of the new issue in a fixed proportion to their shareholding.

Resource mobilisation through primary market by Indian corporate companies is shown in Table 40. 2 for the years 2007-08 to 2010-11. The primary capital market progressed significantly in 2009-10 and 2010-11 after the setback in 2008-09. The amounts of funds raised and the number of new issues which entered the primary market increased in 2009-10 and 2010-11. The total amount of capital raised through equity issues in 2009-10 was ₹ 46,736 crore as against ₹ 2082 crore in 2008-09. Due to global financial crisis in 2008, the primary capital market received a setback in 2008-09. The number of new issues declined sharply in 2008-09. Total amount of capital raised through equity issues during 2010-11 was ₹ 48,654 crore. The total number of initial public offerings (IPOs) in 2010-11 were only 55 as against 85 in 2007-08 and 39 in 2009-10. The amount mobilized by IPOs in 2010-11 was ₹ 35,569 as against ₹ 24,696 crore in the whole year 2009-10. The mean IPO size increased from ₹ 633 crore in 2009-10 to ₹ 671 crore in 2010-11. There was debt issue (*i.e.* issue of corporate bonds and debentures) to the tune of ₹ 2,500 crore in 2009-10 and ₹ 9,451 crore in 2010-11. There was no debt issue in 2007-2008. As will be seen from Table 40.2 the amount of capital mobilised *through private placement* in 2010-11 was ₹ 2,18,785 crore as compared to ₹ 2,12,635 crore in 2009-10. In the financial year 2011-12 resource mobilisation through the primary market was still greater. ₹ 35,611 crore was raised through sale of bonds by the corporate sector (*i.e.*, through debt mode) and ₹ 12,857 crore was raised through issue of equity and ₹ 2,61,282 crore were raised through primary primate placement. In this way the total of ₹ 3,09,750 crore were raised during financial year 2011-12. During the financial year (up to December 2012-13) resource mobilisation through primary market witnessed an upward movement and a total of ₹2,81,667 crores were raised in the first three quarters of 2012-13 (See Table 40.2)

Table 40.2. Resource mobilization through primary market

(₹ *crore*)

	Mode	2007-08	2008-09	2009-10	2010-11*	2011-12	2012-13*
1.	**Debt**	0	1,500	2,500	9,451	35,611	4,974
2.	**Equity**	54,511	2,082	46,736	48,654	12,857	13,050
	of which, IPOs	42,595	2,082	24,696	35,569	5,904	6,043
	Number of IPOs	85	21	39	55	34	20
	Mean IPO size	501	99	633	671	174	302
3.	**Private placement**	1,18,485	1,73,281	2,12,635	2,18,785	2,61,282	2,63,644
4.	**Euro issues (ADR/GDR)**	NA	NA	NA	NA	NA	NA
	Total (1 + 2 + 3 +4)	**2,16,176**	**1,79,066**	**2,81,871**	**2,76,890**	**3,09,750**	

Source : SEBI and RBI (for Euro Issues)

NOTE: NA Indicates Not Available. *As on 31 December 2012.

Initial Public Offer (IPO). As is seen from Table 40.2, the equity capital may be raised through IPO. IPO or Initial public offer is the first issue of shares by a corporate company to the general public to raise capital for expansion of its business. IPO is followed by a listing of its shares in the stock market. The issue of IPO by the Indian companies and the price of share that is fixed is regulated by SEBI. IPOs may be issued through the "Fixed Price Method" or through the book Building Procedure. In 2007-08 there were 85 IPOs but the number of IPOs declined to 39 only in 2009-10. In 2008-09, when global financial crisis hit the Indian economy, the number of IPOs had declined to only 21.

Private Placement. It will be seen from Table 40.2 that a lot of capital is raised through the private placement. An unlisted company which wants to raise equity funds but is not yet prepared to make an IPO may place privately its equity or equity related instruments with one or more sophisticated investors such as financial institutions, mutual funds, venture capital funds, banks etc. The private placements can be made by a company to the investors at any agreed price and quantity as such private equity issues are not regulated by SEBI.

The Securities and Exchange Board of India (SEBI) has effected several reforms in the New Issue Market. These reforms seek improved disclosure standards, prudential norms and simplification of issue procedures.

Improvements in Resource Mobilisation from the Primary Market

During April-May 2013, the total resource mobilisation from the primary equity market more than doubled to ₹ 9.3 billion compared with ₹ 3.9 billion mobilised during April-May 2012 (Table 40.3). The higher resource mobilisation in equity was due to a recovery in the secondary market and the floatation of a mega issue in May 2013. Resource mobilisation *via* the private placement route continued its growth momentum. During April-May 2013, mobilisation through private placements increased by nearly 59 per cent to ₹ 756 billion as compared to ₹ 475 billion in the corresponding period last year. Led by private sector mutual funds, resources mobilised by mutual funds during April-June 2013 also registered an increase to ₹ 956 billion as against net sales of ₹ 4,995 billion during April-June 2012.

Table 40.3. Primary Market Trends

Category		2012-13 (Apr-Mar)	2012-13 (Apr-June)	2013-14 (Apr-June)
1		2	3	4
a.	**Public Issue (*i*) + (*ii*)**	219	4*	11*
	(*i*) Public Issue (Equity)	65	4*	9*
	of which : IPOs	65	4*	9*
	FPOs	0	0*	0*
	(*ii*) Public Issue (Debt)	154	0*	1*
b.	Rights Issue	89	1*	0*
	Total Equity Issues (i + b)	155	4*	9*
c.	Euro Issues (ADR/GDR)	10	2	1
d.	Mutual Fund Mobilisation (net)	765	-4995	956
	(*i*) Private Sector	638	-3985	774
	(*ii*) Public Sector	127	-1010	182
e.	Private Placement in Corporate Debt market	3615	475*	756*
f.	QIP	160	0.3*	32*

Source : SEBI.

* : Data upto May

(*b*) Secondary market

The Secondary Market deals in existing securities. This market provides both liquidity and marketability to such securities. It implies that it is a market where a security can be bought or sold at small transaction cost. Although the Secondary Market deals with the purchase and sale of old securities, the firms issuing new securities get themselves registered on a Stock Exchange by applying for *listing* of shares. Listing offers the investor a 'market' for the sale of his stock.

The Secondary Market of Securities in India functions through its following two segments :

(*a*) Stock Exchange ;

(*b*) Over–the–Counter Market.

Stock Exchange. Stock Exchange is an organised market for the purchase and sale of *second hand* listed industrials and financial (*i.e.*, shares and debentures of corporate companies). Listed securities are those securities which appear on the approved list of a Stock Exchange. Only listed securities are traded on the floor of the Stock Exchange.

It is to be noted that an organised Stock Exchange is an 'auction' type of market, where the prices of traded securities are settled by open bids and offers on the floor of the exchange.

In a Stock Exchange, the transactions in stocks can be classified into two types:

(*a*) Investment transactions; and

(*b*) Speculative transactions.

Investment Transactions. An investment transaction in securities is that transaction which is concerned with the purchase of securities, with a view to investing funds to get an income as annual dividends from these securities and gain from the sale of these securities. The basic feature of an investment transaction is that it involves the *actual delivery* of the security and *payment of its full price.* An investment transaction is motivated by the considerations *of safety of investment* and *security of income.*

Speculative Transactions. The speculative transaction in securities is that transaction which is concerned with the purchase or sale of securities for the sake *of capital appreciation.* The basic feature of a speculative transaction is that the delivery of securities or the payment of the full price are rare. The speculator neither takes delivery of the securities sold by him; instead he only receives or pays the difference between the purchase and sale prices, as the case may be. **The trading in securities, without the intention of taking delivery or making payment, is called forward trading.** Under the Securities Contract (Regulation) Act. 1956 forward trading was perfectly legal till it was suspended in 1969 along with all the regulatory and penal measures. The suspension of forward trading created a real vacuum in the stock market. The stock brokers devised the *extra-legal badla system* to fill up this vacuum. Under this *badla system,* securities contract was turned into a carry-forward instrument merely by closing the contract on the 14th day and replacing it by a new hand-delivery contract between the same buyer and seller in respect of the same securities. Thus, only the difference between the 'contract price' and the 'market price' would change hands between the buyer and the seller. *Badla transactions* became the predominant form of Stock Exchange transactions. Since real transactions involving the transfer of securities became a microscopic minority, serious problem of excessive speculation developed in the stock market. In short, **the badla system led to excessive speculation and short–selling often amounting to gambling.** The Securities and Exchange Board of India (SEBI) banned the badla system in December 1993.

There was an increasing demand for the legitimate forward trading to give boost to the stock market. Since stock market quotations are often considered as the barometers of a country's economy, the SEBI and the Government should stimulate stock market. The SEBI, therefore, reintroduced badla (forward trading) on July 27, 1995. Now, with the **introduction of derivatives** in stock market the same purpose is served by the derivatives called **futures** as the old *badla system.*

The Bombay Stock Exchange is one of the 15 recognised Stock Exchanges in India. This Stock Exchange is popularly known as **Dalal Street Stock Market.** It handles around three-fourth of the total trading in securities in India. The number of companies listed on the Bombay Stock Exchange at the December-end 1993 was 3,585. Thus number of listed companies was even larger than in the developed countries stock markets of Japan, UK, Germany. Canada and France.

During the last two years several reform measures have been taken with regard to the working of secondary market. The important changes are explained below.

Rajiv Gandhi Equity Savings Scheme. On 23rd November 2012, the government notified a new tax saving scheme called the Rajiv Gandhi Equity Savings Scheme (RGESS), exclusively for first-time retail investors in the securities market. This scheme provides 50 per cent deduction of the amount invested from taxable income for that year to new investors who invest up to ₹ 50,000 and whose annual income is below ₹ 10 lakh. The operational guidelines were issued by SEBI on 6 December 2012.

Electronic Voting Facility made mandatory for top listed companies. As mandated in the Union Budget 2012-13 for top listed companies to offer electronic voting facility to their shareholders, SEBI has come out with the necessary amendments in this regard on 13 July 2012, to be incorporated in the equity listing agreement by stock exchanges. To make a beginning, based on market capitalization, electronic voting is now mandatory for the top 500 listed companies at the BSE and NSE, in respect of those businesses to be transacted through postal ballot.

SME Exchange/Platform. Separate trading platforms for SMEs were launched and became functional at the BSE and NSE in March 2012 and September 2012 respectively. As on 14 January 2013, the number of equities listed on the BSE and NSE SME platforms is 12 and 2 respectively.

Reduced Securities Transaction Tax for cash delivery transactions. Following the announcement in Union Budget 2012-13, the rate of the securities transaction tax (STT) has been revised downwards by 20 per cent to 0.1 per cent from 0.125 per cent for delivery-based transactions in the cash market, effective 1 July 2012.

Regulatory framework for governance and ownership of stock exchanges, clearing corporations, and depositories. Based on the recommendations of the Dr. Bimal Jalan Committee, new Securities Contracts (Regulation) (Stock Exchanges and Clearing Corporations) Regulations 2012 were notified on 20 June 2012 to regulate recognition, ownership, and governance in stock exchanges and clearing corporations, Further, the Securities and Exchange Board of India (Depositories and Participants) (Amendment) Regulations 2012 have been brought into effect from 11 September 2012 to regulate ownership and governance norms of depositories.

Expansion of Qualified Foreign Investors (QFIs) Scheme. In Budget 2011-12, the government, for the first time, permitted qualified foreign investors (QFIs), who meet the know-your-customer (KYC) norms, to invest directly in Indian MFs. In January 2012, the government expanded this scheme to allow QFIs to directly invest in Indian equity markets. Taking the scheme forward, as announced in Budget 2012-13, QFIs have also been permitted to invest in corporate debt securities and MF debt schemes subject to a total overall ceiling of US $ 1 billion. In May 2012, QFIs were allowed to open individual non-interest-bearing rupee bank accounts with authorized dealer banks in India for receiving funds and making payment for transactions in securities they are eligible to invest in. In June 2012, the definition of QFI was expanded to include residents of the member countries of the Gulf Cooperation Council (GCC) and European Commission (EC) as the GCC and EC are the members of the Financial Action Task Force (FATF).

Initiatives to attract FII Investment. As regards FII investment in debt securities, there has been progressive enhancement in the quantitative limits for investments in various debt categories. In June 2012, the FII limit for investment in G-Secs (government securities) was enhanced by US $ 5 billion, raising the cap to US $ 20 billion. The scheme for FII investment in long-term infra bonds has been made attractive by gradual reduction in lock-in and residual maturity periods criteria. In November 2012, the limits for FII investment in G- Secs and corporate bonds (non-infra category) have been further enhanced by $ 5 billion each, taking the total limit prescribed for FII investment to US $ 25 billion in G-Secs and US $ 51 billion for corporate bonds (infra + non-infra). FII debt allocation process has also been reviewed for bringing greater certainty among foreign investors and helping them periodically re-balance their portfolios in sync with international portfolio management practices.

Establishment of National Stock Exchange

An important step to provide efficient and transparent stock market culminated into the establishment of National Stock Exchange of India (NSEI) in July 1994. The NSEI opened membership to 13 cities, including Bombay, the commercial capital of India. The NSEI operates in its two segments: (*i*) Wholesale Debt Market (WDM) and (*ii*) Capital Market (CM). In the Wholesale Debt

Market. Government Securities, Treasury Bills, Public Sector Undertaking (PSU) bonds, Certificates of Deposits, Commercial Papers and Corporate Debentures are traded in. The main participants in this market are banks., financial institutions and large corporate firms. The RBI has directed banks to use only the NSEI for all transactions in debt securities instead of using the services of brokers so as to ensure transparent and regulated deals.

In the capital market, segment of NSEI, equities are traded in. In the capital market segment of NSEI, the number of securities admitted to trading has expanded from 200 to start with to 525 by December 1994. Thus, the National Stock Exchange of India (NSEI), with its scripless trading system, can be regarded as a milestone in the development of stock market in India.

In short, stock exchanges, as secondary market in industrial securities, ***furnish an important mechanism of imparting liquidity in Indian capital market.*** Of late, SEBI has evolved certain guidelines of rules and regulations to make stock exchanges to function in accordance with the principle of safety of the market, transparency and investor protection. The liberalisation, privatisation and globalisation (LPG) of Indian economy has led to the increase in volume of business in industrial securities in both the New Issue Market and Secondary Market (stock exchange) of Indian capital market.

TRENDS IN STOCK INDICES IN INDIA

In the secondary market segment, the market activity expanded sharply during 2007-08 with BSE and NSE indices scaling new peaks of 21,000 and 6,300 respectively, in January 2008. Although the indices showed some intermittent fluctuations, reflecting change in the market sentiments, the indices maintained their north-bound trend during the year. **This could be attributed to the larger inflows from Foreign Institutional Investors (FIIs) and wider participation of domestic investors,** particularly the institutional investors. During 2007, on a point-to-point basis, Sensex and Nifty Indices rose by 47.1 and 54.8 per cent, respectively. The buoyant conditions in the Indian bourses were aided by, among other things, India posting a relatively higher GDP growth amongst the emerging economies, continued uptrend in the profitability of Indian corporates, persistence of difference in domestic and international levels of interest rates, impressive returns on equities and a strong Indian rupee on the back of larger capital inflows.

Amongst the NSE indices, both Nifty and Nifty Junior delivered **record annual equity returns** (current year-end index divided by previous year-end index multiplied by 100) of 54.8 per cent and 75.7 per cent, respectively, during the calendar year 2007 . While Nifty gave compounded returns of 34.4 per cent, Nifty Junior recorded compounded returns of 38.4 per cent per year between 2003 and 2007. In terms of month-to-month movement, the NSE indices (Nifty and Nifty Junior) were subdued during February and August 2007, while they showed a rising trend during the rest of the year. The BSE sensex (top 30 stocks) too echoed a similar trend while the climb of BSE sensex during 2007-08 till September 2007 was the fastest, the journey of BSE sensex from 18,000 to 19,000 mark was achieved in just four trading sessions during October 2007.

BSE further crossed the 20,000 mark in December 2007 and 21,000 in an intra-day trading in January 2008. However, BSE and NSE indices declined subsequently reflecting concerns on global developments. BSE Sensex yielded a compounded return of 36.5 per cent per year between 2003 and 2007. In terms of simple average, BSE Sensex has given an annual return of more than 40 per cent during these three years (2007, 2008 and 2009). BSE Sensex 500 recorded compounded annual return of 38 per cent between 2003 and 2007.

As the stock indices scaled new highs, investors' wealth as reflected in market capitalization also rose correspondingly. The market capitalisation in India nearly doubled in 2007. The markets were more stable in 2007 as measured by the standard deviation of daily volatility of the Indian indices as compared to the previous year . The price-to-earnings (P/E) ratio, which partly discounts future corporate earnings reflecting investors' expectations of corporate profit, was higher at around 27 by end-December 2007 as compared to around 21 at end-December 2006. It is, however, noted that in the period January 2006 to December 2007, the volatility of weekly returns of Indian indices was higher as compared to indices outside India such as S&P 500 of United States of America and Kospi of South Korea.

In terms of institutional players, both FIIs and mutual funds leveraged their activity in the equity market during the year. While the net investment by FIIs in both spot and derivative markets witnessed quantum increases during 2007, the corresponding gross buy and sell by FIIs too increased significantly. In 2007 FIIs net activity (gross buy/gross sell) constituted 17.3 per cent of the spot market and 9 per cent of the derivative market . The number of registered FIIs rose to 1,219 at the end of 2007 from 1,044 in the corresponding period of last year; the number of sub-accounts also increased to 3,644 from 3,045 over the same period.

Sharp Decline in Stock Indices in 2008

In the secondary market segment, the market activity began on a bullish note with BSE and NSE indices scaling new peaks of 20,873 and 6,287 on January 8, 2008. However, this momentum could not be sustained and the indices recorded significant downtrend in line with the decline in all the major international indices during the second half of January 2008. *In fact, intra-day fall of 1,968 points in absolute terms in BSE Sensex on January 21, 2008 was the highest recorded fall in the history of Sensex.* Despite intermittent corrections in the stock market, the market sentiment remained bearish due to the rising domestic inflation, increasing oil prices and volatility in international financial markets (in the wake of uncertainties about US sub-prime mortgage market and credit market exposures) and negative portfolio investment flows during February-March 2008. The indices showed some improvement during April 2008 in line with positive cues from the global markets.

Global Financial Crisis and Volatility in Indian Capital Market in 2008. The global financial crisis had an adverse effect on the Indian capital markets though the Indian market started the year 2008 on a highly bullish trend with both BSE and NSE indices touching new peaks of 20,873 and 6,288 points respectively, the sentiments thereafter got adversely affected reflecting the impact of global financial crisis.

On account of the global financial market crisis, the primary market and secondary market remained subdued in 2008. After recording strong growth during 2006 and 2007, the primary capital market received a setback in 2008. Total amount of capital raised through equity issues during 2008 was ₹ 49, 485 crore, recording a decline of 15.7%, against the 2007 level, reflecting the bearish trend, the share prices fell sharply in 2008 and as a result the market capitalisation of shares traded on BSE and NSE declined substantially in 2008. On a year-on-year basis the market capitalisation dipped around 50 per cent at end-December 2008 as compared to end-December 2007 (For example, in case of BSE sensex, market capitalisation declined from 28,61,341 crore at end-Dec. 2007 to 14,63,165 crore at end-Dec. 2008 (see Table 40.4).

The **volatility** of weakly returns of Indian stock indices increased in 2008-09 and was even higher than that of indices outside India such as S & P 500 of the USA and Kospi of South Korea. Reflecting the fall in the share prices in the Indian equity markets, *the market capitalisation* of shares traded on BSE and NSE declined sharply in 2008-09 (See Table 40.4). On a year-on-year basis, the market capitalisation (as per NIFTY) which had reached record levels in 2007-08 of ₹ 12,40,071 crore dipped to 7,71,483 crore in 2008-09 but again rose to 15,25,162 crore in 2009-10 and to ₹ 18,27,097 (till December 2010) in 2010-11 (See Table 40.4).

Table 40.4. Equity Returns, Volatility, Market Capitalization, and P/E ratio

Index	2006-07	2007-08	2008-09	2009-10	2010-2011
NIFTY					
Returns (per cent)	12.3	23.9	–36.2	73.8	17.9
Market Capitalization (₹ crore)	9,27,098	12,40,071	7,71,483	15,25,162	18,27,097
Daily volatility*	1.8	2.0	2.6	1.9	1.0
P/E Ratio	18.4	20.6	14.3	22.2	24.5
Nifty Junior					
Return (per cent)	7.3	16.0	–45.6	148.4	17.8
Market Capitalization (₹ crore)	13,76,826	2,02,809	1,13,523	2,92,316	3,37,573
Daily Volatility*	2.0	2.4	2.8	2.0	1.1
P/E Ratio	18.5	16.7	8.7	15.8	17.6
BSE Sensex					
Return (per cent)	15.9	19.7	–37.9	80.5	17.0
Market Capitalization (₹ crore)	8,31,033	10,71,940	6,95,152	13,28,862	16,32,236
Daily volatility*	1.8	1.9	2.8	1.9	1.0
P/E Ratio	20.3	20.1	13.7	21.3	23.6
BSE 500					
Return (per cent)	9.7	24.3	–42.8	96.4	15.1
Market Capitalization (₹ crore)	4,56,632	19,96,839	11,68,850	24,44,151	29,52,135
Daily Volatility*	1.7	2.0	2.6	1.8	1.0
P/E Ratio	17.7	20.0	13.7	20.4	21.4

Sources : BSE and NSE *Standar Deviation values

Note: $ As on 31 December 2010

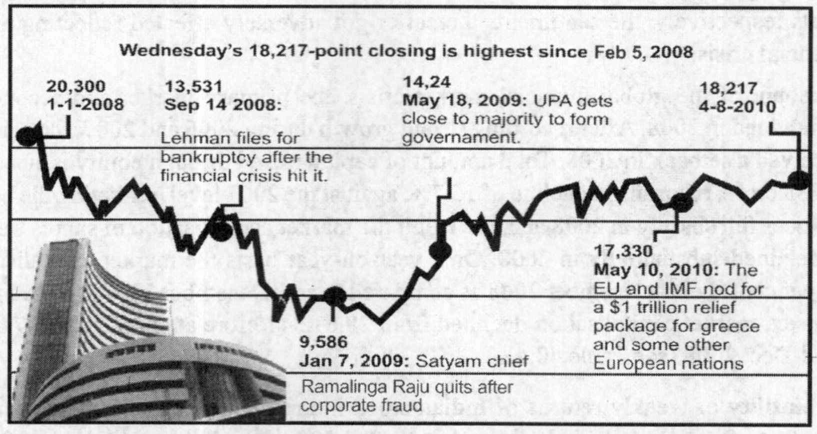

Fig. 40.1. Fall and Rise of BSE Sensex 2008-09 and 2009-10.

Market volatility as measured by the standard deviation of daily volatility of the Indian indices increased significantly in 2008-09. For example, daily volatility in case of BSE sensex which was 1.8 in 2006-07 rose to 2.6 in 2008-09 (see Table 40.4).

Besides, the *price-to-earnings (P/E)* ratio, which partly discounts future corporate earnings reflecting investors' expectations of corporate profit, declined in 2008-09 in all the market segments reflecting the downward trend in stock prices. P/E ratio in India in 2008-09 was 13.7 and was even

Table 40.5. P/E Ratios in Select Emerging Markets

Country	Index	2008-09	2009-10	2010-2011*
Korea	Kospi	25.7	11.1	14.8
Thailand	SET	15.7	12.3	15.0
Indonesia	Jakarta Composite	20.1	16.6	20.9
Malaysia	Ruais lumour comp.	15.0	18.9	17.4
Taiwan	TSEC weighted	65.7	19.1	15.7
India	BSE Sensex	13.7	21.3	23.6
India	S&P Nifty	14.3	22.3	24.5

Source: BSE, NSE and 11

Note: *As on 31 December 2010.

lower than the stock exchange P/E rates of Korea, Thailand, Indonesia, Malaysia, Taiwan. (See Table 40.4.). Even volatility of weekly return in Indian equity markets was quite high in 2008-09 but it fell in 2009-10 and 2010-11. It is worth mentioning that after reaching the bottom in January-March 2009, BSE Sensex started rising after March 2009 as will be seen from Fig. 40.2 and reached 14,284 on May 18, 2009 and 15,500 in the first week of July 2009. On Aug. 21, 2009, it again touched 15,250 and with slight variations during September it crossed 17,000 mark on September 30, 2009. It continued with little variation from time to time its upward journey and reached 17,330 mark on May 10, 2010 when EU and IMF approved a $ trillion relief package for Greece and other European nations. Again with slight weekly variations it rose to 18,217 mark on August 4, 2010 (See Fig. 40.1).

Transactions by FIIs (Foreign Institutional Investors)

Portfolio investment by FIIs has played an important role in bringing capital flows into India in recent years. In fact they have been calling shot in Indian stock market: When in 2006 and 2007 large capital inflows were made by them to purchase shares of the Indian companies the stock indices of India shot up leading to large capital appreciation of Indian stockholders

Table 40.6: Transactions of FIIs

(₹ Crore)

Transactions		Calendar Year	
	2008-09	2009-10	2010-11*
Number of FIIs (actual)	1635	1713	1718
Number of Sub-accounts (actual)	5015	5378	5503
1. Equity market activity (₹ Crore)			
Gross buy	5,54,585	7,05,523	6,03,406
Gross sell	6,02,292	5,95,302	4,90,785
Net	–47,706	1,10,221	1,12,622
2. Debt market activity (₹ Crore)			
Gross buy	59,993	1,40,914	1,54,081
Gross sell	58,098	1,08,477	1,29,241
Net	1,895	32,438	24,839
3. Total Activity (₹ Crore)			
Gross buy	6,14,579	8,46,437	7,57,487
Gross sell	6,60,389	7,03,779	6,20,026
Net	–45,811	1,42,658	1,37,461

Source : SEBI

Note: *As on 31 December, 2010

On the other hand, when following global financial crisis FIIs sold the shares in Indian stock market on a large scale and sent back capital to their home countries in 2008 there was crash in Indian stock market which caused huge losses of wealth of Indians.

It will be seen from Table 40.6 that during 2008-09 FIIs were net sellers in equity market in India to the extent of ₹ 47,706 crore. The overall (both equity and debt) of net outflow investment by FIIs in 2008-09 was ₹ 45,811 crore. In 2009-10 and 2010-11 (up to December 31, 2010) in both the Indian equity set and debt market, FIIs were *net buyers*. In 2009-10, they were net buyers in equity market to the tune of ₹110,221 crore and in 2010-11 (up to December 31, 2010) they were net buyers of equity worth ₹ 1,12,622 crore. Similarly, in 2009-10 and 2010-11 they were net buyers of Indian bonds (*i.e.*, debt) of ₹ 32,438 crore and ₹ 24,839 crore respectively.

The number of registered FIIs increased to 1,718 as on 31 December 2010 from 1,713 on 31 March 2010. The number of registered sub-accounts also increased to 5,503 from 5,378 during the same period.

Resource Mobilisation by Mutual Funds

In India in recent years resource mobilisation through mutual funds has acquired greater importance. It is generally believed that mutual funds cater to the needs of retail investors. However, the capital structure of the mutual funds reveals that over 60 per cent of subscriptions to mutual funds still come from corporates.

In line with the rising trend in resources raised in the primary market, the net inflow of savings into mutual funds increased by 60 per cent in 2007-08 to ₹ 1,53,802 crore as compared to ₹ 93,985 crore in 2006-07. The sharp increase in funds flowing into mutual funds during 2007-08 was partly due to buoyant equity markets and partly to the efforts made by the Indian mutual funds to introduce innovative schemes. The private sector mutual funds outperformed the public sector mutual funds in terms of resource mobilisation in 2007. The share of UTI and other public sector mutual funds in total amount mobilised gradually declined over the years to 17.8 per cent in 2006-07 and further to 12.7 per cent in 2007-08.

Table 40.7: Trends in Resource Mobilisation (Net) by Mutual Funds

(₹ crore)

Sector	*Financial Year*						
	2006-07	**2007-08**	**2008-09**	**2009-10**	**2010-11**	**2011-12**	**2012-13#**
1. UTI	7,326	10,677	–3659	15,653	–16636	–3184	10617
2. Public Sector	7,621	9,820	9,380	12,499	–13555	–3394	8746
3. Private Sector	79,038	1,33,304	–34,018	54,928	–19215	–22024	100906
4. Total (1 + 2 + 3)	**93,985**	**1,53,802**	**–28,296**	**83,080**	–49406	–28602	120269

Source : SEBI

Note : *As on 30 November, 2010

Reflecting the volatile capital market conditions, the net inflow of saving into mutual funds, which had recorded a steady rise during 2005-08, turned negative in 2008-09. The private sector mutual funds witnessed heavy redemption pressure in 2008-09 and recorded a *net outflow* of ₹ 34,018 crore as will be seen from Table 40.7. The Unit Trust of India (UTI) also recorded net redemption to the extent of ₹ 3,659 crore in 2008-09, while the public sector mutual funds (other than UTI) mobilised positive amount of ₹ 9,380 crore in 2008-09. The change reflected changing risk preference of investors towards public sector institutions in times of global financial crisis (see Table 40.7). During 2010-11 and 2011-12 there was large scale redemption from mutual funds, 49,406 crore in 2010-11 and 28,602 crore in 2011-12. After two years of redemption pressures, mutual funds (MF) mobilised ₹ 1,20,269 from the market in 2012-13 (See Table 40.7). The market value of their assets under management stood at ₹ 7,59,995 crore as on 31 December, 2012 compared to ₹ 5,87,217 crore as on 31 December, 2012 indicating an increase of 29.4 per cent.

Movements of Stock Indices in 2010-11 and 2011-12. The year 2010 has been one of strong growth for the Indian capital markets. Bulls tossed off the markets in the year 2010 to a net gain of 18 per cent, following global recovery and with FIIs pumping money into the market on account of solid domestic growth coupled with a resurging corporate sector. Indices achieved record highs during the special one-hour *muhurat* trading on 5 November 2010 with the Sensex touching 21004.96 and Nifty 6312.45. As on 31 December 2010, the markets stood just 3 per cent away from this all-time peak and closed at 20509.09 (+ 17.43 per cent from 31 December 2009 for the Sensex) and 6134.5 (+ 17.95 per cent for Nifty).

Indian markets had been making gains for eight quarters in a row, their longest winning run in at least 20 years. While 2009 was basically a year of recovery from the crisis year of 2008, 2010 was one of consolidation of gains. From 9647 on 31st December 2008, the Sensex climbed to 17464.81 on 31 December 2009 and further consolidated its rally at 20509.09 on 31 December 2010. The total market capitalization as on 31 December 2010 stood at ₹ 72,96,725 crore compared to ₹ 60,81,308 crore as on 31 December, 2009.

Reasons for Stock Market Movements in 2010-11

Markets rose on the strong health of the Indian corporate sector; also advance tax payments by India's top 100 corporate taxpayers rose by 18.7 per cent in December from a year ago, indicating better corporate performance in the third quarter, reinforcing the belief in fundamentals of the Indian economy in the market sphere. India's economy surpassed the Government's growth target for the fiscal year, giving further fillip to bourses on the domestic front. There was 9.3 per cent growth in India's GDP in 2010-11.

FII Inflows at Historical Levels: Historically low yields in developed markets due to accommodative monetary policies and weak economic prospects pushed FII inflows to emerging markets to record highs. The primary market of India got a new lease of life, the calendar year 2010 with Indian companies raising ₹ 69,192 crore through IPOs and FPOs. This was 3.5 times higher than the previous year (₹ 19,567 crore) and 53 per cent higher than the earlier record of ₹ 45,142 crore in 2007. Over 72 per cent of the year's total mobilization was accounted for by public sector units (PSUs). The year also witnessed the largest ever IPO in India–of ₹ 15,199 crore–from Coal India, which single-handedly accounted for 22 per cent of the year's total mobilization.

Global recovery also resulted in an upsurge in the markets. Boosting sentiments across the globe, the US economy expanded at a 2.6 per cent annual rate in the third quarter, marking a pickup in growth as consumers and companies gained confidence to spend. Globally, leaders were striving to keep the pace of growth intact.

Decline in Stock Prices in 2011-12

Concern that Greece might either default on paying back of its debt or unable to meet budgetary deficit targets under austerity programme imposed on it by EU and IMF hit stock markets hard all over the world. Similar sovereign debt crisis spread to Spain and Italy. IMF also came to the rescue of Italy to tide over its payment problem concerning sovereign debt. From April 2011 as revealed by Figure 40.2 BSE sensex started falling. Foreign investors (FIIs) started selling shares in the Indian stock market due to uncertain global environment. In May 2011, BSE Sensex fell to 18,998 and further to 18,763 in June 2011. When in August 2011 the US was downgraded by S&P due to its high sovereign debt, this caused huge slide in BSE Sensex in September and October. BSE Sensex fell to 16821 in September 2011 and further to 16152 on October 3, 2011.

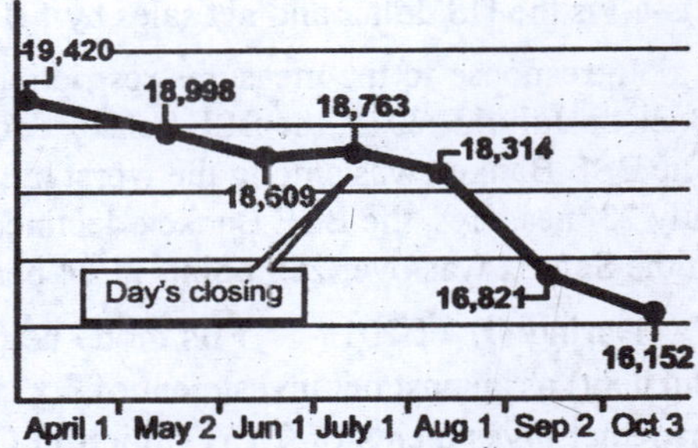

Fig. 40.2. *How the BSE Sensex Moved in the Fiscal Year 2011-12.*

Developments in 2012-13 and Stock Market Changes in 2012 and 2013

During 2012 and early 2013, global bond and equity markets had significantly rallied following central banks' massive quantitative easing (QE) programmes in the US economies. Though global growth remained sluggish, the risk appetite improved and the markets aggressively priced the perceived reduction in risks. However, during Q1 of 2013-14, particularly in May and June, the global financial markets experienced renewed turbulence. This followed the signalling by the Chairman of the US Federal Reserve on May 22, 2013 that the Fed may taper off its bond purchase programme (*i.e.,* QE policy) if economic conditions improve rapidly. The signal was followed by a more explicit forward guidance by the US Fed governor on June 19, 2013 on moderating its bond purchases starting later this year and, in a phased manner, unwinding the QE by mid-2014. The subsequent statement by the Fed of a 'highly accommodative' monetary policy in July appears to have calmed the market to a large extent.

It may be observed in this context that the balance sheets of central banks in advanced economies have expanded significantly since the inception of the crisis in 2007. Therefore, the US Fed's signal of an exit from QE raised the prospects of the global interest cycle turning thus posing the prospects of significant losses on existing bond holdings. Consequently, there was a bond by FII all over the globe. Asian markets came under intense pressure as the bond sell-off was accompanied by the reverse flight of capital back into the US.

Emerging developing economies. As portfolio capital, especially in bond markets, witnessed outflows from emerging developing economies their currencies came under severe pressure. This, in turn, added to the sell-offs in the equity markets by global investors, especially in EMDE markets.

Following Fed. governor's announcement on May 22, 2013, the rupee depreciated to ₹ 61.05 on July 26, 2013. The announcement by RBI some measures to check excessive outflows of foreign exchange rupee further depreciated and touched a record level of ₹ 68.83 on Aug. 28, 2013, share price index (both Sensex and Nifty) sharply declined. But when assured that they are not capital controls on outflows of foreign exchange stock market recovered but showed a good deal of fluctuations

During the financial year 2013-14 (up to July 26, 2013), the BSE Sensex and CNX Nifty recorded gains of 4.8 per cent and 3.6 per cent, respectively (Fig. 40.3). The stock market recorded significant gains at the beginning of the quarter due to sustained FII buying and easing of concerns about the twin deficits due to moderation in commodity prices. However, the market lost some of its earlier gains in June 2013 due mainly to worries over capital outflows arising from the signals of gradual tapering of monetary stimulus by the US Fed and weak industrial output data of the domestic economy. Other ancillary factors such as the weak growth outlook for China, the persistent weakness of the rupee vis-a-vis the US dollar and net sales by FIIs reinforced the pressures.

In response to the measures restricting foreign exchange outflows announced by the Reserve Bank on July 15, 2013, the BSE Sensex declined by over 180 points (0.9 per cent) on July 16, 2013. The BSE Bankex was among the worst hit, declining by nearly 5 per cent. Reflecting the impact of July 23 measures, the BSE Bankex declined by 590 points (4.6 per cent) on July 24, while the drop in the Sensex was over 200 points (1.04 per cent).

During Q1 of 2013-14 FIIs mode net sales of ₹ 90 billion in the capital market (both equity and debt) as against net investment of ₹ 19 billion during Q1 of 2012-13. In the equity market, FIIs made net investments of ₹ 153 billion in Q1 of 2013-14 as against net sales of ₹ 7 billion during Q1 of the previous year, while in the debt market, FIIs made net sales of ₹ 243 billion in Q1 of 2013-14 as against net investment of ₹ 25 billion in Q1 of the previous year (Table 40.8). However, after the response of the US Fed Governor on May 22, 2013, both debt and equity markets recorded net outflows amounting to ₹ 522 billion and ₹ 116 billion, respectively, between May 22 and July 24, 2013.

However, with postponement of tapering of quantitative easing by US Federal Reserve from mid-September 2013 BSE Sensex started rising and on October 18, 2013, it closed at 20,883 – a three year high, raising investors' wealth as measured by BSE's market capitalisation (See Fig. 40.3).

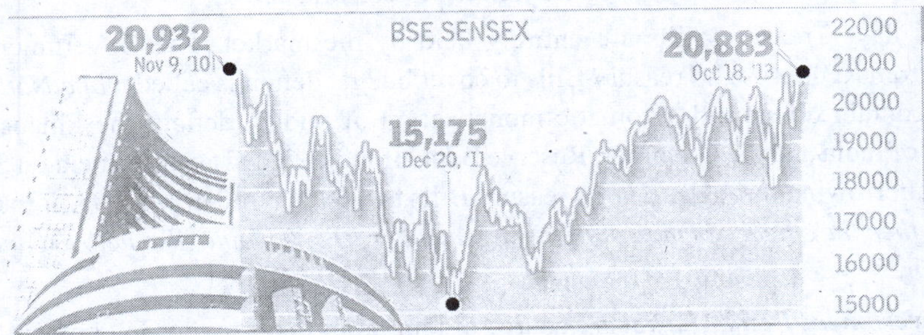

Fig. 40. 3 : Movement of BSE Sensex

Table 40.8 : Investment by FIIs in Equity and Debt Market

(₹ *billion*)

	Equity Market	*Debt Market*	*Total*
1	2	3	4
FII			
Q1 2012-13	–6.6	25.3	18.7
Q2 2012-13	397.5	44.6	442.1
Q3 2012-13	455.4	96.1	551.5
Q4 2012-13	560.1	148.7	708.9
Q1 2013-14	152.9	–243.3	–90.3
Q2 2013-14@	–61.6	–126.9	–188.4

@ Till July 2013

GOVERNMENT SECURITIES MARKET (GILT-EDGED MARKET)

The term 'gilt edged' means the 'best quality'. Since Government Securities are of best quality in the sense of liquidity and zero degree of the risk of default, so these are called gilt-edged securities. In the Gilt-edged Market, the securities of the Government of India and of the State Governments are traded in. The securities guaranteed (as to both principal and interest) by the Government are also traded in this market.

The importance of Government Securities Market, that is, Gilt-edged Market, as a segment of the capital market, emanates from the fact that this market provides a mechanism for the management of public debt and open market operations to the Reserve Bank of India (RBI). It is, therefore, imperative to emphasise that this market has a strong bearing on the formulation of the *fiscal policy* of the Government of India and the *monetary policy* of RBl. The Gilt-edged Market has two segments: *Treasury Bill Market* and *Government Bond Market*.

The *Treasury Bill Market* is a source of short term funds for the Government. A Treasury Bill is a promissory note, that is, a liability of the Government of India. The Treasury Bills are of the maturity period of 91 days, 182 days and 364 days. The RBI sells Treasury Bills on behalf of the Government of India. It is important to point out that RBI is the chief holder of these bills. Outside it, commercial banks hold these bills. Thus, the Treasury Bills Market is a captive market. The

Indian Treasury Bills Market is underdeveloped as compared to U.S.A. and U.K. However, recently RBI has initiated certain reforms in the Treasury Bill Market to transform its captivity character to broad-based market character. The RBI reduces its holdings of Treasury Bills by converting them into dated-Government Securities at market-related interest rates.

The 364 days Treasury Bills are entirely held by the market. The Government of India's borrowings from RBI through Treasury Bills to cover budget deficit is called *monetisation of deficit.* In order to contain direct and automatic monetisation of budget deficit, the Finance Secretary, Government of India and the Governor, Reserve Bank of India signed an agreement on September 9, 1994 to limit borrowing through *ad hoc* Treasury Bills to ₹ 6000 crore in 1994-95. *It is an important step to strengthen the efficacy of monetary management by RBI. It would also help to control inflation in the economy.*

The ***Government Bond Market*** is a source of long-term funds to the Government of India and State Governments. *The Government bonds are dated securities which are floated to raise medium and long–term loans in the open market.* It is significant to note that it is generally the *institutions,* instead of individuals, that are the buyers of Government bonds. It is due to relatively lower interest rate, long maturity period and face value in high denominations that the individuals are found to be reluctant to invest their funds in Government bonds. The institutions like commercial banks, LIC and G1C buy the Government bonds to build up their asset portfolio. These institutions invest in Government bonds as they are required by law to invest a certain minimum proportion of their total funds in these bonds. Left to themselves, they would not like to buy these bonds owing to low interest rate on them. The RBI, as a manager of public debt, operates on the *supply* side of the Government bond market. At the end of the subscription period, RBI holds the stock of unsold Government bonds and keeps them selling on its own account.

The Government bond market is a captive market. The RBI is launching a system of primary dealers for deepening and expanding the Government bond market. The Securities Trading Corporation of India was set up in 1993-94 to develop the secondary market in Government securities.

Growth of Central Government's Securities

The growth of Securities Market is an integral part of the process of economic growth in a free market economy. Of late, the RBI and the Government of India have pursued certain measures to reform the Securities market. These reforms have been introduced in both the New Issue Market and the Secondary Market of industrial securities and Government securities.

The average daily trading volume of central government securities in the secondary market increased to around ₹ 570 billion during Q1 of 2013-14 from ₹ 376 billion during Q4 of 2012-13. The traded volume in G-secs generally varied inversely with G-sec yields.

The gross market borrowings of the

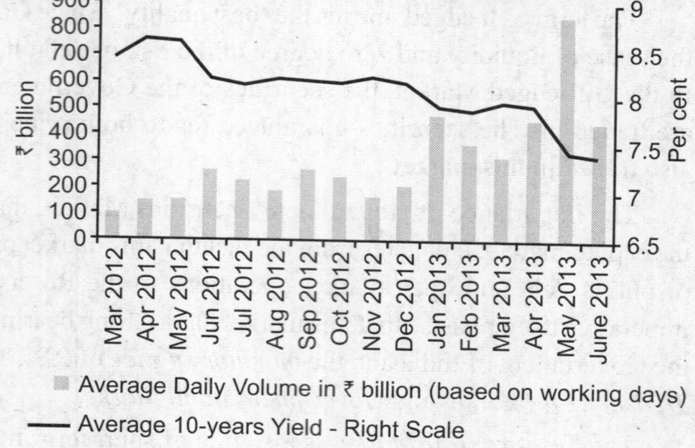

Fig 40.4. *Average Daily Volume and 10-Year Weighted Average*

central government through dated securities during 2013-14 were to the tune of ₹ 2,100 billion (net borrowings of ₹ 1,972 billion) up to July 26, 2013 compared with ₹ 2,340 billion (net borrowings of ₹ 1,594 billion) during the corresponding period of the previous year. The weighted average maturity of the dated securities increased to 14.96 years from 13.62 years during the corresponding period of the previous year. The weighted average yield during the primary auctions eased to 7.64 per cent from 8.52 per cent during the corresponding period of the previous year. The weighted average yield during the primary auctions eased to 7.64 per cent from 8.52 per cent during the corresponding period of the previous year (Table 40.9). The bid-cover ratio stood in the range of 1.41-6.09 as against 1.47-3.59 during the corresponding period of the previous year. The government availed of ways and means advances (WMA) on three occasions up to end-June 2013. As on July 16, 2013 the outstanding WMA position of the government was ₹ 3.06 billion.

Table 40.9 : Issuances of Central and State Government Dated Securities*

Item	2012-13	2013-14
1	2	3
Central Government		
Gross amount raised (₹ billion)	1880	1650
Development on primary dealers (₹ billion)	11.95	Nil
Bid-cover ratio (range)	1.47-3.59	2.38-6.08
Weighted average maturity (years)	13.38	17.92
Weighted average yield (per cent)	8.57	7.57**
State Government		
Gross amount raised (₹ billion)	310.9	379.1
Cut-off yield range (per cent)	8.80-9.31	7.57-8.51
Weighted average yield (per cent)	9.07	7.92

* Up till July 3, 2013. Includes Inflation-Indexed Bond (IIB) issuances.

During 2013-2014 (up to July 16, 2013), 18 states have raised ₹ 401.2 billion on a gross basis (net amount of ₹ 252.3 billion) compared with ₹ 419.8 billion (net amount of ₹ 369.6 billion) raised by 20 states during the corresponding period of the previous year. The weighted average yield eased to 7.98 per cent up to July 16, 2013 from 9.01 per cent during the corresponding period of the previous year.

CORPORATE DEBT MARKET

In pursuance of the guidelines of the High Level Expert Committee on Corporate Bonds and Securitisation (December 2005) and the subsequent announcement made in the Union Budget 2006-07, SEBI authorised BSE (January 2007), NSE (March 2007) and Fixed Income Money Market and Derivatives Association of India (FIMMDA) (August 2007) to set up and maintain corporate bond reporting platforms for capturing all information related to trading in corporate bonds as accurately as possible. In the second phase of development, BSE and NSE put in place corporate bonds trading platforms in July 2007 to enable efficient price discovery in the market. Reflecting these developments, trading in corporate bonds increased significantly in terms of number of issues and amount raised through them.

Economy vibrancy coupled with sophisticated state-of-the-art financial infrastructure has contributed to rapid growth in the equity markets in India. In terms of market features and depth the Indian equity market ranks among the best in the world. In parallel, the Government securities market has also evolved over the years and expanded given the increasing borrowing requirements of the Government. In contrast, the corporate bond market has languished both in terms of market participation and structure. Non-bank finance companies are the main issuers and very small amounts of finance are raised by these companies directly. There are several reasons for this :

(*i*) Predominance of bank loans;

(*ii*) FII's participation is limited;

(*iii*) Pensions and insurance companies and households are limited participants because of lack of investor confidence; and

(*iv*) Crowding out by Government bonds.

The corporate bond market as a result is only about 14 per cent of the total bond market; and market liquidity and infrastructure remain constrained. With the implementation of the Patil Committee recommendations, the corporate bond market is slowly evolving.

With bank finance drying up for long-term infrastructure projects in view of asset liability problems faced by banking system, the need for further development of a deep and vibrant corporate bond market can hardly be overemphasized. The following table shows the status of corporate bond market in India:

Table 40.10. Private Placement of Corporate Bonds Listed on NSE and BSE

(₹ *Crore*)

Year	*No. of Issues*	*Amount*
2007-08	744	1,18,485
2008-09	1041	1,73,281
2009-10	1278	2,12,635
2010-11 (till Nov. 10)	929	1,47,400

Source: SEBI (Includes NBFCs)

Earlier initiatives taken for development of corporate bond market in India

1. Regulatory jurisdiction over corporate bond market has been clearly defined and placed under SEBI. SEBI (Issue and Listing of Debt Securities) Regulations, 2008 simplified disclosures and listing requirements. A minimum market lot criterion has been reduced from ₹ 10 lakhs to ₹ 1 lakh to encourage retail investors.
2. The limit of FIIs investment in corporate bonds has been increased to US$ 20 billion from the existing limit of US$ 15 billion and the incremental limit of US$ 5 billion has to be invested in corporate bonds with residual maturity of over five years.
3. BSE, NSE and FIMMDA have set up reporting platforms. Aggregate data reported on these platforms is disseminated to the public. Summary data is available on SEBI website. Repos in corporate bonds have been permitted, following RBI guidelines, since March 2010. Exchange traded interest rates futures were introduced in August 2009.
4. Draft Credit Default Swap, (CDS) guidelines have been released by RBI in July, 2010.
5. The Finance Act, 2008 (with effect from 01.06.2008) mandated that no TDS (tax deduction at source) would be deducted from any interest payable on any security issued by a company, where such security is issued in dematerialized form and is listed on a recognized stock exchange in India. The stamp duty on items in Central List (debentures and bonds in the nature of promissory note) have been brought down and made uniform.

6. Clearing and Settlement through clearing corporations have been mandated for trades between specified entities, namely, mutual funds, foresight institutional investors, venture capital funds etc. Clearing and Settlement is on DvPI basis.

Suggested initiatives to be taken for further development of corporate bond market (Agency responsible is indicated in bracket) :

1. Clearing and settlement on DvP (Delivery versus Payment) III basis. Market making with primary dealers. Enabling credit default Swap. Allowing banks to do credit enhancement-Guaranteeing of corporate bonds by banks. Relaxing norms on short-selling of Government bonds. (RBI)
2. Relaxing norms for use of shelf prospectus requires amendment to Section 60 of Companies Act (MCA).
3. Empowering bond holder under SARFAESI (Department of Financial Services, RBI).
4. Creating of a comprehensive bond data base (RBI, SEBI, FIMMDA).
5. Amendment to Section 9 of the Stamp Act to lower stamp duties across states and make them uniform (Department of Revenue).

The yield on corporate debt paper (with AAA rating) for five-year maturity ranged between 8.13 per cent and 11.64 per cent during 2008-09.The spread between yield on five-year GoI bonds and Indian corporate debt paper (AAA rating) with five-year maturity, which had moved in a range of 133-223 basis points between April-August 2008, widened thereafter to reach as high as 416 basis points in November 2008, which reflected tight liquidity conditions in the market. However, it narrowed down from December 2008 and was around 200 basis points by the end of March 2009.

GROWTH OF INDIAN CAPITAL MARKET

The planned industrialisation process initiated in 1951 brought into focus the need for the capital market to grow. It was realised that the rapid growth of capital market was an essential condition for the growth of private corporate sector. The present scenario of Indian capital market is radically different from that what it was in 1951. It has undergone structural changes in terms of financial assets traded in and financial intermediaries operating in it. The *various developments in the Indian capital market, removing its basic deficiencies, can be reviewed as follows:*

1. Growth in Financial Intermediation

The Indian capital market has grown due to innovation of the mechanism of *indirect financing.* This innovation has enhanced the efficiency of flow of funds from ultimate savers to ultimate users through newly established financial intermediaries like UTI, LIC and GIC. The LIC has been mobilising the savings of households to build a 'life fund'. It has been deploying a part of 'life fund' to purchase the shares and debentures of the companies. Until 1991 UTI was amongst the top ten shareholders in one out of every three companies listed in the Stock Exchange in which it had a shareholding. Likewise, UTI has been mobilising savings of households through the sale of 'units' to invest in securities of 'blue-chip' companies.

In short, financial intermediaries like LIC, UTI and GIC have activised the growth process of Indian capital market. It is evident from the rising *intermediation ratio.* The *intermediation ratio* is a ratio of the volume of financial instruments issued by the financial institutions, *i.e.,* secondary securities to the volume of primary securities issued by non-financial corporate firms rose from 0.27 during 1951-56 to 0.37 during 1979-80 to 1981-82.

2. Growth in Underwriting of Securities

The New Issue Market as a segment of capital market can be activised through institutional arrangements for the underwriting of new issues of securities. During the pre-independence period, the volume of securities underwritten was quite minimal due to lack of an adequate institutional arrangement for the provision of underwriting. Stock brokers and banks used to perform this function. In recent years, the volume and amount of securities underwritten have tremendously increased owing to increasing participation of specialised financial institutions like LIC and UTI and the developed banks like 1FC1, 1CICI and IDBI in underwriting activities. It is evident from the fact that the amount of securities underwritten was only 55 per cent in 1960-61, whereas at present it is about 99 per cent.

3. Growth in Response to the Offer of Public Issues of Shares and Bonds

Traditionally investors in India being risk-investors had been reluctant to invest in shares of public limited companies. Hence, industrial securities as a form of investment were not popular in India before 1951. However, since 1991 public response to corporate securities has been improving. But equity-cult has yet to be developed in rural areas. It is important to point out that the public response to new issues of shares and bonds depends upon number of factors such as rates of return on industrial securities relative to rates of return on non-marketable financial assets and real assets, government's monetary policy and fiscal policy and above all legal protection to investors in recent years. All the above mentioned factors have contributed to the growth of public response to new issue of corporate securities. In short, growing response to public issues has strengthened the Indian capital market. It is evident from the fact that the number of shareholders rose from 60 lakh in 1985 to 160 lakh in 1994.

4. Growth of Merchant Banking

The role of merchant banking in India's capital market can be traced back to 1969 when Grindlays Bank established a special cell called the 'Merchant Banking'. Since then all the commercial banks have set up the 'Merchant Banking Division' to play an important role in the capital market. The merchant banking division of commercial banks advises the companies about economic viability, financial viability and technical feasibility of the project. They conduct the initial 'spade work' to find out the investment climate to advise the company whether the public issue floated would be fully subscribed or under-subscribed. The merchant banks in India act as the underwriter as well as the manager of new issues of securities. The Securities and Exchange Board of India (SEBI) regulates all merchant banks as far as their operations relating to issue activity are concerned. To sum up, the emergence of merchant banking has strengthened the institutional base of Indian capital market.

5. Growth of Credit Rating Agencies

Of late, credit rating agencies have emerged in the financial sectors. This is an important development for the growth of Indian capital market. Investment Information and Credit Rating Agency of India (ICRA) rates bonds, debentures, preference shares, CDs (Corporate Debentures) and CPs (Commercial Papers). As Credit Rating Information Services of India Ltd. (CRISIL) is a pioneer in credit rating, it *rates* debt instruments of banks, financial institutions and corporate firms. The credit assessment of companies issuing securities helps in the growth of New Issue Market segment of the capital market.

6. Growth of Mutual Funds

Mutual funds companies are investment trust companies. Mutual funds schemes are designed to mobilise funds from individuals and institutional investors, who in exchange get *units* which can be redeemed after a certain lock-in period, at their *Net Asset Value* (NAV). The mutual fund schemes provide tax benefits and buy back facility. The Unit Trust of India (UTI) can be regarded as pioneer in the setting up of mutual funds in India. Of late, commercial banks have also launched in India mutual funds schemes. Canstock scheme of the Canara bank and LIC's scheme, such as Dhanashree, Dhanaraksha and Dhanariddhi are mutual funds schemes. Since mutual funds schemes help to mobilise small savings of the relatively smaller savers to invest in industrial securities, so these schemes contribute to the growth of capital market. The total assets of mutual funds companies increased from ₹ 66,272 crore in 1993-94 to ₹ 99,248 crore in 2005 and to ₹ 4,13,365 crore in 2008. The investment of mutual funds in the secondary market influences the share prices in the stock exchange.

7. Stock Exchange Regulation Act

The growth of capital market would not have been possible had the Government of India not legislated suitable laws to protect the investors and regulate the Stock Exchanges. Under this Act, only recognised stock exchanges are allowed to function. This Act has empowered the Government of India to enquire into the affairs of a Stock Exchange and regulate its working. The Government of India established the Securities and Exchange Board of India (SEBI) on April 12, 1988 through an extra ordinary notification in the Gazette of India. In April 1992, SEBI was granted statutory recognition by passing an Act. Since 1991, SEBI has been evolving and implementing various measures and practices to infuse greater transparency in the capital market in the interest of investing public and orderly development of the securities market.

8. Liberalisation Measures

Foreign Institutional Investors (FII) have been allowed access to Indian capital market. Investment norms for NRIs have been liberalised, so that NRIs and Overseas Corporate Bodies can buy shares and debentures, without prior permission of RBI. This was expected to *internationalise* Indian capital market.

To sum up, the Indian capital market has registered an impressive growth since 1951. However, it is only since the mid-1980s that new institutions, new financial instruments and new regularity measures have led to speedy growth of the capital market. The liberalisation measures under New Economic Policy (NEP) gave a further boost to the growth of Indian capital market.

SECURITIES AND EXCHANGE BOARD OF INDIA (SEBI) AND CAPITAL MARKET REFORMS

The Securities Contract (Regulation) Act, 1956 empowers the Central Government to regulate stock exchanges in India. The Government of India realised the *need for an apex institution to* regulate Stock Exchanges and to promote an orderly growth of securities market. The Securities and Exchange Board of India (SEBI) was accordingly set up on April 12,1988 through an extraordinary notification of the Government of India in the Gazette of India. In April 1992, SEBI was made a statutory body by an Act of Parliament. On January 25,1995, Securities and Exchange Board of India Act, 1992 was amended by an ordinance to provide SEBI additional powers so that it could work even more efficiently.

Objectives of SEBI

In the securities market, the three parties which operate with vested interests are :

(*a*) Issues of securities.

(*b*) Subscribers to securities, that is, investors; and

(*c*) Market intermediaries.

SEBI aims at the development and regulation of securities market in the interests of investing public and healthy development of capital market. The main objectives of SEBI may be spelled out as follows:

(*a*) To safeguard the interest of investors in securities through disclosure of such informations by companies issuing securities, that enable the investing public to form a correct perception of risk and returns; and (*b*) To regulate the work of brokers and sub-brokers in stock exchanges and to regulate the work of bankers to an issue, underwriters, merchant bankers and mutual funds to check all kinds of shady activities relating to securities market.

Capital Market Reforms by SEBI

SEBI has effected the following reforms in the capital market in the last some years :

1. SEBI has issued guidelines to Stock Exchanges to make their governing bodies more broad-based. According to these guidelines, the governing body of a stock exchange should have five elected members, not more than four members nominated by the government or SEBI and three or fewer members nominated as public representatives.
2. SEBI introduced the system of registration of intermediaries, such as brokers and sub-brokers. The registration is on the basis of certain eligibility criteria such as capital adequacy.
3. SEBI has framed rules for making the relationship between client and broker more transparent and also for segregating client and broker accounts.
4. The system of periodical inspection of stock exchanges has been introduced by SEBI. SEBI inspected 8 stock exchanges till January 1993.
5. SEBI has advised stock exchanges to amend the listing agreement to ensure that a listed company furnishes annual statements to them showing variations between financial projections and project utilisation of funds made in the offer documents and actuals. This will enable shareholders to make comparisons between performance and promises..
6. SEBI vets the offer document to ensure that all disclosures have been made by the company in the offer document at the time company applies for listing of its securities (*i.e.*, shares and debentures) to the stock exchanges.
7. The offer document of schemes to be launched by Mutual Funds are required to be vetted by SEBI. SEBI has also specified a procedure for calculating and declaring Net Asset Value (NAV) of each Mutual Funds scheme. This would help investors to judge the performance of mutual funds. Mutual funds have also been allowed to underwrite issues, as a part of their investment activity. Regular monitoring of Mutual Funds is undertaken by SEBI to ensure compliance with these regulations.
8. SEBI has brought merchant banking also under its regularity framework. The merchant bankers are required to follow the code of conduct issued by SEBI in respect of pricing and premium fixation of issues.
9. The abolition of the office of Controller of Capital Issues has led to the removal of control over price and premium of shares to be issued. However, companies can approach capital market, only after clearance by SEBI.
10. SEBI has introduced a code of advertisement for public issues for ensuring fair and truthful disclosures. Companies are required to disclose all material facts and specific risk factors associated with their projects while making public issues.
11. SEBI has issued guidelines for the allotment of new issues . According to the guidelines, preferential allotment is to be made to the extent of 20 per cent for the Mutual Funds, 20 per cent for the domestic financial institutions, 24 per cent for foreign institutional investors and 10 per cent for the issuer company's employees. The balance 25 per cent is to be issued to the general public. However, 50 per cent of the minimum public offering of 25 per cent of the total issue shall be earmarked for the small investors applying for up to 1000 shares. The unsubscribed portion in either category is fully interchangeable.

12. The practice of making preferential allotment of shares at prices unrelated to the prevailing market price has been stopped and fresh guidelines for this purpose have been issued by SEBI.
13. SEBI has relaxed the guidelines for the issue of bonus shares.
14. SEBI has introduced regulations governing substantial acquisition of shares and takeovers.
15. As a part of the process of establishing transparent rules for trading in stock exchanges, the badla system was banned by SEBI in December 1993.
16. SEBI has allowed Foreign Institutional Investors to have an access to Indian capital market after getting registered with it. SEBI registered 286 foreign institutional investors by the January-end 1995.
17. SEBI has notified regulations for primary and secondary market intermediaries, bringing them within its regularity framework.
18. SEBI has taken several initiatives to promote *dematerialised* trading in securities through the promotion of the network of *depositories.* This will eliminate the risks of bad delivery and fake or forged shares. The depositories provide a system to record ownership details of securities in a *book entry* form without physical handling of securities. Thus, dematerialised trading is *paperless trading* in securities.
19. SEBI **put ban on short sale of securities** on June 15, 1998 with a view to containing volatility in share price. It prescribed additional volatility margins (AVM) with effect from July 6, 1998. The daily price band was reduced from 10 per cent to 8 per cent. Weekly 25 per cent band was removed to introduce graded margin system.
20. **Derivatives Trading.** SEBI has accepted the major recommendations of L.C. Gupta Committee on Derivatives Trading. Under this system, derivatives contracts would be treated as 'Securities'. The derivatives trading, as trading in Stock indices, would provide investors a *hedging instrument* to manage risks and help in improving the liquidity of secondary markets in India.
21. SEBI has exempted infrastructure firms from certain norms, while floating a public issue. They would be exempted from making a minimum public offer of 25 per cent of equity, minimum subscription of 90 per cent and five shareholders per ₹ 1 lakh of offer.
22. SEBI has formulated the regulations governing **buy-back of shares** by Indian companies. Buy-back has been permitted for the purpose of capital restructuring but not for treasury operations.
23. SEBI has given freedom to companies to determine the par value of shares issued by them thereby removing the requirement to issue shares at fixed price value of ₹ 10 and ₹ 100.
24. In order to encourage Initial Public Offers (IPOs), the existing SEBI norm for IPO has been relaxed by stipulating "ability to pay" in place of "actual payment of dividend".

Comments

SEBI has attempted to introduce improved trading practices and greater transparency in both the primary and secondary segments of securities market in India. These are imperative in the context of Liberalisation, Privatisation and Globalisation (LPG) of Indian economy. The aforesaid reforms in Indian Capital Market would help to build up a strong financial mechanism, to assist the financing of growing private sector in the liberalised environment of business. Since public sector units are also approaching the capital market instead of State Exchequer to get funds for expansion, so these units would also get support from the strong capital market.

Thanks to the regulations by SEBI, the Indian Equity Market has become highly transparent and liquid attracting investors from all over the world. The National Stock Exchange (NSE) is now the third largest in the world in terms of transactions in a year. However, there has been little progress outside the equity market and the corporate bond market in particular has remained underdeveloped. The investor base in corporate bonds has remained restricted because regulatory guidelines severely restrict the ability of banks and other financial institutions to invest in corporate bonds. Without development of all segments of the capital market, it will be difficult for India to become a global financial centre. Further, our equity market suffers from a great shortcoming. *The frequent changes in stock prices make it quite volatile and therefore risky for small or retail investors*. Therefore, retail investors still continue to invest their savings in traditional mediums like post-office savings, Bank deposits, NSCs and bonds besides traditional commodities like gold and silver. If one were to account for yield or return of investment from these instruments after providing for tax and inflation, they are not good enough to provide adequate returns to the small investors.

A recent survey reveals conclusively that retail investors have been *running away from not only the equity market, but also* from mutual funds. According to the survey, only 3.5 million Indians – from a total working population of 321 million people under 18–59 years age group–*invest in stocks*. Overall, only 7.2 million people invest in stocks, either directly or through mutual funds, which works out to just 2 per cent of the total working population In this context, the RBI data also reveals that only 5 *per cent* of the *total savings finds its way into the securities market including equities, Gilts, MF as against 34 per cent in the USA*.

In our view, to encourage small investors to invest in corporate equity the problem of large volatility has to be tackled.

CHAPTER 41

Planning in India : 1951 to 1991

Introduction

At the time of independence India was a backward underdeveloped country. There was a lot of exploitation of India during the British colonial rule. This made Indian people very poor. The aim of freedom struggle was not mere gaining political freedom from the British rule but also to attain economic freedom for the Indian people. Economic freedom implies the removal of mass poverty that prevailed in India. At the time of independence there was deficiency of good entrepreneurs who could use the natural resource endowment of India for economic development. To improve living standards of the people, it was necessary to accelerate rate of economic growth. It was thought that the private sector lacked the necessary resources and the proper mindset to bring about rapid economic growth. Inspired by the Russian experience, planning as an instrument of economic development was adopted. The Planning Commission was set up to prepare five year plans which would indicate directions in which the Indian economy should move. Resources were to be allocated both at the Centre and in the States according to the plan priorities decided in a five year plan.

The basic objective of Indian planning has been acceleration of economic growth so as to raise the living standards of the people. Further, various five year plans also gave high priority to generation of employment opportunities and removal of poverty. In what follows we will explain the role of planning in India and then explain the development strategies adopted in various plans to achieve the objectives.

ROLE OF PLANNING IN INDIA

Accelerating Economic Growth. There were two main features of India's economic policy that emphasised the role of planning and intervention by the State in the development process of the Indian economy in the first three decades of planning. First, to accelerate economic growth economists and planners recognised that raising the rate of saving and investment was essential to accelerate the rate of economic growth. It was thought that the private sector on its own would not be able to achieve a higher rate of saving and investment required to break the vicious circle of poverty. Therefore, the state had to intervene to raise resources and increase the rate of saving and investment. This made the planning and the expansion of the public sector essential to accelerate economic growth.

Emphasis on Industrialisation, Second, the strategy of development, adopted since the adoption of Second Five Year Plan which was based on Mahalanobis growth model, laid stress on the industrialisation with an emphasis on the development of basic heavy industries and capital goods industries. This model implied allocating a higher proportion of investible resources to capital goods industries than to consumer goods industries. Private sector which is driven by profit motive could not be expected to allocate sufficient resources to the growth of capital goods industries. Therefore, the role of planning and the public sector was considered essential for rapid growth of basic heavy industries. We have explained in a separate chapter how Mahalanobis growth model was wrong in neglecting the role of agriculture and importance of wage goods for accelerating growth of output and employment. In fact, shortage of food, a cheap wage good, rather than machines could act as a constraint on the growth process. This became evident by the time of the Third Plan which laid a relatively greater stress on growth of agriculture to achieve self-reliance.

But rapid growth of agriculture itself requires a good deal of state intervention and planning. The land reforms in agriculture, supply of adequate credit to farmers, development of infrastructure such as irrigation, power, roads were necessary where planning and State could play an important role.

To Compenstate for Market Failures. The dominant view in development economics in the fifties and sixties also laid stress on the planning by the State to compensate for 'market failures'. It was argued that while market mechanism was efficient in distributing a given stock of available goods, *it was quite inefficient in allocating resources over time for investment*. This was because of myopic nature of private sector which guided the working of markets. It was therefore asserted that the State and planning could play an important role in allocating resources for investment to bring about rapid economic growth. Besides, failures of market mechanism and free working of private sector to *allocate adequate amount of resources for investment in infrastructure such as power, transport, communication* created substantial external economies and also where significant economies of scale existed. Therefore, in the development of infrastructure, the State and planning had an important role to play.

Regulatory Role of the State. There is another important aspect of the role of State and planning in the development of the Indian economy which dominated economic thinking in the pre-reform period. Though the private sector was given an important role to play in the framework of mixed economy, to achieve optimal allocation of resources among different industries according to plan priorities, economic activities in the private sector were required to be regulated by the State. Further, to achieve other objectives of planning such as restraining the concentration of economic power in a few big business houses, the private sector was subjected to industrial licensing controls. To quote C. Rangarajan, the former Governor of the Reserve Bank of India, "*while the private sector was given space to operate in keeping with the concept of a mixed economy, in the field of industry particularly the decisions of the private sector were circumscribed by the licensing mechanism. Hence, while foreign trade was subject to control because of the strategy of import substitution, industrial production and investment were subject to control because of the need to direct resources according to plan priorities*"[1].

Tackling the Problems of Poverty and Unemployment. The other problem which makes role of planning and state intervention important is the need to tackle the problems of poverty and unemployment. Since the beginning of the seventies the Indian planners realised, especially in the Fifth, Sixth and Seventh Five Year Plans, that even if growth rate of GDP was raised to 5 to 6 per cent per annum, it was not possible to make a significant dent on the problems of mass poverty and unemployment prevailing in the Indian economy. Some argued that benefits of economic growth did not trickle down to the poor. Others were of the view that even if the poor get benefits from growth by way of more employment opportunities generated by it, mere economic growth was not enough to eradicate poverty and unemployment. Therefore, role of planning and State was necessary to start and implement special poverty and unemployment schemes such as Food for Work Programme and Employment Guarantee Schemes to help the poor and weaker sections of the society.

1. C. Rangarajan, *Indian Planning : Objectives, Strategy and Instrumentality*, Paper presented at the Conference on Planning and Economic Policy in India, at the ISI, Calcutta, June 1993.

DEVELOPMENT STRATEGY IN INDIA'S FIVE YEAR PLANS

In the Second Five Year Plan strategy which continued practically till the Fourth Plan period (1969-74) it was visualised that basic constraints on development was the acute deficiency of physical capital which was responsible for small productive capacity of the Indian economy. It was further thought that the rate of capital formation depended on the domestic rate of saving which could be raised by the adoption of proper fiscal and monetary policies. However, Mahalanobis, author the Second Plan's development strategy, asserted that even if domestic rate of saving could be increased, the non-availability of the domestic capacity to produce capital goods would prevent the transformation of these savings into real productive investment. Note that real investment occurs when savings are spent on purchasing capital goods such as machinery and equipment. The alternative to the expansion of domestic capacity to produce capital goods would be importing capital goods to ensure sustained increase in the rate of real investment.

Mahalanobis ruled out import of capital goods on grounds of lack of foreign exchange earnings from exports. He argued that if large investment was not made in basic heavy industries producing capital goods, the country would ever remain dependent on foreign countries for the import of steel and capital goods. Since it was not possible for India to earn sufficient foreign exchange by increasing exports, the capital goods could not be imported in sufficient quantities owing to foreign exchange constraint. The result will be that the rate of real capital formation and rate of economic growth in the country would remain low. Thus, Mahalanobis was of the opinion that without adequate investment in basic heavy industries, it would not be possible to achieve rapid self-reliant economic growth. According to Mahalanobis, "*The proper strategy would be to bring about a rapid development of the industries producing investment goods in the beginning by increasing appreciably the proportion of investment in basic heavy industries. As the capacity to manufacture both heavy and light machinery and other capital goods increases, the capacity to invest in home produced capital goods would also increase steadily and India would become more and more independent of imports of foreign machinery and capital.*"[2]

Further, according to Mahalanobis, productive employment can be created only by increasing the production of capital goods. To quote him, "*the only way of eliminating unemployment in India is to build up a sufficiently large stock of capital which will enable all unemployed persons being absorbed in productive activity. Increasing the rate of investment is therefore the only fundamental remedy for unemployment in India.*"[3]

Another important element of development strategy adopted in India's earlier Five Year Plans was their emphasis on modern industrialisation, especially of import-substitution type. It was generally believed that industrialisation would generate sufficient employment opportunities which would cause surplus labour currently unemployed in agriculture to be shifted to more productive employment in industries. The underlying assumption was that agriculture was subject to diminishing returns and could not absorb unemployed labour productively whereas industries operated according to increasing returns to scale.

Thus, identifying underdevelopment with dependence on agriculture and thinking industrial growth especially the development of heavy industries as the core of development underlined the approach and strategy of the Second Five Year Plan. To quote from Second Plan again, "low or static

2. P.C. Mahalanobis, "The Approach of Operational Research to Planning in India," *Sankhya*, Vol. 16, Dec. 1953.
3. Mahalanobis, *op. cit.* p. 22.

standards of living, underemployment and unemployment, and to a certain extent even the gap between the average income and the highest income are all manifestations of the basic underdevelopment which characterises an economy depending mainly on agriculture. Rapid industrialisation and diversification of the economy is thus the core of development. But *if industrialisation is to be rapid enough, the country must aim at developing basic industries and industries which make machines to make the machines needed for further development.*"[4]

It is clear from above that in the Second Plan there was a clear shift of priorities from agriculture to industries and within industries to basic heavy industries. As mentioned above, the logic of Mahalanobis in emphasising heavy industries was that the growth of basic heavy industries would enable the economy to accelerate the rate of capital formation and therefore economic growth. In fact, he identified the rate of growth of investment in the economy with the rate of growth of output in the capital goods sector of the economy.

Mahalanobis' Four-Sector Growth Model and Employment Generation

Mahalanobis realised that the basic heavy industries being capital-intensive would not ensure rapid expansion of employment opportunities and to bring the employment aspect into sharp focus he put forward a four-sector growth model in which he kept heavy industry sector (*i.e.* K-sector) intact but divided the C-sector (*i.e.* consumption goods sector) into three sub-sectors : C_1, C_2, and C_3 (sector C_1 represented factory enterprises using mechanised techniques and producing consumer goods; sector C_2 represented the household and small-scale enterprises also producing consumer goods, and sector C_3 represented provision of services). It was sector C_2 representing households and small-scale industries which in Mahalanobis' four-sector model was visualised to ensure the increased supply of consumer goods to meet the rising demand for them and also to ensure, being labour-intensive, expansion of employment opportunities. In keeping with this approach, Second Five Year Plan put restrictions on the growth of capacity in factory enterprises engaged in commodity production. However, since for these household or cottage enterprises, adequate resources were not provided, nor any effort was made to improve their productivity, they could neither fulfil their targets of production of consumer goods nor of generating enough employment opportunities.[5]

Vital Role of the Public Sector. Lastly, the other important element of development strategy pursued in India's Five Year Plans (which continued up to the end of 1980s) was the vital role given to the public sector in economic development of the Indian economy. This was based on the assumption that if private sector and market mechanism were relied upon for development of industries there would be more investment in consumer goods industries catering to the needs of upper income groups while adequate investment in the sectors essential for rapid growth of the economy would not be forthcoming.

In the **Third Plan (1961-66)** also the strategy of Second Plan was continued as is clear from the following: "In the Third Plan, as in the Second, the development of basic industries such as steel, fuel and power and machine building and chemical industries is fundamental to rapid economic growth. These industries largely determine the pace at which the economy can become self-reliant and self-generating."[6] Though, "to achieve self-sufficiency in foodgrains and increase in agricultural

4. Government of India, Planning Commission, *Second Five Year Plan*, 1956.
5. Amlan Datta, *Strategy of Economic Development,* 1973. In the spinning of cotton, main emphasis was on Ambar Charkha. Ambar Charkha experiment failed because productivity and earning capacity per person engaged in it was found to be too low.
6. Government of India, Planning Commission, *Third Five Year Plan,* 1961, p.50..

production to meet the requirements of industry and exports"[7] was stated to be one of the objectives of the Third Plan, actual allocation of resources between agriculture and other sectors did not exhibit any significant difference from that of the Second Plan. Therefore, the concern for food and agriculture in the Third Plan appears to be mere verbal and was not built into the strategy of development.

The **Fourth Five Year Plan** (1969-74) which was prepared under the Deputy Chairmanship of Late Prof. D.R. Gadgil, tried to give a new shape to the planning strategy and emphasis was sought to be placed on the common man, the weaker sections and the less privileged. The Fourth Plan slightly raised the allocation of public sector outlay to agriculture and irrigation to about 23 per cent as against 20 per cent in the Second Plan and the Third Plan. However, a good deal of hangover of the heavy industry biased strategy still prevailed in this plan too.

Thus, the development strategy pursued till the end of the Third Plan was *growth-oriented,* though objectives of increasing employment and reducing income inequalities were mentioned but never seriously pursued and implemented. However, the situation changed dramatically in the mid-sixties. The two wars, one with China in 1962 and the second with Pakistan in 1965, compelled us to increase defence expenditure. During this time foreign aid situation also became unfavourable resulting in foreign exchange crisis. The devaluation of rupee in June 1966 also did not improve the foreign exchange situation. The situation became more grim with the successive two droughts that hit the country in 1966 and 1967.

Worsening economic situation and growing concerns for national security highlighted the two shortcomings of the development strategy adopted in the Second and Third Five Year Plans. They were (1) *relative neglect of agriculture* resulting in the acute food problem for the country, (2) *crucial dependence on foreign aid* which could not be relied upon for accelerating growth in the future plans. This highlighted the importance of pursuing the *objective of self-reliance* which implied reducing the dependence on foreign aid.

In the later half of the sixties, resource situation for the public sector became difficult and uncertain. This resulted in the suspension of planning for three-year period (1966-69). This three-year period (1966-69) is therefore called *period of plan holiday.* Due to non-availability of adequate funds, public sector investment was reduced from the mid-sixties onwards.

Thus, in the 4th Five Year Plan resource allocation to agriculture was increased to achieve self-sufficiency in foodgrains. Besides, new strategy of agricultural development, initiated earlier in 1966-67, was pursued more vigorously during the Fourth Plan period. The new strategy of agricultural development which involved the use of high-yielding varieties (HYV) of seeds, fertilizers, pesticides with appropriate quantity of water was introduced in a few selected districts of the country where assured irrigation facilities were available.

Second, in the Fourth Plan relatively more importance was given to export promotion than before along with the policy of import substitution which was continued. Though the new agricultural development strategy proved to be successful and production of foodgrains, especially wheat, grew at a satisfactory rate, the growth scenario remained dim due to slackening of public sector investment which started in the mid-sixties and continued up till mid-seventies. Average growth in net national product (NNP) achieved during the Fourth Plan was only 3.3 per cent per annum. As a result of *cut-back in public investment, problem of deficiency of aggregate demand emerged* which resulted in slowing down of industrial growth during 1966 to 1978-79. It is important to note that in first four Five Year Plans of India it was never visualised that in the Indian economy level of aggregate demand could possibly be a constraint on the growth process.

---

7. *Ibid*, p. 48.

Development Strategies in the Fifth, Sixth and Seventh Plans

Besides, in the early seventies, it was realised that growth-oriented development strategy adopted in the first over two decades of planned development (1951-74) had not succeeded in alleviating poverty. Statistical evidence revealed that about 321 million people lived below the poverty line in 1973-74 and unemployment problem was mounting. At this time political situation in the country became uncertain with Congress party losing election in some States. Further, while preparing the 5th Five Year Plan it was recognised that trickle down effect of economic growth on the poor and unemployed was not working. Thus, in "**Towards an Approach to Fifth Five Year Plan**" it was stated that "*Economic growth by itself would not lead to the solution of the problem of poverty and unemployment in the foreseeable future*". Therefore, Fifth Plan formulated a programme of making a '*direct attack on poverty*' which visualised special employment such as *Jawahar Rozgar Yojana,* for providing wage employment to the poor, IRDP (Integrated Rural Development Programme) for providing self-employment to the poor. Except for these anti-poverty schemes Firth Plan was not much different from the earlier Five Year Plans. These anti-poverty schemes were merely added to the Fifth Five Year Plan without integrating them with the growth programmes.

But while formulating Fifth Plan (1974-79) the new Planning Minister, Mr. D.P. Dhar, took charge of preparing the final draft. According to the **Approach to Fifth Plan** on which the final draft was made, "*The strategy for elimination of poverty ... rested on two major factors, a rising rate of growth of domestic product combined with declining rate of population growth*". This latter approach was indeed a combination of old planning strategy with emphasis on economic growth though increase in employment was considered to be a desirable objective. Thus *employment-orientation* was not actually given to the planning strategy in the Fifth Five Year Plan. For achieving a higher rate of economic growth Fifth Plan draft was also based on a wrong assumption of incremental capital-output ratio (ICOR) of 3.4 whereas in the previous plan it was actually found to be equal to 4.3.

However, during the period of Fifth Plan (1974-79), the emergency was declared in the country and Prime Minister's 20-Point Programme was given more importance over the implementation of Fifth Plan projects and policies. The Fifth Plan could not be completed as in March 1977, Janata Government came to power and terminated the Fifth Plan in March 1978.

The Sixth Five Year Plan (1980-85). It may be noted that there ware *two* Sixth Five Year Plans. One Sixth Five Year Plan for the period (1978-83) was prepared by Janata Government but it could not be completed as Janata government collapsed and failed to win the new election held in Dec. 1979. The Congress Government again came to power in 1980 and formulated new Sixth Five Year Plan for the period 1980-85. The development strategy of Sixth Plan (1980-85) laid emphasis on promotion of efficiency in resource use and improvement in productivity to achieve 5.2 per cent growth in GDP. Besides, the infrastructure sector was given the topmost priority in the allocation of resources. Further, in the Sixth Plan *employment generation and poverty eradication* were given high priority. In this additional employment opportunities for 46 million persons were planned to be generated during the plan period through IRDS (Integrated Rural Development Scheme), NREP (National Rural Employment Programme) and RLEP (Rural Landless Employment Programme) schemes. The Sixth Plan aimed at reducing the percentage of people below the poverty line to 30 per cent of population.

The infrastructure sector was given the topmost priority in the development strategy of the Sixth Plan whereas, like the earlier plans, agriculture rural development, and special employment programme received allocation of about 13 per cent of total outlay.

The Seventh Plan (1985-90) Strategy. The Seventh Plan's strategy of development was to improve the utilisation of existing productive capacities rather than creating new capacities. It sought to secure more output out of productive assets that had been built up in the previous years. Besides, the plan strategy laid emphasis on a direct attack on the problems of poverty and unemployment by providing a greater outlay on special employment schemes rather than relying on 'trickle -down' effect of economic growth. The other important aspect of development strategy of the Seventh Plan was that it planned for a non-inflationary growth process by laying greater emphases on the production and supply of *mass consumption goods* like foodgrains, edible oils, sugar, cooking fuel and textiles. Thus, the strategy of development for the Seventh Plan accorded a higher priority to wage goods. Another important change in the policy regime during the Seventh Plan period (1985-90) was that process of liberalisation was initiated. In the industrial policy resolution of 1956 amendments were made under which licensing procedures were somewhat relaxed and liberalised, and the existing capacities were allowed to be used liberally by diversification through broad-banding. Besides, measures were taken to give greater role to the private sector in economic development.

INDIA'S ECONOMIC PERFORMANCE IN THE FIRST FOUR DECADES (1951-91) OF DEVELOPMENT PLANNING (PRE-REFORM PERIOD)

The development strategy pursued in the four decades planning (1951-91) has both successes and failures in achieving the objectives and targets. The Indian economy witnessed a profound structural transformation during this period. We became wholly self-sufficient in foodgrains and most other agricultural commodities. Food production grew at a rate faster than that of population. As a result of industrial growth during the first three decades of the Indian industry planning (1950-80) became capable of meeting nearly 100 per cent of our requirements of consumer goods and about 85 per cent of our annual demand for capital goods. The strong base of future industrial growth rate was laid as a result of significant development of basic and heavy industries.

Table 41.1. Economic Growth in the Planning Period (1951 to 2000)

Years	*Average annual growth rates (%)*			
	GDP at Factor Cost (at 1993-94 Prices)	*Agriculture and related activities*	*Industrial Sector (manufact-uring and related activities)*	*Tertiary Sector (Services)*
1950-51 to 1960-61	3.7	2.8	6.2	4.2
1960-61 to 1970-71	3.4	2.1	5.4	4.5
1970-71 to 1980-81	3.4	1.9	4.3	4.5
1980-81 to 1990-91	5.6	3.4	6.6	6.7

Source : Calculated from the data given in GOI, *Economic Surveys*, for the years 2001-02, 2002-03 and 2003-04.

We succeeded in building up a vast reservoir of technical and managerial skills. For three decades, 1951-81, the average annual growth rate of real GDP was 3.5 per cent against a virtual stagnation in real GDP during the first half of the 20th century. However, as compared to international standards the Indian growth rate in the first three decades was quite low. As will be seen from Table 41.1 annual growth rate in GDP was 3.7% during 1951-61, 3.4% during 1961-71 and 1971-81. Further, as is seen from Table 41.1, **growth rate in GDP was pulled down in the decades of sixties and seventies as compared to the fifties by slowdown in both industrial and agricultural growth rates.**

It may be further noted that there was a *significant deceleration in industrial growth rate from mid-sixties to mid-seventies (1965-76)* due to decline in public sector investment. With population growing at the rate of 2.25 per cent per annum, per capita income increased at the rate about 1.5 per cent per year during the period (1951-81). However, during the decades of eighties and nineties growth rate in per capita income accelerated due to higher growth in GDP and also due to decline in growth rate of population.

Table 41.2. Overall GDP Growth, Saving and Investment Rates and Incremental Capital-Output Ratios in the Indian Economy (1951-1991)

Period	GDP (growth rate in plan period)	Saving Rate (% of GDP)	Investment Rate (% of GDP)	ICOR	Current Account Deficit* (% of GDP)
First Plan (1951-1955-56)	3.61	10.28	10.64	2.9	0.36
Second Plan (1956-57 to 1960-61)	4.27	11.73	14.50	3.4	2.77
Third Plan (1961-62 to 1965-66)	2.84	13.21	15.46	5.4	2.25
Plan Period (1966-67 to 1970-71)	4.66	14.35	15.98	3.4	1.63
Plan Period (1971-72 to 1975-76)	3.08	17.98	17.88	5.8	0.6
Plan period (1976-77 to 1980-81)	3.20	21.65	21.46	6.7	–0.19
Sixth Plan 1981-82 to 1985-86	5.20	19.82	21.42	4.1	1.6
Seventh Plan 1985-86 to 1989-90	5.8	20.36	22.74	3.9	2.38

* Current account deficit indicates *foreign savings used.*

Source : CSO, *National Accounts Statistics* and Plan Documents.

In the first three decades (1951-81) of planned development in India the rate of economic growth was not high enough to make a significant dent on the problem of poverty. The proportion of population with level of consumption below a very modest poverty line fluctuated between 50 and 58 per cent of population during the fifties, sixties and seventies (that is, in the first three decades of planning). These estimates clearly show that in the first three decades of planning (1951-81) economic growth did not have any impact on the poverty problem in India. This is because of not only slow rate

Table 41.3. Trends in Poverty in India

Period	*Percentage of Population below the poverty line (HCR)* Rural	Urban	All India	*Number of Poor (in millions)* Rural	Urban	Total
1951-55	54.77	42.70	52.66	170.6	28.1	198.7
1965-66	53.96	47.06	52.74	184.6	34.8	219.5
1961-65	48.59	45.46	48.02	183.0	38.6	221.6
1966-70	60.44	50.90	58.60	251.0	50.7	301.7
1973-74	56.4	49.0	54.9	261	60	321
1977-78	53.1	45.2	51.3	264	68	329
1983	45.7	40.8	44.5	252	71	323
1987-88	39.1	38.2	38.9	232	75	307
1993-94	37.3	32.4	36.3	244	76	320

Source: *Planning Commission* for the data from 1973-74 onwards and from 1951-55 to 1966-70. Gaurav Datt, *Poverty in India, 1951-92, Trends and Decomposition,* World Bank Study 1996. Gaurav Datt's estimates are comparable with Planning Commission data as he uses the same indices for estimating poverty from the data of earlier NSS.

Notes : Poverty line is ₹ 49.1 **per capita per month** (rural) and 56.6 **per capita per month** (urban) in **1973-74. Consumer Price Index** for agricultural labourers (rural) and **Consumer Price Index** for industrial workers (urban) have been used to estimate the poverty line according to the prices prevailing in each year.

of economic growth during this period but also that benefits of whatever economic growth occurred did not trickle down to the poor. As we shall discuss later that it is only in the eighties and nineties when annual rate of economic growth rate accelerated to around 5.6 per cent and 6 per cent respectively and special employment schemes were started on a large scale that there was a significant decline in the incidence of poverty.

In the eighties of the 20th century, two Five Year Plans, the Sixth Plan (1989-85) and Seventh Plan (1985-90) were launched. In the Sixth Plan period (1980-85) and Seventh Plan period (1985-90), average annual growth rate of 5.4 per cent and 5.8 per cent respectively was recorded. This higher growth rate in national income also resulted in a higher growth rate in per capita income of 3.2 per cent and 3.6 in the Sixth Plan and Seventh Plan periods respectively. Favourable result of this higher growth rate in both national income and per capita income was the decline in the ratio of people living below the poverty line. As will be seen from Table 41.3 percentage of population living below the poverty line (All India) which was 51.3 in 1977-78 fell to 44.5 in 1983 and further to 38.9 in 1987-88 and 36.3 in 1993-94.

Now, the question is what caused this acceleration in growth rate in the late seventies and the eighties. The *important factor causing this acceleration in growth rate in the late seventies and early eighties was the increase in public sector investment which remained sluggish earlier since the mid-sixties.* Among other factors bringing about higher growth rate is the *liberalisation measures* of removal of some restrictions and relaxation of licensing procedures by making amendments through industrial policy statements of July 1980 and December 1985. In these industrial policy statements certain changes were made in the industrial licensing policies and procedures which were designed to facilitate capacity expansion in the private sector and create competitive environment. In the later half of eighties (1985-90), contrary to the Mahalanobis strategy of growth, export promotion was given relatively more importance than import substitution which led to higher growth rates of exports of 9.4 per cent, 24.1 per cent, 15.6 per cent, and 18.9 per cent in 1986-87, 1987-88, 1988-89 and 1989-90 respectively which speeded up the overall growth rate of the Indian economy during the later half of the eighties.

But, as mentioned above, *the higher growth rate achieved in the eighties was not sustainable as public sector investment was increased by incurring higher doses of deficit financing leading to higher rates of inflation in the economy and through commercial borrowing on a large scale from abroad which significantly raised external public debt.* External public debt servicing consumed a large part of our export earnings. This created foreign exchange crisis in 1990-91 which brought India to the brink of default.

Since capital-intensive technologies were used in the growth process of both industrial and agricultural sectors, the employment opportunities increased but not large enough to absorb even annual growth of labour force in productive employment. As a result, backlog of unemployment went on increasing with each successive Five Year Plan. At the end of Fourth Plan period (1973-74) unemployment was estimated at 9 per cent of labour force on current daily basis.

Trends in Saving and Capital Formation : 1951 to 1991

Rates of gross saving and capital formation as a per cent of GDP which are important determinants of economic growth showed upward trends with some fluctuations during the period 1951-80. Both rates increased from around 8 per cent in 1950-51 to 13 per cent in 1955-56, the beginning of the second Five Year Plan. Thus the two rates remained in balance during this period (see Table 41.4). However, from 1956 to 1965-66, the gap between the two emerged; gross domestic saving (GDS) falling short of gross domestic capital formulation (GDCF). Besides, the two rates fluctuated a good deal during the decade of 1956-1965. The deficit of gross domestic saving and gross domestic capital formation (GDCF), *i.e.*, gross domestic investment during this decade, was met mostly by obtaining concessional foreign assistance with net capital inflow as percentage of GDFC being equal to 2.12 during 1956-60 and 2.26 during 1961-65.

As will be seen from Table 41.4, during the periods 1966-70 and 1971-73, annual rate of gross domestic capital formation (GDCF) increased to 15 per cent of GDP in 1966-70 and to 15.50 per cent of GDP in 1971-73. This was largely financed by domestic saving which increased only little. The average annual rate of gross domestic saving rose from about 13.2 per cent during 1966-70 to 14.7 per cent during 1971-73. It is mainly due to stagnation of gross capital formation during 1966-70 and 1971-73 that average annual rate of growth of GDP during this period fell to 2.9 per cent per annum during 1966-70 and 1.9 per cent during 1971-73 (See Table 41.4). It may be further noted that after war with Pakistan in 1965 on Kashmir issue and then in 1971 on Bangladesh issue, India could not get much foreign aid. As a result, *capital inflow* during this period declined which also accounted for low rate of capital formation.

From the mid-seventies public sector investment was raised which resulted in higher average rate of capital formation (18.5 per cent of GDP) during 1974-80 and this was fully financed by domestic saving which shot up to 18.6 per cent per annum during this period. In the first half of the eighties, average annual rate of GDCF as per cent of GDP picked up to 19.7 and in the second half (1986-90) of the eighties to 22.6. As a result, annual average growth rate of GDP rose to 5.6 per cent during 1986-90) and to 5.8 per cent during 1986-90. However, in the second half of the eighties (1986-90) annual rate of gross domestic saving (GDS) as per cent of GDP_{FC} was 20.26 resulting in capital inflow of 2.34 per cent of GDP_{FC} which was mostly in the form of commercial borrowing from abroad. This led to a sharp increase in external foreign debt which put pressure on our balance of payments. *In 1990-91, the gap between GDS and GDCF widened and resulted in capital inflow of 3.2 per cent of* GDP_{FC} *causing foreign exchange crisis.*

Table 41.4 Rate of GDS, GDCF and Rate of Growth GDP_{FC} from 1951 to 1991

Period	*GDS at current market prices as % of* GDP_{FC}	*GDCF at current market prices as % of* GDP_{FC} *(at current prices)*	*Net Capital Inflow (+) as % of* GDP_{FC}	*Rate of growth of* GDP_{FC} *at1993-94 prices*
1951-55	8.74	8.96	0.22	3.85
1956-60	11.10	13.22	2.12	3.38
1961-65	11.96	14.22	2.26	5.00
1966-70	13.18	15.00	1.82	2.90
1971-73	14.67	15.50	0.83	1.90
1974-80	18.60	18.46	–0.14	3.40
1981-85	18.36	19.70	1.34	5.66
1986-90	20.26	22.60	2.34	5.84
1990-91	23.10	26.30	3.20	5.30

Source : GOI, *Economic Survey*, Various Issues

A Critical Evaluation of Planning in the First Four Decades (1951-91)

The first three decades of planning in India (1951-81) was characterised by lower rate of economic growth at around 3.6 per cent per annum on an average. There are mainly two explanations of this. First, Late Prof Sukhamoy Chakravarty attributed it to the gross inefficiency of public sector enterprises which were given a crucial role in economic development during this plan period[8]. According to him, there were many areas of public sector production such as transport, steel, fertilizers where gross inefficiency prevailed and this accounted for low productivity and lower

8. Sukhamoy Chakravarty, *Development Planning: The Indian Experience*, 1987, p. 28.

growth rate. Further, according to him, *in Indian planning adequate growth of aggregate demand was taken for granted* and it is due to the decline in aggregate demand caused by decrease in public sector investment from mid-sixties to late seventies that raised incremental capital-output ratio (ICOR) and led to lower growth of output from increase in investment[9].

It is important to note that it is only from mid-eighties when industrial policy was liberalised somewhat and private sector was given relatively greater role that economic growth rate picked up and overall GDP growth rate of 5.6 per cent was achieved in the decade of 1981-91.

Prof. T. N. Shrinivasan and Prof Suresh Tendulkar attributed lower growth rate in the pre-reform period (*i.e.,* before 1991) to the **import-substitution strategy** (which is also called **inward-oriented strategy)** *and inadequate attention paid to expanding exports to generate higher growth of output*. To quote them, "*India's inward-orientation has had significant economic costs to lower overall growth and stagnating living standards. Japan's rapid export growth was associated with very rapid GDP growth and improvement in living standards.*"[10]

Further, Srinivasan and Tendulkar hold Mahalanobis' strategy with its emphasis on basic heavy and capital goods industries and import-substitution industrialisation responsible for lower growth of GDP and the incidence of poverty. Thus they write, "Indian economic performance under this development strategy was poor. For three decades until 1980-81 the average annual rate of growth of real GDP was 3.75 per cent. With the population growing at nearly 2.25 per cent a year income per head grew at about 1.50 per cent. *With such a low rate of growth, it is no surprise that there was little* reduction in poverty—the proportion of population with consumption below a very modest poverty line fluctuated at around an average of more than 50 per cent. *The economy was insulated from world markets—India's* share of world merchandise exports declined from about 2.2 per cent in 1948 to 0.5 per cent in the early eightes[11].

In contrast to the planning in the first three decades. (1951-80), in the decade of eighties growth rate picked up to 5.6 per cent due to revival of public sector investment and along with expansionary fiscal policy financed by commercial borrowing mainly from abroad which proved to be quite unsustainable as it led to balance of payments crisis of 1991. Explaining this consequence of debt-driven unsustainable consequences of policy of fiscal expansionsim Srinivasan and Tendulkar write, "*The current account deficit rose to a record 3.2 per cent of GDP in 1990 and debt-service payments amounted to as much as 35.3 per cent of current foreign exchange receipts*. Foreign exchange reserves were down to a level barely enough to finance imports for $2\frac{1}{2}$ months. Short-term deposits amounted to a dangerously high level of 146.5 per cent of foreign exchange reserves by the end of March 1991. The rate of inflation soared exceeding 10 per cent in 1990. Expectations of an immediate devaluation of the rupee led to withdrawal of deposits by non-resident Indians. A spectre of default on short-term loans and downgrading of India credit rating loomed[12]. Such was the nature of crisis that it compelled India to go in for structural reforms.

The other drawback of planning in the first four decades has been that industrialisation to which a large chunk of resources were allocated failed *to generate adequate employment opportunities* and the goal of transformation of occupational structure by transfer of population from agriculture to organised industries and services remain unfulfilled. The occupational structure remained almost unchanged, Besides, rate of unemployment increased as the increase in employment opportunities could not keep pace with the growth of labour force. No wonder that the change in plan strategy was called for.

9. Sukhamoy Chakravarty, "Development Strategies in the Eighties" in *Economic and Political Weekly,* 1984
10. T.N. Srinivasan and Suresh D. Tendulkar, *'Reintegrating India with the World Economy"*, Oxford University Press. 2003, p. 12.
11. *op. cit.* p. 8
12. Srinivasan and Tendulkar, *op. cit.* pp. 28-29.

CHAPTER 42

Economic Crisis 1991 and Planning in Post-Reform Period

1991 Crisis and Macroeconomic Imbalances

During the whole of the eighties public sector faced a financial crunch as its expenditure on defence, food, fertilizers and imports increased tremendously giving rise to huge budget deficits of the Government. The Government resorted to commercial borrowing from abroad which resulted in heavy debt burden and increased debt service charges. This caused great balance payment crisis in 1990-91. This crisis compelled us to adopt fiscal stabilisation and structural adjustment programme of World Bank and IMF.

As mentioned above, the intervention by the Government was essential to initiate the process of economic development and thereby to break the vicious circle of poverty. As a result, public sector made investment in a big way in basic heavy industries and in irrigation. However, during the seventies and eighties several shortcomings of the working of public sector were noticed.

First, the public sector which was expected to generate adequate resources for the growth of the economy not only failed to do so but in fact was incurring huge losses which raised the expenditure of the Government. The losses of the public sector were said to be due to the *inefficiency in the working of public enterprises.* Secondly, the problem of *macroeconomic imbalances*, both in the internal and external sectors, emerged and assumed serious proportions in 1990-91. The huge deficits in the successive budgets of the government due to the internal imbalance of Government expenditure and revenue led to the creation of more money supply which created the serious problem of rising prices, so much so that annual rate of inflation went up to about 17 per cent during August 1991. This compelled the newly elected Congress government to adopt fiscal policy to reduce budgetary deficits for stabilising prices.

In the external sector, the huge deficits in the balance of payments due to the rising imports and sluggish exports persisted in the eighties and, to meet this deficit, the Government resorted to commercial borrowing from abroad at higher market rates of interest. As a result of persistent deficits on the current account, the foreign exchange reserves declined to a very small sum in June 1991 which were sufficient for payments for necessary imports only for a few weeks. This compelled the Government to approach IMF (International Monetary Fund) for loans to make necessary payments and enhance the foreign exchange reserves.

Thirdly, though the annual growth of national income during the eighties went up to 5.9 per cent and growth rate of the industrial sector to 8 per cent, which was considered to be a good performance, it was feared that due to macroeconomic imbalances which emerged in the economy they would not be sustained any more. In the external sector, the situation became so worse in 1991 that India came to the brink of default. To avoid the default and to win over the confidence of international business community, the Government had to sell a part of its gold reserves and a certain amount of gold was even pledged to obtain the foreign exchange reserves to meet its obligations. Further, it had to approach the IMF for loans to tide over the foreign exchange crisis.

New Economic Policy of Structural Adjustment

However, to evolve a long-term solution to achieve higher rate of economic growth with price stability, to bring about equilibrium in balance of payments the newly elected Congress Government with Dr. Manmohan Singh as Finance Minister adopted what is popularly called *New Economic Policy* on the advice of IMF and World Bank. According to this policy, the Government pruned down its expenditure so as to *reduce budget deficits for achieving price stability. But more important element of new economic policy was the adoption of what are called Structural Adjustment Reforms* which sought to change the nature of Indian economic system by ultimately establishing a *free market economy.* Thus, the economic crisis of 1991 provided an opportunity for the government to undertake major economic reforms aimed at removing restrictive control on the domestic industrial production and investment and foreign trade. Thus Professors T.N. Srinivasan and S. Tendulkar write, "the *reforms indeed heralded a major change in the country's development strategy. India gradually abondoned the use of quantitative controls in economic management in favour of market-based instruments. There was a decisive move away from inward orientation and toward greater integration with the global economy. Finally, the reforms signalled a shift away from an overstretched, over-extended rigid and inefficient public sector and toward greater reliance on the private sector.*"[1]

Under this structural adjustment programme, the role of public sector in economic development has been diluted and that of private sector enhanced and expanded. It may be noted that the policy of free-market economy also got strong stimulus due to the collapse of socialist system in Soviet Russia and other centrally planned socialist economies in Eastern Europe. Accordingly, under the new economic policy initiated in 1991 the idea of the predominant role of the public sector was abandoned and the private sector was given a greater role in promoting economic growth through competition and efficiency. Instead of being directed by the planning and licensing, the private sector was to be governed by the market forces. Besides, there has been liberalisation of imports as tariffs have been drastically cut down. Foreign private investment has been given greater importance and incentives have been provided to attract them. Further, instead of import-substitution, now greater emphasis has been laid on the expansion of exports to achieve growth with self-reliance. In the post-reform period four Five Year Plans have been launched. We discuss them below :

ROLE OF PLANNING AND STATE IN THE POST-REFORM PERIOD

The crisis of 1991 which was the result of fiscal imbalances and balance of payments difficulties proved to be a turning point in Indian planning. Public sector was found to be inefficient. Far from generating resources for investment, it became burden on the national exchequer. Private sector was crippled by various direct bureaucratic controls which prevented its growth. In response to these, policy of economic liberalisation and privatisation was adopted. Licensing was abolished except in case of few industries. The exclusive role of public sector was confined to a few strategic industries. All other industries were thrown open for production and investment by the private sectors. A pertinent question has been raised whether in this regime of liberalisation and privatisation, there was any useful role for planning and State to play in the development of the Indian economy. However, it has been pointed out that even in this regime planning and the State had an important role, though somewhat different one from that envisaged earlier. We explain below the role of planning and the State in the post-reform period.

Creating Social Infrastructure and Promoting Human Development. The first and foremost, planning is needed even after the policy of liberalisation and privatisation for creating the social infrastructure and for human development which are of crucial importance for promoting economic development. We need to build schools, colleges, hospitals, institutions of technical education and

1. T.N. Srinivasan and Suresh D. Tendulkar, *Integrating India with the World Economy*, Oxford University Press, 2003, p.29.

scientific research. We have to impart skills to the youth so that they can be employed in productive activities. These can be built better through planning by the state. Private sector participation in creation of social structure and human development is not capable of taking care of the entire needs of the society, particularly of the poor and weaker sections of the society. Market mechanism which is driven by private profit motive will not be able to bring an equilibrium between the 'need' and 'supply' in this regard. Therefore, planning in this area will remain important.

Poverty Alleviation and Employment Generation. Planning has to play an important role in poverty alleviation and employment generation. Poverty exists because the poor people and downtrodden have little asset endowments with which to engage themselves in productive activities to earn sufficient incomes. Lack of adequate number of jobs on wage basis is another important cause of poverty and unemployment. It is through planning that the assets for the poor can be built. For example, adequate credit supply to the poor farmers is necessary if they have to make improvements in their land, build irrigation facilities and other assets to increase their productivity. Private sector and market mechanism cannot be expected to build and provide assets to the poor.

Special Anti-Poverty Schemes. Besides, due to various factor price distortions such as relatively low price of capital due to various fiscal concessions, over-valued exchange rate of rupee, private sector has a tendency to use more capital-intensive techniques and therefore will not create sufficient employment opportunities. It is due to increasing capital-intensity of the production processes that employment elasticity of output in the industrial and agricultural sectors of the Indian economy has greatly fallen in the last two decades. This has significantly reduced the employment potential of the Indian economy. Planning and State intervention is needed to provide disincentives to the use of capital-intensive technique and to give incentives to use labour-intensive techniques of production.

Further, plans can provide for special anti-poverty schemes and special employment programmes for the poor and unemployed. Anti-poverty programmes such as Food for Work Programme, Employment Guarantee Programme to provide one person of a household living below the poverty line employment for 100 days in a year will be of great help for the poor and unemployed. If the poor and unemployed are used to build *durable assets*, it will enhance the productivity of the economy. It is through planned actions by State that such anti-poverty programmes can be effectively implemented.

Building Physical Infrastructure. It is now well known that private sector is least interested in building physical infrastructure such as power, communication, roads, ports, highways as private benefits are less than social benefits in their case. This is because building of infrastructure generates *external economies*. It is now well-recognised that economic growth is impeded by the lack of these infrastructural facilities. Past experience also shows that except in the field of telecommunication, private sector in India does not feel attracted to make adequate investment in the infrastructure projects. Therefore, to achieve 8 per cent annual growth rate in GDP on a sustained basis, which is the new goal set for the Indian economy, public investment in economic infrastructure in the framework of a well-designed plan is of paramount importance.

Investment in Agriculture. Whereas economic reforms initiated since 1991 had a focus on accelerating industrial growth through liberalisation and privatisation, investment in agriculture was neglected. Much of the resources of the government were spent on providing subsidies to farmers. As a result, capital formation in agriculture has substantially slowed down since the early nineties. The average rate of agricultural growth has been extremely low in the last one decade and a half. This has worsened the employment opportunities in agriculture and in some States, especially Andhra Pradesh, Karnataka and Orissa, several farmers have committed suicide. Agriculture needs adequate investment for which access to credit to farmers at low interest rates are needed. Besides, to enhance the productivity in agriculture investment in irrigation is essential. Only the State in a planned framework can make adequate investment in expanding irrigation facilities and in undertaking flood-control projects.

Regional Balance. Planning is also necessary to remove large disparities in development between regions. The removal of the regional disparities in economic development requires flow of investible resources across regions. With greater freedom and choice of location that is now available to the private sector, it is more likely that some States would be able to attract more private investment than others. As a matter of fact, the past experience has shown that market forces do not work in a way to achieve regional balance in economic development. Therefore, planning is needed to manage the flow of resources across regions for rapid removal of regional disparities. For this plan formulation has to ensure that public investment in infrastructure must be reoriented in favour of the less well-off States. At present plans do provide for special area programmes such as the Hill Area Development Plan, Tribal Area Plan, Plans for development of North East area and Jammu and Kashmir. While these programmes help in development of basic infrastructure in these areas, the backlog of development is large. Therefore, considerable planned efforts and resources are needed for integration of such backward regions into the mainstream of development process in the country.

It may be further noted that the focus regarding the issue of backwardness and regional balance has traditionally been on industrialisation. The evidence, however, suggestes that reduction in regional disparities, particularly in average standards of living, may be better achieved through greater focus on agriculture and other rural activities. For this plan formulation should be such that provides for increasing the productivity of agriculture in backward areas. Besides, planned efforts are needed to improve connectivity of these areas in terms of transport and communication with the rest of the country.

Protecting Environment and Ecology. Finally, there are areas such as protection of environment, forests and ecology in which markets cannot play an efficient allocative role. The intervention of the State is essential to regulate private sector operations and working of market mechanism in respect of activities which adversely affects environment, forest and ecology of the economy. Similarly, working of market mechanism works in a way that leads to the excessive depletion of scarce natural resources like rare minerals, land and water. This harms the prospects of sustainable growth. Proper planning for their optimal use is therefore necessary. In this regard, the observations of the Eighth Five Year Plan are worth quoting. "*Market mechanism is never adequate for protecting environment, forests and ecology. Nor is it adequate in giving guidance about the use of scarce resources like rare minerals, land and water. A long term perspective, and hence planning, is needed in these areas.*"[2]

Allocation of Resources among States. India is a federal state. Both the Centre and States have distinct areas of operation. Investment for development requires resources. Resources from certain taxes levied by the Centre are distributed among the States by the Finance Commission which is appointed every five years to review the situation. Non-tax resources are allocated among the states by the Planning Commission according to their developmental needs and projects submitted by them in this regard.

Indicative Planning

As far as the role of the private sector is concerned under the present regime of economic liberalisation it is regulated through *indicative planning*. Under the indicative planning, Planning Commission has to outline the broad directions in which the economy should be growing. To conclude, the planning has to (a) provide vision of the future, (b) construct medium term economic projections for the entire economy, (c) evolve a system of information pooling and dissemination, (d) identify areas of development where the economy has strengths or where the country needs to build up strengths, (e) evolve appropriate policy measures to achieve the desired goals.

Thus, despite a more deregulated environment as it exists today in India, planning has a useful role to play, especially in policy formulation, to achieve the national goals and objectives.

---

2. Planning Commission, *Eighth Five Year Plan.*

EIGHTH PLAN AND ITS DEVELOPMENT STRATEGY

Eighth Plan which was to start from April 1990 was deferred because of political uncertainty. Finally, when, in June, 1991, Congress government came back to power, Indian economy was in the grip of economic crisis due to balance of payments difficulties. Due to this economic crisis, as mentioned above, the whole approach to economic policy went a sea change. When the final version of Eighth Plan covering the period 1992-97 was formulated in accordance with the new economic policy it laid emphasis on liberalisation, privatisation and globalisation of the Indian economy. The role of public sector, which played a vital role in development strategies of earlier plans, was greatly restricted. The Eighth Five Year Plan visualised the role of public sector in the following terms.

1. The public sector should make investment only in infrastructure such as power, communication, irrigation, and transport where private sector investment is not likely to come forth to an adequate extent within reasonable time perspective. In line with new Industrial Policy of 1991, the public sector was to withdraw from the areas where no public purpose was served by its presence. Thus *public sector disinvestment* was planned to be accelerated. The licensing and other physical controls over the private sector were abolished. The private sector was allowed to invest in those industries which were previously the exclusive concern of the public sector.

2. Public enterprises were expected to accept the principle of market economy as the main operating principle unless the commodities and services that were produced and distributed by them were specifically required for protecting the poorest in the society.

Indicative Planning. In line with the policy of liberalisation and privatisation the Eighth Plan mentioned that planning in India would be increasingly *indicative*. The main purpose of indicative planning is to improve the information available to private enterprises so that they can make optimal decisions regarding investment and production. This information is provided through making forecasts or projections of GDP, demands for various goods, consumer spending, balance of payments, money supply, inflationary trends and other macro aggregates. However, such projections of various macro-aggregates are not regarded as targets as would be the case under centralised planning. Private enterprises face a lot of uncertainties regarding future due to lack of information. Indicative planning is regarded as a way of providing information to the private enterprises. Besides, by using various fiscal and monetary instruments, the government could encourage industries which have a bright future and discourage industries which have no future. Thus, through indicative plans efforts are made to identify so called '*sun-rise*' *industries* and '*sun-set*' industries.

Promoting Competition. The major thrust of the Eighth Plan was to create a more competitive environment as a means to improving the productivity and efficiency of the system. This was sought to be achieved by removing the barriers to entry and restrictions on the growth of firms in the private sector.

Export-oriented Growth Strategy. Another important element of the growth strategy of the Eighth Plan was that it laid greater emphasis on the growth of exports to accelerate rate of economic growth and to achieve self-reliance. Thus, export pessimism of earlier plans was abandoned and it set a target of achieving 13.6 per cent annual growth rate in exports as against the target of 8.4 per cent annual growth in imports.

Realising that investment was a major driving force of economic growth, the Eighth Plan planned an average saving rate of 21.6 per cent of GDP and a foreign saving rate (that is, current account deficit) of 1.4 per cent of GDP, and fixed investment rate of 23 per cent of GDP. With the assumed incremental capital-output ratio (ICOR) of 4.1, it was expected to achieve average annual growth rate of 5.6 per cent during the Eighth Plan period (1992-97). However, in the Eighth Plan higher growth rate of 6.7 per cent per annum was actually achieved. Actual investment rate achieved was 23.3 with 3.5 as incremental capital-output ratio (ICOR).

PLANNING STRATEGY IN THE NINTH PLAN (1997-2002)

In the development strategy adopted in the Ninth Plan, private sector was given a greater role in raising rate of growth and creating employment opportunities in the economy. It was thought that vigorous private sector operating in the macroeconomic environment of competition and free markets would be able to make efficient use of scarce resources. However, the role of government and public sector in providing healthcare, education and safe drinking water, especially in rural areas, was emphasised, since it was believed that private sector would not adequately invest in these social sectors.

In the Ninth Plan a high priority was also given to public investment in economic infrastructure such as power, roads, posts, telecommunications and transport. The higher growth will take place only if adequate infrastructure was available. It was thought that private investment will also rise if infrastructure facilities were available. Further, it was laid down that economic infrastructure in the form of irrigation, rural roads, promotion of agricultural research and creation of organised agricultural markets were quite necessary if broad-based agricultural growth was to be achieved. Besides, exports of agricultural products were planned to be promoted to raise the incomes of the farmers. Like the strategy pursued in the Eighth Plan, ***export-led growth strategy*** was given importance in the Ninth Plan as well. Export orientation was given to the strategy so as to achieve not only self-reliance but also more rapid economic growth. To open up our industrial economy to international competition, phased reduction in import-tariffs was to be carried out. However, to protect Indian industries against foreign competition, anti-dumping measures were planned to be strengthened.

It was stressed that in the Ninth Plan there was no need for retaining majority stake in public sector undertakings except for those that are in the strategic spheres where national security concerns were involved. The resources mobilised from public sector disinvestment in non-strategic enterprises were to be used for much needed investment in social sector, especially health and education. Finally, for keeping inflation under check the need for reduction of *fiscal deficit* of both the Centre and States was emphasised. This was to be achieved through greater tax collection, reduction in subsidies and non-plan expenditure. Besides, subsidies were to the targeted to specific groups who needed help from Government.

In the Ninth Plan (1997-2002), the target of achieving 7 per cent growth rate per annum was fixed which was later revised to 6.5 per cent in view of lower rate of growth actually achieved in the first year (1997-98) of the plan. To achieve this growth rate annual investment rate of 28.2 per cent was planned and incremental capital-output ratio (ICOR) of 4 was assumed.

Rate of growth of GDP actually achieved in the Ninth Plan was 5.5 per cent per annum as against the target of 6.5 per cent. The lower growth of GDP relative to target was due to lower actual growth rate of 2.5 per cent per annum in agriculture as against the target of 3.9 per cent and sharp fall in growth rate of manufacturing which registered 3 per cent annual growth rate as against the target of 8.2 per cent. The lower industrial growth rate in the Ninth Plan was mainly due to demand recession for industry caused by fall in public sector investment and poor performance of agriculture. Another important failure of the Ninth Plan was that it could not generate employment for 50 million persons as per the target fixed. As a matter of fact, it has been found that unemployment rate on current daily status basis which was 7.32 per cent in 1999-2000 went up during the plan period and the backlog of unemployment reached the alarming figure of about 35 million persons at the end of the Ninth Plan.[3]

3. See Planning Commission, *Tenth Five Year Plan* (2002-07), Vol 1, p. 24.

THE TENTH FIVE YEAR PLAN (2002-07)

Objectives and Targets

The Tenth Five Year Plan which covers the period 2002-07 has set an *ambitious growth target of 8 per cent per annum*. In recognising that economic growth cannot be the only objective of a national plan, the Tenth Plan has also set the targets for a few other aspects of human development.

Reduction in Poverty. First, it has envisaged to reduce poverty ratio from 26.1 in 2000 to 21 per cent of population by the year 2007. Second, overall literacy rate (of 7 years +) is to be increased from 65 per cent of population in 2000 to 75 per cent by the end of 2007.

Employment Generation. A significant objective of Tenth Five Year plan is to generate 50 million jobs[4] over the five year period (2002-07) of the Tenth Plan, that is, creation of one crore jobs every year. This is a very ambitious objective and doubts have been rasied about its feasibility. This is significant because no measures have been suggested in the Tenth Plan which would make process of economic growth more labour-intensive.

Balanced Development of States. The Tenth Plan lays stress on the importance of balanced development of all States and includes a State-wise break-up of broad development targets including targets for growth rates and social development consistent with national targets.

Equity and Social Justice. The Tenth Plan also emphasises the goal of achieving equity and social justice. It has been pointed out that rigidities in the Indian economy make poverty-reducing effects of economic growth ineffective. In this regard various poverty alleviation and employment generation programmes such as the Swarnajayanti Gram Swarozgar Yojana (SGSY), Sampoorna Grameen Rozgar Yojana (SGRY), Antyodaya Anna Yojana, drinking water supply projects and housing projects for the poor have been included for effective implementation. These programmes will help to reduce poverty and generate gainful employment opportunities.

Development Strategy of the Tenth Plan

Redefining the Role of Government. The development strategy adopted in the Tenth Plan provides for redefining the role of Government in the context of the emergence of a strong and vibrant private sector. Accordingly, the larger participation of private sector in raising investment and bringing about higher economic growth rate has been provided for in the plan. Besides, the role of public sector for development of infrastructure such as investment in the development of highways, ports, telecommunication, irrigation, transport facilities has been emphasised. Further, the role of Government's fiscal and monetary policies in directing private investment and raising resources for public investment in infrastructure has been given due importance.

Improving Quality of Life. But economic development does not merely mean higher rate of growth in Gross Domestic Product (GDP). Ultimately, economic development means improvement in the *quality of life* of the people. The strategy of the Tenth Five Year Plan lays stress on the greater access to basic social services such as education, health, availability of drinking water and improvement in basic sanitation. In respect of these the Tenth Plan fixes specific targets which are planned to be achieved during the Tenth Plan period. These targets are :

1. Universal access to primary education by 2007.
2. Increase in literacy of the people to 75 per cent of the population by 2007.
3. Reduction of infant mortality rate to 45 per 1000 live births by the end of the Tenth Plan (*i.e.* 2007).
4. Reduction of maternal mortality ratio to 2 per 1000 live births by 2007.

---

4. Planning Commission, *Mid-Term Appraisal of the 10th Plan.*

5. To improve ecology increase in forest and tree cover to 25 per cent by 2007 had been planned.
6. Access to potable drinking water was to be ensured to the people in all villages by the year 2012.
7. Provision for cleaning all major polluted rivers by the year 2007 had been made.

To achieve the above targets adequate amount of resources had been allocated to the social sectors.

Emphasis on Agricultural Development. Another important element of the development strategy of the Tenth Plan was to accelerate agricultural growth. It has been pointed out that higher agricultural growth will benefit the rural poor. In this respect stress has been laid on the *diversification of agriculture* which means farmers should increasingly take to horticulture, fisheries, vegetables apart from growing of crops.

Employment Generation and Services Sector. Besides, the development strategy of the Tenth Plan is to ensure rapid growth of those sectors which will generate more opportunities for gainful employment. For generation of more employment opportunities role of the services sector has been specially highlighted. In this connection mention may be made of such services as construction, tourism, IT enabled services, computer software, transport trade and hotels. However, it has been rightly pointed out that rapid growth of services sector is dependent on higher industrial growth. Therefore, the two cannot be promoted in isolation.

Special Anti-Poverty Programmes. Lastly, as in the previous Five Year Plans, it had been recognised in the Tenth Plan that higher economic growth rate alone is not enough to generate employment opportunities for 50 million workers during the Tenth Plan period and to reduce poverty ratio to 21 per cent of population by 2007. Therefore, special anti-poverty programmes had been planned to supplement the growth efforts to reduce the poverty ratio.

Growth Target and Macroeconomic Parameters

The target of 8 per cent average annual growth rate for the period 2002-07 was considered to be feasibile as it considered that scope for improvements in efficiency in both public and private sectors was very large which would ensure reduction in incremental capital-output ratio (ICOR) from 4.53 during the Ninth Plan to 3.58 in the Tenth Plan. In this regard for utilising the idle capital stock in the economy, the Tenth Plan laid emphasis on completion of on-going projects and privatisation of public enterprises, especially those which are working below capacity.

Table 42.1 : Macro Parameters for the Tenth Plan

	Ninth Plan (1997-2002) (Actuals)	Tenth Plan (2002-07) (Targets)	Tenth Plan 2002-07 (Actuals: Average)
Gross Domestic Saving rate (% of GDP_{mp}) at current market prices)	23.6	26.84	31.4
Investment rate (% of GDP_{mp})	24.3	28.41	31.4
Current account deficit of balance of payments (% of GDP_{mp})	0.7	1.57	0.0
ICOR	4.4	3.58	4.0
GDP_{mp} growth rate (% per annum)	5.4	8.0	7.6

Source. *11th Five Year Plan Document and Economic Surveys,* 2007-08, 2008-09, 2009-10.

The achievement of Tenth Plan target of 8 per cent annual growth rate of GDP depends crucially on the expected reduction in incremental capital-output ratio (ICOR) from then estimated 4.53 during the Ninth Plan to 3.58 in the Tenth Plan. The investment required to achieve this growth target had been estimated to be 28.4 per cent of GDP. This means a sharp acceleration in the investment rate from 24.4 per cent in the base year to 32.3 per cent in the terminal year (2006-07). Of the 7.9 per centage point increase in the investment rate planned in the Tenth Plan, 5.3 percentage increase in the investment rate was to be in the private sector and the remaining 4.5 percentage increase was envisaged for the Government and public sector. For achieving this increase in investment, foreign savings (*i.e.* current account deficit in balance of paymnts) equal to 1.57 per cent of GDP_{mp} had been estimated.

The total outlay envisaged for the Tenth Plan is ₹ 19,68,815 crore for both Central and State plans. Fiscal and revenue deficits had been projected at 4.7 per cent and 2.9 per cent of GDP respectively. It was emphasised that both the Central and State Governments had to take appropriate fiscal measures to achieve the plan targets. The fiscal policy measures suggested by the Planning Commission are effective enforcement of income tax administration, elimination of exemptions under corporation tax, moving towards a single excise duty rate, expansion in the coverage of service tax, implementation of recommendations of the Expenditure Reforms Commission, better targeting of food subsidy so as to reduce expenditure on food subsidy, reduction in the paybill of Central Government, reduction in staff strength, reduction in Government borrowings to reduce interest rate burden. At the State level, implementation of VAT (value added tax) and raising of user charges on power supply had been suggested to increase financial resources for plan projects.

Achievement in the Tenth Plan. As will be seen from Table 42.1, the targets of economic growth and its related macro-variables had been substantially achieved. It was estimated that average annual growth rate in the Tenth Plan period (2002-07) was 7.6% as against the target of 8%, investment rate rose to 31.4% as against target of 28.41. However, the average agricultural growth rate per annum was 2.5% as against the target of 4 per cent. Further, unemployment rate on current daily status basis for the economy rose from 7.3 per cent in 1999-2000 to 8.3 per cent in 2004-05.

Evaluation of Achievements of Tenth Five Year Plan

In the 10th Plan, the Indian economy has made significant progress in terms of GDP growth. As against a target of 8 per cent annual average growth in GDP, the actual growth in rate achieved has been estimated at 7.8 per cent, that is, the target of 10th Plan has been substantially achieved and is much higher than the growth rate of 5.5 per cent achieved during the 9th Plan period. This higher growth rate during the 10th Plan period has been possible due to higher rate of domestic saving and investment and reduction in capital-output ratio in the 10th Plan period. The gross domestic saving rate and investment rate which were 23.1 and 23.8 per cent in the 9th Plan rose to 31.4 and 31.4 per cent on an average in the 10th Plan period respectively. Besides, incremental capital-output ratio (ICOR) improved from 4.4 in the 9th Plan period to 4.0 in the 10th Plan period. Thus we succeeded in achieving overall growth targets in the 10th Plan period. This has inspired the Planning Commission to set a target of average growth rate of 9 per cent per annum in the 11th Plan period.

Increase in Foreign Exchange Reserves. Another significant achievement of 10th Plan is large increase in foreign exchange reserves. It will be remembered that economic crisis of 1991 occurred as a result of drastic fall in foreign exchange reserves. The substantial increase in foreign exchange reserves has been the result of continuing economic reforms initiated in 1991. The increase in foreign exchange reserves has been possible because of increase in capital inflows due to foreign institutional investment (FII), foreign direct investment (FDI) and non-resident Indian (NRI) deposits. Foreign exchange reserves which crossed 100 billion US dollars in December 2003 reached the level of about US $ 192 billion at the end of March 2007.

However, its is worth noting that in the capital inflows the proportion of FDI which enhances productive capacity has been low as compared to FII inflows which are invested in highly speculative activities, especially shares of Indian companies and are very volatile.

In view of the above as compared to the 9th Plan, the pace of growth of the Indian economy accelerated with improvement in major macroeconomic fundamentals.

Lower Growth Rate of Agriculture. A great failure of 10th Plan is its dismal performance regarding growth rate of agriculture. As against the target of 4 per cent annual growth rate in agriculture, the estimate of actual annual growth rate in agriculture is estimated at 2.5 per cent for 10th Plan period. Thus the objective of the 10th Plan has miserably failed to achieve a reversal of declining trend in the growth rate of agriculture and to eventually take it to 4 per cent per annum. It is important to note that rise in inflation rate during 2006-07 and after has been fuelled by supply-side constraints posed by lower growth rate in agriculture.

Failure to Reduce Poverty as per the Target. An important failure of 10th Plan is that it did not achieve the targeted reduction in poverty ratio. It was planned in the 10th Plan period that higher rate of economic growth envisaged in the 10th Plan and introduction of employment guarantee scheme will help in reducing poverty ratio to 19 per cent in 2006-07 as against 26.1 per cent in 1999-2000. However, the 61st Round of NSS finds that on the basis of uniform recall period of 30 days, poverty ratio was 27.5 per cent in 2004-05 as against the comparable figure 36.0 per cent in 1993-94. This means in the years of post-reform period 1993-94 to 2004-05 there was a reduction in poverty by 8.5 percentage points which works out to be 0.74 per cent per annum. The higher growth in GDP in this period, especially 7.6 per cent growth during the 10th Plan, had not resulted in greater reduction in poverty ratio. In absolute number about 302 million persons were found to be below the poverty line in 2004-05. The data also reveal that 55.4 per cent of total poor living below the poverty line were concentrated in five States of Uttar Pradesh, Bihar, Maharashtra, West Bengal and Odisha.

Dismal Performance Regarding Reduction in Unemployment. In the 10th Plan the target of reducing daily status unemployment rate to a level of 5.11 per cent was fixed. The 61st Round of NSS reveals that daily-status unemployment rate which was 6.1 and 7.3 per cent in 1993-94 and 1999-2000 respectively rose to 8.3 per cent in 2004-05. *Rural unemployment on daily status* basis rose from 7.2 per cent in 1999-2000 to 9.1 per cent in 2004-05 whereas *daily status urban unemployment* rose from 7.2 per cent in 1999-2000 to 8.8 per cent in 2004-05. A matter of serious concern is that this had been associated with a sharp increase in unemployment from 9.3 per cent in 1993-94 to 15.3 per cent in 2004-05 among agricultural labour households which represent poorest sections.

Besides, it is worth noting that in the organised sector there had not been any *net* increase in employment opportunities despite a very fast rate of its growth. Actually it is in the unorganised sector where labour productivity is very low that employment of labour has increased. The dismal performance on employment front is a great failure of development strategy of the 10th Plan.

It follows from above that though in the 10th Plan objectives of GDP growth rate, increase in domestic saving and investment rates, expansion of capital flows and foriegn exchange inflows had been achieved, the important objectives of significant reduction in poverty and unemployment remained unfulfilled.

THE ELEVENTH FIVE YEAR PLAN

The Approach Paper of the Eleventh Plan proposes faster and more inclusive growth in the five-year period (2007-12). According to the Approach to the 11th Plan, though annual growth in GDP in the 10th Plan period rose to 7.6 per cent as against 5.5 per cent in the 9th Plan, it failed to be sufficiently inclusive. The failure to achieve inclusive growth implies that all sections of the population were not benefited from higher growth rate achieved. The employment in the organised sector did not increase despite faster growth in GDP. The percentage of population below the poverty line declined but only at a slower pace. Malnutrition levels though appear to have declined but still continue to be very high. Too many people still lack access to basic services such as health, education, clean drinking water and sanitation facilities without which they cannot gain a share in the benefits of economic growth.

Despite the above observations, Approach to the 11th Plan, as in the past, emphasises the achievement of rapid growth in GDP. Thus, according to it, "*Rapid growth is an essential part of our strategy for two reasons: Firstly, it is only in a rapidly growing economy that we can expect to sufficiently raise the incomes of the mass of our population to bring about a general improvement in living conditions. Secondly, rapid growth is necessary to generate the resources needed to provide basic services to all*".[5]

Objectives of the 11th Plan (2007-12)

1. Faster Economic Growth and Related Targets. The foremost objective of the 11th Plan is to achieve a higher annual growth rate of 9 per cent over the 11th Plan period. With population growing at 1.5 per cent per year 9 per cent growth in GDP would double the real per capita income in 10 years. The approach document envisages achievement of higher growth rate by increasing investment rate to 36.7 per cent. It further assumes capital-output ratio of 4.1. Though investment target of 36.7 per cent GDP had already been crossed in the year 2007-08, the 11th Plan target of rate of growth of GDP was revised downward to 7 per cent due to impact of global financial crisis.

To achieve higher rate of investment for generating 9 per cent growth rate, the 11th Plan envisaged increasing the domestic saving rate to 34.8 per cent of GDP and foreign saving to 1.88 per cent of GDP. Further, with overall objective of attaining 9 per cent growth in GDP, the target for agricultural growth was fixed at 4 per cent per annum, for industry at 10.11 per cent and for services at 9.11 per cent per annum. As will be seen from Table 42.2, compared with actual growth rate (2.5%) of

Table 42.2 : Macroeconomic Targets of the 11th Plan and its Achievements

Indicator	*10th Plan (Actuals Average)*	*11th Plan (Targets)*	*2007-08*	*2008-09*	*2009-10*	*2010-11*
(A) Growth Rate	7.8	9.0	9.2	6.7	8.0	8.5
GDP at market prices (%)						
1. Agriculture and Allived Sectors	2.5	4.0	4.7	1.6	0.4	6.6
2. Industry	8.6	10.11	9.3	3.1	10.4	7.3
3. Services	9.0	9.11		9.3	8.3	9.3
(B) Investment Rate			10.4			
(as % of GDP) of which	31.4*	36.7*	37.7	34.9	36.5	36.4
1. Public sector	6.9	8.0	9.1	N.A	–	–
2. Private sector	22.9	28.7	28.5	N.A	–	–
(C) Gross Domestic Saving Rate (% of GDP)	31.4	34.8	36.4	32.5	33.7	33.8
(D) Current Account Deficit (% of GDP), that is, foreign savings	0.0	–1.88	–1.3	–2.4	–2.8	2.6
(E) Government Fiscal Deficit (both Centre and States Combined (as % of GDP)	8.0	6.0	2.6*	6.0*	6.7*	5.1*

Source: (1) Planning Commission, *11th Five Year Plan,* 2007. * indicates of the Centre only
(2) GOI, *Economic Survey* 2008-09, 2009-10, 2010-11.

5. Planning Commission, *Approach to the 11th Plan.*

agriculture attained in the 10th Plan period target for agricultural growth in the Eleventh Five Year Plan was substantially increased to 4 per cent per annum but for industry there is small increase from 8.6 per cent in the 10th Plan to 10.11 per cent and for services from 9 per cent achieved in the 10th Plan to 9.11 per cent in the 11th Plan.

Inclusive Growth : As mentioned above, approach to the 11th Plan lays emphasis on achieving inclusive growth. Inclusive growth means that benefits of economic growth should accrue to all sections of the population. In fact, this is a new term for equitable growth or growth with equity. Thus, the Approach Paper of 11th Plan states, "The higher growth rate must be combined with policies that will ensure that per capita income growth is *broad-based* benefiting all sections of the population, especially those who have thus far remained deprived"[6]. For achieving the objective of inclusive growth, Approach Paper of 11th Plan lays stress on (1) faster agricultural growth, (2) faster generation of employment opportunities, (3) reduction in poverty ratio, and (4) the expansion of education, health and other essential services. Thus, according to 11th Plan Approach Paper, "*The structure of growth should also be such as to promote a widespread of benefits. Doubling agricultural GDP growth rate to around 4 per cent is particularly important in this respect*. This must be combined to promote rapid growth in *non-agricultural employment* so as to create 58 *million jobs* in the 11th Plan period. If these objectives are achieved the percentage of poverty can be reduced by 10 percentage points by the end of the Plan period".[7]

Expansion in Education. Besides, faster agricultural growth and employment generation, the provision of good quality education is very important for attaining inclusive growth. Thus 11th Plan Approach Paper states: "**Education is the most critical input for empowering people with skills and knowledge and for giving them access to productive employment in the future. The 11th Plan should ensure that we move towards raising public spending on education to 6% of GDP....It must fulfil the constitutional obligation of providing free and compulsory elementary education of good quality to all children up to age 14**".[8]

For promoting education the following measures have been suggested by the 11th Plan:

1. Though the enrolment for education of children of the age of 6 to 14 years will be completed by 2007, the 11th Plan envisages that children *must complete* 8 years of schooling and this poses a great challenge. To ensure this drop-out rate in primary school education for both boys and girls of all social groups must be reduced sharply from 52.2 % in 2003-04 to 20% by 2011-12.

2. Literacy rate for persons of age 7 years and above is planned to be raised to 85 per cent by 2011-12. Besides, the *gender gap* in literacy is to be reduced by 10 percentage points.

3. To expand higher education so that the percentage of youth in the relevant age group receiving higher education is to be raised from the present 10 per cent to 15 per cent by the end of 11th Plan.

Health. As regards promoting health of the people, the following targets have been fixed :

1. It is planned to reduce *infant mortality rate* to 28 per cent and maternal mortality rate to 1 per 1000 live births.

2. The target of reduction in total *fertility rate* to 2.1 per cent by 2011-12 has been fixed so as to reduce population growth rate.

3. It is planned to provide clean drinking water facilities to all people in the country by the year 2009.

4. It is planned to reduce malnutrition among children of age group 0–3 years to half its present level.

---

6. *op. cit.*, p. 97
7. *op. cit.*, p. 57
8. *op. cit.*, p.57.

Infrastructure. For the development of infrastructure the following measures are planned to be undertaken:

1. It is planned to ensure connection to all villages and to all households below poverty line (BPL) by 2011-12.

2. It is proposed to ensure all-weather road connections to all habitations with a population of 1000 persons and above (500 and above for hilly areas) by the year 2009.

3. To connect every village by telephone and provide broad-band connectivity to all villages by 2012.

4. It is planned to provide homestead sites to all by the end of 11th Plan and to speed up the pace of housing construction for the poor so as to cover all the poor by 2016-17.

Sectoral Allocation of Resources

A comparison of the total outlay in the 11th Plan with that of the 10th Plan reveals that as compared to the total of ₹ 16,18,460 crores actually spent in the 10th Plan period, in the 11th Plan total outlay of ₹ 36,44,718 is proposed to be spent on various schemes. This was needed to achieve growth rate of 9 per cent per annum.

Table 42.3. Sector Allocation of the 10th and 11th Plans

Sector	10th Plan (Actual) 2002-07		11th Plan 2007-2012 (Proposed)	
	₹ in crores	%	₹ in crores	%
1. Agriculture and Allied	60,702	3.8	1,36,381	3.7
2. Rural Development	1,37,710	8.5	3,01,069	8.3
3. Special Area Programme	16,425	1.0	26,329	0.7
4. Irrigation & flood Control	1,12,415	6.9	2,10,329	5.8
Total Agriculture (1 to 4)	**3,27,250**	**20.2**	**6,74,105**	**18.5**
5. Energy	3,63,635	22.4	8,54,123	23.6
6. Industry and Minerals	64,655	4.0	1,53,600	4.2
7. Transport	2,63,934	16.3	5,72,413	15.7
8. Communication	82,945	5.1	95,380	2.6
9. Science and Technology	28,673	1.8	87,933	2.4
10. General Economic Services	30,349	19	62,523	1.7
11. Social Services*	4,36,529	27.0	11,06,327	30.9
12. General Services	20,489	1.3	42,283	1.2
Total	16,18,460	100	36,44,718	100

* Social services include education, healthcare, water supply and sanitation, housing and urban development

Source : Planning Commission, *Eleventh Five Year Plan* (2007-12)

A look at Table 42.3 will reveal that in absolute terms total outlay on agriculture and allied sectors in the 11th Plan has more than doubled though relative expenditure on it remains almost the same as in the 10th Plan. In respect of irrigation and flood control, the expenditure on it has increased from about 1,12,000 crores in the 10th Plan to about 2,10,000 crores though relative allocation of expenditure on it has been reduced from 6.9 per cent to 5.8 per cent. This is quite disturbing as it is felt by the economists that the growth of irrigation and control of floods are important drivers of agricultural growth.

In keeping with the new thinking about economic development, the *social services* (comprising education, health, drinking water supply etc) has been given a higher priority as allocation of public outlay to it has been increased substantially, both in absolute and relative terms. Similarly, resource allocation to energy generation has been given higher priority; its share in total public outlay has been raised from 22.4 per cent in the 10th Plan to 23.6 per cent in the 11th Plan.

However, in our view, apart from resource allocation much depends on implementation of schemes in various sectors for determining growth of the economy.

Population, Labour Force and Employment Generation

Another important aspect of the 11th Plan is its estimates of growth of population, labour force and employment generation during the plan period. On the basis of its estimates of population growth and participation rate as will be seen from Table 42.4, Planning Commission estimates that population of India would increase from 1,092 million in 2004-05 to 1,208 million in 2011-12 and labour force from about 420 million in 2004-05 to 439 million in 2006-07 and to 483.6 million in 2011-12 i.e. 45 million during the plan period (2007-12). It will be seen from Table 42.4 that employment opportunities for 58 million persons (460–402 = 58) are estimated to be generated during the plan period (2007-2008). On this basis it is calculated that the number of persons unemployed will decline from 36.7 million in 2006-07 to 23.3 milllion in 2011-02. As a result, daily status unemployment rate as per cent of labour force will fall from 8.36 per cent in 2006-07 to 4.83 per cent in 2011-12. However, according National Sample Survey daily status unemployment rate was found to be 5.6 per cent.

Table 42.4. Population, Labour Force and Employment

	2004-05	2006-07	2011-12
1. Population	1092.8	1128.1	1208
2. Labour force	419.6	438.9	483.6
3. Employment opportunities	384.9	402.2	460.3
4. Unemployed (millions)	34.7	36.7	23.3
5. Unemployment Rate (%) on Daily Status Basis	8.28	8.36	4.83

Source : Planning Commission, *Eleventh Five Year Plan,* 2007-08.

Critical Evaluation of the Eleventh Plan

The Eleventh Five Year Plan sets for itself highly ambitious objectives and targets. It not only aims at achieving faster economic growth of 9 per cent per annum but also inclusive growth which ensures rapid reduction in poverty and unemployment and broad-based improvement in the quality of life of the people, especailly of the poor. In our view though the targets of financial outlay, saving and investment rate are likely to be achieved, objectives of higher economic growth (i.e. 9 per cent per annum), employment generation for 58 million person years and reduction in poverty ratio by 10 percentage points from 28 per cent in 2006-07 to 18 per cent in 2011-12 are not likely to be achieved. There are now strong doubts about the achievement of these objectives. First, take the objective of achieving economic growth at the rate of 9 per cent per annum. In the first year (2007-08) of the 11th Plan, growth in GDP_{MP} of 8.7 per cent has been achieved. However in the current year (2008-09), due to global meltdown, especially serious financial crisis in the USA, will adversely affect our growth in exports. It will also decrease capital inflows, especially foreign direct investment (FDI). Rupee will also depreciate increasing our cost of imports which will adversely affect our balance of payments. It has been estimated by PM's Economic Advisory Council that growth rate in 2008-09 will decline to 7.7 per cent. Likewise prospects for 2009-10 are also not bright. Thus economic growth for five years is likely to fall short of the target of 9 per cent per annum.

As regards the employment generation for 58 million persons on current daily status basis during 2007-12, it was too high an objective to be achieved, keeping in view the past record. There was no any specific measures suggested in the 11th Plan which ensures rapid absorption of surplus labour in gainful employment. Whatever new employment opportunities (net) have been created, they happen to be in the unorganised informal sector in which how much employment generated is of productive or gainful type is anybody's guess. In fact in the post-reform period there is net *decrease* in employment in the organised sector (public and private sectors taken together) as is seen from Table 42.4. During the post-reform period (1994-2008) whereas there has been a low positive growth of employment (0.58% per annum) in the private sector there was negative growth of employment in the public sector resulting in net decrease in employment in the organised sector. In the future there is no likelihood of any change in this pattern of employment. As a result, we think that instead of any improvement in this regard unemployment problem will worsen in the 11th Plan period.

Further, the objective of achieving *inclusive growth* is a hollow one. In the post-reform period (1993-2004-05) it has been estimated that reduction in poverty ratio greatly slowed down to only 0.74 per cent per annum as compared to the pre-reform period. This trend is likely to continue in the future. First, due to the tendency on the part of industries to use capital-intensive technologies, sufficient new employment opportunities are not likely to be created. As a result, unemployment will increase. Second, most of the poor live in rural areas and are dependent on agriculture. It is necessary that land reforms should be undertaken so that landless labour and small farmers possess land to generate self-employment and also in case of tenant farmers to ensure security of tenancy at reasonable rate of rent. Besides, the farmers must get loans from banks and other institutions at lower rate of interest as recommended by National Commision on Farmers headed by Dr. M.S. Swaminathan which recommended interest on farm loans be reduced to 4 per cent to promote agricultural investment and production. However the Eleventh Plan neglects the issue of land reforms and peasant agriculture and instead pleads for contract farming which is capital-intensive and not labour-intensive. Further, 11th Plan does not plan to create employment opportunities in agriculture. In view of all these achieving inclusive growth is an unrealistic objective.

Inclusive Growth. Regardless of the impact of the global financial crisis of India, the *fact remains that some of the challenges that India faces are of a continuing nature.* These *inter alia include eradicating poverty, improving its physical and social infrastructure, education and creating productive employment opportunities*. In consonance with the commitment to ensure faster social development and achieving an inclusive pattern of growth, the government continued its focus on several initiatives and programmes towards that end.

Some of the major social sector initiatives for achieving inclusive growth and faster social sector development and to remove economic and social disparities in the Eleventh Five Year Plan include the Bharat Nirman Programme, Mid-day Meal Scheme, National Rural Health Mission, Jawaharlal Nehru National Urban Renewal Mission and the National Rural Employment Guarantee Scheme (NREGS). Central support for the social programmes has continued to supplement efforts made by the States.

A major achievement of the 11th Plan is starting of National Rural Employment Guarantee Scheme (NREGS). Under NREGS, over four crore households were provided employment in 2008-09. This is a significant jump over the 3.39 crore households covered under the scheme during 2007-08. Out of the 215.63 crore person-days of employment created under the scheme during this period, 29 per cent and 25 per cent were in favour of SC and ST population respectively. 48 per cent of the total person-days of employment created went in favour of women. The agriculture debt waiver and relief scheme implemented during the year was able to restore institutional credit to farmers and helped to support demand and revive investment in the rural and the agriculture sector.

MACROECONOMIC PERFORMANCE IN THE POST-REFORM PERIOD

India made a good progress in raising incomes and improving living standards over the two decades (1991-2012) of the post-reform period. During the eighties (1980-90), India achieved a breakthrough from Hindus rate of growth (3.5%) obtained during the first two decades of planned development (1951-70) and achieved 5.6 annual growth in GDP (See Table 42.1) in the eighties. After the 1991 balance of payments crisis which induced the adoption of new economic policy that emphasised liberalisation and privatisation, there has been a change in development strategy from one of *import-substituting* to that of *export-led growth*. Overall Indian economy performed well as a result of economic reforms initiated following the new economic policy. The various aspects of economic performance in the post-reform period are explained below.

Table 42.5. Macroeconomic Trends in the Post-Reform Period

Indicator	8th Plan	9th Plan	10th Plan	Eleventh Plan Period					
	(1992-93 to 1996-97)	(1997-98 to 2001-02)	2002-07 (Average)	2007-08	2008-09	2009-10	2010-11	2011-12	Average
GDP growth (% a year)	6.7	5.5	7.8	9.3	6.7	8.6	9.3	6.2	8.0
Agriculture & Allied Sectors	4.7	1.8	2.5	5.8	0.1	0.8	7.9	3.6	3.7
Industry	7.6	4.5	8.6	9.7	4.4	9.2	9.2	3.5	7.2
Services	7.5	8.1	9.28	10.4	9.3	8.0	9.4	7.9	9.7
Investment rate (% of GDP) at current market prices	23.3	22.5	31.4	38.1	34.5	36.5	36.4	35.0	–
Public Sector	–	8.0	6.6	8.9	9.5	9.2	–	–	–
Private Sector	–	15.3	15.9	28.1	24.6	24.9	–	–	–
Central Govt. Fiscal Deficit (% of GDP)	–	–	4.4	2.6	6.0	6.7	5.1	5.7	–
Fiscal Deficit of Centre and States combined	7.2	9.3	8.0	5.5	8.0	10.0	8.5	8.7	–
Inflation (Average WPI % Change in year)	8.7	4.9	5.1	4.6	8.4	3.6	9.6	5.9	–
Current account balance (% of GDP)	1.2	– 0.7	+1.3	–1.3	–2.3	–2.8	–2.8	–4.2	–

Source : Plan Documents and Central Statistical Organisation (CSO), and World Bank, *India: Sustaining Reform* ; and Reserve Bank of India Annual Report 2009-10

Growth Performance. As will be seen from Table 42.5, the annual growth rate in GDP accelerated during the Eighth Plan period and was estimated to be 6.7 per cent per annum during 1992-93 to 1996-97. After 1996-97, GDP growth relatively showed down and was found to be 5.5% during the Ninth Pan period (1997-98 to 2001-02) but it again went up to average 7.6 per cent per annum during the 10th Plan period. In three successive years, 2005-06, 2006-07, and 2007-08 India's growth rate GDP_{mp} had been on an average more than 9 per cent per annum. After China, Indian economy has become the second highest growing economy of the world. However, in 2008-09 the global financial crisis affected India's economic growth rate which was estimated at 6.7 per cent in 2008-09. The growth rate of GDP picked up and rose to 8.6 per cent in 2009-10 and to 9.3 per cent in 2010-11. However, GDP growth rate fell to 6.2 per cent in 2011-12 and to 5 per cent in 2012-13, the lowest in a decade. It may be noted that average annual growth in the Eleventh Plan (2007-2012) has been 8 per cent which is the highest in any Five Year Plan so far.

Industry in the second half of the nineties was hit by the global slowdown, a fall in rural demand

and decline in public sector investment. Economic growth over the last several years has been driven by both services and industry. But in the five year period of 10th Plan (2002-07) the annual growth of the industrial sector has also been quite high registering 8.6 per cent growth rate.

It may however be noted that economic growth in India has been led by services in the 1980s and by both industry and services in the nineties. During the last two decades (1991-2011) the structure of the Indian economy has changed considerabely with share of agriculture declining to around 14 per cent of GDP and the share of services increasing to nearly 55 per cent.

Slowdown in India's Economic Growth. For the last three years India's growth has been quite sluggish. As is seen from Table 42.5, India's growth, India's GDP growth fell to 6.2 per cent in 2011-12 and further to 5 per cent in 2012-13, the lowest in a decade. Even for 2013-14 Dr. C. Rangarajan, Chairman, Prime Minister's Economic Advisory Council, estimates it to by 5.3 per cent. This slowdown in economic growth is despite the fact that gross capital formation is still 32% of GDP. While we are facing slowdown in economic growth inflation as measured by CPI is around 10%. Besides recent employment and unemployment survey shows that in India there has been jobless growth.

Both domestic and international factors are responsible for slowdown in economic growth. Fragile recovery of the US economy and recessionary conditions in the European countries had impacted India's growth in exports which even became negative for some months in 2012 and 2013. The announcement of the Governor of the US Federal Reserve in May 2013 that it would start tapering of its economic stimulus policy from Sept. 2013 gave rise to capital outflows by FIIs from the emerging economies including India and also affected adversely dollar inflows through foreign direct investment. Decline in foreign direct investment adversely affected India's economic growth. The threat by the US to attack Syria further added to the uncertainties which bad an adverse impact on our capital market and the exchange rate of rupee. Besides, the large current account deficit (CAD) raised doubts about the ability of the government to pay dollars for essential imports and the possibility of default by it in paying its debt. Further, the large fiscal deficit (4.8% of GDP in 2012-13) also affected the sentiments of investors that government would reduce its planned expenditure.

It may also be noted that economic growth in India until recent years has been achieved mostly by increase in gross domestic saving (GDS) and gross domestic investment (GDI). While rate of gross domestic saving which stagnated at around 23 per cent of GDP at current market prices during 1997-2002 showed a significant improvement during 2002-08 which is estimated to have gone up to 34.7 per cent and 36.9 per cent of GDP in 2006-07 and 2007-08 respectively. As a result, gross domestic investment as a per cent of GDP at current market prices increased from 24.8 per cent in 2002-03 to 32.4 per cent in 2004-05 and further to 34.6 and 36.9 per cent of GDP in 2006-07 and 2007-08 respectively Gross investment rate including capital inflows rose to 38.1 per cent of GDP in 2007-08. This increase in rates of gross domestic saving and investment has made it possible to achieve higher growth rate of 9.5, 9.6 and 9.3 per cent in GDP in 2005-06, 2006-07 and 2007-08 respectively. Due to the impact of global financial crisis of 2008, growth rate of GDP fell to 6.7 per cent in 2008-09. But in 2009-10 and 2010-11, growth rate of GDP picked up and rose to 8.6% in 2009-10 and to 9.3 per cent in 2010-11 but it fell to 6.2% in 2011-12 and to 5% in 2012-13.

Inflation

Inflation rate as measured by WPI which was estimated to be 8 per cent in the eighties was brought down to 4.9 per cent on an average per annum during the Ninth Five Year Plan period (1997/98-2001-02). It remained low at 5.1 per cent per annum on an average in the 10th Plan. However, in the last year (2006-07) of 10th Plan, inflation rate as measured by WPI (12 month average) shot up to 6.5 per cent and inflation rate on the basis of CPI(IW) rose to about 6.7 per cent. As a result of measures taken by the Government and RBI, inflation rate came down to 4.8 per cent in 2007-08. However, with effect from April 2008, inflation rate, as measured by WPI, started rising year-on-year basis and crossed 9 per cent mark year-on-year basis in June 2008, and rose to 11 per cent in August and then went up to 12.63% in mid-Sept. 2008. But it started falling afterwards as a result of fiscal and monetary measures adopted by the Government and RBI. The inflation rate as measured by WPI fell to zero at end-March 2009. For the whole financial year 2008-09 the 52 week average inflation (on WPI basis) was found to be 8.0 per cent. During the first half of 2009-10, the headline inflation (i.e. general wholesale price inflation) remained significantly low at 0.36 per cent *on account of sharp increase in prices* recorded in 2008-09, that is, due to the base effect. However, the second half of 2009-10 showed increasing food prices on account of unfavourable agricultural supply conditions with the waning of base effect. Therefore, headline WPI inflation reached 10.23 per cent in March 2010. The average rate of this WPI inflation during the *whole year 2009-10* was estimated at 3.8 per cent but went up to 9.6 per cent in 2010-11.

Table 42.6. Inflation in India

	Year-on-Year Inflation				
	WPI	CPI-IW	CPI-UNME	CPI-AL	CPI-RL
2003-04	5.5	3.9	3.7	3.9	3.8
2004-05	6.5	3.8	3.6	2.6	2.6
2005-06	4.3	4.4	4.7	3.9	3.9
2006-07	6.5	6.7	6.6	7.8	7.5
2007-08	4.8	6.2	5.9	7.5	7.2
2008-09	8.0	9.1	8.9	10.2	10.2
2009-10	3.8	12.4	–	13.9	–
2010-11	9.6	10.5	–	10.6	–
2011-12	8.9	8.4	–	–	–
2012-13	7.6	10.0	–	–	–

UNME : Urban Non-Manual Employees; IW: Industrial workers

Al: Agricultural labourers and RL : Rural Labourers

Financial year 2010-11 started with 11 per cent headline inflation in April 2010. Though during 2010-11 the monsoon situation had been better than the last year but headline inflation remained in double digits. The major contributors to this were (1) *primary articles* whose inflation hovered in the range of 14.7 per cent to 21.5 per cent and (2) *fuel* which recorded inflation in the range of 10.3 per cent to 14.4 per cent. However, the *inflation in the manufactured products remained in lower range* of 4.5 to 6.4 per cent during the year 2010-11 so that overall average WPI inflation was 9.6 per cent (that is, near the double digit level).

The problem of WPI inflation persisted in the year 2011-12 as well and became a matter of concern as it reached double digit level of 10% in September 2011 (Y-O-Y basis). This WPI inflation only marginally fell to 9.73 per cent in Oct. 2011 and to 9.11 per cent in Nov. 2011. The rise in prices of *food, fuel as well as those of manufactured products* which contributed to this headline inflation during the year 2011-12 was 8.4 per cent. It may be noted that marginal decline in WPI inflation in 2011-12 was due to sharp fall in food inflation, although there was rise in prices of fuel and manufactured products.

However, in contrast to food inflation, the *core inflation* which represents the rise in prices of non-food manufactured products had gone up in Nov. 2011 to 7.9 per cent as against 7.7 per cent in Oct. 2011 and 7.6 per cent in April 2011. Besides, fuel inflation had also risen to 15.48 per cent in Nov. 2011 from 14.9 per cent in Oct. 2011. This persistent rise in core inflation during the year 2011-12 was due to both the demand-pull and cost-push factors. Cost-push factors became more prominent from Sept. 2011 onwards due the sharp depreciation of exchange rate of rupee which fell to ₹ 53 per US dollar in Nov. 2011 from ₹ 44 per US dollar in Aug. 2011. This fall in the value of rupee raises the costs of imports of raw materials and fuel for industrial production which will push up the costs of manufactured products.

However, there has been great divergence between inflation as measured by WPI and that measured by different consumer price index (CPI) numbers. As will be seen from Table 42.6 that inflation during 2008-09 as measured by CPI for industrial workers (IW) was 9.1% and as measured by CPI for agricultural labour (AL) and rural labour (RL) it was found to be 10.2 per cent Thus there has been double digit inflation for rural population as measured by CPI. This is a matter of serious concern. Even food-inflation (i.e. rise in price index of foodgrains) based on WPI waś in double-digit number during all quarters of the year 2008-09.

India's Export Performance

In the first three decades of planning, since India followed import substitution strategy accompanied by high level of protection through tariffs and quotas, exports did not register much growth. As a result, the share of India's world exports declined from about 2 per cent in 1951 to 0.5 per cent in 1971-81 and 1981-90. *Average annual growth rate of exports* (in US dollar terms) during the period (1981-90) on BOP basis was 6.1 per cent, went up to 11.4 per cent per annum in 1991-97 but again fell to 6 per cent per annum in the 9th Plan period (1997-2002) but in the 10th Plan period it rose to 28.5, 23.4 and 22.6 per cent in 2004-05, 2005-06 and 2006-07 respectively. In 2007-08 there was 28.9 per cent growth us exports in US dollars (on BOP basis). Similarly, imports also grew in the port-reform period. As compared to 3.9 per average annual growth in imports in the eiglitres (1980-91) imports grew at the annual rate of 14.4 %, but fell to 5.0 per cent in the Ninth Plan period (1997-2002) but as in case of growth in exports, imports also grew at a higher rate during the Tenth Plan period (2002-07) as will be seen from Table 42.7.

Table 42.7. Performance of External Sector in the Post-reform Period : Leading Indicators

	80-91	91-97	97-2002	2002-03	2003-04	2004-05	2005-06	2006-07	2007-08	2008-09	2009-10	2010-11	2011-12
Growth of Exports BOP (%)	6.1	11.4	6.0	20.3	23.3	28.5	23.4	22.6	29	13.6	–3.5	40.5	21.8
Growth of Imports BOP (%)	14.4	14.4	5.0	14.5	24.1	48.6	32.1	21.4	35.5	20.07	–5.0	28.2	32.3
Imports Cover of FER (No. of months)	2.5	–	–	14.2	16.9	14.3	11.6	12.5	14.4	9.8	11.2	9.2	8
					As % of GDP_{mp}								
Exports	6.5	9.9	–	10.6	11.1	11.8	12.6	13.6	13.4	15.4	13.2	–	16.5
Imports	8.8	10.6	–	12.7	13.3	16.5	18.8	20.1	20.8	25.2	21.7	–	–
Current Account Balance	–3.1	–	–	1.3	2.3	– 0.4	–1.2	–1.0	–1.3	–2.3	–2.8	–2.8	–4.2

Source : Government of India, *Economic Surveys, 2005-06, 2006-07, 2007-08 and 2008-09*

Note that these figures of growth of exports and imports in 2008-09 April-Dec. are on BOP basis. On DGCI&S basis during 2008-09 (April-Dec. 2008) the growth of exports was 3.6 per cent and of imports was 21.8 per unit. FER stands for Foreign Exchange Reserves, including gold, SDR_s.

* Data for 2008-09 relate to April-Dec. 2008

However, as will be seen from bottom of Table 42.7 that during 1981-90 on an *average exports constituted 6.5 per cent of* GDP_{mp}. In the post-reform period as a result of opening up of the Indian economy after 1991, India's integration into the world economy increased. The real depreciation of the rupee after the 1991 crisis also promoted exports, and the reduction of import control, allowed more imports of foreign goods into the country. Exports of goods rose from annual 6.5 per cent of GDP_m during 1980-91 to 9.9 per cent during 1991-97 and further to 11.1 per cent in 2003-04 and 12.6 per cent of GDP in 2005-06 and 13.4 per cent in 2007-08. It may be noted that growth of exports and imports remained modest during the Ninth Plan Period (1997-2002) due to slowdown in world economy and sluggish demand growth. In the post-reform period exports of IT services increased sharply and remittances from abroad also edged up.

India's Export Growth

Bolstered by the measures taken by the government to help exports in the aftermath of the world recession of 2008 and also the low base effect, India's export growth in 2010-11 reached an all-time high (40.5 per cent) since Independence. Though it decelerated in 2011-12 to 21.3 per cent, it was still above 20 per cent and higher than the compound annual growth rate (CAGR) of 20.3 per cent for the period 2004-05 to 2011-12. After registering very high growth of 56.5 per cent in July 2011, export growth started decelerating with a sudden fall to single digits in November 2011 as a result of the emerging global situation and then to negative figures from March 2012. Export growth in dollar terms was negative at –4.9 per cent in 2012-13 (April-January), compared to 21.3 per cent growth in 2011-12 (full year).

It is worth noting that India's export growth has almost continuously been above world export growth in the 2000s decade and in 2011. One issue that has been a topic of debate is whether India's export growth rate is dependent on world growth/trade or exchange rate. There is a strong correspondence between India's export growth and world export growth (Figure 42.1). This is clearly visible in 2009 when there was a big dip in both world exports and India's exports. The relationship between changes in real effective exchange rate (REER) and India's export growth is not however as clear-cut as that with world trade.

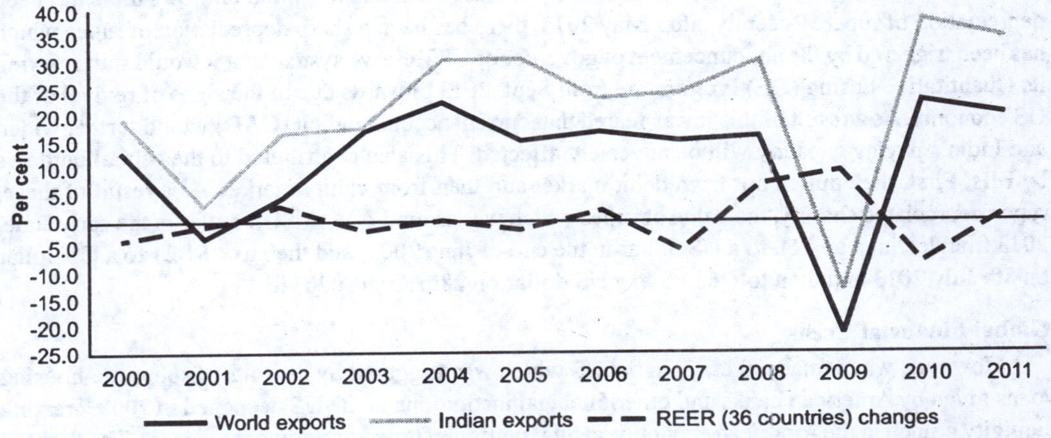

Fig. 42.1. Growth of Exports of World and India and REER changes

The current account balance which showed a large deficit of 3.1% of GDP in 1990-91turned into a surplus of 0.7, 1.3 and 2.3 per cent in 2001-02, 2002-03 and 2003-04 respectively. Current account balance again became negative after 2004-05. But deficit in current account remained within reasonable limits and could be easily met by surplus in capital account of balance of payments. Capital inflows, especially portfolio investment by FIIs, picked up strongly in response to the reforms since 1991. Of special mention is the appreciable increase in our foreign exchange resources which crossed US $ 100 billion in Dec. 2003 and rose to US $ 145 billion in March 2006 and to $ 192 billion at end-March 2007 and further to $ 309 billion at end-March 2008. However, as a result of global financial crisis there was *net capital outflow* from India in 2008-09 and also there was slower growth in exports relatively to that of imports. This caused large deficit in current account of 2.4 per cent of GDP in 2008-09 and also decline in our foreign exchange reserves to $ 252 billion at end-March 2009. As will be seen from Table 42.7 there was negative growth in both exports and imports in 2009-10, the exports registering a higher negative growth. As a result current account deficit increased to 2.8 per cent of GDP_{MP} in 2009-10 and 2010-11. Further due to higher imports of gold and rise in prices of crude oil, current account deficit rose to 4.2 per cent of our GDP in 2011-12 and 4.8 per cent of our GDP in 2012-13. To reduce the current account deficit (CAD) and to finance it through capital inflows is a matter of serious concern and is posing a great challenge for the government.

Adverse Effects of Globalisation

Economic reforms undertaken since 1991 brought about globalisation of the Indian economy as under them the Indian economy was opened up. Trade liberalisation occurred following removal of quantitative restrictions on imports and large reduction in tariffs. Reforms also led to the free flow of foreign capital. This benefited India as its exports increased at a higher rate in the initial years and balance of payments on current account improved. Further foreign investment in India contributed to a higher growth rate achieved in the post-reform period. However, globalisation is not without dangers. These benefits of globalisation were proved to be only temporary.

Foreign Exchange Rate Volatility

The adverse effect of globalisation has been clearly seen recently in the two years, 2007 and 2008, and recently since May 2013. First, the free flow of portfolio capital has created a lot of volatility in exchange rate of rupee. Due to large capital inflows the value of rupee, which was around ₹ 46 to a US dollar in end-March 2004, appreciated to ₹ 44.27 to a US dollar in end-March 2006 and further to ₹ 39.4 to a dollar in Jan. 2008. However, most often due to capital outflows there has been depreciation of rupee. Recently, after May 2013, there has been a sharp depreciation of rupee which has been triggered by the announcement of governor of US Reserve system that it would start relaxing its Quantitative Easing (QE) Programme from Sept. 2013 onwards due to the signs of revival of the US economy. As a result of this it was feared that current account deficit (CAD) would further widen and India's paying capacity will be adversely affected. This also contributed to the capital outflows by FIIs. First, they pulled out from debit market and then from equity market. As a result of these, rupee depreciated sharply, the value of rupee which was around ₹ 56 to a US dollar in the early June, 2013 first declined to ₹ 60 to a US dollar in the end of June 2003, and then to ₹ 61.21 to a US dollar on 8th July 2013 and then to ₹ 68.85 to a US dollar on 28th August 2011.

Global Financial Crisis

However, when financial crisis in the US which was triggered by defaults of subprime-housing loans given by American banks and other financial institutions in the US deepened in 2008, creating liquidity crunch in the American economy, capital outflows started occurring from India. The flight of capital from India led to depreciation of Indian rupee. To meet liquidity requirements in their parent country, foreign financial institutions (FII) started selling shares of Indian corporate companies and got rupee receipts converted into US dollars which they repatriated to their parent country. These outflows of dollars led to the increase in demand for US dollars in the foreign exchange market which caused the depreciation of Indian rupee. The depreciation of rupee will make our imports, especially crude oil, costlier and can adversely affect our balance of payments. The higher prices of imported products, especially capital goods and metals, tended to raise inflation rate in India.

Reduction in Poverty

Another important assessment of economic reforms in the post-reform period is whether there has been a significant decline in poverty during the post-reform period. On the basis of 55th round of NSS (1999-2000) **for all India (both rural and urban) the percentage of population below** the poverty line declined from 36 per cent in 1993-94 to 26 per cent in 1999-2000. However, this data was challenged by Prof. Amartya Sen and Angus Deaton, among others. It was pointed out by them that estimates of the decline in poverty in 1999-2000 *are not comparable* with the pre-1999 estimates because of change in methodology of collecting data in NSS 1999-2000 round where **mixed recalled period** (MRP) was used. After assessing the results Angus Deaton writes, **"the 55th round is not very useful for assessing the trend in poverty"**[9]. Jean Dreze and Amartya Sen also expressed doubts about the finding that poverty in the nineties had more rapidly fallen as compared to the eighties[10]. They pointed to three facts which indirectly refuted the claim that poverty had fallen more rapidly in the nineties as compared to the earlier decades. First, they pointed out that there had been *increase in economic inequalities in the nineties.* They showed that inter-state economic disparities had risen in the nineties. Also, there was a strong evidence of rising rural-urban disparities in the nineties. Furthermore, according to them, there had not been a better performance in the other social indicators in the nineties which should justify the conclusion that there had been more rapid progress in reduction of poverty in the nineties.

Table 42.8 : Trends in Poverty in India

Years	*Poverty Ratio (%)*			*Poor (million)*		
	Rural	*Urban*	*(All India Combined)*	*Urban*	*Rural*	*Total*
1973-74	56.4	49.0	54.9	261	60	321
1977-78	53.1	45.2	51.3	264	65	329
1983	45.7	40.8	44.5	252	71	323
1987-88	39.1	38.2	38.9	232	75	307
1993-94	37.3	32.4	36.0	244	76	320
1999-2000 (MRP)	27.1	23.6	26.1	193	67	260
2004-2005 (URP)	28.3	25.7	27.8	221	80	301

Source : Planning Commission.

A noteworthy fact is that rate of decline in poverty ratio during this period was much lower than the rate of economic growth. Thus while annual growth in GDP in real terms during 1993-94 to 2004-05 was 6.3%, the rate of reduction in poverty was much slower, 0.74 per cent per annum. Secondly, the rate of reduction in poverty ratio slowed down in the period 1993-2004-05, as compared to the pre-reform period. Whereas decline in the poverty ratio was about 1.24 per cent per annum in the pre-reform period 1977-78 to 1987-88, it was only 0.74 per cent per annum during the post-reform period (1993-94 to 2004-05).

Second, the incidence of both rural poverty and urban poverty separately had also declined since 1973-74. Thus, rural poverty ratio which was 56.4 per cent in 1973-74, fell to 45.7 per cent in 1983 and further to 37.3 per cent in 1993-94. In 2004-05, it was estimated to have fallen to 28.3 per cent (URP). Thus there had been a marked decline in the *ratio of poor rural households* when comparing 2004-05 estimates with those of 1973-74 to 40.8 per cent in 1983 and to 32.4 per cent in 1993-94. In 2004-05, poverty ratio (URP) in urban India further fell to 25.7 per cent. *An important fact revealed from these rural and urban poverty ratios is that the incidence of poverty in rural areas is greater*

9. Jean Dreze and Amartya Sen, *op. cit.*
10. *Ibid,* p. 328.

than that in urban areas.

Third, the data regarding the incidence of poverty in various States of India during this period (1973, 2004-05) reveal that the *secular decline in rural poverty ratio (MRD) occurred in every individual state of the country,* although the extent of decline varied. However, it is important to note that in 2004-05 *rural poverty ratio* was still relatively high in Orissa, Bihar, Uttar Pradesh, Madhya Pradesh, Uttarakhand, Jharkhand and West Bengal as compared to 28.3 per cent at the All India level.

It may be noted that the NSS data about incidence of poverty reveal that there has been a *secular decline in urban poverty ratio* in every state of the country, although magnitude of this decline varies a good deal in different states. *It should be further noted that in 2004-05, in Orissa, Madhya Pradesh, Bihar and Uttar Pradesh, urban poverty ratio was relatively much higher than the poverty ratio at the urban national level of 25.7. It was 44.3% in Orissa, 34.6 in Bihar, 42% in Madhya Pradesh, 30.6% in Uttar Pradesh, and 32.6% in Karnataka.*

Latest Estimates of Poverty in India in 68th Round of NSSO

In June 2013 the Planning Commission released the poverty estimates based on special 68th round of NSSO. These estimates gave rise to a lot of controversy about the true extent of poverty prevailing in India. Adjusted for price change the *poverty line* based on Tendulkar Committee methodology was fixed at a daily expenditure of ₹ 27.20 per capita for rural areas and ₹ 33.3 per capita for urban areas for the year 2011-12. Based on this poverty line Planning Commission calculated the poverty ratio and the absolute number of people living below the poverty line based on National Sample Survey on Employment and Unemployment for the year 2011-12. As will be seen from Table 42.9, during the period 2004-05 and 2011-12 there has been massive decline in poverty ratio. According to these estimates, poverty ratio for all India declined from 37.2 per cent in 2004-05 to 21.9 per cent in 2011-12, that is, 15.3 per cent fall in poverty in just seven years which amount to 2.2 per cent per year which is quite a large decline. Further, it will be seen from Table 42.9 that there has been much larger decline in poverty ratio in rural areas, from 41.8 per cent in 2004-05 to 25.7 per cent in 2011-12, that is, 16.1 per cent decline in seven years as compared to 12 per cent in urban areas in these seven years. Based on the poverty line cut-off, there were 270 million poor in India in 2011-12 against 407 million in 2004-05, that is, around 137 million persons were lifted out of below poverty line. This means poverty declined at faster pace of 2.2 per year every year as against the reduction of 0.74 per cent per year during 1993-94 and 2004-05.

Table 42.9 : Estimates of Poverty in 2004-05 and 2011-12 on the Basis of Tendulkar Committee Methodology

	Rural	*Urban*	*Total*
2004-05	41.8	25.7	37.2
2011-12	25.7	13.7	21.9

It may be noted that the previous poverty estimates were based on National Sample Survey 2009-10. However the Government did not consider the poverty number of 2009-10 as correct saying that it was drought year and would not convey the true picture. For calculating, the Planning Commission used Dr. Suresh Tendulkar Committee's methodology which factors in spending on education and health besides calorie intake to arrive at a poverty line in urban and rural areas. Accordingly, those whose daily consumption expenditure per capita on goods and services exceed ₹ 33.33 in urban India and ₹ 27.20 per capita in rural India are not poor.

The recent poverty figures are based on the benchmark set by the controversial committee methodology which was junked by the Planning Commission last year. The commission justified the release of the data, saying the alternative Rangarajan panel recommendation will be available only in mid-2014. Besides, whatever the poverty line, goes the official argument, there will be a decline in poverty in percentage terms. Amid a raging controversy over lower norms of poverty, Planning

Commission Deputy Chairman Montek Singh Ahluwalia acknowledged that the poverty line is very low and represents a large subsistence level.

It was asserted by the Planning Commission Chairman, Dr. Montek Ahluwalia, that *benefits of high economic growth achieved during the period (2004-05 to 2011-12) trickled down to the poor and this resulted in the drastic fall in poverty.* A higher average about 8.5 per cent growth in GDP was achieved during this period which, it is claimed by the Planning Commission, brought down the poverty levels. This is despite the fact that India saw one of the worst droughts in 2009-10 and slowdown in economic growth in 2008-09 due to global financial crisis.

Another factor that accounted for decline in poverty during this period was *larger spending by the government on social welfare programmes* such as Mahatma Gandhi Rural Employment Guarantee Scheme (MGREGS) which was started in 2006. This scheme entitles 100 days of employment for one person per household at minimum of ₹ 100 per day to all rural households. This scheme not only provided employment to the poor households but also helped *pushing up wages in rural areas* and thereby further ensuring reduction in rural poverty. Since no such programme as MGREGS had been started in the urban areas there had been, as seen above, much lower decline in poverty ratio in urban India during this period.

On an all-India basis, there were 217 million poor in rural areas and 53 million poor in urban areas in 2011-12 as against 326 million and 81 million, respectively, in 2004-05. This shows that 138 million person were lifted out of poverty during 2004-05 and 2011-12.

The final figures for 2011-12 are likely to be revised once a government-appointed committee under C. Rangarajan submits its report on a new methodology for fixing the poverty line, but the Planning Commission in its pres release pointed out that this would only change the numbers, not the declining trend. Planning Commission estimates were greatly criticized. It was pointed out that ₹ 27.7 of daily expenditure per capita in rural areas and ₹ 33.3 of daily per capita expenditure in urban areas fixed as poverty line were too low and persons can hardly survive on such low expenditure. Many leaders said, it is *joke on the poor.* In the year 2011, even Supreme Court criticised these criteria of poor in the rural and urban areas. This led the Government to appoint a committee headed by Dr. C. Rangarajan to redefine the poverty line and prepare estimates of poverty ratio on that basis. Rangarajan Committee is expected to submit its report in mid-2014.

Poverty Reduced but Malnutrition Still High

It is important to note that while poverty ratio has declined somewhat, malnutrition has still remained stubbornly high. As was acknowledged by Government's *Economic Survey for 2008-09*, even a 'developed' state such as Punjab having a poverty ratio of 8.4% has 27% children below 3 years as underweight. Similarly, other 'developed' states including Andhra Pradesh, Assam, Gujarat and Haryana have wintnessed high incidence of malnutrition.

Therefore, there is a need for greater focus on mulnutrition issues, while the ability to access such food items depends on household income and is addressed through programmes like MGNREGS, there are other factors which are equally important but have been ignored. The existing policies and programmes are not making a dent on malnutrition and therefore need to be modified. The National Family Health Survey (2005-06) indicated that underweight children constitute 45.9% of those below the age of three years. Though malnutrition cannot be entirely explained by poverty but poverty is the main factor responsible for malnutrition.

Development in Terms of Wide Social Indicators. Prof. Amartya Sen and Jean Dreze have argued for shifting the focus from poverty estimates based on the head-count ratio to a wider range of social indicators such as real agricultural wages, infant mortality rate, total fertility rate, illiteracy rate etc. According to Dreze and Amartya Sen, "*Indeed .... the standard focus on income or expenditure does not do justice to the variety of deprivations we are concerned with, and furthermore, within that narrow approach, the head-count ratio has particularly limited informational value. Looking* *at the broader evidence of social indicators in the nineties a somewhat different picture emerges, with areas of accelerated progress as well as indications of slowdown in some fields.*[11] According to them we have made comparatively lower progress in the fields of healthcare especially with regard to childrens mortality rate and nutrition primary education, decrease in poverty and unemployment. Further, according to them, the potential *benefits of accelerated economic growth in the nineties appear to have been diluted by severe imbalances in growth patterns, growing inequalities and continued state inertia in crucial social field"*[12] According to Dreze and Amartya Sen, *"elimination of deprivation requires not merely more economic growth but also direct public action in social fields."*

Because of greater stress on development of social services for achieving inclusive growth by Prof. Amartya Sen and others, the government in India has stepped up its expenditure on social services. The share of the central government expenditure on social services including rural development in the total government's expenditure has increased from 11.23% in 2002-03 to 19.44% in 2008-09 (as per the budget estimates).[13] The expenditure on social services (education, health and others) by both the central and state governments has increased from ₹ 1,53,454 crore in 2003-04 to ₹ 3,57,381 crore in 2008-09 (as per the budget estimates), a significant rise of 132 per cent.[14]

As mentioned above, an important failure of planning in the last 15 years (1997-2012) is slowdown in agricultural growth. In the Ninth Plan period (1997-2002), agriculture grew at the rate of 1.8 per cent per annum. In the Tenth Plan period (2002-07) agricultural growth did not improve further and is estimated to be not more than 2.5 per cent per year. Therefore, though in 2007-08 agriculture and allied sectors grew by 5.8%, in 2008-09 its growth was negative (–0.1) and in 2009-10 it grew by 0.4 per cent. The low growth in agriculture will constrain the future industrial growth. Therefore, investment in agriculture for building adequate infrastructure for agriculture such as expansion in irrigation facilities, rural roads, flood control projects must be increased on a priority basis.

Finally, a dismal performance of planning in the post-reform period has been the slow growth of employment opportunities resulting in higher rate of unemployment. Unemployment rate on the basis of current daily status rose from 6 per cent in 1993-94 to 7.32 per cent in 1999-2000 and further to 8.3 per cent in 2004-05[15]. The backlog of unemployment in the beginning of Eleventh Plan (April 2007) rose to 36.7 million persons on current daily status basis. This increase in unemployment is not surprising as in the post-reform period growth of employment in the organised sector has been very low. The growth of employment in the organised sector in the post-reform period (1994-2008) has been only 0.05 per cent per annum, whereas in the pre-reform period (1983-94) it was 1.20 per cent per annum[16].

Now, if high economic growth is to be sustained investment in agriculture must be increased both by public and private sectors. Increase in investment in agriculture will lead to increase in supply of agricultural output including cereals, vegetables, fruits which will ensure higher growth rate with price stability. To achieve higher growth of agriculture, public investment in irrigation must rise significantly so as to make agriculture drought-proof. The growth in agriculture will also benefit industrial growth through demand linkage. A clear impact of the Green Revolution has been felt only in certain regions. But to create a second green revolution, many drastic steps will have to taken. Nearly half of the total farm households in India own less than one hectare of land and there is a growing proportion of agricultural labourers as an increaisng number of farmers are selling off their land. Their rising indebtendness has led to hundreds of suicides in Maharashtra, Andhra Pradesh and

11. Jean Dreze and Amartya Sen, *op.cit*, p. 328.
12. Jean Dreze, and Amartya Sen, *India: Development and Participation*, 2002, p. 329
13. GOI, *Economic Survey*, 2008-09
14. *Ibid.*
15. Planning Commission, *An Approach to the 11th Five Year Plan* (December 2006), p.72
16. GOI Economic Survey 2010-11, p.265.

some other parts of the country. There is a severe crisis of rising input costs and stagnant agricultural productivity. Public investment in agriculture has been low and rural employment opportunities have also been declining. This process needs to be reversed.

Besides, to achieve higher growth rate in GDP public investment in infrastructure must be increased. New investments by the private sector are also needed to expand the productive capacity in industries to achieve higher industrial growth. In addition, availability of more credit both for industry and agriculture and more efficient infrastructure is imperative to achieve a higher rate of investment and sustained growth in GDP.

A major failure of planning in India is the problem of inflation which is recent years has become acute. The annual rate of inflation as measured by consumer price index has been around 10 per cent in recent years. This high rate of inflation is hurting the living standards of the people, especially those in low and middle-income brackets. Recently, annual food inflation has risen to 18 per cent which is quite alarming and has made the life of people miserable. Lastly, in the beginning of the 12th plan (i.e., 2012-13, 2013-14) macroeconomic imbalances have occurred. **Current account deficit (CAD)** of balance of payments was estimated at 4.8 per cent in 2012-13 which is quite unsustainable and is an important factor causing sharp depreciation of rupee. Fiscal deficit of the Central Government at around 5 per cent in recent years has also been high in recent years and is an important factor contributing to high rate of inflation in recent years.

APPENDIX TO CHAPTER 42A

Twelfth Plan, 2012-17

Introduction

The Twelfth Plan commenced at a time when the global economy was going through a second financial crisis precipitated by the sovereign debt crisis of Eurozone which arose in the last year of the Eleventh Plan. This crisis affected all countries including India. As a result India's GDP growth rate slowed down to 6.2 per cent in the last year (2011-12) of the Eleventh Plan. Slowdown in economic growth continued in the first year 2012-13 of the 12th Plan when rate of GDP growth fell to 5 per cent. **The Twelfth Plan emphasizes that our first priority is to bring the economy back to rapid growth while at the same time ensuring that growth is both inclusive and sustainable.**

At the very start of the 12th Plan, the Indian economy faces macroeconomic imbalances. First, fiscal deficit increased sharply after 2008 as a result of global financial crisis. Fiscal deficit of the central government rose to 6.2 per cent in 2008-09 and was estimated at 5.7 per cent in 2010-11 and 5.1 per cent in 2011-12. With reduction in plan expenditure by ₹ 90,000 crore, Finance Minister was able to bring down fiscal deficit to 4.8 per cent of GDP in 2012-13. In the first year of the 12th Plan 4.8 per cent of GDP as fiscal deficit is still very high. The second macroeconomic imbalance has been the widening of current account deficit of our balance of payments which has risen to 4.8 per cent of GDP in 2012-13.

In view of the above the Twelfth Plan has proposed a **two-pronged strategy** focusing initially on the need to bring the macroeconomic imbalances under control and to reverse the slowdown in economic growth, while also pushing for structural reforms in many areas that are crucial for maintaining medium-term GDP growth rate.

Sectoral Pattern of Growth

The Twelfth Plan has set a target of average annual 8 per cent GDP growth over the five year plan period, 2012-17. This overall growth rate is to be achieved with target growth rates of 4 per cent in agriculture, 7.6 per cent in industry (which comprises mining and quarrying, manufacturing, electricity, gas and water supply and construction) and 9 per cent in services. Sector-wise break up growth targets in the five year plan period (2012-13 to 2016-17) along with the average growth rates achieved in the Eleventh Plan period is given in Table 42A.1.

The Twelfth Plan has set a target of average annual 8 per cent growth rate in the five-year period of 2012-17 equal to the actual average growth rate achieved in the 11th Plan period. Since in the first two years of the 12th Plan (2012-13 and 2013-14), the actual rate of economic growth achieved is around 5 per cent, it will require a very sharp acceleration in growth rate to 10 per cent in the later three years to achieve an average annual growth rate of 8 per cent. This seems to be quite unfeasible. Therefore, the Deputy Chairman of the Planning Commission, Dr. Montek Singh Ahluwalia, is talking of revising the growth rate target. This might need to revise the target growth rates of all sectors. Thus the whole 12th Plan growth targets are quite uncertain, whereas its first two years are already over. It may be noted that in the 12th Plan, *Planning Commission recognises that though faster economic growth is necessary but not a sufficient condition for raising the living standards of the people as*

Table 42A.1 Annual Growth of GDP by Industry of Origin at Constant (2004-05) Prices

Sector	*11th Plan*	*Twelfth Plan period*					
	Average	2012-13	2013-14	2014-15	2015-16	2016-17	Average
1. Agriculture, Forestry and Fishing	3.7	2.0	4.5	4.5	4.5	4.5	4.0
2. Mining and Quarrying	3.2	1.0	5.0	7.0	7.0	8.5	5.7
3. Manufacturing	7.7	2.2	6.0	8.5	9.5	9.5	7.1
4. Electricity, Gas and Water Supply	6.1	5.2	7.5	8.0	8.0	8.0	7.3
5. Construction	7.7	8.0	8.0	8.5	10.0	11.0	9.1
6. Trade, Hotels, Restaurants	8.3	5.5	6.0	8.0	8.7	8.7	7.4
7. Transport, Storage and Communication	12.0	7.3	11.1	13.0	13.6	14.1	11.8
8. Financing Insurance and Real Estate	11.1	9.8	9.5	10.0	10.0	10.0	9.9
9. Community, Social and Personal Services	8.3	7.3	7.2	7.2	7.2	7.2	7.2
Total GDP	**8.0**	**5.8**	**7.3**	**8.5**	**9.0**	**9.2**	**8.0**
Industry (2–5)	7.2	4.0	6.6	8.4	9.4	9.8	7.6
Services (6–9)	9.7	7.6	8.3	9.4	9.7	9.9	9.0

a whole. This is of course true but Planning Commission has recognised this fact only after several years of planned development in which benefits of economic growth have not trickled down to the poor. We can easily imagine a growth process which may not be sufficiently inclusive to ensure a spread of benefits to the mass of population.

Three Growth Scenarios

Perhaps recognising the uncertainty of achieving overall 8 per cent growth rate in the 12th Plan period, the Planning Commission in the 12th Plan document itself visualises three growth scenarios:

***Scenario 1*: Strong inclusive growth.** This is described as the future of India and will ensure 8 per cent annual growth rate during the Twelfth Plan period along with the objective of 'inclusiveness' if we can implement a well-designed strategy addressing the key constraints holding back the economy. With appropriate steps taken to deal with **implementation and governance problems**, the wheels of government at all levels begin to move more smoothly. Local governance institutions and small enterprises are nurtured and have an opportunity to grow effectively, along with larger enterprises. Livelihood opportunities, along with community-based solutions and enterprises for addressing environmental issues, are seen to be sprouting. Many virtuous circles begin to operate in this scenario, raising confidence and trust.

***Scenario 2*: Insufficient Action.** This scenario reflects the outcome of insufficient policy action. While broad direction of policy may be endorsed at different levels, action is incomplete or implementation is poor, with the result that outcomes are weaker than anticipated. Centralised government systems do not provide sufficient flexibility to cope with demands for decentralisation. Small enterprises and new entrepreneurs need to be encouraged, but unless the business environment necessary for them to flourish is effectively transformed, the outcome will fall short of expectations. The policy conflict between subsidies and financial stability of the economy remains unresolved. In this scenario, growth of 8 per cent is not feasible. Growth could decline to between 6 per cent and 6.5 per cent, and inclusiveness would suffer.

Scenario 3. **Policy Logjam.** This scenario reflects a situation where very little can be done for whatever reason on many of the policy fronts identified in the Twelfth Plan. It will be difficult to build growth momentum if critical supply constraints relating to energy and transport are not overcome. Investor confidence is likely to be severely eroded, and the lack of inclusiveness that results will lead to increased impatience and political logjam, putting the economy under severe stress. Vicious cycles begin to operate and the growth rate can drift down to 5–5.5 per cent with serious loss on the inclusiveness front. In some ways, there is a danger of insufficient action scenario degenerating into a policy logjam scenario, if it persists too long.

Investment

The ability to raise the rate of investment [ratio of gross fixed capital formation, (GFCF) to GDP] is widely recognised as critical for the achievement of high economic growth rate.

For annual output growth to average 8.0 per cent in the Twelfth Plan period, and to cross 9 per cent in the closing year, it is estimated that the fixed investment rate will have to increase by about 1.5 percentage points of GDP over the level in 2011-12. The resulting trajectory of fixed investment over the Plan period is shown in Table 42A.2. The fixed investment rate should increase to 35 per cent of GDP (at constant prices) by the end of the Twelfth Plan, yielding an average fixed investment rate of over 34 per cent of GDP for the Twelfth Plan period as a whole. These levels are marginally higher than what was achieved in the Eleventh Plan but they are broadly consistent with achieving an average

Table 42A.2. Investment as Ratio of GDP at Constant 2004-05 Prices

	11th Plan	*Twelfth Plan period*					
	Average %	2012-13	2013-14	2014-15	2015-16	2016-17	Average
				Ratio to GDP per cent			
(*a*) Fixed Investment Rate	33.7	33.0	33.9	34.4	34.5	35.0	34.2
(*i*) Public	8.3	8.0	8.4	8.4	8.5	8.5	8.4
(*ii*) Private corporate	12.4	11.3	12.5	14.0	14.5	15.0	13.5
(*iii*) Household	13.0	13.5	13.0	12.0	11.5	11.5	12.3
(*b*) Stock	3.0	2.3	2.9	3.1	3.1	3.1	2.9
(*c*) Valuables	1.8	2.2	1.9	1.6	1.6	1.6	1.8
Gross Domestic Capital Formation (GDCF)	38.5	37.5	38.7	39.1	39.2	39.7	38.8
Errors and Omissions	–0.3						
Investment Rate	38.2	37.5	38.7	39.1	39.2	39.7	38.8

real growth rate of little above 8 per cent, allowing for acceleration in growth in the course of the Plan period. This however implies a significant relaxation in the physical constraints that limit the economy in infrastructure and other key sectors.

Composition of Investment: Public Sector Vs. Private Sector. The composition of fixed investment by source is also shown in Table 42A.2. The public fixed investment rate (mostly investment by public enterprises) averaged 8.3 per cent in the Eleventh Plan, with a range of 7.8–8.8 per cent. It is projected to remain roughly in this range in the Twelfth Plan period averaging 8.4 per cent. Household fixed investment (which includes unincorporated business) averaged 13.0 per cent in the Eleventh Plan, with a range of 10.5–14.3 per cent. For the Twelfth Plan, household fixed investment is projected to average 12.3 per cent for the Plan period as a whole, it begins higher at 13.5 per cent in the first two years, slowly reducing to 11.5 per cent in the final two years of the Plan as the corporate sector expands its share.

It is pointed out by the Planning Commission in the 12th Plan that **private corporate investment has now become the major driver of investment in recent years.** In 2003-04 private corporate fixed investment (at constant 1999–2000 prices) was only 6.2 per cent of GDP, while the overall fixed investment rate was 27.1 per cent. It rose to 9.1 per cent (at constant 2004–05 prices) in 2004–05 and to 11.9 per cent in 2005–06. The overall fixed investment rate increased to 28.7 per cent in 2004-05 and to 30.5 per cent in 2005-06. Private corporate investment averaged 12.4 per cent in the Eleventh Plan but it was at a peak of 15.0 per cent in 2007-08, that is, the first year of the Eleventh Plan and declined in subsequent years to 11.6 per cent in 2011-12. If the overall fixed investment rate has to pick up in the Twelfth Plan, there has to be a recovery in private corporate fixed investment. Table 42A.2. shows a gradual build-up in private corporate investment from 11.3 per cent in 2012-13 rising steadily to touch 15.0 per cent—the peak value achieved in 2007–08—in the last year of the Twelfth Plan. This would produce an average of 13.5 per cent for the Twelfth Plan as a whole; higher than the average of 12.4 per cent in the Eleventh Plan.

It is further mentioned that *a large part of private corporate investment is now in the field of infrastructure—power generation, roads, ports, airports and telecommunications–and a lot of it is in the Public–Private Partnership (PPP) mode.* The robust growth in private corporate investment is in part a reflection of the strategy of increasing the share of investment devoted to infrastructure and the recognition that private investment has to play a large part in this. Higher investment in infrastructure is critical for the revival of the investment climate as it would lead to enhanced investment in manufacturing.

Financing the Twelfth Plan

In Table 42A.3 we give the financing pattern in the 12th Plan of financing public sector spending compared to the actual realisation in the Eleventh Plan. It will be seen from the Table 42A.3 that **balance from current revenue** (BCR) of the Centre as per cent of GDP is estimated to be **1.88** per cnt of GDP for the 12th Plan. Note that balance from current revenue represents surplus of tax revenue and other non-tax revenue over the current expenditure of the Central Government. It is worth mentioning that for the Eleventh Plan while Planning Commission had projected BCR at 2.31 per cent but actually it turned out to be negative (–) 0.61 per cent. Now, the Planning Commission visualises unrealistically that with good tax buoyancy in tax revenue and a decline in non-plan expenditure, resources from balance from current revenue (BCR) will be 1.88 per cent of GDP in the 12th Plan.

Table 42A.3 compares the funding pattern in the Twelfth Plan with the Eleventh Plan realisation as percentages of GDP. Balance from current revenue (BCR) as per cent of GDP was projected at 2.31 per cent for the Eleventh Plan which turned negative (–) 0.61 per cent. However, with good buoyancy in tax revenue and decline in non-plan expenditure, BCR is estimted to be 1.88 per cent of GDP for the Twelfth Plan. The target of 3.0 per cent of fiscal deficit for 2016-17 implies that target of borrowing including net miscellaneous capital receipts (MCR) will decline from 5.06 per cent in the Eleventh Plan to 3.35 per cent of GDP in the Twelfth Plan.

Table 42A.3. Resources of the Centre in Eleventh and 12th Plans (as percent of GDP)

Source of Funding	*Eleventh Plan*	*12th Plan*	*% Change*
1. Balance from revenue	– 0.61	1.88	2.49
2. Borrowing including net MCR	5.06	3.35	–1.71
3. Net Capital Flow from Abroad	0.24	0.00	–0.24
4. Gross Budgetary Support (GBS) to Plan (1 to 3)	4.69	5.23	0.54
5. CA to States and UTs' Plan	1.26	1.26	0.00
6. GBS for Central Plan (4 – 5)	3.43	3.97	0.54
7. Resources of BSEs	2.53	2.38	–0.15
8. Resources for Central Plan (6 + 7)	5.96	6.38	0.39

Source: Planning Commission. CA = Central Assistance

Domestic Saving Rate. For the Twelfth Plan period the planning commission has set a saving target of 36.0 per cent of GDP in the last year of the plan. Their projection of **average level of domestic** saving rate for the entire 12th Plan period is 33.6 percent of GDP, slightly higher than the 33.5 per cent recorded in the Eleventh Plan.

Current Account Deficit. On the basis of its projections of exports and imports of goods and also of invisibles, planning commission estimates the current account deficit of average **3.4 per cent of** GDP for the Twelfth Plan period as a whole. It is projected to be higher in the first two years and slightly moderate thereafter. The estimated current account deficit is higher than the normal comfort level of 2.5 per cent of GDP.

To realise this higher than comfort level of current account deficit, namely 3.4 per cent of GDP, the Planning Commission emphasizes that it requires that capital account is managed in a way that façilitates capital inflows.

Gross Budgetary Sources (GBS) of the Centre. The Finance Minister's announcement that fiscal deficit of the Central Government will be reduced to 3 per cent in 2016-17. The 12th Plan proposes to have higher collection of taxes including service tax (GST) so as to contain fiscal deficit to 3 per cent by 2016-17. Given the changed economic scenario, GBS is projected to grow from 5.13 per cent of GDP in 2012-13 to 5.2 per cent of GDP in 2016-17. The average gross budgetary sources for the Central Plan in Twelfth Plan stands at 5.23 per cent of GDP as against 4.69 per cent of GDP realised in the Eleventh Plan.

Gross Tax Revenue. The Gross Tax Revenue as a percentage of GDP is estimated to increase from 10.62 per cent in 2012-13 (BE) to at least the levels achieved in 2007-08. The tax revenue (net of States' share) increases from 7.60 per cent of GDP in 2012-13 to 8.79 per cent of GDP in 2016-17, averaging 8.27 per cent during the Twelfth Plan. Collection of direct tax has remained higher than the indirect tax collection since 2008-09 and is projected to have similar trend during the Twelfth Plan. Corporate tax collection averages 69.37 per cent of direct tax collection during the Twelfth Plan. It increases from 4.25 per cent of GDP in 2012-13 to 4.83 per cent of GDP in 2016-17 averaging 4.57 per cent of GDP, that is, 0.76 percentage points increase over the average Eleventh Plan realisation.

Subsidies. Subsidies in the first year of the Twelfth Plan have been taken as per 2012-13 (BE), which is likely to be somewhat higher when the final figures become available. With the reforms being undertaken, the total subsidies, as a proportion of GDP, are projected to decline to 1.5 per cent by 2016-17. Inability to pass on increases in global oil prices to the consumers would have a substantial impact on resources for the Plan, if this situation is not rectified urgently.

Twelfth Plan Resources of the Centre

Twelfth Plan resources for the Centre and its funding are summarised in Table 42A.4. **The GBS available for the Plan is estimated at ₹35,68,626 crore at current prices.** CA to the States, and UTs' Plan works out to be ₹ 8,57,786 crore. IEBR of Central public sector enterprises (CPSEs) is estimated at ₹ 16,22,899 crore. *The total resources available for the Central Plan outlay are, therefore, projected at ₹ 43,33,739 crore.* This is only an indicative outlay. The actual realisation can change depending on how resources position evolves from year to year.

Borrowing and Fiscal Deficit. 12th Plan projects that borrowing by the government for funding Government budgetary resources for 12th Plan will be higher initially but is planned to decline gradually. The Centre's net borrowing which was 5.9 per cent of GDP in 2011-12 (RE) is estimated to decline to 5.1 per cent of GDP in 2012-13. The fiscal deficit as a percentage GDP is further projected to decline to 4.5 per cent in 2013-14, 3.9 per cent in 2014-15 and 3.2 per cent in 2015-16 and 3.0 per cent of GDP in the last year of the Twelfth Plan.

Table 42A.4. Projections of the Twelfth Plan Resources of the Centre

(*₹ Crore at Current Prices*)

Sources of Funding	Amount Projected
1. Balance from current revenue	13,87,371 (38.88)
2. Borrowing including net MCR	21,81,255 (61.12)
3. Gross Budgetary Support (GBS for Plan (1 + 2)	35,68,626 (100)
4. CA to States and UTs' Plans	8,57,786 (24.04)
5. Total GBS for Central Plan (3-4)	27,10,840 (75.96)
6. Resources of PSE, including Borrowed Resources	16,22,899
7. Total Resources for Central Plan (5 + 6)	43,33,739

Source : Planning Commission.

MCR = Miscellaneous Capital Receipts

Note : Figures in parentheses are percentage of GBS to Plan (S.No. 3)

The financing plan outlined above will pose major challenges. As shown in Table 42A.5, the total resources for the Central and State Plans taken together have to increase from an average of 10.96 per cent of GDP in the Eleventh Plan to an average of 11.80 per cent of GDP in the Twelfth Plan. The increase of 0.84 per cent of GDP in total resources for the Plan has to be achieved keeping borrowing within the stipulated limit and reducing the fiscal deficit of the Centre and States to 3 per cent on each account in the last year of the Twelfth Plan. Taking account of the resources mobilised by the public sector, the combined balance from current revenue (BCR) of the Centre and the States has to increase by more than the projected increase in Plan resources.

Table 42A.5. Plan Resources as per cent of GDP.

S.No.	Item	Eleventh Plan	Twelfth Plan	Increase over Eleventh Plan
I.	**Aggregate Plan Resources**			
	Centre	5.96	6.35	0.39
	States	5.00	5.45	0.45
	Centre and States	10.96	11.80	0.84
II.	**Balance from Current Revenues**			
	Centre	–0.61	1.88	2.49
	States	1.02	1.41	0.39
	Centre and States	0.41	1.29	2.88

Source: Planning Commission

Table 42A.6. Overall Financing Pattern: Eleventh and Twelfth Plans

(₹ crore at Current Prices)

Sources of Funding	Eleventh Plan Realisation			Twelfth Plan Projection		
	Centre	Static and UTs	Total	Centre	States and UTs	Total
1. Balance from Current Revenues	–2,42,390 (–11.97)	3,81,536 (22.11)	1,39,146 (3.71)	13,87,371 (32.01)	9,59,979 (25.83)	23,47,350 (29.16)
2. Borrowings including net MCR	17,51,691 (86.50)	7,52,815 (43.62)	25,04,506 (66.77)	21,81,255 (50.33)	15,18,301 (40.85)	36,99,556 (45.96)
3. Net Inflow from Abroad	80,043 (3.95)	0.00	80.043 (2.13)	—	—	—
4. Centre's GBS (1 + 2 + 3)	15,89,344 (78.48)	— —	15,89,344 (42.37)	35,68,626 (82.35)	— —	35,68,626 (44.33)
5. Resources of PSEs/ Local Bodies	8,57,244 (42.33)	1,70,039 (9.85)	10,27,283 (27.39)	16,22,899 (37.45)	3,80,319 (10.23)	20,03,218 (24.88)
6. State's Own Resources (1 + 2 + 5)	— —	13,04,390 (75.58)	13,04,390 (34.77)	— —	28,58,599 (76.92)	28,58,599 (35.51)
7. CA to States and UTs' Plan	–4,21,458 (–20.81)	4,21,458 (24.42)	— —	–8,57,786 (–19.79)	8,57,786 (23.08)	— —
8. Resources of the Public Sector Plan (1 + 2 + 3 + 5 + 7)	20,25,130	17,25,848	37,50,978	43,33,739	37,16,385	80,50,123

Source: Planning Commission.

Note: Figures in parentheses are percentages of Resources of the Public Sector Plan.

As revealed from the earlier Table 43A.3 the Centre's BCR, realised in the Eleventh Plan, averaged (–) 0.61 per cent of GDP. It is projected to average 1.88 per cent of GDP in the Twelfth Plan, that is, an improvement of 2.49 percentage points of GDP. Similarly, the BCR of the States is also expected to improve from 1.02 per cent of GDP as realised in the Eleventh Plan to 1.41 per cent of GDP in the Twelfth Plan. As can be seen from Table 42A.5, the projected improvement required in the combined BCR of the Centre and States taken together is, therefore, 2.88 percentage points of GDP. It must be emphasised that achievement of these BCR targets is a key element in the financing of the Plan. Underlying the projected BCR is a projection that tax revenues (net to Centre) would grow from 7.60 per cent of GDP in 2012-13 to 8.79 per cent of GDP in 2016-17. NPRE (Non-Plan revenue expenditure) is expected to decline from 8.53 per cent of GDP in 2012-13 to 7.09 per cent in 2016-17. Thus the projected improvement of 2.49 per cent of GDP in BCR of the Centre is expected to come slightly more from contraction in NPRE (Non-plan revenue expenditure) than growth in taxes.

The Planning Commission claims that the assumption of growth in tax revenues of the Centre and the States built into the projections is not unreasonable. Tax revenues recorded in the recent past has shown a lot of swings due to economic slowdown effected by the global financial crisis. The annual growth of gross tax revenue collection which dipped to 2.3 per cent in 2008-09 and 2009-10, returned to a healthy growth of 27 per cent in 2010-11 followed by 13.69 per cent in 2011-12 (RE). With the recovery of the economy and proposal to mobilise additional tax revenues, gross tax revenue is estimated to grow by about 19.5 per cent in 2012-13 (BE) over the previous year. Efforts will continue in the Twelfth Plan period towards achieving the targeted tax-to-GDP ratios. However, the BCR projections are equally dependent upon the ability to moderate the growth in NPRE and this aspect of the projections deserves focused attention.

There are several factors which could make it difficult to contain expenditures to the projected level. There is inevitable upward pressure of increasing expenditure on subsidies, particularly on fertiliser and petroleum due to increasing international crude oil prices, and also on food owing to proposed food security legislation. The subsidy regime needs to be urgently reformed to keep the total subsidy within the ceiling of 1.5 per cent of GDP in 2016-17 that the resources projections have built in.

ALLOCATION OF PUBLIC SECTOR RESOURCES

The projection of the overall resources for the Twelfth Plan has been presented in the preceding section. This section focuses on the allocation of Public Sector Resources for the Twelfth Plan between the Centre and the States/UTs and the proposed sectoral distribution of the resources in keeping with the objective of achieving faster and more inclusive growth.

The projected assessment of resources of the public sector for the Twelfth Plan at ₹80,50,123 crore at current prices comprises the Centre's share at ₹43,33,739 crore and the States/UTs share at ₹37,16,385 crore. The resources for the Central Plan includes the GBS component of ₹27,10,840 crore and the IEBR component of ₹16,22,899 crore at current prices. Table 42A.7 indicates the sources of funding public sector outlays for Centre and States for the Twelfth Plan. The Twelfth Plan resources of the States and UTs are projected at ₹37,16,385 crore at current prices, out of which States' own resources are ₹28,58,599 crore and the CA (Central Assistance) to States and UTs is ₹8,57,786 crore at current prices.

Table 42A.7. Public Sector Allocation for Twelfth Plan

(₹ Crore at Current Prices)

Centre	
Sources of Funding	**Allocation**
1. Budgetary Support	27,10,840
2. IEBR	16,22,899
3. Total Centre (1 + 2)	43,33,739
States and UTs	
Sources of Funding	**Allocation**
4. States' Own Resources	28,58,599
5. CA to State/UT Plan	8,57,786
6. Total States and UTs (4 + 5)	37,16,385
Total Public Sector Outlay	
7. Grand Total (3 + 6)	80,50,123

Source: Planning Commission.

A comparison of the distribution of the total GBS in the Eleventh and the Twelfth Plan has been shown in Table 42A.8. In comparison to the Eleventh Plan realisation, there is an increase of 132.12 per cent in the projected GBS for the Centre for the Twelfth Plan. CA (Central Assistance) to State/UT Plans for State sector programmes is about 103.53 per cent higher than the grant component realised during the Eleventh Plan. The share of the projected grant component of the CA to States/UTs plan in the total GBS for Twelfth Plan has slightly decreased from the level realised in the Eleventh Plan (from 26.52 per cent to 24.04 per cent).

The Twelfth Plan proposes to provide ₹8,57,786 crore at current prices as CA to Stae/UT Plans. Table 42A.8 indicates the details of sector-wise CA (Central Assistance) component of resources of the States/UTs. Out of the total CA to States/UTs of ₹8,57,786 crore at current prices. 20.84 per cent (that is, ₹1,78,739 crore) has been earmarked for the Gadgil-Mukharjee Formula driven NCA. Special Plan Assistance (SPA) for Special Category States and Special Central Assistance (SCA) for the Border Areas Development Programme (BADP)/Hill Area Development Programme (HADP)/ North East Council (NEC) accounts for 14.31 per cent of the total CA. The remaining 64.85 per ent of CA to the States is assigned to Additional Central Assistance (ACA) for various flagship programmes and other schemes in accordance with the priority set for the Twelfth Plan, such as the AIBP, National Social Assistance Programme (NSAP), BRGF, RKVY and JNNURM including MP's Local Area Development Programme.

The projection of GBS allocation to different sectors, Ministries/Departments and the support to the State/UT Plan has been made in tune with the approach adopted for the Twelfth Plan for ***'faster, sustainable and inclusive growth'***. The Twelfth Plan aims at putting the economy on a sustainable growth trajectory with a growth rate of 9.1 per cent by the end of the Plan period by targeting robust growth in agriculture at 4 per cent per year and by creating productive employment at a faster pace than before. The Twelfth Plan focuses on poverty reduction, ensuring access to basic physical infrastructure, health and education facilities to all while giving importance to bridging the regional/ social/gender disparities and attending to the marginalised and the weaker social groups. Accordingly, a major structural shift across sectors has been proposed by allocating more resources to the priority areas identified for ensuring inclusiveness.

A broad picture of the structural change in terms of sectoral allocation of Centre's budgetary resources (GBS including CA to State Plans for major sectoral programmes) in Twelfth Plan as compared to Eleventh Plan has been shown in the Table 42A.9.

Table 42A.8. GBS Allocation in Eleventh and Twelfth Plans

(₹ Crore at Current Prices)

Items	Eleventh Plan Realisation		Twelfth Plan Projections		% Increase over Eleventh Plan
	Amount	% Share in Total GBS	Amount	% Share in Total GBS	
Central Plan (Central Sector and Centrally-sponsored Schemes)	11,67,886	73.48	27,10,840	75.96	132.12
CA to State Plans	4,21,458	26.52	8,57,786	24.04	103.53
Total	15,89,344	100.00	35,68,626	100.00	124.53

Source: Planning Commission.

It may be noted that the biggest increase in allocation of Centre's GBS for Health and Child Development, Urban Development and Education. The share of Health and Child Development in Centre's GBS goes up to 11.45 per cent as compared to 7.09 per cent in the Eleventh Plan. The share of Urban Development increases from 3.99 per cent in the Eleventh Plan to 4.60 per cent in the Twelfth Plan. The share of Education goes up to 12.71 per cent in Twelfth Plan. The percentage increase in GBS for Scientific Departments, Agriculture and Water Resources is also substantial. The increase in budgetary support for Infrastructure in Transport and Energy Sectors is impressive considering that a large proportion of investments in these sectors would be made from the resources of CPSEs (IEBR) and through Public-Private Partnerships (PPPs). The resources for Rural Development Programmes in the areas of Housing Employment and livelihood had been substantially increased during the

Eleventh Plan as compared to the initial allocations. Even a moderate increase in resources for these programmes proposed in the Twelfth Plan over this high base means a substantial budgetary support for these programmes.

Table 42A.9. Allocation of Centre's GBS by Major Sectors—Eleventh Plan Realisation and Twelfth Plan Projection

(₹ Crore at Current Prices)

S. No.	Major Sectors	Eleventh Plan		Twelfth Plan		% Increase over Eleventh Plan
		Realisation	% Share	Projection	% Share	
1.	Agriculture and Water Resources	1,16,554	7.33	2,84,030	7.96	143.69
2.	Rural Development and Panchayati Raj	3,97,524	25.01	6,73,034	18.86	69.31
3.	Scientific Departments	58,690	3.69	1,42,167	3.98	142.23
4.	Transport and Energy	2,04,076	12.84	4,48,736	12.57	119.89
5.	Education	1,77,538	11.17	4,53,728	12.71	155.57
6.	Health and Child Development	1,12,646	7.09	4,08,521	11.45	262.66
7.	Urban Development	63,465	3.99	1,64,078	4.60	158.53
8.	Others	4,58,849	28.87	9,94,333	27.86	116.70
	Total Plan Allocation	15,89,342	100.00	35,68,626	100.00	124.53

The overall plan outlay of all the States and UTs is projected to increase from ₹17,25,848 crore in the Eleventh Plan to ₹37,16,385 crore in the Twelfth Plan (both at current prices), an increase of 115.34 per cent on a comparable basis. The aggregate picture indicates that the States would be allocating more than proportionate increase to social services (41.68 per cent), transport (11.53 per cent) and agriculture and allied activities (6.85 per cent). The aggregate picture, it must be noted, conceals wide inter-State variations in terms of Plan sizes relative to GSDP (Gross State Domestic Product) per capita plan expenditure and percentage sectoral outlays.

A CRITIQUE OF OBJECTIVES AND TARGETS OF THE TWELFTH PLAN

We summarise below the objectives and targets of the Twelfth Plan.

1.Economic Growth. Real growth rate of 8.0 per cent has been set as the target of the Twelfth Plan keeping in view that around 5 per cent growth rate has been achieved in the initial two years (2012-13 and 2013-14), the growth rate in the remaining three years will have to be very 10 per cent per annum on an average which is very difficult to be achieved. Manufacturing growth of 10.0% per annum has been set as target for the 12th Plan period. This also seems to be very ambitious. The return to high growth path requires policy action on numerous fronts by both by the centre and the states. Given the present policy paralysis, the higher growth rate is unlikely to be achieved.

2.Poverty and Employment. The target of reducing head-count ratio of poverty by 10 percentage points from 21.9 per cent to 11.9 per cent in the end-year 2016-17 on the basis of Tendulkar Committee methodology is also too high a target to be achieved. Besides, even poverty line has to be redrawn by a committee headed by Dr. Rangarajan. The Planning Commission has admitted that the poverty line based on Tendulkar Committee methodology is too low and shows a bare-subsistance level.

Regarding employment, it is proposed to generate 50 million new employment opportunities in the **non-farm sector** and provides skill certification to an equivalent numbers during the Twelfth Five Year Plan. The past experience shows that most of employment are generated in the unorganised and informal sectors where productively is very low. In view of the higher capital-intensity, the organised sector generates little wage-employment.

3. Education and Health. The targets of expansion of education and health facilities are:

1.Mean Years of Schooling to increase to seven years by the end of Twelfth Five Year Plan.

2.Enhance access to higher education by creating two million additional seats for each age cohort aligned to the skill needs of the economy.

3.Eliminate gender and social gap in school enrolment (that is, between girls and boys, and between SCs, STs, Muslims and the rest of the population) by the end of Twelfth Five Year Plan.

Health

1. Reduce IMR to 25 and MMR to 1 per 1,000 live births, and improve Child Sex Ratio (0-6 years) to 950 by the end of the Twelfth Five Year Plan.

2. Reduce Total Fertility Rate to 2.1 by the end of Twelfth Five Year Plan.

3. Reduce under-nutrition among children aged 0-3 years to half of the NFHS-3 levels by the end of Twelfth Five Year Plan.

Infrastructure, including Rural Infrastructure

The following targets regarding infrastructure has been set for the Twelfth Plan period.

1. Increase investment in infrastructure as a percentage of GDP to 9 per cent by the end of Twelfth Five Year Plan.

2. Increase the Gross Irrigated Area from 90 million hectare to 103 million hectare by the end of Twelfth Five Year Plan.

3. Provide electricity to all villages and reduce AT&C losses to 20 per cent by the end of Twelfth Five Year Plan.

4. Connect all villages with all-weather roads by the end of Twelfth Five Year Plan.

5. Upgrade national and state highways to the minimum two-lane standard by the end of Twelfth Five Year Plan.

6. Complete Eastern and Western Dedicated Freight Corridors by the end of Twelfth Five Year Plan.

7. Increase rural tele-density to 70 per cent by the end of Twelfth Five Year Plan.

8. Ensure 50 per cent of rural population has access to 40 lpcd piped drinking water supply, and 50 per cent *gram panchayats* achieve Nirmal Gram Status by the end of Twelfth Five Year Plan.

As Planning Commission itself points out that private sector also plays an important role in the development of infrastructure, private sector will undertake investment in infrastructure projects if they think they would yield profits to them. As at present investor confidence is lacking various infrastructure projects will not come up. As a result, economic growth will be held up because of lack of infrastructure facilities.

Environment and Sustainability

1.It is proposed to increase green cover (as measured by satellite imagery) by 1 million hectare every year during the Twelfth Five Year Plan.

2. It is planned that 30,000 MW of renewable energy capacity in the Twelfth Plan will be added.

3.It is planned to reduce emission intensity of GDP in line with the target of 20 per cent to 25 per cent reduction over 2005 levels by 2020.

Conclusion. In our view, the 12th Plan is 'business as usual'. Ambitious targets have been set plan after plan but are not realised. In view of the experience of the first two years of the Twelfth Plan when only 5 per cent rate of GDP growth has been achieved, it does not appear feasible to achieve 8 per cent average annual growth in the Twelfth Plan period. In view of this, various targets regarding increase in education, health and infrastructure are also unlikely to be realised.

The ***Twelfth Plan has not envisaged any strategy to tackle the problem of inflation*** which poses a big challenge for government to tackle it. Inflation erodes the real income of the people and leads to the increase in poverty. The Planning Commission should have come with an effective strategy to tackle the problem of inflation. It is amazing that it does not do so.

CHAPTER 43

Global Financial Crisis and Eurozone Crisis and their Impact on World Economy

Burst of Sub-prime Housing Bubble : The Origin of Crisis

From the second half of 2007 in the United States a financial crisis started with a burst of housing bubble which led to widespread mortgage defaults and hence large losses to banks and other financial institutions. This crisis occurred due to sub-prime housing loans given on a large scale by the American banks in the past several years. Why did this crisis occur ? But the foundations of this crisis were laid earlier. The IT bubble burst in 2000 throwing the American economy into recession. To get the economy out of recession the US Federal Reserve cut interest rates bringing about large increase in liquidity or money supply with the banks. With cheap availability of credit, the households even with poor credit worthiness borrowed funds from the banks to buy cars and houses. Americans went on a home buying spree. Prices of houses and real estate were rising rapidly. This rise in housing prices made both households and banks believe that their prices would continue rising. In view of low interest rates and excess liquidity with them lending for houses by banks was found to be quite attractive. As a results, banks provided housing finance even to sub-prime households, that is, households that had no capacity to pay back the loans on time.

One imprudent and irresponsible financial behaviour on the parts of banks was to provide *Ninja loans*, which stand for providing loans to households or persons which had no income and no assets. All this went on well as long as housing prices were rising. The building of houses in excess during the boom period led to their oversupply in the market which caused house prices to decline in 2006. But, like the IT bubble, housing bubble burst in the second half of 2007. With the fall in prices of houses which were held as mortgage the sub-prime households started defaulting on a large scale in making their installments. This caused heavy losses to the banks. With this the sub-prime housing market which had expanded on a large scale when there were soft interest rates and huge amount of liquidity with the banks tumbled. The size of this sub-prime housing market can be judged from the fact that as large as $1.4 trillion worth of sub-prime loans were given by the banks earlier.

Securitisation of Sub-prime Mortgage Housing Loans

But the above was not the end of the story of crisis. The banks that sold the sub-prime mortgage loans did not keep them with themselves. They sold them to other banks and investors through a financial innovation generally called CDO (collateralised debt obligations) securities which were backed by a host of mortgage assets. Therefore, CDO are also called '**Mortgage Based Securities** (MBS). Investment banks associated with Wall Street in the US repackaged the sub-prime housing mortgage loans into synthetic securities CDO that were quite complex. To make them quite safe for investment and thereby increase their marketability were given AAA, BBB rating by credit agencies. "A complex financial security that has been created by mixing hundreds of thousands of independent loans can fox even the smartest investor. Specialist agencies tell investors how safe a security really is. But these credit rating agencies did not do their job well enough. All sorts of rubbish were sold as good stuff."[1]

The American and European intermediaries such as banks, hedge funds, pension funds, mutual funds invested heavily in these complex securities (CDO) based on sub-prime mortgage loans

1. Niranjan Rajadhaksha, Meltdoion reconstructed, *Hindustan Times*, Delhi, Oct. 2008

being unaware of the risks involved. Further problem arose from leverage. Those who bought these mortgage-backed securities *borrowed heavily* from banks and other financial institutions to make investment in them. It has been reported that some Wall Street Investment Banks had borrowed 40 times more than they were worth. This was quite dangerous and risky adventure.

Huge Losses by American Investment Banks and Liquidity Crunch

The sub-prime mortgage loans burst in 2007 when housing prices fell at the fastest rates leading to defaults in payment schedules by borrowers. As a result, the value of underlying sub-prime housing securities declined along with the prices of special complex securities, CDOs based on them. As a result, the banks and investment funds that had bought billions of dollars worth of these complex securities based on sub-prime mortgages suffered heavy losses leading to the liquidity crunch. Many securities held by them could not the valued at all inflicting heavy losses on banks. As a results of huge losses a number of banks and investment institutions including Lehman Brothers went bankrupt. The other banks and financial intermediataries such as Citi Bank came to the brink of bankruptcy and lacked liquidity. They therefore stopped giving credit to consumers and corporate companies. This led to credit crunch which adversely affected consumption demand and investment and therefore caused slowdown in economic growth. In fact in the second and third quarters of 2008 in the United States there was drop in GDP and therefore the US economy slipped into recession. Paul Krugman the winner of 2008, Novel Prize for economics writes "The current crisis started with a burst of housing bubble which led to widespread mortgage defaults and hence to large losses at many financial institutions. The initial shock was compounded by secondary effects as lack of capital forced banks to pull back leading to further decline in the prices of assets leading to more losses and soon a vicious circle of "de-leveraging". Pervasive loss of trust in banks including on the part of other banks reinforced the vicious circle"[2].

Thus, top five US investment banks which had significantly increased their financial leverage during the 2004-2007 time period increased their vulnerability to the CDO related losses. As these institutions registered mounting Sub-prime losses, the financial markets panicked and liquidity was sucked out of the market, so much so that these institutions found it very difficult to raise capital to provide for the losses. The month of September eventually saw the "Top 5" of Wall Street succumbing to Sub-prime losses, with Lehman Brothers filing for chapter 11 bankruptcy, Merill Lynch being merged with Bank of America and Goldman Sachs and Morgan Stanley coverting into commercial banks, subjecting themselves to much tighter regulations. Bear Sterns had already been acquired by JP Morgan Chase in March 2008.

After the demise of the "Top 5", several other financial institutions who had large exposure to CDO faced closures or opted for hasty mergers to shore up capital. Investor confidence shrank significantly, and the credit markets around the world virtually dried up. The Federal Reserve and other central banks since then have injected substantial liquidity in the markets, either by means of lowering of interest rates or by bailing out distressed financial institutions, thus leading to nationalization of financial institutions on a large scale.

When in Aug. 2008, a very important American investment bank Lehman Brothers which had world-wide financial dealings and investment was allowed to go bankrupt by the US Treasury Department, it caused the world financial crisis, already severe, to get much more worse. This affected not only the confidence in the financial system of the US but also in the whole world financial structure. The redemption pressure on securities added to the liquidity problem of banks not only in the US but it spread to the banks and financial institutions of Europe, Brazil, Japan, China, India and others. The banks of other countries felt the pinch of the liquidity crisis and being risk-averse stopped providing credit to the companies which adversely affected economic growth in Europe, China and others. Recession emerged in Europe, Japan and growth in GDP in India

---

2. Paul Krugman, Moment of Truth, *New York Times*, Oct. 2008

and Japan slowed down. In September 2008, when the financial crisis gripped not only the US but also the whole world, Bush Government realised that rescue measures were needed to prevent the collapse of the financial system. It got $700 billion rescue plan passed by the American Congress to bail out the banks and other financial institutions to restore the confidence of the public. Delivering a note of warning Paul Krugman, Novel Laureate in economics wrote in early Sept. 2, 2008, "The consequences of Lehman's fall were appareat within days, yet the policy makers have largely wasted the past four weeks. *Now they have reached the moment of truth.* They would do better to do some thing soon –in fact they would better a coordinated rescue plan this weekend or the world economy may well experience its worst slump since the Great Depression".[3] In fact, the US Government delayed its rescue operations to salvage the US economy from slipping into recession by the end of 2008, GDP in the US had declined by 6.3 per cent. Not only the US but Europe and Japan also went into recession in the second and third quarters of the year 2008.

Rescue Measures Adopted in the US to Fight Crisis

It is evident from above that when there were defaults on payment of housing loans the prices of complex securities started falling. The erosion of the values of these securities dented banks' investment portfolio and led to the decline in the capital base of the banks. Many American banks lost heavily and called for rescue by the Government. Getting $700 billion rescue plan passed by the US Congress the US government purchased the complex and so called 'toxic' securities called CDO from the banks. This helped some banks from going bankrupt. Later the US Government also purchased the shares of some banks and financial institutions to bail them out.

Besides, the US Government cut direct taxes and sent refunds to the people to boost aggregate spending. However, it has been found that due to great uncertainty about future economic conditions a good part of increase in disposable income as a result of tax cut was saved by the American people and therefore tax reduction did not have the desired effect on stimulating expenditure and demand. Further, a fiscal stimulus package of $783 billion was provided by newly elected US President Barack Obama. This new package contains *increase in Government expenditure* as well as cut in taxes to boost consumption demand and investment by businesses. With the various fiscal measures of increase in public expenditure and tax cuts, fiscal deficit in the US is estimated to rise to 12.5% of GDP for the year 2009.

To overcome recession the US Federal Reserve (which is the Central Bank of the US) cut overnight interest rate to near zero so that credit becomes cheaper and more loans are provided by the US banks to businesses for investment and to consumers for buying durable consumer goods including houses. The Federal Reserve also took measures to increase money supply in the US economy so as increase the availability of credit. However, these monetary measures did not seen to work. Due to uncertain economic environment risk-averse banks were reluctant to give loans due to the risk of defaults by the borrowers. As a result, recession in the US further depend in the last quarter of 2008 and the earlier months of the year 2009. Therefore, in the fourth week of March 2009, a new plan of investing $ 1 trillion for buying *toxic assets* from banks that are blocking lending by banks. This plan involves public-private partnership to clean up the US banking sector to get credit flowing again. It is thought that it will clean up the banking of bad debts and restore provision of credit by them. Therefore, to end the crisis in the US, under this programme the government will provide the lion's share of the funding to purchase toxic assets to encourage private investors to participate.

Failure of Free Market System

It is evident from above that free market economy of the United States did not work well to automatically correct the crisis that *gripped* it following burst of housing loan bubble and therefore the intervention of the Government was called for to rescue the *sagging* financial system. In this regard it is worth noting that the role played by the Federal Reserve of America and policy of unregulated free market pursued by it earlier, especially under the Chairmanship of Greenspan. Since the seventies

---

3. Paul Krugman, *op. cit.*

when Reagan was the president of the United States, a policy of *complete deregulation* of market economy including its financial architecture has been followed. It is this lack of proper regulation of financial institutions, banks and stock market that led to the creation of complex and non-transparent securities (CDO).

Expressing his views about the cause of American financial crisis, Paul Krugman writes, "The real sin both of the Fed and Bush administration was the failure to exercise adult supervision over markets running wild. It was not just Alan Greenspan's unwillingness to admit that there was anything more than a lot of "froth" in housing markets or his refusal to do anything about sub-prime abuses. The fact is that as America's financial system has grown ever more complex *it has also outgrown the framework of banking regulation that used to protect us*-yet instead of an update that framework all we got were paeans to the wonders of free market."[4]

Crash in Stock Market

The problems of liquidity and credit crunch as a result of financial crisis led to the stock market crash in the United States and Europe. Share prices of many companies tumbled which caused heavy decline in the capital value of the companies and inflicted huge losses on the investors leading to the crisis of confidence for making more investment. The crash in Wall Street hit financial firms the hardest. Even cash-rich banks were scared of lending money to other banks and to the corporate companies following failure of Lahman Brothers. Some European banks suddenly went bust leading to severe credit crunch.

Adverse Effect on Flow of Credit, Investment and Growth

As a result of erosion of capital base of banks and other financial institutions, the liquidity problem faced by them adversely affected the flow of credit to the companies for financing working capital and fixed investment and to the consumers for buying durable goods such as cars, houses etc. This affected the real economy and adversely affected economic growth in the United States and Europe. As lines of credit to corporate dried up in the US and Europe even for meeting their needs of working capital, it affected payments to employees and suppliers. Lack of liquidity and credit crunch also stalled the ongoing investment projects. Fears of several banks and corporate companies going bankrupt arose as several companies and banks started laying off workers. As industrial output started falling the recessionery conditions *reminiscent* of Great Depression came to prevail in the developed economies of the US and Europe, Japan and Asian economies could not remain unaffected.

The loss of asset value of consuming households made them poorer and along with the credit crunch led to the decrease in demand for consumer durables such as cars, houses and a host of other goods. When a few years ago there was a boom in stock market prices of made them wealthier and the **wealth effect** brought about increase in consumption demand leading to consumption–led growth in the United States. Now, from the second half of 2007, when there was a drastic slide – down in share prices the *negative wealth effect* worked to lower the demand for consumer goods and through the working of accelerator dampened investment in the economies of the US and European Countries. This caused *first slowdown in their economies and ultimately recession in the second and third quarters of 2008*.

As mentioned above, the downward spiral accelerated after the failure of Lehman Brothers in September 2008. Money markets already badly affected stopped giving credit to consumers and corporate companies. The people and the banks in the United States and Europe started investing only in Government's treasury bills which were considered as quite safe.

As mentioned above, the financial crisis spilled over to the real economy. The failure of companies to get adequate credit for working capital and fixed investment brought the growth engine to a halt in the United States. The US economy went into recession in December 2007 and this downturn continued in 2008. It is estimated that GDP of the US declined by 6.3 per cent in the last quarter of

---

4. Paul Krugman "Dont't cry for me, America" *New York Times*, Jan., 2008

2008, the worst in the last 28 years (that is, since 1982). For a large number of industries, the growth rate year-on-year basis fell. Many companies cut jobs and started laying off workers. As a result of recession unemployment rate in the US rose to a high rate of 6.7 per cent in Nov. 2008 and further to 8.1 per cent in February 2009. Rate of unemployment in the US went on increasing further and cuts in jobs of several lakh persons in March to June 2009 drove the US unemployment rate to 26 years high level of 9.5 per cent in June 2009. Though in the last two quarters of 2009 the US economy recovered and registered a growth of around 3 per cent, unemployment rate still further rose to 10 per cent of labour force in Dec. 2009 worst after the depression of 1929-33. Latest report indicates that the US economy grew at 3.2 per cent year-on-year basis in the first quarter of the year 2010, while in the first quarter of the year 2009, the US economy shrank at a rate of 6.4%. In the whole year 2010, the growth of US economy has been estimated at 2.6 per cent.Thus the US economy recovered after a recession of around 3 years. However, despite the recovery of the US economy in terms of GDP growth, the rate of unemployment still remains high at 9.6% of labour force (Dec. 2010).

However, the US recovery has been short-lived. The rate of economic growth has slipped to 1.7 per cent in the first two quarters of the year 2011. This is despite the fact that the Federal Reserve went in for Quantity Easing 2 (QE2) under which it purchased bonds of the US Government to the extent of $600 billion in 2010-11 (upto June 2011). Besides, due to lower growth rate unemployment has stuck at 9.6 per cent of labour force. Further, in July 2011 due to **excessive *sovereign debt*** of the US S&P rating agency downgraded the US rating from AAA to AA+. This made the matters worse. Along with extremely low economic growth rate and high unemployment, this downgrading of the US rating due to excessive public debt of the US Government, has given rise to the fears of ***double-dip recession*** of the US economy which many economists predicted earlier. The emergence of the recession again, like the previous one in 2008, in the US economy would have adverse effects on the global economy.

How Crisis Spread to Europe and Other Countries

It is often said that "when America sneezes, the whole world catches cold" This has been found true in case of financial crisis too. Therefore, when all powerful US economy experienced severe financial crisis, the rest of the world could not escape from its fall-out. Due to the globalisation with its free flow of capital and goods between the US and other countries, especially the European countries which were closely integrated with the US economy, suffered a lot. In fact the surplus funds in the European countries and Japan were invested in the United States. Directly or indirectly capital flowing into America from global investors ended up financing the housing credit bubble that ultimately burst with painful consequences. Thus investors and banks of European countries and Japan suffered heavy losses and called for their being bailed out by their Governments or Central Banks. Following the cues from the crash in stock prices in Wall Street share prices in stock markets in European countries (and Asian countries including India) also crashed leading to heavy losses to the investors.

Besides, recession in the US economy affected exports of the European countries as well as of Japan and others Asian Countries (including India) to the United States leading to the decline in output of export goods in these countries with heavy job losses. This has caused recessionary conditions in these countries as well.

Summing up. In 2009, the global economy not only experienced a 'great contraction', but there was also significant uncertainty about the impact of the financial crisis in the advanced economies on the real economy. The successive and large revisions in the IMF's growth outlook for 2009 indicated the extent of uncertainty that resulted from the sub-prime financial crisis. In the first quarter of 2010, stronger evidence of recovery in the global economy started to emerge, though the speed of the recovery turned increasingly divergent as the emerging market economies remained ahead of the advanced economies in terms of both pace and strength of the recovery. The global recovery turned out to be fragile subsequently, following the concerns relating to sovereign debt in the Eurozone.

Persistence of high growth in India and China largely moderated the depth of the global recession in 2009, even though these countries also experienced slowdown in growth in relation to their high growth before the onset of global crisis. World trade contracted much sharper than the contraction in GDP in 2009, and is projected to stage a recovery in 2010. Reflecting the impact of weak global demand conditions as also the protectionist measures adopted by many countries, the decline in world merchandise trade volume was as high as 11.8 per cent in 2009. According to WTO, world exports of commercial services also declined for the first time after 1983 by 13.0 per cent during 2009. The impact of recession in the advanced economies was particularly strong on the employment situation in the USA and European countries.

As a result of the crisis, net capital flows to the emerging market economies declined. Unprecedented use of policy stimulus by countries around the world helped in averting another 'Great Depression' but the fiscal conditions of the advanced economies weakened significantly in that process. In managing the financial crisis, the costs of financial excesses in the private sector shifted to the public sector creating in turn the risk of potential sovereign debt crisis.

IMPACT OF GLOBAL FINANCIAL CRISIS ON INDIA

Since 1991 following the policy of globalisation, the Indian economy was also opened up to foreign capital and foreign trade of goods and services and thereby got integrated with the United States and European and other countries to a greater degree than before. Therefore, when financial crises gripped United States and European countries, India could not remain isolated. We explain below some important effects of global financial crisis on the Indian economy.

Stock-market Crash

Following the eruption of financial crisis when the Wall Street of the US and stock markets of the European countries crashed, its effect spilled over to India and our stock market (Dalal Street) was also badly hit. To meet the liquidity requirements or liabilities of their parent companies, Foreign Institutional Investors (FIIs) started selling the shares of the Indian companies held by them. The selling pressure by FIIs brought about a crash in Dalal Street (i.e., Bombay Stock Exchange). In the last few years FIIs had invested on a massive scale in the equity shares of several Indian companies operating in various industries from consumer goods to infrastructure industries. As a result of the buying spree of shares of Indian companies by FIIs, share prices rose to new heights. The Sensex which was around 6000 in 2004 rose to 8000 in Aug.-Sept. 2005 and went on rising further crossing 10,000 mark in 2006, 13000 mark in 2007 and reached the peak of around 21,000 mark in January 2008. At around this time, share prices in the US and European markets started falling sharply and the problems of liquidity and credit crunch assumed grave proportions. As mentioned above, this led FII to sell shares held by them in the Indian stock market to pull out capital from India. This was done to fulfil the needs of redemption pressures on their parent companies who were facing liquidity problem. As a result of this selling pressure, Sensex of Bombay Stock Market (which is called Dalal Street) started tumbling; it fell from around 21000 in Jan. 2008 to 11000 in Sept. 2008 and in its downward march it fell below 10,000 in Oct. 2008 and 9000 mark in Nov. 2008, that is, 60 per cent fall since Jan. 2008. This caused huge losses to the Indian companies and investors whose huge wealth was wiped out in a couple of months in 2008. Foreign institutional investors sold more than $ 13 billion worth of shares of Indian companies upto Nov. 2008 and repatriated them to their home countries. This also led to the decline in foreign exchange reserves held by RBI to $ 250 billion by the end of 2008.

Depreciation of Indian Rupee

But the effect of capital outflow by FIIs was not confined to drastic fall in share prices but was more deeper and devasting. When foreign institutional investors (FIIs) sold their shares in India they got rupees. They had to convert their rupees into dollars to send them abroad. This led to the increase in demand for dollars. Rupee-dollar exchange rate being determined by demand for and supply of currencies, the increase in demand for dollars caused appreciation of US dollar in terms of rupees, that is, rupee depreciated against US dollar. The Indian importers also demanded dollars to pay for the imports of goods. The Indian banks doing foreign exchange operations also bought US dollars at home to keep their foreign exchange operations afloat since due to credit crunch no one in foreign countries was willing to lend dollars to any Indian bank. This further raised the demand for dollars causing fast depreciation of rupee in the months of September, October and November 2008. The Indian rupee whose value had appreciated to ₹ 39.4 for a dollar in Dec. 2007 depreciated to ₹ 49.3 for a dollar in end-Oct. 2008 and further to all time low of ₹ 50.6 for a dollar in mid-Nov. 2008. This depreciation of Indiana rupee though made our exports cheaper, made our imports costlier. In Oct. and Nov. 2008, crude oil price declined from all time high of $ 147 per barrel to around 50 US dollar in Nov. 2008 and to $ 40 per barrel in Feb. 2009.

Liquidity Crunch in the Banking Sector

But the story of impact of capital outflow by FIIs did not end here. As a result of large outflow of dollars fast depreciation of rupee against dollar began. To prevent fast depreciation of rupee and maintain relative exchange rate stability, RBI intervened and supplied dollars from its foreign exchange reserves. With this too much depreciation of rupee was prevented but in this process of supplying more dollars in the foreign exchange market, it got rupees in return. As a result the quantity of rupees with the banking system declined causing liquidity problem in the Indian banking system which affected credit flow to the industry for financing of working capital and fixed investment projects. This problem became so severe that inter-bank credit market was mostly frozen; no bank was willing to lend to other banks as every bank needed liquidity to tide over contigencies and this restricted credit flow to the industries. Risk aversion by banks in India also played an important role in restricting credit flow to consumers for buying cars, houses etc. and companies for making investment.

Thus the cause of liquidity and credit crunch that arose in India was the sale of billions of dollars from its reserves by the RBI which withdrew rupees from the banking system in the process. It is estimated that each sale of a billion US dollars by RBI sucks around ₹ 5000 crores from the domestic market. The call rates, that is, rates at which banks lend to each other for a short period rose to all time high of 23 per cent.

Impact on Indian Economic Growth

When all powerful US economy witnessed slowdown in economic growth and ultimately experienced recessionary conditions as a result of financial crisis, its effect spilled over to Europe, Japan and other Asian countries. Britain, Germany, Italy and 15 nations sharing Euro slumped into recession for the first time after several years. In September 2008 IMF gave the bleak assessment of the global economy whose growth rate was expected to hit 3 per cent in 2008 and near zero in 2009. In September 2008. IMF also predicted lower growth of 7.7 per cent for India for the year 2008-09 which was later further lowered to 7 per cent as against over 9 per cent growth in the previous 4 years (2004-08). Our Finance Minister repeatedly assured that despite stock market crash, the fundamentals of the Indian economy are quite strong and Indian growth story is quite intact. Prime Minister Dr. Manmohan Singh also expressed the similar views and said that global meltdown would have minimal effect on India's economic growth. However, India's growth of GDP fell to 6.8 per cent in 2008-09 as against over 9 per cent per annum in the preceeding three years. In 2009-10 and 2011-11, the Indian economy recovered and its growth of GDP was 8 per cent and 8.6 per cent respectively.

However, as against the 11th plan target of 9 per cent annual growth, fall in India's growth to 6.7 per cent in 2008-09 and 8.0 per cent in 2009-10 will badly affect the targets of employment generation and poverty reduction. It is true that unlike that of China, India's economic growth depends more on domestic demand rather than external demand and is driven mostly by domestic saving and investment. However, at present after 18 years of globalisation, our exports constitute 14 per cent and imports 20 per cent of GDP (2006-07). Therefore, India could not escape from the adverse consequences of global meltdown. This is evident from industrial growth during the second half of the fiscal year 2008-09; India's industrial production (IIP) registered 4.8 per cent growth in September 2008 and a negative growth of 0.41 per cent in October 2008 for the first time in 15 years. For the whole year 2008-09 the growth in industrial production dipped to 3.7 per cent as compared to 10.3

per cent in 2007-08 and 14.9% in 2006-07. There was a fall in output of automobile, aviation and shipping industries. Besides, export-oriented industries such as textiles, leather, gems and jewellery have been badly hit by the global meltdown and registered a fall in production and employment opportunities. Agriculture registered 1.6 per cent growth rate in 2008-09 as compared to 4.7 per cent in 2007-08. There was a very slow growth of 0.4% in agriculture in 2009-10.

The most adverse consequence of global turmoil was that the growth rate of manufacturing in India fell to 3.2% in 2008-09 from 10.3 per cent in 2007-08. Not only did domestic demand come down even export orders fell substantially due to recession in the developed countries. The other important causes of slowdown in manufacturing are that banks were not willing to give credit and lack of adequate power supply and high input costs. It is worth mentioning that though growth rate of Indian economy slowed down under the impact of global financial crisis, its estimated growth rate of 6.8 per cent in 2008-09 and 8 per cent in 2009-10 was still quite high in view of the fact that other countries such as US, UK, Japan, Euro countries, Germany were experiencing severe recession (that is, contraction in GDP). In fact, growth rate of Indian economy is second highest in the world next only to China. However, a matter of serious concern is that employment situation worsend in the fiscal year 2008-09. There were large scale losses in jobs in the sectors like textiles, metals, leather and jewellery. With slowdown in economic growth in India unemployment in India also went up. Another matter of concern is that due to large increase in government expenditure to pull the economy out of recession and slow growth of agriculture, inflation rate as measured by CPI rose to more than 11 per cent in 2008-09. Besides there has been *severe food inflation* which in Feb. 2010 went up to around 20%. In 2009-10 and 2010-11 food inflation spilled over to manufactured products as well. Rate of infaltion based on CPI (for industrial workers) went upto 9.1% 2008-09, 12.4 in 2009-10 and 11% in 2010-11.

Exports and Balance of Payments

As a result of globalisation and the adoption of export-oriented strategy of growth in place of import substitution, the Indian economy now depends to a greater extent on external market to sell our goods and services. In 1990-91 we exported goods to the tune of 5.8 per cent of GDP whereas in 2006-07 our exports of goods rose to 14 per cent and our imports to 20 per cent of our GDP.[5]

Our foreign trade balance worsened during 2008-09. India's foreign trade balance registered a deficit of \$60 billion in the first half of 2008-09 as against \$ 30 billion in the first half of 2007-08. Actually, our exports in Oct. 2008 were not just down but declined 12.8% as compared to the same month of the previous year 2007. This negative trend continued in the remaining years of 2008-09. As a result, our target of exports of 200 billion US dollar for 2008-09 was revised downward to \$ 175 billion. Actually, growth of Indian exports in 2008-09 was around \$ 170 billion, much short of the original target. Due to global financial crisis the growth of our exports were bound to decline as a result of recessionary conditions in the US and the European countries. Besides, due to sharp depreciation of rupee during 2008-09, our imports also costed more despite the fall in international commodity prices and crude oil. Hitherto our export growth was bolstered by rising commodity prices and yet strong demand from emerging markets and oil producing countries. All such contributory factors are no longer there. In 2008-09 and 2009-10 deficit in our balance of payments on current account went up to 2.4% and 2.9% of GDP_{mp} respectively. However, beginning from Nov. 2009, there has been *positive* growth in our exports indicating recovery in the world economy, especially in the US. However, due to high growth in imports our current account deficit has gone up.

INDIAN RESPONSE TO THE FINANCIAL CRISIS

The major effects of global financial crisis were (1) stock market crash, (2) depreciation of Indian rupee due to capital outflows by FIIs and (3) credit crunch in the Indian economy following the drastic decline in the liquidity in the bank system.

5. GOI, *Economic Survey*, 2007-08, p.112

Monetary Policy Measures

Our response to the global financial turmoil has been both monetary and fiscal. The RBI which for several months before had been increasing cash reserve ratio and interest rates to fight against inflation reversed its monetary policy from Oct. 2008. The RBI took several steps to prevent fast depreciation of Indian rupee due to massive capital outflow by FIIs by selling billions of dollars in the foreign exchange market from its reserves. But for RBI intervention, the value of rupee would have gone much below ₹ 52 for a US dollar.

The problem raised by global financial crisis was diagnosed as the lack of liquidity in the money market which adversely affected the flow credit to industries. Therefore, to increase liquidity of the banking system, RBI cut cash reserve ratio (CRR) four times in Oct.2008 to January 2009 by 400 basis points (*i.e.* by 4 percentage points) from 9 per cent to 5 per cent. With this the RBI infused liquidity of ₹ 1,60,000 crores in the banking system. Besides, RBI reduced statutory liquidity ratio (SLR) from 25 per cent to 24 which enabled banks to get ₹ 20,000 crores from RBI against Government securities *for lending* to mutual funds. Besides, RBI released ₹ 25,000 crores to the banks in connection with the farm waiver scheme of the Central Government. It may be noted further that banks can also borrow from RBI through repo window of liquidity adjustment facility (LAF) scheme of RBI. Besides, unwinding of some ***market stabilisation scheme*** was also undertaken to increase liquidity with the banks. In this way about ₹ 2,00,000 crores had been infused into the domestic money market to alleviate the pressures brought on by deterioration in global financial environment. With infusion of this adequate liquidity in the system through various measures the banks could provide credit to the industries for financing working capital and fixed investment projects. This was expected to boost industrial growth which had slackened in the last few months.

However, it was felt that to fullfil the needs of credit of the companies, mere infusion of more liquidity was not enough unless the lending rates of banks were lowered to reduce the cost of borrowing. To achieve this, repo rate – the rate at which banks borrow from RBI for a short time and used as a policy signal – was cut five times by 4 percentage point from 9 per cent to 5 per cent in Oct. 2008. As a result of this various Indian banks (including SBI) reduced their prime lending rate (PLR) to around 12 to 12.5 per cent. With this banks lowerd their lending rates so that cost of borrowing from the banks fell and more credit was created for investment by the companies and there was more demand for durable consumer goods such as houses, cars etc. Besides, RBI cut *reverse repo rate*, which is the overnight rate of interest at which banks park their surplus funds with the RBI to 4 per cent. This was meant to encourage banks to give credit to business enterprises for investment and to consumers for buying houses, cars etc. rather than keeping surplus liquid funds with RBI.

However, reports from banks (in March 2009) revealed that though liquidity had eased in the system and banks had lowered their lending rates but credit to industries did not pick up to the extent it was expected to happen. As a result, most banks were sitting on surplus cash. This showed due to global meltdown and its adverse effects on various sectors of the Indian economy banks became risk averse and were not willing to lend for fear of defaults by the borrowers.

Fiscal Stimulus

Besides easy monetary policy it was emphasized that a fiscal stimulus to overcome recession and slowdown in economic growth was needed. This fiscal stimulus is in keeping with Keynesian macroeconomics as Keynes emphasized increase in government expenditure to get rid of depression in the nineteen thirties. To keep growth momentum and to ensure 7 per cent growth rate in 2008-09 the Indian Government came out with three fiscal stimulus packages which involved increase in Government expenditure and cut in indirect taxes to boost both consumption demand and investment demand. The first fiscal stimulus package announced on Dec. 6, 2008 involved ***increase in Government expenditure by ₹ 30,700 crore.*** This increase in Government expenditure was meant to help growth of infrastrucutre, textiles (which is a major employer of labour force) exports, housing, automobiles, and small and medium enterprises.

An important measure in the first fiscal stimulus package was **all-round cut in excise duty** (CENVAT) to raise the demand for goods and services. This 4% cut in excise duty was estimated to result in revenue loss of ₹ 8700 crore to the Government. Further, to *counter the slump in exports* due to global financial crisis, the first fiscal package provided for ***subsidising interest costs of exporters.*** It was hoped that lower interest costs of exporters would make the Indian exports more competitive. In order to give further boost to the exports, an additional fund of ₹ 1100 crore had also been provided to ensure full *refund of duties including service tax* paid on inputs.

In the first week of January 2009, it was felt that global recessionary conditions were still very strong which would adversely after growth of the Indian economy, the second fiscal stimulus packjage was announced on Jan. 2, 2009. While the first fiscal stimulus package focussed on direct increase in Goivernment expenditure the second fiscal stimulus package sought to improve or facilitate supply of finance to some organizations. For thus purpose in this second package to **increase expenditure on infrastructure** was sought by providing finance to non-banking finance Companies (NBFCs) *dealing exclusively with infrastructure finance.* For this purpose the public sector company Indian Infrastructure Finance Company (IIFC) was allowed to borrow ₹ 30,000 crore from the market by issuing tax-free bonds that would be used to assist in funding of projects worth ₹ 75000 crore.

Secondly, *a higher depreciation rate of 50 per cent for Commercial Vehicles (CVs)* like trucks, buses and vans bought in the period, January-March 2009 was allowed. Besides, an extra line of credit to non-banking financial companies (NBFCs) for purchase of CVs and assistance by it for purchase of buses for urban transport system under governmental urban renewal scheme. All these steps were expected to boost demand for CVs which had been badly hit by economic slowdown.

Further measures taken in this second stimulus package related to providing an indirect push to realty and infrastructure sectors by **removing exemption from countervailing duties** (CVDs) along with special CVDs for steel and cement, the two important inputs for real estate and infrastructure sectors. Besides, in order to ensure that Indian corporate sector get cheaper funds from abroad, in the second stimulus package the **government *increased the limit on investment* by foreign institutional investors (FIIs) in *rupee denominated* corporate bonds** issued by the Indian companies from $8 billion to $15 billion.

It was hoped that the above measures in the second fiscal stimulus package would result in additional credit supply of ₹ 56000 crore.

The Third Fiscal Stimulus Package. In *this third package* announced on Jan. 24, 2009 *the government sought to boost demand by cutting central excise duty, service tax and customs duty.* This was estimated to cost the exchequer ₹ 29,100 crores. The measures announced in this fiscal stimulus were :

1. Central excise duty was slashed further by 2 per cent from 10 per cent to 8 per cent. Along with this the earlier 4% cut in central excise duty announced in Dec. 2008 was extended beyond March 31, 2009. It was expected that if this cut in excise duty was actually passed on to the consumers by manufacturers, this would lead to the reduction in prices and therefore stimulate demand for goods.

2. As a further measure to boost demand, service tax was also cut across the board by 2 percentage point from 12 per cent to 10 per cent.

3. To provide relief to the power sector naptha imported for generation of electricity was fully exempted from basic customs duty beyond March 2009.

Summing up. The above fiscal stimulus packages were bound to increase domestic demand in the economy and helped in achieving 6.8 per cent rate of growth of the Indian economy in the fiscal year 2008-09 and 8 per cent in 2009-10 and 8.6 per cent in 2010-11. This was also expected to help in generating more employment opportunities and thereby prevent the problem of unemployment from getting more worse. Due to fiscal stimulus it was expected that fiscal deficit to rise to more than 6 per cent of GDP. However, in times of recessionary conditions, the higher fiscal deficit is an appropriate counter-cyclical policy. It is worth noting that increase in Government expenditure causes increase in aggregate income not only equal to the amount by which it is increased but has also a multiplier effect. The manifold increase in aggregate income or GDP, as a result of increase in Government expenditure is called *Government expenditure multiplier* which plays an important role in expansion in national income in an economy when productive capacity is not fully utilised due to deficiency of aggregate demand.

Recovery of the Indian Economy

From the slowdown caused by global financial crisis Indian economy recovered in the second-half of the year 2009-10 as a result of Government's fiscal stimulus measures and accomodative expansionary monetary policy of the RBI. The Indian economy recovered from the crisis first due to increase in Government expenditure under fiscal stimulus and later due to pick-up in private consumption and investment demand as a result of multiplier effect of increase in Government expenditure, especially incurred on infrastructre projects.

The growth of GDP which had reached over 9 per cent for three successive years prior to the crisis dipped to 6.7 per cent in 2008-09 but again rose to 8.6 per cent in the year 2009-10 and to 9.3% in 2010-11. However, due to slowdown in the US and other developed countries, lower growth of agriculture due to weak monsoon and European debt crisis India's growth will fell to 6.2 per cent or in 2011-12. The growth of industry which had fallen to 3.7 per cent in 2008-09 rose to 8 per cent in 2009-10 and 2010-11 but again fell to 7 per cent in 2011-12. Agriculture after registering a very low growth of 1.6% in 2008-09 and 0.4 per cent in 2009-10 achieved a high growth of 6.6 per cent in 2010-11. The lower growth of agriculture in 2008-09 and 2009-10 caused high food inflation in India in 2009-10 with which India is still persisting.

Exports and Foreign Investment

India's exports also revived in 2009-10. Exports which *slipped* into negative territory in Oct. 2008 due to global economic slowdown and a resulting fall in demand came out of the red after 13 months in November 2009. Since then every month the growth of our exports has been positive. Our exports during 2009-10 was around $ 182.2 billion as against exports worth $ 189 billion in the previous fiscal year. But for the recovery of our exports since Nov. 2009, decline in our exports during 2009-10 would have been much higher. During 2010-11 our exports recorded on an average 29.5 per cent growth (in US $) year-on-year basis which is quite impressive. This growth in our exports in 2010-11 was helped by global recovery real GDP growth rate in 2010.

Besides exports, foreign capital inflows (both portfolio investment and foreign direct investment, FDI) revived during 2009-10. It is because of portfolio capital inflows during 2009-10, that Indian rupee appreciated to around ₹44 per US $ and BSE Index shot up to around 20,000 mark in September 2010. Though in May 2010, due to Greek debt crisis FIIs got panicky and started selling their shares in the Indian stock market and repatriating dollars to the US. However, after a few months, Capital inflows by FII again started coming.

Global investors are getting better returns from India. Therefore, foreign direct investment inflows (FDI) into India in the year 2009-10 are estimated to be around $ 25.8 billion against $ 27.3 billion in the previous year 2008-09. In a globalised world, a congenial global economic environment and a sustainable balance of payments position are critical for achieving the policy goal of sustained growth of 9% per annum in India. The global recession in 2007-09 operated as a dampener on the prospects of a faster growth. Besides the conventional channels of trade and capital flows for transmission of external shocks to India's real economy, the uncertainty about global recovery continued to affect business confidence and market sentiments, which indirectly affected domestic private consumption and investment demand. India's high degree of resilience and capacity to manage a severe external shock was evident from the strength and pace of recovery in GDP growth rate after 2007-08. India's growth rate fell to 6.7 per cent in 2008-09 but it recovered to 8.6 per cent growth in GDP in 2009-10 and 9.3 per cent in 2010-11. However, due to slow recovery in the US and Eurozone crisis in 2010, 2011 and 2012, India GDP growth rate fell to 6.2 per cent in 2011-12 and to 5 per cent in 2012-13.

EUROZONE CRISIS AND ITS IMPACT

In 2010 the world again found itself in financial turmoil threatening another recession in the developed economies of the world, especially in European Euroland before the effects of global financial crisis (2007-09) had yet to fully wear off. The new crisis emerged not due to hitherto toxic assets as was the case of 2007-09 sub-prime crisis but due to the threat of defaulting on payment of its debt by governments of European countries especially by Greek government. Some economists have put forward the view that this new crisis is continuation of the previous crisis of 2007-09. This is because to overcome recession or slowdown following the financial crisis (2007-09) the governments of various European countries increased their public expenditure by heavily borrowing, especially from foreign sources and thereby increasing significantly their sovereign debt. The problem of Greece and other European Countries is of ***huge sovereign debt*** on which annual interest has to paid and the repayment of the principal sum borrowed. This has created the risk of default on paying debt by these countries.

The global financial system seems to be very fragile. Though Greece accounted for less than 2 per cent of the combined GDP of the European Union (EU), yet it set that entire region in turmoil and terrified investors throughout the world. Greek crisis created a good deal of uncertainty about the returns from their investment by investors in Greece and other Euroland countries bonds. As a result, during the Month of May 2010 stock market prices crashed not only in Europe but also in the USA and throughout Asia. Besides, the fears of *double-dip recession* and consequently large decline in stock market prices caused fall in world prices of commodities, crude oil and petroleum products. The price of crude oil went below $ 70 per barrel in May 2010.

Causes of Greek (Eurozone) Crisis

Governments of Greece and other Euro countries ran up record debts to pull their economies out of the deepest slump in 2007-09 since the Great Depression of 1930s and are new experiencing problem of defaulting on sovereign debt. Countries like India are suffering because of wrong-doings of the developed countries. While the US crisis of 2007-09 had broken out as most of the borrowers could not repay housing loans and therefore started defaulting on loan payments, in Greece and other European Countries, the problem has been created by governments which lived beyond their means and borrowed heavily thereby adding greatly to their debt burden which they are finding it difficult to repay now. Countries like Greece, Spain, Italy, Ireland and UK have been undertaking *double-digit fiscal deficit*. According to a report, the fiscal deficit of Greece in 2009 was 13.6 per cent of GDP, that of UK 11.6 per cent, of Spain 11.2 per cent and Ireland 11 per cent. According to Joseph Stiglitz, such a huge fiscal deficit is clearly unsustainable and was bound to cause problem of defaulting on payment of debt that increased due to heavy borrowing to meet the large deficits.

Debt of Greece and other European countries is very large. At present public debt of Greece stands at 115 per cent of GDP and is estimated to rise to 150 per cent of GDP in 2014. This is in part due to the fact that Greece, Ireland, Spain has been incurring large fiscal deficit in the past and has been adding 14 per cent annually to its sovereign debt and partly because Greece has been experiencing negative growth of 4 to 5 per cent annually. Greece faced dilemma. Getting back to sustainable fiscal path required cutting annual fiscal deficit by 10% by reducing public expenditure and increasing taxes. This was politically infeasible as it would have caused loss of a large number of jobs and therefore would have been resisted by the people who would protest vehemently as was actually revealed by widespread protests in 2010, 2011 and 2012. Besides, attempts to reduce fiscal deficit was likely to hamper economic growth which would lead to lower tax revenue in future. This is because withdrawing fiscal stimulus by cutting public expenditure and raising taxes will lower aggregate demand. These austerity measures in fact caused recession or lower GDP growth in European Countries.

It is worth mentioning that Greece had adopted Euro as its currency and no longer had its own currency. Therefore, because of its being locked into Euro, Greece *could not devalue the currency* so as to switch its aggregate expenditure from imports to exports.

In the absence of defaulting on debt, three possible options were available to Greece to overcome its debt crisis. First, Greece could withdraw from EU and revive its own currency and undertake its *devaluation* to expand exports and stimulate growth and thereby lower its debt burden. With its ending of membership of EU and revival of its currency Greece could print its own currency to pay off a part of its internal debt and thus easing its fiscal burden. This also applies to other countries. However, this scenario was unlikely to happen since no European country including Greece is prepared to see its dismemberment as EU comes to their rescue whenever required.

Secondly, Greece could remain in the EU and adopt harsh **austerity measures imposed by EU and IMF**. Accordingly, it could drastically cut its public expenditure on the one hand and increase its taxes to raise revenue on the other to reduce its annual fiscal deficits which will help in solving its debt problem over time. This, as pointed out above, was bound to be opposed and resisted strongly by the people and was therefore considered as politically infeasible. The third option to be adopted was to take only ***moderate and politically feasible austerity measures*** **along with *rescheduling* of its debt.** Note that austerity measures require ***fiscal compression***, that is, cutting of public expenditure and raising taxes.

It is not only Greece that is affected by heavy debt problem, similar debt crisis is also faced by Spain, Portugal, Ireland, Italy and even UK. If Greece defaulted on its debt, it was likely to cause similar situation in these other European countries. It was to prevent the fears of this **contagion effect** that EU in collaboration with IMF announced $ 1 trillion bail-out package for Greece and other Euro countries facing sovereign debt crisis so that these countries could repay their debt and interest on it. Besides, independent European Central Bank (ECB) was persuaded to announce that it would buy Greek government bonds to ease the pressure on redemption of Government bonds. It would help the Greek government for tackling its debt crisis. It is worth mentioning that EU while announcing its bail-out package put the condition that Greece and other Euro countries would adopt ***austerity measures,*** that is, cut their public expenditure and raise taxes to increase revenue so as to reduce fiscal deficit.

In 2011 again sovereign debt crisis in Greece arose in serious form putting financial markets all over the world in turmoil. European Central Bank (ECB) again came to its rescue and purchased its bonds but put strict conditions that Greece would adopt ***severe austerity measures*** (i.e. cut its expenditure and raise its resources through higher taxes) so that it is able to reduce its debt burden.

Spread of Sovereign Debt Crisis to other European Countries

In 2011 sovereign debt problem spread to other major economies of Eurozone such as Italy and Spain putting the whole Eurozone in the danger zone, that is, to the brink of default on their public debt. After some hesitation, in August 2011, European Central Bank (ECB) took emergency operations to bail them out. ECB purchased Italian and Spanish debt-bonds of the value of 22 billion Euro which was biggest bail-out operation undertaken by it so far. Besides, in Sept. 2011private banks which had given loans to Greece and other debt-ridden European countries agreed to write off 50 per cent of their debt to these countries and thus providing great relief to them.

However, investors realised that bail-out package for Greece and other Euro countries facing sovereign debt crisis would only postpone the date of their being declared insolvent. As a result, investors not willing to take risk started selling the Greek bonds and Government bonds of other Euro countries and sending dollars to the US to invest there which they considered as quite safe. As a result, US dollar greatly appreciated and Euro greatly depreciated.

It is worth mentioning that some economists were of the view that adoption of *harsh* austerity measures by Greece and other European countries and therefore cutting public expenditure and raising taxes as recommended by EU and IMF to solve their debt problem will not only hamper their recovery from the recession/slowdown following the global financial crisis (2002-07) but will also pose a risk to global economic recovery and growth and thus raising spectre of a ***double-dip recession***, especially when the US in 2011 also faced a sovereign debt problem. Barak Obama entered into a deal with the US Congress to raise the country's ***debt ceiling*** and thus managed to avoid the default but the US economy was moving from bad to worse in 2011 and 2012 despite the ***quantitative easing (QE)*** policy pursued by the Federal Reserve.

In 2011 crisis seemed to be spreading to other European countries such as Spain, Ireland, Portugal, Italy, UK and even Hungary. The terrified investors exposed not only to Greek debt and its derivatives but also to the debts of other European countries. This resulted in great volatility in stock markets and foreign exchange markets throughout Europe, US and Asian countries. There was *flight of capital* from Greece and other European countries to the US in 2010 but in 2011, even the US was pushed into danger zone. This caused a great turmoil in financial markets in Europe, US and even in Asia. If this financial turmoil continues, the global economy may again slip into recession. Reports were coming about the slow growth or near stagnation in not only large European countries but also of US. In France, the second-largest economy in the European Union after Germany, growth came to a standstill in 2010-11. The growth in the United States also slowed down in 2010-11 and 2011-12. The second recession was already well under way in Greece and Portugal; growth in Spain, Italy and Britain was quite slow, domestic demand in Europe was weak and growth was dependent on sales from abroad, where signals indicated that they were shrinking. According to a report in the week-end of Aug. 2011 there was 0.7% fall in industrial production in 17 nations of European Union (EU) in June 2011 compared with May 2011. With less economic growth, governments will collect less tax revenue. They will have more trouble in paying their debts. That could make investors even more nervous and add to turmoil in the stock and bond markets, which will undercut business and consumer confidence, and will lead to yet slower growth, and ultimately recession. There is a real risk that there is a self-enforcing cycle under way here.

India did not escape from this new global crisis. The Indian exports to European countries and the US declined which adversely affected India's industrial growth. The decline in India's exports also brought about increase in current account deficit (CAD) to 4.2% of GDP in 2011-12 and further to around 5% GDP in 2012-13. Such a large current account deficit was unsustainable and was a matter of great concern. Besides, the large current account deficit in 2011-12 and 2012-13 put pressure on the Indian rupee which sharply depreciated.

Eurozone Treaty. Eurozone debt problem still remains unresolved threatening the breaking up of European union as well. In the first week of December 2011 European union summit was held in Berlin to make an attempt to solve Eurozone present debt crisis problem and to save Eurozone from splitting by preventing the future debt crisis. At this summit a Eurozone treaty was forged to bring about a deeper integration in Eurozone. However, Britain was not a party to this treaty. In this treaty EU leaders agreed to lend up to $200 billion to an emergency lending facility of the IMF to help it aid eurozone countries gripped by crises. This is in addition to the 440 billion Euro for European Financial Stability Fund (EFSF) already established by European governments, and a permanent € 500 billion facility called the European Stability Mechanism which was to be established by June 2012. This was in addition to the relief to Greece already provided by private banks in writing down and restructuring their loans up to 50%. Greek problem had not yet been solved that Spain, another important country of European Union, was gripped with a crisis in middle of the year 2012. Spain posed a bigger wory than Greece. The Spanish government said that it would infuse 19 billion euros into distressed real estate lender Bankia SA whose troubles had led to a run on Spanish institutions. Also the Bank of Spain warned that the country might sink deeper into a recession. Dealers were worried about Spain because it was a much larger economy and might prove more difficult to bail out by the larger economies of northern Europe.

These arrangements for bailing out stressed economies were expected to go a long way in dealing with the existing debt problem. But they do not deal with the fiscal problem that underlies the debt problem, namely, that most EU governments spend much more than the revenues they raise, especially in a variety of generous entitlement programmes of the welfare state. Unless these governments conform to prudent fiscal rules that align their spending with their revenues, the sovereign debt problem will keep recurring. Hence the most significant achievement of the last EU summit was the agreement by all EU governments, except UK, to commit to a fiscal agreement. While this was a major step forward, details of how this will work are yet to be worked out. However, an adverse development (in Mid-January 2012) has been the downgrading the Standard and Poor of rating of 9 EU countries which affected European Financial Stability Found (EFSE's) credit worthiness and the available funds could fall short of needs again. Standard and Poors downgraded the credit ratings of nine euro zone countries, while stripping France and Austria of their coveted triple-A status but not of EU paymaster Germany. Standard and Poor's rating actions were primarily driven by its assessment that the policy initiatives that have been taken by European policy makers in recent weeks might be insufficient to fully address onging systemic stresses in the eurozone. S&P cut the ratings of Italy, Spain, Portugal and Cyprus by two notches and the standing of France, Austria, Malta, Slovakia and Slovenia by one notch each. The move put highly, indebted Italy on the same BBB + level as Kazakhstan and pushed Portugal into junk status.

Crisis in Cyprus

In March 2013, the important European country Cyprus faced with an acute debt burden problem. It may be noted that Cyprus has a large exposure to Greek debt and the second Greek bailout package in 2012 caused 56.9 billion hole in Cypriot budget. Now, because of its mounting debt burden it sought $ 13 billion from EU for its bail-out. The EU asked the Cyprus government to raise funds of $ 5.8 billion itself before it sanctions its bailout. In order to raise these funds Cyprus government proposed a tax on deposits in its banks. This created a turmoil in stock and foreign exchange markets in the world as two thirds of $ 88.4 billion total deposits in banks of Cyprus was in foreign currency. However, the Cypriot Government said that Cyprus had no choice but to accept the EU's bailout condition with levy on bank deposits or go bankrupt.

Cyprus is a routing centre for offshare investment due to its low tax regime. Before these investments were to be transferred to other countries these investment funds wre deposited in Cypriot banks. Imposition of tax on bank deposits, these investments wre to be affected. The proposed tax on bank deposits set a dangerous precedent for contries needing to be bailed out, especially in the Eurozone area. Depositors' savings were sacrosent and tax on deposits sent a shiver across the entire Eurozone causing Euro to tumble and stock markets to dive.

As a good part of bank deposits in Cyprus amounting to $ 38 billion was Russian, the Russian President Putin opposed the tax on bank deposits describing it quite unfair and setting a dangerous president.

Fortunately, the Cypriot parliament rejected its government proposal of imposing tax on bank deposits calling it as bank robbery. At the time of writing this piece Cyprus is pressing Russia to pump in funds to reduce its debt burden and to extend an existing 2.5 billion Russian loan.

It fellows from above that almost entire Eurozone is in crisis and in a state of stagnation and this Eurozone crisis has created uncertainty and risk which has prevented the investors from investing in bonds and shares of banks of this region. Besides, stagnation in European countries is responsible for slowdown in the Indian exports.

Cyprus Deal. After a good deal of negotiations. Cyprus clinched a deal with international lenders to shut down its second-largest bank and inflict heavy losses on uninsured depositors, including wealthy Russians, in return for a Euro 10-billion ($13 billion) bailout plan.

The deal came hours before a deadline to avert a collapse of the banking system between President Nicos Anastasiades and heads of the European Union, the European Central Bank and the International Monetary Fund. Without a deal, Cyprus banking system would have collapsed and the country could have become the first to crash out of the European single currency (Euro).

Swiftly backed by euro zone finance ministers, the deal will spare the Cyprus a financial meltdown by winding down the largely state-owned Popular Bank of Cyprus, also known as Laiki, and shifting deposits below €100,000 to the Bank of Cyprus to create a "good bank". Deposits above €100,000 in both banks, which are not guaranteed under EU law will be frozen and used to pay Laiki's debts and recapalise Bank of Cyprus through deposit/equity conversion. An EU spokesman said no tax on levy would be imposed on deposits in banks.

How did the Cyprus Crisis Come About ?

Cyprus, the smallest of the eurozone economies, was a robust economy till about two years ago, characterised by relatively high economic growth, low levels of unemployment and healthy state of government finances. Cyprus accounts for a very small fraction of the eurozone economy–about 0.2%. But its banking sector is strongly linked to Greece, which itself has been hit by sovereign debt worries. Cypriot banks had given out loans to top Greek borrowers that had accounted for nearly 160% of Cyprus's GDP. As the Greek economy ran into a crisis in 2010, it was the Cypriot banks that were among the hardest hit. A slowing economy also meant that the government did not have the adequate finances to bail out its banks.

Latest Change in Stance by EU and European Central Bank (ECB)

At long last there was a change in stance or thinking by EU and European Central Bank (ECB) in respect of solving the sovereign debt crisis. After the crises broke out in the late nineties in European countries such as Greece, Spain, Portugal, Italy, Ireland, EU and IMF joined together to bail them out of the crisis so as to keep the members within the union. For this purpose they imposed stringent austerity measures (cutting budget expenditure and raising taxes) so that they are able to pay back the loans taken. The many debt-ridden countries like Greece, Ireland, Portugal, Spain and Italy were forced to accept these conditions in return for bailout loans to reassure the jittery bond markets that they would be able to repay the loans. Accordingly, they slashed their budget expenditure and raised more tax revenue to achieve surplus in their budgets.

However, for austerity measures they had to pay a heavy price as their economies landed in recession or slowdown in economic growth. The evidence grew that cutting government expenditure drastically and raising taxes were less effective in reducing deficits than initially thought and perhaps counter-productive. This is because as growth of the economies slowed down due to austerity measures, it made it difficult to raise enough tax revenue to balance the budget.

EU stance regarding the solution of sovereign debt problem changed in its summit meeting on March 14, 2013 at Brussels where they reviewed the austerity measures regarding their effectiveness in solving the sovereign debt problem. It was found that the unemployment in Eurozone reached a record level of 11.9 per cent (Average of 17 member countries of EU) and slowdown in economic growth in some of them and recession in others. As a result, there was widespread discontent in European Countries such as Greece, Spain, Italy and Portugal which were forced to undertake austerity measures as a condition for their bailout by EU. In its submit at Brussels, leaders of EU agreed to relax the austerity conditions by postponing the budget cuts and higher deficit-cut targets by the debt-ridden European countries. That is, the European Union slowed its enforcement of deficit limit until the region economy turned around. Accordingly, the countries like Greece and Spain which had been bailed out were given more time to repay the loans to the countries such as Germany. This means there was ***rescheduling of debt*** and thereby easing the pressures on then to cut budget deficits sharply through reducing government expenditure and raising taxes.

Thus due to recession that overtook the debt-affilicted European Countries as a result of austerity measures financial leaders of EU and European Central Bank (ECB) realised their previous approach of strong austerity measures were wrong and now *more emphasis was placed on reviving growth*. This represents a clear shift from its earlier emphasis on stringent austerity measures to close budget deficits. However, the new EU stance does not mean that countries have not to follow austerity measures but instead they only need more time to follow austerity measures *that are needed to bring a country's balanced budget* in structural terms, that is, deficit excluding the effects of recession. And the EU commission has been asked to judge the performance of the debt-ridden countries in respect of their progress in reducing structural deficit. This provides the ailing countries more time to get their finances under control.

The change in recent stance of EU and European Central Bank implies that they have realised that their earlier stringent austerity measures imposed on their debt-ridden members did not deliver. As a result of these austerity measures Greece economy went into recession causing huge unemployment. In Greece as a result of this recession unemployment shot up 27 per cent of labour force in January 2013. Portugal's GDP dipped by 3.2 per cent in 2012 as its unemployment reached a record level of 17% of its labour force. Similarly, other European countries such as Spain, Ireland, Portugal, Italy experienced recessionary conditions as a result of adoption of austerity measures imposed by EU and IMF as a condition for their bailout. Prime Minister Mario Monty the supporter of austerity measures lost the elections in Italy held in February 2013.

Predictions by some economists, chiefly by Joseph Stiglitz that the austerity measures would harm growth and even bring about recession in the countries adopting them proved to be true. Austerity measures (cutting government expenditure) and raising taxes they argued would lower economic growth. Not only would they lead to decrease in aggregate demand that adversely affect economic growth but lower growth would also mean loss of revenue for government which will make harder to close the budget gaps. Greece and Spain are running deficit more than their official target limit. A growing number of European countries appear headed in the direction of less austerety no matter what the financial leaders EU decide because most people in their countries are opposed to the austerity policies of EU. Therefore, the new changed stance and rethinking about stringent austerity measures and therefore deciding in relaxing them would come as comfort to millions of Europeans, especially those living in countries that received bailouts, such as Greece, Ireland and Portugal. These countries remain under pressure to keep spending levels down and continue unpopular tax hikes even as they *battle recession.*

The Greek economy is in its sixth year of recession and the unemployment rate there has reached 27%. Portugal's economy contracted 3.2% last year–its severest annual downturn since 1975—and its unemployment rate is at record 17.2%.

The rethinking about strict austerity measures was prompted by recession in Eurozone region which was expected to end in the second half of year 2013. However, Germany which played an important role in bailout of the debt-afflicted countries like Greece and Spain expressed reservation about relaxing austerity measures and decision of about postponting of budget cutting and deficit targets. Germany's Chancellor Angela Merkel said after the EU sumbit meeting that it was necessary to trim the budget deficits to promote growth and investment. But despite Germany's reservations, EU in its sumit meeting at Brussels in March 2013 decided about relaxing of austerity measures to overcome recession and revive growth in the region.

However, it seems this Eurozone treaty has failed to boost sentiments. Analysts are sceptical about long-term steps taken to overcome current crisis. Markets have considered it as too little and too late.

Fall in capital inflows caused a crash in the Indian stock market and led to the sharp depreciation of the Indian rupee. EU's agreement to sign treaty to foster deeper economic integration is definitely the route to take for the longer term but it is unclear how this would unfold in the short term. However, if austerity measures become too stringent it could impact the global economy including India. A week Europe is a reality for at least the middle of the year 2014, though EU leaders have agreed on a treaty. That apart, a lot would depend on the manner of execution of this agreement.

Impact on India

European debt crisis and fragile US recovery have contributed to the growth slowdown of the Indian economy by hurting our exports and affecting capital inflows into India. The capital outflows have resulted in crash in our stock markets that have affected investment sentiments of the corporate world. The rupee's depreciation, while aggravated by domestic speculative activity, is primarily traceable to the ongoing sovereign debt crisis in Europe. The value of rupee which was around 44.50 rupees to a US dollar in August 2011 fell to as low as 54 rupees to a dollar on December 15, 2011 and was around ₹ 54.8 to a US dollar in the first week of April 2013. As observed during the crisis of 2008, the present crisis has again led to a large withdrawal of FII money from the Indian stock market, eroding its value. This large withdrawal of portfolio investments from India also led to the depreciation of the rupee.

The slowdown in GDP growth to 6.2 per cent in 2011-12 and 5 per cent in 2012-13 was partly due to Eurozone crisis. Eurozone debt crisis put a damper on India's exports to Europe, the biggest destination for Indian exports as well as capital inflows into the Indian equity and debt markets. The government blamed European crisis as important reason for India's slowdown in economic growth in recent years.

However, *we think that current slowdown in economic growth is partly a result* as pointed out above, of Eurozone debt crisis and overall global environment, especially slow recovery in the United States and stagnation in the European countries. Besides, increase in interest rates by RBI to fight inflation has led the corporate sector to defer investment has resulted in the drastic fall in output of capital goods. However, in our view, the Indian economy will soon recover once these short-run problems are resolved. Once inflation is brought under control RBI will cut its interest rates which will give a push to investment that will boost industrial growth. If investment in infrastructure increases, as is expected now, this will lead to the expansion in domestic demand for capital goods. This will ensure a higher growth rate in the next year, 2013-14. Besides, we still have the ability to achieve 8% per cent growth rate even on the basis of our domestic market. This is because, *we still, on the supply side, have the fundamentals for higher growth rate. These are high saving and investment rates which even in the year (2013-14) are around 30 per cent and 32 per cent respectively.* However, to ensure higher growth in the next few years productivity of capital has to be raised through better governance and speedy implementation of stalled infrastructure products.

CHAPTER 44

Environment, Climate Change and Sustainable Development

Introduction

In recent years there has been growing concern about degradation and pollution of environment and climate change as they impact on future development of both the developing and developed countries. In 1992, representatives of over 150 countries met at Rio in Brazil to discuss the environmental issues and their implications for future development of the world. This meeting at Rio is called the '**Earth summit**' or the **United Nations Conference on Environment and Development** (UNCED). This conference clearly spelled out the linkages between natural environment and development and put forward the concept of **"sustainable development"**. This has produced greater awareness about environmental issues and facilitated the cooperation between different countries to reduce environmental degradation, particularly to reduce emission of greenhouse gasses (GHG) such as carbon dioxide to prevent adverse climate change, that is, global warning in future which if not prevented will have disastrous consequences for the welfare and development of the population, both in developing and developed countries.

The conflict between economic growth and environment is sharper today than ever before, particularly in developing countries like India with fast growing population and mass poverty. The developing countries are making strenous efforts to balance their need for rapid economic growth with the environmental concerns for keeping their natural base intact. In India, as in other developing countries, the adoption of development strategy based primarily on large-scale industrialisation, energy-intensive technologies and biochemical-based agricultural technology, ignoring indigenous development paradigm based on locally self-sufficient technologies, has led to environmental degradation. In this, chapter, we shall explain various environmental issues and the adverse impact of climate change and explain the need for sustainable development.

In a recent conference state environment ministers held in August 2009, Prime Minister Manmohan Singh said that the ecological crisis that confronts the country has led to **'alarming situation'.** He urged upon the State governments to control environment pollution, clean rivers and fight climate change. This Statement highlights the fact that India's growth is increasingly taking place at the cost of its environment. This shows that we have not been taking adequate efforts to ensure sustainable development. To stop further decline in our natural resources and protect environment from pollution stringent regulations and incentives are needed. But, as the PM has said, due to rampant corruption prevailing in the bureaucracy the rules regarding the use of our natural resources and protection of environment have been flouted with impunity. There are numerous instances when the Ministry of Environment and Forests has flouted all norms to give clearance to dubious projects at the cost of environment and communities that depend on it.

Population and Environment

Concern over environment issues arises because it is thought that the population may increase to a level whose needs cannot be adequately met by earth's natural resources resulting in fall in living standards of the people. This is because increasing population causes environmental degradation. Increases in population cause over-exploitation of natural resources such as forests, water, fisheries and minerals at a rate for greater than their capacity to regenerate. Besides, population pressure on land compels us to cultivate arable land more intensively by using chemical inputs such as fertilizers, pesticides which cause soil degradation. Further, increase in population through its effect on deforestation by the rural and urban population for timber and fuel leads to the increase in carbon dioxide in the atmosphere and therefore causes air pollution. Thus the population impacts on environment primarily through the use and depletion of natural resources and is associated with environmental problems such as air and water pollution and loss of biodiversity and increased pressure on arable land. As an example of estimate of loss, Tata Energy Research Institute (TERI) estimates that economic losses due to soil degradation, diseases caused by pollution and forest degradation is between ₹ 100,000 to 450,000 crore every year and this does not include a series of other losses due to ecological destruction.[1]

Population increases cause over-exploitation of land and water resources and loss of biodiversity and forests and will therefore endanger sustainability of agriculture and food security in the country. According to Prof MS. Swaminathan, a noted agriculture scientist, " the capacity to support even the existing human and animal population has been exceeded in many parts of the world"[2] and if population growth is not checked, it will endanger the attainment of food security. To quote him again, "In the recent years there has been considerable concern about human capacity to produce adequate food to meet the needs of the growing population and the increase in purchasing power resulting in higher consumption of animal products."[3]

It is manifest from above that rapidly increasing population in developing countries will lead to the over-exploitation and degradation of land and depletion of fisheries which will threaten the achievement of food security in the developing countries.

Besides, the growth of urban population in the absence of adequate infrastructure facilities has caused the **lack of clean water to drink** and given rise to **slums with the poor sanitation** which has increased the vulnerability of the people to several diseases. It follows from above that to meet the expanding needs of the developing countries, environment degradation must be halted. For that purpose, reduction in population growth will greatly help in easing the intensification of many environmental problems.

Poverty and Environment

Poverty in developing countries is also said to be responsible for environmental degradation. Poor people rely on natural resources more than the rich. For survival the rural poor are forced to cut forests for timber and fuel as well as graze animals on pasture lands more than the reproductive capacity of these natural resources. Besides, when the cultivable land becomes short relative to population, the poor are forced to make their subsistence by cultivating fragile land on hills and mountains resulting in soil erosion on a large scale. It is in such environment that poverty becomes a vicious circle. Poverty leads to land degradation and land degradation accelerates the process of impoverishment because the poor people depend directly on exploitation of natural resources on which property rights are not properly assigned. Moreover, poverty results in malnutrition and reduces poor people's capacity to do work.

With growing population the poor encroach upon large remote areas of forests and grasslands to make their livelihood. If there are strict regulations to prevent such encroachment, it is opposed with stiff resistance by the poor, especially in the tribal areas.

---

1. Quoted by Ashish Kothari, in "Unsustainable Development, Unfulfilled Promises" in **Survey of Environment.** *The Hindu*, 2002.
2. M.S. Swaminathan, Agriculture : Route to an evergreen revolution " **in the Survey of Environment**. *2002 The Hindu*. P. 34.
3. *Ibid*, P. 33.

The solution to the poverty problem of these teeming millions lies in land reforms, generation of more employment opportunities and improvement in productivity of arable land already in use, for example, shifting the poor from poor resource-based to modern science-based agriculture. This is what has been sought to be achieved through green revolution technology.

However, the green revolution has been criticised for environmental reasons, especially the use of fertilizers and pesticides that increase soil salanity. Besides, ample use of irrigation in green revolution technology without adequate drainage facilitiess results in soil degradation through salinity and water logging. Adequate and appropriate steps should be taken be make the green revolution technology clean and environment-friendly. There can be no two opinions that major efforts must be made to overcome these defects through development of **less poisonous chemicals**, pest and insect control with reduced chemical application and improved drainage facilities. However, if the efforts to develop modern technology were abandoned because of these defects, employment and income-earing opportunities for marginal farmers and agricultural labourer would continue to be reduced under population pressure. As a result, many would be forced to push cultivation frontiers into ecologically fragile lands resulting in increased incidence of food and soil erosion"[4].

It is important to note that the environment representing forests, mines, sources of water, land that provide employment and livelihood to the poor people, especially those living in the tribal regions and it is they who in India are opposing the various development projects, even those cleared by the government Sunita Narain, a noted environmentalist, rightly writes. "Let us be clear, it is not the minister or his ministry, which is opposing development projects - from Vedanta to Posco or Jindal's steel or thermal plant or Nirma's cement plant. It is people, often the poorest, saying these projects will devastate their environment, their forests, which is their source of water, land and livelihood. They are saying, we are poor, but your development will make us poorer. The environmental movement of the country is being led from the bottom today. It is not in the hands of middle-class environmentalists like me."[5]

Business and Natural Environment

In this chapter we study the decline and degradation of natural environment of an economy and its impact on the people. How are business firms concerned with this environmental issue ? The business firms are related to the natural environment in two ways. First, they require natural resources such as land (for setting up industries), energy sources (coal, petroleum, gas—the natural products), wood and water for their production work. In the present state of technological development, the modern industries do not depend on the natural resources to the extent the industries depended on them in the early stages of industrial development in the nineteenth century. Neverthless, they require for land setting up industrial plants and consume energy from fossil fuels-the natural sources.

On the other hand, production in industries leads to degradation and pollution of environment. It is now well-known that industries and vehicular traffic in the urban areas are great polluter of air and water which cause heavy damage to the health of the people which represents social cost imposed on the society. Because of these adverse effects, the industries which pollute air and water need to be regulated to prevent them from causing heavy damage to the health of the people. Bhopal gas tragedy is prime example of polluting industries in the urban areas which pose threat to the life and health of the people. In Bhopal thousands of people died and thousands others suffered severe damage to their health as a result of leakage of gas from pesticides producing industrial unit owned by an MNC (Union Carbide Ltd.) operating in the residential area without proper safeguards.

4. Yujiro Hayami and Yoshihisa Godo, *Development Economics*'. Oxford University Press, 3rd ed. 2005. p. 227.
5. Sunita Narain, "Fix growth, not environment" in *Times of India.*

Again, in Delhi, the capital of India, where thousands of small industrial units were located in the congested residential areas against Master Plan and environment law. It was due to tough stand taken by High Court and Supreme Court that a good number of them has been relocated at the periphery of Delhi where proper infrastructure for prevention of pollution has been created. However, thousands of industrial units are still operating in the residential areas due to political pressure and vote-bank politics and government has authorised them declaring those areas as fully commercial areas.

Delhi is not an isolated case of industries being set up in residential areas and causing air and water pollution. Similar situation prevails in other big Indian cities such Mumbai, Kolkata. Due to rampant corruption in the bureaucracy these unauthorised polluting industrial units even get environment clearance from the Government.

ECONOMIC DEVELOPMENT, URBANISATION AND ENVIRONMENT

Industrialisation of the economy and urban development go together. In the post independence period, especially since the beginning of the Second Five Year Plan (1956 – 61) high priority has been accorded to industrialisation to achieve the goals of rapid growth of output and emplayment. New industrial factories and plants have been set up in the towns and cities or near to them. This industrialisation and urban development may bring about rise in material levels of living but they also cause environmental degradation, especially the pollution of air and water and creation of hazardous wastes. Across the world in both the developed and developing countries air and water pollution are being considered as a matter of serious concern as they not only cause harm to the health of the present population but endanger future generation by causing global warming with disastrous consequences.

It is worth noting that we need various projects, which relate to the manufacture of steel, cars cement, nuclear plants for industrial development of the country. But, as mentioned above, they are opposed by the people, especially the poor ones, because they will be displaced without being sure of the alternative avenues of their livelihood. Though we need these projects for our growth but we cannot build them against the will of the people. While approving the industrial projects we must adopt such strategy that ensure that the people who live on the rich lands with minerals, water and forests and who are displaced by the development projects must benefit from them. In this regard we need urgent reforms in policies for land acquisition, forest management and mineral development. Besides, we must approve the development projects subjects to the conditions that while they take local resources–mineral water or land, the project developors or the government must provide jobs to the people who are displaced so as to provide livelihood to them. It is because of the failure to provide such guarantee that people are opposing and fighting for the setting up projects.

It is worth mentioning that urbanisation, that is, the growth of the urban population has been increasing at a faster rate than industrial growth causing not only air and water pollution but also putting increased stress on the existing water supplies and sanitation facilities which create health hazards for the urban population. The governments of developing countries are generally unable to cope with the vastly increased needs for clean water and sanitation facilities resulting from rapid growth of urban population. Urban population has been increasing not only at the rate of natural population growth but also through rural-urban migration induced by industrialisation. Thus the lack of clean water and sanitation has led to the several diseases from which urban people suffer resulting in their poor health, Besides, due to the poor housing facilities the growth of urban population has led to the **growth of slums** without clean water and hygenic conditions.

Let us understand the Indian urban scene as unfolded by the census 2001. Between 1991 and 2001, the number of towns and cities increased from 3696 to 4368. The total urban population in India rose to 285 million in 2001. Of this 108 million, that is, nearly 40 percent lived in 35 cities with a population of one million or more each. Such a large increase in urban population has led to the growth of slums with acute scarcity of clean drinking water and poor sanitation facilities. Apart from growth of slums, industrialisations and urbanisation has led to the problems of air and water pollution and piles of hazardous wastes which we discuss below in some detail. Though these problems exist both in the developed and developing countries but they are often more serious and acute in developing countries. It is worth mentioning that it is consumption of energy from fossil fuels such as petroleum, coal and gas in various urban activities such as industrial production, vehicular traffic that is the basic source of pollution. In this early stage of industrialisation, as we find today in the case of developing countries, as the share of industry in domestic product increases, it results in energy consumption faster than the growth in national product. If a developing country gives a higher priority to basic heavy and chemical industries, as was the case in India in the second, third and fourth five year plans, consumption of energy takes place at a higher rate resulting in higher degree of pollution.

Air Pollution and Urban Development. Two main urban activities, namely, industrial production and vehicular traffic are the principal man-made source of air-pollution as energy is consumed. Therefore, as more industrial growth takes place in developing countries, it results in more air pollution. Industries emit smoke containing carbon dioxide, carbon monoxide, methane gas in the atmosphere causing air pollution. This air pollution is quite harmful for human beings as it causes tuberculosis, asthma, and other respiratory diseases and, according to world Development Report 1992, causes 3 to 7 lakh premature deaths annually. Besides, respiratory diseases adversely affect health of the people and reduces their productivity and working capacity. The people have to spend a lot of money for treatment of the ill-effects of toxic emissions by the factories which represents social cost which is ignored by the private entrepreneurs in their cost-profit accounting.

Since anti-pollution regulations are quite weak in developing countries the emission of toxic gases and pollution of water have been increasing enormously resulting from increased energy consumption is the industrial sector.

Vehicular Traffic and Environment. Besides industrial production, toxic gases are also emitted from vehicles plying in the urban areas. Motor vehicles causes both air and noise pollutants. Motor vehicles such as cars, buses, trucks, scooters and bikes emit pollutants such as carbon monoxide, hydrocarbon and nitrogen oxide which cause immense damage to the health of the human beings. At present (2009) more than 1.5 mullion registered motor vehicles are there in Delhi alone and about 1,50,000 are being added every year. These emit around 1000 tonnes of toxic gases into Delhi's atmosphere every day. In other metropolitan cities, Mumbai, Kolkata, Chennai, Banglore air pollution due to vehicular transport is also enormous.

In recent years under pressure of high courts and supreme court which have delivered judgements for improvement of environment some success has been achieved towards the use of lead-free fuels, better emission standards for cars and buses plying in the city roads. As a result, new models of cars with more fuel efficiency and lower emission levels have come in the market. In Delhi DTC buses and three-wheelers have been using less toxic CNG gas instead of diesel and petrol. Similarly, government has taken some measures to reduce emission of **lead** by vehicular traffic. It has been found that dangerous level of lead in the blood of young children expose them to the various health problems including neurological deficiencies. Elevated levels of lead in the atmosphere expose even adults to higher blood pressure, higher risk of heart attack and stroke.

Water Pollution and Urban Development. Water pollution is another major environment problem is urban areas. Water is contaminated mostly from wastes of expanding industries in the urban areas. In the towns and cities where industrial growth is taking place, rivers become polluted with toxic chemicals and heavy metals such as lead and mercury thrown into them by expanding industries and mining activities. The rivers like Ganga and Yamuna have become highly polluted over time. It is very difficult to remove pollutants from drinking water with standard purification facilities. Therefore, special measures and instruments are being used to clear rivers from pollutants. As a result, not only there is scarcity of safe drinking water for human beings, even the capacity of rivers to support aquatic life has decreased.

Not only surface water near towns and cities has been contaminated over the years but also ground water has been polluted through seepage of chemical wastes, heavy metals and other hazardous wastes created by industries and thrown into rivers and drains. Water pollution is a very serious problem in the urban areas, especially is cities like Delhi, Mumbai and Kolkata, especially for the urban poor who live in slums with no proper facilities for clean drinking water and sanitation, It is mainly these urban poor who bear the direct impact of water-borne diseases which are responsible for a large number of deaths, especially of children. According to **World Development Report 1992,** in the year 1990 one billion people in developing countries had no access to clean water and 1.7 billion lacked access to proper sanitation. After two decades of development now in 2009 the number of population without access to clean water and proper sanitation must have increased substantially despite good rate of economic growth achieved during this period.

As mentioned above, the various development projects are being vehemently opposed by the people who are affected and displaced by them. Sunita Narain, a noted environmentalist has given the right suggestion that for making environmental assessment of the project the people affected must be heard and their interests protected. If proper inclusive industrial development has to occur, the words of Sunita Narain, we must "Strengthen institutions of regulation and the procedures to listen to people. This will build credibility of the process of governance and it will also mitigate risks for investors. Public hearings held during the environmental impact assessment provide the platform for people to voice their concerns. In most cases today, the effort is to rig and undermine the hearing. The environmental impact assessment is seen by industry as a document, which must clear the project, not seriously assess it. Then even if a project is cleared with environmental conditions (like Posco or Navi Mumbai airport), there is no capacity to monitor compliance."[6]

RURAL AND AGRICULTURAL DEVELOPMENT AND ENVIRONMENT

About 75 per cent of India's population live in rural areas. Agriculture is the main occupation of rural people. Population in India has been increasing at the rate of 1.90 per cent per annum. Adequate food production is needed to feed the teeming millions. In recent years there has been considerable debate about the need to ensure food security for the rising population Food security, as is now generally understood, refers not only to the adequate food production but also sufficient increase in purchasing power of the people for having access to the consumption of required food and animal products. An eminent agricultural scientist, Dr M.S. Swaminathan writes, "*the future of food security depends on the conservation and care of arable land through attention on soil health and replenishment of fertility and the conservation and careful management of all water sources so that more crops can be produced. Improvement of production in perpetuity without associated social or ecological harm is vital to safeguard food security*".[7]

Land degradation is the chief environment problem in rural areas. **Land degradation occurs through soil erosion, salinisation of soil, and water logging.** The land degradation lowers agricultural production and adversely affects the fertility or productivity of the soil. Reduction in agricultural production and productivity threatens the livelihood of the rural people. To quote Dr Swaminathan aganin, "Land degradation, diversion, of arable land and the depletion and pollution of water resources result in the loss of rural livelihood. This triggers unplanned migration of the rural poor to towns and cities resulting in the proliferation of urban slums".[8]

It is worth mentioning that degraded land belongs either to the poor farm households or it is common property which has been overused and overgrazed. To ensure food security and livelihood to the rural population land and water resources ought to be protected from degradation and pollution. Land degradation of various forms in the regions of both the irrigated agriculture and rain-fed

---

6. Sunita Narain op. cit.
7. M.S. Swaminathan, 'Agriculture : Route to an evergreen revolution', in **Hindu Survey of Environment, 2002 p. 34.**
8. op. cit, p.35.

agriculture are causing serious threats to sustainability of agricultural growth. A serous problem that affects the sustainability of ramifed agriculture is the **top-soil erosion** which occurs as a result of rain water draining away the top soil of the land and thereby lowers its fertility. It has been estimated that 6 billion tons of soil in India are eroded from Indian crop land each year[9]. The soil erosion adversely affects agricultural growth and achievement of food security.[10]

Though land degradation due to soil erosion is taking place gradually farmers do not take effective measures to prevent or halt the process of soil erosion, Kerr and Sanghi[10] observe that the most important factor responsible for farmers not adopting the recommended practices to control soil erosion is **due to their perception** about soil erosion and other forms of land degradation It is therefore important that government should integrate the use of technologies for preventing land degradation with its programme and strategy of agricultural growth.

Deforestation: Another important factor causing land degradation is deforestation, that is, cutting of trees for fuel and timber. A good deal of deforestation has also been due to commercial logging Forests are highly useful for protecting environment. Trees of forests during the process of photosynthesis absorb carbon dioxide from atmosphere and give out oxygen. Thus, before station reduces CO_2 in the atmosphere that prevents the increase in temperature of the earth surface. Therefore, deforestation (i.e., cutting of trees) for fuel and timber and for extending cultivation for agricultural crops leads to the increase in CO_2 in the atmosphere which is responsible for global warming. Besides, deforestation causes floods water logging and sail erosion in the local areas and thereby leads to land degradation.

Overgrazing on Common Land. The other factor causing land degradation is **overgrazing on Common land** and intensification of agriculture through use of excess irrigation water and chemicals such as fertilizers and pesticides. According to a global survey conducted by the UN Environmental Programme, land degradation during five decades (1945-95) was of the order of 2 billion hectares of total cultivable land area of the world. Of this 80 per cent of degraded area was located in Asia, Africa and Latin America. According to this global sueney, 30 per cent of land degradation was caused by deforestation ,7 per cent by over-exploitation for getting fodder and fuel, 35 per cent by overgrazing, 28 per cent by agricultural production activities and only 1 per cent by industrialisation. Though agricultural growth with the use of modern agricultural technology such as the use of excess irrigation water, chemical inputs has played a part in causing land degradation, the main factor responsible for land degradation is over-exploitation of natural resources by poverty-driven population.

Water Scarcity. Another important environmental problem facing India is the **decline in underground water resources**. A recent released '**State of the Environment Report**' says that the amount of water being used in India from underground sources is estimated to be 45 per cent more than what natural system can replenish. A National Aeronautics and Space Administration study released in August 2009 found that ground water levels in northern India-Punjab, Haryana and Rajasthan-are declining at an alarming rate as much as one foot per year over the last decade. Its reason is that water is being pumped and consumed by human activities, mainly for irrigation, faster than aquifiers can be replenished by natural processes. The problem of water shortage therefore poses a serious threat to the sustained agricultural growth. Therefore, it is necessary to ensure scientific delivery and usage of water for irrigation besides encouraging the development and use of drought-resistent seeds and change in cropping pattern where necessary. The use of **drip irrigation** should be encouraged as in this water is delivered in measured dozes through slender pipes close to the plant, thereby avoiding waste from spillovers and is being used successfully in some countries where water is carce. Besides, water-intensive crops like sugur-cane and rice ought to be confined to the areas where these crops are grown traditionally because of availability of enough water.

9. See V.V Naryana and Ram Babu, 'Estimation of Soil Erosion in India' in **Journal of Irrigation and Drainage Engineering** ASCE, 109(4) pp 419-33.
10. Kerr T.M. and V. Sanghi, Indigenous Soil and Water Conservation in India's Semi-arid Tropics, Gatekeepers Series 34,1992, International Institute of Environment and Development.

India depends on ground water reserves for most of its agricultural and domestic water requirement. Hence the there is increased stress on ground water reservoirs. Urban and rural **rain water harvesting** therefore should be explored fully. Check dams can be thought of as an alternative to mega dam projects to provide local water support. In our view the way to stop environment degradation in the rural areas is not to curb the use of modern green revolution technology for fear of its defects but efforts should be made to overcome its defects through undertaking new scientific research.

Lack of clean water and sanitation facilities. Another important environmental problem faced by rural population, especially the rural poor, arises due to lack of clean drinking water and sanitations. These greatly contribute to many water-borne diseases such as typhoid, cholera, amoebic infections, bacillary dysentery and diarrhea which account for 80 per cent of all diseases that prevail in developing countries and account for a large number of child deaths each year. Apart from responsible for deaths in rural areas these diseases lower the **health** of the people which in modern economic theory is considered as **human capital** and its deterioration in the rural areas lowers productivity and economic growth.

Similarly, air pollution in the rural areas which arises due to greater dependence on **biomass fuels** such as wood, straw, manure that is closely related to the poverty of the rural population impacts their health. About the harmful effects of air pollution due to greater dependence on biomass fuel, Todaro and Smith[11] write, "the burning of biomass fuels for cooking and boiling of water create dangerously high levels of indoor pollution to which 400 million to 700 million people, mostly women and children, are exposed each year. Smoke and fumes from indoor stoves are believed to contribute significantly to up to 4.3 million childhood deaths each year from respiratory diseases and to an ever-larger number of chronic respiratory illnesses".

SUSTAINABLE DEVELOPMENT

Economists have used the teem **sustainable development** in an attempt to clarify the balance between economic growth on the one hand and conservation and protection of environment on the other. Sustainable development refers to **"meeting the needs of the present generation without compromising the needs of future generation"**[12]. Thus economic growth will be sustainable if the stock of capital assets including land remains constant or increases over time. It may however be noted that future economic development and quality of life crucially depends on the natural resource base and quality of the environment *i.e,*. the quality of land, water and air. To destroy and over-exploit the natural resources indiscriminatly and pollute the environment will though raise the short-term growth rate and living standards of the people will have adverse effect on the long-term future growth and the quality of life of the future generations as the latter will have smaller natural resource base and poor quality of environment. It is therefore necessary that while deciding about growth environmental issues should be factored in. For instance, loss or preservation of important environmental resources should be taken into account while preparing estimates of growth and well -being of the people. Alternatively, economic policy makers may opt for framing a growth strategy of **no net loss of environmental assets** so as to ensure sustainable development. In this later case if environmental resources are destroyed or depleted in one area, an equal or greater amount of environmental resources are replenished or regenerated so that future economic growth is not adversely affected.

Pearce and Warford[13] has put forward a view which takes into account preservation of environment for sustainability of growth. In the overall capital stock they include not only the man- made physical capital (such as machines, factories, roads) but also human capital (education, skills, health care) and environmental capital (such as forests, water resources, climate, arable land,

11. Michael P.Tadoro and Stephen C.Smith, **Economic Development**, 8th edition, 2003, Pearson Education (Singapore): p.471.
12. Sharachandra, A.Lele, "Sustainable Development : A Critical Review" **World Development**, 19 (Jan. 1991) PP. 607-621.
13. David W. Pearce and Jeremy J. Warford, **World without End : Economic Environment and Sustainable Development: A Summary** (Washington DC: World Bank 1993).

soil quality). According to Pearson and Warford, sustainable development implies that overall capital stock, as defined above, does not decrease in the growth process. In this regard, they point out that the sustainable measure of net national product (NNP*) can be obtained as the amount that is consumed during the growth process without any decrease in the overall capital stock during a year, Thus

$$NNP^* = GNP - D_m - D_n - R - A$$

where

NNP* stands for sustainable net national product which does not diminish over the course of a year

GNP stands for gross national product

D_m stands for depreciation of man-made physical capital stock

D_n stands for decrease in money value of destruction of capital over the course of a year.

R is the expenditure required to replenish environmental capital (forests, fisheries etc.) destroyed during a year.

A is the expenditure required to prevent destruction of environmental capital such as air, water, soil quality etc.

In the context of rising consumption standards both in the developing and developed countries along with rapid growth of population in developing countries achievement of the goal of sustainable development is a major challenge facing the world today. It is evident that meeting the consumption needs of future generations when the world population is estimated to increase by an additional 3 billion by 2050 require substantial changes in consumption and production pattern.

Rio conference held in 1992 where 150 countries participated was an important milestone in defining the concept of "sustainable development". This was spelled out in considerable detail in agenda 21, which set out general principles for sustainable development and framed blueprint for conservation and use of forests and suggested important steps that are required to be taken to generate an environmentally stable and sustainable planet.

Over the last two decades there has been increased awareness about the need for preventing environmental degradation, checking pollution and averting global warming as a result of climate change but not significant practical steps have been taken in this regard and another world conference on environment and climate change will take place at Copenhagen in Dec. 2009. This conference is expected to resolve the issues eoncering environmental pollution and climate change between the developing and developed countries. The difficult problem is that the development and technological path pursued by the western developed countries is highly energy-intensive and explaints huge quantities of natural resources and leaves a highly degraded environment with emission of greenhouse gases (GHG) in the atmosphere. It is this path that developing countries are also following for their economic and social development which is quite unsustainable and leads to a large-scale pollution and ecological degradation. To ensure sustainable development in the world today both the developed and developing countries have to take appropriate environment-friendly steps, especially by the developed ones as they have in the past through reckless industrialisation and use of energy-intensive technology has emitted greenhouse gases to a larger extent. A noted Indian environmentalist Sunita Narain rightly writes, "*The process of ecological globalisation is driven by the fact that levels of production and consumption have reached a stage where what one does in one's country can have major impact on neighbouring countries or even on the rest of the world. Even simple things like using a refrigerator or an air-conditioner can today destroy the world's ozone layer, running an automobile or cutting a tree without planting another one can destabilize the world's climate. And, using a persistent organic compound like DDT can mean life threatening pollution for human beings and other life forms in the remote polar regions of the world as these compounds are slowly but steadily carried to these regions by the world's oceanic currents and air streams. Never before have human beings needed to learn to live in 'one world' as now*"[14]

14. Sunita Narain, Southern Challenges: Need for One Version, in the **Hindu, Survey of Environment**, 2002, p-13.

Sustainable Development and Climate Change in the Indian Context

The key environmental challenges in India have been sharper in the past two decades. The State of the Environment Report by the MoEF clubs the issues under five key challenges faced by India, which are climate change, food security, water security, energy security, and managing urbanization. Climate change is impacting the natural ecosystems and is expected to have substantial adverse effects in India, mainly on agriculture on which 50 per cent of the population still depends for livelihood, water storage in the Himalayan glaciers which are the source of major rivers and groundwater recharge, sea-level rise, and threats to a long coastiline and habitations. Climate change will also cause increased frequency of extreme events such as floods, and droughts. These in turn will impact India's food security problems and water security. As per the Second National Communication submitted by India to the UNFCCC, it is projected that the annual mean surface air temperature rise by the end of the century ranges from 3.5°C to 4.3°C whereas the sea level along the Indian cost has been rising at the rate of about 1.3 mm/year on an average. These climate change projections are likely to impact human health, agriculture, water resources, natural ecosystems, and biodiversity.

Wary of the threats imposed by climate change and pressures on natural resources, sustainability and environment are increasingly taking centre stage in the Indian policy domain. India has been part of 94 multilateral environmental agreements. *India has also voluntarily agreed to reduce its emission intensity of its GDP by 20-26 per cent over 2005 levels by 2020, and emissions from the agriculture sector would not form part of the assessment of its emissions intensity.* Indian economy is already moving along a lower carbon and sustainable path in terms of declining carbon intensity of its GDP which is expected to fall further through lower carbon strategies. It is estimated that India's per capita emission in 2031 will still be lower than the global per capita emission in 2005 (in 2031, India's per capita GHG emission will be under 4 tonnes of carbon dioxide equivalent (CO_2 eq.) which is lower than the global per capita emissions of 4.22 tonnnes of CO_2 eq. in 2005). Along with the national efforts in different sectors, India also recognizes that rural areas are equally prone to stress and pressures from natural resource exploitation. In this context, schemes for rural development and livelihood programmes are very relevant. A vast majority of the works under the Mahatma Gandhi National Rural Employment Guarantee Scheme (MGNREGS) are linked to land, soil, and water. There are also programmes for non-timber forest produce-based livelihood, promotion of organic and low-chemical agriculture, and increased soil health and fertility to sustain agriculture-based livelihoods. These schemes help mobilize and develop capacities of community institutions to utilize natural resources in a sustainable manner and their potential can be further developed.

Together with efforts to incorporate sustainability in the rural development process, India is increasingly making efforts to *integrate the three pillars of sustainable development into its national policy space*. In fact, environment protection is enshrined in our Constitution (Articles 48A and 51 A[g]). Various policy measures are being implemented across the domains of forestry, pollution control, water management, clean energy, and marine and costal environment. Some of these are policies like Joint Forest Manatgement, Green Rating for Integrate Habitat Assessment, Coastal Zone Regulation Zone, eco labelling and energy efficinecy labelling, fuel efficiency standards etc. Over a period of time, a stable organizational structure has been developed for environment protection. *The country has been making fast progress in increasing its renewable energy capacity and has displayed the fastest expansion rate of investment of any large renewables market in the world in 2011, with a 62 per cent increase to $12 billion (Frankfurt School of Finance and Management 'Global Trends in Renewable Energy investment 2012'*). The Twelfth Five Year Plan with a prominent focus on sustainability makes provision and provides for many more opportunities like these.

Sustainable Development and Poverty Eradication

Working on the *social and economic pillars of sustainable development policies, programmes and targeted schemes have been introduced* to *eradicate poverty*. This is done either through a direct focus on economic indicators like employment generation, youth mobilization, and building up assets of the poor, or indirectly through social indicators of human development with emphasis on health, education, and women's empowerment. Many parameters on this front have shown improvement. The poverty head-count ratio declined by 15.3 percentage points from 37.2% in 2004-05 to 21.9% in 2011-12, maternal mortality rate (MMR) dropped from 301 per 100,000 live births in 2001-03 to 212 in 2007-09; literacy rates have been constantly rising and are estimated to be 82.14 per cent for men and 66.46 per cent for women as per the 2011 Census of India. However, India is still not on target to meet some key Millennium Development Goals (MDGs) by 2015.

Over the years arguments in favour of looking beyond the conventional measure of GDP and taking into account the environmental damage caused by production of goods and services have received attention. An expert group under the chairmanship of Prof Sir Partha Dasgupta has been set up to develop a framework for '*Green National Account's* for India. In fact, the Central Statistics Office (CSO) under the Ministry of Statistics & Programme Implementation (MOSPI) has been publishing comprehensive environment statistics since 1997. The process of putting in place a system for *natural resources accounting was initiated by* MOSPI way back in 2002.

Despite all these efforts, the challenges that confront us on the environmental front continues to be harsh and complex. Increasing population, urbanization, and growing demand for water and land resources have severely impacted the quality and availability of water and soil resources. Rising energy needs is another area of concern. Besides, rapid growth will require corresponding growth in energy supply. Presently a large share of our energy demand is met through coal and oil and this trend will continue, given the unprecedented surge in energy demand and resource constraints. Energy issues have become more complex with existing energy shortage and rise in energy prices. There is considerable scope for increasing efficiency in the use of energy and water in India together with other development indicators like infant mortality rate, maternal mortality rate (MMR), sanitation facilities, and public health services. Economic instruments, regulatory measures, and market mechanisms can play an important role in helping to achieve development and growth in a sustainable manner.

Why Environment matters to achieve sustainable development in the special and specific context of India

Economic Development without environmental considerations can cause serious environmental damage, in turn impairing the quality of life of present and future generations. Such environmental degradation imposes a cost on the society and needs to be explicitly factored into economic planning, with necessary remedial measures incorporated. The challenge of sustainable development thus requires integration of the country's quest for economic development with its environmental concerns. Environment management in India has, over the years, recognized these sustainable development concerns. The National Environment policy 2006 has attempted to mainstream environmental concerns in all our developmental activities. It underlines that '*while conservation of environmental resources is necessary to secure livelihoods and well being of all, the most secure basis for conservation is to ensure that people dependant on particular resources obtain better livelihoods from the fact of conservation, than from degradation of the resource*'. The Government of India, through its various policies, has been factoring ecological concerns into the development process so that economic development can be achieved without critically damaging the environment. The strong sustainable development agenda followed by India incorporates rigorous environmental safeguards for infrastructure projects, strengthening of the environmental governance system, revitalizing of regulatory institutions, focusing on river conservation, and efforts for improvements in air and water quality, on a continuous basis.

Our environmental standard are set through Government policies aimed at a development process that is environmentally sustainable and ensures well-being of the people. The broad objectives of our environmental policies and programmes are:

1. Conservation of flora, fauna, forests, and wildlife;
2. Prevention and control of pollution;

3. Afforestation and regeneration of degraded areas;
4. Protection of the environment.

As a country, India has been in the forefront of *preserving biodiversity, sustainable management of forests, reducing emissions intensity of the economy*, and following sustainable consumption and production patterns. Specifically, India has been following a development path that takes into consideration the needs of the present generation without compromising the ability of future generations to meet their needs. Suitable attention has been given to protecting and conserving critical ecological systems and resources and invaluable natural and man-made heritage, which are essential for life-support, livelihoods, economic growth, and a broad conception of human well-being. Moreover, the effort has been to ensure equitable access to environmental resources and quality for all sections of society, in particular to ensure that poor communities which are most dependent on environmental resources for their livelihoods are assured secure access to these resources.

THE UNITED NATIONS CONFERENCE ON SUSTAINABLE DEVELOPMENT (UNCSD), RIO +20, 2012

Recognising the well-founded concerns on the need to redress environmental problems, there have been global calls for cooperation, action, and innovation. World leaders in 2012 continued to engage and deliberate in international forums dedicated to climate and environment and also in forums like the G20 where sustainable development and climate change were an integral part of the discussions. Ambition or goal setting to reach targets, provision of finance and technology for developing countries, and institutions and mechanisms for capacity building were the common threads of negotiations running through all these forums. One such event in 2012 was the United Nations Conference on Sustainable Development (UNCSD) which was held at Rio in Brazil in June 2012. This is also known as Rio + 20 Conference since the first United Nations Conference on environment and development was held at Rio in Brazil in 1992. Therefore, the name Rio + 20. It was attended by the heads of states of the member countries.

The objective of the Rio+20 Conference was to secure renewed political commitment for sustainable development, review progress made and identify implementation gaps, and assess new and emerging challenges since the UNCSD held 20 years ago in Rio in 1992. Towards this end, the Conference had two themes, viz, (a) *green economy* in the context of sustainable development & poverty eradication, and (b) *institutional framework for sustainable development*. The most significant outcomes of the Rio Summit have been the ***restoration of the principles of equity and of common but differentiated responsibilities (CBDR) in the global environmental discourse and placing poverty eradication at the centre of the global development agenda. The outcome also ensures the required domestic policy space to countries on a green economy*** **and launched four processes mechanisms,** i.e. developing sustainable development goals (SDGs), financing strategy, technology transfer, and defining the format and organizational aspects of the proposed high-level political forum to follow up on the implementation of sustainable development.

Equity or 'Fairness' as an issue received attention. It is a matter of satisfaction and achievement for India that the Rio outcome document reaffirms equity and the principle of common but differencial responsibility (CBDR) among other Rio principles. India together with other developing countries played an instrumental role in this. CBDR is especially important for developing countries, as it *implies that while all countries should take sustainable development actions, the developed countries have to take the leading role in environmental protection*, as they have contributed the most to environmental problems. Also they should support developing countries with finance and technology in their sustainable development efforts. *India has always held that the eradication of poverty should be the over arching goal of sustainable development*. This was given due recognition in the deliberations at the Rio Summit and in the outcome document.

On the issue of Green economy, the outcome document affirms that there are different approaches, visions, models, and tools available to each country, in accordance with its national circumstances and priorities, for achieving sustainable development. *It identifies green economy in the context of sustainable development and poverty eradications as one of the important tools for achieving sustainable development* but specifies that while it could provide options for policy-making it should not be a rigid set of rules. The outcome document clearly states what green economy policies should result in and what they should not. It is a matter of satisfaction that the document firmly rejects prescriptive policies, unilateral measures, and trade barriers as well as unwarranted conditionality of official developmental assistance in this context.

The Rio+20 Conference will also be remembered for kick-starting the process on developing sustainable development goals (SDGS). The SDGs would address and incorporate in a balanced way, all the three dimensions of sustainable development and their inter-linkages. The SDGs would be universal, global, and voluntary. Since the SDGs are expected to become a part of the past-2015 UN development agenda, they would hopefully guide the international community towards inclusive sustainable development.

From India's point of view, SDGs need to bring together development and environment into a single set of targets. The fault line, as ever in global conferences, is the inappropriate balance between environment and development. Developing countries do not want any bindings on their efforts towards poverty eradication or any agreement that comes with such a price tag. Therefore, we could also view the SDGs and the post 2015 agenda as an opportunity for revisiting and fine-tuning the *millennium development goals* (MDGs) framework and sustainable regaining focus on developmental issues. India and many developing countries are slow or off track in achieving targets under some of the MDGs, which have concrete areas of overlap between environment and development. This is another reason why these MDGs should continue to be a part of the post-2015 global policy architecture.

The Rio Summit did not lead to any specific commitments on the finance and technology front. The developed countries, having obligations and responsibilities, need to commit to provision of adequate public funds including for transfer of technology and capacity building to developing countries.

CLIMATE CHANGE; ISSUE, CAUSES AND EFFECTS

Climate Change : The Issue

The climate change has become one of the most important environmental issues that confronts the human beings both in the developed and developing countries. The issue is that the various economic activities by the people, especially the burning of fossil fuels such as coal, petroleum, natural gas in various productive activities is likely to disturb the planet's heat and radiation balance. It will lead to an increase in earth's temperature (*i.e.* warmer climate) in the next 50 years which would have disatrous consequences not only for the quality of life (*i.e.* clean environment) of the people but also for economic development. Climate change has therefore become a global issue and negotiations among the countries, both developed and developing, are going on to mitigate global warming through reduction in emission of greenhouse gases such as carbaon dioxide (CO_2) and thereby save the humanitty.

What is climate change ?

Now, what is climate change ? 'Climate change' means a change of climate which is attributed directly or indirectly to human activity that alters the composition of the global atmosphere and which is in addition to natural climate variability observed over comparable time periods. Increasing levels of fossil fuel burning and land use changes have emitted, and are continuing to emit, greenhouse gases (mainly carbon dioxide (CO2), methane, and nitrous oxide) into the earth's atmosphere. This increasing level of emissions of greenhouse gases has caused a rise in the amount of heat from the sun trapped in the earth's atmosphere, heat that would normally be radiated back into space. This has led to the **greenhouse effect**, resulting in climate change. The major characteristics of climate change are rise in average global temperature, ice cap melting, changes in precipitation, and increase in ocean temperature. The efforts needed to *address the climate change problem include greenhouse gas emissions on the one hand and building of capacities to cope with the adverse impacts of climate change on various sectors of the society and economy on the other*. Scientists who have been working on the subject for a long time point out that greenhouse gases (GHGs) such as carbon dioxide in the atmosphere trap the incoming heat from the sun and thereby leads to the increase in earth's temperature which is often referred to as **global warming.** Besides carbon dioxide, other greenhouse gases are methane, nitrous oxide and water vapour. This climate change is likey to cause adverse change in weather patterns and extreme events such as cyclones, hurricanes, floods, rise in sea level. How to **reduce the emission of greenhouse gases** and also to **adapt to the changes in climate** are the issues that confront the humanity.

Why does carbon dioxide concentration in the atmosphere increase ? Though human beings also emit carbon dioxide while they breathe, the most important source of carbon dioxide emission is **burning of fossil fuels** such as coal, oil, gas during the process of industrial production. As most of the industrual growth has taken place in the developed countries such as the USA, Europe and Japan over the last more than a century, it is they who have contributed most to the increase in carbon dioxide concentration in the atmosphere. It is the unsustainable consumption pattern of the rich developed countries that are responsible for much of the emission of carbon dioxide and other green- house gases by burning fossil fuels. While 25 per cent of world population live in these rich industrilised countries, they emit more than 70 per cent of total global carbon dioxide emission[15]. In per capita terms disparities in emission of carbon are also very large. Thus, while a citizen of USA on an average emits more than 5.5 tonnes carbon per year, an Indian citizen emits only 0.25 tonnes of carbon per year.[16]

It may be noted that though the developed countries emit more carbon dioxide and other green- house gases (GHGs) into the atmosphere, it is not only their local atmosphere that gets polluted, but the whole **global atmosphere** is adversely affected. The air and winds know no national boundaries; the emission of toxic gases into the air by one nation easily trravels to the whole global atmosphere. Thus, there is climate change for India and other developing countries though it is the rich industrialised nations of the USA, European countries and Japan which have contributed most to the concentration of green house gases (GHGs) in the atmosphere. Similarly, the flow of sea water knows no national boundaries and therefore rise in sea level as a result of climate change will affect the people of coastal areas of many countries. Therefore, global cooperation and efforts are required to mitigate climate change.

The Size of the World Greenhouse Gas Emission Problem

According to the Fourth Assessment Report of the Inter-governmental Panel on Climate Change (IPCC 2007), over the century, atmospheric concentrations of carbon dioxide increased from a pre-industrial value of 278 parts per million to 379 parts per million in 2005, and the average global temperature rose by 0.740C. Projections indicate that global warming will continue and accelerate. Thus climate change represents additional stress on ecological and socio-economic systems that are already facing tremendous pressure due to rapid economic development. With climate change, the type, frequency, and intensity of extreme events, floods, and droughts are expected to increase. Hence addressing climate change is a major challenge in terms of policies and resources needed to address it at domestic and international levels.

15. Jyoti K. Parikh and Kirit Parikh, Climate Change: India's Perceptions, Position, Policies and Possibilities, in *Climate Change and Development*, OECD, 2002, p.5.
16. Ibid, p-5.

While the worldwide emissions of GHGs have increased since 1945, with the largest increases taking place in carbon dioxide (CO_2) emissions, scientists attribute the global problem of climate change not only to the current GHG emissions but also to the stock of historical GHG emissions. Most of the countries, particularly the industrialized countries, having large current emissions, are also the largest historic emitters and the principal contributors to climate change. A relatively small number of such countries are responsible for the largest chunk of the stock of global GHG emissions. The industrialized countries with the largest total emissions also rank among those with the highest per capita emissions. Per capita emissions are generally higher in wealthier countries. Global Greenhouse Gas (GHG) emissions have risen sharply since 1945. As per a working paper published by the World Resources Institute, total GHGs were estimated at 44,153 $MtCO_2$ equivalent (million metric tons) in 2005. As CO_2 is the predominant GHG, an analysis of its emissions across G20 countries in per captia terms in 2009, compared to 2005 presents an interesting picture which can seen from Fig. 56.1. Although the G20 is referred to as a group, there are stark disparities on the ground between member countries int erms of incomes, stages of development as well as respective per capita CO_2 emissions. In 2005, the USA had the highest CO_2 emissions in metric tons per capita at 19.7, followed by Australia (18.0). The lowest per capita emitters in 2005 were Brazil (1.9), Indonsia (1.5), and India (1.2) who continued to be the bottom three in 2009 as well. In 2009, Australia ranked first within the G20 followed by the USA.

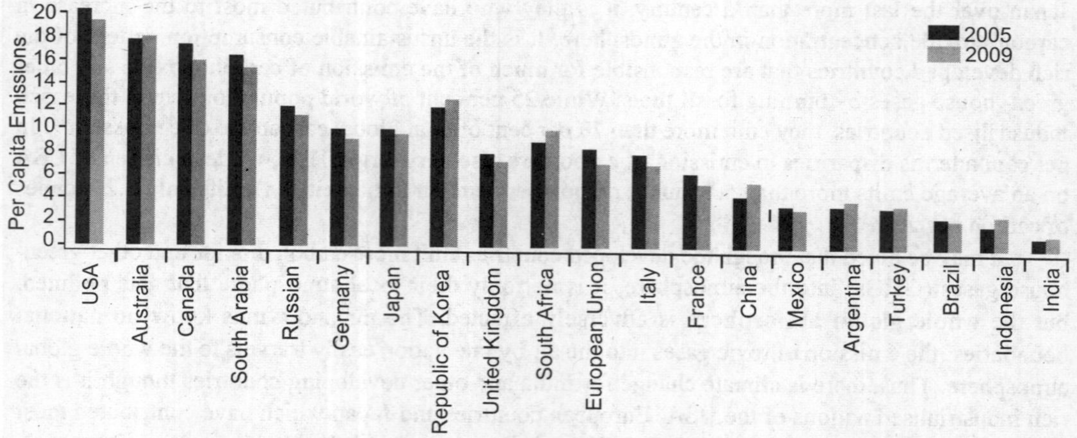

Figure 44.1 Per Capita CO_2 Emission of G.20 Countries in 2005 and 2009

India is a country which will be severely impacted by climate change. This puts additional hurdles in its developmental path in addition to the challenges of poverty eradication and growing population. The projected impacts of climate change cut across water resources, forests, agriculture, and health. With a large agrarian population, India is vulnerable to changes in weather parameters. Further, rainfall, variability and melting of glaciers will impact replenishment of rivers, thereby affecting availability of water in river basins and watersheds. India, most of the rivers flowing in the northern regions are dependent on snow and glacial melt, thus climate change threatens the perennial nature of these rivers. This has huge implications for agriculture and allied activities and resultant livelihoods. This is a serious concern for an economy that is tied to its natural resource base along its developmental path.

Why should India be concerned about climate change ?

India is deeply concerned about climate change because it will have substantial adverse effects on the Indian people. As will be explained later in detail, climate change or global warming will (1) lower agriculture production (2) raise sea level leading to submergence of coastal areas, and (3) will increase the frequencies of extreme events such as cyclones, hurricanes, floods. These are long-term issues. Negotiation at the global level are taking place to reduce global warming. India must play an active role in negotiations so that agreement about the extent of global level reduction in emission of greenhouse gases is reached and just and fair distribution of individual countries' contribûtion to it.

Since the developed countries have made substantial contribution to the concentration of CO_2 and other greenhouse gases (GHGs) they have to accept greater responsibility in reducing emission of these gases in future. Besides, they have to give financial and technical support to the developing countries for reduction of emission of GHGs.

It is worth mentioning here that **India's main energy source is coal which is highly polluting.** With the threat of climate change India is being urged by developed countries to change its energy strategy based on coal and instead use other energy sources such as oil, natural gas, nuclear energy which are more expensive. Thus immediate important issue facing India and other developing countries is to reach an agreement with the developed countries so that we have more freedom to decide which type of energy source we use, how we generate power, how to reduce methane emissions by agricultural practices or forestry and so on. Negotiations are important for us as a means to reduce or postpone future vulnerability by getting the developed countries to reduce their emissions"[17]

Adverse Effects of Climate Change

The climate change or global warming poses a threat to the sustainable economic development and therefore to the future generations. The global warming has the following effects.

1. Risk of lower Agricultural Growth. Climate change has a significant adverse impact on the agricultural growth of developing countries. As regards India, it is a low latitude tropical country highly vulnerable to the consequences of increase in atmospheric temperature (*i.e.* global warming). The global weather variability is a major constraint on agricultural growth and welfare in India. Increase in temperature in the Tibetian plateau, the Hindu Kush and Himalyas will affect the volume and timing of river flows with adverse effect on **crop production.** Kumar and Parikh[18] have shown that even with farm level adaptations, the impact of climate change on Indian agriculture would be significant. According to their estimates a temperature change of + 2°C and accompanying precipitation change of +7 per cent, farm level total-revenue would fall by 9 per cent whereas with a temperature change of +3.5°C cent and precipitation change of +15 per cent the fall in farm level total revenue product would decline by nearly 25 per cent. This is a very large change in agricultural production which can cause much hardship for the Indian people, especially the poor. These estimates reveal that even 2°C increase in temperature will be quite substantial for India.

2. Rise in Sea Level. There is a great risk of rise in sea level as a result of global warming. It is expected that a large coastal area will be submerged with the rise in sea level. This will cause large-scale emigration from the coastal settlements. These climate migrants, often called climate refugees, will create problems for India for their settlement and cause much human hardslip. The Gangces-Brahmputra delta of India has been perceived to be exceptionally vulnerable area as water level in this area well rise submerging most of the land. Early signs of the potential impact can already be seen in the Sunderbans and Bangladesh. In view of this India faces a serious prospect of climate migrants.

According to the estimates of Asian Development Bank (ADB) made in 1995, if there is one meter rise in sea level today, it would displace 7 million people in India. With one meter rise in sea level 35 per cent of land in Bangladesh would be subemerged. The cost of building a wall along the coastal line to prevent submerging is quite enormous.

---

17. Jyoti Parikh and Kirit Parikh, op cit. p.6.
18. See Kumar, K.S. Kavi and Jyoti Parikh, Socio-economic Impacts of Climate Change on Indian Agriculture, **International Review of Environment Strategies, 2(2), 2001.**

3. Rusk of Extreme Events. As a result of climate change extreme events like cyclones, hurricanes will more frequently occur causing a lot of human misery in terms of both death and loss of livelihood of the people. For example, in Andbra pradesh in India the Cyclone of 1996 and again of 2009 caused deaths of more than 1000 people. Further, it caused loss of large properly owned by the people, especially the poor.

4. Climate Change and Economic Growth. Climate change is intimately linked to the process of economic growth and development. Since greenhouse gases (GHGs) are generated by burning fossil fuels for energy use for industrial production and vehicular transport. Industrial factories, power plants, automobiles generate CO_2 and other greenhouse gases, the reduction in their emission will mean lower GDP and economic growth and consequently rise in poverty. Therefore, in developing countries where absolute poverty still prevails on a large scale and the need for sustained economic growth is therefore very necessary, it is very difficult for them to reduces emission of GHGs to achieve the global target. Thus, in case of developing countries the larger reduction in GHGs will come at the expense of economic growth.

On the other hand, the rich developed countries which contributed most to CO_2 and other GHGs emissions in the past and where absolute poverty has been largely eliminated are in a better position to reduce emission of these gases. Besides, they have both the finance and technology to mitigate climate change.

Murthy, Panda and Parikh[19] have shown that reduction in CO_2 emission in developing countries imposes costs in terms of lower GDP and higher degree of poverty. Using a multisectoral and intertemporal model they have estimated the effect of reduction CO_2 emission on GDP and incidence of poverty in developing countries. Their estimates show that in India reduction of emission CO_2 of over the period of 30 years (taking the year 2000 as base line) and using annual emission target will lead to a fall in GDP by 4 per cent and increase in the number of poor by 17.5 per cent. Therefore, in view of this an important problem faced in this regard in democratic countries like India is to get public support for this reduction in CO_2 emission. While the cost will be borne by the present generation in the immediate period, the benefits of climate change will accrue to the future generations. Anand Patwardhan rightly poses this problem when he writes :

"Any serious attempt to cut emission will have clear and immediate costs but the benefits may not appear for a long time. To the extent that the benefets may be disasters that did not happen, they may never be obvious that the costs will be. As the debate develops **much of it is being cast in terms of the restraint that** the present generation owes to future generations"[20]

Mitigating Climate Change

As seen above, climase change or global warming has disastrous consequences. The global negotiations are going on to reach an agreement regarding emission of greenhouse gases by the developed and developing countries as per certain time framework. However, realising that it is in our own interest that India has been for quite some time pursuing environmental-friendly policies and taken steps to reduce emission of GHGs through reduction in energy consumption. It is worth noting that India is committed to eradication of poverty. This requires stepping up rate of economic growth (i.e. increase in GDP). Therefore, emphases of high economic growth to reduce poverty results in higher energy consumption which is likely to adversely affect elimate change. Given this constraint the following steps have been taken in India to mitigate climate change.

1. Promoting energy conservation and efficiency
2. Promotion of renewable energy sources
3. Reduction of air pollution

19. Murthy, NS. Manoj Panda and Jyoti Parikh, Economic Growth, Energy Demand and Carbon Dioxide Emiussion in India, 199-2020 in '*Environment and Development Economics*', Vol. 2, 2009.
20. Anand Patwardhan, Global Warming and India, **Seminar,** 486 Feb. 2000, p.p. 63-69

4. Afforestation and wasteland development
5. Fuel substitution policies

We discuss these policies below in some detail.

1. Energy Conservation and Efficiency. In India energy conservation and greater efficiency in energy use play an important role in national policy to reduce GHGs emissions. It has been estimated by Jyoti Parikh and Kerit Parikh that power sector is the highest direct CO_2 emission in India (48%) followed by transport sector, i.e. road, railways, air transport (10%), iron and steel (10%). Increase in the use of coal and electricity is estimated to result in significant reduction in CO_2 emission. Nag and Jyoti Parikh[21] have found that *greater efficiency in energy* use has been actually achieved in India as a result of government efforts.

Production of Non-Commercial Energy Sources. Apart from energy conservation and increase in efficiency in energy use, the steps have also been taken in India by Ministry of Nn-Conventional Energy Sources to develop and exploit non-conventional energy sources which are clean and renewable. Various renewable sources, namely,. wind farms, micro-hydroelectric plants, biomas and cogeneration power plants, biomass gasfiers system and solar pholovoltic system of aggregate installed capacity of 2302 MW was planned to set up by the end of the Eight Plan in 1997 and this was planned to rise to rise to 6500 MW by the end of Ninth Plan (1997-2002).

According to data furnished by Jyoti Praikh and Kirit Parikh, about 2.6 million family size biogass plants and 25 million improved cooking gas stoves that use less fuelwood and 43,0000 solar cookers had been cumulatively installed by the end of Eighth Plan.[22] The expected energy savings from these non-commercial energy sources amounts to 12 to 15 per cent in total wood consumption which is quite significant.

Reduction of Ait Pollution. Measures taken by the Government to increases efficiency in use of fossil fuels has led to dual benefits. First, they have succeeded to the great extent of reducing local area pollution. Secondly, they have achieved abatement in GHGs emission. Pollution levels have been prescribed for vehicles in cities like Delhi to reduce urban pollution. Thus by providing for more energy efficiency in vehicles attempt has been made to reduce air pollution. This regulation of pollution has also resulted in higher fuel quality. It is estimated that pollution control measures for vehicular traffic have will cause reduction of GHS in the range of 10 to 15 percent by 2015 by which time the current stock of vehicles would be largly replaced.

Afforestation and Wasteland Development. Afforestation and wasteland development can contribute significantly to reduction in emission of CO_2 if proper policy is adopted and enforced. Biomass is widely used in India for various purposes such as fuel, timber and feedstock. This causes degradation of forests and as a result degradation of soil. Recently, Government has initiated programme for afforestation and wasteland development. This programmne is meant not only to halt deforestation but also plant more trees to increase green cover. Under this programme various agencies spend about ₹ 50 billion every year on wasteland development. If we succeed in our efforts to achieve the targets of afforestation and wasteland development there will be significant decline in India's emission of CO_2. Afforestation and regreening of wasteland is also desirable to arrest land degradation, to improve soil fertility to provide renewable source of fuel and timber and non-timber forest products which provide livelihood to the millions of poor people.

Coal Substitution. In India till recently coal was the main source of commercial energy. After the policy of liberalisation initiated in 1991, the use of oil and natural gas has been increasingly made in sectors where its use was not permitted earlier. That is, the use of oil and gas has increasingly substituted coal since 1991. For example, power plants now use natural gas instead of coal. Similarly,

21. Jyoti Parikh and Kerit Parikh, op.at.p.of coal and electriaty use is
22. Nag, Barnali and Jyoti Parikh Indicators of Carbon Emission Intensity from Commercial Energy Use in India, **Energy Economics** Vol. 22, pp. 441-461.

fertilizer plants no longer use coal for its production and instead use other fuels. The use of coal in railways has been completely stopped.

Increases in Energy Efficiency

Due to import liberalisation strong competition from imports has induced the private firms including joint ventures producing consumer goods such as cars, televisions, refrigerators, air conditioners, consumer appliances to become more fuel efficient as price of electricity has been raised by removing subsidy on it.

INDIA'S GREEN HOUSE EMISSIONS AND THEIR IMPACT

Although India ranks in the top five in terms of GHG emissions, the *per capita emissions* are much lower compared to those of the developed countries, even if the historical emissions are excluded. Its high level of emissions is due to large populace, geographical size, and large economy. The most recent data available for India are the assessment carried out by the Indian Network for Climate Change Assessment (INCCA) in May 2010. The key results of the assessment are that the total net GHG emissions from India in 2007 were 1727.71 million tons of CO_2 equivalent (eq.), of which carbon dioxide emissions were 1221.76 million tons; methane 20.56 million tons; and nitrous

Table 44.2: A Comparison of GHG Emissions by Sector between 1994 and 2007

(in million tons of CO_2 equivalent)

	1994	2007	CAGR (per cent)
Electricity	355.03 (28.4)	719.30 (37.8)	5.6
Transport	80.28 (6.4)	142.04 (7.5)	4.5
Residential	78.89 (6.3)	137.84 (7.2)	4.4
Other Energy	78.93 (6.3)	100.87 (5.3)	1.9
Cement	60.87 (4.9)	129.92 (6.8)	6.0
Iron and Steel	90.53 (7.2)	117.32 (6.2)	2.0
Other Industry	125.41 (10.0)	165.31 (8.7)	2.2
Agriculture	344.48 (27.6)	334.41 (17.6)	-0.2
Waste	23.23 (1.9)	57.73 (3.0)	7.3
Total without LULUCF	1251.95	1904.73	3.3
LULUCF	14.29	-177.03	
Total with LULUCF	**1228.54**	**1727.71**	**2.9**

Note: Figures in brackets indicate percentage emissions from each sector with respect to total GHG emissions without LULUCF (*Labour use, land use change and forestry*) in 1994 and 2007 respectively.

Source: GOI, *Economic Survey,* 2010-11

oxide 0.24 million tons. In 1994, the total net GHG emissions for India were 1228.54 million tons of CO_2 eq. This represents a compounded annual growth rate of 2.9 per cent during the period 1994 to 2007 (See Table 41.2). GHG emissions from the energy, industry, agriculture, and waste sectors in 2007 constituted 58 per cent, 22 per cent, 17 per cent, and 3 per cent of the net CO_2 eq. emissions respectively. India's per capita CO_2 eq. emissions including land use, land use change, and forestry (LULUCF) were 1.5 tons per capita in 2007.

Impacts of Climate Change in India

Climate change has enormous implications for the natural resources and livelihoods of the people. It will have wide-ranging effects on the environmental and socio-economic and related sectors.

Various studies indicate that the key sectors in India such as the agriculture, water, natural ecosystem, biodiversity, and health are vulnerable to climate change. This is happening precisely at a time when it is confronted with huge development imperatives. The Indian Network for Climate Change Assessment (INCCA) released a report in November 2010 on assessment of the impact of climate change on key sectors and regions of India in the 2030s. The assessment covers four key sectors of the Indian economy, namely agriculture, water, natural ecosystems and biodiversity, and health in four climate sensitive regions, namely the Himalayan region, the Western Ghats, the Coastal Area, and the North-east region. The report warns of impacts such as sea-level rise, increase in cyclonic intensity, reduced crop yield in rainfed crops, stress on livestock, reduction in milk productivity, increased flooding, and spread of malaria. This calls for urgency of action in reducing vulnerability to adverse impacts of climate change and enhancing adaptive capacity through sector-pecific interventions and efforts.

India's Policies to Tackle Climate Change

India's total CO_2 emissions are about 4 per cent of total global CO_2 emissions and the energy intensity of India's output has been falling with improvements in energy efficiency, autonomous technological changes, and economical use of energy. India's climate modeling studies show that even with 8-9 per cent gross domestic product (GDP) growth every year for the next decade or two, its per capita emissions will be around 3-3.5 tonnes of CO_2 eq. by 2030, as compared to the present 1-1.2 tonnes. These are well below developed country averages by any estimation. India's determination in addressing climate change is evident from the fact that an indicative target of increasing energy efficiency by 20 per cent by 2016-17 was included in the Eleventh Five Year Plan. This has now been supplemented with the domestic mitigation goal of reducing emissions intensity of the GDP by 20-25 per cent of the 2005 level by 2020 through proactive policies.

The resources for the measures required to achieve this objective will need to be mobilized from various sources including the national planning process. Studies in respect of a low carbon strategy for development aimed at ensuring inclusive growth are being conducted with the aim of including this as one of the key pillars in the Twelfth Five Year Plan. Second, India is taking conscious steps to diversify the energy fuel mix such as setting up of 20,000 MW of solar power-generating capacity by 2022, doubling the present share of 3 per cent of nuclear power in the energy mix over the next decade, putting in place a major market-based programme to stimulate energy efficiency, imposing clean energy cess on coal for funding research and development (R&D) of clean energy technologies even though coal will continue to play a key role in our future energy strategy, and aggressively expanding the use of natural gas in power production. Third, India has been pursuing aggressive strategies for forestry and coastal management to increase the quality and quantity of forest cover and has launched a major new programme on coastal zone management to address the adaptation challenges facing over 300 million people in our country who live in vulnerable areas near our coast.

As part of its international obligations under the United Nations Framework Convention on Climate Change (UNFCCC) India periodically prepares the National Communication (NATCOM) that gives an inventory of the GHG emissions in India, assesses the vulnerability and impacts, and makes appropriate recommendations regarding social, economic and technological measures for addressing climate change. The First NATCOM was presented to the UNFCCC in 2004. The Government's NATCOM II, was presented to the UNFCCC in 2011. Preparation of NATCOM is an exercise of high scientific rigour based on an extensive network of research and scientific institutions in India and draws upon expertise and excellence from different institutions. India has set up an elaborate Indian Network for Comprehensive Climate Change Assessment of some 250 scientists and 120 research institutions to assist in this work. This Network has already published India's GHG inventory for the year 2007 and a 4 × 4 assessment of climate change impacts on four key sectors and four key regions of the country for the 2030s, a time frame for which decisive interventions can be made now.

This network is expected to put in place a programme for measuring, monitoring, and modeling the impact of black carbon which could have climate change and public health impacts.

India's strategy for *enhancing its adaptive capacity to climate* variability is reflected in many of its social and economic development programmes. For developing countries like India, adaptation ultimately boils down to assisting the vulnerable population during exigencies and empowering them to build their lives and cope with uncertainties in the long run. Several of India's social-sector schemes, with their emphases on livelihood security and welfare of the weaker sections, aim to do just that. India implements a series of Central sector and centrally sponsored schemes under different Ministries/Departments aimed at achieving social and economic development. Many of these schemes contain elements (objectives and targets) that are decidedly geared to adaptation. In other words, there is substantial adaptaion orientation in many of the sectoral schemes currently under operation. An exercise has been carried out to measure the expenditure on adaptation-related programmes with critical adaptation components: (*a*) crop improvement and research, (*b*) poverty alleviation and livelihood preservation, (*c*) drought proofing and flood control, (*d*) risk financing, (*e*) forest conservation, (*f*) health, and (*g*) rural education and infrastructure. It has been found that India's expenditure on these *adaptationor-ented schemes* has increased from 1.45 per cent of GDP in the year 2000-01 to 2.84 per cent during 2009-10. This is a fairly impressive level of spending and is an obvious reflection of the multiplicity of economic and social welfare.

India announced a **National Action Plan on Climate Change** (NAPCC) in June, 2008 which incorporates its vision of sustainable development and the steps it must take to realize it. The NAPCC is coordinated by the Ministry of Environment and Forests and implemented through the nodal Ministries and is aimed at advancing relevant actions in specific sectors/areas. Eight national missions in the areas of solar energy, enhanced energy efficiency, sustainable agriculture, sustainable habitat, water, Himalayan ecosystem, increasing the forest cover, and strategic knowledge for climate change form the core of NAPCC. State Governments are also preparing, under the advice of the Central Government, State Action Plans aimed at creating institutional and programme-oriented capacities to address climate change. These, together with the National Missions, will enhance climate change-related actions in the public and private domains.

COST OF ENVIRONMENT DAMAGE IN INDIA: WORLD BANK STUDY IN 2009

On the request of government of India World Bank carried out a study of cost of environment damage in India whose report was brought out in July 2013. According to this study outdoor air pollution in urban areas by itself claims 1.09 lakh lives of adults and 7,513 lives of chilldren below 5 years, annually, The study revealed that the annual cost of environmental degradation in India is about ₹ 3.75 lakh crores, which is equivalent to 5.7 of the country's GDP in 2009. However, the report says, India can make green growth a reality by putting in place strategies to reduce the damage at a minimal cost of 0.02% to 0.04% of its average annual GDP growth rate. The World Bank has brought out how urban growth centres are choking and claims that outdoor and indoor air pollution have the maximum share of this annual burden on India's economy. According to the estimates of the bank, outdoor air pollution accounts for 29% of this, followed by indoor air pollution (23%), cropland degradation (19%), water supply and sanitation (14%), pasture (11%) and forest degradation (4%). This is shown in the following see the following Table 56.2.

Table 44.2. India's Environmental Degradation Cost is Pegged ₹ 3.75 Trillion Annually

	Cost of Degradation	
Environmental Categories	₹ Billion	% age of Total Damage
Outdoor Air Pollution	1,100	29%
Indoor Air Pollution	870	23%
Crop Lands Degradation	703	19%
Water Supply, Sanitation & Hygiene	540	14%
Pastures Degradation	405	11%
Forest Degradation	133	4%
Total Environmental Damage	**3.75 lakh crore**	

Besides, according to world bank study environmental degradation and diseases are responsible for 22.8% of *child mortality* in India. As will be seen from Table 56.3, 0.4% of child mortality was due to outdoor air pollution, 9.8 per cent was due to Indoor air pollution and 12.6% of children dealth was caused by polluted water supply, poor sanitation and Hygiene

Table 44.3. Estimated Share of child Mortality Because of Pollution

Cause	% share of child Mortability due to Pollution
Outdoor Air Pollution	0.4
Indoor Air Pollution	9.8
Inadequate Water Supply, Sanitation and Hygiene	12.6
Total	22.8%

Cost of Environmental Degradation in Some Other Countries

It may be noted that the cost of environmental degration on helath related outdoor and indoor air pollution, sanitation and hygiene and cost of natural resource damages as per cent of GDP in India is lower as compared to some other countries such as China, Ghana, Nigeria and Pakistan as will be noticed from the following table.

Table 44.4. Cost of Environmental Degradation

(Health & Natural Resources Damage) % of GDP

Ghana 9.6		India	5.7
Tajikistan 9.5	Nigeria 7.7	Bangladesh	4.0
China 9.0	Pakistan 7.4	Nepal	3.5

It will be seen that cost of environment degradation as per cent GDP was 9 per cent in China, 9.6 per cent in Ghana, 7.4 per cent in Pakistan, 4.0 per cent in Bengladesh and 3.5% in Nepal as against 5.7 % GDP in India.

CLIMATE CHANGE NEGOTIATIONS

Negotiations on climate change began under the auspices of the United Nations to reach an agreement. These negotiations resulted in the **United Nations Framework Convention on Climate Change** (UNFCCC) at the Earth Summit at Rio in 1992. This convention required some binding rules to be pursued by the participating countries regarding GHG emissions. The convention required that the developed countries to formulate and adopt polices that aim stabilising greenhouse gases

Table 44.5: GHG Emissions in Some Countries

Country	Per Capita CO_2 emission (tonnes)
USA	20.01
E U	9.40
Japan	9.87
China	3.60
Russia	11.71
India	1.02
World Average	4.25

Source : GOI, *Economic Survey*, 2008-09

emission at 1990 level. Besides, this convention adopted the notion of **common but differentiated responsibility** to achieve the goal of stabilising GHGs emission. This followed from the recognition that global climate was a common resource and responsibility. It was however emphasized that there were asymmetries between the developed and developing countries regarding the past and present contribution of GHGs emissions and regarding financial resources required to reduce future emissions. It will be seen from Table -1 above that whereas per Capita emission of CO_2 in the USA is 20 tonnes in India it is only 4.25 tonnes. The developed countries had contributed most to GHGs concentration in the atmosphere during the process of industrial growth in the past. Therefore, they should bear substantial part of the cost to be borne by the developing countries to achieve abatement of climate change. Moreover, the developed countries had the necessary technology to reduce GHG emissions.

Berlin Meeting and Kyoto Protocal

After Rio Summit of May 1992, the advocates of more specific and legally binding targets and appropriate timeframe for reducing GHG emission succeeded in 1995 at a meeting of the parties to the convention on Climate Change was held at **Berlin** in Germany which concluded that commitments made in 1992 at Rio to reduce greenhouse gas emission were inadequate to meet the objective of climate change abatement. As a result, parties meeting at Berlin agreed to set forth a process of analysis and assessment of what next steps might be taken to reduce GHGs emissions. This process resulted in negotiation of a protocol and to adopt it a meeting of the parties to the UN Framework Convention on Climate Change was held at **Kyoto** in Japan in Dec. 1997. **This Kyoto protocol Committed rich industrialized countries to specific, legally binding emission targets for six greenhouse gases,** namely, carbon dioxide, methane, nitrous oxide, hydrofluorocarbon and sulphuric hexafluoride. However the USA which is the largest emitter of GHGs refused to sign it pointing to its needs for higher industrial growth which results in higher emission of GHGs. As a result, negotiations about fixing a limit of GHGs emission has remained in a limbo since then. Under UN auspices negotiators have been trying to hammer out a deal to cut global emission of GHGs. Now, a meeting of parties to UN Framework Convention on climate change has been called to be held in Copenhaegen in December 2009 an arrive at an agreement on mitigating climate change.

The adoption of the Kyoto Protocol contains a legally binding quantitative time-bound target for developed countries. The Kyoto Protocol set a target for developed countries (individually or jointly) to reduce overall emissions by at least 5 per cent below 1990 levels in the first commitment period, 2008 to 2012. Recognizing that relying on domestic measures alone to meet the target could be onerous, the Kyoto Protocol offers considerable flexibility through three mechanisms: **Clean Development Mechanisms** (CDM), **Joint Implementation** (JI), and **Emissions Trading** (ET). Through the CDM, industrial countries can finance mitigation projects in developing countries contributing to their sustainable development. *Credits received from such projects can be used to meet* *commitments under the Kyoto Protocol.* Through it, industrialized countries acquire emissions credit by financially supporting projects in other industrialized countries. ET allows countries that expect their emissions to be above target to buy unused quotas from other countries. All major countries except the USA have ratified the Kyoto Protocol.

Bali Action Plan and Copenhagen Accord

The Conference of Parties (CoP), which is the supreme body of the Convention, meets annually. During the 13th CoP held at Bali, Indonesia, in December 2007, a comprehensive process called the Bali Action Plan to enable the full, effective, and sustained implementation of the Convention through Long Term Cooperative Action, now, up to, and beyond 2012 was launched. Currently, international actions for addressing climate change are being pursued under the Bali Action Plan and the mandate of the Kyoto Protocol. The 15th CoP held at Copenhagen in December 2009 made some advance in the form of the 'Copenhagen Accord', which reflects the political understanding reached by a select group of countries. However, this was *noted* and *not adopted by* the parties to the Convention. Copenhangen Climate Accord is discussed below.

Copenhagen Accord. In December 2009 climate talks were held at Copenhagen to arrive at new policy framework on climate change and review the progress under Kyoto Protocol. It may be recalled that Kyoto Protocol requires the developed countries to bring down the emission of greenhouse gases by at least 5 per cent below the 1990 levels. In subsequent negotiations the developed countries took upon themselves the commitment of emission reduction targets of 20 to 25 per cent below 1990 levels to achieve the objective of limiting the rise of global temperature to 2^0 celsius. The developing countries had made no such commitment as they had not contributed much to the global warming and their emission levels were far below those of the rich developed nations due to lack of industrialisation in them.

At Copenhagen, the Indian delegation led by Jairam Romesh and Prime Minister Manmohan Singh went back to their commitment made before Partiament that *no international verfication of their actions for reduction of emission of greenhouse gases would be permitted.* They assured the parliament that only information would be furnished voluntarily to the International Body about its activities for mitigating the emission of greenhouse gases. However, contrary to this commitment before the parliament the Indian delegation agreed for international scruting or verification of its efforts for reduction of emission greenhouse gases. Further, surprisingly, Indian delegation did not insist on the fulfillment of targets of emission reduction committed by the developed nations under Kyoto Protocol. In the Copenhagen accord the developed countries were in fact let off from the legally binding provisions in Kyoto Protocol for penalties against the defaulting states. It also did not insist on provision of funds by the rich developed nations to the developing countries to help them in actions for mitigating emission of greenhouse gases. For example, it was not clear from the Copenhagen accord how the developed countries would finance the stopping of deforestation and encourage, afforastation by the developing countries.

Further, the Indian Government also went back on its assurance to the Indian Parliament that it would not accept the concept of peaking year to be fixed in regard to the emission of greenhouse gases. However, the Indian delegation agreed to the clause in Copenhagen Accord according to which the peaking year will be fixed for the developed countries and a little longer period will be fixed for the emerging economies such as India, China, Brazil.

At Copenhagen not only the developed countries went back on their emission reduction commitment under the Kyoto Protocol, they also succeeded in securing the new framework which is an alternative to Kyoto Protocol. This para 4 of Copenhagen Accord requires the developed countries to commit themselves to emission reduction targets for 2020 which were to be communicated to the UN Secretariat by Jan 31, 2010. This was to be kept as INF document which essentially means 'for information' only. Thus in Copenhagen Accord, the legally binding targets for reduction in emissions by developed countries were given up. Thus the legal obligations of the rich developed nations under Kyoto Protocol were done way with in Copenhagen accord.

It is thus evident from above that at Copenhagen climate conference, the world leaders were unable to translate rhetoric about global warming into actual action. However, world leaders at the Conference agreed to one thing, namely, that a great devastation would follow from increase in global temperature to more than 2°C. They paid some attention to the mounting scientific evidence about the ill-effects of increase in global warming and reaffirmed the principle set out in 1992 Rio Framework convention that various countries have *"common but differential responsibilities"*, which means that the rich developed nations which had contributed more to global warming had greater responsibilities to make larger efforts for reducing emission levels.

Further, at Copenhagen conference, the promise of developed countries were repeated that they would provide adequate, predictable and sustainable financial resources, technology and help for capacity-building to the developing countries. Commenting on dismal failure of Copenhagen Conference on Climate Change to address the problem of saving the planet from global warming Joseph E. Stiglitz write "*The failure of Copenhagen was not the absence of a legally binding agreement. The real failure was that there was no agreement about how to achieve the lofty goal of saving the planet, no agreement about reduction in carbon emission, no agreement on how to share the burden, and no agreement on help for developing countries*. Even the commitment of the accord to provide amount of $ 30 billion for the period 2010-12 for adaptation and mitigation appears paltry next to the hundreds of billions of dollars that have been doled out to the banks in the bailouts of 2008-09. If we can affored that much to save banks, we can affored something more to save the planet".[23] He further writes that "*most ethical principles would suggest that those that have polluted most in the past, especially after the problem was recognised in 1992 should have less right to pollute in the future.* But such an allocation would implicitly transfer hundreds of billions of dollars from rich to poor. Given the difficulty of coming up with even $ 10 billion a year let alone $ 200 billion a year that is needed for mitigation and adaptation it is wishful thinking to expect an agreement along these lines."[24]

Prof Stiglitz puts forward an alternative approach to reduction of emission of greenhouse gases. According to this approach, a carbon tax can be levied or emission cap to an agreed level, say $ 80 per tonne can be prescribed. The revenue so raised can be used as an alternative to other taxes. By raising resources in this way the rich developed countries could use some of the resources so procured to fulfill their obligations to help the developing countries in terms of adaptation and to compensate them for maintaining forests.

With the present attitude of developed countries in climate talks, in all likelihood, these talks are bound to fail. Thus while the efforts to check further global warming are halting, the greenhouse gases are building up in the atmosphere with the disastrous consequences, the possibility of meeting even agreed upon target of linking global warming to 2°C seems to be quite remote.

Negotiations at Cancun Meeting (2010) on Climate Change

As a follow up measure of Copenhagen Accord, a meeting of various ministers of the developed and developing countries were held in Dec. 2010 to deliberate on actions for mitigating greenhouse gases. Like that at Copenhagen India lost much more than it gained at Cancuy Climate Change

23. Joseph E Stiglitz, Overcoming the Copenhagen Failure, Project Syndicate 2010.
24. Ibid.

meeting. *At the meeting India formally commited itself to international scrutiny of its actions for emission reduction.* Not only that, it also let the US off from its obligations for reducing emission under Kyoto Protocol. Thus, the future of Kyoto Protocol which ensures hard targets to cut emission for rich countries has been greatly weakened and diluted. This in fact amounted to abondening Kyoto Protocol and contrary to the earlier agred-upon principle of *"Common but defferentiated responsibility"* of the rich developed and developing countries on a par on emission cut targets. Nitin Sethi, an eminent environmentalist writes, "Without Kyoto Protocol Countries such as India and China would end up having similar commitments as US and Europe. While India has no obligation under the UN Climate Convention, rich countries are mandated to adhere to stiff largets. But under the Cancun deal, the Indian Government admits to be dependent entrely on *domestic will and laws of the concerned countries"*.[25]

Thus, contrary to Kyoto Protocol, at Cancun Conference the developed countries only agreed to indicate their emission targets (which were not negotiated) but pledged by themselves voluntarily but did not specify whether this would be under Kyoto Protocol or Convention.

The result of Cancun meeting was that the emerging economies would all have the similar obligations as the rich developed nations while till date contributed far less to the climate change. Besides this, biggest blow to India's international climate stance, even other provesions of Cancun accord greatly diluted the the greater responsibility of the rich developed nations for making efforts to check global warming. The experts are of the view that at Cancun meeting India's long-held position of an *equal per capita rights for all countries to the global common carbon space in the atmosphere* was breached. This change is likely to have weakening effect on India's growth and access to technology.

Further, at Cancun meeting India's concerns for *easing the intellectual property rights control on technology* were thrown out of the window. Besides, at cancun meeting *India's demand for banning trade sanctions* against the developing countries was diluted substantially which would adversely affect their exports to the developed countries. Furthermore, the important question of provision of funds by the rich developed countries to the developing countries for technology transfer and capacity building for mitigation and adaptation to climate change had not even been addressed to at Cancun meeting.

Climate Negotiation at Bonn (Germany)

To carry forward the talks from Cancun Conference held in December 2010, negotiations were held in Bonn (Germany) in June 2011. In the Bonn meeting the rich developed countries including US, Germany, European community, Japan made attempts to prescribe rules for international scrutinity of actions taken for emission reduction by India and other emerging economies without committing themselves to fix targets of emission reduction and provision of funds under Kyoto Protocol.

It may be noted that Kyoto Protocol had two phases for its implementation of emission reduction targets. Under the first phase, the developed countries had emission reduction targets running up to 2012. The US was not a party to the Kyoto Protocol as it refused to sign it while other developed countries including European union were party to Kyoto Protocol as they had put their signatures on it. It is worth noting that under Kyoto Protocol the developing countries such as India, China, Brazil had made no such commitments about emission reduction targets. Under the second phase of Kyoto Protocol which is to commence from 2012, the new targets for reduction in emissions were to be set. But the rich developed countries now backed out and refused to set their targets for the second phase. They were in fact *demanding a new deal* which puts similar obligations for emission reduction for the emerging economies of India and China, Brazil, as for US and European Union. Therefore, it now appears as one expert opines it will be a empty shell with no targets.

---

25. Nitin Sethi, "Cancun Lost Cause, Government admits" in **Times of India**, June 8, 2011 (italics added).

It is thus evident that talks at Bonn yulded no results. On the other hand, the developing countries found that issues closer to their interests such as Kyoto Protocol had been put on the back while those leading to the *new global treaty* in which emerging economics are to be treated on a par with the rich developed countries were brought to fore on formal agenda in talks about climate change. As a result, at Bonn, negotiations about climate change ended in a political stalement as the rich developed countries were bent upon pushing emerging economies to a higher level of commitments with regard to emission reduction. At Bonn talks European Union and other rich developed countries asked India to first show what it was willing to commit as actions for emission reduction and how it would be verified before EU moves to discuss the targets under the second phase of Kyoto Protocol. India has so far refused to let Kyoto Protocol to die and move towards a new legal treaty that binds all countries, both developed and developing to similar obligations with regard to emission reduction. But when will India give in to the developed countries pressure is anybody guess.

Cancun Agreement. The climate negotiations held at Cancun during 29 November 2010 to 11, December 2010 that resulted in a set of decisions that cover various areas of action, for example mitigation, adaptation, technology and finance as outlined in the Bali Action Plan, while agreeing to work towards an ambitious target of emissions reduction under the Kyoto Protocol. The Cancun Agreements include decisions under both the Convention and Kyoto protocol negotiating tracks. They were widely perceived as a modest, small step forward and a reaffirmation of faith in the multilateral process. As *per the Cancun Agreements, all Parties to the Convention (including the developed and developing countries) have agreed to report their voluntary mitigation goals for implementation.* These will be subject to measurement and verification or international consultation, as appropriate, in accordance with agreed international guidelines. Decisions were taken at Cancun to set up a *Green Climate Fund, a Technology Mechanism*, and an *Adaptation Committee* at global level to support developing country actions for adaptation and mitigation. These decisions are significant because they reflect, to a large degree, the political understanding that was reached by a select group of countries in the form of the Copenhagen Accord in December 2009.

Details of Cancun Agreement (Nov-Dec 2010)

The following decisions were taken at Cancun meeting:

1. Industrialized country targets are officially recognized under the multilateral process and these countries are to develop low-carbon development plans and strategies and assess how best to meet them, including through market mechanisms, and to report their inventories annually.
2. Developing country actions to reduce emissions are officially recognized under the multilateral process. A registry is to be set up to record to finance and technology support from by industrialized countries. Developing countries are to publish progress reports every two years.
3. Parties meeting under the Kyoto Protocol agree to continue negotations with the aim of completing their work and ensuring there is no gap between the first and second commitment periods of the treaty.
4. The Kyoto Protocol's **Clean Development Mechanism** (CDM) has been strengthened to drive more major investments and technology into environmentally sound and sustainable emission reduction projects in the developing world.
5. Parties launched a set of initiatives and institutions to protect the vulnerable from climate change and to deploy the money and technology that developing countries need to plan and build their own sustainable futures.

6. A total of $30 billion in fast start finance from industrialized countries to support climate action in the developing world up to 2012 and the intention to raise $100 billion in long-term funds by 2020 are included in the decisions.
7. In the field of climate finance, a process to design a **'Green Climate Fund'** under the Conference of the Parties, with a Board with equal representation from developed and developing countries, is established.
8. A new Cancun Adaptation Framework was established to allow better planning and impiementation of adaptation projects in developing countries through increased financial and technical support, including a clear process for continuing work on loss and damage.
9. Governments agreed to boost action to curb emissions from deforestation and forest degradation in developing countries with technological and financial support.
10. Parties have established a technology mechanism with a Technology Executive Committee and Climate Technology Centre and Network to increase technology cooperation to support action on adaptation and mitigation.

Efforts to Back Out by Developed Countries

In what could turn into a deal-breaker at the climate talks, US and other indutrialized countries in the Major Economies Forum meet at Washigton in the second week of Sept. 2009 told India that they wanted to do away with the Kyoto Protocol, a move opposed by India. The industrialized countries proposed that the developing world should agree to the Australian proposal, which demands all countries, regardless of development levels, take on commitments and fix timetable by when they start reducing emissions. It demands that all key countries, including India, curb their emissions by 2020. The India's stand is that the official negotiations at UN were already grappling with the question of strong mid-term targets for rich nations under the second phase of Kyoto Protocol and to do away with the protocol was not a part of the mandate of negotiations. US and some other industrialized countries, European Union (EU) have for long opposed strong mid-term targets and demanded China and India get on board on a long-term agreement.

Besides, both the **USA and EU are trying to link foreign trade with mitigating climate change**. The provisions in the US domestic bill on climate change to impose trade tariffs on goods imported from countries that don't agree to emission reductions were like 'sanctions' against 'renegade' countries that did not sign up the international agreements. India has opposed the provisions, which the Indian Government perceives as protectionism hidden in the garb of climate change concerns. It's rather ironic for a US to say so after the US backed out of Kyoto Protocol and now finds it politically improbable to pass even an extremely weak domestic legislation on climate change. The attempts by US to throw up completely unacceptable proposals on the table at the last moment with less than three months left of the final round of negotiations in December as well as becoming aggressive on trade barriers is being seen as a ploy to deflect attention from its failure to move ahead on its domestic climate change bill.

DURBAN CONFERENCE ON CLIMATE CHANGE (DECEMBER 2011)

To carry the talks for climate change further to contain global warming diplomats of 194 countries met at Durban in South Africa in Dec.1 to Dec.14 to deliberate on carbon emission cuts by various countries and to review Kyoto Protocol. As before, the developed countries led by EU, US and Canada were reluctant to agree to any legally-binding emission cuts and were also not in favour of extension of commitment period for reducing emission they had accepted under Kyoto Protocol. They sought similar carbon emission cuts by the major developing countries, especially China and

India beyond 2020, Finally, a new climate treaty called as '*Durban Platform for Enhanced Action*' was signed which describes roadmap for emission cuts to be operational after 2020 both by the developed and developing countries. This treaty will be formally finalised by 2015 and will have '*legal force*'. To accommodate the viewpoint of the developed countries and to secure the second commitment period for Kyoto Protocol from them India diluted its stand on legally binding emission cuts by the developed countries based on the principle of equity and common but differentiated responsibility (CDR) and agreed to emission cuts being binding on all nations, both developed and developing countries, especially India and China after 2020. The Indian delegation led by Environment Minister Jayanti Natarajan changed the wording from '*legally binding*' to the '*agreed outcome with legal force*'. This leaves some vagueness in the climate agreement reached at Durban. While India maintains that Durban agreement does not mean mandatory emission cuts beyond 2020 but other countries including its allies China and South Africa think it differently and interpret the new treaty to be binding on both developed developing countries. Even the European Union which conducted the negotiations at Durban says that Durban agreement "*brings all countries into a common and truly global legal regime to curb emissions*". This Durban agreement was also backed by the United States. China which agreed to the emission cuts beyond 2020 also says that Durban agreement means mandatory emission reductions but its exact nature is yet to be decided by 2015. In the next three years (2012-15) under the Durban roadmap. Country-wise emission cuts will be finally decided on the review of pledges of the rich nations under Kyoto Protocol, voluntary mitigation efforts by the developing countries and the fifth assessment report of '*UN's scientific Inter-governmental Panel on climate change*'.

Durban agreement suits well to the rich nations who have demanding common but differentiated responsibility with respective capabilities by all countries, both developed and developing countries enshrined in the UN Climate Convention. What has given India some scope to interpret the Durban climate agreement differently is vagueness of the language used. The Durban Platform for Enhanced Action talks about "highest possible mitigation efforts by all parties" and nowhere mentions emission reduction or cuts. India has already announced a domestic mitigation goal of reducing emission intensity of its output by 20-25 per cent by 2020 in comparison with 2005 levels. According to Environment Minister Jayanti Natrajan this goal is relative in nature and allows India's emissions to grow," she said, without referring to India's position on emission cuts beyond 2020.

A significant achievement of Durban agreement is the second committment period (2013-2017) secured for Kyoto Protocol which was to expire in 2012. Though no fresh emmission cuts were proposed for the second committment period, the developed countries which were legally bound to certain emission cuts by 2012 under Kyoto Protocol would now have to be fulfilled till 2017. Thus at Durban the Kyoto Protocol got a new lease of life for a few more years. The Kyoto Protocol sets binding targets for 37 industrialised nations and the Europeon Union (EU) to slash carbon emissions to 5% below the 1990 levels by 2012. Until now, China and India have been exempt from any constraints because they are developing countries. Besides, the United States which was not the signatory of Kyoto Protocol came on board in Durban agreement and accepted the transparency of its climate action and to emission cuts that will be decided under the agreement to be operational beyond 2020.

The Durban Conference also decided to hold a **workshop on equity** in 2012 but this did not find reference in the pact on new climate treaty. But one Indian member of the delegation, Sunita Narain says" It is clear from this conference that the fight to reduce emissions effectively in an unequal world will be even more difficult in the years to come.But it is a conference, which has put the issue of equity back into the negotiations. It is for this reason an important move ahead." The new emission cuts regime will be decided on basis of equity, which could mean lower emission reduction for India as compared to China, whose per capita global warming causing carbon dioxide release is almost double of India's. Jayanti Natrajan told Lok Sabha that no emission cuts were agreed to in Durban. She stated, " I must clarify that this decision does not imply that India has to take binding commitments to reduce its emissions in absolute terms in 2020," It will therefore be interesting to watch how India plays its cards in the new working group considering its annual per capita emissions (of 17 tonnes) is even lower than some of the Island nations such as Barbados, which sought binding emission commitments from India and China. In our view at Durban both US and EU have gained from the treaty as it treats all polluters on par. China succeeded in managing to push that new global regime that would be operational only after 2020. To what extent the principle of equity will be finally enshrined in Durban Platform for Enhanced Action will be known when the agreement is finally formalised by 2015. However, Jayanti Natrajan asserts that earning second commitment period for Kyoto Protocol as major achievement. The minister assured the principles of "equity" and " common but differentiated responsibility" (CBDR) would be enshrined in the new climate treaty.

However, China an ally of India, succeeded in securing an important commitment that it would consider legally binding outcome after 2020 if five preconditions including a second commitment period for Kyoto Protocol were met. As far as China is concerned it does not matter if the roadmap is finalised by 2015 provided it is not implemented before 2020.

Green Climate Fund (GCF) and Technology Transfer

A significant achievement at Durban for India, China and other developing countries was that they were able to get commitment about Green Climate Fund (GCF) of $ 100 billion (already committed but not implemented) from rich nations. Under this India will get long -term finance to adapt to climate change, transfer and development of clean technology.

Besides, the Green Climate Fund to finance the adaptation to and mitigation of climate change, **technological transfer talk** gained momentum at Durban India's proposal to break the logjam on transferring green technologies gained centre stage when other intractable issues appeared to be resolved. Under the Cancun Agreements, countries had decided to set up centres that would help transfer technologies from rich countries and develop new ones in collaboration. But the talks on operationalising these centres had got stuck since countries were unable to come to a consensus over several key elements. The key point of dissension had been how the UN convention would control the flow of technologies and ensure they were meeting the need of the developing world that would put forth its requirements .The talks on technology had got stuck since developed countries were not keen to have a review process to assess if they were providing the kind of technological help required and demanded by developing countries.

It was decided to select a panel that would oversee the entire process of technology transfer and guide why it has run into rough weather because developing countries are keen to have clean technologies. The developing Countries want a transparent process of selection of this panel.

Intellectual Property Rights Besides equity, India raised the issue of intellectual property rights for clean technology transfer. India wants intellectual property rights should not be enforced in case of clean technology transfer. However, for this. India was told to take up the issue at '*World Intellectual property organisation*'. In this regard India has China's support but not from other. BRICS nations–Brazil and South Africa.

Unilateral Trade Barriers. Another issue that India raised at Durban was unilateral trade barriers imposed by the developed countries should be done away with. Most countries wanted India to take up the issue at World Trade Organisation (WTO). On the other hand, in this connection a paper on Carbon tax on aviation and maritime transport was approved by a UN Committee despite India's protest.

Conclusion. It is evident from above that at Durban Conference India failed to secure commitment regarding equity in emission cuts. Instead it accepted its clubbing with developed countries which has historically contributed most to the pollution of environment. Besides, its other demands regarding intellectual property rights and unilateral trade barriers were not accepted.

It may be noted that new climate treaty with binding emission cuts after 2020 has important implications for India's economic growth and energy strategy. For both industrial and agricultural growth and energy strategy. For both industrial and agricultural growth we require the use of energy which in India are mostly supplied by thermal power plants which use coal for generation of power. If we accept the larger carbon emission cuts, we will have to restrict the use of coal-based energy generation and make large investment in development of other sources of alternative clean technologies. To conclude in the words of one environmentalist. At Durban Conference "the differentiation between the developed and developing countries - which has been the bedrock of the global climate regime - has already been written out, even before work on the Durban Plan on Enhanced Action could begin. While there are specific timeliness for actions or requirements that developing countries have to meet, there is no time-line for support, neither technology nor finance, from developed countries."[26]

Doha Climate Change Conference 2012

The 18th session of the (COP) Committee of parties to the UNFCCC, that started on 26 November concluded on 8 December 2012 in Doha, Qatar has resulted in a set of decisions (clubbed together as '*Doha Climate Gateway*') aimed at advancing the implementation of the UNFCCC and its Kyoto Protocol (KP). The key issues for the Doha conference were; amending the KP to implement the second commitment period under the Protocol; successfully concluding the worked of the Bali Action Plan (BAP) within which there was urgent need for a clear path to climate finance; and planning the work under the *Durban Platform* (DP) for enhanced action. The Conference addressed all three issues and came out with a package which balanced the interests and obligations of various countries.

At the Doha Conference, the three issues of equity, technology-related IPRs, and unilateral measures raised by India resounded in the decisions. These outstanding or unresolved issues under the (BAP) are now part of the planned or continuing work of various bodies of the Convention. At doha, India also ensured that no hasty decision is taken on aspects related to mitigation in agricultural sector at global level as agriculture is a sensitive sector for developing countries. The Conference has explicitly recognized that the action of Parties will be based on equity and CBDR (Common but Differential Responsibility) including the need for equitable access to sustainable development. The Conference also recognized that issues relating to global peaking that could place a cap on emissions of developing countries and restrict their development space were controversial and best avoided at this stage of development. At the same time, in an effort to cater to the interest of all countries and come up with a balanced package, some elements of the package required compromise or deferral. In many cases, ambitious and strong demands were collectively made by developing countries, but

---

26. Urmi A Goswamy, Only Noble Words, No. Bid to Cut Emissions, *The Economic Times*, Dec.16,2012

in the act of balancing, countries were made to accept the mellowed down and subtle versions of their demands.

Among the key concerns which the Conference could not address were those relating to financing commitments of developed countries and sectorial actions. No specific targets for mid-term financing (2013-2020) were adopted. While the Conference stopped short of giving a mandate to the International Civil Aviation Organization (ICAO) or International Martine Organization (IMO) to initiate steps for curtailing emissions in their respective sectors, the absence of a decision on sectoral framework for such actions has left open the possibility of such actions being initiated in such sectors by the respective international organizations. Considering the fact that some of the leading members of ICAO prefer a global market based mechanism to be the vehicle of such actions, the framework and the principle on the basis of which such actions will be taken are likely to be a bone of contention for quite sometime. Also, despite vociferous demand from vulnerable countries, there could be no satisfactory agreement on a compensation mechanism for loss and damage resulting from climate change.

On the positive rise, the Doha Conference succeeded in carrying out amendments to the Kyoto Protocol (KP) to ensure a second commitment period. The second commitment period will last for a period of eight years as of 1st January 2013. This decision has ensured that there will be no gap between the first commitment period under the Kyoto Protocol (KP) ending on 31 December 2012 and the second one commencing on 1 January 2013. With the exception of Russia, New Zealand, Japan, and Canada, all other countries that were part of the first commitment period entered into the second round, with some new countries joining as well. It has been agreed that the KP Parties will revisits their targets in 2014 with a view to increasing their ambition. The emission reduction obligations undertaken by the Kyoto Protocol Parties are not as ambitious as required by science; however, they provide a relative degree of certainty to the carbon markets. The EU will reduce its emissions by 20 per cent by 2020 compared to 1990. Governments also agreed to speedily work under the Durban Platform (DP) to evolve a new set of arrangements for mitigation commitments and actions applicable to all countries from 2020, and to adopt it by 2015. In a significant and positive advancement, it has been agreed that the work of the DP will be based on the principles of the convention.

Key Outcomes of Doha Conference, 2012 on Climate Change. The Key outcomes of Doha Conference, 2012 on climate change are stated below.

- ✧ It has been agreed that the KP, as the only existing and binding agreement under which developed countries commit to cutting emissions of GHGs, will enter a second commitment period that will run for eight years.
- ✧ Governments have agreed to speedily work toward a climate change agreement under DP applicable to all countries from 2020, to be adopted by 2015. Further governments have decided to find ways to scale up efforts before 2020 to meet the gap in global ambition for emissions reduction.
- ✧ Governments have launched a robust process to review the long-term temperature goal. This will start in 2013 and concluded by 2015 and is a reality check on the advance to the climate change threat and the possible need to mobilize further action.
- ✧ The Work Programme on Long term Finance launched last year has been extended for another year to contribute to the ongoing efforts to scale up mobilization of climate finance. Developed countries have reiterated their commitment to deliver on promises of mobilizing US$100 billion both for adaptation and mitigation by 2020.

- ✧ Decision also encourages developed countries to increase efforts for providing finance between 2013 and 2015, and at least to the average annual level provided during the 2010-2012 fast-start finance period.
- ✧ Finance pledges of about $6 billion for period upto 2015 announced by Germany, the UK, France, Denmark, Sweden and the EU Commission.
- ✧ The selection of the Republic of Korea by the Board of the Green Climate Fund (GCF) to host the GCF has been endorsed.
- ✧ The unresolved issues of Technology-related Intellectual Property Rights (IPRs) and the Unilateral Measures under the BAP (Bali Action Plan) are now part of the planned or continuing work of various bodies of the Convention. Based on the decisions, the Technology Executive Committee (TEC) will initiate exploration of issues relating to enabling environments and barriers, including IPRs in its future work-plan. The TEC has already identified IPRs intellectual property rights one of the key messages on which further work is necessary. Similarly, a decision has been taken for facilitating discussion on the issue of unilateral measures under the existing forum on implementation of response measures.